Catalogue of the snakes in the British Museum (Natural History)

British Museum (Natural History). Dept. of Zoology, George Albert Boulenger

Nabu Public Domain Reprints:

You are holding a reproduction of an original work published before 1923 that is in the public domain in the United States of America, and possibly other countries. You may freely copy and distribute this work as no entity (individual or corporate) has a copyright on the body of the work. This book may contain prior copyright references, and library stamps (as most of these works were scanned from library copies). These have been scanned and retained as part of the historical artifact.

This book may have occasional imperfections such as missing or blurred pages, poor pictures, errant marks, etc. that were either part of the original artifact, or were introduced by the scanning process. We believe this work is culturally important, and despite the imperfections, have elected to bring it back into print as part of our continuing commitment to the preservation of printed works worldwide. We appreciate your understanding of the imperfections in the preservation process, and hope you enjoy this valuable book.

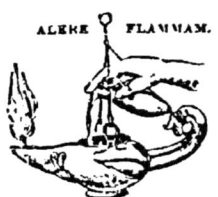

PRINTED BY TAYLOR AND FRANCIS,
RED LION COURT, FLEET STREET

PREFACE.

With this volume is brought to a conclusion a series of works which all zoologists must acknowledge to be of primary importance in the history of science. The series consists of nine volumes, viz. :—The Catalogue of Batrachia Salientia, published in 1882; the Catalogue of Batrachia Gradientia, also in 1882; the Catalogue of Lizards, vol. i. 1885, vol. ii 1885, vol. iii. 1887, the Catalogue of Chelonians, Rhynchocephalians, and Crocodiles, 1889; and the Catalogue of Snakes, vol. i. 1893, vol. ii. 1894, and vol. iii 1896.

These works are not only catalogues in the ordinary sense of the largest general collections of Batrachia and Reptilia ever yet brought together, but are complete monographs of the groups of animals treated of, so far as their zoological characters, geographical distribution, and synonymy are concerned—descriptions being given of every species regarded by the author as valid, whether contained in the Museum or not.

The initiative of the series is due to Dr. Gunther. It was begun and has been carried out almost to its close under his Keepership of the Zoological Department.

Of the unremitting devotion of Mr. Boulenger to the task which has occupied him for more than fifteen years, or of the ability and large anatomical and literary knowledge he has brought to bear upon it, it is not necessary for me to speak—they are known to all zoologists; and I hardly need point out that the value of the work has been greatly increased by the numerous carefully executed figures of new species and of illustrative anatomical details which it contains.

W. H. FLOWER,
Director

April 15, 1896.

INTRODUCTION.

This concluding volume of the Catalogue of Snakes, contains the descriptions of 689 species, 564 of which are represented in the Collection, and the enumeration of 5230 specimens.

The total number of recognized species of Ophidians now amounts to 1639. Duméril & Bibron's 'Erpétologie Générale' (1854) registers 531; Gray and Gunther's Catalogues (1849–58) 544; and 789 (including numerous *nomina nuda*) are enumerated in Jan's 'Elenco' (1863).

The amalgamated index to the three volumes, which is appended, contains 7335 names, thus showing the enormous extent of the synonymy.

With this volume the revision of the entire Herpetological Collection in the British Museum is brought to a close, a work the publication of which has extended over fourteen years. The whole series of Catalogues, consisting of nine Volumes—two of Batrachians (1882), three of Lizards (1885–87), one of Rhyncho-cephalians, Chelonians, and Crocodiles (1889), and three of Snakes (1893–96)—deals with 4,413 species and 28,642 specimens. But the numerous additions to the Collection and to the Literature, made since the appearance of the earlier volumes, raise these numbers as follows:—

INTRODUCTION.

	Described valid species.	Species represented in Collection	Specimens in Collection
REPTILIA			
SQUAMATA.			
Ophidia	1639	1327	11092
Rhiptoglossa	76	58	544
Lacertilia	1893	1413	13524
EMYDOSAURIA	23	20	250
CHELONIA	219	183	1852
RHYNCHOCEPHALIA	1	1	13
BATRACHIA.			
ECAUDATA	1146	778	8950
CAUDATA	130	89	1685
APODA	43	36	176
Total	5170	3905	38086

The Collection in the Museum is not only the largest but also the best-arranged in existence, every specimen in it having been carefully examined and classified according to a modern system after consultation of the whole literature.

The Author begs to express his thanks to the following gentlemen who have assisted him in the preparation of the Catalogue of Snakes, through gift or loan of specimens, or with notes on the types in the Collections under their charge:—Professor Vaillant, Dr Mocquard, and M. Bocourt, of the Paris Museum; Marquis Doria and Dr. Gestro, Genoa; Professor Hertwig, Munich; Professor Ehlers, Gottingen; Professor Barboza du Bocage, Lisbon; M. Dollo, Brussels, Professor Möbius and Dr. Tornier, Berlin; Professor Boettger, Frankfort/M.; Professor Camerano and Count Peracca, Turin; Professor Bavay, Brest, and Professor von Méhely, Kronstadt. To his former Chief, Dr. Gunther, to whose initiative the publication of this work is due, his best thanks are also now offered for the kind encouragement he has bestowed on him for so many years.

G. A BOULENGER

Zoological Department,
March 27, 1896

SYSTEMATIC INDEX.

OPHIDIA

× Fam 7 COLUBRIDÆ

Series B. *Opisthoglypha.*

Subfam. 4. HOMALOPSINÆ

	Page
124. Hypsirhina, *Wagl.*	2
1. indica, *Gray*	4
2. alternans, *Reuss*	5
3 plumbea, *Boie*	5
4 jagorii, *Ptrs*	6
×5. enhydris, *Schn*	6
6 bennettii, *Gray*	8
7 chinensis, *Gray*	8
8. macleavi, *D. Ogilby*	9
9. polylepis, *Fisch.*	9
10 blanfordii, *Blgr*	10
11 bocourti, *Jan*	10
12. albomaculata, *D & B*	11
13. sieboldii, *Schleg*	11
14 punctata, *Gray*	12
15 doriæ, *Ptrs*	13
125. Homalopsis, *Kuhl*	13
× 1. buccata, *L.*	14
126 Cerberus, *Cuv*	15
× 1 rhynchops, *(Schn)*	16
2 australis, *Gray*	18
3 microlepis, *Blgr.*	18
127. Eurostus, *D & B.*	19
1. dussumieri, *D. & B.*	19
128 Myron, *Gray*	19
1 richardsonii, *Gray*	20
129. Gerardia, *Gray*	20
1 prevostiana, *Eyd. & Gerv.*	20
130. Fordonia, *Gray*	21
1. leucobalia, *Schleg.*	21
131. Cantoria, *Gir*	23
1. violacea, *Gir*	23
132. Hipistes, *Gray*	24
×1. hydrinus, *(Cant.)*	24
133 Herpeton, *Lacép*	25
1. tentaculatum, *Lacép.*	25

Subfam 5 DIPSADOMORPHINÆ.

	Page
134 Geodipsas, *Blgr*	32
1 infralineata, *Gthr.*	32
2. boulengeri, *Peracca*	32
135 Hologerrhum, *Gthr.*	33
1 philippinum, *Gthr*	33
136. Ithycyphus, *Gthr.*	34
1 goudoti, *Schleg.*	34
2. miniatus, *Schleg*	35
137. Langaha, *Brugn*	35
1. nasuta, *Shaw*	36
2. intermedia, *Blgr.*	37
3 crista-galli, *D & B.*	37
138 Alluaudina, *Mocq.*	38
1 bellyi, *Mocq.*	26, 38
139 Eteirodipsas, *Jan*	38
1 colubrina, *Schleg*	39
140 Stenophis, *Blgr*	39
1 guentheri, *Blgr.*	40
2 granuliceps, *Bttgr*	41
3. inornatus, *Blgr.*	42
4 gaimardii, *Schleg*	42
5. maculatus, *Gthr.*	43
6. arctifasciatus, *D & B.*	43
7. variabilis, *Blgr.*	43
8 betsileanus, *Gthr.*	44
141. Lycodryas, *Gthr.*	44
1 sancti-johannis, *Gthr.*	45
142 Pythonodipas, *Gthr.*	45
1. carinata, *Gthr*	45
143. Ditypophis, *Gthr.*	46
1. vivax, *Gthr.*	46
144. Tarbophis, *Fleischm.*	47
1 savignyi, *Blgr*	48
2 fallax, *Fleischm.*	48
3. iberus, *Eichw*	49
4. rhinopoma, *Blanf*	50
5 variegatus, *Reinh*	51
6. semiannulatus, *Smith*	51
7 guentheri, *And*	52
8. obtusus, *Reuss*	52
145. Trimorphodon, *Cope*	53
1 biscutatus, *D. & B.*	54
2 upsilon, *Cope*	55

SYSTEMATIC INDEX.

	Page
3. lyrophanes, *Cope*	56
4. tau, *Cope*	56
146. Lycognathus, *D. & B.*	56
1. cervinus, *Laur*	57
2. rhombeatus, *Ptrs*	58
147 Trypanurgos, *Fitz.*	58
1. compressus, *Daud.*	58
148. Dipsadomorphus, *Fitz*	59
1 trigonatus, *Schn.*	62
2. multimaculatus, *Boie*	63
3. gokool, *Gray*	64
x 4. hexagonotus, *(Blyth)*	65
5 ceylonensis, *Gthr*	66
x 6 fuscus, *(Gray)*	67
7. pulverulentus, *Fisch.*	68,649
8. multifasciatus, *Blyth*	69
9. dightonii, *Blgr.*	69
10. dendrophilus, *Boie*	70
11 cyaneus, *D & B*	72
12 nigriceps, *Gthr.*	72
13. jaspideus, *D. & B.*	73
14. barnesii, *Gthr.*	73
15. drapiezii, *Boie*	74
16. angulatus, *Ptrs.*	75
17. irregularis, *Merr.*	75
18. flavescens, *D & B.*	77
19. philippinus, *Ptrs*	77
20. blandingii, *Hallow.*	77
21. cynodon, *Boie*	78
22. forsteni, *D. & B.*	80
bertholdi, *Jan*	81
ornata, *Macleay*	81
149. Dipsadoboa, *Gthr.*	81
1 unicolor, *Gthr*	81
150 Rhinobothryum, *Wagl*	81
1. lentiginosum, *Scop.*	82
151 Himantodes, *D & B.*	83
1 cenchoa, *L*	84
2 elegans, *Jan*	85
3 lentiferus, *Cope*	86
4 gemmistratus, *Cope.*	86
5. gracillimus, *Gthr.*	87
6. inornatus, *Blgr.*	88
7. ? subæqualis, *Fisch*	88
152. Leptodira, *Gthr.*	88
1 hotamboia, *Laur.*	89, 649
2. punctata, *Ptrs.*	91
3. nigrofasciata, *Gthr*	92
4. frenata, *Cope*	92
5. septentrionalis, *Kenn.*	93
x 6. personata, *Cope*	93
7. ocellata, *Gthr.*	94
x 8 albofusca, *Lacép.*	95
9. annulata, *L.*	97
153 Chamætortus, *Gthr.*	98
1. aulicus, *Gthr.*	98

	Page
154 Oxyrhopus, *Wagl.*	99
1. petolarius, *L.*	101
2. rhombifer, *D & B*	103
3. trigeminus, *D. & B*	104
4 bitorquatus, *Gthr.*	104
5. melanogenys, *Tsch.*	105
6 doliatus, *D & B.*	106
7. formosus, *Wied*	106
8. labialis, *Jan*	107
9 clathratus, *D. & B.*	107
10 fitzingeri, *Tsch.*	108
11. cloelia, *Daud*	108
12. maculatus, *Blgr.*	110
13 occipitoluteus, *D & B.*	110
14 rusticus, *Cope*	111
x 15. coronatus, *Schn.*	111
16 neuwiedii, *D. & B*	112
17. guerini, *D & B.*	113
155. Rhinostoma, *Fitz.*	114
1 guianense, *Trosch*	114
2. vittatum, *Blgr*	115
156. Thamnodynastes, *Wagl*	115
1 nattereri, *Mik.*	116
2. punctatissimus, *Wagl*	117
157 Tachymenis, *Wiegm.*	117
x 1. peruviana, *Wiegm.*	118
2. affinis, *Blgr*	119
158 Hemirhagerrhis, *Bttgr.*	119
1. kelleri, *Bttgr.*	119, 649
159. Manolepis, *Cope*	120
1. putnami, *Jan*	120
160. Tomodon, *D. & B*	120
1. dorsatus, *D. & B.*	121
2. ocellatus, *D. & B.*	121, 649
161. Conophis, *Ptrs.*	122
1 lineatus, *D. & B*	123
2 vittatus, *Ptrs*	123
3 tæniatus, *Hens.*	124
162 Amplorhinus, *Smith*	124
1. multimaculatus, *Smith.*	125
2. nototænia, *Gthr.*	125
163. Pseudablabes, *Blgr.*	126
1. agassizii, *Jan*	127
164. Philodryas, *Wagl.*	127
1. æstivus, *Schleg.*	128
x 2. viridissimus, *(L.)*	129
3 olfersii, *Licht.*	129
4. schotti, *Schleg.*	130
5. bolivianus, *Blgr.*	132
6 psammophideus, *Gthr.*	132
7. vitellinus, *Cope*	133
8. elegans, *Tsch*	133
9 nattereri, *Stdr.*	134
10. serra, *Schleg.*	134
11 burmeisteri, *Jan*	135

SYSTEMATIC INDEX.

	Page
12 baroni, *Berg*	136
13. ? inornatus, *D. & B.*	136
165 Ialtris, *Cope*	137
1 dorsalis, *Gthr*	137
166 Trimerorhinus, *Smith*	138
1. rhombeatus, *L.*	138
2. tritæniatus, *Gthr.*	139, 649
3 variabilis, *Gthr.*	140
167 Cœlopeltis, *Wagl*	141
×1 monspessulana,*(Herm.)*	141
2. moilensis, *Reuss*	143
168. Rhamphiophis, *Ptrs.*	144
1 rubropunctatus, *Fisch*	146
2. oxyrhynchus, *Reinh.*	146
3. togoensis, *Matschie*	147
4. acutus, *Gthr*	148
5. multimaculatus, *Smith*	148
169. Dromophis, *Ptrs* ....?	149
1. lineatus, *D & B.*	149
2. præornatus, *Schleg.*	150
170. Taphrometopon, *Brandt.*	151
1. lineolatum, *Brandt*	151
171. Psammophis, *Boie*	152
1 leithii, *Gthr.*	155
2. notostictus, *Ptrs*	156
×3 schokari,*(Forsk.)*	157
4 punctulatus, *D & B*	159
5 trigrammus, *Gthr.*	159
6 subtæniatus, *Ptrs.*	160
7 bocagii, *Blgr.*	161
8 sibilans, *L.*	161
9. furcatus, *Ptrs*	164
10. longifrons, *Blgr*	165
×11. condanarus, *(Merr.)*	165
12. brevirostris, *Ptrs*	166
13 elegans, *Shaw*	167
14. biseriatus, *Ptrs.*	168
15 crucifer, *Daud.*	169
16. pulcher, *Blgr*	169
17 angolensis, *Bocage*	170
172. Mimophis, *Gthr.*	171
1 mahfalensis, *Grand.*	171
173 Psammodynastes, *Gthr.*	172
×1. pulverulentus,*(Boie.)*	172
2. pictus, *Gthr.*	174
174. Macroprotodon, *Guich.*	175
×1 cucullatus,*(I. Geoffr.)*	175
175. Dryophis, *Dalm*	177
1. perroteti, *D & B.*	178
2 dispar, *Gthr.*	179
3 fronticinctus, *Gthr.*	179
4. xanthozona, *Boie*	180
×5 prasinus, *Boie*	180
6. fasciolatus, *Fisch.*	182
7 mycterizans, *L*	182
8. pulverulentus, *D. & B.*	184

	Page
176. Thelotornis, *Smith*	184
1 kirtlandii, *Hallow.*	185
177 Dispholidus, *Duvern.*	186
1. typus, *Smith*	187
178. Oxybelis, *Wagl.*	189
1. brevirostris, *Cope*	190
2 argenteus, *Daud.*	190
3 fulgidus, *Daud*	191
4. acuminatus, *Wied*	192
179. Dryophiops, *Blgr.*	193
1. rubescens, *Gray*	194
2. philippina, *Blgr.*	195
180. Chrysopelea, *Boie*	195
1 rhodopleuron, *Boie*	195
×2 ornata,*(Shaw)*	196
3. chrysochlora, *Reinw.*	198
181. Erythrolamprus, *Wagl.*	199
1. æsculapii, *L*	200
2. decipiens, *Gthr.*	204
3. grammophrys, *Dugès.*	204
4. laterititus, *Cope*	205
5. dromiciformis, *Ptrs.*	205
6. imperialis, *B. & G.*	206
7. fissidens, *Gthr*	207
8. bipunctatus, *Gthr.*	208
9. piceivittis, *Cope*	209
182. Hydrocalamus, *Cope*	209
1. quinquevittatus, *D & B.*	210
183. Scolecophis, *Cope*	210
1. atrocinctus, *Schleg.*	211
2. michoacanensis, *Cope.*	211
3. æmulus, *Cope*	212
184. Homalocranium, *D. & B*	212
1. melanocephalum, *L*	215
2. annulatum, *Bttgr.*	217
3. trilineatum, *Ptrs.*	217
4. longifrontale, *Blgr*	218
5. coronatum, *B. & G.*	218
6. rubrum, *Cope*	219
7. semicinctum, *D. & B*	219
8. fuscum, *Bocourt*	220
9. boulengeri, *Gthr.*	221
10. schistosum, *Bocourt*	221
11. canula, *Cope*	222
12. miniatum, *Cope*	222
13. virgatum, *Gthr.*	223
14. ruficeps, *Cope*	223
15. bocourti, *Gthr.*	224
16. reticulatum, *Cope*	224
17. mœstum, *Gthr*	225
18. vermiforme, *Hallow.*	225
19. breve, *Gthr.*	225
20 atriceps, *Gthr.*	226
21. planiceps, *Blainv.*	226

		Page
22.	calamarinum, *Cope*	227
23.	gracile, *B. & G.*	228
185.	Ogmius, *Cope*	228
1.	acutus, *Cope*	229
186.	Stenorhina, *D. & B.*	229
1.	degenhardtii, *Berth.*	229
187.	Xenopholis, *Ptrs.*	231
1.	scalaris, *Wuch.*	232
188.	Apostolepis, *Cope*	232
1.	coronata, *Sau.*	233
2.	assimilis, *Reinh.*	234
3.	flavitorquata, *D. & B*	234
4.	nigrolineata, *Ptrs.*	235
5.	quinquelineata, *Blgr.*	235
6.	nigroterminata, *Blgr.*	235
7.	dorbignyi, *Schleg*	236
8.	erythronota, *Ptrs.*	236
9.	ambinigra, *Ptrs*	237
189.	Elapomoius, *Jan*	237
1.	dimidiatus, *Jan*	238
190.	Elapomorphus, *D. & B.*	238
1.	blumii, *Schleg.*	239
2.	wuchereri, *Gthr.*	240
3.	lepidus, *Reinh.*	241
4.	tricolor, *D. & B.*	241
5.	lemniscatus, *D. & B.*	242
6.	trilineatus, *Blgr.*	243
7.	bilineatus, *D. & B.*	243
191.	Amblyodipsas, *Ptrs.*	244
1.	microphthalma, *Bianc.*	244
192.	Elapotinus, *Jan*	244
1.	picteti, *Jan*	245
193.	Calamelaps, *Gthr*	245
1.	unicolor, *Reinh.*	245
2.	polylepis, *Bocage*	246
3.	? concolor, *Smith*	246
194.	Rhinocalamus, *Gthr.*	247
1.	dimidiatus, *Gthr.*	247
195.	Xenocalamus, *Gthr.*	247
1.	bicolor, *Gthr.*	248
2.	mechovii, *Ptrs.*	248
196.	Micrelaps, *Bttgr.*	248
1.	muelleri, *Bttgr.*	249
2.	vaillanti, *Mocq.*	249
197.	Miodon, *A. Dum*	249
1.	acanthias, *Reinh.*	250
2.	collaris, *Ptrs.*	251
3.	gabonensis, *A. Dum.*	252
4.	notatus, *Ptrs*	252
5.	neuwiedi, *Jan*	253
198.	Polemon, *Jan*	253
1.	barthii, *Jan*	254
199.	Brachyophis, *Mocq.*	254
1.	revoili, *Mocq*	254
200.	Macrelaps, *Blgr.*	255
1.	microlepidotus, *Gthr.*	255, 512

		Page
201.	Aparallactus, *Smith*	255
1.	jacksonii, *Gthr.*	256, 649
2.	werneri, *Blgr*	257
3.	concolor, *Fisch.*	257
4.	lunulatus, *Ptrs.*	258
5.	guentheri, *Blgr*	259
6.	bocagii, *Blgr.*	259
7.	capensis, *Smith*	259
8.	nigriceps, *Ptrs.*	260
9.	punctatolineatus, *Blgr.*	261
10.	lineatus, *Ptrs*	261
11.	anomalus, *Blgr.*	262
202.	Elapops, *Gthr.*	262
1.	modestus, *Gthr.*	262, 649

Subfam. 6. ELACHISTODONTINÆ.

		Page
203.	Elachistodon, *Reinh.*	263
1.	westermanni, *Reinh.*	264

Series C. *Proteroglypha.*

Subfam. 7. HYDROPHIINÆ

		Page
204.	Hydrus, *Schn.*	266
× 1.	platurus, *L.*	267
205.	Thalassophis, *Schmidt*	268
1.	anomalus, *Schmidt*	269
206.	Acalyptophis, *Blgr*	269
1.	peronii, *D. & B.*	269
207.	Hydrelaps, *Blgr*	270
1.	darwiniensis, *Blgr.*	270
208.	Hydrophis, *Daud*	271
1.	spiralis, *Shaw*	273
2.	polyodontus, *Jan*	274
3.	schistosus, *Daud.*	274
4.	hybridus, *Schleg*	274
5.	longiceps, *Gthr*	275
6.	cærulescens, *Shaw*	275
7.	frontalis, *Jan*	276
8.	kingii, *Blgr.*	276
9.	nigrocinctus, *Daud*	277
10.	mamillaris, *Daud*	277
11.	elegans, *Gray*	278
12.	pacificus, *Blgr*	278
13.	latifasciatus, *Blgr*	279
14.	coronatus, *Gthr.*	279
15.	gracilis, *Shaw*	280
16.	cantoris, *Gthr.*	281
× 17.	fasciatus, *Schn.*	281
18.	brookii, *Gthr.*	282
19.	melanocephalus, *Gray.*	283
20.	torquatus, *Gthr.*	283
21.	obscurus, *Daud.*	284
22.	leptodira, *Blgr.*	285
209.	Distira, *Lacép.*	285
1.	stokesii, *Gray*	288

SYSTEMATIC INDEX.

	Page
2. major, *Shaw*	289
✗ 3. ornata, (*Gray*)	290
4. godeffroyi, *Ptrs*	291
5. melanosoma, *Gthr.*	291
6. semperi, *Garm.*	292
7. subcincta, *Gray*	292
8. brugmansii, *Boie*	292
9. tuberculata, *And.*	292
10. grandis, *Blgr*	293
11. macfarlani, *Blgr*	294
12. cyanocincta, *Daud*	294
13. bituberculata, *Ptrs.*	296
14. belcheri, *Gray*	296
15. pachycercus, *Fisch*	297
16. lapemidoides, *Gray*	297
17. viperina, *Schmidt*	298
18. jerdoni, *Gray*	299
210. Enhydris, *Merr*	300
1. curtus, *Shaw*	300
2. hardwickii, *Gray*	301
211. Enhydrina, *Gray*	302
⋏ 1. valakadien, *Boie*	302
212. Aipysurus, *Lacép.*	303
1. eydouxii, *Gray*	304
2. annulatus, *Krefft*	304
3. lævis, *Lacép*	305
4. australis, *Sauv.*	305
213. Platurus, *Daud*	306
1. laticaudatus, *L.*	307
✗ 2. colubrinus, (*Schn*)	308
3. schistorhynchus, *Gthr*	309
4. muelleri, *Blgr.*	309

Subfam. 8. ELAPINÆ

214. Ogmodon, *Ptrs*	312
1. vitianus, *Ptrs*	313
215. Glyphodon, *Gthr.*	313
1. tristis, *Gthr*	314
216. Pseudelaps, *D & B*	315
1. muelleri, *Schleg.*	316
2. squamulosus, *D. & B.*	317
3. krefftii, *Gthr.*	318
4. fordii, *Krefft*	318
✗ 5. harriettæ, *Krefft*	318
✗ 6. diadema, (*Schleg*)	319
7. warro, *De Vis*	320
8. sutherlandi, *De Vis.*	320
217. Diemenia, *Gray*	320
✗ 1. psammophis, *Schleg*	322
2. torquata, *Gthr.*	323
⋏ 3. olivacea, *Gray*	323
4. ornaticeps, *Macleay*	324
5. modesta, *Gthr.*	324
6. textilis, *D. & B.*	325
7. nuchalis, *Gthr*	326

	Page
218. Pseudechis, *Wagl.*	327
⋏ 1. porphyriacus, *Shaw*	328
2. cupreus, *Blgr*	329
3. australis, *Gray*	330
4. darwiniensis, *Macleay.*	330
5. papuanus, *Ptrs & Doria*	331
6. scutellatus, *Ptrs*	331
7. microlepidotus, *McCoy*	332
8. ferox, *Macleay*	332
219. Denisonia, *Krefft*	334
✗ 1. superba, *Gthr.*	335
2. coronata, *Schleg.*	335
3. coronoides, *Gthr.*	336
4. muelleri, *Fisch.*	337
5. frenata, *Ptrs.*	338
6. ramsayi, *Krefft*	338
✗ 7. signata, (*Jan*)	338
8. dæmelii, *Gthr*	339
9. suta, *Ptrs.*	339
10. frontalis, *D. Ogilby*	340
11. flagellum, *McCoy*	340
12. maculata, *Stdr.*	341
13. punctata, *Blgr.*	341
14. gouldii, *Gray*	342
✗ 15. nigrescens, *Gthr*	343
16. nigrostriata, *Krefft*	343
17. carpentariæ, *Macleay*	344
18. pallidiceps, *Gthr*	344
19. melanura, *Blgr.*	345
20. par, *Blgr*	345
21. woodfordii, *Blgr.*	346
220. Micropechis, *Blgr.*	346
1. ikaheka, *Less.*	347
2. elapoides, *Blgr.*	347
221. Hoplocephalus, *Cuv*	348
1. bungaroides, *Boie*	348
2. bitorquatus, *Jan*	349
3. stephensii, *Krefft*	350
222. Tropidechis, *Gthr.*	350
✗ 1. carinatus, *Krefft*	350
223. Notechis, *Blgr.*	351
✗ 1. scutatus, (*Ptrs.*)	351
224. Rhinhoplocephalus, *F. Mull*	353
1. bicolor, *F Mull.*	353
225. Brachyaspis, *Blgr.*	353
1. curta, *Schleg.*	353
226. Acanthophis, *Daud*	354
✗ 1. antarcticus, *Shaw*	355
227. Elapognathus, *Blgr.*	356
1. minor, *Gthr.*	356
228. Boulengerina, *Dollo*	357
1. stormsi, *Dollo*	357
229. Elapechis, *Blgr*	358
1. guentheri, *Bocage*	359
2. niger, *Gthr.*	359

SYSTEMATIC INDEX.

	Page
3. hessii, *Bttgr.*	360
4. decosteri, *Blgr.*	360
5. sundevallii, *Smith*	360
6. boulengeri, *Bttgr.*	361
230. Rhynchelaps, *Jan*	361
1. bertholdi, *Jan*	362
2. australis, *Krefft*	363
3. semifasciatus, *Gthr.*	363
4. fasciolatus, *Gthr.*	364
231. Bungarus, *Daud.*	365
×1 fasciatus, *(Schn.)*	366
× 2 ceylonicus, *Gthr.*	367
× 3. candidus, *(L.)*	368
4. lividus, *Cant.*	370
5. bungaroides, *Cant.*	370
6. flaviceps, *Reinh.*	371
232. Naia, *Laur*	372
1. haie, *L.*	374
2 flava, *Merr.*	376
3. melanoleuca, *Hallow*	376
4 nigricollis, *Reinh.*	378, 649
× 5. tripudians, *Merr*	380
6. samarensis, *Ptrs*	385
× 7. bungarus, *Schleg.*	386
8. anchietæ, *Bocage*	387
9. goldii, *Blgr.*	387
10. guentheri, *Blgr.*	388
233. Sepedon, *Merr.*	388
1. hæmachates, *Lacép*	389
234. Aspidelaps, *Smith*	390
1. lubricus, *Laur.*	390
2. scutatus, *Smith*	391
235 Walterinnesia, *Lataste*	392
1. ægyptia, *Lataste*	392
236. Hemibungarus, *Ptrs.*	392
1 calligaster, *Wiegm.*	393
2 collaris, *Schleg.*	393
3 nigrescens, *Gthr.*	394
4. japonicus, *Gthr.*	395
237. Callophis, *Gray*	396
1. gracilis, *Gray*	396
2. trimaculatus, *Daud.*	397
3. maculiceps, *Gthr.*	397
× 4 macclellandii, *(Reinh.)*	398
5 bibronii, *Jan*	399
238. Doliophis, *Gir.*	399
1. bivirgatus, *Boie*	400
× 2. intestinalis, *Laur.*	401
3 bilineatus, *Ptrs.*	404
4. philippinus, *Gthr.*	404
239. Furina, *D. & B.*	405
1. bimaculata, *D. & B.*	406
2. calonota, *D. & B*	407
×3. occipitalis, *(D. & B)*	407

	Page
240. Homorelaps, *Jan*	408
1. lacteus, *L.*	409
2 dorsalis, *Smith*	410
241. Elaps, *Schn*	411
1 surinamensis, *Cuv.*	414
2 heterochilus, *Mocq*	414
3. euryxanthus, *Kenn*	415
4. gravenhorstii, *Jan*	415
5 langsdorffii, *Wagl.*	416
6. buckleyi, *Blgr.*	416
7. anomalus, *Blgr.*	417
8 heterozonus, *Ptrs.*	417
9. elegans, *Jan*	418
10 annellatus, *Ptrs.*	418
11. decoratus, *Jan*	419
12. dumerilii, *Jan*	419
13. corallinus, *Wied*	420
14. hemprichii, *Jan*	421
15 tschudii, *Jan*	422
16. dissoleucus, *Cope*	422
× 17. fulvius, *L.*	422
18. psyches, *Daud.*	426
19. spixii, *Wagl.*	427
20 frontalis, *D. & B.*	427
21. marcgravii, *Wied*	428
22. lemniscatus, *L.*	430
23 filiformis, *Gthr.*	430
24. mipartitus, *D. & B.*	431
25. fraseri, *Blgr.*	432
26. mentalis, *Blgr.*	432
27 ancoralis, *Jan*	432
28 narduccii, *Jan*	433
242. Dendraspis, *Schleg.*	434
1. viridis, *Hallow.*	435
2 jamesonii, *Traill*	436
3 angusticeps, *Smith*	437
4 antinorii, *Ptrs.*	437

Fam. 8. AMBLYCEPHALIDÆ

	Page
1. Haplopeltura, *D. & B.*	439
1. boa, *Boie*	439
2. Amblycephalus, *Kuhl*	440
1 lævis, *Boie*	441
2. malaccanus, *Ptrs*	442
3. monticola, *Cant.*	443
4. moellendorffii, *Bttgr.*	443
5. andersonii, *Blgr.*	444
6 modestus, *Theob*	444
7 macularius, *Theob.*	444
8. margaritophorus, *Jan*	445
9 carinatus, *Boie*	445
3. Leptognathus, *D & B*	446
1. catesbyi, *Sentz*	449
2. pavonina, *Schleg.*	450

SYSTEMATIC INDEX.

	Page
3. variegata, *D. & B.*	451
4. albifrons, *Sauv.*	451
5. brevifacies, *Cope*	452
6 andiana, *Blgr.*	452
7. elegans, *Blgr*	452
8 leucomelas, *Blgr.*	453
9. mikani, *Schleg.*	453
10 ventrimaculata, *Blgr*	454
11. inæquifasciata, *D. & B*	455
12. turgida, *Cope*	456
13 alternans, *Fisch.*	456
14. viguieri, *Bocourt*	457
15 annulata, *Gthr*	457
16. articulata, *Cope*	458
17. incerta, *Jan*	458
18 argus, *Cope*	458
19. sanniola, *Cope*	459
20. dimidiata, *Gthr*	459
21. bicolor, *Gthr.*	460
4. Dipsas, *Laur.*	460
1 bucephala, *Shaw*	461
5 Pseudopareas, *Blgr*	462
1 vagus, *Jan*	462
2. atypicus, *Cope*	463

Fam. 9 VIPERIDÆ

Subfam 1 VIPERINÆ.

1. Causus, *Wagl.*	465
× 1 rhombeatus, *Licht*	467
2. resimus, *Ptrs.*	468
3 defilippii, *Jan*	469
4 lichtensteini, *Jan*	470
2 Azemiops, *Blgr*	470
1. feæ, *Blgr*	471
3 Vipera, *Laur.*	471
1. ursinii, *Bp.*	473
2. renardi, *Christ.*	475
× 3. berus, *L*	476
× 4 aspis, *L.*	481
× 5. latastii, *Boscá*	484
× 6. ammodytes, *L*	485
7. raddii, *Bttgr.*	487
8 lebetina, *L.*	487
× 9 russellii, *Shaw*	490
10 superciliaris, *Ptrs.*	491
4. Bitis, *Gray*	492
× 1 arietans, *Merr.*	493
2 peringueyi, *Blgr.*	495
× 3 atropos,(*L*)	495
4. inornata, *Smith*	496
5 cornuta, *L*	497
6 caudalis, *Smith*	498
7. gabonica, *D & B*	499
8. nasicornis, *Shaw*	500

	Page
5 Pseudocerastes, *Blgr*	501
1 persicus, *D. & B*	501
6. Cerastes, *Wagl.*	501
× 1 cornutus, *Forsk*	502
× 2 vipera, *L*	503
7 Echis, *Merr.*	504
γ 1. carinatus, (*Schn*)	505
2. coloratus, *Gthr.*	507
8. Atheris, *Cope*	508
1. chlorechis, *Schleg*	508
2. squamiger, *Hallow.*	509
3 ceratophorus, *Werner*	510
9. Atractaspis, *Smith*	510
1. hildebrandtii, *Ptrs*	512
2. congica, *Ptrs*	513
3. irregularis, *Reinh.*	513
4 corpulenta, *Hallow.*	514
5 rostrata, *Gthr*	514
6. bibronii, *Smith*	515
7. aterrima, *Gthr.*	515
8 dahomeyensis, *Bocage*	516
9. micropholis, *Gthr*	516
10 leucomelas, *Blgr*	517
11. microlepidota, *Gthr.*	517

Subfam 2 CROTALINÆ

10. Ancistrodon, *Pal de Beauv.*	519
× 1. piscivorus,(*Lacép*)	520
2 bilineatus, *Gthr.*	521
× 3 contortrix,(*L.*)	522
4. acutus, *Gth*	524
5 halys, *Pall.*	524
6. intermedius, *Strauch*	525
7. blomhoffii, *Boie*	525
× 8 himalayanus,(*Gthr*)	526
9. rhodostoma, *Boie*	527
10. hypnale, *Merr.*	528
11. Lachesis, *Daud.*	529
× 1. mutus, *L.*	534
2. lanceolatus, *Lacép.*	535
3. atrox, *L*	537
4. pulcher, *Ptrs*	539
5 microphthalmus, *Cope.*	540
6 pictus, *Tsch.*	540
7. alternatus, *D. & B*	541
8. neuwiedii, *Wagl.*	542
9. ammodytoides, *Leyb.*	543
10. xanthogrammus, *Cope*	543
11. castelnaudi, *D & B*	544
12. nummifer, *Rupp*	544
13. godmani, *Gthr.*	545
14 lansbergii, *Schleg*	546
15. brachystoma, *Cope*	547
×16. monticola, *Gthr.*	548
17. okinavensis, *Blgr*	549

VOL. III.

	Page		Page
18 strigatus, *Gray*	549	37. bicolor, *Bocourt*	566
19. flavoviridis, *Hallow.*	550	38 schlegelii, *Berth*	567
20. cantoris, *Blyth*	551	39 nigroviridis, *Ptrs.*	568
21 jerdonii, *Gthr.*	551	40. aurifer, *Salv.*	568
22. mucrosquamatus, *Cant.*	552	12. Sistrurus, *Garm.*	569
23. luteus, *Bttgr*	553	× 1. miliarius, (*L.*)	569
× 24. purpureomaculatus, (*Gray*)	553	× 2 catenatus, (*Raf*)	570
× 25 gramineus, *Shaw*	554	3. ravus, *Cope*	571
26. flavomaculatus, *Gray*	556	13 Crotalus, *L*	572
27. sumatranus, *Raffles*	557	× 1. terrificus, *Laur.*	573
28 anamallensis, *Gthr*	558	2. scutulatus, *Kenn.*	575
29. trigonocephalus, *Daud*	559	× 3 confluentus, *Say*	576
30. macrolepis, *Bedd*	560	× 4 durissus, *L.*	578
× 31. puniceus, *Boie*	560	✓5. horridus, *L.*	578
32. borneensis, *Ptrs.*	561	6. tigris, *Kenn*	580
× 33. wagleri, *Boie*	562	7. mitchelli, *Cope*	580
34. bilineatus, *Wied*	565	8. triseriatus, *Wagl*	581
35 undulatus, *Jan*	565	9 polystictus, *Cope*	582
36 lateralis, *Ptrs.*	566	10 lepidus, *Kenn.*	582
		11. cerastes, *Hallow.*	583

CATALOGUE OF SNAKES.

Fam. 7. COLUBRIDÆ.
(Continued.)

Series B. OPISTHOGLYPHA.

Divided into three subfamilies:—

4. *Homalopsinæ.*—Nostrils valvular, on the upper surface of the snout.
5. *Dipsadomorphinæ.*—Nostrils lateral; dentition well developed.
6. *Elachistodontinæ.*—Teeth rudimentary; maxillary and mandible edentulous in front.

Most, if not all, of the Snakes in this division are poisonous to a slight degree, paralyzing their prey before deglutition.

Subfam. 4. *HOMALOPSINÆ.*

Hydrophidæ, part, *Boie, Isis,* 1827, p 510
Hydridæ, part., *Gray, Cat. Sn.* p. 35, 1849.
Anisodontiens, part, Platyrhiniens, *Duméril, Mém Ac. Sc.* xxiii. p. 427, 1853; *Duméril & Bibron, Erp. Gén.* vii. p. 796, 1854.
Homalopsinæ, part., *Jan, Elenco sist Ofid.* p. 74, 1863.
Homalopsidæ, *Gunther, Rept. Brit. Ind.* p. 275, 1864.
Homalopsinæ, part., *Cope, Proc Amer. Philos. Soc.* xxiii. p. 484, 1886, and *Tr Amer. Philos Soc* xviii p. 209, 1895.
Homalopsinæ, *Boulenger, Faun. Ind., Rept.* p. 372, 1890.

Nostrils valvular, on the upper surface of the snout. Dentition well developed. Hypapophyses developed throughout the vertebral column.

Thoroughly aquatic Snakes, bringing forth their young alive in the water. Inhabitants of Southern China, the East Indies, Papuasia, and North Australia.

COLUBRIDÆ.

Synopsis of the Genera.

I. Ventrals without keels.

   A. Nasals in contact.

      1. Ventrals well developed.

Scales smooth; parietal shields well developed 125

Scales keeled; parietal shields well developed, not distinct from neck 125

Scales keeled; parietals more or less broken up, not very distinct from neck 126

      2. Ventrals very narrow; scales smooth.
                      127. Eurostus, p. 19.

   B. Nasals separated by an internasal.

Loreal present; scales keeled .... 128. Myron, p. 19.

Loreal present; scales smooth; body moderately elongate.   129 Gerardia, p. 20.

Loreal absent; scales smooth; body stout.   130. Fordonia, p. 21.

Loreal present; scales smooth; body extremely elongate.   131. Cantoria, p. 23.

II. Ventrals bicarinate, very narrow.

Scales smooth .... 132. Hipistes, p. 24.

Scales keeled; two rostral appendages.   133. Herpeton, p. 25.

124. HYPSIRHINA.

Hydrus, part., *Schneid Syst. Amph.* i. p 233 (1799).
Hypsirhina, *Wagl. Syst. Amph.* p. 169 (1830), *Gray, Zool. Misc.* p. 66 (1842), and *Cat. Sn.* p. 71 (1849), *Gunth Rept. Brit. Ind.* p. 280 (1864); *Bouleng. Faun. Ind., Rept.* p. 375 (1890).
Homalopsis, part, *Schleg. Phys Serp* ii. p. 332 (1837).
Ferania, *Gray, ll. cc* pp. 67, 68; *Gunth. l. c.* p. 284.
Raclitia, *Gray, ll. cc.* pp. 67, 79.
Miralia, *Gray, ll. cc.* pp. 68, 79.
Phytolopsis, *Gray, Cat.* p. 67.
Hypsiscopus, *Gray, l. c* p. 72
Trigonurus, *Dum. & Bibr. Mém. Ac. Sc.* xxiii. 1853, p. 498, and *Erp. Gén.* vii p. 959 (1854).
Hypsirhina, part, *Dum. & Bibr. ll. cc.* pp. 498, 945; *Jan, Arch. Zool. Anat Phys.* iii. 1865, p. 258.
Eurostus, part., *Dum. & Bibr. ll. cc.* pp. 498, 951.
Tachyplotus, *Reinh. Vidensk. Meddel.* 1860, p. 151.
Feranoides, *Carlleyle, Journ. As. Soc. Beng.* xxxviii. 1869, p. 196.
Pythonopsis, *Peters, Mon. Berl. Ac.* 1871, p. 576.
Homalophis, *Peters, l. c.* p. 577.
Pseudoferania, *Douglas Ogilby, Proc. Linn. Soc. N. S. W.* (2) v. 1890, p. 51.

Maxillary teeth 10 to 16, followed, after an interspace, by a pair of enlarged, grooved teeth; anterior mandibular teeth longest. Head small, not or but slightly distinct from neck; eye small, with round or vertically elliptic pupil; head-shields large; nasals in contact behind the rostral, semidivided, the cleft extending from the nostril to the first labial or the loreal; internasal single or divided; loreal present. Body cylindrical, scales smooth, without pits, in 19 to 31 rows; ventrals rounded. Tail moderate or short; subcaudals in two rows.

South-eastern Asia, Papuasia, Northern Queensland.

Synopsis of the Species.

I. Eye in contact with one, two, or three labials.

  A. Scales in 19 rows.

Two internasals; ventrals 173–175 ...... 1. *indica*, p. 4.
Two internasals; ventrals 125–152 ...... 2. *alternans*, p. 4.
A single internasal; ventrals 120–134 . 3. *plumbea*, p. 5.

  B. Scales in 21 or 23 rows.

    1. Four or five lower labials (on each side) in contact with the anterior chin-shields; only the fourth upper labial entering the eye.

      a. Loreal in contact with the internasal; scales in 21 (rarely 23) rows.

Ventrals 120–128; subcaudals 54–66 .... 4. *jagorii*, p. 6.
Ventrals 150–177; subcaudals 47–78 .... 5. *enhydris*, p. 6.

      b. Loreal not reaching the internasal.

Scales in 21 rows; ventrals 158–163; subcaudals 47–53 .... 6. *bennetti*, p. 8.
Scales in 23 rows; ventrals 143–151; subcaudals 40–49 .... 7. *chinensis*, p. 8.

    2. Three lower labials in contact with the anterior chin-shields.

Fourth and fifth or fourth, fifth, and sixth labials entering the eye; ventrals 147–152 .... 8. *macleayi*, p. 9.
Fifth or fifth and sixth labials entering the eye; ventrals 137–146 .... 9. *polylepis*, p. 9.

  C. Scales in 25 to 33 rows.

    1. A single internasal; ventrals 125–130.

Scales in 25 rows; internasal nearly as long as broad .... 10. *blanfordii*, p. 10.
Scales in 27 rows; internasal about twice as broad as long .... 11. *bocourtii*, p. 10.

2. Two internasals; ventrals 141–156.

Scales in 27 rows; rostral considerably broader than deep .... 12. *albomaculata*, p. 11.
Scales in 29 to 33 rows; rostral nearly as deep as broad .... 13. *sieboldii*, p. 11.

II. Eye separated from the labials.

Scales in 25 or 27 rows; a single internasal; a single pair of lower labials in contact behind the symphysial .... 14. *punctata*, p. 12.
Scales in 31 or 33 rows, two internasals; two pairs of lower labials in contact behind the symphysial .... 15. *doriæ*, p. 13.

1. Hypsirhina indica. (Plate I. fig. 1.)

Raclitia indica, *Gray, Zool. Misc.* p. 67 (1842), *and Cat.* p. 79 (1849)

Rostral broader than deep; internasals distinct; frontal as broad as or narrower than the supraocular (which appears to have fused with an upper postocular), little longer than broad, as long as its distance from the rostral or the end of the snout, shorter than the parietals, loreal longer than deep, in contact with the internasal; one præ- and one postocular; temporals 1+2; eight upper labials, fourth entering the eye; four lower labials in contact with the anterior chin-shields, which are longer than the posterior; the latter separated from each other by scales. Scales in 19 rows. Ventrals 173–175; anal divided; subcaudals 28–34. Dark purplish brown above, with a few interrupted, yellowish, transverse lines on the occiput and anterior part of the body; sides with yellowish (red?) vertical bars; belly yellowish (red?), spotted with black.

Total length 345 millim.; tail 40.

Malay Peninsula?

a, b. ♂ (V. 173; C. 34)   Malay Peninsula?   Gen. Hardwicke [P.].
 & ♀ (V. 175; C. 28).   (Types.)

2. Hypsirhina alternans.

Brachyorrhos alternans, *Reuss, Mus. Senckenb.* i p. 155, pl. ix. fig. 3 (1834).
Homalopsis decussata, *Schleg. Phys. Serp.* ii. p. 344, pl. xiii. figs. 14–16 (1837).
Miralia alternans, *Gray, Zool. Misc.* p. 68 (1842), *and Cat.* p 79 (1849); *Günth. Cat.* p. 277 (1858), *and Proc. Zool. Soc.* 1872, p. 590.
Eurostus alternans, *Dum. & Bibr.* vii. p. 957 (1854).
Hypsirhina alternans, *Jan, Elenco,* p. 78 (1863); *Arch. Zool. Anat. Phys.* iii. 1865, p. 262, *and Icon. Gén.* 30. pl. vi. figs. 1 & 2 (1868); *Boetty. Ber. Offenb. Ver. Nat.* 1892, p. 133.

Rostral broader than deep; internasals distinct; frontal broader than the supraocular, once and one third to once and a half as long as broad, as long as or longer than its distance from the end of the snout, shorter than the parietals; loreal as long as deep, in contact with the internasal; one præ- and one or two postoculars; temporals 1+2; eight upper labials, fourth entering the eye; four or five lower labials in contact with the anterior chin-shields, which are larger than the posterior; the latter separated from each other by scales. Scales in 19 rows. Ventrals 125-152; anal divided; subcaudals 24-36. Dark purplish brown above, usually with more or less distinct light (red?) cross-bars, the first on the occiput; yellowish (red?) beneath, with large alternating transverse black spots or with irregular black cross-bars.

Total length 465 millim.

Java, Borneo.

a. ♀ (V. 152; C.?).   Borneo.   Dr. Bleeker. (*Rabdosoma borneensis*, Blkr.)

b. Hgr. (V 135; C. 24).   Borneo.

3. Hypsirhina plumbea.

Homalopsis plumbea, *Boie, Isis,* 1827, p. 560; *Schleg Phys. Serp.* ii. p. 346, pl. xiii. figs. 12 & 13 (1837); *Cantor, Cat. Mal Rept* p. 101 (1847).

Hypsirhina hardwickii, *Gray, Ill. Ind. Zool.* ii pl lxxxvii. fig. 1 (1834), *and Cat.* p. 72 (1849).

Coluber plumbeus, *Eyd. & Gerv. in Guér. Mag. Zool.* Cl. iii. 1837, pl xvi. fig. 1.

Hypsirhina plumbea, *Gray, Zool. Misc.* p. 66 (1842), *Gunth. Rept. Brit. Ind.* p. 280 (1864), *Jan, Arch Zool. Anat Phys* iii. 1865, p. 261, *and Icon. Gén* 30. pl. v. fig 2 (1868): *Theob. Cat. Rept. Brit. Ind* p. 182 (1876); *Boettg. Ber Offenb Ver. Nat.* 1888, p 83. *Bouleng. Faun. Ind., Rept.* p 376, fig (1890)

Eurostus plumbeus, *Dum. & Bibr.* vii. p. 955, pl lxxxiv. fig. 2 (1854).

Rostral much broader than deep; internasal single, broader than long, frontal once and a half to once and two thirds as long as broad, as long as its distance from the end of the snout, shorter than the parietals; loreal as long as deep or deeper than long; one præ- and two postoculars; temporals 1+2; eight upper labials, fourth or fourth and fifth entering the eye; four or five lower labials in contact with the anterior chin-shields, which are larger than the posterior; latter separated by scales. Scales in 19 rows. Ventrals 120-134; anal divided; subcaudals 29-46. Brownish or greyish olive above, uniform or with a vertebral series of small black spots; upper lip and lower parts white, usually with a blackish line along the middle of the tail; belly sometimes with some blackish spots, or with a median series of blackish dots.

Total length 485 millim.; tail 65.

Burma, Southern China, Indo-China, Malay Peninsula and Archipelago.

a-b. ♂ (V. 128; C. 40)   Formosa.   R. Swinhoe, Esq. [C.].
& ♀ (V. 129; C. 33).

c. Yg (V. 129; C. 36).	Hong Kong.	J. C. Bowring, Esq. [P.].
d–e. ♂ (V. 132; C. 42) & ♀ (V. 126; C. 31).	Hoi How, Hainan.	J. Neumann, Esq. [P.].
f. ♂ (V. 131; C. 40).	China	Intern. Fisher. Exhib. 1883.
g. ♀ (V. 126; C. 33).	Pachebone, Siam.	M. Mouhot [C.].
h–i. ♂ (V. 127; C. 43) & ♀ (V. 121; C. 36).	Pinang.	Dr. Cantor.
k. ♀ (V. 125; C. 35).	Pinang.	Gen. Hardwicke [P.]. (Type of *H. hardwickii.*)
l. ♂ (V. 120; C. 37).	Borneo.	
m–o. Hgr. ♂ (V. 122; C. 45), ♀ (V. 122; C. 37), & yg. (V. 122, C. 43).	Labuan.	L. L. Dillwyn, Esq. [P.]
p. ♂ (V. 121; C. 39).	Java.	A. Scott, Esq. [P.].

4. Hypsirhina jagorii.

Hypsirhina (Eurostus) jagorii, *Peters, Mon. Berl. Ac.* 1863, p. 245.
—— jagorii, *Gunth. Rept. Brit. Ind.* p. 282 (1864).

Rostral nearly twice as broad as deep; internasal single, more than twice as broad as long; frontal broader than the supraocular, once and two thirds as long as broad, as long as its distance from the end of the snout, slightly shorter than the parietals; loreal as long as deep, in contact with the internasal; one præ- and two postoculars; temporals 1+2; eight upper labials, fourth entering the eye; four lower labials in contact with the anterior chin-shields; posterior chin-shields smaller and separated by scales. Scales in 21 rows. Ventrals 120–128; anal divided; subcaudals 54–66. Dark olive above, with small black spots; lower half of upper labials, sides of body, and ventrals yellowish white, with a grey band running along each side of the belly on the outer ends of the ventrals and the two outer rows of scales; subcaudals blackish, spotted with yellowish white.

Total length 510 millim.

Siam.

a. ♀ (V. 128; C.?).	Siam.	M. Mouhot [C.].
b. ♀ (V. 120; C.?).	Siam.	Sir R. Schomburgk [P.].
c. Hgr. (V. 122; C. 54).	Siam.	W. H. Newman, Esq. [P.].

5. Hypsirhina enhydris.

Russell, Ind. Serp. i. pl. xxx. (1796).
Hydrus enhydris, *Schneid. Hist. Amph.* i. p. 245 (1799).
—— atrocæruleus, *Shaw, Zool.* iii. p. 567 (1802).
Enhydris cærulea, *Latr. Rept.* iv. p. 202 (1802).
Coluber pythonissa, *Daud. Rept.* vii. p. 107 (1803).
Homalopsis aer, *Boie, Isis,* 1826, p. 214, and 1827, p. 560; *Schleg. Phys. Serp.* ii. p. 347, pl. xiii. figs. 10 & 11 (1837).
C[.] .[. .] a .. *Eyd. & Gerv. in Guer. Mag. Zool.* Cl. iii. 1837, pl. xvi. figs. 2 & 3.

124. HYPSIRHINA.

Homalopsis olivaceus, *Cantor, Proc. Zool Soc.* 1839, p. 55.
Hypsirhina trilineata, *Gray, Zool. Misc.* p. 66 (1842).
—— bilineata, *Gray, l. c., and Cat.* p. 73.
—— furcata, *Gray, ll cc.*
—— aer, *Gray, Cat.* p. 72.
Homalopsis enhydris, *Cantor, Cat. Mal. Rept.* p. 99 (1847).
Hypsirhina enhydris, *Dum. & Bibr.* vii. p. 946 (1854); *Gunth. Rept. Brit. Ind.* p. 281, pl xxii. fig. K (1864); *Jan, Arch Zool. Anat. Phys.* iii. 1865, p. 261, *and Icon Gén.* 30, pl iii fig 2, & v fig 1 (1868), *Theob. Cat Rept. Brit. Ind.* p. 183 (1876); *Bouleng. Faun. Ind, Rept.* p. 376 (1890).

Rostral twice as broad as deep; internasal single, nearly twice as broad as long; frontal nearly twice as long as broad, as long as or shorter than its distance from the end of the snout, as long as the parietals; loreal as long as deep or a little longer than deep, in contact with the internasal; one præ- and two (rarely one) postoculars; temporals 1+2; eight upper labials, fourth entering the eye; four lower labials in contact with the anterior chin-shields, which are shorter than the posterior; latter widely separated from each other. Scales in 21 rows, rarely 23 (specs. *a, c*). Ventrals 150–177; anal divided; subcaudals 47–78. Dark grey, brown, or olive above, with two more or less distinct light longitudinal bands; lower parts whitish, with a blackish line along each side of the ventrals, and usually a median blackish line or series of dots.

Total length 680 millim., tail 135.

Bengal, Southern India, Ceylon, Burma, Southern China, Cochinchina, Siam, Malay Peninsula and Archipelago.

A. A dark median ventral line. (*H. enhydris*, Schn.; *H. trilineata*, Gray.)

a. ♀ (V. 155; C. ?).	India.	(Type of *H trilineata*.)
b, c ♂ (V. 157, 157; C. 67, 64).	India.	W. Masters, Esq. [P.].
d–e. Yg. (V. 162, 158; C. 66, 67).	Bengal (?).	Dr. Cantor.
f. ♀ (V. 163; C 60).	Darjeeling (?).	T. C. Jerdon, Esq. [P.].
g. ♀ (V. 169; C 71).	Siam.	
h–r. Yg. (V. 170, 168, 172, 170, 177, 166, 168, 166, 171, 164, C. 78, 75, 74, 74, 72, 63, 62, 64, 63, 64)	Siam	Sir R. Schomburgk [P.].
s–t. ♂ (V. 158, C. 64) & ♀ (V. 157; C. 53).	Pinang.	Dr Cantor.
u. Hgr. ♀ (V. 163; C. 69).	Singapore.	R. Swinhoe, Esq. [C.].
v. ♀ (V. 159; C. 63).	Borneo.	Leyden Museum.

B. Median ventral line absent or reduced to a few widely separated dots. (*H. bilineata*, Gray; *H. furcata*, Gray.)

a. ♂ (V. 161; C. 63).	China.	W. Lindsay, Esq. [P.]. (Type of *H. bilineata*.)

b. Hgr. ♀ (V. 155; C. 47).		Hong Kong.	J C. Bowring, Esq. [P].
c–d. Yg. (V. 155, 153; C. 48, 47).		India.	(Types of *H. furcata*.)
e. ♀ (V. 151; C. ?).		—— ?	Zoological Society.

6. Hypsirhina bennetti.

Hypsirhina bennettii, *Gray, Zool. Misc.* p. 67 (1842), *and Cat.* p 74 (1849); *Gunth. Rept. Brit. Ind.* p. 283 (1864).
—— maculata, *Dum. & Bibr.* vii. p. 950 (1854)
—— enhydris, var. maculata, *Jan, Arch. Zool Anat Phys.* iii. 1865, p. 261, *and Icon. Gén.* 30, pl. iv. fig. 1 (1868).

Rostral broader than deep; internasal single, small, not or but little broader than long; frontal broader than the supraocular, once and a half to once and two thirds as long as broad, as long as or a little longer than its distance from the end of the snout, as long as or a little shorter than the parietals; loreal as long as deep; one præ- and two postoculars; temporals 1+2; eight upper labials, fourth entering the eye; four lower labials in contact with the anterior chin-shields; posterior chin-shields smaller and separated by scales[*]. Scales in 21 rows. Ventrals 158–163; anal divided; subcaudals 47–53. Greyish olive above, with large blackish spots, which may form an interrupted zigzag band along the back; upper lip, sides (three or four rows of scales), and lower parts yellowish white; outer row of scales, ventrals, and subcaudals black-edged; a median row of small black spots on the belly.

Total length 530 millim.; tail 95.

China.

a. ♂ (V. 163; C. ?).		China.	G Bennett, Esq. [P]. (Type.)
b. ♂ (V. 161; C. 53).		China.	J. S. Bowerbank, Esq. [P].

7. Hypsirhina chinensis. (PLATE I. fig. 2.)

Hypsirhina chinensis, *Gray, Zool. Misc.* p. 73 (1842), *and Cat.* p. 73 (1849); *Gunth. Rept. Brit Ind.* p. 283 (1864); *Boettg. Ber. Offenb. Ver Nat* 1885, p. 123.

Rostral broader than deep; internasal single, small, broader than long; frontal broader than the supraocular, once and two thirds to twice as long as broad, as long as its distance from the rostral or the end of the snout, a little shorter than the parietals; loreal as long as deep; one præ- and two postoculars; temporals 1+2; eight upper labials, fourth entering the eye; four (rarely five) lower labials in contact with the anterior chin-shields; posterior chin-shields smaller and separated by scales. Scales in 23 rows. Ventrals 143–151; anal divided; subcaudals 40–49. Dark grey or olive above, with small darker spots which may be confluent into

---
[*] Jan represents them as in contact.

three streaks on the occiput and nape; second and third rows of scales yellowish white; ventrals, subcaudals, and outer row of scales dark grey or olive anteriorly, yellowish white posteriorly.

Total length 520 millim.; tail 70.

China; Siam*.

a. ♂ (V. 150, C. 46).	China	J R Reeves, Esq. [P.]. (Type.)
b. ♀ (V. 143; C. 41).	China.	Intern. Fisher. Exhib. 1883.
c. Hgr. ♂ (V. 148; C. 46).	China.	A. Adams, Esq. [C.].
d. ♂ (V. 150; C. 49).	Ichang.	R Swinhoe, Esq [C.]
e. ♂ (V 151; C. 47).	Hoi How, Hainan.	J. Neumann, Esq. [P.].

8. Hypsirhina macleayi.

Pseudoferania macleayi, *Douglas Ogilby, Proc. Linn. Soc. N. S. W.* (2) v. 1890, p 51.

Rostral nearly twice as broad as deep; internasal single or divided, nearly twice as broad as long; frontal a little broader than the supraocular, nearly twice as long as broad, as long as its distance from the end of the snout, a little shorter than the parietals; loreal triangular, longer than deep, in contact with or narrowly separated from the internasal; one or two præ- and one or two postoculars; temporals 1+2; eight or nine upper labials, fourth and fifth, or fourth, fifth, and sixth entering the eye; three lower labials in contact with the anterior chin-shields, which separate the posterior. Scales in 21 or 23 rows. Ventrals 147–152; anal divided; subcaudals 38–47. Grey or brown above, with small black spots, which may be confluent into two streaks on the neck; a blackish stripe on each side of the head, body, and tail, passing through the eye; upper lip, two or three lower rows of scales, and lower parts yellowish white; a blackish streak on each side of the belly, between the ventrals and the first row of scales, and a broad black stripe along the lower surface of the tail.

Total length 635 millim.; tail 105.

Herbert River District, Queensland.

a-c ♂ (Sc. 23; V. 151; C. 43) & yg. (Sc. 23, V. 152, 150, C 47, 39).   Herbert R.   J. A. Boyd, Esq. [P.].

9. Hypsirhina polylepis.

Hypsirhina polylepis, *Fischer, Abh. Nat. Ges. Hamb.* ix. 1886, p. 14.

Rostral broader than deep; internasal single or divided, twice as broad as long; frontal broader than the supraocular, twice as long as broad, slightly longer than its distance from the end of the

---

* I have examined a specimen from Bangkok preserved in the Christiania Museum.

snout, as long as or a little shorter than the parietals; one or two præ- and two postoculars; temporals 1+2 or 1+3; eight upper labials, fifth or fifth and sixth entering the eye; three lower labials in contact with the anterior chin-shields, which separate the posterior. Scales in 21 or 23 rows. Ventrals 137–146; anal divided; subcaudals 39–40. Dark olive or blackish above and on the sides, with a yellowish lateral streak along the second row of scales; belly brown, spotted with yellowish, or with a yellowish spot at the outer end of each ventral shield; tail dark, with a yellowish spot on each subcaudal shield.

Total length 710 millim.; tail 110.

New Guinea.

a, b-c. ♀ (Sc 23; V. 143,   Fly River.   Rev. S. Macfarlane [C.].
C. 40) & hgr. (Sc. 21;
V. 137, 143; C. 39, 40).

10. Hypsirhina blanfordii.

Hypsirhina maculata (non D. & B), *Blanf. Journ. As. Soc. Beng.* xlviii. 1879, p. 130.
—— maculosa, *Blanf. Proc. Zool. Soc.* 1881, p. 226
—— blanfordi, *Bouleng. Faun. Ind., Rept.* p. 377 (1890).

Head short, with broad, square, truncated snout; internasal single, nearly as long as broad; frontal fully twice as long as broad, a little shorter than the parietals; one præ- and two postoculars; temporals 1+2; eight upper labials, fourth entering the eye; only one pair of large chin-shields, the posterior pair scarcely exceeding the adjoining scales in size. Scales in 25 rows. Ventrals 125; anal divided; subcaudals 45. Colour blackish ashy, with a row of large irregular-shaped black spots along the back and another rather less in size, but each spot including several scales, along each side; a blackish band along the margins of the ventrals, caused by the dark edges of the shields and of the first row of scales on each side.

Total length 300 millim.; tail 45

Pegu.

11. Hypsirhina bocourtii.

Hypsirhina bocourti, *Jan, Arch. Zool. Anat. Phys.* iii. 1865, p. 258, and *Icon. Gén.* 28, pl v. fig. 2 (1868).
Ferania sieboldii (non Schleg.), *Gunth. Ann. & Mag N. H.* (3) xviii. 1866, p. 28.
? Hypsirhina multilineata, *Tirant, Notes Rept. Cochinch.* p. 41 (1885).

Rostral broader than deep; a single internasal, about twice as broad as long, frontal narrow, narrower than the supraocular, at least twice as long as broad, as long as its distance from the end of the snout, a little shorter than the parietals; loreal a little longer than deep; one præ- and two postoculars; temporals 1+2; eight upper labials, fourth entering the eye; four or five lower labials in contact with the anterior chin-shields, which are very large; posterior chin-shields very small and separated by scales. Scales in 27 rows. Ventrals 126-130; anal divided; subcaudals 40-48. Pale olive-brown above, with blackish cross-bands separated by narrow interspaces; these cross-bands with roundish spots of the ground-colour in the middle, tapering to vertical bars on the sides of the body, and forming complete or interrupted rings across the belly; upper lip, sides, and belly yellow, the labial shields black-edged.

Total length 1120 millim.; tail 150.

Siam.

a. ♀ (V. 126; C. 40). Siam. Sir R. Schomburgk [P.].

12. Hypsirhina albomaculata.

Homalopsis albomaculatus, *Dum. & Bibr.* vii. p. 974 (1854).
Hypsirhina albomaculata, *Jan, Elenco*, p. 77 (1863), *Arch. Zool. Anat. Phys.* iii. 1865, p. 259, and *Icon. Gén.* 28, pl. v. fig. 1 (1868).

Rostral broader than deep; two internasals; each præfrontal usually longitudinally divided; frontal broader than the supraocular, once and a half to once and two thirds as long as broad, as long as its distance from the end of the snout, as long as or a little shorter than the parietals; loreal a little longer than deep; one præ- and one or two postoculars; temporals 1+2 or 3; nine upper labials, fifth (exceptionally fourth) entering the eye; five or six lower labials in contact with the anterior chin-shields; posterior chin-shields small and separated by scales. Scales in 27 rows. Ventrals 140-150; anal divided; subcaudals 37-48. Dark olive-brown above, with small yellowish or orange spots, one or two more or less distinct yellow cross-bars on the nape, sides and lower parts yellowish or orange, spotted with black.

Total length 500 millim.; tail 60.

Sumatra.

a-c. ♂ (V. 143; C. 47) & ♀ (V. 146, 141; C. 37, 38). Pulo Nias. Hr Sundermann [C.].

13. Hypsirhina sieboldii.

Homalopsis sieboldii, *Schleg. Phys. Serp.* ii. p. 349, pl. xiii. figs. 4 & 5 (1837); *Cantor, Cat. Mal. Rept.* p. 98 (1847).
Ferania sieboldii, *Gray, Zool. Misc.* p. 67 (1842), and *Cat.* p. 66 (1849); *Gunth. Rept Brit. Ind.* p. 284 (1864), *Anders. Proc Zool. Soc.* 1871, p. 180; *Theob Cat. Rept. Brit. Ind.* p 184 (1876), *Murray, Journ. Bomb. Soc* i. 1886, p. 219.
Trigonurus sieboldii, *Dum. & Bibr.* vii. p 960 (1854).
Hypsirhina sieboldii, *Jan, Elenco*, p. 78 (1863), *Arch. Zool. Anat Phys*, iii. 1865, p. 260, and *Icon Gén.* 30, pl iv. fig. 2 (1868), *Bouleng. Faun. Ind., Rept*, p. 377 (1890); *W. Sclater, Journ. As. Soc. Beng*. lx. 1891, p. 245.
Feranoides jamnæticus, *Carlleyle, Journ. As. Soc Beng*. xxxviii. 1869, p. 196.

Rostral nearly as deep as broad; two internasals; frontal broader than the supraocular, as long as its distance from the end of the snout, as long as the parietals; loreal as long as deep or a little deeper than long; one præocular, sometimes with a small subocular below it, two postoculars; temporals small, 1+2; seven or eight upper labials, fourth entering the eye; four lower labials in contact with the anterior chin-shields; posterior chin-shields very small. Scales in 29 to 33 rows. Ventrals 147-156; anal divided; subcaudals 48-56. Whitish or pale brown above, with dark brown black-edged elliptical or rhomboidal transverse spots broader than their interspaces; a series of round spots on each side, alternating with the dorsal spots; head with three dark brown longitudinal bands, confluent between the eyes; lower parts white, checkered with black.

Total length 365 millim.; tail 67. Grows to 600 millim.

India, Burma, Malay Peninsula.

a. Yg (Sc 33, V. 156; C. 56).   Bombay.   Dr. Gunther [P.].
b. Yg. (Sc. 29; V. 147; C. 50).   Pinang.   Dr. Cantor.
c. Hgr. ♂ (Sc. 29; V. 147, C. 51).   ——?

14. Hypsirhina punctata.

Phytolopsis punctata, *Gray, Cat.* p. 68 (1849).
Eurostus heteraspis, *Bleek. Nat. Tydschr. Nederl. Ind.* xvi 1859, p. 440.
Tachyplotus hedemanni, *Reinh. Vidensk. Meddel.* 1866, p. 151, fig.
Pythonopsis borneensis, *Peters, Mon. Berl. Ac.* 1871, p. 576.
—— punctata, *Peters, Ann. Mus. Genova,* iii. 1872, p. 37; *Günth. Proc. Zool. Soc* 1872, p. 590.
Homalophis doriæ, var., *Steind. Sitzb. Ak. Wien,* xcvi. i. 1887, p 71
Hypsirhina hageni, *v. Lidth de Jeude, Notes Leyd. Mus.* xii 1890, p. 20, pl. i.

Rostral slightly broader than deep; a single small internasal; frontal not broader than the supraocular, at least twice as long as broad, as long as its distance from the end of the snout, as long as or a little shorter than the parietals; one or two loreals; one præ- and two postoculars; temporals small, scale-like; twelve to fourteen upper labials, the four or five first deep and narrow, the following divided into small shields between the labials proper and the eye and temporal shields, five or six lower labials in contact with the anterior chin-shields, which are very large; posterior chin-shields small and separated by scales. Scales in 25 or 27 rows. Ventrals 135-156; anal divided; subcaudals 28-41. Dark olive-brown above, uniform or with small yellow spots, which may form cross-bars: one or two yellow cross-bars on the nape: a yellow transverse spot between the eyes; yellow beneath.

Total length 370 millim.; tail 40.
Sumatra, Borneo.

a. ♀ (Sc. 25; V. 135; C. 28). ——? (Type.)
b. Hgr (Sc. 25; V. 156; C. 39). Sinkawang, Borneo Dr. Bleeker. (Type of *Eurostus heteraspis*.)

15. Hypsirhina doriæ.

Homalophis doriæ, *Peters, Mon. Berl. Ac.* 1871, p. 577, *and Ann. Mus Genova,* iii. 1872, p. 38, pl. v. fig. 2.

Rostral as deep as broad; two internasals; frontal once and a half as long as broad, shorter than its distance from the end of the snout, as long as or a little shorter than the parietals; supraocular divided into two or three small shields; two loreals, deeper than long; one præ-, two or three post-, and two or three suboculars; temporals small, scale-like; fifteen upper labials, the five or six first deep and narrow, the following mostly transversely divided; a pair of large chin-shields, separated from the symphysial by the first and second pairs of lower labials. Scales in 31 or 33 rows. Ventrals 141, anal divided; subcaudals 45. Olive-brown above; bright yellow beneath, uniform or spotted or dotted with blackish.

Total length 800 millim.; tail 120. The specimen in the Collection (tail injured) measures 450 millim. from snout to vent.
Borneo.

a. ♀ (Sc. 33; V 141; C. ?). Sarawak. A. Everett, Esq [C.].

125. HOMALOPSIS.

Homalopsis, *Kuhl, Isis,* 1822, p 474; *Gray, Zool. Misc.* p 64 (1842), *and Cat. Sn.* p 66 (1849), *Gunth Rept. Brit Ind* p. 285 (1864); *Bouleng Faun. Ind., Rept.* p. 373 (1890).
Homalopsis, part., *Schleg Phys. Serp.* ii. p. 332 (1837), *Dum. & Bibr. Erp. Gén.* vii. p. 967, *Jan, Arch Zool. Anat. Phys.* in 1865, p. 256.
Pythonia, *Blyth, Journ. As. Soc. Beng* xxviii. 1859, p 297.

Maxillary teeth 11 to 13, decreasing in length posteriorly, followed, after an interspace, by a pair of slightly enlarged, grooved teeth; anterior mandibular teeth much longer than the posterior. Head distinct from neck; eye small, with vertically elliptic pupil; head-shields large; nasals in contact behind the rostral, semidivided, the cleft extending from the nostril to the first labial; internasal single or divided; loreal present. Body cylindrical; scales distinctly striated and keeled, without pits, in 37 to 47 rows, ventrals well developed, not keeled. Tail moderate; subcaudals in two rows.

South-eastern Asia.

Fig. 1.

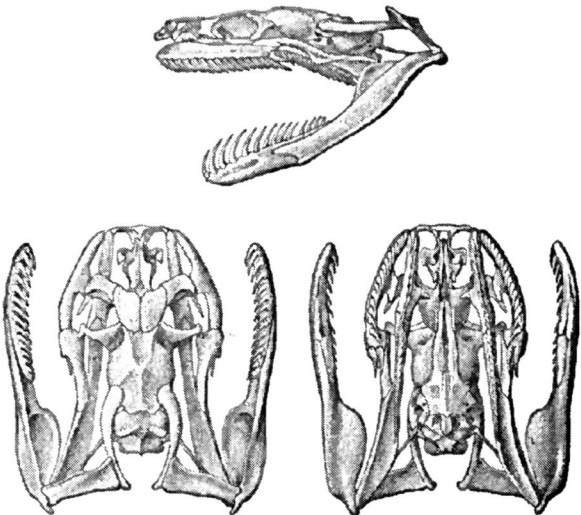

Skull of *Homalopsis buccata*.

1. Homalopsis buccata.

Merr. Beitr. ii, p. 36, pl. x. (1790); *Russell, Ind. Serp.* ii. pl. xxxiii. (1801).
Coluber buccatus, *Linn. Mus. Ad. Frid.* p. 29, pl. xix. fig. 3 (1754), and *S. N.* i. p. 377 (1766).
—— subalbidus, *Gmel. S. N.* i. p. 1103 (1788).
Vipera buccata, *Daud. Rept.* vi. p. 220 (1803).
Coluber monilis, part., *Daud. op. cit.* vii. p. 59 (1803).
—— horridus, *Daud. l. c.* p. 71.
Homalopsis molurus, *Kuhl, Isis*, 1826, p. 213.
—— monilis, *Boie, Isis*, 1827, p. 521.
—— buccata, *Schleg. Phys. Serp.* ii. p. 337, pl. xiii. figs. 1-3 (1837); *Cantor, Cat. Mal. Rept.* p. 96 (1847); *Gray, Cat.* p. 67 (1849); *Dum. & Bibr.* vii. p. 968 (1854); *Günth. Rep. Brit. Ind.* p. 285 (1864); *Jan, Arch. Zool. Anat. Phys.* iii. 1865, p. 256; *Theob. Cat. Rept. Brit. Ind.* p. 185 (1876); *Bouleng. Faun. Ind., Rept.* p. 374, fig. (1890).
—— hardwickii, *Gray, Zool. Misc.* p. 65 (1842), and *Cat.* p. 67.
—— semizonata, *Blyth, Journ. As. Soc. Beng.* xxiv. 1855, p. 187.
Pythonia semizonata, *Blyth, op. cit.* xxviii. 1859, p. 297.

Frontal often broken up into several shields, not much broader, sometimes even narrower than the supraocular; parietals short; loreal sometimes divided into two: one or two præ- and two post-oculars: one to three suboculars sometimes present: temporals small, scale-like; ten to twelve upper labials, fifth or sixth entering the eye or narrowly separated from it by suboculars; two or three pairs of chin-shields in a transverse row, inner in contact with the three first lower labials. Scales in 37 to 47 rows. Ventrals 160–171; anal divided; subcaudals 70–90. Above with broad transverse dark brown, black-edged cross-bands separated by narrow pale brown interspaces, which are whitish in the young; head pale, with a triangular or V-shaped dark brown mark on the snout, a Λ-shaped mark on the vertex, and a dark brown band on each side, beginning in front of and passing through the eye; belly whitish, with a series of dark brown spots along each side; tail brown-spotted inferiorly.

Total length 1050 millim.; tail 230.

Bengal (?), Burma, Indo-China, Malay Peninsula, Sumatra, Borneo. Java.

a. ♂ (Sc. 41, V. 164, C. 83).	India (?).	Gen Hardwicke [P.]. (Type of *H hardwickii*)
b, c, d Yg (Sc 37, 41, 41 V 162, 160, 160; C. 82, 85, 78).	Bengal (?).	Gen. Hardwicke [P.].
e. ♀ (Sc. 47; V. 169; C ?).	Camboja.	M Mouhot [C.].
f–h. ♂ (Sc. 41; V. 168, C. 88) & yg. (Sc. 39, 40, V. 163, 164; C. 90, 86).	Pinang.	Dr. Cantor.
i–l. Yg (Sc 41, 39, 37; V. 165, 167, 161; C 85, 85, 76).	Singapore.	Dr Dennys [P.].
m. ♂ (Sc 40, V 168; C. 77).	Labuan.	L. L. Dillwyn, Esq [P.].
n ♀ (Sc. 37; V. 160; C 71).	Java.	Leyden Mus
o. Yg. (Sc. 39, V. 162; C.81).	Batavia.	
p–q. ♀ (Sc. 45; V. 167; C. 85) & yg. (Sc. 45, V. 170; C. 86).	——?	Haslar Collection.
r. Skull.	Malacca.	

126. CERBERUS.

Hydrus, part., *Schneid. Syst Amph.* i. p. 233 (1799).
Cerberus, *Cuv. Règne Anim* 2nd ed. ii. p. 81 (1829); *Gray, Zool Misc.* p. 64 (1842), and *Cat. Sn.* p. 63 (1849); *Dum. & Bibr. Erp. Gén.* vii. p. 977 (1854); *Günth Rept Brit. Ind.* p. 278 (1864); *Bouleng Faun Ind , Rept.* p 374 (1890).
Homalopsis, part., *Schleg. Phys Serp.* ii. p. 332 (1837), *Jan, Arch. Zool. Anat. Phys.* iii. 1865, p. 256.

Maxillary teeth 12 to 17, followed, after a very short interspace, by two slightly enlarged, grooved teeth; anterior mandibular teeth longest. Head small, not very distinct from neck; eye small, with vertically elliptic pupil; snout covered with shields; parietal shields more or less broken up into scales; nasals in contact behind the rostral, semidivided, the cleft extending from the nostril to the first or second labial; two internasals (rarely united); loreal present. Body cylindrical; scales striated and keeled, without pits, in 23 to 29 rows; ventrals rounded. Tail moderate, slightly compressed, subcaudals in two rows

South-eastern Asia; North Australia.

Synopsis of the Species.

Four lower labials in contact with the anterior chin-shields; scales very strongly keeled, in 23 to 27 rows; ventrals 132-160 ...... 1. *rhynchops*, p. 16.
Three lower labials in contact with the anterior chin-shields; scales moderately keeled, in 25 rows; ventrals 148-149. .... 2. *australis*, p. 18.
Three (rarely four) labials in contact with the anterior chin-shields; scales rather feebly keeled, in 29 rows; ventrals 163-165 3. *microlepis*, p. 18.

1. Cerberus rhynchops.

Russell, Ind. Serp i. pl. xvii. (1796), and ii. pl. xl. (1801).
Hydrus rhynchops, *Schneid. Hist. Amph.* i. p. 246 (1799)
Elaps boæformis, *Schneid. op. cit.* ii p. 301 (1801).
Hydrus cinereus, *Shaw, Zool.* iii p 567 (1802).
Hurria schneideriana, *Daud. Rept.* v. p. 281 (1803).
Coluber cerberus, *Daud op. cit.* vii. p. 167 (1803).
Python rhynchops, *Merr. Tent.* p. 90 (1820).
Homalopsis cerberus, *Fitzing. N Class. Rept.* p. 55 (1826).
—— molurus, *Boie, Isis,* 1826, p. 213.
—— schneideri, *Schleg. Phys. Serp.* ii. p. 341, pl. xiii. figs. 6 & 7 (1837).
Cerberus cinereus, *Cantor, Proc. Zool. Soc.* 1839, p. 54; *Gray, Cat.* p 64 (1849).
Homalopsis rhynchops, *Cantor, Cat. Mal. Rept.* p. 94 (1847).
Cerberus cinereus, part., *Gray, Cat.* p. 64.
—— acutus, *Gray, l. c.* p. 65.
—— unicolor, *Gray, l. c.*
—— boæformis, *Dum. & Bibr.* vii. p. 978 (1854).
Homalopsis boæformis, *Jan, Elenco,* p. 77 (1863), and *Arch. Zool. Anat. Phys.* iii. 1865, p. 257
Cerberus rhynchops, *Gunth. Rept. Brit. Ind.* p. 279 (1864), *Anders. Proc. Zool. Soc.* 1871, p. 179; *Theob. Cat. Rept. Brit. Ind.* p. 185 (1876); *Murray, Zool. Sind,* p. 381 (1884); *Bouleng. Faun. Ind, Rept.* p. 374 (1890).

Rostral nearly as deep as broad; frontal shield distinct or broken up into small shields; loreal usually in contact with the three or four anterior labials and with the internasal, nasal cleft extending to the first upper labial, rarely to the second, eye between four to six shields, viz. a supraocular, a præocular, one or two postoculars, and one, two, or three suboculars; nine or ten upper labials, posterior transversely divided; four lower labials in contact with the anterior chin-shields; posterior chin-shields smaller and wedged in between the anterior and the labials. Scales very strongly keeled, in 23 or

25 (rarely 27 *) rows. Ventrals 132–160, anal divided; subcaudals 49–72. Grey, brown, olive, or blackish above, with more or less distinct black spots or cross-bars; a black streak on each side of the head, passing through the eye, a more or less distinct white or yellow lateral band; beneath whitish or yellowish, spotted or barred with black, or almost entirely black.

Total length 980 millim.; tail 180.

India and Ceylon, Burma, Indo-China, Malay Peninsula and Archipelago, Pelew Islands.

a.	♀ (Sc. 25; V. 145; C. 57)	Ganjam.	F. Day, Esq. [P.].
b.	♀ (Sc. 25; V. 147; C. 56).	Cocanada.	W. T. Blanford, Esq [P.].
c, d, e.	♂ (Sc. 23, 25, V. 145, 146; C. 64, 62) & yg. (Sc. 25, V. 146, C. 63).	Madras.	T. C. Jerdon, Esq. [P.].
f.	♂ (Sc. 25, V. 147; C. 66).	Nilgherries.	W. Theobald, Esq [P.].
g.	♂ (Sc. 25; V. 145; C. 67)	Malabar	Col Beddome [C.].
h.	♂ (Sc. 25; V. 142; C. 64).	India.	Dr. P. Russell.
i, k–m.	♀ (Sc. 25; V. 145; C. 56) & yg (Sc 23, 25, 25; V 146, 143, 146; C 62, 60, 60)	India.	Gen. Hardwicke [P.].
n	♀ (Sc. 25; V. 147; C 57).	India.	College of Surgeons.
o.	♀ (Sc. 25; V 137, C. 53).	Ceylon.	Messrs. v. Schlagintweit [C.].
p	Hgr. (Sc. 25; V.139; C. 55).	Ceylon.	R Templeton, Esq [P.].
q–r.	♂ (Sc. 23, V. 149, C. 58) & yg. (Sc. 23; V 147, C. 56)	Pinang.	Dr. Cantor.
s.	Yg. (Sc. 23; V. 148; C. 67)	Pinang (?).	Dr Cantor.
t–u.	♂ (Sc 23, V. 141, 144; C. 55, 59)	Singapore.	Dr. Dennys [P.].
v.	♂ (Sc. 23; V. 152, C. 58).	Deli, Sumatra.	Mr. Iversen [C].
w	♀ (Sc. 23; V. 125; C. 56).	Engano.	Dr. Modigliani [C.].
x	♂ (Sc. 23, V 145; C 63).	Borneo	Leyden Museum. (Type of *C acutus*.)
y.	Yg. (Sc. 23; V. 150, C. 63).	Borneo.	
z.	♀ (Sc. 25; V. 144, C. 53).	Sarawak.	Sir J. Brooke [P.].

---

* I have examined a specimen from Trevandrum, preserved in the Travancore Museum, with 27 rows of scales.

a, β. ♂ (Sc. 23; V. 154; C. 65) & ♀g. (Sc. 23; V. 155, C. 66).	Labuan.	L. L. Dillwyn, Esq. [P.].
γ. ♀ (Sc. 23; V. 153; C. 60).	Palawan.	A. Everett, Esq [C.].
$\delta-\epsilon$. ♂ (Sc. 23; V. 160; C. 69) & ♀ (Sc. 25; V. 158, C. ?).	Placer, Mindanao.	A. Everett, Esq. [C.]
ζ. ♀ (Sc. 25; V. 151; C. 58).	Negros.	Dr. A B. Meyer [C.].
η. ♂ (Sc. 23; V. 157; C.?).	Philippines.	H. Cuming, Esq. [C.] (Type of *C. unicolor*.)
θ, ι. ♀ (Sc. 25, 23; V. 151, 150; C. 55, 52).	Philippines.	Messrs. Veitch [P.].
κ. ♂ (Sc. 23; V. 153; C. 66).	Java.	G. Lyon, Esq. [P.]
λ ♂ (Sc. 23; V. 151; C. 64).	Batavia.	
μ. ♀ (Sc. 25; V 150; C. 55).	Manado, Celebes	Dr. A. B. Meyer [C].
$\nu-\xi$. ♀ (Sc. 23; V. 145, 145; C. 52, 50).	N. Ceram.	
$o-\rho$. ♂ (Sc. 23; V. 151; C. 61) & ♀ (Sc. 23; V. 147, 147; C. 52, 53).	Pelew Ids.	G L. King, Esq. [P.].
σ. Skeleton.	Sumatra.	
τ. Skull.	Manilla.	
υ. Skull.	Java.	

2. Cerberus australis. (PLATE II. fig. 1.)

Homalopsis australis, *Gray, Zool. Misc.* p. 65 (1842).
Cerberus australis, *Gray, Cat.* p. 65 (1849).

Closely allied to the preceding, but distinguished as follows:— Nasal cleft usually extending to the second upper labial; loreal in contact with the second and third labials, not touching the internasal; three lower labials in contact with the anterior chin-shields. Scales in 25 rows, not so strongly keeled as in *C. rhynchops*. Slate-colour above, with transverse black spots, whitish and blackish beneath, with a regular series of large black blotches along each side of the belly.

Total length 590 millim.; tail 105.

North Australia.

a. ♀ (V. 148; C. 47).	Port Essington.	Mr. Gilbert [C.]. (Type.)
b. ♂ (V. 149, C. 51).	Port Essington.	Sir J. Richardson [P.].

3. Cerberus microlepis. (PLATE II. fig. 2.)

Cerberus cinereus, part., *Gray, Cat.* p. 64 (1849).

Closely allied to *C. rhynchops*, but only three (exceptionally four) lower labials in contact with the anterior chin-shields; loreal not touching the internasal; scales much smaller, in 29 rows, rather feebly keeled; and ventrals more numerous, 163–165. Dark olive above, with darker spots; a dark streak on each side of the head, passing through the eye; yellowish beneath, much spotted or marbled with blackish.

Total length 660 millim.; tail 120.

Philippine Islands.

a–b. ♀ (V. 165, 163; C. 61, 57). Philippines. H. Cuming, Esq. [C.].

127. EUROSTUS.

Eurostus part, *Dum. & Bibr. Mém. Ac. Sc.* xxiii. 1853, p 498, *and Erp. Gén* vii. p 951 (1854)

Hypsirhina, part, *Jan, Arch Zool Anat Phys* iii. 1865, p. 258.

Maxillary teeth 13 or 14, followed, after an interspace, by a pair of enlarged, grooved teeth. Head small, scarcely distinct from neck; eye small, with round (?) pupil; head-shields large; nasal semi-divided, the cleft extending from the nostril to the internasal, in contact behind the rostral, internasals distinct; loreal present. Body cylindrical; scales smooth, without pits, in 27 to 31 rows; ventrals narrow. Tail moderate or short; subcaudals in two rows.

Bengal?

1. Eurostus dussumieri.

Eurostus dussumieri, *Dum. & Bibr.* vii. p 953, pl. lxxxiv. fig. 1 (1854).

Hypsirhina dussumieri, *Jan Elenco*, p 78 (1863), *Arch. Zool Anat. Phys.* iii. 1865, p. 260, *and Icon. Gén* 30, pl iii. fig. 1 (1868)

Rostral broader than deep; internasals broader than long, behind the nasals, frontal once and a half to once and two thirds as long as broad, as long as its distance from the end of the snout, a little shorter than the parietals; loreal nearly as deep as long, one præ- and two postoculars; temporals 1+2; eight upper labials, fourth entering the eye; chin-shields small. Scales in 27 to 31 rows. Ventrals 144–148; anal divided; subcaudals 28–34. Pale brown above, with three blackish stripes; ventrals and subcaudals whitish, with a median series of small black spots which may be confluent into a streak.

Total length 673 millim.; tail 71.

Bengal?

128. MYRON.

Myron, part., *Gray, Cat Sn* p. 70 (1849).

Neospades, *De Vis, Proc. R. Soc. Queensl* vi 1889, p. 238.

Maxillary teeth about 10, followed, after a short interspace, by a pair of enlarged, grooved teeth; anterior mandibular teeth longest. Head small, not or but slightly distinct from neck; eye very small, with vertically elliptic pupil; head-shields large; nasal semi-divided, the cleft extending from the nostril to the first or second labial; a single internasal, separating the nasals; loreal present. Body cylindrical; scales striated and keeled, without pits, in 21 rows; ventrals rounded. Tail short, feebly compressed; subcaudals in two rows.

North Australia.

1. Myron richardsonii.

Myron richardsonii, *Gray, Cat.* p. 70 (1849).
Neospades kentii, *De Vis, Proc. R. Soc. Queensl.* vi. 1889, p. 238, pl. xiv.

Rostral nearly as deep as broad; frontal as long as or a little longer than broad, as long as its distance from the rostral or the end of the snout, shorter than the parietals; loreal a little longer than deep; two præ- and two postoculars: temporals 1+2; eight or nine upper labials, fourth or fifth entering the eye; three pairs of chin-shields in contact on the median line, the anterior in contact with three or four lower labials. Scales rather feebly keeled, in 21 rows. Ventrals 138–140; anal divided; subcaudals 30–35. Grey or olive above, with black cross-bars, head blackish; ventrals yellowish or pale brownish, edged with blackish in front, and with a more or less distinct dusky median streak.

Total length 415 millim.; tail 60.

North Australia.

a. ♀ (V. 140; C. 35) N.W Australia. Sir J Richardson [P.]. (Type.)
b ♀ (V. 140; C. 30). Port Essington.

Both specimens are unfortunately in bad condition.

129. GERARDIA.

Gerarda, *Gray, Cat Sn.* p 77 (1849); *Bouleng Faun. Ind , Rept.* p 379 (1890)
Campylodon, *Dum & Bibr Mém Ac. Sc.* xxiii. 1853, p. 499, *and Erp Gén.* vii. p 963 (1854); *Jan, Arch. Zool Anat. Phys.* iii. 1865, p. 263
Heleophis, *F. Müll. Verh. Nat. Ges. Basel*, vii. 1884, p. 286.

Maxillary teeth 10, very small, followed by a pair of enlarged grooved teeth; mandibular teeth subequal. Head small, not distinct from neck; eye small, with vertically subelliptic pupil; head-shields large; nostril in an undivided nasal, a single internasal, separating the nasals; loreal present. Body cylindrical; scales smooth. without pits, in 17 rows; ventrals rounded. Tail moderate; subcaudals in two rows.

India, Burma and Ceylon.

1. Gerardia prevostiana.

Coluber (Homalopsis) prevostianus, *Eyd. & Gerv in Guér. Mag Zool.*, Cl. iii. 1837, pl. xiii, *and Voy. Favorite*, v. Zool. p. 70, pl. xxix. (1839).
Gerarda bicolor, *Gray, Cat.* p 77 (1849); *Günth. Ann. & Mag. N H.* 4. i 1868, p. 421; *Rept. Brit Ind* p 180 1876).

Campylodon prevostianum, *Dum. & Bibr.* vii. p. 964 (1854); *Jan, Arch. Zool. Anat. Phys* in 1865, p 263, *and Icon. Gén* 30, pl. vi. fig. 3 (1868); *F Mull. Verh. Nat Ges. Basel*, vii. 1885, p. 700.
Heleophis flavescens, *F. Mull. Verh. Nat. Ges. Basel*, vii 1884, p 286, pl. v. fig. 2.
Gerardia prevostiana, *Bouleng. Faun. Ind., Rept.* p. 379 (1890); *Haly, Journ. As. Soc Ceyl.* xi. 1892, p. 197.

Rostral broader than deep; frontal a little longer than broad, as long as or shorter than its distance from the end of the snout, shorter than the parietals; loreal slightly longer than deep, a little smaller than the nasal; one præ- and two postoculars; temporals 1+2 or 3; eight upper labials, fourth entering the eye; four lower labials in contact with the anterior chin-shields, which are much larger than the posterior. Scales in 17 rows. Ventrals 146–148, anal divided; subcaudals 31–34. Uniform dark olive or grey above; three outer series of scales white; upper lip white, rostral dark olive; ventrals and subcaudals grey or whitish, with dark edges.

Total length 520 millim.; tail 65.

Coasts of India, Ceylon, and Burma.

a. ♂ (V. 154; C. 33).   Bandora, Bombay Coast.   H. M. Phipson, Esq. [P.]

b–c. ♂ (V. 153, 148, C. 33, 34).   Bassein R., Pegu.   W. Theobald, Esq. [C.]

d ♂ (V. 146; C.33).   ——?   (Type of *G. bicolor*)

130. FORDONIA.

Homalopsis, part., *Schleg. Phys. Serp.* ii. p. 332 (1837).
Fordonia, *Gray, Zool. Misc.* p. 67 (1842), *and Cat. Sn.* p. 76 (1849); *Gunth Rept. Brit. Ind.* p. 277 (1864); *Bouleng. Faun. Ind., Rept.* p. 378 (1890)
Hemiodontus, *Dum & Bibr. Mém. Ac. Sc.* xxiii. 1853, p. 494, *and Erp. Gén.* vii. p 882 (1854).
Hemiodontus, part., *Jan, Arch. Zool. Anat. Phys.* iii. 1865, p. 263.

Maxillary teeth small, 7 or 8, followed by two enlarged grooved teeth; mandibular teeth subequal. Head small, not distinct from neck; eye very small, with vertically elliptic pupil; head-shields large; nostril in an undivided or semidivided nasal; a single internasal, separating the nasals; no loreal. Body cylindrical; scales smooth, without pits, in 25 to 29 rows; ventrals rounded. Tail short; subcaudals all or part in two rows.

From Burma and Cochinchina to New Guinea and North Australia.

1. Fordonia leucobalia.

Homalopsis leucobalia, *Schleg. Phys. Serp.* ii. p. 345, pl. xiii. figs. 8 & 9 (1837); *Schleg. & Mull. Verh. Nat. Nederl. Overz. Bezitt., Rept.* p. 61, pl viii. (1844), *Cantor, Cat. Mal. Rept.* p. 102, pl xl. fig 5 (1847).

Fordonia leucobalia, *Gray, Zool. Misc.* p 67 (1842), *and Cat.* p. 77 (1849); *Bouleng. Faun. Ind., Rept.* p 378 (1890), *W. L. Sclater, Journ. As. Soc. Beng.* lx. 1891, p. 245.
—— unicolor, *Gray, Cat.* p. 77; *Gunth. Rept. Brit. Ind.* p 277 (1864), *and Zool. Rec.* 1865, p. 154; *Theob. Cat. Rept Brit. Ind.* p. 182 (1876); *Peters & Doria, Ann. Mus. Genova*, xiii. 1878, p 389.
Hemiodontus leucobalia, *Dum. & Bibr.* vii p 884 (1854); *Jan, Arch. Zool Anat. Phys* iii. 1865, p. 264, *and Icon. Gén.* 28, pl. vi. fig. 1 (1868).
—— chalybæus, *Jan, Elenco,* p. 79 (1863), *and ll cc* pl vi fig. 3.
Fordonia bicolor, *Theob. Journ. Linn. Soc.* x 1868, p. 56, *and Cat. Rept. Brit. Ind* p. 181.
—— variabilis, *Macleay, Proc. Linn. Soc. N. S. W.* ii. 1878, p 219

Rostral nearly as deep as broad; frontal a little longer than broad, longer than its distance from the end of the snout, a little shorter than the parietals, one præ- and two postoculars; temporals 1+3 or 2+3; five upper labials, third entering the eye; three lower labials in contact with the anterior chin-shields, which are small and a little larger than the posterior. Scales in 25 to 29 rows. Ventrals 130-156, last frequently divided; anal divided; subcaudals 26-43 Coloration of upper parts very variable; lower parts uniform yellowish white.
Total length 930 millim; tail 110.
Rivers and Coasts of Bengal, Burma, Cochinchina, Malay Archipelago, New Guinea, and North Australia.

A. Black above, with or without small yellowish-white spots (*F. leucobalia,* Schl.)

a. ♀ (Sc. 25; V. 155; C. 29) Nicobars. W. T. Blanford, Esq. [P.]
b-c ♂ (Sc.25; V 148; C. 37) & ♀ (Sc. 25; V. 147; C 28). N. Coast of Australia. H.M.S 'Alert.'
d. ♂ (Sc. 25, V. 148; C. 38). N. Australia. Mrs. Montague Levey [P.].

B. Yellow or pale reddish above, spotted or marbled with black.

a-c. ♂ (Sc 25; V.145, 146; C. 33, 39) & ♀ (Sc.25; V.140; C.32) Port Darwin, N. Australia. R G S. Buckland, Esq [P.]

C. Red above, with a black vertebral stripe; head black.

a. ♂ (Sc. 25; V. 143; C. 39). N. Coast of Australia. H.M S. 'Alert.'

D. Brown above, with or without small black spots, gradually passing to yellowish on the sides. (*F. unicolor,* Gray.)

a. ♀ (Sc. 29; V. 155; C. 30). Burma. H. L. Goertz, Esq. [P.].
b. ♀ (Sc. 27; V. 152; C. 32) Cochinchina. C. E. Cox-Smith, Esq [P.].

c. ♀ (Sc. 29; V 146; C 32). Pinang. Dr. Cantor.
d. ♀ (Sc. 27; V. 153; C. 37). Borneo. Sir E. Belcher [P.].
e. ♂ (Sc. 25, V. 148; C. 43). Borneo.
f. Yg. (Sc. 27; V. 147; C 41). Niah, Borneo. A. Everett, Esq. [C.].
g. ♀ (Sc. 27; V. 156; C 38). Java G. Lyon, Esq. [P.].
h-i. ♀ (Sc. 27, 25; V 144, 146; O. 32, 34) N. Ceram.
k. ♀ (Sc. 25; V. 156; C. 28). Fly R., New Guinea. Rev. S. Macfarlane [C.].
l. ♀ (Sc. 27; V 138, C 34) Port Moresby. Rev. G. Turner [C.].

Fordonia papuensis, Macleay, Proc. Linn. Soc. N. S. W. ii. 1877, p. 35, from Katow, New Guinea, is possibly a synonym of the above species The exclusion of the third labial from the eye may be an individual anomaly; whilst the number (22) of series of scales given in the description may not be the highest to be found on the specimen.

131. CANTORIA.

Cantoria, *Girard, Proc Ac. Philad.* 1857, p 182, *and U S. Explor. Exped., Herp* p. 156 (1858); *Gunth. Rept Brit. Ind.* p. 277 (1864); *Bouleng Faun. Ind., Rept* p 380 (1890).
Hydrodipsas, *Peters, Mon. Berl. Ac.* 1859, p. 270.
Hemiodontus, part., *Jan, Arch. Zool. Anat. Phys.* iii. 1865, p. 263.

Maxillary teeth 10 or 11, last longest and grooved; anterior mandibular teeth longest. Head small, not distinct from neck; eye very small, with round pupil; head-shields large; nostril in a semidivided nasal, the cleft of which extends to the præfrontal; a single internasal, separating the nasals, loreal present. Body extremely elongate, slightly compressed; scales smooth, without pits, in 19 rows; ventrals rounded. Tail moderate; subcaudals in two rows.

Burma, Malay Peninsula, Borneo.

1. Cantoria violacea.

Cantoria violacea, *Girard, Proc Ac Philad.* 1857, p 182, *and U.S. Explor. Exped., Herp.* p 156, pl xi. figs. 7-10 (1858); *Cope, Proc. Ac. Philad* 1866, p. 312; *Lutk Vidensk Meddel.* 1866, p 151; *Bouleng. Faun Ind., Rept.* p. 380, fig. (1890).
Hydrodipsas elapiformis, *Peters, Mon. Berl. Ac.* 1859, p 270, pl. — fig 1.
Cantoria elongata, *Gunth. Rept. Brit. Ind.* p. 277 (1864).
Hemiodontus elapiformis, *Jan, Elenco*, p. 79 (1863), *Arch. Zool. Anat. Phys.* iii. 1865, p. 265, *and Icon Gén* 28, pl. vi. fig. 2 (1868).
Cantoria elapiformis, *Gunth. Zool. Rec.* 1868, p. 124.
—— dayana, *Stoliczka, Journ. As. Soc. Beng.* xxxix. 1870, p. 208,

pl. xi. fig. 5; *Anders. Proc. Zool. Soc.* 1871, p. 178; *Theob. Cat. Rept. Brit. Ind.* p. 181 (1876).

Rostral broader than deep; frontal a little longer than broad, shorter than its distance from the end of the snout or than the parietals; eye between four shields, viz., a præocular, a supraocular, a postocular, and a subocular; loreal longer than deep; one elongate anterior temporal, in contact with the postocular and the subocular; five upper labials; three lower labials in contact with the anterior chin-shields, which are not longer than the posterior. Scales in 19 rows. Ventrals 266-278; anal divided, subcaudals 56-64. Blackish above, with white transverse bands which widen towards the abdomen; these bands are very narrow in the typical form, wider in the var. *dayana* (spec. *a*), but constantly much narrower than the black interspaces, some white spots on the head; lower parts white, with greyish spots, the continuation of the dorsal bands; these bands may form complete rings on the tail.

Total length 830 millim.; tail 110.

Mouth of the Moulmein River, Burma; Singapore; Borneo.

a. ♀ (V 266; C. 57). ——?

132. HIPISTES.

Hipistes, *Gray, Cat Sn* p 77 (1849); *Gunth Rept. Brit. Ind.* p. 286 (1864); *Bouleng Faun. Ind., Rept* p. 381 (1890).

Bitia, *Gray, l. c.* p. 63.

Maxillary teeth 8 or 9, followed, after a short interspace, by a pair of slightly enlarged grooved teeth. Head small, not distinct from neck; eye minute, with vertically elliptic pupil; head-shields small, parietals broken up into numerous shields; nostril a transverse slit between two nasals; a single internasal, separating the nasals, a loreal. Body elongate, slightly compressed; scales smooth, without pits, juxtaposed or subimbricate, in 35 to 43 rows; ventrals narrow, with two sharp keels. Tail short, feebly compressed; subcaudals in two rows.

Coasts of Burma, Siam, and the Malay Peninsula.

1. Hipistes hydrinus.

Homalopsis hydrina, *Cantor, Cat. Mal. Rept.* p. 104, pl. xl. fig. 4 (1847).

Bitia hydroides, *Gray, Cat.* p. 63 (1849).

Hipistes fasciatus, *Gray, l. c.* p. 78.

—— hydrinus, *Gunth Rept Brit Ind.* p 287, pl. xxiv. fig. 11 (1864); *Stoliczka, Journ. As. Soc. Beng.* xxxix. 1870, p. 207; *Anders. Proc. Zool. Soc.* 1871, p. 181; *Theob. Cat. Rept. Brit. Ind.* p. 184 (1876); *Bouleng Faun. Ind., Rept.* p. 382, fig. (1890).

Rostral nearly as deep as broad; frontal narrow, twice as long as broad, as long as or a little longer than its distance from the end of the snout; eye between four shields, viz. a supraocular, a præocular, a subocular, and a small postocular; seven upper labials, five lower labials in contact with the anterior chin-shields; posterior chin-shields extremely small. Scales in 35 to 43 rows. Ventrals 153–165; anal divided; subcaudals 22–35. Pale grey or brownish above, with black cross-bands as broad as the interspaces between them or narrower; lower parts white.

Total length 485 millim.; tail 50.

Mouths of rivers and coasts of Pegu, Siam, and the Malay Peninsula.

a–b. ♂ (Sc. 37; V. 160; C. 34)	Pinang	Dr. Cantor.
& yg. (Sc. 39; V 155; C. 35).		
c. ♀ (Sc. 43, V. 160, C 27).	Pinang	F Day, Esq. [P.]
d. ♂ (Sc 41, V 160, C. 31).	Bangkok.	Christiania Museum.
e ♂ (Sc 39, V. 165; C. 33).	Pegu.	W. Theobald, Esq. [C].
f. ♂ (Sc. 39; V. 157; C. 33).	——?	(Type of *Bitia hydroides*.)
g. ♀ (Sc. 39; V. 161, C. 24).	——?	(Type of *Hipistes fasciatus*.)
h. ♀ (Sc. 41; V. 161, C. 27).	——?	

133. HERPETON.

Erpeton, *Lacép. Bull. Sc. Soc. Philom* ii. 1800, p. 169, *and Ann. Mus* ii 1803, p. 280; *Gray, Cat. Sn* p. 62 (1849); *Dum. & Bibr. Erp. Gén.* vii. p. 983 (1854)

Rhinopirus, *Merr Tent. Syst. Amph.* p. 81 (1820).

Herpeton, *Wagl. Syst Amph* p. 169 (1830), *Gunth. Proc. Zool Soc.* 1860, p. 115, *and Ann. & Mag. N. H* (3) viii. 1861, p 266, *and Rept. Brit. Ind.* p. 288 (1864), *Jan, Arch. Zool. Anat. Phys.* iii. 1865, p. 255.

Homalopsis, part, *Schleg. Phys. Serp.* ii. p. 332 (1837).

Maxillary teeth 12 or 13, followed, after a short interspace, by a pair of slightly enlarged grooved teeth; mandibular teeth subequal. Head distinct from neck, with two long, scaly, rostral appendages; eye small, with vertically elliptic pupil; head-shields large; nostril in a semidivided nasal, which is separated from its fellow by a series of small scales; loreal region covered with small scales; no regular chin-shields. Body cylindrical, scales strongly keeled, in 37 rows; ventrals very narrow, bicarinate. Tail moderate, covered with uniform keeled scales.

Cochinchina and Siam.

1. Herpeton tentaculatum.

Erpeton tentaculatus, *Lacép. Bull. Sc Soc. Philom.* ii 1800, p. 169, *and Ann. Mus* ii 1803, p 280, pl. l.; *Daud. Rept.* vii. p. 246, pl. lxxxvi. (1803); *Guér Icon. R A., Rept.* pl. xx. fig. 3 (1844); *Gray, Cat.* p. 63 (1849), *Dum. & Bibr.* vii. p 984 (1854).

Rhinopirus erpeton, *Merr. Tent.* p. 82 (1820).

Homalopsis herpeton, *Schleg. Phys. Serp.* ii. p. 359 (1837), *and Abbild.* p 50, pl. xvi. (1839).

Herpeton tentaculatum, *Jan, Icon. Gén.* 1, pl. i. (1860); *Gunth. Proc. Zool. Soc.* 1860, p. 114, pl. xxiii.; *Cornalia, Rev. & Mag. Zool.*

(2) xiii. 1861, p. 145; *Peters, Mon. Berl. Ac* 1861, p. 902, and 1863, p. 247 , *Gunth. Rept. Brit. Ind.* p. 288 (1864); *Bocourt, N. Arch Mus.* ii. 1866, *Bull.* p. 6; *Morice, Ann. Sc. Nat.* (6) ii. 1875 art. 5, pl xx ; *Peters, Sitzb. Ges. Naturf. Fr.* 1882, p 74.

Rostral very small; a pair of præfrontals, separated from the nasals by small shields; frontal slightly longer than broad, shorter than the parietals, separated from the supraoculars by a series of small shields; 13 to 15 upper labials, separated from the eye by a series of suboculars; temple covered with small keeled scales. Scales strongly keeled, in 37 rows. Ventrals 110–136, only twice as large as a scale; anal divided. A broad dark brown vertebral band, with more or less regular black transverse lines; a dark brown lateral stripe, extending to the snout and passing through the eye, separated from the vertebral band by a yellowish-brown band; yellowish beneath, with two dark brown longitudinal stripes.

Total length 610 millim.; tail 170

Cochinchina and Siam, in brackish water.

a–b. ♀ (V. 126) & yg. (V. 133). Siam. M. Mouhot [C.]

Alluaudina (*infra*, p. 38) should perhaps be referred to this Subfamily. See *Mocquard, Bull. Soc. Philom.* (8) vii. 1895, p. 124.

Subfam. 5. *DIPSADOMORPHINÆ.*

Coronellæ, part , Colubrini, part , Dendrophidæ, part , *Boie, Isis*, 1827, p. 510.

Oxycéphaliens, Sténocéphaliens, Scytaliens, Dipsadiens, Anisodontiens, part., *Duméril, Mém. Ac. Sc.* xxiii. p. 427, 1853 ; *Duméril & Bibron, Erp Gén.* vii. p 796, 1854.

Calamaridæ, part , Coronellidæ, part , Dryadidæ, part , Psammophidæ, Dendrophidæ, part., Dryiophidæ, Dipsadidæ, part., Scytalidæ, *Gunther, Cat Col Sn.* 1858.

Calamaridæ, part , Probletorhinidæ, part , Coronellidæ, part., Potamophilidæ, part., Psammophidæ, Dryophilidæ, part., Scytalidæ, part., Dipsadidæ, part., *Jan, Elenco sist. Ofid.* 1863

Calamaridæ, part., Colubridæ, part., Psammophidæ, Dendrophidæ, part., Dryiophidæ, Dipsadidæ, *Gunther, Rept. Brit Ind* 1864.

Trimerorhini, part , *Peters, Reise n. Mossamb.* iii. p. 118, 1882.

Calamarinæ, part , Scytalinæ, Philodryadinæ, Dryophidinæ, Psammophidinæ, Dipsadinæ, *Cope, Proc. Amer. Philos Soc.* xxiii. p. 484, 1886.

Dipsadinæ, *Boulenger, Faun. Ind., Rept.* p. 356, 1890.

Dipsadinæ, Scytalinæ, Erythrolamprinæ, *Cope, Trans Amer. Philos. Soc.* xviii. p. 207, 1895.

Nostrils lateral; dentition well developed.

Cosmopolitan, except the northern parts of the Northern Hemisphere. Terrestrial, arboreal, or subaquatic.

Synopsis of the Genera.

I. Hypapophyses present throughout the vertebral column, represented on the posterior dorsal vertebræ by a more or less developed crest or tubercle projecting below the condyle.

   A. Solid maxillary teeth equal or subequal.

      1. Pupil round; body cylindrical; scales smooth.

Mandibular teeth subequal; scales without pits.
                        134. **Geodipsas**, p. 32.

Anterior mandibular teeth strongly enlarged; scales without pits; subcaudals single .... 135. **Hologerrhum**, p. 33.

Anterior mandibular teeth longest; scales with apical pits.
                        136 **Ithycyphus**, p. 34.

      2. Pupil vertical.

         a. Eye moderate; body cylindrical.

Snout ending in a long scaly appendage, scales keeled.
                        137. **Langaha**, p. 35.

Snout without appendage; scales strongly keeled.
                        138. **Alluaudina**, p. 38.

Snout without appendage; scales smooth; a series of suboculars.
                        139. **Eteirodipsas**, p. 38.

         b. Eye large; body compressed; scales smooth.
                        140. **Stenophis**, p. 39.

   B. Solid maxillary teeth very unequal; anterior mandibular teeth strongly enlarged; pupil vertical.

Body compressed; scales smooth; tail long.
                        141. **Lycodryas**, p 44.

Body cylindrical; scales smooth or obtusely keeled; tail moderate, with single subcaudals, nostril between nasal and supranasal.
                        142. **Pythonodipsas**, p. 45.

Body cylindrical; scales smooth; tail short, with single subcaudals.
                        143. **Ditypophis**, p. 46.

II. Hypapophyses absent in the posterior dorsal vertebræ.

   A. Solid maxillary teeth gradually decreasing in length, the anterior much longer than the posterior; head distinct from neck; pupil vertical.

      1. Vertebral scales not enlarged.

Body cylindrical or slightly compressed; scales oblique; no suboculars .... 144. **Tarbophis**, p. 47.

Body compressed; scales slightly oblique; usually a subocular below the præocular and loreal divided.
       145. **Trimorphodon**, p. 53.
Body compressed; scales straight; no suboculars.
       146. **Lycognathus**, p. 56.
  2. Scales of vertebral row enlarged.
       147. **Trypanurgos**, p. 58.

B. Solid maxillary teeth subequal or gradually increasing in length, head more or less distinct from neck; pupil vertical.

  1. Scales more or less oblique, vertebral row more or less enlarged

Subcaudals in two rows........ 148. **Dipsadomorphus**, p. 59.
Subcaudals single .... 149. **Dipsadoboa**, p. 81.

  2. Scales not oblique.

   a. Ventral shields strongly angulate laterally; scales strongly keeled .. 150. **Rhinobothryum**, p. 82.

   b. Ventrals rounded or obtusely angulate.

    a. Nostril between two nasals.

     * Body very slender, strongly compressed; scales very narrow . 151. **Himantodes**, p. 83.

    ** Body cylindrical or moderately compressed.

     † Maxillary teeth gradually and feebly increasing in length; posterior nasal concave.

Body cylindrical or moderately compressed, loreal not entering the eye .... 152. **Leptodira**, p. 88.
Body compressed; loreal entering the eye.
       153. **Chamætortus**, p. 98.

     †† Maxillary teeth equal; body cylindrical or feebly compressed.

Anterior mandibular teeth longest.
       154. **Oxyrhopus**, p. 99.
Mandibular teeth subequal; rostral shield with sharp horizontal edge .... 155. **Rhinostoma**, p. 114.

   β. Nasal entire or semidivided; body cylindrical.

    * Scales with apical pits.

     † Maxillary teeth 10 to 18, subequal.

Mandibular teeth subequal; eye large.
       156. **Thamnodynastes**, p. 115.
Anterior mandibular teeth longest; eye moderate.
       157. **Tachymenis**, p. 117.

†† Maxillary teeth 9 or 10, increasing in length; anterior mandibular teeth strongly enlarged; eye small . 158. **Hemirhagerrhis**, p. 119.

** Scales without pits; maxillary teeth 15, equal; anterior mandibular teeth strongly enlarged.
159. **Manolepis**, p. 120.

C. Solid maxillary teeth subequal or increasing in length to the last; head more or less distinct from neck; pupil round or horizontal; scales with apical pits.

1. Solid maxillary teeth 10 or more, separated from the grooved fangs by an interspace.

   a Pupil round.

   α. Anterior mandibular teeth not enlarged; nasal entire or semidivided.

Maxillary teeth gradually increasing in size.
162. **Amplorhinus**, p. 124.
Maxillary teeth equal . . . . 163. **Pseudablabes**, p. 126.

   β. Anterior mandibular teeth enlarged.

Maxillary teeth subequal; scales more or less oblique; nostril between two nasals . . . . 164. **Philodryas**, p. 127.
Last solid maxillary tooth very large, fang-like.
165. **Ialtris**, p. 137.
Maxillary teeth subequal; nostril between two nasals and the internasal . . . . 166. **Trimerorhinus**, p 138.
Maxillary teeth subequal; nostril in a single or divided nasal; scales more or less distinctly grooved.
167. **Cœlopeltis**, p. 141.

   b. Pupil horizontal; scales very oblique; body compressed.
   176. **Thelotornis**, p. 184

2. Solid maxillary teeth 17 to 20, not separated from the grooved fangs, which are feebly enlarged; scales more or less oblique; body compressed.

Ventrals rounded; pupil round . 178. **Oxybelis**, p. 189.
Ventrals and subcaudals with suture-like lateral keel; pupil horizontal . . . . 179. **Dryophiops**, p. 193.
Ventrals and subcaudals with suture-like lateral keel; pupil round.
180. **Chrysopelea**, p. 195.

3. Solid maxillary teeth 4 to 9, grooved fangs very large.

Eye large; scales oblique . . . . . 160. **Tomodon**, p 120.
Eye moderate, scales forming straight longitudinal series.
168. **Rhamphiophis**, p. 144.
Eye extremely large; scales very oblique.
177. **Dispholidus**, p. 186.

D. Solid maxillary teeth unequal, the middle ones the longest.

1. Solid maxillary teeth forming an uninterrupted series; pupil round.

Maxillary teeth 10 or 11, gradually decreasing in size in front and behind .... 169. **Dromophis**, p. 149.

Maxillary teeth 14, middle ones much enlarged.
170. **Taphrometopon**, p. 151.

2. Longest solid maxillary teeth followed by a gap.

  a. Pupil round; scales with apical pits.

Loreal in contact with the præocular.
171. **Psammophis**, p. 152.

Loreal separated from the præocular by the præfrontal.
172. **Mimophis**, p. 171.

  b. Pupil vertically subelliptic.

Eye rather large; scales without apical pits.
173. **Psammodynastes**, p. 172.

Eye rather small; scales with apical pits.
174. **Macroprotodon**, p. 175.

  c. Pupil horizontal; scales very oblique, with apical pits.
175. **Dryophis**, p. 177.

E. Solid maxillary teeth subequal or increasing in length to the last; head not or but slightly distinct from neck, pupil round; scales without apical pits.

1. Subcaudals in two rows.

  a. Solid maxillary teeth 10 to 15, the grooved fangs below or just behind the vertical of the posterior border of the eye.

    α. Grooved maxillary teeth very large; anterior mandibular teeth longest.
161. **Conophis**, p. 122.

    β. Grooved maxillary teeth feebly or moderately enlarged; mandibular teeth equal.

      * Internasals distinct from nasals; two præfrontals.

      † Loreal present.

Eye moderate; tail moderate or long; nostril between two nasals.
181. **Erythrolamprus**, p. 199.

Eye small; tail moderate; nasal entire or semidivided.
182. **Hydrocalamus**, p. 209.

Eye small; tail short; nostril between two nasals.
183. **Scolecophis**, p. 210.

DIPSADOMORPHINÆ.

†† Loreal absent.

Rostral moderate .... 184. **Homalocranium**, p. 212
Rostral very large, prominent . 185. **Ogmius**, p. 228.

** Internasals united with anterior nasals.
186. **Stenorhina**, p. 229.

*** Internasals distinct; a single præfrontal; vertebræ with shield-like neural expansions.
187. **Xenopholis**, p. 231.

l. Maxillary very short, with 2 to 5 solid teeth; grooved teeth below or in advance of the eye.

α. No anterior temporal; parietals in contact with labials.

* Palate toothed.

No internasals, nasal entire, moderate.
188. **Apostolepis**, p. 232.
No internasals; nasal entire, very small.
191. **Amblyodipsas**, p. 244.
Internasals distinct; nasal divided or semidivided.
193. **Calamelaps**, p. 245.

** Palate toothless.

Internasals distinct; no præocular.
194. **Rhinocalamus**, p. 247.
No internasals; nasal in contact with an elongate præocular.
195. **Xenocalamus**, p. 247.

β. Postocular in contact with a temporal.

* Nasal in contact with the rostral.

† Nasal single.

No internasals; loreal present .. 189. **Elapomoius**, p. 237.
No loreal; a præocular........ 190. **Elapomorphus**, p. 238.
No loreal; no præocular ...... 196. **Micrelaps**, p. 248.

†† Nostril between two nasals.
192. **Elapotinus**, p. 244.

** First labial in contact with the internasal.
197. **Miodon**, p. 249.

2. Subcaudals single.

a. Maxillary very short, with 2 to 4 solid teeth.

α. First labial in contact with the internasal.

No occipital shield .... 198. **Polemon**, p. 253.
A large azygous occipital shield.. 199. **Brachyophis**, p. 254.

β. Nasal in contact with the rostral.
200. **Macrelaps**, p. 255.

b. Maxillary short, with 6 to 10 solid teeth.

Posterior maxillary teeth large and strongly grooved.
201. **Aparallactus**, p. 255.

Posterior maxillary teeth feebly enlarged and feebly grooved.
202. **Elapops**, p 262.

134. GEODIPSAS.

Maxillary teeth 14 or 15, equal, followed, after an interspace, by a pair of enlarged grooved fangs, mandibular teeth subequal. Head distinct from neck; eye moderate, with round pupil. Body cylindrical: scales smooth, without pits, in 19 rows; ventrals rounded. Tail moderate; subcaudals in two rows. Hypapophyses developed throughout the vertebral column.

Madagascar.

1. Geodipsas infralineata. (PLATE III. fig. 1.)

Tachymenis infralineatus, *Gunth. Ann. & Mag. N. N.* (5) ix. 1882, p. 265.

Rostral broader than deep, just visible from above; internasals broader than long, a little shorter than the præfrontals; frontal once and a half to once and two thirds as long as broad, longer than its distance from the end of the snout, shorter than the parietals; loreal trapezoidal, as long as deep; one præ- and two postoculars; temporals 1+2; seven upper labials, third and fourth entering the eye; four lower labials in contact with the anterior chin-shields, which are shorter than the posterior. Scales in 19 rows. Ventrals 172–187; anal entire; subcaudals 55–62. Brown above, uniform or with small blackish spots; a black streak along the upper surface of the tail and the posterior part of the back; a dark streak on each side of the head, behind the eye, and another in the middle, from the frontal to the occiput; lower parts yellow, with some brown dots and a continuous or interrupted brown streak along the middle of the belly and tail.

Total length 760 millim.; tail 150.

Madagascar.

a. ♀ (V. 187; C. 62).   E. Betsilio.   Rev. W. D. Cowan [C.]. (Type.)
b. ♀ (V. 172; C. 55).   E. Imerina.   Rev R. Baron [C.]

2. Geodipsas boulengeri.

Tachymenis boulengeri, *Peracca, Boll. Mus. Torin.* vii. 1892, no 112, p. 3.

Rostral broader than deep, scarcely visible from above; internasals broader than long, a little smaller than the præfrontals; frontal nearly twice as long as broad, longer than its distance from the end of the snout, shorter than the parietals; two superposed loreals; one præ- and two postoculars; temporals 1+2; seven upper labials, third and fourth entering the eye; four lower labials in contact with the anterior chin-shields, which are longer than the posterior. Scales in 19 rows. Ventrals 137; anal entire; subcaudals 31. Brown above, with scattered small yellow spots; lips, sides, and outer ends of ventrals closely dotted with blackish; each labial with a round yellow spot; a crescentic yellow marking on each side of the neck, just behind the head; belly and lower surface of tail bright yellow.

Total length 348 millim.; tail 48.

Andrangoloka, Madagascar.

135. HOLOGERRHUM.

Hologerrhum, *Gunth. Cat. Col. Sn.* p. 186 (1858).

Maxillary teeth 20, equal, followed, after a short interspace, by a pair of enlarged, grooved fangs; anterior mandibular teeth strongly enlarged. Head slightly distinct from neck; eye moderate, with round pupil. Body cylindrical; scales smooth, without pits, in 17 rows, ventrals rounded. Tail moderate; subcaudals single. Hypapophyses developed throughout the vertebral column.

Philippine Islands.

1. Hologerrhum philippinum.

Hologerrhum philippinum, *Gunth. Cat.* p. 186 (1858), *and Proc. Zool. Soc.* 1873, p. 171, pl. xviii fig B *

Cyclochorus maculatus, *Jan, Icon. Gén.* 36, pl. vi fig. 3 (1870).

Rostral broader than deep, scarcely visible from above; internasals as long as broad, a little shorter than the præfrontals; frontal twice as long as broad, longer than its distance from the end of the snout, a little shorter than the parietals; loreal as long as deep; two præ- and two postoculars; temporals 1+1, eight upper labials, third, fourth, and fifth entering the eye; four lower labials in contact with the anterior chin-shields, which are shorter than the posterior. Scales in 17 rows. Ventrals 144; anal entire; subcaudals 40. Brown above, with a few alternating black spots on the anterior part of the back, and one or two black cross-bars behind the head; a black streak on each side of the head; passing through the eye, upper lip yellowish; a black line on each side of the posterior part of the body and of the tail; lower parts yellowish, with a black dot at the outer end of each ventral shield; on the tail these dots are confluent into a line.

---

* The specimen from Placer, Mindanao, referred to this species by Gunther (Proc. Zool. Soc. 1879, p. 78), belongs to *Cyclocorus lineatus*.

Total length 280 millim.; tail 52.
Philippine Islands.

a. ♀ (V. 144; C. 40). Philippines. H. Cuming, Esq. [C.].
(Type.)

136. ITHYCYPHUS.

Coluber, part., *Schleg. Phys. Serp.* ii. p. 125 (1837).
Herpetodryas, part., *Schleg. l. c.* p. 173.
Dryophylax, part, *Dum. & Bibr. Erp. Gén.* vii. p 1103 (1854).
Philodryas, part., *Gunth. Cat. Col. Sn.* p. 123 (1858), *Jan, Elenco sist. Ofid.* p. 83 (1863).
Ithycyphus, *Gunth. Ann. & Mag. N. H.* (4) xi. 1873, p. 374.

Maxillary teeth 15 to 18, subequal, followed, after a short interspace, by a pair of enlarged, grooved fangs; anterior mandibular teeth longest. Head distinct from neck; eye moderate, with round pupil. Body cylindrical, scales smooth, with apical pits, in 21 rows; ventrals obtusely angulate laterally. Tail long; subcaudals in two rows. Hypapophyses developed throughout the vertebral column.

Madagascar; Comoro Islands.

1. Ithycyphus goudoti.

Herpetodryas goudoti, *Schleg. Phys. Serp.* ii. p. 187 (1837).
Dryophylax goudoti, *Dum. & Bibr.* vii. p. 1122 (1854)
Philodryas goudoti, *Gunth. Cat.* p. 125 (1858).
Ithycyphus caudolineatus, *Gunth. Ann. & Mag. N. H.* (4) xi. 1873, p. 374.

Rostral twice as broad as deep, just visible from above; internasals longer than broad, shorter than the præfrontals; frontal bell-shaped, once and one third to once and a half as long as broad, as long as its distance from the end of the snout, shorter than the parietals; loreal twice to thrice as long as deep; one præocular (sometimes divided), in contact with the frontal; three postoculars; temporals 1+2 or 2+2; eight upper labials, fourth and fifth entering the eye; four or five lower labials in contact with the anterior chin-shields, which are much shorter than the posterior. Scales in 21 rows. Ventrals 170–209; anal divided; subcaudals 121–175. Yellowish or pale brown above, uniform or with more or less distinct angular or arrowheaded black markings; some of the scales may be white-edged; upper lip yellow; a black line on each side of the head, passing through the eye; two more or less distinct black streaks on each side of the tail; belly yellowish or pale brown, uniform or spotted with black; tail frequently with a black line along its lower surface.

Total length 830 millim.; tail 340.
Madagascar.

a–d. ♂ (V. 170, 175; S. Madagascar. (Types of *I. caudo-*
C. 128, 165) & ♀ *lineatus*.)
(V. 181, 180); ♂ ♀,
170).

e. ♂ (V. 175; C. 162).	Tamatave.	Rev. W. D. Cowan [C.].
f. ♂ (V. 170; C. 164).	Sahambendrana.	M. Majastre [C.].
g. ♀ (V 176; C. 144).	Antongil Bay.	L. H. Ramsom, Esq. [P.].
h. Skull of e.		

2. Ithycyphus miniatus.

Coluber miniatus, *Schleg. Phys. Serp.* ii. p. 148 (1837), *and Abbild.* p 104, pl. xxviii figs 12-16 (1844)
Dryophylax miniatus, *Dum. & Bibr.* vii. p 1120 (1854).
Philodryas miniatus, *Jan, Elenco*, p 84 (1863); *Boetty. Abh. Senck. Ges.* xi. 1877, p. 13, and 1879, p. 464, and xii. 1881, p. 444.

Rostral broader than deep, just visible from above; internasals as long as broad or longer than broad, a little shorter than the præfrontals; frontal bell-shaped, once and one third to once and a half as long as broad, as long as its distance from the rostral or the end of the snout, as long as or a little shorter than the parietals; loreal once and a half to twice as long as deep; one præocular, not reaching the frontal; two (rarely three) postoculars; temporals 1+2 (rarely 2+3); eight upper labials, fourth and fifth entering the eye; four or five lower labials in contact with the anterior chin-shields, which are as long as or shorter than the posterior. Scales in 21 rows. Ventrals 195-212; anal divided; subcaudals 128-164. Greyish, yellowish, or reddish, uniform or with small darker and lighter variegations; posterior part of body and tail sometimes bright red; sides of head and neck sometimes with a blackish streak, passing through the eye; labials yellowish, sometimes edged with blackish; belly more or less closely speckled with brown.

Total length 1230 millim.; tail 400.

Madagascar; Comoro Islands.

a ♀ (V. 198; C. 153).	Madagascar.	
b-e. ♂ (V. 202, 202; C. 160, 160) & ♀ (V. 207, 195; C. ?, 138).	Imerina.	Rev. R. Baron [C.].

137. LANGAHA.

Langaha, *Brugnière, Journ. de Phys.* xxiv. 1784, p. 132; *Lacép. Serp.* ii. p 469 (1789); *Daud Rept.* vii p. 237 (1803), *Dum. & Bibr Erp Gén* vii p. 802 (1854), *Gunth. Cat. Col. Sn.* p. 161 (1858); *Jan, Elenco sist. Ofid* p. 89 (1863)
Xyphorhynchus, *Wagl. Syst Amph.* p. 184 (1830).
Dryiophis, part, *Schleg Phys Serp.* ii p. 241 (1837)

Maxillary teeth 15 or 16, subequal, followed by a pair of enlarged, grooved fangs; anterior palatine and mandibular teeth very strongly enlarged, fang-like. Head distinct from neck, snout with small shields, ending in a long scaly appendage; eye moderate, with vertical pupil; nasal entire. Body cylindrical; scales keeled, with apical pits, in 19 rows; ventrals rounded or obtusely angulate laterally. Tail long; subcaudals in two rows. Hypapophyses developed throughout the vertebral column.

Madagascar.

Fig. 2.

Maxillary and mandible of *Langaha nasuta*.

Synopsis of the Species.

Rostral appendage twice as long as the snout, ensiform, not serrated .... 1. *nasuta*, p. 36.
Rostral appendage once and a half to once and two thirds as long as the snout, tapering to a sharp point, and serrated above at the end .... 2. *intermedia*, p. 37.
Rostral appendage not more than once and a half as long as the snout, serrated above and beneath .... 3. *crista-galli*, p. 37.

1. Langaha nasuta.

Brugnière, Journ de Phys. xxiv. 1784, p 132, pl ii
Langaha nasuta, *Shaw, Nat. Misc.* xxii. pl. cmlxviii —(?); *Gunth. Cat* p. 162 (1858); *Boettg. Abh. Senck. Ges* xi. 1878, p. 270, and 1879, p. 467, and xii. 1881, p. 447.
Amphisbæna langaha, *Schneid. Hist. Amph.* ii. p. 357 (1801).
Langaha madagascariensis, *Daud. Rept.* vii. p 240 (1803).
Dryiophis langaha, *Schleg. Phys. Serp.* ii. p. 248 (1837), *and Abbild.* p. 20, pl. vii., & pl. viii. figs. 7-11 (1837)
Langaha ensifera, *Dum. & Bibr.* vii. p. 803 (1854); *Jan, Icon. Gén.* 33, pl. vi fig. 2 (1869)

Head narrow and elongate, ending in a long, ensiform, three-edged rostral appendage, covered with imbricate scales, which gradually tapers to a sharp point; the length of this appendage about twice the length of the snout, and five to six times its basal depth; rostral nearly twice as broad as deep; a pair of more or less regular, enlarged præfrontal shields; frontal narrow, its anterior width about equal to the posterior width of the supraocular; one, two, or three loreal shields; two præ- and four postoculars; temporals small, scale-like; eight upper labials, fourth and fifth entering the eye; three pairs of chin-shields bordering the mental groove. Scales rather strongly keeled, in 19 rows. Ventrals 145-152; anal divided (rarely entire); subcaudals 136-153. Pale brown to brick-red above, uniform, or with ill-defined small black spots; upper lip and lower parts yellow or orange, the belly and tail sometimes dotted with blackish; a fine yellowish-white line, edged above with brown or black, extends on each side from below the nasal shield to the anterior third of the body, where it is gradually lost.

Total length 950 millim.; tail 410.

Madagascar.

a. Hgr. (V. 150; C. 141).	Madagascar.	Paris Museum [E.].
b. ♂ (V. 152; C. 148).	Madagascar.	
c-d ♂ (V. 149, C. ?) & yg (V. 148, C 137).	Imerina.	Rev. R. Baron [C.].
e. ♂ (V. 150; C. ?).	Antongil Bay.	L H. Ransome, Esq. [P.].
f. ♂ (V 147, C. 142).	Nossi Bé.	
g. Skull of f.		

2. Langaha intermedia.

Langaha intermedia, *Bouleng. Ann. & Mag. N. H.* (6) i. 1888, p. 105, pl v fig. 6.

Intermediate between *L. nasuta* and *L. crista-galli*. Rostral appendage once and a half to once and two thirds as long as the snout, tapering to a sharp point, feebly serrated at the end, its basal depth contained four to five times in its length. Ventrals 142–147; subcaudals 120–135. Grey-brown above and beneath, speckled with dark brown or black and with more or less distinct traces of lighter, dark-edged cross-bars on the sides; no light lateral streak.

Total length 910 millim; tail 315.

Madagascar.

a. ♀ (V 142; C. 125).	Nossi Bé.	(Type.)
b, c ♀ (V. 146, 147; C. 135, 129).	Madagascar	
d. Yg. (V. 147; C. 120)	Madagascar.	Mr. Last [C.].

3. Langaha crista-galli.

Langaha crista-galli, *Dum. & Bibr.* vii. p. 806, pl. lxxi (1854), *Günth. Cat.* p. 162 (1858), *Jan, Icon Gen.* 33, pl vi fig. 1 (1869); *Boettg. Abh. Senck. Ges.* xi 1879, p 465

Differs from the two preceding in having the rostral appendage much deeper, obtuse or rounded, and strongly serrated at the end; its length once and one third to once and a half that of the snout, its greatest depth two to three times in its length; the serrations forming one crest above and two below the distal half of the appendage. Ventrals 146–149; subcaudals 119–142 Grey-brown or reddish above and beneath, more or less speckled with dark brown, and with a lateral series of more or less distinct whitish, dark-edged spots alternating with those on the other side; no light lateral streak.

Total length 800 millim.; tail 315.
Madagascar.

a. ♂ (V. 146; C. 119).	S.E. Betsileo.	Mr. T. Waters [C.].
b. ♀ (V. 148; C 129).	Madagascar.	Christiania Museum.
c. ♂ (V. 146; C. 142).	Madagascar.	

138. ALLUAUDINA.

Alluaudina, *Mocquard, C.R. Soc. Philom.* 1894, no 17, p. 9.

Mandibular teeth small and equal Head very distinct from neck, eye moderate, with vertically subelliptic pupil; nasal indistinctly divided. Body rounded; scales keeled, without apical pits, in 25 rows; ventrals rounded. Tail moderate; subcaudals single.

Madagascar.

1. Alluaudina bellyi.

Alluaudina bellyi, *Mocquard, l. c.*

Head broad, much depressed. Rostral twice as broad as deep, not extending to the upper surface of the snout; internasals very short, præfrontals very large, as long as broad; frontal as broad as long, shorter than its distance from the end of the snout, shorter than the parietals; supraocular small; loreal a little longer than deep; two præ- and three postoculars; temporals scale-like, keeled, eight upper labials, third and fourth entering the eye, four or five lower labials in contact with the anterior chin-shields. Scales rugose and strongly keeled, in 25 rows. Ventrals 161; anal entire; subcaudals 68. Purplish brown above, with a lateral series of darker spots along the flanks; lower parts greyish white, with square black spots, partly confluent and disposed irregularly.

Total length 312 millim.; tail 73.

Ambre Mt., Saccaranii Valley, Madagascar.

139. ETEIRODIPSAS.

Dipsas, part., *Schleg. Phys. Serp.* ii. p. 357 (1837); *Dum. & Bibr. Erp. Gén.* vii. p. 1133 (1854).
Eteirodipsas, part, *Jan, Elenco sist. Ofid* p. 105 (1863).

Maxillary teeth 14 to 16, equal, followed, after an interspace, by a pair of enlarged grooved fangs; anterior mandibular teeth longest. Head distinct from neck; eye moderate, with vertical pupil, separated from the labials by suboculars. Body cylindrical; scales smooth, with apical pits, in 25 to 29 rows; ventrals rounded. Tail moderate, subcaudals in two rows. Hypapophyses developed throughout the vertebral column.

Madagascar.

1. Eteirodipsas colubrina.

? *Seba, Thes* i. pl. xix. fig. 7 (1734).
? *Coluber nepa, Laur. Syn. Rept* p. 97 (1768).
Dipsas colubrina, *Schleg. Phys. Serp.* ii. p. 273 (1837), and *Abbild.* p. 136, pl xlv figs. 21-26 (1844), *Dum. & Bibr.* vii. p. 1146 (1853), *Boettg. Abh. Senck. Ges.* xii. 1881, p. 448.
Eteirodipsas colubrina, *Jan, Elenco,* p 105 (1863), and *Icon. Gén.* 39, pl i. fig 1 (1872); *Boettg. Abh. Senck. Ges.* xi. 1877, p. 16, 1878, p. 271, & 1879, p 467.

Rostral broader than deep, visible from above; internasals as long as broad or a little broader than long, as long as or a little longer than the præfrontals; frontal once and a half to twice as long as broad, as long as or longer than its distance from the end of the snout, as long as the parietals; loreal nearly as long as deep; two præoculars, upper largest and in contact with or narrowly separated from the frontal; three postoculars; three suboculars, separating the eye from the labials; temporals small, scale-like, 2 or 3 + 2 or 3; eight or nine upper labials; four or five lower labials in contact with the anterior chin-shields; posterior chin-shields narrower and separated from each other by two series of scales. Scales in 25 to 29 rows. Ventrals 176-202, anal divided (rarely entire); subcaudals 44-71, a few of which may be entire. Pale brown, yellowish, or greenish yellow above, with dark brown or black spots arranged quincuncially; a more or less distinct dark streak on each side of the head behind the eye; uniform yellowish white beneath.

Total length 860 millim.; tail 120.

Madagascar, Bourbon (?).

a.	♀ (Sc 27; V 192; A. 2, C. 62)	Madagascar.	Prof. A. Newton [P.].
b	♀ (Sc. 27; V. 189, A. 1, C. ?).	Madagascar.	Rev. T. Ellis [P.].
c-d.	♂ (Sc. 29, V. 200, A. 1; C. 59) & ♀ (Sc. 25, V. 184; A. 2; C. 50).	Madagascar.	J. Caldwell, Esq. [P.].
e	♂ (Sc. 29, V. 194; A. 2; C. 56)	Madagascar.	Rev. R. Baron [C.].
f.	Hgr. (Sc 27; V. 195, A. 2; C. 68).	Tamatave.	M. Majastre [C.].
g.	♀ (Sc. 27; V. 192; A. 2; C. 51).	E. Imerina.	Rev. R. Baron [C.].
h-i.	♂ (Sc. 27; V. 195; A. 2; C 51) & yg (Sc 27; V. 197; A. 2, C. 44).	Imerina.	Rev. R. Baron [C.].
k.	♀ skeleton.	E. Imerina.	Rev. J. Wills [C.].

140. STENOPHIS.

Dipsas, part., *Schleg. Phys Serp* ii p 257 (1837).
Heterurus (*non Hodgs*), part, *Dum. & Bibr Mém Ac. Sc.* xxiii. 1853, p. 538, *and Erp. Gén.* vii. p. 1168 (1854), *Jan, Elenco sist. Ofid.* p 103 (1863).
Dipsadoboa, part., *Gunth Cat Col. Sn* p. 182 (1858).

Maxillary teeth 13 or 14, equal, followed, after an interspace, by a pair of enlarged, grooved fangs; anterior mandibular teeth longest. Head distinct from neck; eye large, with vertical pupil. Body more or less compressed; scales smooth, with apical pits, in 17 to 25 rows, the scales of the middle row slightly, if at all, enlarged; ventrals obtusely angulate laterally. Tail moderate or long; subcaudals single or paired. Hypapophyses developed throughout the vertebral column.

Madagascar; Comoro Islands.

Synopsis of the Species.

I. Scales in 17 or 19 rows; internasals much shorter than the præfrontals.

   A. Scales in 17 rows; ventrals 187; subcaudals 67 pairs.
                          1. *guentheri*, p. 40.

   B. Scales in 17 rows; ventrals 228–276.

Posterior chin-shields a little shorter than the anterior, and in contact with each other; ventrals 229–248; subcaudals 107–122, all or greater part in pairs ..   2. *granuliceps*, p. 41.

Posterior chin-shields larger than the anterior and in contact with each other; ventrals 228; subcaudals 110, greater part in pairs ....   3. *inornatus*, p. 42.

Posterior chin-shields shorter than the anterior and separated by scales; ventrals 255–276; subcaudals 93–116, all or greater part single ....   4. *gaimardii*, p. 42.

   C. Scales in 19 rows; ventrals 243, subcaudals 126, single.
                          5. *maculatus*, p. 43.

II. Scales in 21 to 25 rows; internasals nearly as long as, or a little longer than, the præfrontals.

   A. Loreal separated from the eye by the præocular; subcaudals 152–159, single.

Posterior chin-shields large and in contact with each other; ventrals 225–236 ....   6. *arctifasciatus*, p. 43.
Posterior chin-shields very small or absent; subcaudals 251–265 ....   7. *variabilis*, p. 43.

   B. Loreal entering the eye, ventrals 226; subcaudals 106 pairs.
                          8. *betsileanus*, p. 44.

1. Stenophis guentheri. (PLATE IV. fig. 1.)

Rostral twice as broad as deep, scarcely visible from above; internasals nearly as long as broad, much shorter than the præfrontals; frontal once and one third as long as broad, as long as its distance from the end of the snout, shorter than the parietals; loreal twice as long as deep; one præocular, forming a suture with the frontal; three postoculars; temporals 2 + 3; eight upper labials, third, fourth, and fifth entering the eye; four lower labials in contact with the anterior chin-shields; posterior chin-shields as large as the anterior and in contact with each other anteriorly. Scales in 17 rows. Ventrals 187; anal divided; subcaudals 67 pairs. Pale brown above, with squarish dark brown spots disposed quincuncially, those on the vertebral line much larger than the others, the first spot, on the occiput, produced forwards as a streak to the frontal; a rhomboidal dark brown spot on the snout; an irregular dark streak on each side of the head, passing through the eye: yellowish white beneath, tail with some small brown spots.

Total length 435 millim.; tail 92.

Madagascar.

a. ♀ (V. 187; C. 67).   S.W. Madagascar.   Mr. Last [C.].

2. Stenophis granuliceps.

Dipsas (Heterurus) gaimardi, var granuliceps, *Boettg. Abh. Senck. Ges.* xi. 1877, p. 14, pl i. fig 3, & xii 1881, p. 448.
—— (Heterurus) gaimardi, *Steind. Sitzb. Ak. Wien*, c 1891, p 297.

Rostral twice as broad as deep, scarcely visible from above; internasals not or but slightly broader than long, much shorter than the præfrontals; frontal once and one third to once and a half as long as broad, as long as or a little longer than its distance from the end of the snout, shorter than the parietals; loreal much longer than deep, one præocular (rarely divided) in contact with or narrowly separated from the frontal; two or three postoculars; temporals 1 + 2 or 2 + 3; eight upper labials, fourth and fifth entering the eye; four or five lower labials in contact with the anterior chin-shields; posterior chin-shields a little shorter than the anterior and in contact with each other. Scales in 17 rows. Ventrals 229-248; anal divided; subcaudals 107-122, all divided or a few (2 to 5) entire. Pale brown or yellowish above, with dark brown or black cross-bars, which may be narrower or broader than the interspaces; a ⊥-shaped black marking on the occiput and nape; white beneath, tail with black spots.

Total length 720 millim.; tail 170.

Madagascar.

a. ♂ (V. 233; C. 121).   Nossi Bé.   Senckenberg Mus [E.].
b. ♂ (V. 229; C. 122).   Imerina.   Rev. R. Baron [C.].
c. ♀ (V. 242; C 115).   Madagascar.

3. Stenophis inornatus.

Rostral twice as broad as deep, scarcely visible from above; internasals as long as broad, much shorter than the præfrontals; frontal twice as long as broad, a little longer than its distance from the end of the snout, shorter than the parietals; loreal much longer than deep; one præocular, in contact with or narrowly separated from the frontal; three postoculars; temporals 2+2; eight upper labials, fourth and fifth entering the eye; four or five lower labials in contact with the anterior chin-shields; posterior chin-shields a little longer than the anterior and in contact with each other. Scales in 17 rows. Ventrals 228; anal divided; subcaudals 110, three of the anterior (third to fifth) single, rest divided. Pale brown above, with a series of rather indistinct, small darker spots along the spine, no other markings on the head and body; lower parts brownish white.

Total length 550 millim., tail 145.

Madagascar.

a. ♂ (V. 228; C. 110).   Madagascar.   Mr. Last [C.].

4. Stenophis gaimardii.

Dipsas gaimardii, *Schleg. Phys. Serp.* ii. p. 293 (1837), *and Abbild.* p. 135, pl. xlv. figs. 16–18 (1844).
Heterurus gaimardii, *Dum. & Bibr.* vii. p. 1173 (1854), *Jan, Icon. Gén.* 38, pl ii. fig 2 (1871).
Dipsas (Heterurus) gaimardii, var. comorensis, *Peters, Mon. Berl. Ac.* 1873, p. 794.

Rostral broader than deep, scarcely visible from above; internasals as long as broad, much shorter than the præfrontals; frontal once and one third as long as broad, as long as or a little longer than its distance from the end of the snout, shorter than the parietals; loreal much longer than deep, one præocular, in contact with or narrowly separated from the frontal; three postoculars, temporals 2+2 or 3; eight upper labials, fourth and fifth entering the eye; four lower labials in contact with the anterior chin-shields; posterior chin-shield shorter than the anterior, and separated from each other by scales. Scales in 17 rows. Ventrals 255–276; anal divided; subcaudals 93–116, all or greater part single. Pale brown above, with dark brown or black cross-bars, which are as broad as or narrower than the interspaces; a ⊥-shaped black marking on the occiput and nape; white beneath, uniform or with brown spots.

Total length 660 millim.; tail 135.

Madagascar; Comoro Islands.

a–b ♂ (V. 262; C. 105)   Imerina.   Rev. R. Baron [C.].
& yg. (V. 265; C. 93).

5. Stenophis maculatus. (Plate IV. fig. 2.)

Dipsadoboa maculata, *Günth. Cat.* p. 183 (1858).

Rostral twice as broad as deep, scarcely visible from above; internasals as long as broad, much shorter than the præfrontals; frontal a little longer than broad, as long as its distance from the end of the snout, shorter than the parietals; loreal longer than deep, one præocular, in contact with the frontal; three postoculars; temporals small, scale-like, 2+2; eight upper labials, fourth and fifth entering the eye; four lower labials in contact with the anterior chin-shields; posterior chin-shields narrower and separated from each other by two series of scales. Scales in 19 rows. Ventrals 243; anal entire; subcaudals 126, single. Yellowish, " with small quadrangular black spots."

Total length 655 millim.; tail 165.

Habitat unknown.

a. ♂ (V. 243; C. 126). ——— ? (Type.)

6. Stenophis arctifasciatus.

Heterurus arctifasciatus, *Dum. & Bibr.* vii p. 1176 (1854); *Jan, Icon. Gén* 38, pl. iii. fig. 1 (1871).

Dipsas (Heterurus) arctifasciatus, *Boettg. Abh. Senck. Ges.* xi. 1877, p. 34.

Rostral broader than deep, just visible from above; internasals a little broader than long, nearly as long as the præfrontals; frontal once and one third as long as broad, longer than its distance from the end of the snout, shorter than the parietals, loreal longer than deep; one præocular, not reaching the frontal; two or three postoculars; temporals 1+1, 1+2, or 2+2; eight upper labials, fourth and fifth entering the eye; six lower labials in contact with the anterior chin-shields; posterior chin-shields as long as the anterior and in contact with each other. Scales in 21 or 23 rows. Ventrals 225–236; anal divided; subcaudals 152–159, single. Pale orange or pale brown above, with numerous narrow blackish cross-bars; a black transverse spot on the nape; head without markings; whitish beneath, tail spotted with blackish.

Total length 800 millim.; tail 260.

Madagascar.

a. ♀ (Sc 23; V. 236; C 152). Imerina. Rev. R. Baron [C.].

7. Stenophis variabilis. (Plate IV. fig. 3.)

Rostral broader than deep, just visible from above; internasals a little broader than long, a little shorter than the præfrontals, frontal once and one third as long as broad, longer than its distance from the end of the snout, shorter than the parietals; loreal longer than deep; one præocular, which may be divided, not reaching the frontal; two or three postoculars; temporals 2+2 or 3; eight upper labials, fourth and fifth entering the eye; five lower labials in contact with the anterior chin-shields; posterior chin-shields very small or absent. Scales in 23 or 25 rows. Ventrals 251–265; anal entire; subcaudals 159, single. Greenish yellow or orange above, with small black spots or rather indistinct dark green cross-bars; a series of larger blackish spots along the spine; head bright yellow, spotted or marbled with blackish; a large black nuchal spot; yellow beneath, tail (in the male) with black spots.

Total length 1098 millim.; tail (injured) 260.

Madagascar.

a–b. ♂ (Sc. 23, V. 251, C. ?)   Madagascar.
& yg. (Sc. 25; V. 265, C 159).

8. Stenophis betsileanus. (Plate IV. fig. 4.)

Dipsas betsileana, *Günth. Ann. & Mag. N. H.* (5) vi 1880, p. 238.

Rostral broader than deep, just visible from above; internasals broader than long, a little longer than the præfrontals; frontal once and one third as long as broad, longer than its distance from the end of the snout, shorter than the parietals, loreal longer than deep, entering the eye below the præocular, which is widely separated from the frontal; two postoculars; temporals 1+2; seven upper labials, third and fourth entering the eye; five lower labials in contact with the anterior chin-shields; posterior chin-shields shorter than the anterior, in contact with each other. Scales in 23 rows. Ventrals 226; anal divided; subcaudals 106 pairs. Black, with yellowish-white annuli, widening on the belly; some of the annuli interrupted and alternating on the back; upper labials and throat yellowish white; a yellowish-white bar across the snout.

Total length 400 millim.; tail 90.

Madagascar.

a. Yg. (V. 226; C 106).   S.E. Betsileo.   (Type.)

141. LYCODRYAS.

Lycodryas, *Günth. Ann. & Mag. N. H.* (5) iii. 1879, p. 218.

Maxillary teeth 12 or 13, anterior longest, followed, after a short interspace, by an enlarged, grooved fang; anterior palatine and mandibular teeth longest. Head very distinct from neck, eye rather large, with vertical pupil. Body much elongate, compressed; scales smooth, with apical pits, in 19 rows; ventrals angulate laterally. Tail long; anterior subcaudals single, rest divided. Hypapophyses developed throughout the vertebral column.

Comoro Islands.

1. Lycodryas sancti-johannis. (Plate III. fig. 2.)

Lycodryas sancti-johannis, *Gunth. Ann. & Mag N. H.* (5) iii. 1879, p. 218.

Head much depressed, with broad, truncated snout. Rostral twice as broad as deep, scarcely visible from above; internasals as long as broad, much shorter than the præfrontals, frontal with concave sides, a little longer than broad, as long as its distance from the end of the snout, much shorter than the parietals: nostril between two nasals; loreal twice as long as deep; one præocular, forming a suture with the frontal; three postoculars, temporals small, scale-like, 2+2 or 2+3; eight or nine upper labials, fourth and fifth or third, fourth, and fifth entering the eye; four or five lower labials in contact with the anterior chin-shields, which are larger than the posterior. Scales in 19 rows. Ventrals 243-258; anal divided; subcaudals 75, the 23 or 24 anterior single. Reddish yellow above, uniform or mottled with brown; some rather ill-defined dark cross-bars may be present on the neck; lower parts yellowish, uniform or dotted with blackish.

Total length 770 millim., tail 150.

Comoro Islands.

a. ♂ (V. 258; C ᴾ).	Johanna.	C. E. Bewsher, Esq. [C.]. (Type)
b. ♂ (V. 243; C. 75)	Comoro Ids.	Sir J. Kirk [C.]

142. PYTHONODIPSAS.

Pythonodipsas, *Gunth. Ann. & Mag. N. H.* (4) i. 1868, p. 425.

Maxillary teeth 13, third to sixth longest, followed, after a very short interspace, by a large, grooved fang; second to fifth mandibular teeth strongly enlarged, fang-like. Head distinct from neck, eye moderate, with vertically elliptic pupil; nostrils directed upwards, pierced between a nasal and a supranasal; parietals broken up into small shields. Body cylindrical; scales smooth or very obtusely keeled, with apical pits, in 21 rows; ventrals rounded. Tail moderate; subcaudals single. Hypapophyses developed throughout the vertebral column.

Tropical Africa.

1. Pythonodipsas carinata.

Pythonodipsas carinata, *Gunth Ann & Mag. N. H.* (4) i. 1868, p. 426, pl. xix. fig. K; *Bouleng. Ann. & Mag. N H.* (6) ii 1888, p 140.

Snout broad, truncate, concave above, rostral more than twice as broad as deep, scarcely visible from above; internasals considerably longer than broad, shorter than the præfrontals; frontal as broad as the supraocular, nearly twice as long as broad, with concave sides; one or two small shields between the præfrontals and the frontal; several small loreals, one præocular, three or four suboculars, and three postoculars, temporals small, scale-like, nine upper labials; four or five lower labials in contact with the anterior chin-shields, which are as long as the posterior. Scales in 21 rows, smooth or very obtusely keeled. Ventrals 190-192; anal entire; subcaudals 54-55. Sand-coloured or pale buff above, with a double alternating series of square grey spots, a few of which may coalesce to form transverse bars; lips with vertical grey bars; lower parts white.

Total length 590 millim.; tail 85.

Zambesi; Damaraland.

a. ♂ (V. 190; C. 54).   Zambesi.   J. Chapman, Esq. [C.]. (Type.)

143. DITYPOPHIS.

Ditypophis, *Günth* Proc. Zool. Soc. 1881, p 462.

Maxillary teeth 8 or 9, strongly increasing in length to the last but one, followed, after an interspace, by a large, grooved fang; second to fifth mandibular teeth strongly enlarged, fang-like. Head distinct from neck; eye moderate, with vertically elliptic pupil. Body short, cylindrical; scales smooth, with apical pits, in 21 rows;

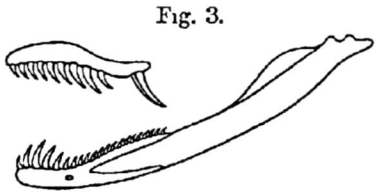

Fig. 3.

Maxillary and mandible of *Ditypophis vivax*.

ventrals rounded. Tail short; subcaudals single. Hypapophyses developed throughout the vertebral column.

Socotra.

1. Ditypophis vivax.

Ditypophis vivax, *Günth.* Proc. Zool Soc 1881, p. 462, pl xl.

Snout short, broad; rostral more than twice as broad as deep, scarcely visible from above; internasals a little longer than broad, longer than the præfrontals; frontal not broader than the supraocular, once and two thirds as long as broad, as long as its distance from the end of the snout, shorter than the parietals; nostril pierced in the upper part of an undivided nasal; loreal slightly longer than deep; one præocular, forming a suture with the frontal; a subocular below the præocular; two postoculars; temporals small, scale-like, 2+3 or 4; eight upper labials, fourth and fifth entering the eye; four lower labials in contact with the anterior chin-shields, which are as long as the posterior. Scales in 21 rows. Ventrals 146; anal entire; subcaudals 37. Reddish sandy above, with indistinct darker cloudy spots on the back; a dark streak on each side of the head, passing through the eye; lower parts white

Total length 345 millim.; tail 50.

Socotra.

a. ♀ (V. 146; C. 37).   ·   ·   Dr. I. B. Balfour C. . (Type.)

144. TARBOPHIS.

Telescopus (*non Montf.*), *Wagl. Syst. Amph.* p. 182 (1830); *Dum. & Bibr. Erp. Gén.* vii. p 1054 (1854), *Jan, Elenco sist. Ofid.* p 102 (1863)
Tarbophis, *Fleischm Dalm nov Serp. Gen.* p. 17 (1831); *Dum. & Bibr. t. c.* p 911, *Jan, l. c.* p. 99.
Trigonophis, *Eichw. Zool. Spec. Ross. Pol.* iii. p. 174 (1831).
Dipsas, part., *Schleg Phys Serp.* ii. p 257 (1837).
Ailurophis, *Bonap. Icon Faun. Ital* ii. (1837).
Tachymenis, part., *Gunth. Cat. Col. Sn.* p. 83 (1858).

Maxillary teeth 10 to 12, anterior longest, gradually decreasing in size posteriorly, and followed, after an interspace, by a pair of enlarged, grooved fangs, situated below the posterior border of the eye, anterior mandibular teeth strongly enlarged. Head distinct from neck; eye moderate, with vertically elliptic pupil. Body cylindrical or slightly compressed; scales smooth, oblique, with apical pits, in 19 to 23 rows, ventrals rounded. Tail moderate; subcaudals in two rows.

Fig 4.

Maxillary and mandible of *Tarbophis fallax*.

South-eastern Europe, South-western Asia, Tropical and North-eastern Africa.

Synopsis of the Species.

I. Loreal entering, or nearly entering, the eye.

A. Scales in 19 or 21 rows.

Posterior chin-shields narrowly separated from each other in front; ventrals 174–190; anal divided.... 1. *savignyi*, p. 48.
Posterior chin-shields widely separated; ventrals 186–222; anal divided ... 2. *fallax*, p. 48.
Posterior chin-shields widely separated; ventrals 203–235; anal entire .... 3. *iberus*, p. 49.

B. Scales in 23 rows; ventrals 268–280; anal entire.
4. *rhinopoma*, p. 50.

II. Loreal separated from the eye by the præocular.

A. Scales in 19 rows; anal divided.

Two labials entering the eye .... 5. *variegatus*, p. 51.
Three labials entering the eye ...... 6. *semiannulatus*, p. 51

B. Scales in 19 or 21 rows; anal entire.
7. *guentheri*, p. 52.

C. Scales in 21 or 23 rows; anal divided.
8. *obtusus*, p. 52.

1. Tarbophis savignyi.

Savigny, Descr. Egypte, Rept., Suppl. pl. iv. fig 2 (1829)
Tachymenis vivax (*non Fitz.*), *Gunth. Proc Zool Soc.* 1864, p. 489.
Tarbophis vivax, *Boettg. Ber. Senck. Ges.* 1878-79, p. 67, and 1879-80, p. 33; *Peracca, Boll. Mus. Tor.* ix. 1894, no 167, p. 15
—— vivax, f. syriaca, part., *Boettg. Ber. Senck. Ges.* 1879-80, p 166.

Very closely allied to *T. fallax*, but snout shorter and broader; internasals broader than long, frontal not more than once and one third as long as broad; nasal entire or semidivided; loreal once and a half to twice and a half as long as deep, usually entering the eye; posterior chin-shields narrowly separated from each other in front. Scales in 19 rows. Ventrals 174-190; anal divided; subcaudals 45-57. Yellowish above, with a dorsal series of 23 to 28 dark brown or black spots on the body, these spots sometimes confluent with a lateral series of spots or vertical bars which usually alternate with the dorsal series; the first blotch largest, covering the nape and descending to the sides of the neck, which it may entirely encircle; head greyish above, dotted with black and with a few small black spots; labials dark-edged; belly black, or much spotted or marbled with dark brown or black.

Total length 465 millim.; tail 65.

Southern Syria, Lower Egypt.

a. ♀ (V 174; C. 51).	Jerusalem	Canon Tristram [C.].
b-c. ♂ (V 187; C. ?) & yg. (V.178; C. 55).	Mt. Tabor	Canon Tristram [C].
d. Yg. (V 190; C. 53).	Lebanon.	Canon Tristram [C.].

2. Tarbophis fallax.

Coluber vivax, *Fitzing. N. Class. Rept.* p. 57 (1826).—Nomen nudum.
Tarbophis fallax, *Fleischm. Dalm. nov. Serp Gen.* p. 18, pl i. (1831).
Dipsas fallax, *Schleg. Phys Serp.* ii. p. 295, pl. xi. figs. 35 & 36 (1837).
Ailurophis vivax, *Bonap. Icon. Faun. Ital.*, Anf. (1837).
Tarbophis vivax, *Dum. & Bibr.* vii. p. 913 (1854), *Schreib. Herp. Eur.* p. 213, fig. (1875); *Boettg. Zeitschr. Ges. Naturw* xlix. 1877, p. 287, *Bedriaga, Bull Soc. Nat. Mosc.* 1881, p 313; *Boettg Sitzb. Ak. Berl.* 1888, p. 178; *Tomasini, Wiss. Mitth. aus Bosn. u. Herzeg.* ii p 657 1894.

Tachymenis vivax, *Gunth. Cat.* p 33 (1858), *and Ann. & Mag. N. H.* (5) v 1880, p. 436.
Tarbophis vivax, part., *Strauch, Schl. Russ. R.* p. 194 (1873).
—— vivax, f. syriaca, part., *Boettg. Ber. Senck. Ges.* 1879–80, p. 166.

Rostral broader than deep, just visible from above; internasals nearly as long as broad, shorter than the præfrontals; frontal once and one fourth to once and a half as long as broad, as long as its distance from the end of the snout, shorter than the parietals; nasal divided or semidivided; loreal twice and a half to thrice as long as deep, entering the eye below the præocular, which is in contact with the frontal; two (rarely three) postoculars; temporals small, scale-like, 2 or 3+3 or 4; eight (rarely seven or nine) upper labials, third, fourth, and fifth (rarely fourth and fifth or fourth, fifth, and sixth) entering the eye; three or four lower labials in contact with the anterior chin-shields; posterior chin-shields very small and widely separated from each other by scales. Scales in 19 or 21 rows. Ventrals 186–222; anal divided, subcaudals 48–73. Greyish above, with 40 to 57 brown or black spots or bars on the body; a lateral series of smaller spots or vertical bars, alternating with the dorsals; the first spot, on the nape, elongate, usually with one or three linear processes in front extending on the head; usually a dark streak from the eye to the angle of the mouth; lower parts whitish, speckled, spotted, or marbled with grey or brown.

Total length 850 millim.; tail 120.

From Illyria and Dalmatia to Greece, the Archipelago, Asia Minor, and Northern Syria.

A. Scales in 19 rows.

a. ♂ (V. 194; C. ?).	Zara, Dalmatia.	Count M. Peracca [P.].
b. ♀ (V. 206; C. 52).	Zara, Dalmatia.	Dr F Werner [E.].
c–g. ♂ (V 201, 204, 204; C. 50, 55, 55) & ♀ (V. 204, 199; C. 48, 51).	Dalmatia.	Lord Lilford [P.].
h. Yg. (V. 210, C. 50).	Dalmatia.	
i. ♀ (V. 208; C. 55).	Cerigo Id.	Dr. Forsyth Major [P.].
k. Hgr (V 201; C. 73).	Xanthus.	Sir C. Fellows [P.].
l. ♂ (V 186, C. 53).	Beyrout	
m. ♀ skeleton.	Dalmatia.	Lord Lilford [P.].

B. Scales in 21 rows.

n. ♀ (V. 199; C. ?).	Cyprus	Gen. Biddulph [P.]
o. ♀ (V. 208; C. 66).	Cyprus.	R. T. Kenyon, Esq. [P.].
p–r. ♂ (V. 199, 203; C. 66, 60) & ♀ (V. 197; C. 60).	Cyprus.	Hr. H. Rolle [C.].

3. Tarbophis iberus.

Trigonophis iberus, *Eichw. Zool. Spec.* iii. p. 175 (1831), *and Faun. Casp.-Cau.* p. 101, pl. xviii. (1842).
Coluber carneus, *Dwigubsky, Nat. Hist Russ., Amph.* p. 27 (1832).— *Teste Strauch.*

Dipsas fallax, *Nordm. in Demid. Voy. Russ. Mér* iii. p 343, *Rept.* pl. iv. fig. 2 (1840); *Berth. in Wagn. Reise n. Kolchis*, p 334 (1850).
Tarbophis vivax, *Jan, Icon. Gén.* 38, pl. i. fig. 2 (1871); *Boettg. in Radde, Faun. Flor Casp.-Geb* p 72 (1886).
—— vivax, part., *Strauch, Schl. Russ. R.* p. 194 (1873).

Agrees in most respects with *T. fallax*, but parietals shorter, slightly longer than the frontal, and anal entire. Nasal semidivided; fourth and fifth, or third, fourth, and fifth labials entering the eye. Scales in 19 rows (exceptionally 21). Ventrals 203–235; subcaudals 55–70. Grey above, with 35 blackish spots on the body, the anterior largest and darkest; a lateral series of smaller spots or vertical bars; lower parts blackish, with small whitish spots and dots.

Total length 650 millim.; tail 100.

Caucasus.

a ♂ (Sc.19; V. 213; C. 61). Evlakh, Gov Elizabethpol, Transcaucasia.

4. Tarbophis rhinopoma.

? Tarbophis sp., *Cope, Proc. Ac. Philad.* 1862, p 338.
Dipsas rhinopoma, *Blanf. Ann. & Mag. N. H.* (4) xiv. 1874, p. 34, and *Zool E. Pers.* p. 424, pl. xxviii fig 2 (1876); *Boettg. in Radde, Faun. Flor. Casp.-Geb.* p. 72 (1886).
Tarbophis rhinopoma, *Bouleng. Journ. Bomb. N. H. Soc.* ix. 1895, p. 325.

Rostral broader than deep, just visible from above; internasals broader than long, shorter than the præfrontals; frontal slightly longer than broad, as long as its distance from the end of the snout, a little shorter than the parietals; nasal semidivided; loreal twice to twice and a half as long as deep, entering the eye below the præocular, which is in contact with the frontal; two postoculars; temporals small, scale-like, 2 or 3+3 or 4; eight to ten upper labials, third, fourth, and fifth, or fourth and fifth, or fourth, fifth, and sixth entering the eye; four or five lower labials in contact with the anterior chin-shields; posterior chin-shields very small and widely separated from each other by scales. Scales in 23 (or 24) rows. Ventrals 268–280; anal entire; subcaudals 76–82. Pale sandy grey above, with a dorsal series of 65 to 85 brown square or transverse spots, larger than the interspaces between them, and an alternating series of smaller spots on each side; on the posterior part of the body the dorsal spots may split up into two alternating series; head with small dark spots or specks; labials dark-edged; throat white; ventrals dark brown

Total length 990 millim.; tail 155.

Persia, Sind.

♂ (V. 268; C. 77). Karman, S. Persia, 5000 ft. W. T. Blanford, Esq. [E]. (One of the types.)
b. Yg. (V. 280; C. 82). Sind. H. M. Phipson, Esq. [P.]

5. Tarbophis variegatus.

Dipsas variegata, *Reinh. Vidensk. Selsk. Skrift.* x. 1843, p. 249, pl. i. figs. 15-17; *F. Mull Verh. Nat. Ges. Basel,* vii 1885, p. 689.

Rostral broader than deep, scarcely visible from above; internasals nearly as long as broad, a little shorter than the parietals; frontal about once and a half as long as broad, longer than its distance from the end of the snout, as long as or a little shorter than the parietals; nasal divided; loreal longer than deep; one præ-[*] and two postoculars; temporals small, 2+3; seven to nine upper labials, third and fourth or fourth and fifth entering the eye; three or four lower labials in contact with the anterior chin-shields; posterior chin-shields small and widely separated from each other, or indistinct. Scales in 19 rows. Ventrals 209-226; anal divided; subcaudals 62-67. Pale brownish above, with 26 to 30 rather irregular dark brown cross-bars, each enclosing a whitish vertebral spot; head spotted or marbled with brown; the sutures between the upper labials dark brown; belly and lower surface of tail yellowish white, spotted with dark brown.

Total length 590 millim.; tail 95.

Guinea.

a, b. ♂ (V. 218; C. 64) &   W. Africa.
    ♀ (V. 226; C. 62).

6. Tarbophis semiannulatus.

Telescopus semiannulatus, *Smith, Ill. Zool. S Afr., Rept.* pl. lxxii. (1849); *Dum. & Bibr* vii. p. 1058 (1854); *Peters, Reise n. Mossamb.* iii p. 127 (1882).

Leptodira semiannulata, *Gunth. Ann & Mag. N. H.* (4) ix. 1872, p 31; *Bouleng The Zool.* 1887, p 179; *Boettg. Ber. Senck. Ges.* 1887, p 162.

Crotaphopeltis semiannulatus, *Bocage, Herp. d'Angola,* p. 122 (1895).

Rostral broader than deep, just visible from above; internasals as long as broad or a little broader than long, usually shorter than the præfrontals; frontal once and one third to once and a half as long as broad, as long as or a little longer than its distance from the end of the snout, a little shorter than the parietals; nasal divided; loreal as long as deep or a little longer than deep; one præocular, not reaching the frontal; two postoculars; temporals 2+2 or 3; eight or nine upper labials, third, fourth, and fifth entering the eye; four or five lower labials in contact with the anterior chin-shields; posterior chin-shields small and widely separated from each other. Scales in 19 rows. Ventrals 206-242; anal divided; subcaudals 51-83. Yellowish or pale brown above, with 24 to 34 dark brown

---

[*] In the specimens in the Collection the præocular does not reach the frontal.

or blackish transverse rhomboidal spots or cross-bars on the body; head without any spots or markings; yellowish white beneath

Total length 700 millim.; tail 120.

Tropical Africa.

a.	♀ (V. 230; C. 63).	Zanzibar Coast.	
b.	♀ (V. 224; C 73).	Mombasa	H. W. Lane, Esq. [C.].
c.	♀ (V. 237; C. 66).	Ugogo.	Mr. Baxter [C.].
d.	♀ (V. 228; C. ?).	Tanganyika.	Sir J. Kirk [C.].
e.	♀ (V. 224; C. 64).	Lake Nyassa.	Miss M. Woodward [C.].
f.	Hgr. ♀ (V. 225; C. 58).	Lake Nyassa	Universities Mission.
g.	♂ (V. 224; C. ?).	Loanda.	(Type of *L. semiannulata*.)

7. Tarbophis guentheri.

? Coluber dhara, *Forsk. Descr. Anim* p. 14 (1775); *Daud. Rept.* vi. p. 257 (1803).

Telescopus obtusus (non Reuss), *Jan, Icon. Gén.* 38, pl i. fig. 4 (1871)

Tarbophis guentheri, *Anders. Proc Zool. Soc.* 1895, p. 656, pl. xxxvi fig. 3.

Agrees with *T. obtusus*, except in having the scales in 19 or 21 rows and the anal entire. Nine or ten upper labials, third, fourth, and fifth, or fourth, fifth, and sixth entering the eye. Ventrals 205-274; subcaudals 69-75.

Total length 1045 millim.; tail 160.

Arabia; East Africa.

a.	♂ (Sc. 21; V. 235; C. ?).	Lahej, near Aden	Col Yerbury [P.].
b.	♀ (Sc. 21; V. 240; C. ?).	Sheikh Othman, near Aden.	Col. Yerbury [P.].
c-d.	♂ (Sc. 21; V. 236; C ?) & hgr. (Sc. 21; V. 239; C. 72.)	Hadramaut.	Dr J. Anderson [P.]. (Types)
e, f.	♂ (Sc. 21; V. 264; C. 69) & ♀ (Sc 21; V. 274; C. 75).	Muscat.	A.S.G. Jayakar, Esq [P.]. (Types)
g.	♂ (Sc. 19; V. 205; C. 72).	Ngatana, E Africa.	Dr. J. W. Gregory [P.].

8. Tarbophis obtusus.

Savigny, Descr. Egypte, Rept., Suppl. pl. v. fig. 1 (1829).

Coluber obtusus, *Reuss, Mus. Senck.* i. 1834, p. 137.

Dipsas ægyptiacus, *Schleg. Phys. Serp.* ii. p. 274 (1837), and *Abbild.* pl. xlv. figs. 19 & 20 (1844).

Telescopus obtusus, *Dum. & Bibr.* vii. p. 1056 (1854); *Mocq. Mém. Cent. Soc. Philom.* p. 133 (1888).

Tarbophis obtusus, *Bouleng. Ann. Mus. Genova*, (2) xv. 1895, p. 15; *Anders. Proc. Zool. Soc.* 1895, p. 658.

Rostral broader than deep, scarcely visible from above; internasals as long as broad or a little broader than long, considerably shorter than the præfrontals; frontal about once and a half as long as broad, as long as or a little longer than its distance from the end of the snout, shorter than the parietals; nasal divided; loreal once and a half to once and three fourths as long as deep; one præocular, in contact with or narrowly separated from the frontal; two post-oculars; temporals small, scale-like, 2+2, 3, or 4; nine to eleven upper labials, third, fourth, and fifth, fourth, fifth, and sixth, or fifth, sixth, and seventh entering the eye, three to five lower labials in contact with the anterior chin-shields; posterior chin-shields small and widely separated from each other, or indistinct. Scales in 23 (rarely 21) rows. Ventrals 213–272; anal divided; subcaudals 65–82. Pale buff or sandy grey above, uniform or with ill-defined brown variegations or cross-bars, lower parts white.

Total length 1870 millim.; tail 165.

Egypt to Somaliland.

a. ♂ (V. 271; C 75).		Nile.	Rev. O. P. Cambridge [P.].
b. ♀ (V. 263; C. 75).		Beltim.	Dr. J. Anderson [P.]
c–d. Hgr (V. 262; C. 77) & yg. (V. 257; C. 79).		Gizeh.	Dr. J Anderson [P.].
e. ♀ (V. 272; C 72).		Tel el Amarna.	Dr. J Anderson [P.].
f. Hgr (V. 263; C.81).		Assouan.	Dr. J. Anderson [P.].
g. ♀ skeleton.		Egypt.	

145. TRIMORPHODON.

Dipsas, part., *Dum. & Bibr Erp. Gén.* vii. p. 1133 (1854).
Dipsadomorphus, part., *Gunth. Cat Col. Sn* p. 174 (1858).
Trimorphodon, *Cope, Proc. Ac. Philad.* 1861, p 297.
Eteirodipsas, part., *Jan, Elenco sist. Ofid.* p. 105 (1863).

Maxillary teeth 10 or 11, anterior much longer than the posterior, which gradually decrease in size, followed, after an interspace, by a pair of enlarged grooved teeth situated below the posterior border of the eye; anterior mandibular teeth strongly enlarged. Head distinct from neck; eye moderate, with vertically elliptic pupil; loreal usually divided; usually a subocular below the præocular. Body compressed; scales smooth, slightly oblique, with apical pits, in 21 to 27 rows; ventrals obtusely angulate laterally. Tail moderate; subcaudals in two rows.

Lower California, Arizona, Mexico, Central America.

Synopsis of the Species.

I. Eight or nine upper labials.

Scales in 25 (rarely 23 or 27) rows; ventrals 234–264; subcaudals 74–94; head with chevron-shaped bands . . . . 1. *biscutatus*, p. 54.
Scales in 21 or 23 rows; ventrals 205–236; subcaudals 61–72 . . . . 2. *upsilon*, p. 55.

Scales in 21 rows; ventrals 236; subcaudals
70; head with a lyre-shaped pattern;
dorsal spots in pairs .... 3. *lyrophanes*, p. 56.

II. Six or seven upper labials; scales in 23 rows.
4. *tau*, p. 56.

1. Trimorphodon biscutatus.

Dipas biscutata, *Dum. & Bibr.* vii. p. 1153 (1854).
Dipsadomorphus biscutatus, *Gunth. Cat.* p. 176 (1858).
Trimorphodon biscutatus, *Cope, Proc. Ac. Philad* 1861, p. 297, and *Proc. Amer. Philos. Soc.* xi. 1869, p. 152, *Dugès, La Naturaleza*, vi. 1882, p. 145, fig.; *Cope, Proc. Amer. Philos. Soc.* xxii. 1886, p. 286; *Gunth. Biol. C.-Amer., Rept.* p 174 (1895).
Eteirodipsas biscutata, *Jan, Elenco*, p. 105 (1863).
Trimorphodon major, *Cope, Proc. Amer. Philos. Soc.* xi 1869, p. 153.
Sibon biscutatum, part., *Garm. N. Amer. Rept.* p. 16 (1883).
? Trimorphodon lambda, *Cope, Proc. Amer. Philos. Soc.* xxiii. 1886, p. 286.

Rostral broader than deep, the portion visible from above measuring one fourth to one half its distance from the frontal; internasals much shorter than the præfrontals, which are usually broader than long; frontal once and one fourth to once and a half as long as broad, as long as or a little longer than its distance from the end of the snout, as long as or slightly shorter than the parietals; two or three loreals, rarely one; two (rarely one) præoculars, usually with a subocular below; the upper præocular in contact with or narrowly separated from the frontal; three postoculars; temporals small, scale-like, 2+3, 3+3, or 3+4; nine (rarely eight) upper labials, fourth and fifth (in one specimen third, fourth, and fifth, owing to the absence of subocular) entering the eye; four or five lower labials in contact with the anterior chin-shields, which are longer than the posterior. Scales in 23 to 27 rows, usually 25. Ventrals 234–264; anal divided; subcaudals 74–94. Pale greyish or brownish above, with dark, black-edged cross-bars or transverse markings with light centre; head with angular dark bands separated by a crescentic transverse light area between the eyes and a ∧- or ⋋-shaped one on the occiput; lower parts whitish, more or less mottled with brown, with large dark brown spots on the sides.

Total length 1200 millim.; tail 230.

Mexico to Panama.

a ♀ (Sc. 25; V. 251; C. 78).	Mazatlan.	Hr. A. Forrer [C.].
b–d, e–g. ♂ (Sc. 25, 25, 24, V. 250, 249, 243; C. 85, 84, 87), ♀ (Sc. 25; V. 255; C. 78), & yg. (Sc. 25, 23; V. 244, 237; C 86, 86).	Presidio.	Hr A. Forrer [C.].
h. Her. ♀ (Sc. 25; V. 223; C. 78).	Oaxaca.	M. Sallé [C.].

i. ♂ (Sc. 25; V. 251; C. 87).   Lanquin, Guatemala.   O. Salvin, Esq. [C.].

k. Hgr. ♀ (Sc. 27; V. 253; C. 81).   Guatemala.   O. Salvin, Esq. [C.].

l. ♀ (Sc. 27; V. 263; C. 79).   Nicaragua.

m. ♂ (Sc. 25; V. 259, C. 89).   Panama   Capt. J. C. Dow [P.].

n. Hgr. ♀ (Sc. 25; V. 256, C. 77).   C. America.   Haslar Collection.

o. Skull.   San Ramon, Mexico.   Dr. A. C. Buller [C.].

2. Trimorphodon upsilon.

Trimorphodon upsilon, *Cope, Proc Amer. Philos. Soc.* xi. 1869, p 152, and xxiii. 1886, p. 286; *Gunth. Biol. C.-Am., Rept.* p 175 (1895).

Dipsas biscutata, var. latifascia, *Peters, Mon. Berl. Ac* 1869, p. 877.

Eteirodipsas biscutata, *Jan, Icon. Gén* 39, pl. i. fig. 3 (1872).

Trimorphodon collaris, *Cope, Journ Ac. Philad.* (2) viii. 1876, p. 131, *and Proc. Amer. Philos Soc.* xxiii. 1886, p. 286.

Sibon biscutatum, part., *Garm. N. Am. Rept.* p. 16 (1883).

—— upsilon, *Garm. l.c.* p. 134.

? Trimorphodon vilkinsonii, *Cope, Proc. Amer. Philos. Soc.* xxiii. 1886, p. 285.

Rostral broader than deep, the portion visible from above measuring one fourth to one third its distance from the frontal; internasals much shorter than the præfrontals, which are nearly as long as broad; frontal once and a half to once and two thirds as long as broad, as long as or a little longer than its distance from the end of the snout, as long as the parietals; two or three loreals; two præoculars and a subocular; upper præocular in contact with or narrowly separated from the frontal; two or three postoculars; temporals 2+2, 2+3, or 3+3; eight or nine upper labials, fourth and fifth entering the eye; five or six lower labials in contact with the anterior chin-shields, which are longer than the posterior. Scales in 21 or 23 rows. Ventrals 205–236; anal divided; subcaudals 61–72. Pale grey-brown above, with dark, black-edged cross-bars narrowing on the sides and descending to the ends of the ventrals, head dark brown above, pale greyish on the occiput, usually with a light cross-bar between the eyes; a V-shaped light marking sometimes present on the parietal shields, embracing the frontal; whitish beneath, more or less mottled with dark and with dark spots on the sides. In the young the dark bars are much wider, separated by narrow whitish interspaces, and they may form complete annuli.

Total length 660 millim.; tail 120.

Mexico.

a. ♂ (Sc. 23; V. 217, C. 71).   La Cumbre de los Arrastrados, Jalisco.   Dr. A. C. Buller [C.].

b. ♀ (Sc. 21; V. 205, C. 61).   Jalapa.   Mr. Hoege [C.].

c–d. Yg. (Sc. 23, 21; V. 223, 220; C. 70, 72).   Ventanas, Durango.   Hr. A Forrer [C]

e–f. Yg (Sc. 23, 23; V. 236, 214; C. 72, 72).   S. Mexico   F. D. Godman, Esq. [P.].

3. Trimorphodon lyrophanes.

Lycodon lyrophanes, *Cope, Proc. Ac. Philad.* 1860, p 343
Trimorphodon lyrophanes, *Cope, Proc. Ac. Philad.* 1861, p. 297, *and Proc. Amer. Philos. Soc.* xi. 1869, p. 152
Sibon biscutatum, part., *Garm. N. Am. Rept.* p. 16 (1883).

Rostral broader than deep, visible from above; præfrontals broader than long; two loreals; two præoculars and a subocular, the upper præocular not in contact with the frontal; three postoculars; nine upper labials, fourth and fifth entering the eye, anterior chin-shields the longer. Scales in 21 rows. Ventrals 236; anal divided; subcaudals 70. Light grey above; snout crossed by an indistinct ashy band; a lyre-shaped brown marking on the head; back with deep brown spots disposed in pairs; an irregular series of lateral spots and another extending on the ends of the ventral shields; under surface whitish.

Total length 710 millim.; tail 110.

Lower California, Arizona.

4 Trimorphodon tau.

Trimorphon tau, *Cope, Proc. Amer. Philos. Soc.* xi. 1869, p. 152, and xxiii. 1886, p. 286.

Snout projecting considerably beyond the mouth. Rostral somewhat produced behind; internasals about one fourth the size of the præfrontals, which are as long as wide; frontal as long as the parietals; three loreals; two præoculars and a subocular; three postoculars; temporals 2+3; six or seven upper labials, fourth and fifth entering the eye. Scales in 23 rows. Grey above, with black rhombs which extend to the ventral shields by their lateral angles; head black as far as the middle of the parietal shields, with two lateral ear-shaped prolongations on the latter; a pale ⊥-shaped mark, the longitudinal limb on the snout, the transverse limb between the eyes.

Total length 236 millim.; tail 35.

Isthmus of Tehuantepec, Mexico.

146. LYCOGNATHUS.

Lycodon, part., *Boie, Isis,* 1827, p. 521; *Schleg. Phys. Serp.* ii. p. 104 (1837).
Lycognathus, part., *Dum. & Bibr. Mém. Ac. Sc.* xxiii. 1853, p. 495 *and Erp. Gén* vii p. 916 (1854).
Siphlophis, *Cope, Proc. Ac. Philad.* 1861, p. 297.
Oxyrhopus, part., *Jan, L'Elenco sist. Ofid.* p. 92 (1863).

Maxillary teeth 14 to 16, anterior much longer than the posterior, which gradually decrease in size, followed, after an interspace, by a pair of enlarged, grooved fangs situated below the posterior border of the eye; anterior mandibular teeth strongly enlarged. Head distinct from neck; eye rather large, with vertically elliptic pupil. Body compressed; scales smooth, with apical pits, in 19 rows; ventrals strongly angulate laterally. Tail long; subcaudals in two rows.

Tropical South America.

1. Lycognathus cervinus.

Seba, Thes. i. pl. c. fig. 4 (1734), and ii. pl. xxxix. figs. 1 & 2, & lxxix fig. 3 (1735).
Coronella cervina, *Laur. Syn Rept.* p 88 (1768).
Coluber cervinus, *Gmel. S. N.* i. p. 1114 (1788).
—— zeylonicus, part, *Gmel. l c.* p. 1106
—— audax, *Daud. Rept* vi p. 345, pl lxxix. (1803).
—— maximiliani, *Merr. Tent.* p. 105 (1820)
Dipsas audax, *Fitzing N Class Rept.* p. 59 (1826).
Lycodon audax, *Boie, Isis,* 1827, p 525; *Schleg. Phys. Serp.* ii. p 121, pl. iv. figs. 18 & 19 (1837).
Lycognathus scolopax, *Dum. & Bibr.* vii. p. 919 (1854).
—— geminatus, *Dum & Bibr. t. c.* p 922.
Oxyrhopus doliatus (non *D & B.*), *Gunth. Cat* p 192 (1858).
Siphlophis scolopax, *Cope, Proc. Ac. Philad.* 1861, p 297.
Oxyrhopus scolopax, *Jan, Elenco,* p. 92 (1863), *and Icon. Gén.* 35, pl. iv figs. 1 & 2 (1870).

Rostral nearly twice as broad as deep, just visible from above; internasals much shorter than the præfrontals; frontal once and a half as long as broad, as long as its distance from the end of the snout, shorter than the parietals; loreal twice as long as deep; one præocular, not reaching the frontal; two or three postoculars; temporals 2+3; eight (rarely nine) upper labials, third, fourth, and fifth (rarely fourth and fifth or fifth and sixth) entering the eye; four lower labials in contact with the anterior chin-shields, which are as long as or a little shorter than the posterior. Scales in 19 rows. Ventrals 205-255; anal entire; subcaudals 98-118. Yellowish above, variegated or irregularly spotted or barred with black; belly yellow, with black spots or irregular cross-bars.

Total length 930 millim.; tail 230.

Brazil, Bolivia, Guianas, Trinidad.

a–b. ♀ (V. 229, 234; C. 98, 103).	Upper Amazon.	Mr. E Bartlett [C.].
c. ♀ (V. 245; C. 113).	Larecaja, Bolivia.	
d. ♀ (V. 238; C. 118).	Yungas, Bolivia.	
e. ♂, bad state (V. 242; C. 116).	Trinidad.	H.M.S. 'Chanticleer.'
f. ♀ (V. 238; C. 105).	——?	College of Surgeons.
g. ♀ (V. 255; C. 114).	——?	
h. Skull.	Bahia.	

2. Lycognathus rhombeatus.

Oxyrhopus rhombeatus, *Peters, Mon. Berl. Ac.* 1863, p. 288.

Rostral twice as broad as deep, just visible from above; internasals much shorter than the præfrontals; frontal once and a half as long as broad, longer than its distance from the end of the snout, as long as the parietals; loreal once and two thirds to twice as long as deep; one præocular, extending to the upper surface of the head but not reaching the frontal; two postoculars; temporals 2+3, eight upper labials, fourth and fifth or third, fourth, and fifth entering the eye; four lower labials in contact with the anterior chin-shields, which are as long as the posterior. Scales in 19 rows. Ventrals 223–230; anal entire; subcaudals 110–115. White, with large black blotches disposed in partly confluent pairs alternating on each side of the vertebral line on the greater part of the body; two black cross-bands on the neck and complete annuli on the posterior part of the body; head dotted with black; lower parts white, some of the black blotches extending on the ventrals.

Total length 820 millim.; tail 220.

Brazil.

a. ♂ (V. 220; C. 115). Bahia. Dr. O. Wucherer [C.].

147. TRYPANURGOS.

Boiga, part., *Fitzing. N. Class. Rept.* p. 29 (1826).
Dipsas, part., *Schleg. Phys. Serp.* ii. p. 257 (1837).
Trypanurgos, *Fitzing. in Tschudi, Faun. Per., Herp.* p. 55 (1845).
Lycognathus, part., *Dum. & Bibr. Erp. Gén.* vii. p. 916 (1854).
Eudipsas, part., *Gunth. Cat. Col. Sn.* p. 168 (1858).
Oxyrhopus, part., *Jan, Elenco sist. Ofid.* p. 92 (1863).

Maxillary teeth 13 to 15, anterior much longer than the posterior, which gradually decrease in size, followed, after an interspace, by a pair of enlarged, grooved teeth situated below the posterior border of the eye; anterior mandibular teeth strongly enlarged. Head distinct from neck; eye large, with vertically elliptic pupil. Body compressed, scales smooth, slightly oblique, with apical pits, in 19 rows, the vertebral row enlarged; ventrals obtusely angulate laterally. Tail long; subcaudals in two rows.

Tropical South America.

1. Trypanurgos compressus.

Coluber compressus, *Daud. Rept.* vi. p. 247 (1803).
—— leucocephalus, *Mikan, Delect. Faun. Flor. Bras.* pl. —. fig. 2 (1820).
Boiga leucocephala, *Fitzing. N. Class. Rept.* p. 60 (1826).
Dipsas compressus, *Boie, Isis,* 1827, p. 560.
—— leucocephala, *Schleg. Phys. Serp.* ii. p. 288 (1837).
Dipsadomorphus compressus, *Tschudi, Faun. Per., Herp.* p. 55 (1845).
Lycognathus leucocephalus, *Dum. & Bibr.* vii. p. 924 (1854).

Eudipsas leucocephalus, *Gunth. Cat.* p. 168 (1858).
Oxyrhopus leucocephalus, *Jan, Elenco,* p. 92 (1863), *and Icon. Gén.* 35, pl. iii. fig. 3 (1870).

Rostral broader than deep, just visible from above; internasals much shorter than the præfrontals; frontal a little longer than broad, as long as its distance from the end of the snout, a little shorter than the parietals; loreal longer than deep; one præocular, in contact with or narrowly separated from the frontal; two postoculars; temporals 2+3; eight upper labials, fourth and fifth entering the eye; four lower labials in contact with the anterior chin-shields, which are as long as or a little longer than the posterior. Scales in 19 rows. Ventrals 228-258; anal entire; subcaudals 110-125. Yellowish or pale brown above, with dark brown crossbars, which may be broken in the middle and alternate, head white; neck blackish brown; uniform whitish beneath.

Total length 1080 millim.; tail 250.

Guianas, Brazil, Bolivia.

a. ♀ (V. 228; C. 116).	Berbice.	
b Yg (V. 248; C. 112).	Berbice.	Lady Essex [P.].
c-d. ♂ (V. 245; C. 124) & hgr. (V. 248; C. 110).	Demerara Falls.	
e. ♂ (V. 247, C. 125).	Para.	
f. ♀ (V. 258; C. 118).	Brazil.	Lord Stuart [P.].
g. ♂ (V. 237; C.?).	Brazil.	

148. DIPSADOMORPHUS.

Hurria, part., *Daud. Rept.* v. p. 275 (1803).
Boiga, part, *Fitzing. N. Class. Rept* p. 29 (1826)
Dipsas, part., *Boie, Isis,* 1827, p. 548; *Schleg. Phys. Serp.* ii. p. 257 (1837); *Gunth. Cat Col. Sn.* p. 169 (1858); *Jan, Elenco sist. Ofid* p. 103 (1863); *Gunth. Rept. Brit. Ind.* p. 307 (1864).
Dipsadomorphus, *Fitzing. in Tschudi, Faun. Per., Herp.* p. 55 (1845).
Opetiodon, *Dum. & Bibr Mém. Ac. Sc.* xxiii. 1853, p. 494, *and Erp. Gén.* vii. p. 905 (1854).
Triglyphodon, *Dum. & Bibr. ll. cc* pp. 507, 1069.
Toxicodryas, *Hallow. Proc. Ac. Philad.* 1857, p. 60.
Dipsadomorphus, part., *Gunth. Cat.* p. 174.
Boiga, *Cope, Proc. Ac. Philad.* 1860, p. 264.
Pappophis, *Macleay, Proc. Linn. Soc. N. S W* ii. 1877, p. 39.
Dipsas, *Bouleng. Faun. Ind., Rept.* p. 357 (1890).
Liophallus, *Cope, Proc. Ac. Philad.* 1894, p. 427 (1895).

Maxillary teeth 10 to 14, subequal in size, followed by two or three enlarged, grooved fangs; anterior mandibular teeth longest. Head very distinct from neck; eye moderate or large, with vertically elliptic pupil; posterior nasal more or less deeply concave. Body more or less compressed; scales smooth, more or less oblique, with apical pits, in 17 to 31 rows, the vertebral row more or less enlarged; ventrals obtusely angulate laterally. Tail moderate or long; subcaudals in two rows.

Tropical Africa, Southern Asia, Papuasia, Australia.

Fig. 5.

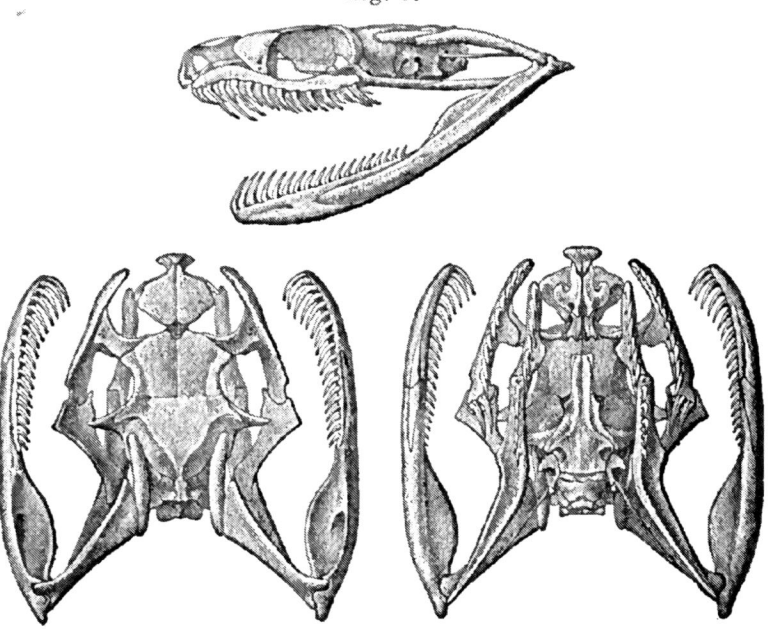

Skull of *Dipsadomorphus cynodon*.

Synopsis of the Species.

I. Anterior palatine teeth not or but feebly enlarged.

  A. Snout longer than the eye.

    1. Præocular not extending to upper surface of head; scales in 17 to 21 rows; ventrals 202–250.

Scales in 21 rows, vertebrals feebly enlarged; subcaudals 76–92	1. *trigonatus*, p. 62.
Scales in 17 or 19 rows, vertebrals strongly enlarged; subcaudals 80–106	2. *multimaculatus*, p. 63.
Scales in 21 rows, vertebrals strongly enlarged; subcaudals 87–94	3. *gokool*, p. 64.
Scales in 19 or 21 rows, vertebrals strongly enlarged; subcaudals 94–140	4. *hexagonotus*, p. 65.

    2. Præocular extending to upper surface of head; scales in 19 to 23 rows; ventrals 209–272.

      a. Posterior chin-shields larger than the anterior; scales in 19 or 21 rows; ventrals 211–268.

Præocular usually in contact with or
narrowly separated from the frontal;
subcaudals 90–125 .... 5. *ceylonensis*, p. 66.
Præocular not reaching the frontal;
subcaudals 87–103 .... 6. *fuscus*, p. 67.

 b. Posterior chin-shields not larger than the anterior.

  a. Scales in 19 rows; ventrals 240–260; subcaudals
   110–124 .... 7. *pulverulentus*, p. 68.

 β. Scales in 21 or 23 rows.

  * Subcaudals 89–110.

Scales in 21 rows, vertebrals feebly
enlarged; ventrals 231–248...... 8. *multifasciatus*, p. 69.
Scales in 23 rows, vertebrals feebly
enlarged; ventrals 241 .... 9. *dightonii*, p. 69.
Scales in 21 (rarely 23) rows, verte-
brals more or less strongly enlarged;
ventrals 209–239 .... 10. *dendrophilus*, p. 70.

  ** Subcaudals 124–144, scales in 21 rows.

Ventrals 237–252; subcaudals 124–
133 .... 11. *cyaneus*, p. 72.
Ventrals 240–263, subcaudals 143–
144......................... 12. *nigriceps*, p. 72.

B. Snout as long as the eye.

 1. Scales in 21 rows, ventrals 243–266; subcaudals 140–166.
  13. *jaspideus*, p. 73.

 2. Scales in 19 rows.

Ventrals 220; subcaudals 99; three
præoculars .... 14. *barnesii*, p. 73
Ventrals 250–276; subcaudals 114–
163; posterior chin-shields not
much smaller than the anterior .. 15. *drapiezii*, p. 74.
Ventrals 254–258, subcaudals 126–
135; anterior chin-shields nearly
thrice as large as the posterior .... 16. *angulatus*, p. 75.

II Anterior palatine teeth strongly enlarged.

 A. Posterior chin-shields larger than the anterior; scales in 19–
  to 23 (rarely 25) rows.

Scales in 19–23 rows; ventrals 217–
270; anal entire; subcaudals 103–
125; one præocular, extending to
upper surface of head .... 17. *irregularis*, p. 75.

Scales in 19 rows; ventrals 260; anal entire; subcaudals 116; one præocular, not extending to upper surface of head .... 18. *flavescens*, p. 77.

Scales in 19 rows; ventrals 240; anal divided; subcaudals 133; two præoculars, extending to upper surface of head .... 19. *philippinus*, p. 77.

Scales in 21–25 rows; ventrals 265–274; anal divided; subcaudals 123–147; one or two præoculars, not extending to upper surface of head. 20. *blandingii*, p. 77.

Scales in 23–25 rows; ventrals 248–290; anal entire; subcaudals 114–156; one præocular, extending to upper surface of head; rostral scarcely visible from above ...... 21. *cynodon*, p. 78.

B. Posterior chin-shields not or but slightly larger than the anterior; scales in 25 to 31 rows; ventrals 254–270; anal entire; subcaudals 103–131.. 22. *forstenii*, p. 80.

TABLE SHOWING NUMBERS OF SCALES AND SHIELDS.

	Sc.	V.	A.	C.	Lab.	Pr. oc.	Pt oc.
trigonatus	21	209–238	1	76–92	8	1	2
multimaculatus	17–19	202–235	1	80–106	8	1	2
gokool	21	224–225	1	87–94	8	1–2	2
hexagonotus ...	19–21	218–250	1	94–140	8–9	1	2
ceylonensis	19–21	214–268	1	90–125	8–9	1–2	2
fuscus	19–21	236–257	1	87–103	8–9	1	2
pulverulentus	19	240–260	1	110–124	8–9	1–2	2–3
multifasciatus ...	21	231–248	1	96–109	8	1	2
dightonii	23	241	1	95	8	1	2
dendrophilus ...	21–23	209–239	1	89–110	8–9	1	2
cyaneus	21	237–252	1	124–133	8	1	2
nigriceps	21	240–263	1	140–144	8	1	2
jaspideus	21	243–266	1	140–166	8	1	2
barnesii	19	220	1	99	8	3	2
drapiezii	19	250–276	1	114–163	8	1	2
angulatus	19	254–258	1	126–135	8	1	2
irregularis	19–23	217–270	1	103–125	'8–10	1	2
flavescens	19	260	1	116	8	1	3
philippinus	19	240	2	133	8	2	2
blandingii	21–25	265–274	2	123–147	8–9	1–2	2–3
cynodon	23–25	248–290	1	114–156	8–10	1	2
forstenii	25–31	254–270	1	103–131	8–11	1	2–3

1. **Dipsadomorphus trigonatus.**

Russell, *Ind. Serp* i pl. xv. (1796).
Coluber trigonatus, Schneid. in Bechst. Uebers. Lacép. iv. p. 156 (1802).

148. DIPSADOMORPHUS.

Coluber sagittatus, *Shaw, Zool.* iii. p 526 (1802).
—— catenularis, *Daud. Rept.* vi. p. 253, pl. lxxv. fig. 2 (1803).
Dipsas trigonata, *Boie, Isis*, 1827, p. 559; *Schleg. Phys. Serp.* ii. p. 267, pl. xi. figs 6 & 7 (1837); *Dum. & Bibr* vii p. 1136 (1854); *Blyth, Journ. As. Soc. Beng.* xxiii. 1855, p. 294; *Gunth. Rept. Brit. Ind.* p. 312 (1864); *Jan, Icon. Gén.* 38, pl. iii. fig. 2 (1871), *Theob. Cat Rept. Brit. Ind.* p. 196 (1876); *Blanf Journ. As. Soc. Beng.* xlviii. 1879, p 131; *Murray, Zool. Sind*, p. 383 (1884); *Bouleng. Faun. Ind, Rept.* p 358 (1890), *and Proc. Zool. Soc.* 1891, p. 633.
Dipsadomorphus trigonatus, *Gunth. Cat.* p. 175 (1858).

Anterior palatine teeth scarcely larger than the posterior; anterior mandibular teeth feebly enlarged. Rostral broader than deep, just visible from above; internasals broader than long, shorter than the præfrontals; frontal once and one fourth to once and one third as long as broad, longer than its distance from the end of the snout, shorter than the parietals; loreal as long as deep or longer than deep; one præocular, not extending to the upper surface of the head; two postoculars; temporals 2+2 or 2+3; eight upper labials, third, fourth, and fifth entering the eye; four or five lower labials in contact with the anterior chin-shields, which are as long as or a little longer than the posterior. Scales in 21 rows, vertebral row feebly enlarged. Ventrals 209–238; anal entire; subcaudals 76–92. Yellowish olive or pale grey above, with a white black-edged zigzag band along the back, or with a dorsal series of white, black-edged spots; head with two brown bands edged with black, diverging posteriorly; belly white, with or without a series of small brown spots along each side.

Total length 970 millim.; tail 175.

Transcaspia, Baluchistan, India.

a. ♂ (V. 225; C. 84).	Puli Hatun, Transcaspia.	M. C Eylandt [C.].
b. Hgr. (V. 230; C. 92).	Gwadar, Baluchistan.	W. T. Blanford, Esq. [P.].
c. ♀ (V. 229; C. 84).	Kurrachee.	Dr Leith [P.].
d. ♀ (V. 223; C. 83).	Kamaon, Himalayas.	Messrs v Schlagintweit [C.]
e. ♀ (V. 235; C. 82).	Bengal.	Gen. Hardwicke [P.].
f. ♀ (V. 225; C. 80)	Vizagapatam.	Dr. P. Russell.
g. ♀ (V. 231; C 83).	Bombay.	Dr. Leith [P.].
h, i, k ♀ (V. 230; C. 79), hgr. (V. 209; C. 85), & yg. (V. 224; C 79)	Madras.	J. Boileau, Esq. [P.].
l, m. ♂ (V. 235; C. 90) & ♀ (V. 232; C. 76).	Anamallays.	Col. Beddome [C.].
n. Skeleton.	India.	
o. Skull.	Pondichery.	

2. Dipsadomorphus multimaculatus.

Russell, Ind. Serp. ii. pl. xxiii. (1801).
Dipsas multimaculata, *Boie, Isis*, 1827, p. 549; *Schleg. Phys. Serp.* ii. p. 265, pl. xi. figs. 4 & 5 (1837), *and Abbild.* pl xlv. figs. 13–15

(1844); *Cantor, Cat. Mal. Rept.* p. 76 (1847); *Dum. & Bibr.* vii. p. 1139 (1854); *Gunth. Cat.* p. 169 (1858), *and Rept. Brit. Ind.* p. 311 (1864); *Jan, Icon. Gén.* 38, pl. iii. fig. 3 (1871); *Theob. Cat. Rept. Brit. Ind.* p. 194 (1876); *Boettg. Ber. Offenb. Ver. Nat.* 1885, p. 124; *Bouleng. Faun. Ind., Rept.* p. 360 (1890).

Boiga multimaculata, *Cope, Proc. Ac. Philad.* 1860, p. 264.

Anterior palatine teeth scarcely larger than the posterior, anterior mandibular teeth moderately enlarged. Rostral broader than deep, just visible from above; internasals broader than long, shorter than the præfrontals; frontal as long as broad or a little longer than broad, as long as or a little longer than its distance from the end of the snout, shorter than the parietals; loreal as long as deep or deeper than long; one præocular, not extending to the upper surface of the head; two postoculars; temporals 2+2 or 2+3 (rarely 1+2); eight upper labials, third, fourth, and fifth entering the eye; four or five lower labials in contact with the anterior chin-shields, which are as long as or a little shorter than the posterior. Scales in 19 (rarely 17) rows, vertebral row strongly enlarged. Ventrals 202-235; anal entire; subcaudals 80-106. Grey-brown above, with two alternating series of roundish dark brown spots and two other series of smaller spots lower down on the sides; two blackish bands on the head, diverging posteriorly; a blackish streak from the eye to the angle of the mouth, lower parts whitish, marbled or spotted with brown, and with a series of brown spots along each side.

Total length 750 millim.; tail 165.

Southern China, Indo-China, Burma, Malay Peninsula, Sumatra, Java, Celebes.

a. ♀ (V. 203; C. 80).	Hong Kong.	J. C. Bowring, Esq. [P.].
b. ♂ (V. 225, C. 100).	Moulmein.	R. C. Beavan, Esq. [P.].
c. ♀ (V. 220; C. 90).	Toungyi, Shan States.	E. W. Oates, Esq [P.].
d-e. ♂ (V. 227, C. 94) & ♀ (V. 220; C. 81).	Fort Steadman, Shan States, 3000 ft.	E. W. Oates, Esq. [P.].
f. ♂ (Sc. 17; V. 225; C. 98).	Pachebon.	M. Mouhot [C.].
g. ♂ (V. 233; C. 106).	Pinang.	Dr. Cantor.
h. ♂ (V. 203, C. 84).	Java.	Leyden Mus.
i. ♂ (V. 211; C. 84).	Java.	A. Scott, Esq. [P.].
k. ♀ (V. 204; C. 88).	Willis Mts., Kediri, Java, 5000 ft	Baron v. Huegel [C].

3. Dipsadomorphus gokool

Dipsas gokool, *Gray, Ill. Ind. Zool.* ii. pl. xxxiii. fig. 1 (1834); *Gunth. Rept. Brit. Ind.* p. 313 (1864), *Theob. Cat. Rept. Brit. Ind* p 197 (1876); *Bouleng. Faun. Ind., Rept.* p. 360 (1890).

Anterior palatine teeth scarcely larger than the posterior; anterior mandibular teeth feebly enlarged. Rostral a little broader than deep, scarcely visible from above; internasals broader than long, much shorter than the præfrontals; frontal as long as broad or slightly longer than broad, as long as its distance from the end of the snout, shorter than the parietals, loreal as long as deep or deeper than long, one or two præoculars, not extending to the upper surface of the head, two postoculars, temporals 2+3; eight upper labials, third, fourth, and fifth entering the eye; four or five lower labials in contact with the anterior chin-shields; posterior chin-shields as long as the anterior and in contact with each other. Scales in 21 rows, the vertebral row strongly enlarged. Ventrals 224–225; anal entire; subcaudals 87–94. Yellowish brown above; head with an arrow-shaped brown, black-edged marking, longitudinally bisected; a black streak on each side of the head, passing through the eye; a yellowish vertebral streak; a series of erect Y-shaped markings on each side of the back; lower parts yellowish, with a series of brown spots along each side.

Total length 830 millim.; tail 170.

Bengal, Assam, Pinang.

a.	♀ (V. 224, C 94).	Bengal.	Gen. Hardwicke [P.].	(Type.)
b.	♀ (V. 225; C. 87).	Pinang.	Dr. Cantor [C.].	

4. Dipsadomorphus hexagonotus.

Dipsas hexagonotus, *Blyth, Journ. As. Soc. Beng.* xxiv. 1856, p. 360; *Stoliczka, Journ. As. Soc. Beng.* xxxix. 1870, p. 198, pl. xi. fig. 4, and xl 1871, p. 439; *Theob. Cat. Rept Brit. Ind.* p. 195 (1876); *Bouleng. Faun. Ind , Rept.* p. 361 (1890).
—— ochracea, *Gunth. Ann. & Mag. N. H.* (4) i. 1868, p. 425; *Theob Journ. Linn. Soc.* x. 1868, p. 53, and l. c p 196
—— hexagonata, part., *Anders Proc. Zool. Soc* 1871, p. 185.

Anterior palatine teeth scarcely longer than the posterior; anterior mandibular teeth considerably enlarged. Rostral broader than deep, just visible from above; internasals broader than long, shorter than the præfrontals; frontal a little longer than broad, as long as its distance from the end of the snout, considerably shorter than the parietals; loreal as long as deep or deeper than long; one præocular, not reaching the upper surface of the head; two postoculars; temporals 2+3; eight (rarely nine) upper labials, third, fourth, and fifth (or fourth, fifth and sixth) entering the eye; four or five lower labials in contact with the anterior chin-shields, which are as long as or a little shorter than the posterior. Scales in 19 or 21 rows, vertebral row strongly enlarged. Ventrals 218–250; anal entire; subcaudals 94–140. Dusky grey, reddish, or ochraceous above, uniform or with ill-defined blackish transverse lines; a more or less distinct dark streak from eye to gape, lower parts yellow, uniform, or clouded with pale brownish in the young.

Total length 1050 millim.; tail 200.

Eastern Himalayas, Bengal, Burma, Andamans.

a, b. ♀ (Sc. 21; V. 238, 241; C. 107, 109).		Darjeeling.	T. C. Jerdon, Esq. [P.].
c. ♂ (Sc. 21, V. 233; C. 109)		Darjeeling.	W. T. Blanford, Esq. [P.].
d–f. ♂ (Sc. 19; V. 227, 228; C. 94, 104) & yg. (Sc. 19; V. 228; C. 102).		Bhamo, Upper Burma.	M. L. Fea [O].
g–h ♂ (Sc 19; V. 242, C. 101) & ♀ (Sc. 19, V. 238; C. 96).		Pegu.	W Theobald, Esq. [O.]. (Types of *D. ochracea*.)
i–k. Yg. (Sc. 21, V 232, 218; C. 109, 113).		Burma.	Col. Beddome [C.].

5. Dipsadomorphus ceylonensis.

Dipsadomorphus ceylonensis, *Gunth. Cat.* p. 176 (1858)
Dipsas ceylonensis, *Gunth Rept. Brit. Ind.* p 314, pl. xxiii. fig. B (1864); *F. Mull. Verh. Nat Ges. Basel*, viii. 1887, p 275; *Bouleng. Faun Ind., Rept.* p. 359 (1890); *W Sclater, Journ As. Soc. Beng.* lx. 1891, p. 243.
—— hexagonata, part., *Anders. Proc. Zool. Soc.* 1871, p. 185.
—— nuchalis, *Gunth. Proc. Zool. Soc.* 1875, p 233.

Anterior palatine teeth scarcely longer than the posterior, anterior mandibular teeth moderately enlarged. Rostral a little broader than deep, just visible from above; internasals broader than long, shorter than the præfrontals; frontal as long as broad or a little longer than broad, as long as or longer than its distance from the end of the snout, shorter than the parietals; loreal as long as deep or deeper than long; one or two præoculars, reaching the upper surface of the head, often in contact with or narrowly separated from the frontal; two postoculars; temporals small, 2 or 3+3 or 4; eight (rarely nine) upper labials, third, fourth, and fifth (or fourth, fifth, and sixth) entering the eye; four or five lower labials in contact with the anterior chin-shields, which are shorter than the posterior. Scales in 19 or 21 rows, vertebral row much enlarged. Ventrals 214–268; anal entire; subcaudals 90–125. Pale brown or greyish above, with a series of dark brown or blackish transverse spots or bands; nape with a dark blotch or three dark longitudinal streaks, or a transverse bar; a more or less distinct dark streak from the eye to the angle of the mouth; lower parts yellowish, dotted with brown, usually with a lateral series of brown spots.

Total length 1320 millim.; tail 250.

Ceylon; hills of the West Coast of India.

a, b–d. ♂ (Sc. 19; V. 235; C. 107), hgr. (Sc. 19, V. 229, 231; C. 110?), & yg. (Sc. 19; V. 232; C. 104).		Ceylon.	
e. ♀ (Sc. 19; V. 219; C. 101).		Ceylon.	A. Paul, Esq. [P.]
f–g. H.-т. · Sc. 19; V. 257, 222; C. 126, 99).		Ceylon.	R. Templeton, Esq. [P.].
(Types.)

h–i Hgr. ♂ (Sc. 19; V. 226, C. 103) & yg. (Sc. 19; V. 220, C. 101).	Ceylon.	Dr. Kelaart
l–m. Yg. (Sc. 19; V. 262, 253, 266; C. 125, 113, 120).	Trincomalee, Ceylon.	Major Barrett [P.].
n. Hgr. ♂ (Sc 19; V. 253; C 122).	Ceylon.	
o. Hgr. ♂ (Sc 19; V. 234; C. 105).	Anamallays.	Col. Beddome [C.].
p. ♂ (Sc. 19, V. 229; C. 100).	North slope of Nilgherries, 4000 ft.	Col Beddome [C.].
q ♀ (Sc. 21, V. 248; C. 90).	Wynad.	Col. Beddome [C.].
r–v. ♂ (Sc. 21; V. 242, 243; C. 100, 104), ♀ (Sc. 21; V. 234; C. 94), & yg. (Sc. 21, V. 234, 249; C. 102, 101).	Forests of W. Coast of India.	Col Beddome [C]. (Types of *D. nuchalis.*)
w Hgr. ♀ (Sc. 19; V. 214, C. 98).	Malabar.	Col. Beddome [C.].
x–y Hgr ♀ (Sc. 19; V. 248, C. 117) & yg. (Sc. 19; V. 235; C. 111).	Matheran, Bombay	Dr. Leith [P.].

6. Dipsadomorphus fuscus.

Dendrophis fusca, *Gray, Zool. Misc* p. 54 (1842).
Dipsas fusca, *Gunth Cat.* p. 171 (1858); *Krefft, Sn Austral.* p. 26, pl. v. fig 7 (1869); *Peters & Doria, Ann. Mus. Genova,* xiii. 1878, p 395; *Boettg. in Semon, Zool. Forsch.* v. p. 118 (1894).
—— boydii, *Macleay, Proc. Linn. Soc. N. S. W.* ix. 1884, p. 548.

Anterior palatine teeth feebly enlarged; anterior mandibular teeth strongly enlarged. Rostral broader than deep, visible from above, internasals as long as broad or broader than long, as long as or shorter than the præfrontals; frontal as long as broad or slightly longer than broad, as long as its distance from the rostral or the end of the snout, shorter than the parietals; loreal as long as deep or longer than deep; one præocular, extending to the upper surface of the head but not reaching the frontal; two postoculars; temporals 1+2, 2+2, or 2+3; eight or nine upper labials, third, fourth, and fifth, or fourth, fifth, and sixth entering the eye; four or five lower labials in contact with the anterior chin-shields, which are shorter than the posterior. Scales in 19 (rarely 21) rows, vertebral row strongly enlarged. Ventrals 236–257; anal entire, subcaudals 87–103. Yellowish or pale reddish brown above, with more or less distinct, more or less regular dark brown or black cross-bands; uniform yellowish or salmon-pink below.

Total length 1500 millim.; tail 290.

Northern and Eastern Australia.

a. ♂ (Sc. 19; V. 251; C. 98).	Port Essington.	(Type.)
b–c. ♀ (Sc 19; V. 254, 250; C. 103, 97).	Port Essington.	Lord Derby [P.].

d, e. ♂ (Sc.19; V.248; C. 94) & ♀ (Sc. 19; V. 252; C. 99).	Port Essington.	Haslar Collection.
f. ♀ (Sc. 19; V. 257; C. 93).	Daly R., N. Australia.	Christiania Museum.
g-h ♂ (Sc.19; V 246; C. 96) & ♀ (Sc. 21; V. 248; C. 92).	Herbert R., N. Queensland.	J. A. Boyd, Esq. [P.].
i. ♂ (Sc 21; V. 253; C.103).	Sydney.	Mrs. Levey [P.].
k. ♂ (Sc. 19; V. 239, C. 90).	New South Wales.	G. Krefft, Esq. [P.].
l. Yg (Sc 19; V. 247; C. 102).	Australia.	Sir J. Richardson [P.].

7. Dipsadomorphus pulverulentus.

Dipsas pulverulenta, *Fisch. Abh. Nat. Ver. Hamb.* iii. 1856, p. 81, pl. iii. fig. 1; *Gunth. Cat.* p 173 (1858); *Jan, Icon Gén.* 38, pl. iv fig. 1 (1871), *F. Müll. Verh. Nat. Ges Basel,* vi. 1878, p. 688; *Bocage, Jorn. Sc. Lisb.* xi 1887, p. 186, *Boettg Ber. Senck. Ges.* 1888, p. 75.

Anterior palatine and mandibular teeth moderately enlarged. Rostral broader than deep, just visible from above; internasals broader than long, shorter than the præfrontals; frontal as long as broad or a little longer than broad, as long as or longer than its distance from the end of the snout, shorter than the parietals; loreal as long as deep or deeper than long; one præocular (rarely divided), widely separated from the frontal; two (rarely three) postoculars; temporals 2+2 (rarely 2+3); eight (rarely nine) upper labials, third, fourth, and fifth (or fourth, fifth, and sixth) entering the eye; four or five lower labials in contact with the anterior chin-shields, which are as large as or a little larger that the posterior. Scales in 19 rows, vertebral row more or less enlarged. Ventrals 240–260, anal entire; subcaudals 110–124. Buff or pale brown above, uniform or with more or less distinct dark brown cross-bars; young with a series of brown rhombs on each side, each enclosing a light ocellar spot; belly and lower surface of tail yellowish, powdered with brown, with two longitudinal dark brown lines.

Total length 850 millim.; tail 185.

West Africa, from the Coast of Guinea to Angola.

a. ♂ (V. 253; C. 118).	Sierra Leone.	
b. ♂ (V. 260, C. 117).	Niger	Dr. J. W. Crosse [P.].
c-d. Yg. (V 259, 240; C.115, 110)	Old Calabar	W. Logan, Esq. [P.].
e. Yg. (V. 250; C. 113).	Fernando Po.	Sir A. Smith [P.].
f. ♀ (V. 250; C. P).	W. Africa.	J. C. Salmon, Esq. [P.].
g. ♂ (V. 254; C. 110)	W. Africa.	Sir A. Smith [P.].

8. Dipsadomorphus multifasciatus.

Dipsadomorphus trigonatus, var. B, *Gunth Cat.* p. 175 (1858).
Dipsas multifasciata, *Blyth, Journ. As. Soc. Beng.* xxix. 1861, p. 114; *Gunth Rept. Brit. Ind.* p 313 (1864); *Stoliczka, Journ. As. Soc. Beng.* xxix. 1870, p. 199, pl. xi. fig. 6, and xl. 1871, p. 440; *W. Sclater, Journ. As. Soc. Beng.* lx. 1891, p. 243.
—— ceylonensis (*non Gunth.*), *Theob. Cat. Rept. Brit. Ind* p. 196 (1876).

Anterior palatine and mandibular teeth feebly enlarged. Rostral broader than deep, just visible from above; internasals broader than long, shorter than the præfrontals; frontal a little longer than broad, as long as its distance from the end of the snout, shorter than the parietals; loreal as long as deep or longer than deep, sometimes entering the eye below the præocular, which is widely separated from the frontal, but reaches the upper surface of the head; two postoculars; temporals 1+2 or 2+2; eight upper labials, third, fourth, and fifth entering the eye; five to seven lower labials in contact with the anterior chin-shields; posterior chin-shields as long as the anterior, separated from each other by scales. Scales in 21 rows, vertebral row feebly enlarged. Ventrals 231–248; anal entire; subcaudals 96–109. Greyish above, with oblique black cross-bars; a more or less distinct series of whitish spots along the vertebral line; a pair of black streaks on the head, from the præfrontals to the occiput, a black streak from the eye to the commissure of the jaws, and another along the nape; upper labials black-edged; lower parts spotted or checkered with dark brown or black.

Total length 875 millim.; tail 180.
Himalayas.

a, b. ♂ (V 245; C. 102)   India.
♀ (V. 240; C. 102).

9. Dipsadomorphus dightonii.

Dipsas dightoni, *Bouleng. Journ. Bomb. N. H. Soc.* viii. 1894, p. 528, pl. —.

Anterior palatine and mandibular teeth moderately enlarged. Rostral broader than deep, just visible from above; internasals broader than long, shorter than the præfrontals; frontal as long as broad, as long as its distance from the end of the snout, shorter than the parietals; loreal longer than deep; one præocular, narrowly separated from the frontal, two postoculars; temporals small, scale-like, 2+3; eight upper labials, third, fourth, and fifth entering the eye; four lower labials in contact with the anterior chin-shields, which are as long as the posterior. Scales in 23 rows, vertebral row feebly enlarged. Ventrals 241; anal entire; subcaudals 95. Pale reddish-brown above, without any dark markings; a series of salmon-red blotches along the back; head pale brown, with minute blackish dots; lower parts yellowish, finely dotted with brown; the outer ends of the ventrals salmon-pink.

Total length 1100 millim.; tail 220.

Travancore.

a. ♀ (V. 241; C. 95).   Peermad, 3300 feet.   S. Dighton, Esq. [C.], H. S. Ferguson, Esq. [P.]. (Type.)

10. Dipsadomorphus dendrophilus.

Seba, Thes. ii pl. xxi. fig. 1 (1735).
Coluber peruvianus, *Shaw, Zool* iii. p. 483, pl cxxii. (1802).
Dipsas dendrophila, *Boie, Isis*, 1827, p. 549; *Wagl. Icon. Amph.* pl. viii. (1828); *Schleg. Phys. Serp.* ii p. 263, pl. xi. figs. 1-3 (1837), *and Abbild.* p. 133, pl. xlv. figs 1-9 (1844); *Cantor, Cat Mal. Rept.* p. 76 (1847); *Motley & Dillwyn, Contr. Nat. Hist. Lab.* p. 47 (1855); *Gunth Cat.* p. 169 (1858), *and Rept. Brit. Ind.* p. 310 (1864); *Jan, Icon. Gén.* 38, pl. iv. fig. 2 (1871).
Triglyphodon dendrophilum, *Dum & Bibr.* vii. p. 1086 (1854).
—— gemmicinctum, *Dum & Bibr. t c.* p. 1091.
Boiga dendrophila, *Cope, Proc. Ac. Philad.* 1860, p. 264.
Dipsas (Triglyphodon) gemmicincta, *Peters, Mon. Berl. Ac.* 1861, p 688.

Anterior palatine teeth scarcely longer than the posterior; anterior mandibular teeth moderately enlarged. Rostral a little broader than deep, just visible from above; internasals broader than long, as long as or shorter than the præfrontals; frontal as long as broad or a little longer than broad, as long as or a little shorter than its distance from the end of the snout; loreal as long as deep or a little longer than deep (in one specimen, E. *a*, much longer than deep and entering the eye below the præocular); one præocular, extending to the upper surface of the head but not reaching the frontal, two postoculars; temporals 2+2 or 2+3; eight (exceptionally nine) upper labials, third, fourth, and fifth entering the eye; four or five lower labials in contact with the anterior chinshields, which are as large as or a little larger than the posterior. Scales in 21 (rarely 23) rows, vertebral row more or less strongly enlarged. Ventrals 209-239; anal entire; subcaudals 89-110. Coloration very variable.

Total length 1900 millim.; tail 370.

Malay Peninsula and Archipelago.

A. Black above, with 40 to 46 narrow yellow cross-bars which are mostly continuous across the back; upper labials yellow, black-edged, ventrals in the anterior third of the body yellow, spotted with black, further back black, uniform or spotted or speckled with yellow. (*D. dendrophila*, Boie.)

a, b, c. ♂ (V. 220. 220: C.P. 08)   V. 226. C. 93).   Java.   Lidth de Jeude Collection.
d. ♂ (V. 210. C. 51).   Java.   Zoological Society.

148. DIPSADOMORPHUS.

B. Black above and below, sides of body with 23 to 36 yellow vertical bars which do not extend across the back; throat and labial shields yellow, the latter black-edged. (Var. *melanotus*, Blkr.)

a. ♀ (V. 224; C. 100).	Kedah.	S. S. Flower, Esq. [P.].
b. ♂ (V. 218; C. 97).	Pinang.	Dr. Cantor.
c ♀ (V. 225; C. ?).	Singapore.	Dr. Dennys [P.].
d ♀ (Sc. 23; V. 213; C. 89).	Singapore ?	Gen Hardwicke [P.].
e. Hgr. (Sc. 23; V. 202; C. 93).	Sumatra.	Dr. Bleeker.
		(*Triglyphodon melanotus*, Blkr.)
f. ♀ (V 222; C. 103).	W. coast of Sumatra.	Mrs. Findlay [P.].
g. Skull.	—— ?	

C. Black above and below, with 47 yellow cross-bars on the body which are mostly continuous across the back; throat and labial shields yellow, the latter black-edged. (Var. *annectens*.)

a. ♀ (V. 232; C. 104) Borneo. Sir H. Low [P.].

D. Like the preceding, but cross-bars more numerous, 60 to 64 on the body. (Var. *regularis*.)

a. ♀ (V. 235; C. 110).	Borneo.	Mr. Stokes [C].
b. ♂ (V. 218; C. ?)	Borneo.	Mr. Wright [C.].
c–d. Hgr. (V. 239, 233; C. 108, 108).	Borneo.	Sir E. Belcher [P.].

E. Like the preceding, but cross-bars more numerous, 70 to 80 on the body. (Var. *multicinctus*.)

a–b. ♂ (V. 224; C. 110) & yg. (V 223; C 107).	Puerta Princesa, Palawan.	A. Everett, Esq. [C.].
c. ♀ (V 226; C. 75).	Palawan.	A. Everett, Esq. [C.].
d. ♂ (V. 227; C. 94).	Philippines.	H. Cuming, Esq. [C.].

F. Black above and below, body with 70 to 90 cross-bands of round yellow spots; belly with round yellow spots, which are not connected with the cross-bands; labials blackish, or with very broad black edges. (Var. *gemmicinctus*, D. & B.)

a. ♀ (V. 231; C. 105). Celebes. Leyden Museum.

G. Body with 37 to 47 broad greenish-white bands alternating with black ones, the light scales all edged with black; labials and ventrals yellowish white, black-edged; the black bands form complete rings on the hinder part of the body and on the tail. (Var. *latifasciatus*.)

a. ♂ (V 216; C. 101).	Zamboanga, Mindanao.	A. Everett, Esq. [C.].
b–c. ♂ (V. 222, 218; C. 99, 93).	Butuan, Mindanao.	A. Everett, Esq. [C.].

11. Dipsadomorphus cyaneus.

Triglyphodon cyaneum, *Dum. & Bibr.* vii p. 1079 (1854).
Dipsas nigromarginata, *Blyth, Journ. As. Soc. Beng.* xxiii. 1855 p. 294.
—— cyanea, *Jan, Elenco*, p. 104 (1863), *Bouleng Faun. Ind.* p. 361 (1890); *W. Sclater, Journ. As. Soc. Beng.* lx. 1891, p 244
—— bubalina, *Gunth. Rept. Brit. Ind.* p. 311, pl xxiv. fig. E (1864); *Stoliczka, Journ. As. Soc. Beng.* xl. 1871, p 441; *Theob. Cat. Rept. Brit. Ind.* p. 107 (1876).

Anterior palatine teeth scarcely larger than the posterior; anterior mandibular teeth considerably larger than the posterior. Rostral a little broader than deep, just visible from above; internasals broader than long, a little shorter than the præfrontals; frontal slightly longer than broad, as long as its distance from the end of the snout, shorter than the parietals; one præocular, extending to the upper surface of the head but not reaching the frontal; two postoculars; temporals 2+3 or 3+3; eight upper labials, third, fourth, and fifth entering the eye; five lower labials in contact with the anterior chin-shields, which are about as long as the posterior. Scales in 21 rows, vertebral row rather strongly enlarged. Ventrals 237–252; anal entire; subcaudals 124–133. Adult uniform green above, the skin between the scales black, uniform greenish yellow beneath. Young olive, with black cross-bars and a black streak behind the eye; belly variegated brown and white.

Total length 1360 millim.; tail 340.

Assam, Cachar, Sikkim, Tenasserim.

a. ♂ (V. 242; C. 129). ——? Dr. Gunther [P.].
b. Yg. (V 237; C.?). Darjeeling. W T. Blanford, Esq. [P.].

12. Dipsadomorphus nigriceps. (PLATE III. fig. 3.)

Dipsas nigriceps, *Gunth. Ann & Mag. N H.* (3) xii 1863, p. 359.
—— hoffmanseggii, *Peters, Mon Berl. Ac.* 1867, p. 27.
—— flavescens, var, *Jan, Icon. Gén.* 38, pl. v. fig. 2 (1871).

Anterior palatine and mandibular teeth moderately enlarged. Rostral broader than deep, just visible from above; internasals broader than long, shorter than the præfrontals; frontal as long as broad or a little longer than broad, as long as its distance from the end of the snout, shorter than the parietals; loreal as long as deep, or longer than deep; one præocular, in contact with or narrowly separated from the frontal; two postoculars; temporals very variable, 1+2 or 2+3 or 3+3; eight upper labials, third, fourth, and fifth entering the eye; four or five lower labials in contact with the anterior chin-shields, which are considerably shorter than the posterior. Scales in 21 rows, vertebral row strongly enlarged. Ventrals 240–263; anal entire; subcaudals 140–144. Reddish or greyish brown above, uniform or irregularly mottled with darker; head uniform b.. .sh .. .. upper lip white; lower parts white or greyish, faintly dotted with darker.

Total length 1650 millim.; tail 410.
Borneo, Java.

a. ♀ (V. 250; C. 144).   Bongon, N. Borneo.   A. Everett, Esq. [C.].
b. ♂ (V. 263, C ?).   —— ?   Zoological Society.
                                (Type.)
c. ♂ (V. 262; C. 143).   —— ?   College of Surgeons.

13. Dipsadomorphus jaspideus.

Dipsas cynodon, part., *Schleg. Phys. Serp.* ii. p. 269 (1837).
Triglyphodon jaspideum, *Dum. & Bibr* vii p. 1093 (1854).
Dipsas fusca (*non Gray*), *Motley & Dillwyn, Contr. Nat. Hist. Lab.* p. 48, pl. — (1855).
—— boops, *Gunth. Cat.* p. 170 (1858), *and Rept. Brit. Ind.* p. 309, pl xxiv. fig G (1864), *F. Mull. Verh. Nat. Ges. Basel,* vii. 1882, p. 151.
—— jaspidea, *Jan, Elenco,* p. 104 (1863).

Anterior palatine and mandibular teeth feebly enlarged. Eye as long as the snout. Rostral broader than deep, scarcely visible from above; internasals broader than long, as long as the præfrontals; frontal about once and one third as long as broad, much longer than its distance from the end of the snout, as long as or a little shorter than the parietals; loreal as long as deep or deeper than long; one præocular, narrowly separated from the frontal; two postoculars; temporals 2+2; eight upper labials, third, fourth, and fifth entering the eye; four or five lower labials in contact with the anterior chin-shields; posterior chin-shields as long as or longer than the anterior, separated from each other by scales. Scales in 21 rows, vertebral row strongly enlarged. Ventrals 243–266; anal entire; subcaudals 140–166. Light brown above, mottled and speckled with black or dark brown, and with more or less distinct blackish cross-bars interrupted on the vertebral line; a series of large whitish spots on each side, partly on the ventrals: all the head-shields spotted with black, the larger spots light-edged; a black, light-edged longitudinal streak on the occiput; yellowish beneath, speckled with brown.

Total length 1400 millim.; tail 370.
Java, Borneo, Pinang.

a. ♂ (V. 266; C. 156).   Java?   Zoological Society.
b. ♀ (V 243; C. 140).   Labuan.   L L Dillwyn, Esq [P.].
                                     (Type of *D fusca*)
c, d. ♂ (V. 248, C. 166)   Bengal (??).   Gen. Hardwicke [P.].
& ♀ (V. 264; C. 157).   (Types of *D. boops.*)

14. Dipsadomorphus barnesii.

Dipsas barnesii, *Gunth. Proc. Zool. Soc* 1869, p. 506, pl. xl. fig. 2; *Bouleng. Faun. Ind., Rept.* p. 359 (1890).

Anterior palatine teeth not enlarged; anterior mandibular teeth feebly enlarged. Eye as long as the snout. Rostral as deep as broad, just visible from above; internasals broader than long, much shorter than the præfrontals; frontal once and a half as long as broad, longer than its distance from the end of the snout, a little shorter than the parietals; loreal a little longer than deep; three præoculars, the upper not reaching the frontal; two postoculars; temporals 1+3 or 2+3; eight upper labials, fourth and fifth entering the eye; four lower labials in contact with the anterior chin-shields, which are nearly as long as the posterior. Scales in 19 rows, scarcely oblique, vertebrals very feebly enlarged. Ventrals 220; anal entire; subcaudals 99. Grey-brown above, with lighter black-edged transverse spots; a series of black spots along each side, near the ventrals; a blackish band behind the eye; labial sutures blackish; lower parts whitish, powdered with brown.

Total length 550 millim.; tail 130.

Ceylon.

a. ♂ (V. 220; C. 99).   Ceylon.   B. H. Barnes, Esq. [P.]. (Type.)

15. Dipsadomorphus drapiezii.

Dipsas drapiezii, *Boie, Isis,* 1827, p. 559; *Schleg. Phys. Serp.* ii. p. 270, pl. xi. figs. 8 & 9 (1837), *and Abbild.* p 48, pl xv (1840); *Gunth. Cat.* p. 171 (1858), *and Ann. & Mag. N. H.* (3) ix. 1862, p. 53; *F. Mull. Verh. Nat. Ges Basel*, viii 1887, p. 275.
Triglyphodon drapiezii, *Dum. & Bibr.* vii. p. 1097 (1854).
Dipsas drapiezii, var. bancana, *Peters, Mon. Berl. Ac.* 1867, p. 20.

Anterior palatine and mandibular teeth moderately enlarged. Eye as long as the snout. Rostral broader than deep, scarcely visible from above; internasals broader than long, shorter than the præfrontals; frontal as long as broad or slightly longer than broad, as long as its distance from the end of the snout, shorter than the parietals; loreal small or absent; one præocular, in contact with or narrowly separated from the frontal; two postoculars; temporals 2+2, 2+3, or 3+3; eight upper labials, third, fourth, and fifth, or fourth and fifth, entering the eye; five or six lower labials in contact with the anterior chin-shields, which are as long as or a little longer than the posterior. Scales in 19 rows, vertebral row strongly enlarged. Ventrals 250-276; anal entire; subcaudals 114-163. Pale brown above with dark transverse spots, or brown with yellowish or reddish, dark-edged pale transverse bands each of which ends in a white spot on the side of the belly; brownish white below, uniform or speckled with brown, with two more or less distinct brown longitudinal lines.

Total length 1300 millim.; tail 350.

Malay Peninsula and Archipelago.

a. Yg. (V. 270; C. 147).   Malacca   D. F. A. Hervey, Esq. [P.].
b. ♀
c. ♀

d, e. ♀ (V. 267; C. 136) Sarawak. Rajah Brooke [P.].
 & yg (V. 250; C 151).
f. ♀ (V. 276; C. 170). Sandakan, N. Borneo. Douglas Cator, Esq. [P.].
g. ♂ (V. 264; C. 145). Java.

In the var. *bancana*, Peters, which is stated to resemble closely the *Dipsas indica* of Laurenti (*D. bucephala*, Shaw), the loreal is well developed, the præocular is divided, and the dark lines along the belly are absent.

16. Dipsadomorphus angulatus.

Dipsas (Dipsadomorphus) angulata, *Peters, Mon. Berl. Ac.* 1861, p 688.
—— (Eudipsas) guiraonis, *Steind. Novara, Rept.* p. 75, pl. iii. figs. 9-10 (1867).

Closely allied to *D. drapiezii*. Frontal longer than broad, longer than its distance from the end of the snout, loreal well developed, as long as deep; præocular nearly reaching the frontal; two postoculars, temporals 2+2 or 2+3; eight upper labials, third, fourth, and fifth entering the eye; anterior chin-shields nearly thrice as large as the posterior. Scales in 19 rows, vertebral row strongly enlarged. Ventrals 254-258; anal entire; subcaudals 126-135. Greyish or yellowish brown above, with dark brown spots and dots and with dark cross-bars which widen on the sides and extend across the belly, but are interrupted on the vertebral line; large whitish spots on the sides, extending on the ventrals, between the dark bars.

Total length 1015 millim.; tail 240.

Leyte, Philippine Islands.

17. Dipsadomorphus irregularis.

Merrem, Beitr. ii. p. 23, pl iv (1790).
Coluber irregularis, *Merr. in Bechst. Uebers. Lacép* iv. p. 239, pl. xxxvii. fig. 1 (1802)
Hurria pseudoboiga, *Daud. Rept.* v. p. 277, pls. lix. figs. 8 & 9, & lxvi. figs. 1 & 3 (1803).
Boiga irregularis, *Fitzing. N. Class. Rept* p. 60 (1826).
Dipsas irregularis, *Boie, Isis,* 1827, p 549; *Schleg. Phys. Serp.* ii. p. 271, pl. xi figs. 12 & 13 (1837); *Günth Cat* p 172 (1858), *Jan, Icon. Gen.* 37, pl. i. (1870); *Peters & Doria, Ann. Mus. Genova,* xiii. 1878, p. 394; *Boettg. Ber. Offenb. Ver. Nat.* 1885, p. 153
Triglyphodon irregularis, *Dum. & Bibr.* vii. p. 1072 (1854).
Dipsas pallida, *Jan, Elenco,* p. 103 (1863), *and Icon. Gén.* 38, pl. v. fig. 1 (1871).
Pappophis laticeps, *Macleay, Proc. Linn Soc N. S W.* ii. 1877, p. 39
—— flavigastra, *Macleay, l c.* p. 40.
Dipsas aruanus, *Gunth. Ann. & Mag. N. H.* (5) xi. 1883, p 137.

Anterior palatine and mandibular teeth strongly enlarged. Rostral broader than deep, just visible from above; internasals broader than long, much shorter than the præfrontals; frontal as long as broad or a little longer than broad, as long as its distance from the rostral, shorter than the parietals; loreal as long as deep or longer than deep; one præocular, in contact with or narrowly separated from the frontal; two postoculars; temporals 2 or 3+3 or 4; nine (rarely eight or ten) upper labials, fourth, fifth, and sixth (or third, fourth, and fifth, or fifth, sixth, and seventh) entering the eye; four or five lower labials in contact with the anterior chin-shields, which are shorter than the posterior. Scales in 19 to 23 rows, vertebral row moderately or strongly enlarged. Ventrals 217–270; anal entire; subcaudals 103–125 (some of which may be single). Coloration very variable. Yellowish, greyish, brown, or olive above, uniform or with more or less distinct darker cross-bands or spots disposed quincuncially; upper labials yellowish, usually dark-edged; a more or less distinct dark streak usually present on each side of the head, behind the eye; belly yellowish, uniform or more or less profusely spotted or speckled with brown, olive, or black; subcaudals more or less spotted or speckled, sometimes entirely black.

Total length 2150 millim.; tail 450.

Celebes, Moluccas, Papuasia, Solomon Islands.

A. Scales in 23 rows.

a. ♂ (V. 259; C. 111).	Celebes.	Leyden Museum.
b. Yg (V. 253; C. 123).	Gorontalo, Celebes	Hr Riedel [C.].
c. ♂ (V. 265, C. 117)	Amboyna.	Leyden Museum
d–e, f. ♂ (V. 263; C. 104) & ♀ (V. 260, 261; C. ?, 109).	Ceram.	
g. ♀ (V. 254, C. 110).	Mysol.	
h. ♂ (V. 258; C. ?).	Wokau, Aru Ids.	H M S. 'Challenger.' (Type of *D. aruanus*.)
i. Hgr. (V. 240; C. 104).	Trobriand Ids.	Mr. A. S. Meek [C.].
k. ♂ (V. 245; C. ?).	Normanby, Louisiade Archipelago.	B. H. Thomson, Esq. [P.].

B. Scales in 21 rows.

a–b. ♂ (V. 267; C. 121) & hgr. (V. 259; C. 119).	N. Celebes.	Dr. A. B. Meyer [C.].
c–d. ♂ (V. 268, C. 118) & yg (V. 260; C. 125).	Manado, Celebes.	Dr. A. B. Meyer [C.].
e. ♀ (V. 248, C. 108).	Sangir Id. (?).	Dr. A. B. Meyer [C.].
f. ♂ (V. 249, C. 113).	N.W. New Guinea.	M. A. Linden [C.].
g–h, i. ♀ (V. 250, 259, 259; C. ?, 106, 115).	New Guinea.	
k. ♀ (V. 253; C. 115).	New Guinea, S. of Huon Gulf.	
l. ♀ (V. 270; C. 109).	Fly River.	Rev. S Macfarlane [C.].
m–n. ♀ (V. 244; C. 109) & hgr (V. 250, C. 104).	Kei Ids.	Capt. Langen [P.].
o. ♂ (V. 20; C. ?).	Murray Id., Torres Straits.	Rev. S. Macfarlane [C.].

p-q. ♂ (V. 266, 262; C. ?, ?).	Cornwallis Id., Torres Straits	Rev. S. Macfarlane [C].	
r. ♂ (V. 257; C. ?).	Fergusson Id., D'Entrecasteaux Group.	Mr A. S. Meek [C].	
s-t. ♂ (V. 258, C. 112) & hgr. (V. 256; C. 117).	Duke of York Id.	Rev. G. Brown [C]	
u-v. ♀ (V. 232; C. 110) & yg. (V. 217; C. 111).	Treasury Id., Solomon Ids.	H B. Guppy, Esq. [P.].	
w. Yg. (V. 238, C. 114).	Alu, Shortland Ids., Solomon Ids	C. M. Woodford, Esq. [C.].	
x-a. ♂ (V. 236, 242, 242; C. 115, ?, 103) & ♀ (V. 241; C ?).	New Georgia, Solomon Ids.	C. M. Woodford, Esq. [C].	
β-δ. Hgr. (V. 233, 234; C. 109, 112) & yg. (V 229; C. 112).	Gela, Solomon Ids.	C. M. Woodford, Esq. [C.].	
ε. ♂ (V. 239; C. ?).	Guadalcanar, Solomon Ids.	C. M. Woodford, Esq. [C.].	

C. Scales in 19 rows.

a. ♀ (V. 263; C 112).	Ternate.	H.M S. 'Challenger.'	
b. Hgr. (V. 244; C. 108).	Gilolo.	Dr. Platen [C.].	

18. Dipsadomorphus flavescens.

Triglyphodon flavescens, *Dum. & Bibr.* vii p. 1080 (1854).
Dipsas flavescens, *Jan, Elenco*, p. 104 (1863).

Closely allied to *D. irregularis*, but præocular not extending to the upper surface of the head, and three postoculars. Eight upper labials. Scales in 19 rows. Ventrals 260; anal entire; subcaudals 116. Yellowish brown above, with mere traces of darker cross-bands; uniform yellowish beneath.

Total length 1121 millim.; tail 234.
Macassar, Celebes.

19. Dipsadomorphus philippinus.

Dipsas philippina, *Peters, Mon Berl Ac* 1867, p 27.

Like *D irregularis*, but præocular divided. Eight upper labials, third, fourth, and fifth entering the eye. Scales in 19 rows, vertebrals strongly enlarged. Ventrals 240; anal divided; subcaudals 133 Brownish yellow above, with black cross-lines; head spotted with black above, but without temporal streak.

Total length 690 millim; tail 155.
Luzon, Philippine Islands.

20. Dipsadomorphus blandingii.

Dipsas blandingii, *Hallow. Proc. Ac. Philad.* 1844, p. 170, & 1854, p 100; *A. Dum. Arch. Mus.* x. 1859, pp. 209 & 211; *Boettg. Ber. Senck. Ges.* 1888, p 74.
Triglyphodon fuscum, *Dum & Bibr.* vii. p. 1101 (1854); *Mocq. Bull. Soc. Philom.* (7) xi. 1887, p. 80

Dipsas fasciata, *Fisch. Abh. Nat. Ver. Hamb* iii. 1856, p. 84, pl. iii.
fig. 5; *Günth. Cat.* p. 173 (1858).
—— valida, *Fisch. l. c.* p 87, fig. 4; *Günth l. c.* p. 172
—— globiceps, *Fisch. l. c.* p. 89, fig 6; *Gunth l. c.* p. 173; *F Mull.
Verh. Nat. Ges Basel*, vii. 1885, p. 687.
Toxicodryas blandingii, *Hallow. Proc. Ac. Philad.* 1857, p. 60.
Dipsas fischeri, *Jan, in A. Dum. l. c.* p. 212.
Boiga blandingii, *Cope, Proc. Ac. Philad.* 1860, p. 264.
—— globiceps, *Cope, l. c.*
Dipsas fusca, *Jan, Elenco,* p. 104 (1863).
—— cynodon, part., *Jan, l. c., and Icon. Gén.* 38, pl. vi. fig. 2 (1871).
—— regalis (*Schleg.*), *Jan, Icon l c*: *F. Mull. l. c.* p. 687.
? Dipsas globiceps, var. tumboensis, *F. Mull. l. c.* p. 688.

Anterior palatine and mandibular teeth strongly enlarged.
Rostral broader than deep, just visible from above; internasals
broader than long, shorter than the præfrontals; frontal as long as
broad or slightly longer than broad, as long as or a little shorter
than its distance from the end of the snout, shorter than the
parietals; loreal nearly as long as deep; two (rarely one) præoculars, widely separated from the frontal; two (rarely three) postoculars; temporals 2+2 or 2+3; nine (rarely eight) upper labials,
fourth, fifth, and sixth (or third, fourth, and fifth) entering the eye;
three or four lower labials in contact with the anterior chin-shields,
which are smaller than the posterior. Scales in 23 (rarely in 21 or
25) rows, vertebral row strongly enlarged. Ventrals 265–274;
anal divided; subcaudals 123–147. Yellowish to dark olive above,
with more or less distinct dark brown or black cross-bars, which
may be interrupted on the vertebral line; some specimens nearly
uniform black; black bars on the posterior border of the upper
labials, the one on the penultimate labials extending on the temple
to the eye; ventrals and subcaudals yellowish to dark olive, with
or without a darker edge.

Total length 2200 millim.; tail 500.

West Africa, from the Senegal to the Congo; Zanzibar.

a–b, c ♂ (V 267, 265; C 133, 125) & yg. (V. 265; C. 130).	Sierra Leone.	
d. ♀ (V. 264, C. 125).	Fantee.	Leyden Museum.
e. ♂ (V. 271, C. 130)	Coast of Guinea.	
f. ♀ (V 274; C ?).	Oil River.	H. H. Johnston, Esq. [P.].
g–h. ♀ (V. 268; C 126) & hgr (Sc 21; V. 266; C 135).	Gaboon.	
i. ♀ (V. 266; C. 123).	W. Africa.	
k Yg. (Sc 25; V. 273; C. 124).	Zanzibar.	

21. Dipsadomorphus cynodon.

Dipsas cynodon, *Boie, Isis,* 1827, p. 559; *Guér. Icon. R. A., Rept.*

Gén. 38, pl. vi. fig. 1 (1871); *W. Sclater, Journ. As. Soc. Beng.* lx. 1891, p. 244, *Boettg. Abh. Mus. Dresd.* 1894-95, no. 7, p. 4 (1895).

Dipsas cynodon, part., *Cantor, Cat. Mal. Rept.* p. 77 (1847).
Opetiodon cynodon, *Dum. & Bibr.* vii. p. 907 (1854).
Eudipsas cynodon, *Gunth. Cat.* p. 168 (1858).
Pareas waandersii, *Bleek Nat. Tijdschr. Nederl. Ind.* xxi. 1860, p. 471, *Edeling, op. cit* xxxi. 1870, p 385.

Anterior palatine and mandibular teeth very strongly enlarged Rostral broader than deep, scarcely visible from above; internasals broader than long, shorter than the præfrontals; frontal as long as broad or slightly longer than broad, as long as or a little longer than its distance from the end of the snout, shorter than the parietals; loreal square, or longer than deep; one præocular, narrowly separated from the frontal; two postoculars; temporals 2+2 or 2+3 or 3+3; eight to ten upper labials, third, fourth, and fifth, fourth and fifth, fourth, fifth, and sixth, or fifth, sixth, and seventh entering the eye; four or five lower labials in contact with the anterior chin-shields, which are smaller than the posterior. Scales in 23 (rarely 25) rows, vertebral row strongly enlarged Ventrals 248-290; anal entire; subcaudals 114-156.

Total length 2050 millim.; tail 480.

Assam, Burma, Malay Peninsula and Archipelago.

A. Yellowish or pale reddish brown above, with dark brown or black transverse spots or cross-bars; a dark streak on each side of the head, behind the eye, belly yellowish, uniform or marbled with brown.

a-b. ♀ (Sc. 25; V. 261; C. 114) & yg (V. 257; C. 129). Toungoo, Burma. E. W. Oates, Esq. [P.].
c. ♀ (V. 283, C. 142). Singapore. Dr. Dennys [P.].
d. Yg. (V. 264; C. 149). Singapore. H. N. Ridley, Esq. [P.].
e Hgr. (V 290, C. ?) Singapore.
f Ad., bad state (V. 267; C. ?). Bali. Dr. Bleeker. (Type of *Pareas waandersii*.)
g. ♂ (V. 277; C. 149). Sandakan, N. Borneo. Douglas Cator, Esq. [P.]
h. ♂ (V. 266; C. 152). Java?
i. ♀ (V 264, C. 129). Philippines. H. Cuming, Esq. [C.].
k. ♀ (V. 269; C 145). ——? Leyden Museum.
l. Skull of *a*.

B. Dark brown or black above, with more or less distinct lighter cross-bars; sides usually with a series of whitish spots on or close to the ventrals, belly black, or yellowish speckled with black; head brown above, speckled with black; a black streak on each side of the head behind the eye; labials with black vertical lines on the sutures.

a. ♀ (V. 270; C. 156). Malacca. D. F. A. Hervey, Esq. [P.].
b. ♂ (V. 285; C. 150). ——? Zoological Society.
c. ♂ (V. 274; C. 144). ——? Dr. Günther [P.].

C. Fawn-colour, without spots or markings, or with traces of darker cross-bands.

a. ♀ (V. 268; C. 132). Mindanao. A. Everett, Esq. [C.].
b. Hgr. ♂ (V. 261; C. 143) Rejang R., Sarawak. Brooke Low, Esq. [P.].

22. Dipsadomorphus forsteni.

Triglyphodon forsteni, *Dum. & Bibr.* vii. p. 1077 (1854).
—— tessellatum, *Dum. & Bibr* t c. p. 1082.
Dipsas forsteni, *Jan, Elenco,* p. 104 (1863); *Gunth. Rept. Brit. Ind.* p. 309 (1864), *Anders. Proc. Zool. Soc.* 1871, p. 187; *Stoliczka, Journ. As. Soc. Beng* xl. 1871, p. 439; *Theob. Cat. Rept. Brit. Ind* p. 198 (1876); *Bouleng. Faun Ind., Rept.* p. 362 (1890).
—— tessellata, *Jan, l. c.*
—— cynodon, var., *F. Müll. Verh. Nat. Ges. Basel,* vi. 1878, p. 689.

Anterior palatine and mandibular teeth strongly enlarged. Rostral broader than deep, just visible from above; internasals broader than long, much shorter than the præfrontals; frontal as long as broad, or a little longer than broad, as long as or a little shorter than its distance from the end of the snout, shorter than the parietals, loreal square, or deeper than long; one præocular, extending to the upper surface of the head but not reaching the frontal; two or three postoculars; temporals very small and numerous, scale-like; eight to eleven upper labials, third, fourth, and fifth, or fourth, fifth, and sixth entering the eye; three or four lower labials in contact with the anterior chin-shields, which are as large as or a little larger than the posterior; latter separated from each other by scales. Scales in 25 to 31 rows, vertebral row feebly enlarged. Ventrals 254–270; anal entire; subcaudals 103–131. Brown above, uniform or with more or less regular, angular, black cross-bars, with or without white spots between them; usually a black band from the frontal shield to the nape, and another on each side behind the eye; lower parts white, uniform or spotted with brown.

Total length 1720 millim.; tail 330.

India and Ceylon.

a–b. Yg., dry. Matheran, Bombay. Dr. Leith [P.].
c, d, e. ♀ (Sc. 29; V. 254; C. 111), hgr. (Sc. 27; V. 259; C. 103), & yg. (Sc. 29; V. 268; C. 119). Anamallays. Col. Beddome [C.].
f–g. ♂ ♀, imperfect. Anamallays. Col. Beddome [C.].
h. ♂ (Sc. 29; V. 263; C. 112). Madras Pres. Sir W. Elliot [P.].
i, k. ♂ (Sc. 27; V. 262; C. 111) & ♀ (Sc. 27; V. 265; C. 103). India.
l. (Sc. 27; V. 257; C. 107). —— ? Zoological Society.

The descriptions of the two following Snakes are insufficient, and as the dentition does not appear to have been examined, it is even doubtful whether they belong to the genus *Dipsadomorphus* as here defined :—

DIPSAS BERTHOLDI, Jan, Elenco, p. 103 (1863), and Icon. Gén. 38, pl. v. fig. 3 (1871).

Rostral broader than deep; internasals shorter than the præfrontals; frontal once and one fourth as long as broad, a little longer than its distance from the end of the snout, shorter than the parietals; loreal as long as deep; one præocular, not reaching the frontal; three postoculars; temporals 2+2; eight upper labials, fourth and fifth entering the eye; five lower labials in contact with the anterior chin-shields. Body strongly compressed. Scales in 15 rows, vertebrals enlarged. Above with dark spots forming interrupted cross-bands; two dark lines running along the belly and tail.

Habitat unknown.—Prof. Ehlers informs me the specimen is no longer to be found in the Gottingen Museum.

DIPSAS ORNATA, Macleay, Proc. Linn. Soc. N. S. W. (2) iii. 1888, p. 416.

Head broad, flat, rounded at the muzzle, and very suddenly contracted behind into a very narrow neck. Body elongate, compressed, and tapering to a very long fine tail. Loreal nearly square; a large præocular; two small postoculars; nine upper labials. Scales in 15 rows. Ventrals 277; anal entire; subcaudals 120. Yellowish-white, closely barred with black.

Total length 610 millim.; tail 230.

King's Sound, N.W. Australia.

149. DIPSADOBOA.

Dipsadoboa, part, *Günth. Cat. Col. Sn* p 182 (1858).
Heterurus, part., *Jan, Elenco sist. Ofid.* p. 103 (1863).
Anoplodipsas, *Peters, Mon. Berl. Ac.* 1869, p. 442.

Maxillary teeth 16 to 18, followed, after a short interspace, by a pair of enlarged grooved fangs situated below the posterior border of the eye; anterior mandibular teeth feebly enlarged. Head distinct from neck; eye rather large, with vertically elliptic pupil; nasals concave. Body compressed, scales smooth, with apical pits, disposed slightly obliquely, in 17 rows, the vertebral row enlarged; ventrals rounded. Tail moderate, subcaudals single.

West Africa.

1. Dipsadoboa unicolor.

Dipsadoboa unicolor, *Günth. Cat.* p. 183 (1858), *and Zool. Rec.* 1872, p. 75.

Heterurus bicolor, *Jan, Icon. Gén.* 38, pl. ii. fig. 3 (1871).
Anoplodipsas viridis, *Peters, Mon. Berl. Ac.* 1869, p. 442, pl. —. fig. 4.
Dipsadoboa assimilis, *Matschie, Sitzb. Ges. Nat. Fr.* 1893, p. 173.

Rostral broader than deep, scarcely visible from above; internasals broader than long, about half as long as the præfrontals; frontal a little longer than broad, as long as or a little longer than its distance from the end of the snout, shorter than the parietals; loreal as long as deep or deeper than long; one præocular, usually in contact with the frontal; two postoculars; temporals 1+2; eight or nine upper labials, fourth and fifth, fifth and sixth, or fourth, fifth, and sixth entering the eye; five or six lower labials in contact with the anterior chin-shields, which are as long as or shorter than the posterior. Scales in 17 rows. Ventrals 186–216; anal entire; subcaudals 66–100. Green or dark purplish brown above, yellowish beneath.

Total length 790 millim.; tail 160.

West Africa.

A. Green above.

a. ♀ (V. 186; C. 68).	W. Africa.	Mr. Rich [C.]	(Type.)
b. ♂ (V. 193; C. 76).	Fernando Po.	Dr. Gunther [P.].	

B. Dark purplish brown above.

a–b. ♀ (V. 199; C. ?) & hgr. (V. 210, C. 93). Rio del Rey. H. H. Johnston, Esq. [P.].
c. ♀ (V. 194, C. 66). Gaboon.

150. RHINOBOTHRYUM.

Rhinobothryum, *Wagler, Syst. Amph.* p. 186 (1830), *Dum. & Bibr. Erp. Gén.* vii. p. 1060 (1854); *Gunth. Cat. Col. Sn.* p. 176 (1858); *Jan, Elenco sist. Ofid.* p. 102 (1863).
Dipsas, part., *Schleg. Phys. Serp.* ii. p. 357 (1837).

Maxillary teeth 14, equal, followed, after an interspace, by a pair of enlarged grooved fangs situated below the posterior border of the eye; anterior mandibular teeth longest. Head distinct from neck; eye large, with vertically elliptic pupil; nostril very large, vertically oval, between two nasals and the internasal; rostral shield very large. Body compressed; scales keeled, with apical pits, in 19 or 21 rows; ventrals angulate and feebly notched laterally. Tail long; subcaudals in two rows.

Tropical South America.

1. Rhinobothryum lentiginosum.

Coluber lentiginosus, *Scopoli, Delic. Flor. Faun. Insubr.* iii. p. 41, pl. xx. fig. 2 (1788).
Rhinobothryum maculatum, *Wagl. Syst. Amph.* p. 188 (1830).

Dipsas macrorhina, *Schleg. Phys. Serp.* ii. p. 289, pl. xi. figs 31. & 3 (1837).
Rhinobothryum lentiginosum, *Dum. & Bibr.* vii. p. 1061 (1854); *Jan, Icon Gén.* 38, pl. i fig. 3 (1871).

Snout broad, truncate. Rostral very large, as deep as broad, separating the internasals, the portion visible from above as long as its distance from the frontal; frontal as long as broad, shorter than its distance from the end of the snout, shorter than the parietals; loreal deeper than long; one præocular, not extending to the upper surface of the head; two postoculars; temporals 2+2; eight to ten upper labials, fourth and fifth or fifth and sixth entering the eye; four or five lower labials in contact with the anterior chin-shields; posterior chin-shields narrower and separated from each other by scales. Scales rather strongly keeled on the back, smooth on the sides, in 19 or 21 rows. Ventrals 245–278; anal divided; subcaudals 114–120. Body with black annuli separated by narrower whitish annuli which are spotted with black in the middle on the back, head-shields black, edged with whitish.

Total length 1380 millim.; tail 300.

Colombia, Guianas, Eastern Peru.

a. ♂ (Sc. 19; V. 257; C. 114).   Yurimaguas, N.E. Peru
b. ♂ (Sc 19; V 275; C. 117).   ——— ?

151. HIMANTODES.

Bungarus, part., *Oppel, Ann. Mus.* xvi 1810, p. 391.
Dipsas, part., *Fitzing. N. Class. Rept.* p. 29 (1826), *Wagl Syst. Amph.* p. 180 (1830); *Schleg. Phys. Serp.* ii. p. 257 (1837); *Gunth. Cat. Col. Sn.* p. 169 (1858).
Imantodes, *Dum & Bibr. Mém. Ac. Sc.* xxiii. 1853, p. 507, *and Erp. Gén.* vii. p. 1064 (1854).
Himantodes, *Cope, Proc Ac Philad.* 1860, p. 264; *Jan, Elenco sist. Ofid.* p. 102 (1863).

Maxillary teeth equal, 12 to 18, followed, after an interspace, by a pair of enlarged grooved teeth situated just behind the vertical of the posterior border of the eye; anterior mandibular teeth longest. Head small, very distinct from neck; eye very large, with vertically elliptic pupil. Body very slender, strongly compressed; scales narrow, smooth, with apical pits, in 15 or 17 rows, vertebral row enlarged or not; ventrals rounded. Tail long; subcaudals in two rows.

Mexico, Central America, Tropical South America.

Synopsis of the Species.

I. Scales in 17 rows, vertebral row strongly enlarged.

Vertebral scales, on the thickest part of
   the body, broader than long . . . . . . 1. *cenchoa*, p. 84.
Vertebral scales, none broader than long   2. *elegans*, p. 85.

II. Scales in 15 rows, vertebral row strongly enlarged.
   3. *lentiferus*, p. 86.
III. Scales in 17 rows, vertebral row not or but very slightly enlarged
   A. Anal divided.
      1. Frontal not twice as long as broad.
Head twice or twice and a half as wide as the neck.............. .... 4. *gemmistratus*, p. 86.
Neck extremely slender, not more than one third the width of the head .... 5. *gracillimus*, p. 87.
      2. Frontal more than twice as long as broad.
   6. *inornatus*, p. 88.
   B. Anal entire .... 7. *subæqualis*, p. 88.

1. Himantodes cenchoa.

Seba, Thes. ii. pl. xvi. figs 2 & 3 (1735).
Coluber cenchoa, *Linn. S. N.* i. p. 389 (1766); *Daud. Rept.* vi. p. 283 (1803).
Bungarus cencoalt, *Oppel, Ann. Mus.* xvi. 1810, p. 392
Dipsas cenchoa, *Wied, Beitr. Nat. Bras.* i. p. 396 (1825); *Günth. Cat* p 174 (1858), and *Biol. C.-Am , Rept.* p. 175 (1895).
—— weigelii, *Fitzing. N. Class. Rept.* p. 50 (1826); *Schleg. Phys. Serp.* ii. p. 278, pl. xi. figs. 19 & 20 (1837).
Imantodes cenchoa, *Dum. & Bibr.* vii p. 1065 (1854).
Himantodes cenchoa, *Cope, Proc. Ac. Philad.* 1861, p. 296, and *Amer. Nat.* 1894, p. 613.
—— leucomelas, *Cope, ll. cc.*
—— anisolepis, *Cope, Amer. Nat.* 1894, p. 613.

Rostral small, broader than deep, scarcely visible from above; internasals much shorter than the præfrontals; frontal once and one fourth to once and a half as long as broad, as long as or a little longer than its distance from the end of the snout, shorter than the parietals; loreal as long as deep or deeper than long, rarely a little longer than deep; one or two (rarely three) præoculars, frequently a small upper and a large lower; two (rarely three) postoculars; temporals 1 or 2+2 or 3; eight upper labials, fourth and fifth or third, fourth, and fifth entering the eye; four or five lower labials in contact with the anterior chin-shields, which are as long as or shorter than the posterior. Scales in 17 rows, vertebrals strongly enlarged, the largest broader than long. Ventrals 220-267; anal divided; subcaudals 122-175. Pale brown or greyish above; head with dark brown spots or bands which may be separated by narrow light lines; body with 26 to 58 dark brown or reddish-brown spots or cross-bands edged with darker and lighter, narrowed on the sides, where they may break up into spots; lower parts whitish, dotted or powdered with brown, with or without a dark streak along the middle of the belly.

Total length 1100 millim.: tail 340.

Mexico, Central America, Tropical South America.

151. HIMANTODES.

A. Posterior dorsal spots broken up on the sides, lateral spots being present. (*C. cenchoa*, L.)

a. ♀ (V. 237; C. 142).	Teapa, Tabasco	F. D. Godman, Esq. [P.].
b-c. ♂ (V. 244; C. 145) & ♀ (V. 238; C. 145).	Hacienda Rosa de Jericho, Nicaragua, 3250 feet.	Dr. Rothschuh [C.].
d. ♂ (V. 235; C. ?).	Irazu, Costa Rica.	F. D. Godman, Esq [P.].
e ♀ (V. 267; C. 162).	Panama.	
f. ♂ (V. 251; C. 163).	Rosario de Cucuta, Colombia	Mr. C. Webber [C.].
g. ♀ (V. 248, C. 150).	Carthagena, Colombia.	Capt. Garth [P.].
h. ♂ (V. 249; C. 171).	Trinidad.	F. W. Urich, Esq. [P.].
i. Hgr. (V. 251; C. 161).	Surinam.	
k. ♀ (V. 254; C. 160).	Moyobamba, N E Peru.	Mr. A. H. Roff [C.].

B. Dorsal spots all extending down to the ventrals. (*H. leucomelas*, Cope.)

a-e. ♂ (V. 243, 231, 232, 239; C 158, 154, 163, 147) & ♀ (V. 220; C. 147).	Mexico.	Mr. Hugo Finck [C.].
f. ♂ (V. 230; C. 164).	Jalapa, Vera Cruz.	F. D. Godman, Esq. [P.].
g Yg. (V. 242; C. 160).	Huatuzco, Vera Cruz.	F. D. Godman, Esq. [P.].
h Yg. (V. 245; C. 159).	Orizaba, Vera Cruz.	
i-l ♂ (V. 253; C. 166) & hgr. (V. 230, 233; C. 152, 145).	Teapa, Tabasco.	F. D Godman, Esq. [P].
m. Hgr. (V. 234; C. 157).	Coban, Vera Paz.	O. Salvin, Esq. [C.].
n. ♂ (V. 240; C 160).	Vera Paz, low forest.	O. Salvin, Esq. [C.].
o-p. ♂ (V. 257; C. 157) & ♀ (V. 236, C. 133).	Hacienda Rosa de Jericho, Nicaragua, 3250 feet	Dr Rothschuh [C.].
q. ♂ (V. 236; C. 145).	Matagalpa, Nicaragua.	Dr. Rothschuh [C.].
r. ♀ (V. 246; C. 158).	Chiriqui.	F. D. Godman, Esq. [P.].
s. ♀ (V. 250; C. 154).	Pebas, Upper Amazon.	H. W. Bates, Esq. [C.].
t. ♀ (V. 248; C. 167).	Madre de Dios, Bolivia.	
u. ♂ skeleton.	Nicaragua.	

2. Himantodes elegans.

Himantodes cenchoa, var. elegans, *Jan, Icon. Gén.* 38, pl. ii fig. 1 (1871).

Leptognathus stratissima, *Cope, Proc. Amer. Philos. Soc.* xxiii. 1886, p. 280.

Himantodes semifasciatus, *Cope, Amer. Nat.* 1894, p. 613.
Dipsas gemmistrata (non *Cope*), *Gunth. Biol. C.-Am., Rept.* p. 175 (1895).

Closely allied to the preceding, the only structural difference being that the vertebral scales are not so large, mostly longer than broad, the largest never broader than long. Ventrals 220–237; subcaudals 122–146. Pale brown above, head with dark brown, black-edged spots or symmetrical markings; forty to sixty dark brown black-edged large transverse spots on the body, the anterior extending right across down to the ventrals, the others confined to the back and accompanied on each side by a smaller spot; lower parts yellowish, dotted or powdered with dark brown.

Total length 810 millim.; tail 240.

Central America.

a–b. Hgr. (V. 228, 220; C. 124, 122).	Pacific Coast of Guatemala.	O. Salvin, Esq. [C.]
c–e. ♂ (V. 237; C. 142) & ♀ (V. 233, 231; C. 137, 146).	Cartago, Costa Rica.	

3. Himantodes lentiferus.

Himantodes lentiferus, *Cope, Amer. Nat.* 1894, p. 613.

Agrees in structure, and particularly in the largest vertebral scales being broader than long, with *H. cenchoa*, but differs in having only 15 rows of scales. Dorsal spots terminating in an angle near the ventrals; no lateral spots.

Total length 622 millim.; tail 189.

Eastern Ecuador.

4. Himantodes gemmistratus.

Himantodes cenchoa (non *L.*), *Cope, Proc. Ac. Philad.* 1860, p. 264.
—— gemmistratus, *Cope, Proc. Ac. Philad.* 1861, p. 296, and *Amer. Nat.* 1894, p. 613.
—— tenuissimus, *Cope, Proc. Ac. Philad.* 1866, p. 317, and *Amer. Nat.* 1894, p. 613.
Dipsas gemmistratus, *Cope, Journ. Ac. Philad.* (2) viii. 1876, p. 131.
—— gemmistrata latistrata, *Cope, Bull. U.S. Nat. Mus.* no. 32, 1887, p. 68.
—— tenuissima, *Cope, l. c.*; *Günth. Biol. C.-Am., Rept.* p. 176 (1895).
—— splendida, *Günth. l. c.* p. 176, pl. lvi. fig. A.

Rostral small, broader than deep, scarcely visible from above; internasals much shorter than the præfrontals; frontal once and one third to once and a half as long as broad, as long as or a little longer than its distance from the end of the snout, shorter than the parietals; loreal as long as deep, or a little longer than deep; one præocular (rarely divided) not reaching the frontal; two postoculars; temporals 1 + 2 (or 2 + 3); eight upper labials, fourth and fifth or third, fourth, and fifth entering the eye; four to six lower labials in contact with the anterior chin-shields, which are as long as or a little longer than the posterior. Scales in 17 rows, vertebrals scarcely enlarged. Ventrals 223–250; anal divided; subcaudals 130–157. Pale brown above; head with dark brown spots or symmetrical markings; 35 to 50 dark brown spots or cross-bars on the body, lighter in the centre and sometimes edged with whitish, often connected by a narrow dark brown line on the middle of the back; lower parts whitish, dotted or powdered with brown.

Total length 830 millim.; tail 270.

Mexico and Central America.

A. 35 dorsal spots, broken up on the sides in the posterior half of the body.

a. ♀ (V. 223, C. ?).   Yucatan.   (Type of *D. splendida.*)

B. 46 dorsal spots, all extending down to the ventrals.

b. ♂ (V. 242, C. 155).   Yucatan

C. 50 dorsal spots, broken up on the sides in the posterior fourth of the body.

c. ♂ (V. 231; C. 130).   Hacienda Santa Gertru-   Dr. A. C. Buller [C.].
dio, Mexico.

5. Himantodes gracillimus.

Dipsas gracillima, *Gunth. Biol. C.-Am*, *Rept.* p. 177, pl. lvi. fig. B (1895).

Neck extremely slender, not more than one third as wide as the head. Rostral small, broader than deep, scarcely visible from above; internasals much shorter than the præfrontals; frontal once and one third as long as broad, longer than its distance from the end of the snout, shorter than the parietals; loreal as long as deep or a little longer than deep; one præocular; two post-oculars; temporals 1+2; eight upper labials, fourth and fifth or third, fourth, and fifth entering the eye; five lower labials in contact with the anterior chin-shields, which are as long as or a little shorter than the posterior. Scales in 17 rows, vertebrals not enlarged. Ventrals 244–253; anal divided; subcaudals 145. Pale brownish above, with 42 to 72 darker spots edged with blackish; these spots being much larger than the interspaces between them, the body appears brown with pale black-edged cross-bars; whitish beneath, dotted or powdered with brown.

Total length 1000 millim; tail 300.

Mexico.

a. ♂ (V. 244, C. ?).   S Mexico.   F. D. Godman, Esq.
[P.]. (Type.)
b. ♂ (V. 253; C. 145).   Tres Marias Ids., W.   Hr. A. Forrer [C.]
Mexico.

6. Himantodes inornatus. (PLATE V. fig. 1.)

Neck extremely slender, one third as wide as the head. Rostral small, broader than deep, scarcely visible from above; internasals much shorter than the præfrontals; frontal twice to twice and one third as long as broad, longer than its distance from the end of the snout, slightly shorter than the parietals; loreal as long as deep; one præocular; two postoculars; temporals 1+2, eight upper labials, third, fourth, and fifth entering the eye; four or five lower labials in contact with the anterior chin-shields, which are a little shorter than the posterior. Scales in 17 rows, vertebrals not enlarged. Ventrals 206; anal divided; subcaudals 112. Pale brown above, with blackish dots and faint traces of black cross-bars; a black line along the occiput; whitish beneath, finely speckled with blackish and with a blackish median line.

Total length 820 millim.; tail 230.

Nicaragua.

a–b. ♀ (V. 206; C. 112) and head & neck of adult.	Hacienda Rosa de Jericho, 3250 ft.	Dr. E. Rothschuh [C.].

7. Himantodes (?) subæqualis.

Dipsas subæqualis, *Fischer, Arch f. Nat.* 1880, p. 224, pl. ix. figs. 18-21.

Neck extremely slender, one third as wide as the head. Rostral small, a little broader than deep, scarcely visible from above; internasals much shorter than the præfrontals; frontal a little longer than broad, longer than its distance from the end of the snout, shorter than the parietals, loreal as long as deep; two præ- and two postoculars; temporals 1+1; eight upper labials, third, fourth, and fifth entering the eye; five lower labials in contact with the anterior chin-shields, which are as long as the posterior. Scales in 17 rows, vertebrals scarcely enlarged. Ventrals 226; anal entire; subcaudals 105. Uniform bluish green above, lighter beneath.

Total length 1050 millim.; tail 250.

Habitat unknown.

152. LEPTODIRA.

Sibon, part., *Fitzing. N. Class. Rept.* pp. 29, 31 (1826)
Coronella, part., *Schleg. Phys. Serp.* ii. p 50 (1837).
Dipsas, part., *Schleg. l. c.* p. 357; *Dum. & Bibr. Erp. Gén.* vii. p. 1133 (1854).
Heterurus, part., *Dum. & Bibr. t. c.* p. 1168.
Leptodeira, *Gunth. Cat. Col. Sn.* p. 165 (1858).
Sibon, *Cope Proc. Ac. Philad.* 1860. p. 268.

Maxillary teeth 15 to 18, gradually and feebly increasing in length, followed, after an interspace, by a pair of enlarged grooved teeth situated just behind the vertical of the posterior border of the eye; mandibular teeth, anterior slightly enlarged. Head distinct from neck; eye large, with vertically elliptic pupil; posterior nasal concave. Body cylindrical or moderately compressed; scales smooth or faintly keeled, with apical pits, in 17 to 25 rows; ventrals rounded. Tail moderate or rather long; subcaudals in two rows.

Tropical and South Africa; Tropical America, northwards to Texas.

Synopsis of the Species.

I. Anal entire; scales in 19 (exceptionally 17) rows; ventrals 144–180; subcaudals 32–54 .... 1. *hotambœia*, p. 89.

II. Anal divided.

    A. Subcaudals 51–72; lateral spots none, or very small.

        1. Scales in 19 rows.

Seven upper labials; ventrals 151–164.   2. *punctata*, p. 91.
Eight upper labials; ventrals 170–196.   3. *nigrofasciata*, p. 92.

        2. Scales in 21 to 25 rows.

Nine upper labials; ventrals 188 ....   4. *frenata*, p. 92.
Eight upper labials; ventrals 194 ....   5. *septentrionalis*, p. 93.
Eight upper labials; ventrals 160–180.   6. *personata*, p. 93.

    B. Subcaudals 71–107.

        1. Scales in 21 or 23 rows; rostral twice as broad as deep; lateral spots present.

Ventrals 158–169 ....   7. *ocellata*, p. 94.
Ventrals 172–211 ....   8. *albofusca*, p. 95.

        2. Scales in 19 (exceptionally 17 or 21) rows; ventrals 175–195; rostral not twice as broad as deep.
                              9. *annulata*, p. 97.

1. Leptodira hotambœia.

Seba, Thes. i pl. xxxiii fig. 6, & lxxv. fig. 3 (1734).
Coronella hotambœia, *Laur. Syn. Rept.* p. 85 (1768).
—— virginica, *Laur. l. c.* p 86
Coluber rufescens, *Gmel. S. N.* i. p. 1094 (1789), *Daud. Rept.* vii. p. 110 (1803).
—— hitambœia, *Gmel. l. c* p. 1113.
—— bicolor, *Leach, in Bowdich, Miss. Ashantee,* p. 493 (1819).
Ophis heterurus, *Duvernoy, Ann. Sc. Nat* xxx 1833, p 9, pl. i. fig. 2.

Ophis albocinctus, *Duvernoy, l c.* p. 10, pl. ii. figs. 1–3.
Coronella rufescens, *Schleg Phys. Serp.* ii. p. 72, pl. ii. figs. 16 & 17 (1837).
Dipsas hippocrepis, *Reinh. Vidensk. Selsk. Skrift.* x. 1843, p. 251, pl. i. figs. 18–20.
Crotaphopeltis rufescens, *Smith, Ill. Zool. S. Afr*, *Rept.* App. p. 18 (1849); *Cope, Proc. Ac. Philad.* 1860, p. 566, *Jan, Icon. Gén.* 39, pl. ii. fig. 1 (1872); *Boettg Abh. Senck. Ges.* xii. 1881, p. 398.
? Dipsas inornatus, *Smith, l. c* p. 20
Heterurus rufescens, *Dum & Bibr*. vii. p. 1170 (1854).
—— hippocrepis, *Dum. & Bibr. t. c.* p. 1177.
Leptodeira rufescens, *Gunth. Cat.* p. 165 (1858); *Boettg. Ber. Senck. Ges.* 1887, p. 162, & 1888, p. 72.
Oxyropus melanocrotaphus, *Cope, Proc. Ac. Philad.* 1860, p. 260.
Crotaphopeltis hitambœia, *Peters, Reise n. Mossamb.* iii. p. 126 (1882).

Rostral broader than deep, scarcely visible from above; internasals shorter than the præfrontals; frontal once and one third to once and two thirds as long as broad, as long as or a little longer than its distance from the end of the snout, shorter than the parietals; loreal as long as deep, or a little longer than deep; one præocular (rarely divided); two (rarely three) postoculars; temporals 1+1 or 2; eight (rarely nine) upper labials, third, fourth, and fifth (exceptionally fourth and fifth or fourth, fifth, and sixth) entering the eye; three or four pairs of large chin-shields, the anterior longer than broad and in contact with four and five lower labials, the others usually broader than long. Scales smooth or faintly keeled, in 19 (exceptionally 17) rows. Ventrals 144–180; anal entire; subcaudals 32–54. Brown, olive, or blackish above, uniform or with whitish dots which may form cross-bars; a black band on the temple, usually connected with its fellow across the occiput; belly whitish.

Total length 610 millim.; tail 90.

Tropical and South Africa, as far north as Senegambia and Nubia.

a. Hgr. (V. 159; C. 38).	Gambia.	T. Mitchell, Esq. [P.]
b. Hgr. (V. 165; C. 39).	Bissao.	V. H. Cornish, Esq. [C.]
c. Hgr. (V. 161; C. 44).	Gold Coast	W. F. Evans, Esq. [C.]
d. ♀ (V. 164; C. ?).	Fantee.	T E Bowdich, Esq. [P.] (Type of *C bicolor*.)
e, f-l. ♂ (V. 164; C. 54), ♀ (V. 160; C. 41), hgr. (V. 155, 156; C. 38, 33), & yg. (V. 161, 162, 159, C. 44, 42, 40).	Asaba, Niger.	J. W. Crosse, Esq. [P.]
m. ♀ (V. 167; C. 42).	Congo.	
n-s. ♀ (V. 159; C. 39), hgr (V. 164, 153, 140, 148; C. 41, 50, 46, 46), & yg. (V. 164; C. 52).	Mkonumbi, E. Africa.	Dr J W. Gregory [P.]

152. LEPTODIRA.

t. ♀ (V 166; C. 34).	Mt Ruwenzori, 5000–6000 ft.	Scott Elliot, Esq. [P].
u–v. Yg. (V. 151, 169, C. 40, 49).	Mt Kilimanjaro.	F. J Jackson, Esq. [P.].
w–z. ♂ (V. 160, C. 38) & yg. (V. 153, 145, 144; C. 43, 42, 39).	Zomba, Brit. C. Africa	H. H. Johnston, Esq. [P.].
a ♂ (V. 159; C. 40).	Shiré highlands	H. H. Johnston, Esq. [P.].
β–δ. ♂ (V 158, C 42) & hgr. (V. 166, 164; C. 37, 41).	Zambesi.	Sir J. Kirk [P.]
ε. ♀ (V. 151; C. 32).	Johannesburg, Transvaal.	Rev. G. H. R. Fisk [P].
ζ. Yg. (V. 159, C. 41).	Pretoria, Transvaal.	W. L. Distant, Esq. [P]
η–θ Hgr (V. 152, 149; C. 44, 43).	Natal.	E. Howlett, Esq. [P.].
ι λ. Yg. (V. 154, 158, 162; C. 46, 41, 40).	Port Elizabeth.	J. M. Leslie, Esq. [P.].
μ ♀ (V 164, C. 42).	Uniondale, Natal	Mr. Drege [P.].
ν, ξ. ♂ (V. 156, C. 45) & ♀ (V. 151; C 37).	Port Natal.	Mr T. Ayres [C.].
ο. Yg. (V. 157; C. 38).	Grahamstown.	Rev. G. H R. Fisk [P.]
π. ♀ (Sc. 17, V. 163, C. 45).	Cape of Good Hope.	Lord Derby [P.]
ρ. ♀ skeleton.	S Africa.	

2. Leptodira punctata.

Crotaphopeltis punctata, *Peters, Mon Berl. Ac* 1866, p. 93
Leptodira pacifica, *Cope, Proc. Ac Philad.* 1868, p. 310; *Gunth. Biol. C-Am, Rept.* p 169 (1895)
Sibon pacificum, *Cope, Bull. U.S. Nat Mus.* no. 32, 1887, p. 67, *and Proc. U.S. Nat. Mus* xiv. 1892, p. 678.
Leptodira punctata, *Bouleng. The Zool.* 1887, p 178.

Rostral twice as broad as deep, scarcely visible from above; internasals much shorter than the præfrontals; frontal once and a half as long as broad, as long as its distance from the end of the snout, shorter than the parietals; loreal as long as deep; one præocular, separated from the frontal, usually with a small subocular below it; two postoculars; temporals 1+2, seven upper labials, third and fourth entering the eye; four lower labials in contact with the anterior chin-shields, which are a little shorter than the posterior. Scales in 19 rows Ventrals 151–164; anal divided; subcaudals 61–65. Pale brown above, with four or five rows of small black spots, head with short black streaks; a light occipital blotch with a short mesial black streak, followed by a pair of large black spots; upper lip yellowish; lower parts uniform white.

Total length 490 millim.
Mazatlan, Mexico.

a. ♀ (V. 163; C. ?)	Presidio, near Mazatlan	Hr. A Forrer [C.].

3. Leptodira nigrofasciata, (Plate V. fig. 2.)

Leptodira nigrofasciata, *Günth. Ann. & Mag. N. H.* (4) i. 1868, p. 425, and *Biol. C.-Am., Rept.* p 169 (1895).
—— mystacina, *Cope, Proc. Amer. Philos. Soc* xi. 1869, p. 151; *Günth. Biol. C.-Am.* p 169
Sibon nigrofasciatum, *Cope, Bull. U S. Nat. Mus.* no. 32, 1887, p. 67, and *Proc. U.S. Nat. Mus.* xiv. 1892, p. 678.
—— mystacinum, *Cope, Bull U.S. Nat Mus.* no. 32, p. 67.

Rostral twice as broad as deep, just visible from above; internasals much shorter than the præfrontals; frontal once and two thirds as long as broad, a little longer than its distance from the end of the snout, shorter than the parietals; loreal as long as deep or a little longer than deep; one præocular, in contact with or narrowly separated from the frontal, with or without a small subocular below it; two postoculars; temporals 1+2; eight upper labials, fourth and fifth or third, fourth, and fifth entering the eye, sixth sometimes touching the parietal; four or five lower labials in contact with the anterior chin-shields, which are as long as or a little shorter than the posterior. Scales in 19 rows. Ventrals 170–196; anal divided; subcaudals 56–70. Above with dark brown spots or semiannuli separated by narrow whitish ones, the first across the occiput; labials black-spotted; a blackish streak on each side of the head, passing through the eye; lower parts white.

Total length 480 millim.; tail 100.

Isthmus of Tehuantepec; Nicaragua.

a.	♂ (V. 170, C. 70).	Nicaragua.	Dr. Seeman [P.]. (Type.)
b.	♂ (V. 196, C. 64).	Tapana, Tehuantepec.	Prof. F Sumichrast [C.]; O. Salvin & F. D. Godman, Esqs. [P.].
c.	♀ (V. 188; C. 56).	Tehuantepec City.	Dr A. C Buller [C.].

4. Leptodira frenata.

Sibon frenatum, *Cope, Proc. U.S. Nat. Mus.* ix. 1886, p. 184, & xiv. 1892, p 677.
Leptodira frenata, *Günth. Biol. C.-Am., Rept.* p. 173 (1895).

Frontal twice as long as broad; loreal subquadrate; one præocular, not reaching the frontal, with a small subocular below it; two postoculars; temporals 1+2; nine upper labials, fourth and fifth entering the eye. Scales in 23 rows. Ventrals 188; anal divided; subcaudals 69. Black above, with narrow grey cross-bands (one scale in width), which may be broken up and alternate on the vertebral line; head grey, densely mottled with blackish, occiput pale greyish; a black streak on each side behind the eye; upper labials with black borders.

Total length 305 millim.; tail 66.

Jalapa, Mexico.

5. Leptodira septentrionalis.

Dipsas septentrionalis, *Kennicott, Rep. U.S. Mex. Bound. Surv.* ii. *Rept.* p. 16, pl. viii. fig. 1 (1859); *Cope, Proc. Ac. Philad.* 1860, p. 266.
Sibon annulatum septentrionale, *Cope, Check-list N. Am. Rept.* p. 38 (1875).
Leptodeira septentrionalis, *Stejneger, Proc. U.S. Nat Mus.* xiv. 1891, p. 505.
Sibon septentrionale, part., *Cope, Proc. U.S. Nat. Mus.* xiv. 1892, p 677.
Leptodira annulata, part., *Gunth. Biol. C-Am., Rept.* p. 170 (1895).

Rostral twice as broad as deep, scarcely visible from above; internasals a little shorter than the præfrontals; frontal once and a half as long as broad, as long as its distance from the end of the snout, shorter than the parietals; loreal as long as deep; two præoculars, upper in contact with the frontal, with a small subocular below them, two postoculars; temporals 1+2; eight upper labials, fourth and fifth entering the eye; five lower labials in contact with the anterior chin-shields, which are as long as the posterior. Scales in 21 or 23 rows. Ventrals 194; anal divided, subcaudals 65-72. Greyish or pale brown above, with large, rhomboidal, transverse black spots descending to the sides; no lateral spots; head spotted with black, occiput whitish; lower parts uniform whitish.

Total length 720 millim.; tail 150.

South-western Texas and North Mexico.

a. ♂ (Sc. 21; V. 194; C. 72). Texas. Smithsonian Institution [P.].

6. Leptodira personata.

Dipsas annulata, var. C, *Dum. & Bibr* vii p 1141 (1854)
Leptodeira annulata, part, *Gunth. Cat.* p. 166 (1858).
Sibon annulata, part, *Cope, Proc. Ac. Philad.* 1860, p 266.
Leptodira personata, *Cope, Proc. Ac. Philad.* 1868, p. 310; *Günth. Biol. C.-Am., Rept.* p 171, pl. liv. figs A & B (1895)
Eteirodipsas annulata, var. septentrionalis, *Jan, Icon. Gén.* 39, pl. 1. fig. 2 (1872).
Leptodira rhombifera, *Gunth. Ann & Mag. N. H* (4) ix. 1872, p. 32, and *l c.* p. 173, pl. liv. fig. C.
Sibon personatum, *Cope, Bull. US. Nat. Mus.* no. 32, 1887, p. 67, and *Proc. U.S. Nat. Mus.* xiv. 1892, p. 677.
—— rhombiferum, *Cope, ll cc*
Leptodira splendida, *Gunth. Biol. C-Am.* p 171, pl. liii. fig. B.

Rostral broader than deep, scarcely visible from above; internasals shorter than the præfrontals; frontal once and a half to once and two thirds as long as broad, shorter than the parietals; loreal as long as deep or longer than deep; one or two præoculars, usually in contact with the frontal, and usually a small subocular; two postoculars; temporals 1+2; eight upper labials, fourth and fifth entering the eye; five (rarely four) lower labials in contact with the anterior chin-shields, which are as long as or a little shorter than the posterior. Scales in 23 or 25 (rarely 21) rows. Ventrals

160–180; anal divided; subcaudals 53–72. Pale brown above, with large dark brown or blackish rhomboidal spots, which may be confluent to form a zigzag band; lateral spots absent or small; head dark brown, with a white or whitish cross-band on the occiput, rarely divided by a blackish median streak; upper labials spotted or edged with brown; belly uniform white, without brown dots.

Total length 780 millim.; tail 135.

Mexico, Guatemala.

a–f. ♂ (Sc. 25, 23, 25; V. 177, 176, 169; C. 65, ?, ?) & ♀ (Sc. 23; V. 180, 172, 167; C. 62, 60, 58).	Mexico.	Mr. Hugo Finck [C.].
g–n, o. ♂ (Sc. 25, 23; V. 160, 166; C. 64, 65) & ♀ (Sc. 23, 23, 23, 25, 23, 23; V. 171, 175, 172, 169, 165, 172; C. 56, 57, ?, ?, 55, 60).	Mexico.	Mr. Warwick [C.].
p, q. llgr ♂ (Sc. 23; V. 173; C. 69) & yg (Sc. 23; V. 180; C. 59).	Mexico.	M. Sallé [C.].
r–s. ♂ (Sc. 21; V. 166; C. 67) & ♀ (Sc. 23; V. 167; C. 66).	Presidio, near Mazatlan.	Hr. A. Forrer [C.].
t–v. ♀ (Sc. 25; V. 171, C. ?) & hgr. (Sc. 23, 25, V. 174, 173; C. 72, 64).	Hacienda Sta. Gertrudio.	Dr. A. C. Buller [C.].
w. Yg (Sc. 23; V. 166; C. 69).	Sto. Domingo de Guzman.	Dr. A. C. Buller [C.].
x–ζ. ♂ (Sc. 23; V. 165; C. 68), ♀ (Sc. 25; V. 169, 166, 168, 166, 161; C. ?, ?, 57, 58, 58), hgr. (Sc. 23; V. 167, 159, C. 66, 68), & yg. (Sc. 23; V. 173; C. 58).	Tampico.	F. D. Godman, Esq. [P.].
η–ξ, o. llgr ♂ (Sc. 23; V. 171, 170, 174; C. 67, 70, 67), ♀ (Sc. 23; V. 163; C. 66), & yg. (Sc. 23, 23, 25, 23, 23; V. 166, 167, 173, 174, 180; C. 65, 68, 55, 56, 58).	Jalapa.	Mr. Hoege [C.]; F. D. Godman, Esq [P.].
π. ♀ (Sc. 23; V. 176; C. 53)	Plateau of Mexico.	P. Geddes, Esq. [P.].
ρ–σ. ♀ (Sc. 21; V. 162; C. 70) & hgr. (Sc. 21; V. 164; C. 67).	Izucar, Mexico.	(Types of *L. splendida*.)
τ. Yg. (Sc. 21; V. 163; C. 67).	S. Mexico.	F. D. Godman, Esq. [P.].
v. ♀ (Sc. 25; V. 170; C. 68).	Rio Chisoy, near Cubulco, Guatemala.	O. Salvin, Esq. [C.]. (Type of *L. rhombifera*.)

7. Leptodira ocellata.

Leptodira ocellata, *Günth. Biol. C.-Am., Rept.* p. 172, pl. lv. fig. B (1895).

? Sibon septentrionale rubricatum, *Cope, Proc. Amer. Philos. Soc.* xxxi. 1894, p. 347.

Intermediate between *L. personata* and *L. albofusca*. Agrees with the former in the stouter body with lower number of ventral shields, with the latter in the length of the tail and number of caudal shields as well as in the coloration. Scales in 23 rows. Ventrals 158–169; subcaudals 74–83.

Total length 500 millim.; tail 135.

Central America.

a. ♂ (V. 166; C. 74)	Chontalez, Nicaragua.	R. A. Rir, Esq. [C.]; W. M. Crowfoot, Esq. [P.].	(Types)
b–d. ♂ (V. 169; C. 76); hgr. (V 164; C. ?), & yg. (V. 158; C. 83).	Cartago, Costa Rica.		
e. ♂ (V. 161, C. 79).	Panama.	Capt. J. C. Dow [P.].	

8. Leptodira albofusca.

Coluber albofuscus, *Lacép. Serp.* ii. pp. 94 & 312 (1789).
—— annulatus, *Merr. Beitr.* iii. p 25, pls iii. & iv. (1821).
Dipsas annulatus, part , *Schleg. Phys. Serp.* ii. p. 294 (1837).
—— annulata, var. B, *Dum. & Bibr.* vii. p. 1141 (1854).
Leptodeira annulata, part., *Gunth Cat* p 166 (1858), and *Biol. C-Am , Rept.* p. 170 (1895).
Sibon annulata, part , *Cope, Proc. Ac. Philad.* 1860, p 266.
Leptodira annulata, *Cope, Proc. Ac. Philad.* 1866, p. 127; *Garm. Bull. Essex Inst.* xxiv. 1892, p. 90.
Sibon annulatum yucatanense, *Cope, Bull. U.S. Nat. Mus.* no. 32, 1887, p. 67.
—— annulatum, *Cope, Proc. U.S. Nat. Mus.* xiv. 1892, p. 677.
—— yucatanense, *Cope, l c.*
Leptodira affinis, *Gunth Biol C-Am* p. 170.
—— yucatanensis, *Gunth. l. c.* p. 171.
—— polysticta, *Gunth. l. c.* p. 172, pl. lv fig A.

Rostral twice as broad as deep, scarcely visible from above; internasals shorter than the præfrontals; frontal once and one fourth to once and two thirds as long as broad, as long as or a little longer than its distance from the end of the snout, shorter than the parietals; loreal as long as deep or a little longer than deep; one or two præoculars, in contact with or narrowly separated from the frontal, and a small subocular; two (rarely three) postoculars; temporals 1+2 or 3; eight upper labials, fourth and fifth (rarely third, fourth, and fifth) entering the eye, four to six lower labials in contact with the anterior chin-shields, which are as long as or a little shorter than the posterior. Scales in 21 or 23 rows. Ventrals 170–211; anal divided; subcaudals 71–95. Pale brown above, with one or two dorsal series of brown, darker edged spots which may be partly confluent into a zigzag band or form cross-bands which do not descend to the ventrals; a lateral series of spots; frequently a dark median line on the occiput; a dark streak behind the eye, lower parts whitish, frequently with fine brown specks.

Total length 950 millim.; tail 220.
Tropical America.

a, b. ♀ (Sc. 23; V. 198, 202; C. 84, 79).	Mexico.	M. Sallé [C.]. (Types of *L. polysticta*.)
c–d. ♂ (Sc. 21; V. 197; C. 81) & ♀ (Sc. 21; V. 197; C. 72).	Mexico.	Mr. Warwick [C.].
e–g. ♀ (Sc. 23, V. 191, 199, 196; C. 83, 84, 87).	Mexico.	Mr. H. Finck [C.].
h. ♀ (Sc. 23; V. 194; C. 71)	Tampico, Tamaulipas.	F. D. Godman, Esq. [P.].
i. ♂ (Sc. 23; V. 200; C. 93).	Huatuzco, Vera Cruz.	F. D. Godman, Esq. [P.].
k. Hgr. ♂ (Sc. 23; V. 197; C. 75).	Jalapa, Vera Cruz.	Mr. Hoege [C.]; F. D. Godman, Esq. [P.]. (Type of *L. polysticta*.)
l. Yg. (Sc. 23; V. 195; C. 85).	Jalapa.	Mr Hoege [C.]; F D Godman, Esq. [P.].
m–n. ♀ (Sc. 21; V. 186; C. ?) & hgr. (Sc. 21; V. 171; C. ?).	Cozumel Id., Yucatan.	Mr. F. Gaumer [C.].
o. Yg. (Sc. 21; V. 198; C. 88).	Yucatan.	
p. ♀ (Sc. 23; V. 204; C. 86).	Honduras.	Mr. Dyson [C.].
q. ♀ (Sc. 21; V. 211; C. 87).	Belize.	F. D. Godman, Esq. [P.].
r ♀ (Sc. 23; V. 192; C. 81).	Panama.	
s–v. ♀ (Sc. 21, V. 193, C. ?), hgr. (Sc. 21, 23; V 177, 179; C. 86, ?), & yg (Sc. 21; V. 192; C. 88).	Chiriqui.	(Types of *L. polysticta*.) F. D Godman, Esq. [P.].
w. ♀ (Sc. 21; V. 189; C. ?).	C. America	Dr. Günther [P.]. (Type of *L. affinis*.)
x. ♀ (Sc. 21; V. 185; C. ?).	W. Ecuador.	Mr. Fraser [C.].
y, z. ♂ (Sc. 21; V. 183, C. ?) & ♀ (Sc. 23; V. 198; C. 75).	Guayaquil.	Mr. Fraser [C.].
α–β. Hgr. (Sc 21; V. 170, 174, C. 90, 95)	Carthagena.	Capt. Garth [P.].
γ–δ. ♀ (Sc. 21; V. 190; C ?) & yg. (Sc. 21; V. 181; C. 91).	Caracas.	
ε. ♂ (Sc. 21; V. 174; C. 79).	Venezuela.	Mr. Dyson [C.].
ζ. ♀ (Sc. 21; V. 191; C. 86).	Brit. Guiana.	Demerara Mus. [P.].
η. ♀ (Sc. 21; V. 182; C. 91).	Demerara.	Mr Snellgrove [C.].
θ. ♂ (Sc. 21; V. 184; C 93).	Demerara.	Dr. Hancock [P.].
ι. Hgr. (Sc. 21; V. 194; C. 82).	Berbice.	Lady Essex [P.].

κ. ♂ (Sc. 21; V. 186; Berbice.
  C. 93).
λ. Hgr. (Sc. 21; V. 190; Pernambuco. J. P. G. Smith, Esq.
  C. 95). [P.].
μ. Yg. (Sc. 21; V. 196; Para. R. Graham, Esq.
  C. 89). [P.]
ν. Hgr. (Sc. 21; V. 176; Asuncion, Paraguay. Dr J. Bohls [C].
  C. 72).
ξ. Hgr. (Sc. 23; V. 203; —— ? Haslar Collection.
  C. 82).
ο. Skull. Mexico.

9. Leptodira annulata.

Coluber annulatus, *Linn. Mus Ad. Frid* p. 34, pl. viii. fig. 2 (1754),
  and *S. N.* i. p. 386 (1766); *Daud. Rept.* vi. p. 369 (1803).
Dipsas annulata, part., *Schleg. Phys. Serp.* ii. p. 294 (1837).
—— annulata, var. A, *Dum. & Bibr.* vii. p. 1141 (1854).
Leptodeira annulata, part, *Gunth. Cat* p. 166 (1858).
Sibon annulata, part., *Cope, Proc. Ac. Philad.* 1860, p. 266.
Eteirodipsas annulata, *Jan, Elenco*, p. 105 (1863).
Dipsas approximans, *Gunth. Ann. & Mag. N. H.* (4) ix. 1872, p. 32.
Eteirodipsas wieneri, *Sauvage, Bull. Soc. Philom.* (7) viii. 1884,
  p. 146*.

Rostral once and a half to once and two thirds as broad as deep, scarcely visible from above; internasals shorter than the præfrontals; frontal once and a half to once and two thirds as long as broad, as long as or a little longer than its distance from the end of the snout, shorter than the parietals; loreal as long as deep or a little deeper than long, one præocular, in contact with or narrowly separated from the frontal, rarely with a very small subocular below it; two (rarely three) postoculars, temporals 1+2; eight (rarely seven) upper labials, third, fourth, and fifth (rarely third and fourth or fourth and fifth only) entering the eye; five or six lower labials in contact with the anterior chin-shields, which are as long as or a little longer than the posterior. Scales in 19 (exceptionally 17 [spec. n] or 21 [spec. h]) rows, the vertebrals sometimes slightly enlarged. Ventrals 175-196; anal divided; subcaudals 78-107. Yellowish or brown above, with a dorsal series of large dark brown or blackish spots often confluent into an undulous or zigzag band; lateral spots usually small or absent, a dark streak behind the eye. occipital region whitish in the young; lower parts white.

Total length 730 millim.; tail 175.

Tropical South America.

a-b. ♂ (V. 183, 182; C. ?, Rio de Cucuta, Mr. C. Webber
  95) Colombia. [C.].
c-d. ♀ (V. 193, 178, C. 80, Chyavetas, N.E. Mr. E. Bartlett
  ?). Peru. [C.]. (Types of
  D. approximans.)

---

* I am indebted to M. Bocourt for notes on the type specimen.

e, f. ♀ (V. 193, 184; C. 89, 88).	Sarayacu, N.E. Peru.	Mr. W. Davis [C.]; Messrs. Veitch [P.].
g–m, n–o. ♂ (V. 191, 189; C. 98, 96), ♀ (V. 192, 189, 190; C. 89, 82, ?), hgr. (V. 194, 182; C. 96, 91), & yg. (V. 175; C. 92).	Moyobamba, N.E. Peru.	Mr. A. H. Roff [C.].
p. ♀ (V. 187; C. 78).	Santarem.	H. W. Bates, Esq. [C.].
q. ♂ (V. 192; C. 94).	Upper Amazon.	
r–t. ♀ (V. 186, 194, 187; C. 87, 82, 82).	Rio Ucayali	Dr. E. A. Goldi [P.].
u. Yg. (V. 190; C. 90).	Upper Amazon.	Mr. E. Bartlett [C.].
v. ♂ (V. 190; C. 97).	Madre de Dios, Bolivia.	
w. ♂ (V. 194; C. 98).	Charobamba, Bolivia.	
x. Hgr. (V. 192; C. 97).	Para.	R. Graham, Esq. [P.].
y–z. ♂ (V. 184, 179; C. 89, 84).	S. America.	E Bowerbank, Esq. [P.].

153. CHAMÆTORTUS.

Chamætortus, *Günth. Proc. Zool. Soc.* 1864, p. 310.

Maxillary teeth 12, gradually and feebly increasing in length, followed, after a short interspace, by a large grooved fang situated below the posterior border of the eye; mandibular teeth subequal. Head distinct from neck; eye large, with vertically elliptic pupil; posterior nasal concave; loreal entering the eye. Body compressed; scales smooth, with apical pits, in 17 rows; ventrals obtusely angulate laterally. Tail long; subcaudals in two rows.

East and Central Africa.

1. Chamætortus aulicus.

Chamætortus aulicus, *Gunth. l. c.* pl. xxvi. fig. 2; *Peters, Reise n. Mossamb.* iii. p. 128 (1882).

Rostral nearly twice as broad as deep, just visible from above; internasals a little broader than long, a little shorter than the præfrontals; frontal once and two thirds to twice as long as broad, longer than its distance from the end of the snout, shorter than the parietals; loreal a little longer than deep, bordering the eye below a small præocular; two postoculars; temporals 1+1; eight upper labials, third, fourth, and fifth entering the eye; five lower labials in contact with the anterior chin-shields, which are a little longer than the posterior. Scales in 17 rows. Ventrals 172–195; anal entire; subcaudals 81–95. Brown above, the back with numerous whitish, dark-edged cross-bars, the sides spotted with whitish; head whitish, spotted and marbled with brown, and with a brown streak on each side, passing through the eye; labials edged with brown; beneath white.

Total length 640 millim.; tail 160.
East and Central Africa.

a. Hgr. (V. 195; C. 81).	Zambesi.	Sir J. Kirk [C.]. (Type.)
b. ♂ (V. 190, C. 95).	Lake Tanganyika.	Sir J. Kirk [C.].

154. OXYRHOPUS.

Pseudoboa, part, *Schneid. Hist. Amph.* ii. p. 281 (1801).
Scytale (*non Latr.*), part., *Merr. Tent.* p. 90 (1820); *Fitzing. N. Class. Rept* p. 29 (1826).
Clelia, part., *Fitzing. l. c.*; *Wagl. Syst. Amph.* p. 187 (1830).
Duberria, part., *Fitzing. l. c.*
Oxyrhopus, part., *Wagl l c* p. 185; *Dum. & Bibr. Erp. Gén.* vii. p 1011 (1854); *Günth Cat. Col Sn.* p. 188 (1858); *Jan, Elenco sist. Ofid.* p. 92 (1863).
Erythrolamprus, part., *Wagl. l. c.* p. 187.
Scytale, *Wagl. l. c.*; *Dum. & Bibr. t. c.* p. 996; *Günth. l. c.* p 187; *Jan, l. c.* p 91.
Lycodon, part., *Schleg. Phys. Serp.* ii. p. 104 (1837).
Coluber, part, *Schleg. t. c.* p. 125.
Sphenocephalus, *Fitzing. in Tschudi, Faun. Per., Herp.* p. 48 (1846).
Siphlophis, *Fitzing. l. c* p. 56
Rhinosimus (*non Latr.*), *Dum. & Bibr. t c.* p. 991; *Günth. l. c.* p. 10.
Brachyruton, *Dum. & Bibr. t. c.* p. 1002; *Jan, l. c.* p. 91.
Olisthenes, *Cope, Proc. Ac. Philad* 1859, p. 296.
Phimophis, *Cope, Proc. Ac. Philad.* 1860, p. 79.

Maxillary teeth 10 to 15, subequal, followed, after an interspace, by a pair of moderately enlarged grooved teeth situated just behind the vertical of the posterior border of the eye; anterior mandibular teeth longest. Head distinct from neck; eye moderate or rather small, with vertically elliptic pupil. Body cylindrical or feebly compressed; scales smooth, with apical pits, in 17 or 19 rows; ventrals rounded or obtusely angulate laterally. Tail moderate or rather long; subcaudals single or in two rows.

Central and South America.

Synopsis of the Species.

I. Subcaudals in two rows.

  A. Normally eight upper labials; præocular reaching the upper surface of the head.

    1. Præocular in contact with, or, exceptionally, narrowly separated from the frontal; ventrals 174–225.

      a Black cross-bars, if present, not disposed in threes.

Eye moderate; subcaudals 78–126 .... 1. *petolarius*, p. 101.
Eye rather small; subcaudals 47–80 . 2. *rhombifer*, p. 103.

      b. Black cross bars, if present, disposed in threes.

Snout rather prominent; subcaudals 55–83 .... 3. *trigeminus*, p. 104.
Snout not prominent; subcaudals 76–89. 4. *bitorquatus*, p. 104.

2. Præocular separated from the frontal.

    a. Ventrals 172–206; subcaudals 51–85.

        α. Eye rather small, not half the length of the snout.

Black cross-bars disposed in threes; head black above .... 5. *melanogenys*, p. 105.
Black cross-bars or annuli not disposed in threes; head black above........ 6. *doliatus*, p. 106.
Complete black annuli round the body; head uniform yellow or orange...... 7. *formosus*, p. 106.

        β. Eye moderate, about half the length of the snout.

Loreal present, at least twice as long as deep .... 8. *labialis*, p. 107.
Loreal often absent; if present, short .. 9. *clathratus*, p. 107.

    b. Ventrals 232–236; subcaudals 77–81.
        10. *fitzingeri*, p. 108.

B. Normally seven upper labials; præocular not or but just reaching the upper surface of the head.

    1. Portion of rostral visible from above measuring one fourth to one third its distance from the frontal.

Frontal a little longer than broad; subcaudals 64–93 .... 11. *cloelia*, p. 108.
Frontal as long as broad; subcaudals 51. 12. *maculatus*, p. 110.

    2. Portion of rostral visible from above measuring about half its distance from the frontal.

Præocular moderate, just reaching the upper surface of the head; subcaudals 67–85.... .... 13. *occipitoluteus*, p. 110.
Præocular very small; subcaudals 44–61. 14. *rusticus*, p. 111.

II. Subcaudals single.

    A. Scales in 17 rows; rostral broader than deep, forming an obtuse angle posteriorly, its upper portion not more than half as long as its distance from the frontal; seven upper labials .... 15. *coronatus*, p. 111.

    B. Scales in 19 rows; normally eight upper labials.

Rostral much broader than deep, forming an obtuse angle posteriorly, its upper portion not more than half as long as its distance from the frontal .... 16. *neuwiedii*, p. 112.
Rostral nearly as deep as broad, forming a right or acute angle posteriorly, its upper portion at least two thirds its distance from the frontal .... 17. *guerini*, p. 113.

154. OXYRHOPUS.

TABLE SHOWING NUMBERS OF SCALES AND SHIELDS.

	Sc.	V.	C.	Lab.
petolarius	19	191–222	78–126	8 (9)
rhombifer	19	174–225	47–80	8
trigeminus	19	174–203	55–83	8
bitorquatus	19	185–206	76–89	8
melanogenys	19	206	79	8
doliatus	19	183–199	61–80	8
formosus	19	182–203	51–73	8
labialis	19	172–201	57–78	8
clathratus	19	190–205	66–85	8
fitzingeri	19	232–236	77–81	8
clælia	17–19	198–237	64–93	7 (8)
maculatus	19	214	51	7
occipitoluteus	19	204–215	67–85	7
rusticus	19	197–223	44–61	7 (8)
coronatus	17	171–208	80–97*	7
neuwiedii	19	177–205	64–96*	8 (7)
guerini	19	185–211	70–99*	8 (7)

* All or most single.

1. Oxyrhopus petolarius.

Coluber petolarius†, *Linn Mus. Ad. Frid.* p. 35, pl. ix. fig. 2 (1754), and *S. N.* i p 387 (1766), *Daud. Rept.* vi. p. 307 (1803).
—— pethola, *Linn. S N.* i. p. 387.
—— digitalis, *Reuss, Mus. Senckenb.* i. 1834, p. 148, pl. ix. fig. 1.
Lycodon petolarius, part., *Schleg. Phys. Serp.* ii. p. 122, pl. iv. figs. 20 & 21 (1837).
—— (Oxyrhopus) semifasciatus, *Tschudi, Faun. Per., Herp.* p. 54, pl. vii. (1846)
Oxyrhopus multifasciatus, *Dum. & Bibr.* vii. p. 1019 (1854).
—— spadiceus, *Dum & Bibr.* t c p. 1028.
—— immaculatus, *Dum & Bibr* t. c p 1029; *Guichen. in Casteln. Anim. Nouv. Amér. Sud, Rept.* p. 64, pl xiii*. (1855); *Günth. Cat.* p. 191 (1858); *Jan, Icon. Gén.* 35, pl. vi. fig. 1 (1870).
—— bipræocularis, *Dum. & Bibr.* t c. p. 1030; *Günth. l. c.*
—— petolarius, *Dum & Bibr.* t. c. p. 1033; *Günth. Proc. Zool. Soc.* 1859, p. 414; *Jan, Icon. Gén.* 35, pl. vi. fig. 2, & 36, pl. i figs. 1 & 2 (1870); *Cope, Journ Ac. Philad.* (2) viii. 1876, p. 132; *Günth. l. C.-Am , Rept.* p. 167 (1895).
—— ...æ, *Dum & Bibr.* t. c. p. 1036.

... moderately large, its diameter about half the length of the snout, which is rounded and scarcely projecting. Rostral broader than deep, just visible from above; internasals much shorter than the præfrontals; frontal once and one fifth to once and one third as long as broad, as long as its distance from the end of the snout, as long as or a little shorter than the parietals; loreal much longer

---

† The name is misspelt "*petalarius*" in the 'Systema Naturæ.'

than deep; one præocular (sometimes divided) usually forming a suture with the frontal, sometimes, however, narrowly separated from it; two (exceptionally one or three) postoculars; temporals 2+3; eight (exceptionally nine) upper labials, fourth and fifth (or fifth and sixth) entering the eye; four or five lower labials in contact with the anterior chin-shields, which are as long as or shorter than the posterior. Scales in 19 rows. Ventrals 191–222; anal entire; subcaudals 78–126 pairs. Coloration variable.

Total length 910 millim.; tail 220.

Mexico, Central America, Tropical South America.

A. Black above, with numerous (50–75) narrow yellow cross-bands, the first on the nape; these bands sometimes interrupted in the middle. (*C. petolarius*, L.)

a. Yg. (V. 206; C. 102).	Rosario de Cucuta, Colombia.	Mr. C. Webber [C.].
b, c. ♂ (V. 204; C. 117) & yg. (V. 119; C. 115).	Venezuela.	Mr. Dyson [C.].
d. ♀ (V. 213; C. 89).	Caracas.	
e–f, g. ♂ (V. 200; C. 89), ♀ (V. 203, C. 104), & hgr. (V. 197; C. 83)	British Guiana.	
h, i. ♂ (V. 192; C. 94) & ♀ (V. 211; C. ?).	Demerara.	Mr. Snellgrove [C.].
k. ♀ (V. 203; C. 87).	Berbice.	
l. ♀ (V. 200; C. 92).	Surinam ?	Lidth de Jeude Coll.

B. Light cross-bars (sometimes reduced to large spots on the sides) fewer (15–25) and far apart.

a. Hgr. (V. 209; C. 115).	Guayaquil.	Mr Fraser [C.].
b. Yg. (V. 202; C. 116).	Ecuador.	Mr. Buckley [C.].
c–d, e, f. Hgr ♀ (V. 212, 208, 205; C. 100, 121, 101) & yg. (V. 216; C. 119).	Moyobamba, N.E. Peru.	Mr. A. H. Roff [C.].
g. ♂ (V. 209; C. 126).	Sarayacu, N.E. Peru.	Mr. W. Davis [C.]; Messrs. Veitch [P.].
h–i. ♀ (V. 222; C. ?) & yg. (V. 210; C. 101).	Yurimaguas, Huallaga River.	Dr. Hahnel [C].
k. ♂ (V. 214; C. 115).	Pebas.	H.W. Bates, Esq [C.].
l. Hgr. (V. 208; C. 89).	Pernambuco.	W. A. Forbes, Esq. [P.].
m. Yg. (V. 191; C. 101).	Bahia.	
n. Hgr. (V. 203; C. 109).	Bahia.	Dr. O. Wucherer [C.].

C. Uniform dark brown above, or with faint traces of light bars as in B.

a. ♀ (V. 220; C. 97).	Moyobamba, N.E. Peru.	Mr. A. H. Roff [C].
b. ♀ (V. 214; C. 98).	Yungas, Bolivia.	
c. ♂ (V. 202; C. 100).	Pernambuco.	

D. Above barred black and red, the red bars, which may be dotted with black, as broad as or a little narrower than the black, and 30 to 40 in number; the black bars usually forming complete annuli on the tail.

a. ♀ (V. 207; C. 80).	Mexico.	Mr. Hugo Finck [C.].
b. ♀ (V. 204; C. 85).	Atoyac, Guerrero.	Mr H. H. Smith [C.]; F. D Godman, Esq. [P.].
c. Hgr (V. 193; C. 78).	Vera Paz (low forest).	O. Salvin, Esq. [C.].
d-e. Hgr. (V. 204, 197; C. 105, 95).	Chontalez, Nicaragua.	
f. ♀ (V. 210; C. 80).	Chontalez, Nicaragua.	R. A. Rix, Esq. [C.]; W. M. Crowfoot, Esq. [P.].
g. Yg. (V. 206; C. 97).	Matagalpa, Nicaragua.	Dr. Rothschuh [C.].
h, i. ♂ (V. 205; C. 88) & hgr. (V. 198; C. 92).	Hacienda Rosa de Jericho, Nicaragua, 3250 ft.	Dr. Rothschuh [C.].
k-l. Hgr. (V. 205, 194; C. 88, 103).	Costa Rica.	
m. Hgr (V. 213; C. 109).	W. Ecuador.	Mr. Fraser [C.].
n. Yg. (V. 210; C. 93).	Quito.	

2. Oxyrhopus rhombifer.

Lycodon formosus, part., *Schleg. Phys. Serp.* ii. p. 113 (1837).
Oxyrhopus rhombifer, *Dum. & Bibr.* vii. p. 1018 (1854); *Jan, Icon. Gén.* 35, pl. v. fig. 2 (1870); *Berg, Act. Ac. Cordoba*, v. 1884, p 95.
—— subpunctatus, *Dum. & Bibr.* t. c. p. 1016.
—— dorbignyi, *Dum. & Bibr.* t. c p. 1024.
—— petolarius, part., *Gunth. Cat.* p. 190 (1858); *Jan, Elenco*, p. 94 (1863).
? Coronella bachmanni, *Weyenb. Period. Zool. Cordoba*, ii. 1876, p. 193.

Eye rather small, its diameter one half (young) to one third the length of the snout, which is rounded and scarcely projecting. Rostral much broader than deep, just visible from above; internasals much shorter than the præfrontals; frontal as long as broad or a little longer than broad, as long as its distance from the end of the snout, shorter than the parietals; loreal much longer than deep; one præocular, forming a suture with the frontal; two postoculars; temporals 2+3; eight upper labials, fourth and fifth entering the eye; four or five lower labials in contact with the anterior chinshields, which are as long as or a little longer than the posterior. Scales in 19 rows. Ventrals 174–225; anal entire; subcaudals 47–80 pairs. Red or pale brown above, the scales tipped with black, with black cross-bands or rhomboidal transverse spots; upper surface of head, as far as the posterior third or fourth of the parietal shields, black; yellow beneath, uniform or dotted with black.

Total length 900 millim.; tail 160.

Southern Brazil, Paraguay, Uruguay, Argentina, Bolivia.

a-b. ♂ (V. 205; C. 68) & ♀ (V. 216; C. 57).	Brazil.	Mr. Clausen [C.].

c, d, e–g, h–m. ♂ (V. 187; C. 67), ♀ (V. 201, 203, 200, 195; C. 60, 59, 56, 55), & yg. (V. 186, 193, 202, 196, 204; C. 71, 63, 56, 60, 51).	Rio Grande do Sul.	Dr. H. v. Ihering [C.].
n. Hgr. (V. 180; C. 47).	Paraguay.	Prof. Grant [P.].
o. Yg. (V. 199; C. 80).	Asuncion, Paraguay.	Dr. J. Bohls [C.].
p. Yg. (V. 174; C. 59).	Uruguay.	
q. ♀ (V. 225; C. 70).	Charocampa, Bolivia.	

3. Oxyrhopus trigeminus.

Lycodon formosus, part., *Schleg. Phys. Serp* ii. p. 113 (1837).
Oxyrhopus trigeminus, *Dum. & Bibr.* vii. p. 1013 (1854), *Gunth. Cat.* p. 191 (1858).
—— tergeminus, part., *Jan, Icon. Gén.* 36, pl. i. fig. 4 (1870).

Eye moderate or rather small, its diameter two fifths to one half the length of the snout, which is obtuse but rather prominent. Rostral broader than deep, just visible from above; internasals much shorter than the præfrontals; frontal a little longer than broad, as long as its distance from the end of the snout, shorter than the parietals; loreal at least twice as long as deep; one præocular, forming a narrow suture with the frontal; two postoculars; temporals 2+3; eight upper labials, fourth and fifth entering the eye; four or five lower labials in contact with the anterior chin-shields, which are as long as or a little longer than the posterior. Scales in 19 rows. Ventrals 174–203; anal entire; subcaudals 55–83 pairs. Red above, some or all of the scales tipped with black, with more or less regular black cross-bars disposed in threes; head yellow or red above with a black blotch on the crown, sometimes extending on the snout; yellow beneath.

Total length 660 millim.; tail 115.

Guianas, Brazil.

a–b. ♂ (V. 179; C. 70) & ♀ (V. 195; C. 56).	Demerara.	Capt. Sabine [P.].
c. ♀ (V. 198; C. 64).	Pernambuco.	W. A. Forbes, Esq. [P.].
d. ♂ (V. 181; C. 73).	Pernambuco.	H. N. Ridley, Esq [P.].
e–f. ♀ (V. 193; C. 57) & hgr. (V. 185; C. 57).	Bahia.	Mr. Ker [P.].
g–h. ♀ (V. 190, 188; C. ?, ?).	Bahia.	Dr. O Wucherer [C.].
i. ♀ (V. 174; C. 67).	Rio Janeiro.	D. Wilson Barker, Esq. [P.].
k–l. ♂ (V. 181, C. 75) & ♀ (V. 193; C. 62).	S. America.	W. F. Evans, Esq. [P.].

4. Oxyrhopus bitorquatus. (PLATE VI. fig. 1.)

Oxyrhopus trigeminus, var., *Peters, Mon. Berl. Ac.* 1871, p. 401.
? Oxyrhopus submarginatus, *Peters, l. c.*
Tachymenis bitorquatus, *Gunth. Ann. & Mag. N. H.* (4) ix. 1872, p. 19.

Eye moderate, its diameter about half the length of the snout;

snout rounded, scarcely projecting. Rostral broader than deep, just visible from above; internasals much shorter than the præfrontals; frontal slightly longer than broad, as long as its distance from the end of the snout, a little shorter than the parietals; loreal much longer than deep; one præocular, usually forming a narrow suture with the frontal; two postoculars; temporals 2+3; eight upper labials, fourth and fifth entering the eye; four or five lower labials in contact with the anterior chin-shields, which are as long as or a little longer than the posterior. Scales in 19 rows. Ventrals 185–206; anal entire; subcaudals 76–89 pairs. Red above, the scales tipped and edged with black; head black above, usually with a light cross-band behind the parietals and one or two black cross-bands on the nape, the snout sometimes yellow; black cross-bands disposed in threes may be present on the body; lower parts yellow.

Total length 890 millim.; tail 175.

Upper Amazon, Bolivia.

a. Yg. (V. 197; C. 85).		Peruvian Amazon.	Mr. E. Bartlett [C.]. (Type.)
b. ♂ (V. 206; C. 76).		Upper Amazon	Mr. E. Bartlett [C.]
c–d. ♂ (V. 187, 185; C. 81, 82).		Moyobamba, Peru.	Mr. A. H. Roff [C.].
e. ♂ (V. 191; C. ?).		Pozuzu, Peru	Mr. W. Davis [C.]; Messrs. Veitch [P.].
f, g. ♂ (V. 196, 185; C. 89, 83).		Sarayacu, Peru.	Mr. W. Davis [C.]; Messrs. Veitch [P.].
h–i. ♂ (V. 194, 197; C. 87, 86).		R. Ucayali.	Dr. E. A. Goldi [P.].
j. Yg. (V. 206; C. 76).		Yungas, Bolivia.	

5. Oxyrhopus melanogenys.

Sphenocephalus melanogenys, *Tschudi, Faun. Per., Herp.* p. 49, pl. iv. (1846).

Oxyrhopus tergeminus, part, *Jan, Icon. Gén.* 36, pl. i. fig. 3 (1870).

Eye small, its diameter not more than one third the length of the snout; snout rounded, scarcely projecting. Rostral broader than deep, just visible from above; internasals shorter than the præfrontals; frontal slightly longer than broad, as long as its distance from the end of the snout, shorter than the parietals, loreal much longer than deep; one præocular, reaching the upper surface of the head but separated from the frontal; two postoculars; temporals 2+3; eight upper labials, fourth and fifth entering the eye; five lower labials in contact with the anterior chin-shields, which are as long as the posterior. Scales in 19 rows. Ventrals 206; anal entire; subcaudals 79 pairs. Red or pale reddish brown above, dotted with blackish brown; head blackish brown above; nape blackish brown or with a pair of black cross-bands; anterior half of body with a few black cross-bands disposed in threes; belly yellowish.

Total length 680 millim.; tail 170.

Chanchamayo, Peru.

6. Oxyrhopus doliatus.

Oxyrhopus doliatus, *Dum. & Bibr.* vii. p. 1020 (1854).
—— formosus (*non Wied*), *Gunth. Cat.* p. 190 (1858).

Eye rather small, its diameter two fifths the length of the snout, which is rounded and scarcely projecting. Rostral broader than deep, just visible from above; internasals much shorter than the præfrontals; frontal a little longer than broad, as long as its distance from the end of the snout, a little shorter than the parietals; loreal much longer than deep; one præocular, just reaching the upper surface of the head and widely separated from the frontal; two postoculars; temporals 2+3; eight upper labials, fourth and fifth entering the eye; four lower labials in contact with the anterior chin-shields, which are as long as or a little longer than the posterior. Scales in 19 rows. Ventrals 183–199; anal entire; subcaudals 61–80 pairs. Above with broad black annuli; the anterior much wider than the red or reddish-brown interspaces between them; head black above, with a light occipital blotch or a narrow collar; the black annuli may be interrupted on the belly; the red scales tipped with black.

Total length 550 millim.; tail 115.
Brazil.

A. Annuli complete, broad.

a. Yg. (V. 199; C. 61). ——? Messrs. Veitch [P.].

B. Annuli interrupted on the belly, all except the six or seven anterior much narrower than the red interspaces.

a, b. ♂ (V. 180, 183; C. 77, 80). ——? Zoological Society.

7. Oxyrhopus formosus.

Coluber formosus, *Wied, N. Acta Ac. Leop. Carol.* x 1820, i. p. 109, *Beitr. Nat. Bras.* i. p. 381 (1825), and *Abbild.* (1825).
Duberria formosa, *Fitzing. N. Class. Rept.* p. 56 (1825).
Lycodon formosus, part., *Schleg. Phys. Serp.* ii. p. 113 (1837).
Oxyrhopus formosus, *Dum. & Bibr.* vii. p. 1022 (1854); *Jan, Elenco,* p. 93 (1863).
? Oxyrhopus leucocephalus, *Dum. & Bibr.* t. c. p. 1038.

Eye rather small, its diameter one third to two fifths the length of the snout, which is rounded and feebly projecting. Rostral broader than deep, just visible from above; internasals much shorter than the præfrontals; frontal slightly longer than broad, as long as its distance from the end of the snout, shorter than the parietals; loreal much longer than deep; one præocular, just reaching the upper surface of the head and widely separated from the frontal; two postoculars; temporals 2+3; eight upper labials, fourth and fifth entering the eye; four lower labials in contact with the anterior chin-shields, which are as long as the posterior. Scales in 19 rows. Ventrals 182–203; anal entire; subcaudals 51–73 pairs. Body greenish in front, red behind, each scale with a black dot, with black annuli which are narrower on the belly than on the back; head uniform orange.

Total length 870 millim.; tail 165.

Brazil.

a. ♀ (V 194; C. 67).	Bahia.	Dr. O. Wucherer [C.].
b. ♀ (V. 203; C. 67).	S. America.	Liverpool Mus. [E.].

8. Oxyrhopus labialis.

Oxyrhopus labialis, *Jan, Elenco,* p 93 (1863), *and Icon. Gén.* 35, pl. ii. fig. 2 (1870).
—— dorbignyi (*non D. & B.*), *Jan, Icon. Gén.* 35, pl iv. fig. 3.

Eye moderate, its diameter about half the length of the snout, which is rounded, scarcely projecting. Rostral broader than deep, just visible from above; internasals much shorter than the præfrontals; frontal once and one third to once and a half as long as broad, as long as its distance from the end of the snout, a little shorter than the parietals; loreal much longer than deep; one præocular, extending to the upper surface of the head but not reaching the frontal; two postoculars; temporals 2+3; eight upper labials, fourth and fifth entering the eye; four (or three) lower labials in contact with the anterior chin-shields, which are as long as or a little longer than the posterior. Scales in 19 rows. Ventrals 172–201; anal entire; subcaudals 57–78. Pale brown or red above, with or without rhomboidal transverse spots; head dark brown or blackish above; yellow beneath.

Total length 760 millim.; tail 130.

Argentina.

A. No dorsal spots; all the scales with a blackish terminal dot.

a. ♂ (V. 172; C. 68). Argentina. E W. White, Esq. [C.].

B. A series of large rhomboidal transverse spots on the body and tail, the interspaces between them dotted with black.

a. ♀ (V. 201; C. 61).	Cosquin, Cordova.	E. W. White, Esq. [C].
b. Yg. (V. 194; C. 64).	Salta.	Herbert Druce, Esq. [P.].

9. Oxyrhopus clathratus.

Oxyrhopus clathratus, *Dum. & Bibr.* vii. p. 1028 (1854), *Guichen. in Casteln. Anim. Nouv. Amér. Sud, Rept.* p 63, pl. xii. *a* (1855); *Jan, Icon Gén.* 35, pl. iii. figs. 1 & 2 (1870).

Eye moderate, its diameter about half the length of the snout, which is rounded and scarcely prominent. Rostral broader than deep, just visible from above; internasals much shorter than the præfrontals; frontal a little longer than broad, as long as its distance from the end of the snout, a little shorter than the parietals; loreal usually fused with the præfrontal; one præocular, just reaching the upper surface of the head but separated from the frontal; two postoculars; temporals 2+3; eight upper labials, fourth and fifth entering the eye; four lower labials in contact with the anterior chin-shields, which are as long as the posterior. Scales in 19 rows. Ventrals 190-205; anal entire; subcaudals 66-85 pairs. Dark brown or blackish above, with yellowish crossbars widening towards the belly and usually more or less interrupted on the back; yellow occipital collar, if present, narrow; yellow beneath, posterior ventrals and subcaudals sometimes spotted with blackish.

Total length 790 millim.; tail 170.

Brazil.

a.	♂ (V. 197; C. 74).	Porto Real, Prov. Rio Janeiro.	M. Hardy du Dréneuf [C.].
b.	Yg. (V. 190; C. 74).	Rio Grande do Sul.	Dr. H. v. Ihering [C.].

10. Oxyrhopus fitzingeri.

Siphlophis fitzingeri, *Tschudi, Faun. Per., Herp.* p. 56, pl. viii. (1846).

Oxyrhopus fitzingeri, *Jan, Elenco,* p. 93 (1863), *and Icon. Gén.* 35, pl. v. fig. 1 (1870).

Eye moderate, its diameter about half the length of the snout; snout rounded, slightly projecting. Rostral broader than deep, the portion visible from above measuring about one fourth its distance from the frontal; internasals much shorter than the præfrontals; frontal once and one third as long as broad, as long as its distance from the end of the snout, shorter than the parietals; loreal much longer than deep; one præocular, just reaching the upper surface of the head and widely separated from the frontal; two postoculars; temporals 2+3; eight upper labials, fourth and fifth entering the eye; four or five lower labials in contact with the anterior chin-shields, which are as long as the posterior. Scales in 19 rows. Ventrals 232-236; anal entire; subcaudals 77-81 pairs. Yellowish above, with numerous small black spots irregularly arranged; upper surface of head speckled with black; a large black blotch on the nape; uniform yellowish beneath.

Total length 980 millim.; tail 190.

Peru.

a.	♀ (V. 232; C. 81).	Peru.	Prof. Nation [P.].

11. Oxyrhopus clœlia.

Coluber clœlia, *Daud. Rept.* vi. p 330, pl lxxviii. (1803).

—— plumbeus, *Wied, Reise n. Bras.* i. p 95 (1820), *Beitr.* i. p 314 (1825), *and Abbild.* (1820); *Schleg. Phys. Serp.* ii. p. 152, pl. vi. figs. 3 & 4 (1837).

Natrix occipitalis, *Wagl. in Spix, Serp. Bras.* p. 21, pl. vi. fig. 2 (1824).

154. OXYRHOPUS.

Clelia daudinii, *Fitzing. N. Class Rept.* p. 55 (1826)
Duberria plumbea, *Fitzing. l. c.* p. 56.
Lycodon clœlia, part , *Schleg. l. c.* p. 114.
Brachyruton plumbeum, part., *Dum. & Bibr.* vii. p. 1005 (1854).
—— clœlia, *Dum. & Bibr. t. c.* p. 1007 , *F. Mull. Verh. Nat. Ges. Basel*, vi. 1878, p. 684.
Oxyrhopus plumbeus, *Gunth. Cat.* p 189 (1858), *and Proc. Zool. Soc.* 1859, p. 414; *Garm. Proc. Amer. Philos. Soc.* xxiv. 1887, p. 285.
—— clœlia, *Gunth Cat.* p. 189; *Peters, Mon. Berl. Ac.* 1873, p. 607; *Cope, Bull. U.S. Nat. Mus.* no. 32, 1887, p. 76.
Scolecophis scytalinus, *Cope, Proc Ac. Philad.* 1866, p. 320.
Brachyrhyton clœlia, part., *Jan, Icon. Gén.* 35, pl. i. fig. 1 (1870).
—— plumbeum, *Jan, l. c.* fig. 3.

Eye rather small, its diameter about one third the length of the snout in the adult, snout rounded, scarcely projecting. Rostral broader than deep, the portion visible from above measuring one fourth to one third its distance from the frontal; internasals much shorter than the præfrontals; frontal a little longer than broad, as long as or a little longer than its distance from the end of the snout, shorter than the parietals; loreal usually longer than deep, sometimes absent; one præocular, not extending to the upper surface of the head; two postoculars; temporals 2+2 or 2+3; seven (exceptionally eight) upper labials, third and fourth (or fourth and fifth) entering the eye; four or five lower labials in contact with the anterior chin-shields, which are as long as or longer than the posterior. Scales in 17 or 19 rows. Ventrals 198–237; anal entire; subcaudals 64–93 pairs. Adult uniform dark grey, olive-grey or blackish above, yellowish white beneath, the subcaudals often spotted or margined with blackish. Young sometimes blackish above, but usually pale brown or red, with or without a dark brown dot on the end of each scale; head and nape blackish, with a more or less broad yellow area across the occiput and temples.

Total length 1550 millim.; tail 340. A larger specimen, with injured tail, measures 2100 millim. to vent.

Mexico and Central America; Tropical South America; Lesser West Indies.

A. Scales in 19 rows.

a. ♀ (V. 237 ; C. 81).	Guatemala.	Institute of Jamaica [P.].
b. Yg. (V. 233 ; C. 82).	Panama.	Zoological Society.
c. Yg. (V. 224 ; C. 93).	Rosario de Cucuta, Colombia.	Mr. C. Webber [C.].
d. ♂ (V. 211 ; C. 79).	Guayaquil.	H. B. James, Esq. [P.].
e, f. ♀ (V. 210 , C. 85) & yg. (V. 203 ; C. 91).	Moyobamba, N.E. Peru.	Mr. A. H. Roff [C.].
g ♂ (V. 214 , C. 73).	Peru.	Warsaw Museum [P].
h. ♂ (V. 220 , C. 90).	Caracas.	
i. ♂ (V. 206 ; C. 76).	Berbice.	
k. Yg. (V. 211 ; C. 71).	Demerara.	Mr. Snellgrove [C.].
l. Yg. (V. 208 ; C 85).	Surinam.	

m, n. ♀ (V. 231; C. ?) & yg. (V. 218; C. 02).	Bahia.	Dr. O. Wucherer [C.].
o ♂ (V. 213; C. 85).	Sta. Catharina.	Dr. F. Werner [E].
p. Yg. (V. 204; C. 64).	Rio Grande do Sul.	Dr. H. v. Ihering [C.].
q, r. Skulls.	Brazil.	

B. Scales in 17 rows.

a–b. Yg. (V. 206, 201; C. 83, 81).	City of Mexico.	Mr. Doorman [C.].
c–e. ♂ (V. 198; C. 75) & ♀ (V. 215, 219; C. ?, ?).	W. Ecuador.	Mr. Fraser [C.].
f. ♀ (V. 232; C. ?)	Demerara.	Capt. Sabine [P.].
g. ♀ (V. 235; C. 72).	Dominica.	G. A. Ramage, Esq. [C.].
h. ♂ (V. 222; C. 82).	St. Lucia.	G. A. Ramage, Esq. [C].

12. Oxyrhopus maculatus. (PLATE VI. fig. 2.)

Snout broad, not prominent; eye small. Rostral broader than deep, the portion visible from above measuring one third its distance from the frontal; internasals shorter than the præfrontals; frontal as long as broad, as long as its distance from the rostral, two thirds the length of the parietals; loreal a little longer than deep; one præocular, not reaching the upper surface of the head; two postoculars; temporals 2+3; seven upper labials, third and fourth entering the eye; five lower labials in contact with the anterior chin-shields, which are as long as the posterior. Scales in 19 rows. Ventrals 214; anal entire; subcaudals 51 pairs. Dark brown above and below, with scattered, irregular, yellowish-white spots.

Total length 1400 millim.; tail 180.

Uruguay.

a. ♀ (V. 214; C. 51).   Uruguay.

13. Oxyrhopus occipitoluteus.

Brachyruton occipitoluteum, *Dum. & Bibr.* vii. p. 1009 (1854); *Guichen. in Casteln. Anim. nouv. Amér. Sud, Rept.* p. 62, pl. xi. (1855); *Jan, Icon. Gén.* 35, pl. i. fig. 2 (1870); *Boettg. Zeitschr. f. Naturw.* (4) iv. 1885, p. 236.

Eye rather small; snout rounded, scarcely projecting. Rostral as deep as broad, the portion visible from above measuring about half its distance from the frontal; internasals much shorter than the præfrontals; frontal slightly longer than broad, as long as or a little shorter than its distance from the end of the snout, shorter than the parietals; loreal a little longer than deep; one præocular, just reaching the upper surface of the head but widely separated from the frontal; two postoculars; temporals 2+3; seven upper labials, third and fourth entering the eye; four or five lower labials in contact with the anterior chin-shields, which are as long as or a

little longer than the posterior. Scales in 19 rows. Ventrals 204–215; anal entire; subcaudals 67–85 pairs. Greyish or brown above, uniform or scales edged with blackish; upper surface of head and nape blackish brown, with or without a yellow band across the temples and occiput; lower parts yellowish white, subcaudals edged with brown.
Total length 820 millim.; tail 145.
Paraguay.

a. ♀ (V. 215; C 67).   Asuncion.   Dr. J. Bohls [C.].

14. Oxyrhopus rusticus.

Brachyruton plumbeum, part, *Dum. & Bibr.* vii p. 1004 (1854).
—— clœlia, part., *Jan, Icon. Gén.* 34, pl vi. fig. 3 (1870).
Oxyrhopus rusticus, *Cope, Proc. Amer. Philos. Soc.* xvii. 1877, p. 92.

Snout more conical and eye smaller than in *O. clœlia*. Rostral a little broader than deep, the portion visible from above measuring about half its distance from the frontal; internasals much shorter than the præfrontals; frontal a little longer than broad, as long as its distance from the end of the snout, a little shorter than the parietals; loreal longer than deep; one præocular, small; two postoculars; temporals 2+2 or 2+3; seven (exceptionally eight) upper labials, third and fourth (or fourth and fifth) entering the eye; four or five lower labials in contact with the anterior chinshields, which are as long as or a little longer than the posterior. Scales in 19 rows. Ventrals 197–223; anal entire; subcaudals 44–61 pairs. Yellowish brown or pale brown above, some or all of the scales edged with blackish brown; uniform yellowish beneath.
Total length 1140 millim.; tail 140.
Southern Brazil, Uruguay, Argentina.

a–b. Hgr. ♀ (V. 223; C. 44) & yg (V. 201; C 61).   S. Lorenzo, Rio Grande do Sul.   Dr. H. v. Ihering [C.].
c. ♂ (V. 197; C. 60).   Buenos Ayres.   E. W. White, Esq. [C.].
d–e. ♂ (V. 211; C. 54) & ♀ (V. 210, C. 45).   Argentina.

15. Oxyrhopus coronatus.

Pseudoboa coronata, *Schneid. Hist. Amph.* ii. p. 286 (1801).
Boa coronata, *Daud. Rept.* v. p. 220 (1803).
Scytale coronata, *Merr. Tent.* p. 91 (1820); *Dum. & Bibr.* vii. p. 999 (1854).
Lycodon clœlia, part., *Schleg. Phys. Serp.* ii. p. 114, pl. iv. figs. 12 & 13 (1837).
Scytale coronatum, part., *Gunth. Cat.* p. 187 (1858).

Eye rather small, about one third the length of the snout in the adult; snout broad, rounded, scarcely projecting. Rostral broader than deep, forming an obtuse angle above, the portion visible from above measuring about one third its distance from the frontal;

internasals much shorter than the præfrontals; frontal as long as broad or slightly longer than broad, as long as or a little longer than its distance from the end of the snout, shorter than the parietals; loreal as long as deep or longer than deep; one præocular, not reaching the upper surface of the head; two postoculars; temporals 1+2, 2+2, or 2+3; seven upper labials, third and fourth entering the eye; four or five lower labials in contact with the anterior chin-shields, which are as long as or a little longer than the posterior. Scales in 17 rows. Ventrals 171-208; anal entire; subcaudals 80-97, single. Reddish or pale brown to blackish above, paler brown or yellowish on the sides; upper surface of head and nape blackish, with or without a yellowish band across the temples and occiput; beneath yellowish white.

Total length 870 millim.; tail 200. A larger specimen, with injured tail, measures 1060 millim. to vent.

Guianas, Brazil.

a. ♂ (V. 171; C 84).	Demerara.	J. J. Quelch, Esq. [P].
b. ♂ (V. 177; C 96).	Para.	Dr. E. A. Goldi [P.].
c. ♀ (V. 190; C. 80).	Para.	
d, e. ♀ (V. 203; C. 83) & yg. (V. 199; C. 82).	Rio Janeiro.	A. Fry, Esq. [P.].
f. ♀ (V 201; C. ?).	Petropolis, Organ Mts.	A H E. Petre, Esq. [P.]
g. ♀ (V. 199; C. 82).	Brazil	Dr. Gardner [C.].

16. Oxyrhopus neuwiedii.

Scytale coronata, *Wied, Abbild.* (1824); *Cope, Proc. Ac. Philad.* 1860, p. 79; *Jan, Icon. Gén.* 34, pl. v. figs. 3 & 4 (1870).
Lycodon clœlia, part., *Schleg. Phys Serp.* ii. p. 114 (1837).
—— clelia, *Trosch. in Schomb Reise Brit Guian* iii. p. 653 (1848).
Scytale neuwiedii, part., *Dum. & Bibr.* vii. p. 1001 (1854).
—— coronatum, part., *Gunth. Cat.* p. 187 (1858).
Olisthenes euphæus, *Cope, Proc. Ac. Philad.* 1859, p. 296.
Pseudoboa neuwiedii, *Cope, Proc. Ac Philad.* 1860, p. 260.
Olisthenes coronatus, *Cope, Proc. Ac. Philad* 1868, p 107.

Eye rather small; snout obtuse, moderately projecting. Rostral broader than deep, forming an obtuse angle above, the portion visible from above measuring about one half its distance from the frontal; internasals much shorter than the præfrontals; frontal a little longer than broad, as long as or a little shorter than its distance from the end of the snout, shorter than the parietals; loreal much longer than deep; one præocular, not reaching the upper surface of the head; two postoculars; temporals 2+2 or 2+3, eight (exceptionally seven) upper labials, fourth and fifth (or third and fourth) entering the eye; four lower labials in contact with the anterior chin-shields, which are as long as or a little shorter than the posterior. Scales in 19 rows. Ventrals 177-205; anal entire; subcaudals 64-96, single. Pale brown or whitish above, uniform or with a few scattered blackish spots; upper surface of head and

nape dark brown or blackish, with or without a yellowish band across the temples and occiput; lower parts uniform yellowish.
Total length 1180 millim.; tail 240.
Tropical South America, Panama.

a. Yg. (V. 190; C. 64).	Cayenne.	H. C. Rothery, Esq [P.].
b, c, d. ♂ (V 185, C 81) & yg (V. 190, 184; C. 71, 78)	Caracas	
e. ♂ (V 189; C. ?).	Trinidad.	
f. ♀ (V 190, C. ?).	Trinidad.	C. Taylor, Esq. [P.].
g. Hgr (V. 198; C. 77).	Bogota.	C. Laverde, Esq. [P.].
h. ♂ (V. 188, C. 96).	Panama	Mr. Fraser [C.].
i, k ♂ (V 197; C 79) & ♀ (V. 205; C. 75).	S America.	

17. Oxyrhopus guerini.

Rhinosimus guerini, *Dum. & Bibr.* vii. p. 991, pl. lxxii. (1854); *Gunth. Cat.* p. 10 (1858).
Scytale neuwiedii, part, *Dum. & Bibr. t. c.* p. 1001.
—— coronatum, part, *Gunth l c* p 187.
Phimophis guerini, *Cope, Proc. Ac. Philad.* 1860, p. 79, and 1862, p. 347.
Scytale guerini, *Jan, Elenco*, p. 91 (1863), *and Icon. Gén.* 34, pl. vi. fig 2 (1870).
—— coronatum, *Wucherer, Proc Zool Soc* 1863, p. 56; *Peracca, Boll Mus. Torin* no. 195, 1895, p 21.
Rhinosimus, sp., *F. Mull. Verh. Nat. Ges. Basel*, vi. 1878, p. 683.

Eye rather small; snout obtusely pointed, strongly projecting. Rostral large, nearly as deep as broad, its upper portion forming a right or acute angle and measuring at least two thirds its distance from the frontal; internasals much shorter than the præfrontals; frontal a little longer than broad, usually shorter than its distance from the end of the snout, shorter than the parietals; loreal much longer than deep; one præocular (rarely divided), not reaching the upper surface of the head; two postoculars; temporals 2+3; eight (exceptionally seven) upper labials, fourth and fifth (or third and fourth) entering the eye; four lower labials in contact with the anterior chin-shields, which are shorter than the posterior. Scales in 19 rows. Ventrals 185–211; anal entire; subcaudals 70–99, single or only a few of the posterior in pairs. Adult dark brown or black above, with or without some large irregular whitish spots, yellowish white beneath; young pale brown above, with the anterior half of the head and the nape blackish, the posterior half of the head yellowish white.
Total length 1120 millim.; tail 250
Brazil, Paraguay.

a. ♂ (V. 200, C. 89).	Corumba, Matto Grosso.	Spencer Moore, Esq. [P.].
b-c. ♂ (V. 189; C. 93) & ♀ (V. 205; C. 83).	Bahia.	Lord Walsingham [P.].

d, e, f. ♂ (V. 197; C. 99), ♀ (V. 203; C. ?), & yg. (V. 194; C. 90).	Bahia.	Dr. O. Wucherer [C.].
g. ♂ (V. 194; C. 98).	Bahia.	
h, i, k, l. ♂ (V. 204; C. 91), ♀ (V. 192, 203; C. 82, 80), & yg. (V. 201; C. 82).	Pernambuco.	J. P. G. Smith, Esq. [P.].
m. Yg. (V. 195; C. 77).	Pernambuco.	

155. RHINOSTOMA.

? Rhinostoma, part., *Fitzing. N. Class. Rept.* p. 29 (1826).
Rhinostoma, *Dum. & Bibr. Erp. Gén.* vii. p. 992 (1854); *Jan, Elenco sist. Ofid* p 91 (1863).
Rhinostoma, part., *Günth. Cat. Col. Sn.* p. 8 (1858).

Maxillary teeth 10, subequal, followed, after an interspace, by a pair of moderately enlarged grooved teeth situated below the posterior border of the eye; mandibular teeth subequal. Head slightly distinct from neck; eye rather small, with vertically elliptic pupil; rostral very large, with sharp horizontal edge. Body cylindrical; scales smooth, with apical pits, in 19 rows; ventrals rounded or obtusely angulate laterally. Tail moderate; subcaudals in two rows.

South America.

1. Rhinostoma guianense.

Heterodon guianensis, *Trosch. in Schomb. Reise Brit. Guian.* iii p. 653 (1848).
Rhinostoma nasuum (*non Wagl**), *Dum. & Bibr.* vii. p 994 (1854); *Günth. Cat.* p. 8 (1858); *Jan, Icon. Gén.* 34, pl. v. figs. 1 & 2 (1870).
Rhinostoma guntheri, *Cope, Proc. Ac. Philad.* 1860, p. 243.

Snout short, turned up. Outline of rostral rounded, the lower surface of the shield broader than long, its upper surface at least as long as its distance from the frontal; internasals a little shorter than the præfrontals; latter forming a short median suture or in contact with their inner angles only, or even narrowly separated from each other; frontal as long as broad or a little longer than broad, as long as or a little shorter than its distance from the end of the snout, as long as the parietals; loreal longer than deep; one præocular (sometimes divided), widely separated from the frontal; two (rarely three) postoculars; temporals 2+3; eight upper labials, fourth and fifth entering the eye; four lower labials in contact with the anterior chin-shields; posterior chin-shields small, scale-like. Scales in 19 rows. Ventrals 168-209; anal entire; subcaudals

---

* The *Vipera (Rhinostoma) nasua* of Wagler, Syst. Amph. p. 171, is, to judge by the definition given, probably identical with *Lystrophis dorbignyi*, D. & B.

56-70. Blackish above, the lateral scales edged with whitish, or pale yellowish brown with numerous small brown spots and a large blackish blotch on the nape; uniform whitish beneath.

Total length 1030 millim.; tail 160.

Colombia, Venezuela, Guianas, Brazil, Paraguay.

a-b, c. ♂ (V. 180; C. 70), ♀ (V. 194; C. 60), & yg. (V. 196, C. 56).	Carthagena, Colombia.	
d. ♂ (V. 189, C. 70).	Sta. Marta, Colombia.	
e. Hgr. ♀ (V. 168; C. 53).	Berbice, Brit. Guiana.	Lady Essex [P.].
f. ♀ (V. 209; C. ?).	Asuncion, Paraguay.	Dr. J. Bohls [O.].

2. Rhinostoma vittatum. (PLATE V. fig. 3.)

Snout acutely pointed. Rostral subtrihedral, obtusely keeled above, its lower surface as long as broad, its upper surface as long as its distance from the frontal; internasals shorter than the præfrontals; frontal a little longer than broad, as long as its distance from the end of the snout, slightly longer than the parietals; loreal longer than deep; one præocular, narrowly separated from the frontal; two postoculars; temporals 2+3; eight upper labials, fourth and fifth entering the eye; four lower labials in contact with the anterior chin-shields, which are a little larger than the posterior. Scales in 19 rows. Ventrals 199; anal entire. Pale yellowish brown above, with two dark brown longitudinal bands uniting on the nape, uniform whitish beneath.

Total length (tail injured) 620 millim.

Argentina.

a. ♂ (V. 199, C. ?).   Buenos Ayres.   E. W. White, Esq. [C.].

156. THAMNODYNASTES.

Dryophylax, *Wagler, Syst Amph.* p. 181 (1830).
Thamnodynastes, *Wagl l. c.* p 182; *Gunth Cat. Col. Sn.* p. 163 (1858); *Jan, Elenco sist. Ofid.* p. 105 (1863).
Dipsas, part., *Schleg. Phys. Serp.* ii. p. 257 (1837), *Dum. & Bibr. Erp Gén.* vii. p. 1133 (1854).
Tomodon, part, *Gunth. l. c.* p. 52.
Mesotes, part, *Jan, Arch. Zool Anat. Phys.* ii. 1863, p. 306.

Maxillary teeth 13-18, subequal, followed, after an interspace, by a pair of enlarged, grooved teeth situated below the posterior border of the eye; mandibular teeth subequal. Head distinct from neck; eye large, with vertically elliptic pupil; nostril in a single or semidivided shield. Body cylindrical; scales smooth or keeled, with apical pits, in 17 or 19 rows; ventrals rounded. Tail moderate or rather long; subcaudals in two rows.

South America.

1. Thamnodynastes nattereri.

Coluber nattereri, *Milan, Delect. Faun. Flor. Bras.* pl. —. fig. 1 (1820); *Wied, Beitr. Nat. Bras.* i. p. 277 (1825), *and Abbild.* (1830).

Tropidonotus nattereri, *Boie, Isis,* 1827, p 535.

Dipsas nattereri, *Schleg. Phys. Serp* ii. p. 290 (1837); *Dum. & Bibr.* vii. p. 1149 (1854).

Thamnodynastes nattereri, *Gunth. Cat.* p. 104 (1858); *Jan, Icon. Gén.* 39, pl. ii. fig. 3 (1872); *Boettg. Zeitschr. f. Naturw.* lviii. 1885, p. 236.

Tomodon strigatus, *Gunth. l. c.* p. 52.

Tachymenis hypoconia, *Cope, Proc. Ac. Philad.* 1860, p. 247; *Gunth. Zool. Rec.* 1866, p 126; *Cope, Proc. Amer. Philos. Soc.* xxii. 1885, p. 192.

Mesotes obtrusus, *Jan, Arch. Zool. Anat Phys* ii. 1863, p 306, *and Icon. Gén.* 18, pl. vi. fig. 1 (1866).

Thamnodynastes punctatissimus (*non Wagl*), *Hensel, Arch f. Nat.* 1868, p. 332.

—— nattereri, var. lævis, *Bouleng. Ann. & Mag. N. H.* (5) xv. 1885, p. 195.

—— strigatus, *Bouleng. Ann. & Mag. N. H.* (5) xviii. 1886, p. 437.

Tachymenis strigatus, *Cope, Proc. Amer. Philos. Soc.* xxiv. 1887, p. 58.

Snout short, convex. Rostral broader than deep, just visible from above; internasals as long as or a little shorter than the præfrontals; frontal once and two thirds to twice as long as broad, longer than its distance from the end of the snout, as long as or a little shorter than the parietals; nasal entire or semidivided; loreal as long as deep or deeper than long; one præocular (sometimes divided), not reaching the frontal; two postoculars; temporals 2 + 2 or 3; eight (rarely seven or nine) upper labials, two or three of which enter the eye; four or five lower labials in contact with the anterior chin-shields, which are as long as or a little longer than the posterior. Scales in 19 rows, smooth or more or less strongly keeled. Ventrals 137–160; anal divided; subcaudals 48–78. Brown or olive above, spotted or striped with darker; a yellowish vertebral stripe or series of spots may be present, head with dark undulous streaks or vermiculations; labial shields sometimes barred with black; an oblique dark streak from the eye to the angle of the mouth; yellowish beneath, speckled and stroaked with blackish.

Total length 760 millim.; tail 170.

South America east of the Andes.

A. Scales strongly keeled.

a. ♂ (V. 153; C. 77).	Santarem.	H W. Bates, Esq. [C.].
b, c. ♂ (V. 160, 143; C. 78, 78).	Tijuca R.	R. Bennett, Esq. [P].
d–e. ♀ (V. 144, 142; C. 63, 59).	Rio Grande do Sul.	Dr. H. v. Ihering [C.].
f. ♀ (V. 145; C. 70).	Brazil.	Capt. J. Parish [P.].
g–h. ♂ (V. 146, 145; C. 72, 75).	Uruguay.	
i. ♂ skeleton.	Uruguay.	

B. Scales moderately keeled.

a, b-c. ♂ (V.151; C.73) & ♀ (V. 150, 143; C. 67, 59).	Rio Janeiro.	Mrs Fry [P.].
d-e. ♂ (V. 145; C. 65) & hgr. (V.139; C.55).	Asuncion, Paraguay.	Dr. J. Bohls [C.].

C. Scales faintly keeled.

a-c. Hgr. (V. 152, 138, 141; C. 70, 60, 60).	Demerara.	Dr. Hancock [P].
d, e ♂ (V. 155; C. 78) & ♀ (V. 148; C. 69).	Rio Janeiro.	A. Fry, Esq. [P.].
f. ♀ (V. 154; C. 69).	Brazil.	Dr. Gardner [P.].

D. Scales smooth.

a. ♀ (V. 144; C. 48).	Aracati, N. Brazil.	D. G. Rutherford, Esq. [P.]
b, c-d ♂ (V. 139, 142; C. ?, 63) & hgr. (V. 136, C 62).	Rio Grande do Sul.	Dr. H. v. Ihering [C.].
e. ♀ (V. 133, C. 56).	—— ?	(Type of *Tomodon strigatus*.)

2. Thamnodynastes punçtatissimus.

Natrix punctatissima, *Wagl. in Spix, Serp. Bras*, p 39, pl. xiv. fig. 1 (1824).
Dipsas punctatissima, *Schleg. Phys. Serp.* ii p 292, pl. xi figs. 33 & 34 (1837); *Dum. & Bibr* vii. p. 1151 (1854).
Sibon punctatissimus, *Berthold, Abh. Ges. Wiss. Gotting.* i. 1843, p. 68, pl. i figs 13 & 14.
Thamnodynastes punctatissimus, *Gunth. Cat.* p. 164 (1858); *Jan, Icon. Gén.* 39, pl. ii. fig. 2 (1872).

Very closely allied to the preceding, but body more slender, eye larger, rostral but little broader than deep, scales smooth, in 17 rows, and anal entire. Ventrals 137-159; subcaudals 80-96.

Total length 550 millim.; tail 150.

Guianas, Brazil.

a. ♂ (V. 159, C. 88).	Demerara.	Mr. W. T. Turner [C.].
b. ♂ (V. 144, C. ?).	Upper Amazon.	Mr. E. Bartlett [C.].
c. ♀ (V. 146, C. 80).	—— ?	

157. TACHYMENIS.

Tachymenis, *Wiegm N Act. Ac. Leop.-Carol* xvii i. 1835, p. 251.
Coronella, part, *Schleg Phys Serp.* ii. p. 50 (1837).
Dipsas, part, *Dum. & Bibr. Erp Gén* vii p. 1133 (1854).
Tachymenis, part., *Gunth. Cat. Col. Sn.* p. 33 (1858).
Mesotes, part, *Jan, Arch. Zool. Anat. Phys.* ii. 1863, p. 306.
Psammophylax, part., *Jan, l. c* p. 309.

Maxillary teeth subequal, 10 to 15, followed, after an interspace, by a pair of large grooved fangs situated below the posterior border of the eye, anterior mandibular teeth longest. Head scarcely distinct from neck; eye moderate, with vertically elliptic or sub-elliptic pupil; nasal shield single or semidivided. Body cylindrical; scales smooth, with apical pits, in 17 or 19 rows; ventrals rounded. Tail moderate; subcaudals in two rows.

Bolivia, Peru, Chili.

1. Tachymenis peruviana.

Tachymenis peruviana, *Wiegm. N. Act. Ac. Leop.-Carol.* xvii. i. 1835, p. 252, pl xx. fig. 1, *Peters, Mon. Berl. Ac.* 1863, p. 275; *Steind. Novara, Rept.* p. 62 (1867).

Coronella chilensis, *Schleg. Phys. Serp.* ii. p. 70 (1837); *Guichen. in Gay, Hist. Chile, Rept.* p. 79, pl. iv. fig. 1 (1854).

Ophis peruana, *Tschudi, Faun. Per., Herp.* p. 58 (1845).

Dipsas chilensis, *Dum. & Bibr.* vii. p. 1159 (1854).

Tachymenis chilensis, *Girard, Proc. Ac. Philad.* 1854, p. 226, *and Gilliss' U.S. Nav. Astron. Exped.* ii. p. 213, pl. xxxvii. figs. 1–6 (1855), *and U.S. Explor. Exped., Herp.* p. 173 (1858), *Gunth. Cat.* p. 34 (1858), *Cope, Proc. Ac. Philad.* 1860, p 247.

Mesotes chilensis, *Jan, Arch Zool. Anat. Phys.* ii. 1863, p. 308, *and Icon Gén* 18, pl. vi. fig. 2 (1866).

Psammophylax assimilis, *Jan, ll. cc.* p. 311, *Icon.* 19, pl. i. fig. 2.

Rostral broader than deep, scarcely visible from above; internasals as long as or shorter than the præfrontals; frontal once and a half to twice as long as broad, a little longer than its distance from the end of the snout, as long as or a little shorter than the parietals; loreal as long as deep; one or two præ- and two postoculars; temporals 1+2 or 2+3; seven or eight upper labials, third and fourth or fourth and fifth entering the eye; four or five lower labials in contact with the anterior chin-shields, which are as long as or longer than the posterior. Scales in 19 rows. Ventrals 135–158; anal divided; subcaudals 33–53. Yellowish or pale brown above, with darker spots or more or less distinct longitudinal streaks; an oblique dark streak from the eye to the angle of the mouth; yellowish or grey beneath, usually with small blackish spots often forming longitudinal series.

Total length 530 millim.; tai 90.

Bolivia, Peru, Chili.

a. ♂ (V. 144; C. 53).	Aschiquiri, Bolivia.	
b. ♀ (V. 142; C. 44).	Larecaja, Bolivia.	
c. ♂ (V. 135; C. 51).	Lake Titicaca.	J. B. Pentland, Esq. [P.]
d ♀ (V. 151; C. 39).	Colchagua, Chili.	
e. ♂ (V. 145; C. 44).	Coquimbo.	Dr. Cunningham [P.].
f–g. ♀ (V. 141; C. 49) & yg. (V. 140, 146; C. 46, 36).	Coquimbo.	Dr. Coppinger [P.].
h ♀ (V. 157; C. 43).	Talcahuana.	Dr. Coppinger [P.].
i–l. ♂ (V. 158; C. 46) & ♀ (V. 147; C. 45).	S. Chili.	Mr A. Lane [C.]; H. B. James, Esq. [P.].
m–n. ♀ (V. 148, 151; C. 38, 33).	Chili.	
o. Yg. (V. 158; C. 46).	Chili.	

2. Tachymenis affinis. (Plate VII. fig. 1.)

Very closely allied to the preceding, but maxillary longer, with more numerous solid teeth, viz. 15 instead of 10 to 12, and scales in 17 rows. One præocular; temporals 2+3; eight upper labials, fourth and fifth entering the eye. Ventrals 153; anal divided; subcaudals 57. Brown above, darker on the four outer rows of scales, with a few small darker spots; a dark oblique streak behind the eye; grey beneath, much spotted with black.

Total length 520 millim., tail 110.

Peru.

a. ♂ (V. 153; C. 57).	Muña.	Mr. W. Davis [C.]; Messrs. Veitch [P.].

158. HEMIRHAGERRHIS.

Hemirhagerrhis, *Boettg. Zool. Anz.* 1893, p. 119.

Maxillary short, with 9 or 10 teeth gradually increasing in length and followed by an enlarged grooved fang situated below the posterior border of the eye; anterior mandibular teeth strongly enlarged. Head distinct from neck; eye small, with vertically subelliptic pupil; nasal semidivided, the cleft horizontal. Body cylindrical; scales smooth, with apical pits, in 17 or 19 rows; ventrals rounded. Tail moderate; subcaudals in two rows.

East Africa.

1. Hemirhagerrhis kelleri.

Hemirhagerrhis kelleri, *Boettg. t. c.* p. 129; *Stejneger, Proc. U.S. Nat. Mus.* xvi. 1893, p. 729.

Rostral nearly twice as broad as deep, scarcely visible from above; internasals shorter than the præfrontals; frontal twice to twice and a half as long as broad, longer than its distance from the end of the snout, as long as or shorter than the parietals; loreal longer than deep; one præocular, extending to the upper surface of the head but not reaching the frontal; two postoculars; temporals 2+2, 2+3, or 2+4; eight upper labials, fourth and fifth entering the eye; four or five lower labials in contact with the anterior chinshields, which are as long as or shorter than the posterior. Scales in 17 (exceptionally 19) rows. Ventrals 148–173; anal divided; subcaudals 61–78. Greyish or yellowish brown above, with a dark grey or olive, black-edged vertebral band and another on each side, passing through the eye; head lineolated with blackish; upper lip blackish; lower parts with brown longitudinal lines disposed in pairs.

Total length 270 millim.; tail 83.

Somaliland, East Africa.

a. ♀ (V. 148; C. 72).	British East Africa.	
b. Hgr. (V. 173, C. 61).	Mombasa.	D. J. Wilson, Esq. [C.]; G. Waller, Esq. [P.].
c. Hgr. (V. 150; C. 66).	Thiriati, E. Kikuyu.	Dr. J. W. Gregory [P.].

159. MANOLEPIS.

Manolepis, *Cope, Proc. Amer. Philos. Soc.* xxii. 1885, p. 176.

Maxillary teeth 15, small, equal, followed, after an interspace, by a pair of enlarged grooved fangs situated behind the vertical of the eye; anterior mandibular teeth much longer than the posterior. Head distinct from neck; eye large, with vertically subelliptic pupil; nasal single; frontal narrow. Body cylindrical; scales smooth, without pits, in 19 rows; ventrals rounded. Tail moderate; subcaudals in two rows.

Mexico.

1. Manolepis putnami.

Dromicus putnami, *Jan, Elenco,* p. 67 (1863), and *Icon. Gén.* 24, pl. vi. fig. 3 (1867); *Garm. N. Am. Rept.* pp. 59, 153 (1883).
Tomodon nasutus, *Cope, Proc. Ac. Philad.* 1864, p. 166, *Bocourt, Miss. Sc. Mex., Rept.* p. 641 (1886).
Manolepis nasutus, *Cope, Proc. Amer. Philos. Soc.* xxii. 1885, p. 176.
Dromicus (Ocyophis) putnami, *Bocourt, op. cit.* p. 714, pl. l. fig. 3 (1890).
Philodryas putnami, *Gunth. Biol. C.-Am , Rept* p. 166 (1895).

Eye about two thirds the length of the snout, which is truncate and rather prominent. Rostral much broader than deep, scarcely visible from above; internasals shorter than the præfrontals; frontal twice to twice and a half as long as broad, longer than its distance from the end of the snout, as long as the parietals; loreal elongate or absent (fused with the præfrontal); one præocular, extending to the upper surface of the head but not reaching the frontal; two postoculars; temporals 1 + 2; eight upper labials, third, fourth, and fifth entering the eye; five lower labials in contact with the anterior chin-shields, which are a little shorter than the posterior. Scales in 19 rows. Ventrals 171–186; anal divided, subcaudals 69–83. Yellowish or pale brownish above, with a brown, darker-edged vertebral stripe three scales wide; head speckled with blackish, more closely on the lip; lower parts whitish, speckled with brown.

Total length 550 millim.; tail 140.—The young specimen in the Collection measures 265 millim.; tail 63.

Mexico.

a. Yg. (V. 176; C. 83).   La Cumbre de los Arrastrados, Jalisco, 8500 feet.   Dr. A. C. Buller [C.].

160. TOMODON.

Tomodon, part., *Dum. & Bibr Mém. Ac. Sc.* xxiii 1853, p. 495, *and Erp. Gén.* vii. p. 932 (1854); *Gunth. Cat. Col. Sn.* p. 52 (1858); *Jan, Arch. Zool. Anat. Phys.* ii. 1862, p. 322.
Opisthoplus, *Peters, Sitzb. Akad. Berl.* 1882, p. 1148.

Maxillary short, with 5 to 8 small teeth increasing in size and followed by a pair of enormous grooved fangs situated below the eye; anterior mandibular teeth a little larger than the posterior.

Head distinct from neck; eye moderate, with round pupil; nasal entire or semidivided. Body cylindrical; scales oblique, smooth, with apical pits, in 17 or 19 rows; ventrals rounded. Tail moderate or short; subcaudals in two rows.

South America.

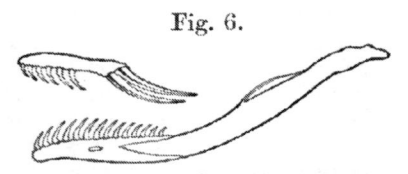

Fig. 6.

Maxillary and mandible of *Tomodon ocellatus*.

1. Tomodon dorsatus.

Tomodon dorsatum, *Dum. & Bibr.* vii. p. 934 (1854); *Günth. Cat.* p. 53 (1858); *Jan, Arch. Zool. Anat. Phys.* ii. 1862, p. 323, *and Icon. Gén.* 19, pl. vi. fig. 1 (1866).
Opisthoplus degener, *Peters, Sitzb. Ak. Berl.* 1882, p. 1149, fig.

Snout short, very convex. Rostral broader than deep, just visible from above; internasals as long as or a little shorter than the præfrontals; frontal once and one third to once and two thirds as long as broad, longer than its distance from the end of the snout, shorter than the parietals; no loreal; nasal elongate and in contact with the præocular, which is single; two or three postoculars; temporals 1+2; seven (exceptionally six) upper labials, third and fourth (or second and third) entering the eye; chin-shields short, the anterior in contact with four or five lower labials. Scales in 17 rows. Ventrals 134–143; anal divided; subcaudals 53–62. Brown or olive above, with a yellow vertebral stripe which may be confined to the nape; small blackish spots may be present on the back; an oblique dark streak from the eye to the angle of the mouth; yellowish or pale olive beneath, uniform or speckled with darker.

Total length 610 millim.; tail 150.

Brazil.

a. ♂ (V. 136; C. 62).	Rio Janeiro.	A. Fry, Esq. [P.].
b–c. ♂ (V. 139; C. ?) & hgr. (V. 134; C. 53).	Rio Grande do Sul.	Dr. H. v. Ihering [C.].

2. Tomodon ocellatus.

Tomodon ocellatum, *Dum. & Bibr.* vii. p. 938 (1854); *Jan, Arch. Zool. Anat. Phys.* ii. 1862, p. 323, *and Icon. Gén.* 19, pl. vi. fig. 2 (1866).

Snout short, very convex. Rostral broader than deep, just visible from above; internasals a little shorter than the præfrontals; frontal once and two thirds to twice as long as broad, longer than its distance from the end of the snout, as long as the parietals; nasal entire or semidivided; loreal as long as deep or deeper than long; one præ-

and two postoculars; temporals 1+2 or 2+3; seven upper labials, third and fourth entering the eye; four or five lower labials in contact with the anterior chin-shields, which are as long as or longer than the posterior. Scales in 19 rows. Ventrals 137–143; anal divided; subcaudals 31–38. Yellowish or pale brown above, with two dorsal series of dark brown, black-edged roundish spots separated by a narrow light vertebral line; smaller spots on the sides; a large angular dark band on the back of the head, and one or two crossbars between the eyes; two oblique dark streaks, one below and the other behind the eye; yellowish beneath, with squarish or roundish black spots.

Total length 460 millim.; tail 70.

Southern Brazil, Paraguay, Uruguay, Argentina.

a. ♂ (V. 143; C. 35).		S Lorenzo, Rio Grande do Sul.	Dr. H. v. Ihering [C.].
b. ♂ (V. 137, C. 38).		Paraguay.	Prof. Grant [P.].
c. ♀ (V. 139; C. 31).		Uruguay.	
d. ♂ (V. 141; C. 36).		S. of R de la Plata.	Lieut. Gairdner [P.].
e. Skull of b.			

161. CONOPHIS.

Tomodon, part., *Dum. & Bibr. Mém. Ac. Sc.* xxiii. 1853, p. 495, *and Erp. Gén.* vii. p. 932 (1854); *Jan, Arch. Zool. Anat. Phys.* ii. 1862, p. 322.

Psammophis, part., *Gunth. Cat. Col. Sn.* p. 135 (1858).

Conophis, *Peters, Mon. Berl. Ac.* 1860, p. 519; *Cope, Proc. Ac. Philad.* 1861, p. 300, *Bocourt, Miss. Sc. Mex., Rept.* p 642 (1886).

Maxillary teeth 10, slightly increasing in size posteriorly, followed, after an interspace, by a pair of very large grooved fangs situated just behind the vertical of the posterior border of the eye; anterior mandibular teeth longest. Head slightly distinct from neck; eye moderate, with round pupil. Body cylindrical; scales smooth, without pits, in 17 or 19 rows; ventrals rounded. Tail moderate; subcaudals in two rows.

Mexico and Central America; Southern Brazil.

Synopsis of the Species.

Scales in 19 rows; snout feebly projecting.	1. *lineatus*, p. 122.
Scales in 19 rows; snout strongly projecting	2. *vittatus*, p. 123.
Scales in 17 rows	3 *tæniatus*, p. 124.

1. Conophis lineatus.

Tomodon lineatus, *Dum. & Bibr.* vii. p. 936, pl. lxxiii (1854); *Jan, Arch. Zool. Anat. Phys.* ii. 1862, p. 234, *and Icon. Gén.* 19, pl. vi. fig. 3 (1866); *Bocourt, Journ. de Zool.* v. 1876, p. 406.

Psammophis lineatus, *Gunth. Cat.* p. 135 (1858).

Conophis concolor, *Cope, Proc. Ac. Philad.* 1866, p. 318; *Bocourt, Miss. Sc. Mex., Rept.* p. 648 (1886).

Conophis lineatus, *Cope, Proc. Ac. Philad.* 1868, p. 308, *and Journ. Ac. Philad.* (2) viii. 1876, p. 137; *Bocourt, Miss. Sc. Mex., Rept.* p. 643, pl. xxxviii. fig. 5, *Gunth Biol. C.-Am., Rept.* p. 165 (1895).

—— pulcher, *Cope, Proc. Ac. Philad.* 1868, p. 308; *Bocourt, Miss. Sc. Mex., Rept.* p. 646, pl. xxxviii. fig. 6.

Tomodon pulcher, *Bocourt, Journ. de Zool.* v. 1876, p. 408.

Tachymenis lineata, *Garm. N. Am. Rept* p. 60 (1883).

Snout projecting. Upper portion of rostral measuring one third to one half its distance from the frontal; internasals as long as broad, a little shorter than the præfrontals; frontal nearly twice as long as broad, a little longer than its distance from the end of the snout, as long as the parietals; loreal square or longer than deep; one præocular (sometimes divided), not reaching the frontal; two postoculars; temporals 2+2 or 3; eight (rarely seven) upper labials, fourth and fifth (or third and fourth) entering the eye; four or five lower labials in contact with the anterior chin-shields, which are as long as the posterior. Scales in 19 rows. Ventrals 158–183; anal divided; subcaudals 66–78. Yellowish, greyish, or pale olive above, usually with six to ten black longitudinal lines, uniting to form three stripes on the head, the outer of which pass through the eyes; a black line or series of spots running along the outer row of scales; chin greyish or olive, spotted with white; rostral and labials greyish or blackish beneath, lower parts white.

Total length 780 millim.; tail 150.

Mexico and Central America.

A. Striped. (*C. lineatus*, D. & B.)

a ♀ (V. 171; C. 68).	Mexico	
b–c, d. ♂ (V. 170; C. 78) & ♀ (V. 171, 183; C. ?, ?).	Dueñas, Guatemala.	O. Salvin, Esq. [C.].
e. ♀ (V. 163; C. 77).	Cartago, Costa Rica	

B. Uniform brownish above, with a dark brown stripe on each side of the head. (*C. concolor*, Cope.)

a. ♀ (V. 158; C. 66).   Yucatan.

2. Conophis vittatus.

Conophis vittatus, *Peters, Mon. Berl. Ac.* 1860, p. 519, pl. —. fig. 3; *Bocourt, Miss. Sc. Mex., Rept.* p. 644, pl. xxxviii. fig. 7 (1886); *Gunth. Biol. C.-Am., Rept.* p. 165 (1895).

—— sumichrasti, *Cope, Journ. Ac. Philad.* (2) viii. 1876, p. 137

? Conophis viduus, *Cope, l. c*

Tomodon vittatus, *Bocourt, Journ. de Zool.* v. 1876, p. 407.

Very closely allied to the preceding, but snout more prominent and shorter, upper portion of rostral measuring at least half its distance from the frontal, and internasals broader than long. Seven upper labials, third and fourth entering the eye. Ventrals 147–163; subcaudals 57–70. Cream-colour, with three dark brown or black stripes extending from the tip of the snout to the end of the tail; the outer stripe passing through the eye and extending along the second, third, and fourth rows of scales, the median stripe sometimes divided into two.

Total length 575 millim.; tail 120

Southern Mexico.

a. ♀ (V. 161; C. 65).	Tehuantepec.	Prof. F. Sumichrast [C.].
b. ♀ (V. 163; C. 65).	Santo Domingo de Guzman.	Dr. A. C Buller [C.].
c. ♂ (V. 158; C. 70).	Tepetlapa, Guerrero.	Mr. H. H. Smith[C.]; F. D. Godman, Esq [P.].

3. Conophis tæniatus.

Philodryas tæniatus, *Hensel, Arch. f. Nat.* 1868, p. 331; *Bouleng. Ann. & Mag. N. H.* (5) xviii. 1886, p 434.

Snout scarcely projecting Rostral nearly as deep as broad, well visible from above; internasals shorter than the præfrontals; frontal twice and a half as long as broad, longer than its distance from the end of the snout, slightly shorter than the parietals; loreal a little longer than deep; one præocular, just reaching the upper surface of the head; two postoculars; temporals 1+2; seven upper labials, third and fourth entering the eye; four lower labials in contact with the anterior chin-shields. Scales in 17 rows. Ventrals 170; anal divided; subcaudals 74. Pale yellowish olive above, with an olive-brown, black-edged vertebral stripe three scales wide; a broader lateral dark stripe, covering the three outer rows of scales and the outer ends of the ventrals, bordered above by a black line running along the fourth row of scales; a fine line right along the outer row of scales; head olive, with darker variegations; a white line from the rostral along the four anterior upper labials; yellowish beneath, with a bluish-grey streak on each side.

Total length 615 millim.; tail 150.

Porto Alegre, Rio Grande do Sul.

162. AMPLORHINUS.

Amplorhinus, *Smith, Ill. Zool. S. Afr., Rept* (1847).
Dipsas, part., *Dum. & Bibr. Erp Gén.* vii. p. 1153 (1854).
Coronella, part, *Gunth. Cat. Col. Sn.* p. 34 (1858).
Psammophylax, part, *Jan, Arch. Zool. Anat. Phys* ii. 1863, p. 309.
Tachymenis, part., *Peters, Reise n. Mossamb* iii. p. 117 (1882).
Amphiophis (*lapsu calami*), *Bouleng. Proc. Zool. Soc.* 1891, p. 307.

Maxillary teeth 12 or 13. gradually increasing in size, followed by an enlarged, grooved tooth; mandibular teeth subequal. Head distinct from neck; eye moderate, with round pupil; nasal semi-divided. Body cylindrical; scales smooth or feebly keeled, with apical pits, in 17 rows; ventrals rounded. Tail moderate; subcaudals in two rows.

Tropical and South Africa.

1. Amplorhinus multimaculatus.

Amplorhinus multimaculatus, *Smith, Ill. Zool. S. Afr., Rept.* pl. lvii. (1847).
Dipsas smithii, *Dum. & Bibr.* vii. p. 1162 (1854).
Coronella multimaculata, *Gunth Cat.* p 38 (1858)
Psammophylax multimaculatus, *Jan, Arch Zool. Anat. Phys.* ii. 1863, p. 310, *and Icon. Gén.* 19, pl. i. fig. 1 (1866); *Boettg. Ber. Senck. Ges.* 1887, p. 157.

Rostral broader than deep, just visible from above; internasals shorter than the præfrontals; frontal about twice as long as broad, longer than its distance from the end of the snout, as long as or a little shorter than the parietals; loreal as long as deep or longer than deep; one præocular, extending to the upper surface of the head but not reaching the frontal; two postoculars; temporals 2+2 (rarely 1+2); eight upper labials, fourth and fifth entering the eye; five lower labials in contact with the anterior chin-shields, which are nearly as long as the posterior Scales in 17 rows, usually feebly keeled on the posterior part of the back and at the base of the tail. Ventrals 133–149; anal entire; subcaudals 60–86, some of the anterior frequently entire. Olive or brown above, with two more or less distinct yellowish stripes and longitudinal rows of black spots; bluish grey or olive beneath; specs. *h–i* uniform bright green above and beneath.

Total length 495 millim.; tail 115.

Cape of Good Hope.

a–e. ♀ (V. 141, 140, 146; C. 66, 67, 60) & hgr. (V. 137, 137; C. 89, 61).	Cape of Good Hope.	Sir A. Smith [P]. (Types)
f. ♀ (V 149; C. 60).	Cape of Good Hope	Lord Derby [P.]
g. ♂ (V. 142, C. 75).	Cape of Good Hope.	
h–i. ♂ (V. 142; C. 76) & hgr. (V. 144; C. 62).	S. Africa.	Dr. Quain [P.].

2. Amplorhinus nototænia.

Coronella nototænia, *Gunth Proc Zool. Soc.* 1864, p. 309, pl xxvi. fig. 1.
Psammophylax rhombeatus?, *Bocage, Jorn. Sc. Lisb.* 1. 1867, p. 224.
——— viperinus, *Bocage, Jorn. Sc. Lisb.* iv. 1873, p 222
Ablabes hildebrandtii, *Peters, Mon. Berl. Ac.* 1878, p 205, pl. ii. fig. 6, *Fischer, Jahrb Hamb. Wiss. Anst.* i 1884, p. 7.
Tachymenis nototænia, *Peters, Reise n. Mossamb.* iii. p. 118 (1882)
Amphiophis nototænia, *Bouleng. Proc. Zool. Soc.* 1891, p. 307.
Hemirhagerrhis hildebrandtii, *Stejneger, Proc. U.S. Nat. Mus.* xvi. 1893, p. 729.
——— nototænia, *Stejneger, l c.* p. 730.
Psammophylax nototænia, *Bocage, Herp. Angola*, p. 109 (1895).

. Rostral broader than deep, just visible from above; internasals shorter than the præfrontals; frontal twice as long as broad, as long as or a little longer than its distance from the end of the snout, as long as or a little shorter than the parietals; loreal as long as deep or a little longer than deep; one præocular, extending to the upper surface of the head but not reaching the frontal; two postoculars; temporals 1+2 or 2+3; eight upper labials, fourth and fifth entering the eye; four or five lower labials in contact with the anterior chin-shields, which are as long as or shorter than the posterior. Scales in 17 rows, all smooth. Ventrals 154–187; anal divided; subcaudals 59–98. Greyish or pale brown above, with two series of small blackish spots connected by a dark vertebral line; the spots and bands unite on the occiput and nape and form a more or less marked zigzag band; a dark streak on each side of the head, passing through the eye; tail with three dark stripes: whitish or pale brownish below, spotted or speckled with brown.

Total length 355 millim.; tail 85.

Tropical Africa south of the Equator, East Africa.

a. ♂ (V. 187; C. 73).	Rios de Sena, Zambesi.	Sir J. Kirk [C.]. (Type.)
b. ♂ (V. 183; C. 77).	Cape McLear, Lake Nyassa.	A. A. Simons, Esq. [C.].
c. ♀ (V. 171; C. 68).	Lake Nyassa.	J. B. Thelwall, Esq. [C.].

The specimen from Caffraria referred by Peters to this species (Reise n. Mossamb. iii. p. 118) is no doubt specifically distinct, as it is stated to have 19 rows of scales and 137 ventrals.

163. PSEUDABLABES.

Maxillary teeth small, equal, 14, followed, after an interspace, by a pair of enlarged grooved fangs situated just behind the posterior border of the eye[*]; mandibular teeth equal. Head small, scarcely distinct from neck; eye moderate, with round pupil; nostril in a single or semidivided nasal. Body cylindrical; scales smooth, with apical pits, in 13 rows; ventrals rounded. Tail moderate; subcaudals in two rows.

Southern Brazil, Uruguay.

1. Pseudablabes agassizii.

For synonymy and description, see Vol. II. p. 259 (*Contia agassizii*), and add :—

Philodryas paucisquamis, *Peters, Mon. Berl. Ac.* 1863, p. 280.

---

[*] These fangs, hidden in the gum, were overlooked by Jan and myself. Their presence, first ascertained by Peters, has been pointed out to me by Count Peracca.

164. PHILODRYAS.

Philodryas, *Wagler, Syst. Amph.* p. 185 (1830).
Chlorosoma, *Wagler, l. c.*
Xenodon, part, *Schleg. Phys. Serp* ii. p. 80 (1837).
Herpetodryas, part., *Schleg. l. c.* p. 173
Lygophis, *Tschudi, Faun. Per., Herp.* p 52 (1845).
Dryophylax, part., *Dum. & Bibr. Erp Gén.* vii. p. 1103 (1854).
Callirhinus (*non Cuv.*), *Girard, Proc. Ac. Philad.* 1857, p. 182, *and U.S. Explor. Exped., Herp.* p. 139 (1858).
Philodryas, part., *Gunth. Cat. Col. Sn.* p. 123 (1858); *Jan, Elenco sist. Ofid.* p. 83 (1863)
Euophrys (*non Koch*), *Gunth. l. c.* p. 139.
Galeophis, *Berthold, Gotting. Nachr.* 1859, p. 181.
Teleolepis, *Cope, Proc. Amer. Philos. Soc.* xi. 1869, p. 153.
Dirrhox, *Cope, Proc. Amer. Philos. Soc.* xxiv. 1887, p. 58.
Atomophis, *Cope, l. c.*

Maxillary teeth 12 to 15, subequal, anterior smallest, followed, after an interspace, by a pair of large grooved fangs situated just behind the vertical of the posterior border of the eye; mandibular teeth, anterior longest. Head distinct from neck, with more or less distinct canthus rostralis; eye moderate or rather large, with round pupil. Body cylindrical or slightly compressed; scales smooth or keeled, with apical pits, disposed more or less obliquely in 17 to 23 rows; ventrals rounded or obtusely angulate laterally. Tail rather long, subcaudals in two rows.

South America.

Synopsis of the Species.

I. Ventrals 157 or more.
   A. Scales strongly keeled, in 21 rows; ventrals 184–201; subcaudals 120–140 .... 1. *æstivus*, p. 128.
   B. Scales smooth or feebly keeled, in 17 or 19 rows.
      1. Ventrals distinctly angulate laterally, 206–228; subcaudals 106–131; scales in 19 rows.. 2. *viridissimus*, p. 129.
      2. Ventrals rounded or indistinctly angulate.
         a. Rostral not much broader than deep.
            α. Internasals not longer than broad, shorter than the præfrontals.

Scales in 19 rows; ventrals 175–198; subcaudals 94–126; green above.... 3. *olfersii*, p. 129.
Scales in 19 rows; ventrals 157–199; subcaudals 74–119; loreal not longer than deep .... 4. *schotti*, p. 130.
Scales in 17 rows; ventrals 168–187; subcaudals 101–104 .... 5. *bolivianus*, p. 132.
Scales in 19 rows; ventrals 184–204; subcaudals 82–96; loreal longer than deep .... 6 *psammophideus*, [p. 132.

β. Internasals longer than broad; scales in 19 rows; ventrals 202; subcaudals 93. 7. *vitellinus*, p. 133.

b. Rostral much broader than deep; scales in 19 rows; ventrals 184-215; subcaudals 97-125.
8. *elegans*, p. 133.

C. Scales smooth or feebly keeled, in 21 or 23 rows; ventrals 194-244.

a. Snout obtuse or obliquely truncate.

Subcaudals 114-124; loreal as long as deep; internasals shorter than the præfrontals.. .... 9. *nattereri*, p. 134.

Subcaudals 88-106; loreal longer than deep; internasals shorter than the præfrontals........... 10. *serra*, p. 134.

Subcaudals 135; loreal, if present, twice as long as deep; internasals as long as the præfrontals . ... 11. *burmeisteri*, p. 135.

b. Snout acutely pointed; subcaudals 132-135.
12. *baroni*, p. 136.

II. Ventrals 145; subcaudals 134 ... 13. *inornatus*, p. 136.

1. Philodryas æstivus.

Herpetodryas æstivus, part., *Schleg. Phys. Serp.* p. 186 (1837).
Dryophylax æstivus, *Dum & Bibr* vii p. 1111 (1854); *Jan, Icon. Gén* 49, pl. iii. fig (1879).
Philodryas æstivus, *Gunth. Cat.* p 125 (1858).
Dryophylax olfersii, part., *Burm. Reise La Plata*, ii. p. 529 (1861).
Philodryas carinatus, *Hensel, Arch. f. Nat.* 1868, p. 332.
Tropidodryas æstivus, *Cope, Proc. Amer. Philos. Soc.* xxii. 1885, p. 192.

Diameter of eye about half length of snout, latter rather pointed, prominent. Rostral nearly as deep as broad, well visible from above; internasals shorter than the præfrontals; frontal once and a half to once and two thirds as long as broad, as long as or a little longer than its distance from the end of the snout, shorter than the parietals; loreal longer than deep; one præocular, in contact with or narrowly separated from the frontal; two postoculars; temporals 1 + 2; eight upper labials, fourth and fifth entering the eye; five lower labials in contact with the anterior chin-shields, which are as long as or longer than the posterior. Scales keeled, with double pits, in 21 rows. Ventrals rounded, 184-201; anal divided; subcaudals 120-140. Uniform green above, yellowish beneath.

Total length 1050 millim.; tail 310.

Southern Brazil, Paraguay, Uruguay, Argentina.

a. ♀ (V. 201; C. 120).	Rio Grande do Sul.	Dr. H. v. Ihering [C.].
b. ♂ (V. 184; C. 121).	Paraguay.	Prof. Grant [P.].
c-e. ♂ (V. 184, 193; C. 126, 120) & ♀ (V. 188; C. ?).	Uruguay.	
f. ♂ (V. 192; C. 140).	Argentina.	Zoological Society.

2. Philodryas viridissimus.

Merrem, Beytr. i. p. 45, pl. xii (1790).
Coluber viridissimus, *Linn. S. N.* i. p. 388 (1766); *Daud. Rept.* vi. p. 302 (1803).
—— janthinus, *Daud t c* p. 273.
Herpetodryas viridissimus, *Schleg. Phys. Serp.* ii. p. 182, pl. vii. figs. 10 & 11 (1837).
Dryophylax viridissimus, *Dum. & Bibr.* vii. p. 1106 (1854).
Philodryas viridissimus, part, *Gunth. Cat* p. 123 (1858).
—— viridissimus, *Gunth. Ann. & Mag. N. H.* (3) ix. 1862, p. 127, pl ix fig 8.
? Philodryas crassifrons, *Cope, Proc. Ac. Philad* 1860, p. 559.

Eye half length of snout. Rostral much broader than deep, just visible from above; internasals as long as or a little shorter than the præfrontals; frontal once and one fourth to once and a half as long as broad, as long as or a little longer than its distance from the end of the snout, shorter than the parietals; loreal longer than deep; one præocular, not quite reaching the frontal; two post-oculars; temporals 1+2 or 1+3; eight upper labials, fourth and fifth entering the eye; five lower labials in contact with the anterior chin-shields, which are as long as or a little longer than the posterior. Scales smooth, with double apical pits, in 19 rows. Ventrals angulate laterally, 206–228; anal divided; subcaudals 106–131. Uniform green above, yellowish green beneath.

Total length 990 millim.; tail 280.

Guianas to Eastern Peru.

a–b, c. ♂ (V. 215, 223, 212, C. 128, 123, 114).	Berbice.	
d. ♀ (V. 218; C. 131).	Demerara.	
e. ♀ (V. 225; C. 126).	Cayenne.	H. C. Rothery, Esq. [P.].
f. ♂ (V. 206; C. 106).	Huallaga R.	

3. Philodryas olfersii.

Coluber olfersii, *Licht. Verz. Doubl* p. 104 (1823).
—— pileatus, *Wied, Beitr. Nat. Bras.* i. p. 344, and *Abbild.* (1825).
—— herbeus, *Wied, l. c.* p. 349
Herpetodryas olfersii, part, *Schleg. Phys. Serp.* ii. p. 183, pl. vii. figs. 14 & 15 (1837).
Dryophylax olfersii, *Dum. & Bibr.* vii. p. 1109 (1854); *Jan, Icon. Gén* 49, pl. iii. figs. 2–4 (1879).
Philodryas viridissimus, part, *Gunth. Cat.* p. 123 (1858)
—— olfersii, *Gunth. l. c.* p. 124; *Boettg. Zeitschr. f. Naturw.* lviii. 1885, p. 234.
Dryophylax olfersii, part., *Burm. Reise La Plata*, ii. p 529 (1861).
Philodryas reinhardti, *Gunth. Ann. & Mag. N. H.* (3) ix. 1862, p. 128, pl. ix. fig. 7.
—— latirostris, *Cope, Proc. Ac. Philad.* 1862, pp 73 & 348.
Dryophylax viridissimus, *Jan, Icon. Gén.* 49, pl. xi. fig. 1 (1879).

Eye about two thirds length of snout. Rostral a little broader than deep, just visible from above; internasals shorter than the præfrontals; frontal once and a half to once and three fourths as long as broad, as long as or a little longer than its distance from the end of the snout, as long as or a little shorter than the parietals; loreal as long as deep or longer than deep; one præocular (rarely divided), usually not reaching the frontal; two postoculars; temporals 1+1 or 1+2; eight upper labials, fourth and fifth entering the eye; four (rarely five) lower labials in contact with the anterior chinshields, which are as long as or a little longer than the posterior. Scales smooth, with single apical pits, in 19 rows. Ventrals rounded, 175–198; anal divided (rarely entire); subcaudals 94–126. Green above, yellowish beneath.

Total length 1160 millim.; tail 330.

Brazil, Paraguay, Uruguay, Eastern Peru, Argentina.

A. Upper surface of head, and a more or less distinct vertebral line pale brown or reddish; a black streak on each side of the head, behind the eye. (*C. olfersii*, Licht.; *C. pileatus*, Wied.)

a, b, c. ♂ (V. 190, 193; C. 115, 112) & ♀ (V. 191; C 104)	Brazil.	Lord Stuart [P.].
d. ♀ (V. 198, C. 101).	Brazil.	Mr. Clausen [C.].
e. ♀ (V. 190; C. 94).	Rio Janeiro.	G. Busk, Esq. [P.].
f. ♂ (V. 189, C. 126).	Rio Grande do Sul.	Dr. H. v. Ihering [C.].
g. ♀ (V. 189; C. 101).	S. America.	Haslar Collection.
h. Skull.	Brazil.	

B. Uniform green; a black streak on each side of the head, behind the eye. (*P. latirostris*, Cope.)

a. ♂ (V 189; C. 112).	Asuncion, Paraguay.	Dr J Bohls [C.].
b. ♀ (V. 193; C. 102).	Argentina.	

C. Uniform green; no postocular streak. (*P. reinhardti*, Gthr.)

a, b. ♀ (V. 194; C 106) & hgr. (V. 189, C. 109).	Bahia.	Dr. O. Wucherer [C.]. (Types of *P. reinhardti*.)
c. ♂ (V. 175; C. 114).	Bahia.	Haslar Collection.
d. ♀ (V. 191; C ?).	Pernambuco.	J. P G. Smith, Esq. [P.]
e Yg. (V. 181; C. 113).	Pernambuco.	W. A Forbes, Esq. [P.].
f-g. ♂ (V. 182; C. 108) & ♀ (V. 190; C. ?).	Moyobamba, N.E. Peru.	Mr. A. H. Roff [C.].
h. ♀ (V. 188; C. 104).	Asuncion, Paraguay.	Dr. J. Bohls [C.].
i. Yg. (V. 178; C. 118).	S. America.	H. A. Evans, Esq. [P.].
k. ♀ (V. 187; C. 103).	S. America.	

(Types of *P. reinhardti*.)

4. Philodryas schotti.

Xenodon schottii, *Schleg. Phys. Serp.* ii. p. 91, pl. iii. figs. 8 & 9 (1837).

Dryophylax schottii, *Dum. & Bibr.* vii. p. 1118 (1854); *Casteln. Anim. nouv. Amér. Sud, Rept.* p. 67 (1855); *Jan, Icon. Gén* 49, pl. i. fig. 2 (1879).

Callirhinus patagoniensis, *Girard, Proc. Ac. Philad.* 1857, p. 182, and *U.S Explor. Exped., Herp* p. 139, pl. xii. figs. 1-6 (1858).
Philodryas schottii, *Gunth. Cat.* p. 125 (1858); *Hensel, Arch. f. Nat.* 1868, p. 332, *Boettg. Zeitschr. f. Naturw* lviii. 1885, p. 235; *Bouleng. Ann. & Mag N. H.* (5) xviii. 1886, p. 434.
Euophrys modestus, *Gunth. l. c.* p. 139, *and Ann. & Mag. N. H.* (4) ix. 1872, p. 29.
Pseudophis schottii, *Cope, Proc. Ac. Philad.* 1862, p. 348.
—— patagoniensis, *Cope, l. c.*
Liophis poecilostictus, *Jan, Arch. Zool. Anat. Phys.* ii. 1863, p. 189, and *Icon Gén.* 13, pl. vi. fig. 2 (1865).
Dirrhox patagoniensis, *Cope, Proc. Amer. Philos. Soc.* xxiv. 1887, p. 58.

Eye about two thirds length of snout. Rostral nearly as deep as broad, well visible from above; internasals shorter than the præfrontals; frontal once and two thirds to twice as long as broad, as long as its distance from the end of the snout, as long as the parietals; loreal as long as deep or deeper than long, rarely a little longer than deep; one præocular, extending to the upper surface of the head but rarely reaching the frontal; two postoculars; temporals 1+1, 1+2, or 2+2; seven or eight upper labials, third and fourth or fourth and fifth entering the eye; four lower labials in contact with the anterior chin-shields, which are as long as or a little longer than the posterior. Scales smooth, with single apical pits, in 19 rows. Ventrals rounded, 157-199; anal divided; subcaudals 74-119. Yellowish or pale olive above, the scales usually edged with darker or lighter, with or without small black spots; two rather indistinct light lines may run along the back; sutures between the head-shields usually blackish; yellow or white beneath, with the shields black-edged on the sides.

Total length 1550 millim.; tail 350.

Brazil, Paraguay, Uruguay, Argentina, Northern Patagonia.

a. ♂ (V. 170; C ?).	Pernambuco	J. P. G. Smith, Esq. [P.].
b. Yg. (V. 164; C. 108).	Bahia.	Dr. O. Wucherer [C.].
c. ♂ (V. 181; C. 119).	Porto Real, Prov. Rio Janeiro.	M. Hardy du Dréneuf [C.].
d. Yg. (V. 193; C. 101).	S. José dos Campos, Prov. S. Paulo.	Mr. A. Thomson [P.].
e-g, h-i ♂ (V. 191, 188; C. 96,?), hgr. (V. 190; C. 96), & yg. (V. 199, 179, C. 101, ?).	S. Lorenzo, Rio Grande do Sul.	Dr. v. Ihering [C].
k. Hgr (V. 177; C. 108).	Rio Grande do Sul.	
l. ♀ (V. 185; C 95).	Asuncion, Paraguay.	Dr. Bohls [C.]
m. ♂ (V. 157; C. 80).	Paraguay.	Prof Grant [P.].
n-p, q-r. ♂ (V 165, 168; C. 101, 80), ♀ (V. 178; C. 94), & yg. (V. 174, 169; C. 88, 75).	Soriano, Uruguay.	R. Havers, Esq. [P.].
s. ♀ (V. 173; C 74).	Uruguay.	
t. ♂ (V. 180; C. 83).	Buenos Ayres.	G. Wilkes, Esq. [P.].

u. ♂ (V. 172; C. 83). Rio Negro, Patagonia. F. Coleman, Esq [P.].
v, w ♂ (V. 171; C. 93) ———? Haslar Collection.
& ♀ (V. 178; C. ?). (Types of *Luophrys modestus*)
x. Skeleton. Uruguay.
y, z. Skulls. Brazil.

5. Philodryas bolivianus. (Plate IX. fig. 1.)

Eye three fifths length of snout. Rostral a little broader than deep, visible from above; internasals shorter than the præfrontals; frontal once and two thirds to twice as long as broad, longer than its distance from the end of the snout, as long as or slightly shorter than the parietals; loreal as long as deep; one præocular, in contact with or narrowly separated from the frontal; one or two postoculars; temporals 1+2; eight upper labials, fourth and fifth entering the eye; five lower labials in contact with the anterior chin-shields, which are as long as the posterior. Scales smooth, with single apical pits, in 17 rows. Ventrals rounded, 168–187; anal divided; subcaudals 101–104. Olive above, with three darker, black-edged stripes; a black streak on the outer border of the parietal shields; lower parts greyish olive, throat white.

Total length 690 millim.; tail 200.

Bolivia.

a–b. ♂ (V. 187; C. 101) & Charobamba.
yg. (V. 168; C. 104).

6. Philodryas psammophideus.

Philodryas psammophideus, *Günth. Ann. & Mag N. H.* (4) ix. 1872, p. 23, pl. iv. fig. A.
Dirrhox lativittatus, *Cope, Proc. Amer. Philos Soc* xxiv. 1887, p. 58.

Eye about three fifths length of snout. Rostral nearly as deep as broad, well visible from above; internasals shorter than the præfrontals; frontal once and two thirds to twice as long as broad, longer than its distance from the end of the snout, as long as or slightly shorter than the parietals, loreal longer than deep; one præocular, extending to the upper surface of the head but usually not reaching the frontal; two postoculars; temporals 1+2 or 3; eight upper labials, fourth and fifth entering the eye; four or five lower labials in contact with the anterior chin-shields, which are as long as or a little shorter than the posterior. Scales smooth, with single apical pits, in 19 rows. Ventrals rounded, 184–204; anal divided; subcaudals 82–96. Yellowish brown or pale olive above, with a brown vertebral stripe three or five scales wide; this stripe edged with a black line or a series of small black spots; a dark lateral stripe, extending to the eye; a whitish lateral stripe on the outer ends of the ventrals and the lower half of the outer row of scales, edged below by a black line or series of dots; lips yellowish, with a few black spots; belly yellowish, uniform or dotted with blackish.

Total length 1080 millim.; tail 280.

Matto Grosso, Uruguay, Argentina.

a. ♀ (V. 195; C. 91). Tucuman. (Type)
b. ♂ (V 204; C ?) Catamarca. Lord Dormer [P.].
c–d. ♂ (V. 188; C.?) Cordova. E. W. White, Esq. [C.].
  & ♀ (V. 197; C. 03).
e ♂ (V. 191; C. 96). Argentina. E. W. White, Esq. [C.].
f ♀ (V. 193; C 95). Uruguay.

7. Philodryas vitellinus.

Dryophylax vitellinus, *Cope, Proc. Amer. Philos. Soc.* xvii. 1878, p. 33.

Rostral as deep as broad, just visible from above; internasals longer than broad; frontal long and narrow, longer than the parietals, loreal a little longer than deep: one præocular, nearly reaching the frontal; two postoculars; temporals 1+1; eight upper labials, fourth and fifth entering the eye; five lower labials in contact with the anterior chin-shields, which are a little shorter than the posterior. Scales smooth, with single apical pits, in 19 rows. Ventrals 202; anal divided; subcaudals 93. Yellow, strongly tinged with brown above, and with orange on the labial plates and lower surfaces.

Pacasmayo, Peru.

8. Philodryas elegans

Lygophis elegans, *Tschudi, Faun. Per , Herp.* p. 53, pl. vi. (1845); *Girard, U S Explor. Exped., Herp* p. 163 (1858).
Dryophylax freminvillei, *Dum. & Bibr.* vii p. 1115 (1854).
Dromicus rufodorsatus, part , *Gunth Cat.* p. 130 (1858).
——— elegans, *Jan, Elenco*, p. 67 (1863), and *Icon. Gén.* 25, pl. i. fig. 2 (1867).
Philodryas freminvilhi, *Jan, ll. cc* p. 83, *Icon* 49, pl. iv. fig 2 (1879).
Tachymenis canilatus, *Cope, Proc. Ac Philad.* 1868, p. 104.
Lygophis pœcilostomus, *Cope, Journ Ac. Philad* (2) viii. 1876, p 180.
Dryophylax elegans, *Cope, Proc. Amer. Philos. Soc.* xvii. 1878, p. 34.
Tachymenis elegans, *Boettg. Ber. Senck. Ges.* 1889, p 312.

Eye about half as long as the snout. Rostral much broader than deep, just visible from above; internasals as long as the præfrontals; frontal twice to twice and a half as long as broad, as long as or a little longer than its distance from the end of the snout, as long as or slightly shorter than the parietals; loreal longer than deep; one præocular (sometimes divided), extending to the upper surface of the head but not reaching the frontal; two (exceptionally three) postoculars; temporals 1+1, 1+2, or 2+2; eight upper labials, fourth and fifth entering the eye; five lower labials in contact with the anterior chin-shields, which are a little shorter than the posterior. Scales smooth, with single apical pits, in 19 rows. Ventrals rounded, 184–215; anal divided; subcaudals 97–125. Yellowish, greyish, or pale brown above, with darker, black-edged spots disposed in paired or single longitudinal series on the back; these spots may be accompanied or replaced by a dark vertebral stripe; a dark streak on each side of the head, passing through the eye, sometimes continued along the body; upper lip yellowish, usually with dark dots; lower parts yellowish, uniform or dotted or speckled with blackish.

Total length 1020 millim.; tail 300.

Ecuador, Peru, Northern Chili.

a–b. ♀ (V. 202, 203; C. 102, 97).	Tacna, Peru.	J. G. Fischer Collection.
c–e. Yg. (V. 209, 215, 207; C. 112, 123, 117).	Lima.	J. M. Cowper, Esq. [P.].
f. Hgr. (V. 213; C. 123).	Id. of San Lorenzo, Peru.	College of Surgeons.
g–i. ♂ (V. 208; C. 125) & ♀ (V. 200, 200; C. 112, 107).	Peru	T. Scott, Esq. [P.].
k–m. ♂ (V. 200; C. 109), ♀ (V. 201; C. 102), & yg. (V. 184; C. 108).	Peru.	
n. Yg. (V. 190; C. ?).	Chili.	
o. ♂ (V. 207, C. ?).	——?	Haslar Coll. (Types of *D. rufodorsatus*.)
p. ♀ (V. 210, C. 111).	——?	

9. Philodryas nattereri.*

Philodryas nattereri, *Steind. Sitzb. Ak. Wien*, lxii. 1870, p. 345, pl. vii figs. 1–3.

Eye two thirds the length of the snout. Rostral a little broader than deep, visible from above; internasals shorter than the præfrontals; frontal twice as long as broad, longer than its distance from the end of the snout and than the parietals; loreal as long as deep; one præocular, not reaching the frontal; two or three postoculars; temporals 2+2 or 3, eight upper labials, fourth and fifth entering the eye; five lower labials in contact with the anterior chin-shields, which are as long as the posterior. Scales in 21 rows. Ventrals 203–225; anal divided; subcaudals 114–124. Olive above; a yellow line on each side bordering the upper surface of the head; a yellow, black-edged streak along the upper lip; yellowish beneath, with a blackish line along each side of the belly; throat brown, with small yellowish spots.

Total length 895 millim.; tail 275.

Matto Grosso.

10. Philodryas serra.

Herpetodryas serra, *Schleg. Phys. Serp.* ii. p. 180, pl. vii. figs. 1 & 2 (1837).

Dryophylax serra, *Dum. & Bibr.* vii. p. 1113 (1854); *Jan, Icon. Gén.* 49, pl. iv. fig. 1 (1879).

Philodryas serra, *Gunth. Cat.* p. 125 (1858).

? Galeophis jani, *Berthold, Gotting. Nachr.* 1859, p. 181.

Teleolepis striaticeps, *Cope, Proc. Amer. Philos. Soc.* xi. 1869, p. 153.

Tropidodryas serra, *Cope, Proc. Amer. Philos. Soc.* xxii. 1885, p. 192.

---

* I have examined a male specimen (V. 203, C. 124), the type of *Philodryas molorchinus* (Berthold), Jan, Elenco, p. 84, preserved in the Göttingen Museum, and for the loan of which I am indebted to the kindness of Prof. Ehlers. A description of it has never been published, so far as I am aware.

Eye about half the length of the snout; latter truncate, with more or less concave lores. Rostral a little broader than deep, just visible from above; internasals shorter than the præfrontals; frontal once and a half to once and two thirds as long as broad, as long as or a little longer than its distance from the end of the snout, as long as or a little shorter than the parietals; loreal longer than deep; one præocular (rarely divided), twice as broad above as below, in contact with or narrowly separated from the frontal; three postoculars; temporals small, scale-like, 2 or 3+3 or 4; eight upper labials, fourth and fifth entering the eye, five lower labials in contact with the anterior chin-shields, which are as long as or a little longer than the posterior. Scales with double apical pits, in 21 rows, smooth or more or less distinctly keeled. Ventrals rounded, 194–244; anal entire or divided; subcaudals 88–106. End of tail, in the young, somewhat swollen, with the scales raised. Greyish or brown above, with large dark transverse angular spots or bars, which may be bordered with whitish on the sides; head with interrupted longitudinal dark streaks and a dark lateral streak passing through the eye; lips spotted with blackish; belly brownish or greyish, with darker or lighter spots; end of tail whitish in the young.

Total length 1010 millim.; tail 200.

Brazil.

a. Hgr. (V. 205; A. 2; C. 101).	Porto Real, Prov. Rio Janeiro.	M. Hardy du Dréneuf [C.]
b. Yg. (V. 194, A. 2; C. 104).	Theresopolis, Prov. Rio Janeiro.	Dr. E. A. Goldi [P.].
c-d. Yg. (V. 230, 233; A. 1, 2; C. 106, 103).	Bahia.	Dr. O. Wucherer [C.].
e. ♀ (V. 226; A. 1; C. 98).	Brazil.	Zoological Society.
f. ♀ (V. 213; A. 1; C. 88).	Brazil.	Liverpool Museum.

11. Philodryas burmeisteri.

Herpetodryas trilineatus, *Burmeister, Reise La Plata,* i. p. 309 (1861).—No proper description.

Dryophylax burmeisteri (*Jan*), *Burm. op. c.* ii. p. 529 (1861); *Jan, Elenco,* p. 84 (1863), *and Icon. Gén.* 49, pl. v. (1879).

Atomophis trilineatus, *Cope, Proc. Amer. Philos. Soc.* xxiv. 1887, p. 59.

Eye about half as long as the snout, which is prominent, obliquely truncate. Rostral as deep as broad, just visible from above; internasals as long as the præfrontals; frontal twice as long as broad, a little longer than its distance from the end of the snout, as long as the parietals; loreal twice as long as deep, usually fused with the præfrontal; one præocular, in contact with or narrowly separated from the frontal; two postoculars; temporals 1 or 2+2 or 3; eight upper labials, fourth and fifth entering the eye; four or five lower labials in contact with the anterior chin-shields, which are as long as or shorter than the posterior. Scales smooth, with partly single, partly double pits, in 23 rows. Ventrals obtusely angulate laterally, 211; anal entire; subcaudals 135. Young cream-colour above, with three dark brown stripes, the outer extending to the end of the snout, passing through the eyes; rostral and labials white; the stripes may disappear in the adult, lower parts whitish.

Total length (young) 410 millim.; tail 120.

Mendoza, Catamarca.

a. Yg. (V. 211; C. 135).   Catamarca.   Lord Dormer [P.].

12. Philodryas baroni.

Philodryas baroni, *Berg, An. Mus. Buen. Ayres*, iv. 1895, p. 189, fig.

Eye not one third the length of the snout, which is very prominent and acutely pointed. Rostral deeper than broad, confined to the lower surface of the snout, the upper surface being occupied by two or more small shields in front of the internasals; frontal once and two thirds to once and three fourths as long as broad, longer than the parietals; loreal thrice as long as deep; one præocular, in contact with or narrowly separated from the frontal; two postoculars; temporals 1+2 or 2+2; eight (exceptionally seven or nine) upper labials, fourth and fifth entering the eye; five lower labials in contact with the anterior chin-shields, which are shorter than the posterior. Scales smooth, with single pits, in 21 or 23 rows. Ventrals 224–231; anal entire; subcaudals 132–135. Green or reddish above, the scales and shields sometimes edged with black; a black line on each side of the head, passing through the eye; upper lip white; a black vertebral line may be present on the anterior half of the body; greenish white beneath, the shields sometimes edged with black.

Total length 1430 millim.; tail 410.

Argentina (Tucuman and Chaco).

13. Philodryas ? inornatus.

Dryophylax inornatus, *Dum. & Bibr.* vii. p. 1127 (1854).*

Rostral well visible from above; internasals a little smaller than the præfrontals; frontal much elongate; two loreals; one præ- and three postoculars; temporals 1+2; eight upper labials. Scales in 18 rows, dorsals keeled. Ventrals 145; anal entire; subcaudals 134. Head yellowish brown above, spotted with black on the sides; body greyish olive, finely speckled with black; a few black blotches on the neck.

Total length 935 millim.; tail 355.

Habitat unknown.

---

* The specimen, I am informed, is not to be found in the Paris Museum. On p 754 Duméril & Bibron identify the snake with Boie's *Xenodon inornatus*, which does not at all agree with their description

165. IALTRIS.

Philodryas, part., *Günth. Cat. Col. Sn.* p. 123 (1858).
Ialtris, *Cope, Proc. Ac. Philad.* 1862, p. 73.

Maxillary teeth 14, increasing in size, the last large and fang-like and followed, after a considerable interspace, by a pair of large grooved fangs situated just behind the posterior border of the eye; the five or six anterior mandibular teeth increasing in length and followed by a toothless space. Head distinct from neck, with distinct canthus rostralis; eye rather large, with round pupil. Body cylindrical; scales smooth, with apical pits, in 19 rows; ventrals rounded. Tail long; subcaudals in two rows.

Santo Domingo.

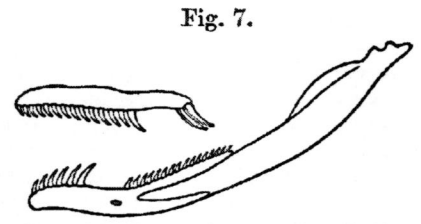

Fig. 7.

Maxillary and mandible of *Ialtris dorsalis*.

1. Ialtris dorsalis. (Plate VII. fig. 2.)

Philodryas dorsalis, *Günth. Cat.* p. 126 (1858).
Ialtris vultuosa, *Cope, Proc. Ac. Philad.* 1862, p. 73; *Garm. Proc. Amer. Philos. Soc.* xxiv. 1887, p. 284.
Dromicus mentalis, *Günth. Ann. & Mag. N. H.* (3) ix. 1862, p. 128, pl. ix. fig. 9.
Jaltris dorsalis, *Cope, Proc. Amer. Philos. Soc.* xviii. 1879, p. 273.

Rostral nearly twice as broad as deep, scarcely visible from above; internasals as long as broad, nearly as long as the præfrontals; frontal once and two thirds to twice as long as broad, longer than its distance from the end of the snout, shorter than the parietals; loreal a little longer than deep; one præocular, not reaching the frontal; two postoculars; temporals 1+2; seven upper labials, third and fourth entering the eye; four lower labials in contact with the anterior chin-shields, which are much shorter than the posterior. Scales in 19 rows. Ventrals 180–188; anal divided; subcaudals 102–110. Olive above, with large black blotches anteriorly which may be wholly or partially confluent, posteriorly with small irregular light spots; yellowish beneath, speckled with olive, with or without small blackish spots.

Total length 1090 millim.; tail 350.

Santo Domingo.

a. ♂ (V. 180; C. 102). S. Domingo. M. Sallé [C.]. (Type.)
b. ♂ (V. 181; C. 110). ——? (Type of *D. mentalis*.)

166. TRIMERORHINUS.

Coronella, part., *Schleg. Phys. Serp.* ii. p. 50 (1837).
Trimerorhinus, *Smith, Ill. Zool. S. Afr., Rept.* (1847).
Dipsas, part., *Dum. & Bibr. Erp. Gén.* vii. p. 1133 (1854).
Psammophylax, *Gunth. Cat. Col. Sn.* p. 31 (1858).
Psammophylax, part., *Jan, Arch. Zool. Anat. Phys.* ii. 1863, p. 309.

Maxillary teeth 10 to 12, subequal, followed, after an interspace, by a pair of enlarged grooved fangs, situated below the posterior border of the eye; anterior mandibular teeth strongly enlarged. Head distinct from neck; eye moderate, with round pupil; nostril crescentic, between two nasals and the internasal. Body cylindrical; scales smooth, with apical pits, in 17 rows; ventrals rounded. Tail moderate; subcaudals in two rows.

Africa south of the Equator; East Africa.

Synopsis of the Species.

Rostral at least as deep as broad; eye as
  long as its distance from the nostril.... 1. *rhombeatus*, p. 138.
Rostral as deep as broad; eye shorter than
  its distance from the nostril .... 2. *tritæniatus*, p. 139.
Rostral slightly broader than deep; eye
  shorter than its distance from the nostril. 3. *variabilis*, p. 140.

1. Trimerorhinus rhombeatus.

Seba, Thes ii pp. 17, 20, 84, pls. xv fig. 2, xix figs. 3 & 4, lxxix. fig. 2 (1735)
Coluber rhombeatus, *Linn. Mus. Ad Frid.* p. 27, pl. xxiv fig 2 (1754), *and S. N.* i. p. 380 (1766); *Daud. Rept.* vii. p. 119 (1803).
Coronella tigrina, *Laur. Syn. Rept.* p. 87 (1768).
Coluber tigrinus, *Gmel. S. N.* i. p. 1113 (1788).
Coronella rhombeata, *Boie, Isis,* 1827, p. 539; *Schleg. Phys. Serp.* ii. p. 70, pl. ii. figs. 14 & 15 (1837).
Cœlopeltis rhombeata, *Wagl. Icon. Amph.* pl. xxxii. (1833).
Trimerorhinus rhombeatus, *Smith, Ill. Zool. S. Afr., Rept.* pl. lvi. (1847).
Dipsas rhombeata, *Dum. & Bibr.* vii p. 1154 (1854).
Psammophylax rhombeatus, *Gunth. Cat.* p. 31 (1858); *Jan, Arch. Zool. Anat. Phys.* ii. 1863, p. 309; *Bocage, Herp. Angola,* p. 108 (1895).
—— ocellatus, *Bocage, Jorn. Sc. Lisb.* iv 1873, p. 221.
—— rhombeatus, var. trilineatus, *Boettg. Ber. Offenb. Ver. Nat.* 1883, p. 156.
—— rhombeatus, var. biseriata, *F. Müll. Verh. Nat. Ges. Basel,* x. 1892, p. 202.

Snout rather prominent, with obtusely angular canthus. Rostral very variable in shape, at least as deep as broad, frequently much deeper than broad, more or less deeply wedged in between the internasals, which it often entirely separates; frontal once and two thirds to twice as long as broad, as long as or longer than its distance from the end of the snout, usually longer than the parietals;

loreal as long as deep or a little longer than deep; one præocular, in contact with or narrowly separated from the frontal; two postoculars; temporals 1 or 2+2 or 3; eight (rarely seven or nine) upper labials, fourth and fifth entering the eye, four or five lower labials in contact with the anterior chin-shields, which are as long as or longer than the posterior. Scales in 17 rows. Ventrals 140–183; anal divided; subcaudals 62–79. Coloration very variable. Greyish, yellowish, or pale olive-brown above, with brown black-edged markings, which may form three or four longitudinal series of round or rhomboidal spots or be partially or entirely confluent into three undulous or straight longitudinal bands; a yellow vertebral line sometimes present; a dark band on each side of the head, passing through the eye, widening behind and often joining its fellow on the occiput, sometimes broken up into spots; upper lip yellowish white, uniform or with black spots; tail with three dark stripes; lower parts white, dotted or spotted with bluish grey or black.

Total length 850 millim., tail 170.

South Africa.

a–e. ♀ (V. 160, 149, 151; C. 71, 68, 71) & yg. (V. 152, 162; C. 70, 69).	Cape of Good Hope.	
f. Hgr. (V. 153; C. 77).	Cape of Good Hope.	Rev. G. H. R. Fisk [P.].
g–i. ♂ (V. 142; C. 70), ♀ (V. 148; C. 67), & yg. (V. 161; C. 72).	Simon's Bay.	H.M.S. 'Challenger'
k–l. ♂ (V. 162, 156, C. ?, 71).	Port Elizabeth.	Mr. J. L. Drege [P.].
m. ♀ (V. 171; C. 66).	Port Natal.	Rev. H. Callaway [P.].
n. Hgr. (V. 160; C. 66).	Johannesburg, Transvaal.	Rev. G. H. R. Fisk [P.].
o. ♀ (V. 177; C. 62).	Humbe, Angola.	Prof. Barboza du Bocage [P.].
p–v, w–α. ♂ (V. 157, 147; C. 69, 68), ♀ (V. 155, 159, 154, 170, 172, 176, 162, 153), & hgr.(V. 171, 151; C. 75, 69)	S. Africa.	
β, γ. Skulls.	S. Africa.	

2. **Trimerorhinus tritæniatus.**

Rhagerrhis tritæniata, *Gunth. Ann & Mag N. H.* (4) i. 1868, p. 423, pl. xix. fig. II; *Bocage, Herp. Angola,* p. 110, pl. x a. fig. 1 (1895).

Coronella tritænia, *Gunth. in Oates, Matabele Land,* p. 329, pl. C (1881).

Psammophylax tritæniatus, *Peters, Reise n. Mossamb.* iii. p. 119 (1882).

Agrees in structural characters with *T. rhombeatus* except in having a smaller eye, the diameter of which is less than its distance from the nostril. The rostral shield, which is as deep as broad, is wedged in between the nasals, but does not separate them behind; its upper portion measuring at least half its distance from the frontal. Ventrals 149-170; subcaudals 53-66. Greyish or pale brown above, with two or three dark brown, black-edged bands originating on the head and extending to the end of the tail, the outer passing through the eye, the vertebral sometimes rather indistinct or absent; a fine yellowish line sometimes divides the vertebral band; the sides below the bands white, with a pale brown or red streak running along the outer row of scales; upper lip and lower parts white.

Total length 740 millim.; tail 150.

Tropical Africa south of the Equator; East Africa.

a. ♂ (V. 160; C. 60).	S.E. Africa.		(Type.)
b. Yg. (V. 163; C. 58).	Waterberg District, Transvaal.		W. L. Distant, Esq. [P.].
c. ♂ (V. 152; C. 60).	Pietersburg, Transvaal.		C. H. Jones, Esq. [P.].
d. ♀ (V. 162; C. 58).	Matabeleland.		F. Oates, Esq. [P.]. (Type of *Coronella tritænia*.)
e-g. ♂ (V. 160; C. 65) & ♀ (V. 162, 153; C. 56, 53).	Halamabeeli, Kalahari Desert.		R. J. Cuninghame, Esq. [P.].
h-i. ♂ (V. 156, 149; C 61, 57)	Zomba, Brit. Central Africa.		Sir H. H. Johnston [P.].
k-l. ♀ (V. 162, 150; C 55, 54).	Chiradzulu, Brit. Central Africa.		Sir H. H. Johnston [P.].
m. Hgr. (V. 149; C. 55).	Fwambo, Brit. Central Africa.		A. Carson, Esq. [C.].
n-o. ♀ (V. 165, 166; C. 66, ?).	Mpwapwa, E. Central Africa.		
p. Hgr. (V. 170; C. 63).	Kibibi Basin, E. Africa.		Dr. J. W. Gregory [P.].
q. Skull of o.			

3. Trimerorhinus variabilis.

Psammophylax variabilis, *Gunth. Proc. Zool. Soc.* 1892, p. 557, pl. xxxv.

Agrees with *T. tritæniatus*, but rostral shield slightly broader than deep, its upper portion measuring about one third its distance from the frontal. Ventrals 157-169; subcaudals 52-60. Pale olive to blackish above, uniform or with three dark, black-edged longitudinal bands and a fine yellowish vertebral line; belly olive-to lead-grey.

Total length 770 millim.; tail 130.

Nyassaland.

a-d. ♂ (V 157; C. 55) & ♀ (V. 169, 162, 163; C. 57, ?, 60).	Shiré highlands		Sir H. H. Johnston [P.]. (Types.)
e. ♀ (V. 162; C. 52).	Zomba, Brit. Central Africa.		Sir H. H. Johnston, [P.].

167. CŒLOPELTIS.

Malpolon, part., *Fitzing. N. Class. Rept.* p. 29 (1826).
Psammophis, part., *Boie, Isis,* 1827, p. 521; *Schleg. Phys. Serp.* ii. p. 201 (1837).
Cœlopeltis, *Wagler, Syst. Amph.* p. 189 (1830); *Dum. & Bibr. Erp. Gén.* vii. p. 1129 (1854); *Günth. Cat. Col. Sn.* p. 138 (1858); *Jan, Elenco sist. Ofid.* p. 89 (1863); *Bouleng. Tr. Zool. Soc.* xiii. 1891, p. 151.
Rhabdodon, *Fleischm. Dalm. nov. Serp. Gen.* p. 26 (1831).
Bothriophis, *Eichw. Reise Kasp. M. u. Kauk.* i. p. 748 (1837).
Rhagerhis, *Peters, Mon. Berl. Ac.* 1862, p. 274.
Cœlopeltis, part., *Jan, Elenco sist. Ofid.* p. 89 (1863).

Maxillary teeth 10 to 17, subequal, followed by one or two very large grooved fangs situated below the posterior border of the eye; anterior mandibular teeth strongly enlarged. Head distinct from neck, with more or less prominent snout, angular canthus rostralis, and projecting supraocular; eye large, with round pupil; nostril a crescentic slit in a single or divided nasal; frontal narrow. Body cylindrical; scales smooth, more or less distinctly grooved longitudinally in the adult, with apical pits, in 17 or 19 rows; ventrals rounded. Tail moderate or rather long; subcaudals in two rows.

Southern Europe, South-western Asia, North Africa.

Fig. 8.

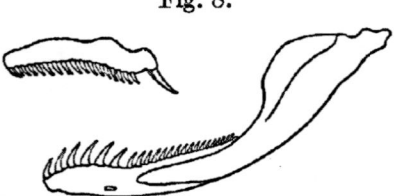

Maxillary and mandible of *Cœlopeltis monspessulana*.

1. Cœlopeltis monspessulana.

Coluber monspessulanus, *Hermann, Obs. Zool.* i. p. 283 (1804); *Dugès, Ann. Sc. Nat.* (2) iii. 1835, p. 137, pl. V b. figs. 1-6.
Natrix lacertina, *Wagl. in Spix, Serp. Bras.* p. 18, pl. v. (1824).
Malpolon lacertinus, *Fitzing. N. Class. Rept.* p. 59 (1826).
Coluber rupestris, *Risso, Hist. Nat. Eur. Mér.* iii. p. 91 (1826).
—— insignitus, *I. Geoffr. Descr. Egypte, Rept.* pp. 147, 151, pl. vii. fig. 6, *and Suppl.* pl. v. figs. 2 & 3 (1827).
—— æsculapii, *Dugès, Ann. Sc. Nat.* xii. 1827, p. 394, pl. xlvi. fig. 17.
Rhabdodon fuscus, *Fleischm. Dalm. nov. Serp. Gen.* p. 26, pl. ii. (1831).
Coluber fuscus, *Dwigubsky, Nat. Hist. Russ., Amph.* p. 26 (1832).
—— virens, *Dwigubsky, l. c.*
—— vermiculatus, *Ménétr. Cat. Rais.* p. 72 (1832).
—— flexuosus, *Fisch. de Waldh. Bull. Soc. Nat. Mosc.* iv. 1832, p. 574.

Cœlopeltis monspessulana, *Ranzani, Nov. Comm. Acad. Bonon.* ii. 1830, p. 229, pl. x.; *Bonap. Icon. Faun. Ital.* (1838); *Bedriaga, Bull. Soc. Nat. Mosc.* 1881, p. 311; *Boettg. Sitzb. Ak. Berl.* 1888, p. 177, *Camerano, Mon. Ofid. Ital., Colubr.* p. 5, pl. ii. figs. 12 & 13 (1891); *Bedriaga, Instituto,* xxxviii. 1890, p. 136.

Psammophis lacertinus, *Schleg. Phys. Serp.* ii. p. 203, pl. viii. figs. 1-3 (1837).

Bothriophis distinctus, *Eichw. Reise Kasp. M. u. Kauk.* i. p. 748 (1837).

Cœlopeltis lacertina, *Eichw. Faun. Casp.-Cauc.* p. 154 (1841), *Guichen. Explor. Sc. Alg., Rept.* p. 23 (1850); *Günth. Cat.* p. 138 (1858); *Strauch, Erp. Alg.* p. 67 (1862), *and Schl. Russ. R.* p. 179 (1873); *Schreib. Herp. Eur.* p. 221, fig. (1875); *Boettg. Zeitschr. f. Ges. Naturw.* xlix. 1877, p. 287, *Ber. Senck. Ges.* 1879-80, p. 162, *and Abh. Senck. Ges* xiii. 1883, p. 103; *Tristram, Faun. Palest.* pl xiv. (1884); *Bouleng. Tr. Zool. Soc.* xiii. 1891, p. 151; *Tomasini, Mitth Bosn. Herz.* ii. p. 630 (1894).

—— vermiculata, *Eichw. l. c.* p. 155, pl. xxix.

Coluber monspessulana, var. neumayeri, *Bonap. l. c.*

—— monspeliensis, *Gerv. Ann. Sc. Nat.* (3) x. 1848, p. 205.

Cœlopeltis insignitus, *Dum. & Bibr.* vii. p. 1130 (1854); *Jan, Icon. Gén.* 34, pl. i figs. 2 & 3 (1870); *Boettg. Abh. Senck Ges.* ix. 1874, p. 161, *De Betta, Faun. Ital., Rett. Anf.* p. 50 (1874).

Snout projecting, rounded, with angular raised canthus. Rostral as deep as broad, just visible from above; internasals much shorter than the præfrontals; frontal very narrow, twice to twice and a half as long as broad, longer than its distance from the end of the snout, as long as or a little longer than the parietals; two loreals; præocular large, forming a suture with the frontal, encroaching on the supraocular; two (rarely three) postoculars; temporals 2+3 or 4; eight (rarely nine) upper labials, fourth and fifth (or fifth and sixth) entering the eye; four or five lower labials in contact with the anterior chin-shields, which are as long as or shorter than the posterior. Scales longitudinally grooved, in 17 or 19 rows. Ventrals 160-189; anal divided, subcaudals 68-102. Olive, brown, yellowish, or reddish above, with or without dark, light-edged spots; sides often blackish, with whitish dots; head, in the young, with dark symmetrical markings; yellowish white beneath, uniform or spotted, clouded, or streaked with brown or olive.

Total length 1800 millim.; tail 350.

Borders of the Mediterranean (in the Italian Peninsula only in Liguria), eastwards to the Caucasus and Persia.

a, b. ♀ (Sc. 19: V 184; C. 91) & yg. (Sc. 19; V. 177; C. 87)	Valencia, Spain.	Lord Lilford [P.].
c-d. Hgr. (Sc. 19; V. 181; C. ?) & yg. (Sc. 19; V. 176; C. ?).	Nice.	Count Peracca [P.].
e. ♀ (Sc. 17; V. 163; C. 75)	Zara, Dalmatia.	Dr. F. Werner [E.].

f. ♀ (Sc. 19; V. 174; C. ?).	Tangier.	Mr. Fraser [C.].
g–h. Hgr. (Sc. 19; V. 171; C. 83) & yg. (Sc. 19; V. 175; C 90)	Tangier.	M. H. Vaucher [C.].
i, k. ♂ (Sc. 19; V. 180, C. ?) & hgr. (Sc. 19; V. 174; C 94)	Mogador.	Zoological Society.
l. Yg. (Sc. 19; V. 169; C. 93).	Algiers.	
m, n, o. ♂ (Sc. 19; V. 167; C. 87) & ♀ (Sc. 19; V. 174, 170; C. 90, 92)	Tunis.	Mr. Fraser [C.].
p. ♀ (Sc. 19; V. 169; C. 102).	Duirat, S. Tunisia.	Dr. J. Anderson [P].
q, r, s Hgr (Sc. 19; V. 169, 174, 170; C. 93, 83, 95).	Tripoli.	J. Ritchie, Esq. [P.].
t–u. ♂ (Sc. 19; V. 171; C. 95) & ♀ (Sc. 19; V. 170; C. 93).	Alexandria.	Dr. J. Anderson [P.].
v–γ. ♂ (Sc. 17, 19, V. 161, 165; C ?, 82), ♀ (Sc. 17; V. 164; C. 85), hgr. (Sc. 17; V. 164, 163, 160; C. 82, 80, 97), & yg. (Sc. 19, 17; V. 166, 161; C. ?, 84).	Cyprus.	Lord Lilford [P.]
δ. ♀ (Sc. 19; V. 173; C. 88).	Jerusalem.	Canon Tristram [C.].
ε, ζ. ♀ (Sc. 19; V. 177, 168; C. 89, ?).	Galilee.	Canon Tristram [C.].
η. ♀ (Sc. 19; V. 176; C. 83).	Mt. Carmel.	Canon Tristram [C.].
θ. ♂ (Sc. 17; V. 171; C. 84).	Shiraz, Persia.	
ι Skeleton.	Morocco.	
κ. Skull.	Montpellier.	
λ. Skull.	Algiers.	

2. Cœlopeltis moilensis.

Coluber moilensis, *Reuss, Mus. Senckenb.* i. p. 142, pl. vii. fig. 1 (1834).
Cœlopeltis producta, *Gerv. Mém. Ac. Montp.* iii. 1857, p. 512, pl. v. fig. 5; *Strauch, Erp. Alg* p. 68 (1862); *Jan, Icon. Gén.* 34, pl. ii. fig. 2 (1870), *Bouleng. Tr. Zool. Soc.* xiii. 1891, p 151; *Anders. Proc. Zool. Soc.* 1892, p. 20; *Werner, Verh zool.-bot. Ges. Wien,* xliv 1894, p 85.
Rhagerhis producta, *Peters, Mon. Berl. Ac.* 1862, p. 275, pl. —. fig 3, *Murray, Ann. & Mag. N. H.* (5) xiv. 1884, p 104.
Cœlopeltis moilensis, *Anders. Proc. Zool. Soc.* 1895, p. 656.

Snout projecting, obtusely pointed, with angular canthus. Rostral at least as deep as broad, wedged in between the internasals, its upper surface one half to two thirds as long as its distance from the frontal; internasals as long as or a little shorter than the præfrontals; frontal as broad as the supraocular, twice as long as broad, as long as or a little longer than its distance from the end of the snout, as long as or a little longer than the parietals; loreal as long as deep or deeper than long; one præocular (rarely divided), usually not reaching the frontal; two (rarely three) postoculars; temporals 2+2 or 3 (rarely 1+2); eight (rarely seven) upper labials, fourth and fifth (or third and fourth) entering the eye; four or five lower labials in contact with the anterior chin-shields, which are shorter than the posterior. Scales very indistinctly grooved, in 17 rows. Ventrals 159–176; anal divided; subcaudals 48–73. Pale buff or sandy grey above, with brown or blackish spots; one or two oblique brown or blackish bars on each side of the head behind the angle of the mouth; lower parts white, uniform or spotted with brick-red.

Total length 430 millim.; tail 190.

Northern Sahara, from Algeria to Egypt, Nubia, Arabia, Western Persia.

a.	♀ (V. 159; C. 48).	Duirat, S. Tunisia.	Dr J. Anderson [P.].
b.	Hgr. (V. 159; C 54).	Abu Roash, nr. Cairo.	Dr. J. Anderson [P.].
c.	♀ (V. 173; C. 55).	Dooroor, N. of Suakin.	Dr. J. Anderson [P.].
d.	♀ (V. 174; C. 54).	Suakin.	Dr. J. Anderson [P.].
e.	Hgr. (V. 176; C 59).	Nubia.	Prof. Peters [P.].
f.	♀ (V. 176; C. 53).	Aden.	Col. Yerbury [P.].
g.	♂ (V. 176; C. 73).	Hadramaut.	Dr. J. Anderson [P.].
h.	♀ (V. 172, C. 64).	Muscat.	A. S. G. Jayakar, Esq. [P.].
i.	♀ (V. 168; C. 52).	Bushire.	Mr. J. A. Murray [P.].

168. RHAMPHIOPHIS.

Rhamphiophis, *Peters, Mon. Berl. Ac.* 1854, p. 624, *and Reise n. Mossamb.* iii p. 123 (1882).
Dipsina, *Jan, Arch Zool. Anat. Phys.* ii. 1862, p. 1313.
Cœlopeltis, part., *Jan, Elenco sist. Ofid.* p. 89 (1863).

Maxillary short, with 6 to 9 teeth gradually increasing in length and followed, after an interspace, by a pair of very large grooved fangs situated below the eye; anterior mandibular teeth longest. Head distinct from neck, with projecting snout; rostral large, hollowed out beneath; eye moderate, with round pupil; nostril crescentic, in a divided or a semidivided nasal. Body cylindrical; scales smooth, with apical pits, in 17 or 19 rows; ventrals rounded. Tail moderate or long; subcaudals in two rows.

Tropical Africa.

Fig. 9.

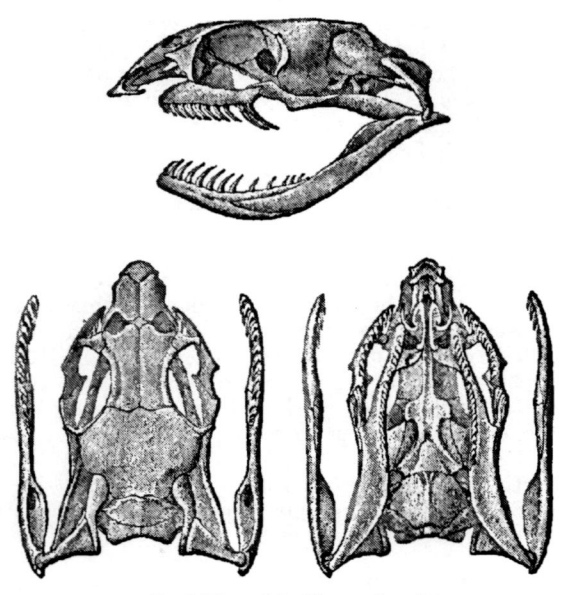

Skull of *Rhamphiophis oxyrhynchus.*

Synopsis of the Species.

I. Præocular not reaching the frontal.

Scales in 19 rows on the body; ventrals 230–241; subcaudals 154–160; upper portion of rostral measuring two thirds its distance from the frontal .... 1. *rubropunctatus*, [p. 146.

Scales in 17 rows on the body; ventrals 148–192; subcaudals 90–110; upper portion of rostral as long as or a little shorter than its distance from the frontal .... 2. *oxyrhynchus*, [p. 146.

Scales in 17 rows on the body; ventrals 171–182; subcaudals 66–88; upper portion of rostral half as long as its distance from the frontal .... 3. *togoensis*, p. 147.

II. Præocular forming a suture with the frontal; scales in 17 rows on the body.

Ventrals 172–185; subcaudals 59–63 .... 4. *acutus*, p. 148.
Ventrals 155–168; subcaudals 31–40 .... 5. *multimaculatus*, [p. 148.

1. Rhamphiophis rubropunctatus.

Dipsina rubropunctata, *Fischer, Jahrb. Hamb. Wiss. Anst.* i. 1884, p. 7, pl. i. fig. 3.
Rhagerrhis rubropunctatus, *Günth. Ann. & Mag. N. H.* (6) i. 1888, p. 327.

Snout rounded, with obtusely angular horizontal edge. Rostral broad above, measuring two thirds its distance from the frontal, narrowed and T-shaped beneath; internasals much broader than long, much shorter than the præfrontals; frontal twice as long as broad, slightly shorter than its distance from the end of the snout, longer than the parietals; loreal as long as deep; præocular single or divided, not reaching the frontal, its upper portion resting on the loreal; two postoculars; temporals 2 or 3+4; eight (rarely nine) upper labials, fourth and fifth (or fifth and sixth) entering the eye; four or five lower labials in contact with the anterior chin-shields, which are a little longer and much broader than the posterior. Scales in 19 rows (21 or 23 on the neck). Ventrals 230–241; anal divided; subcaudals 154–160. Brown or reddish brown above, uniform or dotted with red, head reddish, without dark markings; upper lip and lower parts yellowish.

Total length 1020 millim.; tail 340.

Kilimandjaro, E. Africa.

a. ♂, bad state (V. 230; C. 154). Kilimandjaro. Sir H. H. Johnston, [P.].

2. Rhamphiophis oxyrhynchus.

Psammophis oxyrhynchus, *Reinh. Vid. Selsk. Skrift.* x. 1843, p. 244, pl. i. figs. 10–12.
Rhamphiophis rostratus, *Peters, Mon. Berl. Ac.* 1854, p. 624, and *Reise n. Mossamb.* iii. p. 124, pl. xix. fig 1 (1882).
Cœlopeltis oxyrhynchus, *Jan, Elenco,* p. 89 (1863), and *Icon Gén.* 34, pl. i fig. 1 (1870), *F. Müll. Verh. Nat. Ges. Basel,* vi 1878, p 682.
Rhagerrhis unguiculata, *Günth. Ann. & Mag. N. H.* (4) i. 1868, p. 422, pl. xix. fig. G.
Cœlopeltis porrectus, *Jan, Icon. Gén.* 34, pl. ii. fig. 1.
Rhamphiophis oxyrhynchus, *Peters, Reise n. Mossamb.* iii. p. 126.
Rhagerrhis oxyrhynchus, *Günth. Ann. & Mag. N. H.* (6) i 1888, p. 327.

Snout obtusely pointed, with angular horizontal edge, somewhat hooked in profile. Upper portion of rostral as long as or a little shorter than its distance from the frontal; internasals broader than long, shorter than the præfrontals; frontal about twice as long as broad, nearly as long as its distance from the end of the snout, shorter than the parietals; loreal as long as deep; two or three præoculars, upper not reaching the frontal; two or three postoculars; temporals small, 2 or 3 + 3 or 4; eight (rarely seven) upper labials, fifth or fourth and fifth entering the eye; four or five lower labials in contact with the anterior chin-shields, which are as long as or shorter than the posterior. Scales in 17 rows (21 or 23 on the neck). Ventrals 148–192; anal divided; subcaudals 90–110. Yellowish or pale brown above, uniform or with small red or dark brown spots, or with dark brown margins to the scales; a blackish shade in front of and behind the eye; upper lip and lower parts yellowish white.

Total length 1380 millim.; tail 420.

Tropical Africa.

a–b. ♂ (V. 151, 148; C. 94, 100).	Lamu, E. Africa.	F. J. Jackson, Esq. [P.]
c. Yg. (V. 183; C. ?).	Taveta, E. Africa.	K. Anstruther, Esq. [P.]
d ♂ (V. 171; C. ?).	Taro Plains, E. Africa.	Dr. J. W. Gregory [P.]
e. Yg. (V. 177; C. 99).	Zanzibar.	Sir J. Kirk [C.]. (Type of *R. unguiculata*.)
f–g. ♂ (V. 178; C 108) & ♀ (V. 157; C 103).	Coast of Zanzibar.	
h. Yg. (V. 168, C. 103).	Coast of Zanzibar.	F. Finn, Esq. [P.].
i. Hgr. (V. 192, C. 110).	Mpwapwa, interior of East Africa.	
k. Hgr. (V. 170; C 90).	Fort Johnston, Brit. C. Africa.	Sir H. H. Johnston, [P.]
l Skull.	Mombasa.	
m. Skull.	Kavironda, E. Africa.	F. J. Jackson, Esq. [P.]

3. Rhamphiophis togoensis.

Psammophis acuta (*non Gunth.*), *Matschie, Zool. Jahrb.* v. 1890, p. 615.

—— togoensis, *Matschie, Mitth. Deutsch. Schutzgeb* vi. 1893, p. 212.

Snout obtusely pointed. Rostral nearly as deep as broad, its upper portion half as long as its distance from the frontal; internasals broader than long, a little shorter than the præfrontals; frontal twice as long as broad, longer than its distance from the end of the snout, as long as the parietals; loreal as long as deep; two præoculars, upper not reaching the frontal; two postoculars; temporals 1 or 2+3; eight upper labials, fourth and fifth entering the eye, five lower labials in contact with the anterior chin-shields, which are longer than the posterior. Scales in 17 rows (19 on the neck). Ventrals 171–182, anal divided; subcaudals 66–88. Olive-brown above, with a darker vertebral line, and a black lateral stripe extending to the end of the snout and passing through the eye; upper lip, sides below the black lateral stripe, and lower parts white, a black line along each side of the belly.

Total length 220 millim.

Togoland, West Africa.

a. Yg. (V. 182; C. ?)	Togoland.	Berlin Museum [E.].

4. Rhamphiophis acutus.

Psammophis acutus, *Günth. Ann. & Mag. N. H.* (6) i 1888, p. 327, pl. xix. fig. D.
Rhagerhis acuta, *Bocage, Herp Angola*, p. 111, pl. x *a* fig. 2 (1895).

Snout short, acutely pointed Rostral tetrahedral, its upper portion nearly as long as its distance from the frontal; internasals as long as broad, as long as the præfrontals; frontal nearly twice as long as broad, longer than its distance from the end of the snout, longer than the parietals; loreal a little deeper than long; one præocular, in contact with the frontal; two postoculars; temporals 2+3; eight upper labials, fourth and fifth entering the eye; four lower labials in contact with the anterior chin-shields, which are longer than the posterior. Scales in 17 rows (19 or 21 on the neck). Ventrals 172–185; anal divided; subcaudals 59–63. Pale brown above, with two dark brown, black-edged bands passing through the eyes and extending to the end of the tail; a third band is confined to the head and nape; lateral band edged with white below; upper lip and lower parts white.

Total length 925 millim.; tail 160.

Angola.

a. ♂ (V. 185; C. 59).   Pungo Andongo.   Dr. Welwitsch [P.]. (Type.)

5. Rhamphiophis multimaculatus

Coronella multimaculata, *Smith, Ill. Zool. S. Afr., Rept.* pl. lxi. (1847).
Dipsina multimaculata, *Jan, Arch. Zool. Anat Phys.* ii. 1862, p 1313, and *Icon. Gén.* 19, pl. ii. fig. 1 (1866); *Boettg. Ber. Senck. Ges.* 1886, p. 4
Rhagerrhis multimaculata, *Gunth. Ann. & Mag. N. H.* (3) xviii. 1866, p. 25.

Snout pointed. Rostral as deep as broad, its upper portion nearly half as long as its distance from the frontal; internasals a little longer than broad, nearly as long as the præfrontals; frontal twice as long as broad, as long as its distance from the end of the snout, as long as the parietals; loreal much longer than deep; one præocular (rarely divided), forming a suture with the frontal, two or three postoculars; temporals 2 + 3; eight (rarely nine) upper labials, fourth and fifth (or fifth and sixth) entering the eye; four or five lower labials in contact with the anterior chin-shields, which are as long as or a little longer than the posterior. Scales in 17 rows. Ventrals 155–168; anal divided; subcaudals 31–40. Pale buff or sandy grey above, with three or five series of regular brown spots, the vertebrals broader than long; a Λ-shaped brown marking on the occiput; an oblique brown streak behind the eye; lower parts white.

Total length 395 millim.; tail 45.

Damaraland and Namaqualand.

a–d. ♀ (V. 156, 160, 158, 155;   Damaraland.
      C. 31, 39, 40, 40).

169. DROMOPHIS.

Dryophylax, part., *Dum. & Bibr. Erp. Gén.* vii. p. 1103 (1854).
Psammophis, part., *Gunth. Cat. Col. Sn* p. 135 (1858).
Chrysopelea, part., *Gunth. l c.* p 145; *Jan, Elenco sist. Ofid.* p. 86 (1863).
Philodryas, part., *Jan, l. c.* p 83.
Dromophis, *Peters, Mon. Berl. Ac.* 1869, p. 447.

Maxillary teeth 10 or 11, unequal in size, middle longest, and gradually decreasing in size in front and behind, followed, after a short interspace, by a pair of large grooved fangs situated below the posterior border of the eye; anterior mandibular teeth longest. Head distinct from neck; eye moderate, with round pupil; frontal narrow. Body cylindrical; scales smooth, more or less oblique, with apical pits, in 15 or 17 rows; ventrals rounded. Tail long; subcaudals in two rows.

Tropical Africa.

Fig. 10.

Maxillary and mandible of *Dromophis lineatus*.

1. Dromophis lineatus.

Dryophylax lineatus, *Dum. & Bibr.* vii. p. 1124 (1854).
Psammophis sibilans, part., *Gunth. Cat.* p. 136 (1858).
Philodryas lineatus, *Jan, Elenco,* p. 83 (1863).
Dromophis lineatus, *Bouleng. Ann. & Mag. N. H.* (6) xvi. 1895, p. 33.

Snout once and a half to once and two thirds as long as the eye. Rostral as deep as broad, visible from above; nostril between two shields; internasals one third to one half as long as the præfrontals; frontal once and two thirds to twice as long as broad, not or but slightly narrower, in the middle, than the supraocular, as long as its distance from the end of the snout, as long as or a little shorter than the parietals; loreal once and a half to once and two thirds as long as deep; one præocular, not reaching the frontal; two (rarely three) postoculars, temporals 1+1 or 2; eight upper labials, fourth and fifth entering the eye; four (rarely five) lower labials in contact with the anterior chin-shields, which are as long as or a little shorter than the posterior. Scales in 17 rows. Ventrals 140–159; anal divided, subcaudals 78–105. Olive, most of the scales black-edged, with three greenish-yellow longitudinal lines, one on the vertebral row of the scales, the others on the fourth and fifth rows; outer row of scales greenish yellow, like the belly, its upper border black; young with light cross-bars on the occiput and nape; præ- and postoculars and upper lip greenish yellow; some of the labials with the sutures black; belly and tail below greenish yellow or pale green, uniform or with a series of black dots or short lines on the outer ends of the ventrals.

Total length 1090 millim.; tail 330.

Tropical Africa.

a–d. Hgr. (V 151; C.?) & yg. (V 141, 152, 146; C. 103, 105, ?).	Niger.	J. W. Crosse, Esq [P.].
e. ♂ (V. 146; C.?).	Liberia	Dr. Buttikofer [C.].
f. ♂ (V. 149; C. 78).	Coast of Zanzibar.	
g. ♀ (V. 149; C. 99).	Lado.	Dr. Emin Pasha [P.].
h. ♀ (V. 159; C.?).	Central Africa.	Lieut. Chippendale [P].
i, k. ♂ (V. 147; C. 101) & ♀ (V. 140, C. 98).	Africa.	Mr. Argent [C.].
l. Yg. (V. 146; C. 98).	Africa.	
m. Skull of h.		

2. Dromophis præornatus.

Dendrophis præornata, *Schleg Phys. Serp.* ii. p. 236 (1837).
Oxyrhopus præornatus, *Dum. & Bibr.* vii. p. 1039 (1854).
Chrysopelea præornata, *Günth. Cat.* p. 147 (1858), and *Ann. & Mag. N. H.* (3) xv. 1865, p. 95; *Jan, Icon. Gén.* 33, pl. ii. fig. 2 (1869).
Dromophis præornatus, *Peters, Mon. Berl. Ac.* 1869, p. 447; *Steind. Sitzb. Ak. Wien*, lxii. 1870, p. 353.

Snout once and a half to once and two thirds the diameter of the eye. Rostral a little broader than deep, visible from above; nostril between two shields; internasals rather more than half as long as the præfrontals; frontal twice to twice and a half as long as broad, nearly as broad as the supraocular, longer than its distance from the end of the snout, shorter than the parietals; loreal once and a half to once and two thirds as long as deep; one præocular, in contact with or narrowly separated from the eye; two postoculars; temporals 1+2; eight upper labials, fourth and fifth entering the eye; four or five lower labials in contact with the anterior chinshields, which are as long as the posterior. Scales in 15 rows. Ventrals 161–180; anal divided; subcaudals 110–122. Pale olive above, with black cross-bands anteriorly, black spots or a red vertebral stripe in the middle, and three black stripes posteriorly; the cross-bands most regular on the head; lower parts uniform white.

Total length 550 millim.; tail 175.

West Africa.

a. ♀ (V. 177; C. 110).	Niger.	W. A. Forbes, Esq. [P.].
b–c. ♀ (V. 161, C 111) & yg. (V. 180, C.?).	W. Africa.	Mr. Argent [C].
d. Yg. (V. 167; C.?).	W. Africa.	Mr. Dalton [C.].
e. ♂ (V. 177; C.?).	W. Africa.	

170. TAPHROMETOPON.

Taphrometopon, *Brandt, Bull. Ac. St. Pétersb* iii. 1838, p. 243; *Peters, Proc. Zool. Soc.* 1861, p. 48; *Strauch, Schl. Russ. R.* p. 186 (1873).
Chorisodon, *Dum. & Bibr Mém. Ac Sc.* xxiii. 1853, p. 494, *and Erp. Gén.* vii p. 901 (1854)
Psammophis, part., *Jan, Elenco sist. Ofid.* p. 90 (1863).

Maxillary teeth 14, very unequal in size, the middle ones much enlarged, but not separated from the rest; the solid teeth followed, after an interspace, by one or two very large grooved fangs; anterior mandibular teeth strongly enlarged. Head narrow, distinct from neck, with raised canthus and projecting supraocular; eye large, with round pupil; nostril crescentic, between two nasals; frontal narrow. Body cylindrical; scales smooth, some feebly grooved, with apical pits, in 17 rows; ventrals rounded. Tail long, subcaudals in two rows

Central Asia and Persia.

1. Taphrometopon lineolatum.

Coluber trabalis (*non Pall*), *Lichtenst. in Eversm. Reise*, p. 146 (1823).
—— (Taphrometopon) lineolatus, *Brandt, Bull. Ac. St. Pétersb.* iii. 1838, p. 243.
Chorisodon sibiricum, *Dum & Bibr* vii p 902 (1854).
Taphrometopon lineolatum, *Peters, Proc. Zool. Soc.* 1861, p 48, figs; *Strauch, Schl. Russ R* p 185, pl. v. (1873), *and Voy. Przewalski, Rept* p 51 (1876), *Blanf. Zool. E. Pers.* p. 422 (1876), *and 2nd Yark. Miss., Rept.* p. 23 (1878)
Psammophis doriæ, *Jan, in De Filippi, Viag. Pers.* p. 356 (1865).

Snout moderately prominent, grooved above and on the sides. Rostral broader than deep, just visible from above; internasals much shorter than the præfrontals, separated from the loreal by the nasal; frontal very narrow except in front, nearly twice as long as broad, as long as or a little longer than its distance from the end of the snout, as long as or a little shorter than the parietals; loreal about twice as long as deep; one præocular, forming a suture with the frontal; two or three postoculars; temporals 2+2 or 3; nine upper labials, fourth, fifth, and sixth entering the eye; five lower labials in contact with the anterior chin-shields, which are shorter than the posterior. Scales in 17 rows. Ventrals 175–197; anal divided; subcaudals 72–107. Yellowish or pale grey above, with longitudinal series of blackish dots or with four olive or brown, black-edged stripes, the median pair of stripes prolonged to between the eyes, the outer pair to the nostrils, passing through the eyes; a dark median streak from the interorbital region to the occiput; upper lip white, the anterior shields sometimes with a blackish spot;

lower parts white, dotted with greyish or olive, and with one or two dark lines on each side.

Total length 870 millim.; tail 190.

Aralo-Caspian Steppes, Turkestan, Afghanistan, Eastern Persia.

a. ♂ (V. 192, C. ?).	C. Asia.	Prof. Peters [P].
b–c. ♂ (V. 187; C. 101) & ♀ (V. 182; C. 86).	Syr Daria.	M. Serverzow [O.].
d. ♂ (V. 184; C. 94).	Daryalyk.	M. Serverzow [C.].
e–i. ♂ (V. 181; C 87), hgr. (V. 181, 178; C. 85, ?) & yg (V. 180, 188; C. 83, 90).	Chinas, Turkestan.	St. Petersburg Mus. [E.].
k–l. ♂ (V. 188; C. ?) & ♀ (V. 188, C. 99).	N. side of Humboldt Mts., E. Turkestan	St. G. Littledale, Esq. [P.].
m–p. ♂ (V. 194, 184; C. 98, 82) & ♀ (V. 175, 176; C. 72, 82)	Tirphul, Afghanistan.	Dr. J. Aitchison [C.]; Afghan Boundary Commission.
q. ♂ (V. 179; C. 82).	Helmand.	Dr. J. Aitchison [C.]; Afghan Boundary Commission

Skull of d.

171. PSAMMOPHIS.

Psammophis, part., *Boie, Isis,* 1827, p. 521; *Schleg Phys. Serp.* ii. p 201 (1837), *Dum. & Bibr Erp. Gén.* vii p 887 (1854); *Gunth. Cat. Col. Sn.* p. 135 (1858), *Jan, Elenco sist. Ofid.* p. 90 (1863).

Psammophis, *Wagler, Syst. Amph.* p. 189 (1830); *Gunth. Rept. Brit Ind.* p. 290 (1864); *Bouleng. Faun. Ind., Rept.* p. 365 (1890).

Phayrea, *Theob Cat. Rept. As Soc. Mus.* p. 51 (1868).

Amphiophis, *Bocage, Jorn. Sc. Lisb.* iv. 1872, p. 81.

Maxillary teeth 10 to 13, one or two in the middle much enlarged, fang-like, preceded and followed by an interspace, the last or last two large and grooved and situated below the posterior border of the eye: anterior mandibular teeth very strongly enlarged. Head distinct from neck, with angular canthus rostralis; eye moderate or large, with round pupil; frontal narrow. Body cylindrical; scales smooth, more or less oblique*, with apical pits, in 11 to 19 rows; ventrals rounded. Tail long; subcaudals in two rows.

Africa and Southern Asia.

The skull of this genus, as well as that of the two preceding genera, is remarkable for the wide vacuity between the frontal and sphenoid bones, a condition which approaches that of the Lacertilia. Quite in front, however, the frontals descend to join the sphenoid.

---

* Scarcely oblique in *P. crucifer* and *P. angolensis*

171. PSAMMOPHIS.

Fig. 11.

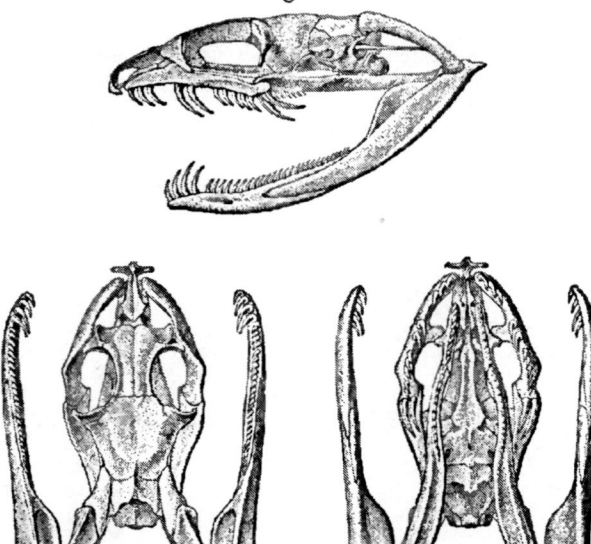

Skull of *Psammophis schokari.*

Synopsis of the Species.

I. Scales in 17 rows, exceptionally 19.
   A. Rostral a little broader than deep, well visible from above.
      1. Anal entire; eight upper labials, fourth and fifth entering the eye.

One præocular; five lower labials in contact with the anterior chin-shields; ventrals 170–185; subcaudals 92–97 .. 1. *leithii*, p. 155.

Two præoculars; four lower labials in contact with the anterior chin-shields; ventrals 157–171; subcaudals 81–104. 2. *notostictus*, p. 156.

      2. Anal divided.
         a. Five or six lower labials in contact with the anterior chin-shields; usually nine upper labials, fifth and sixth entering the eye; præocular in contact with the frontal; ventrals 162–197.

Sixth upper labial shorter than the eye, which is more than half the length of the snout; subcaudals 93–149 ...... 3. *schokari*, p. 157.

Sixth (exceptionally fifth) upper labial as long as the eye, which is more than half

the length of the snout; subcaudals
130-158 .... 4. *punctulatus*, p. 159.
Sixth upper labial as long as the eye,
which is half the length of the snout;
subcaudals 132 .... 5. *trigrammus*, p. 159.

    b. Four lower labials in contact with the anterior chin-shields, eight or nine upper labials; ventrals 151-168; subcaudals 100-108 ...... 6. *subtæniatus*, p. 160.

B. Rostral as deep as broad, well visible from above.

    1. Nine upper labials, three entering the eye; ventrals 161-173; subcaudals 109-127 .... 7. *bocagii*, p. 161.

    2. Eight upper labials, exceptionally seven or nine, two entering the eye.

        a. Frontal, in the middle, narrower than the supraocular; ventrals 155-198; subcaudals 90-116.

Præocular narrowly in contact with or
separated from the frontal, which is as
long as or longer than its distance from
the end of the snout............... 8. *sibilans*, p. 161.
Præocular extensively in contact with the
frontal; snout short, forehead strongly
grooved .... 9. *furcatus*, p. 164.
Præocular separated from the frontal, which
is considerably shorter than its distance
from the end of the snout .... 10. *longifrons*, p. 165.

        b. Frontal, in the middle, nearly as broad as the supraocular; præocular not reaching the frontal.

Snout nearly twice as long as the eye;
ventrals 156-182, subcaudals 75-90 .. 11. *condanarus*, p. 165.
Snout once and a half to once and two
thirds as long as the eye; ventrals 153-
163; subcaudals 64-95 .... 12. *brevirostris*, p. 166.

    C. Rostral a little broader than deep, scarcely visible from above; snout twice to twice and a half as long as the eye; nine upper labials, fifth and sixth entering the eye; ventrals 179-202, subcaudals 144-161 ...... 13. *elegans*, p. 167.

II. Scales in 15 rows.

Nine or ten upper labials (rarely eight);
ventrals 142-164; subcaudals 100-131. 14. *biseriatus*, p. 168.
Eight upper labials (rarely seven), ventrals
136-155; subcaudals 62-81 .... 15. *crucifer*, p. 169.

III. Scales in 13 rows; ventrals 144; subcaudals 108.
                                16. *pulcher*, p. 169.

IV. Scales in 11 rows; ventrals 141-155; subcaudals 57-81.
                                17. *angolensis*, p. 170.

171. PSAMMOPHIS.

TABLE SHOWING NUMBERS OF SCALES AND SHIELDS.

	Sc.	V.	A.	C.	Lab.	Ant Temp.	Præoc.
leithii	17	170-185	1	92-97	8	1	1
notostictus	17	157-171	1	81-104	8	2 (1)	2
schokari	17 (19)	162-195	2	93-149	9 (8-10)	2 (1)	1 (2)
punctulatus	17	177-190	2	130-158	9 (8)	2	1
trigrammus	17	182	2	132	9	1-2	2
subtæniatus	17	151-168	2	100-108	8-9	2	1
bocagii	17	161-173	2	109-127	9	1-2	1
sibilans	17	155-198	2	90-116	8 (9)	2 (3)	1 (2)
furcatus	17	158-179	2	95-114	8	2	1
longifrons	17	173	2	93	8	2	1
condanarus	17	156-182	2	75-90	8	1 (2)	1
brevirostris	17	153-163	2	64-95	8 (7)	2	1
elegans	17	179-202	2	144-161	9	2 (1)	1
biseriatus	15	142-164	1-2	100-131	9-10 (8)	2	1-2
crucifer	15	136-155	2	62-81	8 (7)	2	1
pulcher	13	144	2	108	8	1	2
angolensis	11	141-155	2	57-81	8	1	1

1. Psammophis leithii.

Psammophis leithii, *Gunth. Proc Zool. Soc.* 1869, p 505, pl. xxxix; Stoliczka, *Proc. As. Soc. Beng.* 1872, p. 83, Murray, *Zool. Sind*, p 382 (1884); Bouleng. *Proc. Zool Soc* 1895, p 538.
—— condanarus (non Merr.), Blanf *Journ. As. Soc Beng.* xlviii. 1879, p 126.
—— leithii, part., Bouleng. *Faun. Ind*, *Rept*. p. 365 (1890).

Snout once and a half to once and two thirds as long as the eye. Rostral broader than deep, visible from above; nostril between two or three shields; internasals about half the length of the præfrontals; frontal twice to twice and a half as long as broad, much narrower, in the middle, than the supraocular, longer than its distance from the end of the snout, nearly as long as the parietals; loreal about twice as long as deep; one præocular, in contact with the frontal; two postoculars; temporals 1+2; eight upper labials, third deeper than second and fourth, fourth and fifth entering the eye; five lower labials in contact with the anterior chin-shields, which are a little shorter than the posterior. Scales in 17 rows. Ventrals 170-185; anal entire, subcaudals 92-97. Yellowish above, with four longitudinal brown bands edged with black, the median pair extending to the supraoculars, the outer to the end of the snout, passing through the eye, a dark streak on the vertex; lower parts white.

Total length 730 millim.; tail 210.

Sind, Cutch, Rajputana, Scindia, Baluchistan.

a. ♂ (V. 177, C. 97).	Sind.	Dr. Leith [P.]. (Type)	
b. ♀ (V. 170; C. ?)	Ajmere.	W. T. Blanford, Esq. [P.].	

c. ♀ (V 179; C. 92). Gwalior. C. Maries, Esq. [E.].
d. ♀ (V. 185; C. 94). Munro Khalat, Baluchistan. R. H. C. Tufnell, Esq. [P.].

2. Psammophis notostictus.

Psammophis sibilans, part, *Gunth. Cat.* p. 136 (1858); *Mocquard, Bull. Soc. Philom.* (7) xi. 1887, p. 78.
—— moniliger, var notostictus, *Peters, Mon. Berl. Ac.* 1867, p 237.
—— sibilans, var. stenocephalus, *Bocage, Jorn. Sc. Lisb.* xi. 1887, p. 205, *and Herp. Angola*, p. 116 (1895).
—— notosticta, *Matschie, Mitth. deutsch Schutzgeb.* v. 1893, p. 212; *Bouleng. Proc. Zool Soc.* 1895, p. 538.
—— sibilans, var. notosticta, *Boettg. Ber. Senck. Ges.* 1894, p. 92.

Snout once and a half to once and two thirds as long as the eye. Rostral broader than deep, visible from above; nostril between two or three shields; internasals shorter than the præfrontals; frontal twice to twice and a half as long as broad, in the middle not more than half as broad as the supraocular, longer than its distance from the end of the snout, as long as or a little shorter than the parietals; loreal twice to twice and a half as long as deep; two præoculars, upper in contact with the frontal; two (rarely three) postoculars; temporals 2+2 or 3 (rarely 1+2); eight upper labials, third deeper than second and fourth, fourth and fifth entering the eye. four lower labials in contact with the anterior chin-shields, which are much shorter than the posterior. Scales in 17 rows. Ventrals 157–171; anal entire; subcaudals 81–104. Pale brown or olive above, with a pair of more or less distinct lighter stripes, and with or without small black spots; each vertebral scale often yellow in its posterior half; head with dark spots but no longitudinal streaks; upper labials and usually præ- and postoculars yellowish white; anterior labials often spotted with black; lower parts and whole or part of outer row of scales yellowish white, or olive with a lateral yellowish stripe; anterior ventrals often with small black spots.

Total length 785 millim.; tail 225.

South Africa, Angola, Lower Congo.

a. ♂ (V. 170, C 88). Cape of Good Hope. Lord Derby [P].
b. ♂ (V. 169; C. 85.) Lions Hill, Cape Town. Rev. G. H. R. Fisk [P.].
c. ♂ (V. 161; C. 87). Caffraria. J. P. M. Weale, Esq [P.].
d, e. ♂ (V. 165; C. 86) & yg. (V. 171, C. 88). Orange R. Dr. Kannemeyer[P.].
f-g. ♀ (V. 162, 157; C 83, 81). San Nicolao R., Little Fish Bay. J. J. Monteiro, Esq. [C.].
h. ♀ (V 168; C 91). S. Africa. Zoological Society.

3. Psammophis schokari.

Coluber schokari, *Forsk Descr. Anim.* p. 14 (1775).
—— lacrymans, *Reuss, Mus. Senck.* i. p. 139 (1834)
Psammophis moniliger, part., *Dum & Bibr.* vii p 891 (1854)
—— punctatus, *Dum & Bibr* t c. p 896; *Gerv. Mém. Ac Montp* iii. 1857, p 512, pl. v. fig. 3; *Strauch, Erp Alg.* p. 66 (1862); *Peters, Mon. Berl. Ac.* 1862, p. 274, pl. —. fig. 2.
—— sibilans, *Blyth, Journ. As. Soc. Beng* xxiv. 1855, p. 306.
—— sibilans, part., *Gunth Cat.* p. 136 (1858); *Strauch, l. c.*; *Schreib. Herp. Eur.* p. 217 (1875); *Bouleng Tr. Zool. Soc.* xiii. 1891, p. 150.
—— sibilans, var. hierosolimitana, *Jan, Elenco,* p. 90 (1863), *and Icon. Gén* 34, pl. iii. fig. 2 (1870).
—— sibilans, var. punctata, *Jan, Elenco,* p. 90; *Boettg. in Kobelt, Reis. Alg. Tun.* p. 462 (1885).
—— sindanus, *Stoliczka, Proc As Soc Beng.* 1872, p 83.
—— leithii (*non Gunth.*), *Blanf Zool E. Pers* p. 421 (1876).
—— moniliger, var. hierosolymitana, *Boettg Ber. Senck. Ges.* 1879-80, p. 163.
—— moniliger, var punctata, *Boettg. l. c* p. 164
—— leithii, part., *Bouleng, Faun. Ind , Rept.* p. 365 (1890).
—— lacrymans, *Bouleng. Proc. Zool. Soc.* 1895, p. 538; *Anders. Proc. Zool. Soc.* 1895, p. 655.

Snout once and a half to once and two thirds as long as the eye. Rostral broader than deep, visible from above; nostril between two or three shields; internasals much shorter than the præfrontals; frontal twice to twice and a half as long as broad, about half as broad, in the middle, as the supraocular, as long as or a little longer than its distance from the end of the snout, as long as the parietals; loreal three to four times as long as deep; one præocular (rarely divided), in contact with the frontal; two (rarely three) postoculars; temporals 2+2 or 3 (rarely 1+2); nine (rarely eight or ten) upper labials, third or fourth deepest, usually third, fourth, and fifth in contact with the præocular, fifth and sixth (rarely fourth and fifth or sixth and seventh) entering the eye, five or six lower labials in contact with the anterior chin-shields, which are shorter than the posterior. Scales in 17 (rarely 19) rows. Ventrals 162–195, anal divided; subcaudals 93–149. Yellowish, greyish, pale olive, or reddish above, uniform or spotted or striped with darker; a dark streak on each side of the head, passing through the eye; lips usually with dark dots or spots, belly usually with dark dots and with one or two interrupted dark lines on each side.

Total length 1210 millim.; tail 430.

Borders of the Sahara, Arabia, Syria, Persia, Baluchistan, Afghanistan, Sind.

A. Regularly striped, the stripes brown or olive with a fine black edge, series of vertebral scales yellowish.

a. ♀ (V. 183; C 119).   Biskra.   J. Brenchley, Esq. [P.].

b. ♂ (V. 179; C. 131).	Duirat, S. Tunisia.	Dr. J. Anderson [P.].
c. ♀ (V. 168; C. 149).	Aden.	Col. Yerbury [P.].
d. ♂ (V. 174; C. ?).	Muscat.	A. S. G. Jayakar, Esq [P.].
e–f. ♀ (V. 182, 183; C. 127, ?).	Jask, S Persia	S. Butcher, Esq. [P.].
g. Hgr. (V. 188; C. 122).	Candahar.	Col. Swinhoe [P.].

B. Stripes more indistinct, partially replaced by series of blackish spots.

a–b. ♂ (V. 173; C. 100) & ♀ (V. 169; C 93).	Suakin.	Col. Sir C. Holled Smith & Dr. J. Anderson [P]
c–d. ♀ (V. 164; C. 96) & hgr. (V. 174; C. 105).	Suakin.	Dr. J. Anderson [P.].
e. Hgr (V. 185; C. ?).	Helmand.	Dr. J. Aitchison [C.]; Afghan Boundary Commission.
f–g. ♂ (V. 194, C. ?) & yg. (V. 185; C. 126).	Between the Hamoon and Khusa, Afghanistan.	Dr. J. Aitchison [C.]; Afghan Boundary Commission.

C. No stripes, body uniform or dotted with blackish.

a–b ♂ (V. 185; C. 104) & ♀ (V. 185, C. ?).	Egypt.	M. Lefebvre [P.].
c. ♀ (V. 177; C. ?).	Abbassiyeh, near Cairo.	Dr. J. Anderson [P.].
d. Hgr. (V. 170, C. 113).	Gizeh.	Dr. J. Anderson [P.].
e. ♂ (Sc. 19; V. 188; C. 113).	Oasis of Karhgeh.	Dr. J. Anderson [P.].
f. Hgr. (V. 195; C. 111).	Assouan.	Dr. J. Anderson [P.].
g. ♀ (V. 173; C. ?).	Dooroor.	Dr. J. Anderson [P.].
h. ♀ (V. 176; C. 114).	Ras Gharib.	Dr. J. Anderson [P.].
i. Ad., bad state (V. 190; C. 121).	Chartoum.	Consul Petherick [P].
k. ♂ (V. 177; C. 119).	East of Suez Canal.	Dr. J. Anderson [P.].
l. Hgr. (V. 179; C. 103).	Moses Wells, Suez.	Dr. J. Anderson [P.].
m. ♂ (V. 168; C. 110).	Shaloof, near Suez.	Dr. J. Anderson [P.].
n. ♀ (Sc. 19; V. 192; C. 116)	Island of Shadwan, Gulf of Suez.	Dr. J. Anderson [P.].
o. ♂ (V. 178; C. ?).	Aden.	Col. Yerbury [P.].
p. Hgr. (V. 170; C. 141).	Hadramaut.	Dr. J. Anderson [P.].
q–r. ♀ (V. 185, 196; C. 129, 140).	Muscat.	A. S. G. Jayakar, Esq. [P.].
s–t. ♂ (V. 194, 185; C. 126, 110).	Karman, Persia.	W. T. Blanford, Esq. [C.].
u. Yg. (V. 186; C. 138).	Kurrachee.	Kurrachee Mus. [E.].
v. ♂ (V. 177; C. ?).	Sind.	F. Day, Esq. [P.].
w. Skull.	Egypt.	

4. Psammophis punctulatus.

Psammophis punctulatus, *Dum. & Bibr.* vii. p. 897 (1854); *Peters, Reise n. Mossamb.* iii. p 123 (1882); *Boettg Zool Anz.* 1893, p. 119; *Bouleng. Ann. Mus. Genova*, (2) xv. 1895, p. 14, pl. iv. fig. 1, *and Proc. Zool. Soc.* 1895, p. 537.

Dendrophis furcatus, *Bianconi, Spec Zool. Mosamb.* p. 276, pl. xiii. (1859)

Psammophis punctulatus, var. trivirgatus, *Peters, Mon. Berl. Ac.* 1878, p. 206.

Snout once and a half to once and two thirds as long as the eye. Rostral a little broader than deep, visible from above; nostril between two or three shields, internasals nearly half as long as the præfrontals, frontal nearly twice as long as broad, much narrower, in the middle, than the supraocular, as long as or a little longer than its distance from the end of the snout, as long as or slightly shorter than the parietals; loreal nearly twice to twice and a half as long as deep; one præocular, in contact with the frontal and with the third, fourth, and fifth upper labials; two postoculars; temporals 2+2 or 2+3; nine (exceptionally eight) upper labials, third deepest, fifth and sixth (or fourth and fifth) entering the eye, sixth (or fifth) largest, as long as the eye; five lower labials in contact with the anterior chin-shields, which are shorter than the posterior. Scales in 17 rows. Ventrals 177–190; anal divided; subcaudals 130–158. Yellow or brownish white above, greenish or greyish on the sides and beneath, head and nape olive-grey or reddish, speckled with black, three black stripes along the body, the median broadest and bifurcating on the neck, its branches extending, as brown streaks, to the end of the snout after passing through the eyes; the stripes on the body may be reduced to the vertebral.

Total length 1660 millim; tail 580.

Arabia; East Africa, from Somaliland to Mozambique.

a. ♂ (V. 185; C. 146)	Ogaden, Somaliland.	Capt. Bottego [C]; Marquis G. Doria [P.].
b. ♀ (V. 184; C 136).	Lake Rudolf.	Dr Donaldson Smith [C.].

5. Psammophis trigrammus.

Psammophis trigrammus, *Gunth. Ann. & Mag. N. H.* (3) xv. 1865, p. 95, pl. ii. fig. E, *Bouleng. Proc Zool. Soc.* 1895, p. 538.

Snout twice as long as the diameter of the eye. Rostral broader than deep, visible from above; nostril between three shields; internasals about half as long as the præfrontals; frontal twice as long as broad, half as broad, in the middle, as the supraocular, as long as its distance from the end of the snout, a little shorter than the parietals; loreal thrice as long as deep; two præoculars, upper not quite reaching the frontal; two postoculars; temporals 1+1 or 2+1; nine upper labials, third deeper than second and fourth, third, fourth, and fifth in contact with the præocular, fifth and sixth entering the eye; five lower labials in contact with the anterior chin-shields, which are much shorter than the posterior. Scales in 17 rows. Ventrals 182; anal divided; subcaudals 132. Pale olive above, yellowish posteriorly, the scales on the vertebral line black-edged, forming a stripe posteriorly; a rather indistinct dark lateral stripe, running along the outer row of scales; upper lip, præ- and postoculars yellowish white; lower parts and lower half of outer row of scales yellowish white, the ventrals clouded with olive in the middle.

Total length 1180 millim; tail 430.

Namaqualand.

a. ♂ (V. 182, C. 132).	R. San Nicolao, Little Fish Bay.	J. J. Monteiro, Esq. [P.]. (Type.)

6. Psammophis subtæniatus.

Psammophis sibilans, var. subtæniata, *Peters, Reise n. Mossamb* iii. p. 121 (1882); *Fischer, Jahrb. Hamb. Wiss. Anst.* i. 1884, p. 12
—— subtæniatus, *Bouleng. Proc. Zool. Soc.* 1895, p. 538.

Snout once and a half to once and two thirds as long as the eye. Rostral a little broader than deep, visible from above; nostril between two shields; internasals about half as long as the præfrontals; frontal narrower, in the middle, than the supraocular, a little longer than its distance from the end of the snout, as long as or a little shorter than the parietals; loreal twice and a half to thrice as long as deep; one præocular, in contact with or narrowly separated from the frontal; two postoculars, temporals 2+2 or 3; eight or nine upper labials, third deeper than second and fourth, fourth and fifth, fifth and sixth, or fourth, fifth, and sixth entering the eye; four lower labials in contact with the anterior chin-shields, which are as long as or shorter than the posterior. Scales in 17 rows. Ventrals 151-168; anal divided; subcaudals 100-108. Brown or olive above, the seven middle rows of scales usually darker and black-edged and separated from the sides by a more or less distinct pale streak; usually a black lateral streak, running along the outer row of scales; upper labials yellowish, with black dots and a black line along their upper border which is continued across the rostral; yellowish below, with a black line along each side of the belly.

Total length 1030 millim.; tail 350.

East Africa, from Zanzibar to Mozambique.

a. Hgr. (V. 151; C. 104).	Zanzibar.	Sir J. Kirk [C.].
b. ♀ (V 161; C. 103).	Zanzibar.	Dr. J. G. Fischer.
c-d. ♀ (V. 163; C. 108) & yg. (V. 164; C. 105).	Cape McLear, Lake Nyassa.	Mr. F. A. Simons [C.].
e. ♀ (V. 162; C. ?).	Lake Nyassa.	Miss S. C McLaughlin [P.].
f-g. ♂ (V. 156, 165; C. 103, ?).	Lake Nyassa.	Universities Mission.
h, i. ♂ (V. 169; C. ?) & ♀ (V. 167; C. 104).	Zomba, Nyassaland.	Sir H. H. Johnston, [P.].

k. Yg. (V. 158; C 100).	E. Central Africa.	Dr. Livingstone [C.]; Lord Russell [P.].
l. ♀ (V. 168; C. ?).	Zambesi Expedition.	Sir J. Kirk [C.].

7. Psammophis bocagii. (Plate VIII. fig. 1.)

Psammophis sibilans, var. A, *Bocage, Herp Angola*, p. 115 (1895)
—— bocagii, *Bouleng. Proc. Zool. Soc.* 1895, p. 538.

Snout nearly twice as long as the eye. Rostral as deep as broad, visible from above; nostril between two shields; internasals half as long as the præfrontals; frontal rather more than twice as long as broad, much narrower in the middle than the supraocular, longer than its distance from the end of the snout, as long as the parietals, loreal twice as long as deep; one præocular, not quite reaching the frontal; two postoculars; temporals 1+2, 2+2, or 2+3; nine upper labials, third deeper than second and fourth, fourth, fifth, and sixth entering the eye; four or five lower labials in contact with the anterior chin-shields, which are shorter than the posterior. Scales in 17 rows. Ventrals 161–173; anal divided; subcaudals 109–127. A broad reddish-brown, black-edged vertebral band, seven scales broad, separated from the sides, which are grey or reddish brown, by a yellow streak; a black line along the middle of the outer row of scales; head with rather indistinct yellow, black-edged cross-bars; a black line along the upper border of the labials, which are dotted with black; lower half of outer row of scales and lower parts pale yellow, with a black line on each side.

Total length 820 millim.; tail 295.

Angola.

a. ♂ (V. 166; C. 112).	Benguella.	Prof. B. du Bocage [P.].

8. Psammophis sibilans.

Seba, Thes ii. pl. lvi. fig. 4 (1735); *Linn Amœn. Acad.* i. p. 302 (1749); *Lacép. Serp.* ii p. 246, pl. xii fig. 1 (1879).
Coluber sibilans, part., *Linn S. N.* i. p. 383 (1766).
—— momliger, *Daud. Rept.* vii p. 69 (1803).
—— auritus, *I. Geoffr Descr. Egypte, Rept.* pp. 147, 151, pl. viii. fig 4 (1827), and *Suppl* pl. iv fig. 5 (1829).
Psammophis sibilans, *Boie, Isis,* 1827, p. 547; *Jan, Icon. Gén.* pl. iii. fig. 3 (1870); *Boettg Abh. Senck. Ges.* xii. 1881, p. 395, and *Ber. Senck. Ges.* 1887-88, p. 53; *Boulenger, Proc. Zool. Soc.* 1895, p. 538.
Coluber phillipsii, *Hallow. Proc. Ac. Philad.* 1844, p. 169.
Psammophis momliger, part., *Schleg Phys. Serp* ii. p. 207, pl viii. figs. 4 & 5 (1837), *Dum. & Bibr.* vii. p 891 (1854).
—— phillipsii, *Hallow. Proc. Ac Philad.* 1854, p. 100, and 1857, p 69; *Cope, Proc. Ac. Philad.* 1860, p. 554, *F. Mull. Verh. Nat. Ges. Basel,* vii. 1885, p. 686.
—— irregularis, *Fischer, Abh. Nat. Ver. Hamb.* iii. 1856, p. 92, pl ii. fig. 4; *Gunth Cat.* p. 137 (1858), *A. Dum. Arch. Mus.* x. 1859, p 208, pl. xvii. fig. 9; *Jan, l c.* pl. iv. figs. 1 & 2.

Psammophis sibilans, part., *Gunth. Cat.* p 136; *Schreib. Herp. Eur.* p. 217 (1875).

—— moniliger, var. bilineatus, *Peters, Mon Berl. Ac.* 1867, p. 237.

—— sibilans, var. mossambica, *Peters, Reise n. Mossamb.* iii. p. 122 (1882).

—— sibilans, var intermedius, *Fischer, Jahrb. Hamb Wiss Anst.* i. 1884, p. 14.

—— sibilans, var. leopardina, *Bocage, Jorn Sc. Lisb.* xi. 1887, p. 205.

—— irregularis, *Matschie, Mitth. deutsch. Schutzgeb.* vi. 1893, p. 212.

—— sibilans, var. C, *Bocage, Herp. Angola*, p 116 (1895).

Snout once and a half to twice as long as the eye. Rostral as deep as broad; nostril between two or three shields; internasals about half as long as the præfrontals; frontal once and three fourths to twice and one third as long as broad, narrower, in the middle, than the supraocular, as long as or longer than its distance from the end of the snout, as long as or a little longer than the parietals, loreal once and two thirds to twice and a half as long as deep; one præocular (rarely divided), in contact with or narrowly separated from the frontal; two (rarely three) postoculars; temporals 2+2 or 3 (rarely 3+3); eight (rarely nine) upper labials, fourth and fifth (or fifth and sixth) entering the eye; four or five lower labials in contact with the anterior chin-shields, which are as long as or shorter than the posterior. Scales in 17 rows. Ventrals 155-198; anal divided; subcaudals 90-116. Coloration very variable.

Total length 1210 millim.; tail 380.

Tropical Africa and Egypt.

A. Olive or brown above, the scales mostly black-edged; a more or less distinct, narrow yellow vertebral line and a broader yellow streak along each side of the back; head with yellow, black-edged longitudinal streaks in front, and transverse ones behind, which markings, however, may become very indistinct in the adult; upper lip yellowish white, uniform or with a few brown or black dots on the anterior shields; lower parts, including lower half of outer row of scales, yellowish white, uniform or with a faint brown lateral line.

a ♂ (V. 165; C. 103).	Beltim, between Rosetta and Damietta.	Dr. J. Anderson [P.].
b. ♂ (V. 166; C. ?).	Abassiyeh, near Cairo.	Dr. J. Anderson [P.].
c–d. ♂ (V. 164; C. 108) & ♀ (V. 158; C. ?).	Abu Roash, Gizeh.	Dr. J. Anderson [P.].
e–f. ♂ (V. 167, C. 109) & ♀ (V. 166; C. 109).	Fayoum.	Dr. J. Anderson [P.].
g. ♀ (V. 169; C. 114).	Minia.	Dr. J. Anderson [P.].
h. Hgr. (V. 170; C. ?).	Anseba Valley, Abyssinia.	W. T. Blanford, Esq. [P.]

B. As in A, but no trace of a light vertebral line.

a–b. ♂ (V. 167, 167; C. 116, ?). Minia. Dr. J. Anderson [P.]

C. Uniform brown or greyish olive above, the markings on the head very indistinct; upper lip and lower parts, including lower third of outer row of scales, uniform yellowish white.

a. ♀ (V. 168; C. ?). Egypt. J. Burton, Esq. [P.].
b. Hgr. ♂ (V. 168; C. 109). Mekalla el Kobra. Dr. J. Anderson [P.].
c. ♂ (V. 159; C 103). Fayoum. Dr. J. Anderson [P.].
d. ♀ (V. 172; C. 114). Luxor. Dr. J. Anderson [P.].

D. Brown or olive above, with lateral streaks and head-markings as in A; vertebral line absent or reduced to a series of yellow dots, one on each scale; upper lip with brown or black dots; lower parts, including lower half of outer row of scales, white, with a continuous or interrupted black longitudinal line on each side of the belly.

a. ♀ (V. 165; C. ?). Mekalla el Kobra. Dr. J. Anderson [P.].
b. Hgr. (V. 180; C. ?). Wadelai. Dr. Emin Pasha [P.].
c Hgr. (V 167; C. 102). Mt. Elgon, 6000–7000 ft. F. J. Jackson, Esq. [P.].
d. Yg. (V. 159, C. 110). Kilimandjaro. F. J Jackson, Esq. [P.]
e–f ♂ (V. 157; C 106) & ♀ (V 159; C. 102). Mouths of Niger. Alvan Millson, Esq [P.].
g. Yg (V 157; C. 105) Lagos Sir A Moloney [P.].
h. ♀ (V 172, C. ?). Gambia. Lord Derby [P].
i. Yg. (V. 164; C 106). W Africa Mr. Rich [C.].
k. Yg. (V. 161; C. 97). W. Africa. Mr. Raddon [C.].
l. Hgr. (V. 166; C. 97). ——?

E. Uniform brown or olive above, with more or less distinct traces of the markings on the head; upper lip yellowish, with brown or blackish dots; lower parts, including lower third or lower half of outer row of scales, yellowish, with a brown or black line on each side of the belly.

a Hgr. (V. 155; C. ?). Inland of Berbera, Somaliland. E Lort Phillips, Esq. [P.].
b. ♀ (V. 163; C. ?). Kilifi, E Africa. G. D. Trevor-Roper, Esq. [P.].
c. Hgr. (V. 170; C ?). Bolama, Senegambia. R. Kitching, Esq. [P.].

F. Olive above, which colour extends down to the ends of the ventrals, uniform or dotted with blackish, or with most of the scales black-edged; sometimes, in the young, with traces of light longitudinal stripes and of the head-markings; upper lip yellowish, spotted or speckled with black; belly yellowish or pale olive, uniform or dotted with black on the sides, the dots sometimes confluent into longitudinal lines.

a–b. Yg. (V. 169, 173; C. 97, 93). Wadelai. Dr. Emin Pasha [P.].

c. ♂ (V. 164, C. ?).	Ndi, Teita Mts., E. Africa.	Dr. J. W. Gregory [P.]
d. Hgr. (V. 158; C. 93).	W. of Mombasa.	Dr. J. W. Gregory [P.]
e-f. Yg. (V. 162, 169, C. ?, 101).	Kilimandjaro.	F. J. Jackson, Esq. [P.]
g-h. Hgr. (V. 160; C. 90) & yg (V. 161; C. 90).	Zanzibar.	Sir J. Kirk [C.].
i-k. ♂ (V. 198; C. 104) & ♀ (V. 160, C. 96).	Zanzibar.	Dr. J. G. Fischer.
l, m. Hgr. (V. 169, 170; C. ?, 94).	Zomba, Nyassaland.	Sir H. H. Johnston [P.].
n. Ad., head & neck.	Zambesi.	Sir J. Kirk [C.].
o. Hgr., skin, bad state.	Ungora, Upper Nile.	Capt. Speke [C.].
p-q. Hgr. (V. 176, 170; C. 100, 107) & yg. (V. 181; C. 116).	Asaba, 180 miles up the Niger.	J. W. Crosse, Esq. [P.].
r. ♀ (V. 171; C. ?).	Sierra Leone.	H. C. Hart, Esq. [P.].
s. Hgr. (V. 166, C. ?).	Cette Cama, Gaboon.	
t-u. Yg. (V. 168, 169; C. 100, ?)	Ambriz, Angola.	Mr. Rich [C.].
v. Yg. (V. 170; C. ?).	W. Africa.	Mr. Rich [C.].
w. ♀ (V. 172; C. ?).	W. Africa.	Mr. Fraser [C.].
x. ♂ (V. 179; C. 110).	W. Africa.	Mr. Dalton [C.].
y. Skull.	Asaba, Niger.	J. W. Crosse, Esq. [P.].
α. Skull.	Egypt.	

9. Psammophis furcatus.

Psammophis moniliger, var. furcatus, *Peters, Mon. Berl. Ac.* 1867, p. 236.
—— sibilans, *Boettg. Ber. Senck. Ges.* 1886, p. 5.
—— sibilans, var. furcata, *Boettg. Ber. Senck. Ges.* 1894, p. 92.
—— furcatus, *Bouleng. Proc. Zool. Soc.* 1895, p. 538.

Snout once and a half as long as the eye; forehead strongly grooved. Rostral as deep as broad, visible from above; nostril between two shields; internasals half as long as the præfrontals; frontal nearly twice as long as broad, much narrower, in the middle, than the supraocular, longer than the parietals; loreal once and two thirds as long as deep; one præocular, extensively in contact with the frontal; two or three postoculars; temporals 2+3; eight upper labials, third deeper than second and fourth, fourth and fifth entering the eye, fifth nearly as long as the eye; four lower labials in contact with the anterior chin-shields, which are shorter than the posterior. Scales in 17 rows. Ventrals 158–179; anal divided; subcaudals 95–114. Brown above, the scales edged with darker, a narrow yellow vertebral line, bifurcating on the occiput, its branches extending to the anterior border of the frontal shield; a broader yellow streak on each side, from the eye to the end of the tail; upper lip, lower half of outer row of scales, and lower parts yellowish white, with or without an interrupted blackish line on each side of the ventrals.

Total length 880 millim.; tail 250.

South Africa.

a. ♂ (V. 158; C. 95).   Port Natal.   Mr T. Ayres [C.].

10. Psammophis longifrons. (PLATE VIII. fig. 2.)

Psammophis longifrons, *Bouleng. Faun. Ind., Rept.* p. 366 (1890); Dreckmann, *Journ. Bomb. N. H. Soc.* vii 1892, p. 406; *Gleadow, op. cit.* viii. 1894, p. 553.

Snout nearly twice as long as the eye. Rostral as deep as broad, visible from above; nostril between one anterior and two superposed posterior nasals; internasals hardly half as long as the præfrontals, which are only a little shorter than the frontal; latter shield very narrow, much narrower in the middle than the supraocular, shorter than its distance from the end of the snout, a little shorter than the parietals; loreal slightly more than twice as long as deep; one præocular, not extending to the frontal; two postoculars; temporals 2+3; eight upper labials, third deeper than second and fourth, fourth and fifth entering the eye; five lower labials in contact with the anterior chin-shields, which are as long as the posterior. Scales in 17 rows. Ventrals 173; anal divided; subcaudals 93. Olive above; head with symmetrical undulating black lines; scales on the vertebral line, or on the whole back, with broad black margins; uniform white beneath.

Total length 1320 millim.; tail 375.

Hills of South Western India.

a. Ad. (head and neck only)   Cuddapah Hills.   Col. Beddome [C.].
                                                   (Type.)

11. Psammophis condanarus.

Russell, Ind. Serp i pl xxvii. (1796).
Coluber condanarus, *Merr. Tent.* p. 107 (1820).
Leptophis? bellii, *Jerdon, Journ As. Soc. Beng.* xxii. 1853, p 529.
Psammophis condanarus, *Blyth, Journ. As Soc Beng* xxiii. 1854, p 293; *Günth Rept. Brit Ind.* p. 291 (1864), *Stoliczka, Journ. As. Soc Beng.* xxxix. 1870, p. 196, and xl. 1871, p. 438; *Anders. Proc. Zool. Soc.* 1871, p 182; *Stoliczka, Proc. As. Soc. Beng.* 1872, p 83; *Theob. Cat Rept Brit. Ind.* p. 187 (1876), *Murray, Zool. Sind,* p 382 (1884); *Bouleng. Faun. Ind., Rept.* p, 365, fig. (1890).
—— sibilans, var. E, *Gunth Cat.* p. 137 (1858).
—— indicus, *Beddome, Madras Quart. Journ. Med. Sc.* 1863
Phayrea isabellina, *Theob Cat Rept. As. Soc. Mus.* 1868, p. 51.
Psammophis sibilans, var quadrilineata, *Jan, Icon. Gén.* 34, pl. iii. fig. 1 (1870).

Snout nearly twice as long as the eye. Rostral as deep as broad, visible from above; nasal divided or semidivided; internasals rather more than half the length of the præfrontals; frontal twice as long as broad, nearly as broad, in the middle, as the supraocular, as long as or longer than its distance from the end of the snout, as long as the parietals; loreal about twice as long as deep; one præocular, not extending to the frontal; two postoculars; temporals 1+2 or 1+3, rarely 2+3; eight upper labials, third longer than second and fourth, fourth and fifth entering the eye; four lower labials in contact with the anterior chin-shields, which are as long as the posterior. Scales in 17 rows. Ventrals 156-182; anal divided; subcaudals 75-90. Pale olive above, with two pairs of more or less distinct dark bands each two scales wide; these bands, the lower of which passes through the eye, often black-edged; upper lip and lower parts uniform yellowish, with a dark line along each side of the ventrals and subcaudals.

Total length 920 millim.; tail 220.

Northern India and Burma.

a. Hgr. (V. 165; C. 78).	Kotree, Sind.	Dr. Leith [P.].
b. Hgr. (V. 176; C. 88).	Chillianwallah.	Dr. Cantor.
c. ♀ (V. 182; C. ?).	Bengal.	
d-g. ♂ (V. 156, 164; C. 75, ?), ♀ (V. 168; C. ?), & hgr. (V. 166; C. 87).	Pegu.	W. Theobald, Esq [C.].
h. Hgr. (V 166; C. ?).	Toungyi, S. Shan States.	E. W. Oates, Esq. [P.].

12. Psammophis brevirostris.

Psammophis brevirostris, *Peters, Sitzb. Ges Naturf. Fr.* 1881, p. 89; *Matschie, Zool Jahrb.* v. 1890, p. 609; *Bouleng. Proc. Zool. Soc.* 1895, p. 539.

? Psammophis sibilans, var. tettensis, *Peters, Reise n. Mossamb.* iii. p. 122 (1882), *Matschie, l. c.*

Psammophis sibilans, var. brevirostris, *Bocage, Herp. Angola,* p. 118 (1895).

Snout once and a half to once and two thirds as long as the eye. Rostral as deep as broad, visible from above, nostril between two or three shields; internasals half as long as the præfrontals; frontal twice as long as broad, as broad as or a little narrower, in the middle, than the supraocular, as long as its distance from the end of the snout, as long as the parietals; loreal once and a half to twice as long as deep; one præocular, not reaching the frontal; two postoculars; temporals 2+2 or 3; eight (rarely seven) upper labials, third deeper than second or fourth (or second deeper than first and third), fourth and fifth (or third and fourth) entering the eye; three or four lower labials in contact with the anterior chin-shields, which are shorter than the posterior. Scales in 17 rows. Ventrals 153-163; anal divided; subcaudals 64-95. Brown or dark olive on the back (7 rows of scales), pale olive on the sides down to the ventrals, the two shades separated by a more or less distinct lighter streak; a yellowish black-edged spot usually present on each vertebral scale; head uniform olive-brown in the adult, in the young with a yellowish streak along the frontal and yellowish cross-bars behind; yellowish white beneath, with a series of olive or blackish dots or short streaks along each side.

Total length 1300 millim.; tail 370.

South Africa; Angola.

a. ♂ (V. 161, C. ?).	Pretoria, Transvaal	W. L. Distant, Esq. [P.].
b, c. ♂ (V. 159, C. 77) & ♀ (V. 153, C. 94).	Port Natal.	Mr. T. Ayres [C.]
d-e. Hgr. (V. 158, C. 91) & yg. (V. 153; C. 91).	Natal	E. Howlett, Esq. [P.].
f. ♂ (V. 157; C. 95).	Port Elizabeth.	Mr Drege [P.].
g. Hgr. (V. 162, C. 86).	S. Africa.	J. H. Gurney, Esq. [P.].
h. Yg. (V. 157; C. 70).	Angola.	Prof. Barboza du Bocage [P.].

13. Psammophis elegans.

Seba, Thes. ii. pl. lx. fig 1 (1735).
Coluber elegans, *Shaw, Zool.* iii p. 536 (1802).
Macrosoma elegans, *Leach, in Bowdich, Miss. Ashantee*, p. 493 (1819).
Psammophis elegans, *Boie, Isis*, 1827, p. 533; *Schleg. Phys Serp.* ii. p 216 (1837), *and Abbild.* p. 130, pl. xliii. figs. 15 & 16 (1844); *Dum. & Bibr.* vii p. 894 (1854); *Gunth. Cat.* p. 138 (1858); *A Dum Arch. Mus* x. 1859, p. 208, pl. xvii. fig. 10; *Boettg. Abh. Senck Ges.* xii. 1881, p. 395, *F. Mull. Verh Nat. Ges Basel*, vii. 1885, p. 687; *Bouleng. Proc. Zool. Soc.* 1895, p. 539.

Snout twice to twice and a half as long as the eye, obliquely truncate at the end. Rostral a little broader than deep, scarcely visible from above; nostril between two shields; internasals a little longer than broad, about half as long as the præfrontals, frontal twice as long as broad, narrower, in the middle, than the supraocular, slightly longer than the præfrontals, or as long as its distance from the end of the snout, as long as or shorter than the parietals; loreal three to four times as long as deep, one præocular, usually not reaching the frontal; two or three postoculars; temporals 2+2 or 3, rarely 1+2, nine upper labials, third deeper than second and fourth, third, fourth, and fifth in contact with the præocular, fifth and sixth entering the eye; five lower labials in contact with the anterior chin-shields, which are shorter than the posterior. Scales in 17 rows. Ventrals 179-202; anal divided; subcaudals 144-161. Yellow or pale olive above, with three longitudinal bands, between black lines formed by black-edged scales, the median band five scales wide, the outer narrower and extending to the end of the snout after passing through the eyes; head olive above, punctulated with black; upper lip and sides of belly yellow, the rest of the belly olive, lineolated with black.

Total length 1230 millim.; tail 480.

Senegambia and Guinea.

a–b, c. ♀ (V. 199, 200, 195; C. 151, 148, ?).	W. Africa.	(Types.)
d. Hgr. (V. 196; C. 154).	W. Africa.	Mr. Rich [P.].
e. Hgr (V. 188; C. 155).	W. Africa.	Mr Argent [C.].
f–g. ♂ (V. 179; C. 144) & ♀ (V. 198; C. ?).	W. Africa.	Haslar Collection.
h, i. ♂ (V. 185; C. 152) & hgr. (V. 193; C. 149).	Fantee.	T. E. Bowdich, Esq. [P.].
k. Yg. (V. 190; C. 154).	Ashantee.	
l. Skull.	Senegal.	

14. Psammophis biseriatus.

Psammophis biseriatus, *Peters, Sitzb. Ges. Naturf. Fr.* 1881, p. 88; *Fischer, Jahrb. Hamb. Wiss. Anst.* i. 1884, p. 13, pl. i fig. 4; *Bouleng. Ann. Mus. Genova,* (2) xii. 1892, p 15; *Boettg. Zool. Anz.* 1893, p. 119; *Stejneger, Proc. U.S Nat Mus.* xvi. 1894, p. 731; *Bouleng. Proc. Zool Soc* 1895, p. 537.

Snout once and two thirds to twice as long as the eye. Rostral a little broader than deep, visible from above; nostril between two shields; internasals much shorter than the præfrontals; frontal twice to twice and a half as long as broad, much narrower, in the middle, than the supraocular, longer than its distance from the end of the snout, a little shorter than the parietals; loreal three to four times as long as deep; one præocular, sometimes divided, extensively in contact with the frontal; two postoculars; temporals 2+2 or 3; nine or ten (rarely eight) upper labials, third deepest, fourth, fifth, and sixth or fifth and sixth (or third, fourth, and fifth) entering the eye; five lower labials in contact with the anterior chin-shields, which are much shorter than the posterior. Scales in 15 rows. Ventrals 142–164, anal entire or divided; subcaudals 100–131. Greyish or pale brown above, with a darker vertebral band and two series of reddish-brown or black spots; head with dark brown or reddish-brown, black-edged spots, and usually a dark cross-band on the occiput; a dark streak on each side of the head, passing through the eye; lips with black or brown spots, belly greyish, speckled with black and spotted with white, sometimes with a rusty median stripe.

Total length 1050 millim.; tail 400.

Central and East Africa.

a. ♀ (V. 142; A. 2; C. 113).	Between Obbia and Berbera, Somaliland.	Signor A. B. Robecchi [C.]; Marquis G. Doria [P.].
b. ♀ (V. 154; A. 2; C. 100).	Inland of Berbera, Somaliland.	E. Lort Phillips, Esq. [P.].
c. ♀ (V. 149, A. 1; C. 120).	Kurawa, E. Africa.	Dr. J. W. Gregory [P.].
d. Yg., bad state.	Ungoro, Upper Nile.	Capt. Speke [C.].
e. Yg. (V. 148; A. 2; C. 106).	S shore of Victoria Nyanza.	Dr Emin Pasha [P.].

15. Psammophis crucifer.

Seba, *Thes.* ii. pl. liii. fig. 2, & cvii fig 4 (1735); *Merr. Beytr.* i. p. 13, pl. iii. (1790)

Coluber sibilans, part., *Linn. S. N.* i. p. 383 (1766).

―― crucifer, *Daud. Rept.* vii p 189 (1803)

Psammophis crucifer, *Boie, Isis,* 1827, pp 525, 547; *Dum. & Bibr.* vii p. 892 (1854); *Gunth. Cat* p. 135 (1858); *Jan, Icon Gén.* 34, pl iv fig. 3 (1870); *Bouleng. Proc. Zool Soc.* 1895, p. 539

―― moniliger, part., *Schleg. Phys Serp* ii. p. 209, pl. viii. figs. 6 & 7 (1837).

Snout once and a half as long as the eye. Rostral a little broader than deep, visible from above; nostril between two shields; internasals shorter than the præfrontals; frontal twice to twice and a half as long as broad, as broad as or a little narrower than the supraocular, much longer than its distance from the end of the snout, as long as the parietals; loreal about once and a half as long as deep; one præocular, not reaching the frontal; two postoculars; temporals 2+2 or 3, eight (rarely seven) upper labials, fourth and fifth (or third and fourth) entering the eye; four lower labials in contact with the anterior chin-shields, which are as long as or shorter than the posterior. Scales in 15 rows. Ventrals 136-155; anal divided; subcaudals 62-81. Pale olive or brownish above, with a black-edged dark vertebral band, three scales wide, which extends to the head, giving off one or two transverse bars on the nape, and enclosing a light spot or streak on the suture between the parietal shields; sides of head with large dark blotches, the præ- and postoculars yellowish, a more or less distinct dark band along each side of the body, with a white streak below it on the lower half of the outer row of scales and the outer ends of the ventrals; lower parts yellow or orange, uniform or finely speckled with blackish, with a dark streak or series of small spots on each side.

Total length 640 millim.; tail 160.

South Africa.

a ♀ (V. 150, C. 73).	Simon's Bay.	H.M.S. 'Challenger.'
b-c ♂ (V. 143, 143; C. 81, 70).	Port Elizabeth.	H. A. Spencer, Esq. [P].
d. Hgr. (V. 151; C 80).	Namaqualand.	
e-f ♀ (V. 144; C. 74) & yg. (V. 148, C 73).	Matabeleland.	C. Beddington, Esq. [P.].
g. ♀ (V. 145, C. 66).	S. Africa.	Haslar Collection
h. ♀ (V. 155, C 73).	S. Africa.	

16. Psammophis pulcher.

Psammophis pulcher, *Bouleng. Proc. Zool Soc.* 1895, p. 537, pl xxx. fig 6.

Snout once and two thirds as long as the eye. Rostral broader than deep, visible from above; nostril between two shields; internasals much shorter than the præfrontals; frontal twice and a half as long as broad, a little narrower than the supraocular, longer than its distance from the end of the snout, nearly as long as the parietals; loreal once and two thirds as long as deep; two præoculars, upper not reaching the frontal; two postoculars; temporals 1+2; eight upper labials, third deeper than fourth, fourth and fifth entering the eye, fifth as long as the eye; four lower labials in contact with the anterior chin-shields, which are a little shorter than the posterior. Scales in 13 rows. Ventrals 144; anal divided; subcaudals 108. Pale brownish above, with an orange black-edged vertebral stripe and a black lateral streak, running along the second row of scales and extending to the end of the snout after passing through the eye; upper lip, outer row of scales, and outer ends of ventrals white; ventrals yellow in the middle, with an orange line on each side.

Total length 435 millim.; tail 160.

Western Somaliland.

a. ♀ (V. 144; C. 108).   Webi Shebeli   Dr. Donaldson Smith [P.].
(Type.)

17. Psammophis angolensis.

Amphiophis angolensis, *Bocage, Jorn. Sc. Lisb.* iv. 1872, p. 82; *Peters, Sitzb. Ges. Naturf. Fr.* 1881, p. 149; *Bocage, Herp. Angola,* p 113, pl xi. fig. 3 (1895).
Ablabes homeyeri, *Peters, Mon. Berl Ac.* 1877, p. 620.
Dromophis angolensis, *Boettg. Ber. Senck. Ges.* 1888, p. 55
Psammophis angolensis, *Bouleng. Proc. Zool. Soc.* 1891, p. 307, and 1895, p. 539.

Snout about once and a half the diameter of the eye. Rostral slightly broader than deep, visible from above; nostril between two shields; internasals one half to two thirds as long as the præfrontals; frontal twice to twice and a half as long as broad, nearly as broad as the supraocular, longer than its distance from the end of the snout, nearly as long as the parietals; loreal once and a half to twice as long as deep; one præocular, usually not reaching the frontal; two postoculars; temporals 1+2; eight upper labials, third usually deeper than second and fourth, fourth and fifth entering the eye; four or five lower labials in contact with the anterior chin-shields, which are shorter than the posterior. Scales in 11 rows. Ventrals 141–155; anal divided; subcaudals 57–81. Pale olive above with a dark olive or blackish vertebral stripe, three scales wide, finely edged with black and yellow; head dark olive in front, blackish behind, with three yellow transverse lines, the first behind the eyes, the third behind the parietal shields; two black cross-bands may be present on the nape and neck, separated by a yellowish interspace; labials and præoculars yellowish white; one or two more or less distinct dark lines or series of dots along each side; lower parts whitish.

Total length 375 millim.; tail 110.

Tropical Africa, south of the Equator.

a. ♂   Sir J. Kirk [C.].
b. ♀   Dr. Emin Pasha [P.].

c. ♀ (V. 155; C. 58).	Lake Tanganyika.	E. Coode-Hore, Esq. [C.].
d-e. ♀ (V. 149; C. 71) & hgr. (V. 141; C. 68).	Cape McClear, Lake Nyassa.	Mr. F. A. Simons [C.]
f. ♀ (V. 147; C. 68).	Fort Johnston, Brit. C. Africa.	Sir H. H. Johnston [P].

172. MIMOPHIS.

Mimophis, *Gunth. Ann. & Mag. N. H* (4) i. 1868, p. 421.

Maxillary teeth 10 or 11, two or three in the middle much enlarged, fang-like, followed by an interspace, last large and grooved; anterior mandibular teeth very strongly enlarged. Head distinct from neck; eye rather large, with round pupil; frontal narrow; nostril in an entire or semidivided nasal, followed by a short loreal, which is separated from the præocular by the præfrontal. Body cylindrical; scales smooth, with apical pits, in 17 rows; ventrals rounded. Tail rather long; subcaudals in two rows.

Madagascar.

1. Mimophis mahfalensis.

Psammophis mahfalensis, *Grandid. Rev. & Mag. Zool.* xix. 1867, p. 234.
Mimophis madagascariensis, *Gunth. Ann. & Mag N. H* (4) i. 1868, p. 421, pl. xviii; *Boettg Abh. Senck. Ges* xii. 1881, p. 445, *Steind. Sitzb. Ak Wien*, c. 1891, p. 294
—— mahfalensis, *Mocquard, Bull. Soc. Philom.* (8) vii. 1895, pp. 103 & 124.

Rostral broader than deep, scarcely visible from above; internasals as long as broad or longer than broad, a little shorter than the præfrontals; frontal twice and a half to three times as long as broad, much narrower than the supraocular, longer than its distance from the end of the snout, as long as or shorter than the parietals; one præocular, extending to the upper surface of the head but not reaching the frontal; two postoculars; temporals 2+3; eight upper labials, second or second and third in contact with the præfrontal, third, fourth, and fifth entering the eye; four (rarely three or five) lower labials in contact with the anterior chin-shields, which are shorter than the posterior. Scales in 17 rows. Ventrals 140–164, anal divided; subcaudals 61–102. Pale fawn-colour above, with a dark brown vertebral band or a zigzag series of spots which may be divided by a narrow pale line running along the spine; head with undulous dark lines above and a dark streak on each side, passing through the eye.

Total length 760 millim.; tail 195.

Madagascar.

A. A dark brown dorsal stripe, four scales wide, and two or three brown streaks along the sides; belly yellowish, with more or less distinct brown longitudinal streaks.

a-c ♂ (V 149, 140, C. 70, 61) & ♀ (V 152, C. 65).	Madagascar	Rev W. Ellis [P.]. (Types.)

d–e. ♀ (V. 149, 140; C. 63, 66). Imerina. Rev. J. Wills [C.].
f Yg. (V. 146; C. 71). Imerina. Rev. R. Baron [C.].

B. Dorsal stripe with dentated borders or replaced by spots, and with a more or less distinct light median line; sides and belly spotted or irregularly lineolated.

a ♂ (V. 156; C. 80). Betsileo. Rev. G. Shaw [C.].
b. Hgr. (V. 151; C 80). S.W Madagascar. Mr. Last [C.].
c–g. ♂ (V. 154; C. 87) & ♀ (V. 150, 152, 159, 154; C. 81, 81, ?, 83). Madagascar.
h. Yg. (V. 164; C. 102). ——? Zoological Society.
i. Skull of a.

173. PSAMMODYNASTES.

Psammophis, part., *Boie, Isis*, 1827, p 521; *Schleg. Phys. Serp* ii. p. 201 (1837); *Dum. & Bibr. Erp. Gén.* vii. p. 887 (1854); *Peters, Mon. Berl. Ac.* 1868, p. 452.
Psammodynastes, *Gunth. Cat Col. Sn.* p. 140 (1858); *Jan, Elenco sist. Ofid.* p. 90 (1863); *Gunth. Rept. Brit. Ind.* p. 292 (1864); *Mocquard, Bull. Soc. Philom.* (7) xi. 1887, p. 172, *Bouleng Faun. Ind., Rept.* p. 363 (1890).

Maxillary teeth 9 to 11, third or third and fourth much enlarged, fang-like, followed by a short interspace, last enlarged and grooved anterior mandibular teeth strongly enlarged. Head distinct from neck, with angular canthus rostralis; eye rather large, with vertically elliptic or subelliptic pupil; nostril in a single nasal; frontal very narrow. Body cylindrical; scales smooth, without pits, in 17 or 19 rows; ventrals rounded. Tail moderate or rather short; subcaudals in two rows.

South-eastern Asia.

1. Psammodynastes pulverulentus.

Psammophis pulverulenta, *Boie, Isis*, 1827, p 547; *Schleg. Phys. Serp.* ii. p. 211, pl viii. figs 10 & 11 (1837), and *Abbild.* pl. xliii. figs. 1-4 (1844); *Dum. & Bibr.* vii. p. 895 (1854).
Dipsas ferruginea, *Cantor, Proc. Zool. Soc* 1839, p. 53, *Blyth, Journ. As. Soc Beng.* xxiii. 1854, p. 293, and xxiv. 1855, p 715.
Psammodynastes pulverulentus, part., *Gunth. Cat.* p. 140 (1858).
—— pulverulentus, *Gunth. l. c.* p. 251, *Rept. Brit. Ind.* p. 292 (1864), and *Zool. Rec* 1867, p. 188: *Theob. Cat. Rept. Brit. Ind.* p. 188 (1876); *Fischer, Arch. f. Nat.* 1885, p 62; *Mocquard, Bull. Soc. Philom.* (7) xi. 1887, p. 172, pl iii, and xii. 1888, p. 104; *Bouleng. Faun. Ind., Rept.* p. 363 (1890).
Lycodon bairdi, *Steind. Novara, Rept.* p. 90 (1867).

Snout short, profile truncate or somewhat turned up in the adult. Rostral broader than deep, scarcely visible from above; internasals much shorter than the præfrontals; frontal twice to twice and a half as long as broad, much narrower, in the middle, than the supraocular, much longer than its distance from the end of the snout, a little shorter than the parietals, loreal about as long as deep, often transversely divided into two; one or two præ- and two to four postoculars; temporals 2+3 (rarely 2+2); eight upper labials, third, fourth, and fifth entering the eye; three (rarely four) lower labials in contact with the anterior chin-shields, which are followed by two smaller pairs. Scales in 17 (rarely 19) rows. Ventrals 146-175; anal entire, subcaudals 44-66. Dark brown or ochraceous above, with or without small darker and lighter spots; head usually with symmetrical longitudinal markings; a more or less distinct dark streak on each side of the head, passing through the eye; usually a dark brown band along each side; lower parts powdered with brown, and with dark brown spots or longitudinal lines.

Total length 610 millim.; tail 130.

Eastern Himalayas, Khasi and Assam hills, Burma, Indo-China, Formosa, Malay Peninsula and Archipelago.

a. ♂ (V. 164; C. 64).	Sikkim.	Messrs. v. Schlagintweit [C.].
b-d. ♂ (V. 167, 161; C. 65, 61) & ♀ (V. 157; C. ?).	Khasi Hills.	Sir J. Hooker [P.].
e. ♀ (V. 171; C. 60).	Assam.	Dr Griffith.
f ♀ (V. 174; C. 59).	Assam.	Dr. Cantor. (Type of *Dipsas ferruginea*?)
g-h. Hgr. (V. 156; C. 54) & yg. (V. 161; C. 44).	Toungyi, S. Shan States.	Lieut. Blakeway [C.].
i. ♀ (V. 168; C. 55).	Toungyi, S. Shan States.	E. W. Oates, Esq. [P.].
k. ♂ (V. 153; C. 58).	Lao Mountains.	M. Mouhot [C.].
l. ♀ (V. 175; C. 60).	Taiwanfoo, Formosa.	Mr. Holst [C]
m. ♂ (V. 160; C. 64).	Kuita, Perak.	L. Wray, Esq. [P.].
n ♀ (V. 159, C. 49).	Sumatra.	
o-q. ♂ (V. 165, 162, C. 66, 65) & yg. (V. 173; C. 64).	Engano.	Dr. Modigliani [C.].
r. Yg. (V. 160; C. 55)	Great Natuna.	A. Everett, Esq. [C.].
s. ♀ (V. 159, C. 61).	Barabei, S.E. Borneo.	Hr. Grabowsky [C.]; J. G. Fischer Collection.
t. ♀ (V. 157; C. 61).	Balabac.	A. Everett, Esq. [C.].
u. ♂ (V. 149, C. 64).	Palawan.	A. Everett, Esq. [C].
v-w. ♂ (V. 160, 158; C. 57, 59).	Placer, Mindanao.	A. Everett, Esq. [C].
x. ♂ (V. 155; C. ?).	N. Mindanao.	A. Everett, Esq. [C.].
y. ♀ (V. 166; C. 55).	Dinagat.	A. Everett, Esq. [C.].
z. ♂ (V. 155; C. 64).	Albay, S.E. Luzon.	J. Whitehead, Esq. [C.].
a. ♂ (V. 150, C. 50).	Willis Mts, Kediri, Java.	Baron v Huegel [C.].

β. ♀ (V. 160; C. 53). Flores. Dr. Bleeker (*Psammophis floresianus*, Blkr.).

γ. ♀ (V. 161; C. 55). N. Celebes. Dr A. B. Meyer [C.].
δ. Skull of σ.

2. Psammodynastes pictus.

Psammodynastes pulverulentus, part., *Gunth. Cat.* p. 140 (1858).
—— pictus, *Gunth. l. c.* p 251; *Fischer, Arch f. Nat.* 1885, p. 62; *Mocquard, Bull Soc. Philom.* (7) xii. 1888, p. 105; *v. Lidth de Jeude, Notes Leyd. Mus.* xii. 1890, p. 23.
Psammophis (Psammodynastes) conjunctus, *Peters, Mon. Berl. Ac.* 1868, p. 451.
—— pictus, *Peters, l. c.* p. 452.
Psammodynastes conjunctus, *Mocquard, Bull. Soc. Philom* (7) xi. 1887, p. 178, pl. iv.

Rather more slender, and tail longer than in the preceding. Internasals as long as broad or longer than broad, as long as or a little shorter than the præfrontals; frontal twice and a half to thrice as long as broad; two or three præ- and three or four postoculars; third lower labial very large, bordering the mental groove behind the small anterior chin-shields. Scales in 17 rows. Ventrals 152-169; anal entire; subcaudals 60-78. Pale brown, yellowish, or reddish above, anteriorly with dark transverse spots or bars between two light stripes, posteriorly with a dark brown or blackish vertebral band; this band, in some specimens, extending forwards to the head; a dark streak on each side of the head, passing through the eye and across the rostral shield; this streak edged above with a whitish line in the young; all these markings may become quite indistinct in old specimens. Lower parts whitish, more or less finely speckled with brown, with or without scattered black dots.

Total length 475 millim.; tail 90.

Sumatra, Billiton, Borneo.

a. Hgr. ♂ (V. 166; C. 78). Deli, Sumatra. Prof. Moesch [C.].

b, c. Hgr. ♂ (V. 168, 163; C. 73, 77). Sumatra. Sir S. Raffles [C.]; Zoological Society. (Types.)

d, e. Hgr ♂ (V. 167, 169; C. 72, 74). Borneo. Sir E. Belcher [P.].

f–h. ♂ (V. 152, 156; C. 74, 77) & yg. (V. 157; C. 60). Telang, S.E. Borneo. Hr. Grabowsky [C.]; J. G. Fischer Collection.

i–k. ♀ (V. 159; C. ?) & yg. (V. 154; C. 65). S.E. Borneo.

l. Hgr. (V. 164; C. 76). Sarawak. Rajah Brooke [P.].

m. ♀ (V. 164; C. 63). Mt. Dulit, Sarawak. C. Hose, Esq. [C.].

n. ♂ (V. 158; C. 75). Labuan. L. L. Dillwyn, Esq. [P.]

174. MACROPROTODON.

Coronella, part., *Schleg. Phys. Serp.* ii. p. 50 (1837); *Günth. Cat. Col. Sn.* p. 34 (1858).
Macroprotodon, *Guichen. Explor. Sc. Alg., Rept.* p. 22 (1850); *Bouleng. Tr. Zool. Soc.* xiii. 1891, p. 143.
Lycognathus, part., *Dum. & Bibr. Mém. Ac. Sc.* xxiii. 1853, p. 495, *and Erp. Gén.* vii. p. 916 (1854).
Psammophylax, part., *Jan, Arch. Zool. Anat. Phys.* ii. 1862, p. 309.

Maxillary teeth 10 or 11, fourth and fifth or fifth and sixth enlarged, followed by an interspace, the two posterior again enlarged and grooved, and situated just behind the eye; mandibular teeth increasing in size to the sixth, which is fang-like and followed by an interspace, the posterior teeth small. Head slightly distinct from neck; eye rather small, with vertically subelliptic pupil. Body cylindrical; scales smooth, with apical pits, in 19 to 25 rows; ventrals rounded. Tail moderate; subcaudals in two rows.

Spain and North Africa.

Fig. 12.

Maxillary and mandible of *Macroprotodon cucullatus*.

1. Macroprotodon cucullatus.

Coluber cucullatus, *I. Geoffr. Descr. Egypte, Rept.* pp. 148 & 151, pl. viii. fig. 3 (1827).
Coronella lævis, part., *Schleg. Phys. Serp.* ii. p. 65 (1837).
Macroprotodon mauritanicus, *Guichen. Explor. Sc. Alg., Rept.* p. 22, pl. ii. fig. 2 (1850).
Lycognathus cucullatus, *Dum. & Bibr.* vii. p. 926 (1854); *Gervais, Mém. Ac. Montpell.* iii. 1857, p. 511, pl. v. fig. 2.
—— tæniatus, *Dum. & Bibr. l. c.* p. 930.
—— textilis, *Dum. & Bibr. l. c.* p. 931.
Coronella cucullata, *Günth. Cat.* p. 35 (1858); *Strauch, Erp. Alg.* p. 55 (1862); *Schreib. Erp. Eur.* p. 296, fig. (1875); *Bœttg. Abh. Senck. Ges.* xii. 1880, pp. 374 & 387, and xiii. 1883, p. 96, *and in Kobelt, Reis. Alg. Tunis,* p. 457 (1885).
—— brevis, *Günth. Ann. & Mag. N. H.* (3) ix. 1862, p. 58.
—— tæniata, *Strauch, l. c.* p. 57.
—— textilis, *Strauch, l. c.*
Psammophylax cucullatus, *Jan, Arch. Zool. Anat. Phys.* ii. 1862, p. 312, *and Icon. Gén.* 19, pl. i. figs. 3 & 4 (1866).
Macroprotodon maroccanus, *Peters, Sitzb. Ges. Naturf. Fr.* 1882, p. 27.
—— cucullatus, *Bouleng. Tr. Zool. Soc.* xiii. 1891, p. 143.

Snout broad, much depressed. Rostral at least twice as broad as deep, scarcely visible from above; internasals as long as or a little shorter than the præfrontals; frontal once and two thirds to twice as long as broad, longer than its distance from the end of the snout, shorter than the parietals; loreal once and a half to twice as long as deep; one præocular, extending to the upper surface of the head but not reaching the frontal; two postoculars (exceptionally one or three); temporals 1+2; eight upper labials, fourth and fifth entering the eye, sixth usually in contact with the parietal; four or five lower labials in contact with the anterior chin-shields, which are as long as or a little shorter than the posterior. Scales in 19 to 25 rows. Ventrals 153–192; anal divided; subcaudals 40–54. Pale brown or greyish above, with small brown spots or with more or less distinct darker and lighter longitudinal streaks, some large dark-brown or black markings, or a large blotch usually present on the occiput and nape, descending on the sides of the neck; head and nape sometimes entirely black above; upper lip whitish, with an oblique blackish streak below the eye; lower parts yellowish or coral-red, uniform or more or less spotted with black, the spots sometimes confluent along the middle of the belly.

Total length 550 millim.; tail 90.

Southern Spain, Baleares, Lampedusa, North Africa.

a-b.	♀ (Sc. 21; V. 182; C. 47) & yg. (Sc 21; V. 171; C. 50).	Algeciras.	Lieut. Boger [P.].
c.	♂ (Sc. 23; V. 164; C. 50).	Andalusia.	Lord Lilford [P].
d.	♂ (Sc. 21; V. 177; C. 48).	Tangier.	M. H. Vaucher [C.].
e	Hgr. (Sc. 21; V. 173; C. 50).	Tangier.	
f.	♀, bad state (Sc. 23).	Island off Coast of Mogador.	Rev. R. T. Lowe [P.]. (Type of *C. brevis*.)
g-n.	♀ (Sc. 25; V. 176; C. 48) & yg. (Sc. 23, 23, 23, 23, 23, 21; V. 162, 171, 178, 177, 180, 173; C. 46, 44, 41, 40, 42, 41).	City of Morocco.	J. G. Fischer Collection
o.	♂ (Sc. 21; V. 169; C. 49).	Morocco.	
p.	♀ (Sc. 20; V. 192; C. ?).	Algiers.	P. L. Sclater, Esq. [P.]
q.	♀ (Sc. 19; V. 180; C. 44).	Algiers.	
r.	♂ (Sc. 19; V. 171; C. 54).	Hammam Meskoutine, Algeria.	Dr. J. Anderson [P.].
s.	♂ (Sc. 19; V. 172; C. 50)	Algeria.	Canon Tristram [C.].
t-v.	♀ (Sc. 21, 19; V. 165, 176; C. 50, 48) & hgr. (Sc. 19; V. 184; C. 51).	Tunis.	Mr. Fraser [C.].

w–y. ♂ (Sc. 19; V. 153; C. 45), ♀ (Sc. 19; V. 168; C. 43), & hgr. (Sc. 19; V. 169; C. 45).	Tripoli.	Zoological Society.
z. ♂ (Sc. 19; V. 154; C. 48).	Maryut, Alexandria.	Dr. J. Anderson [P.].
a. ♀ (Sc. 19; V. 165; C. 42).	Between Aboukir and Ramleh, near Alexandria.	Dr. J. Anderson [P.].

β. Skull of *d*.

175. DRYOPHIS.

Dryinus (*non Fabr.*), part., *Merr. Tent. Syst. Amph.* p. 136 (1820); *Bell, Zool. Journ.* ii. 1825, p. 324; *Dum. & Bibr. Erp. Gén.* vii. p. 808 (1854).

Dryophis, *Dalman, Œfvers. of Zool. Arb.*, Stockholm, 1822*; *Fitzing. N. Class. Rept.* p. 29 (1826); *Bouleng. Faun. Ind., Rept.* p. 367 (1890).

Passerita, *Gray, Ann. Phil.* x. 1825, p. 208; *Günth. Cat. Col. Sn.* p. 160 (1858); *Cope, Proc. Ac. Philad.* 1860, p. 554; *Günth. Rept. Brit. Ind.* p. 305 (1864).

Dryophis, part., *Boie, Isis*, 1827, p. 520; *Schleg. Phys. Serp.* ii. p. 241 (1837); *Günth. Cat.* p. 156; *Jan, Elenco sist. Ofid.* p. 88 (1863).

Psammophis, part., *Dum. & Bibr. t. c.* p. 887.

Tropidococcyx, *Günth. Ann. & Mag. N. H.* (3) vi. 1860, p. 428, *and Rept. Brit. Ind.* p. 301.

Gephyrinus, *Cope, Proc. Amer. Philos. Soc.* xxiii. 1886, p. 492.

Maxillary teeth 12 to 15, one or two in the middle much enlarged, fang-like, and followed by an interspace, after which the teeth are very small; one or two posterior grooved fangs, situated below the posterior border of the eye; mandibular teeth increasing in length to the third or fourth, which is very large, fang-like; the posterior small. Head elongate, distinct from neck, with strong

Fig. 13.

Maxillary and mandible of *Dryophis mycterizans*.

canthus rostralis and concave lores; eye rather large, with horizontal pupil; nostril in the posterior part of a single nasal; frontal narrow, more or less bell-shaped. Body much elongate and compressed; scales smooth, without apical pits, in 15 rows, disposed obliquely, vertebral row slightly enlarged; ventrals rounded. Tail long; subcaudals in two rows.

South-eastern Asia.

---

* I have not been able to refer to this work.

Synopsis of the Species.

I. Snout without dermal appendage.

  A. Ventral shields less than 200.

One postocular; no loreal; two labials entering the eye; subcaudals 69–82..	1. *perroteti*, p. 178.
Two postoculars; one or two loreals; one labial entering the eye; subcaudals 82–106	2. *dispar*, p. 179.
Two postoculars; three or four loreals; one labial entering the eye; subcaudals 115–151	3. *fronticinctus*, p. 179.
Two postoculars; two to four loreals; two or three labials entering the eye; subcaudals 115–156	4. *xanthozona*, p. 180.

  B. Ventrals 203–235; subcaudals 158–207.

Anal divided (rarely entire)	5. *prasinus*, p. 180.
Anal entire	6. *fasciolatus*, p. 182.

II. Snout ending in a dermal appendage; no loreal.

Rostral appendage formed entirely by the rostral	7. *mycterizans*, p. 182.
Rostral appendage covered with small scales above	8. *pulverulentus*, p. 184.

1. Dryophis perroteti.

Psammophis perroteti, *Dum. & Bibr.* vii. p. 899 (1854).
Leptophis ? canariensis, *Jerdon, Journ. As. Soc. Beng.* xxii. 1855, p. 530.
Dryiophis tropidococcyx, *Günth. Cat.* p 157 (1858)
Tropidococcyx perroteti, *Günth Ann. & Mag. N. H.* (3) vi. 1860, p. 428, pl. vii. figs. 5–7, and *Rept. Brit. Ind.* p. 301 (1864).
Dryophis perroteti, *Jan, Elenco,* p. 89 (1863); *Peters, Mon. Berl. Ac.* 1868, p. 452; *Jan, Icon. Gén.* 33, pl. v. fig. 2 (1869); *Bouleng. Faun. Ind., Rept.* p. 368 (1890).
Tragops perroteti, *Theob. Cat. Rept. Brit. Ind.* p. 191 (1876).

Snout obtusely pointed and projecting, without dermal appendage, not quite twice as long as the eye. No loreal, internasals and præfrontals in contact with the labials; frontal longer than its distance from the end of the snout, as long as the parietals; one præocular, in contact with the frontal; one postocular; temporals 1+2 or 2+2; eight (rarely nine) upper labials, fourth and fifth entering the eye; five lower labials in contact with the anterior chin-shields, which are as long as the posterior. Scales in 15 rows, those on sacral region keeled. Ventrals 135–147; anal divided; subcaudals 69–82. Bright green above; yellowish or pale green beneath, with a green lateral line.

Total length 560 millim.; tail 135.

North Canara and Nilgherries.

♀ (V. 144; C. 70).	Madras Presidency.	T. C. Jerdon, Esq. [P.].
b-f ♂ (V. 142, 138, 142, 140, 141; C. 79, 82, 80, 75, 80).	India.	Sir J. MacGregor [P.].
g-i. ♂ (V. 141, 135; C. 80, 70) & ♀ (V. 147; C. 69).	India.	Zool. Society. (Types of *D. tropidococcyx*.)
k-l. ♂ (V. 140, 135; C. 77, 76).	India.	

2. Dryophis dispar.

Tragops dispar, *Gunth. Rept. Brit. Ind* p. 303, pl. xxiii fig. A (1864); *Theob. Cat Rept. Brit. Ind.* p 192 (1876).
Dryophis dispar, *Bouleng Faun. Ind., Rept.* p. 368 (1890).

Snout pointed and projecting, without dermal appendage, not quite twice as long as the eye. Internasals or internasals and præfrontals usually in contact with the labials; one or two small loreals; frontal as long as or longer than its distance from the end of the snout, as long as the parietals; one præocular, in contact with the frontal, with one or two suboculars below it; two postoculars; temporals 2+2 or 2+3; eight upper labials, fifth entering the eye; four lower labials in contact with the anterior chin-shields, which are as long as or a little shorter than the posterior. Scales in 15 rows, those on sacral region more or less distinctly keeled. Ventrals 142–156; anal divided; subcaudals 82–106. Bright green or bronzy olive above, the skin between the scales black; pale green or pale olive beneath, with a yellow line on each side.

Total length 650 millim.; tail 200.

Hills of Southern India.

a-f ♀ (V. 151, 149, 151, 145, 156; C. 97, 100, 97, 97, 105) & hgr. (V. 153; C 106).	Anamallays.	Col Beddome [C]. (Types.)
g-i ♀ (V. 142, 150, 147; C. 90, 82, 95)	Anamallays.	Col. Beddome [C.].
k. ♂ (V. 157; C. 92).	Madras Presidency.	Col. Beddome [C.].
l. ♂ (V. 153; C. ?).	High Range, Travancore.	H. S. Ferguson, Esq. [P.].

3. Dryophis fronticinctus.

Dryiophis fronticinctus, *Gunth. Cat.* p. 158 (1858); *Bouleng. Faun. Ind., Rept.* p 368 (1890); *W. Sclater, Journ. As. Soc. Beng.* lx. 1891, p. 244.
Tragops fronticinctus, *Gunth Rept Brit. Ind.* p. 304, pl. xxiii. fig. E (1864), *Theob. Journ Linn. Soc.* x 1868, p. 52; *Stoliczka, Journ. As. Soc. Beng* xxxix. 1870, p. 197; *Theob. Cat. Rept. Brit. Ind.* p. 192 (1876).
—— javanicus (*non Steind.*), *Gunth. Ann. & Mag. N. H.* (4) i. 1868, p. 424; *Theob. l. c* p. 193.

Snout pointed and projecting, without dermal appendage, measuring about twice the diameter of the eye. Nasals usually forming a suture behind the rostral; frontal as long as its distance from the end of the snout, as long as or a little longer than the parietals; usually two superposed pairs of loreals; two præoculars, upper usually in contact with the frontal; two postoculars; temporals 2+2 or 2+3; seven or eight upper labials, fifth or sixth entering the eye; three or four lower labials in contact with the anterior chin-shields, which are much shorter than the posterior. Scales in 15 rows, those on sacral region keeled. Ventrals 183-195, anal divided; subcaudals 115-151. Bright green, olive, or bronze-brown above; pale green or olive beneath, with a white or black-and-white lateral streak.

Total length 820 millim.; tail 265.

Assam, Arrakan, Pegu.

a-c. ♂ (V. 190; C. 143) & ♀ (V. 188, 192; C. 136, 128).	—— ?	(Types.)
d-g, h-k. ♂ (V. 192, 188, 190, 195, C. 120, 149, 141, 144) & ♀ (V. 187, 192, 183, C. 135, ?, 115).	Pegu.	W. Theobald, Esq. [C.].

4. Dryophis xanthozona.

Dryophis xanthozona, *Boie, Isis*, 1827, p 545.
Dryiophis prasina, part., *Schleg. Phys. Serp.* ii. p. 250, pl. x. figs. 11-13. (1837).
Drymus prasinus, var. A, *Cantor, Cat. Mal. Rept.* p. 82 (1847).
Tragops javanicus, *Steind. Novara, Rept.* p. 72, pl iii. fig. 15 (1867).

Snout pointed, feebly projecting, without appendage, nearly twice as long as the eye. Internasals in contact with the rostral; frontal a little longer than its distance from the end of the snout, as long as the parietals; a series of three or four small loreals, one præocular, in contact with the frontal; two postoculars; temporals 2+2; eight or nine upper labials, fourth and fifth, or fourth, fifth, and sixth entering the eye; four lower labials in contact with the anterior chin-shields, which are much shorter than the posterior. Scales in 15 rows. Ventrals 186-195; anal entire (rarely divided); subcaudals 115-156. Green above; a yellow streak on each side of the belly and a pair of more indistinct ones in the middle, separated by a purplish streak.

Total length 1080 millim.; tail 410.

Java, Pinang.

a. Hgr. ♀ (V. 195; C. 115).	Java.	A. Scott, Esq. [P.].
b. ♀ (V. 186; C. 156).	Pinang.	Dr. Cantor.

5. Dryophis prasinus.

Russell. Ind. Serp. ii. pl. xxiv. (1801).
[Dryinus nasutus (Merr.), *Bell, Zool. Journ.* ii. 1825. p. 327.

Dryophis prasinus, *Boie, Isis*, 1827, p. 545; *Schleg. Abbild.* pl. viii. figs 1-6 (1837); *Gunth Cat.* p. 159 (1858); *Jan, Icon. Gén.* 33, pl. v. fig. 1 (1869); *Bouleng. Faun. Ind., Rept.* p. 369 (1890).
—— prasinus, part., *Schleg. Phys. Serp.* ii. p. 250, pl. x. figs 9-11 (1837).
Dryinus prasinus, part., *Cantor, Cat. Mal Rept.* p 81 (1847).
Oxybelis fulgidus, part., *Dum & Bibr.* vii. p. 817 (1854).
Tragops prasinus, *Dum & Bibr. t c* p. 824; *Gunth Rept. Brit. Ind.* p. 303 (1864), *Anders. Proc. Zool. Soc* 1871, p. 185; *Theob. Cat. Rept. Brit Ind* p. 191 (1876).
—— xanthozonius, *Dum. & Bibr. t. c.* p. 826

Snout acuminate, projecting, without dermal appendage, rather more than twice as long as the eye. Internasals usually in contact with the labials; one to four small loreals between the præfrontal and the labials; frontal as long as or a little longer than its distance from the end of the snout, a little longer than the parietals; one præocular, in contact with the frontal; two postoculars; temporals 2+2 or 3+3, rarely 1+2; nine upper labials, fourth, fifth, and sixth entering the eye; four lower labials in contact with the anterior chin-shields, which are shorter than the posterior. Scales in 15 rows, usually faintly keeled on sacral region. Ventrals 203-235; anal divided (rarely entire); subcaudals 158-207. Bright green, pale olive, or grey-brown, with a yellow line along each side of the lower parts; interstitial skin of the neck black and white.

Total length 1790 millim.; tail 600.

Eastern Himalayas, Assam, Burma, Indo-China, Malay Peninsula and Archipelago.

a. ♀ (V. 219, C. 159).	Bengal (?).	Gen. Hardwicke [P.].
b. ♀ (V. 206, C. 165).	Salween Valley, Burma.	R. C Beavan, Esq. [P.].
c. ♂ (V. 207, C 177)	Bassein, Burma.	Major Bingham [P.].
d. ♀ (V. 213; C. 173).	Rangoon.	Major Bingham [P.].
e. ♀ (V. 208, C. 176).	Pegu.	W. Theobald, Esq. [C.].
f ♀ (V. 213; C. 172).	Toungoo.	E. W. Oates, Esq [P].
g. ♀ (V. 209; C. 158).	Mergui.	Prof. Oldham [P.].
h ♀ (V. 208; C. 175).	Camboja.	M. Mouhot [C.].
i, k. ♀ (V 227; C. ?) & yg (V. 227; C. 186).	Singapore.	Dr. Dennys [P].
l. ♀ (V. 225; C. 166).	Pinang.	Dr. Cantor
m. ♀ (V. 223; C. 186).	Sumatra.	Sir S. Raffles.
n. ♀ (V. 215; C. 175).	Nias	Hr. Sundermann [C].
o. ♂ (V. 229, C. 196).	Great Natuna	A. Everett, Esq [C.].
p. ♂ (V. 220, C. 173).	Borneo	Sir E. Belcher [P.].
q, r. ♂ (V 235, 206; C. 180, 165)	Sarawak.	Sir H. Low [P.].
s. Yg. (V. 229; C. 177)	Sarawak.	Rajah Brooke [P.].
t. Yg. (V. 209, C. 188).	Mt. Dulit, Sarawak.	C. Hose, Esq. [C].
u. ♂ (V. 228; C. 189).	Baram R., Sarawak.	C. Hose, Esq. [C]
v. ♂ (V 223; C. ?).	Sibutu Is.	A. Everett, Esq. [C.].
w. ♂ (V. 213; C. 186).	Java.	Dr. Horsfield.
x. ♀ (V. 209; C. 170).	Java.	G. Lyon, Esq. [P.].

γ. Yg. (V. 212; C. 184).	Willis Mts., Kediri, Java.	Baron v. Huegel [C.].
ε. ♀ (V. 227, C. 175).	Celebes.	Leyden Museum.
α. ♀ (V. 216; C. 179).	Manado.	Dr. A. B. Meyer [C.].
β. Yg. (V. 226; C. 207).	N. Celebes.	Dr A. B Meyer [C.].
γ, δ, ε. ♂ (V. 216, 217; C. 170, 167) & hgr. (V. 220; C. 178).	Philippines.	H. Cuming, Esq. [C.].
ζ. ♀ (V. 226, C. 172).	Mindanao	A Everett, Esq. [C.].
η. ♀ (V. 226; C. 195).	Zamboanga.	A. Everett, Esq [C.].
θ. ♂ (V. 231; C. 195).	Zamboanga.	H.M.S. 'Challenger.'
ι. Hgr. (V. 212; C. 182).	Cape Engano, N. Luzon.	Whitehead Exped.
κ. Hgr. (V. 211; C. 174).	Ternate.	H.M.S. 'Challenger.'
λ. ♀, skeleton.	Java.	

6. Dryophis fasciolatus.

Tragops fasciolatus, *Fischer, Arch. f. Nat* 1885, p. 66, pl. v. fig. 4.
Dryophis fasciolatus, *v. Lidth de Jeude, Notes Leyd. Mus.* xii. 1890, p. 23.

Snout acuminate, projecting, without appendage, about twice as long as the eye. Internasals in contact with the first or second labial; frontal as long as or a little shorter than its distance from the end of the snout, as long as the parietals; a series of two or three loreals; one præocular, in contact with the frontal; two postoculars; temporals 2+2 or 3; nine upper labials, fourth, fifth, and sixth entering the eye; four lower labials in contact with the anterior chin-shields, which are much shorter than the posterior. Scales in 15 rows. Ventrals 221-231; anal entire, subcaudals 185-194. Grey above, spotted with black, the spots forming more or less regular cross-bars anteriorly; belly with a grey, black-edged band in the middle and a white streak on each side.

Total length 1400 millim.; tail 500.

Borneo, Sumatra, Natuna Islands.

a. ♀ (V. 221; C. 187).	S.E. Borneo.	Hr. Grabowsky [C]; J. G. Fischer Collection. (Type.)
b-c. Hgr. (V. 226, 229; C. 194, 189).	Baram R., Sarawak.	C. Hose, Esq. [C.].
d. Hgr. (V. 231; C. 185).	Great Natuna	C. Hose, Esq. [C.].

This form should perhaps be regarded as a variety of *D. prasinus* instead of a distinct species.

7. Dryophis mycterizans.

Russell, Ind. Serp. i. pls. xii., xiii. (1796).
Coluber mycterizans, *Linn. Mus. Ad. Frid.* p. 28, pl. v. fig. 1 and pl. xix. fig. 2 (1754), *and S. N.* i. p. 389; *Daud. Rept.* vii. p. 9, pl. lxxxi. fig. 1 (1803).
—— nasutus, *Lacép. Serp.* ii. pp 100, 277, pl. iv. fig. 2 (1789).
Dryinus mycterizans, *Merr. Tent.* p. 136 (1820).

Dryinus nasutus, *Merr. l. c , Guér. Icon R. A , Rept.* pl. xxii. fig. 2 (1830); *Dum. & Bibr.* vii. p. 809 (1854).
—— oxyrhynchus, *Bell, Zool. Journ.* ii. 1825, p. 326.
—— russellianus, *Bell, l. c.* p. 327.
Passerita mycterizans, *Gray, Ann. Phil.* x. 1825, p. 208 ; *Cope, Proc. Ac. Philad.* 1860, p. 554; *Gunth. Rept. Brit. Ind.* p. 305 (1864); *Theob. Cat. Rept. Brit. Ind.* p. 193 (1876).
Dryophis pavoninus, *Boie, Isis,* 1827, p. 545.
—— nasutus, *Schleg. Phys Serp.* ii p. 246, pl x. figs. 1–5 (1837); *Jan, Icon. Gén* 32, pl. v. fig. 2 (1869).
Dryinus fuscus, *Dum & Bibr. t. c.* p 812.
Passerita mycterizans, part., *Gunth Cat.* p. 160 (1858).
—— fusca, *Cope, Proc. Ac. Philad.* 1860, p. 554.
Dryophis mycterizans, *Bouleng. Faun. Ind., Rept.* p. 370, fig. (1890); *W. Sclater, Journ. As. Soc. Beng.* lx. 1891, p. 244.

Snout pointed, terminating in a dermal appendage which is shorter than the eye and formed entirely by the rostral; the length of the snout, without the appendage, about twice the diameter of the eye or rather more. No loreal; internasals and præfrontals in contact with the labials; frontal as long as or a little longer than its distance from the rostral, as long as or a little longer than the parietals; two præoculars and a small subocular, or one præocular and two suboculars; præocular in contact with the frontal; two postoculars; temporals 1+2 or 2+2; eight upper labials, fifth entering the eye; four lower labials in contact with the anterior chin-shields, which are shorter than the posterior. Scales in 15 rows. Ventrals 172–203; anal divided; subcaudals 140–174. Bright green or pale brownish, the interstitial skin black and white on the anterior part of the body, which appears barred when distended; a yellow line along each side of the lower surfaces.

Total length 1500 millim.; tail 560.

India, Ceylon, Burma, Siam.

a	♀ (V. 193; C. 149).	Allahabad, N.W. Provinces.	Messrs. v. Schlagintweit [C.].
b–c.	♂ (V. 184; C. 156) & ♀ (V. 179; C. 147).	Calcutta.	Messrs. v. Schlagintweit [C].
d.	♂ (V. 189; C. ?).	Deccan	Col. Sykes [P.].
e–f.	♀ (V. 182, C. 150) & yg (V. 180; C 157).	Matheran, Bombay.	Dr. Leith [P.].
g.	♂ (V. 180; C. 159).	Mahabaleshwur, Bombay.	Dr. Leith [P.].
h–m.	♀ (V. 186; C ?) & yg. (V. 185, 180, 182, 184; C. 164, 164, 150, 165).	Madras.	Sir W. Elliot [P.].
n–o	♂ (V. 175, 173; C. 167, 174).	Madras.	J. E. Boileau, Esq. [P.].
p.	♀ (V. 174; C. ?).	Madras.	T. C. Jerdon, Esq. [P.].
q.	♀ (V. 179, C. 145).	Anamallays.	Col. Beddome [C]
r.	♂ (V. 176; C. 156).	Peermad, Travancore.	H. S Ferguson, Esq. [P.].

s-u, v. ♂ (V. 180, 187; C. 159, 173) & ♀ (V. 181, 174; C. 140, 152).	Ceylon.	R. Templeton, Esq. [P.].
w, x-y ♀ (V. 172, 174; C. 163, 142) & hgr. (V. 181; C. 153).	Ceylon.	
z. ♂ (V. 203; C. 155).	Assam (?).	Dr. Cantor.
α. Yg. (V. 190; C. 144).	Rangoon.	
β. ♂ (V. 200; C. 156).	Toungoo.	E. W. Oates, Esq. [P.].
γ. ♂ (V. 199; C. 153).	Toungyi, S. Shan States, 5000 ft.	Lieut. Blakeway [C.]
δ. ♂ (V. 193; C. 146).	Siam.	J. Bowring, Esq [P.].
ε, ζ, η. Skulls.	Bengal.	

8. Dryophis pulverulentus.

Dryinus pulverulentus, *Dum. & Bibr.* vii. p. 812 (1854).
Passerita mycterizans, part., *Gunth. Cat.* p. 160 (1858).
Dryophis pulverulentus, *Jan, Elenco*, p. 88 (1863), and *Icon. Gén.* 32, pl. v fig. 1 (1869); *Bouleng. Faun. Ind., Rept.* p. 371 (1890).
Passerita purpurascens, *Gunth. Rept. Brit. Ind.* p. 306, pl. xxiii. fig. F (1864); *Theob. Cat. Rept. Brit Ind.* p. 194 (1876).

Snout pointed, terminating in a dermal appendage which is longer than the eye, formed below by the rostral and covered above with numerous small scales or warts; the length of the snout, without the appendage, more than twice the diameter of the eye. Nasals in contact behind the rostral appendage, or narrowly separated; no loreal; internasals and præfrontals in contact with the labials; frontal as long as its distance from the nasals, as long as or a little longer than the parietals; two præoculars, with one subocular below them; upper præocular in contact with the frontal; two postoculars; temporals 2+2 or 2+3; eight upper labials, fifth entering the eye; four lower labials in contact with the anterior chin-shields, which are shorter than the posterior. Scales in 15 rows. Ventrals 180-191; anal divided; subcaudals 154-173. Greyish, powdered with brown, with blackish transverse spots above; a dark brown rhomboidal spot on the upper surface of the head, and a brown band on each side, passing through the eye.

Total length 1730 millim.; tail 710.

Ceylon and Southern India.

a, b, c. ♀ (V. 182, 180, 190; C 164, 154, 152).	Ceylon.	(Types of *P. purpurascens*.)
d, e. ♀ (V. 191; C. 172) & hgr. (V. 182; C.109).	Anamallays.	Col. Beddome [C.].
f. Skull.	Anamallays.	Col. Beddome [C.].

176. THELOTORNIS.

Thelotornis, *Smith, Ill. Zool. S. Afr., Rept.*, App. p. 19 (1849); *Peters, Reise n. Mossamb.* iii. p. 131 (1882).
Dryophis, part., *Dum. & Bibr. Erp. Gén.* vii. p. 814 (1854).

176. THELOTORNIS.

Dryiophis, part, *Gunth. Cat. Col. Sn.* p. 155 (1858); *Jan, Elenco sist. Ofid.* p. 88 (1863).
Cladophis, *A. Dum. Arch. Mus* x. 1859, p. 204.

Maxillary teeth 16 or 17, gradually increasing in length, followed, after a short interspace, by two or three enlarged grooved teeth situated below the posterior border of the eye; anterior mandibular teeth strongly enlarged. Head distinct from neck, with strong canthus rostralis; eye large, with horizontal pupil; nasal entire. Body cylindrical, very slender; scales narrow, very oblique, feebly keeled, with apical pits, in 19 rows; ventrals rounded. Tail long; subcaudals in two rows.

Tropical and South Africa.

In this genus, as in the following, the ectopterygoid bone is forked, the two branches articulating with the maxillary (see fig. 14, p. 187), a structure not found in any other type of Snakes. *Thelotornis* and *Dispholidus* further agree in having the brain-case widely open in front, as in *Cœlopeltis, Dromophis, Taphrometopon, Psammophis*, and *Dryophis*.

1. Thelotornis kirtlandii.

Leptophis kirtlandii, *Hallow. Proc. Ac Philad.* 1844, p. 62, and 1854, p. 100.
Thelotornis capensis, *Smith, Ill. Zool. S. Afr., Rept.*, App. p. 19 (1849); *Peters, Mon. Berl. Ac* 1867, p. 235.
Oxybelis lecomtei, *Dum. & Bibr* vii. p. 821 (1854).
Tragops rufulus, *Dum. & Bibr.* t. c. p 827.
Oxybelis kirtlandii, *Hallow Proc. Ac. Philad.* 1857, p. 59.
—— violacea, *Fischer, Abh. Naturw. Hamb.* iii. 1856, p. 91, pl. ii. fig. 7
Dryiophis kirtlandii, *Gunth. Cat.* p. 156 (1858), *and Ann & Mag. N. H.* (3) xi. 1863, p 22, *Boettg. Ber Senck. Ges.* 1888, p. 65, *Jan, Icon Gén* 32, pl vi. fig. 2 (1869); *Bocage, Herp. Angola*, p. 119 (1895).
Cladophis kirtlandii, *A. Dum. Arch. Mus.* x. 1859, p. 204, pl. xvii. fig. 8
Dryiophis oatesii, *Gunth. in Oates, Matabeleland*, p. 330, pl D (1881).
Thelotornis kirtlandii, *Peters, Reise n. Mossamb.* iii. p. 131, pl. xix. fig. 2 (1882).

Rostral broader than deep, visible from above; internasals as long as broad, nearly as long as the præfrontals, sometimes reaching the labials between the nasal and the loreal; frontal once and two thirds to twice as long as broad, as long as its distance from the rostral or the end of the snout, as long as or slightly shorter than the parietals, which are followed by a pair of large occipitals separated by a smaller shield; one, two, or three loreals; one præocular, not reaching the frontal, three postoculars; temporals 1+2 (rarely 1+1); eight or nine upper labials, fourth and fifth or fifth and sixth entering the eye; three to five lower labials in contact with the anterior chin-shields, which are shorter than the posterior. Scales feebly keeled, in 19 rows. Ventrals 147–181; anal divided; subcaudals 117–170. Greyish or pinkish brown above, uniform or with more or less distinct darker and lighter spots and cross-bands; head green above, with or without some patches of pinkish speckled with black and a pinkish black-dotted streak on each side of the head, passing through the eye; upper lip cream-colour, or pink, uniform or spotted with black; one or several black blotches on each side of the neck; greyish or pinkish beneath, speckled or striated with brown.

Total length 1180 millim.; tail 400.

Tropical and South Africa.

A. Head uniform green above and on the sides; black blotches usually forming cross-bands on the neck. (*L. kirtlandii*, Hallow.; *O. lecomtei*, D. & B.; *O. violacea*, Fisch.)

a. ♀ (V. 174; C. 139).	Sierra Leone.	
b. ♀ (V. 161; C. ?).	Adjah Bippo, Wassau, Gold Coast.	G. A. Higlett, Esq. [P.].
c. ♂ (V. 168, C. 150).	Fantee.	
d. ♂ (V. 165; C. 139).	Ashantee.	
e. ♀ (V. 181; C. 146).	Oil River.	Sir H. H. Johnston [P.].
f, g. ♂ (V. 170, 168; C. 167, 152).	Gaboon.	
h. ♀ (V. 177; C. 160).	Eloby district, Gaboon.	H. Ansell, Esq. [P.].
i. ♂ (V. 175; C. 170).	Mouth of the Loango.	Mr. H. J. Duggan [C.].
k. ♀ (V. 165; C. 137).	Taveta, E. Africa.	Keith Anstruther, Esq. [P.].
l. Skull.	Cameroons.	

B. Head with black dots above and on the sides; no cross-bands on the neck. (*T. capensis*, Smith; *D. oatesii*, Gthr.)

a. Hgr., bad state.	Victoria Nyanza.	Dr. Emin Pasha [C.].
b. ♂ (V. 159; C. ?).	Mpwapwa, E. Africa.	
c. Yg. (V. 155; C. 137).	Mandala, Brit. C. Africa.	Scott Elliot, Esq. [P.].
d. ♀ (V. 155; C. 130).	L. Nyassa.	Universities Mission.
e. ♀ (V. 147, C. ?).	L. Nyassa.	Miss M. Woodward [C.]; Miss. S. C. McLaughlin [P.].
f, g–k ♂ (V. 161, 151, 156; C. 136, 124, 117) & ♀ (V. 163, 152; C. 118, 124).	Zomba, Brit. C. Africa.	Sir H. H. Johnston [P.].
l–m. ♂ (V. 163; C. 146) & hgr. (V. 148; C. 124).	Milangi, Brit. C. Africa.	Sir H. H. Johnston [P.].
n. ♀ (V. 161; C. ?).	Matabele-land.	C. G. Oates, Esq. [P.]. (Type of *D. oatesii*.)

177. DISPHOLIDUS.

Bucephalus (non Baer), Smith, *Zool. Journ.* iv 1820, p 441; *Dum. & Bibr. Erp. Gén.* vii. p. 875 (1854); *Gunth. Cat. Col. Sn.* p. 143 (1858); *Jan, Elenco sist. Ofid.* p. 86 (1863); *Peters, Reise n. Mossamb.* iii. p. 132 (1882).

Dispholidus, *Duvernoy, Ann Sc. Nat.* xxvi. 1832, p. 150.

Dendrophis, part., *Schleg Phys. Serp.* ii. p. 220 (1837).

Maxillary short, widening behind, where it articulates with the forked ectopterygoid; teeth small, 7 or 8, followed by three very large grooved fangs situated below the eye; mandibular teeth subequal. Head distinct from neck, with distinct canthus rostralis; eye very large, with round pupil; nasal entire. Body slightly compressed; scales very narrow, oblique, more or less strongly keeled, with apical pits, in 19 or 21 rows; ventrals rounded or obtusely angulate laterally. Tail long; subcaudals in two rows.

Tropical and South Africa.

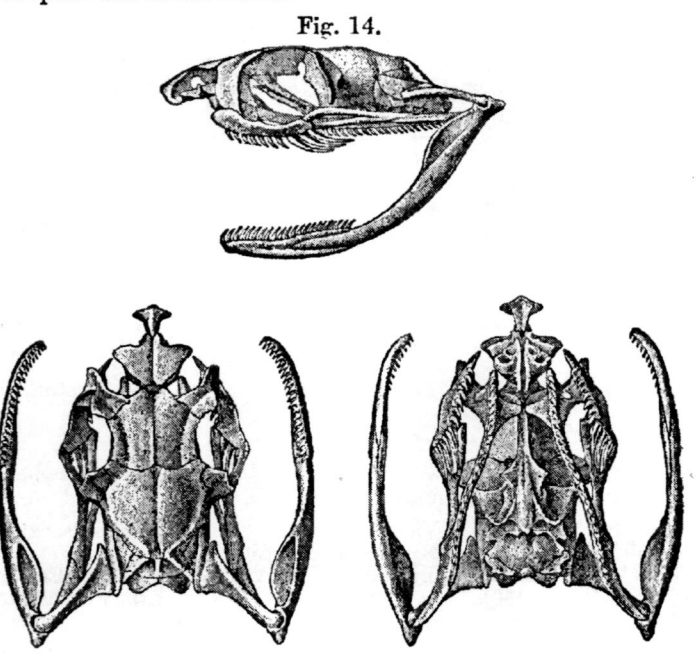

Fig. 14.

Skull of *Dispholidus typus*.

1. Dispholidus typus.

Bucephalus typus, *Smith, Zool. Journ.* iv. 1829, p. 441; *Dum. & Bibr.* vii. p. 877 (1854); *Jan, Icon. Gén.* 32, pl. iv. (1869); *Peters, Reise n. Mossamb.* iii. p. 132 (1882).
—— jardinii, *Smith, l. c.* p. 442.
—— gutturalis, *Smith, l. c.*
—— bellii, *Smith, l. c.*
Dispholidus lalandii, *Duvernoy, Ann. Sc. Nat.* xxvi. 1832, p. 150, and xxx. 1833, p. 24, pl. iii.
Dendrophis colubrina, *Schleg. Phys. Serp.* ii. p. 238, pl. ix. figs. 14–16 (1837).
Bucephalus capensis, *Smith, Ill. Zool. S. Afr., Rept.* pls. x.–xiii. (1841); *Günth. Cat.* p. 143 (1858); *Boettg. Abh. Senck. Ges.* xii. 1881, p. 397.
—— viridis, *Smith, l. c.* pl. iii.
Dendrophis pseudodipsas, *Bianconi, Spec. Zool. Mosamb.* p. 40, pl. iv. fig. 2 (1849).

Snout short, not much longer than the eye. Rostral nearly as deep as broad, visible from above; internasals much shorter than the præfrontals; frontal once and one fourth to once and a half as long as broad, as long as or a little longer than its distance from the end of the snout, as long as the parietals; loreal as long as deep or longer than deep; one præocular (rarely divided), not reaching the frontal; three postoculars; temporals 1+2; seven or eight upper labials, third and fourth or fourth and fifth entering the eye; three or four lower labials in contact with the anterior chin-shields, which are smaller than the posterior. Scales in 19 or 21 rows. Ventrals 164–201; anal divided; subcaudals 91–131. Coloration very variable.

Total length 1500 millim.; tail 380.

Tropical and South Africa.

A. Brown above, upper lip and lower parts yellowish or greyish; young with darker and lighter spots, and the belly speckled with brown. (*B. typus*, Smith.)

a. ♀ (Sc. 19; V. 191; C. 122). Port Natal. Rev. H. Calloway [P.]

b–d. Hgr. ♂ (Sc. 19; V. 185; C. 117), ♀ (Sc. 19, V. 192; C. 120), & yg. (Sc. 19; V. 171; C. 115). Natal. Mr. T. Ayres [C.].

e. Yg. (Sc. 21, V. 187; C. 117). Natal. J. H. Gurney, Esq. [P.]

f. Yg (Sc. 21; V. 169; C. 116). S. Africa. Chatham Mus.

g. Yg (Sc. 19, V. 176; C. 118). Zambesi. Sir J. Kirk [C.].

h. Yg. (Sc. 19; V. 180; C. 123). Zomba, Brit. C. Africa. Sir H. H. Johnston [P.].

i. ♂ (head and tail only). Between the E. Coast and Unyamwezi. Capt. Speke [P.].

k. Hgr. (Sc. 19; V. 183; C. 109). Mpwapwa, interior of E. Africa.

l. Hgr. (Sc. 21; V. 188, C. 98). Anseba Valley, Abyssinia. W. T. Blanford, Esq. [P.]

B. Olive-brown above, yellowish beneath, scales and shields edged with blackish. (*B. jardinii*, Smith.)

a. ♂ (Sc. 19; V. 179; C. 112). Africa. Mr. Argent [C.].

C. Green above, uniform or scales narrowly edged with black. (*B. viridis*, Smith.)

a. ♀ (Sc. 19; V. 164; C. 111). Barberton, Transvaal. S. African Mus. [P.].

b. ♀ (Sc. 19; V. 182; C. ?). Mpwapwa, E. Africa.

c. ♂ (Sc. 19; V. 185; Ugogo, E. Africa. Mr. Baxter [C.].

d. ♀ (Sc. 19 ; V. 184 ;   Africa.
C. 102).

D. Green or olive above, all the scales and shields edged with black ; head often much spotted with black.

a. ♂ (Sc. 19 ; V. 183 ;   Natal   E. Howlett, Esq. [P.].
C. 121).
b. ♂ (Sc. 19 ; V. 190 ;   Natal.   Mr. T. Ayres [C.].
C. 131).
c. Hgr. ♂ (Sc. 19 ; V. 182 ; W. Africa.
C. 107).
d Skeleton

E. Black above, each scale with a yellowish or greenish spot ; head spotted or marked with black ; ventrals and subcaudals yellowish, edged with black. (*B. belli*, Smith.)

a. ♂ (Sc. 21 , V. 176 ;   Port Elizabeth.   Mr. Drege [P.].
C. 110).
b–c. ♂ (Sc 19, 21 , V. 185,   Africa.   Haslar Collection.
180 , C. 108, 113).
d. ♂ (Sc. 19 ; V. 186 ;   Africa.
C. ?).

F. Uniform black above, blackish grey beneath.

a. ♂ (Sc. 21 ; V. 179 ;   Ushambola, Zanzibar   Sir J. Kirk [C.].
C. 125).

178. OXYBELIS.

Dryinus, part., *Bell, Zool. Journ.* ii. 1825, p. 324.
Dryophis, part., *Boie, Isis*, 1827, p. 520 ; *Schleg. Phys. Serp* ii. p. 241 (1837) ; *Gunth. Cat. Col. Sn* p 155 (1858).
Oxybelis, *Wagl. Syst. Amph.* p. 183 (1830) ; *Jan, Elenco sist. Ofid.* p. 88 (1863)
Dryophis, *Wagl l. c.*
Oxybelis, part., *Dum. & Bibr. Erp. Gén.* vii. p. 813 (1854).

Maxillary teeth 20 to 25, subequal, the last three to five a little enlarged and grooved on the outer side ; anterior mandibular teeth strongly enlarged. Head elongate, distinct from neck, with distinct

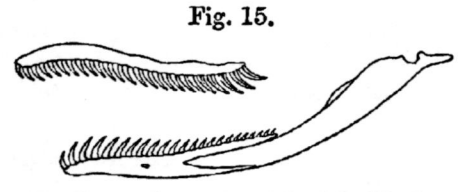

Fig. 15.

Maxillary and mandible of *Oxybelis fulgidus*.

canthus rostralis ; eye rather large, with round pupil ; nasal entire or semidivided ; loreal usually absent ; frontal narrow. Body slender, compressed ; scales smooth or feebly keeled, with apical pits, more or less oblique, in 15 or 17 rows; ventrals rounded. Tail long; subcaudals in two rows.

Tropical America.

Synopsis of the Species.

I. Snout not thrice as long as the eye; anal entire.

Scales in 15 rows; two labials entering
   the eye .... 1. *brevirostris*, p. 190.
Scales in 17 rows; a single labial bordering
   the eye .... 2. *argenteus*, p. 190.

II. Snout thrice as long as the eye; anal divided.

Dorsal scales keeled; green above ...... 3. *fulgidus*, p. 191.
Scales smooth or faintly keeled .... 4. *acuminatus*, p. 192.

1. Oxybelis brevirostris.

Dryophis brevirostris, *Cope, Proc. Ac. Philad.* 1860, p. 555, and *Journ. Ac. Philad.* (2) viii 1876, p. 132, pl xxvi. fig. 2.
Oxybelis cærulescens, *Jan, Elenco*, p. 88 (1863).

Snout once and a half as long as the snout, which scarcely projects beyond the lower jaw. Rostral twice as broad as deep, scarcely visible from above; internasals nearly as long as the præfrontals; frontal twice to twice and a half as long as broad, narrower than the supraocular, as long as its distance from the end of the snout, as long as the parietals; no loreal, præfrontal in contact with two labials; one præocular, in contact with or narrowly separated from the frontal; one or two postoculars; temporals very large, 1+2; six upper labials, third and fourth entering the eye; four lower labials in contact with the anterior chin-shields, which are much shorter than the posterior. Scales smooth or faintly keeled, in 15 rows. Ventrals 167–183; anal entire; subcaudals 170–174. Olive or purplish above, pale green beneath; a dark streak on each side of the head, passing through the eye.

Total length 925 millim.; tail 385.

Central America, Colombia, Ecuador.

a. ♂ (V. 183; C. 174).   Chontalez, Nicaragua.   R. A. Rix, Esq. [C];
                                                 W. M. Crowfoot,
                                                   Esq [P.]
b. ♂ (V. 167; C. 172).   Pallatanga, Ecuador.   Mr. C. Buckley [C.].

2. Oxybelis argenteus.

Coluber argenteus, *Daud Rept.* vi. p. 336 (1803).
—— argentatus, *Merr Tent.* p. 116 (1820).
Dryiophis argentea, *Schleg Phys. Serp.* ii. p. 253, pl. x. figs. 14 & 15 (1837); *Günth. Cat.* p. 155 (1858).

Snout rather more than twice as long as the eye. Rostral much broader than deep, scarcely visible from above; internasals as long as or a little shorter than the præfrontals; frontal twice to twice and a half as long as broad, not broader than the supraocular, as long as or shorter than its distance from the end of the snout or the parietals; loreal elongate, often fused with the præfrontal; one præocular, widely separated from the frontal; two postoculars; temporals 1+2; six upper labials, fourth entering the eye; four lower labials in contact with the anterior chin-shields, which are much shorter than the posterior. Scales smooth, in 17 rows. Ventrals 189-207; anal entire, subcaudals 150-188. Pale greyish brown or purplish above, with three darker longitudinal streaks, the outer of which extend to the end of the snout, passing through the eyes; upper lip whitish; throat bluish grey, dotted with black; yellowish beneath, with two olive-green stripes and a narrow median line of the same colour.

Total length 1060 millim.; tail 410.

Guianas, Brazil, Eastern Peru.

a. ♀ (V. 198; C. 156). Cayenne
b. ♂ (V. 206; C. 150). Pebas, Upper Amazons. H. W. Bates, Esq. [P.].
c. ♂ (V. 204; C. 185). Yurimaguas, N.E. Peru.

3. Oxybelis fulgidus.

Natrix flagelliformis, part, *Laur. Syn. Rept.* p 79 (1768).
Coluber fulgidus, *Daud Rept.* vi. p. 352, pl lxxx. (1803).
Dryophis fulgidus, *Fitzing N Class Rept.* p. 60 (1826); *Boie, Isis,* 1827, p. 546; *Wagl. Icon. Amph.* pl x. (1829); *Günth Cat.* p. 158 (1858); *Cope, Proc Ac Philad.* 1860, p. 555; *Günth. Biol. C.-Am., Rept.* p. 178 (1895).
Dryiophis catesbyi, *Schleg. Phys. Serp.* ii. p. 252, pl. x. figs. 6-8 (1837), *and Abbild.* p 114, pl xxxvi. (1844).
Oxybelis fulgidus, part, *Dum & Bibr* vii. p 817 (1854).
—— flagelliformis, *Steind. Novara, Rept.* p. 73 (1867).
—— fulgidus, *Jan, Icon. Gén.* 33, pl. iv. fig 1 (1869).

Snout about thrice as long as the eye, flat at the end and very prominent. Rostral a little broader than deep, scarcely visible from above; internasals shorter than the præfrontals; frontal once and a half to twice as long as broad, not broader than the supraocular, as long as or a little longer than the præfrontals, as long as or a little shorter than the parietals; no loreal, præfrontal in contact with two or three labials; one præocular, narrowly separated from the frontal; two postoculars (rarely one); temporals very large, 1+2; nine or ten upper labials, fourth, fifth, and sixth or fifth, sixth, and seventh entering the eye; four lower labials in contact with the anterior chin-shields, which are much shorter than the posterior. Scales in 17 rows, dorsals feebly keeled. Ventrals 198-217; anal divided; subcaudals 139-165. Bright green above, yellowish green beneath and on the upper lip; a yellowish-white line along each side of the belly and tail.

Total length 1550 millim.; tail 510.

Tropical America.

a. ♂ (V. 205; C. 165).   Yucatan.
b. ♀ (V. 217; C. ?).   British Honduras.
c. ♂ (V. 214; C. 151).   Panama.   Capt. J. C. Dow [P.].
d. ♀ (V. 205; C. 157).   Para.
e. ♀ (V. 206; C. 156).   Caballo Cocha, N.E. Peru.   Mr. W. Davis [C]; Messrs. Veitch [P.].
f. ♀ (V. 209; C. 139).   ——?
g. ♀, skeleton.   Para.

4. Oxybelis acuminatus.

Coluber acuminatus, *Wied, Abbild. Nat. Bras* (1822), and *Beitr.* 1. p. 322 (1825).
Dryinus æneus, *Wagl. in Spix, Serp. Bras.* p. 12, pl. iii. (1824).
—— auratus, *Bell, Zool. Journ.* ii. 1825, p. 325, pl. xii.
Dryiophis aurata, *Schleg. Phys. Serp.* ii p. 255, pl. x. figs. 16–18 (1837).
Oxybelis æneus, *Dum. & Bibr.* vii. p. 819 (1854); *Jan, Icon Gén.* 33, pl. iv. fig. 2 (1869).
Dryophis vittatus, *Girard, U.S. Nav. Astron. Exped., Rept.* p. 211, pl. xxxvi. (1855).
Dryiophis acuminata, *Gunth. Cat.* pp. 156 & 252 (1858); *Cope, Proc. Ac. Philad* 1860, p 555; *Boettg. Ber. Sench. Ges.* 1889, p. 314; *Gunth Biol. C.-Am , Rept.* p. 177 (1895)
Oxybelis acuminatus, *Steind. Novara, Rept.* p. 72 (1867)
Dryiophis æneus, *Garm. Proc. Am. Philos. Soc.* xxiv. 1887, p. 284.

Snout thrice to thrice and a half as long as the eye, prominent. Rostral nearly as deep as broad or broader than deep, scarcely visible from above; internasals shorter than the præfrontals; frontal once and two thirds to thrice as long as broad, not broader than the supraocular, as long as or a little longer than the præfrontals, as long as or shorter than the parietals; no loreal, præfrontal in contact with two or three labials, one præocular, in contact with or separated from the frontal; two (rarely three) postoculars; temporals very large, 1+2; eight or nine (rarely ten) upper labials, fourth and fifth, fourth, fifth, and sixth, or fifth, sixth, and seventh entering the eye; four (rarely five) lower labials in contact with the anterior chin shields, which are much shorter than the posterior. Scales smooth or faintly keeled, in 17 rows *. Ventrals 174–203; anal divided; subcaudals 150–188. Bronzy, greyish, or reddish above, uniform or freckled with brown, usually with scattered black dots, or with black edges to some of the scales; a black line on each side of the head, passing through the eye; upper lip and lower surface of head yellowish white; yellowish, pale brownish, or reddish beneath, speckled or streaked with brown,

---

* Garman has a specimen from Trinidad with 15 rows.

often with scattered black dots, sometimes with two dark brown longitudinal lines.

Total length 1520 millim.; tail 620.

Tropical America.

a–e. ♂ (V. 190, 184; C. 165, ?) & ♀ (V. 179, 190, 180; C. ?, 160, 157).	Presidio, near Mazatlan.	Hr. A. Forrer [C.].
f. ♀ (V. 194; C 185).	Tres Marias Ids.	Hr. A. Forrer [C.]
g. ♀ (V. 190; C. 183).	Tetepetla, Guerrero.	Mr. H. H Smith [C.]; F.D.Godman, Esq. [P.].
h–k. ♂ (V. 174, 176, 179; C. 160, 169, ?).	Santo Domingo de Guzman, Oaxaca.	Dr. A. C. Buller [C.].
l. ♀ (V. 187; C. 168).	Sarabia, Oaxaca.	Dr A. C. Buller [C.].
m–n. ♂ (V. 183; C. 162) & ♀ (V. 192; C. 187).	Yucatan.	
o ♀ (V. 187; C. 168).	Rio Motagua, Guatemala.	O. Salvin, Esq. [C.].
p–q. ♀ (V. 189, 192; C. 150, 173).	Honduras.	
r–x ♂ (V. 191, 189, 188, 185; C. 188, 180, 188, 170) & ♀ (V. 194, 192, 186, C. 182, 180, 177).	Ruatan Id., Honduras.	Mr. Gaumer [C.]; F. D. Godman, Esq. [P.].
y–a ♂ (V 193, 188; C. 184, 176) & ♀ (V. 194, C. 180).	Bonacca Id., Honduras	Mr Gaumer [C]; F. D. Godman, Esq [P]
β. ♂ (V. 187; C ?).	Hacienda Rosa de Jericho, Nicaragua, 3250 feet.	Dr. E. Rothschuh [C.].
γ. ♂ (V. 179; C 173).	Irazu, Costa Rica.	Mr. Rogers [C.]; F. D. Godman, Esq. [P.].
δ. Hgr (V. 178; C. ?).	Guayaquil.	Mr. Fraser [C.].
ε. ♂ (V. 184; C. 168).	Carthagena.	
ζ. ♂ (V. 175; C. ?).	Venezuela.	Mr Dyson [C.].
η–θ. ♀ (V. 188, 192, C. ?, 172).	Para.	R. Graham, Esq. [P.].
ι. ♀ (V 182; C. 171).	Pernambuco.	W. A. Forbes, Esq. [P.].
κ. ♂ (V. 186; C. 150).	Bahia.	Dr O. Wucherer [C.]

179. DRYOPHIOPS.

Chrysopelea, part., *Günth. Cat. Col. Sn.* p. 88 (1858), *and Rept. Brit. Ind.* p. 298 (1864)

Dryophis, part., *Jan, Elenco sist. Ofid.* p. 88 (1863).

Maxillary teeth 20, subequal, the last two or three a little enlarged and grooved; anterior mandibular teeth enlarged. Head elongate, distinct from neck, with distinct canthus rostralis; eye rather large, with horizontal pupil; nasal entire; frontal narrow, bell-shaped. Body slender, compressed; scales smooth, oblique, with apical pits, in 15 rows; ventrals with suture-like lateral keel and a notch on each side corresponding to the keel. Tail long; subcaudals in two rows, keeled and notched like the ventrals.

South-eastern Asia.

1. Dryophiops rubescens.

Dipsas rubescens, *Gray, Ill. Ind. Zool.* ii. pl. lxxxiv. fig. 2 (1834).
Leptophis rubescens, *Blyth, Journ. As. Soc. Beng.* xxiii. 1855, p. 293.
Chrysopelea rubescens, part., *Gunth. Cat.* p 145 (1858), and *Rept. Brit. Ind* p. 299 (1864).
Dryophis rubescens, *Jan, Elenco,* p. 88 (1863), and *Icon. Gén.* 32, pl. vi. fig. 1 (1869).
Chrysopelea rubescens, *Stoliczka, Journ. As. Soc. Beng.* xxxix. 1870, p 195.

Rostral twice as broad as deep, just visible from above; internasals shorter than the præfrontals; frontal once and a half to once and two thirds as long as broad, as long as its distance from the end of the snout, shorter than the parietals, loreal much elongate; one præocular, forming a suture with the frontal; two or three postoculars; temporals 2+2; nine upper labials, fourth, fifth, and sixth entering the eye; four or five lower labials in contact with the anterior chin-shields, which are much shorter than the posterior. Scales in 15 rows. Ventrals 188–199, anal divided; subcaudals 111–136. Bronzy or reddish brown above, with small black spots; upper surface of head with undulous longitudinal markings; a dark streak on each side of the head, passing through the eye; a median dark streak on the occiput and neck; labials with a few small black spots; lower parts yellow in front, reddish behind, dotted with darker, with or without scattered small black spots.

Total length 750 millim.; tail 210.

Siam, Malay Peninsula, Sumatra, Borneo, Natuna Islands.

a.	♀ (V. 189; C. 115).	Malay Peninsula?	Gen. Hardwicke [P.]. (Type)
b.	♀* (V. 192; C. ?).	Malay Peninsula?	Gen Hardwicke [P.].
c.	♂ (V. 192; C. 119).	Sumatra.	Dr. Bleeker. (*Dendrophis sumatranus*, Blkr.)
d–e.	♂ (V 191; C. 125) & ♀ (V 199; C. 112)	Sarawak.	Sir H. Low [P.].
f.	♀ (V. 188, C. 118).	Sandakan, N. Borneo.	Douglas Cator, Esq. [P.].
g.	♀ (V. 191; C. 111).	Sirhassen, Natuna Ids.	A Everett, Esq [C.].

---

* The specimen contains a *Draco melanopogon*, Blgr., which species was first described from Malacca, and has since been found in the Natuna Islands

2. Dryophiops philippina. (PLATE IX. fig. 2.)

Chrysopelea rubescens, part., *Günth. Cat.* p. 145 (1858), *and Rept. Brit. Ind.* p. 299 (1864).

Agrees in structure with the preceding, except that the loreal is absent, and the præocular only just touches or is narrowly separated from the frontal. Ventrals 177–184; subcaudals 118–123. Pale olive or pale brown above, some of the scales black-edged, yellow or pale olive beneath, dotted with darker; some large black dots on the head and neck; a dark streak on each side of the head, passing through the eye.

Total length 750 millim.; tail 250.

Philippine Islands.

a. ♂ (V. 177; C. 123).	Cape Engano, N. Luzon.	Whitehead Exped.
b, c. ♀ (V. 184, 182; C. 121, 118).	Philippines.	H. Cuming, Esq. [C.]

180. CHRYSOPELEA.

Chrysopelea, *Boie, Isis,* 1827, p. 520; *Wagl. Syst. Amph.* p. 188 (1830); *Dum. & Bibr. Erp. Gén.* vii. p. 1040 (1854), *Bouleng. Faun. Ind., Rept.* p. 371 (1890).
Tyria, part., *Fitzing. N. Class. Rept.* p. 29 (1826).
Dendrophis, part., *Schleg. Phys. Serp.* ii. p. 220 (1837).
Chrysopelea, part, *Günth. Cat. Col. Sn.* p. 145 (1858); *Jan, Elenco sist. Ofid.* p. 86 (1863), *Günth. Rept. Brit. Ind.* p. 298 (1864).

Maxillary teeth 20 to 22, subequal, the last three a little longer and grooved; anterior mandibular teeth longest. Head distinct from neck; eye rather large, with round pupil. Body elongate, compressed; scales smooth or feebly keeled, oblique, with apical pits, in 17 rows; ventrals with suture-like lateral keel and a notch on each side corresponding to the keel. Tail long: subcaudals in two rows, keeled and notched like the ventrals.

South-eastern Asia.

Synopsis of the Species.

Three or more rows of dorsal scales feebly but distinctly keeled, ventrals 202–221.	1. *rhodopleuron,* p. 195.
Scales smooth or faintly keeled; ventrals 200–238	2. *ornata,* p. 196.
Scales smooth; ventrals 181–198	3. *chrysochlora,* p. 198.

1. Chrysopelea rhodopleuron.

Chrysopelea rhodopleuron, *Boie, Isis,* 1827, p. 547; *Dum. & Bibr.* vii. p. 1045 (1854), *Günth. Cat.* p. 145 (1858); *Jan, Icon. Gén.* 33, pl. ii. fig. 1 (1869).
Dendrophis rhodopleuron, *Schleg. Phys. Serp.* ii. p. 233, pl. xi. figs. 11–13 (1837).
Chrysopelea vicina, *Günth. Ann. & Mag. N. H.* (4) ix. 1872, p. 27.
—— viridis, *Fischer, Arch. f. Nat.* 1880, p. 222, pl. ix figs. 13–17.

Snout much depressed, squarely truncate. Rostral broader than deep, just visible from above; internasals shorter than the præfrontals; frontal once and a half to once and three fourths as long as broad, as long as its distance from the end of the snout, shorter than the parietals; loreal much elongate; one præocular, in contact with or separated from the frontal; two postoculars; temporals 2+2; nine upper labials, fifth and sixth entering the eye; five (rarely four) lower labials in contact with the anterior chin-shields, which are shorter than the posterior. Scales in 17 rows, three or more median rows feebly but distinctly keeled. Ventrals 202–221; anal divided; subcaudals 146–180. Pale olive-brown or greenish to blackish above; a darker streak on each side of the head, passing through the eye; upper lip whitish; ventrals yellowish or pale greenish.

Total length 1160 millim.; tail 380.

Moluccas, Sangir Island, Ceram, Tenimber Islands.

A. Dark brown or blackish above, the scales lighter in the centre; outer row of scales red, black-edged, ends of ventrals above the keel red; a black streak along the lower surface of the tail. (*C. rhodopleuron*, Boie.)

a. ♀ (V. 213; C. 167).	Amboyna.	Leyden Museum.
b-c. ♂ (V. 203, C. 164) & ♀ (V. 205, C. ?).	Mysol.	
d. ♀ (V. 218; C. 155).	N. Ceram.	
e. ♂ (V. 204; C. 173).	Timor Laut.	H. O. Forbes, Esq. [C.].

B. Uniform olive above, yellow beneath. (*C. vicina*, Gthr.)

a. ♀ (V. 221; C. 146).   Mysol.   (Type of *C vicina*.)

2. Chrysopelea ornata.

Seba, Thes i. pl. xciv fig. 7 (1734), and ii. pl vii. fig. 1, pl. lvi. fig. 1, and pl. lxi. fig. 2 (1735); *Russell, Ind. Serp.* ii pl. ii. (1801).

Coluber ornatus, *Shaw, Zool.* iii p. 477 (1802).

—— ibibiboca, *Daud. Rept.* vi. p 327 (1803).

Tyria ornata, *Fitzing. N. Class. Rept* p. 60 (1837)

Chrysopelea ornata, *Boie, Isis*, 1827, p 546; *Dum. & Bibr.* vii. p. 1042 (1854); *Jan, Icon. Gén.* 33, pl. i. fig. 1 (1869); *Stoliczka, Journ. As. Soc. Beng.* xxxix. 1870, p. 194; *Theob. Cat. Rept. Brit. Ind.* p. 101 (1876); *Anders. An. Zool. Res. Yunnan*, p. 825 (1878); *Boettg. Ber. Offenb. Ver. Nat.* 1888, p. 84; *Bouleng. Faun. Ind., Rept.* p. 371 (1890)

—— paradisi, *Boie, l. c.* p. 547.

Dendrophis ornata, part., *Schleg. Phys. Serp.* ii. p. 234, pl. ix. figs. 8–10 (1837), *and Abbild.* p. 19, pl. vi figs. 3–10 (1837).

Leptophis ornatus, part. *Cantor, Cat. Mal Rept.* p 87 (1847).

Dendrophis paradisii, *Motley & Dillwyn, Nat. Hist. Labuan*, p 46, pl. —— (1855).

Chrysopelea ornata, part., *Gunth. Cat.* p. 146 (1858), *and Rept. Brit. Ind.* p. 298 (1864).

—— rubescens, part., *Gunth. Rept. Brit. Ind.* p. 299.

180. CHRYSOPELEA.

Snout much depressed, squarely truncate. Rostral broader than deep, visible from above; internasals nearly as long as the præfrontals; frontal once and one third to once and two thirds as long as broad, nearly as long as its distance from the end of the snout, as long as or slightly shorter than the parietals; loreal small and elongate (rarely fused with the præfrontal); one præocular, often in contact with the frontal; two postoculars; temporals 2+2; nine or ten upper labials, fifth and sixth or fourth, fifth, and sixth entering the eye; five lower labials in contact with the anterior chin-shields, which are shorter than the posterior. Scales smooth or faintly keeled, in 17 rows. Ventrals 200–238, last usually divided; anal divided; subcaudals 106–138. Coloration very variable; head black with yellow cross-bars and spots.

Total length 1120 millim.; tail 310.

Ceylon, Hills of Southern India, Bengal, Assam, Burma, Southern China, Indo-China, Malay Peninsula and Archipelago.

A. Black above, each scale with a round greenish-yellow spot; usually with larger coral-red spots on the back, resembling a series of tetrapetalous flowers; ventrals greenish yellow, edged with black.

a. ♂ (V. 221; C. 135).	Anamallays, S. India.	Col. Beddome [C.].
b, c ♂ (V. 215; C 132) & ♀ (V. 236; C. 135).	Pinang.	Dr Cantor.
d. ♂ (V. 238, C. ?).	Kedah, Malay Peninsula.	B. E. Mitchell, Esq. [P.].
e ♂ (V. 228; C. 130).	Singapore.	Dr. Dennys [P.].
f. ♀ (V 213; C 124).	Sumatra.	
g ♀ (V. 221; C. 132).	Borneo	Sir E. Belcher [P.].

B. Like the preceding, but ventrals not black-edged.

a ♀ (V. 222; C. 124).	Malabar.	Dr. Packmann [P.].
b. ♂ (V. 218, C 106).	Batavia.	
c. Hgr. ♂ (V. 204; C. 126).	Tawi-Tawi, Sooloo Is.	A. Everett, Esq. [C.].
d Hgr. ♂ (V. 203; C. ?).	Philippines.	H Cuming, Esq. [C.].

C. Like the preceding, but vertebral spots confluent into a stripe, at least on the anterior part of the body.

a, b, c–d. ♂ (V 221; C. ?), ♀ (V. 227, 225; C. 134, 125), & hgr. (V. 217; C. 131).	Labuan.	L L. Dillwyn, Esq. [P.].
e. ♂ (V. 227; C. 119).	Mt. Dulit, Sarawak.	C. Hose, Esq. [C.].

D. Greenish yellow or pale green above, each scale edged and mesially streaked with black, with more or less distinct black cross-bars; ventrals yellow, with a small black spot on each side.

a. ♀ (V. 232; C. ?).	India (?).	Gen. Hardwicke [P.].

198 COLUBRIDÆ.

b–c, d. ♂ (V. 211, 212; C. 131, 129) & hgr. (V. 222; C. 138).	Anamallay Hills, S. India.	Col. Beddome [C.].
e. ♀ (V. 210; C. ?).	Assam (?).	Dr Griffith.
f–g. ♂ (V. 213, 222; C. 122, 118).	Ruby Mines, Upper Burma.	Major Bingham [P.].
h–i. ♂ (V 213; C. 132) & ♀ (V. 214; C. 120).	Toungoo.	E W. Oates, Esq. [P.].
k–l. ♂ (V. 222, 223; C. ?, 136).	Siam.	J. Bowring, Esq. [P.].
m. ♂ (V. 229; C. 125).	Lao Mountains.	M. Mouhot [C.].

E. Like the preceding, but with a series of large coral-red or orange blotches along the back.

a. ♂ (V. 224; C. ?).	Ceylon.	Sir E Tennant [P.].
b ♂ (V. 226; C 126).	Ceylon.	E. W. H. Holdsworth, Esq. [C.].
c. ♀ (V. 217; C. 127).	Ceylon	
d–e. Hgr. (V. 206, 214; C. ?, 110).	Bengal.	Dr. Cantor.
f–h. ♂ (V. 211, 210; C. 108, 123) & ♀ (V. 218; C. ?).	India.	Gen. Hardwicke [P.].

F. Pale olive above, with regular black cross-bars; some of the black scales with yellow shafts; whitish olive beneath, with a small black spot on the side of each ventral.

a. Hgr. ♂ (V. 204; C. 123).	Ceylon.	
b. Yg. (V. 203; C. 111).	Ceylon.	E. W. H. Holdsworth, Esq [C].
c. Hgr. (V. 200; C. 121).	Ceylon.	Haslar Collection.

G. Black above, with narrow yellowish cross-bars; whitish olive beneath, with a small black spot on the side of each ventral.

a. Yg. (V. 209; C. 141).	Negros, Philippines.	Dr. A. B. Meyer [C].

H. Olive above, with the markings much effaced; pale yellow beneath.

a. ♀ (V. 218; C. 139).	Philippines.	H. Cuming, Esq. [C.].
b ♀ (V. 227; C. ?).	Negros, Philippines.	Dr. A. B. Meyer [C.].
c–d. ♀ (V. 214, 220; C. 121, 122).	Manado, Celebes.	Dr. A. B. Meyer [C.].

a, b. Skeletons.	——?
c. Skull.	Java.

3. Chrysopelea chrysochlora.

Dendrophis ornata, part., *Schleg. Phys. Serp.* ii. p. 234 (1837), *and Abbild.* p. 19, pl. vi. figs. 1 & 2 (1837)
—— chrysochloros *(Reinw), Schleg. ll. cc.*
Leptophis ornatus, part., *Cantor. Cat. Mal. Rept.* p. 87 (1847)

Chrysopelea ornata, part., *Günth. Cat.* p. 146 (1858), *and Rept. Brit. Ind* p. 298 (1864).
—— hasseltii, *Bleek. Nat. Tijdschr. Nederl. Ind.* xxi. 1860, p. 332.

Head rather shorter and snout less depressed than in *C. ornata*. Rostral broader than deep, visible from above; internasals as long as or a little shorter than the præfrontals; frontal once and a half to once and two thirds as long as broad, a little longer than its distance from the end of the snout, a little shorter than the parietals; loreal once and a half to twice as long as deep; one præocular, in contact with or narrowly separated from the frontal; two postoculars; temporals 2+2; nine upper labials, fifth and sixth or fourth, fifth, and sixth entering the eye; five lower labials in contact with the anterior chin-shields, which are shorter than the posterior. Scales smooth, in 17 rows, less oblique than in *C. ornata*. Ventrals 181-198, last usually divided; anal divided; subcaudals 99-120. Back red or orange, with pairs of black cross-bars enclosing a whitish cross-bar; sides olive, some of the scales black-edged; head dark olive-brown above, with two or three orange cross-bars; pale green to olive beneath, the lateral keels black, the portion of the shields above the keel whitish.

Total length 700 millim.; tail 190.

Burma, Malay Peninsula, Sumatra, Borneo, Natuna Islands.

a. ♀ (V. 188; C. 100).	Rangoon.	Dr. J. E. Gray [P.].
b. ♀ (V 194; C 99).	Singapore.	Dr Dennys [P.].
c. ♂ (V. 187; C. 107).	Banka.	Dr. Bleeker. (Type of *C. hasseltii*)
d. ♀ (V. 186; C 99).	Nias.	Hr. Sundermann [C.].
e. ♂ (V. 181; C. 106).	Sarawak.	Sir H. Low [P.].
f. ♂ (V. 196; C. 120).	Great Natuna Id.	A. Everett, Esq. [C.].

181. ERYTHROLAMPRUS.

Erythrolamprus, part., *Wagler, Syst Amph.* p. 187 (1830).
Coronella, part, *Schleg. Phys. Serp.* ii. p. 50 (1837); *Günth. Cat. Col. Sn.* p. 34 (1858).
Erythrolamprus, *Dum. & Bibr. Erp. Gén.* vii. p. 845 (1854); *Günth. l. c.* p. 47; *Jan, Arch. Zool Anat Phys.* ii. 1863, p 314; *Bocourt, Miss. Sc Mex, Rept.* p. 658 (1886); *Cope, Bull U.S. Nat. Mus.* no. 32, 1887, p. 55.
Coniophanes, *Cope, Proc. Ac. Philad.* 1860, p. 248; *Hallow. t. c.* p. 484; *Bocourt, l. c.* p 649.
Glaphyrophis, *Jan, l. c.* p. 304.
Tachymenis, part, *Peters, Mon. Berl. Ac.* 1869, p. 876.

Maxillary teeth subequal, 10 to 15, followed, after an interspace, by a pair of feebly enlarged grooved teeth* situated below the posterior border of the eye; mandibular teeth subequal. Head more or less distinct from neck; eye moderate, with round pupil.

---

* The groove is exceptionally absent in specimens of *E. æsculapii* (see footnote, p. 202).

Body cylindrical; scales smooth, without pits, in 15 to 25 rows; ventrals rounded or obtusely angulate laterally. Tail moderate or long; subcaudals in two rows.

Tropical America, Mexico, Texas.

Synopsis of the Species.

I. Scales in 15 rows; ventrals 172–204; subcaudals 38–61; seven upper labials .... 1. *æsculapii*, p. 200.

II. Scales in 17 rows; ventrals 166–173; subcaudals 50 or more; seven upper labials.

Loreal as long as deep .... 2. *decipiens*, p. 204.
Loreal much longer than deep .... 3. *grammophrys*, p. 204.

III. Scales in 19 rows; ventrals 120–143; subcaudals 67–94.

Seven upper labials; frontal nearly as broad as long; loreal square ...... 4. *lateritius*, p. 205.
Eight or nine upper labials; frontal much longer than broad; loreal deeper than long .... 5. *dromiciformis*, p. 205.
Eight (exceptionally seven) upper labials; frontal longer than broad .... 6. *imperialis*, p. 206.

IV. Scales in 21 rows; ventrals 117–142; subcaudals 64–94; eight upper labials.

Internasals more than half the length of the præfrontals .... 7. *fissidens*, p. 207.
Internasals not more than half the length of the præfrontals .... 8. *bipunctatus*, p. 208.

V. Scales in 25 rows; ventrals 158–169; subcaudals 82–93; eight upper labials .... 9. *piceivittis*, p. 209.

1. Erythrolamprus æsculapii.

Coluber æsculapii, *Linn. Mus. Ad. Frid.* p. 29, pl xi. fig. 2 (1754), and *S. N.* i. p. 380 (1766); *Duvernoy, Ann. Sc Nat.* xxvi. 1832, p. 151, and xxx. 1833, p. 15, pl. iv. fig. A.
—— agilis, *Linn l.cc.* p. 27, pl. xxi. fig. 2, and p. 381.
Natrix æsculapii, *Laur. Syn. Rept.* p. 76 (1768).
Coluber nigrofasciatus, *Lacép. Serp.* ii. pp. 98 & 188 (1789).
—— atrocinctus, *Daud. Rept.* vi. p. 380 (1803).
—— venustissimus, *Wied, Reise Bras.* ii. p. 75 (1821), *and Abbild.* (1825).
—— binatus, *Licht. Verz. Doubl.* p. 105 (1823).
Elaps venustissimus, *Wagl. in Spix, Serp. Bras* p. 6, pl ii. a. fig. 2 (1824).
Coronella venustissima, *Schleg. Phys. Serp.* ii. p. 53, pl. ii. figs. 1–3 (1837).
Erythrolamprus æsculapii, *Dum. & Bibr.* vii. p 845 (1854), *Cope, Proc. Ac. Philad.* 1860, p. 259; *Jan, Arch. Zool. Anat. Phys* ii. 1863, p. 315. *and Icon Gén.* 19, pl. ii. figs. 2 & 3 (1866); *Günth. Biol. C. Am., Rept.* p. 100 (1885).

Erythrolamprus beauperthuisii, *Dum. & Bibr.* t. c p. 850.
—— venustissimus, *Dum. & Bibr.* t. c. p. 851, pl. lxxiv.; *Gunth. Cat.* p. 47 (1858), *Girard, U S Explor. Exped., Herp.* p. 169 (1858); *Cope, l. c.*; *Bocourt, Miss. Sc. Mex., Rept.* p. 658, pl xxxviii. fig. 4 (1886).
—— milberti, *Dum. & Bibr.* t. c. p. 854.
—— intricatus, *Dum. & Bibr.* t. c. p. 855.
—— albostolatus, *Cope, l. c.*
—— æsculapii, vars monozona, dicranta, bizona, confluentus, tetrazona, *Jan, l. c.*
—— ocellatus, *Peters, Mon Berl Ac.* 1868, p 642.
—— guentheri, *Garm. N. Am. Rept.* p. 154 (1883).

Snout very short, convex, rounded. Rostral broader than deep, just visible from above; internasals shorter than the præfrontals; frontal once and a half to once and two thirds as long as broad, longer than its distance from the end of the snout, shorter than the parietals; loreal deeper than long, one præocular (rarely divided), two postoculars; temporals 1+2 (rarely 1+1); seven upper labials, third and fourth entering the eye; four or five lower labials in contact with the anterior chin-shields, which are longer than the posterior. Scales in 15 rows. Ventrals 172–204, anal divided; subcaudals 38–61. Coloration very variable; body usually with black annuli.

Total length 780 millim.; tail 105.

Tropical America.

A. Annuli single, wide apart, 11 or 12 on the body; the scales on the red interspaces tipped with black; head-shields all spotted or margined with black; two black bands across the head, the first passing through the eyes, the second on the occiput. (*E. monozona*, Jan.)

a. ♂ (V. 192; C. 50).	Bahia.	
b–c. ♂ (V. 195; C. 51) & yg. (V. 201; C 53).	Brazil.	Sir C. Stuart [P.].

B. As in the preceding, but annuli in pairs (11 to 15 pairs on the body). (*C. venustissimus*, Wied.)

a ♂ (V. 194; C. 49).	Rio Janeiro.	Haslar Collection.
b. ♂ (V. 197; C. 51).	Brazil.	G Lennox Conyngham, Esq. [P.].
c. Yg. (V. 191; C. 60).	Venezuela.	Mr. Dyson [C.].
d ♀ (V. 186; C. 51).	Cali, Columbia, 3200 ft.	Mr. W. F. H. Rosenberg [C.].
e. ♀ (V. 197; C. 50).	Irazu, Costa Rica.	F. D Godman, Esq. [P.].
f–g Yg. (V. 198, 198; C. 60, 61).	Chiriqui.	G. Champion, Esq. [C.]; F.D.Godman, Esq. [P.].
h. Ad. skeleton.	Brazil.	G. Lennox Conyngham, Esq. [P.].

C. Annuli in pairs, 11 to 14 on the body, the pairs separated from one another by red interspaces, which are about as long as or a little longer than one annulus; red scales tipped with black; head yellow, with a black cross-band passing through the eyes and another on the occiput. (*O. æsculapii*, L.)

a. ♂ (V. 186; C. 46).	Demerara.	Dr. Hancock [P.].
b–c. ♀ (V. 190, 182; C. 45, 39).	Demerara.	Mr. Snellgrove [C.].
d. ♂ (V. 187; C. 38).	Para.	
e. ♀ (V. 194; C. 40).	Brazil.	J. C. Taunton, Esq. [P.].
f. ♀ (V. 178; C. 39).	Upper Amazon.	Mr. E. Bartlett [C.].
g. Hgr. ♀ (V. 188; C. ?).	Cayaria, N.E. Peru.	Mr. W. Davis [C.]; Messrs. Veitch [P.].

D. Annuli in pairs, 12 or 13 on the body, but the pairs incompletely divided, and separated by broad red interspaces; the red scales tipped with black; head black in front and behind, with a yellow band across the temples and occiput.

a–b. ♂ (V. 175; C. ?) & yg. (V. 172; C. 49).	Chontalez, Nicaragua *.	R. A. Rix, Esq [C.]; W. M. Crowfoot, Esq [P.].

E. Like C, but annuli in two approximated pairs separated by wide interspaces; 8 double pairs of annuli on the body. (*E. tetrazona*, Jan.)

a Yg. (V. 191; C. 47).	Mapuri R., Upper Beni, Bolivia.	Senckenberg Mus. [E.].

F. Intermediate between C and D. Each annulus has a tendency to divide into two, the scales in the middle bearing each a light spot; 8 pairs of annuli on the body.

a. Hgr. (V. 174; C. 46).	Huallaga R., N.E. Peru.	

G. Annuli in pairs, very broad, with a tendency to divide, each bearing some light spots; the wider interspaces not broader than the black annuli and unspotted, the narrower interspaces with the scales black-tipped; 9 pairs of annuli on the body;

---

* Dr. Günther has noticed (Biol. C.-Am., Rept. p. 106) that the groove on the posterior maxillary tooth is absent in these specimens. At his suggestion one of the specimens has been handed over to Mr. G. S. West, who is now engaged in investigating the poison-glands of Opisthoglyphous Snakes, and I have been favoured with the following report:—"The buccal glands of *Erythrolamprus æsculapii* and of the *Erythrolamprus* from Nicaragua are precisely identical in disposition and extent, and they have the same structure. The maxillæ only differ in the former possessing on the two posterior slightly larger teeth a very shallow groove, which does not extend more than two-thirds

head yellow, with a few small black spots and a black cross-bar passing through the eyes; no occipital cross-bar.

a. ♂ (V. 193, C. ?).   Cayaria, N.E. Peru.   Mr. W. Davis [C.];
Messrs. Veitch [P.].

H. Annuli in pairs, with a tendency to divide, broader than the interspaces between them, which bear some scanty black dots; 12 pairs of annuli on the body; head yellow, with a black cross-bar passing through the eyes, and another on the occiput.

a ♂ (V. 197 ; C. 46).   British Guiana.

I. Annuli in pairs, the interspaces not broader than the single annuli and unspotted; 11 pairs of annuli on the body; head yellow, with a black occipital cross-band; the anterior cross-band much reduced and interrupted on the frontal shield.

a. ♂ (V. 191; C. ?).   Surinam.   C. W. Ellascombe, Esq. [P.].

K. Annuli in pairs, the interspaces broader than the single annuli and unspotted; 11 pairs of annuli on the body; head yellow, with a black cross-bar passing through the eyes, and a small transverse black blotch behind the occiput.

a. Yg. (V. 190, C. 41).   British Guiana.

L. Annuli in pairs, separated by narrow interspaces, 13 to 20 pairs; head with the two black cross-bars as in C. (*C. agilis*, L.)

a–e,f,g. ♂ (V. 175, 180, 179, 176, 176 ; C. 43, 44, 44, 42, 42) & ♀ (V. 182, 180 ; C. 42, 38).   Berbice.

h. ♂ (V. 181, C. 46).   British Guiana
i. ♀ (V. 180 ; C. 43).   W. Indies (?).   Miss Saul [P.].

M. Annuli equidistant and very numerous (30 to 35), edged with yellowish and separated by dark reddish-brown or nearly black interspaces; head black, with a yellow blotch across the parietal and temporal regions.

a–b ♂ (V. 196, C 48) & ♀ (V. 187, C. 40).   Moyobamba, E. Peru.   Mr. A. H. Roff [C.].

N. Intermediate between M and O. The body entirely black above (through darkening of the red interspaces), with 42 whitish cross-lines ; head as in L.   (*E. guentheri*, Garm.)

a. Yg. (V. 193, C. 42).   Mexico (?).

O. Body black, with 62 whitish cross-lines; head entirely black above. (*E. confluentus*, Jan.)

a. ♀ (V. 182; C. 46).   Moyobamba, E. Peru.   Mr. A. H. Roff [C.]

P. Reddish above, scales tipped with black, without annuli on the body, but a dorsal series of 25 or 26 large roundish black spots with light centre; tail with black annuli; head and nape black above. (*E. ocellatus*, Peters.)

a. ♀ (V. 178, C. 40).   ——?   Zoological Society.
b. ♀ (V. 177; C. 46).   ——?   College of Surgeons.

2. Erythrolamprus decipiens.

Tachymenis decipiens, *Gunth. Biol. C.-Am., Rept.* p. 163, pl. liii. fig. A (1895).

Snout very short, moderately depressed, rounded. Rostral nearly twice as broad as deep, scarcely visible from above; internasals half as long as the præfrontals; frontal once and one fourth to once and one third as long as broad, longer than its distance from the end of the snout, much shorter than the parietals; loreal as long as deep; one præocular; one or two postoculars; temporals 1+1, the first usually absent, fused with the sixth upper labial, which then forms a suture with the parietal; seven upper labials, third and fourth entering the eye; four lower labials in contact with the anterior chin-shields, which are as long as the posterior. Scales in 17 rows. Ventrals 166–173; anal divided; subcaudals 85 or more. Dark brown, with a yellow, black-edged lateral streak from behind the temple to the end of the tail, and another along the outer row of scales, the lower black border of which extends on the ends of the ventral shields; an elliptical yellow, black-edged spot on each parietal shield behind the eye; upper lip yellowish, black-edged; lower parts yellowish white.

Total length 630 millim.; tail (end missing) 190.

Costa Rica.

a–c. ♂ (V 168; C ?)   Irazu, Costa Rica.   F. D. Godman, Esq.
& ♀ (V. 173, 166;   [P.] (Types.)
C. ?, ?).

3. Erythrolamprus grammophrys.

Erythrolamprus grammophrys, *Dugès, Proc. Amer. Philos. Soc.* xxv. 1888, p. 181, fig., and *La Naturaleza*, (2) i. 1890, p. 402, pl. xxvii. fig. 13.
Tachymenis grammophrys, *Gunth. Biol. C.-Am., Rept.* p. 162 (1895).

Allied to *E. imperialis*, but loreal much longer than deep, only seven upper labials, third and fourth entering the eye, and scales in 17 rows. Ventrals 175; subcaudals 50 or more. Back greyish brown, with reddish brown; a whitish line on each side of the upper surface of the head; rostral and upper labials brown above and grey beneath, the two colours separated by a white line; lower parts uniform yellowish white.

Total length 360 millim.

Michoacan, Mexico.

4. Erythrolamprus lateritius.

Coniophanes lateritius, *Cope, Proc. Ac. Philad.* 1861, p. 524.
Tachymenis melanocephala, *Peters, Mon. Berl. Ac* 1869, p 876.
—— lateritia, *Garm N. Am. Rept.* p. 61 (1883), *Gunth. Biol. C-Am., Rept.* p. 162 (1895).
Erythrolamprus melanocephalus, *Cope, Bull. U.S. Nat. Mus.* no. 32, 1887, p. 78.
—— lateritius, *Cope, l. c.*

Snout acute and prominent, head broad behind. Frontal shield nearly as broad as long; loreal square, one præ- and two postoculars; seven upper labials, third and fourth entering the eye. Scales in 19 rows. Bright vermilion above, punctulated with brown, passing through orange to golden on the belly; head and nape black, the labials bordered and traversed by yellow lines, and the parietals dotted with the same; throat and chin yellow, black-spotted.

Guadalajara, Mexico.

5. Erythrolamprus dromiciformis.

Tachymenis dromiciformis, *Peters, Mon. Berl. Ac.* 1863, p. 273
Coniophanes dromiciformis, *Cope, Proc. Ac. Philad,* 1866, p. 128, and 1868, p. 104.
Erythrolamprus dromiciformis, *Cope, Proc. U.S. Nat. Mus.* xiv. 1892, p. 676.
Coniophanes signatus, *Garm. Bull. Essex Inst.* xxiv. 1892, p 91.

Snout moderate, rather strongly depressed, rounded. Rostral broader than deep, just visible from above; internasals shorter than the præfrontals; frontal once and a half to once and two thirds as long as broad, longer than its distance from the end of the snout, shorter than the parietals; loreal deeper than long; one præocular (sometimes divided); two postoculars; temporals 1+2; eight or nine upper labials, fourth and fifth entering the eye; four lower labials in contact with the anterior chin-shields, which are as long as or shorter than the posterior. Scales in 19 rows. Ventrals 123–128; anal divided; subcaudals 71–80. Yellowish above, speckled with brown and with a brown vertebral stripe, five scales wide, and a dark brown lateral streak extending to the head and passing through the eye; lips speckled with brown, yellowish beneath, outer ends of ventrals dark brown or with a dark brown dot.

Total length 335 millim.; tail 105.

Western Ecuador.

a–b. (V. 126, 128; C. 71, ?).   Guayaquil.

6. Erythrolamprus imperialis.

Coronella fissidens, part., *Gunth. Cat.* p. 36 (1858), *and Zool. Rec.* 1866, p. 126.
Tæniophis imperialis, *Baird & Gir. Rep. U.S Mex. Bound Surv.* ii. Rept. p. 23, pl. xix. fig. 1 (1859); *Cope, Proc. Ac. Philad.* 1861, p. 74.
Coniophanes proterops, *Cope, Proc. Ac. Philad.* 1860, p. 249; *Bocourt, Miss. Sc. Mex., Rept.* p. 654 (1886).
Glaphyrophis lateralis, *Jan, Arch. Zool. Anat. Phys.* ii. p. 304, *and Icon. Gén.* 18, pl. v. fig. 3 (1866).
Tachymenis fissidens, part , *Peters, Mon. Berl. Ac.* 1869, p. 876; *Garm. N. Am. Rept.* p 62 (1883); *Gunth. Biol. C.-Am., Rept.* p. 161 (1895).
Coniophanes imperialis, *Cope, Check-list N. Am Rept.* p 38 (1875), *and Journ. Ac. Philad* (2) viii. 1876, p 183; *Stejneger, Proc. U.S. Nat. Mus.* xiv 1891, p 505.
—— lateralis, *F. Mull. Verh Nat. Ges. Basel*, vi. 1878, p. 598.
Tachymenis imperialis, *Garm. N. Am. Rept* p. 61 (1883).
Rhadinæa proterops, *Cope, Proc. Amer. Philos. Soc.* xxii. 1885, p. 381.
—— imperialis, *Cope, l. c.* p. 382.
Erythrolamprus imperialis, *Cope, Bull. U.S. Nat. Mus.* no. 32, 1887, p. 77.
—— proterops, *Cope, l. c.*

Head as in *E. fissidens*, but smaller. Rostral once and a half to once and two thirds as broad as deep, just visible from above; internasals not more than half as long as the præfrontals; frontal once and one third to once and a half as long as broad, as long as or a little longer than its distance from the end of the snout, shorter than the parietals; loreal as long as deep or a little longer than deep; one præocular; two postoculars; temporals 1+2; eight (exceptionally seven) upper labials, fourth and fifth (or third and fourth) entering the eye; five lower labials in contact with the anterior chin-shields, which are as long as or a little shorter than the posterior. Scales in 19 rows. Ventrals 120–143; anal divided; subcaudals 67-94. Brown above, sides, down to the ends of the ventrals, darker; a blackish vertebral line or stripe often present; a blackish lateral streak edged above with yellowish on the anterior part of the body, and preceded by a yellow round or oval spot on the nape; a light line may be present along the outer row of scales; a yellow, black-edged line on each side of the head, from the canthus rostralis to the temple; upper lip white, dotted with black and edged with black above; lower parts white, uniform, or with black dots, which are most numerous on the throat and neck.

Total length 405 millim.; tail 160.

Texas, Mexico, Central America.

a. ♀ (V. 126, C. ?).	Mexico.	M. Sallé [C.].
b. ♀ (V. 123; C. 78)	Mexico.	
c, d-e. Yg. (V. 126, 135, 131; C. 69, 73, 75).	Jalapa.	Mr. Hoege [C.].

f. ♂ (V. 131 ; C. 75).	Tampico	Mr H.H Smith [C] ; F. D.Godman, Esq. [P.].
g. ♀ (V. 123 ; C. ?).	Hacienda del Hobo.	P. Geddes, Esq. [P.].
h. ♂ (V. 128 ; C. ?).	Tehuantepec.	
i. ♂ (V. 123 ; C. 94).	Vera Paz.	O Salvin, Esq. [C.].
k ♀ (V. 135 ; C. ?).	Belize.	'O. Salvin, Esq. [C.].
l–n, o. ♂ (V. 121; C. 86), ♀ (V. 130, 130 ; C. ?, 78), & hgr. (V.129 ; C. 78).	Stann Creek, Brit. Honduras	Rev. J. Robertson [C.].
p–r. ♂ (V 120 ; C. 93) & ♀ (V. 132, 132 ; C. 81, 79).	Brit. Honduras.	
s–t. ♂ (V. 123, 123 ; C. 89, 87).	—— ?	(Two of the types of *C. fissidens*.)

7. Erythrolamprus fissidens.

Coronella fissidens, part., *Gunth Cat.* p. 36 (1858).
Coniophanes punctigularis, *Cope, Proc Ac Philad.* 1860, p. 248, *and Journ Ac Philad* (2) viii. 1876, p. 138 ; *F. Mull. Verh. Nat Ges. Basel,* vi. 1878, p. 666.
—— fissidens, *Cope, ll. cc.* ; Bocourt, *Miss. Sc. Mex., Rept.* p 650, pl. xli. fig. 3 (1886)
Dromicus chitalonensis, *F. Mull. Verh. Nat. Ges. Basel,* vi. 1877, p. 407
Tachymenis fissidens, part, *Garm. N. Am. Rept.* p. 62 (1883) ; *Gunth. Biol C.-Am., Rept.* p 161 (1895).
Erythrolamprus fissidens, *Cope, Bull. U.S. Nat. Mus.* no. 32, 1887, p 77.
—— violaceus, *Cope, l. c.*

Snout moderate, rather strongly depressed, rounded. Rostral once and a half to nearly twice as broad as deep, scarcely visible from above ; internasals much shorter than the præfrontals ; frontal once and a half to once and two thirds as long as broad, as long as or longer than its distance from the end of the snout, shorter than the parietals ; loreal nearly as long as deep ; one præocular (rarely divided) ; two postoculars ; temporals 1+2 ; eight upper labials, fourth and fifth entering the eye ; four or five lower labials in contact with the anterior chin-shields, which are as long as or a little longer than the posterior. Scales in 21 rows. Ventrals 117–140 ; anal divided ; subcaudals 64–89. Brown above, with or without longitudinal series of small dark spots, or an ill-defined dark vertebral stripe ; a dark lateral streak ; a pair of more or less distinct fine yellowish lines on the neck, broken up into small spots anteriorly or preceded by a small roundish spot ; labials grey or brown, speckled with black, with a yellow, above black-edged line running along their upper border ; this line extends to the side of the neck ; throat speckled with blackish ; lower parts white, with more or less numerous black dots, which may form a regular series on each side of the belly.

Total length 525 millim. ; tail 145.

Mexico and Central America.

a–f. ♂ (V. 128; C. ?), ♀ (V. 129, 134, 129, 123; C. 69, ?, 67, 71), & yg. (V. 135, C. 69).	Mexico.	M. Sallé [C.] ⎫ ⎬ (Types.) ⎭
g. ♀ (V. 131; C. 64).	Mexico.	
h–i. ♂ (V. 119, 118; C. ?, ?).	Teapa, Tabasco.	F. D. Godman, Esq. [P.].
k. Yg. (V. 124; C. ?).	Orizaba.	
l. Hgr. (V. 121; C. 89).	Tehuantepec.	
m–n ♀ (V. 121, 119; C. 77, 70).	Vera Paz.	O. Salvin, Esq. [C.]
o–p. ♂ (V. 117, C ?) & ♀ (V. 126; C. 81).	Pacific Coast of Guatemala.	O. Salvin, Esq [C.]
q–t. ♂ (V. 121; C ?) & ♀ (V. 128, 130, 129; C. 67, 70, ?).	Hacienda Rosa de Jericho, Nicaragua, 3250 ft.	Dr. Rothschuh [C.].
u. ♀ (V. 129; C 73).	Matagalpa, Nicaragua.	Dr. Rothschuh [C.].

8. Erythrolamprus bipunctatus.

Coronella bipunctata, *Gunth. Cat.* p. 36 (1858), *and Zool. Rec.* 1866, p. 126

Glaphyrophis pictus, *Jan, Arch. Zool. Anat. Phys.* ii. 1863, p. 304, *and Icon. Gén.* 18, pl. v fig. 4 (1866).

Coniophanes bipunctatus, *Cope, Proc. Ac. Philad.* 1866, p 128, *and Journ. Ac. Philad.* (2) viii. 1876, p. 137, *Bocourt, Miss. Sc. Mex., Rept.* p. 653, pl. xl. fig. 8 (1886).

Tachymenis bipunctata, *Garm. N. Am. Rept.* p 63 (1883); *Gunth. Biol. C-Am., Rept.* p. 161 (1895).

Erythrolamprus bipunctatus, *Cope, Bull. U.S. Nat. Mus.* no. 32, 1887, p. 77.

Snout moderate, rather strongly depressed, rounded. Rostral nearly twice as broad as deep, scarcely visible from above; internasals not more than half as long as the præfrontals; frontal once and a half to once and two thirds as long as broad, as long as or longer than its distance from the end of the snout, shorter than the parietals; loreal as long as deep; one præocular, two postoculars; temporals 1+2; eight upper labials, fourth and fifth entering the eye; five lower labials in contact with the anterior chin-shields, which are as long as or a little shorter than the posterior. Scales in 21 rows Ventrals 135–142; anal divided; subcaudals 85–94. Brown or reddish above, with a more or less distinct darker vertebral line and a dark lateral streak, some white, black-edged dots on the head; lips white, spotted or marbled with blackish; a white, black-edged line from the eye to the angle of the mouth through the three last upper labials; belly and lower surface of tail whitish (red?), with two regular series of round black spots or ocelli; a brown dot on the outer end of each ventral shield.

Total length 550 millim.; tail 190.

Honduras.

a. Hgr. (V. 140; C. 94).	Belize.	F. D Godman, Esq. [P.].
b–d. ♂ (V. 137; C. 91), ♀ (V. 142; C. ?), & hgr. (V. 139; C. 85).	Stann Creek, Brit. Honduras.	Rev. J. Robertson [C.].
e. Hgr. ♂ (V. 135; C. 93).	——?	(Type.)

9. Erythrolamprus piceivittis.

Coniophanes piceivittis, *Cope, Proc. Amer. Philos. Soc.* xi. 1869, p 149, *Bocourt, Miss. Sc. Mex., Rept.* p. 656, pl. xli. fig. 2 (1886).

Tachymenis tæniata, *Peters, Mon. Berl. Ac.* 1869, p 876.

—— piceivittis, *Gunth. Ann. & Mag. N. H.* (4) ix. 1872, p. 20, and *Biol. C.-Am, Rept.* p. 160 (1895).

Erythrolamprus piceivittis, *Cope, Bull. U.S. Nat. Mus.* no. 32, 1887, p. 77.

Snout moderate, rather strongly depressed, rounded. Rostral nearly twice as broad as deep, visible from above, internasals much shorter than the præfrontals; frontal once and a half as long as broad, as long as its distance from the end of the snout, shorter than the parietals; loreal a little longer than deep; one præocular, with a subocular below it; two postoculars; temporals 1+2; eight upper labials, fourth and fifth entering the eye; five lower labials in contact with the anterior chin-shields, which are as long as or a little longer than the posterior. Scales in 25 rows. Ventrals 158–169; anal divided, subcaudals 82–93. Dark brown above, with two whitish longitudinal streaks which extend to the canthi rostrales; these streaks may be interrupted on the occiput; upper lip and sides brownish white, lower parts uniform white.

Total length 520 millim.; tail 150.

Mexico.

a. ♂ (V. 162; C. 91).	Yucatan.	
b. ♀ (V. 164; C. 93).	Mexico.	

182. HYDROCALAMUS.

Homalopsis, part., *Dum. & Bibr. Erp. Gén.* vii. p. 967 (1854).

Hydrocalamus, *Cope, Proc Amer. Philos. Soc.* xxii. 1885, p. 176; *Bocourt, Miss Sc Mex., Rept.* p 811 (1895).

Maxillary teeth 12, gradually increasing in size and followed, after an interspace, by a pair of feebly enlarged grooved fangs situated behind the vertical of the eye; mandibular teeth subequal. Head slightly distinct from neck; eye small, with round pupil; nasal entire or semidivided. Body cylindrical; scales smooth, without apical pits, in 21 rows, ventrals rounded. Tail moderate; subcaudals in two rows.

Central America.

1. Hydrocalamus quinquevittatus.

Homalopsis quinquevittatus, *Dum. & Bibr.* vii. p. 975 (1854).
Calopisma quinquevittatum, *Jan, Arch. Zool. Anat. Phys.* iii. 1865,
   p. 244, *and Icon Gén* 30, pl. ii. (1868).
Hydrops lubricus, *Cope, Proc. Ac. Philad.* 1871, p. 217.
—— quinquevittatus, *Garm. N. Am. Rept.* p. 36 (1883).
Hydrocalamus quinquevittatus, *Cope, Proc. Amer. Philos. Soc.* xxii.
   1885, p. 176, *Günth. Biol. C.-Am*, *Rept.* p. 164 (1895); *Bocourt,
   Miss. Sc. Mex., Rept.* p. 811, pls. lv. fig. 6 & lx. fig. 3 (1895).

Head much depressed; snout short, rounded. Rostral broader than deep, just visible from above; internasals narrowed in front, a little longer than broad, a little shorter than the præfrontals, frontal twice as broad as the supraocular, once and two thirds as long as broad, longer than its distance from the end of the snout, shorter than the parietals; loreal, if present, longer than deep; one præ- and two postoculars, temporals 1+2; eight upper labials, fourth and fifth entering the eye; five lower labials in contact with the anterior chin-shields, which are as long as or shorter than the posterior. Scales in 21 rows. Ventrals 151–164; anal divided; subcaudals 65–71. Dark brown or blackish, with two pale brown longitudinal bands, or brown with a black lateral band; outer row of scales and a portion of the second white; lips white, each shield with a round black spot; ventral shields white, each with two transversely oval black spots forming two regular longitudinal series; on the posterior half of the tail the spots unite to form a zigzag line

Total length 710 millim; tail 160.

Mexico and Guatemala.

a. ♀ (V. 164, C. 68).   Mexico.   Christiania Museum.

183. SCOLECOPHIS.

Calamaria, part, *Schleg. Phys. Serp.* ii. p. 25 (1837).
Homalocranium, part., *Dum. & Bibr. Erp. Gén.* vii. p. 855 (1854).
Scolecophis, *Cope, Proc. Ac. Philad.* 1860, p. 259, and 1861, p. 74;
   Bocourt, Miss Sc. Mex., Rept. p. 577 (1883)
Platycranion, *Jan, Elenco sist. Ofid.* p. 40 (1863).
Procinura, *Cope, Proc. Amer. Philos. Soc.* xviii. 1879, p. 262.

Maxillary teeth 13 to 15, small, equal, followed by a pair of feebly enlarged grooved teeth situated below the posterior border of the eye; mandibular teeth equal. Head slightly distinct from neck; eye small, with round pupil. Body cylindrical; scales smooth or feebly keeled, without apical pits, in 15 rows; ventrals rounded or obtusely angulate laterally. Tail short; subcaudals in two rows.

Central America.

This genus connects *Erythrolamprus* with *Homalocranium*, being distinguished from the former by its smaller eye and shorter grooved teeth and from the latter by the presence of a loreal.

183, SCOLECOPHIS.

Synopsis of the Species.

Scales smooth; nostril between two nasals; ventrals 181–198 .... 1. *atrocinctus*, p. 211.
Scales smooth; nasal single; ventrals 152–170 . ... 2. *michoacanensis*, p. 211.
Posterior dorsal and caudal scales keeled; nostril between two nasals; ventrals 148... .... 3. *æmulus*, p. 212.

1. Scolecophis atrocinctus.

Calamaria atrocincta, *Schleg Phys. Serp* ii. p 47 (1837).
Homalocranium atrocinctum, *Dum. & Bibr.* vii. p 864 (1854); *Jan, Icon Gén* 15, pl. u. fig. 7 (1866).
Elaps zonatus, *Hallow. Proc Ac Philad.* 1855, p 35.
Scolecophis atrocinctus, *Cope, Proc. Ac. Philad* 1860, p. 259; *Bocourt, Miss Sc. Mex, Rept.* p. 577, pl xxxvii. fig. 2 (1883); *Gunth. Biol C.-Am., Rept.* p. 156 (1895).
—— zonatus, *Cope, l. c.*

Eye not quite half as long as the snout. Rostral broader than deep, just visible from above; internasals not more than half as long as the præfrontals; frontal longer than broad, as long as or longer than its distance from the end of the snout, much shorter than the parietals; nostril between two nasals; loreal as long as deep or a little longer than deep; one præ- and two postoculars; temporals 1+1; seven upper labials, third and fourth entering the eye; four lower labials in contact with the anterior chin-shields, which are longer than the posterior. Scales in 15 rows. Ventrals angulate laterally, 181–198; anal divided; subcaudals 45–54. Annulate black and yellow, the black annuli broader than the yellow ones; head black above, with a yellow cross-bar on the snout, and a yellow spot behind the eye.

Total length 370 millim.; tail 47.

Guatemala.

a–c. ♂ (V. 181; C. 47) & ♀ (V 198, 188; C. 45, 50).	Dueñas, Guatemala.	O. Salvin, Esq. [C.].
d. Yg (V. 193, C 47).	—— ?	Dr Günther [P.].

2. Scolecophis michoacanensis.

Contia michoacanensis, *Cope, Proc. Amer Philos. Soc.* xxii. 1885, p. 178
Homalocranium michoacanense, *Gunth. Biol. C.-Am., Rept.* p. 150, pl. xxxvi. figs. B & C (1895).
Elapomorphus michoacanensis, *Cope, Trans. Amer. Philos. Soc.* xviii. 1895, p 218.

Eye nearly half as long as the snout. Rostral broader than deep, visible from above; internasals more than half as long as the præfrontals; frontal longer than broad, longer than its distance from the end of the snout, shorter than the parietals; nasal entire; loreal a little longer than deep; one præ- and two postoculars; temporals 1+2; seven upper labials, third and fourth entering the eye; four lower labials in contact with the anterior chin-shields, which are longer than the posterior. Scales in 15 rows. Ventrals 152-170; anal divided; subcaudals 37-45. Red above, with pairs of black cross-bars enclosing yellow ones; a large black spot on the head, behind the snout; lower parts whitish.

Total length 285 millim.; tail 55.

Mexico.

a–b. ♂ (V. 166; C. 45)   Mezquital del Oro.   Dr. A. C. Buller [C.].
& ♀ (V. 170; C. 42).

3. Scolecophis æmulus.

Procinura æmula, *Cope, Proc. Amer. Philos. Soc.* xviii. 1879, p. 262.

Rostral visible from above; frontal broad, acutely pointed behind; parietals short; nostril between two nasals; loreal quadrangular; one præ- and two postoculars; temporals 1+2; seven upper labials, third and fourth entering the eye; anterior chin-shields much longer than the posterior. Scales in 15 rows, keeled on the posterior dorsal region; caudal scales keeled, tubercular. Ventrals 148; anal divided; subcaudals 41. Body encircled with black annuli, which are broadly bordered with yellow and separated by red interspaces of twice their width; the red scales with a central black spot; a large black spot covering the frontal, parietal, and supraocular shields.

Total length 364 millim.; tail 61.

Southern Chihuahua, Mexico.

184. HOMALOCRANIUM.

Duberria, part., *Fitzing. N. Class. Rept.* p. 29 (1826).
Clœlia, part., *Wagl. Syst. Amph.* p. 187 (1830).
Calamaria, part., *Schleg. Phys. Serp.* ii. p. 25 (1837).
Homalocranium, part., *Dum. & Bibr. Mém. Ac. Sc.* xxiii. 1853, p. 490, *and Erp. Gén.* vii. p. 855 (1854); *Gunth. Cat. Col. Sn.* p. 18 (1858).
Tantilla, *Baird & Gir. Cat. N. Am. Rept.* p. 131 (1853); *Cope, Proc. U.S. Nat. Mus.* xiv. 1892, p. 597.
Lioninia, *Hallow. Proc. Ac. Philad.* 1860, p. 484.
Homalocranium, *Jan, Arch. Zool. Anat. Phys.* ii. 1862, p. 50; *Bocourt, Miss. Sc. Mex., Rept.* p. 778 (1883).
Microdromus, *Gunth Ann. & Mag. N. H.* (4) ix. 1872, p. 17.
Pogonaspis, *Cope, Proc. Ac. Philad.* 1894, p. 204.

Maxillary teeth small, equal, 12 to 14, followed by a pair of feebly-enlarged grooved teeth, situated below the posterior border of the eye, mandibular teeth equal. Head small, not or but slightly distinct from neck; eye small, with round pupil; no loreal shield. Body cylindrical; scales smooth, without pits, in 15 rows; ventrals rounded. Tail moderate or short; subcaudals in two rows.

Southern North America; Central America; Tropical South America.

Synopsis of the Species.

I. Frontal not more than twice as broad as the posterior border of the supraocular, seven upper labials; two postoculars.

  A. Frontal hexagonal.

    1. Ventrals 120 or more.

      a. Two pairs of chin-shields.

        α. Rostral much broader than deep; frontal considerably longer than broad.

          * Eye about half as long as the snout.

            † Frontal not more than once and a half as long as broad; subcaudals 46-71.

First lower labial usually in contact with its fellow; seven upper labials; body uniform or with dark stripes . . 1. *melanocephalum*, [p. 215.

First lower labial in contact with its fellow, seven upper labials; body with dark transverse spots or bars . . 2. *annulatum*, p. 217.

Symphysial in contact with the anterior chin-shields; eight upper labials; body with three light stripes . . . . 3. *trilineatum*, p. 217.

            †† Frontal twice as long as broad; subcaudals 85.
                4. *longifrontale*, p. 218.

          **. Eye not half as long as the snout.

            † Posterior nasal in contact with or narrowly separated from the præocular.

Ventrals 138-158; subcaudals 40-58.. 5. *coronatum*, p. 218.
Ventrals 149-179; subcaudals 59-70.. 6. *rubrum*, p. 219.

            †† Posterior nasal very small and widely separated from the præocular.. 7. *semicinctum*, p. 219.

        β. Rostral a little broader than deep.

          * First lower labial broadly in contact with its fellow; eye not half as long as the snout.

Frontal considerably longer than broad . 8. *fuscum*, p. 220.
Frontal scarcely longer than broad . . . . 9. *boulengeri*, p. 221.

          ** First lower labial separated from or narrowly in contact with its fellow.

            † Eye not half as long as the snout; ventrals 121-135; subcaudals 32-38.
                10. *schistosum*, p. 221.

†† Eye about half as long as the snout; ventrals 147-175; subcaudals 55-65.

Nostril much nearer the internasal than the first labial	12. *miniatum*, p. 222.
Nostril not nearer the internasal than the first labial	13. *virgatum*, p. 223.
b. A single pair of chin-shields..	14. *ruficeps*, p. 223.
2. Ventrals 110................	11. *canula*, p. 222.

B. Frontal pentagonal, or very slightly angulate in front.

Anterior chin-shields shorter than the posterior and separated from the symphysial........	15 *bocourti*, p. 224.
Anterior chin-shields longer than the posterior and in contact with the symphysial.......	16. *reticulatum*, p. 224.

II. Frontal more than twice as broad as the posterior border of the supraocular.

  A. Rostral small, scarcely visible from above; seven upper labials; two postoculars ...... 17. *mœstum*, p. 225.

  B. Rostral large, well visible from above.

    1. Seven upper labials.

      a. Anal entire .... 18. *vermiforme*, p. 225.

      b. Anal divided.

Frontal scarcely longer than broad; upper portion of rostral about half as long as its distance from the frontal	19. *breve*, p. 225.
Frontal considerably longer than broad; upper portion of rostral about half as long as its distance from the frontal..	20. *atriceps*, p. 226.
Upper portion of rostral about two thirds as long as its distance from the frontal	21. *planiceps*, p. 226.

    2. Six upper labials; one postocular.

Upper portion of rostral much shorter than its distance from the frontal....	22. *calamarinum*, [p. 227.
Upper portion of rostral nearly as long as its distance from the frontal......	23. *gracile*, p. 228.

184. HOMALOCRANIUM.

Table showing Numbers of Shields.

	V.	O.	Postoc.	Lab.
melanocephalum	133–171	46–71	2	7
annulatum	149	54	2	7
trilineatum	145–163	63–69	2	8
longifrontale	158	85	2	7
coronatum	138–158	40–58	2	7
rubrum	149–179	59–70	2	7
semicinctum	143–180	50–72	2	7
fuscum	136–159	44–49	2	7
boulengeri	161	46	2	7
schistosum	121–135	32–38	2	7
canula	110	37	2	7
miniatum	147–152	55	2	7
virgatum	154–175	57–65	2	7
ruficeps	146	?	2	7
bocourti	172–176	55	2	7
reticulatum	148	67	2	7
maestum	140–148	55–63	2	7
vermiforme	122	26	2	7
breve	111	?	2	7
atriceps	123–125	55–59	2	7
planiceps	121–153	42–58	1–2	7
calamarinum	119–132	27–35	1	6
gracile	112–133	41–51	1	6

1. Homalocranium melanocephalum.

Coluber melanocephalus, *Linn. Mus Ad. Frid.* p. 24, pl. xv. fig. 2 (1754), *and S N* i. p 378 (1766)
Elaps melanocephalus, *Wagl. in Spix, Serp. Bras.* p. 8, pl ii. *b* fig. 1 (1824).
Duberria melanocephala, *Fitzing. N Class. Rept.* p 55 (1826).
Cloelia dorsata, *Wagl. Syst. Amph.* p. 187 (1830).
Calamaria melanocephala, *Schleg. Phys. Serp* ii. p. 38, pl. i. fig. 30 (1837), *Trosch. in Schomb. Reise Brit. Guian.* iii p. 652 (1848).
Homalocranium melanocephalum, *Dum & Bibr.* vii. p. 859 (1854); *Bocourt, Miss Sc Mex*, Rept. p 588, pl. xxxvii. fig. 4 (1883).
—— melanocephalum, part., *Gunth Cat* p 18 (1858), *Jan, Arch Zool Anat Phys.* ii. 1862, p. 51, *and Icon. Gén.* 15, pl. ii fig 5 (1866); *Gunth. Biol. C.-Am*, Rept. p. 147 (1895)
Tantilla melanocephala, *Cope, Proc. Ac. Philad.* 1861, p. 74, and 1868, p. 102
Elapomorphus mexicanus, *Gunth Ann & Mag. N H* (3) ix. 1862, p. 57, pl ix. fig 1
Tantilla melanocephala, part, *Cope, Proc. Ac Philad.* 1866, p. 126.
—— capistrata, *Cope, Journ Ac Philad.* (2) viii. 1876, p. 181.
Homalocranium melanocephalum, vars fraseri and pernambucense, *Gunth. Biol. C.-Am.* p 148.
—— armillatum, part, *Gunth l. c.* p. 149, pl. lii. fig. C.
—— mexicanum, *Gunth. l c* p. 153.

Eye about half as long as the snout. Rostral much broader than deep, visible from above; internasals not more than half as long as the præfrontals; frontal hexagonal, obtuso-angled in front, acute-angled behind, once and one third to once and a half as long as broad, longer than its distance from the end of the snout, shorter than the parietals; nostril between two nasals (which may be fused), the posterior of which is in contact with or more or less widely separated from the præocular; two postoculars; temporals 1+1; seven upper labials, third and fourth entering the eye; first lower labial in contact with its fellow behind the symphysial; four lower labials in contact with the anterior chin-shields, which are longer than the posterior. Scales in 15 rows. Ventrals 133–171; anal divided; subcaudals 46–71. Red or pale brown above, with or without three or five more or less dark longitudinal lines; head and nape dark brown or black, with the sides of the snout and the lip behind the eye yellow; occiput with two more or less distinct yellow spots or a yellow cross-bar; lower parts uniform yellowish white.

Total length 500 millim.; tail 100.

Central and Tropical South America.

a. Hgr. (V. 171; C. 52).	Cartago, Costa Rica.	
b. ♂ (V. 161; C. 68).	Tobago.	W. J. A. Ludlow, Esq [P.].
c. ♀ (V. 158; C. ?).	W. Indies.	Col. Reid [P.].
d. ♂ (V. 142; C. 58).	Berbice.	
e-g, h. ♂ (V. 137, 140; C. 55, 58), ♀ (V. 136; C. ?), & yg. (V. 142; C. 52).	Para.	
i. ♀ (V. 145; C. ?).	Pernambuco.	W. A. Forbes, Esq. [P.]. (Type of var. *pernambucense*)
k. ♀ (V. 144; C. 46).	Asuncion, Paraguay.	Dr. J. Bohls [C.].
l. ♂ (V. 135; C. ?).	Palmeira, Parana.	Dr. S. F. Grillo [C.]; Marquis G. Doria [P.].
m. ♀ (V. 136; C. 47).	Charobamba, Bolivia.	
n. ♀ (V. 139; C. 49).	Moyobamba, N.E. Peru.	Mr. A. H. Roff [C.].
o. Hgr. (V. 133; C. 48).	Sarayacu, N.E. Peru.	Mr. W. Davis [C.]; Messrs. Veitch [P.].
p-q. ♂ (V. 146, 149; C. 60 ?).	Quito.	
r, s, t. ♂ (V. 149; C. 53) & ♀ (V. 154, 150; C. ?, 52).	W. Ecuador.	Mr. Fraser [C.].
		(Types of var. *fraseri*)
u. Hgr. (V. 157; C. 58).	S. America.	E. Laforest, Esq. [P.].
v. ♀ (V. 158; C. 52).	Mexico (?).	M Sallé [C.]. (?) (Type of *E. mexicanus*)

The latter specimen agrees so completely with Ecuador specimens, that I cannot refer it to a distinct species although the nasal shield is single.—The specimen is probably not from M. Sallé's Mexican Collection.

Tantilla pallida, Cope, Proc Amer. Philos. Soc. xxiv. 1887, p. 56, from Matto Grosso, Brazil, appears to agree in every respect with *H. melanocephalum*, except in having the first lower labial separated from its fellow by the symphysial. This is probably merely an individual variation, as the condition described by Cope is nearly attained by two of the specimens from Para in the Museum.

2. Homalocranium annulatum.

Tantilla annulata, *Boettg Zool. Anz* 1892, p 419.
Homalocranium annulatum, *Gunth. Biol. C.-Am., Rept.* p. 150 (1895).

The description does not give any structural characters by which this form may be distinguished from *H melanocephalum*, but the coloration is very different. Head black, snout to the middle of the præfrontals yellow; fifth upper labial yellow; two narrow yellow collar-bars, each broadly edged with black, the anterior crossing the extremity of the parietal shields; anterior third of body dark grey-brown, with alternating yellow, black-edged transverse spots or bars extending from the vertebral line to the outer ends of the ventrals; lower parts uniform yellow.

Total length 484 millim.; tail 99.

Nicaragua.

3. Homalocranium trilineatum.

Leptocalamus trilineatus, *Peters, Mon. Berl. Ac.* 1880, p. 221, pl. —. fig. 2.
Homalocranium tæniatum, *Bocourt, Miss. Sc. Mex., Rept.* p 587, pl xxxvii fig. 3 (1883), *Gunth Biol. C.-Am , Rept.* p 151 (1895).
—— trivittatum, *F. Mull. Verh. Nat. Ges. Basel*, vii. 1885, p. 678.
Tantilla tæniata, *Cope, Bull U.S Nat. Mus.* no. 32, 1887, p. 83.

Eye half as long as the snout. Rostral much broader than deep, visible from above, internasals half as long as the præfrontals; frontal hexagonal, obtuse-angled in front, acute-angled behind, once and a half as long as broad, longer than its distance from the end of the snout, shorter than the parietals, nostril between two nasals, the posterior in contact with the præocular; two postoculars; temporals 1+1; eight upper labials, third and fourth entering the eye; first lower labial separated from its fellow, the symphysial being in contact with the anterior chin-shields; four lower labials in contact with the anterior chin-shields, which are longer than the posterior. Scales in 15 rows. Ventrals 145-163; anal divided; subcaudals 68-69. Brown above, with three yellowish, dark-edged longitudinal lines; a yellowish cross-band on the occiput, not connected with the longitudinal lines, a yellowish spot on each side of the head behind the eyes; lower parts whitish.

Total length 275 millim.; tail 65.

Guatemala, Honduras.

a. ♀ (V. 163 ; C. 69)   Bonacca Id., Honduras.   F. D. Godman, Esq. [P].

4. Homalocranium longifrontale. (Plate IX fig. 3.)

Homalocranium longifrontale, *Bouleng. Ann. & Mag. N. H.* (6) xvii. 1896, p. 17.

Eye about half as long as the snout. Rostral broader than deep, just visible from above; internasals not half as long as the præfrontals; frontal hexagonal, obtuse-angled in front, acute-angled behind, twice as long as broad, much longer than its distance from the end of the snout, shorter than the parietals; nostril between two nasals, the posterior widely separated from the præocular; two postoculars; temporals 1+1; seven upper labials, third and fourth entering the eye; first lower labial in contact with its fellow behind the symphysial; four lower labials in contact with the anterior chin-shields, which are shorter than the posterior. Scales in 15 rows. Ventrals 158; anal divided; subcaudals 85. Pale brown above, with five dark brown longitudinal lines; head and nape black; a yellow band across the snout; a yellow blotch on each side of the head behind the eye, a round yellow spot on each side of the vertex, between the supraocular and the parietal, another pair on the back of the head between the parietal and the second temporal, and a yellow dot on each parietal near the median suture; the black of the nape bordered with yellow behind; a series of blackish dots along the outer row of scales; lower parts white.

Total length 280 millim.; tail 83.

Colombia.

a. ♂ (V. 158; C. 85).   Cali, 3200 feet.   Mr. W. F. H. Rosenberg [C.]. (Type.)

5. Homalocranium coronatum.

Tantilla coronata, *Baird & Gir. Cat. N. Am. Rept.* p 131 (1853), and *Rep. U S Explor. R. R.* x pt iii. pl xxxiii. fig. 96 (1859); *Garm. N. Am. Rept.* p. 88 (1883); *Cope, Proc. U S Nat. Mus.* xiv. 1892, p. 598; *Loennberg, Proc. U.S. Nat. Mus.* xvii. 1894, p. 333.

? Homalocranium wagneri, *Jan, Arch. Zool. Anat. Phys.* ii. 1862, p 51, *and Icon. Gén.* 15, pl. ii. fig. 3 (1866).

Homalocranium melanocephalum, part, *Jan, l. c.* p. 51.

Eye not half as long as the snout. Rostral broader than deep, visible from above; frontal longer than broad, hexagonal, shorter then the parietals; nostril between two nasals, the posterior in contact with the præocular; two postoculars; temporals 1+1; seven upper labials, third and fourth entering the eye; first lower labial in contact with its fellow behind the symphysial; anterior chin-shields longer than the posterior. Scales in 15 rows. Ventrals 133-158; anal divided; subcaudals 40-58. Uniform reddish brown above; head deep chestnut-brown, with a yellowish crossbar on the occiput, edged with black behind; lower parts whitish.

Total length 220 millim.; tail 35.

South Carolina, Georgia, Alabama, Florida, and Mississippi.

H. wagneri, Jan, from Florida, which is referred to the synonymy of *H. coronatum* by Cope, differs in having the symphysial in contact with the anterior chin-shields, and an undivided anal shield. Loennberg also notes a specimen from Florida in which the first pair of lower labials do not come in contact on the median line, although very close together.

6. Homalocranium rubrum.

Tantilla rubra, *Cope, Journ. Ac. Philad.* (2) viii. 1876, p. 144.
Homalocranium rubrum, *Bocourt, Miss. Sc. Mex., Rept.* p. 590, pl. xxxvii. fig. 6 (1883), *Gunth. Biol. C.-Am., Rept.* p. 155 (1895).

Eye not half as long as the snout. Rostral much broader than deep, visible from above, internasals about half as long as the præfrontals; frontal hexagonal, obtuse-angled in front, acute-angled behind, once and one third to once and a half as long as broad, longer than its distance from the end of the snout, shorter than the parietals, nostril between two nasals, the posterior of which is in contact with or more or less narrowly separated from the præ-ocular; two postoculars, temporals 1+1; seven upper labials, third and fourth entering the eye, first lower labial in contact with its fellow behind the symphysial; four lower labials in contact with the anterior chin-shields, which are longer than the posterior. Scales in 15 rows. Ventrals 149–179; anal divided; subcaudals 59–70. Uniform red above; back of head and nape black, with a yellow bar across the occiput, snout and upper lip behind the eye yellow; lower parts yellowish white.

Total length 390 millim.; tail 90.

Mexico.

a. ♂ (V. 179, C. 70). Orizaba.
b. Yg. (V. 154; C. 59). Tapana, Tehuantepec. M. Sumichrast [C]; F. D. Godman and O. Salvin, Esqrs. [P]
c–d ♀ (V. 155, 153; C. ?, 65). S. Mexico. F. D. Godman, Esq. [P.].

7. Homalocranium semicinctum.

Homalocranium semicinctum, *Dum. & Bibr.* vii. p 862 (1854), *Jan, Arch. Zool. Anat. Phys* ii 1862, p. 53, *and Icon. Gén.* 15, pl. ii. fig. 6 (1866).
—— laticeps, *Gunth. Proc Zool. Soc.* 1860, p 240.
—— supracinctum, *Peters, Mon Berl. Ac* 1863, p. 272.
Tantilla laticeps, *Cope, Proc. Ac Philad* 1866, p. 74.
—— semicincta, *Cope, l. c.*
Homalocranium lineatum, *Fischer, Oster-Progr. Akad Gymn. Hamb.* 1883, p. 6, pl. — figs. 6–8

Eye not half as long as the snout. Rostral much broader than deep, visible from above; internasals not more than half as long as the præfrontals; frontal hexagonal, obtuse-angled in front, acute-angled behind, once and one third to once and a half as long as broad, as long as or longer than its distance from the end of the snout, shorter than the parietals; nostril between two nasals, the posterior very small and widely separated from the præocular; two postoculars; temporals 1+1, seven upper labials, third and fourth entering the eye; first lower labial in contact with its fellow behind the symphysial; four lower labials in contact with the anterior chin-shields, which are longer than the posterior. Scales in 15 rows. Ventrals 143–180; anal divided; subcaudals 50–72. Whitish above, with large black spots or irregular cross-bands, or with two broad black stripes separated by a white vertebral line, or blackish, with whitish cross-bands; end of snout whitish; a white occipital cross-bar, usually interrupted in the middle; lower parts white.

Total length 470 millim.; tail 80.

Venezuela, Colombia, Ecuador.

a–c. ♀ (V. 150; C. ?). & yg. (V. 180, 168; C. 50, 57)	Colombia.	Dr. J. G. Fischer.
d. ♀ (V. 168; C. ?).	Carthagena	Capt. Garth [P] (Type of *H. laticeps*.)
e. ♀ (V. 166; C. ?).	Rosario de Cucuta.	Mr C. Webber [C.].

8. Homalocranium fuscum.

Homalocranium melanocephalum, part., Jan, *Arch. Zool. Anat. Phys.* ii. 1862, p. 51, and *Icon. Gén.* 15, pl. ii. fig. 4 (1866); Günth. *Biol. C.-Am., Rept.* p. 147 (1895).

—— melanocephalum, var. fuscum, Bocourt, *Miss. Sc. Mex., Rept.* p. 589 (1883).

—— jani, Günth. *l. c.* p. 148, pl. lii. fig. D.

—— armillatum, part., Günth. *l. c.* p. 149.

Eye not half as long as the snout. Rostral a little broader than deep, visible from above; internasals about half as long as the præfrontals; frontal hexagonal, obtuse-angled in front, acute-angled behind, once and one third as long as broad, longer than its distance from the end of the snout, shorter than the parietals; nostril between two nasals, the posterior of which is in contact with or separated from the præocular; two postoculars; temporals 1+1; seven upper labials, third and fourth entering the eye; first lower labial in contact with its fellow behind the symphysial; four lower labials in contact with the anterior chin-shields, which are longer than the posterior. Scales in 15 rows. Ventrals 136–159; anal divided; subcaudals 44–49. Brown above, with or without a light, dark-edged lateral line, with or without a blackish vertebral line; head dark brown or blackish above, with yellow markings as in *H. melanocephalum*.

Total length 245 millim.; tail 50.

Guatemala, Nicaragua.

a. ♀ (V. 159; C. 44).	Dueñas, Guatemala.	O. Salvin, Esq. [C.]	
b. ♀ (V. 147; C. 49).	Guatemala	F. D Godman, Esq. [P].	
c. ♀ (V. 136, C. P).	Hacienda Rosa de Jericho, Nicaragua.	Dr. Rothschuh [C.].	

(Types of *H. jani.*)

9. Homalocranium boulengeri.

Homalocranium boulengeri, *Gunth. Biol. C.-Am., Rept.* p. 148, pl. lii fig F (1895).

Eye not half as long as the snout. Rostral a little broader than deep; internasals more than half as long as the præfrontals; frontal hexagonal, obtuse-angled in front, acute-angled behind, scarcely longer than broad, longer than its distance from the end of the snout, shorter than the parietals; nostril between two nasals, the posterior of which is in contact with the præocular; two post-oculars; temporals 1+1; seven upper labials, third and fourth entering the eye; first lower labial in contact with its fellow behind the symphysial, four lower labials in contact with the anterior chin-shields, which are longer than the posterior. Scales in 15 rows. Ventrals 161; anal divided; subcaudals 46. Uniform red above; head black, with the sides of the snout, a spot on the lip behind the eye, and a cross-bar on the occiput yellowish; lower parts whitish.

Total length 240 millim.; tail 40.

Mexico.

a. ♂ (V. 161; C. 46). Huatuzco, Vera Cruz. F. D. Godman, Esq. [P.] (Type.)

10. Homalocranium schistosum.

Homalocranium schistosum, *Bocourt, Miss Sc. Mex., Rept.* p. 584, pl. xxxvi. fig 10 (1883), *Gunth. Biol. C.-Am., Rept.* p 152 (1895).
Tantilla schistosa, *Cope, Bull U S. Nat. Mus.* no. 32, 1887, p. 83

Eye not half as long as the snout Rostral a little broader than deep, visible from above; internasals about half as long as the præ-frontals; frontal hexagonal, obtuse-angled in front, acute-angled behind, scarcely longer than broad, a little longer than its distance from the end of the snout, shorter than the parietals; nostril between two nasals, the posterior of which is in contact with the præocular; two postoculars; temporals 1+1; seven upper labials, third and fourth entering the eye; first lower labial widely separated from its fellow, the symphysial being in contact with the anterior chin-shields; three or four lower labials in contact with the anterior chin-shields, which are longer than the posterior. Scales in 15 rows. Ventrals 121–135, anal divided; subcaudals 32–38. Dark brown above, snout and a cross-bar on the occiput yellowish; lower parts yellowish.

Total length 220 millim.; tail 42.

Mexico, Guatemala, Nicaragua.

a. ♂ (V. 135; C. 38).   Guatemala.   F. D. Godman, Esq.[P.].
b. Hgr. ♂ (V. 130; C. 32).   Matagalpa, Nicaragua.   Dr. Rothschuh [C.].

11. Homalocranium canula.

Tantilla canula, *Cope, Journ. Ac. Philad.* (2) viii. 1876, p. 144.
Homalocranium canulum, *Gunth. Biol. C.-Am., Rept.* p. 153 (1895).

Snout rather wide, but projecting beyond the mouth. Frontal rather small, hexagonal, longer than its distance from the rostral; two postoculars; temporals 1+1; seven upper labials, third and fourth entering the eye; first lower labial separated from its fellow by the symphysial; four lower labials in contact with the anterior chin-shields, which are longer than the posterior. Scales in 15 rows. Ventrals 110; anal divided; subcaudals 37. Colour leaden, darker above; head-shields with paler borders and centres.

Total length 172 millim.; tail 37.

Yucatan.

12. Homalocranium miniatum.

Tantilla miniata, *Cope, Proc. Ac. Philad.* 1863, p. 100, *Journ. Ac. Philad.* (2) viii 1876, p. 144, and *Proc. U.S. Nat. Mus* xiv. 1892, p. 597
Homalocranium deppii, *Bocourt, Miss. Sc. Mex., Rept.* p. 584, pl. xxxvi. fig. 11 (1883); *Gunth. Biol. C.-Am, Rept.* p. 151 (1895).
Tantilla deppei, *Cope, Bull. U.S. Nat Mus.* no. 32, 1887, p. 83
Homalocranium miniatum, *Gunth l c.* p 146

Eye about half the length of the snout. Rostral a little broader than deep, visible from above: internasals about half as long as the præfrontals; frontal hexagonal, obtuse-angled in front, acute-angled behind, once and one third as long as broad, longer than its distance from the end of the snout, shorter than the parietals; nostril between two nasals, much nearer the internasal than the first labial; posterior nasal in contact with the præocular; two postoculars; temporals 1+1; seven upper labials, third and fourth entering the eye; first lower labial separated from its fellow, the symphysial reaching the anterior chin-shields; four lower labials in contact with the anterior chin-shields, which are a little longer than the posterior. Scales in 15 rows. Ventrals 147–152; anal divided; subcaudals 55. Pale brown above, with five dark brown longitudinal lines; head dark brown above, yellowish on the sides; a yellow bar across the occiput, divided in the middle by the dark vertebral line; lower parts yellowish white (red in life).

Total length 270 millim.; tail 65.

Mexico.

a. ♂ (V. 152; C. 55).   S. Mexico.   F. D. Godman, Esq. [P.].

13. Homalocranium virgatum.

Microdromus virgatus, *Gunth. Ann. & Mag. N. H.* (4) ix. 1872, p. 17, pl. iv. fig. B.
Homalocranium sexfasciatum, *Fischer, Abh. Nat. Ver. Bremen*, vii. 1882, p. 225, pl. xiv figs 8-10.
—— virgatum, *Bocourt, Miss. Sc. Mex , Rept* p. 584, pl. xxxvi. fig. 4 (1883); *Gunth Biol. C.-Am., Rept.* p. 154, pl. lii. fig. A (1895).
Tantilla sexfasciata, *Cope, Bull. U.S. Nat. Mus.* no. 32, 1887, p. 83.
—— virgata, *Cope, l. c.* p. 84.

Eye about half the length of the snout. Rostral a little broader than deep, visible from above; internasals about half as long as the præfrontals; frontal hexagonal, obtuse-angled in front, acute-angled behind, once and one third to once and a half as long as broad, longer than its distance from the end of the snout, shorter than the parietals; nostril in a single or divided nasal, which is in contact with or narrowly separated from the præocular; two postoculars; temporals 1+1; seven upper labials, third and fourth entering the eye; first lower labial separated from or narrowly in contact with its fellow, the symphysial usually reaching the anterior chin-shields; four lower labials in contact with the anterior chin-shields, which are longer than the posterior. Scales in 15 rows. Ventrals 154-175; anal divided; subcaudals 57-65. Pale brown above, with four darker stripes edged with blackish; a blackish line along each side of the belly; a yellow, black-edged cross-bar on the occiput, interrupted in the middle; upper lip and end of snout yellowish, with a black spot below the eye and another on the rostral shield; lower parts yellowish white.

Total length 315 millim.; tail 75.

Costa Rica.

a-d. ♂ (V 154; C. 57) & ♀   Cartago, Costa Rica.   (Types.)
(V 173, 175, 167; C. ?, 63, 59).

14. Homalocranium ruficeps.

Pogonaspis ruficeps, *Cope, Proc. Ac. Philad.* 1894, p. 204.

Rostral visible from above; frontal elongate, hexagonal; nostril between two nasals, the posterior not reaching the præocular; two postoculars; temporals 1+1; seven upper labials, third and fourth entering the eye; first lower labial in contact with its fellow behind the symphysial, a single pair of chin-shields, in contact with four lower labials. Ventrals 146; anal divided. Light brown above; median row of scales deep brown; a narrow yellow line on the adjacent borders of the third and fourth rows of scales, which is bounded above by a dark brown line; upper surface of head light reddish brown, with a pale spot at the extremity of each parietal shield; upper lip yellow, with a black spot below the eye; lower parts yellow.

Total length 223 millim.

Costa Rica.

15. Homalocranium bocourti.

Homalocranium coronatum (*non B. & G.*), *Bocourt, Miss. Sc. Mex., Rept.* p. 589, pl. xxxvii. fig. 5 (1883).
—— bocourti, *Gunth. Biol. C.-Am , Rept.* p. 149 (1895).

Eye half as long as the snout. Rostral a little broader than deep, visible from above; internasals more than half as long as the præfrontals; frontal pentagonal, or very slightly angulate in front, acute-angled behind, once and one third to once and a half as long as broad, longer than its distance from the end of the snout, shorter than the parietals; nostril between two nasals, the posterior in contact with the præocular; two postoculars; temporals 1+1; seven upper labials, third and fourth entering the eye; first lower labial in contact with its fellow behind the symphysial; three or four lower labials in contact with the anterior chin-shields, which are shorter than the posterior. Scales in 15 rows. Ventrals 172–176; anal divided; subcaudals 55. Pale reddish above, without spots or markings; head black, with a yellowish cross-bar on the snout and a yellowish, black-edged occipital cross-bar just behind the parietals; upper lip and lower parts white.

Total length 245 millim ; tail 50.
Mexico.

a. ♂ (V. 172 , C. 55).   Guanajuato.   Paris Mus. [E.].   (Type)

16. Homalocranium reticulatum.

Tantilla reticulata, *Cope, Proc. Ac. Philad.* 1860, p. 77, and *Proc. U.S. Nat. Mus.* xiv. 1892, p. 598.
Homalocranium reticulatum, *Gunth. Biol. C.-Am., Rept.* p. 152 (1895).

Rostral broad, visible from above; frontal broad, slightly angulate in front, acute-angled behind; nostril between two nasals, the posterior of which is in contact with the præocular; two postoculars; temporals 1+1; seven upper labials, third and fourth entering the eye; two pairs of chin-shields, the anterior in contact with the symphysial. Scales in 15 rows. Ventrals 148; anal divided; subcaudals 67. Chestnut-brown above, much darker posteriorly, the colour extending on the ends of the ventrals; anteriorly, the scales are edged with darker, presenting a reticulated pattern; central row of scales lighter, forming a vertebral line; third and fourth rows on each side also lighter, forming indistinct lines; a yellowish-brown collar crosses the ends of the parietal shields; head-shields clouded and edged with darker; a deep brown mark extending from the parietals to the mouth across the yellowish labials; beneath pale yellow, deepening posteriorly.

Total length 260 millim.; tail 80.
Panama.

17. Homalocranium mœstum.

Homalocranium mœstum, *Gunth. Ann. & Mag. N. H.* (3) xii. 1863, p. 352; *Bocourt, Miss. Sc. Mex., Rept.* p. 583, pl. xxxvi. fig. 9 (1883), *Gunth. Biol. C.-Am, Rept.* p. 152, pl. lii. fig. E (1895).
Tantilla mœsta, *Cope, Proc. Ac. Philad.* 1866, p 126.

Eye nearly half as long as the snout. Rostral small, a little broader than deep, scarcely visible from above; internasals not half as long as the præfrontals; frontal hexagonal, obtuse-angled in front, acute-angled behind, longer than its distance from the end of the snout, shorter than the parietals; nostril between two nasals, the posterior of which is in contact with the præocular; two postoculars; temporals 1+1; seven upper labials, third and fourth entering the eye, first lower labial separated from its fellow, the symphysial in contact with the anterior chin-shields; four lower labials in contact with the anterior chin-shields, which are longer than the posterior. Scales in 15 rows. Ventrals 140-148; anal divided; subcaudals 55-63. Blackish brown above and below, throat, temples, and occiput yellowish white.

Total length 300 millim.
Guatemala.

a. ♀ (V. 148; C.?).   Peten.   O. Salvin, Esq. [C.]. (Type.)

18. Homalocranium vermiforme.

Lioninia vermiformis, *Hallow. Proc Ac. Philad.* 1860, p. 484.
Tantilla vermiformis, *Cope, Proc. Ac. Philad.* 1861, p. 74, *and Journ. Ac. Philad.* (2) viii. 1876, p. 145.

Snout prominent. Rostral large, acute behind; frontal hexagonal, large, somewhat longer than broad; nostril between two nasals; two postoculars; seven upper labials, third and fourth entering the eye; symphysial in contact with the anterior chin-shields. Scales in 15 rows. Ventrals 122; anal single; subcaudals 26. Whitish above, with numerous small brown spots; sometimes a narrow black vertebral line; head brown above, lighter on the snout, with a whitish blotch on the occiput; lower parts white.

Total length 130 millim.; tail 18.
Nicaragua.

19. Homalocranium breve.

Homalocranium breve, *Gunth. Biol. C.-Am., Rept.* p. 150 (1895).

Eye not half as long as the snout. Rostral a little broader than deep, well visible from above; internasals more than half as long as the præfrontals; frontal hexagonal, obtuse-angled in front, acute-angled behind, scarcely longer than broad, longer than its distance from the end of the snout, shorter than the parietals; nostril between two nasals, the posterior in contact with the præocular;

two postoculars; temporals 1+1; seven upper labials, third and fourth entering the eye; first lower labial in contact with its fellow behind the symphysial; four lower labials in contact with the anterior chin-shields, which are longer than the posterior. Scales in 15 rows. Ventrals 111; anal divided. Pale brown above, speckled with darker; head and nape darker, whitish beneath.

Total length 140 millim.

British Honduras.

a. ♂ (V. 111; C. ?).   British Honduras   O. Salvin, Esq. [P.].
(Type.)

20. Homalocranium atriceps.

Homalocranium atriceps, *Günth. Biol. C.-Am., Rept.* p. 146, pl. lii. fig. B (1895).

Eye not half as long as the snout. Rostral broader than deep, well visible from above; internasals half as long as the præfrontals; frontal hexagonal, obtuse-angled in front, acute-angled behind, once and one third to once and a half as long as broad, longer than its distance from the end of the snout, shorter than the parietals; nostril between two nasals, the posterior in contact with or narrowly separated from the præocular; two postoculars; temporals 1+1; seven upper labials, third and fourth entering the eye; first lower labial in contact with its fellow behind the symphysial; four lower labials in contact with the anterior chin-shields, which are longer than the posterior. Scales in 15 rows. Ventrals 123–125; anal divided; subcaudals 55–59. Pale reddish brown above; upper surface of head blackish, bordered behind by a whitish crossbar; lower parts white.

Total length 170 millim.; tail 47.

North Mexico.

a–b. ♂ (V. 123, 125; C. 55, 59).   Nuevo Leon.   W. Taylor, Esq. [P.].
(Types.)

21. Homalocranium planiceps.

Coluber planiceps, *Blainv. Nouv. Ann. Mus.* iv. 1835, p. 294, pl. xxvii. fig. 3.
Homalocranium planiceps, *Dum. & Bibr.* vii. p. 857 (1854); *Jan, Arch. Zool. Anat. Phys.* ii. 1862, p 51, *and Icon. Gén.* 15, pl. ii. fig. 2 (1866); *Bocourt, Miss. Sc. Mex., Rept.* p. 581, pl. xxxvi. fig. 7 (1883); *Günth. Biol. C.-Am., Rept.* p. 145 (1895).
Tantilla nigriceps, *Kennicott, Proc. Ac. Philad.* 1860, p. 328; *Cope, Proc. U.S. Nat. Mus.* xiv. 1891, p. 598.
Scolecophis fumiceps, *Cope, Proc. Ac. Philad.* 1860, p. 371.
Tantilla planiceps, *Cope, Proc. Ac. Philad.* 1861, p. 74, *and Proc. U.S. Nat. Mus.* xiv. 1891, p. 597.
Homalocranium præoculum, *Bocourt, Miss. Sc. Mex., Rept.* p. 582, pl. xxxvi. fig. 8.

Eye not half as long as the snout, which is much depressed and very prominent. Rostral large, broader than deep, its upper portion measuring about two thirds its distance from the frontal; internasals about half as long as the præfrontals; frontal hexagonal, obtuse-angled in front, acute-angled behind, a little longer than broad, longer than its distance from the end of the snout, shorter than the parietals; nostril in a divided or semidivided nasal, which is in contact with or narrowly separated from the præocular; latter exceptionally divided; one or two postoculars *; temporals 1+1; seven upper labials, third and fourth entering the eye; first lower labial in contact with or separated from its fellow; four lower labials in contact with the anterior chin-shields, which are longer than the posterior. Scales in 15 rows. Ventrals 121-153; anal divided; subcaudals 42-58. Pale brown above, head dark brown or black; lower parts white.

Total length 260 millim.; tail 50

Lower California to Western Texas and North Mexico.

a-c, d ♂ (V. 127, 126; C. ?, Duval Co., Texas. W. Taylor, Esq. [P.].
58), ♀ (V 153; C. 45), &
yg. (V. 121; C. 57).

22. Homalocranium calamarinum.

Tantilla calamarina, *Cope, Proc. Ac. Philad.* 1866, p. 320, *and Journ. Ac. Philad.* (2) viii. 1876, p. 143.
—— bimaculata, *Cope, Journ. Ac. Philad.* (2) viii. 1876, p. 143.
Homalocranium bimaculatum, *Bocourt, Miss. Sc. Mex., Rept.* p 580, pl. xxxvi. fig 6 (1883); *Günth. Biol. C.-Am., Rept.* p. 154 (1895).

Eye not half as long as the snout, which is prominent. Rostral broader than deep, well visible from above; internasals about half as long as the præfrontals; frontal hexagonal, slightly longer than broad, longer than its distance from the end of the snout, shorter than the parietals; nostril between two nasals, the posterior in contact with or narrowly separated from the præocular; one postocular; temporals 1+1, the anterior sometimes separated from the postocular by the contact of the parietal and fifth labial; six upper labials, third and fourth entering the eye; first lower labial separated from its fellow by the symphysial; four lower labials in contact with the anterior chin-shields, which are longer than the posterior. Scales in 15 rows. Ventrals 119-132; anal divided; subcaudals 27-35. Pale brown above, with three brown longitudinal lines, the vertebral extending to the head, which is dark brown, and dividing a yellowish occipital blotch, end of snout yellowish; lower parts white.

Total length 195 millim.; tail 25.

Mexico.

---

* Two of the specimens in the Collection have one postocular on each side, the third has one on the left side and two on the right; whilst in the fourth the postocular is fused with the supraocular.

a–c. ♂ (V. 122; C. 31), ♀   San Blas.   Hr. A. Forrer [C.].
(V. 126; C. 27), & hgr. (V.
132; C. 27).

23. Homalocranium gracile.

Tantilla gracilis, *Baird & Gir.* Cat. N. Am. Rept. pp. 132, 161 (1853); *Hallow.* Proc. Ac. Philad. 1856, p. 246; *Garm.* N. Am. Rept. p. 87, pl. vi. fig. 3 (1883); *Cope*, Proc. U.S. Nat. Mus. xiv. 1892, p. 598.

—— hallowellii, *Cope*, Proc. Ac. Philad. 1860, p. 77.

Homalocranium gracile, *Jan*, Arch. Zool. Anat. Phys. ii. 1862, p. 50, and Icon. Gén. 15, pl. ii fig. 1 (1866); *Bocourt*, Miss. Sc. Mex., Rept. p. 579, pl. xxxvi. fig. 5 (1883), *Gunth.* Biol. C.-Am., Rept. p. 146 (1895).

Eye not half as long as the snout, which is much depressed and very prominent. Rostral large, a little broader than deep, the portion visible from above nearly as long as its distance from the frontal; internasals at least half as long as the præfrontals; frontal hexagonal, obtuse-angled in front, acute-angled behind, a little longer than broad, as long as or longer than its distance from the end of the snout, shorter than the parietals; nostril in a single or divided nasal, which is in contact with or narrowly separated from the præocular; one postocular; temporals 1+1, the first sometimes narrowly separated from the postocular by the contact of the parietal and the fifth labial; six upper labials, third and fourth entering the eye; first lower labial usually separated from its fellow by the symphysial; four lower labials in contact with the anterior chin-shields, which are longer than the posterior. Scales in 15 rows. Ventrals 112–133; anal divided; subcaudals 41–51. Pale brown or reddish above, uniform or speckled with dark brown, sometimes with a dark vertebral line; upper surface of head darker brown; yellowish or orange below.

Total length 195 millim.; tail 44.

Texas.

a. ♂ (V. 122; C. ?)   Texas.   Smithsonian Institution.
b, c, d–g, h–i. ♂ (V. 115, 114,   Duval Co.,   W. Taylor, Esq. [P.].
114, 115, 114, 112; C. 48,   Texas.
46, 47, 51, 49, ?) & ♀ (V.
117, 126; C. ?, 43).

185. OGMIUS.

Ogmius, *Cope*, Proc. Amer. Philos. Soc. xi. 1869, p. 162, and Journ. Ac. Philad. (2) viii. 1876, p. 142.

Dentition as in *Stenorhina*. Head small, not distinct from neck; eye small, with round pupil; snout pointed and projecting; nostril in a single nasal; no loreal. Scales smooth, in 17 rows; ventrals rounded. Tail short; subcaudals in two rows.

Mexico.

1. Ogmius acutus.

Ogmius varians (*non Jan*), *Cope, Proc. Amer. Philos. Soc.* xi. 1869, p. 162.
—— acutus, *Cope, Proc. U.S Nat. Mus.* ix. 1886, p 189, *and Bull. U.S. Nat. Mus.* no 32, 1887, p. 82.

Rostral plate produced, acute-angled, flat above; frontal longer than broad; one præ- and two postoculars; temporals 1+2; seven upper labials, third and fourth entering the eye. Scales in 17 rows. Ventrals 127; anal divided; subcaudals 32. Greyish above, with a dorsal series of transverse dark spots; sides and head, including lips, unspotted.
Total length 249 millim.; tail 40.
W. Tehuantepec.

186. STENORHINA.

Stenorhina, *Dum. & Bibr. Mém Ac. Sc.* xxiii. 1853, p. 490, *and Erp. Gén.* vii. p. 865 (1854), *Gunth. Cat. Col. Sn.* p. 246 (1858); *Jan, Arch. Zool. Anat. Phys.* ii. 1862, p. 63; *Bocourt, Miss. Sc. Mex., Rept.* p. 592 (1883).
Microphis, *Hallow Proc. Ac. Philad.* 1854, p. 97.
Bergenia, *Steind Novara, Rept* p. 92 (1867).

Maxillary teeth small, equal, 13 or 14, followed by a pair of feebly enlarged grooved teeth situated below the posterior border of the eye; mandibular teeth equal. Head small, not distinct from neck; eye small, with round pupil; nostril between two nasals, the anterior of which is fused with the internasal; loreal often absent. Body cylindrical; scales smooth, without pits, in 17 rows; ventrals rounded. Tail moderate or short; subcaudals in two rows.
Mexico, Central America, Colombia, Ecuador.

1. Stenorhina degenhardtii.

Calamaria degenhardtii, *Berthold, Abh Ges. Wiss. Gotting.* iii. 1846, p. 8, pl. i. figs. 3 & 4; *Peters, Mon Berl. Ac.* 1861, p. 461.
Stenorhina ventralis, *Dum. & Bibr.* vii. p. 867 (1854); *Gunth. Cat.* p. 246 (1858); *Cope, Proc. Amer. Philos. Soc.* xi. 1869, p. 162.
—— freminvillii, *Dum. & Bibr t. c.* p 868, pl. lxx. figs. 1 & 2; *Gunth. l. c.*; *Garm. N. Am. Rept.* p 85 (1883); *Bocourt, Miss. Sc. Mex., Rept.* p. 596, pl. xxxvii fig. 8 (1886).
Microphis quinquelineatus, *Hallow. Proc. Ac. Philad.* 1854, p. 97, *and Journ. Ac. Philad.* (2) iii. 1855, p 33, pl iv.
Stenorhina kennicottiana, *Cope, Proc. Ac. Philad.* 1860, p. 242, *and Journ. Ac. Philad.* (2) viii. 1876, p. 142.
—— quinquelineata, *Cope, l. c.* p. 243; *Bocourt, l. c.* p. 597, pl. xxxvii. fig 11.
—— lactea, *Cope, Proc. Ac. Philad.* 1861, p. 303.
—— degenhardtii, *Jan, Arch. Zool. Anat. Phys.* ii. 1862, p. 63, *and Icon. Gén.* 48, pl. ii figs. 5 & 6 (1876), *Cope, Journ. Ac Philad.* (2) viii 1876, p 142; *Bocourt, l. c.* p. 594, pl. xxxvii. figs. 8 & 9; *Gunth. Biol. C-Am., Rept.* p. 158 (1895).
Bergenia mexicana, *Steind Novara, Rept.* p. 92, figs. (1867).

Stenorhina degenhardtii apiata, *Cope, Journ. Ac. Philad.* (2) viii. 1876, p. 142.
Chilomeniscus mexicanus, *Cope, Bull. U.S. Nat. Mus.* no. 32, 1887, p. 81.

Snout short, obtusely pointed, prominent. Rostral large, broader than deep, the portion visible from above measuring one half to two thirds, or even equal to, its distance from the frontal; internasals as long as or a little shorter than the præfrontals; frontal once and one third to once and a half as long as broad, as long as or longer than its distance from the end of the snout, as long as or a little longer than the parietals; loreal, if present, small, if absent fused with the posterior nasal or with the præfrontal; one præ- and two postoculars; temporals 1+2 (rarely 2+3 or 4); seven upper labials, third and fourth entering the eye; three (rarely four) lower labials in contact with the anterior chin-shields, which are longer than the posterior. Scales in 17 rows. Ventrals 136–174; anal divided; subcaudals 28–49. Coloration very variable.

Total length 750 millim.; tail 100.

Mexico to Ecuador.

A. Belly more or less spotted with blackish; upper parts brown with more or less distinct darker spots and irregular crossbars; these markings may entirely disappear in the adult, which is then uniform dark brown above.

a. ♂ (V. 148; C. 43).	Mexico.	
b–c. ♀ (V. 156, 161; C. 33, 33).	Atoyac, Vera Cruz.	Mr. H. H. Smith [C.]; F. D. Godman, Esq. [P.].
d. ♀ (V. 159; C. 33).	Vera Paz, Low Forest.	O. Salvin, Esq. [C.].
e. ♂ (V. 141; C. 42).	Pacific Coast of Guatemala.	O. Salvin, Esq. [C.].
f. ♀ (V. 160; C. 31).	Chontales, Nicaragua.	R. A. Rix, Esq. [C.]; W. M. Crowfoot, Esq. [P.].
g. ♀ (V. 158, C.?).	Cartago, Costa Rica.	
h. ♂ (V. 136; C. 40).	Buenaventura, Colombia.	Mr. W. F. H. Rosenberg [C.].
i–k. Yg. (V. 152, 145; C. 33, 39).	Zaruma, Ecuador.	J. F. Gunter, Esq. [C.].

B. Belly uniform yellowish; back pale brown.

    a. With five black longitudinal lines on the back.

a. ♂ (V. 162; C. 40).	Mexico.	
b. Hgr. (V. 171; C. 32).	Jalapa, Mexico.	Mr. Hoege [C.].
c. ♀ (V. 171; C. 31).	Plain of Zacapa, Guatemala.	O. Salvin, Esq. [C.].

    b. A feebly-marked blackish vertebral line and a black streak behind the eye.

d. ♂ (V. 157; C. 40).   Putla, Mexico.

c. No well-defined markings.

e–f. ♂ (V. 170; C. 33) & ♀ (V. 173; C. 28).	Yucatan.		M. Sumichrast [C.]; F. D. Godman & O. Salvin, Esqrs. [P.].
g. ♂ (V. 162; C. 38).	Tapana, Tehuantepec.		
h. ♂ (V. 171; C. 36).	Cartago, Costa Rica.		
i. ♂ (V. 151; C. 46).	——?		Prof. Grant [P.].
k. ♂, skeleton.	Yucatan.		

187. XENOPHOLIS.

Xenopholis, *Peters, Mon. Berl. Ac.* 1869, p. 440.
Gerrhosteus, *Cope, Proc. Ac. Philad.* 1874, p. 71.
Elapomorphus, part., *Strauch, Bull. Ac. St. Pétersb.* xxix. 1884, p. 549.

Maxillary teeth 14, small, followed after a short interspace by a pair of moderately enlarged, grooved fangs situated just behind the vertical of the eye; mandibular teeth subequal. Head slightly

Fig. 16.

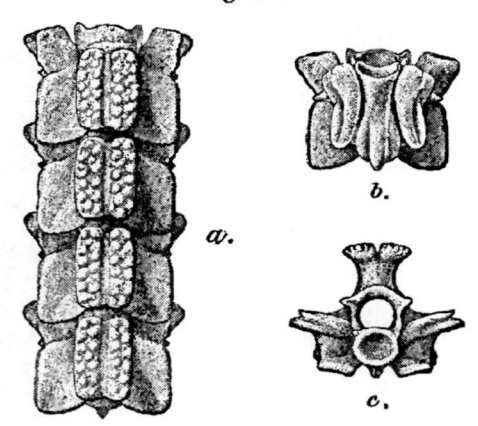

Vertebræ of *Xenopholis scalaris*.
a. Four middle dorsal vertebræ, seen from above.
b. Middle dorsal vertebræ, lower view. c. Ditto, front view.

distinct from neck; eye rather small, with round pupil; nasal entire; præfrontals fused to a single shield. Body cylindrical; scales smooth, without pits, in 17 rows; ventrals rounded. Tail rather short; subcaudals in two rows. Neural spines of the vertebræ expanded above, forming shields which are rugose and divided by a median groove.

South America.

1. Xenopholis scalaris.

Elapomorphus scalaris, *Wucherer, Proc. Zool. Soc.* 1861, p. 325; *Strauch, Bull. Ac. St. Pétersb.* xxix. 1884, p. 573.
Xenopholis braconnieri, *Peters, Mon. Berl. Ac.* 1869, p. 441, pl. —, fig. 3.
Gerrhosteus prosopis, *Cope, Proc. Ac. Philad.* 1874, p. 71.

Rostral slightly broader than deep, hardly visible from above; internasals small; præfrontal large *; frontal large, as broad as long, nearly as long as its distance from the end of the snout, much shorter than the parietals; supraocular small; nasal large; loreal longer than deep; præocular single, larger than the supraocular, extending to the upper surface of the head and forming an extensive suture with the frontal; two postoculars, lower in contact with the anterior temporal; temporals 1+2; eight upper labials, fourth and fifth entering the eye; four lower labials in contact with the anterior chin-shields, which are longer than the posterior. Scales in 17 rows. Ventrals 128-141; anal entire; subcaudals 28-39. Pale brown above, with a dark brown vertebral line separating large blackish-brown transverse spots or cross-bands; upper lip and lower parts yellowish white.

Total length 330 millim.; tail 55.

Brazil, Bolivia, Eastern Ecuador.

a. ♂ (V. 129; C. 34).	Bahia		Dr. O. Wucherer [C.]. (Type)
b. ♀ (V. 141; C. 28).	Yungas, Bolivia.		
c. ♀ (V. 138, C. 34).	Canelos, E. Ecuador.		Mr. C. Buckley [C.].

188. APOSTOLEPIS.

Calamaria, part., *Schleg. Phys. Serp.* ii. p. 25 (1837).
Elapomorphus, part., *Dum. & Bibr. Mém. Ac. Sc.* xxiii. 1853, p. 489, and *Erp. Gén.* vii. p. 832 (1854); *Jan, Arch. Zool. Anat. Phys.* ii. 1862, p. 41; *Strauch, Bull. Ac. St. Pétersb.* xxix. 1884, p. 549.
Apostolepis, *Cope, Proc. Ac. Philad.* 1861, p. 524.
Rhynchonyx, *Peters, Mon. Berl. Ac.* 1869, p. 437.

Maxillary very short, with four or five small teeth, followed, after a short interspace, by a pair of large grooved fangs situated below the eye; mandibular teeth subequal. Head small, not distinct from neck; eye small or minute, with round pupil, internasals fused with the præfrontals; nostril in a single nasal; no loreal; no anterior temporal. Body cylindrical. Scales smooth, without pits, in 15 rows; ventrals rounded. Tail short, obtuse; subcaudals in two rows.

South America.

---

* The type specimen of *Xenopholis braconnieri* is anomalous in having the præfrontal split up into three shields.

188. APOSTOLEPIS.

Synopsis of the Species.

I. A single labial in contact with the parietal; the diameter of the eye nearly equal to the distance between the eye and the oral margin.

Two postoculars; ventrals 199.. ... 1. *coronata*, p. 233.
A single postocular; ventrals 265 .. 2. *assimilis*, p. 234.

II. Two or three labials in contact with the parietal; eye minute.

  A. Fourth and fifth labials in contact with the parietal; ventrals 250–260.

Anal divided .... 3. *flavitorquata*, p. 234
Anal entire .... 4. *nigrolineata*, p. 235.

  B. Fourth, fifth, and sixth labials in contact with the parietal; ventrals 213 .... 5. *quinquelineata*, p. 235.

  C. Fifth and sixth labials in contact with the parietal.

   1. Symphysial in contact with the anterior chin-shields; ventrals 207 .... 6. *nigroterminata*, p. 235.

   2. First lower labial in contact with its fellow behind the symphysial.

Snout feebly projecting; four lower labials in contact with the chin-shields, fourth largest; ventrals 260 .... 7. *dorbignyi*, p. 236.
Snout feebly projecting; five lower labials in contact with the chin-shields, fifth largest; ventrals 244–251 .... 8. *erythronota*, p. 236.
Snout strongly projecting; five lower labials in contact with the chin-shields, ventrals 224–242 ...... 9. *ambinigra*, p. 237.

1. Apostolepis coronata *.

Elapomorphus coronatus, *Sauvage, Bull. Soc. Philom.* (7) i. 1877, p. 110, *Strauch, Bull. Ac. St. Pétersb.* xxix. 1884, p. 582; *Bocourt, Miss. Sc. Mex, Rept.* pl. xxxvi. fig. 1 (1886).

Snout scarcely projecting; eye small, its diameter nearly equalling its distance from the oral margin. Rostral broader than deep, the portion visible from above nearly half as long as its distance from the frontal; latter shield a little longer than broad, as long as its distance from the end of the snout, shorter than the parietals; nasal in contact with the præocular; two postoculars; six upper labials, second and third entering the eye, fifth in contact

---

* M. Bocourt has kindly supplied me with notes on the type specimen.

with the parietal; five lower labials in contact with the chin-shields, which are equal in size; first lower labial in contact with its fellow behind the symphysial. Scales in 15 rows. Ventrals 199; anal divided; subcaudals 47. Yellowish above, with three dark brown longitudinal streaks; anterior half of head blackish, posterior half yellow, with a black cross-band behind the parietals; lower parts white.

Total length 403 millim.; tail 63.

Habitat unknown.

2. Apostolepis assimilis.

Elapomorphus assimilis, *Reinh. Vidensk. Meddel.* 1869, p. 235, pl. iv. figs. 1-5 (1861); *Jan, Arch. Zool. Anat. Phys.* ii. 1862, p. 43, *and Icon. Gén.* 14, pl. i. fig. 4 (1865); *Strauch, Bull. Ac. St. Pétersb.* xxix. 1884, p. 586.

Snout feebly projecting; eye small, its diameter equalling its distance from the oral margin. Rostral a little broader than deep, just visible from above; frontal about once and three fifths as long as broad, as long as its distance from the end of the snout, shorter than the parietals; nasal not in contact with the præocular; a single postocular; six upper labials, second and third entering the eye, fifth in contact with the parietal; five lower labials in contact with the chin-shields, first in contact with its fellow behind the symphysial, fifth largest; chin-shields subequal in size. Scales in 15 rows. Ventrals 265; anal divided; subcaudals 33. Red above; head and nape black, separated by a white collar; præfrontals, nasal, and fourth upper labial white; end of tail black; lower parts white.

Total length 530 millim.; tail 50.

Minas Geraes, Brazil.

3. Apostolepis flavitorquata.

Elapomorphus flavotorquatus, *Dum. & Bibr.* vii. p. 836 (1854); *Guichen. in Casteln. Anim. Nouv. Amér. Sud, Rept.* p. 55, pl. x. (1855); *Jan, Arch. Zool. Anat. Phys.* ii. 1862, p. 43, *and Icon. Gén.* 14, pl. i. fig. 3 (1865); *Strauch, Bull. Ac. St. Pétersb.* xxix. 1884, p. 583.

Apostolepis flavotorquata, *Cope, Proc. Ac. Philad.* 1861, p. 524.

Snout feebly projecting; eye minute. Rostral as deep as broad, the portion visible from above measuring about two thirds its distance from the frontal; latter shield once and a half as long as broad, as long as its distance from the end of the snout, shorter than the parietals, which are twice as long as broad; nasal in contact with the præocular; a single postocular; six upper labials, second and third entering the eye, fourth and fifth in contact with the parietal; five lower labials in contact with the chin-shields, which are subequal in size; first lower labial in contact with its fellow behind the symphysial. Scales in 15 rows. Ventrals 250; anal divided: subcaudals 27. Red above, yellow beneath; head black above, with a yellow spot on each præfrontal and a pair on each side of the upper lip behind the eye; a yellow, black-edged nuchal collar; end of tail black, the terminal shield white

Total length 500 millim.; tail 40.

Goyaz, Brazil.

4. Apostolepis nigrolineata.

Elapomorphus nigrolineatus, *Peters, Mon. Berl. Ac.* 1869, p. 439; *Strauch, Bull. Ac. St. Pétersb.* xxix. 1884, p. 585.

Agrees with *A. flavitorquata*, except in the smaller rostral shield and the undivided anal. Ventrals 260; subcaudals 26. Brownish yellow above, with five black longitudinal lines, the outer broadest and on the fourth and fifth rows of scales; snout brownish yellow, rest of head black; a yellow spot on the third and fourth upper labials; end of tail black, except the terminal shield, which is whitish; lower parts dirty yellow.

Total length 375 millim.; tail 27.

Habitat unknown.

5. Apostolepis quinquelineata. (Plate X. fig. 1.)

Snout scarcely projecting; eye minute. Rostral broader than deep, just visible from above; frontal a little longer than broad, as long as its distance from the end of the snout, half as long as the parietals; nasal in contact with the præocular; a single postocular; six upper labials, second and third entering the eye, fourth, fifth, and sixth in contact with the parietal; five lower labials in contact with the chin-shields, which are subequal in length, first in contact with its fellow behind the symphysial, fifth largest. Scales in 15 rows. Ventrals 213; anal divided; subcaudals 28. Pale reddish above, with five dark brown longitudinal lines, the outer broadest and on the second, third, and fourth rows of scales; head dark brown, with a large yellowish blotch on the forehead and a small round yellowish spot below the eye; whitish beneath.

Total length 165 millim.; tail 13.

British Guiana.

a. Hgr. ♂ (V. 213, C. 28). Demerara. J. Quelch, Esq. [P.].

6. Apostolepis nigroterminata. (Plate X. fig. 2.)

Snout scarcely projecting, eye minute. Rostral a little broader than deep, just visible from above; frontal longer than broad, longer than its distance from the end of the snout, much shorter than the parietals; nasal in contact with the præocular; a single postocular, six upper labials, second and third entering the eye, fifth and sixth in contact with the parietal; symphysial in contact with the anterior chin-shields, which are longer than the posterior; five lower labials in contact with the chin-shields. Scales in 15 rows. Ventrals 207; anal divided; subcaudals 26. Pale reddish above, with a dark brown vertebral line and a dark brown lateral streak on the second, third, and fourth rows of scales; a pair of rather indistinct brown lines on the fifth and sixth rows of scales; head dark brown above, with a round yellowish spot on the snout and a yellowish spot on the third and fourth upper labials; a yellowish nuchal collar; end of tail black; lower parts white.

Total length 217 millim.; tail 18.

North-eastern Peru.

a. ♂ (V. 207, C. 26).   Cayaria.   Mr. W. Davis [C.];
                                             Messrs. Veitch [P.].

7. Apostolepis dorbignyi.

Calamaria d'orbignyi, *Schleg. Phys. Serp.* ii. p. 30 (1837).
Elapomorphus orbignyi, *Dum. & Bibr.* vii. p. 834 (1854); *Jan, Arch. Zool Anat. Phys,* ii 1862, p. 43, *and Icon. Gén.* 14, pl. i. fig. 2 (1865), *Strauch, Bull. Ac. St. Pétersb* xxix. 1884, p 578.
Apostolepis orbignyi, *Cope, Proc. Ac. Philad.* 1861, p. 524.

Snout feebly projecting; eye minute. Rostral a little broader than deep, the portion visible from above measuring about half its distance from the frontal; latter shield once and a half as long as broad, as long as its distance from the end of the snout, shorter than the parietals; nasal not in contact with the præocular; a single postocular; six upper labials, second and third entering the eye, fifth and sixth in contact with the parietal; symphysial nearly touching the anterior chin-shields, which are as long as the posterior; four lower labials in contact with the chin-shields, fourth largest. Scales in 15 rows. Ventrals 160; anal divided; subcaudals 37. Red above; head and nape black, separated by a white collar; snout and fourth upper labials whitish; end of tail black, except the terminal shield which is white; lower parts white.

Total length 384 millim.; tail 49.

Chili (?) *.

8. Apostolepis erythronota.

Elapomorphus erythronotus, *Peters, Mon. Berl. Ac.* 1880, p. 222; *Strauch, Bull. Ac. St. Pétersb.* xxix. 1884, p. 579.
Apostolepis erythronotus lineatus, *Cope, Proc. Amer. Philos. Soc.* xxiv. 1887, p. 56.

Form and lepidosis as in *A. dorbignyi*, but rostral larger, as in *A. flavitorquata*, nasal in contact with the præocular, and five lower labials in contact with the chin-shields. Ventrals 244–251;

---

* As in many other specimens brought home by d'Orbigny, the locality is doubtful. I have recorded the species from Paraguay through confusion with *A. ambinigra*.

anal divided, subcaudals 28. Red above, head, sides, and end of tail black; terminal caudal shield white; ventrals whitish, with two series of black spots. The latter spots absent in the variety described as *lineata*, which differs besides in the presence of five brown longitudinal lines on the body.

Total length 595 millim.; tail 60.

S. Paulo and Matto Grosso, Brazil.

9. Apostolepis ambinigra.

Rhynchonyx ambiniger, *Peters, Mon. Berl. Ac.* 1869, p. 438, pl. —, fig. 2.
—— ambiniger vittatus, *Cope, Proc. Amer. Philos. Soc.* xxiv. 1887, p. 56.
Elapomorphus erythronotus, *Peracca, Boll. Mus Torino*, x. 1895, no 195, p. 20.

Snout strongly projecting; eye minute. Rostral large, the portion visible from above much longer than its distance from the frontal; latter shield once and one fourth to once and one third as long as broad, as long as its distance from the end of the snout, shorter than the parietals; nasal in contact with the præocular; a single postocular, six upper labials, second and third entering the eye, fifth and sixth in contact with the parietal; five lower labials in contact with the chin-shields, which are subequal in size; first lower labial in contact with its fellow behind the symphysial. Scales in 15 rows. Ventrals 224–242, anal divided, subcaudals 21–33. Red above, yellowish white beneath; head, nape, and a gular band black; a yellowish spot on the third and fourth upper labials; end of tail black, the terminal shield whitish. In the var *vittata*, Cope, five dark brown streaks run along the body, on the vertebral row of scales and on the fourth and sixth.

Total length 620 millim.; tail 45.

Paraguay and Matto Grosso.

a–d. ♂ (V 231, 230, 229; C. 30, 28, 29) & ♀ (V. 242; C. 26). Asuncion, Paraguay. Dr. J Bohls [C.].

189. ELAPOMOIUS.

Elapomorphus, part, *Jan, Arch. Zool. Anat. Phys* ii. 1862, p. 41, *Strauch, Bull. Ac St. Pétersb.* xxix. 1884, p. 549.
Elapomojus, *Jan, l. c.* p. 42.

Dentition apparently as in *Apostolepis* and *Elapomorphus*. Head small, not distinct from neck; eye very small, with round pupil; internasals fused with the præfrontals; nasal single, separated from the præocular by a loreal; three pairs of chin-shields. Body cylindrical, scales smooth, without pits, in 15 rows; ventrals rounded. Tail short, obtuse; subcaudals in two rows.

Brazil.

1. Elapomoius dimidiatus.

Elapomorphus dimidiatus, *Jan, Arch. Zool. Anat. Phys.* ii. 1862, p. 47, *and Icon. Gén.* 14, pl. iii. fig. 3 (1865); *Strauch, Bull. Ac. St. Pétersb.* xxix. 1884, p. 587.

Rostral a little broader than deep, the portion visible from above about half as long as its distance from the frontal; latter shield slightly longer than broad, as long as its distance from the end of the snout, shorter than the parietals; loreal longer than deep; a single præocular; a single postocular; temporals 1+1; six upper labials, second and third entering the eye, fifth very small; five lower labials in contact with the chin-shields. Scales in 15 rows. Ventrals 246; anal divided; subcaudals 26. Yellowish above (five rows of scales); sides blackish, the scales edged with whitish; head black above; upper lip white; yellowish white beneath, posterior ventrals and subcaudals spotted with black; end of tail black, the terminal shield whitish.

Total length 580 millim.; tail 40.

Brazil.

190. ELAPOMORPHUS.

Fig. 17.

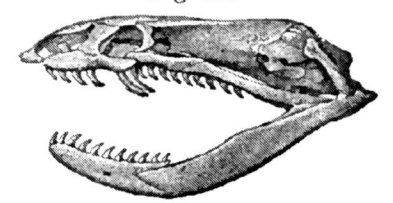

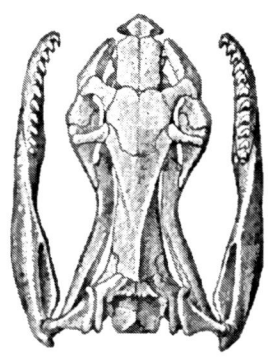

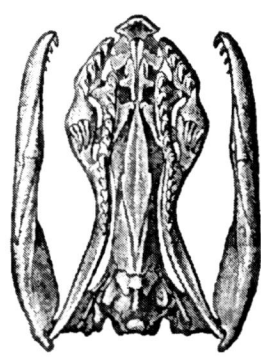

Skull of *Elapomorphus lemniscatus*.

Calamaria, part., *Schleg. Phys. Serp.* ii. p. 25 (1837).
Elapomorphus (*Wiegm.*), part., *Dum. & Bibr. Mém. Ac. Sc.* xxiii. 1853, p. 489, *and Erp. Gén.* vii. p. 832 (1854); *Jan, Arch. Zool. Anat. Phys.* ii. 1862, p. 41; *Strauch, Bull. Ac. St. Pétersb.* xxix. 1884, p. 649.

Elapocephalus, *Günth. Cat. Col. Sn.* p. 276 (1858).
Elapomorphus, *Cope, Proc. Ac. Philad.* 1861, p. 524.
Phalotris, *Cope, l. c*

Maxillary short, with four or five small teeth, followed, after an interspace, by a pair of large grooved fangs situated below the eye; mandibular teeth subequal. Head small, not distinct from neck; eye minute, with round pupil; nostril in a single nasal, which is in contact with a præocular. Body cylindrical; scales smooth, without pits, in 15 rows; ventrals rounded Tail short, obtuse; subcaudals in two rows.

South America.

Synopsis of the Species.

I. Præfrontals paired.

Parietals not twice as long as broad; ventrals 169–188	1. *blumii*. p. 239.
Parietals at least twice as long as broad; ventrals 176–184	2. *wuchereri*, p. 240.
Parietals not twice as long as broad; ventrals 190–234	3. *lepidus*, p. 241.

II. A single præfrontal.

A. Internasals forming a suture behind the rostral.

Portion of the rostral visible from above not longer than the suture between the internasals; ventrals 202–240 ..	4. *tricolor*, p. 241.
Portion of the rostral visible from above longer than the suture between the internasals; ventrals 185–212	5. *lemniscatus*, p. 242.

B. Internasals not forming a median suture.

Internasals meeting with their inner angles behind the rostral; ventrals 203	6. *trilineatus*, p. 243.
Internasals completely separated by the rostral; ventrals 218	7. *bilineatus*, p. 243.

1. Elapomorphus blumii.

Calamaria blumii, *Schleg. Phys. Serp.* ii p. 45 (1837)
Elapomorphus blumii, *Dum. & Bibr.* vii. p. 841 (1854); *Guichen. in Casteln Anim Nouv. Amér. Sud, Rept.* p. 56 (1855); *Gunth. Ann. & Mag. N H.* (3) ix. 1862, p 57; *Jan, Arch. Zool. Anat. Phys.* ii. 1862, p. 45, *and Icon. Gén.* 14, pl. iii. fig. 1 (1865); *Strauch, Bull. Ac. St. Pétersb.* xxix. 1884, p. 551; *Bocourt, Miss. Sc. Mex, Rept.* pl. xxxvi. fig. 2 (1886).
Elapocephalus tæniatus, *Gunth. Cat.* p. 276 (1858).

Rostral a little broader than deep, the portion visible from above measuring one third to one half its distance from the frontal;

internasals shorter than the præfrontals; frontal once and one third to once and a half as long as broad, as long as its distance from the end of the snout, shorter than the parietals, which are not twice as long as broad; one præ- and two postoculars; temporals 1+1; six upper labials, second and third entering the eye; four lower labials in contact with the anterior chin-shields, which are as long as or a little shorter than the posterior. Scales in 15 rows. Ventrals 169-188; anal divided; subcaudals 24-43. Pale yellowish brown above, with five dark brown or black longitudinal streaks; head much spotted with dark brown or black; a yellowish-white occipital collar, which may be interrupted in the middle or confined to the sides; a large yellowish-white blotch on the upper lip, occupying the third, fourth, and fifth labials; lower parts white, with or without a blackish dot on the outer end of each ventral.

Total length 760 millim.; tail 65.

Guianas, Brazil.

a. Yg. (V. 169; C. 42). Cayenne.
b. Yg. (V. 185; C. 30). Tijuca R. R. Bennett, Esq. [P.].
c. ♀ (V. 178, C. 24). Porto Real, Prov. Rio Janeiro. M. Hardy du Dréneuf [C.].
d. Yg. (V. 184; C. 28). Theresopolis. Dr. E. A. Goldi [P.].
e, f. Yg (V. 170, 184; C. 31, 32). Rio Janeiro. G. Busk, Esq. [P].
g. ♀ (V. 179; C. 27). S. America. Zoological Society.
(Type of *Elapocephalus tæniatus*.)

2. Elapomorphus wuchereri.

Elapomorphus wuchereri, part., *Gunth. Ann. & Mag. N. H.* (3) vii. 1861, p. 415, fig., and *Proc. Zool. Soc.* 1861, p. 15, fig.; Strauch, *Bull Ac. St. Pétersb.* xxix. 1884, p. 555.

—— accedens, Jan, *Arch. Zool. Anat. Phys.* ii. 1862, p. 46; Strauch, *l. c.* p. 560.

Rostral broader than deep, just visible from above; internasals shorter than the præfrontals; frontal once and a half to once and two thirds as long as broad, as long as or a little longer than its distance from the end of the snout, much shorter than the parietals, which are at least twice as long as broad; one præ- and two (exceptionally one) postoculars; temporals 1+1; six upper labials, second and third entering the eye; four lower labials in contact with the anterior chin-shields, which are as long as or a little shorter than the anterior. Scales in 15 rows. Ventrals 176-184; anal divided; subcaudals 27-45. Pale yellowish brown above, young with three dark brown longitudinal lines, which disappear in the adult; sides of head dark brown or blackish, with a large yellow blotch on the upper lip on the third to sixth labials; rostral and anterior labials each with a blackish spot; lower parts white.

Total length 1180 millim.; tail 120.

Brazil.

a, b. ♀ (V. 179, C. 35) & hgr ♀ (V. 183; C. 35).	Bahia.	Dr. O. Wucherer [C.]. (Types)
c Yg. (V. 176; C 41).	Bahia.	Dr O. Wucherer [C].
d Hgr. ♀ (V 181; C. 34).	Bahia.	Lord Walsingham [P.].

3. Elapomorphus lepidus.

Elapomorphus lepidus, *Reinh Vidensk. Meddel.* 1860, p. 239, pl. iv. figs. 6–9 (1861); *Jan, Arch. Zool Anat. Phys* ii. 1862, p 46, *and Icon. Gén* 14, pl iii. fig. 2 (1865); *Strauch, Bull. Ac St. Pétersb.* xxix. 1884, p. 558.

―― wuchereri, part., *Gunth. Ann & Mag. N. H.* (3) vii. 1861, p. 415, fig., *and Proc. Zool. Soc.* 1861, p 15, fig.; *Strauch, l. c.* p 555.

Apostolepis lepida, *Cope, Proc. Ac. Philad.* 1861, p. 524.

Rostral broader than deep, just visible from above; internasals shorter than the præfrontals; frontal a little longer than broad, as long as its distance from the end of the snout, shorter than the parietals, which are not twice as long as broad; one præ- and two (exceptionally one) postoculars; temporals 1+1; six upper labials, second and third entering the eye; four lower labials in contact with the anterior chin-shields, which are as long as or a little longer than the posterior. Scales in 15 rows. Ventrals 190–234; anal divided; subcaudals 30–45. Pale brown above, with three more or less distinct darker longitudinal lines; snout, vertex, and nape black; back of head and temples yellowish white; lower parts whitish.

Total length 500 millim.; tail 55.

Brazil.

a, b. ♂ (V. 204; C. 45) & ♀ (V. 201; C. 33)	Bahia	Dr O Wucherer [C.]. (Types of *E. wuchereri*)
c. Hgr. (V. 190; C. 30).	Brazil.	Dr. Gardiner [P.].

4. Elapomorphus tricolor.

Elapomorphus tricolor, *Dum & Bibr.* vii p 837 (1854); *Jan, Arch. Zool. Anat. Phys.* ii 1862, p. 44, *and Icon. Gén.* 14, pl ii fig 2 (1865); *Strauch, Bull. Ac. St. Pétersb.* xxix. 1884, p. 565; *Boettg Abh Nat. Ges. Nurnb* viii. 1891, p. 91; *Peracca, Boll. Mus. Torino,* x 1895, no 195, p 21.

Phalotris tricolor, *Cope, Proc. Ac. Philad* 1861, p. 524.

Rostral broader than deep, just visible from above; suture between the internasals one third to one half the length of the single præfrontal; frontal once and a half as long as broad, as long as its distance from the end of the snout, much shorter than the parietals, which are at least twice as long as broad; one præ- and two (rarely one) postoculars; temporals 1+1; six upper labials, second and third entering the eye; four lower labials in contact with the anterior chin-shields, which are as long as or a little shorter than the posterior. Scales in 15 rows. Ventrals 202–240;

anal divided; subcaudals 22-30. Red above, white beneath; upper surface of head and nape black, separated by a yellowish-white cross-band.

Total length 370 millim.; tail 25. Grows to 938 millim.

Bolivia, Paraguay, Southern Brazil, Uruguay.

a–b. Hgr. (V. 223; C. 23)   Uruguay.
    & yg. (V. 226; C. 26).

5. Elapomorphus lemniscatus.

Elapomorphus lemniscatus, *Dum. & Bibr.* vii. p 840 (1854); *Jan, Arch. Zool. Anat Phys.* ii. 1862, p. 45, *and Icon. Gén* 14, pl ii. fig. 3 (1865); *Strauch, Bull. Ac. St. Pétersb* xxix. 1884, p. 567; *Bouleng. Ann. & Mag. N. H.* (5) xv. 1885, p. 321, pl. x., and xvi. 1885, p. 296.

—— reticulatus, *Peters, Mon. Berl. Ac.* 1860, p. 518, pl. —. fig. 2; *Strauch, l c.* p. 569.

Phalotris lemniscatus, *Cope, Proc. Ac. Philad.* 1861, p. 524.

—— reticulatus, *Cope, l. c.*

Elapomorphus iheringi, *Strauch, l c* p. 571

Phalotris melanopleurus, *Cope, Proc. Amer. Philos. Soc.* xxii. 1885, p. 189.

Rostral a little broader than deep, the portion visible from above measuring about half its distance from the frontal; suture between the internasals one fourth to one third the length of the single præfrontal; frontal once and one third to once and two thirds as long as broad, shorter than its distance from the end of the snout, much shorter than the parietals, which are at least twice as long as broad; one præ- and two postoculars; temporals 1+1; six upper labials, second and third entering the eye; four lower labials in contact with the anterior chin-shields, which are as long as or a little longer than the posterior. Scales in 15 rows. Ventrals 185–212; anal divided; subcaudals 21–34. Red to greyish brown above, with or without a black vertebral stripe; head blackish, usually with a yellowish, black-edged occipital collar which may be much reduced or even entirely absent; lateral scales and ventrals and subcaudals black, light-edged, the outer or the two outer rows of scales often yellowish white; a black bar across the base of the tail.

Total length 700 millim.; tail 60.

Southern Brazil, Paraguay, Uruguay, Argentina.

a–b, c, d–f, g–k. ♂ (V. 202; C. 25), ♀ (V. 207, 208, 209; C. 23, 25, 26), & yg. (V. 186, 185, 211; C. 28, 34, 24).   Rio Grande do Sul.   Dr. H. v. Ihering [C.].

l. ♀ (V. 204; C. 22).   Paraguay.   Prof. Grant [P.].

m–o. ♂ (V. 185; C. 25), ♀ (V. 208; C. 22), & yg (V. 192; C. 26).   Uruguay.

p. ♀ (V. 212; C. 24).		High Pampas of San Luis, Mendoza.	E. W. White, Esq. [C.]
q Skeleton.		Rio Grande do Sul.	

6. Elapomorphus trilineatus. (Plate X. fig. 3.)

Elapomorphus trilineatus, *Bouleng. Ann. & Mag N. H.* (6) iv. 1889, p. 266.

Rostral as deep as broad, the portion visible from above measuring two thirds its distance from the frontal, in contact with the anterior angle of the single præfrontal; internasals meeting with their inner angles; frontal once and a half as long as broad, not quite so long as its distance from the end of the snout, much shorter than the parietals, which are twice as long as broad; one præ- and two postoculars; temporals 1+1; six upper labials, second and third entering the eye, fifth largest; four lower labials in contact with the anterior chin-shields, which equal the posterior in size. Scales in 15 rows. Ventrals 203; anal divided; subcaudals 26. Cream-colour; above with three black streaks interrupted by the pale borders of the scales, the middle one on the vertebral row of scales, the lateral between the fourth and fifth rows, a blackish transverse band on the base of the tail; ventrals and subcaudals black antero-mesially.

Total length 530 millim., tail 45.

Southern Brazil.

a. ♀ (V. 203; C. 26)		Camaquam River, Rio Grande do Sul.	Dr. H. v Ihering [C.] (Type.)

7. Elapomorphus bilineatus.

Elapomorphus bilineatus, *Dum. & Bibr.* vii. p 839 (1854), *Jan, Arch. Zool. Anat. Phys* ii. 1862, p 44, *and Icon. Gén.* 14, pl 11 fig. 1 (1865); *Strauch, Bull. Ac. St. Pétersb.* xxix. 1884, p. 563; *Bocourt, Miss. Sc. Mex., Rept.* pl. xxxvi fig. 3 (1886).
Phalotris bilineatus, *Cope, Proc. Ac. Philad.* 1861, p. 524.

Rostral as deep as broad, the portion visible from above a little shorter than its distance from the frontal and entirely separating the internasals; præfrontal single; frontal a little longer than broad, shorter than its distance from the end of the snout, much shorter than the parietals, which are not twice as long as broad; one præ- and two postoculars; temporals 1+1, six upper labials, second and third entering the eye; four lower labials in contact with the anterior chin-shields, which are as large as the posterior. Scales in 15 rows. Ventrals 218; anal divided; subcaudals 21. Brownish yellow above, with a blackish line on each side of the back, between the fourth and fifth rows of scales; head blackish above and beneath; ventrals and subcaudals blackish, edged with whitish.

Total length 348 millim.; tail 20.

Corrientes, Argentina.

191. AMBLYODIPSAS.

Amblyodipsas, *Peters, Mon. Berl. Ac.* 1856, p. 592, *and Reise n. Mossamb* iii. p. 109 (1882).
Amblyodipsas, part, *Jan, Arch. Zool. Anat. Phys.* ii. 1862, p 40.

Maxillary very short, with five teeth gradually increasing in size and followed, after an interspace, by a large grooved fang situated below the eye; mandibular teeth decreasing in size posteriorly. Head small, not distinct from neck; eye minute, with round pupil; nostril in a single very small nasal; no internasals; no loreal; no præocular; no anterior temporal. Body cylindrical; scales smooth, without pits, in 15 rows; ventrals rounded. Tail very short, obtuse; subcaudals in two rows.

Mozambique.

1. Amblyodipsas microphthalma.

Calamaria microphthalma, *Bianconi, Spec. Zool. Mosamb.* p 94, pl. xii fig. 1 (1852).
Amblyodipsas microphthalma, *Peters, Mon. Berl. Ac.* 1856, p. 592; *Jan, Arch. Zool Anat. Phys.* ii. 1862, p 41, *and Icon. Gén.* 14, pl i fig 1 (1865): *Peters, Reise n. Mossamb.* iii p. 109 (1882).

Rostral broader than deep, the portion visible from above measuring about two thirds its distance from the frontal; præfrontals longer than broad; frontal large, nearly twice as long as broad, acutely pointed behind, much longer than its distance from the end of the snout, a little shorter than the parietals; supraocular very small; a minute postocular; a single temporal; four upper labials, second and third entering the eye, fourth largest and in contact with the parietal; four lower labials in contact with the anterior chin-shields, fourth very large and narrowly separated from its fellow by the posterior chin-shields. Scales in 15 rows. Ventrals 142, anal divided; subcaudals 19. Dark brown above; upper lip, two outer rows of scales, outer ends of ventrals, and lower surface of head and tail white; a dark brown stripe along the middle of the belly.

Total length 300 millim.; tail 24.

Mozambique.

192. ELAPOTINUS.

Elapotinus, *Jan, Arch. Zool Anat. Phys* ii. 1862, p. 31.

Dentition as in *Amblyodipsas*, but the groove on the posterior fang probably less distinct[*]. Head small, not distinct from neck; eye minute, with round pupil; nostril between two nasals; no

---

[*] Jan describes the Snake as aglyphodont, but he has overlooked the groove on the tooth in so many unquestionably opisthoglyphous Colubrines that we may well be permitted to doubt the accuracy of his statement in this particular case.

loreal. Body cylindrical; scales smooth, without pits, in 17 rows; ventrals rounded. Tail short; subcaudals in two rows.

Tropical Africa?

1. Elapotinus picteti.

Elapotinus picteti, *Jan, l. c., and Icon. Gén.* 13, pl. iii. fig. 1 (1865).

Rostral broader than deep, just visible from above, internasals as long as broad, shorter than the præfrontals; frontal once and a half as long as broad, as long as its distance from the end of the snout, shorter than the parietals; supraocular nearly as broad as long; præocular minute; a small postocular, temporals 1+2; seven upper labials, third in contact with the præfrontal, third and fourth entering the eye; four lower labials in contact with the anterior chin-shields, which are a little longer than the posterior. Scales in 17 rows. Ventrals 175; anal divided; subcaudals 36. Blackish above, with a white lateral line; a white occipital collar; upper lip white, brown beneath, outer ends of ventrals and outer row of scales white.

Total length 290 millim.; tail 40.

Habitat unknown.

193. CALAMELAPS.

? Choristodon (non Jonas), *Smith, Ill. Zool S. Afr., Rept*, App. p 18 (1849); *Peters, Mon Berl. Ac.* 1867, p. 235.
Amblyodipsas, part, *Jan, Arch. Zool Anat Phys.* ii. 1862, p. 40.
Calamelaps, *Gunth. Ann. & Mag N. H.* (3) xviii. 1866, p. 26

Maxillary very short, with three or four teeth gradually increasing in size and followed, after an interspace, by a large grooved fang situated below the eye; anterior mandibular teeth enlarged. Head small, not distinct from neck; eye minute, with round pupil; nostril in a divided or semidivided nasal; no loreal; no præocular; no anterior temporal. Body cylindrical. Scales smooth, without pits, in 17 to 21 (or 13?) rows; ventrals rounded. Tail very short, obtuse; subcaudals in two rows.

Tropical Africa; South Africa?

Synopsis of the Species.

Scales in 17 rows...................	1. *unicolor*, p. 245.
Scales in 21 rows.....................	2. *polylepis*, p. 245.
Scales in 13 rows.....................	3. *concolor*, p. 246.

1. Calamelaps unicolor.

Calamaria unicolor, *Reinh. Vidensk. Selsk. Skrift.* x. 1843, p. 236, pl. i. figs 1–3.
Amblyodipsas unicolor, *Jan, Arch. Zool Anat. Phys.* ii. 1862, p. 41.
Calamelaps unicolor, *Gunth. Ann. & Mag. N. H.* (3) xviii. 1866, p. 25.

Rostral large, a little broader than deep, the portion visible from above nearly as long as its distance from the frontal; internasals much broader than long, much shorter than the præfrontals; frontal once and a half to once and two thirds as long as broad, longer than its distance from the end of the snout, shorter than the parietals; supraocular small; nasal divided or semidivided; a very small postocular, sometimes fused with the supraocular; a single temporal; six upper labials, third in contact with the præfrontal, third and fourth entering the eye, fifth largest and in contact with the parietal; four lower labials in contact with the anterior chin-shields, fourth very large and narrowly separated from its fellow by the posterior chin-shields. Scales in 17 rows. Ventrals 173–208; anal divided; subcaudals 21–38. Uniform blackish brown.

Total length 365 millim.; tail 27.

West Africa.

a. ♂ (V. 182; C. 34).	Sierra Leone.	
b. ♂ (V. 173; C. 33).	Niger	J. W. Crosse, Esq. [P.].
c. ♀ (V. 208, C. 21)	W. Africa.	

2. Calamelaps polylepis.

Calamelaps polylepis, *Bocage. Jorn. Sc. Lisb* iv. 1873, p. 216, *and Herp Angola*, p. 126, pl. ix. fig. 2 (1895).
—— miolepis, *Gunth. Ann. & Mag. N. H.* (6) i. 1888, p. 323.

In every respect like *C. unicolor*, except that the scales are in 21 rows. Ventrals 163–212; subcaudals 16–27.

Total length 400 millim.; tail 23.

Angola, Nyassaland.

a ♀ (V. 208; C 18)   Cape McLear, Lake   A. A. Simons, Esq. [C.].
                     Nyassa.   (Type of *C. miolepis*.)

3. Calamelaps? concolor.

Choristodon concolor, *Smith, Ill. Zool. S. Afr., Rept.*, App. p. 18 (1849).

Rostral triangular; internasals small; frontal subrhomboidal, the hinder portion most prolonged; supraocular very small, subtriangular, forming the supero-posterior border of the eye; postocular very small; third and fourth upper labials entering the eye; two pairs of narrow chin-shields, the second pair longest. Scales in 13 rows. Ventrals 134; subcaudals 38. Greenish black above, with purple gloss; pale blackish purple beneath, the shields margined behind with livid white.

Total length 190 millim., tail 28.

Caffraria.

194. RHINOCALAMUS.

Rhinocalamus, *Gunth. Ann. & Mag. N. H.* (6) i. 1888, p. 322.

Maxillary very short, with four teeth gradually increasing in size and followed, after an interspace, by a pair of large grooved fangs situated below the eye; anterior mandibular teeth slightly enlarged; palate toothless. Head small, not distinct from neck; snout much depressed and very prominent; rostral very large, with obtuse horizontal edge, concave below; eye minute, with round pupil; nostril in a semidivided nasal; no loreal; no præocular; no anterior temporal. Body cylindrical; scales smooth, without pits, in 17 rows; ventrals rounded. Tail very short, obtuse; subcaudals in two rows.

East Africa.

1. Rhinocalamus dimidiatus.

Rhinocalamus dimidiatus, *Gunth. l. c.* pl. xix. fig. C.

Rostral very large, capping the end of the snout, the portion visible from above longer than its distance from the frontal; internasals more than twice as broad as long, shorter than the præfrontals; frontal large, a little longer than broad, as long as or a little longer than its distance from the end of the snout, as long as or a little shorter than the parietals; supraocular very small; a minute postocular; a single temporal; six upper labials, third in contact with the nasal and the præfrontal, third and fourth entering the eye, fifth largest and in contact with the parietals; four lower labials in contact with the anterior chin-shields, fourth very large and narrowly separated from its fellow by the posterior chin-shields. Scales in 17 rows. Ventrals 192–215; anal divided; subcaudals 20–27. Black above; upper lip, three lower rows of scales, and lower parts white.

Total length 470 millim.; tail 30.

Interior of East Africa.

a–c. ♂ (V 202, 195, 192 : C 26, 26, 27). Mpwapwa (Types.)
d–e. ♂ (V. 207; C. 25) & ♀ (V. 215; Ugogo. Mr. Baxter [C.].
C. 20).

195. XENOCALAMUS.

Xenocalamus, *Gunth. Ann. & Mag. N. H.* (4) i. 1868, p 414, and (6) xv. 1895, p 526

Maxillary very short, with five teeth gradually increasing in size and followed, after an interspace, by a pair of larger grooved fangs situated below the eye; anterior mandibular teeth a little larger than the posterior; palate toothless. Head small, not distinct from neck; snout much depressed, very prominent, pointed; rostral very large, with obtuse horizontal edge, flat below; eye minute, with round pupil; nostril between two nasals, the posterior very large; no loreal; præfrontals absent (fused with the frontal); no anterior temporal. Body cylindrical; scales smooth, without pits, in 17 rows; ventrals rounded. Tail very short, obtuse; subcaudals in two rows.

Tropical Africa.

1. Xenocalamus bicolor.

Xenocalamus bicolor, *Günth. l. c.* p. 415, pl. xix. fig. A.

Upper portion of rostral nearly half as long as the frontal, which is extremely large and more than half as long as the shielded part of the head; internasals large, forming a short median suture; supraocular very narrow; a large, elongate præocular, in contact with the posterior nasal, the internasal, the frontal, and the third labial; a minute postocular, a single temporal; six upper labials, first very small, third and fourth entering the eye, fifth very large and in contact with the parietal, third lower labial extremely large; a single pair of narrow chin-shields, in contact with three lower labials. Scales in 17 rows. Ventrals 218; anal divided; subcaudals 24. Black above; upper lip, two outer rows of scales, and lower parts white.

Total length 430 millim.; tail 30.

Zambesi.

a. ♀ (V. 218; C. 24).   Zambesi.   Mr. Chapman [C.].   (Type.)

2. Xenocalamus mechovii.

Xenocalamus mechowii, *Peters, Sitzb. Ges. Naturf. Fr.* 1881, p. 147; *Boettg. Ber. Senck. Ges.* 1888, p. 47.

As in the preceding, but supraoculars absent and usually two postoculars instead of one. Ventrals 229–239; anal divided; subcaudals 31–36. Yellowish, with large dark brown spots above; some of these spots are disposed in alternating, partly confluent pairs, others form cross-bands; upper lip, sides, and lower parts unspotted.

Total length 225 millim.; tail 23.

Congo.

a. Hgr. (V. 239, C. 35).   Stanley Falls.

196. MICRELAPS.

Micrelaps, *Boettg. Ber. Senckenb. Ges.* 1879–80, p. 136.
Elaposchema, *Mocquard, Mém. Cent. Soc. Philom.* 1888, p. 122.

Maxillary very short, with two teeth followed, after an interspace, by a very large grooved fang situated below the eye; anterior mandibular teeth longest. Head small, not distinct from neck; eye minute, with round or vertically subelliptic pupil; nostril in a single nasal; no loreal; no præocular; præfrontal entering the eye. Body cylindrical; scales smooth, without pits, in 15 rows; ventrals rounded. Tail short; subcaudals in two rows.

Palestine; Somaliland.

1. Micrelaps muelleri.

F. Müll Verh. Nat. Ges. Basel, vi. 1878, p. 655.
Micrelaps mulleri, *Boettg. Ber Senck. Ges.* 1879-80, p. 137, pl. iii.
  fig. 2, *Lortet, Arch Mus. Lyon,* iii. 1883, p 184, pl xix fig. 2.

Head much depressed; rostral nearly twice as broad as deep, just visible from above; internasals a little broader than long, shorter than the præfrontals; frontal small, not broader than the supraocular, once and two thirds as long as broad, hardly as long as its distance from the rostral, half as long as the parietals; supraocular as long as broad; a small postocular, in contact with the first temporal; temporal 1+1 or 1+2; seven upper labials, third and fourth entering the eye; three or four lower labials in contact with the anterior chin-shields, which are as long as the posterior. Scales in 15 rows. Ventrals 251-275; anal divided; subcaudals 26-32. Black, with whitish annuli, which may be narrower or broader than the interspaces between them, mostly interrupted beneath.

Total length 405 millim.; tail 30.
Palestine.

a ♀ (V. 251; C. 30).   Jerusalem.   Senckenberg Mus. [E.].

2. Micrelaps vaillanti.

Elaposchema vaillanti, *Mocq. l. c.* p. 123, pl. xii. fig. 1.
Calamelaps vaillanti, *Boettg. Zool. Anz.* 1893, p 117.

Head much depressed; rostral large, twice as broad as deep, the portion visible from above about two thirds as long as its distance from the frontal; internasals twice as broad as long, twice as long as the præfrontals; frontal small, once and a half as long as broad, as long as its distance from the end of the snout, much shorter than the parietals; supraocular as long as broad; a very small postocular; temporals 1+1; seven upper labials, third in contact with the præfrontal, third and fourth or third, fourth, and fifth entering the eye; two pairs of chin-shields, subequal in size, the anterior in contact with four lower labials. Scales in 15 rows (17 on the neck). Ventrals 171-203; anal divided; subcaudals 23-27. Brown above, the centre of each scale greyish white; ventrals brown in the middle, whitish on the sides.

Total length 282 millim.; tail 32.
Somaliland.

197. MIODON.

Microsoma (*non Macq.*), *Jan, Rev. & Mag. Zool.* (2) x. 1858, p. 519, and *Elenco sist. Ofid.* p. 111 (1863); *Peters, Mon Berl. Ac.* 1863, p. 369.
Miodon, *A. Dum. Arch. Mus.* x. 1859, p. 206.
Urobelus, *Reinh. Vidensk. Meddel.* 1860, p. 229.

Maxillary very short, with two or three small teeth followed, after an interspace, by a very large grooved fang situated in advance of the eye; second and third or third and fourth mandibular teeth large, fang-like. Head small, not distinct from neck; eye very small, with round pupil; nostril in a single or divided nasal, which does not touch the rostral, the internasal forming a suture with the first labial; no loreal. Body cylindrical; scales smooth, without pits, in 15 rows; ventrals rounded. Tail very short; subcaudals in two rows.

West Africa.

Fig. 18.

Maxillary and mandible of *Miodon acanthias*.

Synopsis of the Species.

I. Anal entire; ventrals 190–216 .. 1. *acanthias*, p. 250.
II. Anal divided.

  A. Frontal longer than broad.

Internasals considerably shorter than the
  præfrontals; ventrals 201–228...... 2. *collaris*, p. 251.
Internasals as long as or slightly shorter
  than the præfrontals; ventrals 214–
  249.................................. 3. *gabonensis*, p. 252.
Internasals as long as or slightly shorter
  than the præfrontals; ventrals 181–
  200.................................. 4. *notatus*, p. 252.

  B. Frontal as long as broad; ventrals 238.
                                           5. *neuwiedii*, p. 253.

1. Miodon acanthias.

Urobelus acanthias, *Reinh. Vidensk. Meddel.* 1860, p. 229, pl. iii.
Elapomorphus acanthias, *Jan, Arch. Zool. Anat. Phys.* ii. 1863, p. 47,
  and *Icon. Gén.* 14, pl. iii. fig. 4 (1865)
—— acanthias, part., *Günth. Ann. & Mag. N. H.* (6) i. 1888, p. 323.
? Microsoma collare, var. D, *Bocage, Herp. Angola*, p. 126 (1895).

Diameter of eye less than its distance from the oral margin. Rostral broader than deep, just visible from above; internasals shorter than the præfrontals; frontal once and a half as broad as the supraocular, once and a half to once and two thirds as long as broad, as long as its distance from the end of the snout, shorter than the parietals; nasal divided; one præocular, in contact with the posterior nasal; one or two postoculars; temporals 1+1; seven upper labials, third and fourth entering the eye; first lower labial forming a suture with its fellow behind the symphysial; four lower labials in contact with the anterior chin-shields, which are longer than the posterior. Scales in 15 rows. Ventrals 190-216; anal entire; subcaudals 16-21. Whitish or pale reddish above, with five black stripes, the median broadest and occupying one and two half scales, the outer running between the second and third rows of scales; top of head black; a whitish occipital bar edged with black behind; end of snout, upper lip, tip of tail, and lower parts white.

Total length 550 millim.; tail 30.

Guinea; Congo?

a. Hgr. (V.190; C. 21).	Ashantee.	Mr. McCarthy [C.].
b ♀ (V. 210; C. 17).	W. Africa.	J. C. Salmon, Esq. [P.].

c. Skull of b.

2. Miodon collaris.

Polemon barthii (*non Jan*), *Gunth. Ann & Mag. N. H.* (3) xv. 1865, p. 90.

Microsoma collare, *Peters, Sitzb. Ges. Naturf. Fr.* 1881, p. 148, *Bocage, Jorn. Sc. Lisb.* xi. 1887, p. 182, *and Herp. Angola*, p. 124, pl. xiv. figs. 1 & 2 (1895).

Elapomorphus acanthias, part., *Gunth. Ann. & Mag. N. H.* (6) i. 1888, p. 323.

Diameter of eye about three fifths its distance from the oral margin. Rostral broader than deep, just visible from above; internasals considerably shorter than the præfrontals; frontal slightly broader than the supraocular, once and a half as long as broad, as long as its distance from the rostral, much shorter than the parietals; nasal divided, in contact with the præocular; two (rarely one *) postoculars; temporals 1+1 (or 1+2); seven upper labials, third and fourth entering the eye; first lower labial forming a suture with its fellow behind the symphysial; four or five lower labials in contact with the anterior chin-shields, which are longer than the posterior. Scales in 15 rows. Ventrals 201–228; anal divided; subcaudals 16–22. Blackish above and on the sides down to the outer end of the ventrals and subcaudals, or dark grey with the scales edged with black; head and nape pale brown, with some black blotches on the crown and below the eye; lower parts and terminal caudal shield white.

Total length 550 millim.; tail 32.

West Africa (Old Calabar, Congo, Angola).

a. ♀ (V. 204; C. 18).   Old Calabar.

---

* The specimen in the Collection has a single postocular on one side.

3. Miodon gabonensis.

Elapomorphus gabonensis, *A. Dum. Rev. & Mag. Zool.* (2) viii. 1856,
p. 468, *and Arch Mus.* x. 1859, p. 206, pl. xvi. fig 2.
—— gabonicus, *Jan, Arch Zool. Anat. Phys.* ii. 1862, p 47.
—— (Urobelus) gabonicus, *Jan, Icon. Gén.* 15, pl. i. fig. 1 (1866).
Microsoma fulvicollis, *Mocq. Bull. Soc. Philom.* (7) xi. 1887, p. 65.
Urobelus gabonicus, *Bouleng. Proc. Zool. Soc.* 1887, p. 127.
Elapomorphus acanthias, part., *Gunth. Ann. & Mag N. H.* (6) i. 1888, p. 323.
—— cæcutiens, *Gunth. l. c.* pl. xix. fig B.

Diameter of eye one third to one half its distance from the oral margin. Rostral broader than deep, just visible from above; internasals as long as or slightly shorter than the præfrontals; frontal slightly broader than the supraocular, once and one third to once and a half as long as broad, as long as its distance from the rostral, much shorter than the parietals; one præocular, in contact with the nasal, which is entire or imperfectly divided, one or two postoculars; temporals 1+1; seven upper labials, third and fourth entering the eye; first lower labial forming a suture with its fellow behind the symphysial; four lower labials in contact with the anterior chin-shields, which are longer than the posterior. Scales in 15 rows. Ventrals 214–249; anal divided; subcaudals 16–24. Dark brown or olive above, with three more or less distinct darker longitudinal lines, or almost uniform blackish; a pale brownish band across the occiput; upper lip, ventrals, subcaudals, and terminal caudal scute white.

Total length 510 millim.; tail 23.

West Africa, from the Old Calabar to the Congo.

a. ♀ (V. 214; C. 17).	Old Calabar.		D.G Rutherford, Esq. [O.]
b–c. ♀ (V. 231, 230; C. 16, 18).	Cameroon Mts, 2000 ft.		Sir H. H. Johnston [P.]. (Types of *E. cæcutiens*.)
d. ♀ (V. 215; C. 17).	Rio del Rey.		Sir H. H. Johnston [P.].

4. Miodon notatus *.

Microsoma notatum, *Peters, Sitzb. Ges. Naturf. Fr.* 1882, p. 127;
Mocq. Bull. Soc. Philom. (7) xi. 1887, p. 64.

Diameter of eye about half its distance from the oral margin. Internasals as long as or slightly shorter than the præfrontals; frontal a little longer than broad, much shorter than the parietals; nasal divided, in contact with the single præocular; one or two postoculars; temporals 1+1; seven upper labials, second in contact with the præocular, third and fourth entering the eye; first lower

---

* I am indebted to Prof. Boettger for notes on a specimen from Cameroon, preserved in the Lubeck Museum.

labial forming a suture with its fellow behind the symphysial; three lower labials in contact with the anterior chin-shields, which are a little longer than the posterior. Scales in 15 rows. Ventrals 181-200; anal divided; subcaudals 14-18. Pale brown above, with two series of round black spots, which may be light-edged; upper surface of head, a nuchal collar, and upper surface of tail black; ventrals, subcaudals, and terminal caudal shield white.

Total length 317 millim.; tail 29.

West Africa (Cameroon, Congo).

5. Miodon neuwiedii.

Microsoma neuwiedi, *Jan, Rev. & Mag. Zool.* (2) x. 1858, p. 519, & xi. 1859, pl iv

Elapomorphus (Urobelus) neuwiedi, *Jan, Icon. Gén.* 15, pl. i. fig. 2 (1866).

Diameter of eye less than its distance from the oral margin. Rostral a little broader than deep, just visible from above; internasals shorter than the præfrontals; frontal nearly twice as broad as the supraocular, as long as broad, as long as its distance from the rostral, much shorter than the parietals; nasal entire, in contact with the single præocular; one postocular; temporals 1+1; seven upper labials, third and fourth entering the eye; first lower labial forming a suture with its fellow behind the symphysial; three lower labials in contact with the anterior chin-shields, which are nearly as long as the posterior. Scales in 15 rows. Ventrals 238; anal divided; subcaudals 21. Pale brown above, with three black longitudinal lines; upper surface of head and base of tail black; lower parts white.

Total length 172 millim.; tail 10.

Guinea (Christiansburg).

198. POLEMON.

Polemon, *Jan, Rev. & Mag. Zool.* (2) x. 1858, p. 520, *and Elenco sist. Ofid.* p 111 (1863), *Peters, Mon. Berl. Ac.* 1863, p. 368

Maxillary very short, with three small teeth followed, after an interspace, by a very large grooved fang situated in advance of the eye; third and fourth mandibular teeth large, fang-like. Head small, not distinct from neck; eye minute, with round pupil; nostril in a divided nasal, which does not touch the rostral, the internasal forming a suture with the first labial; no loreal; parietal narrowly in contact with a labial. Body cylindrical; scales smooth, without pits, in 15 rows; ventrals rounded. Tail very short; subcaudals single.

West Africa.

1. Polemon barthii.

Polemon barthii, *Jan, Rev. & Mag. Zool.* (2) x. 1858, p. 520, and xi. 1859, pl. v; *Peters, Mon Berl. Ac.* 1863, p. 368, pl. —. fig. 7; *Jan, Icon. Gén.* 15, pl. i. fig. 3 (1866).

Rostral twice as broad as deep, just visible from above; internasals a little longer than broad, shorter than the præfrontals; frontal small, a little longer than broad, hardly as long as its distance from the rostral, about half as long as the parietals; a small præocular, in contact with or narrowly separated from the posterior nasal; one postocular; temporals 1+1; seven upper labials, third and fourth entering the eye, fifth forming a short suture with the parietal; four lower labials in contact with the anterior chin-shields, which are longer than the posterior. Scales in 15 rows. Ventrals 221–226; anal entire; subcaudals 16–18. Olive-grey above, the scales edged with black; back of head and lower parts yellowish white.

Total length 810 millim.; tail 40.

Guinea.

a. ♀ (V. 221, C. 18).   Ashantee.   Mr. McCarthy [C.].

199. BRACHYOPHIS.

Brachyophis, *Mocquard, Mém. Cent. Soc Philom.* 1888, p. 125.

Maxillary very short, with two or three small teeth followed, after an interspace, by a large grooved fang; mandibular teeth increasing in length to the third. Head small, not distinct from neck, with depressed, sharp-edged snout; eye minute, with round pupil; nostril in a single nasal, which does not touch the rostral, the internasal forming a suture with the first labial; no loreal; no temporals; a large azygous occipital shield. Body remarkably short, cylindrical, scales smooth, without pits, in 15 rows; ventrals obtusely angulate laterally. Tail extremely short; subcaudals single.

Somaliland.

1. Brachyophis revoili.

Brachyophis revoili, *Mocq. l. c.* pl. xi. fig. 3.

Rostral large, the portion visible from above at least as long as its distance from the frontal and wedged in between the internasals, which are shorter than the præfrontals; frontal hexagonal, longer than broad, longer than its distance from the end of the snout, shorter than the parietals, between which the point of a large pentagonal occipital is wedged in; a small præocular and two small postoculars; seven upper labials, second and third in contact with the præfrontal, third and fourth entering the eye, fifth and sixth largest and in contact with the parietals; two pairs of large chin-shields, separated from each other on the median line by two series of small scales. Scales in 15 rows. Ventrals 104-115; anal divided; subcaudals 11-13. Greyish white above, with irregular brown cross-bands, or dark brown with irregular white cross-bands; ventrals broadly edged with brown in front.

Total length 255 millim.; tail 15.

Somaliland.

a. ♀ (V. 115; C. 11). Somaliland. Paris Museum [E.]. (One of the types.)

200. MACRELAPS.

Maxillary short, with 4 moderately large teeth followed by a very large grooved fang situated below the eye; anterior mandibular teeth enlarged, third to fifth longest. Head small, not distinct from neck, eye minute, with round pupil; nasal divided; no loreal; no præocular; præfrontal entering the eye. Body cylindrical; scales smooth, without pits, in 25 or 27 rows; ventrals rounded Tail short; subcaudals single.

South Africa.

1. Macrelaps microlepidotus.

Uriechis microlepidotus, *Günth. Ann. & Mag. N. H.* (3) v. 1860, p. 168, pl. ix.; *Gurney, t c* p. 342

Rostral broader than deep, the portion visible from above nearly half as long as its distance from the frontal; internasals shorter than the præfrontals; frontal as long as broad, as long as its distance from the end of the snout, much shorter than the parietals; postocular small, single, in one specimen (young) in contact with the first temporal; temporals 1+2; seven upper labials, third and fourth entering the eye, fifth largest; three or four lower labials in contact with the anterior chin-shields, which are a little longer than the posterior. Scales in 25 or 27 rows. Ventrals 163-166; anal entire; subcaudals 37-48. Uniform black.

Total length 850 millim.; tail 105.

Natal.

a, b. ♀ (Sc. 25; V. 166; C. 37) Durban. Mr. T. Ayres [C.]; J. H.
& yg (Sc. 27; V. 163; C. 48).   Gurney, Esq. [P.]. (Types.)

201. APARALLACTUS.

Aparallactus, *Smith, Ill. Zool S. Afr., Rept.*, App. p. 15 (1849).
Elapomorphus (*non Wiegm.*), *Smith, l c* p. 16.
Uriechis, *Peters, Mon. Berl' Ac.* 1854, p 623; *Jan, Arch. Zool. Anat. Phys.* ii. 1862, p. 48; *Peters, Reise n. Mossamb.* iii. p. 110 (1882).
Cercocalamus, *Günth. Ann. & Mag. N. H.* (3) xi. 1863, p. 21, *and Biol. C.-Am., Rept* p. 157 (1895).

Maxillary short, with 6 to 9 small teeth followed by a large grooved fang situated below the eye; anterior mandibular teeth longest. Head small, not distinct from neck; eye small, with round pupil; nasal entire or divided; no loreal. Body cylindrical: scales smooth, without pits, in 15 rows; ventrals rounded. Tail moderate or short, subcaudals single.

Tropical and South Africa.

Synopsis of the Species.

I. Two præfrontals.

  A. Symphysial not in contact with the chin-shields.

    1. Two postoculars, in contact with a temporal; nasal entire, in contact with the præocular.

Third and fourth upper labials entering the eye .... 1. *jacksonii*, p. 257.
Second and third upper labials entering the eye .... 2. *werneri*, p. 257.

    2. A single postocular; one labial in contact with the parietal.

Nasal entire, not in contact with the præocular .... 3. *concolor*, p. 257.
Nasal divided, in contact with the præocular .... 4. *lunulatus*, p. 258.

  B. Symphysial in contact with the chin-shields.

    1. Third and fourth upper labials entering the eye.

Nasal divided; ventrals 154–180; subcaudals 51–59 .. . . 5. *guentheri*, p. 259.
Nasal entire; ventrals 191; subcaudals 44 .... 6. *bocagii*, p. 259.
Nasal entire; ventrals 138–166; subcaudals 37–53 .... 7. *capensis*, p. 259.

    2. Second and third upper labials entering the eye.

Ventrals 110–149; subcaudals 21–40. 8. *nigriceps*, p. 260.
Ventrals 160–161; subcaudals 36–41. 9. *punctatolineatus*, p. 261.

II. A single præfrontal.

Frontal as long as its distance from the end of the snout .... 10 *lineatus*, p. 261.
Frontal longer than its distance from the end of the snout .... 11. *anomalus*, p. 262.

1. Aparallactus jacksonii.

Uriechis jacksonii, *Gunth. Ann & Mag. N. H.* (6) i. 1888, p. 325, pl. xix. fig E.
Aparallactus jacksonii, *Bouleng. Ann. & Mag. N. H.* (6) xvi. 1895, p. 172.

Diameter of eye greater than its distance from the oral margin. Rostral broader than deep, the portion visible from above half as long as its distance from the frontal; internasals much shorter than the præfrontals; frontal once and a half as long as broad, much longer than its distance from the end of the snout, slightly shorter than the parietals; nasal entire, in contact with the præocular, two postoculars, in contact with the anterior temporal, temporals 1+1; seven upper labials, third and fourth entering the eye; first lower labial in contact with its fellow behind the symphysial; two pairs of chin-shields, subequal in length, the anterior broader and in contact with three lower labials Scales in 15 rows. Ventrals 142; anal entire; subcaudals 36. Pale reddish brown above, with a black vertebral line; upper surface of head and nape black, the nuchal blotch edged with yellow and extending to the sides of the neck; a pair of yellow spots behind the parietal shields, sides of head yellow, the shields bordering the eye black; lower parts uniform yellowish.

Total length 180 millim.; tail 30.

East Africa.

a. Hgr ♀ (V. 142; C. 36). Foot of Mt. Kilimanjaro   F J. Jackson, Esq. [P]. (Type)

2. Aparallactus werneri. (PLATE XI. fig. 1.)

Aparallactus werneri, *Bouleng Ann & Mag. N. H.* (6) xvi. 1895, p. 172

Diameter of eye greater than its distance from the oral margin. Rostral twice as broad as deep, the portion visible from above nearly half as long as its distance from the frontal; internasals much shorter than the præfrontals; frontal once and a half as long as broad, longer than its distance from the end of the snout, as long as the parietals; nasal entire, in contact with the præocular; two postoculars, in contact with the anterior temporal; temporals 1+1; six upper labials, second and third entering the eye; first lower labial in contact with its fellow behind the symphysial; two pairs of chin-shields, the anterior broader and a little longer and in contact with three lower labials. Scales in 15 rows. Ventrals 147–160; anal entire; subcaudals 32–41. Blackish above, with a deep black, somewhat light-edged nuchal collar; upper lip blackish below the eye, yellowish in front and behind; lower parts uniform yellowish.

Total length 390 millim.; tail 65.

East Africa.

a–b. ♂ (V. 147; C. 41) &   Usambara.   Dr. F. Werner [E].
♀ (V. 160, C. 32).   (Types.)

3. Aparallactus concolor.

Uriechis concolor, *Fischer, Jahrb. Hamb. Wiss. Anst* i. 1884, p. 4, pl 1. fig. 1; *Gunth. Ann. & Mag. N. H.* (6) 1. 1888, p. 325.

Aparallactus concolor, *Bouleng. Ann. & Mag. N. H.* (6) xvi. 1895, p. 172.

Diameter of eye equal to or greater than its distance from the oral margin. Rostral broader than deep, the portion visible from above one half to two thirds as long as its distance from the frontal; internasals shorter than the præfrontals, frontal once and a half to twice as long as broad, much longer than its distance from the end of the snout, as long as or slightly shorter than the parietals; nasal entire, not in contact with the præocular; one postocular; temporals 1+1; seven upper labials, third and fourth entering the eye, second in contact with the præfrontal, fifth in contact with the parietal; first lower labial in contact with its fellow behind the symphysial; two pairs of chin-shields, posterior longest, anterior in contact with four labials. Scales in 15 rows. Ventrals 145-158; anal entire; subcaudals 55-71. Uniform dark brown or black, somewhat lighter beneath.

Total length 460 millim.; tail 110.

Eastern Central Africa.

a.	♀ (V. 152; C. 55).	Lado.	Dr. Emin Pasha [P.].
b.	Hgr. (V. 145; C. 61).	Steppes E. of Izavo.	Dr. J. W. Gregory [P.].
c.	♀ (V. 158; C. 71).	Boran Country.	Dr. Donaldson Smith [C.].

4. Aparallactus lunulatus

Uriechis lunulatus, *Peters, Mon. Berl. Ac.* 1854, p. 623, *and Reise n. Mossamb.* iii. p. 113, pl. xviii. fig. 2 (1882); *Gunth. Ann. & Mag. N. H.* (6) i. 1888, p. 324.

Aparallactus lunulatus, *Bouleng. Ann. & Mag. N. H.* (6) xvi. 1895, p. 172.

Diameter of eye equal to or greater than its distance from the oral margin. Rostral broader than deep, the portion visible from above measuring about one third its distance from the frontal; internasals shorter than the præfrontals; frontal once and two thirds as long as broad, much longer than its distance from the end of the snout, as long as the parietals; nasal divided, in contact with the præocular; one postocular; temporals 1+1; seven upper labials, third and fourth entering the eye, fifth in contact with the parietal; first lower labial in contact with its fellow behind the symphysial; two pairs of chin-shields, subequal in size, the anterior in contact with four lower labials. Scales in 15 rows. Ventrals 151-158; anal entire; subcaudals 52-58. Olive or pale brown above, each scale edged with darker, anteriorly with several blackish cross-bars followed by small spots; the first cross-bar largest and forming a collar; whitish beneath.

Total length 390 millim.; tail 85.

Eastern Central Africa, Mozambique.

a.	♂ (V. 155; C. 52).	Lake Tanganyika.	Sir J. Kirk [C.].
b.	♂ (V. 151; C. 57).	Lake Nyassa.	

5. Aparallactus guentheri. (Plate XI. fig. 2.)

Uriechis capensis, part, *Gunth. Ann & Mag. N. H.* (6) i. 1888, p. 324, *Bocage, Herp Angola*, p. 128 (1895).
Aparallactus guentheri, *Bouleng Ann. & Mag. N. H.* (6) xvi. 1895, p. 172.

Diameter of eye greater than its distance from the oral margin. Rostral broader than deep, the portion visible from above nearly half as long as its distance from the frontal; internasals shorter than the præfrontals, frontal once and a half as long as broad, much longer than its distance from the end of the snout, a little shorter than the parietals, nasal divided, in contact with the præocular; one postocular; temporals 1+1, seven upper labials, third and fourth entering the eye, fifth in contact with the parietal; symphysial in contact with the anterior chin-shields, which are as long as and a little broader than the posterior and in contact with four lower labials. Scales in 15 rows. Ventrals 154-180; anal entire *; subcaudals 51–59. Blackish brown above, a little lighter beneath, chin and throat yellowish white; a deep black collar, edged with yellowish white in front and behind, narrowly interrupted on the throat.

Total length 330 millim; tail 80.
East Africa, Eastern Central Africa, Angola.

a.	♀ (V. 154; C. 59).	Lake Nyassa.	A. A. Simons, Esq. [C.]
b.	Yg (V. 164, C. 51).	Shiré highlands.	Sir H. H. Johnston [P.]
c.	Yg. (V. 156; C. 52).	Zanzibar.	F. Finn, Esq. [P.]
			(Types)

6. Aparallactus bocagii.

Uriechis capensis, part, *Bocage, Herp Angola*, p. 128 (1895).
Aparallactus bocagii, *Bouleng. Ann & Mag. N. H.* (6) xvi. 1895, p. 173.

Head-shields as in *A. capensis*. Ventrals 191; subcaudals 44. Reddish brown above, with a small brown spot in the centre of each scale; these spots forming longitudinal lines; a black spot on each side of the head, round the eye, and on two or three labial shields, and another on the first temporal shield; a black nuchal bar, separated from the head by a yellowish interspace; uniform yellowish white beneath.

Total length 272 millim.
Angola.

7. Aparallactus capensis.

Aparallactus capensis, *Smith, Ill. Zool. S. Afr., Rept*, App. p. 16 (1849); *Bouleng. Ann. & Mag. N. H* (6) xvi. 1895, p. 173.
Elapomorphus capensis, *Smith, l. c.*

---

* Bocage (*l c.*) describes his *Uriechis capensis* as with divided anal and paired subcaudals, a statement due, no doubt, to an oversight.

Cercocalamus collaris, *Gunth. Ann. & Mag. N. H* (3) xi. 1863,
p. 21, pl. iii fig A, *and Biol. C.-Am , Rept.* p. 157 (1895).
Uriechis capensis, *Gunth. Ann & Mag. N. H.* (3) xv. 1865, p. 89;
Jan, Icon Gén 15, pl. i. fig. 5 (1866), *Peters, Reise n. Mossamb.*
iii. p. 112 (1882).
—— capensis, part., *Gunth. Ann. & Mag N. H* (6) i. 1888,
p. 324.

Diameter of eye a little greater than its distance from the oral margin. Rostral broader than deep, the portion visible from above about one third as long as its distance from the frontal; internasals shorter than the præfrontals; frontal once and a half to once and two thirds as long as broad, much longer than its distance from the end of the snout, a little shorter than the parietals; nasal entire, in contact with the præocular: one postocular; temporals 1+1; seven upper labials, third and fourth entering the eye, fifth in contact with the parietal; symphysial in contact with the anterior chin-shields, which are as long as or a little longer than the posterior and in contact with three lower labials. Scales in 15 rows. Ventrals 138–166, anal entire; subcaudals 37–53. Yellow or pale reddish brown above, with or without a blackish vertebral line, yellowish white beneath; upper surface of head and nape black, with or without a yellowish cross-bar behind the parietal shields, the black of the nape descending to the sides of the neck; sides of head yellowish, the shields bordering the eye black.

Total length 335 millim.; tail 70.

East and South Africa.

a. Hgr. ♀ (V. 158; C. 40)	Caffraria.	Sir A. Smith [P.]. (One of the types)
b ♀ (V. 159; C. 47).	De Kaap Goldfields, Transvaal.	Dr. P. Rendall [C].
c–l. ♂ (V. 138, 139; C. 45, 44) & ♀ (V. 150, 150, 152, 148, 149, 155, 149; C. ?, 44, ?, 42, 41, 43, 41).	Zanzibar.	Sir J. Kirk [C.].
m. ♀ (V. 141; C. ?).	——?	Dr. Günther [P.]. (Type of *Cercocalamus collaris*)

8. Aparallactus nigriceps.

Uriechis nigriceps, *Peters, Mon. Berl. Ac.* 1854, p. 623, *and Reise n. Mossamb.* iii p. 111, pl. xviii. fig. 1 (1882).
—— atriceps, *Jan, Arch Zool Anat. Phys.* ii. 1862, p. 49, *and Icon. Gén.* 15, pl i. fig 4 (1866)
Aparallactus nigriceps, *Bouleng. Ann. & Mag. N. H.* (6) xvi. 1895, p 173.

Diameter of eye greater than its distance from the oral margin. Rostral broader than deep, the portion visible from above about one third as long as its distance from the frontal; internasals much shorter than the præfrontals; frontal once and one third as long as broad, much longer than its distance from the end of the snout, a little shorter than the parietals; nasal entire, in contact with the præocular; one postocular; temporals 1+1 (the first sometimes absent); six upper labials, second and third entering the eye, fourth (or fourth and fifth) in contact with the parietal; symphysial in contact with the anterior chin-shields, which are slightly larger than the posterior and in contact with three lower labials. Scales in 15 rows. Ventrals 110–149; anal entire; subcaudals 21–40. Reddish brown above, whitish beneath; upper surface of head and nape black, the black on the nape edged with yellowish; a pair of yellowish spots may be present behind the parietal shields; sides of head yellowish, the shields bordering the eye black.

Total length 103 millim; tail 17. Grows to 255 millim.

Mozambique, Nyassaland.

a. Yg. (V. 149; C. 40).   Zomba, Brit. C. Africa.   Sir H. H. Johnston [P.].

9. Aparallactus punctatolineatus.

Uriechis capensis, part., *Bocage, Herp. Angola*, p 129 (1895).
Aparallactus punctatolineatus, *Bouleng. Ann. & Mag. N. H.* (6) xvi. 1895, p 173.

Similar to *A. capensis*, but six or seven upper labials, second and third entering the eye, fifth or fourth and fifth in contact with the parietal. Ventrals 160–161; subcaudals 36–41. Yellowish brown above, each scale darker in the centre, with three longitudinal series of large black dots; upper surface of head and a nuchal cross-bar black.

Total length 125 millim.; tail 20.

Angola and Nyassaland.

a. Hgr. (V. 160, C. 36).   Chiradzulu, Brit.   Sir H. H. Johnston [P.] C. Africa

10. Aparallactus lineatus.

Uriechis (Metopophis) lineatus, *Peters, Mon. Berl. Ac.* 1870, p. 643, pl. i. fig. 3
Aparallactus lineatus, *Bouleng. Ann. & Mag. N. H.* (6) xvi. 1895, p. 173.

Diameter of eye greater than its distance from the oral margin. Rostral broader than deep, the portion visible from above one third as long as its distance from the præfrontal; a single præfrontal, forming a suture with the præocular; frontal once and a half as long as broad, as long as its distance from the end of the snout, shorter than the parietals; nasal entire, in contact with the præocular, one postocular; a single temporal; seven upper labials, third and fourth entering the eye, fifth and sixth in contact with the parietal; first lower labial in contact with its fellow behind the symphysial; two pairs of subequal chin-shields, the anterior in contact with three lower labials. Scales in 15 rows. Ventrals 168; anal entire; subcaudals 41. Olive above, with three dark longitudinal lines, each scale of the outer series with a yellow spot; ventrals and subcaudals closely speckled with dark grey.

Total length 440 millim.; tail 57.

Keta, Guinea.

11. Aparallactus anomalus. (Plate XI. fig. 3.)

Uriechis anomala, *Bouleng. Ann. & Mag. N. H.* (6) xii. 1893, p. 273.
Aparallactus anomalus, *Bouleng. Ann. & Mag. N. H.* (6) xvi. 1895, p. 173.

Diameter of eye greater than its distance from the oral margin. Rostral twice as broad as deep, the portion visible from above one third as long as its distance from the frontal, a single præfrontal; internasal nearly reaching the supraocular; frontal once and two thirds as long as broad, longer than its distance from the end of the snout, shorter than the parietals: nasal entire, in contact with the præocular; one postocular, a single temporal; seven upper labials, third and fourth entering the eye, fifth and sixth in contact with the parietal; first lower labial in contact with its fellow behind the symphysial; anterior chin-shields as long as but broader than the posterior and in contact with four lower labials. Scales in 15 rows. Ventrals 170; anal entire; subcaudals 52. Pale brown above, speckled with darker; two dorsal series of small dark brown spots; posterior half of each scale of the outer row yellowish, surrounded by crowded dark brown dots; ventrals yellowish, speckled with dark brown in the middle; subcaudals closely speckled with dark brown.

Total length 440 millim.; tail 80.

Gold Coast.

a. ♂ (V. 170; C. 52). Gold Coast. L. Greening, Esq. [P.]. (Type.)

202. ELAPOPS.

Elapops, *Gunth. Ann. & Mag. N. H.* (3) iv. 1859, p. 161; Jan, *Arch. Zool. Anat. Phys.* ii. 1862, p. 32.
Pariaspis, *Cope, Proc. Ac. Philad.* 1860, pp. 241 & 566.

Maxillary teeth 11 or 12, the last two a little enlarged and feebly grooved on the inner side; anterior mandibular teeth longest. Head small, not distinct from neck; eye small, with round pupil; nostril between two nasals, no loreal; parietal in contact with labials. Body cylindrical; scales smooth, without pits, in 15 rows; ventrals rounded. Tail moderate; subcaudals single.

West Africa.

1. Elapops modestus.

Elapops modestus, *Gunth. Ann. & Mag. N. H.* (3) iv. 1859, p. 161, pl. iv. fig. C; *Cope, Proc. Ac. Philad.* 1860, p. 566; *Gunth. Zool. Rec.* 1865, p. 152.
Pariaspis plumbeatra, *Cope, Proc. Ac. Philad.* 1860, p. 242.
Elapops plumbeater, *Cope, t.c.* p. 566.
—— petersii, *Jan, Arch. Zool. Anat. Phys.* ii. 1862, p. 32, and *Icon. Gén.* 13, pl. iii. fig. 2 (1865).

Diameter of eye equal to or a little exceeding its distance from the oral margin. Rostral broader than deep, the portion visible from above about half as long as its distance from the frontal; internasals shorter than the præfrontals; frontal once and one third to once and a half as long as broad, as long as or longer than its distance from the end of the snout, shorter than the parietals; one præocular, in contact with the posterior nasal; one or two postoculars; a single temporal; seven upper labials, third and fourth entering the eye, sixth or fifth and sixth in contact with the parietal; four lower labials in contact with the anterior chinshields, which are a little longer than the posterior. Scales in 15 rows. Ventrals 138–158; anal entire; subcaudals 36–45. Dark olive-grey above, the scales more or less distinctly edged with black; ventrals and subcaudals yellowish, olive-grey, or yellowish dotted or spotted with grey, the spots sometimes forming a median series.

Total length 540 millim ; tail 75.

West Africa, from Liberia to the Congo.

a. ♀ (V. 158; C. 41).	W Africa.	Mr. Rich [C.]. (Type)
b–d. ♀ (V. 154, 150, 151; C. 37, 37, 36).	W. Africa	J. C. Salmon, Esq [P.].
e. ♂ (V. 144; C. ?).	Lagos.	Sir A. Moloney [P.].
f. ♀ (V. 141; C. 44)	Niger	J. W. Crosse, Esq. [P.].
g. ♂ (V 138, C 45).	Gaboon.	
h–k. ♂ (V 139, 140, C. 44, ?) & yg. (V. 156; C 41).	Cette Cama, Gaboon.	
l. ♀ (V. 155; C. 37).	Mouth of the Loango.	Mr. H. J. Duggan [C.].

Subfam. 6. ELACHISTODONTINÆ.

Only a few teeth on the posterior part of the maxillary and dentary bones and on the palatines and pterygoids. Some of the anterior thoracic vertebræ with the hypapophysis much developed, directed forwards, and capped with enamel.

A single genus, the opisthoglyphous analogue of the aglyphous *Dasypeltis*.

203. ELACHISTODON.

Elachistodon, *Reinh Overs. Dansk. Vid Selsk. Forh.* 1863, p. 206; Bouleng. *Faun. Ind*, Rept. p. 362 (1890).

Maxillary and mandible edentulous in front; two minute maxillary teeth followed by a pair of small grooved teeth; eight mandibular teeth. Head scarcely distinct from neck; eye rather small, with vertically elliptic pupil; posterior nasal deeply concave. Body elongate, somewhat compressed; scales smooth, in 15 rows, vertebral row enlarged. Tail short; subcaudals in two rows.

Bengal.

1. Elachistodon westermanni.

Elachistodon westermanni, *Reinh. Overs. Dansk Vid. Selsk. Forh.* 1863, p. 206; *Gunth. Rept. Brit. Ind.* p. 444 (1864); *Blanf. Journ. As. Soc. Beng.* xliv. 1875, p 207; *Bouleng. Faun Ind., Rept.* p 363 (1890)

Rostral twice as broad as deep, just reaching the upper surface of the head; internasals and præfrontals subequal in size; frontal rather longer than broad, as long as its distance from the end of the snout, shorter than the parietals; loreal small, longer than deep, entering the eye; a small præocular above the loreal; two postoculars; two very long temporals; six or seven upper labials, third and fourth entering the eye, three pairs of large chin-shields. Scales in 15 rows. Ventrals 210–217; anal entire; subcaudals 59–65. Brown above, with a yellowish vertebral stripe; a yellowish stripe commences on the snout and runs along each side of the head to the temporals and the angle of the mouth; an angular yellowish cross-band on the nape; lower parts yellowish.

Total length 784 millim.; tail 114.

Bengal.

Series C. PROTEROGLYPHA.

Divided into two subfamilies:—

7. *Hydrophiinæ.*—Tail strongly compressed, with the neural spines and hypapophyses very much developed.

8. *Elapinæ.*—Tail cylindrical.

Poisonous, the poison being conveyed mainly through the anterior maxillary teeth, which are so folded as to appear hollow or perforated.

Subfam. 7. *HYDROPHIINÆ.*

Hydri, *Oppel, Ordn. Rept.* p. 49, 1811.
Hydrophidæ, part., *Boie, Isis,* 1827, p. 510.
Nauticophes, part., *Lesson, in Bélanger, Voy. Ind. Or, Rept.* p. 320, 1834.
Hydridæ, *Bonaparte, Mem. Acc. Torin.* (2) ii. p. 393, 1839.
Hydridæ, part., *Gray, Cat. Sn.* p. 35, 1849.
Platycerques, *Duméril, Mém. Ac. Sc.* xxiii. p. 519, 1853; *Duméril & Bibron, Erp. Gén.* vii. p. 1507, 1854.
Hydrophidæ, *Cope, Proc. Ac. Philad.* 1859, p. 333.
Hydrophidæ, *Jan, Elenco sist. Ofid* p. 107, 1863.
Hydrophidæ, *Gunther, Rept. Brit. Ind.* p 352, 1864.
Hydrophidæ, *Cope, Proc. Amer. Philos. Soc.* xxii. p 480, 1886.
Hydrophiinæ, *Boulenger, Faun Ind., Rept.* p. 393, 1890.

Tail strongly compressed, oar-shaped, with the neural spines and hypapophyses very much developed. Hypapophyses not developed throughout the vertebral column.

Body more or less compressed, eye small or very small, with round pupil. Rostral shield with two notches in the oral border, only the cleft portion of the tongue being protrusible.

Marine (with the exception of one species of *Distira*, confined to a freshwater lake in Luzon), entering tidal streams. With the exception of *Platurus*, specimens of which have repeatedly been found at some distance from water, these snakes are exclusively aquatic; all are viviparous. They are confined to the Indian and Pacific Oceans, one species (*Hydrus platurus*) being widely distributed, but do not seem to occur on the East Coast of Africa. The habitat of the greater number extends from the Persian Gulf to the Western Tropical Pacific.

Synopsis of the Genera.

I. Maxillary not extending forwards beyond the palatine; ventral shields small or absent; nostrils on the upper surface of the snout.

  A. Symphysial shield triangular, not concealed in a mental groove.

    1. Maxillary longer than the lower aspect of the ectopterygoid, with 4 to 18 small teeth in addition to the poison-fangs.

    a. No ventral shields.

Nostril in the nasal shield .... 204. **Hydrus**, p. 266.
Nostril between two nasals and an internasal.
         205. **Thalassophis**, p. 268.
Nostril between two nasals and the præfrontal.
         206. **Acalyptophis**, p. 269.

    b. Ventral shields distinct, at least on the anterior part of the body.

      α. No præocular .... 207. **Hydrelaps**, p. 270.

      β. Præocular present.

Small maxillary teeth not grooved; body often very slender anteriorly................. 208. **Hydrophis**, p. 271.
All the maxillary teeth grooved ...... 209. **Distira**, p. 285.

    2. Maxillary not longer than the ectopterygoid, with 2 to 5 small grooved teeth in addition to the poison-fangs.
         210. **Enhydris**, p. 300.

  B. Symphysial shield narrow, partly concealed in a deep groove in the chin .... 211. **Enhydrina**, p. 302.

II. Maxillary extending forwards beyond the palatine: ventral shields large.

Nostrils on the upper surface of the snout; nasal shields in contact with each other; maxillary a little longer than the ectopterygoid, with 8 to 10 grooved teeth in addition to the poison-fangs.
212. Aipysurus, p. 303.

Nostrils lateral; nasals separated by the internasals; maxillary much shorter than the ectopterygoid, with one or two small solid teeth in addition to the poison-fangs 213. Platurus, p. 306.

204. HYDRUS.

Hydrus, part., *Schneid Hist. Amph.* i. p 233 (1799).
Pelamis, part., *Daud. Hist. Rept* vii. p. 357 (1803); *Fischer, Abh. Naturw. Hamb.* iii. 1856, p 61.
Pelamis, *Fitzing. N. Class. Rept.* p. 29 (1826); *Wagl. Syst. Amph.* p. 165 (1830), *Gray, Cat. Sn* p. 41 (1849); *Dum. & Bibr. Erp. Gén.* vii. p. 1333 (1854); *Günth. Rept. Brit. Ind.* p. 382 (1864).

Fig. 19.

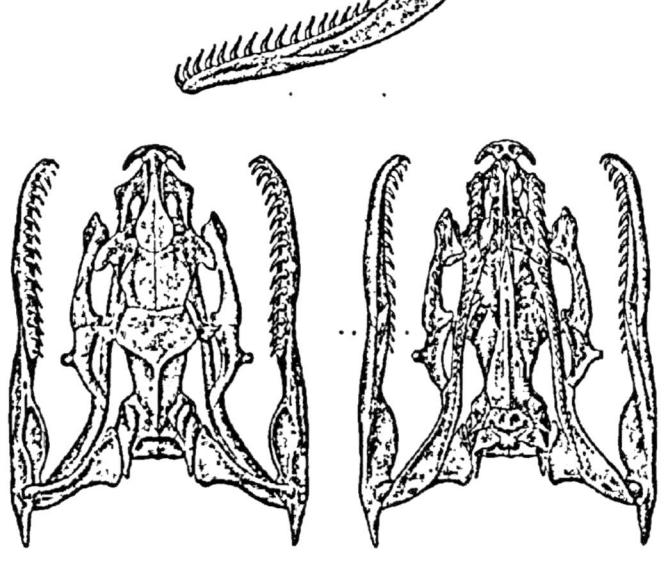

Skull of *Hydrus platurus*.

Hydrophis, part., *Schleg. Phys. Serp.* ii. p. 488 (1837); *Jan, Elenco sist. Ofid* p. 109 (1863)

Maxillary longer than the ectopterygoid, not extending forwards as far as the palatine; poison-fangs rather short, followed, after a short interspace, by 7 or 8 solid teeth. Nostrils superior; snout long; head-shields large, nasals in contact with each other; a præocular; no loreal. Body rather short; scales hexagonal or squarish, juxtaposed; no distinct ventrals.

Indian and Pacific Oceans.

1. Hydrus platurus

Russell, Ind. Serp. i. pl. xli. (1796).
Anguis platura, *Linn S N.* i p 391 (1766).
Hydrus bicolor, *Schneid Hist. Amph* i p. 242 (1799); *Cantor, Cat. Mal Rept.* p. 135 (1847).
Hydrophis platura, *Latr. Rept.* iv. p. 197 (1801).
Pelamis bicolor, *Daud Rept.* vii. p 366, pl lxxxix. (1803); *Gray, Cat.* p. 41 (1849); *Dum. & Bibr.* vii. p. 1335 (1854); *Gunth. Rept Brit. Ind* p. 382 (1864), *Krefft, Sn Austral* p 98, pl xii fig 19 (1869); *Strauch, Schl Russ R* p. 199 (1873); *Fayrer, Thanatoph. Ind* pl xvii. (1874); *Peters & Doria, Ann. Mus. Genova,* xiii 1878. p. 416, *Murray, Zool. Sind,* p. 397 (1883); *Fisk, Proc Zool. Soc.* 1885, p. 482.
Hydrophis pelamis, *Schleg. Phys Serp.* ii. p. 508, pl xviii figs. 13-15 (1837), and *Faun Japon , Rept.* p. 90, pl viii. (1838).
Pelamis ornata, *Gray, Zool. Misc* p. 60 (1842), and *Cat.* p. 43.
Hydrophis bicolor, *Fischer, Abh Naturw Hamb.* iii. 1856, p. 61; *Jan, Icon. Gén.* 40, pls. ii. & iii. (1872).
Pelamis platurus, *Stoliczka, Proc. As Soc Beng.* 1872, p. 92; *Garm. Bull. Essex Inst* xxiv. 1892, p. 88.
Hydrus platurus, *Bouleng Faun Ind , Rept.* p 397 (1890), *Boettg Ber. Offenb. Ver. Nat.* 1892, p. 88

Rostral as deep as broad or a little broader than deep; frontal large, at least as long as the snout or the parietals; one or two præ- and two or three postoculars; one or two suboculars sometimes present; temporals small and numerous; seven or eight upper labials, second in contact with the præfrontal, fourth, fifth, or fourth and fifth usually entering the eye; chin-shields small or indistinct. 45 to 47 scales round the body, smooth in the female and young, laterals and ventrals rough with one, two, or three small tubercles in the male. Black or brown and yellow, the markings very variable.

Total length 700 millim.; tail 80.

Indian Ocean; Tropical and Subtropical Pacific.

A. Yellow, with brown, black-edged cross-bands; black bars between the cross-bands, on the sides of the belly. (*P. ornata,* Gray.)

a. Yg.   Borneo.   (Type of *P. ornata.*)
b. Yg.   . India (?).

B. Anterior third of body with a black dorsal stripe; further back, a series of transverse dorsal rhombs on the back, and black spots on the sides and belly. (Var. *maculata,* Jan.)

a. Yg.   —— ?   Zoological Society.

C. Dorsal region black; sides and belly yellow, with a lateral series of black spots, which may be partly confluent into a stripe; tail with dorsal and lateral spots.

a. ♀.	India.	Gen Hardwicke [P.]
b. Hgr.	Panama.	Haslar Collection

D. Dorsal region black, ventral region brown, the two separated by a yellow lateral stripe; tail spotted as in the preceding.

a. ♂.	Bombay.	Dr Leith [P.].
b. Yg.	Oo Sima, Loo Choo Is.	M Ferrié [C.]; M R Oberthur [P.].
c. Hgr.	Australia.	J. Baines, Esq. [P.]

E. Black above, sides and belly yellow; tail spotted as in the preceding. (*H. bicolor*, Schn.)

a–d. ♂.	Madagascar.	Sir E. Belcher [P.].
e. ♀.	Kurrachee.	Kurrachee Museum [P.].
f. Hgr.	Trevandrum, Travancore.	H. S. Ferguson, Esq. [P.].
g. Hgr.	Madras.	T C. Jerdon, Esq. [P.].
h, i. ♀ & yg.	India.	Gen Hardwicke [P.].
k. Yg.	Ceylon.	Miss Layard [P.].
l. ♂.	Formosa.	R. Swinhoe, Esq. [C.].
m–n. ♂.	Siam.	
o. Hgr.	Gulf of Siam.	H.M.S. 'Herald'
p–q. Hgr.	Borneo.	Sir E. Belcher [P.].
r. ♀.	Australia.	G. Krefft, Esq [P.].
s. Hgr.	New Georgia, Solomon Is.	H M S. 'Penguin.'
t. ♂.	Lat. 0° 4′ S., Long. 130° 20′ E.	H.M.S. 'Challenger.'
u. Yg.	Samoa.	Rev. S. J. Whitmee [P.].
v, w Hgr.	New Zealand.	
x. ♀.	Salina Cruz, Mexico.	Dr. A. C. Buller [C.].
y. ♂.	Off coast of Ecuador.	J. W. Warburton, Esq. [P.].
z. Skeleton.	Indian Ocean.	
α. Skull of *l*.		

F. Yellow, with a black vertebral stripe, broken up into spots posteriorly; no lateral spots on the body or tail.

a. Hgr.	China.	
b. ♀.	Sumatra.	
c. Hgr.	——?	

G. Yellow, with a vertebral band and spots on the tail pale brown or olive.

a–b. ♂ & yg.	Trevandrum, Travancore.	H. S. Ferguson, Esq. [P.].

205. THALASSOPHIS.

Thalassophis, part., *Schmidt, Abh. Naturw. Hamb.* ii. 1852, p 75
Hydrophis, part., *Fischer, Abh. Naturw. Hamb* iii. 1856, p. 41; *Jan, Elenco sist. Ofid.* p. 109 (1863); Günth. *Rept. Brit. Ind.* p. 361 (1864).

Poison-fangs followed by 5 small teeth, the anterior of which are grooved. Snout short, nostrils superior, between two nasals and an internasal, a pair of elongate internasals separating the nasals; frontal and parietal shields large; præocular present; no loreal. Body rather elongate; scales hexagonal, juxtaposed; no distinct ventrals.

Coast of Java.

1. Thalassophis anomalus.

Thalassophis anomalus, *Schmidt, Abh. Naturw. Hamb.* ii. 1852, p 81, pl. iv

Hydrophis anomala, *Fischer, Abh. Naturw Hamb* iii. 1856, p 58, *Gunth. Rept. Brit Ind* p 379 (1864), *Jan, Icon. Gén* 40, pl. iv. fig 1 (1872).

Rostral broken up into several small shields; internasals narrow, elongate, longer than the præfrontals, as long as the frontal; latter shorter than its distance from the end of the snout; one præ- and two postoculars; temporals small, scale-like, seven or eight upper labials, second largest and in contact with the præfrontal, third entering the eye, fourth and fifth separated from the eye by suboculars; two pairs of small chin-shields, the posterior separated from each other by two scales. Scales with a strong tubercular keel, which is double on the median ventral row, 31 to 33 round the body Body with dark annuli, wider on the back.

Total length 810 millim.; tail 84.

Java.

206. ACALYPTOPHIS.

Acalyptus (*non Schonh*), *Dum & Bibr Mém Ac. Sc* xxiii. 1853, p. 522, *and Exp. Gén* vii. p. 1339 (1854), *Fischer, Abh. Naturw Hamb* iii. 1856, p 37, *Jan, Elenco sist Ofid.* p 103 (1863); *Gunth. Rept Brit Ind* p. 359 (1864).

Maxillary longer than the ectopterygoid, not extending forwards as far as the palatine; poison-fangs moderate, followed, after a short interspace, by 8 or 9 solid teeth Snout short; nostrils superior, between two nasals and the præfrontal, the larger nasals in contact with each other; frontal and parietal shields broken up into scales; præocular present; no loreal. Body rather elongate; scales subimbricate; no distinct ventrals.

Western Tropical Pacific Ocean.

1. Acalyptophis peronii.

Acalyptus peronii, *Dum. & Bibr. Mém. Ac. Sc.* xxiii. 1853, p 522.
—— superciliosus, *Dum. & Bibr.* vii. p. 1340 (1854); *Gunth. Rept. Brit. Ind.* p. 359 (1864); *Jan, Icon. Gén.* 40, pl. ii. fig. 2, (1872).

Head rather small. Diameter of neck one third to two fifths the greatest depth of the body. Eye a little longer than its distance from the mouth. Rostral nearly twice as broad as deep; nasals as long as the præfrontals; supraocular raised, its free border pointed; one præ- and three postoculars; six or seven upper labials, third and fourth entering the eye; two pairs of small chin-shields, in contact with each other. 22 to 24 scales round the neck, 25 to 30 round the body; scales with a short keel, which is strong and tubercular in the males. Greyish or pale olive above, whitish beneath, with dark cross-bands, narrower than the interspaces between them, tapering to a point on the sides of the belly; belly uniform or with a series of dark cross-bars alternating with spots.

Total length 890 millim.; tail 115.

Western Tropical Pacific.

a. ♂.	Hong Kong.	Dr. J. G. Fischer.
b. ♀.	—— ?	Dr. Günther [P.].

207. HYDRELAPS.

Maxillary longer than the lower aspect of the ectopterygoid, not extending forwards as far as the palatine; poison-fangs moderate, followed, after an interspace, by 6 solid teeth. Snout short; nostrils superior, in a single nasal which is in contact with its fellow; head-shields large; no loreal or præocular, the præfrontal bordering the eye. Body moderately elongate, feebly compressed; scales imbricate; ventrals small but well-developed.

North Coast of Australia.

1. Hydrelaps darwiniensis. (Plate XII. fig. 1.)

Eye extremely small, about half as long as its distance from the mouth. Rostral broader than deep, scarcely visible from above; frontal longer than broad, nearly as long as its distance from the end of the snout, as long as or a little shorter than the parietals, its lateral sides diverging posteriorly; a single postocular; temporals 1+2, anterior very large and descending between the fifth and sixth labials; six upper labials, third and fourth entering the eye; two pairs of small chin-shields, in contact with each other, the anterior shorter than the posterior. Scales perfectly smooth, imbricate, in 27 to 29 rows on the neck as well as on the body. Ventrals 170–172. Annulate blackish and yellowish white, the black rings broader than the white above, narrower beneath; head dark olive, spotted with black.

Total length 435 millim.; tail 43.

North Australia.

a–b. ♀ (V. 170, 172). Port Darwin. R. G. S. Buckland, Esq. [P.].

208. HYDROPHIS.

Hydrus, part., *Schneid. Hist. Amph.* i. p. 233 (1799); *Wagler, Syst. Amph.* p. 165 (1830).
Hydrophis, part., *Daud. Hist. Rept.* vii. p. 372 (1803); *Wagler, l c.*; *Schleg. Phys. Serp.* ii. p 488 (1837), *Gray, Cat. Sn.* p. 49 (1849); *Dum. & Bibr. Erp. Gén.* vii. p. 1341 (1854); *Fischer, Abh Naturw. Hamb.* iii 1856, p 41; *Jan, Elenco sist. Ofid.* p 109 (1863); *Gunth. Rept. Brit. Ind.* p. 360 (1864).
Pelamis, part., *Merrem, Tent. Syst. Amph.* p. 138 (1820).
Enhydris, part., *Merr. l. c.* p. 140.
Disteira, part., *Fitzing. N. Class Rept* p 29 (1826).
Microcephalophis, *Lesson, in Bélang Voy Ind Or, Rept.* p 320 (1834); *Gray, Cat* p 46
Liopala, *Gray, Zool Misc* p. 60 (1842).
Aturia, part., *Gray, l c* p. 61.
Thalassophis, part., *Schmidt, Abh. Naturw. Hamb.* ii. 1852, p 75.
Hydrophis, *Bouleng Faun. Ind., Rept.* p 398 (1890).

Maxillary longer than the ectopterygoid, not extending forwards as far as the palatine; poison-fangs large, followed by a series of 7 to 18 solid teeth. Head small; nostrils superior, pierced in a single nasal shield, which is in contact with its fellow; head-shields large; præocular present; loreal usually absent. Body long, often very slender anteriorly, scales on the anterior part of the body imbricate; ventrals more or less distinct, very small.

Indian and Pacific Oceans, from the Persian Gulf to Southern China and Northern Australia.

Synopsis of the Species.

I. Head moderately small; neck moderately slender, its diameter not less than half the greatest depth of the body.

A. A single anterior temporal.

Scales imbricate, 33–35 round the body	1. *spiralis*, p. 273.
Scales juxtaposed, 45 round the body .	2. *polyodontus*, p. 274.

B. Two superposed anterior temporals.

1. 32 scales round the neck, 43–47 round the body

Frontal slightly longer than broad, about as long as the nasals	3. *schistosus*, p. 274.
Frontal much longer than broad, as long as its distance from the end of the snout	4. *hybridus*, p. 274.

2. 28–30 scales round the neck, 34 round the body.
5. *longiceps*, p. 275.

II. Head very small; neck very slender, its diameter not half the greatest depth of the body.

A. Two superposed anterior temporals; ventrals 285–331.

1. 34–38 scales round the neck.

Frontal shorter than its distance from the rostral; 48–50 scales round the body .... 6. *cœrulescens*, p. 275.
Frontal as long as its distance from the end of the snout; 42 scales round the body .... 7. *frontalis*, p. 276.

2. 25–29 scales round the neck, 35–39 round the body.

    a. Scales all imbricate; posterior chin-shields separated by scales.

Rostral as deep as broad .... 8. *kingii*, p. 276.
Rostral broader than deep......... 9. *nigrocinctus*, p. 277.

    b. Scales on the body juxtaposed; posterior chin-shields in contact with each other.. 10. *mamillaris*, p. 277.

B. A single anterior temporal.

    1. 27–31 scales round the neck, 40–48 round the body; ventrals 345–500.

Rostral broader than deep; frontal a little longer than broad; scales imbricate; seven upper labials .. 11. *elegans*, p. 278.
Rostral deeper than broad; frontal longer than broad; scales on body juxtaposed .... 16. *cantoris*, p. 281.
Rostral nearly as deep as broad; frontal much longer than broad .. 17. *fasciatus*, p. 281.
Rostral a little broader than deep; frontal slightly longer than broad; scales imbricate; six upper labials. 18. *brookii*, p. 282.

    2. 19–23 scales round the neck, 29–33 round the body ventrals 225–337.

        a. Seven or eight upper labials; rostral as deep as broad; frontal twice as long as broad.
            12. *pacificus*, p. 278.

        b. Six upper labials.

Rostral broader than deep; posterior chin-shields separated by scales .. 13. *latifasciatus*, p. 279.
Rostral broader than deep; posterior chin-shields in contact with each other .... 14. *coronatus*, p. 279.
Rostral as deep as broad; posterior chin-shields in contact with each other .... 15. *gracilis*, p. 280.

    3. 25 scales round the neck, 35 round the body; ventrals 329.
            19. *melanocephalus*, p. 283.

    4. 33–40 scales round the neck, 40–50 round the body.

Frontal shorter than its distance from the r........ .... 20. *t...gnatus*, p. 283.

Frontal as long as its distance from
the rostral; ventrals 310–438 .... 21. *obscurus*, p. 284.

5. 31 scales round the neck, 58 round the body; ventrals 483.
22. *leptodira*, p. 285.

TABLE SHOWING NUMBERS OF SCALES AND SHIELDS.

	Sc. neck.	Sc. body.	V.	Lab. ent. eye.	Ant. temp.
spiralis	28–29	33–35	270–334	2	1
polyodontus	?	45	?	2	1
schistosus	32	47	235–306	2	2
hybridus	32	43	?	2	2
longiceps	28–30	34	271	2	2
cærulescens	35–38	48–50	285–309	2	2
frontalis	34	42	291	2	2
kingii	27	37	314	2	2
nigrocinctus	27–29	39	310–331	2	2
mamillaris	25–27	35	287–316	2	2
elegans	27–30	41–43	350–385	2	1
pacificus	27–29	37–39	310	3	1
latifasciatus	21	33	322	2	1
coronatus	19–23	20–33	278–337	2	1
gracilis	19–21	29–33	225–297	2	1
cantoris	23–25	41–43	412–456	2	1
fasciatus	25–31	40–48	345–500	2	1
brookii	30	42	416	2	1
melanocephalus	25	35	329	2–3	1
torquatus	33–35	43–45	240–285	2	1
obscurus	33–40	40–50	310–438	2	1
leptodira	31	58	483	2	1

1. Hydrophis spiralis.

Hydrus spiralis, *Shaw, Zool.* iii. p. 564, pl. cxxv. (1802).
Enhydris spiralis, *Merr. Tent.* p. 140 (1820).
Hydrophis melanurus, *Wagl. Icon. Amph.* pl. iii. (1828).
—— nigrocincta, part., *Schleg. Phys. Serp.* ii. p. 505 (1837).
—— spiralis, *Gray, Cat.* p. 54 (1859); *Günth. Rept. Brit. Ind.* p. 366, pl. xxv. fig. D (1864); *Anders. Proc. Zool. Soc.* 1872, p. 397; *Murray, Zool. Sind,* p. 390 (1884); *Bouleng. Faun. Ind., Rept.* p. 401 (1890); *Boettg. Ber. Offenb. Ver. Nat.* 1892, p. 88.
—— nigrocinctus, *Jan, Icon. Gén.* 41, pl. ii. fig. 2 (1872).

Head moderately small; body moderately elongate. Rostral broader than deep; frontal longer than broad, as long as its distance from the rostral, a little shorter than the parietals; one præ- and one postocular; a single anterior temporal, descending to the labial border; six or seven upper labials, second largest, third and fourth entering the eye; two pairs of subequal chin-shields, in contact. 28 or 29 scales round the neck, 33 to 35 round the body; scales imbricate, smooth in the young, with a central tubercle in the adult. Ventrals distinct, but feebly enlarged, 270–334. Olive above, yellowish beneath, with black rings connected by a black ventral band in the young; a more or less distinct series of round black dorsal spots between the rings; head black above, with a horse-shoe-shaped yellow mark, the convexity of which rests on the præfrontal shields; end of tail black.

Total length 400 millim. Grows to 1800 millim.

Coasts of India and the Malay Archipelago.

a. Yg. (V. 310).	Indian Ocean.	(Type.)
b–c, d–e. Yg (V. 300, 270, 302, 273).	Indian Ocean.	Sir J. McGrigor [P.].

2. Hydrophis polyodontus.

Hydrophis polydontus, *Jan, Icon. Gén.* 41, pl. i. fig. 1 (1872).

Head moderately small; body moderately elongate. Rostral broader than deep; frontal a little longer than broad, as long as its distance from the rostral, much shorter than the parietals; one præ- and two postoculars; a single anterior temporal; seven upper labials, second largest, third and fourth entering the eye; a single pair of small chin-shields. Scales juxtaposed, with a small tubercle, 45 round the middle of the body. Body with transverse rhomboidal black spots; head black.

Habitat unknown.

3. Hydrophis schistosus.

Russell, Ind. Serp. ii. pl x. (1801).
Hydrophis schistosus, *Daud. Rept.* vii. p. 386 (1803); *Bouleng. Faun. Ind., Rept.* p. 399 (1890).
Pelamis schistosus, *Merr. Tent.* p. 139 (1820).
Hydrophis nigra, *Anders. Proc. Zool. Soc.* 1872, p. 399; *Fayrer, Thanatoph. Ind.* pl. xxv. (1874).

Head moderate; body moderately elongate. Rostral broader than deep; nasals about as long as the frontal, more than twice as long as the suture between the præfrontals; frontal slightly longer than broad, shorter than the parietals; one præ- and one post-ocular; two superposed anterior temporals, seven upper labials, second largest, third and fourth entering the eye; two pairs of subequal chin-shields, posterior separated by one scale. 32 scales round the neck, 47 round the body; scales elongate-rhomboidal, smooth or feebly keeled, feebly imbricate anteriorly, juxtaposed posteriorly. Ventrals distinct anteriorly, 235–306. Uniform blackish.

Total length 465 millim.; tail 50.

Bengal and Cuttack coasts.

a. Hgr. (V. 235).	Poorie, Orissa.	Sir J. Fayrer [P.].

4. Hydrophis hybridus.

Hydrophis hybrida, *Schleg. Abbild.* p. 115, pl. xxxvii. (1844); *Jan, Ic. Gén.* ii. pl. -, f. 1 (1872).

Head moderate; body moderately elongate. Rostral broader than deep; nasals more than twice as long as the suture between the præfrontals; frontal much longer than broad, as long as its distance from the end of the snout, a little shorter than the parietals; one præ- and one postocular; two superposed anterior temporals; seven upper labials, third and fourth entering the eye; two pairs of small chin-shields, posterior separated from each other by scales. 32 scales round the neck, 43 round the body; scales with a small tubercle or short keel, feebly imbricate anteriorly, juxtaposed posteriorly. Yellowish, with a dorsal series of transverse rhomboidal black spots; head black above.

Total length 665 millim.; tail 85.

Molucca Sea.

5. Hydrophis longiceps.

Chitulia fasciata, *Gray, Cat* p. 56 (1829).
Hydrophis longiceps, *Gunth. Rept. Brit. Ind.* p. 375, pl. xxv. fig O (1864).

Head moderate; body moderately elongate. Rostral broader than deep; nasals shorter than the frontal, nearly thrice as long as the suture between the præfrontals; frontal much longer than broad, slightly shorter than its distance from the end of the snout, shorter than the parietals; one præ- and two postoculars; two superposed anterior temporals; eight upper labials, second largest and in contact with the præfrontal, third and fourth entering the eye; two pairs of chin-shields, in contact with each other. 28 to 30 scales round the neck, 34 round the body; scales smooth and imbricate on the neck, juxtaposed and with a short tubercular keel on the body. Ventrals very small but distinct throughout, 271. Greyish above, with dark olive cross-bars separated by narrow interspaces; sides and lower parts uniform white.

Total length 780 millim.; tail 95.

Indian Ocean.

a. ♀ (V. 271) Indian Ocean. Sir E. Belcher [P] (Type)

6. Hydrophis cærulescens.

Hydrus cærulescens, *Shaw, Zool.* iii. p. 561 (1802).
Enhydris cærulescens, *Merr. Tent.* p. 140 (1820).
Hydrophis cærulescens, *Gray, Zool. Misc* p. 62 (1842), *and Cat.* p. 55 (1849); *Gunth. Rept. Brit. Ind.* p. 365, pl. xxv. fig. C (1864); *Bouleng. Faun. Ind., Rept.* p. 400 (1890).

Head very small; anterior part of the body very slender, its diameter about one third the depth of the posterior part. Rostral broader than deep; frontal longer than broad, shorter than its distance from the rostral, much shorter than the parietals; one præ- and one postocular; two superposed anterior temporals; seven upper labials, third and fourth entering the eye; chin-shields very small, posterior pair separated by scales. 35 to 38 scales round the neck, 48 to 50 round the body; scales rhomboidal, imbricate, with a strong short keel. Ventrals distinct throughout, 285-309. Grey above, with black cross-bands, broadest on the back, which form complete rings or are interrupted on the belly; head uniform black.

Total length 665 millim.; tail 75.

Bombay Coast, Bay of Bengal, Straits of Malacca.

a. ♂ (V. 294).	Bombay.	Dr Leith [P].
b. ♂ (V. 298).	Vizagapatam.	Dr. P. Russell [P.]. (Type.)
c. ♀ (V. 285).	Bengal.	Gen. Hardwicke [P.].
d. ♀ (V. 294).	Bengal.	
e. ♂ (V. 293).	Pinang.	Dr Cantor.
f, g–h. ♀ (V. 309, 285) & hgr. (V. 300).	—— ?	Zoological Society.

7. Hydrophis frontalis.

Hydrophis frontalis, *Jan, Elenco,* p. 110 (1863), and *Icon. Gén.* 39, pl. v. fig. 2 (1872).

Head very small; anterior part of body very slender, its diameter one third the depth of the posterior part. Rostral broader than deep; frontal longer than broad, as long as its distance from the end of the snout, a little shorter than the parietals, its point separating the præfrontals; one præ- and one postocular; two superposed anterior temporals; seven upper labials, third and fourth entering the eye; chin-shields very small, posterior separated by scales. 34 scales round the neck, 42 round the body; scales rhomboidal, imbricate, with a strong short keel. Ventrals 291. Whitish, with olive-grey cross-bars, broad on the back, tapering towards the belly; head blackish, with a yellow streak above and behind the eye.

Total length 560 millim.; tail 70.

Indian Ocean.

a. ♂ (V. 291). —— ? Zoological Society.

8. Hydrophis kingii.

Disteira doliata (*non Lacép.*), *Gray in King, Narr. Surv. Austral.* ii. p. 432 (1827).
Hydrophis doliata, part., *Gray, Cat.* p. 51 (1849).
—— elegans, part., *Günth. Rept. Brit. Ind.* p. 369 (1864).

Head small; anterior portion of body slender, its diameter one third the depth of the posterior part. Rostral as deep as broad; nasals shorter than the frontal, thrice as long as the suture between the præfrontals; frontal nearly twice as long as broad, as long as its distance from the end of the snout, as long as the parietals; one præ- and two postoculars; seven upper labials, second largest and in contact with the præfrontal, third and fourth entering the eye, fifth separated from the eye by a subocular; posterior chin-shields separated by a large scale. 27 scales round the neck, 37 round the body; scales all imbricate and keeled, the keels feeble on the neck, strong on the body. Ventrals very distinct throughout, 314, smooth or with two tubercles. Greyish white above, yellowish white beneath, with olive cross-bands on the back, wider than the interspaces; a black streak along the ventrals; head entirely black.

Total length 1200 millim.; tail 90.

North Coast of Australia.

a. ♀ (V. 314).   N Australia.   Capt. King [P.].

9. Hydrophis nigrocinctus.

Russell, Ind. Serp. ii. pl. vi. (1801)
Hydrophis nigrocinctus, *Daud Rept.* vii. p. 380 (1803); *Gray, Cat.* p. 51 (1849); *Gunth. Rept. Brit. Ind.* p. 368, pl. xxv fig. L (1864); *Fayrer, Thanatoph. Ind.* pl. xxv. (1874), *Bouleng. Faun. Ind., Rept.* p 400 (1890).
Enhydris nigrocinctus, *Merr Tent* p 140 (1820).
Hydrus nigrocinctus, *Boie, Isis*, 1827, p. 553.
Hydrophis nigrocinctus, part, *Schleg. Phys Serp* ii p. 505 (1837); *Dum. & Bibr.* vii. p. 1350 (1854).

Head small; anterior part of body slender, its diameter one third to two fifths the depth of the posterior part. Rostral broader than deep; nasals shorter than the frontal, about twice as long as the suture between the præfrontals; frontal longer than broad, as long as its distance from the end of the snout, shorter than the parietals; one præ- and one or two postoculars; a small loreal sometimes present; seven upper labials, third and fourth entering the eye, second and fourth largest; two superposed anterior temporals; two pairs of subequal chin-shields, posterior separated by scales. 27 or 29 scales round the neck, 39 round the body; scales imbricate, rhombic, keeled. Ventrals distinct, but feebly enlarged, 310–331. Pale olive above, yellowish inferiorly, with black annuli, which are broader on the back.

Total length 1000 millim.; tail 100.

Bay of Bengal and Straits of Malacca.

a. ♀ (V. 323).   Sunderbunds, Bengal.   Dr. P. Russell, College of Surgeons [E.]. (Type).
b. ♂ (V. 323).   Bengal.   Gen. Hardwicke [P.].
c. ♀ (V. 310).   India.   Gen. Hardwicke [P.].
d. Hgr. (V. 310).   Malay Archipelago.   Dr. Bleeker.

10. Hydrophis mamillaris.

Russell, Ind. Serp. i. pl. xliv. (1796).
Anguis mamillaris, *Daud. Rept* vii p. 340 (1803).
Hydrophis fasciata (*non Schn.*), *Gunth. Rept. Brit. Ind.* p. 374, pl. xxv. fig. Q (1864).
—— mamillaris, *Bouleng. Faun. Ind., Rept.* p. 401 (1890).

Head very small; anterior part of body very slender, its diameter about one third the depth of the posterior part. Rostral broader than deep; frontal longer than broad, as long as its distance from the end of the snout, a little shorter than the parietals; one præ- and two postoculars; two superposed anterior temporals; seven upper labials, third and fourth entering the eye; two pairs of chin-shields, in contact with each other. 25 to 27 scales round the neck, 35 round the body; scales rhomboidal and imbricate on the neck, hexagonal and juxtaposed on the body, with a tubercle or short keel. Ventrals distinct throughout, 287–316. Black, with yellowish annuli, which are interrupted on the belly.

Total length 650 millim.; tail 60.
Coasts of India.

a. Hgr. (V. 287).	Bombay.	Dr Leith [P].
b. ♂ (V. 316).	Vizagapatam.	Col. Beddome [C].

11. Hydrophis elegans.

Aturia elegans, *Gray, Zool Misc.* p. 63 (1842).
Hydrophis doliata, part., *Gray, Cat.* p. 51 (1849).
—— elegans, part., *Gunth. Rept. Brit. Ind.* p. 369, pl. xxv. fig. K' (1864).

Head small; anterior part of body slender, its diameter two fifths the depth of the posterior part. Rostral broader than deep; nasals nearly as long as the frontal, more than twice as long as the suture between the præfrontals; frontal a little longer than broad, as long as its distance from the rostral, much shorter than the parietals; one præ- and two postoculars, a single anterior temporal; seven upper labials, second largest and in contact with the præfrontal, third and fourth entering the eye; two pairs of chin-shields, posterior in contact with each other or separated by one scale. 27 to 30 scales round the neck, 41 to 43 round the body; scales imbricate, feebly keeled. Ventrals distinct throughout, 350–385. Yellowish white, back with transverse rhomboidal black spots, which may extend downwards to form annuli round the neck; transverse series of small black spots between the rhombs; belly with black spots or cross-bars, with or without a black streak running along the ventrals; head blackish, with a more or less distinct light crescentic marking across the snout, from above the eyes.

Total length 710 millim.; tail 60.
North Coast of Australia.

a. Yg. (V. 385).	Port Essington.	Mr. Gilbert [C]. (Type.)
b. Hgr. (V. 350).	Nicol Bay, N.W. Australia.	
c. Yg. (V. 352).	Rockhampton, Queensland	

12. Hydrophis pacificus. (Plate XII. fig. 2.)

Head small; body long, very slender anteriorly, the diameter of the neck one third the greatest depth of the body. Rostral as deep as broad; frontal twice as long as broad, as long as its distance from the rostral, shorter than the parietals; one præ- and two postoculars; a single, large anterior temporal; seven or eight upper labials, second largest and in contact with the præfrontal, third, fourth, and fifth entering the eye; two pairs of small chin-shields, in contact with each other. 27 to 29 scales round the neck, 37 to 39 round the body; scales imbricate or subimbricate, with a feeble short keel. Ventrals feebly enlarged, 310. Greyish olive above, white beneath, with 51 dark annuli.

Total length 940 millim.; tail 100.
New Britain.

a. ♂ (V. 310). New Britain. Museum Godeffroy.

13. Hydrophis latifasciatus. (Plate XIII.)

Hydrophis latifasciata, *Gunth. Rept. Brit. Ind.* p. 372, pl. xxv. fig. T (1864); *Blanf. Journ As. Soc Beng.* xlviii. 1879, p. 132; *Bouleng. Faun. Ind, Rept* p 401 (1890).

Head small; anterior part of body slender, its diameter about one third the depth of the posterior part. Rostral broader than deep; nasals slightly longer than the frontal, more than twice as long as the suture between the præfrontals; frontal small, longer than broad, much shorter than the parietals or than its distance from the rostral; one præ- and one postocular; præfrontal in contact with the second labial; a single large anterior temporal; six upper labials, second largest, third and fourth entering the eye, two pairs of chin-shields, posterior separated by scales; 21 scales round the neck, 33 round the body, scales imbricate and keeled. Ventrals distinct, but feebly enlarged, 322. Dark olive, sides with vertical yellowish bars; these bars continuous across the neck.

Total length 720 millim.; tail 75.
Mergui; Pegu.

a. ♀ (V. 322). Mergui Prof. Oldham [P.]. (Type.)

14. Hydrophis coronatus.

Hydrophis fasciata, part, *Gray, Cat* p. 50 (1849).
—— coronata, *Gunth Rept. Brit. Ind.* p. 372, pl. xxv. fig. M (1864); *Anders. Proc. Zool. Soc.* 1871, p. 192; *Fayrer, Thanatoph. Ind.* pl xxvi. (1874); *Bouleng. Faun. Ind., Rept.* p. 402 (1890).

Head very small, narrow; body long, extremely slender anteriorly. Rostral broader than deep; frontal small, a little longer than broad, hardly as long as its distance from the rostral; one præ- and one postocular; a single anterior temporal, descending to the labial border; six upper labials, third and fourth entering the eye; two pairs of chin-shields, in contact with each other. 19 to 23 scales round the neck, 29 to 33 round the body; all the scales rhomboidal and imbricate, dorsals with a keel, laterals with a central tubercle. Ventrals hardly distinct, 278–337. Head and neck blackish or dark green, the former with a horseshoe-shaped yellow mark above, the convexity on the snout, the latter with regular yellow cross-bands; body likewise with yellow cross-bands or rings, which may be interrupted on the back.

Total length 930 millim.; tail 80.

Bay of Bengal.

a, b. ♂ (V. 321) & ♀ (V. 337)	Bengal.	Gen Hardwicke [P.]. (Types.)
c–d. Yg. (V. 278, 278).	Bay of Bengal.	W. Theobald, Esq. [C.].

15. Hydrophis gracilis.

Russell, Ind. Serp. ii. pl xiii (1801).
Hydrus gracilis, *Shaw, Zool* iii p. 560 (1802).
Enhydris gracilis, *Merr. Tent* p. 141 (1820)
Disteira gracilis, *Fitzing. N. Class. Rept.* p. 55 (1826).
Microcephalophis gracilis, *Less. in Bélang. Voy. Ind. Or., Rept.* pl. iii. (1834); *Gray, Cat.* p. 46 (1849).
Liopala gracilis, *Gray, Zool. Misc* p. 60 (1842).
Thalassophis microcephala, *Schmidt, Abh. Naturw. Hamb.* ii. 1852, p. 78, pl. ii.
Hydrophis gracilis, part., *Dum. & Bibr.* vii. p. 1352 (1854).
—— microcephala, *Dum. & Bibr. t. c.* p 1356; *Fischer, Abh Naturw. Hamb.* iii. 1856, p. 52; *Jan, Icon. Gén* 41, pl. v fig. 2 (1872).
—— gracilis, *Gunth. Rept. Brit. Ind.* p. 373 (1864); *Murray, Zool. Sind*, p 395 (1884); *Bouleng. Faun. Ind, Rept.* p. 404 (1890); *Boettg. Ber. Offenb. Ver. Nat.* 1892, p 89
—— guentheri (*non Theob.*), *Murray, l. c.* p. 396, pl. —.

Head very small, narrow; body long, extremely slender anteriorly. Snout strongly projecting beyond the lower jaw; rostral as deep as broad; frontal very small, longer than broad, hardly as long as its distance from the rostral; one præ- and one postocular, a single anterior temporal, followed by a second equally large shield; six upper labials, third and fourth entering the eye; two pairs of small chin-shields, in contact with each other. 19 to 21 scales round the neck, 29 to 33 round the body; scales smooth, rhomboidal and imbricate anteriorly, elsewhere hexagonal, juxtaposed, each with two or more tubercles, which are feeble in the female and very strong in the male. Ventrals distinct only anteriorly, very feebly enlarged or split into two posteriorly, 225–297. Bluish black or greyish olive above in the adult, with more or less distinct lighter cross-bands anteriorly. Young with the head and neck black, the latter region with light transverse bands; body with rhombic black cross-bands continued to the belly or subinterrupted on the sides; or black, with a series of elliptical vertical whitish spots on each side.

Total length 1020 millim.; tail 90.

Coasts of Persia, India, and Burma; Malay Archipelago.

a. Yg. (V. 233).	Jask, Persia.	W. T. Blanford, Esq. [P.].
b. ♀ (V. 252).	Malabar.	Col. Beddome [C.].
c. ♂ (V. 257).	Ceylon	E. W. H Holdsworth, Esq. [C.].

d–e. ♂ (V. 228) & ♀ (V. 297).	Madras.	T. C. Jerdon, Esq. [P.].
f–g. ♂ (V. 246, 225).	Madras.	F. Day, Esq. [P.].
h. Yg. (V. 231).	Madras	J E. Boileau, Esq. [P.].
i. Yg (V. 262).	Madras	Col. Beddome [C.].
k. H( )(V. 254).	India.	
l. Skull.	Indian Ocean.	

16. Hydrophis cantoris. (PLATE XIV.)

? Liopala fasciata, *Gray, Zool. Misc.* p. 60 (1842).
Hydrus gracilis, part., *Cantor, Cat. Mal Rept.* p. 130 (1847).
Hydrophis fasciata, part., *Gray, Cat* p. 50 (1849)
—— cantoris, *Gunth. Rept. Brit. Ind* p. 374, pl. xxv. fig. U (1864); *Anders. Proc Zool. Soc.* 1871, p. 192; *F. Müll. Verh. Nat. Ges. Basel*, viii 1887, p. 278; *Boettg Ber Senck. Ges.* 1889, p. 304; *Bouleng. Faun. Ind., Rept.* p. 405 (1864).

Head very small, narrow; body long, extremely slender anteriorly. Rostral considerably deeper than broad, frontal small, longer than broad, hardly as long as its distance from the rostral; one præ- and one postocular, a single anterior temporal, followed by a second equally large shield; six upper labials, third and fourth entering the eye; two pairs of small chin-shields, in contact with each other. 23 to 25 scales round the neck, 41 to 43 round the body; scales smooth, rhomboidal and imbricate anteriorly, elsewhere hexagonal, juxtaposed, each with two or three tubercles one before the other. Ventrals hardly enlarged, 412–456. Body dark olive or blackish anteriorly, with yellowish cross-bands above; posterior part of body olive above, yellowish on the sides; tail with olive vertical bars; a blackish streak along the belly.

Total length 1100 millim.; tail 90.

Bay of Bengal.

a. ♂ (V. 440).	Pinang	Dr. Cantor. (Type.)
b. ♂ (V 424)	Ganjam	F. Day, Esq. [P.].
c. Yg, bad state.	Indian Ocean.	

17. Hydrophis fasciatus.

Hydrus fasciatus, *Schneid. Hist Amph.* i p. 240 (1799).
Pelamis fasciatus, *Merr. Tent* p. 139 (1820).
Disteira fasciata, *Fitzing. N. Class. Rept.* p. 55 (1826).
Hydrophis gracilis, part, *Schleg Phys. Serp.* ii. p. 507 (1837); *Dum. & Bibr.* vii. p. 1352 (1854); *Fischer, Abh. Naturw. Hamb.* iii. 1856, p. 54; *Jan, Icon. Gén.* 41, pl. iv. fig. 2 (1872).
—— chloris (*non Daud.*), *Gunth. Rept. Brit. Ind.* p. 370 (1864); *Anders. Proc Zool Soc.* 1871, p 191, and 1872, p. 396; *Fayrer, Thanatoph Ind.* pl xxvii. (1874); *Murray, Zool. Sind*, p. 392 (1884).
Aturia lindsayi, *Gray, Zool Misc* p 61 (1842).
Hydrophis obscura, part., *Gray, Cat.* p. 49 (1849).
—— lindsayi, *Gray, l. c* p. 50; *Gunth. l. c.* p. 371; *Anders ll. cc.* pp. 396, 191; *Murray, l. c.*
—— atriceps, *Gunth. l. c.* p. 371, pl. xxv. fig. I.

Hydrophis fasciatus, *Peters, Mon. Berl. Ac.* 1872, p 849, pl. i. fig. 1; *Bouleng. Faun. Ind., Rept.* p. 404 (1890); *Boettg. Ber. Offenb. Ver. Nat.* 1892, pp. 89 & 155.

Head very small; body long, very slender anteriorly. Rostral nearly as deep as broad; frontal longer than broad, as long as its distance from the rostral; one præ- and one or two postoculars; a single anterior temporal, followed by a second equally large; six or seven upper labials, third and fourth entering the eye, second largest and usually in contact with the præfrontal; two pairs of small chin-shields, in contact with each other. 25 to 31 scales round the neck, 40 to 48 round the body; all the scales rhomboidal and imbricate, or scales subimbricate or juxtaposed on the posterior part of the body, on the neck smooth, on the body with a small tubercle or short keel. Ventrals feebly enlarged, 345–500. Head and neck black, the latter with yellowish cross-bands; body pale, with black cross-bands or annuli, which are broadest on the back.

Total length 1000 millim.; tail 85.

From the coasts of India to China and New Guinea.

a.-♂ (V. 402).	Malabar.	
b. ♀ (V. 447).	Madras.	T. C. Jerdon, Esq. [P.].
c. ♂ (V. 364).	Siam.	(Type of *H. atriceps*.)
d. ♀ (V. 412).	Siam.	
e. Yg. (V. 452).	China.	W. Lindsay, Esq. [P.].
		(Type of *A. lindsayi*.)
f. Yg. (V. 430).	Pinang.	Dr. Cantor.
g-h. Yg. (V. 370, 400).	Malay Archipelago.	Dr Bleeker.
i. ♀ (V. 500).	East Indies	T. C Eyton, Esq [P.].
k-l. Hgr (V. 435) & yg. (V. 458).	East Indies.	East India Company [P.].
m. ♀ (V. 425).	——?	Haslar Collection.
n. ♂ (V. 353).	——?	Dr Gunther [P.].
		(Type of *H. atriceps*.)

18. Hydrophis brookii.

Hydrophis brookii, *Gunth. Proc. Zool. Soc.* 1872, p. 597, fig.

Head very small; body long, extremely slender anteriorly. Rostral a little broader than deep; frontal slightly longer than broad, as long as its distance from the end of the snout, much shorter than the parietals; one præ- and one postocular; a single anterior temporal, followed by a second equally large; six upper labials, third and fourth entering the eye, second largest and in contact with the præfrontal; two pairs of small chin-shields, in contact with each other. 30 scales round the neck, 42 round the body; all the scales rhomboidal and imbricate, on the neck smooth, on the body with a small tubercle or short keel. Ventrals feebly enlarged, 416. Head and anterior part of body black, the former with a horseshoe-shaped yellowish marking on the head, the latter with yellow rings, the anterior of which are interrupted below;

further back the body annulate with black, the interspaces narrow and pale olive above, broader and yellow beneath.

Total length 970 millim.; tail 95.

Borneo.

a. ♀ (V. 416). Borneo. (Type.)

The specimen contains fully developed young, which differ from the mother in the præfrontals forming a suture, instead of being separated by the frontal.

19. Hydrophis melanocephalus. (PLATE XV.)

Hydrophis sublævis, var. melanocephala, part., *Gray, Cat.* p 53 (1849).

Head very small; body long, very slender anteriorly. Rostral a little broader than deep; frontal nearly twice as long as broad, as long as its distance from the rostral, a little shorter than the parietals; one præ- and one postocular; a single anterior temporal; seven or eight upper labials, third and fourth or third, fourth, and fifth entering the eye, second largest and in contact with the præfrontal; two pairs of small chin-shields, in contact with each other. 25 scales round the neck, 35 round the body, all the scales rhomboidal and imbricate, on the neck smooth, on the body with a small tubercle or short keel. Ventrals feebly enlarged, 329. Head and anterior part of body black, the former with a yellowish spot on the forehead and a yellowish streak behind the eye, the latter with yellow rings interrupted below; body olive above, yellow beneath, with black annuli, which are broader on the back.

Total length 1070 millim.; tail 85.

Indian Ocean.

a. ♀ (V. 329). Indian Ocean. Sir E. Belcher [P.]. (Type.)

20. Hydrophis torquatus.

Hydrophis nigrocincta, part., *Schleg Phys. Serp.* ii. p. 506, pl. xviii. figs. 11 & 12 (1837).

Hydrus nigrocinctus, *Cantor, Cat Mal. Rept.* p. 128 (1847).

Hydrophis torquata, *Gunth Rept Bit Ind* p. 369, pl. xxv. fig. H (1864); *Bouleng. Faun. Ind., Rept.* p 402 (1890).

Head small; anterior part of body slender, its diameter about one third the depth of the posterior part. Rostral broader than deep; nasals longer than the frontal, at least twice as long as the suture between the præfrontals; frontal small, as long as broad or a little longer than broad, shorter than its distance from the rostral, much shorter than the parietals; one præ- and one postocular; præfrontal in contact with the second labial; a single, large anterior temporal; six or seven upper labials, second largest, third and fourth entering the eye; two pairs of subequal chin-shields, in contact with each other. 33 or 35 scales round the neck, 43 or 45 round the body; scales imbricate and keeled.

Ventrals distinct, but feebly enlarged, 240–285. Pale greyish olive, with blackish cross-bands tapering on the sides.

Total length 560 millim.; tail 50.

Bay of Bengal and Straits of Malacca.

a–e. ♀ (V. 283, 285) & yg. (V. 282, 252, 240).	East Indies.	East India Co. [P.]. (Types.)

21. Hydrophis obscurus.

Russell, Ind. Serp. pls. vii. & viii. (1801).
Hydrophis obscurus, *Daud. Rept.* vii. p. 375 (1803); *Bouleng Faun. Ind., Rept.* p. 403 (1890); *Boettg. Ber. Offenb. Ver. Nat.* 1892, p. 88.
—— chloris, *Daud. t. c.* p. 377, pl. xc.
Pelamis obscurus, *Merr. Tent* p. 139 (1820).
—— chloris, *Merr. l c*
Hydrophis diadema, *Günth. Rept. Brit. Ind.* p. 373, pl. xxv. fig. S (1864).
—— stricticollis, *Günth. l. c.* p. 376, pl. xxv. fig. R; *Anders. Proc. Zool. Soc.* 1872, p. 397; *Fayrer, Thanatoph. Ind.* pl. xxviii. (1874), *Gunth. Ann & Mag. N. H.* (4) ix. 1872, p. 33; *Peters, Mon. Berl. Ac.* 1872, p. 858.

Head very small; body very long, extremely slender anteriorly. Rostral broader than deep; frontal longer than broad, as long as its distance from the rostral or the end of the snout; one præ- and one or two postoculars; a single anterior temporal; seven or eight upper labials; second largest, third and fourth entering the eye; two pairs of chin-shields, posterior smallest and usually separated by scales. 33 to 40 scales round the neck, 40 to 50 round the body; scales rhomboidal, imbricate, feebly keeled in the female, strongly in the male, the keels often broken up into tubercles. Ventrals very feebly enlarged, longer than broad under the neck, bicarinate in the male, 310–438. Olive or dark green above, with yellowish cross-bars, which form complete rings round the slender part of the body; on the other two-thirds of the body these bands are interrupted on the back; a yellow spot on the snout and a yellow streak on each side of the upper surface of the head; or pale olive, with dark cross-bands forming rings on the anterior part of the body.

Total length 970 millim.; tail 105.

Bay of Bengal; Malay Archipelago.

a. ♂ (V. 338).	Sunderbunds, Bengal.	Dr. P. Russell, College of Surgeons [E.]. (Type).
b. ♀ (V. 332).	Sunderbunds.	Dr P. Russell, College of Surgeons [E.]. (Type of *H. chloris*).
c. ♀ (V. 370).	Sandheads, Bengal.	Sir J. Fayrer [P.].
d–e ♀ (V. 401, 438).	Bassein R.	W. Theobald, Esq. [C.].
f, g. ♂ (V. 384) & yg. (V. 342).	Pegu.	W. Theobald, Esq. [C.].
h. Yg. (V. 398).	Bay of Bengal.	East India Co. [P.]. (Type of *H. stricticollis*.)
i. ♀ (V. 310).	Borneo	
k–l. Hgr. (V. 318, 315).	——?	Haslar Collection. (Types of *H. diadema*.)
m. Hgr. V. 371	——	

22. Hydrophis leptodira.

Hydrophis gracilis (*non Shaw*), *Cantor, Trans. Zool. Soc.* ii. 1840, p. 311, pl lvi.

Head very small, narrow; body long, extremely slender anteriorly. Snout strongly projecting beyond the lower jaw; rostral broader than deep; frontal very small, longer than broad, hardly as long as its distance from the rostral; one præ- and one post-ocular; a single anterior temporal, followed by a second equally large shield; six upper labials, second largest and in contact with the præfrontal, third and fourth entering the eye, two pairs of small chin-shields, in contact with each other. 31 scales round the neck, 58 round the body; scales smooth, rhomboidal, and imbricate anteriorly, hexagonal, juxtaposed and with a short keel posteriorly. Ventrals very small but distinct throughout, 483. Black, with yellow cross-bars on the neck and complete annuli on the body, the bars and annuli numbering 77.

Total length 525 millim.; tail 40.

Mouths of the Ganges.

a. Hgr. (V. 483). Mouths of the Ganges. Dr. Cantor.

This is the actual specimen figured by Cantor in 1840. Until quite lately it was preserved in the Museum of the University of Oxford.

209. DISTIRA.

Hydrophis, part, *Daud. Hist Rept.* vii. p. 372 (1803); *Wagler, Syst. Amph.* p. 165 (1830), *Schleg. Phys. Serp* ii. p 488 (1837); *Gray, Cat. Sn.* p. 49 (1849), *Dum. & Bibr. Erp. Gén.* vii. p. 1341 (1854); *Fischer, Abh. Naturw Hamb* iii. 1856, p. 40, *Jan, Elenco sist. Ofid.* p 109 (1863); *Günth. Rept. Brit. Ind* p. 360 (1864).
Disteira, *Lacép Ann. Mus.* iv. 1804, p. 210; *Dum. & Bibr. t. c.* p. 1329; *Cope, Proc. Ac. Philad.* 1859, p. 346, *Jan, l c* p. 109, *Gunth. l. c.* p. 358; *Bouleng. Faun. Ind., Rept.* p. 407 (1890).
Leioselasma, *Lacép l. c.*
Pelamis, part., *Merrem, Tent. Syst Amph* p. 138 (1820).
Enhydris, part., *Merr. l. c.* p 140.
Aturia, part., *Gray, Zool. Misc.* p 61 (1842).
Aturia, *Gray, Cat Sn* p. 45 (1849).
Chitulia, *Gray, l c.* p 56.
Kerilia, *Gray, l. c.* p. 57.
Hydrus, *Gray, l. c.* p. 58.
Thalassophis, part., *Schmidt, Abh. Naturw. Hamb.* ii. 1852, p. 75
Astrotia, *Fischer, Abh. Naturw. Hamb.* iii. 1856, p. 38; *Jan, l. c.* p. 108.

Maxillary longer than the lower aspect of the ectopterygoid, not extending forwards as far as the palatine; poison-fangs large, followed by 4 to 10 grooved teeth; anterior mandibular teeth usually grooved. Head moderate or rather small; nostrils superior, pierced in a single or divided nasal shield, which is in contact with its fellow; head-shields large; præocular present, loreal usually absent. Body more or less elongate; scales on the anterior part of the body imbricate; ventrals more or less distinct, very small.

Indian and Pacific Oceans, from the Persian Gulf to Japan and New Caledonia.

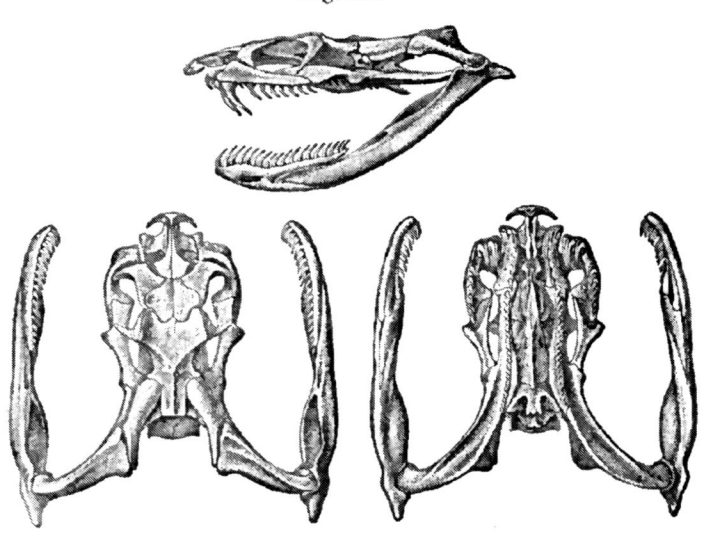

Fig. 20.

Skull of *Distira stokesii*.

Synopsis of the Species.

I. All the scales strongly imbricate; ventrals usually in pairs and pointed, except quite anteriorly; no chin-shields; 39–47 scales round the neck, 48–57 round the body; ventrals 230–267.
                                1. *stokesii*, p. 288.

II. Scales on posterior part of body feebly imbricate, or juxtaposed; 23–42 scales round the neck, 32–50 round the body; one or two pairs of chin-shields.

  A. Frontal shield longer than broad.

    1. Second pair of chin-shields, if distinct, separated by several scales.

      a. Two or three superposed anterior temporals; ventrals 200–300.

Rostral as deep as broad; 31–36 scales round the neck, 36–41 round the body .... 2. *major*, p. 289.

Rostral broader than deep; 35–42 scales round the neck, 40–50 round the body............ .... 3. *ornata*, p. 290.

Rostral broader than deep; 28–33 scales round the neck, 38–43 round the body. .... 4. *godeffroyi*, p. 291.

  b. A single anterior temporal; 27 scales round the neck, 38 round the body; ventrals 329–335.

Two postoculars; two labials entering the eye .... 5. *melanosoma*, p. 291.

One postocular; three labials entering the eye .... 6. *semperi*, p. 292.

 2. Two pairs of chin-shields in contact on the middle line or the posterior separated by a single scale.

  a. A single anterior temporal.

   α. Rostral broader than deep; ventrals 300–354.

23–25 scales round the neck; frontal hardly as long as its distance from the rostral .... 7. *subcincta*, p. 292.

27–31 scales round the neck; frontal as long as its distance from the rostral or the end of the snout.... 8. *brugmansii*, p. 292.

38 scales round the neck .... 9. *tuberculata*, p. 293.

   β. Rostral as deep as broad; ventrals 372–400; 27–29 scales round the neck.. 10. *grandis*, p. 293.

  b. Two or three superposed anterior temporals.

   α. Scales all imbricate.

31–35 scales round the neck, 43–45 round the body; ventrals 220–256. 11. *macfarlani*, p. 294.

27–33 scales round the neck, 39–45 round the body; ventrals 281–385. 12. *cyanocincta*, p. 294.

26–27 scales round the neck, 48–49 round the body; ventrals 278 .... 13. *bituberculata*, p. 296.

   β. Scales on posterior part of body juxtaposed.

25 scales round the neck, 34 round the body; ventrals 317..... .. . 14. *belcheri*, p. 296.

27–29 scales round the neck, 38 round the body, ventrals 258–260...... 15. *pachycercus*, p. 297.

30–33 scales round the neck, 43–47 round the body; ventrals 300–387. 16. *lapemidoides*, p. 297.

 B. Frontal shield as broad as long; anterior ventrals relatively large; 27–29 scales round the neck, 37–43 round the body.
           17. *viperina*, p. 298.

 III. Scales slightly imbricate, 15–17 round the neck, 19–21 round the body................... 18. *jerdonii*, p. 299.

TABLE SHOWING NUMBERS OF SCALES AND SHIELDS.

	Sc. neck.	Sc. body.	V.	Lab	Ant. temp.
stokesii	39–47	48–57	230–267	9–10	2–3
major	31–36	36–41	200–236	7–8	2
ornata	35–42	40–50	210–300	7–8	2–3
godeffroyi	28–33	38–43	238–294	7	2
melanosoma	27	38	335	7	1
semperi	?	38	329	8	1
subcincta	23–25	35	342	7	1
brugmansii	27–31	32–40	300–354	7	1
tuberculata	38	?	321	?	1
grandis	27–29	41–45	372–400	7	1
macfarlani	31–35	43–45	220–256	7–8	2
cyanocincta	27–33	39–45	281–385	7–8	2
bituberculata	26–27	48–49	278	8	2
belcheri	25	34	317	5–6	2
pachycercus	27–29	38–39	258–260	8	2
lapemidoides	30–33	43–47	300–387	8	2–3
viperina	27–29	37–43	235–267	7–8	1–2
jerdonii	15–17	19–21	224–238	5	1

1. **Distira stokesii.**

Hydrus major, part., *Shaw, Zool.* iii. p. 558 (1802).
—— stokesii, *Gray, in Stokes, Discov. Australia,* i. p. 502, pl iii.(1846)
—— major, *Gray, Cat.* p. 58 (1849).
Hydrophis schizopholis, *Schmidt, Abh. Naturw. Hamb.* i. 1852, p. 166, pl xv.; *Dum. & Bibr.* vii p. 1357 (1854).
—— annulatus, *Gray, l. c.* p 59
Astrotia schizopholis, *Fischer, Abh. Naturw. Hamb* iii. 1856, p. 38; *Jan, Icon. Gén.* 39, pl. iii. (1872)
Hydrophis stokesii, *Gunth. Rept. Brit. Ind.* p. 363 (1864); *Peters & Doria, Ann. Mus. Genova,* xiii. 1878, p. 415.
? Hydrophis guentheri, *Theob. Cat. Rept. As. Soc. Mus.* 1868, p. 69.
? Hydrophis granosa, *Anders. Proc. Zool. Soc.* 1871, p. 190.
Hydrophis guttata, *Murray, Journ. Bomb. N. H. Soc.* ii. 1887, p. 34.
Distira stokesii, *Bouleng. Faun. Ind., Rept.* p. 408 (1890).

Head moderate; body stout. Rostral as deep as broad; nasals shorter than the frontal, more than twice as long as the suture between the præfrontals; frontal longer than broad, as long as or slightly longer than its distance from the rostral; one præ- and two postoculars; nine or ten upper labials, fourth, fifth, and sixth entering the eye, if not divided to form a series of suboculars; two or three superposed anterior temporals; no chin-shields. 39 to 47 scales round the neck, 48 to 57 round the body; scales much imbricate, pointed, keeled, the keels frequently broken up into two tubercles. Ventrals usually distinct only quite anteriorly, then in pairs and not larger than the adjoining scales, 230–267. Yellowish or pale brownish, with broad black dorsal cross-bands, or with complete black annuli.

Total length 1510 millim.; tail 200.

From the Mekran Coast and the Chinese Sea to the North Coast of Australia.

209. DISTIRA.

a. ♂ (V. 250).	Mekran Coast.	Capt. E. Bishop [C.]. (Type of *H. guttata*.)
b. ♀ (V. 240).	Singapore.	(Type of *H. annulatus*.)
c. ♂ (V. 256).	Singapore.	Haslar Collection.
d. ♀ (V. 235.)	Indian Ocean.	(One of the types of *H. major*.)
e. ♂ (V. 249).	Indian Ocean.	
f. ♀ (V. 267).	Coast of Australia.	Capt. Stokes [P.].
g. ♂ (V. 240).	Coast of Australia.	Capt. Drevar [C.].
h. Ad., skin.	Port Walcott, N.W. Australia.	Capt. Beckett [P.].
i, k. Hgr. (V. 260) & yg. (V. 230).	Port Essington.	Lord Derby [P.].
l. Ad., skin.	Torres Straits.	W. Wykeham Perry, Esq. [P.]
m. Skull.	Holothuria Bank, N.W. Australia.	J. J. Walker, Esq. [P.].

2. Distira major.

Hydrus major, part., *Shaw, Zool.* iii. p. 558, pl. cxxiv. (1802).
Disteira doliata, *Lacép. Ann. Mus.* iv. 1804, pp. 199 & 210, pl lvii. fig. 2; *Dum & Bibr.* vii. p. 1331 (1854), *Gunth. Rept. Brit. Ind.* p. 359 (1864).
Pelamis shawii, *Merr. Tent.* p. 139 (1820).
Hydrophis mentalis, *Gray, Zool. Misc.* p. 62 (1842), and *Cat.* p. 53 (1849).
Disteira dumerilii, *Jan, Rev. & Mag. Zool.* 1859, p. 149, *Cope, Proc. Ac. Philad.* 1859, p. 347; *Jan, Icon. Gén.* 39, pl. iv. (1872).
Hydrophis protervus, *Jan, l. c* p. 150, and *Prodr* pl D (1859); *Bavay, Mém. Soc. Linn. Norm.* xv. no. 5, 1869, p. 36.
—— lacepedei, *Jan, Prodr.* pl. D.
—— major, *Gunth. l. c.* p. 363, pl. xxv. fig. G.
Hydrophis, sp., *Forné, Note Serp. Mer, Nouméa*, p. 6, pl. —. figs. 1–5 (1888).
Distira major, *Bouleng. Faun. Ind., Rept.* p. 407 (1890).

Head moderate; body stout. Rostral as deep as broad; nasals shorter than the frontal, more than twice as long as the suture between the præfrontals; frontal longer than broad, as long as its distance from the end of the snout; one præ- and one or two post-oculars; two superposed anterior temporals; seven or eight upper labials, third and fourth entering the eye; one pair of small chin-shields. 31 to 36 scales round the neck, 36 to 41 round the body; scales keeled, imbricate, strongly on the neck, feebly on the body. Ventrals distinct, but very small, smooth or bicarinate, 200–236. Yellowish or pale brownish above, regularly barred with blackish or with alternately broad and narrow dark bars; white beneath, with or without small dark brown spots.

Total length 1050 millim.; tail 120.

North Coast of Australia to New Caledonia.

a. ♂ (V. 236).	Indian Ocean.	(One of the types of *H. major*. Type of *H. mentalis*.)
b. Yg. (V 215).	Nicol Bay, N.W. Australia.	Mr. Duboulay [C.].

c. ♂ (V. 217).	Holothuria Bank, N.W. Australia.		J. J. Walker, Esq. [P.].
d. Hgr. (V. 233).	Cape York.		
e. Hgr. (V. 200).	Off Cooktown, N. Queensland.		Capt. Drevar [C.].

3. Distira ornata.

Aturia ornata, *Gray, Zool. Misc.* p 61 (1842), *and Cat.* p. 45 (1849).
Hydrophis ocellata, *Gray, Cat* p 53, *Gunth. Rept. Brit Ind.* p. 378, pl. xxv. fig. P (1864); *Peters & Doria, Ann. Mus. Genova,* xiii. 1878, p. 416.
Chitulia inornata, *Gray, Cat.* p. 56.
Thalassophis schlegelii, *Schmidt, Abh. Naturw. Hamb.* ii. 1852, p. 83, pl. v.
Hydrophis striatus, part., *Dum. & Bibr.* vii. p. 1347 (1854).
—— schlegelii, *Fischer, Abh. Naturw. Hamb.* iii. 1856, p. 50; *Jan, Icon. Gén.* 40, pl. vi. fig 1 (1872).
—— lævis, *Lutken, Vidensk Meddel.* 1862, p 309, pl i. fig 6.
—— ornata, *Gunth. l. c.* p. 376, pl. xxv. fig. V; *Boettg. Zool. Anz.* 1888, p. 397.
—— elliotti, *Gunth. l. c.* p. 377, pl. xxv. fig. N.
—— striatus, *Jan, l. c.* pl. v. fig. 1.
Distira ornata, *Bouleng. Faun. Ind., Rept.* p. 411 (1890).

Head moderate; body moderately elongate. Rostral broader than deep; nasals shorter than the frontal, two or three times as long as the suture between the præfrontals; frontal longer than broad, as long as or a little longer than its distance from the rostral or the end of the snout, shorter than the parietals; one præ- and two or three postoculars; seven or eight upper labials, second largest, third and fourth entering the eye; two or three superposed anterior temporals; anterior chin-shields in contact, posterior chin-shields, if distinct, separated by two or three scales. 35 to 42 scales round the neck, 40 to 50 round the middle of the body; scales juxtaposed and hexagonal in the middle of the body, feebly imbricate anteriorly, smooth in the young, with a central tubercle or short keel in the adult. Ventrals distinct, but feebly enlarged, 210–300. Young with blackish cross-bands, tapering on the sides, and with one or more lateral series of roundish dark spots; the bands may become confluent in some specimens, which are uniform blackish olive above and white beneath.

Total length 1200 millim.; tail 130.

From the mouth of the Persian Gulf and the coasts of India and Ceylon to New Guinea and North Australia.

a. Yg. (V. 232).	Indian Ocean.	(Type.)	
b. ♂ (V. 240).	Indian Ocean.	Sir E. Belcher [P.].	
		(Type of *C. inornata*.)	
c. ♀ (V. 265)	Muscat.	A. S. G. Jayakar, Esq. [P.].	
d. Hgr. (V. 235).	India.	J. Kempe, Esq. [P.].	
e. ♀ (V. 220).	Trevandrum, Travancore.	H. S. Ferguson, Esq. [P.].	
f. Yg. (V. 218).	Ceylon.	Sir A. Smith [P.].	
g. Yg. (V. ...).	...	T. C. Jerdon, Esq. [P.].	
h. ♀ (V. ...).	...		

i. ♂ (V. 275).	Holothuria Bank, N.W. Australia.	J. J. Walker, Esq. [P.].
k. Hgr. (V. 200).	Australia.	J. Macgillivray, Esq. [C.], Lord Derby [P.]. (Type of *H ocellata*.)
l. ♀ (V. 274).	Australia.	J. Baines, Esq [P.].
m, n–o. ♂ (V. 280) & yg. (V. 228, 215).	—— ?	College of Surgeons.
p. Yg. (V. 210).	—— ?	

4. Distira godeffroyi.

Hydrophis godeffroyi, *Peters, Mon. Berl. Ac.* 1872, p. 856, pl. i. fig 3

Head moderate; body stout. Rostral broader than deep; nasals shorter than the frontal, twice as long as the suture between the præfrontals; frontal longer than broad, as long as its distance from the rostral, shorter than the parietals; one præ- and two post-oculars; two superposed anterior temporals; seven upper labials, third and fourth entering the eye; two pairs of chin-shields, posterior separated by a pair of scales. 28 to 33 scales round the neck, 38 to 43 round the body; scales subimbricate on the neck, juxtaposed on the body, with a tubercle or short keel, which is very strong in the male. Ventrals distinct, bituberculate, 238–294. Yellowish or pale brown above, yellowish white beneath, with broad blackish cross-bars narrowing on the sides and encircling or nearly encircling the body; head dark olive above.

Total length 740 millim.; tail 85.

Kingsmill Islands.

a–b. ♂ (V. 238) & ♀ (V. 249).	—— ?	Dr. J. G. Fischer.

5. Distira melanosoma.

Hydrophis melanosoma, *Gunth. Rept. Brit. Ind.* p. 367, pl xxv fig. E (1864).

Head rather small and short; body elongate. Rostral a little broader than deep; nasals shorter than the frontal, twice as long as the suture between the præfrontals; frontal much longer than broad, as long as its distance from the rostral, shorter than the parietals; one præ- and one postocular; a single large anterior temporal; seven upper labials, second largest and in contact with the præfrontal, third and fourth entering the eye; two pairs of chin-shields, the posterior separated by a pair of scales. 27 scales round the neck, 38 round the body; scales imbricate, strongly keeled. Ventrals distinct throughout, bicarinate, 335. Black above, with 66 narrow light rings, more or less interrupted, on the belly, greenish beneath, bright yellow on the sides.

Total length 1250 millim.; tail 130.

Habitat unknown.

a. ♀. (V. 335).	—— ?	College of Surgeons [E.]. (Type.)

6. Distira semperi.

Hydrophis semperi, *Garm. Bull. Mus. Comp. Zool.* viii. 1881, p. 85.

Rostral nearly as deep as broad; nasal grooved from the nostril to the second labial; frontal little less than twice as long as broad; one præ- and two postoculars; a single, large anterior temporal; eight upper labials, third, fourth, and fifth entering the eye; two pairs of chin-shields, anterior larger. Scales smooth, imbricate, 38 round the middle of the body. Ventrals small, 329. Black, crossed by 57 narrow white bands which do not meet on the belly.

Lake Taal, Luzon.

Perhaps specifically identical with the preceding.

7. Distira subcincta.

Hydrophis subcinctus, *Gray, Zool. Misc* p. 63 (1842), *and Cat.* p. 52 (1849): *Gunth. Rept. Brit. Ind.* p. 368, pl. xxv. fig. F (1864).

Head small; body much elongate; neck slender, its diameter about one third the greatest depth of the body. Rostral broader than deep; nasals as long as the frontal, more than twice as long as the suture between the præfrontals; frontal much longer than broad, hardly as long as its distance from the rostral, much shorter than the parietals; one præ- and two postoculars; a single, large anterior temporal, descending nearly to the border of the mouth; seven upper labials, second largest, third and fourth entering the eye; two pairs of chin-shields, in contact with each other. 23 to 25 scales round the neck, 35 round the body; scales feebly imbricate, feebly keeled. Ventrals very distinct, 342. "Trunk with 41 broad dark cross-bands, about as broad as the interspaces, not extending downwards to the middle of the side; a series of small, roundish, blackish spots along the lower part of the sides."

Total length 1070 millim.; tail 100.

Indian Ocean.

a. ♀ (V. 342).   Indian Ocean.   (Type.)

8. Distira brugmansii.

Hydrophis brugmansii, *Boie, Isis,* 1827, p. 554.
—— nigrocincta, part., *Schleg Phys. Serp.* ii. p. 505, pl. xviii. figs. 8–10 (1837).
—— sublævis, *Gray, Zool. Misc.* p. 62 (1842).
Hydrus striatus, part., *Cantor, Cat. Mal. Rept.* p. 126 (1847).
Hydrophis sublævis, part., *Gray, Cat.* p. 52 (1849).
—— nigrocincta (*non Daud.*), *Fischer, Abh. Naturw. Hamb.* iii. 1856, p. 46, pl. i.
—— cyanocincta, part., *Günth. Rept. Brit. Ind.* p. 367 (1864).
—— robusta, *Gunth. l. c.* p. 364; *Fayrer, Thanatoph. Ind.* pl. xxi. (1874); *Murray, Zool. Sind,* p. 394 (1884); *Anders. Journ. Linn. Soc.* xxi. 1889, p. 347.
—— rappii, *Jan, Icon. Gén.* 41, pl. iv. fig. 1 (1872).
—— temporalis, *Blanf. Proc. Zool. Soc.* 1881, p. 680, fig.
—— bishopii, *Murray, l. c.* p 391, pl. —.
Distira robusta, *Bouling. Faun. Ind., Rept.* p. 400 (1890).

Head moderate, body elongate. Rostral broader than deep, nasals shorter than the frontal, about twice as long as the suture between the præfrontals; frontal much longer than broad, as long as its distance from the rostral or the end of the snout, shorter than the parietals; one præ- and one or two postoculars; a single large anterior temporal, sometimes descending to the labial margin; seven upper labials, second largest, third and fourth or third, fourth, and fifth entering the eye; two pairs of subequal chin-shields, in contact on the middle line. 27 to 31 scales round the neck, 32 to 40 round the body; scales rhomboidal and subimbricate, smooth or each with a more or less distinct central tubercle or short obtuse keel. Ventrals distinct throughout, smooth or bitubercular, 300–354. Greenish yellow above, dorsal scales with black margins, with black crossbands or annuli, which are narrower than the interspaces between them; sides and lower parts yellow; end of tail black.

Total length 1800 millim.; tail 120.

Persian Gulf and coasts of India, Burma, and the Malay Archipelago.

a. ♀ (V. 354).	Gangestun, Persia.	(Type of *H. temporalis*.)
b–c. ♀ (V. 348) & hgr. (V. 320).	Muscat.	A. S. G. Jayakar, Esq. [P.].
d. ♂ (V. 323).	Kurrachee.	Mr J. A. Murray [C.].
e. ♀ (V. 312).	Malabar.	Col. Beddome [C.].
f. ♀ (V. 331).	Madras.	T. C. Jerdon, Esq. [P.].
g–h. Hgr. (V. 322) & yg. (V. 300.).	Madras.	Dr. J. R. Henderson [P.].
i. ♀ (V. 330).	Pinang.	Dr. Cantor.
k. ♀ (V. 336).	Indian Ocean.	(Type of *H. sublævis*.)
l. ♀ (V. 310).	——?	(Type of *H. robusta*.)

9. Distira tuberculata.

Hydrophis tuberculata, *Anders Journ. As. Soc. Beng.* xl, 1871, p. 18; *Murray, Zool. Sind*, p. 393 (1884).

Distira tuberculata, *Bouleng. Faun. Ind., Rept.* p. 409 (1890).

Head moderate, neck not very slender. Rostral broader than deep; head-shields studded with minute granules; fourth and fifth labials below the eye; one præ- and two postoculars; anterior temporal large and almost entering the labial margin, two pairs of large square chin-shields in contact with each other. 38 rows of slightly imbricate scales round the neck, each with two prominent tubercles, one before the other. Ventrals 321, small, irregular; each ventral with several minute tubercles on either side. Body encircled by black bands, broadest and blackest on the back; ground-colour olive-yellow above, bright gamboge-yellow below.

Total length 1200 millim.

Persian Gulf, coast of Sind, tidal streams at Calcutta.

10. Distira grandis. (PLATE XVI.)

Head rather small; body much elongate, its greatest depth twice and a half to three times the diameter of the neck. Rostral as deep as broad; nasals shorter than the frontal, twice to thrice as long as the suture between the præfrontals; frontal longer than broad, as long as or a little longer than its distance from the rostral, shorter than the parietals; one præ- and two postoculars; a single anterior temporal; seven upper labials, second largest and in contact with the præfrontal, third and fourth entering the eye; two pairs of chin-shields, in contact with each other. 27 to 29 scales round the neck, 41 to 45 round the body; scales feebly imbricate, keeled, the keels very feeble in the female. Ventrals very small, smooth in the female, with two tubercles in the male, 372–400. Greyish olive above, yellowish white on the sides and beneath; neck with dark olive or blackish cross-bars, which become very indistinct or disappear on the body.

Total length 2300 millim.; tail 160.

Malay Archipelago and North Coast of Australia.

a–b. ♂ (V. 389) & ♀ (V. 400).	Malay Archipelago.	Dr. Bleeker.
c. ♀ (V. 372).	Queensland.	Prof. M. A. Thomson [P.].

11. Distira macfarlani. (Plate XVII. fig. 1.)

Head moderate; body moderately elongate. Rostral a little broader than deep; nasals shorter than the frontal, about thrice as long as the suture between the præfrontals; frontal once and three fourths to twice as long as broad, as long as or a little longer than its distance from the end of the snout, shorter than the parietals; one præ- and two postoculars, two superposed anterior temporals; seven or eight upper labials, second largest and in contact with the præfrontal, third and fourth entering the eye; fifth upper labial also entering the eye, if not, with a detached upper portion forming a subocular; two pairs of chin-shields, in contact with each other. 31 to 35 scales round the neck, 43 to 45 round the body; scales feebly imbricate, smooth, or dorsals faintly keeled. Ventrals very small, 220–256. Whitish, with a dorsal and a ventral series of black rhomboidal transverse spots or cross-bars opposite to each other; on the neck, the ventral spots are confluent in the middle and unite with the dorsals on both sides; head black above and beneath, with a yellow spot on the forehead and a yellow streak from the eye along the temple.

Total length 460 millim.; tail 40.

Torres Straits.

a–b. Yg. (V. 256, 220).	Murray Id.	Rev. S. Macfarlane [C.].

12. Distira cyanocincta.

Russell, Ind. Serp. ii. pl. ix. (1801).

Hydrophis cyanocinctus, *Daud.* Rept. vii. p. 383 (1803); *Peters,* Mon. Berl. Ac. 1872, p. 852, pl. i. fig. 2; *Fayrer,* Thanatoph. Ind. pl. xxiii. (1874); *Murray,* Zool Sind, p 391 (1884).

Leioselasma striata, *Lacép.* Ann. Mus. iv 1804, pp. 198, 210,

Enhydris striatus, *Merr. l. c*
Hydrus cyanocinctus, *Boie, Isis,* 1827, p. 354.
Hydrophis striata, *Schleg. Faun. Japon., Rept* p. 89, pl. vii. (1837), *and Phys. Serp.* II. p. 502, pl. xviii. figs. 4 & 5 (1837); *Fischer, Abh. Naturw. Hamb.* iii. 1856, p. 41.
Hydrus striatus, part., *Cantor, Cat. Mal. Rept.* p. 126 (1847).
Hydrophis subannulata, *Gray, Cat.* p 54 (1849)
—— aspera, *Gray, l. c.* p. 55; *Günth. Rept. Brit. Ind.* p. 365 (1864).
—— cyanocincta, part., *Günth. l. c.* p. 367.
—— trachyceps, *Theob. Cat Rept. As. Soc. Mus.* 1868, p. 70.
—— crassicollis, *Anders. Journ. As Soc. Beng.* xl 1871, p. 19.
—— westermanni, *Jan, Icon. Gén.* 39, pl. v. fig. 1 (1872).
—— phipsoni, *Murray, Journ. Bomb. N. H. Soc.* II. 1887, p. 32, pl. —.
—— taprobanica, *Haly, Taprobanian,* ii 1887, p. 107
Distira cyanocincta, *Bouleng. Faun. Ind., Rept.* p. 410 (1890); *W. Sclater, Journ As. Soc. Beng.* lx. 1891, p. 247; *Boettg. Ber. Offenb. Ver. Nat.* 1892, p. 90.

Head moderate; body elongate. Rostral slightly broader than deep; nasals shorter than the frontal, twice, or rather more than twice, as long as the suture between the præfrontals; frontal much longer than broad, as long as its distance from the rostral or the end of the snout, shorter than the parietals, one præ- and two post-oculars; seven or eight upper labials, second largest, third and fourth, fourth and fifth, or third. fourth, and fifth, entering the eye; two superposed anterior temporals; two pairs of subequal chin-shields, in contact on the middle line, or posterior pair separated by one scale. 27 to 33 scales round the neck, 39 to 45 round the middle of the body; scales rhomboidal and subimbricate, with a short keel which is very strong, and broken up into two or three tubercles in adult males. Ventrals distinct throughout, smooth or with two or more tubercles, 281–385. Greenish olive above, with dark olive or black cross-bars or annuli, broadest on the back, and sometimes joined by a black band running along the belly; or yellowish with a black vertebral stripe sending off a few bar-like processes on the neck.

Total length 1500 millim.; tail 140.

From the Persian Gulf and the coasts of India to China and Japan and Papuasia.

A. Black annuli complete and connected by a black band along the belly.

a–b. ♂ (V 343) & hgr. (V. 326).	Bushire.	E. Lort Phillips, Esq. [P.].
c. Yg (V. 306).	Persian Gulf.	
d Hgr (V. 344).	Malabar.	Col. Beddome [C.].
e. ♀ (V. 315)	Madras.	F. Day, Esq. [P.].
f. ♀ (V. 296).	Sunderbunds, Bengal.	Dr. P. Russell, College of Surgeons [E].
g, h–k. ♀ (V. 310) & yg. (V. 308, 305, 303).	Formosa.	R. Swinhoe, Esq. [C.].

B. Black annuli complete but not connected by a band along the belly.

a. Yg. (V. 339).   Malabar.   Col. Beddome [C.].

b. Hgr. (V. 370). Madras beach. Dr. J. R. Henderson [P.].
c. ♂ (V. 342). China. J. R. Reeves, Esq. [P.].

C. Annuli feebly marked or interrupted on the sides and beneath.

a–b. ♂ (V. 352) & ♀ (V. 374). Khor Abdulla, head of Persian Gulf. W. D. Cumming, Esq. [P.].
c. ♂ (V. 360). Bushire. E. Lort Phillips, Esq. [P.].
d. ♂ (V. 377). Kurrachee. Kurrachee Mus. [E].
e. ♀ (V. 314). Ceylon. R. Templeton, Esq. [P.].
f. Hgr. (V. 296). Mergui. Dr. J. Anderson [P.].
g. ♂ (V. 325). Singapore. (Type of *H. aspera*.)
h. ♀ (V. 330). Formosa. R. Swinhoe, Esq. [P.].
i. ♂ (V. 343). Near Zebu, Philippines. H.M.S. 'Challenger.'
k. ♀ (V. 348). ——?

D. Dark cross-bars, confined to the back.

a. ♀ (V. 281). Muscat. A. S. G. Jayakar, Esq. [P.].
b. Hgr. (V. 360). ——?

E. A dark stripe along the back; cross-bars absent or confined to the nape.

a. ♀ (V. 330). Bombay. H. M. Phipson, Esq. [P.]. (As *H. phipsoni*, Murr.)

13. Distira bituberculata.

Hydrophis bituberculatus, *Peters, Mon. Berl. Ac.* 1872, p. 855, pl. ii. fig. 2.
Distira bituberculata, *Bouleng. Faun. Ind.*, Rept. p. 411 (1890).

Very closely allied to *D. lapemidoides*, but scales imbricate, with the keels mostly broken up into two tubercles; 26 or 27 scales round the neck, 48 or 49 round the deepest part of the body. Ventrals distinct, 278. Dark brown above, yellowish on the sides and beneath, the skin between the scales black.

Total length 1090 millim.; tail 100.
Ceylon.

14. Distira belcheri. (Plate XVII. fig. 2.)

Aturia belcheri, *Gray, Cat.* p. 46 (1849).
Hydrophis belcheri, *Günth. Rept. Brit. Ind.* p. 364 (1864).

Head rather small; body elongate; diameter of neck two fifths greatest depth of body. Rostral as deep as broad; nasals shorter than the frontal, twice as long as the suture between the præfrontals; frontal nearly twice as long as broad, as long as its distance from the rostral, shorter than the parietals; one præ- and two postoculars; two superposed anterior temporals; five or six upper labials, fourth bordering the eye; two pairs of chin-shields, in contact with each other. 25 scales round the neck, 34 round the body; scales feebly imbricate on the anterior part of the body, juxtaposed on the posterior part, feebly keeled. Ventrals very distinct throughout, smooth, 317. Olive above, yellowish beneath; neck with dark cross-bands, which gradually disappear on the body; head dark olive, lighter on the crown.

Total length 810 millim.; tail 75.

New Guinea.

a. ♀ (V. 317).   New Guinea.   Sir E. Belcher [P.]. (Type.)

15. Distira pachycercus.

Hydrophis pachycercos, *Fischer, Abh. Naturw Hamb.* iii. 1856, p. 44, pl. ii; *Gunth. Rept. Brit. Ind.* p. 378 (1864); *Jan, Icon. Gén.* 39, pl. vi. (1872).

Head rather small; body stout. Rostral as deep as broad, nasals shorter than the frontal, more than twice as long as the suture between the præfrontals; frontal longer than broad, as long as its distance from the rostral, shorter than the parietals; one præ- and two postoculars; two superposed anterior temporals; eight upper labials, fourth or third and fourth entering the eye, fifth divided, its upper portion forming a subocular; two pairs of chin-shields, in contact with each other. 27 to 29 scales round the neck, 38 or 39 round the body; scales feebly imbricate on the neck, juxtaposed on the body, with strong keels each formed of two tubercles. Ventrals very distinct, 258-260. Yellowish above, with feebly marked dark cross-bands, white beneath; upper surface of head and nape brown, end of tail black.

Total length 930 millim.; tail 110.

Malay Archipelago.

a. ♂ (V 258).   Malay Archipelago.   Dr. Bleeker.

16. Distira lapemidoides.

Aturia lapemoides, *Gray, Cat* p. 46 (1849).
Hydrophis lapemoides, *Gunth Rept. Brit. Ind.* p. 375 (1864); *Blanf. Journ. As. Soc Beng.* xlviii. 1879, p. 132
—— holdsworthii, *Gunth. Ann. & Mag N. H.* (4) ix. 1872, p. 33.
—— stewartii, *Anders Proc. Zool. Soc.* 1872, p 399; *Fayrer, Thanatoph Ind.* pl xxiv. (1874), *Murray, Zool Sind,* p. 390 (1884).
—— dayanus, *Stoliczka, Proc. As. Soc Beng.* 1872, p. 89, *Murray, l. c.* p. 393.
Distira lapemidoides, *Bouleng Faun. Ind., Rept.* p. 412 (1890).

Head rather small; body elongate, slender anteriorly, diameter of neck two fifths to one third the greatest depth. Rostral slightly broader than deep; nasals shorter than the frontal, more than twice as long as the suture between the præfrontals; frontal much longer than broad, as long as or a little shorter than its distance from the end of the snout, shorter than the parietals; one præ- and two or three postoculars; eight upper labials, second largest, third and fourth entering the eye; two or three superposed anterior temporals; two pairs of subequal chin-shields, in contact, or posterior separated by one scale. 30 to 33 scales round the neck, 43 to 47 round the body; scales rhomboidal and subimbricate on the neck, hexagonal and juxtaposed on the body, of young smooth, of adult female with a feeble tubercle or keel, of adult male with a strong spinose tubercle. Ventrals distinct throughout, 300-387. Young yellowish or greyish olive above, white beneath, with complete black rings which are broadest on the back; head black, with an angular yellow (vermilion) band above, the apex on the snout; tail black, with light vertical bands at the base. In the adult the bands become more obsolete and are not continued across the body, and the head is uniform olive-brown.

Total length 940 millim.; tail 90.

Coasts of Baluchistan, India, and Ceylon.

a.	Yg. (V. 305).	Madras.	T. C. Jerdon, Esq [P.]. (Types.)
b.	Hgr. (V. 332).	Ceylon.	Zoological Society.
c.	♂ (V. 387).	Ceylon.	E. W. H. Holdsworth, Esq. [C.].
d.	Hgr. (V. 328).	Ceylon.	E. W. H. Holdsworth, Esq. [C.]. (Type of *H. holdsworthii*.)
e.	Hgr. (V. 300).	Ceylon.	Miss Layard [P].
f.	♀ (V. 362).	Poorie, Orissa.	Sir J Fayrer [P.].
g.	Yg. (V. 345).	Gwadar, Baluchistan.	W. T. Blanford, Esq. [P.].

17. Distira viperina.

Thalassophis viperina, *Schmidt, Abh. Naturw. Hamb.* ii. 1852, p. 79, pl. iii.
Disteira præscutata, *Dum. & Bibr.* vii. p. 1331 (1854).
Hydrophis doliata, *Fischer, Abh. Naturw. Hamb.* iii. 1856, p. 56.
? Hydrophis obscurus (non *Daud.*), *Jan, Rev & Mag. Zool.* 1859, p. 151, *Prodr.* pl. D (1859), and *Icon. Ophid.* 40, pl. vi fig. 2 (1872).
Hydrophis viperina, *Günth. Rept. Brit Ind.* p. 378 (1864); *Anders. Proc. Zool. Soc* 1872, p. 400; *Boettg. Ber. Offenb. Ver. Nat.* 1888, p. 91; *Bouleng. Ann. & Mag. N. H.* (6) ii. 1888, p. 44.
—— jayakari, *Bouleng. Ann. & Mag. N H.* (5) xx. 1887, p 408; *Anders. Journ. Linn. Soc.* xxi. 1889, p. 348.
—— plumbea, *Murray, Journ. Bomb. N. H Soc.* ii. 1887, p. 34.
Distira viperina, *Bouleng. Faun. Ind., Rept.* p. 413 (1890).

Head rather small; body moderately elongate, rather slender anteriorly. Rostral as deep as broad; nasals as long as or a little shorter than the frontal; suture between the præfrontals very short; frontal as broad as long, as long as its distance from the rostral or the end of the snout, shorter than the parietals; one or two præ- and one or two postoculars; seven or eight upper labials, second largest, fourth or third and fourth entering the eye; one or two anterior temporals; two pairs of chin-shields, in contact with each other, posterior longest. 27 to 29 scales round the neck, 37 to 43 round the body; scales juxtaposed, obtusely keeled. Ventrals relatively large anteriorly, bituberculate in the male, 235-267. Slaty grey above, with rhomboidal transverse black spots, white or pink on the sides and inferiorly; some specimens uniform dark grey above; in the young the black spots are continued down the sides of the body; end of tail black.

Total length 920 millim.; tail 100.

From the Persian Gulf and the Mekran Coast, round the coasts of India and Burma to Java, Hong Kong, and Hainan.

a. ♀ (V. 260).	Muscat.	A. S G Jayakar, Esq [P.]. (Type of *H jayakari*)
b. ♀ (V. 248).	Bombay.	H. M. Phipson, Esq. [P.].
c. Hgr. (V. 245).	Malabar.	Col. Beddome [O.].
d. Yg. (V. 237).	Madras.	T. C. Jerdon, Esq. [P.].
e. ♀ (V 245).	Hong Kong.	City Hall Museum [E.].
f. ♀ (V 235).	Indian Ocean.	

18. Distira jerdonii.

Russell, Ind. Serp. ii pl. xii. (1801).

Hydrus nigrocinctus, var., *Cantor, Cat. Mal. Rept.* p. 129, pl. xl. fig. 8 (1847).

Kerilia jerdonii, *Gray, Cat.* p 57 (1849).

Hydrus cantori, *Jerdon, Journ. As Soc Beng.* xxii 1854, p. 526.

Hydrophis jerdonii, *Gunth. Rept. Brit. Ind.* p. 362, pl. xxv. fig. B (1864); *Anders Proc Zool Soc* 1871, p 190; *Fayrer, Thanatoph Ind.* pl. xx. (1874).

Distira jerdonii, *Bouleng. Faun. Ind., Rept.* p. 408 (1890); *Boettg. Mitth. Geogr. Ges. u. Nat. Mus. Bremen*, (2) v 1893, p —.

Head short; snout declivous and rather pointed; body moderately elongate. Rostral as deep as broad; nasals shorter than the frontal, more than twice as long as the suture between the præfrontals; frontal longer than broad, nearly as long as its distance from the end of the snout, shorter than the parietals; one præ- and one postocular; five upper labials, third and fourth entering the eye; a single large anterior temporal, descending to the labial margin. 15 or 17 scales round the neck, 19 or 21 round the body; scales broader than long, slightly imbricate, strongly keeled. Ventrals distinct, but feebly enlarged, more or less distinctly bituberculate, 224-238. Olive above, yellowish beneath, with black cross-bands, which form complete rings in young and half-grown specimens; a black spot may be present between each pair of annuli.

Total length 910 millim.; tail 100.

Bay of Bengal, Straits of Malacca, Borneo

a. ♂ (V. 238).	Madras.	T. C Jerdon, Esq [P] (Type.)
b. ♂ (V. 228).	Madras.	F. Day, Esq [P.].
c. Hgr., dry.	Pinang.	Dr. Cantor.
d. ♀ (V. 224).	—— ?	Haslar Collection.

210. ENHYDRIS.

Enhydris, part, *Merrem, Tent Syst Amph.* p. 140 (1820).
Hydrophis, part, *Schleg. Phys. Serp.* ii. p. 488 (1837); *Dum. & Bibr. Erp Gén.* vii. p. 1341 (1854); *Jan, Elenco sist. Ofid.* p. 109 (1863); *Gunth. Rept. Brit. Ind.* p. 360 (1864).
Lapemis, *Gray, Zool. Misc.* p. 60 (1842), *and Cat. Sn.* p. 43 (1849).
Pelamis, part, *Fischer, Abh. Naturw. Hamb.* iii. 1856, p. 61.
Enhydris, *Bouleng. Faun Ind., Rept* p. 396 (1890).

Maxillary as long as the ectopterygoid, extending forwards as far as the palatine, with two large poison-fangs and 2 to 4 small feebly-grooved teeth. Nostrils superior; head-shields large; nasals in contact with each other; a præocular; loreal present or absent. Body short and stout; scales hexagonal or squarish, juxtaposed; ventrals very feebly developed, if at all distinct.

From the coasts of India to the Chinese Sea and New Guinea.

1. Enhydris curtus.

Hydrus curtus, *Shaw, Zool.* iii. p. 562 (1802).
Enhydris curtus, *Merr. Tent.* p. 140 (1820); *Bouleng. Faun. Ind., Rept.* p. 396 (1890).
Lapemis curtus, *Gray, Zool. Misc.* p. 60 (1842), *and Cat.* p. 44 (1849).
Hydrophis propinquus, *Jan, Rev. & Mag. Zool.* 1859, p. 151, *Prodr.* pl E (1859), *and Icon. Gén.* 41, pl. i. fig. 2 (1872).
— curta, *Gunth. Rept. Brit. Ind.* p. 379 (1864); *Fayrer, Thanatoph. Ind.* pl. xxiv. (1874); *Stoliczka, Proc. As. Soc. Beng.* 1872, p. 91; *Murray, Zool. Sind,* p. 395 (1884).

Rostral broader than deep; internasals twice to thrice as long as the suture between the præfrontals; parietals broken up into small shields; one præ- and one or two postoculars; no loreal; two or three superposed anterior temporals; seven upper labials, fourth, third, and fourth, or third, fourth, and fifth entering the eye; chin-shields very small and separated by scales, or quite indistinct. 30 to 38 scales round the anterior part of the body, 33 to 42 round the middle, with a very feebly-developed tubercle or short keel; the scales on the lower surface, in the male, with a very strong spinose tubercle. Ventrals distinct in the anterior half of the body, with two spinose tubercles in the male, 150–200. Above with dark transverse bands, broadest in the middle; these bands are usually very dark, nearly black, but in some old specimens rather indistinct; end of tail black.

Total length 750 millim.; tail 75.

Coasts of India and Ceylon.

a. Yg. (V. 152).	India.	(Type.)
b. Hgr. (V. 152).	India.	
c. ♂ (V. 157).	Malabar.	Col. Beddome [C.].
d. ♀ (V. 194).	Mangalore, S. Canara.	E. Pringle, Esq. [P.].
e-f. ♀ (V. 169)	Trevandrum, Travan-	H. S. Ferguson, Esq.
(V. 1.		P.

g. Hgr. (V. 150). Madras. T. C Jerdon, Esq. [P.].
h, i. ♂ (V. 153, 157). Ceylon. E W. H. Holdsworth, Esq. [C].
k. ♂ (V. 155). Ceylon.
l. ♂, skeleton. Ceylon.

2. Enhydris hardwickii.

Lapemis hardwickii, *Gray, Ill. Ind. Zool.* ii. pl. lxxxvii. f. 2 (1834), and *Cat.* p. 44 (1849).
Hydrophis pelamidoides, *Schleg. Phys. Serp* ii. p. 512, pl. xviii. figs. 16 & 17 (1837), *and Faun. Japon*, *Rept.* pl. ix. (1838); *Dum. & Bibr.* vii. p. 1345 (1854); *Jan, Icon. Gén.* 41, pl. iii. fig. 1 (1872).
Lapemis loreatus, *Gray, Ann & Mag. N. H.* xi. 1843, p. 46.
Hydrophis (Pelamis) pelamidoides, *Fischer, Abh. Naturw. Hamb.* iii. 1856, p. 64, pl. iii.
—— problematicus, *Jan, Rev. & Mag. Zool.* 1859, p 150, *and Prodr.* pl. D (1859).
—— hardwickii, *Gunth. Rept. Brit. Ind* p. 380, pl. xxv. fig. W (1864); *Anders. Journ. Linn Soc.* xxi. 1889, p. 348.
—— loreata, *Gunth. l. c.* p 380; *Boettg. Zool. Anz.* 1888, p. 396
—— fayreriana, *Anders Journ. As. Soc. Beng.* xl. 1871, p 19.
—— abbreviatus, *Jan, Icon. Gén.* 40, pl. iv. fig. 2, & v. fig. 2.
—— brevis, *Jan, l. c.* pl. iv. fig. 2.
Enhydris hardwickii, *Bouleng. Faun. Ind., Rept.* p. 397 (1890).

Rostral as deep as broad or slightly broader than deep; parietals large; one præ- and one to three postoculars; a loreal sometimes present; two or three superposed anterior temporals; seven upper labials, fourth, or third and fourth entering the eye; chin-shields very small and separated by scales, or quite indistinct. 25 to 33 scales round the anterior part of the body, 34 to 37 round the middle, with tubercles as in the preceding species. Ventrals usually very indistinct, 130–200. Coloration as in the preceding, but the dark bands often forming complete rings round the body.

Total length 750 millim.; tail 80.

From the Bay of Bengal to the Chinese Sea and the coast of New Guinea.

a. ♀ (V. 150). India. Gen. Hardwicke [P.]. (Type.)
b–c. ♂ (V. 130) & ♀ (V. 153). Singapore. R. Swinhoe, Esq. [C.].
d. ♂ (V. 135). Borneo. Sir E. Belcher [P.]. (Type of *L. loreatus.*)
e, f. ♀ (V. 136, 142). Borneo. Sir E. Belcher [P.].
g ♂ (V. 140). Philippines.
h. Hgr. (V. 175). Manilla.
i–l. ♀ (V. 180, 156, 140.) Negros. Dr. A. B. Meyer [C.].
m–q. ♂ (V. 155, 138), ♀ (V. 200, 146), & yg. (V. 130). Malay Archipelago.

211. ENHYDRINA.

Disteira, part., *Fitzing N. Class. Rept.* p. 29 (1826).
Polyodontus (non *Lacép.*), *Lesson, in Bélang. Voy. Ind. Or., Rept.* p. 325 (1834).
Hydrophis, part., *Schleg. Phys. Serp.* ii. p. 488 (1837); *Dum. & Bibr. Erp. Gén.* vii p. 1341 (1854); *Fischer, Abh. Naturw. Hamb.* iii. 1856, p. 41; *Jan, Elenco sist. Ofid.* p 109 (1863).
Enhydrina, *Gray, Cat. Sn.* p. 47 (1849); *Günth. Rept. Brit. Ind* p. 381 (1864); *Bouleng. Faun. Ind., Rept* p. 405 (1890).

Maxillary scarcely longer than the ectopterygoid, not extending forwards quite as far as the palatine, with two large poison-fangs followed by 4 solid teeth. Nostrils superior, head-shields large, nasals in contact with each other; a præocular; no loreal. Body moderately elongate; scales imbricate; ventrals distinct but very small *.

From the Persian Gulf to New Guinea.

1. Enhydrina valakadien.

Russell, Ind. Serp. ii pl. xi (1801).
Hydrus valakadyn, *Boie, Isis,* 1827, p. 554
Disteira russellii, *Fitzinger, Isis,* 1827, p. 733.
Polyodontus annulatus, *Lesson, in Bélang. Voy. Ind. Or., Rept.* p. 325, pl. iv. (1834)
Hydrophis schistosa (non *Daud.*), *Schleg. Phys. Serp* ii. p. 500, pl. xviii. figs. 1-3 (1837), *Dum. & Bibr.* vii. p. 1344 (1854); *Fischer, Abh. Naturw Hamb.* iii. 1856, p. 48; *Jan, Icon. Gén* 41, pl. ii fig. 1 (1872).
—— bengalensis, *Gray, Zool. Misc.* p. 62 (1842).
—— subfasciata, *Gray, l. c.*
Hydrus schistosus, *Cantor, Cat. Mal. Rept.* p. 132 (1847).
Enhydrina bengalensis, *Gray, Cat.* p. 48 (1849); *Günth. Rept. Brit. Ind.* p 381 (1864); *Fayrer, Thanatoph Ind.* pl. xviii. (1874), *Murray, Zool. Sind,* p. 396 (1884).
—— valakadyen, *Gray, Cat.* p. 48; *Stoliczka, Journ. As. Soc. Beng.* xxxix. 1870, p 213, and *Proc. As. Soc. Beng.* 1872, p. 91; *Bouleng. Faun Ind., Rept* p. 406, fig. (1890).
—— schistosa, *Stoliczka, l. c.*; *Anders. Proc. Zool. Soc.* 1871, p. 193.
Hydrophis fasciatus, *Jan, Icon. Gén.* 41, pl. iii. fig. 2.

Rostral deeper than broad; frontal small, longer than broad, shorter than its distance from the end of the snout or than the parietals; one præ- and one or two postoculars; seven or eight upper labials, fourth or third and fourth entering the eye; usually a single anterior temporal; chin-shields small or indistinct. 40 to 60 scales round the neck, 50 to 70 round the body, scales feebly imbricate, with a small tubercle or short keel, which is stronger in the males. Ventrals very slightly enlarged, 230-314. Young olive or grey above, with black transverse bands, broadest in the middle and tapering to a point on the sides; in the adult these

---

* They begin to be distinguishable at a considerable distance behind the head.

bands are usually less distinct, some specimens being uniform dark grey above; sides and lower parts whitish.

Total length 1300 millim.; tail 190.

From the Persian Gulf along the coasts of India and Burma to the Malay Archipelago and Papuasia.

a–b. ♂ (V. 310) & ♀ (V. 268).	Muscat.	A S. G Jayakar, Esq. [P.].
c–d ♂ (V. 268) & ♀ (V. 250).	Kurrachee.	Kurrachee Museum [E]
e–f ♀ (V. 256) & yg. (V. 260).	Malabar.	Col Beddome [C].
g. ♂ (V. 297).	Malabar.	
h. ♂ (V 268).	W. Ceylon.	E Both, Esq. [P.].
i, k. ♀ (V. 243, 255).	Madras.	T C. Jerdon, Esq. [P.].
l–m. ♂ (V. 240) & yg. (V. 233).	Sandheads, Bengal.	Sir J. Fayrer [P.]
n. ♂ (V. 255).	Bengal.	Gen. Hardwicke [P.]. (Type of *E bengalensis*.)
o. ♀ (V. 249),	Bengal.	Gen. Hardwicke [P].
p. Hgr. (V. 239).	India.	Gen. Hardwicke [P.].
q. ♂ (V. 235)	Mergui.	Prof. Oldham [P].
r–s. ♂ (V 230) & ♀ (V 240).	Mergui.	Dr. J. Anderson [P.].
t. ♀ (V. 236)	Pinang.	Dr. Cantor.
u. ♂ (V. 254).	Siam.	W. H. Newman, Esq. [P.].
v. Yg. (V. 230)	Malay Archipelago.	Dr Bleeker.
w. Yg. (V 238).	S. coast of New Guinea.	J. B. Jukes, Esq. [P].
x. ♀ skeleton.	Madras.	F. Day, Esq. [P.].

212. AIPYSURUS.

Aipysurus, *Lacép. Ann. Mus.* iv. 1804, p. 197; *Dum. & Bibr. Erp. Gén.* vii. p. 1323 (1854), *Fischer, Abh. Naturw. Hamb.* iii. 1856, p 31; *Jan, Elenco sist. Ofid.* p. 108 (1863); *Gunth. Rept. Brit. Ind* p 357 (1864).

Stephanohydra, *Tschudi, Arch. f. Nat.* 1837, p. 331; *Gray, Cat Sn.* p. 59 (1849)

Hydrophis, part, *Schleg. Phys. Serp.* ii. p. 488 (1837).

Hypotropis, *Gray, Ann & Mag. N. H.* xviii 1846, p 284.

Tomogaster, *Gray, Cat.* p 59.

Thalassophis, part, *Schmidt, Abh. Naturw. Hamb.* ii. 1852, p 75.

Emydocephalus, *Krefft, Proc. Zool. Soc.* 1869, p. 321.

Pelagophis, *Peters & Doria, Ann Mus. Genova*, xiii. 1878, p. 413.

Maxillary a little longer than the ectopterygoid, extending forwards beyond the palatine; poison-fangs moderate, followed, after a short interspace, by 8 to 10 grooved teeth; anterior mandibular teeth feebly grooved. Snout short; nostrils superior; head-shields large or broken up into scales, nasals in contact with each other. Body moderate; scales imbricate; ventrals large, keeled in the middle.

Malay Archipelago and Western Tropical Pacific Ocean.

As in *Distira*, the præfrontal nearly reaches the postfrontal.

COLUBRIDÆ.

Synopsis of the Species.

A. Scales in 17 rows; head shielded above.

Six upper labials, fourth entering the eye.. 1. *eydouxii*, p. 304.
Two or three upper labials, second covering nearly the whole lip .... 2. *annulatus*, p. 304.

B. Scales in 19 to 25 rows.

Upper head-shields distinct, more or less broken up; scales in 21 to 25 rows.... 3. *lævis*, p. 305.
Head covered with small scales, scales in 19 rows .... 4. *australis*, p. 305.

1. Aipysurus eydouxii.

Tomogaster eydouxii, *Gray, Cat.* p. 59 (1849).
Thalassophis anguillæformis, *Schmidt, Abh. Naturw. Hamb.* ii. 1852, p. 76, pl i.
—— murænæformis, *Schmidt, l. c.* p 77.
Aipysurus lævis (non *Lacép.*), *Guichen. Voy. Pôle Sud, Zool* iii. *Rept.* p 21, pl vi. (1853), *Dum. & Bibr.* vii. p. 1326, pl. lxxvii b. fig. 4 (1854); *Fischer, Abh. Naturw. Hamb.* iii. 1856, p. 32; *Jan, Icon. Gén.* 40, pl. ii. fig. 1 (1872).
—— margaritophorus, *Bleek. Nat. Tijdschr. Nederl. Ind.* xvi. 1858, p. 49.
—— anguillæformis, *Gunth. Rept. Brit. Ind.* p. 357 (1864); *Boettg. Zool. Anz.* 1892, p. 420.

Eye a little longer than its distance from the mouth. Rostral a little broader than deep; upper head-shields regular; frontal large, once and two thirds to twice as long as broad, longer than its distance from the end of the snout, as long as or a little longer than the parietals; nasal in contact with or narrowly separated from the præocular; one præ- and two postoculars; temporals 1+2 or 2+2; six upper labials, fourth entering the eye; anterior chin-shields shorter than the posterior, which are separated by an azygous shield. Scales smooth, in 17 rows. Ventrals 140-142. Dark brown above, with cross-bands of yellow, black-edged scales, often broken up on the vertebral line; these bands widening towards the belly, which is yellow, with or without dark brown spots.

Total length 490 millim.; tail 70.

Coasts of Singapore, Java, and the Philippines.

a. ♀ (V. 142).	Indian Ocean.	(Type.)
b. ♀ (V. 142).	Java.	Dr. Bleeker. (Type of *Ai. margaritophorus.*)
c. ♀ (V. 140).	Java.	

2. Aipysurus annulatus.

Emydocephalus annulatus, *Krefft, Proc. Zool. Soc.* 1869, p. 322, and *Sn. Austral.* p. 92 (1869).
—— tuberculatus, *Krefft, l. c.* pp. 322, 93.
Aipysurus chelonicephalus, *Bavay, Mém. Soc. Linn. Norm.* xv. no. 5, 1869. p. 34.

Head more or less regularly shielded, the shields granulate, a large frontal; supraocular undivided; one præ- and two postoculars; second upper and lower labial extremely large, covering nearly the whole upper and lower lip. Scales in 17 rows, rough with five or more tubercles. Ventrals 135-144 Purplish brown or black, some of the scales lighter or forming whitish annuli.

Total length 800 millim.

Loyalty Islands.

3. Aipysurus lævis.

Aipysurus lævis, *Lacép. Ann. Mus* iv. 1804, pp. 197, 210, pl. lvi. fig. 3; *Gunth. Rept. Brit. Ind.* p. 358 (1864).
Stephanohydra fusca, *Tschudi, Arch. f. Nat.* 1837, p 331, pl. viii.; *Gray, Cat.* p. 60 (1849), *Gunth. Cat.* p. 272 (1858).
Hydrophis pelamidoides, part., *Schleg. Phys. Serp.* ii. p. 512 (1837), *and Abbild.* p. 115 (1844).
Hypotropis jukesii, *Gray, Ann. & Mag. N. H.* xviii. 1846, p. 284, *and in Jukes, Voy Fly*, ii p. 333, pl. i. (1847).
Aipysurus fuliginosus, *Dum. & Bibr.* vii. p 1327, pl. lxxvii. b. figs. 1 & 2 (1854); *Fischer, Abh. Naturw. Hamb.* iii. 1856, p. 33; *Bavay, Mém. Soc. Linn. Norm.* xv. no. 5, 1869, p 33; *Jan, Icon. Gén.* 40, pl. i fig. 3 (1872); *Sauvage, Bull. Soc. Philom.* (7) i. 1877, p. 112.
—— fuscus, *Fischer, l. c.*
—— duboisii, *Bavay, l. c.*

Eye shorter than its distance from the mouth. Head with distinct shields above, which are more or less divided and often very irregular; rostral broader than deep; frontal a little longer than broad, often longitudinally bisected; supraocular divided into two; one or two præ- and two or three postoculars; eight to ten upper labials, fourth, fifth, and sixth entering the eye if not broken up; chin-shields small or indistinct. Sales in 21 to 25 rows, smooth, vertebrals often more or less enlarged. Ventrals 137-162. Brown, uniform or with small darker spots.

Total length 1720 millim.; tail 170.

Pacific Ocean, from Celebes to the Loyalty Islands.

a. Ad., skin (V. 143).	Arafura Sea.	J. J. Walker, Esq. [P.].
b. ♂ (V. 148).	Kei Is.	Capt. Langen [P].
c. ♂ (V. 146).	New Guinea.	Mrs. Stanley [P.].
d. ♀ (V 151)	Torres Straits.	Mr. Comrie [C.].
e. ♀ (V. 153)	Baudin I.	J. J Walker, Esq. [P.].
f. Yg. (V. 137).	Rockhampton, Queensland.	Museum Godeffroy.
g. ♀, skin (V. 151).	Darnley I.	J. B. Jukes, Esq [P.]. (Type of *Hypotropis jukesii*.)
h. ♂ (V. 155).	—— ?	
i. Skull of *g*.		

4. Aipysurus australis.

Aipysurus fuscus (*non Tschudi*), *Gunth. Rept. Brit. Ind.* p. 358 (1864), *Krefft, Sn. Austral.* p. 91 (1869).

Aipysurus australis, *Sauvage, Bull Soc. Philom.* (7) i. 1877, p. 114.
Pelagophis lubricus, *Peters & Doria, Ann. Mus Genova,* xiii. 1878, p. 414.

Head-shields broken up into small irregular scales with numerous small granular tubercles; eye rather small, surrounded by 8 or 9 small shields; rostral a little broader than deep; eight or nine upper labials, fifth sometimes entering the eye; chin-shields small, indistinct. Scales smooth or obtusely keeled, in 19 rows. Ventrals 156-166. Brown, or cream-colour with brown spots on the scales forming more or less distinct cross-bars.

Total length 930 millim., tail 110.

Coasts of New Guinea and Australia.

a. ♂ (V. 165).	Australia.	Capt. Stokes [P]
b. ♂ (V. 156).	Australia.	G. Krefft, Esq. [P.]
c ♂ (V 166).	Australia.	Mr. Barrow [P.].

213. PLATURUS.

Laticauda, *Laur Syn. Rept.* p. 109 (1768).
Hydrus, part., *Schneid Hist. Amph* i p 233 (1799)
Platurus, *Daud. Rept* vii. p. 223 (1803); *Wagl. Syst Amph* p. 166 (1830); *Dum. & Bibr. Erp. Gén.* vii. p. 1318 (1854); *Fischer, Abh. Naturw. Hamb.* iii. 1856, p. 27; *Jan, Elenco sist. Ofid.* p. 108 (1863), *Gunth. Rept. Brit. Ind.* p. 355 (1864); *Bouleng. Faun. Ind., Rept.* p 394 (1890).
Hydrophis, part., *Schleg Phys. Serp.* ii p. 488 (1837).

Maxillary much shorter than the ectopterygoid, extending forwards beyond the palatine, with two large poison-fangs; one or two small solid teeth near the posterior extremity of the maxillary. Head-shields large; nostrils lateral, the nasals separated by internasals; præocular present, no loreal. Body much elongate; scales smooth and imbricate; ventrals and subcaudals large.

Eastern parts of the Indian Ocean and West Pacific.

Synopsis of the Species.

I. No ventral keel; ventrals 195-240.

No azygous shield on the snout; scales
  in 19 rows .... 1. *laticaudatus*, p. 307.
An azygous shield between the præ-
  frontals; scales in 21-25 rows.... 2. *colubrinus*, p. 308.

II. A keel along the posterior half of the belly.

An azygous shield between the præfrontals; scales in 21-23 rows;
  ventrals 178-198 .... 3. *schistorhynchus*, p. 309.
No azygous shield on the snout; scales
  in 19 rows; ventrals 229 .... 4. *muelleri*, p. 309.

Fig. 21.

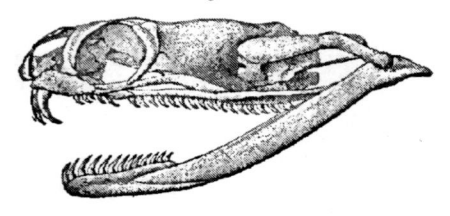

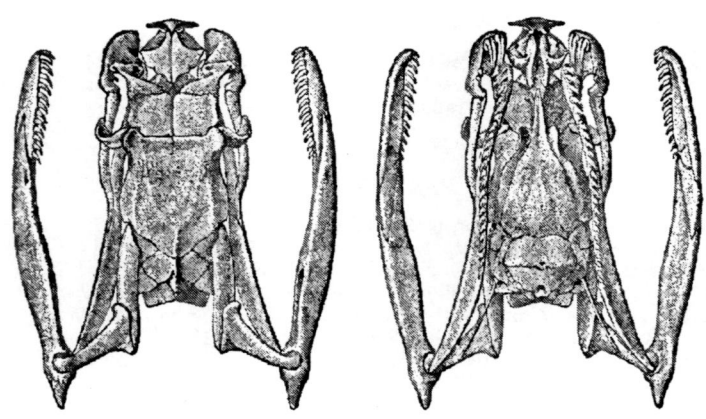

Skull of *Platurus colubrinus.*

1. Platurus laticaudatus.

Coluber laticaudatus, *Linn. Mus. Ad. Frid.* p. 31, pl. xvi. fig. 1 (1754), *and S. N.* i. p. 383 (1766).
Laticauda scutata, *Laur. Syn. Rept.* p. 109 (1768).
Platurus fasciatus, part., *Daud. Rept.* vii. p. 226 (1803); *Dum. & Bibr.* vii. p. 1321 (1854); *Fischer, Abh. Naturw. Hamb.* iii. 1856, p. 28.
Hydrophis colubrinus, part., *Schleg. Phys. Serp.* ii. p. 514 (1837).
Platurus laticaudatus, *Girard, U.S. Explor. Exped., Herp.* p. 180 (1858); *Peters, Mon. Berl. Ac.* 1877, p. 417; *Bouleng. Faun. Ind., Rept.* p. 395, fig. (1890).
—— laticaudatus, var. A, *Günth. Cat.* p. 272 (1858).
—— fischeri, *Jan, Rev. & Mag. Zool.* 1859, p. 149, *and Prodr.* pl. D (1859); *Günth. Rept. Brit. Ind.* p. 356, pl. xxv. fig A (1864); *Anders. Proc. Zool. Soc.* 1871, p. 189; *Jan, Icon. Gén.* 40, pl. i. fig. 2 (1872); *Fayrer, Thanatoph. Ind.* pl. xix. (1874).
—— affinis, *Anders. l. c.* p. 190.

Rostral deeper than broad; no azygous shield on the snout; frontal not longer than the parietals; one præ- and two postoculars; seven or eight upper labials, third and fourth entering the eye;

temporals 1+2. Scales in 19 rows. Ventrals not keeled, 210-240; subcaudals 25-45. Olive above, yellowish beneath, with 29-48 black annuli which are as broad as or broader than the interspaces between them.

Total length 970 millim.; tail 90.

From the Bay of Bengal to the Chinese Sea and the Western South Pacific Ocean.

a. ♂ (V 222; C. 43).	Bengal.	Gen. Hardwicke [P.].
b. Hgr. (V. 231; C 43).	Chartaboum.	
c-d ♀ (V.233; C. 30) & vg. (V. 232; C. 31).	Loo Choo Islands.	H. Pryer, Esq. [P.].
e. Hgr. (V. 231; C. 42).	New Guinea.	
f. Hgr. (V. 223; C. 31).	New Guinea?	Sir E. Belcher [P.].
g. Hgr (V. 210; C. 32).	Duke of York Is.	Rev. G. Brown [C].
h. Hgr. (V. 230, C. 32).	Fiji Is.	H.M.S. 'Herald.'
i. Hgr. (V. 224, C. 35).	Aneiteum, New Hebrides.	J Macgillivray, Esq. [C.].
k. ♂ (V. 237; C. 45).	Australia	G. Krefft, Esq. [P.].
l ♂ (V 234; C. 44).	Tasmania.	Haslar Collection.
m. ♀ (V. 229; C. 33).	S. Pacific.	Museum of Economic Geology.

2. Platurus colubrinus.

Hydrus colubrinus, *Schneid Hist. Amph.* i p. 238 (1799).

Platurus fasciatus, part, *Daud. Rept.* vii p. 226, pl. lxxxv. fig. 1 (1803); *Dum. & Bibr.* vii p. 1321 (1854).

Hydrophis colubrinus, part., *Schleg Phys. Serp* ii. p. 514, pl. xviii figs 21 & 22 (1837).

Laticauda scutata, *Cantor, Cat. Mal. Rept.* p. 125 (1847).

Platurus colubrinus, *Girard, U S. Explor. Exped, Herp.* p. 178 (1858); *Peters, Mon. Berl Ac.* 1877, p. 418; *Fischer, Jahrb. Hamb. Wiss Anst.* v. 1888, p. 18; *Bouleng Faun. Ind., Rept.* p. 395 (1890).

—— laticaudatus, var. B, *Gunth. Cat.* p. 272 (1858).

—— fasciatus, *Jan, Rev. & Mag. Zool.* 1859, p. 149, and *Icon. Gén.* 40, pl. i fig. 1 (1872).

—— scutatus, *Gunth. Rept. Brit. Ind* p. 356 (1864).

Rostral deeper than broad; an azygous shield between the præfrontals and sometimes one or two between the internasals; frontal as long as or slightly shorter than the parietals; one præ- and two postoculars; temporals 1+2 (rarely 2+2); six or seven upper labials, third and fourth entering the eye. Scales in 21 to 25 rows. Ventrals not keeled, 195-240; subcaudals 30-45. Olive above, yellowish below, with 28 to 54 black annuli, which are as wide as the interspaces between them or narrower; some or all of the annuli may be interrupted on the belly.

Total length 1270 millim.; tail 125.

From the Bay of Bengal to the Chinese Sea and the Western South Pacific Ocean.

a-b, c-d. ♂ (V 229, C. 45), ♀ (V. 235; C. 33), & hgr. (V. 202, 240; C. 12, 34).	India.	Sir E. Belcher [P.].

e. Yg. (V 228, C. 33).	Pinang.	Dr. Cantor.
f. ♀ (V 233; C. 33).	Engano I., S.W. Sumatra	Dr. Modigliani [P.]
g. Hgr. (V. 225; C. 45).	Sooloo Is.	Sir E. Belcher [P.].
h. ♀ (V. 220; C 33).	Amboyna.	Sir E. Belcher [P.].
i-k. Yg. (V. 218, 221; C. 44, 34).	Kei Is.	Capt. Langen [P.].
l. Yg. (V. 209; C. 42.)	Pelew Is.	G. L. King, Esq. [P.].
m. Yg. (V. 216, C 34).	Ugi, Solomon Is.	H.M.S. 'Penguin.'
n-p. ♂ (V. 225; C. 45) & yg. (V. 201, 205, C. 45, 34).	New Georgia, Solomon Is.	H.M.S. 'Penguin.'
q. ♀ (V. 225; C. 32)	Pigeon Isle, Admiralty Is	H.M.S. 'Challenger.'
r-s. ♂ (V. 209, 221; C. 36, 37).	Aneiteum, New Hebrides.	J. Macgillivray, Esq. [C.].
t. Yg. (V. 197, C 33)	New Hebrides.	D. McNab, Esq [P.]
u-v. ♀ (V. 220; C 30) & yg. (V. 206; C. 37).	Isle of Pines, New Caledonia.	J. Macgillivray, Esq [C.].
w-x. Hgr. (V 216; C. 37) & yg (V 203, C. 34)	Fiji Is.	J. Macgillivray, Esq. [C].
y. ♀ (V. 228; C 33)	Kandavu, Fiji Is.	H M S. 'Challenger.'
z. Hgr. (V. 213, C. 36).	Australia.	Capt. Stokes [P.].
α. Yg. (V. 208; C. 33).	Australia.	G. Krefft, Esq. [P.].
β. ♂ (V. 207; C. 43).	New Zealand	Sir G Grey [P.].
γ. Skeleton.		

3. Platurus schistorhynchus.

Hydrophis colubrina, part., *Schleg. Faun. Japon., Rept.* p. 92, pl. x (1838)

Platurus schistorhynchus, *Gunth Proc. Zool. Soc* 1874, p. 297, pl xlv. fig. A , *Bouleng. Faun. Ind , Rept.* p. 395 (1890).

Rostral broader than deep; an azygous shield separating the nasals behind the rostral and another between the præfrontals; frontal longer than the parietals; one præ- and two postoculars; seven upper labials, third and fourth entering the eye; temporals small, scale-like, 2+3. Scales in 21 to 23 rows. Ventrals 178–198, on the posterior half of the body with a median keel; subcaudals 32–40. Coloration as in the preceding; 25 to 45 annuli.

Reaches the same size as *P. colubrinus*.

Western Tropical Pacific.

a-d. Yg. (V. 178, 177, 189, 179; C. 38, 40, 32, 37).	Savage I.	Dr. Gunther [P.]. (Types.)
e. ♀ (V. 188; C. 36).	Loo Choo Is.	H. Pryer, Esq. [P].

4. Platurus muelleri.

Platurus, n. sp.?, *F. Mull. Verh. Nat. Ges. Basel*, x. 1892, p. 207.

Head-shields as in *P. laticaudatus*. Scales in 19 rows. Ventrals 229, keeled as in *P. schistorhynchus*. 62 black annuli, some of which are interrupted on the belly.

South Pacific.

Subfam. 8. *ELAPINÆ.*

Elapidæ, *Boie, Isis,* 1827, p. 510.
Holochalina, part., *J Muller, Zeitschr. f. Physiol.* iv. p. 270, 1831.
Najidæ, *Bonaparte, Mem. Acc. Torin.* (2) ii. p. 393, 1840.
Conocerques, *Duméril, Mém. Ac. Sc.* xxiii. p. 514, 1853; *Duméril & Bibron, Erp Gén.* vii. p. 1187, 1854
Eurystomata Iobola, part, *Stannius, Zoot. Amph.* p. 5, 1856.
Dendrechides, *A. Duméril, Rev. & Mag. Zool.* viii. p 555, 1856.
Elapsidæ, Dendraspididæ, *Gunther, Cat. Col. Sn.,* 1858.
Najidæ (Najinæ, Dendraspidinæ), *Cope, Proc. Ac. Philad.* 1859, p 342.
Elapidæ, part, *Jan, Elenco sist. Ofid.* p. 111, 1863.
Elapidæ, *Gunther, Rept. Brit. Ind.* p. 337, 1864.
Elapida, part, *Strauch, Syn Viper.* p. 18, 1869.
Elapidæ, Najidæ, Dendraspididæ, *Cope, Proc. Amer. Philos. Soc.* xviii p. 480, 1886.
Elapinæ, *Bouleng Faun Ind., Rept.* p. 382, 1890.

Tail cylindrical. Hypapophyses more or less developed throughout the vertebral column.

Distributed over Africa, Southern Asia, the Southern parts of North America, Central and South America, and Australia. In the latter Continent they constitute the great majority of the Ophidian fauna and present the greatest variety of forms. Mostly viviparous.

Synopsis of the Genera.

I. Maxillary bone without posterior process; no isolated anterior mandibular tooth.

  A. Maxillary bone not extending forwards beyond the palatine, vertebral scales not enlarged.

    1. Poison-fangs followed by 6 or 7 grooved teeth; subcaudals in two rows; eye very small; head not distinct from neck.

Maxillary and mandibular teeth gradually decreasing in size; first upper labial bordering the nostril .. 214. Ogmodon, p. 312.
Anterior maxillary and mandibular teeth abruptly enlarged.
                              215. Glyphodon, p. 313.

    2. Poison-fangs followed by 7 to 15 small grooved teeth; subcaudals in two rows; head more or less distinct from neck.

No canthus rostralis, eye small, with vertical pupil; tail moderate or short .... 216. Pseudelaps, p. 315.
Canthus rostralis distinct; eye moderate or large, with round pupil; tail moderate or long .... 217. Diemenia, p. 320.

    3. Poison-fangs followed by 1 to 5 small teeth, which may be indistinctly grooved.

      a. Head more or less distinct from neck.

a. Habit colubriform or elapiform.

    * Internasals distinct; rostral moderate.

      † Scales not oblique, smooth.

        ‡ Ventrals rounded.

Eye moderate or rather small; canthus rostralis distinct; subcaudals all or part in two rows . 218. **Pseudechis**, p. 327.

Eye moderate or small; canthus rostralis feebly marked or absent; subcaudals single (with one exception). 219. **Denisonia**, p. 332.

Eye very small; subcaudals in two rows. 220. **Micropechis**, p. 346.

        ‡‡ Ventrals angulate and notched laterally; subcaudals single.. 221. **Hoplocephalus**, [p. 348.

      †† Scales not oblique, strongly keeled; subcaudals single .... 222. **Tropidechis**, p. 350.

      ††† Scales oblique, smooth, laterals shorter than dorsals; subcaudals single
          223. **Notechis**, p. 351.

    ** Internasals absent; rostral very large; subcaudals single .... 224. **Rhinhoplocephalus**, [p. 352.

β. Habit viperiform.

Scales smooth; subcaudals single .. 225. **Brachyaspis**, p. 353.

Scales more or less distinctly keeled; posterior subcaudals paired; end of tail compressed, terminating in a long spine.
          226. **Acanthophis**, p 354.

    b. Head not distinct from neck; subcaudals in two rows.

Scales not oblique, tail moderate; nasal divided
          228. **Boulengerina**, p. 357.

Scales oblique; tail very short; nasal divided.
          229. **Elapechis**, p. 358.

Scales not oblique; tail very short; nasal entire.
          230. **Rhynchelaps**, p. 361.

    4. No maxillary teeth beyond the poison-fangs; nasal entire; subcaudals single .... 227. **Elapognathus**, p. 356.

  B. Maxillary bone not extending forwards beyond the palatine; vertebral scales enlarged . .. 231. **Bungarus**, p. 365.

  C. Maxillary bone extending forwards beyond the palatine; vertebral scales not enlarged.

    1. Internasal bordering the nostril.

      a. Poison-fangs followed by one or more small teeth; scales oblique .... 232. **Naia**, p. 372.

　　　　b. No small maxillary teeth.

Scales oblique, strongly keeled; rostral moderate.
　　　　　　　　　　　233. **Sepedon,** p. 388.

Scales oblique; rostral very large, detached on the sides.
　　　　　　　　　　　234. **Aspidelaps,** p. 390.

Scales not oblique; rostral large .... 235. **Walterinnesia,**
　　　　　　　　　　　　　　　　　　　　　　　[p. 392.

　　2. Internasal not bordering the nostril.

　　　　a. Nasal divided; scales in 13 or 15 rows; one to three small maxillary teeth in addition to the poison-fangs.
　　　　　　　　　　　236. **Hemibungarus,**
　　　　　　　　　　　　　　　　　　　　　　　[p. 392.

　　　　b. Nasal divided; scales in 13 rows; no small maxillary teeth.

Poison-gland not extending beyond the head.
　　　　　　　　　　　237. **Callophis,** p. 396.

Poison-gland extending along each side of the anterior third of the body; heart shifted back to the second third of the body.
　　　　　　　　　　　238. **Doliophis,** p. 397.

　　　　c. Nasal entire; scales in 15 rows; postfrontal bone absent.

One or two small maxillary teeth in addition to the poison-fangs.
　　　　　　　　　　　239. **Furina,** p. 405.

No small maxillary teeth ... . 240. **Homorelaps,** p. 408.

　　　　d. Nasal divided; scales in 15 rows; postfrontal bone absent; no small maxillary teeth.
　　　　　　　　　　　241. **Elaps,** p. 411.

II. Maxillary bone with a strong posterior process, directed backwards and outwards; a large, fang-like anterior mandibular tooth, followed by a considerable toothless space; no solid maxillary teeth; head narrow; body slender, with the scales disposed very obliquely .... 242. **Dendraspis,** p. 434.

214. OGMODON.

Ogmodon, *Peters, Mon. Berl. Ac.* 1864, p. 274.
Labionaris, *Brocchi, Bull. Soc. Philom.* (6) xii. 1876, p. 94.

Maxillary extending forwards as far as the palatine, with 8 grooved teeth gradually decreasing in length; mandibular teeth gradually decreasing in length. Head small, not distinct from neck; eye very small, with round pupil; nostril pierced between the first upper labial, two small nasals, and the internasal; præfrontal entering the eye; an elongate præocular, separated from the nasal by the second labial; no anterior temporal. Body cylindrical; scales smooth, without pits, in 17 rows; ventrals rounded. Tail short; subcaudals in two rows.

Fiji Islands.

1. Ogmodon vitianus.

Ogmodon vitianus, *Peters, Mon Berl. Ac.* 1864, p 275, pl — fig 4, and 1880, p. 223.
Labionaris filholi, *Brocchi, Bull. Soc. Philom.* (6) xii. 1876, p. 94.

Snout elongate, pointed, projecting. Rostral deeper than broad, visible from above, internasals small, about one third the length of the præfrontals; frontal twice as broad as the supraocular, once and a half to once and two thirds as long as broad, as long as or a little longer than its distance from the end of the snout, shorter than the parietals; præocular at least twice as long as deep (in one specimen fused with the third labial); one postocular; six upper labials, second in contact with the præfrontal, fourth and fifth entering the eye, sixth very large and in contact with the parietal, three lower labials in contact with the anterior chin-shields, which are larger than the posterior. Scales in 17 rows. Ventrals 139-152; anal divided; subcaudals 27-38. Dark brown or blackish above, lighter brown on the sides; young with a yellow blotch on the parietal shields; belly brown or white, more or less spotted with black; tail black.

Total length 360 millim.; tail 45.

Fiji Islands.

a-b. ♂ (V. 152; C. 38) & yg. (V 139; C. 38).	Viti Levu.	Dr. J. G. Fischer.
c. ♀ (V. 146, C. 33).	Fiji Islands.	Christiania Museum.
d. ♀ (V. 140; C. 35).	Fiji Islands.	Museum Godeffroy.
e. ♂ (V. 141, C. 35).	Fiji Islands	Dr Gunther [P.].
f. ♀ skeleton.	Viti Levu.	

215. GLYPHODON.

Glyphodon, part., *Gunth Cat. Col. Sn* p. 210 (1858).
Brachysoma, part., *Krefft, Sn. Austral.* p 48 (1869).

Maxillary extending forwards as far as the palatine, with a pair of large grooved poison-fangs, followed, after a wide interspace, by 6 small grooved teeth; mandibular teeth feebly grooved, anterior strongly enlarged, fang-like. Head small, not distinct from neck; eye very small, with round or vertically subelliptic pupil; nostril pierced between two nasals; no loreal. Body cylindrical; scales smooth, without pits, in 17 rows; ventrals rounded. Tail short; subcaudals in two rows.

New Guinea and North Australia.

In this genus the præ- and postfrontals meet, excluding the frontal from the orbital periphery, as in the Sea-snakes of the genera *Distira* and *Enhydris*, which are likewise distinguished by feeble grooves on all the maxillary teeth.

Fig. 22.

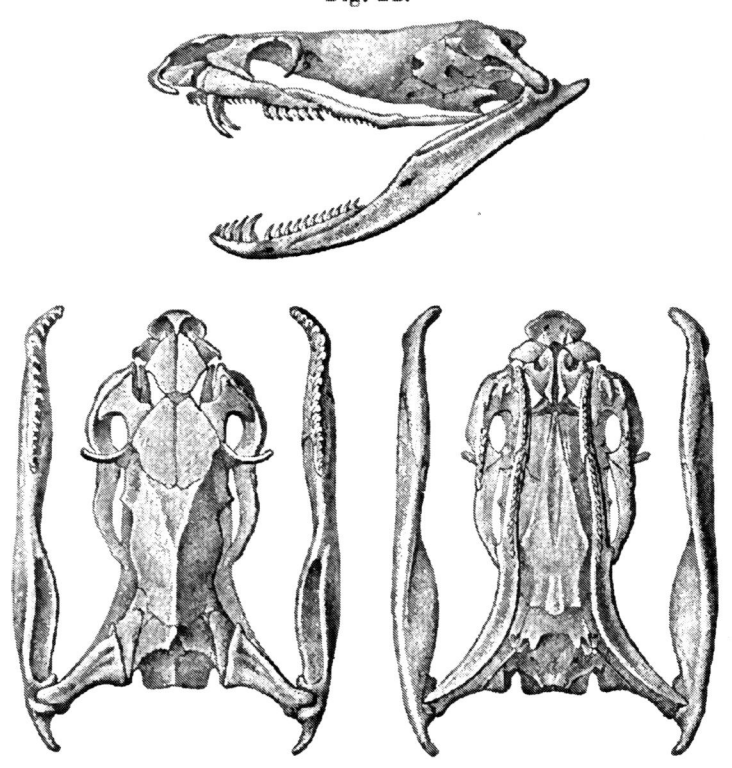

Skull of *Glyphodon tristis.*

1. Glyphodon tristis. (PLATE XVIII. fig. 1.)

Glyphodon tristis, *Günth. Cat.* p. 211 (1858).
Brachysoma triste, *Günth. Ann. & Mag. N. H.* (3) xi. 1863, p. 24; *Krefft, Sn. Austral.* p. 50 (1869); *Ramsay, Proc. Linn. Soc. N. S. W.* ii. 1877, p. 113; *Douglas-Ogilby, Rec. Austral. Mus.* i. 1890, p. 97.

Snout rounded. Eye very small, about half as long as its distance from the mouth. Rostral twice as broad as deep, visible from above; internasals one half to two thirds the length of the præfrontals; frontal once and one fifth to once and a half as long as broad, at least twice as broad as the supraocular, as long as its distance from the rostral or the end of the snout, three fifths to two thirds the length of the parietals; posterior nasal widely separated from the single præocular; two postoculars; temporals 2+2, lower anterior wedged in between the fifth and sixth upper labials; six upper labials, second or second and third in contact with the præfrontal, third and fourth entering the eye; four lower labials in contact with the anterior chin-shields, which are as long as or a little shorter than the posterior. Scales in 17 rows. Ventrals 165–179; anal divided;

subcaudals 38–52, all in pairs or a few of the anterior single Dark-brown or blackish above, the scales edged with lighter; occiput and nape often yellowish or pale reddish brown; belly yellow, outer ends of the ventrals dark brown, subcaudals dark brown in front, yellow behind.

Total length 900 millim.; tail 125.

North-eastern Australia and South-eastern New Guinea.

a. ♂ (V. 179; C. 48).	N.E. Australia.	J. Macgillivray, Esq. [C.]. (Type)	
b. ♂ (V. 175; C 52).	N.E Australia	G. Krefft, Esq. [P]	
c. Hgr. (V. 165; C. 42).	Torres Straits.	Rev S Macfarlane [C.].	
d. ♀ (V. 166; C. 41).	Cornwallis I., Torres Straits.	Rev. S. Macfarlane [C.].	
e–i ♂ (V. 172, 172, 170, 169, C. 46, 43, 47, 45, 46).	Murray I, Torres Straits.	Rev. S. Macfarlane [C.].	
k ♂ (V. 170; C. 47).	Murray I., Torres Straits.	Prof. A. C. Haddon [P.].	
l–m. ♀ (V. 169, 171, C. 40, 38).	S E New Guinea.	Rev. S. Macfarlane [C].	
n–o. ♂ (V. 174, C. 46) & hgr. (V 168; C.43).	Fly River.	Rev S. Macfarlane [C.].	
p. Skull of g.			

216. PSEUDELAPS.

Elaps, part, *Schleg Phys. Serp* ii. p 435 (1837)
Pseudelaps, part., *Dum & Bibr. Mém. Ac Sc* xxiii 1853, p 517, *and Erp. Gén* vii p 1231 (1854); *Jan, Elenco sist. Ofid* p 115 (1863).
Furina, part, *Dum. & Bibr. ll. cc* pp. 517, 1236.
Glyphodon, part., *Gunth. Cat. Col. Sn.* p 210 (1858).
Diemansia, part, *Gunth l. c* p. 211.
Brachysoma, part., *Gunth. l. c.* p. 228; *Krefft, Sn. Austral.* p. 48 (1869).
Cacophis, *Gunth Ann. & Mag. N. H.* (3) xii. 1863, p. 361, *Krefft, l c.* p 73.
Petrodymon, *Krefft, Sn. Sydney*, p. 55 (1865), *and l. c* p. 72.

Maxillary extending forwards as far as the palatine, with a pair of large grooved poison-fangs followed, after a wide interspace, by 8 to 12 small grooved teeth; anterior mandibular teeth strongly enlarged, fang-like. Head slightly distinct from neck; eye small,

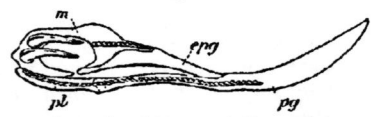

Fig. 23.

Left maxillo-palatal bones of *Pseudelaps muelleri*.
epg Ectopterygoid. *m*. Maxillary. *Pg*. Pterygoid. *pl*. Palatine.

with vertically elliptic pupil; nasal single or divided; no loreal. Body cylindrical; scales smooth, without pits, in 15 or 17 rows; ventrals rounded. Tail moderate or short; subcaudals in two rows.

Australia, Moluccas, Papuasia.

The maxillary develops an inner backward process, which reaches or nearly reaches the ectopterygoid and the posterior portion of the maxillary, the two bones together being loop-shaped in front. The præfrontal is narrowly separated from the postfrontal.

Synopsis of the Species.

I. Scales in 15 rows.

   A. Nasal in contact with or narrowly separated from the præocular.

     1. Nasal divided.

Temporals 2+2; ventrals 139-176; subcaudals 21-35 .... 1. *muelleri*, p. 316.
Temporals 1+2; ventrals 170-183; subcaudals 34-52 .... 2. *squamulosus*, p. 317.

     2. Nasal entire; temporals 1+2; subcaudals 26-38.

Ventrals 146-156 .... 3. *krefftii*, p. 317.
Ventrals 167-172 .... 4. *fordii*, p. 318.
Ventrals 176-193 .... 5. *harriettæ*, p. 318.

   B. Nasal widely separated from the præocular; temporals 2+2.

Third and fourth upper labials entering the eye; ventrals 164-203 .... 6. *diadema*, p. 319.
Fourth and fifth upper labials entering the eye; ventrals 143 .... 7. *warro*, p. 320.

II. Scales in 17 rows .... 8. *sutherlandi*, p. 320.

1. Pseudelaps muelleri.

Elaps muelleri, *Schleg. Phys. Serp.* ii. p. 452, pl. xvi. figs. 16 & 17 (1837); *Schleg & Müll. in Temminck, Verh. Nat. Nederl. Ind., Zool.* p. 66, pl. ix. figs. 1 & 2 (1844).
Pseudelaps muelleri, *Dum. & Bibr.* vii. p. 1233 (1854).
Demansia muelleri, *Gunth. Cat.* p 213 (1858).
Diemenia muelleri, *Gunth. Ann & Mag N. H.* (4) ix 1872, p. 84; *Peters & Doria, Ann. Mus Genova,* xiii. 1878, p. 408; *Boettg. in Semon, Zool. Forsch.* v. p. 121 (1894); *Méhely, Term Fuzet.* xviii. 1895, p. 135.
—— schlegelii, *Gunth. l. c.* p. 35; *Peters & Doria, l. c.*
Trimeresurus ikaheka, juv., *Sauvage, Bull Soc. Philom.* (7) i. 1878, p. 44.

Eye as long as or slightly longer than its distance from the mouth (larger in the young). Rostral twice as broad as deep, scarcely visible from above; internasals shorter than the præfrontals; frontal once and two thirds to twice as long as broad, longer than its distance from the end of the snout, shorter than the parietals; nasal divided, in contact with the single præocular; two postoculars; temporals 2+2, lower anterior wedged in between the fifth and sixth upper labials; six upper labials, third and fourth entering the eye; three or four lower labials in contact with the anterior chin-shields, which are as long as or shorter than the posterior. Scales in 15 rows. Ventrals 139-176; anal divided; subcaudals 21–35. Brown above; a light vertebral line sometimes present on the anterior part of the body; head sometimes spotted or variegated with dark brown; a more or less distinct dark, light-edged streak on each side of the head, passing through the eye, sometimes continued along the neck; a dark brown nuchal collar may be present in the young; belly yellowish or coral-red, uniform or more or less profusely spotted or speckled with brown or black; gular region brown or black.

Total length 500 millim.; tail 70.

Moluccas, New Guinea, New Britain.

a. ♀ (V. 173; C. 33).	N. Ceram.	
b, c ♀ (V. 149, 155; C. 24, 21).	Mysol.	(Types of *D schlegelii*.)
d–e, f ♂ (V. 150; C. 29) & ♀ (V. 169, 151, C. 29, 25).	Mansinam, New Guinea.	M. L. Laglaize [C.].
g–i. ♂ (V. 139; C. 31), ♀ (V. 152; C. 30), & yg. (V. 145; C. 28).	Trobriand Is., E. New Guinea.	Mr. A. S. Meek [C.].
k–n. ♀ (V. 150, 156, 154, 152; C. 35, 34, 33, 30).	Fergusson I., E. New Guinea.	Mr A. S. Meek [C.].
o. Hgr. (V. 160, C. 32).	Duke of York I.	Rev. G. Brown [C.].
p. Yg. (V. 160; C. 31).	New Britain.	Museum Godeffroy.
q. Skull of g.		

2. Pseudelaps squamulosus.

Pseudelaps squamulosus, *Dum. & Bibr.* vii. p. 1235 (1854) *.
Diemansia cucullata, *Gunth. Ann. & Mag N. H.* (3) ix. 1862, p. 129, & xi. 1863, p 24.
Petrodymon cucullatum, *Krefft, Sn. Sydney*, p 55 (1865), *and Sn. Austral.* p. 72, pl. vi. fig 10 (1869).
Pseudelaps atropolios, *Jan, Icon. Gén.* 43, pl. v. fig. 1 (1873).

Eye nearly as long as its distance from the mouth. Rostral twice as broad as deep, just visible from above; internasals shorter than the præfrontals; frontal once and a half to once and two thirds as long as broad, as long as its distance from the end of the snout, shorter than the parietals; nasal divided, in contact with the single præocular; two postoculars; temporals 1+2; six upper labials, third and fourth entering the eye, sixth very large; four lower labials in contact with the anterior chin-shields, which are a little shorter than the posterior. Scales in 15 rows. Ventrals 170–183; anal divided; subcaudals 34–52. Dark brown above, with a yellowish streak round the snout and through the eyes to the nape, where it widens and approaches its fellow; lower parts whitish, closely spotted with black, the spots sometimes confluent into transverse lines, one to each shield.

Total length 375 millim.; tail 55.

New South Wales.

---

* Dr. Mocquard has kindly supplied me with notes on the type specimen.

a. Hgr. (V. 176; C. 47).	Near Sydney.	G. Krefft, Esq. [P.].	
		(Type of *D. cucullata.*)	
b, c. ♂ (V. 178; C. 52)	Port Macquarie.	G. Krefft, Esq [P.].	
& ♀ (V. 183; C. 34).			

3. Pseudelaps krefftii.

Cacophis krefftii, *Günth. Ann. & Mag. N. H.* (3) xii. 1863, p. 361; *Krefft, Sn Austral.* p. 74, pl xi. fig. 5 (1869).

Eye as long as its distance from the mouth. Rostral twice as broad as deep, scarcely visible from above; internasals shorter than præfrontals; frontal once and one fourth as long as broad, a little longer than its distance from the end of the snout, shorter than the parietals; nasal entire, in contact with the single præocular; two postoculars; temporals 1+2; six upper labials, third and fourth entering the eye, three or four lower labials in contact with the anterior chin-shields, which are as long as or shorter than the posterior. Scales in 15 rows. Ventrals 146-156; anal divided; subcaudals 26-38. —Dark brown or blackish above, each scale with a light longitudinal line; a yellowish cross-band on the occiput, connected with the yellowish colour of the sides of the head and end of snout; lateral head-shields spotted and streaked with dark brown; ventrals whitish, edged with black, at least on the sides; subcaudals whitish, with a black longitudinal streak running between them.

Total length 255 millim.; tail 33.

Queensland.

a. Yg. (V. 146; C. 38).	North of the Clarence R.	G. Krefft, Esq. [P.].
		(Type.)
b. Hgr. (V. 151; C. 26).	North of the Clarence R	G. Krefft, Esq. [P.].

4. Pseudelaps fordii.

Cacophis fordei, *Krefft, Proc. Zool Soc.* 1869, p. 318, fig., *and Sn. Austral.* p. 75, pl. xii. fig. 8 (1869).

Appears to agree in almost every respect with *P. krefftii* and *P. harriettæ*, but the ventrals number 167-172 and are yellow, with a dark edge.

Ipswich, Queensland.

5. Pseudelaps harriettæ.

Cacophis harriettæ, *Krefft, Proc. Zool. Soc.* 1869, p. 319, fig., *and Sn Austral.* p. 76, pl. xi. fig. 13 (1869).

Eye hardly as long as its distance from the mouth. Rostral twice as broad as deep, scarcely visible from above; internasals shorter than the præfrontals; frontal once and a half as long as broad, a little longer than its distance from the end of the snout, shorter than the parietals; nasal entire, in contact with or narrowly separated from the single præocular; two postoculars; temporals 1+2; six upper labials, third and fourth entering the eye; four lower labials in contact with the anterior chin-shields, which are as long as the posterior. Scales in 15 rows. Ventrals 176–193; anal divided, subcaudals 29–35. Dark brown above, each scale with a light longitudinal line; a large yellowish blotch on the nape, connected with the yellowish colour of the sides of the head and end of snout; lateral head-shields spotted and streaked with dark brown; ventrals and subcaudals brown or blackish, edged with whitish

Total length 415 millim.; tail 45.

Queensland.

a–b. ♀ (V. 178; C. 29) & yg. (V 176; C 34). Gayndah. Museum Godeffroy

6. Pseudelaps diadema.

Calamaria diadema, *Schleg Phys. Serp.* ii. p. 32 (1837).
Elaps ornatus, *Gray, Zool. Miscell* p. 55 (1842).
Furina diadema, *Dum. & Bibr.* vii. p. 1239 (1854); *Jan, Rev. & Mag. Zool* 1859, p 124.
Rabdion occipitale, *Girard, Proc. Ac. Philad.* 1857, p. 181, and *U.S Explor Exped., Herp.* p. 120 (1858).
Glyphodon ornatus, *Gunth. Cat.* p. 210 (1858).
Pseudelaps diadema, *Jan, Elenco,* p. 116 (1863), and *Icon. Gen.* 43, pl. v. fig. 4 (1873).
Brachysoma diadema, *Gunth. Ann. & Mag. N H* (3) xi. 1863, p. 23, *Krefft, Sn. Austr.* p. 48, pl. xii. fig. 12 (1869)
Cacophis blackmanni, *Krefft, Proc. Zool. Soc.* 1869, p. 320, fig., and *l. c.* p. 77, pl. xii fig 9.
Brachysoma simile, *Macleay, Proc. Linn. Soc. N. S. W.* ii. 1878, p 221.

Eye longer than its distance from the mouth. Rostral not quite twice as broad as deep, just visible from above; internasals shorter than the præfrontals; frontal once and one fifth to once and two thirds as long as broad, as long as or a little longer than its distance from the end of the snout, shorter than the parietals, nasal entire, widely separated from the single præocular; two postoculars; temporals 2+2, lower anterior wedged in between the fifth and sixth upper labials, sometimes reaching the lip and forming an additional labial; six (or seven) upper labials, second or second and third in contact with the præfrontal, third and fourth entering the eye; three or four lower labials in contact with the anterior chin-shields, which are as long as or a little shorter than the posterior. Scales in 15 rows. Ventrals 164–203; anal divided; subcaudals 40–62. Pale brown or reddish above, each scale edged with dark brown, forming a reticulate pattern, or uniform dark brown; head and nape dark brown or black above, with a yellow cross-band on the occiput or a transversely oval yellow blotch surrounded with dark brown; lower parts uniform white.

Total length 600 millim.; tail 80.

Eastern, Northern, and Western Australia.

a. ♂ (V. 169; C. 62). W. Australia. W. Buchanan, Esq. (Type of *E. ornatus*.)
b. Yg. (V. 177; C. 53). N. Australia. Dr. J. R. Elsey [P.]

c-d. ♂ (V. 174; C. 54) & yg. (V. 164; O. 50).	N.E. Australia.	
e. ♂ (V. 168; C. 47).	Queensland.	
f. Yg. (V. 175; C. 44).	Parramatta, N.S.Wales.	A G. Butler, Esq. [P.].
g. ♂ (V. 166; C. ?).	New South Wales.	ImperialInstitute[P.].
h, i, k. ♂ (V. 168; C. 43), ♀ (V. 179; C. 41), & yg. (V. 168; C. 42).	New South Wales (?).	G. Krefft, Esq. [P.].
l. ♀ (V. 191; C. 43).	Australia.	Sir J. Richardson [P.].
m, n. ♀ (V. 203, 193; C 40, 45).	Australia.	Haslar Collection.

7. Pseudelaps warro.

Cacophis warro, *De Vis, Proc. R. Soc Queensl.* i. 1884, p. 139.

Rostral broad and low; frontal broad, acute-angled behind; nasal single, short, widely separated from the præocular; two postoculars; temporals 2+2; seven upper labials, third and fourth in contact with the præfrontal, fourth and fifth entering the eye. Scales in 15 rows Ventrals 143; anal divided; subcaudals 15 (?). Brown, many of the scales irregularly edged with darker; a very broad lunate blackish collar on the nape; upper surface of head, except the tips of the parietal shields, dark, but paler than the nuchal collar.

Port Curtis, Queensland.

8. Pseudelaps sutherlandi.

Brachysoma sutherlandi, *De Vis, Proc. R Soc. Queensl.* i. 1884, p. 139.

Rostral broad; frontal acute-angled behind; nasal single, in contact with the præocular; a single anterior temporal; six upper labials. Scales in 17 rows. Ventrals 160; anal divided; subcaudals 40. Red-brown above, yellow beneath, a broad lunate blackish nuchal collar, edged with lighter; faint bars across the head, body, and tail.

Norman River, Queensland.

217. DIEMENIA.

Elaps, part., *Schleg. Phys. Serp.* ii. p. 435 (1837).
Demansia, *Gray, Zool. Miscell.* p. 54 (1842).
Pseudelaps, part., *Dum. & Bibr. Mém. Ac. Sci.* xxiii. 1853, p. 517, and *Erp. Gén.* vii. p. 1231 (1854); *Jan, Elenco sist. Ofid.* p. 115 (1863).
Furina, part., *Dum. & Bibr ll. cc.* pp. 517, 1236.
Demansia, part., *Gunth. Cat. Col. Sn.* p. 211 (1858).
Pseudonaja, *Gunth. l. c.* p. 227.
Diemansia, *Gunth. l. c.* p. 254.
Diemenia, *Gunth. Ann. & Mag. N. H.* (3) xii. 1863, p. 350; *Krefft, Sn. Austral.* p. 38 (1869).

217. DIEMENIA.

? Elapocephalus (*non Gunth*), *Macleay, Proc. Linn. Soc. N. S. W.* ii. 1878, p 221.
? Elapocranium, *Macleay, Proc. Linn Soc. N. S. W.* ix. 1884, p 560.

Maxillary extending forwards as far as the palatine, with a pair of large grooved poison-fangs followed, after an interspace, by 7 to 15 small grooved teeth; anterior mandibular teeth strongly enlarged, fang-like. Head slightly distinct from neck, with distinct canthus rostralis; eye moderate or large, with round pupil; nasal entire or divided; frontal elongate; no loreal. Body cylindrical; scales smooth, without pits, in 15 to 19 rows (more on the neck); belly rounded. Tail moderate or long; subcaudals all or most in two rows.

Australia and New Guinea.

Fig. 24.

Maxillary and mandible of *Diemenia psammophis*.

Synopsis of the Species.

I. Scales in 15 rows; rostral just visible from above.
   A. Anal divided.

Rostral nearly as deep as broad; internasals at least half as long as the præfrontals	1. *psammophis*, p. 322.
Rostral a little broader than deep; internasals more than half as long as the præfrontals	2. *torquata*, p. 323.
Rostral considerably broader than deep; internasals not more than half as long as the præfrontals	3. *olivacea*, p. 323.
B. Anal entire	4. *ornaticeps*, p. 324.

II. Scales in 17 or 19 rows.

Portion of rostral visible from above measuring about half its distance from the frontal; ventrals 154–165	5. *modesta*, p. 324.
Portion of rostral visible from above measuring one half to two thirds its distance from the frontal; ventrals 190–232	6. *textilis*, p. 325.
Portion of rostral visible from above as as long as its distance from the frontal; ventrals 184–224	7. *nuchalis*, p. 326.

1. Diemenia psammophis.

Elaps psammophis, *Schleg. Phys. Serp* ii p 455 (1837), *and Abbild.* p 137, pl xlvi. fig 14 (1844).
Lycodon reticulatus, *Gray, Zool. Miscell.* p. 54 (1842).
Demansia reticulata, *Gray, l. c.*; *Gunth. Cat.* p. 212 (1858).
Pseudelaps psammophidius, *Dum. & Bibr.* vii. p. 1234 (1854).
Demansia psammophis, *Gunth. l. c.*
Pseudelaps psammophis, *Girard, U S Explor Exped., Herp.* p. 178 (1858); *Jan, Icon Gén.* 43, pl. iii. fig. 3 (1873).
Diemenia psammophis, *Krefft, Sn. Sydney,* p 42 (1865); *Steind. Novara, Rept.* p 80 (1867); *Krefft, Proc Zool. Soc.* 1868, p. 3, *and Sn. Austral* p. 38 (1869).
—— reticulata, *Krefft, Sn. Austral.* p 40, pl xii. fig. 10
—— papuensis, *Macleay, Proc. Linn. Soc. N. S. W.* ii. 1877, p. 40.

Eye large. Rostral nearly as deep as broad, visible from above; internasals one half to two thirds the length of the præfrontals; frontal not broader than the supraocular, twice to twice and a half as long as broad, as long as or longer than its distance from the end of the snout, a little shorter than the parietals; nasal divided, in contact with the single præocular; two (rarely three) postoculars; temporals 2+2, lower anterior wedged in between the fifth and sixth upper labials; six upper labials, third and fourth entering the eye; three lower labials in contact with the anterior chin-shields, which are shorter than the posterior. Scales in 15 rows (17 to 20 on the neck). Ventrals 170–225; anal divided; subcaudals 69–105. Coloration very variable; lower surface of tail, at the end, yellow or orange; young with a dark line across the rostral, gradually disappearing with age, and two oblique dark-edged yellow streaks, one in front, the other behind the eye.

Total length 1420 millim.; tail 340.

South-eastern New Guinea and Australia.

A. Olive-brown above, the scales narrowly edged or tipped with black; belly greyish or pale olive, darker along the median line. (*D. psammophis,* Schleg.)

a. ♀ (V. 176; C 72). Sydney. G. Krefft, Esq [P.].
b. ♀ (V. 176; C. 74). ——?

B. Olive or reddish brown to blackish above, the scales narrowly edged or tipped with black, some with light outer edge; ventrals olive or dark plumbeous-grey, darker along the margins. (*D. psammophis,* Gthr.; *D. papuensis,* Macl.)

a–b. ♂ (V. 173; C. 73) & ♀ (V. 173; C. ?). Fly R., Brit. New Guinea. Rev. S. Macfarlane [C.].
c. ♂ (V. 173; C. 81). Port Moresby, Brit. New Guinea. Rev. W. G. Turner [C.].
d ♂ (V. 175; C. 79). Somerset, Cape York. H.M.S. 'Challenger.'
e, f ♂ (V. 179, 210; C. 78, 105). Port Essington. Lord Derby [P.].
g. ♂ (V. 193; C. 85). Daly River. Dr. Dahl [C.]; Christiania Mus. [E.].

h. Skull of *a.*

C. Pale olive above, each scale edged with black, the black forming a reticulate pattern; uniform yellowish white beneath. (*D. reticulata*, Gray.)

a, b-c, d-e. ♂ (V 181, 176; C 78, 72) & ♀ (V. 188, 180, 189, C. 71, 70, 70₁.	Australia.	(Types of *D. reticulata*.)
f. ♀ (V. 186, C. 72).	N.W. Australia.	
g. ♂ (V 177; C 75).	W. Australia	
h. ♀ (V. 188; C. 69).	Swan River.	

2. Diemenia torquata.

Demansia torquata, *Gunth. Ann. & Mag. N. H.* (3) ix. 1862, p. 130, pl. ix. fig. 10.
Diemenia torquata, *Krefft, Sn. Austral.* p. 43, pl xii. fig. 11 (1869).

Eye large. Rostral a little broader than deep, visible from above; internasals three fifths to two thirds the length of the præfrontals; frontal not broader than the supraocular, twice to twice and a half as long as broad, considerably longer than its distance from the end of the snout, a little shorter than the parietals; nasal divided, in contact with the single præocular; two postoculars; temporals 2+2, lower anterior wedged in between the fifth and sixth upper labials; six upper labials, third and fourth entering the eye; three or four lower labials in contact with the anterior chin-shields, which are shorter than the posterior. Scales in 15 rows (17 on the neck) Ventrals 191–203; anal divided; subcaudals 75–81. Olive above, most of the scales black at the base; head dark olive or black above, the sides of the snout and the postoculars yellowish white, a black streak from eye to eye across the rostral; a black streak from below the eye to the commissure of the mouth; labials black-edged, a black or dark olive band, edged with yellow, across the nape; lower surface of head variegated with black, belly olive or plumbeous, with a darker median streak, end of tail orange.

Total length 580 millim.; tail 145.

N.E. Australia.

a. ♀ (V. 203; C. 81).	Percy Id.	F. M. Rayner, Esq. [P.]. (Type)	
b. Yg. (V. 196; C. 75).	Rockhampton.		
c. Yg. (V. 191; C. 76).	Queensland.	Dr. Coppinger [C.]; H.M S. 'Alert.'	

3. Diemenia olivacea. (PLATE XVIII. fig. 2.)

Lycodon olivaceus, *Gray, Zool Miscell.* p. 54 (1842).
Demansia olivacea, *Gunth. Cat.* p. 212 (1858).
Diemenia olivacea, *Krefft, Sn. Austral* p. 39, pl. vi. fig. 9 (1869); *Peters & Doria, Ann. Mus. Genova*, xiii. 1878, p. 408.
? Diemenia atra, *Macleay, Proc. Linn. Soc. N. S W.* ix. 1884, p. 549.
Diemenia angusticeps, *Macleay, Proc. Linn. Soc. N. S. W.* (2) iii. 1888, p 417

Eye large. Rostral broader than deep, visible from above;

internasals not more than half the length of the præfrontals; frontal not broader than the supraocular, twice to twice and a half as long as broad, considerably longer than its distance from the end of the snout, a little shorter than the parietals; nasal divided, in contact with the single præocular; two postoculars; temporals 2+2, lower anterior wedged in between the fifth and sixth upper labials, and sometimes reaching the lip; six upper labials, third and fourth entering the eye; three or four lower labials in contact with the anterior chin-shields, which are a little shorter than the posterior. Scales in 15 rows (17 on the neck). Ventrals 162-215; anal divided; subcaudals 79-99. Olive, reddish brown, or dark brown above, most of the scales black at the base, some with light edges; snout and sides of the head speckled or vermiculated with dark brown, and with an oblique dark streak below the eye to beyond the commissure of the jaws; these markings disappearing in full-grown specimens; lower parts yellowish, uniform or speckled with olive, throat and anterior ventrals spotted with blackish in the young; tail yellow or reddish.

Total length 1010 millim.; tail 240.

Northern Australia and New Guinea.

a, b ♂ (V. 163, 174; C. 95, 86).	N E Australia.	Sir J Richardson [P]. (Types)
c-d. ♂ (V. 175; C. 97) & ♀ (V. 215; C. 99).	Port Darwin.	R. G. S. Buckland, Esq. [C.].
e. Yg. (V. 162; C. 79)	Australia.	

Diemenia atra of Macleay is probably founded on a melanotic specimen of this species.

4. Diemenia ? ornaticeps.

Elapocephalus ornaticeps, *Macleay, Proc. Linn Soc. N.S.W.* ii. 1878, p. 221.

Elapocranium ornaticeps, *Macleay, Proc. Linn. Soc. N.S.W.* ix. 1884, p. 560.

Eye large. Scales in 15 rows. Ventrals 187; anal entire; subcaudals 90. Pale slate-colour above, each scale tipped with red; head brown, each shield beautifully marked with variously shaped white-margined black patches; an orange collar on the nape; slaty white beneath, head and neck barred and spotted with black; end of tail yellow.

Total length 255 millim.; tail 65.

Port Darwin, Northern Australia.

5. Diemenia modesta.

Cacophis modesta, *Gunth. Ann. & Mag N. H.* (4) ix. 1872, p. 35, pl. iii fig. C.

Furina ramsayi, *Macleay, Proc. Linn. Soc N S W.* x 1885, p. 61.

Eye moderate. Rostral a little broader than deep, the portion visible from above about half as long as its distance from the frontal; internasals one half to two thirds as long as the præfrontals; frontal not broader than the supraocular, once and two thirds to twice as long as broad, as long as or a little longer than its distance from the end of the snout, a little shorter than the parietals; nasal entire, in contact with the single præocular; one or two postoculars; temporals 1+2; six upper labials, third and fourth entering the eye, sixth largest; four lower labials in contact with the anterior chin-shields, which are as long as the posterior. Scales in 17 rows (19 or 20 on the neck). Ventrals 154-165; anal divided; subcaudals 38-51 pairs. Pale olive above, with or without a few widely separated blackish cross-lines; young with a black band across the head and another across the nape, separated by a yellow band, and a yellow blotch in front of the eye; these markings becoming indistinct with age; yellowish white beneath, with or without small dark spots.

Total length 435 millim.; tail 80.

Western Australia.

a. Hgr. ♂ (V. 154; C 48). Perth. Mr. Duboulay [C].
b. Hgr. ♂ (V. 157; C. 49). W. Australia. Dr Gunther [P.]. (Types.)
c. Hgr. ♀ (V. 165; C. 42). N W. Australia.
d. Yg. (V. 156, C. P). N.W. Australia Capt. Beckett [P.].
e-f. ♂ (V. 158, 156; C. 51, 50). Geraldton, W. Australia. Mr. E. H. Saunders [C.].

6. Diemenia textilis.

Furina textilis, *Dum. & Bibr.* vii. p. 1242 (1854); *Steind. Novara, Rept.* p. 79 (1867).
Pseudoelaps superciliosus, *Fischer, Abh. Naturw. Humb.* iii. 1856, p. 107, pl. ii. fig. 3; *Jan, Rev. & Mag. Zool.* 1859, p. 511, *and Icon Gén* 43, pl iv fig. 1 (1873).
Demansia annulata, *Gunth. Cat.* p. 213 (1858), *and Ann. & Mag. N. H.* (3) xi. 1863, p. 24.
Pseudoelaps sordellii, *Jan, Rev. & Mag. Zool.* 1859, p. 127, *and Prodr.* pl C (1859).
—— kubingii, *Jan, ll. cc.*
Pseudonaja textilis, *Krefft, Proc. Zool. Soc.* 1862, p. 149.
Diemansia kubingii, *Gunth. Ann. & Mag. N. H* (3) ix. 1862, p. 53.
Diemenia superciliosa, *Gunth. Proc. Zool. Soc.* 1863, p 17, fig., *and Zool. Rec.* 1867, p 142; *Krefft, Sn. Austral* pp. 41 & 51, pl vii. & pl. xi. fig 10 (1869); *McCoy, Prodr. Zool Vict*, Dec. 3, p. 11, pl. xxiii. fig 1 (1879); *Zietz, Trans R Soc S Austral.* x. 1888, p. 300; *F. Mull. Verh. Nat. Ges Basel*, viii. 1889, p. 696.
Diemansia (Pseudelaps) superciliosa, *Peters, Mon. Berl. Ac.* 1863, p. 234.
Cacophis guentherii, *Steind. l. c.* p. 91, fig.
Pseudoelaps beckeri, *Jan, Icon. Gen.* 43, pl. iv. fig. 2 (1873).
—— textilis, *Jan, l. c.* pl. v, fig. 5.
Furina cucullata, *McCoy, op. cit.*, Dec 4, p. 13, pl. xxxii. (1879).

Eye moderate, rather large in the young. Rostral nearly as deep as broad, the portion visible from above measuring one half to two thirds its distance from the frontal; internasals one half to two thirds the length of the præfrontals; frontal not broader than the supraocular, once and three fourths to twice as long as broad, as long as or a little longer than its distance from the end of the snout, a little shorter than the parietals; nasal entire (rarely divided), in contact with the single præocular; two (rarely three) postoculars; temporals 1+2; six upper labials, third and fourth entering the eye, sixth largest; four lower labials in contact with the anterior chin-shields, which are nearly as long as the posterior. Scales in 17 rows (20 to 23 on the neck). Ventrals 190–232; anal divided; subcaudals 46–73, all or most in pairs Adult uniform pale brown or dark olive-brown above, whitish or olive beneath; young with a black blotch on the crown, separated from a large black blotch on the nape by an orange cross-band; belly spotted with brown or black.

Total length 1700 millim.; tail 290.

Eastern Australia, from Cape York to Victoria.

A. No cross-bars on the body.

a	♂ (V. 215; C. 69).	New South Wales.	Imperial Institute [P.].
b.	Hgr. (V. 220; C. 67).	New South Wales.	G. Krefft, Esq. [P.].
c	Hgr (V 207; C. 67)	Sydney.	G. Krefft, Esq. [P.].
d	Hgr. (V. 202; C. 64).	Sandhurst, Victoria.	Col Beddome [C.].
e.	Yg. (V 202; C. 66).	Adelaide.	G Krefft, Esq. [P]
f.	Yg (V. 197; C. 67).	Adelaide.	Prof Peters [P.].
g.	Yg. (V. 213; C. 52).	Adelaide	Rev. T. S. Lea [P.].
h.	♀ (V. 213; C. 68).	Norfolk Id.	Sir A. Smith [P.].

B. Body with black cross-bars.

a–b.	Yg. (V. 200, 194; C. 66, 61).	New South Wales.	Imperial Institute [P].
c.	Yg. (V. 195; C. 60).	Sydney.	G. Krefft, Esq. [P.].
d	Yg. (V. 194; C. 68).	Sydney.	Dr. Corrie [P.].
e.	Yg. (V. 193; C. 71).	Australia.	R W. Willan, Esq [P]. (Type of D. annulata.)
f.	Yg. (V. 191; C. 64).	Australia.	Capt. Stokes [P.].

7. Diemenia nuchalis.

Pseudonaja nuchalis, Gunth. Cat. p. 227 (1858), and Proc. Zool. Soc. 1863, p. 17, fig.; McCoy, Ann & Mag. N. H. (3) xx. 1867, p 182; Krefft, Sn. Austral p. 44, pl. xii. fig. 13 (1869); Macleay, Proc. Linn. Soc. N.S. W. ii. 1878, p. 219; De Vis, Proc. R. Soc. Queensl. i. 1884, p 58

—— affinis, Gunth. Ann & Mag. N. H. (4) ix. 1872, p. 35. pl. iv. fig. C.

Diemenia aspidorhyncha, McCoy, Prodr. Zool. Vict., Dec. 3, p. 13, pl. xxiii. fig. 4 (1879).

Eye moderate. Rostral deeper than broad, the portion visible from above as long as its distance from the frontal; internasals shorter than the præfrontals; frontal broader than the supraocular, once and a half to once and two thirds as long as broad, as long as or a little shorter than its distance from the end of the snout, two thirds to three fourths the length of the parietals; nasal entire or semidivided, in contact with the single præocular; two postoculars; temporals 1+2; six upper labials, third and fourth entering the eye, sixth very large. Scales in 17 or 19 rows (20 to 23 on the neck). Ventrals 184–224; anal divided; subcaudals 55-65 pairs. Adult uniform brown above, or blackish with pale brown crossbands, yellowish beneath, uniform, or with small red spots; young with a dark brown blotch covering the crown and followed by another on the nape, and small brown spots on the belly.

Total length 1400 millim.; tail 200.

Australia.

A. Body with cross-bands.

a. ♂, skin (Sc. 17, V. 202, Port Essington.   Lord Derby [P.]. C 63)   (Type)

b. Yg. (Sc 17; V. 220; N.W. Australia.   Sir J. Richardson [P.]. C. 65).   (Type.)

B. No cross-bands on the body.

a ♂ (Sc 17; V. 184; N.W. Australia.   R Bynoe, Esq. [C]; C. 59).   Sir J Richardson [P.]. (Type)

b. ♀ (Sc. 17; V. 223; C. Geraldton, W.   Mr. E. H. Saunders [C.]. 61).   Australia.

c Yg. (Sc. 19; V. 224; Swan River.   Dr. Gunther [P]. C. 61)

d. ♀ (Sc. 19; V. 216; Australia.   G. Krefft, Esq. [P.] C. 63).   (Type of *P affinis*)

218. PSEUDECHIS.

Trimeresurus, part, *Lacép. Ann. du Mus.* iv. 1804, p. 209; *Dum. & Bibr. Erp. Gén.* vii. p. 1244 (1854); *Jan, Elenco sist. Ofid.* p. 118 (1863)

Hurria, part., *Merr. Tent. Syst Herp.* p 92 (1820).

Pseudechis, *Wagl. Syst. Amph.* p. 171 (1830); *Günth. Cat. Col. Sn.* p 217 (1858), *Krefft, Sn Austral.* p 45 (1869).

Naja, part, *Schleg Phys Serp* ii. p. 461 (1837).

Maxillary extending forwards as far as the palatine, with a pair of large grooved poison-fangs followed by 2 to 5 small solid teeth; mandibular teeth, anterior longest. Head distinct from neck, with distinct canthus rostralis; eye moderate or rather small, with round pupil; nostril between two nasals; no loreal. Body cylindrical; scales smooth, without pits, in 17 to 23 rows (more on the neck); belly rounded. Tail moderate; subcaudals in two rows or partly single, partly in two rows.

Australia and New Guinea.

Synopsis of the Species.

I. Anal divided; anterior subcaudals single (exceptionally divided); scales in 17 to 21 rows on the body.

A. Scales in 17 rows on the body.

1. Frontal longer than broad.

Frontal once and one fourth to once and two thirds as long as broad, as

long as its distance from the rostral;
latter shield scarcely broader than
deep; ventrals 180-200; sub-
caudals 50-60 .... 1. *porphyriacus*, p. 328.

Frontal nearly twice as long as broad,
longer than its distance from the
end of the snout; rostral scarcely
broader than deep; ventrals 199-
210; subcaudals 57-72 .... 2. *cupreus*, p. 329.

Frontal once and two thirds to twice
as long as broad, as long as its
distance from the rostral; latter
shield considerably broader than
deep; ventrals 199-220; sub-
caudals 57-70 .... 3. *australis*, p. 330.

2. Frontal quite as broad as long; ventrals 212, subcaudals
54-64 .... 4. *darwiniensis*, p. 330.

B. Scales in 19 or 21 rows on the body; frontal once and a half as long as broad, shorter than its distance from the end of the snout; rostral considerably broader than deep; ventrals 221-224; subcaudals 49-55.. 5. *papuanus*, p. 331.

II. Anal entire; subcaudals all in pairs; scales in 23 rows on the body; ventrals 230-237, subcaudals 61-78.

Frontal twice as long as broad, as long
as its distance from the rostral or the
end of the snout .... 6. *scutellatus*, p. 331.

Frontal once and a half as long as
broad, as long as its distance from
the rostral .... 7. *microlepidotus*, p. 332.

III. Anal divided; subcaudals all in pairs; scales in 23 rows on the body; ventrals 235; subcaudals 60.

8. *ferox*, p. 332.

1. Pseudechis porphyriacus.

Coluber porphyriacus, *Shaw, Zool. N. Holl.* p. 27, pl. x. (1794), *and Zool.* iii. p. 423, pl. cx. (1802).
Trimeresurus leptocephalus, *Lacép. Ann. du Mus.* iv. 1804, pp. 196 & 209, pl lvi. fig 1.
Coluber (Hurria) porphyreus, *Merr. Tent.* p. 92 (1820).
Duberria porphyriaca, *Fitzing. N. Class. Rept.* p. 56 (1826).
Acanthophis tortor, *Lesson, Voy. Coquille, Zool.* ii. p. 55, Rept. pl. vi. (1830).
Naja porphyriaca, *Schleg. Phys. Serp.* ii. p. 479, pl. xvii. figs. 6 & 7 (1837).
Trimeresurus porphyricus, *Guér. Icon. R. A , Rept.* p. 15, pl. xxiv. fig. 1 (1844).

Naja porphyrea, *Schleg. Abbild.* p. 139, pl. xlviii. figs. 11–13 (1844).
Trimeresurus porphyreus, *Dum. & Bibr.* vii. p. 1247 (1854); *Jan, Icon Gén.* 44, pl. vi. fig. 1 (1873).
Pseudechis porphyriacus, part., *Gunth. Cat.* p. 218 (1858).
—— porphyriacus, *Gunth Ann. & Mag N. H.* (3) xii. 1863, p. 362; *Krefft, Sn Sydney*, p. 46 (1865); *Gunth Zool. Rec.* 1865, p 156; *Krefft, Sn. Austral.* p. 46, pl viii (1869); *McCoy, Prodr Zool. Vict*, Dec. 1, p. 5, pl. i. (1878), and Dec. 15, p. 159, pl. clxii. fig. 2 (1887).

Eye rather small, its diameter nearly equalling its distance from the mouth (larger in the young). Rostral as deep as broad or slightly broader than deep, the portion visible from above half as long as its distance from the frontal; internasals one half to two thirds as long as the præfrontals; frontal rather small, not broader than the supraocular, once and one third to once and two thirds as long as broad, as long as its distance from the rostral, three fifths to two thirds the length of the parietals; posterior nasal in contact with the single præocular; two postoculars; temporals 2+2 or 3, first lower very large and wedged in between the fifth and sixth labial; six upper labials, third and fourth entering the eye, third deeper than fourth; three lower labials in contact with the anterior chinshields, which are as long as or shorter than the posterior. Scales in 17 rows (18 to 21 on the neck). Ventrals 180–200; anal divided; subcaudals 50–60, first 5 to 20 entire, rest in pairs (exceptionally all divided). Black above; outer row of scales red at the base; ventrals red, edged with black.

Total length 1580 millim.; tail 210.

Eastern, Western, and Southern Australia.

a.	♂ (V. 190; C. 55).	New South Wales.	Imperial Institute [P.].
b.	♂ (V. 189; C. 56).	New South Wales.	Christiania Museum.
c.	♀ (V. 181, C.?)	Australia.	Capt Stokes [P].
d.	♂ (V. 191; C. 59).	Australia.	J. B. Jukes, Esq. [P.].
e.	♀ (V 187; C.?).	Australia.	College of Surgeons.
f–h, i.	♀ (V. 184, 187; C. 56, 53) & hgr. (V. 180, 183; C. 58, 55)	Australia.	
k.	Skull.	Australia.	

2. Pseudechis cupreus.

Pseudechis australis (*non Gray*), *Krefft, Vert. Low Murray*, p. 32 (1865), *McCoy, Prodr. Zool. Vict*, Dec. 15, p. 159, pl. cxlii. (1887).
—— australis, part, *Krefft, Proc. Zool. Soc* 1868, p. 3, and *Sn. Austral.* p. 47 (1869).

Intermediate between *P. porphyriacus* and *P. australis*. Rostral slightly broader than deep; internasals half as long as the præfrontals; frontal nearly twice as long as broad, as broad as the supraocular, longer than its distance from the end of the snout, shorter than the parietals; posterior nasal in contact with the single præocular; two postoculars; temporals 1+2; six upper labials, third and fourth entering the eye, third deeper than fourth, sixth largest; three lower labials in contact with the anterior chin-shields. Scales in 17 rows (25 on the neck). Ventrals 199-210; anal divided; subcaudals 57-72, 11 to 34 anterior entire, rest in pairs. Reddish or coppery brown above, brownish white or orange below, all the scales and shields edged with brown.

Total length 1830 millim.; tail 300.

Murray River.

3. Pseudechis australis.

Naja australis, *Gray, Zool. Miscell.* p. 55 (1842).
Pseudechis porphyriacus, part., *Gunth. Cat.* p. 218 (1858).
—— australis, *Gunth Ann & Mag N. H* (3) xii 1863, p 362
—— australis, part., *Krefft, Proc. Zool. Soc.* 1868, p. 3, *and Sn. Austral* p. 47, pl vi fig 11 (1869).

Eye rather small, its diameter nearly equalling its distance from the mouth. Rostral broader than deep, visible from above; internasals about half as long as the præfrontals; frontal small, not or but slightly broader than the supraocular, once and two thirds to twice as long as broad, as long as its distance from the rostral, two thirds the length of the parietals; posterior nasal in contact with the single præocular; two postoculars, temporals 2+2, lower anterior large and wedged in between the fifth and sixth labials; six upper labials, third and fourth entering the eye, third deeper than fourth; three lower labials in contact with the anterior chin-shields, which are shorter than the posterior. Scales in 17 rows (19 or 20 on the neck). Ventrals 199-220; anal divided; subcaudals 57-70, 26 to 41 anterior single, rest in pairs. Uniform pale brown above, yellowish beneath.

Total length 1080 millim.; tail 170.

Northern Australia.

a. ♀ (V. 206; C 65).   N.E. Australia.   (Type.)
b. Hgr. ♀ (V. ?; C. 60).   Victoria R., N. Australia.   Dr. Dahl [C.]; Christiania Museum *[E.].
c. ♂ (V. 220; C. 70).   —— ?

4. Pseudechis darwiniensis.

Pseudechis darwiniensis, *Macleay, Proc. Linn Soc. N.S.W.* ii. 1878, p. 220, & (2) iii. 1888, p. 410.

Of more elongate form than *P. porphyriacus*. Head-shields much the same as in that species, but frontal quite as broad as long and much wider than the supraocular. Scales in 17 rows. Ventrals

---

* A second specimen, 825 millim long, was obtained by Dr. Dahl on the Daly River, and is preserved in the Christiania Museum. It is a female, with 205 ventrals and 59 subcaudals, 37 of which are single.

212; subcaudals 54-64 (34-49 single and 15-30 pairs). Upper surface of head pale brown, of body and tail reddish brown, the middle of each scale being of a lighter colour than the apex; lower parts uniform yellowish white.

Total length 910 millim.; tail 140.

Port Darwin, Northern Australia.

5. Pseudechis papuanus.

Pseudechis papuanus, *Peters & Doria, Ann. Mus. Genova,* xiii. 1878, p. 409.

Eye small, its diameter less than its distance from the mouth. Rostral broader than deep, the portion visible from above measuring one third its distance from the frontal; internasals two thirds the length of the præfrontals; frontal small, as broad as the supraocular, once and a half as long as broad, as long as the præfrontals, half as long as the parietals; posterior nasal in contact with the single præocular; two postoculars; temporals 2+2, lower anterior very large and wedged in between the fifth and sixth labials; six upper labials, third and fourth entering the eye, third deeper than fourth, three lower labials in contact with the anterior chin-shields, which are a little shorter than the posterior. Scales in 19 or 21 rows (26 or 27 on the neck). Ventrals 221-224; anal divided; subcaudals 49-55 (26-27 single and 23-28 pairs). Uniform blackish, chin whitish.

Total length 1900 millim.; tail 21.

South-eastern New Guinea.

a Head and neck of adult   Port Moresby.   Rev. W. G. Turner [C.].

6. Pseudechis scutellatus.

Pseudechis scutellatus, *Peters, Mon. Berl. Ac.* 1867, p 710.

Eye moderate, its diameter exceeding its distance from the mouth. Rostral as deep as broad or slightly broader than deep, visible from above, internasals shorter than the præfrontals; frontal nearly as broad as the supraocular, twice as long as broad, as long as its distance from the rostral or the end of the snout, as long as or shorter than the parietals; posterior nasal in contact with or narrowly separated from the præocular, which is single or divided; two postoculars; temporals 2+3, first lower wedged in between the fifth and sixth upper labials; six upper labials, third and fourth entering the eye; three lower labials in contact with the anterior chin-shields, which are as long as the posterior. Scales in 23 rows (25 to 30 on the neck). Ventrals 230-233; anal entire, subcaudals 61-78 pairs. Pale brown or blackish brown above; snout and sides of head paler brown or yellowish; belly yellowish, with very indistinct small dark spots in the young.

Total length 1070 millim.; tail 240. The type measures 2230 millim.

South-eastern New Guinea, Queensland, Northern Australia *.

a-b. ♀ (V. 233, 230; C. 63, 61). Fly River. Rev. S. Macfarlane [C.].

7. Pseudechis microlepidotus.

Diemenia microlepidota, *McCoy, Prodr. Zool. Vict.,* Dec. 3, p 12, pl xxiii figs 2 & 3 (1879).

Rostral broader than deep, visible from above; internasals half as long as the præfrontals, not in contact with the præocular; frontal broader than the supraocular, once and a half as long as broad, as long as its distance from the rostral, two thirds the length of the parietals; posterior nasal in contact with the single præocular; two postoculars; six upper labials, third and fourth entering the eye. 30 to 36 scales across the neck, 23 across the middle of the body. Ventrals 232-237; anal entire; subcaudals 61-66 pairs. Dark brown above, yellowish grey below, the ventral shields edged and blotched with dark grey; head sometimes blackish.

Total length 1850 millim; tail 250.

Northern Victoria.

8. Pseudechis ferox.

Diemenia ferox, *Macleay, Proc. Linn. Soc. N. S. W.* vi. 1881, p. 812.

Snout very broadly rounded. Rostral broad and low; internasals very much smaller than the præfrontals; frontal longer than broad, broader than the supraocular; one præocular, deeply grooved; two postoculars; second upper labial touching the præfrontal; last upper labial very large. Scales in 23 rows on the body. Ventrals 235, anal divided; subcaudals 60 pairs. Glossy black above, yellowish white beneath.

Total length 2030 millim.; tail 300.

Fort Bourke, New South Wales.

219. DENISONIA.

Elaps, part., *Schl. Phys. Serp.* ii. p. 435 (1837).
Alecto (*non Wagl*) part., *Dum. & Bibr. Erp. Gén.* vii. p. 1249 (1854); *Jan, Elenco sist. Ofid.* p. 116 (1863).
Hoplocephalus, part., *Günth. Cat. Col. Sn.* p. 213 (1858); *Krefft, Sn. Austral.* p. 53 (1869).
Denisonia, *Krefft, Proc. Zool. Soc.* 1869, p. 321, and l. c. p. 82.

Maxillary extending forwards as far as the palatine, with a pair of large grooved poison-fangs followed by 3 to 5 small solid teeth; mandibular teeth, anterior longest. Head more or less distinct from neck; eye moderate or small, with round or vertically elliptic pupil;

---

* I have examined a young specimen (V. 230; C. 78) from Mt. Showbridge, N. Australia, collected by Dr. Dahl for the Christiania Museum.

nasal entire or divided; no loreal. Body cylindrical, scales smooth, without pits, in 15 to 19 rows; belly rounded. Tail moderate or short; subcaudals single (in one species in two rows).

Australia, Tasmania, Solomon Islands.

Synopsis of the Species.

I. Anal entire; frontal not much broader than the supraocular, once and a half to twice and two thirds as long as broad, pupil round.

  A. Scales in 15 or 17 rows; nasal in contact with the præocular.

    1. Ventrals 136-160; subcaudals 38-57; scales in 15 (exceptionally 17) rows.

Frontal once and three fourths to twice as long as broad; ventrals 145-160 ..	1. *superba*, p. 335.
Frontal once and two thirds to twice as long as broad; ventrals 138-151; a black nuchal collar	2. *coronata*, p. 335.
Frontal twice to thrice as long as broad; scales striated; ventrals 136-151	3. *coronoides*, p. 336.

    2. Ventrals 118; scales in 17 rows.   4. *muelleri*, p. 337.

  B. Scales in 19 rows; nasal not reaching the præocular, ventrals 167; subcaudals 35 .... 5 *frenata*, p. 338.

II. Anal divided; frontal much longer than broad; pupil round.

  A. Scales in 15 rows; nasal not reaching the præocular; ventrals 164; subcaudals 51............ 6. *ramsayi*, p. 338.

  B. Scales in 17 rows; nasal in contact with the præocular.

Frontal once and two thirds to twice as long as broad; ventrals 153-170; subcaudals 41-56	7. *signata*, p. 338.
Frontal once and a half as long as broad; ventrals 147-168; subcaudals 33-45..	8. *dæmelii*, p. 339.

III. Anal entire; frontal much broader than the supraocular, once and one fifth to once and three fourths as long as broad, pupil often vertically elliptic or subelliptic.

  A. Scales in 19 rows; ventrals 154-164; subcaudals 25-30.

Nasal in contact with the præocular ....   9. *suta*, p. 339.
Nasal not reaching the præocular ..... . 10. *frontalis*, p. 340.

  B. Scales in 17 rows; ventrals 121-138, subcaudals 20-30.

Anterior chin-shields as long as the posterior	11. *flagellum*, p. 340.
Anterior chin-shields shorter than the posterior	12. *maculata*, p. 341.

C. Scales in 15 rows.

1. Frontal once and three fourths as long as broad; ventrals 160; subcaudals 25 .... 13. *punctata*, p. 341.

2. Frontal not more than once and a half as long as broad.

   a. Eye at least as long as its distance from the mouth.

   α. Nasal in contact with the præocular.

Ventrals 140–170; subcaudals 22–33 .. 14. *gouldii*, p. 342.
Ventrals 170–200; subcaudals 30–46 .. 15 *nigrescens*, p. 343.
Ventrals 180–184; subcaudals 50–64 . 16. *nigrostriata*, p. 343.

   β. Second labial in contact with the præfrontal; ventrals 166–183; subcaudals 31–43.
   17. *carpentariæ*, p. 344.

   b. Eye hardly as long as its distance from the mouth; ventrals 170–178; subcaudals 37–38.
   18. *pallidiceps*, p. 344.

IV. Anal divided; frontal much broader than the supraocular, as long as broad or a little longer than broad; ventrals 164–172; subcaudals 38–49.

Scales in 15 or 17 rows; subcaudals single .... 19. *melanura*, p. 345.
Scales in 16 rows; subcaudals single.... 20. *par*, p. 345.
Scales in 17 rows; subcaudals paired .. 21. *woodfordii*, p. 346.

TABLE SHOWING NUMBERS OF SCALES AND SHIELDS.

	Sc	V.	A.	O.	Lab.
superba	15 (17)	145–160	1	41–50	6
coronata	15	138–151	1	38–51	6
coronoides	15	136–151	1	42–57	6
muelleri	17	118	1	38	6
frenata	19	167	1	35	6
ramsayi	15	164	2	51	6
signata	17	153–170	2	41–56	6
dæmelii	17	147–168	2	33–45	6
suta	19	157–164	1	25–30	6
frontalis	19	154	1	30	6
flagellum	17	132–138	1	25–27	6
maculata	17	121–136	1	20–30	6
punctata	15	160	1	25	6
gouldii	15	140–170	1	22–33	6
nigrescens	15	170–200	1	30–46	6
nigrostriata	15	180–184	1	50–64	6
carpentariæ	15	166–183	1	31–43	6
pallidiceps	15	170–178	1	37–38	6
melanura	15–17	165–171	2	38–48	7
par	16	164–166	2	40–49	7
woodfordii	17	166–172	2	41–45	7

1. Denisonia superba.

Alecto curta, part., *Dum. & Bibr.* vii. p. 1252 (1854).
Hoplocephalus superbus, part., *Gunth. Cat* p. 217 (1858).
—— superbus, *Krefft, Sn. Austral.* p 54, pl xi. fig. 9 (1869);
McCoy, Prodr. Zool. Vict, Dec. 1, p 7, pl. ii. (1878).
Alecto schmidtii, *Jan, Icon. Gén.* 44, pl. i. fig 4 (1873).
Hoplocephalus bransbyi, *Macleay, Proc. Linn. Soc. N. S. W.* iii. 1878, p. 52.
? Hoplocephalus vestigiatus, *De Vis, Proc. R Soc Queensl.* i. 1884, p. 138.

Eye as long as or a little longer than its distance from the mouth (larger in the young). Rostral a little broader than deep, just visible from above; internasals one half to two thirds as long as the præfrontals; frontal once and three fourths to twice as long as broad, as broad as the supraocular, as long as or a little longer than its distance from the end of the snout, shorter than the parietals, nasal entire, in contact with the single præocular; two postoculars, temporals 2+2, lower anterior large and wedged in between the fifth and sixth upper labials; six upper labials, third and fourth entering the eye; three or four lower labials in contact with the anterior chin-shields, which are as long as or shorter than the posterior. Scales in 15 (rarely 17) rows. Ventrals 145–160; anal entire; subcaudals 41–50. Brownish to dark olive above, the scales often edged with darker; lateral scales often yellow or salmon-red; ventrals yellowish or greyish olive, blackish at the base. Young with a black nuchal blotch or collar, which may be bordered behind with yellow, lips yellow, largely spotted with black.

Total length 1010 millim.; tail 160.

New South Wales, Southern Australia, Tasmania.

a, b, c. ♂ (V. 153, 148, C. 48, 45) & ♀ (V. 155; C. 45).	Australasia.	'Erebus & Terror' Exped.	
d. ♂ (V. 149; C 41).	Tasmania.	A. J. Smith, Esq. [P.]	
e–f. ♂ (V. 150, 147; C. 47. 46).	Tasmania.	R. Gunn, Esq. [P.]	(Types.)
g–i. ♂ (V. 150; C. 45), ♀ (V 153, C. 48), & yg. (V. 153, C. 45).	Australia.		
k. Yg. (V. 145, C 44).	Australia.	College of Surgeons.	
l. Yg. (V. 150; C 49).	Burrawang, New South Wales.	J J. Fletcher, Esq. [P.].	
m. 10 embryos.	Mt. Monda, Victoria.	P. L. Sclater, Esq. [P].	
n. Skull.	Australia.		

2. Denisonia coronata.

Elaps coronatus. *Schleg. Phys. Serp.* ii. p. 454 (1837), *and Abbild.* p 137, pl. xlvi. figs 12 & 13 (1844); *Gray, in Grey's Trav. Austral.* ii. pl. v. fig. 2 (1841).

Trimesurus olivaceus, *Gray, l c* p. 443.
Alecto coronata, *Dum. & Bibr.* vii. p. 1255, pl. lxxvi *b.* fig. 2 (1854); *Jan, Icon. Gén.* 44, pl. i. fig. 3 (1873).
Hoplocephalus coronatus, *Gunth. Cat* p. 215 (1858); *Krefft, Sn. Austral.* p. 62, pl. vi. fig 3 (1869).

Eye longer than its distance from the mouth. Rostral broader than deep, just visible from above; internasals about two thirds the length of the præfrontals; frontal once and two thirds to twice as long as broad, not broader than the supraocular, as long as its distance from the end of the snout, shorter than the parietals; nasal entire, in contact with the single præocular; two postoculars; temporals 2+2, lower anterior wedged in between the fifth and sixth upper labials, and sometimes nearly reaching the mouth; six upper labials, third and fourth entering the eye; three lower labials in contact with the anterior chin-shields, which are shorter than the posterior. Scales in 15 rows. Ventrals 138–151; anal entire; subcaudals 38–51. Olive above, scales sometimes black-edged; a black streak on each side of the head, passing through the eye and extending across the rostral, and a black cross-band on the nape; upper lip, below the black streak, yellowish, with some blackish dots, yellowish or pale olive beneath, ventrals olive at the base.

Total length 480 millim.; tail 95.

Western Australia and New South Wales.

a–b.	♂ (V. 145, 146; C. 45, 47)	Houtman's Abrolhos	Mr. Gilbert [C.].
c.	♂ (V. 145, C. 44).	W. Australia.	Sir J. Macgregor [P].
d.	♀ (V. 151, C 41).	W. Australia.	G. F Moore, Esq. [P.].
e–f, g–h.	♂ (V. 145, 141; C. 41, 51), ♀ (V. 140; C. 42), & yg. (V. 144; C 43).	W. Australia.	
i.	♀ (V. 150; C. 38).	Swan River.	Sir A. Smith [P.].
k.	♀ (V. 150; C. 48).	Sydney.	G. Krefft, Esq. [P.].
l.	♂ (V. 138; C. 49).	New South Wales.	Imperial Institute [P.].

3. Denisonia coronoides.

Hoplocephalus coronoides, *Gunth. Cat.* p. 215 (1858); *Krefft, Sn. Austral.* p. 62, pl. xii. fig. 1 (1869), *McCoy, Prodr. Zool. Vict*, Dec. 2, p 8, pl. xi fig. 2 (1878).
Alecto labialis, *Jan, Rev. & Mag. Zool.* 1859, p. 128, *and Icon. Gén.* 44, pl. i. fig. 1 (1873).
Hoplocephalus mastersii, *Krefft, Proc. Zool. Soc.* 1866, p. 370, *and l. c.* p. 63, pl. xii. fig. 6.
Alecto rhodogaster, *Jan, Icon.* 44, pl. ii. fig. 2
Hoplocephalus labialis, *F. Müll. Verh. Nat. Ges. Basel*, vii. 1885, p. 690.
—— collaris, *Macleay, Proc Linn. Soc. N.S.W.* (2) i. 1887, p. 1111.

Eye longer than its distance from the mouth. Rostral a little broader than deep, just visible from above; internasals about half as long as the præfrontals; frontal twice to thrice as long as broad, not broader than the supraocular, as long as or longer than its distance from the end of the snout, shorter than the parietals; nasal entire, in contact with the single præocular; two postoculars; temporals 2+2 (rarely 2+3), lower anterior wedged in between the fifth and sixth upper labials and sometimes nearly reaching the mouth; six upper labials, third and fourth entering the eye; three (rarely four) lower labials in contact with the anterior chin-shields, which are shorter than the posterior. Scales distinctly striated, in 15 rows. Ventrals 136-151; anal entire; subcaudals 39-57. Brown or olive above, with or without black edges to the scales; a black streak on each side of the head, passing through the eye; a yellow streak on the upper lip, below the black streak; salmon-red to dark olive-grey beneath, speckled with darker, exceptionally with a few black spots; end of tail salmon-red.

Total length 440 millim.; tail 80.

Southern Australia and Tasmania.

A. No collar. (*H. coronoides*, Gthr.; *A. labialis*, Jan.)

a-b, c, d-e, f-i. ♂ (V. 151, 142, 142, 140, 148, 144; C 45, 50, 49, 53, 57, 45), & hgr. (V. 144, 143, 141; C. 49, 49, 54).	Tasmania.	R. Gunn, Esq. [P.]	
k-l. ♀ (V. 147, 143; C. 54, 42)	Tasmania.	A. J. Smith, Esq. [P.].	(Types)
m. ♂ (V. 148; C. 56).	Tasmania.	Zoological Society.	
n. ♀ (V. 147; C. 48).	Swan R.		
o ♀ (V 141; C. 41).	Australia.	Lord Derby [P.].	
p-q ♀ (V. 144, 147; C. 46, 47).	Australasia.	Lords of the Admiralty [P.].	

B. A yellow nuchal collar. (*H. mastersii*, Krefft; *A. rhodogaster*, Jan; *H. collaris*, Macleay.)

a. ♀ (V 140; C. 39).   Flinders Range, S. Australia.   G. Krefft, Esq. [P]. (One of the types of *H. mastersii*.)

4. Denisonia muelleri.

Hoplocephalus muelleri, *Fischer, Jahrb. Wiss Anst. Hamb.* ii 1885, p. 109.

Rostral little broader than deep, visible from above; internasals half as long as the præfrontals; frontal twice as long as broad; nasal entire, in contact with the single præocular; two postoculars; temporals 2+2, lower anterior large and wedged in between the fifth and sixth labials; six upper labials, third and fourth entering the eye; anterior chin-shields nearly as long as the posterior. Scales in 17 rows. Ventrals 118, anal entire, subcaudals 38. Grey-brown above; lips and chin with yellow spots, which extend on the sides of the neck; grey beneath, with four or five longitudinal series of elongate blackish spots.

Total length 292 millim.; tail 52.

Queensland.

Denisonia frenata.

Hoplocephalus frenatus, *Peters*, Mon. Berl. Ac. 1870, p. 646.

Frontal nearly twice as long as broad; nasal not reaching the præocular; two postoculars; temporals 2+2; six upper labials. Scales in 19 rows. Ventrals 167; anal entire; subcaudals 35. Olive-brown above; upper lip yellow, a yellow line on each side of the head, passing through the eye; white beneath.

Total length 390 millim.; tail 54.

Lake Elphinstone, Queensland.

6. Denisonia ramsayi.

Hoplocephalus ramsayi, *Krefft*, Proc. Zool. Soc. 1864, p. 181, *and Sn. Austral.* p. 66, pl. xi. fig. 2 (1869).

Eye moderate. Rostral just reaching the upper surface of the head; internasals shorter than the præfrontals; frontal twice as long as broad, not broader than the supraocular, longer than its distance from the end of the snout, shorter than the parietals; nasal entire, not reaching the single præocular, two postoculars; six upper labials, second and third in contact with the præfrontal, third and fourth entering the eye. Scales in 15 rows. Ventrals 164; anal divided; subcaudals 51. Dark olive-green above, each scale tipped with reddish, crown and a narrow vertebral line somewhat darker, upper labials whitish, marked with olive-brown in the upper corners; beneath yellow, each ventral shield with a blackish margin; subcaudals nearly black.

Total length 265 millim.; tail 50.

Braidwood, New South Wales.

7. Denisonia signata.

Alecto signata, *Jan*, Rev. & Mag. Zool. 1859, p. 128, *an Icon. Gén.* 43, pl. vi. fig. 5 (1873).

Hoplocephalus signatus, *Krefft*, Sn. Austral. p. 64, pl. xii. fig. 5 (1869).

Eye longer than its distance from the mouth. Rostral broader than deep, just visible from above; internasals about two thirds the length of the præfrontals; frontal once and two thirds to twice as long as broad, not or but slightly broader than the supraocular, as long as or a little longer than its distance from the end of the snout, shorter than the parietals; nasal entire, in contact with the single præocular; two postoculars; temporals 2+2, lower anterior wedged in between the fifth and sixth upper labials; six upper labials, third and fourth entering the eye; three or four lower labials in contact with the anterior chin-shields, which are shorter than the posterior. Scales in 17 rows. Ventrals 153–170, anal divided; subcaudals 41–56. Dark olive or black above; head olive-brown, with two yellowish streaks on each side, one along the upper lip, the other from behind the eye along the temple; dark grey or black beneath.

Total length 640 millim.; tail 120.

Queensland, New South Wales.

a. ♂ (V. 160, C. 56).	Cape York.	
b, c. Hgr. ♂ (V. 163, C. 55) & ♀ (V. 165, C. 49).	Clarence R.	G. Krefft, Esq. [P.].
d–e. ♂ (V. 163, 153; C. ?, 49).	Macquarie R.	G. Krefft, Esq. [P.].
f. Yg (V. 170; C. 47).	New South Wales.	G. Krefft, Esq. [P.].
g. Yg. (V. 156, C. 41).	Australia.	Haslar Collection.

8. Denisonia dæmelii. (PLATE XVIII. fig. 3.)

Hoplocephalus dæmelii, *Gunth. Journ. Mus. Godeffroy*, xii. 1876, p. 46; *F. Müll. Verh. Nat. Ges. Basel*, vi. 1878, p. 695.
——— suboccipitalis, *Douglas Ogilby, Rec. Austral. Mus.* ii. 1892, p. 23.

Eye longer than its distance from the mouth. Rostral broader than deep, scarcely visible from above; internasals two thirds the length of the præfrontals; frontal once and a half as long as broad, not twice as broad as the supraocular, a little longer than its distance from the end of the snout, shorter than the parietals; nasal single, in contact with the single præocular; two postoculars; temporals 2+2, lower anterior wedged in between the fifth and sixth upper labials; six upper labials, third and fourth entering the eye; three or four lower labials in contact with the anterior chin-shields, which are as long as or shorter than the posterior. Scales in 17 rows. Ventrals 147–168; anal divided; subcaudals 33–45. Olive above, head darker, blackish on the temples, entirely black in the young; yellowish white beneath.

Total length 380 millim.; tail 60.

Queensland.

a–b. ♂ (V 160; C. 39) & hgr. (V 147; C. 33).	Peak Downs.	Museum Godeffroy. (Types.)
c. Yg. (V 153, C. 45).	Queensland.	

9. Denisonia suta.

Hoplocephalus sutus, *Peters, Mon. Berl. Ac.* 1863, p. 234.

Eye longer than its distance from the mouth. Rostral twice as broad as deep, just visible from above; internasals half as long as the præfrontals; frontal once and one third as long as broad, twice as broad as the supraocular, as long as its distance from the end of the snout, nearly as long as the parietals; nasal entire, in contact with the single præocular; two postoculars; temporals 2+2, lower anterior wedged in between the fifth and sixth labials; six upper labials, third and fourth entering the eye; three lower labials in contact with the anterior chin-shields, which are as long as the posterior. Scales in 19 rows. Ventrals 157-164; anal entire; subcaudals 25-30. Pale olive-brown above, scales edged with dark brown; head dark brown above, nape black; a black streak on each side of the head, passing through the eye; a yellow spot on the præocular, and another on the postoculars; upper lip and lower parts yellowish white.

Total length 200 millim.; tail 23.

Southern Australia.

a ♀ (V. 164; C. 25).   Adelaide.   Rev. T. E. Lea [P.].

10. Denisonia frontalis.

Hoplocephalus frontalis, *Douglas Ogilby*, Proc. Linn. Soc. N.S W. (2) iv. 1889, p. 1027.

Eye small. Rostral twice as broad as deep, slightly bent backward between the internasals, which are much shorter than the præfrontals; frontal a little longer than broad; nasal not reaching the single præocular; two postoculars; temporals 2+2; six upper labials, second in contact with the præfrontal, third and fourth entering the eye; anterior chin-shields rather larger than the posterior. Scales in 19 rows. Ventrals 154; anal entire; subcaudals 30. Light brown above, scales narrowly margined with black; a broad black nuchal collar, extending forwards over portions of the upper labials, temporals, and the lower postocular to the eye; a black spot in front of the eye on the second and third labials; a black vertebral line; pearly white beneath, with a broad bronze-coloured median band.

Total length 400 millim.; tail 50.

Narrabri, New South Wales.

11. Denisonia flagellum.

Hoplocephalus flagellum, *McCoy*, Prodr. Zool. Vict., Dec. 2, p. 7, pl. xi. fig. 1 (1878).

Eye longer than its distance from the mouth. Rostral twice as broad as deep, visible from above; internasals shorter than the præfrontals; frontal once and one fourth to once and a half as long as broad, broader than the supraocular, as long as its distance from the end of the snout, shorter than the parietals; nasal entire, in contact with the single præocular; two postoculars; temporals 2+2, lower anterior wedged in between the fifth and sixth labials; six upper labials, third and fourth entering the eye; three lower labials in contact with the anterior chin-shields, which are as long as the posterior. Scales in 17 rows. Ventrals 132-138; anal entire; subcaudals 25-27. Pale brown above; vertex, occiput, and nape black; upper lip and lower parts white.

Total length 380 millim.; tail 40.

Victoria

12. Denisonia maculata.

Hoplocephalus maculatus, *Steind. Novara, Rept.* p. 81 (1867); *Gunth. Journ. Mus. Godeffr* xii. 1876, p. 46.

Denisonia ornata, *Krefft, Proc. Zool. Soc.* 1869, p. 321, fig., *and Sn. Austral.* p. 82, pl. xi fig. 4 (1869).

Eye longer than its distance from the mouth. Rostral nearly twice as broad as deep, just visible from above; internasals much shorter than the præfrontals; frontal once and a half to once and two thirds as long as broad, as long as or a little longer than its distance from the end of the snout, shorter than the parietals; nasal divided (rarely entire), in contact with the single præocular; two postoculars: temporals 2+2, lower anterior wedged in between the fifth and sixth upper labials; six upper labials, third and fourth entering the eye; three or four lower labials in contact with the anterior chin-shields, which are shorter than the posterior. Scales in 17 rows. Ventrals 121–136; anal entire; subcaudals 20–30. Dark grey-brown or brown above, lateral scales spotted with black; a large dark brown blotch on the head, with some lighter spots or variegations, with a black crescentic border on the nape; sides of head and end of snout pale brown, spotted with black; gular region spotted with black; ventrals whitish, with a dark brown or black spot at the outer end of each ventral.

Total length 400 millim.; tail 55.

Queensland.

a–d. ♂ (V. 122, 121, C 30, 28),   Rockhampton.   Museum Godeffroy.
♀ (V 131; C. 22), & hgr.
(V. 129; C. 20).

e–g, h. ♂ (V. 125; C. 29) & ♀   Rockhampton.
(V. 126, 129, 134; C. 21, 22, 20).

i. Skull of *a.*

Hoplocephalus ornatus, De Vis, *Proc. R. Soc. Queensl.* i. 1884, p. 100, pl. xv., appears to agree in all structural characters with the preceding species, but the body is barred by about 50 dark cross-bands with irregular edges; below the cross-bands, alternating angular blotches.

Near Surat, Queensland.

13. Denisonia punctata. (PLATE XVIII. fig. 4.)

Eye longer than its distance from the mouth. Rostral twice as broad as deep, visible from above; internasals two thirds the length of the præfrontals; frontal once and three fourths as long as broad, acutely angular behind, twice as broad as the supraocular, longer than its distance from the end of the snout, shorter than the parietals, nasal entire, in contact with the single præocular, two postoculars; temporals 2+2, lower anterior wedged in between the fifth and sixth labials; six upper labials, third and fourth entering the eye; three lower labials in contact with the anterior chin-shields, which are shorter than the posterior. Scales in 15 rows. Ventrals 160; anal entire, subcaudals 25. Pale brown above, each scale with a dark brown spot; head and nape orange, with blackish-brown symmetrical markings; a blackish streak on each side of the head, passing through the eye, and terminating on the anterior temporals; upper lip and lower parts yellowish white.

Total length 350 millim.; tail 36.

North-western Australia.

a. ♀ (V. 160; C. 25). Port Walcott. Capt Beckett [C.].

14. Denisonia gouldii.

Elaps gouldii, *Gray, in Grey's Trav. Austral.* ii. p. 444, pl. v. fig. 1 (1841)
Hoplocephalus gouldii, *Gunth. Cat* p. 215 (1858); *Krefft, Proc. Zool Soc.* 1866, p. 370, *and Sn. Austral.* p. 60, pl xii. fig. 2 (1869).
Alecto gouldii, *Jan, Rev. & Mag Zool.* 1859, p. 128, *and Icon. Gén.* 44, pl 1. fig. 5 (1873)
Hoplocephalus nigriceps, *Gunth. Ann & Mag N. H.* (3) xii. 1863, p. 362; *Krefft, Sn. Austral.* p. 68, pl. xii fig. 7
—— spectabilis, *Krefft, l. c.* p. 61, pl. xii. fig. 4.

Eye as long as or a little longer than its distance from the mouth. Rostral twice as broad as deep, visible from above; internasals at least two thirds as long as the præfrontals; frontal a little longer than broad, at least twice as broad as the supraocular, as long as or a little longer than its distance from the end of the snout, shorter than the parietals; nasal entire, in contact with the single præocular: two postoculars; temporals 2 + 2, lower anterior wedged in between the fifth and sixth labials; six upper labials, third and fourth entering the eye; three or four lower labials in contact with the anterior chin-shields, which are as long as or a little shorter than the posterior. Scales in 15 rows. Ventrals 140–170; anal entire; subcaudals 22–33. Yellow to brown above; head and nape black, or black and yellow above; upper lip and lower parts yellowish.

Total length 435 millim; tail 50.

Western and Southern Australia.

A. Yellowish above, scales edged with brown. (*E gouldii*, Gray.)

a ♀ (V. 162; C. 30). W. Australia. Sir G. Grey [P.]. (Type.)
b–c. ♂ (V. 170; C. 33) & ♀ (V. 163; C 31). Swan R. Sir A Smith [P.].
d. ♀ (V. 161; C. 31). Swan R.
e. ♂ (V. 147; C. 33). Flinders Range, S. Australia G. Krefft, Esq. [P.].
f. ♀ (V. 152; C. 22). Port Lincoln, S. Australia. G Krefft, Esq. [P.].
g ♂ (V. 143, C. 28). S. Australia. Prof. Stirling [P.].
h–i. ♀ (V. 140; C. 26) & yg. (V. 146; C. 24). Australia.

B. Yellowish above, without dark edges to the scales.

a. ♀ (V. 155, C. 25).   Swan R.

C. Brown above.   (*H. nigriceps*, Gthr.)

a ♂ (V. 150; C. 30).   ——— ?   Dr Gunther [P.].
(Type of *H. nigriceps*.)
b. ♀ (V. 160; C. 28).   Champion Bay, N W Australia.   Mr. Duboulay [C.]
c. ♀ (V. 156; C. 25).   S. Australia.   Prof. Stirling [P.].

15. Denisonia nigrescens.

Hoplocephalus nigrescens, *Gunth Ann & Mag. N. H.* (3) ix. 1862, p. 131, pl. ix. fig. 12, *Krefft, Sn. Austral.* p. 68, pl. vi. fig. 4 (1869).
——— assimilis, *Macleay, Proc. Linn. Soc. N. S. W.* x. 1885, p. 68.

Eye as long as or slightly longer than its distance from the mouth. Rostral twice as broad as deep, just visible from above; internasals not more than half as long as the præfrontals; frontal once and one fifth to once and a half as long as broad, at least twice as broad as the supraocular, as long as or a little longer than its distance from the end of the snout, shorter than the parietals, nasal entire, in contact with the single præocular; two (rarely one or three) postoculars; temporals 2+2, lower anterior wedged in between the fifth and sixth labials; six upper labials, third and fourth entering the eye, three or four lower labials in contact with the anterior chin-shields, which are as long as or a little shorter than the posterior. Scales in 15 rows. Ventrals 170–200, anal entire; subcaudals 30–46. Dark olive-brown to black above, yellowish below; head black above and below; ventrals and subcaudals sometimes dark-edged.

Total length 545 millim.; tail 75.

New South Wales and Queensland.

a. ♂ (V. 170; C. 35).   Sydney.   G. Krefft, Esq. [P]
(Type)
b. ♀ (V. 186, C 44).   Port Macquarie.   G Krefft, Esq. [P].
c, d. ♀ (V. 180; C. 39) & hgr (V. 172; C. 36).   New South Wales..   G. Krefft, Esq. [P.].
e. ♀ (V 171; C. 39)   Queensland.   H M.S 'Challenger.
f. Hgr (V. 179; C. 34).   Australia.

16. Denisonia nigrostriata.

Hoplocephalus nigrostriatus, *Krefft, Proc Zool Soc.* 1864, p. 181, and *Sn Austral.* p. 70, pl. xii fig 3 (1869); *F. Mull. Verh. Nat. Ges. Basel*, vii. 1885, p. 690.
Alecto dorsalis, *Jan, Icon. Gén.* 44, pl. ii. fig. 1 (1873).

Eye slightly longer than its distance from the mouth. Rostral twice as broad as deep, just visible from above; internasals half as long as the præfrontals; frontal a little longer than broad, twice as broad as the supraocular, as long as its distance from the end of the snout, shorter than the parietals; nasal entire, in contact with the single præocular; two postoculars; temporals 2+2, lower anterior wedged in between the fifth and sixth labials; six upper labials, third and fourth entering the eye; four lower labials in contact with the anterior chin-shields, which are as long as the posterior. Scales in 15 rows. Ventrals 180–184; anal entire; subcaudals 50–64. Yellowish above, the scales edged with brown, with a dark brown vertebral stripe; head dark brown above; upper lip and lower parts yellowish white.

Total length 380 millim.; tail 52.

Queensland.

a. ♀ (V. 184; C. 50).   Rockhampton.   Museum Godeffroy.

17. Denisonia carpentariæ.

Hoplocephalus carpentariæ, *Macleay, Proc. Linn. Soc. N.S. W.* (2) ii. 1887, p. 403.

Eye slightly longer than its distance from the mouth. Rostral twice as broad as deep, just visible from above; internasals hardly half as long as the præfrontals; frontal once and one fourth as long as broad, twice as broad as the supraocular, a little longer than its distance from the end of the snout, shorter than the parietals; nasal entire, not reaching the single præocular; two postoculars; temporals 2+2, lower anterior wedged in between the fifth and sixth labials; six upper labials, second in contact with the præfrontal, third and fourth entering the eye; three or four lower labials in contact with the anterior chin-shields, which are as long as the posterior. Scales in 15 rows. Ventrals 166–183; anal entire; subcaudals 31–43. Brown above, each scale lighter in the centre; upper lip, outer row of scales, and lower parts yellowish white.

Total length 285 millim.; tail 47.

Northern Queensland.

a ♀ (V. 183; C. 31).   Peak Downs.   Museum Godeffroy.

18. Denisonia pallidiceps.

Hoplocephalus pallidiceps, *Gunth. Cat.* p. 214 (1858); *Cope, Proc. Ac. Philad.* 1859, p. 343.
—— pallidiceps, part., *Krefft, Sn. Austral* p. 59 (1869).
Alecto permixta, *Jan, Icon. Gén.* 44, pl. 1 fig 2 (1873).

Eye small, hardly as long as its distance from the mouth. Rostral twice as broad as deep, visible from above; internasals one half to two thirds the length of the præfrontals; frontal once and one fourth to once and a half as long as broad, twice as broad as the supraocular, as long as or a little longer than its distance from the end of the snout, about two thirds the length of the parietals;

posterior nasal in contact with or narrowly separated from the single præocular; two postoculars; temporals 2+2, lower anterior wedged in between the fifth and sixth upper labials; six upper labials, third and fourth entering the eye; three or four lower labials in contact with the anterior chin-shields, which are nearly as long as the posterior. Scales in 15 rows. Ventrals 170–178; anal entire; subcaudals 37–38. Dark olive-brown above, head somewhat paler; yellowish beneath, subcaudals brown in the middle.

Total length 590 millim.; tail 80.

Northern Australia.

a–b. ♀ (V. 178, 170; C. 38, ?) Port Essington. Lord Derby [P.].
c Hgr. (V. 170; C. 37). N E Australia.
(Types.)

19. Denisonia melanura.

Hoplocephalus melanurus, *Bouleng. Proc. Zool. Soc.* 1888, p. 88, and 1890, p. 30, pl. ii. fig. 1.

Eye nearly as long as its distance from the mouth. Rostral broader than deep, just visible from above; internasals half as long as the præfrontals; frontal as long as broad or slightly longer than broad, twice as broad as the supraocular, a little longer than the præfrontals, not much more than half as long as the parietals; posterior nasal in contact with the single præocular, two postoculars; temporals 1+2; seven upper labials, third and fourth entering the eye, sixth largest; four lower labials in contact with the anterior chin-shields, which are shorter than the posterior. Scales in 15 or 17 rows. Ventrals 165–171; anal divided; subcaudals 38–48. Head and sides usually reddish, dorsal region dark brown; some or all of the scales black-edged; tail black; some specimens nearly entirely black, others with traces of black crossbands; ventrals yellow, on the hind part of the body with dark brown or black margin.

Total length 1000 millim.; tail 140.

Guadalcanar, Solomon Islands.

a–f ♂ (V. 168, C. 48) & ♀ (V. 168, 167, 171, 167, 165; C. 38, 45, ?, 38, 43). Guadalcanar. C. M. Woodford, Esq. [C.]. (Types.)
g. Skeleton. Guadalcanar.

20. Denisonia par.

Hoplocephalus par, *Bouleng Proc. Zool Soc.* 1884, p. 210, *Trans. Zool. Soc.* xii. 1886, p 46, pl. vii fig. 4, *and Proc. Zool. Soc.* 1890, p. 30; *Douglas-Ogilby, Rec. Austral. Mus.* i. 1890, p. 5.

Eye nearly as long as its distance from the mouth. Rostral broader than deep, just visible from above; internasals half as long as the præfrontals; frontal a little longer than broad, broader than the supraocular, a little longer than the præfrontals, much shorter than the parietals; posterior nasal in contact with the single præocular; two postoculars; temporals 1+2; seven upper labials, third and fourth entering the eye, third deeper than fourth; four lower labials in contact with the anterior chin-shields, which are shorter than the posterior. Scales in 16 rows. Ventrals 164–166; anal divided; subcaudals 40–49. Body with broad reddish-brown bands, separated by narrow white interspaces; most of the scales black-edged, head blackish brown; lower parts white, the red and black extending on the sutures of the posterior ventrals, tail with complete red annuli.

Total length 750 millim.; tail 110
Faro and Howla Islands, Bougainville Straits, Solomon Islands.

a ♀ (V. 166; C. 43).	Faro Id.	H B Guppy, Esq. [P.]. (Type.)
b-c. ♂ (V. 164; C. 49) & ♀ (V. 165; C. 40).	Faro Id.	C. M. Woodford, Esq. [C.].
d. Skull of *c*.		

21. Denisonia woodfordii.

Hoplocephalus woodfordii, *Bouleng. Proc. Zool. Soc.* 1888, p. 89, and 1890, p. 30, pl. ii. fig 2.

Eye nearly as long as its distance from the mouth. Rostral broader than deep, just visible from above; internasals half as long as the præfrontals; frontal slightly longer than broad, nearly twice as broad as the supraocular, as long as its distance from the rostral, much shorter than the parietals; posterior nasal in contact with the single præocular; two postoculars; temporals 1+2, seven upper labials, third and fourth entering the eye; four lower labials in contact with the anterior chin-shields, which are shorter than the posterior Scales in 17 rows. Ventrals 166–172; anal divided; subcaudals 41–45 pairs. Brownish white above, each scale with a blackish-brown border, forming a reticulate pattern; head dark brown; lower parts white, subcaudals edged with dark brown.

Total length 670 millim.; tail 100.
New Georgia, Solomon Islands.

a. ♀ (V. 166; C. 45).	Rubiana, New Georgia	C. M. Woodford, Esq. [C.] (Type)
b. Yg. (V. 172, C. 41).	New Georgia.	H.M.S. 'Penguin.'

220. MICROPECHIS.

Naja, part., *Schleg. Phys. Serp.* ii. p. 461 (1837).
Trimeresurus, part., *Dum. & Bibr. Erp. Gén.* vii. p. 1244 (1854); *Jan, Elenco sist. Ofid.* p. 118 (1863).

Maxillary extending forwards as far as the palatine, with a pair of large grooved poison-fangs followed by three small solid teeth;

mandibular teeth, anterior longest. Head distinct from neck; eye extremely small, with round pupil; nostril between two nasals; no loreal. Body cylindrical; scales smooth, without pits, in 15 or 17 rows. Tail short; subcaudals in two rows.

New Guinea and Solomon Islands.

1. Micropechis ikaheka.

Coluber ikaheka, *Lesson, Voy. Coquille, Zool.* ii p 54, *Rept* pl. v. (1830).
Naja elaps, *Schleg. Phys. Serp.* ii. p. 485 (1837), *and Abbild.* p. 139, pl. xlviii. figs. 14-16 (1844)
Trimeresurus ophiophagus, part , *Dum & Bibr.* vii. p. 1245 (1854).
—— elaps, *Jan, Rev. & Mag Zool.* 1859, p. 129
—— ikaheka, *Jan, Elenco,* p. 118 (1863), *and Icon. Gén.* 44, pl. v. (1873); *Sauv. Bull Soc. Philom.* (7) i. 1878, p 43.
Ophiophagus elaps, *Meyer, Mon. Berl Ac* 1874, p. 137.
—— ikaheka, *Peters & Doria, Ann. Mus Genova,* xiii. 1878, p. 410.
—— ikaheka, var fasciatus, *Fischer, Abh. Nat. Ver. Hamb* viii. 1884, p 10, pl. vii fig. 3.
Diemenia ikaheka, *F. Müll. Verh. Nat Ges Basel,* x. 1892, p 207.
——, sp., *Boettg Ber. Offenb. Ver Nat.* 1892, p. 154.

Eye hardly half as long as its distance from the mouth. Rostral much broader than deep, visible from above; internasals one half to two thirds the length of the præfrontals, frontal once and one fifth to once and a half as long as broad, broader than the supraocular, as long as its distance from the rostral or the end of the snout, three fifths the length of the parietals; posterior nasal in contact with the single præocular; two postoculars; temporals 2+2, anterior very large, the lower wedged in between the fifth and sixth upper labials; six upper labials, third and fourth entering the eye; three or four lower labials in contact with the anterior chin-shields, which are as long as or a little shorter than the posterior. Scales in 15 rows. Ventrals 180-223; anal divided; subcaudals 39-55. Particoloured yellow and black, the two colours sometimes forming irregular cross-bars; the black scales edged with yellow; head and tail black above, lower parts yellow, uniform or with some of the shields black-edged.

Total length 1550 millim.; tail 180.

New Guinea.

a-b ♀ (V. 185; C. 43) &   Mansinam.   M. L. Laglaize [C].
  hgr. (V. 180 ; C 45)
c. Skull of *b.*

2. Micropechis elapoides.

Hoplocephalus elapoides, *Bouleng. Proc. Zool. Soc.* 1890, p. 30, pl. ii. fig. 3.

Eye hardly half as long as its distance from the mouth. Rostral much broader than deep, just visible from above; internasals two thirds the length of the præfrontals; frontal small, much longer than broad, once and a half as broad as the supraocular, as long as its distance from the rostral, two thirds the length of the parietals, posterior nasal in contact with the single præocular; two postoculars; temporals 1+2; seven upper labials, third and fourth entering the eye; four lower labials in contact with the anterior chin-shields, which are as long as the posterior. Scales in 17 rows. Ventrals 208; anal entire; subcaudals 35. Cream-colour, with 22 black bands, broader than the interspaces between them, interrupted on the belly, encircling the tail; on the posterior three-fourths of the body series of small black spots form a streak along each side of the back; end of snout and ocular region black.

Total length 750 millim.; tail 75.

Florida Island, Solomon Group.

a. ♀ (V 208; C. 35).   Florida Id.   C. M. Woodford, Esq. [C.].
(Type.)

221. HOPLOCEPHALUS.

Oplocephalus (*Cuv.*), *Voigt, Thierr.* iii. p. 143 (1832).
Naja, part., *Schleg. Phys. Serp.* ii. p. 461 (1837).
Alecto (*non Wagl.*), part., *Dum. & Bibr. Ep. Gén.* vii. p. 1249 (1854); *Jan, Elenco sist. Ofid.* p. 116 (1863).
Hoplocephalus, part., *Gunth. Cat. Col. Sn.* p. 213 (1858), *Krefft, Sn. Austral.* p. 53 (1869).

Maxillary extending forwards as far as the palatine, with a pair of large grooved poison-fangs followed by two or three small solid teeth; mandibular teeth, anterior longest. Head distinct from neck; eye rather small, with round pupil; nasal entire or divided; no loreal. Body cylindrical; scales smooth, without pits, in 21 rows; ventrals angulate and notched laterally. Tail moderate; subcaudals single.

Australia.

Synopsis of the Species.

Ventrals obtusely angulate, 204–221; subcaudals 40–56 .... 1. *bungaroides*, p. 348.
Ventrals strongly angulate, 191–227; subcaudals 44–59 .... 2. *bitorquatus*, p. 349.
Ventrals strongly angulate, 239; subcaudals 60 .... 3. *stephensii*, p. 350.

1. Hoplocephalus bungaroides.

Naja bungaroides, *Boie, Isis,* 1828, p. 1034; *Schleg. Phys. Serp.* ii. p. 477 (1837), *and Abbild.* p. 140, pl. xlviii. figs. 17 & 18 (1844).
Alecto variegata, *Dum. & Bibr.* vii. p. 1254, pl. lxxvi. b. fig. 1 (1854).
—— bungaroides, *Dum. & Bibr. t. c.* p. 1257; *Jan, Elenco,* p. 116 (1863), *and Icon. Gén.* 43, pl. vi. fig. 2 (1873).
Hoplocephalus bungaroides, *Gunth. Cat.* p. 213 (1858).

Hoplocephalus variegatus, *Gunth l. c.* p. 214; *Krefft, Sn. Austral.* p 56, pl. vi. fig. 6 (1869).

Eye as long as or slightly longer than its distance from the mouth (larger in the young). Rostral broader than deep, just visible from above; internasals shorter than the præfrontals; frontal once and a half as long as broad, once and a half as broad as the supraocular, as long as its distance from the end of the snout, shorter than the parietals; nasal entire or divided, in contact with or narrowly separated from the single præocular; two postoculars; temporals 2+2, lower anterior very large, wedged in between the fifth and sixth upper labials, and nearly reaching the lip; six upper labials, third and fourth entering the eye; three lower labials in contact with the anterior chin-shields, which are as long as the posterior. Scales in 21 rows. Ventrals obtusely angulate laterally, 204-221; anal entire; subcaudals 40-56. Black above, with yellow spots forming more or less regular cross-bands on the body; upper labials yellow, margined with black; ventrals blackish, yellow on the sides.

Total length 1620 millim.; tail 210.

New South Wales:

a.	♀ (V. 212; C. 45).	New South Wales.	G Krefft, Esq. [P.].
b.	♀ (V. 221; C. 42).	Australia.	Lord Derby [P].
c.	♂ (V. 204, C. 52).	Australia.	Dr. Bennett [P].
d.	Hgr (V. 210; C. 56).	Australia.	Capt Stokes [P.].
e.	♂ (V. 210, C. 51).	Australia.	Zoological Society.
f.	Yg. (V. 204, C. 47).	Australia.	

2 Hoplocephalus bitorquatus.

Alecto bitorquata, *Jan, Rev & Mag. Zool.* 1859, p. 128, *and Icon. Gén* 43, pl. vi. fig 6 (1873).

Hoplocephalus pallidiceps, part., *Krefft, Sn. Austral.* p 59, pl. xi. fig. 1 (1869).

—— sulcans, *De Vis, Proc R Soc. Queensl* i 1884, p. 138.

—— waitii, *Douglas Ogilby, Proc. Linn. Soc. N. S. W.* (2) ix. 1894, p 261.

Eye as long as or slightly longer than its distance from the mouth (larger in the young). Rostral broader than deep, just visible from above; internasals one half to two thirds as long as the præfrontals; frontal once and one third to once and two thirds as long as broad, a little broader than the supraocular, as long as or a little longer than its distance from the end of the snout, shorter than the parietals; nasal entire, in contact with the single præocular; two postoculars, temporals 2+2, lower anterior large and wedged in between the fifth and sixth upper labials and sometimes reaching the lip; six (or seven) upper labials, third and fourth entering the eye; three lower labials in contact with the anterior chin-shields, which are as long as or a little shorter than the posterior. Scales in 21 rows. Ventrals strongly angulate laterally, 191-227; anal entire; subcaudals 44-59. Dark olive above, with or without a darker vertebral streak; head pale olive, with a bright yellow occipital blotch, edged with black behind and sometimes bearing a few black spots; a black bar across the forehead in front of the frontal; sides of head with black spots; lower labials and chin usually spotted with black; lower parts greyish olive or brown.

Total length 510 millim.; tail 95.

Queensland, New South Wales.

a-b ♂ (V 191; C. 58) & yg. (V. 197; C. 44).	Rockhampton.	Museum Godeffroy.
c. Hgr. (V. 201; C. 52).	Rockhampton.	
d Yg (V 192; C. 59).	Clarence R.	G. Krefft, Esq. [P.].
e Head of adult.	Clarence R.	G. Krefft, Esq. [P.].

3. Hoplocephalus stephensii.

Hoplocephalus stephensii, *Krefft, Sn. Austral* p 58, pl. vi. fig. 7 (1869).

Head-shields as in *H. bungaroides*, but frontal broader and parietals longer. Scales in 21 rows. Ventrals 239, flat beneath, notched and strongly angulate laterally; anal entire; subcaudals 60. Body barred alternately with black and white; the black bars twice the size of the white ones, and reaching down to ventral keel; head dark, spotted with yellow; a ⨆-shaped yellow streak on the back of the head.

Total length 760 millim.

Port Macquarie, New South Wales.

222. TROPIDECHIS.

Tropidechis, *Gunth. Ann. & Mag. N. H.* (3) xii. 1863, p. 363; *Krefft, Sn. Austral.* p. 71 (1869).

Maxillary extending forwards as far as the palatine, with a pair of large grooved poison-fangs followed by four small solid teeth; mandibular teeth, anterior longest. Head distinct from neck; eye rather small, with round pupil; nasal entire; no loreal. Body cylindrical; scales strongly keeled, without pits, in 23 rows; ventrals rounded. Tail moderate; subcaudals single.

Australia.

1. Tropidechis carinatus. (PLATE XIX. fig. 1.)

Hoplocephalus carinatus, *Krefft, Proc. Zool. Soc.* 1863, p. 86.
Tropidechis carinata, *Gunth. Ann. & Mag. N. H.* (3) xii. 1863, p 350; *Krefft, Sn. Austral.* p. 71 (1869).

Eye as long as its distance from the mouth. Rostral broader than deep, just visible from above, internasals shorter than the præfrontals; frontal once and a half as long as broad, once and a half as broad as the supraocular, as long as its distance from the end of the snout, two thirds the length of the parietals; nasal in contact with the single præocular; temporals 1+2 or 2+2, the lower anterior, if not converted into a labial, wedged in between the fifth and sixth upper labials; six or seven upper labials, third and fourth entering the eye; three lower labials in contact with the anterior chin-shields, which are shorter than the posterior. Scales in 23 rows, strongly keeled, outer smooth. Ventrals 165–171, anal entire; subcaudals 52–54. Dark olive above, with darker cross-bands, which may be broken up on the vertebral line, yellowish below, more or less obscured with olive.

Total length 730 millim.; tail 120.

New South Wales; Queensland.

a. ♀ (V. 171; C. 52). Clarence River. G. Krefft, Esq. [P.].
(One of the types.)

223. NOTECHIS.

Alecto (*non Wagl*), part., *Dum. & Bibr. Erp. Gén.* vii. p. 1249 (1854); *Jan, Elenco sist. Ofid* p. 116 (1863).
Hoplocephalus, part., *Günth. Cat. Col. Sn.* p. 213 (1858); *Krefft, Sn. Austral.* p. 53 (1869).

Maxillary extending forwards as far as the palatine, with a pair of large grooved poison-fangs followed by four or five small, feebly grooved teeth; mandibular teeth, anterior longest and feebly grooved. Head distinct from neck, with distinct canthus rostralis; eye rather small, with round pupil; nasal entire; no loreal. Body cylindrical; scales smooth, without pits, disposed obliquely, in 15 to 19 rows, the lateral scales shorter than the dorsals, belly rounded. Tail moderate; subcaudals single.

Australia and Tasmania.

1. Notechis scutatus.

? Boa lævis, *Lacép Ann. du Mus.* iv. 1804, p 209.
Alecto curta (*non Schleg*), part., *Dum. & Bibr.* vii. p. 1252 (1854).
Hoplocephalus curtus, *Günth Cat* p. 216 (1858), *Krefft, Sn. Austral* p. 53, pl ix. & pl. xi fig 6 (1869); *McCoy, Prodr. Zool. Vict.*, Dec 1, p. 11, pl iii. (1878).
Naja (Hamadryas) scutata, *Peters, Mon. Berl. Ac.* 1861, p. 690.
Hoplocephalus fuscus, *Steind. Novara, Rept* p. 82 (1867).
—— ater, *Krefft, Proc. Zool. Soc.* 1866, p. 373 (1867), and *l.c.* p. 55, pl. xi. fig. 11.
Alecto fasciolata, *Jan, Icon. Gén.* 43, pl. vi. fig. 4 (1873).

Eye as long as or a little shorter than its distance from the mouth in the adult, larger in the young. Rostral a little broader than deep, the portion visible from above measuring one third to one half its distance from the frontal; frontal as long as broad or longer than broad, not more than once and a half as long as broad, once and a half to twice as broad as the supraocular, as long as its distance from the rostral or the end of the snout, one half to two thirds the length of the parietals; nasal in contact with the single præocular; two postoculars; temporals 2+2, lower anterior very large and wedged in between the fifth and sixth upper labials and sometimes nearly reaching the lip; six (rarely seven) upper labials, third and fourth entering the eye; three lower labials in contact with the anterior chin-shields, which are as long as or a little shorter than the posterior. Scales in 15 to 19 rows. Ventrals 146-185; anal entire; subcaudals 39-61. Olive-brown to blackish above, the skin between the scales black; young with dark cross-bands, which may disappear in the adult; belly yellowish or olive, the shields often dark-edged.

Total length 1280 millim.; tail 170.

Australia and Tasmania.

A. Scales in 15 rows.

a. ♀ (V. 168, C. ?).	Tasmania.	G. Krefft, Esq [P.].
b–e. ♂ (V. 172, 172, 164; C. 54, 50, 53) & ♀ (V. 174; C. 48).	Tasmania.	

B. Scales in 17 rows.

f–h, i–k, l, m. Hgr. (V. 173, 173, 170, 173; C. 50, 52, 51, 55) & yg. (V. 169, 166, 159, C. 55*, 54, 49)	Tasmania.	R. Gunn, Esq. [P.].
n. Yg (V. 179; C. 50).	Hobart.	J. B. Jukes, Esq. [P.].
o. ♀ (V. 160; C. 45).	Kangaroo Id.	Zoological Society.
p. Yg. (V. 154; C. 51).	S. Australia.	Dr. Fleming [P.].
q. ♀ (V. 169; C ?).	Australia.	Haslar Collection.
r. ♀ (V. 150, C. 39).	Australia.	Zoological Society.

C. Scales in 19 rows.

s. ♀ (V. 175; C. 56)	Sydney.	Dr. Bennett [P.].
t. ♀ (V. 179; C 54).	Sydney.	Prof. G. B. Howes [P.].
u. ♂ (V. 185; C. 61)	New South Wales.	Imperial Institute [P.].
v. ♀ (V 178; C. 54).	Kangaroo Id.	Zoological Society.
w. ♀ (V. 161; C. 52).	Australia.	Haslar Collection.
x. Yg (V. 162; C. 48).	Australia.	Sir J. Macgregor [P.].
y. ♀ (V. 160; C. 49)	Australia.	Zoological Society.
z. ♀, skeleton.	Australia.	Zoological Society.
α. Skull of u		

224. RHINHOPLOCEPHALUS.

Rhinoplocephalus, *F. Müll Verh Nat. Ges. Basel*, vii. 1885, p. 690

Dentition as in *Hoplocephalus*. Head feebly distinct from neck; eye small, with round pupil; rostral very large, detached on the sides, as in *Aspidelaps*; no internasals; nostril in an undivided nasal; no loreal. Body cylindrical, rigid; scales smooth, in 15 rows; ventrals rounded. Tail short; subcaudals single.

Australia.

---

* 19 of the subcaudals are divided.

1. Rhinhoplocephalus bicolor.

Rhinoplocephalus bicolor, *F. Müll. l. c.* pl. ix. figs. *f–i.*

Snout broad, truncate; eye a little shorter than its distance from the mouth. Upper portion of rostral subquadrangular, nearly twice as broad as long, as long as the præfrontals; frontal a little longer than broad, twice as broad as the supraocular, as long as its distance from the end of the snout, shorter than the parietals; nasal in contact with the lower præocular; two præoculars, upper small; two postoculars; temporals 1+2; six upper labials, third and fourth entering the eye; four lower labials in contact with the anterior chin-shields, which are a little longer than the posterior. Scales in 15 rows. Ventrals 159; anal entire; subcaudals 34. Greyish olive above, lateral scales dark-edged, yellowish white beneath, tongue white.

Total length 395 millim.; tail 55.

Australia.

225. BRACHYASPIS.

Naja, part, *Schleg. Phys Serp* ii. p 461 (1837).
Hoplocephalus, part, *Gunth. Cat. Col Sn.* p 213 (1858).

Maxillary extending forwards as far as the palatine, with a pair of large grooved poison-fangs followed by two or three small teeth; anterior mandibular teeth strongly enlarged, fang-like. Head distinct from neck; eye small, with vertically elliptic pupil; nostril between two nasals; no loreal Body stout, cylindrical; scales smooth, without pits, slightly oblique, in 19 rows; belly rounded Tail short; subcaudals single.

Australia.

1. Brachyaspis curta.

Naja curta, *Schleg. Phys. Serp* ii. p 486 (1837), *and Abbild.* p. 140, pl. xlviii figs 19 & 20 (1844).
Hoplocephalus curtus, part, *Gunth Cat.* p. 216 (1858)
—— temporalis, *Gunth Ann & Mag. N H.* (3) ix. 1862, p. 130, pl. ix. fig. 11, *Krefft, Sn. Austral.* p 65, pl. vi fig. 5 (1869).

Eye scarcely longer than its distance from the mouth. Rostral a little broader than deep, just visible from above; internasals shorter than the præfrontals; frontal once and a half to twice as long as broad, broader than the supraocular, as long as or longer than its distance from the end of the snout, as long as or a little shorter than parietals; nasal in contact with or narrowly separated from the single præocular; two postoculars; temporals 2+4 or 3+3; six or seven upper labials, third and fourth entering the eye; three lower labials in contact with the anterior chin-shields, which are shorter than the posterior. Scales in 19 rows. Ventrals 128–136; anal entire; subcaudals 30–35. Uniform olive-brown above, yellowish beneath.

Total length 490 millim.; tail 70.

Western Australia.

354   COLUBRIDÆ.

a–b. ♀ (V. 131, 134, C. 33, 32).   N.W. Australia.   Museum Godeffroy.
c. ♀ (V. 136; O. 30).   Port Lincoln.   G. Krefft, Esq. [P.].
d–f. ♂ (V. 134; C. 35) & yg. (V. 128, 129; C 34, 31).   S Australia.   Dr. Fleming [P.].
(Types of *H. temporalis*.)
g. Skull of *c*.

226. ACANTHOPHIS.

Acanthophis, *Daud Hist Rept.* v. p. 287 (1803); *Wagl. Syst. Amph.* p 172 (1830), *Gray, Cat Sn.* p. 34 (1849); *Dum. & Bibr. Erp. Gén.* vii. p. 1388 (1854), *Cope, Proc. Ac. Philad.* 1859, p. 343; *Jan, Elenco sist Ofid.* p. 120 (1863); *Krefft, Sn. Austral.* p. 79 (1869).
Ophryas, *Merrem, Tent. Syst. Amph.* p. 146 (1820).
Vipera, part., *Schleg. Phys. Serp.* ii. p. 573 (1837).

Maxillary extending forwards as far as the palatine, with a pair of large grooved poison-fangs followed by two or three small teeth; anterior mandibular teeth strongly enlarged, fang-like. Head distinct from neck; eye small, with vertically elliptic pupil; nostril in the upper part of a single nasal; no loreal. Body stout, cylindrical; scales more or less distinctly keeled, without pits, in 21 or 23 rows, belly rounded. Tail short, compressed at the end and terminating in a long spine turned upwards; anterior subcaudals single, posterior in two rows.

Moluccas, Papuasia, Australia.

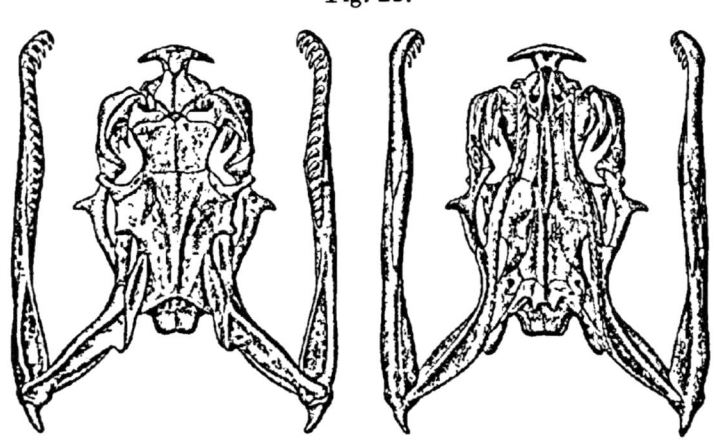

Fig. 25.

Skull of *Acanthophis antarcticus*.

This skull is remarkable for the presence of a strong outer process, directed downwards and backwards, on the ectopterygoid. Such a process is present, but less developed, in some of the Hydrophinæ (*Hydrus, Distira*).

1. Acanthophis antarcticus.

Merrem, Beitr. ii p. 20, pl. xiii. (1790).
Boa antarctica, *Shaw, Nat. Misc.* pl ccccxxxv. (1794).
—— palpebrosa, *Shaw, Zool* iii p. 362 (1802).
Acanthophis cerastinus, *Daud Rept.* v. p 289, pl. lxyii. (1803); *Guér Icon. R. A., Rept.* pl. xxii. (1844); *Dum. & Bibr.* vii. p. 1389 (1854).
—— brownii, *Leach, Zool. Misc.* i. pl. iii. (1814).
Ophryas acanthophis, *Merr. Tent.* p 147 (1820).
Vipera acanthophis, *Schleg. Phys. Serp.* ii. p. 605, pl xxi figs. 21-23 (1837)
Acanthophis antarctica, *Gray, Zool. Misc.* p. 71 (1842), *and Cat.* p 34 (1849); *Krefft, Sn. Austral* p. 80, pl. x & pl. xi. fig 7 (1869); *McCoy, Prodr. Zool Vict.*, Dec 2, p. 11, pl. xii. (1878), *Peters & Doria, Ann. Mus. Genova,* xiii. 1878, p. 91; *McCay, Proc. Linn. Soc. N. S W.* (2) iv 1890, p. 893, pls. xxv.–xxvii.; *Boettg. Ber. Offenb Ver. Nat* 1892, p. 155.
—— lævis, *Macleay, Proc Linn. Soc N. S. W.* ii. 1877, p. 40; *Douglas Ogilby, Rec. Austral. Mus.* i. 1890, p. 99.
—— prælongus, *Ramsay, Proc. Linn. Soc. N. S. W.* ii. 1877, p. 72.

Head with elevated sides, the lores very oblique. Eye much shorter than its distance from the mouth. Rostral large, twice as broad as deep, with horizontal edge, its upper portion measuring one half to two thirds its distance from the frontal; internasals as long as broad, or a little broader than long, as long as or shorter than the præfrontals; frontal narrower than the supraocular, twice as long as broad, as long as or a little shorter than its distance from the end of the snout, as long as or a little longer than the parietals; supraocular often raised and angular, horn-like (*Boa palpebrosa,* Shaw, *A. lævis,* Macl.); upper head-shields more or less rugose or striated; nasal large, in contact with the single præ-ocular; two postoculars; two or three suboculars, separating the eye from the labials; temporals 2-3+2-4; six or seven upper labials; four lower labials in contact with the anterior chin-shields, which are as long as or a little shorter than the posterior. Scales in 21 or 23 rows, dorsals more or less distinctly, sometimes very faintly keeled. Ventrals 113-130, anal entire; subcaudals 41-51, the 5 to 27 last divided Yellowish, reddish, or greyish brown above, with more or less distinct dark cross-bands, with or without small black spots; lips with black or blackish spots or bars; sides spotted with black; belly yellowish white, uniform or more or less spotted with brown or black; end of tail yellow or black.

Total length 850 millim.; tail 150.

Moluccas, New Guinea, Australia.

a. ♂ (Sc. 21; V. 114; C. 46).	Ceram.	Dr Bleeker.
b–d ♂ (Sc. 21; V. 116; C 50), ♀ (Sc. 21, V. 120, C. 44), & yg. (Sc. 21, V. 121; C.?).	N. Ceram.	

e-i. ♂ (Sc. 21; V. 115, 115; C. 50, 46), ♀ (Sc. 21; V. 119, 119; C. 45, 43), & yg (Sc. 21; V. 116; C. 45)	Kei Ids.	Capt. Langen [P.].
k. ♀ (Sc. 23; V. 126; C. 46).	New Guinea, South of Huon Gulf.	Mr. Comrie [C.]
l. Hgr. ♀ (Sc. 21; V. 121; C. 51).	Cape York.	H.M.S. 'Challenger.'
m ♂ (Sc. 23; V. 118; C. 48).	Cape York.	
n. Yg. (Sc. 21; V. 125; C. 45).	Cardwell, Queensland.	H.M S. Challenger'
o. Yg. (Sc 23; V 118; C. 48).	Gulf of Carpentaria.	G. Krefft, Esq. [P.].
p ♀ (Sc 23; V. 130; C. 42)	Port Essington.	Lord Derby [P].
q ♂ (Sc. 23; V. 131; C. ?).	N.W. Australia.	Sir J. Richardson [P.].
r. ♀ (Sc. 21; V. 121; C. 41)	Sydney.	G. Krefft, Esq [P].
s. ♀ (Sc. 21; V 122; C. 44).	New South Wales.	Major Bray [P]
t. ♀ (Sc. 21; V. 123; C. 43).	New South Wales.	G. Krefft, Esq. [P.].
u-v. ♀ (Sc 21; V. 122, 123; C. ?, 48).	New South Wales.	Imperial Institute [P.].
w. ♀ (Sc. 21; V. 115; C. 47).	Australia.	Capt. Stokes [P.].
x. ♀ (Sc. 21; V. 119; C. 43)	——?	(*Boa aculeata*, Shaw.)
y, z. ♂ (Sc. 21; V. 119, C. 48) & hgr. ♀ (Sc 23; V. 119; C 46).	——?	Haslar Collection.
a. ♀ skeleton.	Australia.	Dr. Bennett [P.].

227. ELAPOGNATHUS.

Maxillary extending forwards as far as the palatine, with a pair of moderately large grooved poison-fangs; no other maxillary teeth; mandibular teeth subequal. Head small, not or but slightly distinct from neck; eye moderate, with round pupil; nasal entire; no loreal. Body cylindrical; scales smooth, without pits, in 15 rows; ventrals rounded. Tail moderate; subcaudals single.

Australia.

1. Elapognathus minor. (PLATE XIX. fig. 2.)

Hoplocephalus superbus, part., *Günth Cat* p. 217 (1858).
—— minor, *Günth. Ann & Mag N. H.* (3) xii. 1863, p. 362; *Krefft, Sn. Austral.* p. 67 (1869)

Eye much longer than its distance from the mouth. Rostral as deep as broad or a little broader than deep, the portion visible from above measuring one third to one half its distance from the frontal;

internasals two thirds the length of the præfrontals; frontal once and a half to once and two thirds as long as broad, a little broader than the supraocular, as long as or a little longer than its distance from the end of the snout, shorter than the parietals; nasal in contact with the single præocular; two postoculars, temporals 2+2; six upper labials, third and fourth entering the eye; three lower labials in contact with the anterior chin-shields, which are shorter than the posterior. Scales finely striated, in 15 rows. Ventrals 120–128; anal entire; subcaudals 52–60. Dark olive above; some of the sutures between the upper labials black; a black occipital blotch in the young; yellowish or greyish olive beneath, the ventrals black at the base.

Total length 460 millim.; tail 95.
South-west Australia.

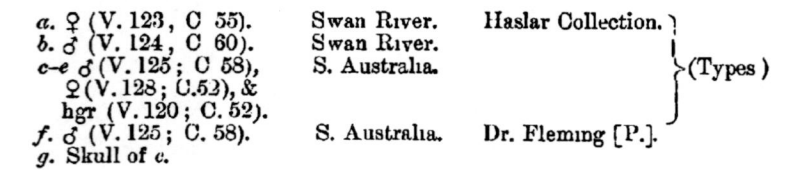

a. ♀ (V. 123, C 55). Swan River. Haslar Collection.
b. ♂ (V. 124, C 60). Swan River.
c-e ♂ (V. 125; C 58), S. Australia. (Types.)
♀ (V. 128; C. 52), &
hgr (V. 120; C. 52).
f. ♂ (V. 125; C. 58). S. Australia. Dr. Fleming [P.].
g. Skull of c.

228. BOULENGERINA.

Boulengerina, *Dollo, Bull. Mus. Belg.* iv. 1886, p 159; *Bouleng. Proc. Zool. Soc.* 1895, p. 866.

Maxillary bone extending forwards as far as the palatine, with a pair of large grooved poison-fangs followed by three or four small teeth; mandibular teeth, anterior longest. Head not distinct from neck; eye small, with round pupil, nostril between two nasals; no loreal. Body cylindrical, scales smooth, without pits, in 21 rows; ventrals rounded. Tail moderate; subcaudals in two rows.
Central Africa.

1. Boulengerina stormsi.

Boulengerina stormsi, *Dollo, Bull. Mus. Belg.* iv. 1886, p. 160, fig.; *Bouleng. Proc. Zool. Soc.* 1895, p. 866, pl. xlviii.

Rostral nearly as deep as broad, the portion visible from above measuring half its distance from the frontal; internasals shorter and a little broader than the præfrontals, extensively in contact with the præocular; frontal small, slightly longer than broad, as broad as the supraocular, as long as its distance from the rostral, slightly more than half the length of the parietals; posterior nasal in contact with the single præocular; two postoculars; temporals 1+2; seven upper labials, third and fourth entering the eye, fourth, fifth, and sixth in contact with the lower postocular, third and sixth deepest, four lower labials in contact with the anterior chin-shields, which are much longer than the posterior. Scales in 21 rows. Ventrals 193; anal entire; subcaudals 67. Brown above; four black cross-bars on the nape and neck, the second and third forming complete rings, followed by five irregular black spots: further back, the body darker brown with the scales black-edged; tail black; belly white anteriorly, brown further back, with the shields black-edged, blackish brown towards the tail.

Total length 240 millim.; tail 85.

Lake Tanganyika.

229. ELAPECHIS.

Elapsoidea [*], *Bocage, Jorn. Sc. Lisb.* i. 1866, p. 70; *Peters, Mon. Berl Ac.* 1880, p. 797.

Maxillary bone extending forwards as far as the palatine, with a pair of large grooved poison-fangs followed by two to four small teeth; mandibular teeth, anterior longest. Head not distinct from neck; eye small, with round pupil; nostril between two nasals; no loreal. Body cylindrical; scales oblique, smooth, without pits, in 13 or 15 rows; ventrals rounded. Tail very short; subcaudals all or most in two rows.

Tropical and South Africa.

Synopsis of the Species.

I. Scales in 13 rows.

  A. Snout broadly rounded.

    1. First lower labial in contact with its fellow behind the symphysial.

Internasals much shorter than the præfrontals; frontal at least three fourths the length of the parietals	1. *guentheri*, p. 359.
Internasals three fourths the length of the præfrontals; frontal two thirds the length of the parietals	2. *niger*, p. 359.

    2. Symphysial in contact with the anterior chin-shields.
                                     3. *hessii*, p. 360.

  B. Snout obtusely pointed.

Portion of rostral visible from above nearly half as long as its distance from the frontal	4. *decosteri*, p. 360.
Portion of rostral visible from above as long as its distance from the frontal	5. *sundevallii*, p. 360.

II. Scales in 15 rows . . . . 6. *boulengeri*, p. 361.

---

[*] The correct form would be *Elapoidea*, which name is preoccupied (*Elapoides*, Boie).

1. Elapechis guentheri.

Elapsoidea guentheri, *Bocage, Jorn. Sc. Lisb.* i p 1866, p. 70, pl i. fig. 3, and iv 1873, p 224; *Sauvage, Bull Soc Zool. France*, ix. 1884, p. 201; *Boettg. Ber. Senck. Ges.* 1888, p. 82; *Gunth. Ann. & Mag N H.* (6) xv 1895, p. 525, pl. xxi. fig. C; *Bocage, Herp. Angola*, p. 129, pl xiv fig 3 (1895).
—— semiannulata, *Bocage, Jorn. Sc Lisb* viii. 1882, p. 303.

Snout rounded. Rostral broader than deep, the portion visible from above measuring about one third its distance from the frontal; internasals much shorter than the præfrontals, frontal once and a half as long as broad, as long as or longer than its distance from the end of the snout, a little shorter than the parietals, posterior nasal in contact with, or narrowly separated from, the single præocular; two postoculars; temporals 1+2, seven upper labials, third and fourth entering the eye, sixth largest; three or four lower labials in contact with the anterior chin-shields, which are separated from the symphysial; posterior chin-shields nearly as large as the anterior. Scales in 13 rows. Ventrals 142–166, anal entire; subcaudals 13–25, all or most in two rows. Whitish or grey above, with black, white-edged cross-bands, or blackish with whitish cross-bars or lines formed by the edges of some of the scales; lower parts dirty white or brownish, grey, or blackish.

Total length 520 millim.; tail 50.

Gaboon, Congo, Angola, Central Africa.

a ♂ (V. 153, C. 25). Stanley Pool.
b. Hgr. (V.166; C 25). Foot of Mt. Ruwenzori. Scott Elliot, Esq [P].
c. Yg (V. 143; C. 21). Shiré Highlands. Sir H. H. Johnston [P.].

2. Elapechis niger. (PLATE XX. fig 1.)

Elapsoidea nigra, *Gunth. Ann & Mag N H.* (6) i. 1888, p 332; *Werner, Verh. zool.-bot. Ges Wien*, xlv. 1895, p 193

Snout rounded. Rostral broader than deep, the portion visible from above measuring about one fourth its distance from the frontal; internasals three fourths the length of the præfrontals; frontal once and one third as long as broad, as long as its distance from the end of the snout, two thirds the length of the parietals, posterior nasal in contact with the single præocular; two postoculars; temporals 1+2; seven upper labials, third and fourth entering the eye, sixth largest; three lower labials in contact with the anterior chin-shields, which are separated from the symphysial; posterior chin-shields as large as the anterior. Scales in 13 rows. Ventrals 153; anal entire; subcaudals 16–20. Black above and below; lower surface of head and anterior ventrals whitish Young with transverse series of white dots.

Total length 420 millim; tail 30.

Zanzibar.

a ♀ (V. 153, C. 16). Ushambola. Sir J. Kirk [C.]. (Type.)

3. Elapechis hessii.

Elapsoidea hessei, *Boettg. Zool. Anz.* 1887, p. 651, *and Ber. Senck. Ges.* 1888, p. 83, pl. ii. fig. 6.

Snout rounded. Rostral broader than deep, the portion visible from above about half as long as its distance from the frontal; internasals one third the length of the præfrontals; frontal a little longer than broad, longer than its distance from the end of the snout, shorter than the parietals; posterior nasal in contact with the single præocular; two postoculars; temporals 1+2; seven upper labials, third and fourth entering the eye; three lower labials in contact with the anterior chin-shields, which are extensively in contact with the symphysial; posterior chin-shields as large as the anterior. Scales in 13 rows. Ventrals 147; anal entire; subcaudals 22. Greyish above, with black cross-bars, much narrower than the interspaces between them, narrowing down the sides; a series of black spots on each side, between the cross-bars; a large black blotch on the nape, produced as a streak along the suture between the parietal shields; lower parts white.

Total length 160 millim.; tail 12.

Banana, Congo.

4. Elapechis decosteri.

Elapsoidea decosteri, *Bouleng. Ann. & Mag. N. H.* (6) ii. 1888, p. 141.

Snout obtusely pointed. Rostral broader than deep, the portion visible from above measuring nearly half its distance from the frontal; internasals half as long as the præfrontals; frontal once and a half as long as broad, as long as its distance from the end of the snout, shorter than the parietals; posterior nasal in contact with, or narrowly separated from, the single præocular; two postoculars; temporals 1+2; seven upper labials, third and fourth entering the eye, sixth largest; three lower labials in contact with the anterior chin-shields, which are separated from the symphysial; posterior chin-shields a little longer than the anterior. Scales in 13 rows. Ventrals 138–142; anal entire; subcaudals 25–26. Dark grey above, each scale edged with black; outer row of scales and lower parts white.

Total length 380 millim.; tail 38.

Delagoa Bay.

a. ♀ (V. 142; C. 26). Delagoa Bay. South African Museum [P.].

5. Elapechis sundevallii.

Elaps sunderwallii, *Smith, Ill. Zool. S. Afr., Rept.* pl. lxvi. (1848).
Elapsoidea sundevallii, *Peters, Mon. Berl. Ac.* 1880, p. 797, pl —. fig. 2.

Snout obtusely pointed. Rostral large, the portion visible from above as long as its distance from the frontal; internasals much shorter than the præfrontals; frontal once and one third as long as broad, as long as or longer than its distance from the end of the snout, a little shorter than the parietals; posterior nasal in contact with the single præocular; two postoculars, temporals 1+2; seven upper labials, third and fourth entering the eye, sixth largest. Scales in 13 rows. Ventrals 163; anal entire, subcaudals 22. Reddish brown above, with yellow cross-bands, the scales on which are edged with reddish brown; upper lip, outer row of scales, and lower parts yellow.

Total length 510 millim.; tail 43.

Caffraria.

6. Elapechis boulengeri.

Elapsoidea boulengeri, *Boettg. Zool. Anz.* 1895, p. 62.

Rostral broader than deep, visible from above; internasals hardly half as long as the præfrontals; frontal once and one third as long as broad, longer than its distance from the end of the snout, much shorter than the parietals; posterior nasal in contact with the single præocular; two postoculars; temporals 1+2; seven upper labials, third and fourth entering the eye; three or four lower labials in contact with the anterior chin-shields, which are separated from the symphysial; posterior chin-shields as long as or slightly longer than the posterior. Scales in 15 rows. Ventrals 141; anal entire, subcaudals 20. Black above, with narrow white cross-bars; head white, black along the suture between the parietal shields, blackish grey beneath.

Total length 170 millim., tail 14.

Zambesi.

230. RHYNCHELAPS.

Rhynchoelaps, *Jan, Rev. & Mag. Zool* 1858, p. 518, *and Prodr. Icon. Gén* p. 7 (1859).
Simoselaps, *Jan, Rev & Mag. Zool.* 1859, p 123, *and Prodr* p 16.
Brachyurophis, *Gunth Ann & Mag N. H.* (3) xi 1863, p. 21; *Krefft, Sn. Austral.* p. 51 (1869)
Elaps, part., *Jan, Elenco sist. Ofid.* p. 112 (1863).
Pseudelaps, part, *Jan, l. c.* p 116.
Rhinelaps, *Gunth Ann & Mag N. H.* (4) ix. 1872, p 33

Maxillary extending forwards as far as the palatine; a pair of moderately large grooved poison-fangs, and two small teeth near the posterior extremity of the maxillary; mandibular teeth, anterior longest. Head small, not distinct from neck, with more or less projecting snout; eye small, with vertically elliptic pupil; nostril in a single nasal, no loreal. Body short, cylindrical; scales smooth, without pits, in 15 or 17 rows; ventrals rounded. Tail very short; subcaudals in two rows.

Australia.

The præfrontal bones are produced posteriorly over the orbit, reaching the parietals in *R. semifasciatus*. A small outer process is present on the ectopterygoid in *R. bertholdi*.

Synopsis of the Species.

I. Scales in 15 rows; rostral much broader than deep; nasal in contact with the præocular; ventrals 112-126.
          1. *bertholdi*, p. 362.

II. Scales in 17 rows; ventrals 143-170.

 A. Nasal in contact with the præocular; upper portion of rostral longer than its distance from the frontal.

Frontal a little longer than broad, twice as
 broad as the supraocular.............. 2. *australis*, p. 363.
Frontal as broad as long, at least thrice as
 broad as the supraocular............ 3. *semifasciatus*, p. 363.

 B. Nasal widely separated from the præocular; upper portion of rostral a little shorter than its distance from the frontal.
          4. *fasciolatus*, p. 364.

1. Rhynchelaps bertholdi*.

Elaps bertholdi, *Jan, Rev. & Mag. Zool.* 1859, p. 123, *Prodr.* p. 16, pl. B (1859), and *Icon. Gén.* 43, pl. ii. fig. 5 (1873).
Vermicella bertholdi, *Gunth Ann. & Mag. N. H.* (3) xv. 1865, p. 89; *Zietz, Tr. R. Soc S. Austral* x 1888, p. 300; *Douglas Ogilby, Rec. Austral Mus.* i. 1890, p. 80.
Elaps mattazoi, *Ferreira, Jorn. Sc. Lisb.* (2) ii. 1891, p. 93.

Snout much depressed, moderately prominent, with obtusely angular edge. Eye measuring about two thirds its distance from the mouth. Rostral much broader than deep, obtuse-angled behind, its upper portion one half to three fourths as long as its distance from the frontal; internasals shorter than the præfrontals; frontal once and a half to twice as long as broad, a little longer than its distance from the end of the snout, shorter than the parietals; nasal elongate and in contact with the præocular, which is widely separated from the frontal; two postoculars; temporals 1+1, anterior sometimes descending to the edge of the mouth; six upper labials, third and fourth entering the eye; three lower labials in contact with the anterior chin-shields; posterior chin-shields in contact with each other or separated by one scale. Scales in 15 rows. Ventrals 112-126, anal divided; subcaudals 15-25. Yellowish, with 19 to 40 black annuli, which are usually narrower than the interspaces; head speckled with brown, with a large dark blotch on the parietals and temples.

Total length 270 millim.; tail 22.

Southern and Western Australia.

---

     * Type (Gottingen Museum) examined.

a. Yg. (V 118; C. 22). Adelaide. Rev. T E. Lea [P.].
b. ♀ (V. 119, C. 15). Swan R. Sir A. Smith [P.].
c-d. ♂ (V. 121; C 23) & Swan R.
   ♀ (V. 126; C. 16).
e. ♀ (V. 116; C. 20) Perth. Mr. Duboulay [C].
f. Yg. (V. 120, C. 19). Geraldton, W. Australia. Mr. E. H. Saunders [C.].
g-i. ♂ (V. 117, 120, C. 21, 24) & hgr (V. 117, C 21) Australia
k. Skull of *d.*

2. Rhynchelaps australis.

Simotes australis, *Krefft, Proc Zool. Soc.* 1864, p. 180.
Brachyurophis australis, *Gunth. Ann. & Mag. N. H.* (3) xv. 1865, p. 97, and (4) ix 1872, p. 33, *Krefft, Sn. Austral.* p. 52, pl xi. fig. 3 (1869).

Snout very prominent, obtusely pointed, with sharp horizontal edge. Eye a little shorter than its distance from the mouth. Rostral as deep as broad, its upper portion forming an acute angle behind and longer than its distance from the frontal; internasals as long as the præfrontals; frontal a little longer than broad, twice as broad as the supraocular, as long as its distance from the end of the snout, as long as the parietals; nasal elongate, in contact with the præocular, which is widely separated from the frontal, two postoculars; temporals 1+1; six upper labials, third and fourth entering the eye; three lower labials in contact with the anterior chin-shields, which are very small; posterior chin-shields indistinct. Scales in 17 rows. Ventrals 152-163, anal divided; subcaudals 18-20. Red above, with ill-defined cross-bars formed of yellowish, black-edged scales; a blackish cross-band on the head, involving the eyes, and another on the nape; snout and occiput yellowish; lower parts whitish.

Total length 290 millim.; tail 25.
Queensland.

a. ♀ (V. 152; C. 20). Clarence R. G. Krefft, Esq. [P.].

3. Rhynchelaps semifasciatus.

Brachyurophis semifasciata, *Gunth. Ann. & Mag. N. H.* (3) xi. 1863, p. 21, pl iii fig. B, and xv. 1865, p 97.
Pseudoelaps rhinostomus, *Jan, Icon Gén* 43, pl. vi. lig 1 (1873)
Furina rhinostoma, *F. Müll. Verh Nat Ges. Basel*, vii. 1865, p. 692.

Snout very prominent, obtusely pointed, with sharp horizontal edge. Eye measuring about two thirds its distance from the mouth Rostral as deep as broad, its upper portion forming an acute angle behind and longer than its distance from the frontal; internasals as long as or shorter than the præfrontals; frontal as long as broad, at least thrice as broad as the supraocular, as long as its distance from the end of the snout, as long as or a little longer than the parietals, nasal elongate, in contact with the præocular, which is narrowly separated from the frontal, two postoculars, temporals 1+1; five or six upper labials, third and fourth entering the eye; three lower labials in contact with the anterior chin-shields, which are very small; posterior chin-shields indistinct. Scales in 17 rows. Ventrals 143–170; anal divided; subcaudals 17–25. Yellowish above, with brown cross-bands; a large brown blotch on the head, covering the frontal, supraoculars, and parietals, and another on the nape; lower parts white.

Total length 300 millim ; tail 30.

West Australia.

a–b ♂ (V.143; C. 22) & hgr. (V 154, C. 22).	West Australia?	(Types.)
c–d. Yg. (V. 168, 161; C. 19, 25).	West Australia.	Mr. Duboulay [C]
e–f ♂ (V. 150, C. 23) & ♀ (V.170, C. 17).	Chapman R, W. Australia.	Mr. E H. Saunders [C.].
g. Skull of f.		

4. Rhynchelaps fasciolatus.

Rhinelaps fasciolatus, *Günth. Ann. & Mag. N. H* (4) ix. 1872, p 34, pl. v. fig. B.

Vermicella fasciata, *Stirling & Zietz, Tr. R. Soc. S. Austral.* xvi 1893, p. 175, pl. vi. fig. 4.

Snout much depressed, prominent, rounded, with angular edge. Eye measuring two thirds its distance from the mouth. Rostral large, broader than deep, obtuse-angled behind, the portion visible from above a little shorter than its distance from the frontal; internasals shorter than the præfrontals; frontal once and one fourth to once and a half as long as broad, as long as or a little longer than its distance from the end of the snout, a little shorter than the parietals: nasal widely separated from the præocular, which nearly reaches the frontal; two postoculars; temporals 1+1; six upper labials, second and third in contact with the præfrontal, third and fourth entering the eye, three lower labials in contact with the anterior chin-shields; an azygous scale between the four chin-shields, which are small. Scales in 17 rows. Ventrals 145–161; anal divided; subcaudals 22–27. Reddish above, with numerous transverse series of blackish-brown spots, the anterior of which are confluent into cross-bars; a large blackish-brown blotch on the head, from the posterior part of the præfrontals to the posterior border of the parietals; two broad blackish-brown cross-bands on the nape; uniform white beneath.

Total length 335 millim.; tail 30.

West Australia.

a. ♀ (V. 161; C. 22).   Perth.   Mr. Duboulay [C.]. (Type.)

231. BUNGARUS.

Pseudoboa, part., *Schneid. Hist. Amph.* ii. p. 281 (1801).
Bungarus, *Daud. Hist. Rept.* v. p. 263 (1803); *Schleg. Phys. Serp.* ii. p. 456 (1837); *Dum. & Bibr. Erp. Gén.* vii. p. 1265 (1854); *Günth. Cat. Col. Sn.* p. 219 (1858); *Jan, Elenco sist. Ofid.* p. 117 (1863); *Günth. Rept. Brit. Ind.* p. 342 (1864); *Bouleng. Faun. Ind., Rept.* p. 387 (1890).
Pseudoboa, *Oppel, Ordn. Rept.* p. 68 (1811).
Aspidoclonion, *Wagler, Icon. Amph.* (1828), *and Syst. Amph.* p. 192 (1830).
Megærophis, *Gray, Ann. & Mag. N. H.* (2) iv. 1849, p. 247; *Günth. Rept. Brit. Ind.* p. 346.
Xenurelaps, *Günth. l. c.* p. 345.

Maxillary extending forwards as far as the palatine, with a pair of large grooved poison-fangs followed by one to four small feebly grooved teeth; mandibular teeth, anterior longest and faintly grooved. Head not or but slightly distinct from neck; eye small,

Fig. 26.

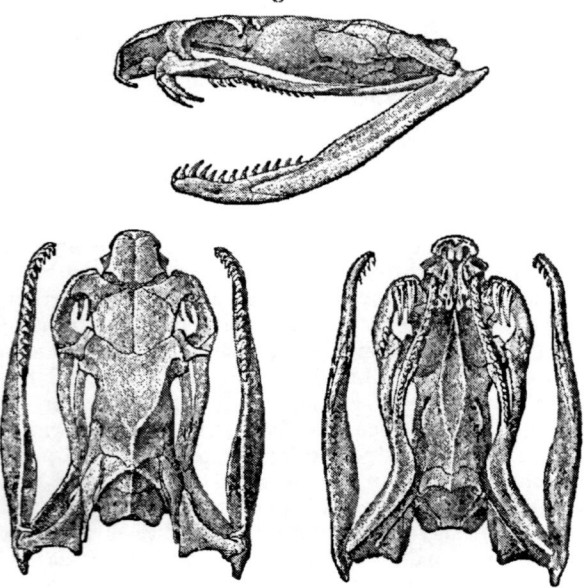

Skull of *Bungarus candidus*.

with round or vertically subelliptic pupil; nostril between two nasals; no loreal *. Scales smooth, oblique, without pits, in 13 to 17 rows, vertebral row enlarged, hexagonal; ventrals rounded. Tail moderate or short; subcaudals single or in two rows.

South-eastern Asia.

---

* Mr. W. L. Sclater records a specimen of *B. bungaroides* with a well-marked loreal shield on either side.

Synopsis of the Species.

I. Subcaudals single; scales in 15 (rarely 17) rows.

  A. A dorsal ridge; tail ending very obtusely; anterior temporal shield scarcely longer than deep .. 1. *fasciatus*, p. 366.

  B. No dorsal ridge; tail tapering to a point, anterior temporal much longer than deep.

Frontal little longer than broad; rostral a little broader than deep; vertebral scales strongly enlarged .... 2. *ceylonicus*, p. 367.

Frontal longer than broad; rostral considerably broader than deep; vertebral scales strongly enlarged .... 3. *candidus*, p. 368.

Frontal longer than broad; rostral nearly as deep as broad; vertebral scales feebly enlarged......................... 4. *lividus*, p. 370.

II. Subcaudals in pairs, or partly single partly in pairs.

Scales in 15 rows .... 5. *bungaroides*, p. 370.
Scales in 13 rows .... 6. *flaviceps*, p. 371.

1. Bungarus fasciatus.

Seba, Thes. ii. pl. lviii. fig. 2 (1735); *Russell, Ind. Serp.* i. pl. iii. (1796).

Pseudoboa fasciata, *Schneid Hist. Amph.* ii. p. 283 (1801).

Boa fasciata, *Shaw, Zool* iii. p. 353 (1802).

Bungarus annularis, *Daud Rept.* v. p. 265, pl lxv. figs. 1 & 3 (1803); *Schleg. Phys. Serp* ii. p. 457, pl xvi. figs. 21 & 22 (1837), *and Abbild.* pl. xviii. figs. 1-5 (1839); *Dum. & Bibr.* vii. p. 1260 (1854); *Jan, Icon Gén.* 44, pl. ii. fig. 3 (1873).

—— fasciatus, *Cantor, Cat Mal. Rept* p 113 (1847); *Gunth. Cat.* p 221 (1858), *and Rept. Brit. Ind.* p. 343 (1864); *Fayrer, Thanatoph. Ind* pl ix (1874); *Theob Cat. Rept. Brit. Ind.* p. 216 (1876); *Boettg Ber. Offenb. Ver Nat.* 1885, p. 16, and 1888, p. 86, *Bouleng. Faun. Ind., Rept.* p. 388 (1890).

Rostral much broader than deep, visible from above; internasals shorter than the præfrontals; frontal longer than broad, as long as or longer than its distance from the end of the snout, as long as or a little shorter than the parietals; one præ- and two postoculars; temporals 1+2, anterior scarcely longer than deep; seven upper labials, third and fourth entering the eye; two pairs of short, subequal chin-shields. An obtuse keel or ridge along the back and tail; latter ending very obtusely. Scales in 15 rows, vertebrals much enlarged, broader than long. Ventrals 200–234; anal entire; subcaudals single, 23–39. Bright yellow, with black annuli as broad as the interspaces between them or broader; a black band, widening behind, on the head and nape, beginning between the eyes snout brown.

Total length 1450 millim.; tail 130.

Bengal, Southern India, Assam, Burma, Southern China, Indo-China, Malay Peninsula, Sumatra, Java.

a. Yg. (V. 220; C. 36).	Anamallays.	Col. Beddome [C.].
b. ♂ (V. 228, C. 37)	Bengal.	Gen.-Hardwicke [P].
c. Yg. (V 225; C. 33).	India.	W. Masters, Esq [P.].
d. Yg. (V. 218; C. 37).	Ruby Mines, Upper Burma.	Major Bingham [P.].
e, f-g. ♂ (V. 213; C. 28) & ♀ (V. 217, 204; C. 26, 23).	Toungoo.	E. W. Oates, Esq. [P.].
h. ♂ (V. 216; C. 33).	S China.	J C Bowring, Esq [P.].
i. ♀ (V. 222; C. 34)	Siam.	W. H. Newman, Esq. [P.].
k. ♂ (V. 220; C. 37).	Siam.	Sir R. Schomburgk [P.].
l. ♀ (V. 227; C 34).	Pinang.	Dr. Cantor.
m. ♂ (V. 234; C. 39).	Deli, Sumatra.	Mr. Iversen [C.].
n. Hgr. (V. 207; C. 36).	Java.	A Scott, Esq. [P.].
o ♂ skeleton.	India.	

2. Bungarus ceylonicus. (PLATE XIX. fig. 3.)

Bungarus fasciatus, var. B., *Gunth Cat.* p. 221 (1858)
—— ceylonicus, *Gunth Rept. Brit. Ind.* p 344 (1864), *Theob. Cat. Rept Brit. Ind* p. 216 (1876); *F Mull. Verh. Nat. Ges. Basel,* viii 1887, p. 276; *Bouleng. Faun. Ind., Rept* p. 388 (1890).

Rostral a little broader than deep, just visible from above; internasals shorter than the præfrontals; frontal a little longer than broad, as long as or a little shorter than its distance from the end of the snout, much shorter than the parietals; one præ- and two postoculars; temporals 1+2; seven upper labials, third and fourth entering the eye; two pairs of short, subequal chin-shields, the anterior in contact with three lower labials. Scales in 15 rows, vertebrals much enlarged, broader than long. Ventrals 219-235; anal entire; subcaudals single, 33-40. Black, with whitish annuli which may be very indistinct and broken up on the back in the adult lower parts uniform white in the young.

Total length 1000 millim.; tail 90.
Ceylon.

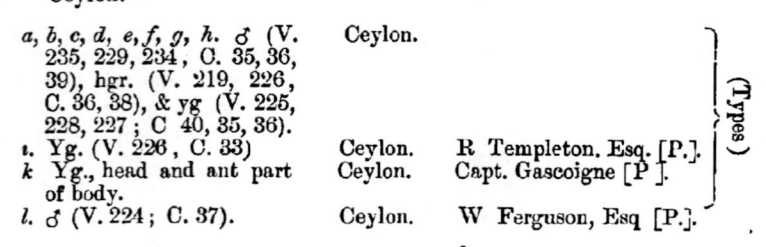

a, b, c, d, e, f, g, h. ♂ (V. 235, 229, 234, C. 35, 36, 39), hgr. (V. 219, 226, C. 36, 38), & yg (V. 225, 228, 227; C 40, 35, 36).	Ceylon.	⎫
i. Yg. (V. 226, C. 33)	Ceylon.	R Templeton. Esq. [P.]. (Types)
k Yg., head and ant part of body.	Ceylon.	Capt. Gascoigne [P].
l. ♂ (V. 224; C. 37).	Ceylon.	W Ferguson, Esq [P.]. ⎭

3. Bungarus candidus.

Seba, *Thes.* ii. pl. lvi. figs. 1, 3, 4 (1735); Russell, *Ind. Serp.* i. pl. i (1796).
Coluber candidus, Linn *Mus. Ad. Frid.* p. 33, pl. vii. fig. 1 (1754), and *S. N.* i. p. 384 (1766); Daud. *Rept.* vi. p 288 (1803).
Pseudoboa cærulea, Schneid. *Hist. Amph* ii. p. 284 (1801).
—— krait, Schneid *l. c.* p. 288.
Boa lineata, Shaw, *Zool* iii. p. 356 (1802).
Bungarus cæruleus, Daud. *Rept.* v. p. 270, pl. lxv. fig 2 (1803); Dum. & Bibr. vii p. 1273 (1854), Stoliczka, *Journ. As. Soc Beng.* xxix. 1870, p 209; Jan, *Icon. Gén* 44, pl iii. figs 2 & 3 (1873), Fayrer, *Thanatoph Ind.* pl. x. (1874); Murray, *Zool. Sind*, p. 387 (1884); Bouleng. *Faun. Ind, Rept.* p. 388 (1890), W. Sclater, *Journ. As. Soc Beng.* lx. 1891, p 245
—— semifasciatus, Boie, *Isis*, 1827, p. 552; Schleg. *Phys Serp* ii. p. 459, pl xvi. figs. 18-20 (1837), and *Abbild.* p. 38, pl. xviii. figs. 6-10 (1839); Dum. & Bibr. *t. c.* p. 1271; Gunth. *Cat.* p. 221 (1858), and *Rept Brit. Ind* p 344 (1864); Jan, *l. c* pl. ii. fig. 4; Boettg *Ber. Offenb. Ver Nat.* 1885, p. 16; F. Mull. *Verh. Nat. Ges Basel*, viii. 1887, p 276
Aspidoclonion semifasciatum, Wagl *Icon Amph.* pl ii (1828).
Bungarus candidus, Cantor, *Cat. Mal. Rept.* p. 113 (1847)
—— arcuatus, Dum. & Bibr. *t c.* p. 1272
—— lineatus, Gunth. *Cat* p 219.
—— multicinctus, Blyth, *Journ As. Soc. Beng.* xxix 1861, p 98; Boettg *Ber. Offenb. Ver. Nat* 1888, p. 86
—— cæruleus, part., Gunth. *Rept. Brit. Ind.* p. 343; Theob. *Cat. Rept. Brit. Ind.* p. 215 (1876).

Rostral broader than deep, visible from above; internasals shorter than the præfrontals; frontal longer than broad, as long as its distance from the end of the snout, shorter than the parietals: one præ- and two postoculars; temporals 1+1 or 1+2; seven upper labials, third and fourth entering the eye; two pairs of subequal chin-shields, anterior in contact with three (rarely four) lower labials. Scales in 15 (rarely 17) rows, vertebrals much enlarged, broader than long on the hinder half of the body. Ventrals 195–237; anal entire, subcaudals single, 37–56 Dark brown or bluish-black above, with narrow transverse white streaks or with small white spots, or alternately barred with dark brown and yellow, lower parts uniform white.

Total length 1080 millim.; tail 160.

India, Burma, Southern China, Indo-China, Malay Peninsula, Java, Celebes.

A. Forma TYPICA (*C. candidus*, L., *B. semifasciatus*, Boie).—27-34 dark brown or blackish bars on the body and tail, the first continuous with the dark colour of the head, narrowed and rounded on the sides; separated by broad yellowish-white interspaces, which may be spotted with black.

a-e. ♂ (V. 215, 216, 215, 212, C. 49, 48, 50, 46) & ♀ (V. 222; C. 45).   Java.   Lidth de Jeude Collection.

231. BUNGARUS.

f. ♀ (V. 210; C. 42).   Java.   A. Scott, Esq [P.].
g. ♂ (V. 217; C. 46).   Java.   Dr Ploem [C].
h Hgr. (V. 217; C. 42). Manado, Celebes.   Dr. A. B Meyer [C.]

B. Var. MULTICINCTUS.—As in the preceding, but the dark bars more numerous, 42–60, and the light interspaces narrower.

a. ♂ (V. 213, C 50).   Toungoo.   E. W. Oates, Esq. [P.].
b. ♂ (V. 214; C. 46).   Mountains North of   A. E. Pratt, Esq. [C.[.
                          Kiu Kiang.
c. ♀ (V. 207; C. 46).   Formosa.   R. Swinhoe, Esq [C].
d. ♀ (V. 216; C. 44).   Hoi How, Hainan.   J. Neumann, Esq. [P.]
e–f. ♀ (V. 210; C. 50) China.
   & hgr. (V. 198; C. 47).
g. ♂ (V. 221; C. 52).   ——— ?   Haslar Collection.

C. Var. CÆRULEUS.—Dark brown to bluish-black above, with narrow transverse white streaks, which may be disposed in pairs, or with small white spots. This variety is almost completely connected with the preceding.

a. Yg. (V. 195; C 39).   Sind.   Dr. Leith [P.].
b. ♀ (Sc. 17, V. 237,   Umarkot, Sind.   H. E. Watson, Esq
   C. 49)   [P.].
c Hgr. (V. 207; C. 45)   Ajmere, Rajputana   Sir O. B. St John [C];
                                                        W. T. Blanford, Esq.
                                                        [P.].
d. ♀ (V. 201, C. 48).   Gwalior.   C. Maries, Esq. [E.].
e. ♀ (V. 207; C. 54).   Benares.   Dr Sayer [P.].
f–h, i. ♀ (V. 225, 209, Bombay.   Dr. Leith [P.].
   C 51, 48) & yg
   (V. 214, 210; C 40,
   49).
k. ♂ (V. 220; C 48).   Matheran.   Dr. Leith [P]
l. Hgr. (V 208; C. 47). Deccan.   Col. Sykes [C.]
m. Hgr. (V. 200; C.   Anamallays.   Col Beddome [C.].
   39).
n–o. ♂ (V. 215, 219;   Trevandrum, Travan-   H. S. Ferguson, Esq.
   C. 40, 37).   core.   [P].
p ♂ (V. 207; C. 45).   India   Dr P. Russell [P].
q, r, s. ♂ (V. 204; C.   India   Gen. Hardwicke [P.].
   47) & hgr. (V. 200,
   211; C. 51, 49).
t. ♂ (V. 205; C 53).   India.
u–x. ♂ (V. 205; C.   Malay Peninsula.   Dr Cantor
   50) & hgr. (V. 214,
   207, 219; C. 56, 47,
   43).
y. ♀ (V. 215; C. 46).   Pinang.   Dr. Cantor.
z. Skull.   India.

4. Bungarus lividus.

Bungarus lividus, *Cantor, Proc Zool. Soc.* 1839, p. 32; *Bouleng. Faun. Ind., Rept.* p. 389 (1890); *W. Sclater, Journ. As. Soc. Beng.* lx. 1891, p. 246.
—— candidus, var. lividus, *Cantor, Cat. Mal. Rept.* p. 113 (1847).
—— lineatus, var. C, *Gunth Cat.* p 219 (1858).
—— cœruleus, part., *Gunth. Rept. Brit. Ind.* p. 343 (1864); *Anders. Proc. Zool. Soc.* 1871, p. 189; *Theob. Cat. Rept. Brit. Ind* p. 215 (1876).

Rostral nearly as deep as broad, visible from above; internasals shorter than the præfrontals; frontal longer than broad, as long as its distance from the end of the snout, shorter than the parietals; one præ- and two postoculars; temporals 1+2; seven upper labials, third and fourth entering the eye; two pairs of chin-shields, anterior longest and in contact with three lower labials. Scales in 15 rows, vertebrals but feebly enlarged and not broader than long. Ventrals 212-225; anal entire; subcaudals single, 37-56. Uniform black or brown above; upper lip white; lower parts white or pale brown.

Total length 940 millim.; tail 100.

Assam, Bengal.

a-c. ♂ (V. 215; C. 37) & yg. (V. 214, 212; C. 40, 37).	Assam.	East India Co. [P.].
d. Hgr. (V. 212; C. 42).	India.	Gen. Hardwicke [P.].

5. Bungarus bungaroides. (Plate XVIII. fig. 5.)

Elaps bungaroides, *Cantor, Proc. Zool. Soc.* 1839, p. 33
Xenurelaps bungaroides, *Gunth. Rept. Brit. Ind.* p. 345 (1864); *Jerdon, Proc As. Soc Beng.* 1870, p. 82; *Theob. Cat. Rept. Brit. Ind.* p. 215 (1876); *Blanf. Journ. As Soc. Beng* xxxviii. 1879, p. 131.
Bungarus bungaroides, *Bouleng. Faun. Ind , Rept.* p. 389 (1890); *W. Sclater, Journ. As Soc. Beng.* lx. 1891, p. 246.

Rostral broader than deep, just visible from above; internasals shorter than the præfrontals; frontal a little longer than broad, longer than its distance from the end of the snout, shorter than the parietals; one præ- and two postoculars; temporals 1+2; seven upper labials, third and fourth entering the eye; two pairs of short, subequal chin-shields, the anterior in contact with three labials. Scales in 15 rows, vertebrals much enlarged, broader than long on the hinder half of the body. Ventrals 220-237; anal entire; subcaudals 44-51, all in pairs, or a few of the anterior single. Black, with white (yellow?) transverse lines, the anterior angular and pointing forwards, these lines widen beneath, forming broad bands across the belly; a yellow line across the snout and a curved one on each side, from the frontal shield to behind the angle of the mouth; a third from the postoculars to the lip.

Total length 800 millim.; tail 100.

Khasi hills and Darjeeling.

a. Hgr. (V. 237, C. 46).	Cherra Pungi, Khasi Hills.	Dr. Cantor. (Type.).
b. ♀ (V. 233; C. 51).	Darjeeling, 6800 ft.	W. T. Blanford, Esq. [P].
c. Yg. (V. 220; C. 44).	Darjeeling	T. C. Jerdon, Esq. [P.].

6. Bungarus flaviceps.

Bungarus flaviceps, *Reinh. Vidensk. Selsk. Skrift.* x. 1843, p. 267, pl. iii. fig. 4; *Cantor, Cat. Mal. Rept.* p. 112 (1847); *Dum. & Bibr.* vii. p. 1274 (1854); *Gunth. Cat.* p. 221 (1858).
Megærophis formosus, *Gray, Ann. & Mag N. H.* (2) iv 1849, p 247.
—— flaviceps, *Gunth. Rept. Brit. Ind.* p. 346 (1864); *Tirant, Rept. Cochinch.* p. 33 (1885), *W. Sclater, Journ. As. Soc. Beng.* lx. 1891, p. 245.

Rostral broader than deep, visible from above; internasals much shorter than the præfrontals; frontal as broad as long or slightly longer than broad, as long as its distance from the end of the snout, shorter than the parietals; one præ- and two postoculars; temporals 1+2; seven upper labials, third and fourth entering the eye; three or four lower labials in contact with the anterior chin-shields, which are as long as the posterior. Scales in 13 rows, vertebrals strongly enlarged. Ventrals 193–226; anal entire; subcaudals 42–54, partly single, partly double. Black above, with or without a yellow vertebral line, two outer rows of scales black and yellow; head red or yellow; tail and sometimes posterior part of body orange-red.

Total length 1850 millim.; tail 220.

Tenasserim, Cochinchina, Malay Peninsula, Sumatra, Borneo, Java.

A. Body uniform black above, brown below; posterior part of body and tail red.

a ♀ (V 220; C. ?).	Sumatra.	Zoological Society.

B. A series of small yellow dots along the vertebral line; a yellow lateral streak along the two outer rows of scales; belly brown; tail red; an elongate black marking on the back of the head.

a Yg. (V. 207, C. 54).	Pinang.	Dr. Cantor.
b. Yg. (V. 193, C. 48).	Java.	Dr. Ploem [C.].

C. A yellow vertebral stripe, a yellow lateral streak; belly yellow, the shields edged with brown; posterior part of body and tail uniform red.

a, b. ♂ (V. 219, C. 52) & yg. (V 217; C 51).	Sarawak	Sir J. Brooke [P.]. (Types of *M. formosus*.)
c, d. ♂ (V. 226, 225; C. 52, 47).	Sarawak	Sir H. Low [P.].

D. Anterior half of body as in C; posterior half of body and tail red, with pairs of black annuli enclosing a yellowish-white, black-spotted area.

a. ♀ (V. 206; C. 42).   Kina Balu, N. Borneo.   A. Everett, Esq. [C.].

232. NAIA.

Naja, *Laur. Syn. Rept.* p. 90 (1768); *Dum. & Bibr. Erp. Gén.* vii. p. 1275 (1854); *Gunth. Cat. Col. Sn.* p. 220 (1858); *Jan, Elenco sist. Ofid.* p. 119 (1863); *Gunth. Rept Brit. Ind.* p. 338 (1864), *Bouleng. Faun. Ind., Rept.* p. 390 (1890).

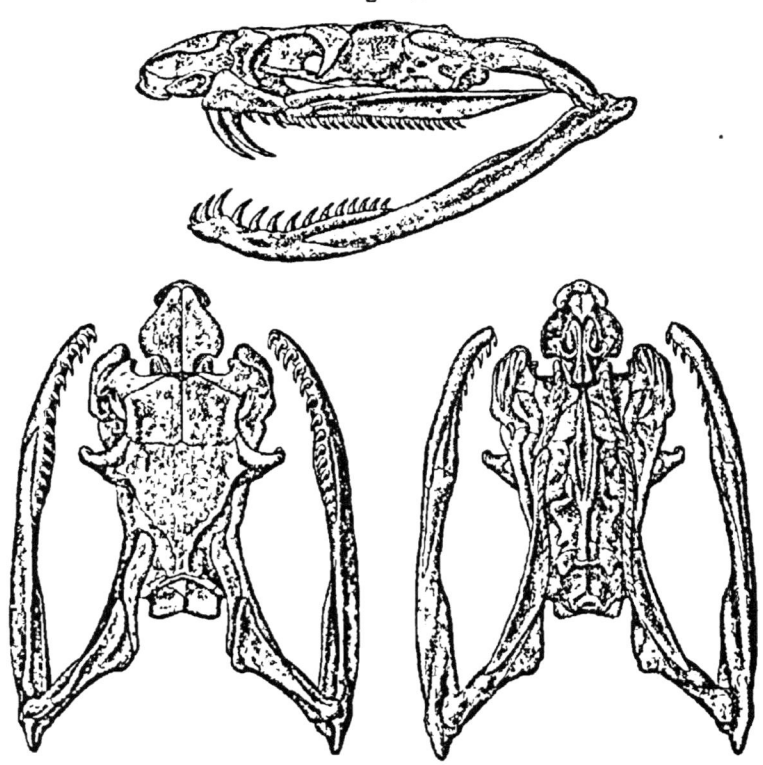

Fig. 27.

Skull of *Naia tripudians.*

Uræus, *Wagler, Syst. Amph.* p. 173 (1830).
Aspis, *Wagl l. c.*
Tomyris, *Eichw. Zool. Spec.* iii. p. 171 (1831).
Hamadryas (non Hübn.), *Cantor, Asiat. Res.* xix. 1836, p. 87; *Gunth. Cat.* p. 218.

232. NAIA.

Naja, part., *Schleg. Phys. Serp* ii. p. 461 (1837).
Trimeresurus, part., *Dum & Bibr. l. c.* p. 1244, *Jan, l. c.* p. 118.
Pseudohaje, *Günth Cat.* p 222
Ophiophagus, *Gunth. Rept. Brit Ind.* p. 340.

Maxillary extending beyond the palatine, with a pair of large grooved poison-fangs, and one to three small, faintly grooved teeth near its posterior extremity, mandibular teeth, anterior longest. Head not or but slightly distinct from neck; eye moderate or rather large, with round pupil, nostril between two nasals and the internasal; no loreal. Body cylindrical, scales smooth, without pits, disposed obliquely, in 15-25 rows (or more on the neck); ventrals rounded. Tail moderate; subcaudals all or greater part in two rows.

Africa and Southern Asia.

Synopsis of the Species.

I. Scales in 19–35 rows on the neck, which is more or less dilatable

  A. 17–25 scales across the middle of the body.

    1. Sixth or seventh upper labial largest and deepest, in contact with postoculars.

Eye separated from the labials by suboculars; rostral as deep as broad or slightly broader than deep ....   1. *haie*, p. 374.

Third and fourth labials entering the eye; rostral as deep as broad .. ..   2. *flava*, p. 376.

Third and fourth labials entering the eye; rostral considerably broader than deep .   3. *melanoleuca*, p 376.

    2. Third upper labial deepest, sixth and seventh not in contact with postoculars.

Rostral once and a half as broad as deep; usually six upper labials; posterior chin-shields much narrower than the anterior and widely separated from each other ....   4. *nigricollis*, p. 378.

Rostral once and one fourth to once and a half as broad as deep; seven upper labials; posterior chin-shields as broad as the anterior and in contact with each other or narrowly separated in front ..   5. *tripudians*, p. 380.

Rostral once and two thirds as broad as deep; usually seven upper labials; posterior chin-shields as broad as the anterior and in contact with each other in front ....   6. *samarensis*, p. 385.

B. 15 scales across the middle of the body ; a pair of large shields behind the parietals .. .. 7. *bungarus*, p. 386.

II. Scales in 15 or 17 rows on the neck.

Rostral as deep as broad ; eye separated from the labials by a series of suboculars; scales in 17 rows on the body. 8. *anchietæ*, p. 387.

Rostral broader than deep ; fourth or third and fourth labials entering the eye; scales in 15 rows on the body ...... 9. *goldii*, p. 387.

Rostral broader than deep; third and fourth labials entering the eye; scales in 13 rows on the body ... ... 10. *guentheri*, p. 388.

1. Naia haie.

Seba, Thes. ii. pl. xv. fig. 1 (1735).
Coluber haje, *Linn in Hasselq. Reise Palest.* p. 366 (1762), *and S. N.* i. p. 387 (1766), *Forsk. Descr. Anim* p. 14 (1775).
—— niveus, *Linn. S. N.* i. p. 384.
Cerastes candidus, *Laur. Syn. Rept.* p. 83 (1768).
Coluber candidissimus, *Lacép. Serp.* ii. pp. 76 & 118 (1789).
Vipera nivea, *Daud. Rept.* vi. p. 39 (1803).
—— haje, *Daud. t. c* p. 41 ; *I. Geoffr. Descr. Egypte, Rept* p. 157, pl. vii. figs 2, 4, & 5 (1827), and *Suppl.* p. 184, pl. iii. (1829).
Naja haje, *Merr. Tent.* p. 148 (1820) , *Jan, Rev. & Mag Zool.* 1859, p 129 ; *Peters, Reise n Mossamb* iii. p. 137, pl. xx. figs. 7 & 8 (1882); *Boettg. Abh. Senck Ges.* xiii. 1883, p 104 ; *Tristram, Faun. Palest* p. 146 (1884); *Valery Mayet, C.R. Ac. Sc.* xcviii. 1884, p. 1206.
—— haje, part , *Dum. & Bibr.* vii. p. 1298; *A. Dum Rev. & Mag. Zool.* 1856, p. 554.
—— haje, var. annulifera, *Peters, Mon. Berl. Ac.* 1854, p 624; *Bouleng Tr. Zool. Soc.* xiii. 1891, p 152.
—— haje, var. A, *Günth. Cat.* p. 226 (1858).
—— haje, var. viridis, *Peters, Mon. Berl Ac* 1873, p. 411, pl. i. fig. 1 ; *Reichen Arch f. Nat.* 1874, p. 293.

Eye moderate, two fifths to one half the length of the snout. Rostral a deep as broad or slightly broader than deep, its upper portion measuring one half to two thirds its distance from the frontal; internasals as long as the præfrontals; frontal once and one fifth to once and a half as long as broad, as broad as the supraocular, shorter than its distance from the end of the snout, one half to two fifths the length of the parietals ; one or several more or less enlarged occipital shields behind the parietals; one præocular, not in contact with the internasal ; two or three postoculars ; two or three suboculars, separating the eye from the labials ; temporals 1+2 or 3 : seven (rarely eight) upper labials, third deeper than fourth, sixth (or seventh) largest and in contact with the lower postocular ; four lower labials in contact with the anterior chin-shields; posterior chin-shields nearly as long as but narrower than the anterior, and separated from each other by scales. 21-23 scales across the neck, 19-21 across the middle of the body. Ventrals

191–214; anal entire; subcaudals 53–64. Yellowish or olive to dark brown or black above, uniform or with darker or lighter spots; lower parts yellowish, with a brown or black band on the neck, or dark brown to blackish; head sometimes blackish.

Total length 1180 millim.; tail 290.

Countries bordering the Sahara; Southern Palestine; East Africa, southwards to Mozambique.

A. Brown above, yellowish beneath, with or without brown spots.

a. Hgr. (Sc. $\frac{23}{21}$, V. 202; C. 64). Beltim, between Rosetta and Damietta. Dr. J. Anderson [P.]

b. Yg. (Sc. $\frac{23}{21}$; V. 207, C. 61). Gizeh. Dr. J. Anderson [P.].

c–d. ♂ (Sc. $\frac{23}{21}$; V. 197; C. 61) & ♀ (Sc. $\frac{23}{21}$; V. 205, C. 56). Fayoum. Dr. J. Anderson [P.].

e. Yg. (Sc. $\frac{23}{19}$; V. 211; C. 63). Maryut. Dr. J. Anderson [P.].

f. ♀ (Sc. $\frac{21}{21}$; V. 208; C. 64). Beni Hassan, Upper Egypt. Dr. J. Anderson & W. M. Blackden, Esq. [P.]

g. ♂ (Sc. $\frac{23}{21}$; V. 204; C. 63). Tel-el-Amarna, Upper Egypt. Dr. J. Anderson [P.].

h. ♀ (Sc. $\frac{21}{21}$; V. 209, C. 63). Egypt. J. Burton, Esq. [P.].

i–l, m. ♂ (Sc. $\frac{21}{21}$, $\frac{21}{21}$, $\frac{23}{21}$; V. 197, 200, 208; C ?, 62, 62) & ♀ (Sc. $\frac{21}{21}$, V. 214, C 53). Egypt. Sir J. G. Wilkinson [P.].

n. ♀ (Sc. $\frac{21}{21}$; V. 209; C. 58). ——?

o. Skull. Egypt

B. Dark brown above, with yellowish spots; dark brown beneath.

a. ♂ (Sc. $\frac{23}{21}$; V. 205; C. ?). Beni Hassan, Upper Egypt. Dr. J. Anderson & W. M. Blackden, Esq. [P.].

b. ♂ (Sc. $\frac{23}{21}$; V. 199, C. ?). ——? Zoological Society.

C. Blackish brown above and beneath.

a. ♀ (Sc. $\frac{21}{21}$; V. 200, C. 58). Morocco. Zoological Society.

2. Naia flava.

Sparrman, Reise Afr. p. 190 (1784).
Vipera (Echidna) flava, *Merr. Tent.* p. 154 (1820).
Naja nivea, *Boie, Isis,* 1827, p. 557
—— haje, var, *Schleg. Phys Serp.* ii. p. 471, pl. xvii. figs. 4 & 5 (1837); *Jan, Rev. & Mag. Zool.* 1859, p. 129.
—— nigra, *Smith, Mag. N. H.* ii. 1838, p. 92.
—— gutturalis, *Smith, l. c.*
—— haje, *Smith, Ill. Zool. S. Afr., Rept.* pls. xviii.-xxi. (1839); *Boettg. Ber. Senck. Ges* 1894, p. 92.
—— haje, part., *Dum & Bibr* vii. p. 1298 (1854); *Gunth. Cat.* p. 225 (1858); *Bocage, Herp Angola,* p. 132 (1895).
—— haje, var. capensis, *Jan, Elenco,* p. 119 (1863).

Eye moderate, two fifths to one half the length of the snout. Rostral as deep as broad, its upper portion measuring one half to two thirds its distance from the frontal; internasals as long as the præfrontals; frontal as long as broad to once and two thirds as long as broad, as broad as the supraocular, shorter than its distance from the end of the snout, three fifths to two thirds the length of the parietals; one præocular, narrowly in contact with or separated from the internasal; three postoculars (one of which may be regarded as subocular); temporals 1 or 2+2 or 3; seven upper labials, third and fourth entering the eye, sixth largest and in contact with the lower postoculars; four lower labials in contact with the anterior chin-shields; posterior chin-shields nearly as long as but narrower than the anterior, and separated from each other by scales. 23 scales across the neck, 19 or 21 across the middle of the body. Ventrals 200–227; anal entire; subcaudals 50–67. Coloration very variable, yellowish, reddish, or brown to black, uniform or with lighter and darker spots; a blackish band sometimes present across the lower surface of the neck.

Total length 1470 millim.; tail 230.

South Africa.

a. ♂ (Sc. $\frac{23}{21}$, V. 204; C. 65)	Simons Bay.	H.M.S. 'Challenger.'
b. ♂ (Sc. $\frac{23}{19}$, V. 207; C. 57).	Port Elizabeth.	J. M. Leslie, Esq. [P.].
c. ♀ (Sc. $\frac{23}{21}$, V. 200; C. 61).	Port Elizabeth.	Mr. J. L. Drege [P.].
d. Hgr. (Sc. $\frac{23}{21}$; V. 216, C. 50).	—— ?	Haslar Collection.

3. Naia melanoleuca.

Seba, Thes. ii. pl. lxxxiii. fig. 2 (1735).
Naja haje, part., *Schleg Phys. Serp* ii. p. 471 (1837); *Bocage, Herp. Angola,* p. 132 (1895).
—— haje, var. melanoleuca, *Hallow. Proc. Ac. Philad.* 1857, pp. 61 & 72; *A. Dum. Arch. Mus.* x. 1859, p. 218; *Boettg. Ber. Senck. Ges.* 1888, p. 80.
—— haje, vars. B & C, *Gunth. Cat.* p. 226 (1858).
—— annulata, *Buchh. & Peters, Mon. Berl. Ac.* 1876, p. 119;

Mocquard, *Bull. Soc. Philom.* (7) xi 1887, p. 84; *Bocage, l. c.* p 137.

Aspidelaps bocagii, *Sauvage, Bull. Soc. Zool. France*, 1884, p. 205, pl vi. fig. 2.

Naja haje, var. leucosticta, *Fischer, Jahrb. Hamb. Wiss. Anst.* ii. 1885, p. 115, pl iv fig 11.

—— melanoleuca, *Matschie, Mitth. Deutsch. Schutzgeb.* vi. 1893, p. 214.

Eye moderate, two fifths to one half the length of the snout. Rostral once and one third to once and a half as broad as deep, its upper portion measuring one fourth to one third its distance from the frontal, internasals shorter than the præfrontals, frontal as long as broad or a little longer than broad, as broad as the supraocular, not longer than its distance from the rostral, one half to three fifths the length of the parietals, one præocular, rarely in contact with the internasal; two or three postoculars; temporals $1+2$ or 3; seven upper labials, third and fourth entering the eye, sixth largest and in contact with the lower postoculars; three or four lower labials in contact with the anterior chin-shields, posterior chin-shields as long as or a little shorter than the anterior, and in contact with each other anteriorly. 23-29 scales across the neck, 19-21 across the middle of the body. Coloration very variable. Sides of head yellowish or whitish, some or all of the labials with posterior black edge.

Total length 2400 millim.; tail 400.

Tropical Africa.

A. Black, with a lighter angular marking or ring on the hood; anterior ventral region with yellowish cross-bars alternating with black ones.

a. ♂ (Sc. $\frac{27}{19}$; V. 213; C. ?). Niger Expedition.

b. ♂ (Sc. $\frac{29}{19}$; V. 217; C. 67). Oil River. Sir H H Johnston [P.].

c. Ad., skin (Sc. $\frac{25}{19}$; V. 212, C. ?). Uganda. Mr. Baxter [C.].

B As in the preceding (of which it is no doubt the young), but with white dots or edges to the dorsal scales, the white may be disposed in cross-bars.

a–b Yg. (Sc. $\frac{29}{19}$, $\frac{27}{19}$, V. 219, 215; C. 68, 67). Eloby, Gaboon. J. G. Fischer Collection

c Yg (Sc. $\frac{25}{19}$; V. 208; C. ?). W. Africa. Mrs. Burton [P.].

d. Yg. (Sc. $\frac{23}{19}$; V. 204; C. 67). W Africa.

C. Uniform black (sides and under surface of head excepted).

a. ♂ (Sc. $\frac{23}{19}$; V. 207;   Coast of Guinea.
   C. 60).

D. Anterior half of body pale brown above and white beneath, with blackish annuli, which are broader on the back; posterior part of body and tail black.

a. Yg. (Sc. $\frac{25}{19}$, V. 208;   Gambia.   J Mitchell, Esq. [P].
   C. 70).

E. Brown above, with small black spots; uniform yellowish beneath.

a. ♂ (Sc. $\frac{25}{19}$; V. 207;   Oil River.   Sir H. H. Johnston
   C. 60).   [P].

b. Ad., skin (Sc. $\frac{23}{19}$; V.   Shiré Valley, Brit
   208; C. 65).   C. Africa

4. Naia nigricollis.

Vipera haje, part., *I Geoffr. Descr. Egypte, Rept.* pl vii fig 3 (1827).
Naja nigricollis, *Reinh. Vidensk. Selsk. Skrift.* x. 1843, p. 269, pl. iii. figs. 5-7; *Bocage, Jorn. Sc. Lisb.* 1 1866, pp. 51 & 71, pl. i. fig. 4; *Peters, Mon. Berl. Ac.* 1867, p 237; *Jan, Icon. Gén.* 45, pl. i. fig. 1 (1874); *Peters, Reise n. Mossamb* iii. p. 138, pl. xx. figs. 9 & 10 (1882); *Mocq. Bull. Soc. Philom* (7) xi. 1887, p 83; *Boettg. Ber. Senck. Ges.* 1888, p 81; *Stejneger, Proc U S. Nat. Mus.* xvi. 1893, p. 734, *Bouleng. Ann. & Mag. N. H.* (6) xvi. 1895, p. 168, *Bocage, Herp Angola,* p 135 (1895)
—— mossambica, *Peters, Mon. Berl. Ac.* 1854, p. 625.
—— nigricollis, var. crawshayi, *Gunth. Proc. Zool Soc* 1893, p. 620.

Eye moderate, two fifths to one half the length of the snout in the adult. Rostral once and a half as broad as deep, the portion visible from above measuring one third to one half its distance from the frontal; internasals as long as or shorter than the præfrontals, in contact with or narrowly separated from the præocular; frontal once and one fifth to twice as long as broad, as broad as or narrower than the supraocular, as long as or shorter than its distance from the end of the snout, shorter than the parietals; two (rarely one) præ- and three postoculars; temporals 2 or 3+4 or 5; six (rarely seven) upper labials, third (or third and fourth) deepest and entering the eye, last longest; four lower labials in contact with the anterior chin-shields; posterior chin-shields narrow, as long as or longer than the anterior, and widely separated from each other. 21-29 scales across the neck, 17-25 across the middle of the body. Ventrals 183-228; anal entire; subcaudals 55-68. Coloration very variable.

Total length 2000 millim.; tail 300.

Africa, from Senegambia and Upper Egypt to Angola and the Transvaal.

232. NAIA.

A. Var. MOSSAMBICA, Peters.—Brown or olive above, some or all of the scales black-edged, the skin between the scales black; yellowish beneath, the ventrals speckled or edged with brown or blackish; lower surface of neck with black cross-bars.

a. ♀ (Sc. $\frac{29}{25}$; V. 228; C. ?).		Assouan.	Dr J. Anderson [P.].
b. ♀ (Sc. $\frac{25}{21}$; V. 186; C. 58).		Zomba, Brit C. Africa.	Sir H. H. Johnston [P.].
c. ♀ (Sc. $\frac{27}{23}$; V. 194; C. ?)		Shiré Valley.	
d–e Heads & tail.		Zambesi.	Sir J. Kirk [C.].
f. Yg. (Sc. $\frac{27}{23}$, V. 183; C. 56).		De Kaap Goldfields, Transvaal.	Dr P. Rendall [C.].

B. Var. PALLIDA.—Uniform brown above, yellowish beneath; lower surface of neck brown in the adult; young with a broad black ring round the neck.

a. Yg. (Sc. $\frac{27}{25}$; V. 201; C. 68).		Inland of Berbera, Somaliland.	E. Lort Phillips, Esq [P.].
b ♂, head & anterior part of body & tail (Sc. $\frac{25}{21}$).		Lake Rudolf.	Dr. Donaldson Smith [C.].

C. Forma TYPICA.—Dark olive to black above; lower surface of head and neck black; subcaudals and posterior ventrals black, the remainder black and yellow.

a ♂ (Sc. $\frac{23}{21}$; V. 201; C. ?).		Gambia.	Sir A. Moloney [P.].
b. ♀ (Sc. $\frac{21}{19}$; V. 193; C. 66).		Bissao.	Prof. B. du Bocage [P.].
c. ♀ (Sc. $\frac{25}{23}$; V. 196, C. 61).		W. Africa.	Mr. Rich [C.].
d–e Hgr. (Sc. $\frac{23}{21}$; V. 196, 193; C. 66, 60).		W. Africa.	College of Surgeons.
f. Hgr. (Sc. $\frac{25}{23}$; V. 196; C 57.)		W. Africa.	
g. Ad., skin (Sc $\frac{23}{19}$; V. 184; C 63).		L. Mweru, Brit. C. Africa.	Sir H. H. Johnston [P.]. (Type of var. *crawshayi*.)
h Ad., skin (Sc. $\frac{21}{19}$, V. 186; C. 65).		Zongomero, interior of E. Africa	Capt. Speke [P.].
i. Skull of g.			

5. Naia tripudians.

Seba, Thes. i. pl. xliv. fig. 1 (1734), and ii pls lxxxix figs. 1–4, xc. figs. 1 & 2, and xcvii. figs 1 & 2 (1735); *Russell, Ind. Serp.* i. pls. v. & vi. (1796), & ii. pls. i & xxxvi. (1801).

Coluber naja, *Linn. Mus. Ad. Frid.* p. 30, pl. xxi. fig. 1 (1754), and *S. N.* i. p. 382 (1767).

Naja lutescens, *Laur. Syn. Rept.* p. 91 (1768); *Cantor, Cat. Mal. Rept.* p. 117 (1847).

—— fasciata, *Laur. l. c.*

—— brasiliensis, *Laur. l. c.*

—— siamensis, *Laur. l c*

—— maculata, *Laur. l. c.*

—— non naja, *Laur. l. c.* p. 92.

Coluber cæcus, *Gmel. S. N.* i. p. 1104 (1788).

—— rufus, *Gmel. l. c* p. 1105.

—— peruvii, *Lacép. Serp.* ii. pp. 90 & 102 (1789).

—— brasiliæ, *Lacép. l. c* pp 90 & 104.

Vipera naja, *Daud Rept.* vi. p. 61, pl lxxi (1803).

Elaps fuscus, *Merr. Tent.* p. 144 (1820).

Naja tripudians, *Merr l. c.* p. 147, *Gray, Ill Ind. Zool.* ii. pls. lxxvii.–lxxix. (1834); *Schleg. Phys Serp* ii. p. 406, pl. xvii. figs. 1–3 (1837); *Dum. & Bibr.* vii. p. 1293 (1854); *Gunth. Rept. Brit. Ind.* p 338 (1864), *Stoliczka, Journ. As Soc Beng.* xxxix. 1870, p. 211; *Fayrer, Thanatoph. Ind.* pls i.–vi. (1874); *Jan, Icon. Gén.* 45, pl. i. fig. 3 (1874), *Theob. Cat. Rept. Brit. Ind.* p. 208 (1876); *Blanf. Journ As. Soc. Beng.* l. 1881, p. 241; *Murray, Zool. Sind*, p. 387 (1884); *Tirant, Rept. Cochinch* p. 30 (1885); *Boettg. Zool. Jahrb.* iii. 1888, p. 943; *Bouleng. Proc. Zool. Soc.* 1890, p. 35, and *Faun. Ind., Rept.* p. 391, fig. (1890); *v. Lidth de Jeude, Notes Leyd Mus* xii 1890, p 26, and in *M. Weber, Zool. Ergebn.* i. p. 191 (1891); *W. Sclater, Journ. As Soc. Beng.* lx. 1891, p. 246; *Bouleng. Ann & Mag. N H.* (6) xiv. 1894, p. 84.

—— sputatrix, *Boie, Isis,* 1827, p 557, *Bouleng Faun. Ind., Rept.* p. 391.

Tomyris oxiana, *Eichw Zool. Spec.* iii. p. 171 (1831), and *Faun. Casp.-Cauc.* p. 104, pl. xx. (1841).

Naja tripudians, vars. fasciata & nigra, *Gray, Ill. Ind. Zool.*

—— kaouthia, *Lesson, in Bélang. Voy. Ind Or., Rept.* p. 312, pl. ii. (1834).

—— larvata, *Cantor, Proc. Zool. Soc* 1839, p. 32.

—— atra, *Cantor, Ann. & Mag. N. H.* ix. 1842, p 482

—— tripudians, var. sondaica, *Schleg. Abbild* p. 139, pl. xlviii. figs. 1–10 (1844).

—— tripudians, part., *Günth. Cat.* p. 228 (1858).

—— tripudians, var. scopinucha, *Cope, Proc. Ac. Philad.* 1859, p 343.

—— oxiana, *Strauch, Bull. Ac. St. Pétersb.* xiii. 1868, p. 87, and *Schl. Russ. R.* p. 204 (1873); *Nikolsky, Tr. St. Petersb. Soc. Nat.* xvii. 1886, p. 405; *Bouleng Tr. Zool. Soc.* (2) v. 1889, p. 103, pl. xi. fig. 2.

—— tripudians, var unicolor, *Peters, Preuss. Exped. O.-As., Zool.* i. p. 382 (1876).

Eye moderate, one third to one half the length of the snout. Rostral once and one fourth to once and a half as broad as deep, its upper portion measuring one fourth to one half its distance from the frontal; internasals as long as or shorter than the præfrontals, in contact with the præocular; frontal as long as broad or longer than broad, as broad as or little broader than the supraocular, as long as or a little longer than its distance from the rostral; one præocular; three (rarely two) postoculars; temporals 2+3 or 3+3; seven upper labials, third deepest, seventh largest, third and fourth entering the eye; four lower labials in contact with the anterior chin-shields, which are as long as or longer than the posterior. Neck dilatable. 21-35 scales round the neck, 17-25 round the middle of the body. Ventrals 163-205, anal entire; subcaudals 42-75. Coloration very variable.

Total length 1550 millim; tail 230.—A skin from Mysore measures 1900 millim.

Southern Asia, from Transcaspia to China and the Malay Archipelago.

This species, as here understood, varies very considerably, and the forms enumerated hereafter might be regarded as distinct species but for the absence of any sharp demarcation-lines between them. The author has taken a conservative view in this case and provisionally maintained intact the association which has so long been known under the name of *Naja tripudians*. It is nevertheless advisable to recognize some of the forms as subspecies.

A. Forma TYPICA (*C. naja*, L.; *N. lutescens, fasciata, brasiliensis, siamensis*, Laur.; *C. rufus*, Gmel.).—Yellowish to dark brown above, with black-and-white spectacle-mark on the hood and a black-and-white spot on each side of the lower surface of the hood. 25-35 scales across the neck, 23-25 across the middle of the body.

a. One or two dark brown cross-bands on the belly behind the hood.

a–d. ♀ (Sc. $\frac{31}{23}$; V. 181, C. 55), hgr. (Sc. $\frac{31}{23}$, V. 183; C 57), & yg. (Sc. $\frac{31}{23}$, $\frac{31}{23}$; V. 177, 170, C. 57, 56).	Deccan.	Colonel Sykes [P.].
e. Yg. (Sc. $\frac{33}{23}$; V. 182; C. 58).	Anamallays.	Colonel Beddome [C.].
f. ♀ (Sc. $\frac{35}{25}$; V. 193; C. 64).	Madras.	T. C. Jerdon, Esq. [P].
g. Yg. (Sc. $\frac{31}{23}$; V. 170 C. 60)	Madras.	J. E. Boileau, Esq. [P.].
h Ad., skin (Sc. $\frac{35}{25}$ 190; C. 56).	Mysore.	Sir J. Fayrer [P.].

i. Ad., skin (Sc. $\frac{31}{23}$; V. 188; C. ?).   Bengal.   F Enoch, Esq. [P.].

k. ♀ (Sc. $\frac{31}{23}$; V. 187; C. 53).   Pinang.   Dr. Cantor.

b. Body variegated with darker and lighter; belly with several dark cross-bands, which may extend across the back.

a–b. ♀ (Sc. $\frac{31}{23}$; V. 189; C. 63) & hgr. (Sc. $\frac{33}{25}$; V. 191; C. 61).   Near Candy.   Capt. Gascoigne [P.].

c. Yg. (Sc. $\frac{31}{23}$; V. 185; C. 60).   Ceylon.   Sir E. Tennant [P.].

d–e. Yg. (Sc. $\frac{35}{25}$, $\frac{35}{25}$; V. 174, 184; C. 65, 60).   Ceylon.   R. Templeton, Esq. [P.].

f–g. Yg. (Sc. $\frac{35}{25}$, $\frac{33}{23}$; V. 179, 185; C. 62, 55).   Ceylon.

B. Var. CÆCA (*N. non-naja*, Laur.; *C. cæcus*, Gmel.; *T. oxiana*, Eichw.).—Uniform pale brown or grey to blackish; no marking on the hood; one or more dark cross-bands on the anterior part of the belly; young sometimes with dark rings. 25–31 scales across the neck, 21–25 across the middle of the body.

a. ♀ (Sc. $\frac{25}{21}$; V. 197; C. 62)   Togly-olum, Transcaspia.   Dr. Radde [C.].

b–d. ♀ (Sc. $\frac{25}{21}$, V. 198; C. 63), and heads of adults.   Chinkilok & Karabagh.   Dr. Aitchison [C.]. Afghan Boundary Commission.

e–f, g. ♂ (Sc. $\frac{25}{23}$, $\frac{27}{25}$; V. 195, 203; C. 73, 71) & yg. (Sc. $\frac{27}{25}$; V. 203; C. 75)   Gilgit.   Colonel Biddulph [P.].

h. ♀ (Sc. $\frac{27}{21}$; V. 192; C. ?).   Sikkim.   Messrs. v. Schlagintweit [C.].

i. ♂ (Sc. $\frac{27}{21}$; V. 184; C. 68).   Kurrachee.   Kurrachee Museum [C.].

k. Ad., stfld. (Sc. $\frac{29}{21}$).   Saugor, Central Provinces.   N. E. Robin, Esq. [P.].

l. Ad , skin (Sc. $\frac{31}{23}$; V. 186; C. 58).   Bengal.   F. Enoch, Esq. [P.].

m. ♀ (Sc. $\frac{25}{21}$; V. 172; C. 48).   Java.   A. Scott, Esq. [P.].

232. NAIA.

n. ♀ (Sc. $\frac{25}{21}$; V. 180; C. 48). Java.

o. ♂, skin (Sc. $\frac{25}{21}$; V. 194; C. ?). Highlands of Lepauto, N. Luzon. Whitehead Expedition.

p. ♂ (Sc. $\frac{29}{23}$, V. 180; C. 60). ——? Mrs. Mauger [P.].

C. Var. FASCIATA, Gray (*N. kaouthia*, Less., *N. larvata*, Cant., var. *scopinucha*, Cope).—Brown, olive, or blackish above, often with more or less distinct light, black-edged cross-bars; hood with a whitish, black-edged ring or U, or with a mask-shaped figure; a black spot on each side under the hood. 25–31 scales across the neck, 19–21 across the middle of the body.

a. Body dark brown behind, with light variegations; two to four blackish cross-bars under the anterior part of body.

a, b. ♂ (Sc $\frac{31}{21}$, $\frac{27}{21}$; V. 181, 181; C ?, 54). Sikkim. Messrs. v. Schlagintweit [C].

c. ♂ (Sc. $\frac{29}{21}$, V. 176; C. ?). Deccan. Col. Sykes [P.].

d. ♂ (Sc. $\frac{27}{19}$; V. 176; C. 56). Calcutta. Messrs. v. Schlagintweit [C.].

e. ♂ (Sc. $\frac{27}{21}$; V. 177, C. ?). Bengal? E. India Co.

f, g. Yg. (Sc. $\frac{29}{21}$, $\frac{31}{21}$; V. 186, 177, C. 51, 48). India. Gen. Hardwicke [P.].

h–i, k. ♂ (Sc. $\frac{29}{21}$; V. 185; C. 55), ♀ (Sc. $\frac{27}{21}$; V. 190; C. 53), & yg. (Sc. $\frac{27}{19}$, V. 179; C. 57). India.

b. Olive to blackish above, the skin between the scales black; lower surface of neck white, with a black cross-bar, rest of lower parts dark brown or blackish.

a ♀ (Sc. $\frac{25}{21}$; V. 166; C. 48). Kiu Kiang. J. Walley, Esq. [P.].

b. ♀ (Sc. $\frac{25}{21}$; V. 170, C. ?). Canton. Haslar Collection.

c. ♀ (Sc $\frac{25}{21}$, V. 168; C. 43). Hoi How, Hainan. J. Neumann, Esq. [P.].

d–e. ♂ (Sc. $\frac{27}{21}$; V. 170; C. 48) & ♀ (Sc. $\frac{27}{21}$; V. 174; C. 47). Siam.

f. Hgr. (Sc. $\frac{29}{21}$; V. 179; C. 59). Kedah, Malay Peninsula. B E. Mitchell, Esq. [P.].

D. Var. SPUTATRIX (*N. sputatrix*, Boie, var. *nigra*, Gray, *N. atra*, Cantor).—Black or dark brown above and beneath, with some yellow or orange on the sides of the head and neck; young with a pale U or O-shaped marking on the hood, and the chin and throat whitish. 25 scales across the neck, 19–21 across the middle of the body.

a. ♂ (Sc. $\frac{25}{21}$; V. 167; C. ?). Chusan Ids. J. J. Walker, Esq [P].

b. Yg. (Sc. $\frac{25}{21}$; V. 177; C. 47). China. R. Lindsay, Esq. [P.].

c. ♀ (Sc. $\frac{25}{19}$; V. 185; C. 49). Pinang. Dr. Cantor.

d. ♀ (Sc. $\frac{25}{19}$; V. 191; C. 48). Singapore. Dr. Dennys [P.]

e. Yg. (Sc. $\frac{25}{21}$; V. 174; C. 46). Sumatra.

f. Yg. (Sc. $\frac{25}{19}$; V. 163; C. 44). Batavia. R. Kirkpatrick, Esq. [P.].

E. Var. LEUCODIRA.—Brown or blackish; no marking on the hood; lower surface of neck yellowish white, followed by a black cross-band, and usually with an azygous black spot anteriorly and one or two on each side. 21–25 scales across the neck, 17 or 19 across the middle of the body.

a–d. ♀ (Sc. $\frac{25}{19}$, $\frac{23}{17}$; V. 186, 191, C. 52, 50) & yg (Sc. $\frac{23}{19}$, $\frac{23}{17}$; V. 192, 183; C. 52, 51). Deli, Sumatra. Mr. Iversen [C.].

e. ♀ (Sc. $\frac{21}{17}$; V. 193; C. 51). Malay Peninsula? Gen. Hardwicke [P.].

F. Var. MIOLEPIS.—Dark brown or black; sides of head and throat yellowish, whitish in the young, no marking on the hood; young with whitish rings completely encircling the body and tail, and with the white of the sides of the neck extending backwards towards its fellow to form an angular band behind the hood. 21–23 scales across the neck, 17–19 across the middle of the body.

a, b, c. ♂ (Sc. $\frac{21}{17}$, $\frac{23}{17}$; V. 185, 188, C. ?, 51) & ♀ (Sc. $\frac{21}{17}$; V. 192; C. 48). Sarawak. Sir J. Brooke [P.].

d. Yg. (Sc. $\frac{21}{17}$; V. 199; C. 46). Sarawak. Rajah Brooke [P.].

Hgr. (Sc. $\frac{23}{17}$; V. 192, C. 45). Rejang R., Sarawak. Brooke Low, Esq [P.]

f–g. ♂ (Sc. $\frac{23}{17}$; V. 181; C. 47) & ♀ (Sc. $\frac{21}{19}$; V 182; C. ?).		Labuan.	L. L. Dillwyn, Esq [P.].
h. Yg. (Sc. $\frac{21}{17}$; V. 186; C. 49).		Mt. Kina Balu, N. Borneo.	A. Everett, Esq. [C].
i. Yg. (Sc. $\frac{23}{17}$; V. 186; C. 46).		Limbawan, Lower Padas R., N. Borneo.	A. Everett, Esq. [C.].
k ♀ (Sc. $\frac{21}{19}$, V. 186, C. 50).		Borneo.	Sir E Belcher [P.].
l. ♀ (Sc. $\frac{23}{17}$; V 199; C. 42).		Borneo	
m. Yg. (Sc. $\frac{23}{19}$; V. 185; C. 47).		Palawan.	A. Everett, Esq [P.].
a. Skeleton.		India.	
b, c. Skulls.		India.	

6. Naia samarensis

Naja tripudians, var. F, part., *Gunth. Cat* p. 225 (1858).
—— tripudians, var. samarensis, *Peters, Mon. Berl. Ac.* 1861, p. 690

Eye moderate, about half as long as the snout in the adult. Rostral once and two thirds as broad as deep, the portion visible from above measuring one fourth to one third its distance from the frontal; internasals shorter than the præfrontals, in contact with or narrowly separated from the præocular; frontal as long as broad or slightly longer than broad, as broad as the supraocular, as long as or shorter than its distance from the rostral, one half to three fifths the length of the parietals; one or three enlarged occipital shields may be present behind the parietals; one præ- and three postoculars; temporals 2+2 or 2+3, seven upper labials (exceptionally six through fusion of the third and fourth), third deepest, third and fourth entering the eye; four lower labials in contact with the anterior chin-shields, which are longer than the posterior. 21 or 23 scales across the neck, 17 or 19 across the middle of the body. Ventrals 159–175; anal entire; subcaudals 45–50. Black above, uniform or variegated with yellowish; yellowish or pale brownish beneath, the neck (14 shields or more) black.

Total length 1000 millim.; tail 160.
Philippine Islands.

a. ♂ (Sc. $\frac{21}{19}$; V. 170; C. 49).	Philippines.	H. Cuming, Esq. [C.].
b. ♀ (Sc. $\frac{21}{17}$, V. 174; C. ?).	N. Mindanao.	A. Everett, Esq. [C.].
c. Yg. (Sc. $\frac{23}{19}$, V. 159; C. 50.)	S. Leyte.	A. Everett, Esq [C.].

7. Naia bungarus.

Hamadryas hannah, *Cantor, As. Res.* xix. 1836, p. 87, pls x.-xii.
Naja bungarus, *Schleg. Phys. Serp.* ii. p. 476, pl. xvii. figs. 8 & 9 (1837); *Schleg. & Mull. in Temm. Verh. Overz. Bez. Nederl Ind*, *Rept.* p. 71, pl. x. (1844); *Peters, Mon. Berl Ac.* 1861, p. 690; *Bouleng. Faun. Ind*, *Rept* p 392, fig. (1890).
Hamadryas ophiophagus, *Cantor, Proc. Zool. Soc.* 1839, p. 32, and *Cat. Mal. Rept* p. 116 (1847).
Trimeresurus ophiophagus, part., *Dum. & Bibr.* vii. p. 1245 (1854).
Hamadryas elaps, *Gunth. Cat* p 219 (1858).
Trimeresurus bungarus, *Jan, Rev. & Mag. Zool.* 1859, p. 129, and *Icon. Gén.* 44, pl. iv. (1873).
Naja fasciata, *Peters, Mon. Berl. Ac.* 1861, p. 689.
Ophiophagus elaps, *Gunth Rept Brit Ind* p. 341 (1864); *Stoliczka, Journ. As. Soc. Beng.* xxxix. 1870, p. 210, pl. xi fig. 7; *Anders. Proc. Zool. Soc.* 1871, p. 188, *Fayrer, Thanatoph. Ind.* pls. vii. & viii. (1874); *Boettg. Ber. Offenb. Ver. Nat.* 1888, p. 86.
Naja elaps, *Theob Cat. Rept. Brit. Ind.* p. 209 (1876).
—— ingens, *v. Hasselt, Versl Ak Amsterd.* xvii 1882, p. 140.
—— tripudians, var. sumatrana, *F Mull Verh Nat Ges. Basel*, viii. 1887, p. 277.

Eye moderate, two fifths to one half the length of the snout in the adult. Rostral once and a half to once and two thirds as broad as deep, just visible from above; internasals as long as or a little shorter than the præfrontals, separated from the præocular, frontal once and one fourth to once and a half as long as broad, as broad as the supraocular, as long as its distance from the end of the snout, much shorter than the parietals; a pair of large occipital shields; one præocular (rarely two); three postoculars; temporals 2+2; seven upper labials, third deepest, seventh longest, third and fourth entering the eye; four lower labials in contact with the anterior chin-shields, which are as long as or a little longer than the posterior. 19 or 21 scales across the neck, 15 across the middle of the body. Ventrals 215-262; anal entire; subcaudals 80-117, the anterior usually single. Coloration very variable. Yellowish, brown, or olive to black, with or without more or less marked dark cross-bands.

Total length 3900 millim.; tail 630.

India, Burma, Indo-China, Southern China, Malay Peninsula and Archipelago.

A. With dark cross-bands or annuli, of which at least traces persist in old specimens. Young annulate black and yellow.

a. Ad., skin.	Near Collem, Goa.	W. F. Hamilton, Esq. [P.].
b. Head of adult.	S Canara.	Col. Beddome [C.].
c. Yg. (V. 246; C. 91).	Anamallays.	Col. Beddome [C.].
d. Ad. stffd.	Madras.	Sir W. Elliot [P.].
e. ♀ (V. 254; C. 83).	Pegu.	W. Theobald, Esq. [C.].
f-g. ♂ (V. 237; C. 95) & ♀ (V. 251; C. 86).	Siam.	W. H Newman, Esq. [P.].

h. Yg. (V. 236; C. 93).   Cochinchina.   E. Cox-Smith, Esq [P.].
i. Ad., skeleton.   Burma.

B. Black above, with narrow white cross-bars; whitish beneath, all the shields black-edged.

a. Yg. (V. 250; C 117).   ——?

C. Olive above, scales and shields black-edged; young blackish, with a yellow spot on each scale.

a ♂ (V. 244; C. 82).   N. Canara.   T. A. Bulkley, Esq. [P].
b. Yg. (V 257; C. 114).   Singapore   Dr Dennys [P].
c. Yg. (V. 248; C. 118).   Malay Archipelago   Dr. Bleeker (*Trimeresurus boiei*, Blkr.)
d. ♀ (V. 261; C. 81).   Philippines.   H Cuming, Esq. [C.]
e Ad., head & tail.   Isabella, N.E. Luzon.   Whitehead Expedition.

D. Dark brown above and beneath; lower surface of head and neck yellow.

a. ♂ (V. 254; C ?)   Borneo.   Sir E. Belcher [P.].
b. ♂ (V. 256, C. 113).   Claudetown, Baram R., Sarawak.   C Hose, Esq [C.]

8. Naia anchietæ.

Naia anchietæ, *Bocage, Jorn. Sc. Lisb.* vii. 1879, pp. 89 & 98, *and Herp. Angola*, p 133, pl xvi. fig. 2 (1895).
Naja haje, *Boettg. Ber Senck. Ges.* 1887, p. 164.

Eye moderate, about half the length of the snout. Rostral as deep as broad, its upper portion forming an acute angle wedged in between the internasals, and measuring nearly its distance from the frontal; internasals shorter than the præfrontals; frontal once and a half as long as broad, shorter than its distance from the end of the snout, half as long as the parietals; one præ- and two postoculars, three or four suboculars, separating the eye from the labials; temporals 2+3; seven upper labials, sixth largest and in contact with the lower postocular; four lower labials in contact with the anterior chin-shields, which are longer than the posterior. Neck non-dilatable. Scales in 17 rows on the neck as well as on the body. Ventrals 181–192; anal entire; subcaudals 52–62. Brown to blackish above; end of snout and sides of head yellow; yellow or pale brownish beneath, with or without brown spots and with a brown or black cross-band under the neck.

Total length 1800 millim.; tail 340.

Angola and Ovamboland.

9. Naia goldii. (PLATE XX. fig. 2.)

Naia goldii, *Bouleng. Ann. & Mag N H* (6) xvi 1895, p. 34.

Eye large, two thirds the length of the snout in the adult. Rostral broader than deep, the portion visible from above one third to one half as long as its distance from the frontal; internasals as long as the præfrontals, not reaching the præocular; frontal once and a half as long as broad, as long as its distance from the end of the snout, as long as the parietals; one or two præ- and two postoculars; one, two, or three suboculars, temporals 1+2 or 3; seven upper labials, fourth or third and fourth entering the eye, sixth largest and in contact with the lower suboculars; four lower labials in contact with the anterior chin-shields, which are as long as or a little longer than the posterior. Scales in 15 rows on the neck as well as on the body. Ventrals 194–195; anal entire; subcaudals 88. Black above, uniform or with transverse series of small whitish spots; sides of head and end of snout white, with most of the sutures between the shields black, ventrals white, with a black edge, which becomes gradually broader until, on the posterior fourth of the body, the shields are entirely black; subcaudals black.

Total length 1750 millim.

Lower Niger.

a. ♂ (V. 195; C. ?).	Asaba.	W. H. Crosse, Esq. [P.] (Type.)
b. Yg. (V 194, C 88)	Mouths of the Niger.	A. Millson, Esq [P].

10. Naia guentheri. (Plate XXI.)

Pseudohaje nigra, *Gunth. Cat.* p. 222 (1858), *nec* Naia nigra, *Smith*.

Eye large, about two thirds the length of the snout. Rostral broader than deep, the portion visible from above measuring one third its distance from the frontal; internasals as long as the præfrontals, not reaching the præocular; frontal once and one third as long as broad, as long as its distance from the end of the snout, two thirds the length of the parietals; one præocular; three postoculars, one of which may be termed a subocular; seven upper labials, third and fourth entering the eye, sixth largest and in contact with the lower postoculars; four lower labials in contact with the anterior chin-shields, which are as long as the posterior. Scales in 15 rows on the neck, in 13 rows on the body. Ventrals 185; anal entire, subcaudals 74. Black above, brown beneath.

Total length 2130 millim.; tail 470.

West Africa?

a. ♂ (V 185; C. 74). ——? Lord Derby [P.] (Type.)

233. SEPEDON.

Sepedon, *Merrem, Tent Syst. Amph* p. 146 (1820); *Wagler, Syst Amph.* p. 173 (1830); *Gray, Cat. Sn.* p. 32 (1849); *Dum. & Bibr. Erp. Gén* vii p. 1258 (1854).
Naja, part., *Schleg. Phys. Serp.* ii. p. 461 (1837).
Aspidelaps, part., *Jan, Rev & Mag. Zool.* 1859, p. 510.

Maxillary extending forwards beyond the palatine, with a pair of large grooved poison-fangs; no other maxillary teeth; mandibular teeth, anterior longest. Head not distinct from neck; canthus rostralis distinct; eye moderate, with round pupil; nostril between two nasals and the internasal; no loreal. Body cylindrical; scales oblique, keeled, without pits, in 19 rows; ventrals rounded. Tail moderate; subcaudals in two rows.

South Africa.

1. Sepedon hæmachates.

Seba, Thes ii pl. lxxv fig 1 (1735).
Coluber hæmachata, *Lacép. Serp.* ii. pp. 121 & 115, pl. iii. fig 2 (1789).
—— hæmachates, *Bonnat. Encycl. Méth*, *Ophiol.* p. 31 (1789).
Vipera hæmachates, *Latr. Rept.* iv p 30 (1802); *Daud Rept.* vi. p. 207 (1803)
Sepedon hæmachates, *Merr. Tent* p 146 (1820); *Gray, Cat.* p. 33 (1849); *Dum. & Bibr.* vii. p. 1259 (1854).
Naia capensis, *Smith, Edinb N. Philos Journ* i 1826, p 252
Naja hæmachates, *Schleg Phys Serp* ii p. 481, pl xvii. figs 10 & 11 (1837); *Smith, Ill. Zool S. Afr*, *Rept.* pl. xxxiv (1843)
Aspidelaps hæmachates, *Jan, Elenco*, p. 118 (1863), *and Icon. Gén.* 44, pl. vi. fig 4 (1873).

Snout prominent, obtusely pointed. Rostral nearly as deep as broad, its upper portion nearly as long as its distance from the frontal; internasals longer than the præfrontals; frontal once and a half to once and three fourths as long as broad, shorter than its distance from the end of the snout, as long as or a little shorter than the parietals; one præocular, in contact with the internasal and the posterior nasal; three postoculars; temporals 2+3, lower anterior very large; seven upper labials, third deepest, third and fourth entering the eye; four lower labials in contact with the anterior chin-shields, which are longer than the posterior Scales strongly keeled, in 19 rows. Ventrals 116-150; anal entire; subcaudals 33-44. Black above, spotted, variegated, or irregularly barred with yellowish white or pale brown, or brown spotted with black; black beneath, often with one or two whitish cross-bands on the neck.

Total length 650 millim.; tail 120.

Cape of Good Hope and Namaqualand.

a. ♀ (V. 137; C. 43).	Table Mt, Cape Town.	H. A. Spencer, Esq. [P]
b. ♂ (V. 118; C. 40).	Cape of Good Hope.	Lords of the Admiralty [P.].
c. Hgr. (V.141; C. 39).	Cape of Good Hope.	Dr. Statham [P.].
d. ♀ (V. 133; C. 38).	Namaqualand.	
e. ♀ (V. 130, C. 33).	S. Africa	College of Surgeons
f, g-h. ♂ (V 116, 117; C. 37, 38) & ♀ (V. 121; C. 35).	S Africa.	Haslar Collection.
i. Skull.	Cape of Good Hope.	

234. ASPIDELAPS

Naja, part , *Schleg. Phys. Serp.* ii. p. 461 (1837).
Aspidelaps, *Smith, Ill. Zool. S Afr., Rept.* App. p. 21 (1849).
Cyrtophis, *Smith, l. c.* p. 22; *Gunth. Cat. Col. Sn.* p. 226 (1858);
 Peters, Reise n Mossamb. iii. p. 139 (1882)
Elaps, part., *Dum. & Bibr. Erp. Gén* vii p. 1191 (1854).
Aspidelaps, part., *Jan, Rev. & Mag. Zool.* 1859, p. 510

Maxillary extending forwards beyond the palatine, with a pair of large grooved poison-fangs; no other maxillary teeth; mandibular teeth, anterior longest. Head slightly distinct from neck; eye moderate, with round or vertically elliptic pupil; rostral shield very large, detached on the sides; nostril between two or three nasals and the internasal; no loreal. Body cylindrical; scales oblique, smooth or keeled, without pits, in 19 to 23 rows, ventrals rounded. Tail short, obtuse; subcaudals in two rows.

South Africa and Mozambique.

1. Aspidelaps lubricus.

Seba, *Thes* ii. pl xxxiv. fig. 4, & pl xliii. fig. 3 (1735); *Merr. Beytr.*
 i. p. 9, pl. ii. (1790).
Natrix lubrica, *Laur. Syn. Rept.* p. 80 (1768).
Coluber latonia, *Daud Rept* vii. p 156 (1803).
Elaps lubricus, *Merr. Tent.* p 143 (1820); *Dum. & Bibr.* vii p. 1218 (1854).
Naia somersetta, *Smith, Edinb. N. Philos. Journ.* i. 1826, p. 253.
Naja lubrica, *Schleg Phys Serp.* ii. p. 484, pl. xvii figs. 14 & 15 (1837).
Aspidelaps lubricus, *Smith, Ill Zool S. Afr*, Rept. App p. 21 (1849); *Jan, Icon Gén* 44, pl. vi. fig. 2 (1873); *Boettg. Abh Nat. Ges Nurnberg,* viii 1891, p. 93
Cyrtophis scutatus, *Gunth. Cat* p. 227 (1858), *and Proc. Zool. Soc.* 1859, p. 88.

Rostral as deep as broad, one third the width of the head, forming a right or acute angle above; internasals much longer than the præfrontals; frontal once and one third to once and two thirds as long as broad, shorter than its distance from the end of the snout, shorter than the parietals; internasal and posterior nasal in contact with the single præocular; two or three postoculars; temporals 2+2 or 3, lower anterior very large and reaching or nearly reaching the mouth; six (rarely seven) upper labials, third and fourth entering the eye; three or four lower labials in contact with the anterior chin-shields, which are as long as or longer than the posterior. Scales smooth, in 19 (or 21) rows. Ventrals 146-167; anal entire; subcaudals 20-28. Whitish (orange or red in life), with black annuli which are slightly angular on the back; a black bar below the eye; sometimes a black cross-bar between the eyes and an oblique band on the temple; upper surface of head sometimes entirely black.

Total length 590 millim.; tail 55.

Cape Colony and Great Namaqualand.

A. 20-32 black annuli, much narrower than the interspaces.

a. Hgr. (V. 151, C. 21).	Cape of Good Hope.	Mr. O'Halloran [C.].
b. ♀ (V. 147; C. 22).	S. Africa.	Mr. Goldschmidt [C.]
c–d, e–f. ♂ (V. 152, 146; C. 27, 25), ♀ (V. 161; C 26), & hgr. (V. 155; C 27).	S. Africa.	

B. 42-47 black annuli, much narrower than the interspaces; white scales black-edged.

a. ♀ (V 167; C. 24).	Cape of Good Hope.	Sir A Smith [P.].
b. ♀ (V. 159; C. 23).	Caffraria.	J. P. M. Weale, Esq. [P.].

C. 38-42 black annuli, broader than the interspaces.

a. ♀ (V. 160; C 26)	Cape of Good Hope.	Sir A Smith [P.].
b. ♀ (V. 150; C. 28).	Cape of Good Hope.	Officers of the Chatham Museum [P.].

2. Aspidelaps scutatus.

Cyrtophis scutatus, *Smith, Ill. Zool. S. Afr., Rept.* App. p. 22 (1849), *Peters, Reise n Mossamb* iii. p. 139, pl. xx. figs 1-6 (1882).

Naia fula-fula, *Bianconi, Spec. Zool. Mossamb., Rept.* p. 41, pl. iv. fig. 1 (1849).

Aspidelaps scutatus, *Jan, Elenco*, p. 118 (1863), *and Icon. Gén.* 44, pl. vi. fig. 3 (1873).

Rostral broader than deep, two fifths to half as broad as the head, forming an obtuse angle above, separating the internasals; frontal small, as long as broad or broader than long, as long as the præfrontals, shorter than the parietals, internasal and posterior nasal in contact with the præocular, which is single or divided; three postoculars; temporals 2+4, lower anterior very large; six upper labials, fourth entering the eye; three or four lower labials in contact with the anterior chin-shields, which are longer than the posterior. Scales in 19 to 23 rows, smooth or faintly keeled, tubercularly keeled on the posterior part of the body and on the tail. Ventrals 115-135; anal entire; subcaudals 24-38. Pale greyish brown above, with transverse dark spots or cross-bands: a ∧-shaped black marking on the head; a black nuchal collar encircling the neck, followed by a large black blotch; a black vertical streak below the eye; belly whitish.

Total length 190 millim; tail 22. Grows to 520 millim.

South-east Africa (Natal, Delagoa Bay, Inhambane).

a. Yg. (Sc. 21; V. 123; C. 25).		Natal.	Sir A. Smith [P.]. (One of the types.)

235. WALTERINNESIA.

Walterinnesia, *Lataste, Le Naturaliste,* 1887, p. 411.

Maxillary extending forwards beyond the palatine, with a pair of large grooved fangs; no other maxillary teeth; mandibular teeth, anterior largest. Head distinct from neck, with distinct canthus rostralis; eye rather small, with round pupil; rostral large; nostril between two or three nasals and the internasal; no loreal. Body cylindrical; scales smooth or feebly keeled, without pits, in 23 rows (more on the neck); ventrals rounded. Tail rather short; subcaudals all or most in two rows.

Egypt.

1. Walterinnesia ægyptia.

Walterinnesia ægyptia, *Lataste, l. c.*

Rostral broader than deep, the portion visible from above half as long as its distance from the frontal; internasals as long as the præfrontals; frontal once and a half as long as broad, as long as its distance from the rostral, two thirds the length of the parietals; posterior nasal in contact with the single præocular, which is more than twice as long as deep; two postoculars and a subocular; temporals 2+3, lower anterior very large; seven upper labials, third and fourth entering the eye, third, fourth, and fifth deepest; four lower labials in contact with the anterior chin-shields, which are longer than the posterior. Scales in 23 rows (27 on the neck), feebly keeled on the posterior part of the body and on the tail. Ventrals 189–197; anal divided; subcaudals 45–48, first 2 to 8 single, rest divided. Blackish brown above, paler brown beneath.

Total length 1170 millim.; tail 170.

Egypt.

a. ♂ (V. 189; C. 48).   Cairo.   Dr. Walter Innes [P.].

236. HEMIBUNGARUS.

Elaps, part., *Dum. & Bibr. Erp. Gén.* vii. p. 1191 (1854); *Günth. Cat. Col. Sn.* p. 229 (1858); *Jan, Rev. & Mag. Zool.* 1858, p. 516.
Callophis, part., *Günth. Proc. Zool. Soc.* 1859, p. 81.
Hemibungarus, *Peters, Mon. Berl. Ac.* 1862, p. 637.

Maxillary bone extending forwards beyond the palatine, with a pair of large grooved poison-fangs and one to three small solid teeth; mandibular teeth subequal. Præfrontal bones in contact with each other on the median line. Head small, not distinct from neck; eye small, with round pupil; nostril between two nasals; no loreal. Body cylindrical, much elongate; scales smooth, without pits, in 13 or 15 rows; ventrals rounded. Tail short; subcaudals in two rows.

South-eastern Asia.

236. HEMIBUNGARUS.

Synopsis of the Species.

I. Scales in 15 rows; ventrals 219-260; subcaudals 12-22.

Temporals 2+3; six upper labials ...... 1. *calligaster*, p. 393.
No anterior temporals, sixth upper labial forming a suture with the parietal; seven upper labials .... 2. *collaris*, p. 393.

II. Scales in 13 rows.

Ventrals 218-251; subcaudals 33-44; a single temporal .. .. 3. *nigrescens*, p. 394.
Ventrals 190-216; subcaudals 28-29; temporals 1+1 .... 4. *japonicus*, p. 395.

1. Hemibungarus calligaster.

Elaps calligaster, *Wiegm. N. Act Ac. Leop.-Carol* xvii. i 1835, p. 253, pl xx fig 2; *Dum. & Bibr.* vii p 1226 (1854); *Gunth. Cat.* p 231 (1858), *Jan, Rev & Mag Zool.* 1859, pp. 509, 510, *and Icon. Gén.* 43, pl. ii fig. 2 (1873).
Callophis calligaster, *Gunth. Proc. Zool. Soc.* 1859, p. 83.
Hemibungarus calligaster, *Meyer, Mon. Berl. Ac.* 1869, p 213; *Peters, Mon. Berl Ac.* 1872, p 587.
—— gemianulis, *Peters, l. c.*
Callophis gemianulis, *F. Mull. Verh. Nat. Ges. Basel*, vii. 1883, p. 289.

Rostral a little broader than deep; frontal once and one third to once and a half as long as broad, as long as its distance from the end of the snout, shorter than the parietals; one præ- and two postoculars; temporals 2+3; six upper labials, third and fourth entering the eye; four lower labials in contact with the anterior chin-shields, which are longer than the posterior Scales in 15 rows. Ventrals 219-260; anal entire; subcaudals 17-22. Purplish brown to black above, with narrow whitish cross-bars; red beneath, with black cross-bars, most of which are divided by a light cross-bar; end of snout yellowish; a black bar on the upper lip below the eye; end of tail red.

Total length 520 millim.; tail 30.

Philippine Islands.

a. ♀ (V. 219; C. 22). Philippines. H Cuming, Esq [C.].
b-d. ♀ (V. 229, 235, C. 22, 19) & yg. (V. 260; C. 17) Philippines. Museum Godeffroy.
e. ♀ (V. 221, C. 19). Albay, S.E Luzon. Whitehead Expedition.
f. Skull of *e*.

2. Hemibungarus collaris.

Elaps collaris, *Schleg. Phys Serp.* ii. p 448 (1837), *and Abbild.* p. 137, pl. xlvi figs 10 & 11 (1844), *Jan, Elenco*, p. 114 (1863), *and Icon. Gén.* 43, pl. i fig. 1 (1873).
—— gastrodelus, *Dum. & Bibr* vii p 1212 (1854).
Hemibungarus collaris, *Boettg. Ber. Senck. Ges.* 1886, p. 117.

Rostral broader than deep, just visible from above; internasals shorter than the præfrontals; frontal once and a half as long as broad, as long as its distance from the rostral, as long as the parietals; one præ- and two postoculars; seven upper labials, third and fourth entering the eye, sixth largest and forming a suture with the parietal; anterior chin-shields in contact with the symphysial and with four lower labials; posterior chin-shields as long as the anterior. Scales in 15 rows. Ventrals 228-230; anal divided; subcaudals 12-22. Blackish above, barred black and red below; a yellowish occipital collar.

Total length 430 millim.; tail 15.

Philippine Islands.

3. Hemibungarus nigrescens.

? Elaps malabaricus, *Jerdon, Journ As. Soc. Beng.* xxii. 1853, p. 522.
Callophis nigrescens, *Günth Ann & Mag N. H.* (3) ix. 1862, p 131, and *Rept Brit. Ind* p. 351, pl. xxiv fig. F (1864), *Theob. Cat. Rept Brit Ind.* p 213 (1876); *Phipson, Journ. Bomb N. H. Soc.* ii. 1887, p. 248; *Bouleng. Faun. Ind, Rept.* p. 384 (1890).
Callophis concinnus, *Beddome, Madras Quart. Journ. Med. Sc.* 1863.
—— pentalineatus, *Beddome, Madras Monthly Journ. Med. Sc* 1871.

Rostral broader than deep; frontal as long as its distance from the end of the snout, much shorter than the parietals; one præ- and two postoculars; a single temporal; seven upper labials, third and fourth entering the eye; anterior chin-shields as long as the posterior or a little shorter, in contact with four labials. Scales in 13 rows. Ventrals 218-251; anal usually divided; subcaudals 33-44 Falls into several colour-varieties, which are connected by insensible gradations, head and nape black, with an oblique yellow band, sometimes broken up into spots, on each side from the parietals to behind the angle of the mouth; upper lip yellow in front of and behind the eye; lower parts uniform red.

Total length 1100 millim.; tail 115.

Hills of Western India, from Bombay to Travancore.

A. Dark purplish brown above, with three or five longitudinal series of black, light-edged spots.

a. Hgr. (V. 218; C. 32).   Shevaroys, 4000 ft.   Col. Beddome [O.].

B. The spots confluent and forming three or five longitudinal black bands edged with whitish. (*C. nigrescens*, Gthr.)

a. ♀ (V. 241; C. 34)   India.   Officers of the Chatham Mus. [P.]. (Type)
b. ♂ (V. 241; C. 43).   Nilgherries.   Col. Beddome [O.].
c. ♂ (V. 244; C. 42).   Kotagiri, Nilgherries.   Dr. J. R. Henderson [P.].
d Hgr. (V. 242; C. 34).   Wynad.   Col. Beddome [O.].

C. Intermediate between A and B.

a–b. ♂ (V. 240; C. ?) & ♀   Nilgherries.   W. Theobald, Esq.
(V. 241, C. 35).   [C.].

D. Dark purplish brown above, with three or five more or less distinct black stripes, which are not light-edged. (*C. concinnus*, Bedd.)

a. ♂ (V. 246; C. 41).   Nilgherries, 6000 ft.   Col. Beddome [C.].

b, c–d. ♂ (V. 248, 225, 235; C. 43, 38, 42).   Wynad.   Col. Beddome [C.].

E. Pale reddish brown or red above, with five black stripes. (*C. pentalineatus*, Bedd.)

a–c. ♂ (V. 238, 247; C. 39, 35) & ♀ (V 241; C. 35)   Anamallays.   Col Beddome [C.].

d–e, f–g. ♂ (V. 251, 245; C. 44, 40), ♀ (V. 236; C. 34), & yg. (V. 249; C. 34)   Anamallays, 4700 ft.   W. Davison, Esq. [C].

h. ♂ (V. 249; C. 43).   N. Travancore Hills   Col. Beddome [C.].

i–k ♂ (V. 243; C. 36) & hgr. (V 234, C. 37).   Tinnevelly Hills.   Col. Beddome [C.]

l Skull of *d*.

4. Hemibungarus japonicus.

Callophis japonicus, *Gunth. Ann. & Mag. N H* (4) i. 1868, p. 428, pl. xvii. fig. C, *Bouleng. Ann. & Mag. N. H.* (6) x. 1892, p 302, and *Zool. Rec* 1894, *Rept.* p. 31.
—— boettgeri, *Fritze, Zool. Jahrb.* vii. 1894, p 861.

Rostral broader than deep; frontal as long as or longer than its distance from the end of the snout, much shorter than the parietals; one præ- and two postoculars; temporals 1+1; seven upper labials, third and fourth entering the eye; two pairs of subequal chin-shields, anterior in contact with four lower labials. Scales in 13 rows. Ventrals 190–216; anal divided; subcaudals 28–29. Red above, with one, three, or five black stripes crossed by black bars edged with yellowish; snout and sides of head black; yellowish beneath, with large black spots alternating with black cross-bars, which may form annuli with the dorsal bars.

Total length 520 millim.; tail 40.

Loo Choo Islands; Japan (?)*.

a. Yg. (V. 205; C. 29).   Nagasaki.   Mr. Whitely [C.]. (Type.)
b. ♂ (V. 190; C. 28).   Great Loo Choo.   Mr Holst [C.]
c–d. ♀ (V 216; C 28) & yg (V. 211; C 28).   Oo Sima.   M. Ferrié [C.]; M. R. Oberthur [P.].

---

* The type is stated to be from Nagasaki The species has not been rediscovered in Japan, and the fact that the companion snake purchased from Mr. Whitely (*Cyclophis nebulosus*) belongs to a Loo Choo species (see Cat. ii. p 278) renders it probable that an error of locality has taken place.

237. CALLOPHIS.

Elaps, part., *Wagler, Syst. Amph.* p. 193 (1830), *Schleg Phys. Serp.* ii. p. 435 (1837); *Dum. & Bibr. Erp. Gén.* vii. p. 1191 (1854); *Günth Cat. Col. Sn.* p. 229 (1858), *Jan, Rev. & Mag. Zool.* 1858, p. 516.
Calliophis, *Gray, Ill Ind. Zool.* ii. (1834)
Helminthoelaps, part., *Jan, l. c.* p. 518.
Callophis, part., *Günth. Proc. Zool. Soc* 1859, p 81; *Peters, Mon. Berl. Ac.* 1862, p. 636; *Günth. Rept. Brit. Ind.* p. 346 (1864); *Meyer, Mon. Berl. Ac.* 1869, p 211; *Reinh. Vid. Meddel.* 1869, p. 117; *Meyer, Proc. Zool. Soc.* 1870, p. 368.
Callophis, *Peters, Mon. Berl. Ac.* 1871, p. 579; *Meyer, Sitzb. Ak. Berl.* 1886, p. 614; *Bouleng. Faun. Ind, Rept.* p 383 (1890).

Maxillary extending forwards beyond the palatine, with a pair of large grooved poison-fangs but no other teeth; mandibular teeth subequal. Præfrontal bones in contact with each other on the median line. Head small, not distinct from neck; eye small, with round pupil; nostril between two nasals; no loreal. Body cylindrical, much elongate; scales smooth, without pits, in 13 rows; ventrals rounded. Tail short; subcaudals in two rows.

South-eastern Asia.

Synopsis of the Species.

I. One præ- and two postoculars.

  A. Six upper labials.

Ventrals 303–320 .... 1. *gracilis*, p. 396.
Ventrals 240–274 . ... 2. *trimaculatus*, p. 397.

  B. Seven upper labials; ventrals 182–247.

A single temporal .. .. 3. *maculiceps*, p. 397.
Temporals 1+1 .... 4. *macclellandii*, p. 398.

II. No præocular; one postocular; ventrals 222–226.
                         5. *bibronii*, p. 399.

1. Callophis gracilis.

Calliophis gracilis, *Gray, Ill. Ind. Zool* ii pl. lxxxvi fig. 1 (1834); *Günth. Proc. Zool. Soc.* 1859, p. 83, and *Rept. Brit. Ind.* p. 349 (1864); *Meyer, Sitzb. Ak. Berl.* 1886, p.614.
Elaps nigromaculatus, *Cantor, Proc. Zool. Soc.* 1839, p. 33, and *Cat. Mal. Rept.* p. 108, pl. xl. fig. 7 (1847).
—— gracilis, *Günth. Cat* p. 230 (1858).

Eye minute, about half as long as its distance from the mouth. Rostral broader than deep; frontal as long as its distance from the rostral or the end of the snout, much shorter than the parietals; one præ- and two postoculars; a single temporal; six upper labials, third and fourth entering the eye; two pairs of subequal chin-shields, the anterior in contact with four lower labials. Scales in 13 rows. Ventrals 303–320; anal divided; subcaudals 21–28.

Reddish or pale brown above, with three dark brown or black longitudinal lines passing through distant round dark brown or black spots, the lateral spots alternating with the vertebrals; two outer rows of scales dark brown or black with a yellow longitudinal streak; belly and lower surface of tail barred black and yellow.

Total length 740 millim.; tail 35.

Pinang, Singapore, Sumatra.

a. ♀ (V 309; C. 23)	Pinang.	Dr. Cantor.	(Type of *C nigromaculatus*)
b-c. Hgr (V 305, 303, C 28, 23).	Pinang.	E India Co. [P.]	
d. ♀ (V. 320; C 21).	——?	E India Co. [P].	
e. ♀ (V. 303; C. 22).	——?	Haslar Collection	

2. Callophis trimaculatus.

Russell, Ind Serp. i pl viii. (1796).
Coluber melanurus, *Shaw, Zool.* iii p. 552 (1802)
Vipera trimaculata, *Daud. Rept.* vi. p. 25 (1803).
Elaps trimaculatus, *Meir Tent* p. 143 (1820)
—— melanurus, *Jerd. Journ As Soc. Beng* xxii. 1856, p 522.
Callophis trimaculatus, *Gunth. Proc. Zool. Soc.* 1859, p 83, pl xvi fig E, and *Rept. Brit Ind.* p 350 (1864), *Theob. Cat. Rept. Brit. Ind.* p. 212 (1876); *Phipson, Journ. Bomb. N. H Soc.* ii. 1887, p. 248; *Bouleng. Faun. Ind, Rept.* p. 384 (1890).

Eye as long as or a little shorter than its distance from the mouth. Rostral a little broader than deep; frontal as long as its distance from the end of the snout, much shorter than the parietals; one præ- and two postoculars, a single temporal, six upper labials, third and fourth entering the eye, two pairs of subequal chinshields, the anterior in contact with three or four labials. Scales in 13 rows. Ventrals 240-274; anal divided; subcaudals 24-35. Light bay above, each scale with a brown dot; sometimes a fine dark vertebral line; head and nape black, with a yellow spot on each side of the occiput; lower parts uniform red; tail with two black rings.

Total length 335 millim.; tail 21.

India and Burma.

a. Hgr. (V. 240; C. 32).	Nerva, Bengal.	Dr. P. Russell. (Type.)
b. ♀ (V. 264; C 26)	Trichinopoly.	Col. Beddome [C.].
c-d ♀ (V. 263, 266; C. 24, 27).	Anamallays.	Col. Beddome [C.].
e. Hgr. (V. 266, C. P).	India.	W. Masters, Esq. [P.].

3. Callophis maculiceps.

Elaps melanurus (*non Shaw*), *Cantor, Cat. Mal Rept* p. 106, pl. xl fig. 6 (1847).
—— maculiceps, *Gunth. Cat* p. 232 (1858).
Callophis maculiceps, *Gunth. Proc. Zool. Soc.* 1859, p. 84, pl. xvi. fig D, and *Rept Brit. Ind.* p. 351 (1864), *Theob Cat. Rept.*

Brit. Ind. p. 213 (1876); *Bouleng. Faun Ind., Rept.* p. 384 (1890).
Elaps atrofrontalis, *Sauvage, Bull Soc. Philom* (7) i. 1877, p 111.

Eye measuring at least two thirds its distance from the mouth. Rostral broader than deep; frontal as long as its distance from the end of the snout, much shorter than the parietals; one præ- and two postoculars; a single temporal; seven upper labials, third and fourth entering the eye; two pairs of subequal chin-shields, the anterior in contact with four or five labials. Scales in 13 rows. Ventrals 205-247; anal divided; subcaudals 21-32. Light bay above, with a distant series of black dots along each side of the back; head and nape black, with one or two yellow bands on each side; lower parts red; tail with two black rings.

Total length 485 millim.; tail 30.

Burma, Cochinchina, Malay Peninsula.

a. ♀ (V. 205; C 23).	Rangoon	W. Theobald, Esq. [C.].
b. Hgr (V. 178; C. 20).	Cochinchina.	E. Cox-Smith, Esq. [P.].
c. ♀ (V. 204; C. 24).	——?	Zoological Society. (Type)

4. Callophis macclellandii.

Elaps macclellandii, *Reinh. Calc. Journ. N. H.* iv. 1844, p. 532, *and Vid. Meddel.* 1860, p. 247.
—— personatus, *Blyth, Journ. As. Soc. Beng.* xxiii. 1855, p. 298
—— univirgatus, *Gunth Cat.* p. 231 (1858).
Callophis univirgata, *Gunth. Proc. Zool. Soc.* 1859, p. 83, pl. xvii.
—— macclellandii, *Gunth. Proc. Zool. Soc.* 1861, p. 219, *and Rept. Brit. Ind* p. 349 (1864); *Theob Cat Rept. Brit Ind.* p. 214 (1876); *Bouleng. Faun. Ind., Rept.* p. 385 (1890), *and Ann. Mus. Genova,* (2) xiii. 1893, p. 327.
—— annularis, *Gunth. Rept. Brit. Ind.* p. 350, pl. xxiv. fig. I; *Theob. l. c.* p. 212.

Eye as long as or a little shorter than its distance from the mouth. Rostral broader than deep; frontal as long as or a little longer than its distance from the end of the snout, as long as or slightly shorter than the parietals; one præ- and two postoculars; temporals 1+1; seven upper labials, third and fourth entering the eye; two pairs of small subequal chin-shields, anterior in contact with three or four lower labials. Scales in 13 rows. Ventrals 182-240; anal divided; subcaudals 25-34. Reddish brown above, with regular, equidistant, black, light-edged transverse bars or rings; belly yellowish, with black cross-bands or quadrangular spots; head with two black cross-bands separated by a yellow one. A variety distinguished by the presence of a black vertebral line; the transverse bars are replaced by transverse spots or altogether absent.

Total length 620 millim.; tail 55.

Nepal, Sikkim, Assam, Burma, Southern China.

A. Forma TYPICA. No vertebral line.

a. ♂ (V. 212, C. 28).	Assam.	
b ♀ (V 219, C. 28).	Pegu.	W. Theobald, Esq. [C].
c. Hgr. (V. 215; C 26).	Mountains N. of Kiu Kiang.	A. E. Pratt, Esq [C].
d. ♂ (V. 240; C. 34).	Formosa.	R. Swinhoe, Esq. [C.]
e. ♂ (V. 212; C. 32).	S. China.	J. C. Bowring, Esq [P.]. (Type of *C. annularis*.)

B. Var. UNIVIRGATUS, Gthr. A black vertebral line

a–b ♀ (V. 214, 231; C 28, 25).	Nepal.	B. H. Hodgson, Esq. [P]. (Types of *E univirgatus*)
c, d–e. ♂ (V 210, 210; C. 30, 30) & yg. (V. 182; C. 28).	Darjeeling.	W. T. Blanford, Esq. [P.].

5 Callophis bibronii.

Elaps bibroni, *Jan, Rev. & Mag Zool.* 1858, p. 526, *Prodr*. pl. B (1859), *and Icon. Gén.* 43, pl. ii. fig. 1 (1873).
—— cerasinus, *Beddome, Proc Zool. Soc.* 1864, p. 179.
Callophis cerasinus, *Beddome, Madras Quart Journ. Med Sc* 1867, p. 16, pl ii. fig 5; *Theob. Cat. Rept Brit. Ind.* p 213 (1876).
—— bibronii, *Bouleng. Faun Ind., Rept.* p. 386 (1890).

Eye minute, about half as long as its distance from the mouth. Rostral broader than deep; frontal nearly as long as its distance from the end of the snout, much shorter than the parietals, no præocular; præfrontal in contact with the third labial; one very small postocular; temporals 1+1; seven upper labials, third and fourth entering the eye; first lower labial much elongate, forming a long suture with its fellow; anterior chin-shields small, much shorter than the posterior, in contact with the third and fourth labials. Scales in 13 rows. Ventrals 222–226; anal entire; subcaudals 27–34. Cherry-red to dark purplish brown above, red beneath, with black transverse bands which are sometimes continuous across the belly; anterior part of head black above.

Total length 640 millim.; tail 50.

Wynad, Malabar.

a. ♀ (V 224; C. 34).	Wynad, 3000 ft.	Col Beddome [C.]. (Type of *C. cerasinus*.)
b–c, d ♀ (V. 222, 226; C. 27, 32) & hgr. (V. 223; C. 30).	Wynad.	Col. Beddome [C.].

238. DOLIOPHIS.

Elaps, part., *Schneid. Hist. Amph.* ii. p. 289 (1801), *Wagl. Syst. Amph.* p 193 (1830), *Schleg. Phys. Serp.* ii. p. 435 (1837); *Dum. & Bibr. Erp. Gén.* vii. p. 1191 (1854); *Gunth. Cat. Col. Sn.* p. 229 (1858), *Jan, Rev & Mag Zool.* 1858, p 516.
Maticora, *Gray, Ill Ind Zool.* ii (1834)—No definition
Doliophis, *Girard, Proc. Ac. Philad.* 1857, p. 182, *and U S. Explor. Exped., Herp.* p. 175 (1858).
Helminthoelaps, part., *Jan, l. c.* p. 518.

Callophis, part., *Günth Proc. Zool. Soc.* 1859, p. 81 ; *Peters, Mon. Berl Ac.* 1862, p. 636; *Günth Rept. Brit. Ind.* p 346 (1864); *Meyer, Mon. Berl. Ac.* 1869, p 211 ; *Reinh. Vid. Meddel.* 1869, p. 117 : *Meyer, Proc. Zool. Soc.* 1870, p. 368.
Adeniophis, *Peters, Mon. Berl. Ac.* 1871, p. 578 ; *Meyer, Sitzb. Ak. Berl* 1886, p 614; *Bouleng. Faun. Ind., Rept* p. 386 (1890).

Characters of *Callophis*, except that the poison-glands, instead of being confined to the temporal region, extend along each side of the body for about one third of its length, gradually thickening and terminating in front of the heart with club-shaped ends. The presence of these glands may be detected without dissection by feeling the thickening and rigidity of the cardiac region in the second third of the body, the heart being shifted further back than in other snakes owing to the extension of the glands.

Burma, Cochinchina, Malay Peninsula and Archipelago.

Synopsis of the Species.

I. Subcaudals 34–50 .... 1. *bivirgatus*, p. 400.
II. Subcaudals 15–33.

A. Eye much more than half as long as its distance from the mouth.

Frontal at least as long as its distance
from the end of the snout........ .. 2. *intestinalis*, p. 401.
Frontal as long as its distance from the
rostral .... 3. *bilineatus*, p. 404.

B. Eye about half as long as its distance from the mouth.
4. *philippinus*, p. 404.

1. Doliophis bivirgatus.

Elaps bivirgatus, *Boie, Isis*, 1827, p. 556; *Schleg Phys. Serp.* ii. p 451, pl xvi figs 10 & 11 (1837), *and Abbild* p. 138, pl xlvii (1844); *Dum. & Bibr.* vii. p 1230 (1854), *Günth. Cat.* p. 230 (1858); *Jan, Icon. Gén.* 43, pl. 1. fig. 2 (1873).
—— flaviceps, *Cantor, Proc. Zool. Soc.* 1839, p. 33, *and Cat. Mal. Rept.* p. 109 (1847).
Doliophis flaviceps, *Girard, Proc. Ac. Philad.* 1857, p. 182, *and U.S. Explor Exped., Herp.* p 176, pl. x. figs. 1–5 (1858).
Callophis bivirgatus, *Günth. Proc Zool. Soc.* 1859, p. 81, *and Rept. Brit. Ind* p 348 (1864); *Tirant, Rept. Cochinch.* p 33 (1885).
Elaps tetrataenia, *Bleek. Nat. Tijdschr Nederl. Ind* xx 1859, p. 201.
—— bivirgatus, var quadrivirgatus, *Jan, Elenco*, p. 114 (1863).
Adeniophis bivirgatus, *Meyer, Sitzb. Ak. Berl.* 1886, p. 614 ; *Bouleng Ann. Mus Genova*, (2) xiii. 1893, p. 327.
—— flaviceps, *Meyer, l. c.*
—— tetrataenia, *Meyer, l. c.*

Eye nearly as long as its distance from the mouth. Rostral a little broader than deep ; frontal large, longer than broad, as long as or longer than its distance from the end of the snout, as long as or a little shorter than the parietals; one præ- and two postoculars; temporals 1+1 or 1+2; six upper labials, third and fourth entering the eye; anterior chin-shields a little longer than the posterior and in contact with three or four lower labials. Scales in 13 rows. Ventrals 244–293; anal entire; subcaudals 34–50. Dark purple or black above; head, tail, and lower parts red.

Total length 1610 millim.; tail 190.

Burma, Cochin-China, Malay Peninsula, Sumatra, Borneo, Java.

A. A fine white lateral line between the borders of the two outer rows of scales. (*E. bivirgatus*, Boie.)

a. ♂ (V. 274; C 40). Pinang. Gen. Hardwicke [P.].
b. ♂ (V. 281; C. 49). Java.

B. Four white lines along the body, the outer broader and running along the adjacent halves of the two outer rows of scales. (*E. tetratænia*, Blkr.)

a. ♂ (V. 280; C. 44). Sintang, Borneo. Dr. Bleeker. (Type of *E tetratænia*)
b. ♀ (V. 244, C. 44). Matang, Borneo.
c. ♀ (V. 246, C. 38). Bongon, N. Borneo. A. Everett, Esq [C.].

C. A pale blue lateral stripe, occupying the two outer rows of scales. (*E. flaviceps*, Cant.)

a. ♀ (V. 252; C. 38). Pinang. Dr. Cantor.
b. ♂ (V. 293; C. 50). Pinang.
c. ♀ (V. 253; C 37). Kedah, Malay Peninsula. B. E Mitchell, Esq. [P].
d. Hgr. (V. 244, C. 43). Singapore. Dr Dennys [P.].
e. ♀ (V. 263; C. 43) Deli, Sumatra. Mr. Iversen [C.].
f–g. ♀ (V. 246; C. 37) & hgr. (V. 272; C. 47). ——? East India Co. [P].
h. ♀ (V. 249; C. 34). ——?

2. Doliophis intestinalis.

Seba, Thes. ii. pl. ii. fig. 7 (1735); *Russell, Ind. Serp.* ii. pl. xix. (1801).
Aspis intestinalis, *Laur. Syn. Rept.* p. 106 (1768).
Elaps furcatus, *Schneid. Hist Amph* ii p 303 (1801); *Schleg. Phys. Serp.* ii. p. 450, pl xvi. figs. 12 & 13 (1837), *and Abbild.* pl. xlvi. figs. 1–8 (1844); *Cantor, Proc. Zool. Soc.* 1839, p 34; *Dum. & Bibr.* vii. p 1228 (1854); *Motley & Dillwyn, Nat. Hist. Labuan,* p. 45 (1855); *Jan, Icon Gén.* 43, pl. i fig 3 (1873).
Vipera furcata, *Daud. Rept* vi. p. 22 (1803).
Maticora lineata, *Gray, Ill. Ind. Zool.* ii. pl. lxxxvi. fig. 2 (1834).
Elaps intestinalis, *Cantor, Cat. Mal Rept.* p. 107 (1847); *Günth. Cat* p. 230 (1858).
—— trilineatus, *Dum. & Bibr.* t c. p. 1227; *v. Lidth de Jeude, in M. Weber, Zool Ergebn* i. p. 191, pl. xvi. fig. 10 (1890).
—— thepassi, *Bleek. Nat. Tijdschr. Nederl. Ind.* xx. 1859, p. 201.

Callophis intestinalis, *Gunth. Proc. Zool. Soc.* 1859, p. 82, pl. xvi. figs. B & C, *and Rept. Brit. Ind.* p. 348 (1864); *Meyer, Mon. Berl Ac.* 1869, p. 204, pls. i & ii.; *Stoliczka, Journ. As. Soc. Beng.* xxxix. 1870, p. 212; *Theob. Cat. Rept. Brit. Ind.* p. 211 (1876).

—— furcatus, var. nigrotæniatus, *Peters, Mon. Berl. Ac.* 1863, p. 404.

—— intestinalis, var. malayana, *Gunth. l. c.* p. 349.

Adeniophis nigrotæniatus, *Peters, Mon. Berl. Ac.* 1871, p. 578.

Callophis maclellandii (*non Reinh.*), *Fayrer, Thanatoph. Ind.* pl. x. (1874).

Adeniophis intestinalis, *Meyer, Sitzb. Ak. Berl.* 1886, p. 614; *Bouleng. Faun. Ind, Rept.* p. 386 (1890).

—— malayanus, *Meyer, l. c.*

Elaps sumatranus, *v Lidth de Jeude, in M. Weber, Zool. Ergebn.* i. p. 190 (1890)

Callophis intestinalis, var. suluensis, *Steind. Sitzb. Ak. Wien.* c. i. 1891, p. 295.

Eye as long as or a little shorter than its distance from the mouth. Rostral a little broader than deep; frontal as long as broad or slightly longer than broad, as long as or longer than its distance from the end of the snout; one præ- and two postoculars; temporals 1+2; six upper labials, third and fourth entering the eye; three or four lower labials in contact with the anterior chin-shields, which are as long as or a little longer than the posterior. Scales in 13 rows. Ventrals 197-273; anal entire; subcaudals 15-33. Brown or blackish above, with darker or lighter longitudinal streaks, tail pink or red beneath; belly with black cross-bars.

Total length 580 millim.; tail 45.

Burma, Malay Peninsula, Sumatra, Borneo, Java, Celebes.

A. Forma TYPICA (*A. intestinalis*, Laur., *E. furcatus*, Schn.).—Dark brown above, blackish towards the middle of the back; a narrow orange or yellow vertebral line, forked on the head and extending on each side to the upper lip behind the nostril; a large subtriangular yellow temporal blotch usually present; a black stripe along each side, divided by a yellow line running between the two outer series of scales; barred black and yellow beneath, the black bars as broad as or a little narrower than the yellow.

a. ♂ (V. 255; C. 22). Java.
b-d. ♂ (V. 249, 242, 231; C. 26, 24, 25). Willis Mt., Kediri, Java, 5000 ft. Baron v. Huegel [C.].
e. ♂ (V. 224, C. 26). Labuan. Dr. Collingwood [P].

B. Var. ANNECTENS. As in the preceding, but vertebral line not bifurcating on the head This variety completely connects the preceding and the following. Specimen *d* black above and on the sides, with three yellow lines.

a. ♂ (V. 235; C. 25). Singapore. H. N. Ridley, Esq. [P].
b. ♀ (V. 247; C 20). Labuan. L. L. Dillwyn, Esq. [P.].

c. Hgr. (V. 257, C. 19). Matang, Borneo.
d. ♀ (V. 266; C. 17). Tandjong, S.E. Borneo.
e. ♀ (V. 229; C. 28). ———? East India Co. [P.].

C. Var. LINEATA, Gray (*E. thepassi*, Blkr., var. *malayanus*, Gthr.).—Pale greyish or reddish brown above, with a pair of dark brown or blackish dorsal lines bordering a light vertebral stripe; the latter may be obscured in some specimens, which thus lead to the var. *nigrotæniatus*; sides and belly as in the preceding varieties, but black bars sometimes broader than the interspaces between them.

a. ♀ (V. 218; C. 26). Pinang. Gen. Hardwicke [P.]. (Type of *M. lineata*.)
b. ♂ (V 229; C 24). Pinang. Dr. Cantor.
c. ♀ (V. 230, C 24). Singapore. Dr. Cantor.
d–f. ♂ (V. 233; C. 28), ♀ (V. 239; C. 24), & hgr. (V. 273; C. 15). Singapore. Dr. Dennys [P.].
g–h. ♂ (V. 232; C. 25) & ♀ (V. 233; C. 23). E. Coast of Sumatra. Mrs. Findlay [P.].
i–l ♂ (V 235, 233; C 28, 27) & ♀ (V 243; C 21). Nias. Hr. Sundermann [C.].
m ♀ (V. 263; C. 16). Sintang, Borneo. Dr. Bleeker. (Type of *E. thepassi*.)

D. Var. TRILINEATUS, D. & B.—As in the preceding, but the yellow vertebral stripe broken up by dark brown spots at regular intervals.

a. Hgr. (V. 256, C. 22). Sumatra. Dr. Bleeker.

E. Var. NIGROTÆNIATUS, Ptrs.—A dark brown or blackish vertebral band three scales wide, separated from the dark colour of the sides by a pale reddish-brown streak two scales wide; a pale brown line between the two outer rows of scales; belly with black bars which are as wide as or wider than the interspaces between them, and confluent with the black of the sides.

a. ♀ (V. 232, C. 20). Sumatra. Dr. Bleeker. (*Elaps melanotænia*, Blkr.)
b. ♀ (V. 229; C. 22). Sarawak. D. Davies, Esq. [P.].

F. Var. SUMATRANUS, Jeude.—As in the preceding, but black bars on the belly narrower than the interspaces between them and not connected with the dark colour of the sides.

a–c. ♂ (V. 231; C 25) & ♀ (V. 237, 235; C. 22, 25). Labuan. L. L. Dillwyn, Esq. [P.].
d–e. ♂ (V. 213; C. 25) & ♀ (V 226; C 24). Mt. Dulit, Sarawak. C. Hose, Esq. [P.].
f. ♂ (V. 239; C. 23). Manado, Celebes. Dr. A. B. Meyer [C.].

G. Var. EVERETTI.—Black, with traces of a light vertebral stripe, with two pale grey longitudinal streaks two scales wide, separated by three series of scales; belly with black bars narrower than the interspaces and connected with the black of the sides.

a–b. ♀ (V. 244, 240; C. 21, 22). Kina Balu, N. Borneo. A. Everett, Esq. [C.].

a. Skeleton. ——? Zoological Society.

3. Doliophis bilineatus.

Callophis bilineatus, *Peters, Sitzb. Ges. Nat. Fr.* 1881, p. 109.
Adeniophis bilineatus, *Bouleng. Ann. & Mag. N. H.* (6) xiv. 1894, p. 84; *Boettg. Abh. Mus. Dresd.* 1894–95, no 7, p. 5.

Eye a little shorter than its distance from the mouth. Rostral a little broader than deep; frontal as long as broad, as long as its distance from the rostral, considerably shorter than the parietals; one præ- and two postoculars; temporals 1+2; six upper labials, third and fourth entering the eye; chin-shields two pairs, subequal, the anterior in contact with four labials. Scales in 13 rows. Ventrals 225–268, anal entire; subcaudals 24–30. Black above, with two white streaks along the body, commencing on the parietal shields, and running along the fourth and fifth series of scales; outer row of scales white, with a black longitudinal streak or a series of black dots; upper lip and a blotch across the præfrontal shields white; belly with black cross-bars, each involving two or three ventral shields and separated from each other by two to four white shields; tail orange or pink, with two or three black blotches or rings.

Total length 710 millim.; tail 45.

Philippine Islands.

a. ♀ (V. 268; C. 25). Puerta Princesa, Palawan. A. Everett, Esq [C.].
b. ♂ (V. 245; C. 29). Balabac. A. Everett, Esq. [C.].
c–d. ♂ (V. 225, 244; C. 30, 30). Mindanao. Dr A. B. Meyer [C.].

4. Doliophis philippinus.

Elaps intestinalis, var., *Günth. Cat.* p. 230 (1858).
Callophis intestinalis, var. C, *Günth. Proc. Zool. Soc.* 1859, p. 82, pl. xvi. fig. A
—— intestinalis, var. philippina, *Günth. Rept. Brit. Ind.* p. 349 (1864).
Adeniophis philippinus, *Meyer, Sitzb. Ak. Berl* 1886, p. 614.

Eye about half as long as its distance from the mouth. Rostral a little broader than deep; frontal nearly as broad as long, as long as its distance from the end of the snout, a little shorter than the parietals; one præ- and two postoculars; temporals 1+2; six upper labials, third and fourth entering the eye; four lower labials in contact with the anterior chin-shields, which are as long as the posterior. Scales in 13 rows. Ventrals 218; anal entire; subcaudals 26. Above with dark brown cross-bands, continuous with the black ventral bars, separated by narrower yellowish interspaces and divided by two pale reddish-brown stripes; beneath, barred black and yellow (red?); head brown above, with a few small yellow spots; a black blotch on each side, involving the eye and edged with yellow.

Total length 430 millim.; tail 35.

Philippine Islands.

a. ♂ (V. 218; C. 26).   Philippines.   H. Cuming, Esq. [C.].   (Type.)

239. FURINA.

Fig. 28.

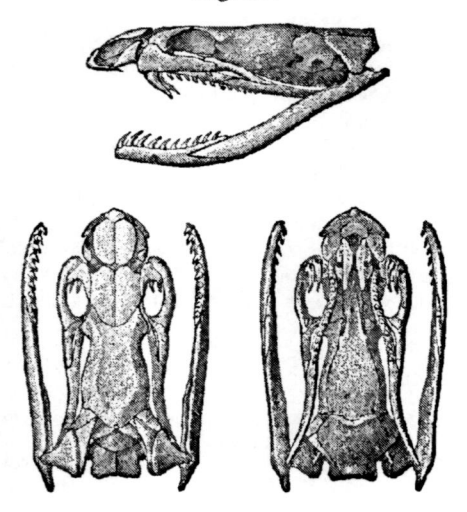

Skull of *Furina occipitalis*.

Furina, part., *Dum. & Bibr. Mém. Ac. Sc.* xiii. 1853, p. 517, *and Erp. Gén.* vii. p. 1236 (1854).
Elaps, part., *Dum. & Bibr. Erp. Gén.* vii. p. 1191; *Jan, Elenco sist. Ofid.* p. 112 (1863).
Brachysoma, *Günth. Cat. Col. Sn.* p. 228 (1858).
Vermicella, *Günth. l. c.* p. 236, *and Proc. Zool. Soc.* 1859, p. 87; *Krefft, Sn. Austral* p. 78 (1869).
Homaloselaps, *Jan, Rev. & Mag. Zool.* 1858, p. 518.
Furina, *Günth. Ann. & Mag. N. H.* (3) xi. (1863), pp. 23 & 24; *Krefft, l. c.* p. 50.
Neelaps, *Günth. l. c.* p. 24.
Pseudelaps, part., *Jan, Elenco sist. Ofid.* p. 115.

Maxillary extending forwards beyond the palatine; a pair of moderately large, grooved poison-fangs, and one or two small solid teeth near the posterior extremity of the maxillary; mandibular teeth subequal. Head small, not distinct from neck; eye very small, with round pupil; nostril in a single nasal, no loreal. Body cylindrical; scales smooth, without pits, in 15 rows; ventrals rounded. Tail very short, obtuse; subcaudals in two rows.

Australia.

The skull agrees with *Elaps* and *Homorelaps*, and differs from all other Elapines in the absence of postfrontal bone; the præfrontals, which are widely separated from each other, are produced backwards towards the parietals so as to nearly exclude the frontals from the orbital periphery.

Synopsis of the Species.

Upper portion of rostral at least as long as its distance from the frontal; five upper labials; frontal more than twice as broad as the supraocular; ventrals 181–200 ..	1. *bimaculata*, p. 406.
Upper portion of rostral shorter than its distance from the frontal; six upper labials; frontal more than twice as broad as the supraocular; ventrals 126–131 ..	2. *calonota*, p. 407.
Upper portion of rostral shorter than its distance from the frontal; six upper labials; frontal not more than twice as broad as the supraocular; ventrals 180–234............................	3. *occipitalis*, p. 407.

1. Furina bimaculata.

Furina bimaculata, *Dum. & Bibr.* vii. p. 1240 (1854); *Jan, Rev. & Mag. Zool.* 1859, p. 125, pl. vi.; *Gunth Ann. & Mag N. H.* (3) xi. 1863, p. 24; *Krefft, Sn. Austral.* p. 51 (1869).
Brachysoma diadema (non *Schleg*), *Gunth Cat.* p. 229 (1858).
—— bimaculatum, *Gunth. l. c.*
Pseudelaps bimaculatus, *Jan, Elenco*, p. 116 (1863), and *Icon. Gén.* 43, pl. v. fig. 2 (1873).

Rostral large, as deep as broad, the portion visible from above at least as long as its distance from the frontal; internasals a little shorter than the præfrontals; frontal nearly as broad as long, thrice as broad as the supraocular, as long as its distance from the end of the snout, shorter than the parietals; nasal elongate, in contact with the præocular; two postoculars; temporals 1+1; five upper labials, third and fourth entering the eye, fifth very large; two pairs of very small chin-shields, with an azygous shield between them. Scales in 15 rows. Ventrals 181–200, anal divided; subcaudals 21–25. Yellowish above, each scale edged with black or with a small black spot; end of snout, a large blotch covering the frontal, supraocular, and parietals, and a broad cross-bar on the nape, black; lower parts white.

Total length 330 millim.; tail 25.

W. Australia.

a. ♂ (V. 181, C. 25).   W. Australia.
b. ♀ (V. 191; C. 21).   Australia.

2. Furina calonota.

Furina calonotos, *Dum. & Bibr* vii. p. 1241, pl lxxv b. (1854); *Jan, Rev & Mag. Zool.* 1859, p. 125, pl. vi.; *Krefft, Sn. Austral.* p. 50 (1869).
Brachysoma calonotos, *Gunth Cat* p. 229 (1858)
Neelaps calonotus, *Gunth. Ann. & Mag. N. H* (3) xi. 1863, p. 24, and xv. 1865, p. 97.
Pseudelaps calonotus, *Jan, Elenco*, p. 116 (1863), and *Icon. Gén.* 43, pl. v. fig. 3 (1873).

Rostral moderately large, broader than deep, its upper portion shorter than its distance from the frontal; internasals shorter than the præfrontals; frontal a little longer than broad, nearly thrice as broad as the supraocular, as long as its distance from the end of the snout, shorter than the parietals; nasal elongate, in contact with the præocular; latter reaching or nearly reaching the frontal; two postoculars; temporals 1+1; six upper labials, third and fourth entering the eye; a pair of small chin-shields. Scales in 15 rows. Ventrals 126–131; anal divided; subcaudals 29–30. Yellowish, with a black vertebral stripe, each scale on which bears a white dot; a bar across the end of the snout, a large blotch covering the frontal, supraocular, and parietals, and a black crossband on the nape, black; lower parts white.

Total length 215 millim., tail 33.

W. Australia.

a. ♂ (V. 131; C. 30)   W. Australia? *

3. Furina occipitalis.

White, Journ. Voy. N. S. Wales, p 259, pl. —. fig. 2 (1790).
Elaps occipitalis, *Dum. & Bibr.* vii p. 1220 (1854); *Jan, Rev. & Mag. Zool.* 1858, p. 518, and *Icon. Gén.* 43, pl. ii fig 4 (1873).
Vermicella annulata, *Gunth Cat.* p. 236 (1858); *Krefft, Sn. Austral.* p. 78, pl xi fig 12 (1869); *McCoy, Prodr. Zool. Vict.*, Dec. 6, p. 11, pl. lii (1881).
—— occipitalis, *Gunth Proc. Zool. Soc.* 1859, p. 87, pl. xvii. fig. B.
—— lunulata, *Krefft, l. c.* p. 79, pl. xii. fig. 14.

Rostral moderately large, broader than deep, its upper portion shorter than its distance from the frontal; internasals much shorter than the præfrontals †; frontal once and one third to once

---

* The specimen was purchased as from Baranquilla, Colombia, together with a specimen of the W Australian *Rhynchelaps semifasciatus*

† In two specimens, the internasal on each side is fused with the præfrontal.

and two thirds as long as broad, not more than twice as broad as the supraocular, as long as or a little shorter than its distance from the end of the snout, shorter than the parietals; nasal not longer than and in contact with the præocular, two postoculars; temporals 1 + 1, six upper labials, third and fourth (exceptionally, third only) entering the eye, sixth large; two pairs of small chin-shields, with an azygous shield between them. Scales in 15 rows. Ventrals 180-234; anal divided; subcaudals 14-25. Annulate black and white, the annuli narrower beneath *; head black above, with a white band across the snout and another across the occiput.

Total length 590 millim.; tail 36.

Australia.

a. ♀ (V. 210; C. 18)	Swan R.	(Type of *V. annulata*.)
b. ♂ (V. 207; C 25).	Sydney.	G. Krefft, Esq. [P.].
c-d, e. ♀ (V. 210, 207; C. 21, 18) & yg. (V. 222; C. 16).	New South Wales.	Imperial Institute [P.].
f-g. Hgr. (V. 200, 180; C. 18, 20).	Moreton Bay, Queensland.	
h. ♀ (V. 234; C. 18).	Herbert R., N. Queensland.	J. A. Boyd, Esq. [P.].
i-l. ♂ (V. 205; C. 21) & ♀ (V. 219, 221; C. 14, 19).	Queensland.	
m. ♀ (V. 206; C. 18).	Queensland.	Col. Beddome [C.].
n ♂ (V. 227; C. 25).	N. Australia.	Rev. T. S. Lea [P.].
o. ♀ (V. 215; C. 20).	Australia.	Haslar Collection.
p. Skull of c.		

240. HOMORELAPS.

Elaps, part., *Schneid. Hist. Amph.* ii. p. 289 (1801); *Wagl. Syst. Amph.* p. 193 (1830); *Schleg. Phys. Serp.* ii. p. 435 (1837); *Dum. & Bibr. Erp. Gén* vii p 1191 (1854); *Gunth. Cat. Col. Sn.* p. 229 (1858); *Jan, Rev. & Mag Zool* 1858, p 516.

Homoroselaps, *Jan, l. c.* p. 518.

Pœcilophis (non Kaup), *Gunth. Proc. Zool Soc* 1859, p. 88; *Peters, Mon. Berl. Ac.* 1862, p. 636.

Maxillary extending forwards beyond the palatine, with a pair of large poison-fangs without groove, pterygoids toothless; mandibular teeth few, subequal. Head small, not distinct from neck; eye very small, with round pupil; nostril in a single nasal; no loreal. Body cylindrical; scales smooth, without pits, in 15 rows; ventrals rounded. Tail short; subcaudals in two rows.

South Africa.

No postfrontal bone; præfrontals widely separated from each other and in contact with the parietals, excluding the frontals from the orbital periphery.

---

* Interrupted on the belly in *V. lunulata*, Krefft, which is probably only a colour-variety.

1. Homorelaps lacteus.

Seba, Thes. ii. pl. xxxiv. fig. 5, xxxv. fig. 2, xlv. fig. 1 (1735); *Merr. Beytr.* i. pl. vi. (1790).
Coluber lacteus, *Linn. Mus. Ad. Frid.* p. 28, pl. xviii. fig. 1 (1754), and *S. N.* i. p. 381 (1766)
—— domicella, *Linn. S. N.* i. p. 376.
Cerastes lacteus, *Laur. Syn. Rept.* p. 83 (1768).
Coluber guineensis, *Bonnat. Encycl Méth , Ophiol.* p. 20 (1789).
—— siamensis, *Donnd. Zool. Beitr* iii p 203 (1798).
Elaps lacteus, *Schneid Hist Amph.* ii. p 293 (1801).
Vipera lactea, *Latr. Rept.* iv. p 29 (1801).
Coluber hygeiæ, *Shaw, Zool.* iii. p. 487 (1802).
—— iphisa, *Daud Rept.* vi. p. 416 (1803).
Elaps hygeæ, *Merr Tent* p 144 (1820); *Schleg Phys. Serp.* ii. p 446, pl. xvi. figs 14 & 15 (1837); *Smith, Ill. Zool. S. Afr., Rept.,* App. p. 21 (1849), *Dum. & Bibr.* vii. p. 1213 (1854); *Gunth. Cat.* p. 232 (1858); *Jan, Icon Gén.* 43, pl. ii. fig. 3 (1873); *F. Mull Verh Nat. Ges Basel,* vi. 1878, p 693.
—— punctatus, *Smith, Edinb N Phil Journ.* i. 1825, p. 254.
—— bipunctiger, *Dum. & Bibr. t c.* p. 1227.
Pœcilophis hygiæ, *Gunth. Proc. Zool. Soc* 1859, p. 88.
Aspidelaps lacteus, *Steind Novara, Rept.* p 78 (1867).
Pœcilophis lacteus, *Peters, Mon. Berl. Ac.* 1870, p. 114.
Elaps (Pœcilophis) hygiæ, var chrysopeleoides, *F. Mull. Verh. Nat. Ges. Basel,* viii. 1887, p 276, pl. ii

Rostral broader than deep; internasals shorter than the præfrontals; frontal not broader than the supraocular, once and a half to twice and a half as long as broad, as long as or a little longer than its distance from the end of the snout, usually shorter than the parietals; one præ- and one postocular, temporals 1+2; six upper labials, first and second small, third and fourth entering the eye, fifth in contact with the parietal, three lower labials in contact with the anterior chin-shields, which are longer than the posterior. Scales in 15 rows. Ventrals 160–209; anal divided; subcaudals 26–42. Coloration very variable, but vertebral line constantly bright yellow, orange or red, even if crossed by black annuli; head black, with yellow or orange markings, sometimes with two yellow dots close together behind the frontal shield.

Total length 460 millim., tail 50.
South Africa.

A. Yellowish white, with more or less regular black bars or annuli; belly black or with a continuous or interrupted black stripe. (*C. lacteus,* L., *C. hygiæ,* Shaw.)

a–c. ♀ (V. 198, C. 30) & hgr. (V. 173, 177; C 38, 39).		Simon's Bay.	H.M.S. 'Challenger.'
d–f. ♂ (V. 182; C. 36) & ♀ (V. 202, 200, C. 33, 31).		Cape of Good Hope.	Sir J. MacGregor [P.]
g. Yg. (V. 186; C. 37).		Cape of Good Hope	Mr. Ford [P.].
h, i ♀ (V 192; C. 33) & hgr. (V. 187; C. 32).		Cape of Good Hope.	

k–l. Hgr. (V. 191, 192; C. 42, 37). S Africa.
m. Skull. Cape of Good Hope

B. As in the preceding, but ventrals uniform white.

a. ♂ (V. 176; C. 41). ——?

C. Black, with small round yellow spots forming various markings a series of large orange spots along the spine, more or less confluent into a band; ventrals black at the base, yellow behind. (*E. punctatus*, Smith.)

a ♀ (V. 191; C. 29).	Cape of Good Hope.	Dr. Lee [P.].
b. Yg. (V. 209; C. 26).	Caffraria.	J. P. M. Weale, Esq. [P.].
c–d. ♂ (V. 165, 160; C. 37, 38).	S. Africa.	Dr. Quain [P.].
e. ♀ (V. 195; C. 27).	S. Africa.	

D. Black, each scale with a yellow dot; an orange or citrine vertebral stripe, ventrals black at the base, yellow behind. (Var. *chrysopeleoides*, F. Müll.)

a ♀ (V. 195; C. 29).	Cape of Good Hope	Officers of the Chatham Museum [P.].
b. ♀ (V. 188; C. 28).	Umtentu, Tembuland.	Mr. G. E. Nightingale [C.].
c. ♀ (V. 200; C. 30).	Port Elizabeth.	H. A. Spencer, Esq. [P.].
d. ♀ (V. 207; C. 31).	Durban.	Captain Munn [P.].
e. ♂ (V. 176; C. 39).	Natal.	E. Howlett, Esq. [P.].
f. ♀ (V. 184; C. 25).	S. Africa.	

2. Homorelaps dorsalis.

Elaps dorsalis, *Smith, Ill. Zool. S. Afr., Rept.*, App. p. 21 (1849).
Pœcilophis dorsalis, *Günth. Proc. Zool. Soc.* 1859, p. 88.

Rostral broader than deep; internasals half as long as the præfrontals; frontal once and a half as long as broad, a little longer than its distance from the end of the snout, much shorter than the parietals; one præ- and one postocular; a single temporal; six upper labials, the three anterior equal in size, third and fourth entering the eye, fifth in contact with the parietal; three lower labials in contact with the anterior chin-shields, which are slightly longer than the posterior. Scales in 15 rows. Ventrals 219–226; anal divided; subcaudals 25–28. Black above, with a yellow vertebral stripe extending to the tip of the snout; lower parts and three outer rows of scales white.

Total length 240 millim.; tail 21.

Caffraria and Natal.

a. Hgr. (V. 226; C. 25) King William's Town.

241. ELAPS.

Elaps, part., *Schneid. Hist. Amph.* ii. p. 289 (1801); *Wagler, Syst. Amph.* p. 193 (1830); *Schleg. Phys. Serp.* ii. p. 435 (1837); *Dum. & Bibr. Erp. Gén.* vii. p. 1191 (1854); *Günth. Cat. Col. Sn.* p. 229 (1858); *Jan, Rev. & Mag. Zool.* 1858, p. 516.
Micrurus, *Wagler, in Spix, Serp. Bras.* p. 48 (1824).
Elaps, *Günth. Proc. Zool. Soc.* 1859, p. 84; *Peters, Mon. Berl. Ac.* 1862, p. 636; *Cope, Proc. U. S. Nat. Mus.* xiv. 1892, p. 679; *Stejneger, Rep. U. S. Nat. Mus.* f. 1893, p. 358 (1895).

Maxillary very short, extending beyond the palatine, with a pair of large poison-fangs with obsolete grooves; pterygoid teeth few or absent; mandibular teeth subequal. No postfrontals; præfrontals meeting, or narrowly separated on the median line. Head small,

Fig. 29.

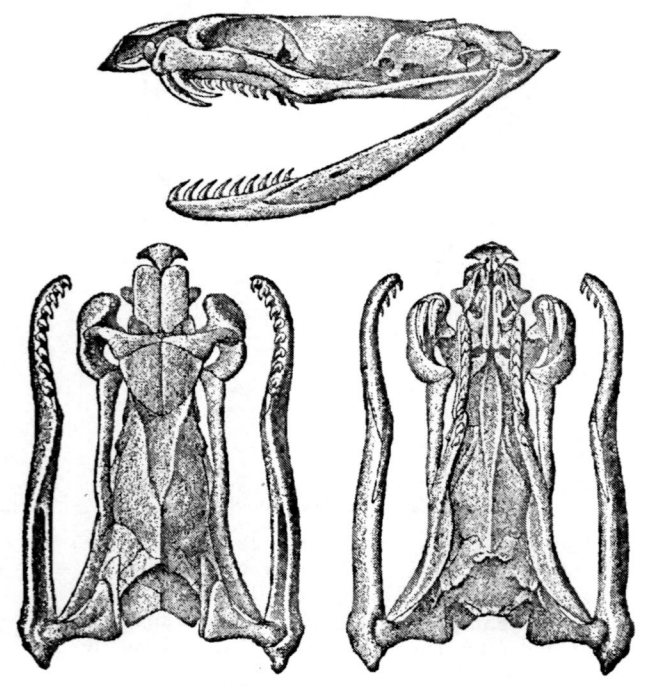

Skull of *Elaps marcgravii*.

not distinct from neck; eye small, with vertically elliptic or subelliptic pupil; nostril between two nasals; no loreal. Body cylindrical; scales smooth, without pits, in 15 rows; ventrals rounded. Tail short; subcaudals in two rows or partly single, partly in two rows.

America.

Synopsis of the Species.

I. Seven upper labials, fourth entering the eye; frontal very narrow; ventrals 167–182 ...... 1. *surinamensis*, p. 414.

II. Six upper labials, second and third entering the eye; snout narrow; ventrals 209 .... 2. *heterochilus*, p. 414.

III. Seven upper labials, third and fourth entering the eye.

  A. Seventh upper labial very small, rostral large, its upper portion nearly as long as its distance from the frontal; internasals nearly as long as the præfrontals; ventrals 215–241; subcaudals 21–29 ...... 3. *euryxanthus*, p. 415.

  B. Seventh labial well developed; rostral moderate, just visible from above; internasals much shorter than the præfrontals.

    1. First lower labial in contact with its fellow; posterior nasal not reaching the præocular; ventrals 191; subcaudals 23 .... 4. *gravenhorstii*, p. 415.

    2. First lower labial in contact with its fellow; posterior nasal in contact with the præocular.

      a. Eye nearly as long as or a little longer than its distance from the mouth; frontal as long as or slightly shorter than the parietals, which are not longer than their distance from the internasals; ventrals 189–227.

        α. Frontal once and one third to once and two thirds as long as broad.

          * Frontal longer than its distance from the end of the snout; anterior chin-shields as long as or a little shorter than the posterior.

Subcaudals 37–54; temporals 1+1.... 5. *langsdorffii*, p. 416.
Subcaudals 39–43; temporals 1+2.... 6. *buckleyi*, p. 416.
Subcaudals 29; temporals 1+1 ...... 7. *anomalus*, p. 417.

          ** Frontal as long as its distance from the end of the snout, anterior chin-shields shorter than the posterior.

Subcaudals 16–23; rostral a little broader than deep .... 8. *heterozonus*, p. 417.
Subcaudals 29–47; rostral much broader than deep .... 9. *elegans*, p. 418.

        β. Frontal not or but slightly longer than broad; nearly twice as broad as the supraocular; rostral little if at all broader than deep; subcaudals 29–45.

Temporals 1+1; third upper labial not or but scarcely larger than fourth .. 10. *annellatus*, p. 418.

No anterior temporal; sixth labial large
and forming a suture with the parietal;
third upper labial larger than fourth..   11. *decoratus*, p. 419.

    b. Eye shorter than its distance from the mouth (in the adult); parietals not longer than their distance from the internasals; ventrals 179–231, subcaudals 30–53.

Frontal as long as the parietals ......   12. *dumerilii*, p. 419.
Frontal shorter than the parietals ... . ·13. *corallinus*, p. 420.

    c. Eye shorter than its distance from the mouth (in the adult), frontal shorter than the parietals, which are longer (even if but slightly) than their distance from the internasals.

      a. Anal entire; ventrals 168–181; subcaudals 22–29.
                 14. *hemprichii*, p. 421.

      β. Anal divided (very rarely entire).

         * Snout obtusely pointed, projecting considerably beyond the mouth; ventrals 200–221; subcaudals 19–28.

Parietals a little longer than their
distance from the internasals .. ...   15. *tschudii*, p. 422.
Parietals very elongate... .. ..   16. *dissoleucus*, p. 422.

         ** Snout broadly rounded, scarcely projecting.

          † Ventrals 180–240; anterior temporal large and deep.

Subcaudals 30–59; frontal usually more
than once and a half as long as broad,
anterior chin-shields shorter than the
posterior ....   17. *fulvius*, p. 422.
Subcaudals 32–47; frontal not more than
once and a half as long as broad;
anterior chin-shields shorter than the
posterior ....   18. *psyches*, p. 426.
Subcaudals 22–29; eye measuring two
thirds its distance from the mouth in
the adult; anterior chin-shields shorter
than the posterior ....   19. *spixii*, p. 427.
Subcaudals 15–26; eye measuring two
thirds to three fourths its distance from
the mouth in the adult ....   20. *frontalis*, p. 427.
Subcaudals 23–42; eye measuring two
fifths to three fifths its distance from
the mouth in the adult; anterior chin-
shields not or but slightly shorter than
the posterior ....   21. *marcgravii*, p. 428.

†† Ventrals 241 or more; anterior temporal large and deep.

Ventrals 241-262; subcaudals 30-39 .. 22. *lemniscatus*, p. 430.
Ventrals 290-308; subcaudals 35-45 .. 23. *filiformis*, p. 430.

††† Ventrals 210 or more, anterior temporal very narrow, sometimes absent.

Ventrals 210-278 .... 24. *mipartitus*, p. 431.
Ventrals 303 .... 25. *fraseri*, p. 432.

3. Symphysial in contact with the anterior chin-shields.

Ventrals 255-268; temporals 1+1; frontal much broader than the supraocular........................ 26. *mentalis*, p. 432.
Ventrals 258; temporals 1+1; frontal little broader than the supraocular .. 27. *ancoralis*, p. 432.
Ventrals 240-315; no anterior temporal. 28. *narducci*, p. 433.

1. Elaps surinamensis.

Seba, Thes ii. pl. lxxxvi. fig. 1 (1735).
Elaps surinamensis, *Cuv. R. An.* ii. p. 84 (1817), *Schleg. Phys. Serp.* ii. p. 445, pl. xvi. figs. 8 & 9 (1837), *and Abbild.* p. 137, pl. xlvi. fig. 9 (1844); *Dum. & Bibr.* vii. p. 1224 (1854); *Gunth. Cat.* p. 234 (1858); *Jan, Icon. Gén.* 42, pl. iii. fig. 1 (1872); *Cope, Journ. Ac. Philad.* (2) viii. 1876, p. 182.

Eye measuring a little more than half its distance from the mouth. Rostral a little broader than deep; frontal very narrow, narrower than the supraocular, at least twice as long as broad, as long as its distance from the rostral or the end of the snout, shorter than the parietals; latter longer than their distance from the internasals; one præ- and two postoculars; temporals 1+2; seven upper labials, fourth entering the eye; four lower labials in contact with the anterior chin-shields, which are as long as or longer than the posterior. Scales in 15 rows. Ventrals 167-182; anal divided; subcaudals 33-37. Red, with black annuli disposed in threes, the middle one broad, separated by narrow yellow interspaces; 7 or 8 sets of annuli on the body; the red scales dotted with black; head red above, with the shields black-edged, followed by a black crossband behind the parietals.

Total length 740 millim.; tail 95. Grows to 1900 millim.

Venezuela, Guianas, Northern Brazil, N.E. Peru.

a. ♂ (V. 170; C. 37).   British Guiana.
b. llgr. ♂ (V. 167; C. 36).   Para.   Dr. E. A. Göldi [P.].

2. Elaps heterochilus.

Elaps heterochilus, *Mocquard, Bull. Soc. Philom.* (7) xi. 1887, p. 39.

Snout narrow. Rostral broader than deep; frontal once and a

half as long as broad; one præ- and two postoculars; temporals 1 or 1+1; six upper labials, second and third entering the eye; first lower labial formed by the fusion of two. Scales in 15 rows Ventrals 209; anal entire; subcaudals 29. Coloration as in *E. marcgravii*.

Total length 553 millim.; tail 43.

Brazil.

3. Elaps euryxanthus.

Elaps fulvius, part., *Gunth. Ann. & Mag. N. H.* (3) iv. 1859, p. 170.
—— euryxanthus, *Kennicott, Proc. Ac. Philad.* 1860, p. 337; *Cope, Proc. Ac. Philad.* 1861, p. 296; *Cragin, Bull. Washburn Laborat.* i. 1884, p 8, *Cope, Proc US Nat. Mus.* xiv. 1892, p 681; *Stejneger, Rep. U.S. Nat Mus.* f. 1893, p. 362, pl. ii. (1895).

Eye much shorter than its distance from the mouth Rostral large, nearly as deep as broad, its upper portion nearly as long as its distance from the frontal, internasals nearly as long as the præfrontals. frontal small and narrow; parietals small; one præ- and two postoculars; temporals 1+2; seven upper labials, third and fourth entering the eye, seventh very small; chin-shields very short, the anterior in contact with three lower labials. Scales in 15 rows. Ventrals 215–241; anal divided; subcaudals 21–29. Body with 11 or more black annuli edged with yellow and separated by broad red interspaces; head black to the posterior border of the parietals.

Total length 400 millim.; tail 33.

Arizona, Sonora, and North-western Mexico,

a. ♀ (V. 220; C. 29).   ——?   Haslar Collection.

4. Elaps gravenhorstii.

Elaps gravenhorstii, *Jan, Rev & Mag. Zool.* 1858, p. 523, *and Prodr.* pl. A (1859).

Eye a little shorter than its distance from the mouth. Frontal longer than broad; parietals as long as their distance from the internasals; one præ- and two postoculars; temporals 1+1, posterior nasal separated from the præocular, which is very small; seven upper labials, third in contact with the præfrontal, fourth and fifth entering the eye. Scales in 15 rows. Ventrals 191; anal divided; subcaudals 23. Body with black annuli disposed in threes, the median broadest; seven sets of annuli; head black, with a yellow transverse band behind the eyes covering the anterior two-thirds of the parietals and the posterior extremity of the frontal.

Total length 550 millim.; tail 50.

Brazil.

5. Elaps langsdorffii.

Elaps langsdorffii, *Wagl. in Spix, Serp. Bras.* p. 10, pl. ii. fig. 2 (1824); *Jan, Arch. f. Nat.* 1859, p. 273.
—— batesii, *Günth. Ann & Mag. N. H.* (4) i. 1868, p. 428, pl. xvii. fig. D.
—— imperator, *Cope, Proc. Ac. Philad.* 1868, p. 110, *and Proc. Amer. Philos. Soc.* xi. 1869, p. 156.

Eye as long as or a little longer than its distance from the mouth. Rostral broader than deep; frontal broader than the supraocular, once and two thirds as long as broad, longer than its distance from the end of the snout, as long as or slightly shorter than the parietals; latter as long as their distance from the internasals; one præ- and two postoculars; temporals 1+1; seven upper labials, third little larger than fourth, third and fourth entering the eye; four lower labials in contact with the anterior chin-shields, which are as long as or a little shorter than the posterior. Scales in 15 rows. Ventrals 204–225; anal divided; subcaudals 37–54. Dark brown above, the scales lighter at the base, with 63 transverse series of small cream-coloured spots, each occupying one scale; yellowish beneath, with red cross-bands; a yellow dot on each supraocular shield.

Total length 300 millim.

Upper Amazon.

a. Hgr. ♂ (V. 204; C. 54). Pebas, N.E. Peru. Mr. Hauxwell [C.].
(Type of *E. batesii*.)

Thanks to the kindness of Prof. Hertwig, I have been able to examine the type specimen (♂), from the R. Japura, preserved in the Museum of Munich.

E. imperator, which is identified with *E. batesii* by Cope, forms a colour-variety distinguished by the spaces between the transverse series of yellow spots, on the back, being alternately black and red, the red ventral cross-bars extending to the upper surface.

6. Elaps buckleyi. (PLATE XXII. fig. 1.)

Elaps corallinus, part, *Günth. Cat.* p 233 (1858), *and Ann & Mag. N. H.* (3) iv 1859, p. 171.

Eye nearly as long as or a little longer than its distance from the mouth. Rostral broader than deep; frontal broader than the supraocular, once and one third to once and a half as long as broad, longer than its distance from the end of the snout, as long as or slightly shorter than the parietals; latter as long as their distance from the internasals; one præ- and two postoculars; temporals 1+2; seven upper labials, third not larger than the fourth, third and fourth entering the eye; four lower labials in contact with the anterior chin-shields, which are shorter than the posterior. Scales in 15 rows. Ventrals 202–211; anal divided; subcaudals 39–43. Orange (red?), with 48–60 black annuli on the body, on the back the annuli edged with small yellow spots, each occupying one scale; the annuli close together on the tail; head black above, as far as the posterior third of the parietals; a small yellow spot on each supraocular; temples yellow.

Total length 505 millim.; tail 70.

Northern Brazil, Eastern Ecuador.

a. ♂ (V 202, C. 43).   Para.
b. Yg. (V. 211, C. 39).   Canelos, E. Ecuador.   Mr. Buckley [C.].

7. Elaps anomalus. (PLATE XXII. fig. 2.)

Eye as long as its distance from the mouth. Rostral broader than deep; frontal broader than the supraocular, once and a half as long as broad, a little longer than its distance from the end of the snout, as long as the parietals; latter as long as their distance from the internasals; a narrow azygous shield separating the præfrontals*; one præ- and two postoculars; temporals 1+1, seven upper labials, third scarcely larger than fourth. third and fourth entering the eye; four lower labials in contact with the anterior chin-shields, which are as long as the posterior. Scales in 15 rows. Ventrals 227; anal divided; subcaudals 29. Body with 55 black cross-bands separated by narrow brownish-white, black-dotted interspaces two or three scales wide; the black bands taper to a point on the sides, only a few extending across the belly to form complete rings; belly yellowish (red?), anterior half of head black, posterior half yellow; tail yellow (red?) with four black rings.

Total length 280 millim.; tail 23.

Colombia.

a. Yg (V. 227; C. 29).   Colombia.   Mr. F. A. Simons [C.].

8. Elaps heterozonus.

Elaps heterozonus, *Peters, Sitzb Ges. Naturf. Fr. Berl.* 1881, p. 52.
? Elaps corallinus, var. obscura, *Jan, Icon. Gén.* 41, pl. vi. fig. 3 (1872).

Eye nearly as long as or a little longer than its distance from the mouth. Rostral a little broader than deep; frontal broader than the supraocular, once and a half as long as broad, as long as its distance from the end of the snout, as long as the parietals; latter as long as their distance from the internasals; one præ- and two postoculars; temporals 1+1; seven upper labials, third larger than fourth, third and fourth entering the eye; four lower labials in contact with the anterior chin-shields, which are shorter than the posterior. Scales in 15 rows. Ventrals 210–219, anal divided; subcaudals 16–23. Red or brown, most of the scales tipped with black, with 17 to 23 subequal black rings mostly narrower than the interspaces; the first annulus with an angular prolongation reaching the occiput; shields on the snout edged and spotted with

---

* Probably an individual anomaly

ack; a more or less distinct black band on the head passing through the eye and across the supraocular and frontal shields; a large black spot on each parietal shield.

Total length 900 millim.; tail 40.

Eastern Ecuador, Eastern Peru, Bolivia.

a. Yg. (V. 218, C. 16).	Canelos, Ecuador.	Mr. Buckley [C.].
b, c–d. ♀ (V. 219, 214, 210; C. 16, 17, 18).	Moyobamba, Peru	Mr. A. H. Roff [C.].
e. ♂ (V. 219; C. 23).	Jungas, Bolivia.	

9. Elaps elegans.

Elaps elegans, *Jan, Rev. & Mag. Zool.* 1858, p. 524, *Prodr.* pl. B (1859), and *Icon. Gén.* 42, pl. v. fig. 2 (1872).

Eye nearly as long as its distance from the mouth. Rostral much broader than deep; frontal broader than the supraocular, once and a half to once and two thirds as long as broad, as long as its distance from the end of the snout, slightly shorter than the parietals; latter as long as their distance from the internasals; one præ- and two postoculars; temporals 1+1; seven upper labials, third larger than fourth, third and fourth entering the eye; four lower labials in contact with the anterior chin-shields, which are shorter than the posterior. Scales in 15 rows. Ventrals 189–221; anal divided; subcaudals 29–47. Body with black annuli disposed in threes, subequal in size, separated, within each set, by two series of alternately black and yellow scales; the sets, 12 to 17 in number, narrowly separated by reddish-brown interspaces which may be divided by a black cross-bar; head black, with a yellow blotch on each side behind the eye, widening on the lip.

Total length 730 millim.; tail 70.

Mexico and Guatemala.

a–b. ♂ (V. 189, C. 40) & ♀ (V. 206; C. ?).	Huatuzco, Vera Cruz.	F. D. Godman, Esq. [P.].
c. ♂ (V. 205; C. 47).	Teapa, Tabasco.	F. D. Godman, Esq. [P.].
d–e. ♀ (V. 221, 220; C. 35, ?).	Vera Paz, low forest.	O. Salvin, Esq. [C.].

10. Elaps annellatus.

Elaps annellatus, *Peters, Mon. Berl. Ac.* 1871, p. 402.
? Elaps imperator, var., *Cope, Journ. Ac. Philad.* (2) viii 1876, p. 181.

Eye as long as its distance from the mouth. Rostral a little broader than deep; frontal nearly twice as broad as the supraocular, slightly longer than broad, as long as its distance from the end of the snout, a little shorter than the parietals; latter as long as their distance from the internasals; one præ- and two postoculars; temporals 1+1; seven upper labials, third not or but scarcely larger than fourth, third and fourth entering the eye; three or four lower labials in contact with the anterior chin-shields, which are shorter than the posterior. Scales in 15 rows. Ventrals 200-211; anal divided; subcaudals 30-45. Black, with narrow white rings (one scale and one shield wide), some of which are approximate in pairs, the others equidistant; 41-49 white rings on the body, 4 to 7 on the tail; a white ring on the head, crossing the parietals.

Total length 490 millim.; tail 70.

Eastern Peru.

a. ♂ (V. 200; C. 45).	Sarayacu.	Mr. W. Davis [C]; Messrs Veitch [P.]
b. ♂ (V 201; C. 42).	Cueva Blanca.	Messrs. Veitch [P].

11. Elaps decoratus.

Elaps decoratus, *Jan, Rev. & Mag. Zool* 1858, p. 525, *and Prodr.* pl. B (1859); *Gunth. Proc. Zool. Soc* 1859, p. 85, pl. xviii. fig. A; *Jan, Icon. Gén.* 42, pl. vi. fig. 4 (1872).

Eye as long as or a little shorter than its distance from the mouth. Rostral nearly as deep as broad; frontal nearly twice as broad as the supraocular, not or but slightly longer than broad, as long as its distance from the end of the snout, a little shorter than the parietals; latter as long as their distance from the internasals; one præ- and two postoculars; a single temporal; seven upper labials, third larger than fourth, third and fourth entering the eye, sixth very large and forming a suture with the parietal, three or four lower labials in contact with the anterior chin-shields, which are as long as or shorter than the posterior. Scales as in 15 rows. Ventrals 196-213; anal divided; subcaudals 29-37. Body with black annuli disposed in threes, the middle one broader, enclosing two yellow rings, and separated by broad red, black-dotted interspaces; 15 or 16 sets of annuli on the body; head yellow, with the end of the snout and a band passing through the eyes black.

Total length 625 millim.

Brazil

a. ♂ (V. 205; C. ?).	Rio Janeiro.	Mrs Fry [P].
b. ♂ (V. 202; C. ?).	Brazil.	Dr. Gardiner [C.].
c. ♂ (V. 196, C. ?).	Brazil.	

12. Elaps dumerilii.

Elaps marcgravi (*non Wied*), *Dum. & Bibr.* vii. p. 1209 (1854).
—— dumerilii, *Jan, Rev. & Mag Zool* 1858, p. 522, *Prodr.* pl A (1859), *and Icon. Gén.* 42, pl. i fig. 3 (1872).

Eye measuring two thirds its distance from the mouth. Rostral nearly as deep as broad; frontal broader than the supraocular, once and three fourths as long as broad, longer than its distance from the end of the snout, as long as the parietals; latter as long as their distance from the internasals; one præ- and two postoculars; temporals 1+1; seven upper labials, third a little larger than fourth, third and fourth entering the eye; four lower labials in contact with the anterior chin-shields, which are slightly shorter than the posterior. Scales in 15 rows. Ventrals 197-204; anal divided; subcaudals 50-53. Body with 8 or 9 sets of three black annuli separated by very broad red interspaces, the scales on which are tipped with black; the median black annulus much broader than the outer, from which it is separated by a yellow annulus, head black above, separated from the black of the nape by a yellow crescentic band extending to below the eyes and covering the temples, the outer border of the parietals, and the occiput.

Total length 410 millim.; tail 65.

Colombia

a. ♂ (V. 197; C. 50).   Carthagena.   Capt. Garth [P.].

13 Elaps corallinus.

Elaps corallinus, *Wied, N. Acta Ac. Leop.-Carol.* x. i. 1820, p. 108, pl. iv., and *Abbild. Nat. Bras.* (1825).
—— corallinus, part., *Schleg. Phys. Serp.* ii. p. 440 (1837), *Dum. & Bibr.* vii. p 1207 (1854); *Gunth. Cat.* p. 233 (1858), and *Ann. & Mag. N. H.* (3) iv. 1859, p. 173.
—— ornatissimus, *Jan, Rev. & Mag. Zool* 1858, p. 521, *Prodr.* pl. A (1859), and *Icon. Gén.* 42, pl. 1. fig 1 (1872).
—— riisii, *Jan, ll. cc.* p. 525, pl. B, and *Icon.* pl vi fig 3
—— bocourtii, *Jan, Icon.* pl. vi. fig. 2.
—— circinalis, *Cope, Journ. Ac. Philad.* (2) viii. 1876, p. 182
—— corallinus, var. gastrosticta, *Boetty. Ber. Senck. Ges* 1889, p. 315.

Eye measuring two thirds to three fourths its distance from the mouth in the adult. Rostral broader than deep; frontal a little broader than the supraocular, once and a half to twice as long as broad, as long as its distance from the end of the snout, a little shorter than the parietals; latter as long as their distance from the internasals; one præ- and two (rarely one) postoculars; temporals 1+1, the anterior sometimes fused with the sixth labial; six upper labials, third as large as or a little larger than fourth, third and fourth entering the eye; three or four lower labials in contact with the anterior chin-shields, which are shorter than the posterior. Scales in 15 rows. Ventrals 179-231; anal divided; subcaudals 30-47. Body with black annuli edged with yellow, separated by red interspaces which may be more or less profusely spotted with black; head black above, temples, and often a more or less broad band behind or partly on the parietals, yellow.

Total length 790 millim., tail 70.

Tropical South America and Lesser Antilles (St. Thomas, St. Vincent, Martinique).

A. 21–31 black annuli on the body (*E. corallinus*, Wied).—The black dots on the red areas may be so crowded together near the yellow borders of the annuli as to form additional annuli (*E. bocourti*, Jan).

a–b. ♂ (V. 195; C. 47) & ♀ (V. 231; C. 37).	Brazil.	
c. ♀ (V. 209; C. 37).	Rosario de Cucuta, Colombia.	Mr. C. Webber [C.].
d. ♀ (V. 194; C. 32).	Trinidad.	C. Taylor, Esq. [P.].
e. ♀ (V. 199, C. 35).	Trinidad.	L Guppy, Esq. [P.].
f, g ♂ (V. 193; C. 43) & h gr (V 179; C 45)	Trinidad.	W Wright, Esq. [P.].
h. ♀ (V. 201; C. 32).	Trinidad.	Mus. Guilding.
i. ♂ (V. 183; C. 45).	St. Vincent.	Mus. Guilding.
k ♂ (V. 181; C. 46).	W. Indies.	Mus. Guilding.
l. ♀ (V. 193; C. 30).	——?	Haslar Collection.
m–o, p. ♂ (V. 186; C. 46) & ♀ (V. 196, 192, 192; C. 33, 30, 30).	——?	

B. 15 to 20 black annuli on the body.

a. ♂ (V 193; C. 43).	Interior of Brazil.	Dr. Gardiner [C.].
b. Yg. (V. 194; C. 45).	Brazil.	J. O W. Fabert, Esq. [P.].
c. ♂ (V 198; C 44).	Brazil.	G. Busk, Esq [P.].
d. ♀ (V 216; C. 32).	Brazil.	
e. ♀ (V. 221; C. 31).	——?	Haslar Collection.

14. Elaps hemprichii.

Elaps lemniscatus, part., *Gunth Cat* p 233 (1858).
—— hemprichii, *Jan, Rev & Mag Zool* 1858, p 523, *and Prodr.* pl A (1859); *Cope, Proc Ac. Philad.* 1860, p. 72; *Jan, Icon. Gén.* 42, pl. iv. fig. 3 (1872).

Eye measuring about two thirds its distance from the mouth. Rostral scarcely broader than deep; frontal broader than the supraocular, once and a half to once and two thirds as long as broad, as long as or a little longer than its distance from the end of the snout, a little shorter than the parietals; latter as long as their distance from the internasals; one præ- and two postoculars; temporals 1+1, seven upper labials, third larger than fourth, third and fourth entering the eye; four lower labials in contact with the anterior chin-shields, which are as long as the posterior. Scales in 15 rows. Ventrals 168–181; anal entire; subcaudals 22–29. Black above, with yellowish (red?) annuli, one broad one between two narrow ones; upper head-shields black; upper lip, temples, and occiput behind parietal shields yellowish; the yellowish scales black-edged; the yellowish annuli widening on the belly.

Total length 720 millim.; tail 65.
Guianas, Colombia, Peru.

a. ♀ (V. 168; C 29).	Surinam.	
b. ♂ (V. 176; C. 27).	——?	

15. Elaps tschudii.

Elaps tschudii, *Jan, Rev. & Mag. Zool.* 1858, p. 524, *Prodr.* pl. B (1859), *and Icon. Gén.* 42, pl. vi. fig. 1 (1872); *Boettg. Ber. Senck. Ges.* 1889, p. 316.

Snout obtusely pointed, projecting considerably beyond the mouth. Eye shorter than its distance from the mouth. Rostral broader than deep; frontal broader than the supraocular, once and two thirds as long as broad, as long as or a little longer than its distance from the end of the snout, shorter than the parietals; latter longer than their distance from the internasals; one præ- and two postoculars; temporals 1+1; seven upper labials, third much larger than fourth, third and fourth entering the eye; three or four lower labials in contact with the anterior chin-shields, which are shorter than the posterior. Scales in 15 rows. Ventrals 207–221; anal divided; subcaudals 21–28. Body with black annuli broader than the interspaces; the black annuli disposed in threes, a broad one between two narrow ones; the interspaces yellow and red, all or only the red ones dotted with black; snout black; frontal, supraoculars, and anterior half of parietals and temples yellow; occiput black.

Total length 430 millim.; tail 35.

Peru.

a. ♀ (V. 216; C. 28).	Andes of Peru.	Prof. W. Nation [P.].
b. ♀ (V. 221; C. 28).	Lima.	Christiania Museum.

16. Elaps dissoleucus.

Elaps dissoleucus, *Cope, Proc. Ac Philad.* 1859, p. 345

Snout obtusely pointed, projecting; eye very small. Frontal small, elongate; parietals very elongate; seven upper labials. Scales in 15 rows. Ventrals 200; anal divided; subcaudals 19. Body red, with seven sets of three black rings; the central ring not twice as wide as the outer ones; head black above, sides behind the eyes red.

Total length 1070 millim.; tail 35.

Venezuela.

17. Elaps fulvius.

Coluber fulvius, *Linn. S. N.* i. p. 381 (1766); *Daud. Rept.* vi. p. 300 (1803); *Say, Amer. Journ.* i. 1819, p. 262; *Harl. Med. Phys. Res.* p. 180 (1835).
Elaps fulvius, *Fitzing. N. Class Rept.* p. 61 (1826); *Holbr. N. Am. Herp.* iii. p. 49, pl. x. (1842); *Baird & Gir. Cat. N. Am. Rept.* p. 21 (1853), *Dum & Bibr.* vii. p. 1215 (1854); *Salvin, Proc. Zool Soc* 1860, p. 458; *Matthes, Denkschr. Ges. Isis,* 1860, p. 52, pl. —. figs. 1–5; *Jan, Icon. Gén* 41, pl i. fig. 2, & 42, pl. ii. figs. 2 & 3 (1872); *Bocourt, Miss. Sc. Mex., Rept.* pl. xxiii. (1874); *Garm N. Am Rept.* p. 105, pl. viii. fig. 3 (1883); *Cope, Proc. U.S Nat. Mus.* xiv 1892, p 680; *Hay, Rept. Indiana,* p 121 (1893); *Loennberg, Proc U S. Nat. Mus* xvii. 1894, p. 334; *Stejneger, Rep. U.S. Nat. Mus. f.* 1893, p. 359, pl. i. (1895).

Vipera fulvia, *Harl. Journ. Ac. Philad.* v. 1827, p. 364.
Elaps tenere, *Baird & Gir. Cat N. Am Rept.* pp. 22 & 156, *and Rep U S Mex Bound. Surv.* ii. x., *Rept.* p 15, pl. vii. fig. 1 (1859).
—— tristis, *Baird & Gir. Cat.* p. 23.
—— circinalis, *Dum. & Bibr t c* p. 1210
—— diastema, *Dum & Bibr t. c* p. 1222.
—— epistema, *Dum. & Bibr. t. e.* p. 1222.
—— nigrocinctus, *Girard, Proc. Ac Philad* 1854, p. 226, *and U.S. Nav. Astron. Exped.* ii. *Zool* p. 210, pl. xxxv. (1855).
—— divaricatus, *Hallow. Journ. Ac. Philad.* (2) iii. 1855, p. 36.
—— fulvius, part., *Gunth. Cat.* p. 235 (1858), *Ann. & Mag. N. H.* (3) iv 1859, p 169, *and Biol. C.-Am., Rept.* p. 182 (1895)
—— fitzingeri, *Jan, Rev. & May. Zool.* 1858, p. 521, *and Prodr.* pl A (1859).
—— apiatus, *Jan, ll cc* p 522, pl. A
—— affinis, *Jan, ll. cc.* p. 525, pl. B
—— aglæope, *Cope, Proc. Ac. Philad.* 1859, p. 344; *Gunth. Biol. C-Am., Rept.* p. 184.
—— distans, *Kennicott, Proc. Ac. Philad.* 1860, p. 338; *Cope, Proc. U S. Nat. Mus.* xiv. 1892, p. 681.
—— corallinus, *Salvin, Proc. Zool. Soc.* 1861, p. 228; *Dugès, Naturaleza*, vii. 1885, p 201.
—— hippocrepis, *Peters, Mon. Berl Ac* 1861, p 925.
—— corallinus, var. crebripunctatus, *Peters, Mon. Berl. Ac.* 1869, p 877.
—— marcgravi, var laticollaris, *Peters, l. c.*
—— corallinus, var. circinalis, *Jan, Icon. Gén.* 41, pl. vi. fig. 1 (1872).
—— laticollaris, *Garm. l c.* p 107.
—— ephippifer, *Cope, Proc Amer. Philos. Soc.* xxiii 1886, p. 281
—— bernardi, *Cope, Bull. U.S Nat Mus* no 32, 1887, p. 87.
—— diastema, var. michoacanensis, *Dugès, Naturaleza*, (2) i. 1891, p. 487, pl xxxii.
—— lemniscatus, part., *Gunth Biol. C.-Am., Rept.* p. 185.
—— ruatanus, *Gunth. l. c.* p. 185, pl. lvii. fig. B.

Eye shorter than its distance from the mouth (one half to two thirds) in the adult. Rostral broader than deep; frontal as broad as or broader than the supraocular, once and a half to twice as long as broad, as long as or a little shorter than its distance from the end of the snout, shorter than the parietals; latter longer than their distance from the internasals; one præ- and two postoculars; temporals 1+1 (rarely 1+2), seven upper labials, third usually larger than fourth, third and fourth entering the eye; three or four lower labials in contact with the anterior chin-shields, which are shorter than the posterior. Scales in 15 rows. Ventrals 180–237; anal divided (rarely entire), subcaudals 30–59. Body annulate, black and red or black, yellow, and red; tail annulate black and yellow; snout black; parietal shields usually entirely or greater part yellow, the first black annulus just behind or encroaching a little upon the parietals.

Total length 990 millim.; tail 85.

Eastern North America, from Southern Virginia, the Ohio River, and the Missouri to the Rio Grande; Mexico; Central America.

A. Body with 12 to 19 broad black annuli edged with yellow, separated by red, black-spotted interspaces of nearly equal extent; the black spots may be so crowded as to nearly entirely obscure the red colour; the black of the anterior part of the head extending to the posterior third or the posterior extremity of the frontal; the first black annulus just behind the parietals. (*E fulvius*, L., *E. tenere*, B. & G., *E. tristis*, B. & G.)

a-b. ♀ (V. 219, 224; C. 34, 35).	Marion Co., Florida.	A. Erwin Brown, Esq. [P]
c-d ♂ (V. 213; C. 41) & ♀ (V. 226; C. ?).	Duval Co., Texas.	W. Taylor, Esq [P.].
e. ♂ (V. 211, C. 43).	Texas.	Smithsonian Institution.
f, g. ♂ (V. 218; C. 43) & ♀ (V 223; C 31).	Texas.	
h. ♂ (V. 212; C. 38).	Mexico.	
i. ♂ (V. 200; C. 40).	—— ?	College of Surgeons.
k, l ♂ (V. 212; C. 41) & hgr. (V. 209; C. 38).	—— ?	
m. Skull.	Mexico.	

B. Body with 9 to 17 widely separated, narrow black rings more or less distinctly edged with yellow; the rest of the body red, uniform or dotted with black; black of the anterior part of the head extending to the middle or to the posterior point of the frontal, first black annulus behind the parietals or extending on the posterior extremity of the latter (*E nigrocinctus*, Gir, *E. diastema*, D. & B., *E. affinis*, Jan, *E. distans*, Kenn)

a-d, e. ♂ (V. 197, 197, C. 44, 41) & ♀ (V. 206, 210, 206; C. 35, 36, 36).	Mexico	Mr Hugo Finck [C].
f. ♀ (V. 207, C. 36).	Mexico.	M. Sallé [C.].
g i. ♂ (V. 186, 195; C. 44, 45) & ♀ (V. 211; C 31).	Mexico.	
h ♂ (V. 216; C 52).	Presidio, W. Mexico.	Hr. A. Forrer [C.].
l m ♂ (V 201; C. 49) & ♀ (V 218, C. 34).	Jalisco, N. of Rio de Santiago.	F. D. Godman, Esq. [P.].
n Hgr (V. 207; C. 50).	Omilteme, Guerrero.	F. D Godman, Esq. [P.].
o-q. ♀ (V. 211; C. 37) & yg. (V. 209; C. 33).	Atoyac, Guerrero.	F. D Godman, Esq. [P.].
r-s ♂ (V. 203, 205; C. 54, 53).	Teapa, Tabasco.	F. D. Godman, Esq. [P]
t-u ♂ (V. 200, 207; C. 45, 55) & ♀ (V. 220, C. 38)	British Honduras.	Colonial Exhibition.
v. ♀ (V. 213; C. 38).	Stann Creek, Brit. Honduras.	Rev. J Robertson [C.].
w. Hgr (V. 198; C 51).	Guatemala.	O. Salvin, Esq. [C.].
x. ♂ (V 191; C. 54).	Chontalez, Nicaragua.	R. A. Rix, Esq. [C.]; W. M. Crowfoot, Esq. [P.].

y–z.	Yg. (V. 204, 203; C. 34, 33).	Metagalpa, Nicaragua	Dr. E. Rothschuh [C.].
a–β	♂ (V. 188; C 48) & yg. (V. 187; C. 48).	Costa Rica.	O Salvin, Esq. [C].
γ.	♂ (V. 191, C?)	Chiriqui.	F. D. Godman, Esq [P.]

This form is nearly completely connected with the typical, and leads through *E. affinis*, Jan, to *E epistema*, D. & B., in which the annuli are reduced to a few dorsal spots. *E. distans*, Kenn., and *E. hippocrepis*, Ptrs., connect it with *E apiatus*, Jan The var. *laticollaris*, Ptrs., is, I am almost certain, based on an individual of this division in which the yellow margins of the annuli are edged with black; hence the annuli are triad, and the specimen has been referred to *E. marcgravi* and *E. lemniscatus*.

C. As in the preceding, but annuli numbering 21 to 24 on the body.

a.	♀ (V. 220, C. 35).	Vera Paz, low forest.	O. Salvin, Esq. [C]
b	♂ (V. 206; C. 56).	Belize	O Salvin, Esq. [C.].
c.	Yg. (V. 216, C. 42).	Honduras.	
d–e.	♂ (V. 205, C. 47) & ♀ (V. 219, C. 41).	——?	

D. Body with 20 to 27 black annuli edged with yellow, separated by red interspaces which are as broad as or a little narrower than the black annuli, the black of the anterior part of the head extending to the posterior third or nearly to the end of the frontal; the first black annulus extending on the posterior extremity of the parietals. (*E. fitzingeri*, Jan.)

a.	♀ (V. 228, C. 37).	City of Mexico.	Mr. Doorman [C]
b.	♀ (V. 221, C 36).	Dueñas, Guatemala.	O. Salvin, Esq [C.].
c.	Yg. (V. 213; C. 51).	Belize.	Rev. J. Gegg [P.].

E. Body with 40 to 52 black annuli, which are nearly as broad as the red interspaces, or alternately broader and narrower; snout black, rest of head yellow. (*E. ruatanus*, Gthr.)

a–h.	♂ (V 187, 180, 188, 186, 186, 191; C. ?, 47, 46, 47, 48, 46) & ♀ (V. 205, 201; C. 38, 38).	Ruatan Id., Honduras.	Mr. Gaumer [C.], F. D Godman, Esq. [P.]. (Types of *E. ruatanus*)

F. Body with 19 or 20 black annuli separated by brown (dark red?) interspaces which are nearly twice as broad; the black of the anterior part of the head extending nearly to the posterior point of the frontal; the first black annulus extending on the posterior extremity of the parietals; the space between the black areas on the head pale brown.

a.	♂ (V. 212; C. 59).	Guatemala.	O. Salvin, Esq. [C.].
b–c.	♂ (V. 212, 209; C 52, 56).	Dueñas, Guatemala.	O. Salvin, Esq [C.].

G. Body with 12 black annuli separated on the back by long dark mahogany-red interspaces; belly bright red, with the black bars edged with yellow, head and nape entirely black, with a faint trace of the light occipital cross-band of the typical form.

a. ♂ (V. 199; C. 47).   San José, Costa Rica.   Mr. C. F. Underwood [C.].

H. Body with 19 black annuli, edged with yellow, separated by broader red, black-dotted interspaces; the black of the head extends to the posterior extremity of the parietals, where it is fused with the first black annulus.

*a. Hgr. ♂ (V. 195; C. 52).   Yucatan.

I. Body with 24 to 62 more or less regular narrow black annuli which may be edged with yellow; the red spaces dotted or spotted with black, these spots often arranged in regular transverse series; head black as far as the posterior third of the frontal, with a yellow spot on the snout; the first black annulus extends on the posterior extremity of the parietals. (*E. apiatus*, Jan, *E. aglæope*, Cope.)

a, b-c, d-e ♂ (V. 212; C. 56), ♀ (V. 229, 226; C. 44, 41), & yg.(V. 198, 204; C 49, 35).	Vera Paz, low forest.	O. Salvin, Esq. [C.].
f. ♀ (V. 210; C. 40).	Lanquin, Vera Paz.	O. Salvin, Esq. [C.].
g. Hgr. ♂ (V. 207; C. ?)	Yzabal, Guatemala.	O. Salvin, Esq. [C.]
h. Yg. (V. 199, C. 51).	Stann Creek, Brit. Honduras.	Rev. J. Robertson [C.].

18. Elaps psyches.

Vipera psyches, *Daud. Rept.* viii. p. 320, pl. C. fig. 1 (1803).
Elaps psyches, *Merr. Tent.* p. 144 (1820), *Dum. & Bibr.* vii. p. 1212 (1854); *Jan, Icon. Gén.* 41, pl. vi. fig. 4 (1872).

Eye measuring two thirds its distance from the mouth. Rostral broader than deep; frontal broader than the supraocular, once and one third to once and a half as long as broad, as long as its distance from the end of the snout, shorter than the parietals; latter longer than their distance from the internasals; one præ- and two postoculars; temporals 1+1 (or 1+2), seven upper labials, third a little larger than fourth, third and fourth entering the eye; four lower labials in contact with the anterior chin-shields, which are shorter than the posterior. Scales in 15 rows. Ventrals 188–214; anal divided; subcaudals 32–47. Body annulate alternately black and dark brown, with 48 to 52 more or less distinct narrow yellowish rings; head black, with a triangular yellow spot on each side behind the head, the point touching the parietal shield.

Total length 495 millim.; tail 80.

Guianas.

a. ♀ (V. 214; C 32).   Demerara Falls.
b. ♂ (V. 197, C. 47).   ——?   Dr. Gunther [P.].

19. Elaps spixii.

Micrurus spixii, *Wagl. in Spix, Serp. Bras.* p. 48, pl xviii. (1824).
Elaps lemniscatus, part., *Gunth. Cat.* p. 234 (1858), and *Ann. & Mag. N. H.* (3) iv. 1859, p. 168.
? Elaps melanogenys, *Cope, Proc. Ac. Philad.* 1860, p. 72.
Elaps isozonus, *Cope, l. c.* p 73.
—— corallinus, *Jan, Icon. Gén* 41, pl. vi. fig 2 (1872)
—— marcgravi, *Jan, op. cit* 42, pl. iii fig. 2*.

Eye measuring two thirds its distance from the mouth in the adult, as long as its distance from the mouth in the young. Rostral broader than deep; frontal as broad as or a little broader than the supraocular, once and two thirds to twice as long as broad, as long as or a little longer than its distance from the end of the snout, shorter than the parietals; latter a little longer than their distance from the internasals; one præ- and two postoculars; temporals 1+1; seven upper labials, third larger than fourth, third and fourth entering the eye; four lower labials in contact with the anterior chin-shields, which are shorter than the posterior. Scales in 15 rows. Ventrals 201–219; anal divided (exceptionally entire); subcaudals 22–29 Red, the scales mostly tipped with black, with 20 to 38 subequal black rings on the body, as broad as or narrower than the interspaces, disposed more or less distinctly in threes; the first black ring extends to the posterior border of the parietals; upper head-shields black or largely spotted with black, with a more or less distinct black cross-band passing through the eyes; a black occipital collar, followed by a wide red space.

Total length 1400 millim.; tail 70.

Venezuela, Northern Brazil.

a. Hgr. ♂ (V. 204; C. 27).   Venezuela.   Mr. Riise [C.].
b ♀ (V. 218, C 22)   R. Capin, Para
c. Hgr. ♀ (V. 219, C. 26).   ——?

20. Elaps frontalis.

Elaps frontalis, part, *Dum & Bibr.* vii p. 1223 (1854)
—— frontalis, *Guichen. in Casteln Anim. Nouv. Amér. Sud, Rept* pl. xiv. (1855); *Cope, Proc. Ac. Philad.* 1862, p. 347.
—— lemniscatus, part, *Gunth. Cat* p 234 (1858), and *Ann. & Mag. N. H.* (3) iv. 1859, p. 168.
—— altirostris, *Cope, Proc. Ac. Philad* 1859, p. 345, 1860, p. 73, and 1862, p. 347.
—— baliocoryphus, *Cope, ll. cc* pp. 346 & 73
—— lemniscatus, *Hensel, Arch. f. Nat* 1868, p. 333.
—— marcgravi, *Jan, Icon. Gén.* 42, pl iii fig 2 (1872)

Eye measuring two thirds to three fourths its distance from the mouth in the adult, as long as its distance from the mouth in the young. Rostral a little broader than deep; frontal as broad as or slightly broader than the supraocular, once and two thirds to twice as long as broad, as long as its distance from the end of the snout, shorter than the parietals; latter a little longer than their distance from the internasals; one præ- and two postoculars; temporals 1+1 (rarely 1+2); seven upper labials, third larger than fourth, third and fourth entering the eye; three or four lower labials in contact with the anterior chin-shields, which are as long as or shorter than the posterior. Scales in 15 rows. Ventrals 197–230; anal divided; subcaudals 15–26. Tail ending very obtusely. Body with black annuli disposed in threes, the red and yellow interspaces tipped with black; upper surface of head, as far as the posterior border of the parietals, black, the shields edged or spotted with yellow or red; parietals often red in front.

Total length 1350 millim.; tail 70.

Southern Brazil, Uruguay, Paraguay, Argentina.

A. 10 to 12 sets of annuli on the body; red spaces large; labials yellow, black-edged.

a–b, c. ♂ (V. 225, 227; C. 22, 21) & Lgr. (V. 224, C. 18). Brazil. Mr. Clausen [C].

B. 12 to 15 sets of annuli on the body; red spaces large; labials and temporals black and yellow.

a–b ♀ (V. 216, 211; C. 24, 22). Rio Grande do Sul.
c. ♀ (V. 213; C. 21). Rio Grande do Sul. Dr. H. v. Ihering [C.].
d ♂ (V. 223; C. 21). S. Lorenzo, Rio Grande do Sul. Dr. H. v. Ihering [C].
e. ♂ (V. 230; C. 20) Asuncion, Paraguay. Dr. J. Bohls [C.].
f. ♀ (V. 224; C. 24). Argentina. Zoological Society.
g. ♂ (V. 220; C. 23). —— ? Zoological Society.

C. 12 to 15 sets of annuli on the body; red spaces small; labials, temporals, and chin-shields black, light-edged.

a–f. ♂ (V. 213, 204, 197, 203; C. 18, 18, 16, 16) & ♀ (V. 197, 204; C. 17, 15). Soriano, Uruguay. R. Havers, Esq. [P.].

21. Elaps marcgravii.

Elaps lemniscatus, part., *Schneid. Hist. Amph.* ii. p. 291 (1801); *Schleg. Phys. Serp.* ii. p. 444 (1837); *Dum. & Bibr.* vii. p. 1217 (1854); *Günth. Cat.* p. 234 (1858), and *Ann. & Mag. N. H.* (3) iv. 1859, p. 167.

Vipera lemniscata, part., *Daud. Rept.* vi. p. 13 (1803).

Elaps marcgravii, *Wied, N. Acta Ac. Leop.-Carol.* x. i. 1820, p. 109, and *Abbild. Nat. Bras.* (1825).

—— ibibiboca, *Merr. Tent.* p. 142 (1820).

Elaps corallinus, part., *Schleg Phys. Serp* ii. p. 440 (1837).
—— frontalis, part., *Dum. & Bibr t. c.* p. 1223
—— pyrrhocryptus, *Cope, Proc. Ac. Philad.* 1862, p. 347; *Peracca, Boll. Mus. Torin* x. no. 195, 1895, p. 19.

Eye measuring two fifths to three fifths its distance from the mouth. Rostral broader than deep; frontal as broad as or broader than the supraocular, once and a half to twice as long as broad, as long as its distance from the end of the snout, shorter than the parietals; latter a little longer than their distance from the internasals; one præ- and two postoculars; temporals 1+1, anterior usually much longer than the second; seven upper labials, third much larger than fourth, third and fourth entering the eye; four lower labials in contact with the anterior chin-shields, which are as long as or a little shorter than the posterior. Scales in 15 rows. Ventrals 210-240; anal divided, subcaudals 23-42 Body with black annuli disposed in threes, the middle one usually wider; 6 to 10 sets of annuli, separated by broad red interspaces which, like the narrow greenish-white annuli within each set, may be dotted, or the scales edged with black; snout yellow, the end usually black; a more or less regular black band across the middle of the head; back of the head red; the upper head-shields sometimes all black, edged with yellow.

Total length 1120 millim.; tail 100.

Tropical South America.

a. ♀ (V. 239, C. 34)	Trinidad	Mus Guilding.
b. ♀ (V. 220; C. 35)	Trinidad.	Hr. A. H Ruse [C.]
c. ♂ (V. 224; C. 34).	British Guiana.	
d. ♂ (V. 218; C. 27).	Pernambuco.	J. P. G. Smith, Esq. [P.]
e. ♂ (V. 225; C. ?).	Pernambuco.	W A Forbes, Esq. [P]
f, g. ♂ (V 237, C. ?) & yg. (V. 237; C. ?).	Bahia.	Haslar Collection.
h. Yg (V 222; C. 25)	Bahia.	Dr. O. Wucherer [C.].
i. ♀ (V. 223; C.?).	Bahia.	
k ♀ (V. 223, C. 28).	Rio Janeiro	D. Wilson Barker, Esq. [P.]
l. Yg. (V. 232; C. 40).	Charobamba, Bolivia.	
m-n, o, p. ♂ (V. 227; 229; C. 42, 39), ♀ (V. 236; C. 37), & yg. (V. 221; C. 36).	Moyobamba, E Peru.	Mr. A H Roff [C.].
q. Hgr. (V. 230; C 37).	Canelos, E. Ecuador.	Mr. Buckley [C.].
r. ♂ (V. 225, C. 36).	——?	
s, t. Skulls.	Santa Cruz.	

I regard *E. pyrrhocryptus*, Cope, a specimen of which has been kindly sent to me by Count Peracca, as a colour-variety, distinguished from the typical *E. marcgravii* of Wied in having the upper surface of the head entirely black, and the middle black annuli very much broader.

22. Elaps lemniscatus.

Coluber lemniscatus, *Linn. Mus. Ad Frid.* p. 34, pl xiv. fig 1 (1754), *and S. N.* i p 386 (1766).
Natrix lemniscata, *Laur. Syn. Rept* p. 76 (1768).
Elaps lemniscatus, part, *Schneid. Hist. Amph.* ii. p. 291 (1801); *Schleg Phys. Serp.* ii. p. 444, pl. xiv. figs. 6 & 7 (1837), *and Abbild.* p. 138, pl. xlvi. figs. 15-18 (1844), *Dum. & Bibr.* vii. p. 1217 (1854); *Gunth. Cat.* p. 234 (1858), *and Ann. & Mag. N. H.* (3) iv. 1859, p. 167.
Vipera lemniscata, part., *Daud. Rept.* vi p. 13 (1803).
Elaps lemniscatus, *Jan, Icon Gén* 42, pl. v. fig 1 (1872)

Eye measuring about half its distance from the mouth (three fifths in the young). Rostral broader than deep; frontal broader than the supraocular, once and a half to once and two thirds as long as broad, as long as its distance from the end of the snout, shorter than the parietals, latter longer than their distance from the internasals; one præ- and two postoculars; temporals 1+1, anterior usually much longer than second; seven upper labials, third much larger than fourth, third and fourth entering the eye, four lower labials in contact with the anterior chin-shields, which are as long as or a little longer than the posterior. Scales in 15 rows. Ventrals 241-262, anal divided, subcaudals 30-39. Body with black annuli disposed in threes, subequal in width or middle ones a little larger; 11 to 14 sets of annuli, separated by more or less broad red interspaces which, like the narrow yellow annuli within each set, may be dotted or the scales edged with black, head yellow, end of snout and a band across the middle of the head black; often a roundish black spot on the occiput.

Total length 1000 millim.; tail 80.

Guianas, Brazil.

a. ♂ (V 253; O. 31).	Brazil.	Mr. Clausen [C.].
b. Yg. (V. 243; C. 36).	Bahia.	Dr. O. Wucherer. [C.].
c. Yg. (V. 254; O. 34).	Macasseema, Brit. Guiana.	W. L Sclater, Esq. [P.].
d Yg (V. 262; O. 39).	British Guiana.	
e,f. ♀ (V. 257; O. 37) & yg.(V. 261; O.37).	—— ?	

23. Elaps filiformis.

Elaps filiformis, *Gunth. Proc. Zool. Soc.* 1859, p. 86, pl. xviii. fig. B; *Cope, Proc. Ac. Philad.* 1860, p 73; *Gunth. Ann. & Mag. N. H.* (4) i. 1868, p. 428; *Jan, Icon. Gén.* 42, pl. iv. fig. 1 (1872).

Eye not half as long as its distance from the mouth. Rostral broader than deep; frontal at least twice as broad as the supraocular, once and one fourth to once and two thirds as long as broad, as long as or longer than its distance from the end of the snout, much shorter than the parietals; latter as long as their distance from the end of the snout; one præ- and one or two postoculars; temporals 1+1; seven upper labials, third and fourth entering the eye; three or four lower labials in contact with the anterior chin-shields, which are shorter than the posterior. Scales in 15 rows. Ventrals 290-308; anal divided; subcaudals 35-45. Black annuli disposed in threes, with red interspaces as broad as or broader than a single annulus; the red scales may be dotted or edged with black; head yellow; end of snout black; a black cross-band passing through the eyes.

Total length 575 millim.; tail 40.

Amazon, Colombia.

a. Hgr (V 290; C. 45).	Para.	(Type.)	
b. ♀ (V. 298, C. 36).	Para	Dr. E. A. Goldi [P.].	
c. ♀ (V. 291; C. 35).	Bogota.		

24. Elaps mipartitus.

Elaps mipartitus, *Dum & Bibr.* vii. p. 1220 (1854); *Gunth. Ann & Mag N. H* (3) iv. 1859, p. 172, *Cope, Proc Ac. Philad.* 1868, p. 110.
—— decussatus, *Dum. & Bibr. t. c.* p. 1221.
—— semipartitus, *Jan, Rev. & Mag. Zool.* 1858, p. 516, *Elenco,* p 113 (1863), and *Icon Gén.* 42, pl. ii. fig. 1 (1872).
—— multifasciatus, *Jan, l c.* p. 521, *and Prodr.* pl. A (1859); *Cope, Proc. Ac. Philad* 1871, p. 209, *Gunth Ann & Mag. N. H.* (4) ix 1872, p 36, *and Biol. C.-Am., Rept* p. 184 (1895).

Eye about half or three fifths as long as its distance from the mouth Rostral broader than deep; frontal broader than the supraocular, once and two thirds to once and two thirds to once and three fourths as long as broad, as long as or a little longer than its distance from the end of the snout, shorter than the parietals; latter slightly longer than their distance from the internasals, one præ- and two postoculars; temporals 1+1, anterior very narrow, sometimes absent; seven upper labials, third much larger than fourth, third and fourth entering the eye; three or four lower labials in contact with the anterior chin-shields, which are as long as or a little shorter than the posterior. Scales in 15 rows. Ventrals 210-278; anal divided; subcaudals 24-34. Black above, with 40 to 68 narrow white crossbars; these widen on the belly, which is barred black and white; the white dorsal scales often each with a black spot; tail red, with 2 to 5 black annuli; head black to between the eyes, then yellow to the posterior border of the parietal shields.

Total length 610 millim.; tail 50.

Central America and Tropical South America.

a-b, c. ♂ (V 237, 239; C. 33, 31) & ♀ (V. 264, C. 26).	Chontalez, Nicaragua.	
d. ♂ (V. 261, C. 33).	Panama.	Christiania Museum.
e. ♂ (V. 246; C. 28).	Bogota.	C. Laverde, Esq.[P].
f. Yg. (V. 277; C 24).	Bogota.	

g. ♂ (V 210; C 33) Caracas. Prof. Peters [P.].
h. ♀ (V 238; C. 27). Venezuela. Mr. Dyson [C.].
i. ♀ (V. 233; C. 27). Venezuela

25. Elaps fraseri. (Plate XXII. fig. 3.)

Eye nearly half as long as its distance from the mouth. Rostral broader than deep; frontal a little broader than the supraocular, once and two thirds as long as broad, as long as its distance from the end of the snout, shorter than the parietals; latter as long as their distance from the internasals; one præ- and two postoculars; temporals 1+1, anterior very narrow; seven upper labials, third much larger than fourth, third and fourth entering the eye; four lower labials in contact with the anterior chin-shields, which are a little shorter than the posterior. Scales in 15 rows. Ventrals 303; anal divided; subcaudals 25. Black above, with 75 narrow whitish cross-bars with broken outlines; the cross-bars widen on the belly, which is barred black and yellow (red?); anterior half of head black, posterior half yellow; tail with black and yellow (red?) annuli.

Total length 780 millim,; tail 40.

Ecuador.

a. ♂ (V. 303; C. 25). W. Ecuador. Mr. Fraser [C].

26. Elaps mentalis. (Plate XXII. fig. 4.)

Eye measuring about three fifths its distance from the mouth. Rostral much broader than deep; frontal broader than the supraocular, once and a half to once and two thirds as long as broad, as long as its distance from the end of the snout, shorter than the parietals; latter as long as their distance from the internasals; one præ- and two postoculars; temporals 1+1, anterior very narrow; seven upper labials, third much larger than fourth, third and fourth entering the eye; anterior chin-shields in contact with the symphysial and with three lower labials, shorter than the posterior. Scales in 15 rows. Ventrals 255-268; anal divided; subcaudals 30-31. Black, with 58-70 narrow white annuli; these annuli wider on the belly, where they cover two shields, the black bars covering two or three shields; snout black, back of head yellow; tail annulate black and orange.

Total length 490 millim.; tail 30.

Colombia and Ecuador.

a. ♂. V. 260; C. 30). Pallatanga,E Ecuador. Mr. Buckley [C.].
b. Yg.(V. 255; C. 31). Cali,Colombia,3200 ft. Mr.W. F. H. Rosenberg [C.].

27. Elaps ancoralis.*

Elaps marcgravi, var. ancoralis, *Jan, Icon. Gén.* 42, pl. iv. fig. 2.

Eye about half as long as its distance from the mouth. Rostral much broader than deep; frontal broader than the supraocular, once

---

* Described from the type specimen (♂) in the Museum of Munich, kindly entrusted to me by Prof. Hertwig

and one third as long as broad, little broader than the supraocular, as long as its distance from the end of the snout, shorter than the parietals; latter as long as their distance from the internasals; one præ- and two postoculars; temporals 1+1; seven upper labials, third larger than fourth, third and fourth entering the eye; anterior chin-shields in contact with the symphysial and with four lower labials, as long as the posterior. Scales in 15 rows. Ventrals 258; anal divided; subcaudals 31. Body with 16 sets of black annuli disposed in threes, the middle one a little wider; the scales of the interspaces black, light-edged; head light in front, dotted and spotted with black; an anchor-shaped black marking on the occiput and nape, the transverse branch nearly covering the parietals and extending to the throat.

Total length 780 millim.; tail 57.

Ecuador.

28. Elaps narduccii.

Elaps narduccii, *Jan, Arch. Zool. Anat. Phys.* ii. 1863, p. 222, *and Icon. Gén.* 42, pl. vi. fig. 5 (1872).
—— scutiventris, *Cope, Proc. Amer Philos. Soc* xi 1869, p 156.
—— melanotus, *Peters, Sitzb. Ges. Naturf. Fr* 1881, p. 51.

Eye hardly half as long as its distance from the mouth. Rostral broader than deep; frontal nearly as broad as the supraocular, once and a half to once and two thirds as long as broad, as long as its distance from the end of the snout, shorter than the parietals; one præ- and two postoculars; temporals 1+1; seven upper labials, third and fourth entering the eye; anterior chin-shields in contact with the symphysial and with three or four lower labials; posterior chin-shields as long as the anterior. Scales in 15 rows. Ventrals 240–315; anal divided; subcaudals 15–33. Black, beneath with yellow (red?) cross-bands or transversely oval spots, as broad as or narrower than the interspaces and sometimes extending as triangular blotches up the sides; a yellow cross-band on the head, covering the temples, the frontal, supraoculars, and anterior half of the parietals.

Total length 720 millim.; tail 50.

Eastern Ecuador, North-eastern Peru, Bolivia.

a–b ♂ (V. 315, 304; C. 33, 27).	Canelos, Ecuador.	Mr. Buckley [C.].
c–d. ♂ (V. 240; C. 24) & ♀ (V. 270; C. 19).	Moyobamba, N.E. Peru.	Mr. A. H. Roff [C.].
e. ♂ (V. 302, C. 32)*.	Chyavetas, N.E. Peru	Mr. E. Bartlett [C].

---

* This specimen has been referred to *E. gastrodelus*, D. & B, by Gunther Ann. & Mag. N. H. (4) i. 1868, p 413.

242. DENDRASPIS.

Dendraspis, *Schleg. Versl. Zool. Gen. Amsterd.* 1848, p. — * ; *Gunth. Cat. Col. Sn.* p. 238 (1858); *A. Dum. Arch. Mus.* x. 1859, p. 215; *Cope, Proc. Ac. Philad.* 1859, p. 346; *Jan, Elenco sist. Ofid.* p. 120 (1863).
Dinophis, *Hallow. Proc. Ac. Philad.* 1852, p. 203; *Peters, Reise n. Mossamb* iii p. 136 (1882).
Drendroechis, *Fischer, Mich. Progr. Hamb. Realsch.* 1855, p. 20.

Maxillary bone curved upwards, with a strong posterior process directed backwards and outwards; a pair of large poison-fangs, not fissured, not followed by other teeth; a large, fang-like anterior mandibular tooth, followed by a considerable toothless space. Head narrow, elongate; eye moderate, with round pupil; nostril between two shields; no loreal. Body slightly compressed; scales smooth, narrow, very oblique, without pits, in 13 to 23 rows; ventrals rounded. Tail long; subcaudals in two rows.

Tropical and South Africa.

Fig. 30.

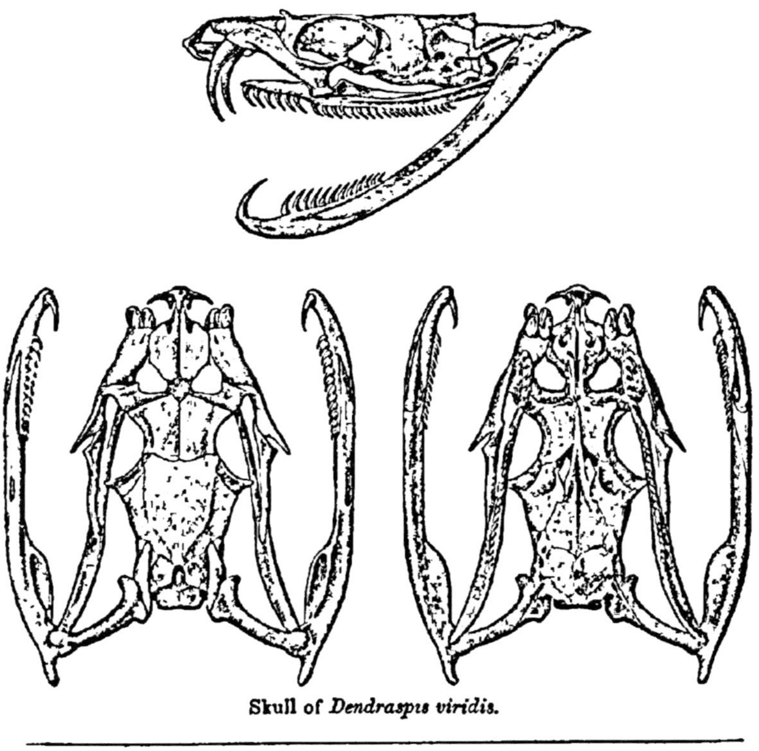

Skull of *Dendraspis viridis*.

---

* I have not been able to refer to this paper.

Synopsis of the Species.

I. A large upper temporal, in contact with the whole outer border of the parietal.

Scales in 13 rows, outer half as long as dorsals .... 1. *viridis*, p. 435.

Scales in 15 to 19 rows, outer not shorter than dorsals .... 2. *jamesonii*, p. 436.

II. Temporals 2+3 or 4, two in contact with the outer border of the parietal; scales in 19 to 23 rows, outer not shorter than dorsals.

Second upper labial much deeper than first .... 3. *angusticeps*, p. 437.

Second upper labial not deeper than first 4. *antinorii*, p. 437.

1 Dendraspis viridis.

Leptophis viridis, *Hallow. Proc Ac. Philad.* 1844, p. 172.

Naja jamesonii (*non Traill*), *Schleg. Versl. Ak. Amsterd.* iii. 1855, p. 313.

Dinophis hammondii, *Hallow. Proc. Ac. Philad.* 1852, p. 203, *and Journ. Ac. Philad* (2) ii. 1854, p. 304, pl. xxix.

Dendroechis reticulata, *Fisch. Mich Progr Hamb. Realsch.* 1855, p. 20.

Dendraspis jamesonii, *Fisch. Abh. Naturw. Hamb.* iii. 1856, p. 115, pl. i.; *A. Dum. Rev. & Mag. Zool.* 1856, p. 557; *Gunth. Cat.* p. 238 (1858); *A. Dum. Arch. Mus.* x. 1859, p. 215, pl. xvii. fig. 11; *Gunth. Ann. & Mag. N. H.* (3) xv. 1865, p. 97, *F. Mull. Verh. Nat. Ges Basel*, vii 1885, p. 692; *Boettg Ber. Senck. Ges.* 1887, p 63; *Bocage, Jorn Sc. Lisb.* xii. 1888, p. 139, figs., (2) ii. 1892, p. 265, *and Herp. Angola*, p. 138, pl. xv. fig. 1 (1895).

Dendraspis angusticeps (*non Smith*), *Bedriaga, Instituto*, 1892, no. 6, p. 432.

Rostral broader than deep; internasals shorter than the præfrontals; frontal as long as broad or a little broader than long; shorter than its distance from the end of the snout, much shorter than the parietals, in contact with the upper præocular; two or three præoculars, with a subocular below them, the latter sometimes fused with the third labial; two or three postoculars with a subocular below them; two very large temporals, the upper longest and in contact with the entire outer border of the parietal, the lower usually descending to the lip, between the sixth and seventh labials; the large upper temporal separated from its fellow on the other side by three occipital shields; seven or eight upper labials, fourth (or third and fourth) entering the eye, second and third much deeper than third and usually both, sometimes only the second, in contact with the præfrontals; four lower labials in contact with the anterior chin-shields, which are as long as or shorter than the posterior. Scales in 13 rows, outer much shorter than the others, one dorsal scale corresponding to two laterals or to two ventral shields. Ventrals 211–225; anal divided; subcaudals 107–119. Olive-green above, uniform or each scale brown at the end; head-shields finely edged with blackish; lips yellowish, the shields edged with black; belly yellowish, the shields finely edged with brown or black; tail yellow, scales and shields edged with black.

Total length 1830 millim.; tail 460.

West Africa, from the Senegal to the Niger; S. Thome Island.

a. ♂ (V. 214; C. 114)	Gambia.	Sir A. Smith [P.].
b. ♂ (V. 221; C. 111).	Sierra Leone.	Sir A. Kennedy [P.].
c-d. ♂ (V. 219; C. 118) & hgr. (V. 214; C. 119).	Sierra Leone.	H. C. Hart, Esq [P.].
e. ♂ (V. 214; C. 112).	Ancobra R., Gold Coast.	Major Burton & Capt. Cameron [P.].
f. ♀ (V. 225; C. 107).	Coast of Guinea.	
g. ♂ (V. 215; C. 119).	W. Africa.	
h. ♂ skeleton.	Axim, Gold Coast.	

2. Dendraspis jamesonii.

Elaps jamesonii, *Traill, in Schleg Phys. Serp, Engl. Transl.* p. 179, pl. ii. figs 19 & 20 (1843).

Dendraspis angusticeps (*non Smith*), *A. Dum Rev. & Mag. Zool.* 1856, p. 558, *and Arch. Mus* x. 1859, p. 216, pl. xvii. fig. 12; *Bocage, Jorn. Sc. Lisb.* 1 1866, p. 52; *Mocq. Bull Soc. Philom.* xi. 1887, p 88.

—— angusticeps, part., *Gunth Cat.* p. 238 (1858), *and Ann & Mag. N. H.* (3) xv. 1865, p. 98, pl. iii. fig. B.

—— welwitschii, *Gunth. Ann. & Mag. N. H* (3) xv. 1865, p. 97, pl. iii. fig. A, and (6) xv. 1895, p. 529.

Dinophis fasciolatus, *Fisch Jahrb. Nat. Ver. Hamb.* ii. 1885, p. 111, pl. iv. fig. 10

Dendraspis jamesonii, *Boettg. Ber. Senck. Ges.* 1888, p. 85.

—— neglectus, *Bocage, Jorn. Sc. Lisb.* xii. 1888, p. 141, figs.

Head-shields and coloration as in the preceding. Scales in 15 to 19 rows (19 to 21 on the neck), the outer not shorter than the dorsals. Ventrals 210–235; subcaudals 99–121. Young with chevron-shaped black cross-bars. Tail sometimes black.

Total length 2100 millim.; tail 560.

West Africa, from the Niger to Angola; Central Africa.

a. ♂ (Sc. 17; V. 214; C. 110).	150 miles up the Niger.	W. H. Crosse, Esq. [P.].
b. Yg. (Sc. 19; V. 220; C. ?).	Niger.	Mr. Fraser [C.].
c. ♀ (Sc. 17; V. 216; C. 113).	Cameroon Mts., 2000 ft.	Sir H. H. Johnston [P].
d. Yg. (Sc. 19; V. 218; C. 105).	Fernando Po	H. Veitch, Esq. [P.].
e. Yg. (Sc. 17; V 226; C. 111).	Fernando Po.	Mrs. Burton [P.]
f. ♀ (Sc. 19; V. 222; C. 106).	Fernando Po.	
g. Yg. (Sc. 17; V. 219; C 120)	Gaboon.	Dr. J. G. Fischer. (Type of *D. fasciolatus*)
h. Hgr. (Sc. 17; V. 215; C. 113).	Eloby, Gaboon.	H. Ansell, Esq. [P.].
i-k. Hgr. (Sc. 17; V. 225; C. 108) & yg. (Sc. 19; V. 214; C. 110).	Mouth of the Loango.	Mr. H. J. Duggan [C.].
l. ♂ (Sc. 15, V. 219; C. 107).	Golungo Alto, Angola.	Dr. Welwitsch [P.]. (Type of *D. welwitschii*.)
m. Hgr. (Sc. 17; V. 227; C. 115).	W. Africa.	Mr. Rich [C.].
n. ♀ (Sc. 19; V. 227; C. 121).	W. Africa.	

o. Hgr., skin (Sc. 15; V. 210; Kavirondo, E. F. J. Jackson, Esq.
C. ?).   Central Africa.   [P.].
p ♂, imperfect, head missing —— ?   (One of the types*.)
   (Sc. 17).
q. Skull.   W. Africa.

3. Dendraspis angusticeps.

Naja angusticeps, *Smith, Ill. Zool S Afr., Rept.* pl. lxx. (1849);
   Dum. & Bibr. vii. p. 1301 (1854).
Chloroechis angusticeps, *Peters, Mon. Berl Ac.* 1854, p. 625.
Dendraspis angusticeps, part, *Gunth Cat.* p. 238 (1858).
—— polylepis, *Gunth. Proc. Zool. Soc.* 1864, p. 310, *and Ann. & Mag. N. H.* (3) xv. 1865, p. 98, pl. iii. fig. D.
—— intermedius, *Gunth. Ann. & Mag. N. H* (3) xv. 1865, p. 97, pl. iii. fig. C
—— angusticeps, *Peters, Mon. Berl. Ac* 1878, p. 207; *Bocage, Jorn. Sc Lisb* xii. 1888, p. 143, figs; *Boettg. Ber. Senck. Ges.* 1889, p 295; *Bocage, Herp. Angola*, p. 140, pl. xv. fig. 3 (1895).
Dinophis angusticeps, *Peters, Reise n. Mossamb.* iii p 136, pl. xix A. fig. 4 (1882).

Head-shields as in the preceding, but upper temporal much smaller, not longer than the lower, followed by a second, and separated from its fellow on the other side by five or more scales or shields. Scales in 19 to 23 rows (21 to 27 on the neck), outer not shorter than dorsals. Ventrals 202–270; subcaudals 99–121. Green, olive or blackish, uniform or some of the scales edged with black; yellowish or pale green beneath; caudal scales and shields not black-edged.

Total length 2000 millim.; tail 430.

West Africa south of the Congo, Central Africa, East Africa, Transvaal, Natal.

a. ♂ (Sc. 19; V. 202; C. 116).   Kelifi, E. Africa.   G. Trevor-Roper, Esq. [P.]
b. Hgr. (Sc. 19; V. 205, C. 105) Taveta, E Africa.   G Trevor-Roper, Esq. [P.].
c. Ad., skin (Sc. 23; V 248;   Mombasa.
   C. 116).
d. ♂ (Sc. 23; V. 249; C. 105).   S. of Kiboko,   Dr. J. W. Gregory
                                 E. Africa.   [P.]
e. ♂, skin (Sc. 19; V. 202;   L. Tanganyika.   Sir J. Kirk [C.].
   C. 113)
f–g. Heads.   C. Africa.   Capt. Speke [P.].
h. Ad., skin (Sc. 23; V. 258;   Zambesi.   Sir J. Kirk [C.].
   C. 120).   (Type of *D polylepis*)
i. ♂ (Sc. 19; V. 204; C. 110).   Zambesi.   (Type of *D. intermedius*.)
k. ♂ (Sc. 19; V. 203; C. 99).   Pondoland.

4. Dendraspis antinorii.

Dendraspis antinorii, *Peters, Mon Berl. Ac* 1873, p. 411, pl. i. fig. 2, *Bocage, Jorn. Sc. Lisb.* xii. 1888, p. 145.

Head-shields as in the preceding, but second upper labial small,

---

* Dr. Traquair has been so kind as to send me notes on the other type specimen, preserved in the Museum of Science and Art, Edinburgh.

not larger than first, and in contact with the posterior nasal only;. third upper labial large, forming a short suture with the præfrontal. Scales in 21 or 23 rows. Ventrals 248; anal divided; subcaudals 117. Olive above, yellowish beneath.

Total length 2690 millim.; tail 545.

Anseba, Abyssinia.

Fam. 8. AMBLYCEPHALIDÆ.

Aglyphodontes Paréasiens, part, Leptognathiens, part, *Duméril, Mém Ac. Sc.* xxiii. p 427, 1853, *Duméril & Bibron, Erp. Gén.* vii. 1854.

Dipsadidæ, part., *Günther, Cat. Col Sn* p. 162, 1858.

Amblycephalidæ, *Günther, Rept. Brit. Ind.* p. 324, 1864.

Colubridæ, part. (Leptognathinæ, part.), *Cope, Proc. Amer. Philos. Soc.* xxiii. p. 484, 1886.

Amblycephalidæ, *Boulenger, Faun. Ind., Rept.* p. 414, 1890.

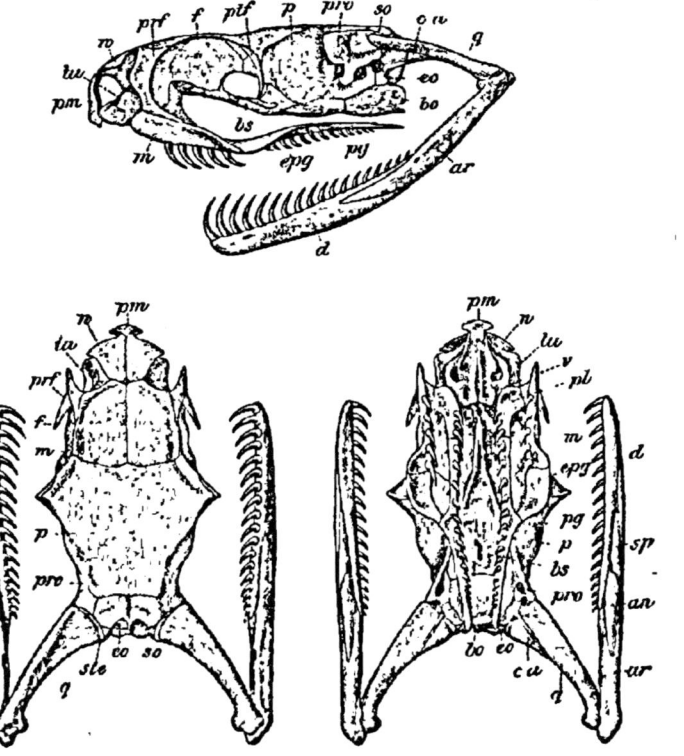

Fig. 31.

Skull of *Amblycephalus carinatus.*

Facial bones slightly movable; præfrontal not in contact with nasal; ectopterygoid (transpalatine) present; pterygoid short, not extending to quadrate or mandible; supratemporal rudimentary; maxillary horizontal, parallel with or converging posteriorly towards the palatine. Mandible without coronoid bone. Solid teeth in both jaws.

The hypapophyses disappear in the anterior third of the dorsal vertebral column.

These Snakes, which inhabit South-eastern Asia and Central and South America, may be readily distinguished from the *Colubridæ*, without an examination of the skull, by the absence of a mental groove, the mouth being susceptible of but slight expansion, and by the free termination of the pterygoid bones, which do not diverge behind, as may be seen on the back of the palate when the mouth is fully open.

Synopsis of the Genera.

I. Body more or less compressed.

A. Maxillary very short, with 5 or 6 teeth.

Subcaudals single .. .. 1. **Haplopeltura,** p. 439.
Subcaudals in two rows .. .. 2. **Amblycephalus,** p. 440.

B. Maxillary rather short, turned inwards, with 11 to 18 teeth.

Pterygoids toothed ... . 3. **Leptognathus,** p. 446.
Pterygoids toothless .... 4. **Dipsas,** p. 460.

II. Body cylindrical .... 5. **Pseudopareas,** p. 462.

1. HAPLOPELTURA.

Dipsas, part., *Schleg. Phys. Serp.* ii. p. 257 (1837).
Aplopeltura, *Dum. & Bibr Mém Ac Sc.* xxiii. 1853, p. 463, *and Erp. Gén.* vii p 444 (1854).
Amblycephalus, *Gunth. Cat. Col. Sn.* p. 184 (1858); *Jan, Elenco sist. Ofid.* p. 100 (1863); *Gunth. Rept. Brit. Ind.* p. 325 (1864)

Maxillary bone very short, deep, with five subequal teeth; maxillary and mandibular teeth decreasing in size posteriorly. Head distinct from neck, eye large, with vertical pupil; nasal entire. Body strongly compressed; scales smooth, without pits, oblique, in 13 rows, vertebral row strongly enlarged; ventrals rounded. Tail moderate; subcaudals single.

Pinang, Malay Archipelago.

1. Haplopeltura boa.

Amblycephalus boa, *Boie, Isis,* 1828, p. 1034; *Gunth. Cat.* p. 184 (1858), *and Rept. Brit. Ind* p. 325 (1864), *Jan, Icon. Gén.* 37, pl. iii. fig 2 (1870), *Modigliani, Ann. Mus. Genova,* (2) vii. 1889, p. 120.

Dipsas boa, *Schleg. Phys. Serp.* ii. p. 284, pl. xi. figs. 29 & 30 (1837); *Cantor, Cat. Mal. Rept.* p. 78, pl. xl. fig. 3 (1847).
Aplopeltura boa, *Dum. & Bibr.* vii. p. 444 (1854).
Haplopeltura boa, *Boettg. Ber. Offenb. Ver. Nat.* 1892, p. 134.

Snout very short and deep. Rostral narrow, once and a half to twice as deep as broad, just visible from above; internasals shorter than the præfrontals; frontal not broader than the supraocular, once and two thirds to twice as long as broad, longer than its distance from the end of the snout, as long as or a little longer than the parietals; two or three enlarged occipitals; two or three superposed loreals, the lower often entering the eye, which is bordered by six to eight shields in addition to the supraocular; temporals 3+3 or 4; eight to ten upper labials, none entering the eye; two pairs of lower labials in contact on the median line behind the symphysial; three or four pairs of large chin-shields, the anterior pair sometimes fused to a single azygous shield or preceded by an azygous shield. Scales in 13 rows, vertebrals strongly enlarged.. Ventrals 148–170; anal entire; subcaudals 88–120. Yellowish or pale brown above, yellowish beneath, mottled with dark brown; usually with large dark brown blotches, which may extend across the belly; a large dark brown blotch on the head; sides of head yellowish white, with three or more dark streaks radiating from the eye.

Total length 750 millim.; tail 220.

Pinang, Borneo, Philippines, Java, Moluccas.

a–b. ♀ (V. 167, 160; C. 106, 108).	Pinang.	Dr Cantor.
c. Hgr. (V. 165; C. 107).	Sarawak.	Sir H. Low [P.].
d. ♂ (V. 158, C. 120).	Baram, Sarawak.	C. Hose, Esq. [C.].
e. ♀ (V 163, C. 116).	Borneo.	
f. ♀ (V. 156; C 100).	Palawan.	A. Everett, Esq. [C.].
g. ♂ (V 162; C. 88).	Balabac.	A. Everett, Esq. [C.].
h. ♀ (V. 148; C. 98)	Philippines.	H. Cuming, Esq. [C.].
i. ♀ (V 150; C 99).	Java.	Leyden Museum
k. Hgr. (V. 155; C. 97).	Java	Dr. Horsfield [P].
l. ♀ skeleton.	Sarawak.	A. Everett, Esq [C.].

2. AMBLYCEPHALUS.

Amblycephalus, *Kuhl, Isis*, 1822, p. 474; *Boie, Isis*, 1827, p. 519; *Bouleng. Faun. Ind., Rept.* p. 514 (1890).
Pareas, *Wagler, Syst. Amph.* p. 181 (1830); *Dum. & Bibr. Erp. Gén.* vii. p 438 (1854); *Gunth. Cat. Col. Sn.* p. 184 (1858), and *Rept. Brit. Ind.* p. 326 (1864).
Dipsas, part, *Schleg. Phys. Serp.* ii. p. 257 (1837).
Leptognathus, part., *Jan, Elenco sist. Ofid.* p. 100 (1863).
Asthenodipsas, *Peters, Mon. Berl Ac.* 1864, p. 273.

Maxillary bone very short, deep, with 5 or 6 subequal teeth; mandibular teeth gradually decreasing in length. Head distinct from neck; eye moderate, with vertical pupil; nasal single. Body more or less compressed; scales smooth or feebly keeled, without pits, more or less oblique, in 15 rows, vertebral row enlarged or not. Ventrals rounded. Tail moderate or short; subcaudals in two rows.

South-eastern Asia

Synopsis of the Species.

I. A single shield between the nasal and the eye, præfrontal entering the eye; one or two labials entering the eye.

   A. Frontal at least as broad as long; symphysial in contact with an azygous chin-shield; second or third lower labial very large, usually in contact with its fellow; ventrals 148–176; subcaudals 26–55.

Six upper labials .... 1. *lævis*, p. 441.
Seven upper labials .... 2. *malaccanus*, p. 442.

   B. Frontal longer than broad; symphysial in contact with a pair of chin-shields; ventrals 188–194; subcaudals 70–87.
      3. *monticola*, p. 443.

II. Loreal and præocular distinct; eye separated from the labials by suboculars.

   A. Præfrontal entering the eye.

      1. Scales smooth; eye bordered by four or five shields, ventrals 136–151; subcaudals 37–47.
         4. *moellendorffii*, p. 443.

      2. Dorsal scales feebly keeled.

Eye bordered by five shields; ventrals 153–155; subcaudals 38–46 ...... 5. *andersonii*, p. 444.
Eye bordered by six shields . ... 6. *modestus*, p. 444.
Eye bordered by seven or eight shields; ventrals 164; subcaudals 51 ...... 7. *macularius*, p. 444.

   B. Præfrontal excluded from the eye.

Ventrals 138; subcaudals 53 .... 8. *margaritophorus*, [p. 445.
Ventrals 161–183; subcaudals 57–80 .. .. 9. *carinatus*, p. 445.

1. Amblycephalus lævis.

Amblycephalus lævis, *Boie, Isis*, 1827, p. 520; *Bouleng. Faun. Ind., Rept.* p. 415 (1890).
Dipsas lævis, *Schleg. Phys. Serp.* ii. p. 287, pl. xi. figs. 24 & 25 (1837).
Pareas lævis, *Dum. & Bibr.* vii. p. 442 (1854); *Gunth. Cat.* p. 185

(1858), and *Rept. Brit. Ind* p. 328 (1864); *Theob. Cat. Rept. Brit. Ind.* p. 203 (1876).

Leptognathus lævis, *Jan, Elenco*, p. 101 (1863), *and Icon. Gén.* 37, pl. vi. fig. 4 (1870).

Rostral a little broader than deep; internasals small, about one third the length of the præfrontals; latter entering the eye; frontal as long as broad or a little broader than long, as long as or a little longer than its distance from the end of the snout, two thirds the length of the parietals; supraocular very small; no præocular; loreal entering the eye; one or two postoculars; temporals 2+2; six upper labials, third and fourth, or third, fourth, and fifth entering the eye, sixth very long; symphysial in contact with a small azygous chin-shield; third lower labial very large, forming a suture with its fellow; two pairs of large chin-shields, broader than long. Scales in 15 rows, smooth, vertebrals enlarged. Ventrals 148–176; anal entire; subcaudals 34–69. Brown above, with irregular transverse blackish cross-bands; lower parts brownish or yellowish, spotted with brown or with transverse brown spots on the sides.

Total length 545 millim.; tail 65.

Java, Borneo, Natuna Islands, and Malacca.

a.	♀ (V. 167; C. 40).	Sarawak.	Rajah Brooke [P.]
b.	♂ (V. 156; C. 55).	Sarawak.	A. Everett, Esq. [C].
c.	♀ (V. 172; C. 34).	Mt. Kina Balu, N. Borneo.	A. Everett, Esq. [C.].
d.	♂ (V. 160; C. 50).	Borneo.	Sir E. Belcher
e.	♀ (V. 176; C. 46).	Borneo.	
f.	Yg. (V 148; C. 47).	Sirhassen, Gt. Natuna Id	A. Everett, Esq. [C.].
g.	♂ (V. 163, C. 55).	Java.	Leyden Museum.
h.	♂ (V. 170; C. 69).	Java	Hr. Fruhstorfer [C.].

2. Amblycephalus malaccanus.

Asthenodipsas malaccana, *Peters, Mon. Berl. Ac.* 1864, p. 273, pl. —. fig. 3; *v. Lidth de Jeude, in M. Weber, Zool. Ergebn.* i. p. 189, pl. xv. figs. 4–6 (1890).

Pareas dorsopictus, *Edeling, Nat. Tijdschr. Nederl. Ind.* xxxi. 1870, p. 383.

Amblycephalus malaccanus, *Bouleng. Proc. Zool. Soc.* 1892, p. 507.

Rostral a little broader than deep; internasals not more than half as long as the præfrontals; latter entering the eye; frontal as long as broad or a little broader than long, as long as or a little longer than its distance from the end of the snout, much shorter than the parietals; supraocular small; no præocular; loreal short, entering the eye; two postoculars; temporals 2+2, the two upper sometimes fused; seven upper labials, third and fourth entering the eye, seventh large; symphysial in contact with a small azygous shield; second or third lower labial very large, usually in contact with its fellow; two pairs of large chin-shields, broader than long. Scales smooth, in 15 rows; three median rows a little enlarged. Ventrals

154–170; anal entire; subcaudals 26–55. Yellowish or pale brown above, with rather irregular dark brown cross-bars, which are interrupted on the spine; vertebral scales yellowish; head sometimes whitish; sides and lower surface of neck black; belly whitish, uniform or speckled with dark brown.

Total length 440 millim.; tail 50.

Malay Peninsula, Sumatra, Borneo.

a.	♀ (V. 168; C. 40).	Sarawak.	A. Everett, Esq. [C.].
b.	♂ (V. 169; C. 55).	Mt. Dulit, Sarawak.	C. Hose, Esq. [C.].
c.	♀ (V. 170; C. 37).	Bongon, N. Borneo.	A. Everett, Esq. [C.].

3. Amblycephalus monticola. (PLATE XXIII. fig. 1.)

Dipsas monticola, *Cantor, Proc Zool. Soc.* 1839, p. 53.
Pareas monticola, *Gunth. Rept. Brit Ind* p. 327 (1864); *Anders. Proc. Zool. Soc.* 1871, p. 188, *Theob. Cat. Rept. Brit. Ind.* p. 203 (1876).
Amblycephalus monticola, *Bouleng. Faun. Ind., Rept.* p. 415, fig. (1890), *W. L. Sclater, Journ. As. Soc. Beng* lx. 1891, p. 247.

Rostral as deep as broad; internasals not more than half as long as the præfrontals; latter entering the eye; frontal a little longer than broad, longer than its distance from the end of the snout, a little shorter than the parietals; loreal entering the eye; a præocular below the loreal; two postoculars; temporals 2+3; seven upper labials, fourth or fourth and fifth entering the eye; three pairs of large chin-shields, anterior longer than broad and in contact with the symphysial. Scales in 15 rows, smooth; vertebrals enlarged, hexagonal. Ventrals 188–194; anal entire; subcaudals 70–87. Brown above, with vertical blackish bars on the sides; a black line from above the eye to the nape, and another from behind the eye to the angle of the mouth; yellowish below, dotted with brown.

Total length 600 millim.; tail 135.

Eastern Himalayas, Khasi and Naga hills, Nicobar Islands.

a.	♂ (V. 193; C. 84).	Naga hills, Assam.	Dr. Cantor. (Type.)
b.	♂ (V. 194; C. 87).	Khasi hills.	Dr. Griffith.
c.	♂ (V. 188; C. 75).	Darjeeling.	W. T. Blanford, Esq. [P.].

4. Amblycephalus moellendorffii.

Pareas carinata, part, *Gunth. Rept. Brit. Ind.* p. 326 (1864).
—— moellendorffii, *Boettg. Ber. Offenb. Ver.* 1885, p. 125, *and* 1888, p. 84, pl. ii. fig 1; *Cope, Proc. Ac. Philad.* 1894, p. 424 (1895).
Amblycephalus moellendorffii, *W. L. Sclater, List Sn Ind. Mus.* (1891).

Rostral nearly as deep as broad; internasals not more than half as long as the præfrontals; latter entering the eye; frontal as long as broad or a little longer than broad, longer than its distance from the end of the snout, shorter than the parietals; supraocular small;

loreal longer than deep; one præocular; a crescentic subocular; a small postocular sometimes present; temporals elongate, 2+3; seven or eight upper labials; three pairs of large chin-shields, anterior longer than broad and in contact with the symphysial. Scales smooth, equal, in 15 rows. Ventrals 136-151; anal entire; subcaudals 37-47. Brown or dark grey above, with irregular transverse series of black and white spots; a white nuchal collar may be present; lower parts white, spotted or dotted with black on the sides.

Total length 350 millim.; tail 57.

Canton, Hong Kong, Hainan, Cochinchina, Siam, Tenasserim.

a. Hgr. (V. 136; C. 44).	Hong Kong.	Indian Museum [E.].
b. ♀ (V. 136, C. 42).	Lao Mountains.	M. Mouhot [C.].
c. ♀ (V. 154; C. 38).	Camboja.	

5. Amblycephalus andersonii.

Pareas andersonii, *Bouleng. Ann. Mus. Genova,* (2) vi. 1888, p. 601, pl. v. fig 3.
Amblycephalus andersonii, *Bouleng. Faun. Ind., Rept.* p. 416 (1890).

Internasals about one third the length of the præfrontals; latter entering the eye; frontal slightly longer than broad, two thirds the length of the parietals; supraocular moderate, not quite half the width of the frontal; a small loreal; a præocular, a postocular, and a crescentic subocular, excluding the labials from the eye; temporals 2+3; seven upper labials, seventh very long; three pairs of large chin-shields. Scales in 15 rows, dorsals feebly keeled. Ventrals 153-155; anal entire; subcaudals 38-46. Dark brown above, with distant small black spots with a white dot; labial region spotted black and white; lower parts white, with closely-set squarish black spots.

Total length 350 millim.; tail 52.

Upper Burma.

6. Amblycephalus modestus.

Pareas modestus, *Theob. Journ. Linn. Soc* x. 1868, p. 55, *and Cat. Rept Brit. Ind.* p. 204 (1876).
Amblycephalus modestus, *Bouleng. Faun. Ind., Rept.* p. 416 (1890).

Internasals small; præfrontals large, entering the eye; supraocular small; loreal moderate; præoculars two, very small; postocular one, very small; a band-like subocular, excluding the labials from the orbit; two anterior temporals; seven upper labials, seventh very long; three pairs of large chin-shields. Scales in 15 rows, dorsals faintly keeled. Colour above uniform brown; below pale yellowish.

Pegu.

7. Amblycephalus macularius.

Pareas macularius, *Theob. Journ. Linn. Soc.* x. 1868, p. 54.
—— berdmorii, part., *Theob. Cat. Rept. As. Soc. Mus* 1868, p. 63.

Pareas margaritophorus (non Jan), *Theob. Cat. Rept. Brit. Ind.* p. 203 (1876)
Amblycephalus macularius, *Bouleng. Faun Ind., Rept* p 416 (1890); *W L Sclater, Journ As Soc. Beng.* lx. 1891, p. 248

Rostral a little broader than deep; internasals about half the length of the præfrontals; latter entering the eye; frontal a little longer than broad, longer than its distance from the end of the snout, a little shorter than the parietals; supraocular moderate, nearly half the width of the frontal; a small loreal; one præocular, one postocular, and three or more suboculars, excluding the labials from the eye; temporals much elongate, 2+2; seven upper labials, seventh very large; three pairs of large chin-shields. Scales in 15 rows, dorsals feebly keeled. Ventrals 164; anal entire; subcaudals 50. Pale brown or reddish brown above, with transverse series of dark brown and white spots; lower parts brownish white, spotted with brown.

Total length 405 millim.; tail 70
Tenasserim.

a. ♂ (V. 164; C. 50). Tenasserim. W Theobald, Esq. [C.] (Type)

8. Amblycephalus margaritophorus.

Leptognathus margaritophorus, *Jan, N. Arch. Mus.* ii. 1866, *Bull.* p. 8.

Loreal separated from the eye by the præocular; eye surrounded by four shields and the supraocular; seven upper labials, none entering the eye. Scales smooth, in 15 rows. Ventrals 138; anal entire; subcaudals 53. Blackish above, with transverse series of white spots; a white, black-edged nuchal collar.

Total length 250 millim.; tail 56.
Siam.

9. Amblycephalus carinatus.

Amblycephalus carinatus, *Boie, Isis,* 1828, p. 1035, *W. L. Sclater, Journ. As. Soc. Beng.* lx. 1891, p. 248; *Boettg Ber. Offenb. Ver. Nat.* 1892, p. 135.
Dipsas carinata, *Schleg. Phys. Serp.* ii. p. 285, pl. xi. figs. 26-28 (1837), *and Abbild* p. 135, pl. xlv. figs. 10-12 (1844)
Pareas carinata, *Dum. & Bibr.* vii. p. 439 (1854), *Gunth. Cat.* p. 185 (1858).
Leptognathus carinatus, *Jan, Elenco,* p. 101 (1863), *and Icon. Gén.* 37, pl iv fig 3 (1870)
Pareas carinata, part., *Gunth. Rept Brit. Ind.* p 326 (1864).[1]
—— berdmori, part., *Theob. Cat. Rept. As. Soc. Mus.* 1868, p. 63

Rostral small, deeper than broad; internasals two thirds the length of the præfrontals; frontal as long as broad or a little longer than broad, longer than its distance from the end of the snout, as long as or a little shorter than the parietals, loreal deeper than long; eye surrounded by five to seven shields in addition to the supraocular, viz., one or two præoculars, two or three suboculars, one or two postoculars; temporals 2+3 or 3+4; seven or eight upper labials; last very long, none entering the eye; first lower labial in contact with its fellow behind the symphysial; three pairs of large chin-shields, broader than long. Scales in 15 rows, three dorsal rows slightly enlarged and more or less distinctly keeled, the keels sometimes hardly distinguishable. Ventrals 161-183; anal entire; subcaudals 57-80. Yellowish or reddish brown above, with blackish transverse spots or more or less regular cross-bars interrupted on the spine; a black line on each side of the head behind the eye, confluent with an X-shaped black blotch on the nape; an oblique black line from below the eye to the anterior border of the last upper labials; yellow beneath, dotted or striolated with blackish, or with a median blackish line.

Total length 500 millim.; tail 115.

Cochinchina, Burma, Java.

a. ♂ (V. 163; C. 65).	Java.	Leyden Museum.	
b. ♂ (V. 175; C. 76).	Java.	J. C. Bowring, Esq. [P.]	
c, d. ♂ (V. 165, 178; C. 69, 80).	Java.		
e. ♀ (V. 162; C. 57)	Willis Mts., Kediri, Java.	Baron v. Huegel [C.].	
f. ♂ (V. 166; C. 71)	Lao Mountains.	M. Mouhot [C.].	
g. ♂ skeleton.	Batavia.	R. Kirkpatrick, Esq [P.].	

3. LEPTOGNATHUS.

Dipsas, part., *Wagler, Syst. Amph.* p. 180 (1830), *Schleg. Phys. Serp.* ii. p 257 (1837); *Cope, Proc. Ac. Philad.* 1860, p. 265.
Leptognathus, *Dum. & Bibr. Mém. Ac Sc.* xxiii. 1853, p 467, and *Erp. Gén.* vii. p. 473 (1854)
Cochliophagus, *Dum. & Bibr ll cc.* pp. 467, 478.
Stremmatognathus, *Dum. & Bibr. ll cc.* pp. 468, 520
Anholodon, *Dum. & Bibr. Erp. Gén.* vii. p. 1165.
Leptognathus, part., *Gunth. Cat Col. Sn* p. 177 (1858); *Jan, Elenco sist. Ofid.* p. 100 (1863); *Cope, Proc. Ac. Philad.* 1868, p. 107.
Dipsadomorus, part, *Jan, l. c.* p. 99
Mesopeltis, *Cope, Proc. Ac. Philad.* 1866, p. 318.
Asthenognathus, *Bocourt, Bull. Soc. Philom* (7) viii. 1884, p. 141.
Neopareas, *Gunth. Biol. C.-Am., Rept.* p. 178 (1895).

Maxillary bone with the toothed border more or less turned inwards; teeth 11 to 18, equal or middle longest; mandibular teeth, anterior longest, gradually decreasing in length. Head distinct from neck; eye moderate or large, with vertical pupil; nasal entire or divided. Body more or less compressed; scales smooth, without pits, more or less oblique, in 13 or 15 rows, vertebral row enlarged or not; ventrals rounded. Tail moderate or long; subcaudals in two rows.

Central and South America.

3. LEPTOGNATHUS.

Synopsis of the Species.

I. Scales in 13 rows, vertebrals enlarged

Eight (rarely nine) upper labials; ventrals 162-190; subcaudals 82-108 .   1. *catesbyi*, p. 449.
Ten or eleven upper labials; ventrals 186-220; subcaudals 112-145 ....   2. *pavonina*, p. 450.

II. Scales in 15 rows.

    A. First two or three pairs of lower labials in contact behind the symphysial; ventrals 162-192; subcaudals 85-91.

        1. Vertebral scales moderately enlarged.

Nine or ten upper labials   ....   3. *variegata*, p. 451.
Seven upper labials...............   4. *albifrons*, p. 451.

        2. Vertebral scales scarcely enlarged; nine or ten upper labials   ....   5. *brevifacies*, p. 452.

    B. First lower labial in contact with its fellow behind the symphysial.

        1. Vertebral scales very strongly enlarged, the largest nearly twice as broad as long; ventrals 184-188; subcaudals 82-94.

            a. Eight upper labials.

Rostral broader than deep; no præocular ....   6. *andiana*, p. 452.
Rostral nearly as deep as broad; one præocular .. ..   7. *elegans*, p. 452.

            b. Seven upper labials . .... .   8. *leucomelas*, p. 453.

        2. Vertebral scales moderately enlarged.

            a. Ventrals 156-180; subcaudals 45-90.

Subcaudals 53-90; three labials behind those entering the eye.... ....   9. *mikani*, p. 453.
Subcaudals 45-52; two labials behind those entering the eye............   10. *ventrimaculata*, p. 454.
Subcaudals 61; five labials behind those entering the eye........ ...   11. *inæquifasciata*, p. 455.

            b. Ventrals 164-197; subcaudals 110-114.

Two præoculars . . ..   13. *alternans*, p. 456.
No præocular ....   14. *viguieri*, p. 457.

c. Ventrals 204-215; subcaudals 122-135.

No præocular; two labials entering the
eye .... 16. *articulata*, p. 458.
A præocular above the loreal; three
labials entering the eye .... 17. *incerta*, p. 458.

3. Vertebral scales not enlarged.

Ventrals 149-159; subcaudals 41-51;
no azygous chin-shield ...... 12 *turgida*, p. 456.
Ventrals 195, subcaudals 129; three
azygous chin-shields .... 21. *bicolor*, p. 460.

C. Lower labials all separated by chin-shields.

1. No azygous anterior chin-shield, vertebral scales moderately enlarged.

Ventrals 164; subcaudals 113 ...... 15. *annulata*, p. 457.
Ventrals 212; subcaudals 121 ...... 18. *argus*, p. 458.

2. An azygous chin-shield in contact with the symphysial; vertebral scales not enlarged.

Ventrals 156; subcaudals 55 .... 19. *sanniola*, p. 459.
Ventrals 186-193; subcaudals 98-126. 20. *dimidiata*, p. 459.

TABLE SHOWING NUMBERS OF SCALES AND SHIELDS.

	Sc	V.	C.	Lab.
catesbyi	13	162-190	82-108	8-9
pavonina	13	186-220	112-145	10-11
variegata	15	180-192	88-91	9-10
albifrons	15	168	85	7
brevifacies	15	162-171	86-89	9-10
andiana	15	184	82	8
elegans	15	185	94	8
leucomelas	15	188	85	7
mikani	15	156-180	53-90	6-8
ventrimaculata	15	156-167	45-52	5-6
inæquifasciata	15	174	61	10
turgida	15	149-159	41-51	7
alternans	15	197	110	9
vigueri	15	196	114	9
annulata	15	164	113	7-8
articulata	15	215	135	9
incerta	15	204	122	9
argus	15	212	121	7
sanniola	15	156	55	8-9
dimidiata	15	185-195	98-126	9
bicolor	15	195	129	11

1. Leptognathus catesbyi.

Coluber catesbyi, *Sentzen, Meyer's Zool. Arch* ii. 1796, p. 66.
Dipsas catesbœi, *Boie, Isis*, 1827, p. 560, *Schleg. Phys Serp.* ii. p 279, pl. xi. figs. 21-23 (1837); *Tschudi, Faun. Per., Herp.* p. 57 (1845).
Stremmatognathus catesbyi, *Dum. & Bibr.* vii. p. 522 (1854); *Guichen in Casteln Anim Nouv Amér. Sud*, ii. *Rept.* p. 47, pl. ix. (1855)
Leptognathus catesbyi, part., *Gunth. Cat* p. 180 (1858).
—— catesbyi, *Cope, Proc. Ac. Philad.* 1868, p. 107; *Jan, Icon. Gén.* 37, pl ii. fig 2 (1870)
—— pavoninus (*non D. & B.*), *Jan, l. c.* pl. iv. fig. 1

Body slender, strongly compressed. Eye large. Rostral much broader than deep, scarcely visible from above; internasals one half to two thirds as long as the præfrontals; frontal as long as broad, as long as or a little longer than its distance from the end of the snout, shorter than the parietals; nasal entire or semidivided; loreal as long as deep or deeper than long, usually separated from the eye by two (rarely three) præoculars, sometimes fused with the lower præocular; two postoculars (rarely three, or fused into one); temporals 1+2, rarely 2+2, eight (rarely nine) upper labials, fourth and fifth, fifth and sixth, or fourth, fifth, and sixth entering the eye, first lower labial usually in contact with its fellow behind the symphysial; three pairs of chin-shields, the anterior longer than broad and rarely in contact with the symphysial. Scales in 13 rows, vertebrals very strongly enlarged, largest twice as broad as long. Ventrals 162-190; anal entire; subcaudals 82-108. Yellowish or reddish brown to dark brown above, whitish beneath, with large round or oval, white-edged dark brown or black spots disposed in pairs or alternating and extending from the vertebral line to the sides of the belly, head and neck blackish brown, with white or pale brownish cross-bars or annuli, the first forming a collar; belly more or less spotted or speckled with dark brown or black.

Total length 670 millim.; tail 200
Tropical South America.

a–c ♂ (V 179; C 94) & hgr (V. 179, 175, C. 87, 94).	Demerara Falls.	
d–e ♂ (V. 173; C. 93) & ♀ (V 175; C. 83)	Surinam.	Lidth de Jeude Collection.
f Hgr (V. 181, C. 93).	Para.	
g ♀ (V. 183; C. 96).	Para.	Dr. E. A. Goldi [P.]
h–i ♂ (V. 190; C. ?) & ♀ (V 178; C 97).	Pebas, Peru.	Mr. Hauxwell [C.].
k–l ♂ (V. 180, C. 87) & ♀ (V. 162; C. 80).	Moyobamba, Peru.	Mr. A. H Roff [C].
m–n. ♂ (V. 185, 180; C. 95, 94).	Sarayacu, Peru.	Mr. W. Davis [C.]; Messrs Veitch [P.].

o. ♀ (V. 179; C. 95).	Pozuzu, Peru.	Mr. W. Davis [C.]; Messrs. Veitch [P.].
p. Hgr. (V. 179; C. 91).	Pampa del Sacramento, Peru.	Mr W. Davis [C]; Messrs. Veitch [P.].
q. Hgr. (V. 178; C. 92).	Madre de Dios, Bolivia.	
r-s. ♂ (V. 189; C. 108) & hgr. (V. 171; C. 90).	Canelos, Ecuador.	Mr. Buckley [C.].
t. ♂ (V. 176; C. 97).	Guayaquil.	Mr Fraser [C.]
u. Skull of o.		

2. Leptognathus pavonina.

Dipsas pavonina, *Schleg. Phys. Serp.* ii. p. 280 (1837).
Leptognathus pavoninus, *Dum. & Bibr.* vii. p. 474 (1854); *Günth. Cat.* p. 179 (1858); *Cope, Proc Ac. Philad.* 1868, p. 107.
—— catesbyi, part., *Gunth l c* p 180
—— copii, *Gunth. Ann. & Mag. N. H.* (4) ix. 1872, p. 30.

Body slender, strongly compressed. Eye large. Rostral broader than deep, not or but scarcely visible from above; internasals one half to two thirds as long as the præfrontals; frontal as long as broad, nearly as long as its distance from the end of the snout, much shorter than the parietals; nasal entire or semidivided; loreal deeper than long, bordering the eye, sometimes fused with the nasal or with a præocular; a præocular above the loreal; two or three postoculars; temporals 1+2 or 2 or 3; ten or eleven upper labials, fifth and sixth, fourth to sixth, or fifth to seventh entering the eye; first lower labial in contact with its fellow behind the symphysial; three pairs of chin-shields, anterior longer than broad. Scales in 13 rows, vertebrals more or less enlarged, largest not twice as broad as long. Ventrals 186–220; anal entire; subcaudals 112–145. Yellowish brown or cream-colour above, with very large elongate, dark brown, white-edged spots, disposed, singly or in pairs, at regular distances, the interspaces much shorter than the spots; these descend to the sides of the belly, the anterior even coalescing beneath and forming complete rings; head dark brown, spotted with white, or snout and temples white.

Total length 700 millim.; tail 230.

Guianas, Brazil, Ecuador, Bolivia.

a. ♀ (V. 190; C. 112).	Berbice.	Lady Essex [P.].
b-c. ♂ (V. 210, 217; C. 129, 125).	Demerara.	
d. ♂ (V. 218; C. 140).	Surinam.	Lidth de Jeude Collection. (Type of *L. copii.*)
e. Hgr. (V. 203; C. 114).	Para.	Dr. E. A. Goldi [P.].
f. ♀ (V. 186, C. 113).	W. Ecuador.	Mr. Fraser [C.].
g. ♂ (V. 210; C. 131).	Madre de Dios, Bolivia.	

3. Leptognathus variegata.

Leptognathus variegatus, *Dum. & Bibr* vii. p. 477 (1854); *Gunth. Cat.* p. 179 (1858); *Cope, Proc. Ac. Philad.* 1868, p 107.
Dipsadomorus variegatus, *Jan, Elenco,* p. 100 (1863), *and Icon. Gén.* 37, pl. iii. fig. 1 (1872).

Body strongly compressed. Eye large. Rostral broader than deep, scarcely visible from above; internasals about half as long as the præfrontals; frontal nearly as long as broad, as long as its distance from the end of the snout, shorter than the parietals; nasal semidivided; loreal deeper than long, bordering the eye; no præocular; præfrontal entering the eye; two or three postoculars; temporals 2+3; nine or ten upper labials, third, fourth, and fifth, or third, fourth, fifth, and sixth entering the eye; first two pairs of lower labials forming a suture behind the symphysial; two pairs of chin-shields, broader than long. Scales in 15 rows, vertebrals moderately enlarged. Ventrals 180–192; anal entire; subcaudals 88–91. Brown above, with narrow dark brown cross-bands formed of confluent spots, some dark brown spots on the back of the head; labials dark-edged; lower parts whitish, dotted or spotted with brown and with a large dark brown spot on each side as a prolongation of the dorsal cross-bands.

Total length 640 millim.; tail 170.

Guianas.

a, b. ♂ (V. 180; C 91) & hgr   British Guiana
    (V. 186, C. 90)

4. Leptognathus albifrons.

Dipsadomorus albifrons, *Sauvage, Bull. Soc. Philom.* (7) viii. 1884, p. 145.

Body slender, strongly compressed. Eye large. Rostral broader than deep, scarcely visible from above; internasals half as long as the præfrontals; frontal slightly longer than broad, longer than its distance from the end of the snout, shorter than the parietals; nasal divided; loreal as long as deep, bordering the eye; a small præocular above the loreal; two postoculars; temporals 1+2 or 2+2; seven upper labials, fourth and fifth or third, fourth, and fifth entering the eye; two or three pairs of lower labials in contact with each other behind the symphysial; three pairs of chin-shields, anterior a little broader than long. Scales in 15 rows, vertebrals rather feebly enlarged. Ventrals 168; anal entire; subcaudals 85. Pale brownish above, with brown dark and light edged transverse spots or cross-bands, some of which are broken on the vertebral line and alternate; a brown spot on each side between every two bands, head whitish, with two elongate brown spots on the parietal shields; belly whitish, speckled with brown.

Total length 450 millim.; tail 115.

Brazil

a ♂ (V. 168; C. 85).   Blumenan, Santa Catharina.

5. Leptognathus brevifacies.

Tropidodipsas brevifacies, *Cope, Proc. Ac. Philad.* 1866, p. 127.
Leptognathus brevifacies, *Cope, Proc. Ac. Philad.* 1868, p. 108.
Dipsadomorus fasciatus, *Bocourt, Bull. Soc. Philom.* (7) viii. 1884, p. 135.
Leptognathus torquatus, *Cope, Proc. Amer. Philos. Soc.* xxii 1885, p. 172.

Eye large. Nasal divided; loreal usually entering the eye; one or two præoculars; three postoculars; nine or ten upper labials, fourth and fifth entering the eye; two anterior pairs of lower labials in contact with each other behind the symphysial; four pairs of chin-shields. Scales in 15 rows, vertebrals scarcely enlarged. Ventrals 162–171; anal entire; subcaudals 86–89. Black, with narrow whitish annuli.

Total length 153 millim.; tail 57.

Yucatan.

6. Leptognathus andiana. (Plate XXIII. fig. 2.)

Body strongly compressed. Eye large. Rostral broader than deep, scarcely visible from above; internasals half as long as the præfrontals; frontal as long as broad, as long as its distance from the end of the snout, shorter than the parietals, nasal divided; loreal as long as deep, bordering the eye; no præocular; præfrontal entering the eye; two postoculars; temporals 2+3; eight upper labials, third and fourth entering the eye; first lower labial in contact with its fellow behind the symphysial; two pairs of chinshields, first as long as broad. Scales in 15 rows, vertebrals strongly enlarged, the largest twice as broad as long, many divided into two. Ventrals 184; anal entire; subcaudals 82. Yellowish above, with interrupted fine black longitudinal lines; large vertically elliptic black, white-edged blotches on the side extending to the vertebral line and alternating with those on the other side, a large ∩-shaped black marking on the head; lower parts uniform white.

Total length 255 millim.; tail 60.

Ecuador.

a. Yg. (V. 184; C. 82). Quito.

7. Leptognathus elegans. (Plate XXIII. fig. 3.)

Leptognathus mikanii (*non Schleg.*), *Gunth. Biol. C.-Am., Rept.* p. 141 (1895).

Body strongly compressed. Eye large. Rostral nearly as deep as broad, not visible from above; internasals one third the length of the præfrontals; frontal slightly broader than long, as long as its distance from the end of the snout, much shorter than the parietals; nasal entire; loreal once and a half as long as deep, bordering the eye; a præocular above the loreal; two postoculars; temporals

2+3; eight upper labials, fourth and fifth entering the eye; first lower labial in contact with its fellow behind the symphysial; four pairs of chin-shields, anterior slightly longer than broad. Scales in 15 rows, vertebrals strongly enlarged, the largest twice as broad as long. Ventrals 185; anal entire; subcaudals 94. Pale brown above, with numerous blackish-brown cross-bands, lighter in the middle, the anterior as if divided into two; head much spotted and marbled with blackish; lower parts whitish, spotted with blackish brown.

Total length 310 millim.; tail 80.

Isthmus of Tehuantepec.

a. Hgr. (V. 185; C. 94). Tehuantepec. M. F. Sumichrast [C.].

8. Leptognathus leucomelas. (PLATE XXIV. fig. 1.)

Leptognathus leucomelas, *Bouleng. Ann. & Mag. N. H.* (6) xvii. 1896, p 17.

Body strongly compressed. Eye large. Rostral a little broader than deep, not visible from above; internasals half as long as the præfrontals; frontal as long as broad, as long as its distance from the end of the snout, shorter than the parietals; nasal divided; loreal once and a half as long as broad, bordering the eye; no præocular; præfrontal entering the eye; two postoculars; temporals 1+2; seven upper labials, third and fourth entering the eye; first lower labial in contact with its fellow behind the symphysial; three pairs of chin-shields, first longer than broad Scales in 15 rows, vertebrals strongly enlarged, the largest nearly twice as broad as long. Ventrals 188; anal entire; subcaudals 85. Dark grey above, spotted with black, with black, white-edged annuli. some of which are broken on the vertebral line; head blackish, speckled with white; belly white, speckled and spotted with black and irregularly barred by the black annuli.

Total length 570 millim.; tail 130.

Colombia.

a. ♀ (V. 188; C. 85). Near Buenaventura Mr. W. F. H. Rosenberg [C.]. (Type).

9. Leptognathus mikani.

Dipsas mikanii, *Schleg Phys. Serp.* ii. p. 277 (1837).
Anholodon mikanii, *Dum & Bibr* vii p 1165 (1854).
Leptognathus mikanii, *Gunth Cat.* p. 178 (1858), *Cope, Proc. Ac. Philad.* 1868, pp 108 & 135; *Jan, Icon. Gén.* 37, pl. vi. fig. 3 (1870); *Gunth. Ann. & Mag. N. H.* (4) ix. 1872, p. 49; *Bouleng. Ann & Mag N H.* (5) xviii. 1886, p. 436
—— oreas, *Cope, l. c* pp 108 & 109.
—— andrei, *Sauvage, Bull. Soc. Philom.* (7) viii. 1884, p. 146 *.
—— garmani, *Cope, Proc. Amer. Philos Soc.* xxiv. 1887, p. 60.

Body feebly compressed. Eye moderate. Rostral broader than

---

* I am indebted to M. Bocourt for notes on the type specimen.

deep, scarcely visible from above; internasals not more than half as long as the præfrontals; frontal as long as broad, or slightly broader than long, as long as or shorter than its distance from the end of the snout, much shorter than the parietals; nasal entire or semidivided, rarely divided; loreal as long as deep or a little longer than deep, bordering the eye; a præocular rarely present; præfrontal usually entering the eye; two or three postoculars; temporals 1 or 2+2 or 3; seven or eight, rarely six, upper labials, third, third and fourth, fourth and fifth, or third, fourth, and fifth entering the eye; first lower labial in contact with its fellow behind the symphysial; two to four pairs of chin-shields, anterior as long as broad or a little longer than broad. Scales in 15 rows, vertebrals feebly or moderately enlarged. Ventrals 156–180; anal entire (rarely divided); subcaudals 53–90. Pale brown above, with small darker spots and dots, and with light-edged blackish-brown cross-bands or alternating transverse spots; head with dark brown, light-edged spots; yellowish beneath, spotted or dotted with dark brown.

Total length 720 millim.; tail 170.

Brazil, Ecuador, Colombia.

A. Dark cross-bands wide; belly dotted with brown, or with two series of small brown spots. (*L. milani*, Schleg.)

a, b ♂ (V. 160; C. 61) & ♀ (V. 168; C. 55).	Rio Grande do Sul	Dr. H. v. Ihering [C.].
c. Yg. (V. 167, C. 70).	Brazil.	

B. Cross-bands narrow; belly as in the preceding.

a, b-c. ♂ (V. 163; C. 65), hgr. (V. 172; C. 62), & yg. (V. 177; C. 60).	Pernambuco.	Zoological Society.
d, e. ♀ (V. 170, 172; C. 61, 63).	Bahia.	Dr. O. Wucherer [C.].
f. Hgr. (V. 156; C. 63).	Rio Janeiro.	A. Fry, Esq. [P.].
g. ♀ (V. 158; C. 73).	Porto Real, Prov. Rio Janeiro.	M. Hardy du Dréneuf [C.].
h. Hgr. (V. 161; C. 63).	Brazil.	
i. ♀ skeleton.	Brazil.	Dr. Günther [P.].

C. Ventrals with large dark brown or black spots. (*L. oreas*, Cope.)

a–c. ♀ (V. 179, 175, 173; C. 73, 66, 76).	W. Ecuador.	Mr. Fraser [C.].
d. ♀ (V. 164; C. 65).	Pallatanga, Ecuador.	Mr. C. Buckley [C.].

10. **Leptognathus ventrimaculata.** (Plate XXIV. fig. 2.)

Leptognathus ventrimaculatus, *Bouleng. Ann. & Mag. N. H.* (5) xvi. 1885, p. 87; *Peracca, Boll. Mus. Torino*, x. 1895, no. 195, p. 21

Body feebly compressed. Eye moderate. Rostral broader than

deep, scarcely visible from above; internasals not more than half as long as the præfrontals; frontal as long as broad, as long as or a little shorter than its distance from the end of the snout, much shorter than the parietals; nasal entire or semidivided; loreal once and a half to twice as long as deep, bordering the eye; a præocular rarely present, the præfrontal usually entering the eye; two postoculars; temporals 1+2; five or six upper labials, third or third and fourth entering the eye; first lower labial in contact with its fellow behind the symphysial; three or four pairs of chin-shields, anterior as long as broad. Scales in 15 rows, vertebrals strongly enlarged, the largest not twice as broad as long Ventrals 156–167; anal entire; subcaudals 45–52. Body with large dark brown or blackish-brown transverse spots, or with two alternating series of such spots, separated by narrow pale brownish or whitish interspaces; head with the dark spots so crowded as to appear dark brown or blackish, veined with brownish white; lower parts white, largely spotted with dark brown or black.

Total length 525 millim.; tail 105.

Southern Brazil, Paraguay.

a–b.	♂ (V. 156, C. 48) & ♀ (V. 161; C. 45).	Rio Grand do Sul.	Dr. H. v. Ihering [C.]. (Types)
c.	♂ (V. 158; C. 49).	Rio Grande.	Dr. H. v. Ihering [C.].
d–f.	♀ (V. 158, 156, 164, C. 51, 51, 50).	Asuncion, Paraguay.	Dr. J. Bohls [C.].

11. Leptognathus inæquifasciata.

Cochliophagus inæquifasciatus, *Dum. & Bibr.* vii p. 480 (1854).
Legtognathus inæquifasciatus, *Jan, Elenco*, p. 100 (1863), *and Icon. Gén.* 37, pl. iv. fig. 2 (1870).

Body feebly compressed. Eye moderate. Rostral nearly as deep as broad; internasals two thirds the length of the præfrontals, scarcely visible from above; frontal as long as broad, as long as its distance from the end of the snout, shorter than the parietals; nasal divided; loreal once and a half as long as deep, bordering the eye; no præocular, præfrontal entering the eye; three or four postoculars; temporals 1+3; ten upper labials, fourth and fifth entering the eye; first lower labial in contact with its fellow behind the symphysial; two pairs of chin-shields, anterior a little longer than broad. Scales in 15 rows, vertebrals moderately enlarged. Ventrals 174; anal entire; subcaudals 61 Pale brown above, with large irregular transverse dark brown spots anteriorly and narrow dark brown cross-bars posteriorly; upper head-shields marbled with brown; a round dark spot on the occiput; whitish beneath, with a lateral series of small brown spots.

Total length 445 millim.; tail 76.

Brazil (?).

12. Leptognathus turgida.

Cochliophagus inæquifasciatus (*non D. & B*), *Cope, Proc. Ac. Philad.* 1862, p. 347.
Leptognathus turgida, *Cope, Proc Ac. Philad* 1868, pp. 108 and 136.
—— mikanii (*non Schleg.*), *Boettg. Zeitschr. ges. Naturw.* lviii. 1885, p. 238; *Peracca, Boll. Mus. Torin.* x. 1895, no. 195, p. 21.

Body feebly compressed. Eye moderate. Rostral broader than deep, scarcely visible from above; internasals two thirds the length of the præfrontals; frontal slightly broader than long, as long as its distance from the end of the snout, much shorter than the parietals; nasal divided; loreal once and a half as long as deep, bordering the eye; no præocular, præfrontal entering the eye; two postoculars; temporals 1+2; seven upper labials, third and fourth entering the eye; first lower labial in contact with its fellow behind the symphysial; four pairs of chin-shields, anterior a little longer than broad. Scales in 15 rows, vertebrals not enlarged. Ventrals 149–159; anal entire; subcaudals 41–51. Pale brown above, with a dorsal series of large transverse black, white-edged spots not extending down the sides, and a lateral series of smaller spots—the first spot forming a collar, descending to the sides of the neck; a cross-shaped black marking on the head, with two large spots on each side of it; lower parts white, with an irregular series of small black spots on each side.

Total length 255 millim.; tail 43.

Paraguay, Matto Grosso.

a. Hgr. (V. 150; C. 44). Asuncion, Paraguay. Dr J. Bohls [C.].
b. Yg. (V. 152; C 45). Corumba, Matto Grosso. S. Moore, Esq. [P.].

13. Leptognathus alternans.

Leptognathus alternans, *Fischer, Jahrb. Hamb. Wiss Anst.* ii. 1885, p. 105, pl. iv, fig. 8.

Body slender, strongly compressed. Eye large. Rostral broader than deep, scarcely visible from above; internasals half as long as the præfrontals; frontal as long as broad, as long as its distance from the end of the snout, much shorter than the parietals; nasal entire; loreal deeper than long, separated from the eye by two præoculars; two postoculars; temporals 1+2; nine upper labials, fourth, fifth, and sixth entering the eye; first lower labial in contact with its fellow behind the symphysial, three pairs of chinshields, anterior a little longer than broad. Scales in 15 rows, vertebrals feebly enlarged. Ventrals 197; anal entire; subcaudals 110. Pale reddish brown above, with two series of elongate oval, dark brown, light-edged spots, opposed to each other or alternating, narrowly separated on the vertebral line, and descending to the sides of the ventrals; neck dark brown above; head pale brown, with a large, oval, dark brown, white-edged spot on each parietal shield; lower parts whitish, dotted and lineolated with dark brown.

Total length 630 millim.; tail 195.

Brazil.

a. ♂ (V. 197; C. 110).   Santos.   Dr. J. G. Fischer. (Type.)

14. Leptognathus viguieri.

Leptognathus viguieri, *Bocourt, Bull. Soc. Philom.* (7) viii. 1884, p. 136.

? Leptognathus brevis, *Dum. & Bibr.* vii. p. 476 (1854) *.

Eye large. Nasal divided; loreal bordering the eye; no præocular, but a small subocular below the loreal; three postoculars; nine upper labials, fourth and fifth entering the eye; first lower labial in contact with its fellow behind the symphysial; two pairs of chin-shields. Scales in 15 rows, vertebrals feebly enlarged. Ventrals 196; anal entire; subcaudals 114. Reddish yellow above, with large brown spots, mostly forming complete annuli; head purplish black above; temples and nape yellow.

Total length 570 millim., tail 170.

Isthmus of Darien.

15. Leptognathus annulata.

Leptognathus annulatus, *Gunth. Ann. & Mag. N. H.* (4) ix. 1872, p. 30, and *Biol. C.-Am., Rept.* p. 141, pl. xlix. fig. C (1895).

Body very slender, strongly compressed. Eye large. Rostral small, nearly as deep as broad, not visible from above; internasals one third the length of the præfrontals; frontal a little longer than broad, a little longer than its distance from the end of the snout, much shorter than the parietals; nasal entire; loreal once and a half as long as deep, bordering the eye; no præocular; præfrontal entering the eye; a small subocular below the loreal; two postoculars; temporals 1+2; seven or eight upper labials, fifth and sixth entering the eye; four pairs of chin-shields, the anterior very small and in contact with the symphysial, the second pair large and much longer than broad. Scales in 15 rows, vertebrals moderately enlarged. Ventrals 164; anal entire; subcaudals 113. Body with dark brown rings, separated by interspaces of pale brown above, of white beneath; head spotted with brown, with two elongate large brown spots on the parietal shields.

Total length 440 millim.; tail 150.

Costa Rica.

a. Hgr. (V. 164; C. 113).   Cartago.   (Type.)

---

* M. Bocourt, who has kindly supplied me with additional information on the type of *L. viguieri*, informs me that the type of *L. brevis* had disappeared from the Paris Museum as early as 1862.

16. Leptognathus articulata.

Dipsas brevis (non *D. & B.*), *Cope, Proc. Ac. Philad.* 1860, p. 266.
Leptognathus articulata, *Cope, Proc. Ac. Philad.* 1868, pp. 107 & 135.

Body very slender, strongly compressed. Eye large. Loreal bordering the eye; no præocular; præfrontal entering the eye; two postoculars; temporals 2+3, nine upper labials, fourth and fifth entering the eye; first lower labial in contact with its fellow behind the symphysial; four pairs of chin-shields. Scales in 15 rows, vertebrals enlarged. Ventrals 215; anal entire; subcaudals 135. Yellow, with broad brown entire annuli, which are wider anteriorly than posteriorly, and wider than the interspaces between them; top of head, sides, and upper labials in front of the eye, and all the lower labials, brown; rest of head with numerous short lines on the snout, yellow or white.

Total length 675 millim.; tail 225.

Costa Rica.

17. Leptognathus incerta.

Leptognathus incertus, *Jan, Elenco*, p. 101 (1863), and *Icon. Gén.* 37, pl. vi. fig. 1 (1870).

Body slender, strongly compressed. Eye large. Rostral broader than deep, scarcely visible from above; internasals two thirds the length of the præfrontals; frontal slightly longer than broad, as long as its distance from the end of the snout, shorter than the parietals; nasal entire; loreal slightly deeper than long, bordering the eye; a præocular above the loreal; two postoculars; temporals 1, 2, or 3+2 or 3; nine upper labials, fourth, fifth, and sixth entering the eye; first lower labial in contact with the symphysial; three pairs of chin-shields, anterior a little longer than broad. Scales in 15 rows, vertebrals moderately enlarged. Ventrals 204; anal entire; subcaudals 122. Pale brown above, with large dark brown, black-edged cross-bars or alternating spots; a dark brown spot on each parietal shield; pale brown beneath, with interrupted darker streaks.

Total length 720 millim.; tail 220.

Guianas, Brazil.

a. ♂ (V. 204; C. 122). S. José dos Campos, Prov. S. Paulo, Brazil. Mr. A. Thomson [P.].

18. Leptognathus argus.

Leptognathus argus, *Cope, Journ. Ac. Philad.* (2) viii. 1876, p. 130.

Rostral very small, triangular, as deep as broad; loreal and præfrontal bordering the eye in front; two postoculars; temporals 1+2; seven upper labials, fourth, fifth, and sixth entering the eye; three pairs of chin-shields, anterior longer than broad and in contact with the symphysial. Scales in 15 rows, vertebrals not abruptly enlarged. Ventrals 212; anal entire; subcaudals 121. Greenish-ash above, with two series of alternating light ocelli with black borders; a large black-bordered ocellus on the nape; head vermiculated with black; lips yellow, with black specks; below yellow, with a lateral series of black-edged ocelli, like those of the back.

Total length 345 millim., tail 104.

Costa Rica.

L. pictiventris, Cope, *l. c.*, from the same locality, appears to agree in structure with the preceding, differing, however, considerably in coloration. The specimen is besides stated to be in bad condition.

19. Leptognathus sanniola.

Mesopeltis sanniolus, *Cope, Proc. Ac. Philad* 1866, p. 318.

Snout contracted from under the orbit; eye large. Rostral not visible from above; frontal nearly twice as long as broad in the middle, nearly as long as the parietals; nasal divided, loreal narrow, erect; two very narrow præoculars, the inferior very small; eight or nine upper labials, fourth and fifth entering the eye; anterior chin-shields united into an azygous ovoid shield which is in contact with the symphysial; posterior chin-shields quite small. Scales in 15 rows, vertebrals not enlarged. Ventrals 156; anal divided; subcaudals 55. Above light brown, with one series of small dark brown spots on the spine, separated by intervals nearly equal to their diameter; a broad nuchal band continued to middle of frontal shield; lips and sides with numerous pale brown spots; beneath with minute brown punctulations.

Total length 280 millim. (tail not included).

Yucatan.

20. Leptognathus dimidiata.

Leptognathus dimidiatus, *Gunth. Ann. & Mag. N. H.* (4) ix. 1872, p. 31.

Petalognathus multifasciatus, *Bocourt, Bull. Soc. Philom* (7) viii. 1884, p. 139.

Mesopeltis multifasciatus, *Cope, Proc. Amer. Philos. Soc.* xxii. 1885, p. 172.

Leptognathus (Asthenognathus) grandoculis, *F Mull. Verh. Nat. Ges. Basel*, viii 1887, p 271, pl i fig. 2.

Mesopeltis dimidiatus, *Gunth. Biol. C.-Am*, *Rept.* p. 143, pl. li figs. A & B (1895).

Body very slender, strongly compressed. Eye large. Rostral as deep as broad, scarcely visible from above; internasals not more than half as long as the præfrontals; frontal a little longer than broad, as long as its distance from the end of the snout, shorter than the parietals, nasal entire; loreal once and a half as long as deep, bordering the eye; no præocular; præfrontal entering the eye; two postoculars, temporals 1+2; nine upper labials, fifth and sixth or fifth, sixth, and seventh entering the eye; symphysial in contact with a small azygous chin-shield followed by three pairs of chin-shields, the anterior longer than broad. Scales in 15 rows, vertebrals not enlarged. Ventrals 185-195; anal entire; subcaudals 98-126. Body with blackish-brown or reddish dark-edged annuli separated by narrower interspaces which may be whitish, black-spotted, or dark brown above and whitish powdered with brown beneath; head dark brown above.

Total length 620 millim.; tail 205.

Central America.

a	♀ (V. 186; C. 100).	Mexico.	(Type.)
b.	♂ (V. 188; C 114).	Hacienda Rosa de Jericho, Nicaragua, 3250 ft.	Dr. E. Rothschuh [C.].

21. Leptognathus bicolor.

Neopareas bicolor, *Gunth. Biol. C.-Am., Rept.* p. 178, pl. lvi. fig. C (1895).

Body very slender, very strongly compressed. Eye large. Rostral broader than deep, scarcely visible from above; internasals two thirds the length of the præfrontals; frontal as long as broad, as long as its distance from the end of the snout, shorter than the parietals; nasal entire; loreal as long as deep, bordering the eye; a præocular above the loreal; three postoculars; temporals 2+3; eleven upper labials, fourth to seventh entering the eye; first lower labial in contact with and partially fused with its fellow behind the symphysial; three large azygous chin-shields, followed by a pair. Scales in 15 rows, vertebrals not enlarged. Ventrals 195; anal entire; subcaudals 129. Annulate black and white, the white annuli much narrower than the black ones, the first across the occiput; the snout, chin, and upper head-shields black.

Total length 565 millim., tail 190.

Nicaragua.

a	♂ (V. 195; C. 129).	Chontalez, Nicaragua.	R. A. Rix, Esq. [C.]; W. M. Crowfoot, Esq. [P.]. (Type.)

4. DIPSAS.

Dipsas, *Laur. Syn. Rept.* p. 89 (1768).
Bungarus, part., *Oppel, Ann. Mus.* xvi. 1810, p. 391.
Dipsas, part., *Boie, Isis*, 1827, p 548; *Wagl Syst Amph.* p. 180 (1830); *Schleg. Phys Serp.* ii. p. 257 (1837); *Cope, Proc. Ac. Philad.* 1860, p. 265.
Dipsadomorus, *Dum. & Bibr. Mém. Ac. Sc.* xxiii. 1853, p. 407, and *Erp. Gén.* vii. p 468 (1854).
Leptognathus, part., *Gunth. Cat. Col Sn.* p. 177 (1858); *Cope, Proc. Ac. Philad.* 1868, p. 107.
Dipsadomorus, part., *Jan, Elenco sist. Ofid.* p. 99 (1863).

Maxillary bone with the toothed border turned inwards, forming a suborbital lamina, widening behind; teeth 13 or 14, subequal; mandibular teeth, anterior longest, gradually decreasing in length; pterygoids toothless. Head distinct from neck; eye large, with vertical pupil; nasal entire. Body strongly compressed; scales smooth, without pits, oblique, in 13 rows, vertebral row enlarged; ventrals rounded. Tail long; subcaudals in two rows.

South America.

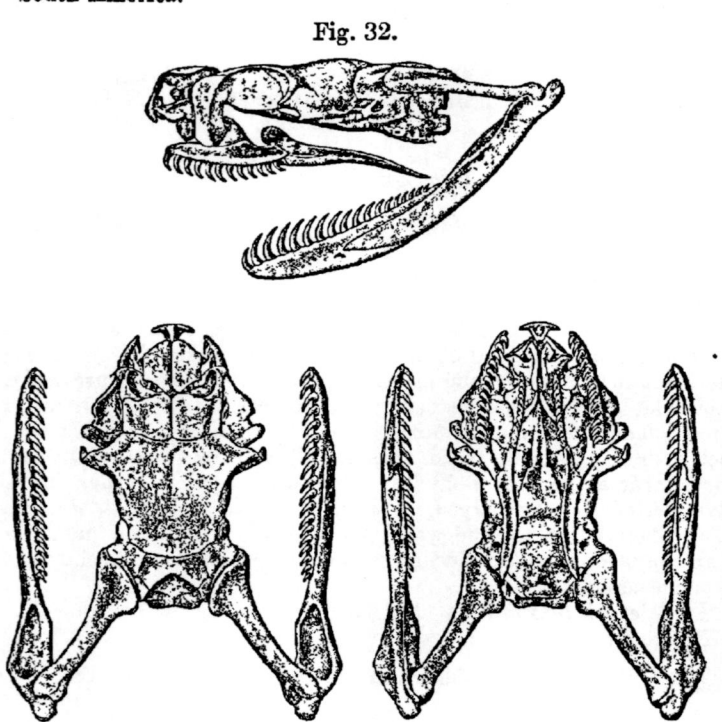

Fig. 32.

Skull of *Dipsas bucephala*.

1. Dipsas bucephala.

Seba, Thes. i. pl. xliii. fig. 4 (1734).
Dipsas indica, *Laur. Syn. Rept.* p. 90 (1768).
Coluber bucephalus, *Shaw, Zool.* iii p. 422, pl. cix. (1802).
Bungarus bucephalus, *Oppel, Ann Mus.* xvi 1810, p. 392.
Dipsas bucephala, *Schinz, Cuv. Thierr.* ii. p 117 (1822); *Schleg. Phys. Serp.* ii. p. 281, pl. xi. figs. 16–18 (1837).
Dipsadomorus indicus, *Dum. & Bibr.* vii. p. 470, pl. lxvii. (1854).
Leptognathus indicus, *Gunth Cat.* p. 180 (1858).
Dipsadomorus bucephalus, *Jan, Elenco,* p. 99 (1863), *and Icon. Gén.* 37, pl. ii. fig. 1 (1870).
Leptognathus bucephalus, *Cope, Proc. Ac. Philad.* 1868, p. 107.

? Leptognathus (Dipsadomorus) cisticeps, *Boettg. Zeitschr. ges. Naturw.* lviii 1885, p 237.

Rostral as deep as broad or a little deeper than broad, scarcely visible from above; internasals not more than half the length of the præfrontals; frontal as long as broad or slightly longer than broad, as long as or shorter than its distance from the end of the snout, much shorter than the parietals; nasal entire; loreal not or but scarcely longer than deep, entering the eye; a præocular above the loreal; two postoculars; temporals 1 or 2+2 or 3, eight to ten upper labials, fourth and fifth, fifth and sixth, or fourth, fifth, and sixth entering the eye; two lower labials in contact with each other behind the symphysial; two to four pairs of chin-shields. Scales in 13 rows, vertebral row strongly enlarged. Ventrals 171–200; anal entire; subcaudals 91–116. Yellowish, greyish, or reddish brown above, with more or less distinct dark cross-bands or triangular spots on the sides; a series of whitish spots, corresponding to the light interspaces along each side, partly upon the ventral shields; head with dark, light-edged spots; lower parts brownish, speckled with white.

Total length 680 millim.; tail 250.

Tropical South America.

a. ♂ (V 198, C. 116).	Demerara.		Zoological Society.
b. Hgr. (V. 185; C. 105).	Bahia.		Dr. O. Wucherer [C.].
c. Hgr. (V. 191; C. 106).	Ecuador.		Mr. C. Buckley [C.].
d-e ♂ (V 171; C. 92) & ♀ (V. 177; C. 91).	Moyobamba, Peru.	N E.	Mr A H. Roff [C].
f. ♀ (V. 191; C. 99).	Charocampa, Bolivia.		
g. ♀ (V. 194; C. 101).	—— ?		Dr. Günther [P.].
h. Skull of e.			

5. PSEUDOPAREAS.

Leptognathus, part., *Jan, Elenco sist. Ofid.* p. 100 (1863).

Head distinct from neck; eye moderate, with vertical pupil. Body cylindrical; scales smooth, in 15 rows, vertebral row slightly enlarged; ventrals rounded; subcaudals in two rows.

South America.

1. Pseudopareas vagus.

Leptognathus vagus, *Jan, l. c., and Icon. Gén.* 37, pl. vi. fig. 2 (1870); Cope, *Proc. Ac. Philad.* 1868, p 136.
Pareas vagus, *Boettg. Ber. Offenb. Ver. Nat* 1888, p. 145.

Rostral nearly as deep as broad; internasals shorter than the præfrontals; frontal a little longer than broad, as long as its distance from the end of the snout, much shorter than the parietals; loreal twice as long as deep, entering the eye; a small præocular between the loreal and the supraocular; two postoculars; temporals 1+2; eight upper labials, fourth and fifth entering the eye; first lower labial in contact with its fellow behind the symphysial; three pairs of chin-shields, anterior longer than broad and in contact with four labials. Scales in 15 rows, vertebrals a little enlarged. Anal entire; subcaudals 51. Above wood-brown, with irregular narrow dark cross-bars interrupted on the spine; upper labials dark-edged; lower parts with squarish light-edged black spots.

Hong Kong (?).

2. Pseudopareas atypicus.

Leptognathus atypicus, *Cope, Proc Ac Philad.* 1874, p 65.

Rostral subtriangular; frontal and parietals broad and short; a subquadrate loreal; no præocular; two postoculars; temporals 2+3; six upper labials, third and fourth entering the eye, first lower labial in contact with its fellow behind the symphysial; four pairs of chin-shields, all except the first broader than long. Scales in 15 rows, equal. Colour pale, with black transverse spots, which are wide anteriorly and become gradually narrower posteriorly, where their lateral ends are broken off and alternate with the dorsal portion; a few small blotches on the ends of the ventrals.

Total length 243 millim.; tail 47.

Andes of Peru.

Fam. 9 VIPERIDÆ.

Holochalina, part., *J Muller, Zeitschr f Physiol* iv. p 270, 1831.
Viperidæ, *Bonaparte, Mem Acc. Torin* (2) ii p. 393, 1840.
Thanatophides, *Duméril & Bibron, Erp. Gén.* vi. p. 70, 1844.
Viperina, part, *Gray, Cat Snakes*, p. 3, 1849
Solénoglyphes, *Duméril, Mém Ac Sc* xxiii p. 523, 1853; *Duméril & Bibron, Erp Gén.* vii. p. 1359, 1854.
Eurystomata Iobola, part, *Stannius, Zoot. Amph.* p. 5, 1856.
Viperidæ, *Cope, Proc. Ac. Philad.* 1859, p 333.
Viperiformes, *Gunther, Rept. Brit Ind* p 383, 1864.
Solenoglypha, *Cope, Proc. Ac. Philad.* 1864, p 231
Viperidæ, *Boulenger, Faun. Ind., Rept.* p. 417, 1890.

Facial bones movable; præfrontal not in contact with nasal; ectopterygoid (transpalatine) present, extending to mandible; supratemporal present, attached scale-like to the skull and suspending quadrate, maxillary much abbreviated, erectile perpendicularly to ectopterygoid, supporting a pair of large poison-fangs without external groove. Mandible without coronoid bone. Hypapophyses developed throughout the vertebral column.

Poisonous.—All except *Atractaspis* are ovoviviparous.

This family includes terrestrial, semiaquatic, arboreal, and burrowing types. In the Crotalines, the passage from terrestrial to arboreal species is so gradual as to preclude their being referred to distinct genera.

Europe, Asia, Africa (absent from Madagascar), America.

Fig. 33.

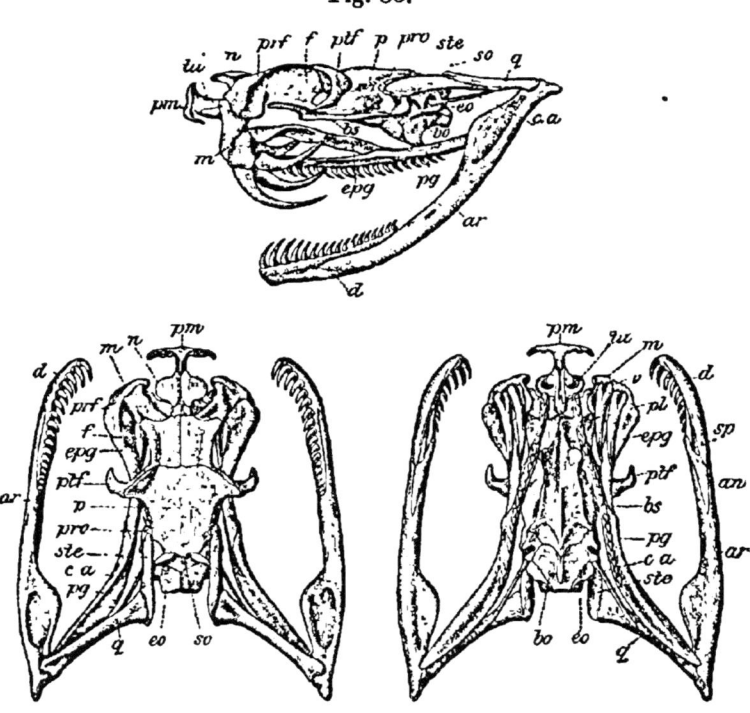

Skull of *Vipera lebetina.*

Divided into two subfamilies:—

1. *Viperinæ.*—No pit on the side of the snout; maxillary not hollowed out above.
2. *Crotalinæ.*—A deep pit on each side of the snout, between the nostril and the eye; maxillary hollowed out above.

Subfam. 1. *VIPERINÆ.*

Viperoidea, part., *Fitzinger, Neue Classif. Rept.* p. 11, 1826.
Viperidæ, part., *Boie, Isis,* 1827, p. 511.
Viperina, *Bonaparte, Mem. Acc. Tor.* (2) ii. p. 393, 1840.
Viperidæ, part., *Gray, Zool. Miscell.* p. 68, 1842, *and Cat. Sn.* p. 22, 1849.
Vipériens, *Duméril, Mém. Ac. Sc.* xxiii. p. 528, 1853; *Duméril & Bibron, Erp. Gén.* vii. p. 1375, 1854.
Atractaspididæ, *Gunther, Cat. Col. Sn.* p. 239, 1858.
Viperinæ, Causinæ, Atractaspidinæ, *Cope, Proc. Ac. Philad.* 1859, p. 334.
Viperidæ, *Gunther, Rept. Brit. Ind.* p. 395, 1864.

Viperidæ, Causidæ, Atractaspididæ, *Cope, Proc. Ac. Philad.* 1864, p. 231.
Viperida, *Strauch, Syn Viper.* p 18, 1869
Abothrophera, *Garman, N. Amer Rept.* p 104 (1883)
Viperinæ, *Boulenger, Faun. Ind., Rept.* p. 418, 1890.

Europe; Asia; Africa.

Synopsis of the Genera.

I. Head covered with large symmetrical shields as normal in the *Colubridæ*; mandibular teeth well developed, eye moderate.

Nostril between two nasals and the internasal; pupil round; scales oblique on the sides .... **1. Causus**, p. 465.
Nostril in a single nasal; pupil vertical; scales not oblique.
2. Azemiops, p. 470.

II. Some or all of the head-shields broken up into small shields or scales; mandibular teeth well developed; eye moderate or small, with vertical pupil.

A. Lateral scales not smaller than dorsals, without serrated keels; ventrals rounded; subcaudals in two rows.

Nasal in contact with the rostral or separated by a naso-rostral shield; postfrontal bone small .... **3. Vipera**, p. 471.
Nasal separated from the rostral by small scales; a crescentic supranasal; postfrontal bone very large.. **4. Bitis**, p. 492.
Nasal separated from the rostral by small scales; no supranasal.
5. Pseudocerastes, p. 501.

B. Lateral scales smaller than dorsals, disposed obliquely, with serrated keels.

Ventrals angulate laterally; subcaudals in two rows.
6. Cerastes, p. 501.
Ventrals rounded; subcaudals single . **7. Echis**, p. 504.

C. Lateral scales smaller than dorsals, slightly oblique, the keels not serrated; subcaudals single; tail prehensile.
8. Atheris, p. 508.

III. Head covered with large symmetrical shields; mandibular teeth reduced to two or three in the middle of the dentary bone; eye minute, with round pupil; postfrontal bone absent.
9. Atractaspis, p 510.

1 CAUSUS.

Causus, *Wagler, Syst. Amph* p. 172 (1830); *Gray, Cat. Sn* p. 33 (1849), *Dum. & Bibr. Erp. Gén.* vii p. 1262 (1854), *Cope, Proc. Ac. Philad* 1859, p. 342, *Peters, Reise n. Mossamb.* iii. p. 143 (1882).
Naja, part., *Schleg. Phys. Serp.* ii p. 461 (1837).
Distichurus, *Hallow. Journ. Ac. Philad.* viii. 1842, p. 337.

Aspidelaps, part., *Jan, Rev. & Mag. Zool.* 1859, p. 510.
Heterophis, *Peters, Mon. Berl. Ac.* 1862, p. 276.
Dinodipsas, *Peters, Sitzb. Ak. Berl.* 1882, p. 893; *Cope, Proc. Ac. Philad.* 1883, p. 57.

Head distinct from neck, covered with symmetrical shields; nostril between two nasals and the internasal; loreal present; eye moderate, with round pupil, separated from the labials by suboculars. Body cylindrical; scales smooth or keeled, with apical pits, oblique on the sides, in 15–22 rows; ventrals rounded. Tail short, subcaudals in two rows or single.

Tropical and South Africa.

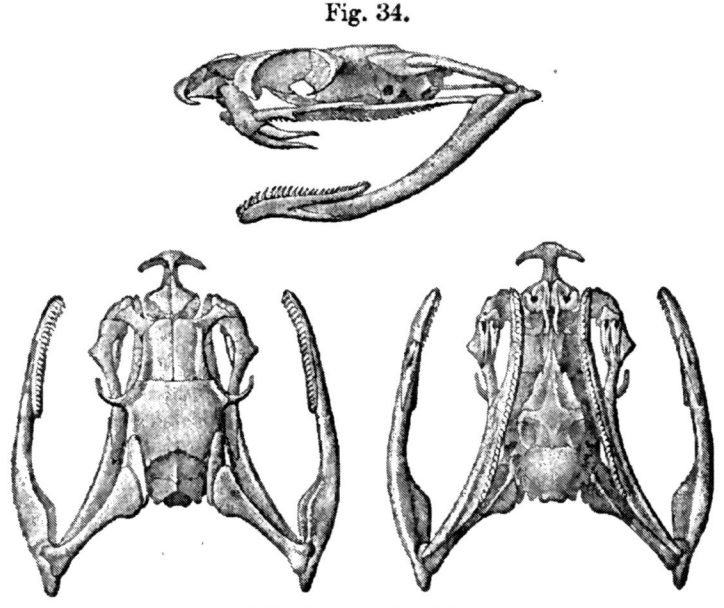

Fig. 34.

Skull of *Causus rhombeatus*.

Synopsis of the Species.

I. Scales in 17 rows or more; subcaudals all or greater part in two rows.

Snout obtuse, moderately prominent; scales in 17–21 rows; ventrals 120–155; subcaudals 15–29 .... 1. *rhombeatus*, p. 467.
Snout prominent, often more or less distinctly turned up at the end; scales in 19–22 rows; ventrals 134–152; subcaudals 17–25 .... 2. *resimus*, p. 468.

Snout prominent, more or less turned up
at the end, scales in 17 rows; ventrals
113–125; subcaudals 10–18 .... 3. *defilippii*, p 469.

II. Scales in 15 rows; subcaudals single. 4. *lichtensteinii*, p. 470.

1. Causus rhombeatus.

Sepedon rhombeatus, *Lichtenst. Verz. Doubl. Mus. Berl.* p. 106 (1823).
Naja V-nigrum, *Boie, Isis*, 1827, p. 556.
—— rhombeata, *Schleg Phys. Serp* ii. p. 483, pl. xvii. figs. 12 & 13 (1837).
Distichurus maculatus, *Hallow. Journ. Ac. Philad.* viii. 1842, p. 337, pl. xix.
Causus rhombeatus, *Gray, Cat.* p. 33 (1849); *Dum. & Bibr.* vii p 1263 (1854); *Hallow. Proc Ac. Philad.* 1854, p 101; *Peters, Reise n. Mossamb.* iii. p. 144 (1882); *Boettg. Ber. Senck. Ges.* 1887, p 63, and 1888, p 88; *Stejneg Proc U S. Nat. Mus* xvi. 1893, p 735; *Bocage, Herp Angola*, p. 145 (1895).
Aspidelaps rhombeatus, *Jan, Rev & Mag. Zool.* 1859, p.511; *Bcettg. Abh. Senck. Ges.* xii. 1881, p. 399.

Snout obtuse, moderately prominent. Rostral rounded, its upper portion forming a right or obtuse angle behind and measuring one half to two thirds its distance from the frontal; internasals as long as or a little longer than the præfrontals, often forming a suture with the loreal; frontal once and a half to once and three fourths as long as broad, as long as or longer than its distance from the end of the snout, longer than the parietals; two or three præoculars, one or two postoculars, and one or two suboculars separating the eye from the labials; temporals 2+3 or 4; six upper labials; three or four lower labials in contact with the anterior chin-shields; posterior chin-shields small or indistinct. Scales in 17 to 21 rows, dorsals more or less distinctly keeled. Ventrals 120–155; anal entire; subcaudals 15–29, all or greater part in pairs. Olive or pale brown above, rarely uniform, usually with a dorsal series of large rhomboidal or V-shaped dark brown spots which may be edged with whitish; usually a large dark Λ-shaped marking on the back of the head, the point on the frontal, and an oblique dark streak behind the eye; labials usually dark-edged; lower parts yellowish white or grey, uniform or the shields edged with black.

Total length 700 millim.; tail 75.

Tropical and South Africa.

a.	♀ (Sc 19; V. 131; C. 21).	Gambia.	Lord Derby [P.].
b.	Yg. (Sc 17, V. 138; C. 17).	Gambia.	J. Mitchell, Esq. [P.].
c.	♀ (Sc. 18; V. 136; C. 19).	Axim, Gold Coast.	G. A. Higlett, Esq [P.].
d, e.	Yg (Sc 21, 18; V. 135, 125, C. 17, 21)	Gold Coast.	W. H. Evans, Esq. [P.].

f. Yg. (Sc. 18; V. 131; C. 17).	Sierra Leone.	H. C. Hart, Esq. [P.].
g–h. ♀ (Sc. 19, 20; V. 129, 133; C. 17, 16).	Mouths of the Niger.	A. Millson, Esq. [P.].
i–m. ♂ (Sc 19 ; V. 132; C. 21), ♀ (Sc. 18, 19 ; V. 136, 129; C. 18, 17), & yg. (Sc. 19 ; V. 131 ; C. 17).	150 miles up the Niger.	W. H. Crosse, Esq. [P.].
n–o. ♂ (Sc. 18, 18; V. 136, 132; C. 21, 20).	Fernando Po.	H. Veitch, Esq. [P.]
p. ♀ (Sc. 19 ; V. 147 ; C. 19)	Stanley Falls, Congo.	
q. ♀ (Sc. 19; V. 140; C. 19).	Congo.	
r–s. ♂ (Sc. 17, 17 ; V. 134, 128 ; C 28, 30).	Huilla, Angola.	Dr. Welwitsch [P.].
t. ♂ (Sc. 19; V. 150; C. 28).	Golungo Alto, Angola.	Dr. Welwitsch [P.].
u. ♀ (Sc 19 ; V. 125 ; C. 15).	W. Africa.	Mr Raddon [C.]
v. ♂ (Sc. 19; V. 155; C. 25).	Kavirondo, E. C Africa	F. J. Jackson, Esq. [P.]
w–x, y–a ♂ (Sc. 18; V. 141; C. 29) & ♀ (Sc. 18, 18, 19, 18; V. 139, 138, 142, 143; C. 22, 23, 23, 23).	Zomba, Brit. C. Africa.	Sir H H. Johnston [P.].
β. Yg. (Sc. 18 ; V. 144 ; C. 29).	Mandala, Brit. C. Africa.	Scott Elliot, Esq. [P.].
γ ♂ (Sc. 18; V. 140, C. 27)	Blantyre, Brit. C. Africa.	A. A. Simons, Esq. [C.].
δ ♂ (Sc. 17, V. 141 ; C. 27).	Blantyre.	J. Grant, Esq. [P.].
ε. ♀ (Sc. 19; V. 134; C. 26).	Pretoria, Transvaal.	W. L. Distant, Esq. [P.].
ζ–θ ♂ (Sc. 19, 19, 19 ; V. 133, 133, 130; C. 25, 23, 26).	Natal.	E. Howlett, Esq. [P.].
ι ♂ (Sc. 19; V. 139; C. 20).	Port Natal	Rev H. Calloway [P.].
κ. ♂ (Sc. 20; V. 130; C. 24).	Port Natal.	Mr. T. Ayres [C.].
λ. ♀ (Sc. 19 ; V. 140 ; C. 22).	Port Elizabeth.	J. M. Leslie, Esq. [P.].
μ. Yg. (Sc. 20, V. 144 ; C. 23).	Grahamstown.	Rev. G H. R. Fisk [P]
ν. Yg. (Sc. 20; V. 138; C. 27).	Cape of Good Hope.	Dr. Lee [P.].
ξ. ♀ (Sc. 19; V. 139 ; C. 23).	S. Africa.	
ο. Skeleton	Niger.	W. H. Crosse, Esq. [P.].

2. Causus resimus.

Heterophis resimus, *Peters, Mon. Berl. Ac.* 1862, p. 277, pl.—. fig. 4.
Causus resimus, *Bocage, Jorn. Sc. Lisb.* x. 1887, p. 211, *and Herp. Angola*, p. 146 (1895).
—— jacksonii, *Gunth. Ann. & Mag. N. H.* (6) i. 1888, p 331.
—— nasalis, *Stejneger, Proc. U.S. Nat. Mus.* xvi. 1893, p. 735.
—— resimus, var. angolensis, *Bocage, Herp. Angola*, p. 148.

Snout more prominent than in *C. rhombeatus*, often more or less distinctly turned up at the end, the rostral with obtuse horizontal edge. Rostral broader than deep, forming nearly a right angle above, its upper portion measuring one half to two thirds its distance from the frontal; internasals longer than the præfrontals, separated from or just touching the loreal; frontal once and a half as long as broad, as long as or longer than its distance from the end of the snout, longer than the parietals; two præoculars, two postoculars, and one or two suboculars separating the eye from the labials; temporals 2+3 or 4; six upper labials; four lower labials in contact with the anterior chin-shields; posterior chin-shields very small or indistinct. Scales smooth or faintly keeled, in 19 to 22 rows. Ventrals 134–152; anal entire; subcaudals 17–25 pairs. Greyish olive above, uniform or with curved or chevron-shaped black cross-bars pointing backwards; uniform white beneath.

Total length 470 millim.; tail 40.

Sennar, East and Central Africa, Angola.

a. ♀ (Sc. 22; V. 146; C. 18). Ngatana, E. Africa. Dr. J. W. Gregory [P.]
b. Yg. (Sc 22; V. 143; C. 23). Mkonumbi, E. Africa. Dr. J. W. Gregory [P.]
c–d. ♀ (Sc. 22; V. 145; C. 18) & yg. (Sc. 21; V. 146, C. 18). Lamu, E. Africa. F. J. Jackson, Esq. [P.]
e. ♀ (Sc. 22; V 144; C. 19). L. Tanganyika. Sir J. Kirk [C.].

(Types of *C. jacksonii.*)

f. Yg (Sc. 19; V. 144; C. 22). Golungo Alto, Angola. Dr Welwitsch [P.].

3. Causus defilippii.

Heterodon defilippii, *Jan, Arch. Zool. Anat. Phys.* ii. 1862, p. 225, and *Icon Gén.* 11, pl. iv. fig. 3 (1865).
Causus (Heterophis) rostratus, *Gunth. Ann. & Mag. N. H.* (3) xii. 1863, p 363, *and Proc Zool Soc.* 1864, p 115, pl. xv.
—— rostratus, *Mocq. Le Natur.* xiv. 1892, p. 35, *Bocage, Herp. Angola*, p. 147 (1895).
—— defilippii, *Mocq. t. c.* p. 64.

Snout obtusely pointed, prominent, more or less turned up at the end. Rostral large, T-shaped, with obtuse horizontal edge; its upper portion forming a right or acute angle behind and quite as long as its distance from the frontal; internasals longer than the præfrontals and forming a suture with the loreal; frontal once and a half to once and two thirds as long as broad, as long as its distance from the end of the snout, longer than the parietals, two præ-oculars, two postoculars, and one or two suboculars separating the eye from the labials; temporals 2+3; six or seven upper labials; three or four lower labials in contact with the very short anterior chin-shields; posterior chin-shields very small or indistinct. Scales in 17 rows, dorsals feebly keeled. Ventrals 113–125; anal entire; subcaudals 10–18 pairs. Grey or pale brown above, vertebral region darker, with a series of large rhomboidal or V-shaped dark brown spots; a large ∧-shaped dark brown marking on the occiput, the point on the frontal; an oblique dark streak behind the eye; upper labials black-edged; yellowish white beneath, uniform or with small greyish-brown spots.

Total length 400 millim., tail 22.

East and Central Africa, Transvaal.

a. ♂ (V. 120; C. 14).	Ugogo	Capt. Speke [P.]. (Type of *C. rostratus.*)
b. ♂ (V. 117; C. 16).	Rabai hills, Mombas.	Rev. W. E. Taylor [P.].
c-d. ♂ (V. 118; C. 17) & ♀ (V. 125; C. 12).	Zomba, Brit. C. Africa	Sir H. H. Johnston [P.]
e. ♂ (V. 123, C. 15).	Shiré highlands.	Sir H. H Johnston [P.]
f. ♀ (V. 120; C. 10).	Murchison Range, Transvaal.	C. R. Jones, Esq. [P.].
g. ♂ (V. 119, C. 15)	Barberton, Transvaal	S. African Mus [P.].

4. Causus lichtensteinii.

Aspidelaps lichtensteinii, *Jan, Rev. & Mag. Zool.* 1859, p. 511, *and Icon. Gén.* 44, pl. vi. fig 5 (1873); *Mocq. Bull Soc Philom.* (7) xi. 1887, p 86.

Causus lichtensteinii, *A. Dum. Arch. Mus.* x. 1859, p. 217, *Stejneger, Proc. U.S. Nat. Mus.* xvi. 1893, p. 736.

Dinodipsas angulifera, *Peters, Sitzb. Ak Berl.* 1882, p. 893, pl. xv

Snout obtuse. Rostral a little broader than deep, obtuse-angled above, its upper portion not half as long as its distance from the frontal; internasals longer than the præfrontals, separated from the loreal; frontal once and one third as long as broad, as long as its distance from the end of the snout, as long as the parietals; two præoculars, two postoculars, and one or two suboculars separating the eye from the labials; temporals 2+3; six upper labials, four lower labials in contact with the anterior chin-shields; posterior chin-shields very small. Scales in 15 rows, dorsals feebly keeled. Ventrals 142-144; anal entire; subcaudals 15-21, single. Greyish above, with rather indistinct darker chevron-shaped cross-bands pointing forwards

Total length 413 millim.; tail 35.

West Africa (Gold Coast, Congo).

2 AZEMIOPS.

Azemiops, *Bouleng. Ann. Mus. Genova*, (2) vi. 1888, p. 602, *and Faun. Ind., Rept.* p. 418 (1890).

Head distinct from neck, covered with symmetrical shields; nostril in a single nasal; loreal present; eye moderate, with vertical pupil. Body cylindrical; scales smooth, in 17 rows; ventrals rounded. Tail short; subcaudals in two rows.

Upper Burma.

1. Azemiops feæ.

Azemiops feæ, *Bouleng. Ann. Mus. Genova,*(2) vi. 1888, p. 603, pl. vii., and *Faun. Ind., Rept.* p. 418, fig. (1890).

Head elliptical, snout short and broad. Rostral moderate, broader than deep; internasals and præfrontals subequal in length; frontal a little broader than long, nearly thrice as broad as the supraocular; parietals as long as their distance from the end of the snout; loreal small, pentagonal, as deep as long; two (or three) præoculars; two postoculars; two large superposed anterior temporals, the upper alone in contact with the postoculars; six upper labials, third entering the orbit, first and second smallest, fourth and fifth largest; seven lower labials, first large and forming a long suture with its fellow, second small; a pair of short chin-shields. Scales in 17 rows. Ventrals 180; anal entire; subcaudals 42. Blackish above, the scales being dark grey in the centre and black on the borders, with fifteen transverse white bands, one scale wide, some of which are disconnected in the middle and alternate with those on the other side; upper surface of head, from the præfrontals, black, with a yellow median line, which is very narrow anteriorly and widens posteriorly, ending on the neck on the eleventh transverse series of scales; end of snout and sides of head yellow; a blackish streak from below the eye to the lower border of the fourth upper labial; another from the postoculars to the upper border of the sixth labial. Lower parts olive-grey, with some small lighter spots; chin and throat variegated with yellow

Total length 610 millim.; tail 90.

Kakhyen Hills, Upper Burma.

3. VIPERA.

Vipera, part., *Laur. Syn. Rept.* p. 99 (1768); *Merr. Tent. Syst. Amph.* p. 149 (1820); *Jan, Elenco sist. Ofid.* p. 120 (1863); *Strauch, Syn. Viper.* p. 21 (1869); *Bouleng. Faun. Ind., Rept.* p. 419 (1890).
Pelias, *Merr. l c.* p. 148, *Wagl. Syst. Amph.* p. 177 (1830); *Gray, Cat. Sn.* p. 31 (1849); *Dum. & Bibr. Erp. Gén.* vii. p. 1393 (1854).
Echidna, part, *Merr. l c.* p. 150, *Dum & Bibr l. c.* p 1420.
Cobra, part, *Fitzing. N. Class. Rept.* p 33 (1826).
Vipera, *Fitzing. l.c.*, *Wagl. l.c.*; *Gray, l.c.* p. 30; *Dum. & Bibr. l.c.* p. 1403.
Rhinaspis (*non Wagl*), *Bonap Icon Faun. Ital., Anf.* (1834)
Daboia, *Gray, Zool. Miscell.* p. 69 (1842), and *Cat.* p. 23, *Günth. Rept. Brit. Ind.* p. 395 (1864).
Echidnoides, *Mauduyt, Herp Vienne,* p. 29 (1844).

Head distinct from neck, covered with small scales, with or without small frontal and parietal shields; eye moderate or small, with vertical pupil, separated from the labials by scales; nostrils lateral; nasal in contact with the rostral or separated by a naso-rostral shield. Body cylindrical; scales keeled, with apical pits, in 19–31 rows; ventrals rounded. Tail short; subcaudals in two rows.

Europe, Asia, North and Tropical Africa.

Synopsis of the Species.

I. Supraocular shield large, bordering the eye; scales on crown and snout smooth or faintly keeled; nostril in a single or irregularly divided nasal, which is separated from the rostral by a naso-rostral; scales in 19–23 rows (very rarely 25); ventrals 120–169.

  A. Snout not turned up at the end, supraocular usually extending posteriorly beyond the vertical of the posterior border of the eye; frontal and parietal shields usually well developed; usually a single series between the eye and the labials, rarely two.

Snout obtusely pointed, flat above, or with the canthus slightly raised; rostral usually in contact with a single apical scale, rarely with two; 6 to 9 upper labials, usually 7 or 8; scales in 19 rows, rarely 21; ventrals: ♂ 120–135, ♀ 125–142 .... 1. *ursinii*, p. 473.

Snout pointed, with raised canthus; rostral in contact with a single apical scale; 8 or 9 upper labials; scales in 21 rows, rarely 19; ventrals: ♂ 130–148, ♀ 130–150 .... 2. *renardi*, p. 475.

Snout truncate or broadly rounded, flat above or with very slightly raised canthus; rostral in contact with two apical scales, rarely with one; scales in 21 rows, rarely 19 or 23; ventrals: ♂ 132–150, ♀ 132–158 .... 3. *berus*, p. 476.

  B. Snout usually more or less turned up at the end or produced in a scaly dermal appendage; supraocular not extending posteriorly beyond the vertical of the posterior border of the eye; crown usually covered with small scales, frontal and parietals, however, sometimes well developed; two or three series of scales between the eye and the labials; 9 to 13 upper labials; scales in 21–23 rows, rarely 19 or 25.

Snout simply turned up, the raised portion bearing two or three (apical) scales; rostral not more than once and a half as deep as broad; ventrals: ♂ 134–158, ♀ 144–169 .... 4. *aspis*, p. 481.

Snout simply turned up or produced in an appendage, the raised portion with five or six (rarely three) scales; rostral once and a half to twice as deep as broad; ventrals: ♂ 125-146, ♀ 135-147........................ 5. *latastii*, p. 484.

Snout produced in an appendage covered with 10 to 20 scales; rostral not deeper than broad; ventrals: ♂ 133-158, ♀ 135-162 .... 6. *ammodytes*, p. 485.

II. Supraocular shield large, erectile, the free border angular, separated from the eye by a series of small scales; nostril in a single nasal, which is partially fused with the naso-rostral; scales in 23 rows; ventrals 150-180.
7. *raddii*, p. 487.

III. Supraocular shield moderately large or narrow, not erectile, or broken up into scales, upper surface of head covered with small, imbricate, usually keeled scales; scales in 23-31 rows; ventrals 142-180.

A. Supranasal shield present.

Scales in 23-27 rows; supranasal usually not bordering the nostril .... 8. *lebetina*, p. 487.

Scales in 27-33 rows; supranasal bordering the nostril .... 9. *russellii*, p. 490.

B. No supranasal; nostril pierced between two nasals, the anterior in contact with the rostral; scales in 27 rows.
10. *superciliaris*, p. 491.

1. Vipera ursinii.

Pelias chersea (*non L*), *Bonap. Icon. Faun. Ital. Anf.* (1835).
—— ursinii, *Bonap. l. c.*
—— berus, var ursinii, *Cope, Proc. Ac. Philad.* 1859, p. 342.
Vipera berus, part., *Tournev Bull Soc. Zool. Fr.* 1881, p. 41. pl. i. fig 785; *Camerano, Mon. Ofid Ital., Vip.* p. 35, pl. i figs. 16-18 (1888)
—— berus, var. rakosiensis, *Méhely, Zool Anz* 1893, p. 190.
—— ursinii, *Bouleng. Proc. Zool. Soc* 1893, p. 596, pl. li., and *Feuille Jeunes Natur.* 1893, p. 8, *Méhely, Zool. Anz.* 1894, pp. 57 & 86; *Werner, Verh. zool.-bot. Ges. Wien*, xliv. 1894, p 237, *Méhely, Math. Term. Kozl. Budapest*, xxvi. 1895, p. 85, pls. i. & ii
—— berus, *Werner, Zool. Anz* 1893, p. 423.
—— rakosiensis, *Méhely, Math Term. Ert. Budapest*, xii. 1894, p. 87.

Snout obtusely pointed, flat above or with the canthus slightly raised; eye very small, usually smaller than the nasal shield, its horizontal diameter not exceeding its distance from the posterior border of the nostril, its vertical diameter equal to or less than its distance from the mouth. Rostral as deep as broad or slightly deeper than broad, visible from above, in contact with one, rarely with two apical shields, distinct frontal and parietal shields, the former once and a half to once and two thirds (rarely once and one third) as long as broad, as long as its distance from the rostral or the end of the snout, and nearly always longer than the parietals; supraocular well developed, separated from the frontal by one to three shields; 6 to 10 scales round the eye, usually 8 or 9, the upper præocular usually in contact with the nasal; a single series of scales between the eye and the labials; nasal single, separated from the rostral by a naso-rostral; temporal scales smooth; 6 to 9 upper labials, usually 7 or 8; 3 (rarely 4) lower labials in contact with the chin-shields. Scales in 19 (rarely 20 or 21) rows, strongly keeled on the back, less strongly on the sides, outer row smooth. Ventrals 120-135 in ♂, 125-142 in ♀; anal entire; subcaudals 30-37 in ♂, 20-28 in ♀. Yellowish or pale brown above, grey or dark brown on the sides, sometimes uniform brown; a vertebral series of more or less regular, transversely oval, elliptic or rhomboidal dark brown, black-edged spots, some or all of which may be confluent and form an undulous or zigzag band; two or three longitudinal series of dark brown or black spots along the sides, the lowermost on the outer row of scales; small dark spots and one or two ∧-shaped markings on the upper surface of the head; an oblique dark stripe from the eye to the angle of the mouth; rostral and labials uniform white, rarely with a few small blackish spots, or with brownish borders; chin and throat yellowish white, rarely with some blackish spots; ventrals and subcaudals black, with transverse series of small white spots, grey, checkered with black and white, or whitish with small round black spots; tail but rarely tipped with yellow. No sexual differences of coloration.

Total length: ♂ 420 millim.; tail 55. ♀ 500; 50.

S.E. France (Basses-Alpes); Italy (Abruzzi); Istria (Veglia Id.); Mountains of Bosnia; Plains of Lower Austria, Hungary.

a. ♀ (V 134; C. 25).	Basses-Alpes.	M. E. Honnorat [P.].
b–g, h. ♂ (V. 130, 131, 126; C. 33, 30, 35) & ♀ (V. 134, 133, 134, 132; C. 24, 25, 26, 27)	Laxenburg, near Vienna.	Dr. F. Werner [E.].
i, k. Many specimens, ♂ (V 120-135; C. 30-37) & ♀ (V.125-142; C. 20-28).	Laxenburg	Hr. F. Henkel [E.]
l. ♀ (V. 134; C. 24).	Parndorf, near Bruck.	Hr. F. Henkel [E.].
m ♀ (V. 137; C 24).	Rakos, near Buda-Pest.	Prof. L. v. Méhely [E.].
n. ♀ skull.	Laxenburg.	

2. Vipera renardi.

Pelias renardi, *Christoph, Bull. Soc. Nat. Mosc.* xxxiv 1861, ii. p. 599.
Vipera berus, part., *Strauch, Syn Vip* p 32 (1869), *and Schl. Russ. R.* p 206 (1873)
—— berus, *Boettg Ber. Senck. Ges.* 1892, p. 149
—— renardi, *Bouleng. Proc. Zool Soc* 1893, pp 598 & 757, pl lxiv ; *Méhely, Zool. Anz.* 1894, p. 69.

Snout pointed, flat above, with raised canthus, eye as in *V. berus*. Rostral as deep as broad or a little deeper than broad, just visible from above and in contact with a single apical shield, distinct frontal and (usually) parietal shields, the former once and two thirds to once and one third as long as broad, as long as or longer than its distance from the end of the snout, usually longer than the parietals; supraocular well developed, separated from the frontal by one to three shields; 9 to 11 scales round the eye, the upper præocular usually in contact with the nasal; a single series of scales between the eye and the labials, or two series except under the centre of the eye, which is separated from the fourth labial by a single scale; nostril pierced in the lower half of a single nasal, which is separated from the rostral by a naso-rostral; temporal scales smooth or upper faintly keeled; 8 or 9 upper labials; 4 (rarely 5) lower labials in contact with the chin-shields. Scales in 21 rows (19 in specimen *n*), strongly keeled on the back, smooth or feebly keeled on the outer row. Ventrals 130–148 in ♂, 130–150 in ♀; anal entire; subcaudals 31–37 in ♂, 24–30 in ♀. Coloration much as in *V. ursinii*, and likewise the same in both sexes, but rostral and labials spotted, speckled, or margined with black or brown.

Total length : ♂ 620 millim.; tail 75. ♀ 395; 40.

Southern Russia and Central Asia.

a. ♀ (V. 142; C. 24).	Sarepta.	Dr. F. Muller [P.].
b–c. ♂ (V 145, 146; C. 37, 35).	Uralsk.	M. Borodine [C.]
d. ♂ (V. 142; C. 36).	Saratov	St Petersburg Mus. [E]
e. ♂ (V. 144; C. 35).	L. Ourkatsch, Kirghiz Steppes.	M Nazarow [E.]
f. ♂ (V. 148, C 36).	R Emba, Kirghiz Steppes.	St. Petersburg Mus. [E.].
g. Yg. ♂ (V. 145; C. 35).	Kirghiz Steppes.	St. Petersburg Mus. [E.].
h. ♂ (V. 142; C. 35).	Smeinogorsk, Gov. Tomsk	St. Petersburg Mus. [E.]
i–l, m. ♂ (V. 137, 136; C 36, 32), ♀ (V. 137; C. 30), & yg. ♂ (V. 130; C. 36)	Chinas, Turkestan	St. Petersburg Mus. [E.].
n. Yg. ♀ (V. 130, C. 30).	Kunges, R Ili, E. Turkestan.	St. Petersburg Mus. [E].

o–p. ♂ (V. 134; C. 31) & ♀ (V. 141; C. 27).		Wernensky Ujesd, Varnoe, E. Turkestan.	St. Petersburg Mus. [E.].
q–r. ♂ (V. 133, 138; C. 34, 32).		Kuldja, E. Turkestan.	St. Petersburg Mus. [E.].

3. Vipera berus.

Coluber berus, *Linn. Faun. Suec.* p. 104 (1761), and *S. N.* i. p. 377 (1766); *Laur. Syn. Rept.* p. 97, pl. ii. fig. 1 (1768); *Van Lier, Verh. Schl. Add Drenthe,* p 84, pl ii. (1781); *Reider & Hahn, Faun. Boica,* iii. (1832); *Collett, Vidensk. Selsk. Forh. Christ* 1878, no. 3, p. 4.

—— chersea, *Linn. ll. cc* pp 103, 377; *Wolf, in Sturm, Deutschl. Faun.* iii II 3 (1802) & II 4 (1805).

—— prester, *Linn. ll. cc.* pp. 104, 377; *Wolf, l c.* H 4; *Reider & Hahn, l. c.*

—— vipera, *Laur. l. c.* p. 98, pl. iv. fig. 1.

—— melanis, *Pall. Reise,* i. p 460 (1771).

—— scytha, *Pall. op. cit* ii. p. 717 (1773).

—— aspis, *Mull. Zool. Dan. Prodr.* p 36 (1776)

Vipera prester, *Latr Rept.* iii. p. 309 (1802); *Daud. Rept.* vi. p. 161 (1803); *Linck, Voigt's Mag. Nat.* xii. 1806, p. 295.

—— melanis, *Latr. t c.* p. 311; *Daud t. c.* p 191.

—— schyta, *Latr. t. c* p. 312; *Daud. t c.* p. 150

—— berus, *Daud. t. c.* p. 89, pl lxxii fig 1; *Linck, l c.* p. 291, pl. v. figs. 1 & 2; *Meisner, Mus. Nat. Helv.* p 89, pl. i. fig. 1 (1820), *Brandt & Ratzeb. Med. Zool.* i. p. 171, pl xx. (1829); *Schleg. Phys. Serp.* ii. p. 591, pl. xxi. figs. 14 & 15 (1837); *Berth. in Wagn. Reise n. Kolchis,* p. 335 (1850); *Viaud-Grandm. Serp Vend.* p. 37 (1867), *Jan, Icon. Gén.* 45, pl. ii. (1874); *Ninni, Atti Soc. Ital Sc. Nat.* xxii. 1879, p. 175, *Leydig, Abh. Senck. Ges.* xiii 1883, p 187; *F Mull. Verh. Nat Ges Basel,* vii 1884, p. 300, & 1885, p 695; *Bouleng. The Zool.* 1885, p 373; *Notthaft, Zool. Anz.* 1886, p. 450; *Blum, Abh. Senck Ges* xv. 1888, p. 128; *Meyer & Helm, Jahresb. Ornith. Beob. Sachsen,* vi. 1892, p. 55; *Bouleng. The Zool.* 1892, p. 87; *Méhely, Beitr. Mon. Kronstadt, Herp.* p. 37 (1892); *Bedriaga, CR. Congr. Int Zool* 1892, i. p. 240; *Dürigen, Deutschl. Amph. u. Rept.* p. 337, pl ix (1894), *Nobre, Ann. Sc. Porto,* i. 1894, p. 123, *Bouleng. The Zool.* 1895, p. 60; *Bedriaga, Ann. Sc. Porto,* ii. 1895, p. 114; *Méhely, Math. Term Kozl Budapest,* xxvi. 1895, p 4, pls i & ii.

Coluber cæruleus, *Sheppard, Trans. Linn. Soc* vii 1804, p. 56.

Vipera chersæa, *Linck, l. c.* p. 294.

—— communis, *Leach, Zool. Miscell.* iii p. 7, pl. cxxiv. (1817).

Pelias berus, *Meri. Tent.* p. 148 (1820); *Frivaldsky, Mon. Serp, Hung.* p. 35 (1823); *Bonap. Icon Faun. Ital, Anf* (1835); *Bell, Brit. Rept.* p. 58, figs. (1839); *Steenstr. Nat. Tidsskr. Copenh* ii. 1839, p. 542; *Gray, Cat.* p. 31 (1849); *Dum. & Bibr.* vii. p. 1395, pl lxxix b. fig. 2 (1854); *De Betta, Erp. Venet.* p. 229 (1857); *Cook, Our Rept* p 66, pl. v. (1865); *Blanche, Bull. Soc. Amis Sc. Nat. Rouen,* i. 1865, p. 100; *Fatio, Vert Suisse,* iii. p. 210 (1872); *De Betta, Faun Ital, Rett Anf.* p. 53 (1874); *Schreib. Herp. Eur* p. 202 (1875), *Lessona, Atti Acc. Torin.* xiv. 1879, p. 748; *De Betta, Atti Ist Ven.* (5) vi. 1880, p. 301; *Dalla Torre, Progr. Gymn. Innsbr.* 1891, p. 7.

Vipera limnæa, *Bendiscioli, Giorn. Fis. Stor. Nat.* (2) ix. 1826, p. 431.
—— trilamina, *Millet, Faune Maine et Loire,* ii. p 651, pl. v fig. 2 (1828).
Pelias chersea, *Ménétr. Cat. Rais* p 73 (1832).
Vipera torva, *Lenz, Schlangenk* p 133, pls i–iv. & viii. (1832).
Pelias prester, *Steenstr. Nat Tidsskr. Copenh.* ii. 1839, p. 542.
—— dorsalis, *Gray, Zool Miscell.* p. 71 (1842).
Echidnoides trilamina, *Mauduyt, Herp Vienne,* p. 29 (1844).
Vipera pelias, *Soubeiran, De la Vipère,* p 30 (1855), *and Bull. Soc. Acclim.* x. 1863, p 397
—— berus, part, *Strauch, Syn Viper* p 32 (1869) *and Schl. Russ. R* p 206 (1873); *Tournev Bull. Soc Zool France,* 1881, p. 53, pl. i. figs. 728 & 1030; *Camerano, Mon. Ofid. Ital., Viper.* p 35, pl. i. figs. 8, 19, 20, 21, 26–29 (1888); *Méhely, Zool. Anz.* 1893, p. 186.
—— berus seoanci, *Lataste, Bull. Soc. Zool France,* 1879, p. 132; *Tournev l. c.* p. 41, pl i. figs. *u, v, z*

Snout broadly rounded or truncate, with strong canthus which is very rarely slightly raised; eye usually larger in males than in females, its vertical diameter equal to or greater than its distance from the mouth. Rostral as deep as broad, or slightly broader than deep, or a little deeper than broad, not or but scarcely visible from above, in contact with two apical shields, rarely with one; frontal and parietal shields usually distinct, the former as long as broad or a little longer than broad, usually shorter than its distance from the rostral, as long as or a little shorter than the parietals; supraocular well developed, sometimes in contact with the frontal, usually separated from it by a series of two to four scales; 6 to 13 scales round the eye, usually 8 to 10; the upper præocular only exceptionally in contact with the nasal; one, rarely two, series of scales between the eye and the labials; nasal single, not or but slightly larger than the eye, separated from the rostral by a naso-rostral: temporal scales smooth, rarely feebly keeled; 6 to 10 upper labials, usually 8 or 9; three or four (rarely five) lower labials in contact with the chin-shields. Scales in 21 rows (exceptionally 19 or 23), strongly keeled, outer row smooth or feebly keeled. Ventrals 132–150 (usually 137–147) in ♂, 132–158 (usually 140–150) in ♀; anal entire; subcaudals 33–46 (usually 35–40) in ♂, 24–38 (usually 28–33) in ♀. Coloration very variable: grey, yellowish, olive, brown, or red above, usually with a dark undulating or zigzag band along the spine and a series of lateral spots, a ∧-, ✕-, or ⋏-shaped dark marking on the back of the head, and a dark postocular streak; upper labials whitish or yellowish, the anterior at least edged with brown or black; grey to brown or black beneath, uniform or spotted with darker or lighter; end of tail usually yellow or coral-red. Some specimens entirely black, either through darkening of the ground-colour (♀) or through extension of the black markings (♂). Males usually distinguishable from females by darker, deep black markings and lighter ground-colour.

Total length: ♂, 660 millim.; tail 90. ♀, 700; 75.

Europe, generally distributed in the North, mostly confined to the mountains in the Centre, irregularly distributed in the South (North of Spain and Portugal, Northern Italy, Bosnia); Caucasus; Siberia, eastwards to Sachalien Island.

a. ♀ (V. 145; C. 29).	Near Freswick, Canisbay, Caithness.	Dr MacGregor [P.].
b-c. ♂ (V. 143, C. 38) & ♀ (V. 145; C. 33).	Betty Hill, Sutherlandshire.	Capt. S. G. Reid [P].
d. ♀ (V. 142; C. 32).	W. Ross-shire.	W. Eagle Clarke, Esq. [P].
e. ♂ (V. 141; C. 35).	Pluscarden Abbey, nr. Forres, Morayshire.	D. Charleson, Esq. [P.].
f-g. ♂ (V. 138, C. 35) & ♀ (V. 144; C. 29).	Braemar, Aberdeenshire.	Dr. J. Anderson [P.].
h. ♀ (V. 142; C. 28)	Nr. Aberdeen	G Sim, Esq. [P.].
i-o. ♂ (V. 137, 138, 137; C. 40, 33, 38) & ♀ (V. 142, 140, 143; C 33, 32, 31).	Cromlix, Dunblane, Stirling, 800–1000 ft	W. R Ogilvie Grant, Esq. [P.].
p. ♀ (V 148; C. 29)	Crichton, W. Edinburgh-shire.	W. Evans, Esq. [P.].
q, r. ♀ (V. 144, 141, C. 28, 32).	I of Arran	W. Leach, Esq. [P].
s-t. ♂ (V. 141, 145; C. 36, 41).	Newby Bridge, N. Lancashire.	Mr. G Smith [P.].
u-v. Hgr. & yg. ♀ (V. 136, 144; C. 30, 28).	Newby Bridge, N. Lancashire.	Mr. J. Paul [P.].
w-y. Yg. ♂ (V. 144; C. 35) & yg. ♀ (V. 141, 140; C 33, 32).	Somersetshire.	W. Leach, Esq. [P.].
z. ♀ (V. 146, C. 28).	Woolhope, Herefordshire.	Col Yerbury [P.].
α. ♀ (V. 142, C. 30).	Nr. Penzance.	Mr. F. W Terry [P.].
β, γ, δ, ε. ♂ (V 138, C. 37), ♀ (V 139, 154; C. 29, 28), & yg. ♀ (V. 138, C. 30).	Devonshire.	W. Leach, Esq. [P.].
ζ. Yg. ♀ (V. 142, C. 31).	Dorsetshire.	Rev. W. Rackett [P.]
η. ♂ (V. 141; C. 35).	Morecomb, Dorsetshire.	W Eagle Clarke, Esq. [P.].
θ. ♀ (V. 149; C. 32).	Hampshire.	Zoological Society.
ι. Hgr. ♀ (V. 143, C. 31).	Milton, Hampshire.	R. Kirkpatrick, Esq. [P].
κ. ♂ (V. 140; C. 38)	Ventnor, I. of Wight.	Mrs Mowatt [P.].
λ-μ. ♀ (V. 140, 150; C. 29, 33).	Brockenhurst, Hampshire.	W R. Ogilvie Grant, Esq. [P.].
ν. ♀ (V. 145; C. 35).	Ringwood, Hampshire.	G. A. Boulenger, Esq. [P.].
ξ-τ. ♂ (V. 140, 145, 140; C. 39, 36, 37) & ♀ (V. 146, 145, 140; C. 32, 31, 31).	New Forest, Hampshire.	Mr. J. L. Monk [P.].

v. Many specimens, ♂ (V. 137-146, C. 35-40) & ♀ (V 143-150, C. 28-32).	Near Petersfield, Hampshire.	Mrs. Mowatt [P].	
φ-ψ. ♂ (V. 146, 142, 140; C. 36, 39, 36).	Nr. Haslemere, Surrey	Mrs. Mowatt [P].	
ω-b'. ♂ (V 140; C 36) & ♀ (V. 147. 145; C. 32, 33).	Reigate, Surrey.	Rev. E. P. Larkin [P.].	
c'. ♀ (V. 148; C. 29).	Oxted, Surrey	G. A. Boulenger, Esq. [P].	
d'. ♂ (V 146, C. 37).	Lancing, Sussex.	R. G. Rye, Esq. [P.].	
e'. ♀ (V. 150, C. 30).	Kent.	Sir J Lubbock [P.].	
f'. ♂ (V. 139, C. 36).	Epping Forest, Essex.	L. N. Jekyll, Esq [P.].	
g'. ♀ (V. 146; C. 32).	Waulsort, Prov. Namur, Belgium.	G. A. Boulenger, Esq. [P].	
h'. ♀ (V. 146; C. 29).	Orival, nr. Elbeuf, Normandy.	M. H Gadeau de Kerville [P.].	
i'-k'. ♂ (V. 142; C 40) & ♀ (V 150; C. 28)	Forêt de Lyons, Normandy.	M H Gadeau de Kerville [P.].	
l' ♂ (V 143, C. 38).	Nr. St Malo, Brittany.	G A. Boulenger, Esq [P.].	
m'-r'. ♂ (V 139; C 38), ♀ (V. 149, 147; C 33, 29), yg. ♂ (V. 146, 143; C. 37, 37), & yg. ♀ (V 150; C. 30).	Nr. Rennes, Brittany.	Dr. L. Joubin [P.].	
s'. ♀ (V. 147; C. 31).	France.		
t'. ♀ (V. 144; C. 29).	Burbia, nr. Villafranca, Santander, 2700 ft	Dr. H. Gadow [P.].	
u'. Yg. ♂ (139, C 40).	Potes, nr. Santander, 1300 ft.	Dr. H. Gadow [P.].	
v'-z', a^2-c^2, d^2. ♂ (V. 133, 137, 138 C. 39, 33, 36) & ♀ (V. 135, 141, 135, 138, 135, 147; C. 29, ?, 29, 28, 31, 29).	Galicia, Spain.	M. V. L. Scoane [P.]	
e^2. ♀ (V. 150; C 30).	Walkmuhle, near Eisenberg, Altenburg.	Hr. J. Geithe [C.].	
f^2. ♀ (V. 149; C. 32).	Marktleithen, Fichtel Mts	Hr J Geithe [C.].	
g^2. ♂ (V. 148; C. 38).	Hohenleipisch, near Elsterwenden, Prov. Saxony	Hr. J Geithe [C.].	
h^2. ♀ (V. 150; C. 28).	Hohenleipisch.	Hr W. Wolterstorff [P.]	
i^2. ♀ (V. 154; C. 30).	Croldilzer Wald, nr. Grimma, Saxony.	Hr J. Geithe [C.].	
k^2. ♀ (V. 152; C. 31).	Lichtenberg, nr Pulsnitz, Upper Lausitz, Saxony.	Hr J Geithe [C.].	
l^2-m^2 ♀ (V 151, 150; C 26, 29)	Selmutz, Saxon Switzerland.	Hr. J. Geithe [C.].	

480   VIPERIDÆ.

n^2–r^3. ♂ (V. 144; C. 40), ♀ (V. 146, 144; C. 31, 29), yg ♂ (V. 140; C. 35), & yg. ♀ (V. 147; C. 32).	Frauenstein, Saxony.	Dr. A. B. Meyer [P.].
s^3–w^3. ♂ (V. 150, 138; C. 35, 46) & ♀ (V. 144, 147, 149; C. 33, 32, 30).	Saxony.	Dr. A. B. Meyer [P.].
x^3. ♀ (V. 146; C. 32).	Saxony.	Hr. F. Henkel [E.].
y^3–z^3. ♀ (V. 149, 152; C. 34, 36).	Nr. Berlin.	Hr W. Wolterstorff [P.].
a^3. ♂ (V. 141; C. 41).	Silesia.	Dr. F. Werner [E.].
b^3. Many specimens, ♂ (V. 139–147; C. 36–46), & ♀ (V. 142–153; C. 26–35).	Nr. Konigsberg, E. Prussia.	Dr. R. Klebs [P.].
c^3–e^3. ♂ (V. 138, 143; C. 36, 38) & ♀ (V. 151, C 32).	Mecklenburg.	Dr. F. Werner [E.].
f^3–g^3, h^3–i^3 ♂ (V. 146, 147; C. 39, 38) & ♀ (V. 146, 145; C. 31, 30).	Seeland, Denmark	Prof. Lutken [P.]
k^3. ♂ (V. 145, C. 35).	Nr. Copenhagen	Mr. G. L. F. Sarauw [P.].
l^3, m^3 Many specimens, ♂ (V. 139–145; C. 36–39) & ♀ (V. 145–154; C. 28–33).	Knudskov, S. Seeland.	Mr. G. L. F. Sarauw [P.].
n^3. ♂ (V. 145; C. 37).	Skaarup, S. Fyen.	Mr. G. L. F. Sarauw [P.].
o^3–u^3. ♂ (V. 142, 142, 137; C. 42, 41, 38) & ♀ (V. 148, 147, 150, 144; C. 33, 32, 32, 34).	Glamsbjerg, S.W. Fyen	Mr. G. L. F. Sarauw [P.].
v^3. ♂ (V. 144; C. 38).	Bónnelykke, Langeland.	Mr G L. F. Sarauw [P.].
w^3. ♀ (V. 145, C. ?).	Nr. Aalborg, N. Jutland.	Mr. G. L. F. Sarauw [P.].
x^3. Many specimens, ♂ (V. 136–144, C. 34–39) & ♀ (V. 142–146; C. 30–38)	Nr. Viborg, C Jutland.	Mr. G. L. F. Sarauw [P.].
y^3. ♂ (V. 141; C. 42).	Trust, C. Jutland.	Mr G L. F. Sarauw [P.].
z^3–b^4. ♂ (V. 135, 137; C. 30, 35) & ♀ (V. 140; C 33).	Skarrild, C. Jutland.	Mr. G. L. F. Sarauw [P.].
c^4, d^1–h^4. ♂ (V. 145, 146, 143, 147, C. 38, 40, 40, ?) & yg. ♀ (V. 149; C. 33).	S. Norway.	Prof. R. Collett [P.].
i^4 ♂ (V. 147; C. 40).	Bohuslän, Sweden.	Prof. A W. Malm [P.].
k^4–l^4. ♂ (V. 143, C. 40) & ♀ (V. 151; C. 34).	Sweden.	Mr. C. J. A. Thuden [P.].
m^4. ♀ (V. 146; C. 32).	Rauhe Alp, Würtemberg.	Dr. Günther [P.].

3. VIPERA.

n^4. ♀ (V. 151; C. 30).	Sardasca Valley, Switzerland.	Dr. F. Muller [P.].
o^4, p^4. ♂ (V. 139, 136; C. 39, 35),	Fort of Chioggia, Prov. Venice.	Hr. F. Henkel [E.].
q^4, r^4. ♂ (V. 145, 142; C. 38, 38).	Ferrara, Italy.	Prof. J. J. Bianconi [P.].
s^4. ♀ (V. 143; C. 28).	Travnik, Bosnia	Dr F. Werner [E].
t^4. ♂ (V. 144; C. 37).	Schneeberg, Carniola.	Dr. F. Werner [E.].
u^4–y^4. ♂ (V. 138, 142, C. 34, 36) & ♀ (V. 145, 150, 147, 144; C. 26, 26, 26, 28).	St Peter, nr. Grafenbrunn, Carniola.	Hr. F. Henkel [E.].
z^4–a^5. ♂ (V. 149; C. 37) & ♀ (V. 145, C 24).	Malborgeth, Carinthia.	Hr. F. Henkel [E].
b^5 ♀ (V. 145; C. 28).	Spieglitzer Schneeberg, Bohemia	Dr. F. Werner [E.].
c^5, d^5. ♀ (V. 140, 145; C. 28, 28)	Schneeberg, Lower Austria.	Dr. F. Werner [E.].
e^5–f^5, g^5–h^5, i^5, k^5, l^5. ♂ (V. 144, 140, 137, C. 37, 38, 34) & ♀ (V. 143, 138, 151, 145; C. 34, ?, 32, 29)	Schneeberg, Lower Austria.	Hr. F. Henkel [E].
m^5–n^5. ♂ (V. 146; C. 35) & ♀ (V. 146, C. 27).	Iglau, Moravia.	Dr F. Werner [E].
o^5–p^5. ♂ (V. 142; C. 38) & ♀ (V. 145, 144, 142; C. 33, 31, 30).	Moravia.	Hr. F. Henkel [E.].
q^5–r^5. ♀ (V. 145, 148, C 29, 28).	Rothwasser, Moravia.	Hr. F. Henkel [E].
s^5. ♂ (V. 142; C. 36).	Near Kronstadt, Transylvania.	Prof. L. v. Méhely [C].
t^5. ♀ (V. 145; C 30)	Transylvania	Dr F. Werner [C].
u^5. ♂ (V. 142, C. 39).	Terioki, Finland	Norman Douglass, Esq [P]
v^5. ♀ (V. 153; C. 32).	Nr. St. Petersburg.	St. Petersburg Mus [E.].
w^5. ♀ (V. 155; C. 33).	Charkov.	Dr. J. de Bedriaga [P.].
x^5. ♂ (V. 142, C. 39).	Iekaterinburg, Gov. Perm.	St. Petersburg Mus [E.].
y^5. ♂ (V. 146, C. 38).	Newelskoi Ujesd, Gov. Vitebsk	St. Petersburg Mus [E.]
z^5. ♀ (V. 146; C. 33).	Smeinogorsk, Gov. Tomsk, N Altai.	Dr. O. Finsch [C.]
a^6–b^6. ♀ (V. 158, 143; C. 33, 32).	Sachalien Id.	St. Petersburg Mus [E.].
c^6. Hgr. ♂ (V. 143, C.39).	—?	(Type of *P dorsalis*.)
d^6, e^6. ♂ ♀. skeletons.	Nr Haslemere, Surrey.	Mrs. Mowatt [P].
f^6, g^6. Skulls.	France.	

4. Vipera aspis.

Coluber aspis, *Linn S. N.* i. p. 378 (1766).
Vipera francisci redi, *Laur Syn. Rept.* p. 99 (1768).
—— mosis charas, *Laur l. c.* p. 100.

Coluber redi, *Gmel. S N* i. p. 1091 (1789).

—— charasii, *Shaw, Zool.* iii. p. 379 (1802).

Vipera vulgaris, *Latr. Rept.* iii. p. 212 (1802).

—— ocellata, *Latr.* t. c. p. 292; *Daud. Rept.* vi. p 140, pl lxxii. fig 2 (1803).

—— chersea (*non L.*), *Latr. t. c.* p. 297; *Daud. t c* p. 144; *Metaxa, Mon. Serp. Rom* p. 43 (1823); *Bendiscioli, Giorn Fis. Stor. Nat.* (2) ix. 1826, p 429.

—— redi, *Latr. t. c* p 304; *Daud. t. c.* p. 152; *Metaxa. l. c.* p. 42; *Bendiscioli, l. c.* p. 428, *Lenz, Schlangenk* p. 332 (1832), *Schaefer, Moselfaun.* p. 263 (1844); *Meisn. Mus. Nat. Helv.* p. 90, pls. i. fig. 3, & ii. fig. 1 (1820), and *in Wyder, Serp Suisse*, p. 17, pl. i. fig 3, & ii. fig. 1 (1823).

—— berus (*non L.*), *Meisn. ll. cc.* pp. 89, 17, pl. i. figs. 1 & 2; *Metaxa, l. c.* p. 42; *Bendiscioli, l c.* p. 424; *Guér. Icon. R. A., Rept.* pl. xxiii. fig. 1 (1844).

—— atra, *Meisn. ll cc.* pp. 93, 18, pl ii. fig. 2

—— prester (*non L*), *Meisn. ll. cc.* pp. 93, 18, pl. ii. fig. 3; *Metaxa, l. c.* p 43.

—— aspis, *Merr. Tent.* p 151 (1820), *Metaxa, l. c.* p. 42; *Bendiscioli, l c.* p. 426; *Bonap. Icon Faun. Ital, Anf.* (1834); *Schleg. Phys Serp.* ii. p 599, pl. xxi. figs. 16–18 (1837), *Gray, Cat.* p. 30 (1849); *Dum. & Bibr.* vii p. 1406, pl. lxxix. *b.* fig. 3 (1854); *Soubeiran, De la Vipère*, p. 31 (1855), *De Betta, Erp. Ven.* p. 238 (1857), *Soubeiran, Bull Soc. Acclim.* x 1863, p 397, *Viaud-Grandm. Serp. Vend* p 30 (1867); *Strauch, Syn. Viper.* p. 55 (1869); *Fatio, Vert. Suisse*, iii. p. 220 (1872), *Jan, Icon. Gén.* 45, pl. iii. figs. 2-7 (1874); *De Betta, Faun Ital., Rett. Anf.* p. 54 (1874); *Lataste, Act. Soc Linn. Bord.* 1875, (3) x. CR. p. xxi; *Schrieb. Herp. Eur.* p. 193 (1875); *Lataste, Herp Gironde*, p. 166, pl. viii. fig. 7 (1876); *F. Müll. Verh. Nat. Ges. Basel*, vi. 1877, p. 415, & 1878, p 695, pl. iii. fig. B, *De Betta, Atti Ist. Ven.* (5) v. 1879, p. 399, and vi. 1880, p 379; *Tournev. Bull. Soc. Zool. France*, 1881, p 53; *F Müll. op. cit* vii. 1882, p. 153; *De Betta, Atti Ist. Ven.* (7) i. 1883, p. 935; *Leydig, Abh Senck. Ges.* xiii. 1883, p. 192; *F. Müll. op. cit.* vii. 1884, p. 300, & 1885, p. 692; *Blum, Abh. Senck. Ges* xv 1888, p. 128, *and Zool. Gart* 1892, pp 12 & 265; *Dalla Torre, Progr Gymn. Innsbr.* 1891, p 12; *Bedriaga, CR. Congr Int. Zool* 1892, i. p. 241; *Durigen, Deutschl. Rept u. Amph.* p. 360, pl x. fig. 1 (1894).

—— communis, *Millet, Faune Maine et Loire*, ii. p. 646, pl. v. fig. 1 (1828); *Mauduyt, Herp. Vienne*, p. 33 (1844).

—— hugyi, *Schinz, Nat. Rept.* p 179, pl lxxviii. fig. 2 (1833).

—— berus, subsp. aspis, *Camerano, Mon. Ofid. Ital., Viper.* p. 41, pl. i. figs. 1-7, 22-32 (1888); *Mina-Palumbo, Nat. Sicil.* xi. 1892, p. 110, *Caruccio, Boll. Soc. Rom. Zool.* iii. 1894, p. 77.

Snout flat above, more or less distinctly turned up at the end, with sharp, not or but very feebly raised canthus; vertical diameter of the eye nearly equal to its distance from the mouth; supraocular region more or less slanting forwards, the posterior border of the supraocular usually not extending beyond the vertical of . the posterior border of the eye. Rostral usually deeper than broad, its width $\frac{1}{2}$ to $\frac{2}{3}$ its depth, extending to the upper edge of the snout; two or three apical shields; upper surface of head usually covered with small, subimbricate, smooth or feebly keeled scales, in 4 to 7 series between the supraoculars; frontal and parietal shields usually absent, sometimes distinct, but small and rather irregular, the former separated from the supraoculars by two series of scales; supraocular well developed; 8 to 13 scales round the eye, usually 10 to 12; two (rarely three) series of scales between the eye and the labials; nasal single, separated from the rostral by a naso-rostral; temporal scales smooth or feebly keeled; 9 to 13 upper labials, usually 9 to 11, 4 (rarely 5) lower labials in contact with the chin-shields. Scales in 21 or 23 rows (exceptionally 19 or 25), strongly keeled, outer row more or less distinctly keeled, rarely perfectly smooth. Ventrals 134–158 in ♂, 142–169 in ♀; anal entire; subcaudals 32–49 in ♂, 30–43 in ♀. Coloration very variable: grey, yellowish, brown, or red above, with dark markings in the form of paired spots or cross-bars, or with a zigzag band as in *V. berus*; usually a ∧-shaped dark marking on the back of the head and a dark streak behind the eye; upper lip whitish, yellowish, or pinkish, with or without dark vertical bars on the sutures between the labials; yellowish, whitish, grey, or black beneath, with or without darker and lighter markings. Some specimens entirely black.

Total length. ♂, 675 millim.; tail 95. ♀, 620; 75.

France, as far north as Southern Brittany and Paris; Pyrenees, Alsace-Lorraine; Southern Black Forest; Switzerland; Italy and Sicily; Southern Tyrol.

a. Many specimens, ♂ (V. 143–150; C. 39–43) & ♀ (V. 142–157, C. 32–36).	Nr. Nantes	Messrs. H & T. Piel de Churchville [P.].
b–d, e. ♂ (V. 145, 144, 144; C 38, 35, 38) & ♀ (V. 150, C 33)	Argenton, Indre.	M. R. Parâtre [P].
f–l. ♂ (V. 150, 151; C.44, 44) & ♀ (V.157, 148, 153, 156; C. 38, 36, 34, 33).	Argenton, Indre.	M. R. Rollinat [P].
m–o. ♂ (V. 151, C. 44), ♀ (V. 145; C 33), & yg ♀ (V. 141, C. 38).	Cadillac and Talais, Gironde.	M F Lataste [P].
p. ♂ (V 137, C. 37).	Pau, Pyrenees.	H. A. Hammond, Esq [P.].
q. ♂ (V. 152; C 45).	France	
r–v. ♀ (V. 151, 157; C. 34, 35) & yg ♂ (V. 151, 155, 148, 157; C.40,42,44,41).	Nr Geneva.	G A. Boulenger, Esq. [P.].
w–z. ♂ (V 152, 153, 151, C 43, 38, 41) & ♀ (V. 152, C. 32).	Lausanne.	W. Morton, Esq [P].
α. ♂ (V. 158; C. 45)	Château d'Oex, 3450 ft.	Dr F. Muller [P].
β. ♂ (V. 156; C. 43).	Binn, Upper Wallis, 3900 ft.	Dr. F. Muller [P.].
γ. Yg. ♂ (V. 152, C. 48)	Alps.	Rev S. W. King [P.].
δ–ζ, η–ι ♂ (V. 148, 153, 155; C. 45, 44, 43) & ♀ (V. 147,156, C. 32, 38).	Viu, Alps of Piedmont	Count Peracca [P.].

κ, λ. ♂ (V. 153, 156, C. ?, 43).   Italian Alps.   Prof. Bonelli [P.].

μ. ♂ (V. 147; C. 37).   Ferrara, Prov. Venice.   Prof. Bianconi [P.].

ν, ξ. ♀ (V. 147; C. 43) & vg. ♀ (V. 147; C. 35).   Bozen, S. Tyrol.   Hr. F Henkel [E.].

ο–τ. ♂ (V. 141, 148, 146, 148, 147; C. 43, 47, 43, 42, 43).   Nr Pisa.   Prof. C E. Della Torre [P.].

υ. ♀ (V. 150; C. 32).   Mondragone, nr. Naples.   Dr. Monticelli [P.].

φ. ♂ (V. 136; C. 39)   Serra S. Bruno, Calabria.   Florence Museum [E.]

χ. ♂ skeleton.   N. Italy.

5. Vipera latastii.

Coluber aspis (non L.), *Vandelli, Mem. Acc Lisb.* i. 1797, p 69.
Vipera ammodytes, part., *Schleg Phys. Serp* ii p 602, pl. xxi. figs 19 & 20 (1837), *Gray, Cat.* p. 31 (1849); *Schreib. Herp Eur.* p. 187 (1875); *De Betta, Atti Ist. Ven.* (5) vi. 1880, p. 385.
—— aspis, part, *Strauch, Erp. Alg.* p. 70 (1862).
—— latastei, *Boscá, Bull Soc. Zool. France*, 1878, p. 116, pl. iv, and 1880, p. 261; *De Betta, Atti Ist. Ven.* (5) v. 1879, p 612, *Tournev Bull. Soc Zool. France*, 1881, p 56; *Boettg. Abh. Senck. Ges.* xiii. 1883, p. 106; *Bouleng Trans. Zool. Soc.* xiii 1891, p. 147; *Bedriaga, Amph & Rept Portug, Istituto*, xxxviii. 1890, p. 138, *and CR Congr. Int. Zool.* 1892, i p. 239; *Ferreira, Jorn Sc Lisb* (2) iii 1894, p 167
—— berus, subsp. aspis, var., *Camerano, Mon. Ofid. Ital, Viper.* p 48 (1888).

Intermediate between *V. aspis* and *V. ammodytes*. Snout sometimes merely turned up as in the former, sometimes ending in a dermal appendage or 'horn' which is but little less developed than in the latter. Rostral once and a half to twice as deep as broad, nearly reaching the tip of the rostral wart; 5 or 6 (rarely 3) scales on the posterior aspect of the latter; head covered with small, smooth, or feebly keeled, subimbricate scales, among which a slightly enlarged frontal may sometimes be distinguished; 5 to 7 longitudinal series of scales between the supraoculars, which are well developed; 9 to 13 scales round the eye, usually 10 to 12, two or three series of scales between the eye and the labials; nasal entire, separated from the rostral by a naso-rostral; temporal scales smooth or feebly keeled; 9 to 11 upper labials; 4 or 5 lower labials in contact with the chin-shields. Scales in 21 rows, strongly keeled, outer row smooth or feebly keeled. Ventrals 125–146 in ♂, 135–147 in ♀; anal entire; subcaudals 35–43 in ♂, 32–35 in ♀. Grey or brown above, with a dark brown, usually black-edged undulous or zigzag band along the spine and a lateral series of spots; head with or without small dark markings above, and a dark streak behind the eye; labials more or less speckled or spotted with black; lower parts grey, spotted with black and white, or blackish speckled with white; end of tail usually yellow or with yellow spots.

Total length: ♂ 550 millim.; tail 85. ♀ 610; 80.

Spain and Portugal, Morocco and Algeria North of the Atlas.

a–b, c–d ♂ (144, C. 42), ♀ (V. 147; C. 34), yg ♂ (V 142; C. 41), & yg. ♀ (V. 141; C. 35).	Serra de Gerez, Portugal.	Dr. H. Gadow [C.].
e. ♂ (V. 146, C. 40).	Serra de Gerez.	Dr. Lopez Vieira [P].
f–g. ♂ (V. 129; C. 42) & ♀ (V. 138; C. ?).	Coimbra.	Dr Lopez Vieira [P].
h–i. ♂ (V. 131; C. 43) & ♀ (V. ?, C 35)	Seville.	Prof. Calderon [E].
k. ♀ (V. 135; C. 35).	Costo del Rey, Andalusia.	H.R.H. Comte de Paris [P.].
l–m. Yg. ♂ (V. 133, 133, C. 38, 42).	Andalusia.	Zoological Society.
n. ♂ (V. 125, C 35).	Nr. Tangier.	M. H. Vaucher [C.].
o. ♀ (V. 135; C. 32).	Mt. Edough, nr. Bona, Algeria.	M. F. Lataste [P.].
p. Yg. ♂ (V. 133, C. 42)	Mt. Edough.	Dr F. Muller [E.].
q ♂ (V. 128, C. 38).	——?	

6. Vipera ammodytes.

Coluber ammodytes, *Linn. Amœn Acad* 1. p 506, pl. xii. fig 2 (1749), *and S N* 1. p. 376 (1766), *Wolf, in Sturm, Deutschl. Faun.* iii. H. 2 (1799); *Reider & Hahn, Faun. Borca,* iii. (1832).

Vipera illyrica, *Laur Syn Rept.* p 101 (1768).

—— ammodytes, *Latr. Rept.* iii p. 306 (1802); *Daud Rept* vi. p. 193, pl. lxxiv fig. 2 (1803); *Lenz, Schlangenk.* p 403 (1832); *Bibr. & Bory, Expéd. Sc Morée,* iii. Rept. p. 74, pl xii. fig. 3 (1833), *Bonap Icon. Faun Ital., Anf.* (1834), *Dum. & Bibr.* vii. p. 1414, pl. lxxviii. b. fig. 1 (1854); *De Betta, Erp. Venet* p. 253 (1857), *and Atti Ist. Ven.* (3) xiii. 1868, p 943, *Strauch, Syn. Viper.* p. 66 (1869), *and Schl Russ R.* p. 214 (1873), *Jan, Icon Gén.* 45, pl. iii. fig. 1 (1874); *De Betta, Faun. Ital, Rett Anf.* p. 56 (1874), *and Atti Ist. Ven* (5) v. 1879, p. 589, *Bedriaga, Bull Soc Nat. Mosc.* lvi 1881, p. 322, *Tournev. Bull Soc. Zool. France,* 1881, p. 65, *Leydig, Abh. Senck. Ges.* xiii. 1883, p 196, *Boettg Sitzb Ak Berl* 1888, p. 179, *Camerano, Mon Ofid. Ital, Viper* p. 46 (1888); *Parona, Atti Ist Ven.* (6) vi 1888, p 1165; *Dalla Torre, Progr Gymn Innsbr* 1891, p 13, *Bedriaga, CR. Congr. Int Zool.* 1892, 1. p. 239, *Werner, Zool Anz.* 1893, p 424; *Tomasini, Wiss. Mitth. Bosn Herzeg.* ii. p. 638 (1894).

Echidna ammodytes, *Frivaldsky, Mon Serp. Hung.* p. 33 (1823).

Cobra ammodytes, *Fitzing. N. Class. Rept.* p. 62 (1826).

Vipera ammodytes, part., *Schley. Phys Serp.* ii. p. 602 (1837); *Gray, Cat.* p 31 (1849), *Schreib. Herp Eur.* p 187 (1875), *De Betta, Atti Ist Ven.* (5) vi. 1880, p. 385.

Rhinechis ammodytes, *Fitzing. Gesch Menag. Œsterr. Hof.* p. — (1855).

Snout produced into an erect, horn-like dermal appendage covered with 10 to 20 small scales; canthus rostralis strong; vertical diameter of eye less than its distance from the mouth in the adult. Rostral as deep as broad or broader than deep; upper surface of head covered with small smooth or faintly keeled scales, among which an enlarged frontal or a frontal and a pair of parietals are sometimes distinguishable; 5 to 7 longitudinal series of scales between the supraoculars; latter large, usually not extending posteriorly beyond the vertical of the posterior border of the eye: 10 to 13 scales round the eye; two series of scales between the eye and the labials; nasal entire, separated from the rostral by a naso-rostral; temporal scales smooth or feebly keeled; 8 to 12 upper labials, usually 9 or 10; 4 or 5 lower labials in contact with the chin-shields. Scales in 21 or 23 rows, strongly keeled, outer row smooth or feebly keeled. Ventrals 133-158 in ♂, 135-162 in ♀; anal entire; subcaudals 27-38 in ♂, 24-34 in ♀. Grey, brown, or reddish above, with an undulous or zigzag black or dark brown, usually black-edged dorsal band, a lateral series of dark spots present or absent; head with or without symmetrical markings above; a dark streak behind the eye usually present; belly greyish or pink, powdered with black, with or without black and white spots; end of tail yellow, orange, or coral-red. Males usually distinguishable from females by darker markings.

Total length: ♂ 550 millim.; tail 80 ♀ 640; 70.

From the Southern Tyrol, Carinthia, Styria, and Hungary to Greece, Turkey, Asia Minor, Transcaucasia, and Syria.

a-b ♀ (V 154; C. 30) & hgr. ♂ (V. 154; C. 30).	Friesach, Carinthia	Dr. F. Werner [E.].
c-d. ♂ (V. 153; C. 38) & ♀ (V. 150, C. 31).	Landskron, Carinthia.	Dr. F. Werner [E.].
e. ♀ (V. 160, C 33).	Feldkirche, Carinthia.	Hr F. Henkel [E].
f-h, i-n. ♂ (V. 157, 153, 157; C. 27, 36, 35) & ♀ (V. 159, 151, 150, 153, 154; C. 29, 34, 24, 30, 29).	Carinthia.	Hr. F. Henkel [E.].
o. Hgr. ♂ (V. 156; C. 33).	Bozen, S Tyrol.	Dr F. Werner [E.].
p. ♂ (V. 154; C. 36).	St. Peter, Carniola.	Hr. F. Henkel [E.].
q-r, s. ♂ (V. 155, 149; C. 38, 36) & ♀ (V. 154; C. 30).	Travnik, Bosnia.	Dr. F. Werner [E].
t. Yg. (V. 151; C. 33).	Dinaric Alps, Bosnia, 7500 feet.	Dr. F. Werner [E.].
u Hgr. ♀ (V 147; C. 28)	Zara, Dalmatia.	Dr. F. Werner [E.].
v-w. ♂ (V. 145; C. 33) & ♀ (V. 155; C P).	Zara.	Hr. Spada Novak [C.].
x ♂ (V. 154; C. 35).	Dalmatia.	Christiania Museum.
y. ♀ (V. 160, C. 30).	Herkulesbad, Hungary.	Prof. v. Móhely [E.].
z Hgr. ♀ (V. 135; C. 27).	Nr. Tarsos, N. Morea.	Norman Douglas, Esq. [P.].

α–β. Yg (V. 137; C. 30) Xenochori, N. Euboia. Senckenberg Mus.
& head of adult [E.].
γ. Hgr. ♀ (V. 139; Delos. J. Ince, Esq. [P.]
C. 26).
δ. Hgr. ♀ (V. 138; Lebanon. Canon Tristram [C.].
C. 24).
ε–ζ. Hgr. ♂ (V. 133, Mediterranean. J. Miller, Esq. [P.]
C. 35) & ♀ (V. 137;
C. 26).
η–θ. ♂ (V. 156, 158; S. Europe.
C 37, 34)
ι. Skull. Morea

7. Vipera raddii.

Vipera aspis, var ocellata (non Latr.), Berth. in Wagn. Reise n
Kolchis, p. 337 (1850)
—— xanthina (non Gray), Strauch, Syn. Viper p 73, pl. i. (1869),
and Schl. Russ R. p. 216 (1873)
—— raddei, Boettg Zool. Anz. 1890, p. 62.

Snout rounded; vertical diameter of eye measuring hardly half
its distance from the mouth. Rostral somewhat deeper than broad,
not extending to the upper surface of the snout; head covered
above with small feebly keeled scales; supraocular well developed,
erectile, the free edge angular, separated from the eye by small
scales, the eye being surrounded by a complete circle of 14 to 17
scales; eye separated from the labials by two series of scales;
nostril pierced in a single nasal, which is imperfectly separated
from the naso-rostral; temporal scales keeled; 9 or 10 upper
labials. Scales in 23 rows, strongly keeled. Ventrals 150–180;
anal entire; subcaudals 23–32. Pale brown or greyish above,
with a dorsal series of somewhat lighter reddish roundish spots
which are dark-edged on the sides; these spots may be in pairs
and alternating; sides with two series of dark brown spots; a
dark /\-shaped marking on the back of the head and a dark streak
behind the eye; yellowish beneath, powdered with black, each
shield with a transverse series of black and white spots.

Total length 740 millim.; tail 50.
Armenia.

8. Vipera lebetina.

Coluber lebetinus, Linn S. N i. p 378 (1766), Forsk. Descr. Anim.
p. 13 (1775)
Vipera lebetina, Daud. Rept. vi. p. 137 (1803); Strauch, Erp. Alg.
p. 71 (1862); Jan, Elenco, p. 121 (1863), and Icon Gén. 46, pl. vi.
fig. 1 (1874); Boettg Zeitsch. Ges. Naturw. xlix. 1877, p. 288;
Bouleng. Faun. Ind., Rept. p. 421 (1890), and Trans Zool. Soc.
xiii. 1891, p. 148; Bedriaga, CR. Congr. Int. Zool. 1892, i.
p 239.
—— obtusa, Dwigubsky, Essay Nat Hist Russ. Emp p. 30 (1832),
Blanf. Zool. E. Pers. p. 428 (1876), and Zool. 2nd Yark. Miss.,
Rept p. 24 (1878); Boettg. Zool. Jahrb iii. 1888, p. 946.

Vipera euphratica, *Martin, Proc. Zool. Soc.* 1838, p. 82; *Strauch, Schl. Russ. R.* p. 221, pl. vi. (1873), *Boettg Ber Senck. Ges* 1880, p. 267; *Bedriaga, Bull Soc Nat. Mosc* lvi 1881, p. 315.
—— echis?, *Schleg. in Wagn. Reis Reg. Alg.* iii. p. 131 (1841).
Echidna mauritanica, *Guichen Explor. Sc. Alg, Rept.* p 24, pl iii. (1848); *Dum. & Bibr.* vii. p. 1431 (1854).
Daboia xanthina, *Gray, Cat.* p. 24 (1849), *Gunth. Proc. Zool. Soc.* 1864, p. 489; *Tristram, Faun. & Flor. Palest.* pl. xv. (1884).
Clotho? mauritanica, *Gray, l c* p. 27
Daboia euphratica, *Gray, l. c.* p. 116.
Vipera minuta, *Eichw. Nouv. Mém. Soc Nat. Mosc.* ix. 1851, p 438.
Bitis mauritanica, *Gunth Cat* p. 268 (1858).
Vipera confluenta, *Cope, Proc Zool. Soc.* 1863. p 229, fig
—— mauritanica, *Strauch, Syn. Viper.* p. 79 (1869).
—— xanthina, *F. Mull. Verh. Nat. Ges. Basel*, vi. 1878, p. 700, pl. iii fig. A; *Boettg. Sitzb. Ak. Berl.* 1888, p. 180, and *Zool. Jahrb.* iii. 1888, p. 947, *Bedriaga, CR Congr Int Zool.* 1892, i. p. 239.
—— euphratica, var. mauritanica, *Boettg. Abh. Senck. Ges.* xiii. 1883, p. 105.
—— lebetina, var. deserti, *Anders. Proc. Zool. Soc.* 1892, p. 20, pl. i. figs. 6 & 7.

Snout rounded and obtuse or subacuminate, usually with well-marked canthus; vertical diameter of eye shorter than its distance from the mouth in the adult. Rostral as deep as broad, a little broader than deep, or slightly deeper than broad, reaching or nearly reaching the upper surface of the snout and in contact with two or three apical scales; scales on upper surface of head small, subimbricate, feebly or strongly keeled, rarely smooth on the forehead and snout; 7 to 12 longitudinal series of scales between the eyes (supraoculars included); supraocular well developed or narrow, or broken up into two or more small shields; 12 to 18 scales round the eye; two or three series of scales between the eye and the labials, sometimes only a single scale between the eye and the fourth labial; nostril in a single nasal *, which is usually partially fused with the naso-rostral; a well-developed supranasal; temporal scales keeled; 9 to 12 upper labials; 4 or 5 lower labials in contact with the chin-shields. Scales in 23 to 27 rows, strongly keeled, outer row smooth or feebly keeled. Ventrals 147–177 in ♂, 152–180 in ♀; anal entire; subcaudals 38–51 in ♂, 29–48 in ♀. Coloration varying to the same extent as in *V. aspis*. Grey or pale brown above, with a dorsal series of large dark brown spots, often edged with blackish, which may be confluent into an undulous band, or with small dark spots or cross-bars; small dark lateral spots and vertical bars; a large ∧-shaped marking on the upper surface of the head, and a /\-shaped one on the occiput, may be present; a dark streak behind the eye to the angle of the mouth, and usually a dark blotch or bar below the eye; whitish beneath, powdered with grey-brown, with or without dark brown

---

* The nasal being often strongly hollowed out, the nostril may appear pierced between three shields, as in *V. russellii*.

spots; end of tail yellow. All the markings sometimes very indistinct.

Total length: ♂ 960 millim.; tail 120   ♀ 1350; 170.

This species may be divided into several ill-defined varieties, the two extremes being the var. *xanthina*, Gray, from Asia Minor and Syria, and the var. *deserti*, Anders., from the confines of the Tunisian Sahara—the former characterized by an obtusely pointed snout covered with strongly keeled scales, the latter with a very short and broad snout without canthus and covered with smooth scales. Certain specimens approach the var. *hugyi* of *V. aspis*, and the species is to a certain extent connected with *V. russellii* through the var. *xanthina*.

Morocco, Algeria, Tunisia, Egypt (?), Syria, Cyprus, Greek Archipelago, Asia Minor, Transcaspia, Persia, Mesopotamia, Afghanistan, Baluchistan, Cashmir.

a. ♀ (Sc. 27; V. 157; C. 48).	Oran, Algeria.	M. Doumergue [E.].
b, c ♂ (Sc. 25, V.156; C. 43) & ♀ (Sc. 25; V. 157; C. 38).	Algeria.	
d. ♂ (Sc. 27; V. 167; C 51).	Duirat, S Tunisia	Dr. J Anderson [P]. (Type of var. *deserti*.)
e ♀ (Sc. 25, V. 154, C. 43).	Cyprus.	Gen. Biddulph [P.].
f–g, h–k. ♀ (Sc. 25, V. 156, 158, 153, C. 43, 43, 39) & yg (Sc. 25, V. 148, 147; C 44, 42).	Cyprus.	Lord Lilford [P.].
l. ♀ (Sc. 25; V. 170; C 44).	Galilee.	Canon Tristram [C.].
m, n ♂ (Sc. 25; V.160, 157, C. 40, 41)	Plain of Acre and Tiberias.	Canon Tristram [C.].
o. ♀ (Sc. 25; V. 152; C 31).	Xanthus, Asia Minor.	Sir C. Fellows [P.]. (Type of *V. xanthina*.)
p. Hgr ♀ (Sc. 23; V. 158; C 34).	Budrum, Ruins of Halicarnassus.	H.M S. 'Supply.'
q. Yg. (Sc. 23; V. 162; C. 30).	Smyrna.	
r. Yg. (Sc 23, V. 152, C. 29)	Asia Minor.	A.C Christy, Esq.[P.]. (Type of *V. xanthina*)
s–t. ♀ (Sc. 25; V. 172, C. 44) & yg (Sc 25; V. 163; C. 49)	Nuhar, Transcaspia.	Dr Radde [C.]
u ♂ (Sc 25, V 177; C. 50).	Teheran Hills.	
v, w ♀ (Sc. 25, V 173, 180; C. 46, 47).	Persia.	
x. Head and neck of adult.	Sang Hadji.	Dr. Aitchison [C.]; Afghan Boundary Commission.
y. Head and neck of adult.	Shoré Kaltegai.	Dr. Aitchison [C.]; Afghan Boundary Commission.

z. ♀ (Sc. 25; V. 175; C. 45).   Quetta, Baluchistan   Mr J A. Murray [P.].
a. ♀ (Sc. 27; V. 173; C. 46).   ——?   Zoological Society.
(One of the types of *V. confluenta*)
β. ♀ (Sc. 27; V. 178; C. 46).   ——?   Zoological Society.
γ. Skull.   Cyprus.

9. Vipera russellii.

Russell, Ind. Serp. i. pl. vii. (1796) & ii. pl. xxxii. (1801).
Coluber russellii, *Shaw, Nat Miscell.* viii. pl ccxci., *and Zool.* iii. p. 418, pl. cviii (1802).
—— trinoculus, *Bechst. Lacép Naturg. Amph.* iv. p. 245 (1802).
Vipera elegans, *Daud Rept.* vi. p. 124, pl. lxxiii. (1803); *Schleg. Phys. Serp.* ii p. 588, pl. xxi. figs. 4 & 5 (1837); *Jan, Icon. Gén* 45, pl. vi. fig. 2 (1874)
Coluber triseriatus, *Herm. Obs. Zool.* i. p. 278 (1804).
Daboia elegans, *Gray, Zool. Miscell.* p 69 (1842), *and Cat.* p. 23 (1849).
—— russellii, *Gray, ll cc* pp. 69 & 24, *Gunth. Rept. Brit. Ind.* p 396 (1864); *Stoliczka, Journ. As Soc. Beng.* xxxix. 1870, p 226; *Fayrer, Thanatoph. Ind.* pl. xi (1874); *Theob. Cat. Rept Brit. Ind.* p. 217 (1876); *Anders. An. Zool. Res. Yunnan*, p. 833 (1879).
—— pulchella, *Gray, Zool. Miscell.* p. 69
Echidna elegans, *Dum. & Bibr.* vii p 1435 (1854)
—— russellii, *Steind. Novara, Rept* p. 88 (1867).
Vipera russellii, *Strauch, Syn. Viper* p 85 (1869); *Bouleng Faun Ind., Rept.* p. 420, fig. (1890), *Brook-Fox, Journ. Bomb. N H Soc.* viii 1894, p. 565.

Snout obtuse, with distinct canthus; vertical diameter of the eye shorter than its distance from the mouth in the adult. Rostral as deep as broad or a little broader than deep, in contact with two or three apical scales; scales on upper surface of head small, imbricate, strongly keeled; 6 to 9 longitudinal series of scales between the supraoculars, which are very narrow; 10 to 15 scales round the eye; three or four series of scales between the eye and the labials; nostril very large, pierced in the nasal and bordered by a supranasal and a naso-rostral; temporal scales strongly keeled; 10 to 12 upper labials; 4 or 5 (rarely 3) lower labials in contact with the chin-shields. Scales in 27–33 rows, strongly keeled, outer row smooth. Ventrals 154–176; anal entire; subcaudals 43–64. Pale brown above, with three longitudinal series of black, light-edged rings or rhombs, which may encircle reddish-brown spots; the vertebral spots may join or even form an undulous band; in some specimens, however, these elegant markings may be replaced by faint dark spots; head with large symmetrical dark markings and two light streaks uniting on the snout and diverging behind; yellowish white beneath, uniform or with crescentic small black spots.

Total length 1250 millim.; tail 170. Grows to 1670 millim.

India, Ceylon, Burma, Siam; Sumatra and Java (?).

a.	♀ (Sc. 29 ; V. 164 ; C. 48)	India.	Dr. P. Russell [P.].
b.	♀ (Sc. 31 ; V. 165 ; C. 43).	India.	Gen. Hardwicke [P.].
c, d.	♀ (Sc. 29, 33 ; V. 176, 173 ; C. 52, 45).	India.	
e	Yg (Sc 31 ; V. 160 ; C. 46).	Kulu, Himalayas.	Messrs v. Schlagintweit [C.].
f.	♂ (Sc. 29 ; V. 164 ; C. 46).	Almorah.	R. Hearsey, Esq. [P].
g.	♂ (Sc 30 ; V. 164 ; C. 49).	Almorah.	Dr. Cantor.
h.	♀ (Sc. 29 ; V 172 ; C. 49).	Bombay.	Dr. Leith [P.].
i.	♀ (Sc. 29 ; V. 163 ; C 49).	Anamallays.	Col. Beddome [C.].
k–l.	Yg. (Sc. 29, 28 , V. 167, 175 ; C. 52, 54).	Trincomalee.	Major Barrett [P.]
m.	Yg , bad state.	Ceylon.	Capt. Gascoigne [P.]. (Type of *D pulchella*)
n, o.	♀ (Sc. 29, V. 163 ; C 43) & yg (Sc. 30 , V. 160 ; C. 45).	Ceylon	R Templeton, Esq. [P.].
p.	Yg. (Sc 28 , V. 164 ; C. 54)	Ceylon.	W. Ferguson, Esq. [P.].
q	Many specimens, yg. (Sc. 28–31 , V. 154–168 ; C. 43–64).	Ceylon.	Miss Layard [P.]
r.	Yg. (Sc. 29 ; V. 172 , C. 53).	Java (?)	
s.	Skull	Bombay.	

10. Vipera superciliaris.

Vipera superciliaris, *Peters, Mon. Berl. Ac.* 1854, p 625, *Strauch, Syn. Viper.* p. 84 (1869); *Peters, Reise n. Mossamb.* III p 144, pl. xxi. (1882); *Pfeffer, Jahrb. Hamb. Wiss. Anst.* x. 1893, p. 21.

Snout rounded, with distinct canthus; vertical diameter of the eye a little shorter than its distance from the mouth. Rostral broader than deep; head covered with small, imbricate, keeled scales; a large supraocular shield, 12 scales round the eye, which is separated from the labials by two series of scales; nostril very large, between two nasals, the anterior of which is in contact with the rostral; temporal scales keeled; nine upper labials. Scales in 27 rows, strongly keeled, outer row feebly keeled. Ventrals 142; anal entire; subcaudals 40. Pale reddish brown or orange above, with blackish cross-bars broken by an interrupted yellowish longitudinal streak on each side; head with blackish symmetrical markings; whitish beneath, spotted with blackish.

Total length 570 millim.; tail 77.

Coast of Mozambique.

4. BITIS.

Cobra, *Laur. Syn. Rept.* p. 103 (1768).
Vipera, part., *Merr. Tent. Syst. Amph.* p. 149 (1820); *Schleg. Phys. Serp.* ii. p. 573 (1837); *Dum. & Bibr. Erp. Gén.* vii. p. 1403 (1854); *Jan, Elenco sist. Ofid.* p. 120 (1863); *Strauch, Syn. Viper.* p. 21 (1869).
Echidna (*non Forst.*), part., *Merr. l. c.* p. 150; *Dum. & Bibr. l. c.* p. 1420 (1854).
Echidna, *Wagl. Syst. Amph.* p. 177 (1830).
Cerastes, part., *Wagl. l. c.* p. 178; *Gray, Zool. Miscell.* p. 70 (1842); *Dum. & Bibr. t. c.* p. 1438.
Clotho (*non Fauj.*), *Gray, l. c.* p. 69, and *Cat. Sn.* p. 24 (1849).
Bitis, *Gray, ll. cc.* pp. 69, 25; *Peters, Mon. Berl. Ac.* 1866, p. 891, and *Reise n. Mossamb.* iii. p. 145 (1882).
Calechidna, *Tschudi, Faun. Per., Herp.* p. 60 (1845).

Head very distinct from neck, covered with small imbricate scales; eye moderate or rather small, with vertical pupil, separated

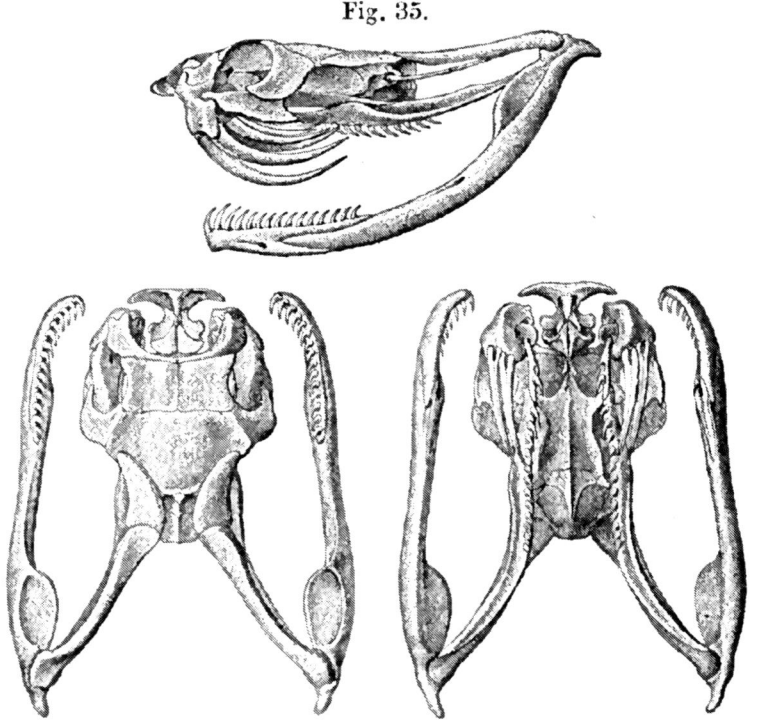

Fig. 35.

Skull of *Bitis arietans*.

from the labials by small scales; nostrils directed upwards or upwards and outwards, pierced in a single or divided nasal, with a deep pit or pocket above, closed by a valvular, crescentic supranasal. Postfrontal bone very large, in contact with the ectopterygoid, which has an outer, hook-shaped process. Scales keeled, with apical pits, in 22-41 rows; lateral scales in some species slightly oblique; ventrals rounded. Tail very short; subcaudals in two rows.

Africa.

Synopsis of the Species.

I. Nostrils directed upwards; no nasal or palpebral raised scales; one or two series of scales between the nasal and the rostral; scales in 29-41 rows. .... 1. *arietans*, p. 493.

II. Nostrils directed upwards and outwards.

   A. No enlarged raised scales between the supranasals; two or three series of scales between the nasal and the rostral; scales in 22-31 rows.

      1. Supraocular region not raised, no horn-like scales; subcaudals well developed and smooth in both sexes.

Outer row of scales smooth .... 2. *peringueyi*, p. 495.
Outer row of scales keeled .... 3. *atropos*, p. 495.

      2. Supraorbital region raised, but without horn-like scales; subcaudals well developed and smooth in both sexes.
                                                      4. *inornata*, p. 496.

      3. Supraorbital "horns" usually present; subcaudals, in females, small and scale-like, more or less distinctly keeled.

Several supraorbital "horns" .... 5. *cornuta*, p. 497.
Supraorbital "horn," if present, single .. 6. *caudalis*, p. 498.

   B. Enlarged, more or less raised or horn-like scales between the supranasals; four or five series of scales between the nasal and the rostral; scales in 33-41 rows.

A single enlarged scale above the supranasal, in contact with its fellow ...... 7. *gabonica*, p. 499.
Two or three enlarged scales above the supranasal, usually with small scales between them and their fellows ...... 8. *nasicornis*, p. 500.

1. Bitis arietans.

Seba, Thes. ii. pls. xxx. fig. 1, liv. fig. 4, & xciv. fig. 2 (1735).
? Cobra clotho, *Laur. Syn. Rept.* p. 104 (1768).
Cobra lachesis, *Laur. l. c.*
Coluber lachesis, *Gmel. S. N.* i. p 1085 (1788).
? Coluber clotho, *Gmel. l. c* p. 1086
? Coluber bitin, *Bonnat. Encycl. Méth., Ophiol.* p. 22 (1789).

Coluber intumescens, *Donnd. Zool. Beytr.* iii. p. 209 (1798).
Vipera severa, part, *Latr. Rept.* iii. p. 335, pl. —. fig. 1 (1802); *Daud. Rept.* vi. p. 115 (1803).
—— (Echidna) arietans, *Merr. Tent.* p. 152 (1820), and *Beitr.* iii. p. 121 (1821).
—— inflata, *Burchell, Trav. S. Afr.* i. p. 469 (1822); *Smith, Edinb. N. Philos. Journ* i 1826, p. 250.
Echidna arietans, *Wagl Icon Amph.* pl. xi. (1828); *Dum. & Bibr.* vii. p. 1425, pl. lxxix b. fig. 1 (1854).
Vipera brachyura, *Cuv. R. A.* 2nd ed. ii. p. 90 (1829).
—— arietans, *Schleg. Phys Serp.* ii p. 577, pl xxi. figs 1-3 (1837), *Strauch, Syn. Viper.* p. 93 (1869); *Jan, Icon Gén* 45, pl vi figs. 3 & 4 (1874), *Boettg. Abh Senck. Ges.* ix. 1874, p. 163, and *Ber Senck. Ges.* 1888, p. 89; *Bouleng. Tr Zool. Soc.* xiii 1891, p. 148; *Boettg. Zool. Anz.* 1893, p 130; *Bocage, Herp. Angola*, p. 149 (1895).
Clotho arietans, *Gray, Zool. Miscell.* p. 69 (1842), and *Cat.* p. 25 (1849).
—— lateristriga, *Gray, ll. cc.* pp. 69 & 26.
Bitis arietans, *Gunth. Cat.* p. 263 (1858); *Peters, Reise n. Mossamb.* iii. p. 145 (1882).
Echidna clotho, *Steind. Novara, Rept.* p. 88 (1867).

Nostrils on the upper surface of the spout. Rostral small, twice to twice and a half as broad as deep; head covered with small imbricate scales, 8 to 11 across the vertex, from eye to eye; 12 to 16 scales round the eye, three or four series of scales between the eye and the labials; two (rarely three) series of scales between the supranasals; one or two series of scales between the nasal and the rostral; 12-16 upper labials; 3-5 lower labials in contact with the chin-shields. Scales in 29-41 rows, strongly keeled, outer row smooth or feebly keeled. Ventrals 131-145; anal entire; subcaudals 16-34. Yellowish, pale brown, or orange above, marked with regular chevron-shaped dark brown or black bars pointing backwards, or black with yellow or orange markings; a large dark blotch covering the crown, separated from a smaller interorbital blotch by a transverse yellow line, an oblique dark band below and another behind the eye; yellowish white beneath, uniform or with small dark spots.

Total length 1350 millim.; tail 160.

Africa, from Southern Morocco, Kordofan, and Somaliland to the Cape of Good Hope; Southern Arabia.

a. Yg. (Sc. 32; V. 136; C. 18)	Hadramaut, S. Arabia.	Dr. J. Anderson [P.].
b. Ad., skin.	Somaliland.	Lord Wolverton [P].
c. Yg. (Sc. 35; V. 140; C. 21)	Senegal.	
d. Ad., stuffed.	Gambia.	(Type of *C. lateristriga*)
e. Yg. (Sc. 31; V. 140; C. 28).	Kilimanjaro.	F. J. Jackson, Esq. [P.].
f Yg. (Sc. 35; V. 133; C. 20).	Zanzibar.	Sir J. Kirk [C.].
g Ad. skin.	Uzaramo.	Capt. Speke [P.].

h–i Yg. (Sc. 35, 33; V. 139, 137; C. 16, 18).	Zomba, Brit. C. Africa.	Sir H. H. Johnston [P.].
k ♂ (Sc. 35, V. 134, C. 33)	Chiradzulu, Brit. C. Africa, 3000–5000 ft	Sir H. H. Johnston [P.].
l Yg. (Sc. 37; V. 131; C. 18).	L. Nyassa.	Miss M. Woodward [C.]; Miss S. C. McLaughlin [P.].
m. Yg (Sc. 31; V. 132; C. 17).	Zambesi.	Sir J. Kirk [P.].
n Yg (Sc. 31; V. 132; C. 28).	Ambriz, Angola.	Mr. Rich [C.].
o. Yg (Sc. 36; V. 140; C. 20).	Mossamedes.	Dr. Welwitsch [P.].
p ♂ (Sc. 33; V. 133; C. 29).	Pretoria, Transvaal	W. L. Distant, Esq. [P.].
q, r–s. ♂ (Sc. 33, V. 140, C. 28) & hgr. ♀ (Sc. 39, 37; V. 134, 132; C. 17, 18)	Port Natal.	Rev. H. Calloway [P.]
t. ♀ (Sc. 37; V. 144, C. 16)	Natal.	Zoological Society.
u–w. ♂ (Sc. 37, 39; V. 138, 141, C. 34, 29) & ♀ (Sc. 41, V. 142, C. 22).	Simon's Bay.	H.M.S. 'Challenger'
x, y, z Ad, stffd.	Cape of Good Hope	
α, β. Skeletons	Senegal.	
γ. Skull.	Cape of Good Hope.	

2. Bitis peringueyi.

Vipera peringueyi, *Bouleng. Ann. & Mag. N. H.* (2) ii. 1888, p. 141.
—— heraldica, *Bocage, Jorn. Sc. Lisb* (2) i. 1889, p. 127, fig, *and Herp. Angola*, p. 151, pl. xvi. fig. 1 (1895).

Nostrils turned upwards and outwards. Rostral small, broad, crescentic. Head covered with small, strongly keeled scales, smallest on the vertex; 11 scales round the eye; three series of scales between the eye and the labials; nasal separated from the rostral by two series of scales, 11 to 14 upper labials. Scales in 25 or 27 rows, strongly keeled, outer row smooth. Ventrals 130–132; anal entire; subcaudals 19–28. Pale buff or greyish olive above, with three longitudinal series of grey or blackish spots, the outer ocellar, enclosing a white centre; head sometimes (*V. heraldica*) with a trident-shaped dark marking on the crown followed by a cross and two large markings on the occiput; whitish beneath, with small dark spots.

Total length 325 millim.; tail 26.

Angola and Damaraland.

3. Bitis atropos.

Coluber atropos, *Linn. Mus. Ad. Frid* p. 22, pl xiii. fig. 1 (1754), *and S. N.* i p. 375 (1766).
Cobra atropos, *Laur Syn. Rept.* p. 104 (1768).

Vipera atropos, *Latr. Rept.* iii. p. 334 (1802); *Daud. Rept.* vi. p. 210 (1803); *Schleg. Phys. Serp.* ii. p. 581, pl. xxi. figs. 6 & 7 (1837), *Smith, Ill. Zool. S. Afr., Rept.* pl lii (1846); *Strauch, Syn. Viper.* p. 93 (1869); *Jan, Icon. Gén.* 45, pl iv. figs. 1 & 2 (1874).
—— montana, *Smith, Edinb N Philos. Journ* i. 1826, p 252
Clotho atropos, *Gray, Zool. Miscell.* p. 69 (1842), *and Cat.* p. 26 (1849)
Echidna ocellata, *Tschudi, Faun. Per., Herp.* p 60 (1845).
Calechidna ocellata, *Tschudi, l. c.* pl. ix.
Echidna atropos, *Dum. & Bibr.* vii. p. 1432 (1854).
Bitis atropos, *Gunth. Cat.* p. 268 (1858).

Nostrils turned upwards and outwards. Rostral small, once and two thirds to twice as broad as deep; head covered with small, imbricate, strongly keeled scales, 13 to 16 across the vertex from eye to eye, 13 to 16 scales round the eye; two or three series of scales between the eye and the labials; two to five series of scales between the supranasals; two series of scales between the nasal and the rostral; 10–12 upper labials; three or four lower labials in contact with the chin-shields. Scales in 29–31 rows, all strongly keeled. Ventrals 124–145; anal entire; subcaudals 18–29 Brown or grey-brown above, with four longitudinal series of large, dark brown, black-and-white edged spots, formed by the breaking up into two of two series of subcircular spots; a continuous or interrupted whitish streak running between and dividing the spots on each side of the back, and another lower down on the sides; two large dark markings on the head, from the nape to between the eyes; an oblique, light, dark-edged streak from behind the eye to the mouth; belly grey or brown, spotted with darker.

Total length 350 millim.; tail 25.
Cape of Good Hope.

a. ♀ (Sc. 31; V. 137; C 22).	Table Mt, near Cape Town.	H. A Spencer, Esq [P.].
b. ♀ (Sc. 31, V. 128; C. 21).	Cape of Good Hope.	Dr. Lee [P.].
c. ♀ (Sc. 29; V. 128; C. 19).	S. Africa.	Sir H. Sloane [P.].
d, e. ♀ (Sc 31; V. 131, C. 18) & yg. (Sc. 29, V. 130, C. 25).	S. Africa.	

4. Bitis inornata.

Echidna inornata, *Smith, Ill. Zool. S. Afr., Rept.* pl. iv. (1838).
Vipera atropoides, *Smith, op. cit.* pl liii. (1840).
Clotho atropos, part, *Gray, Cat.* p. 26 (1849).
Clotho ? inornata, *Gray, l. c.*
Vipera inornata, *Strauch, Syn. Viper.* p. 97 (1869).

Intermediate between *B. atropos* and *B. cornuta*. Eye smaller than in the former and separated from the labials by four series of scales; supraorbital region raised as in the latter, but without erect, horn-like scales; 15–17 scales across the head from eye to eye; 13 or 14 upper labials; three lower labials in contact with the chin-shields. Scales in 27–29 rows, all keeled. Ventrals 126–140; subcaudals 19–26. Markings, if present, as in *B. cornuta*. Total length 350 millim.; tail 30.

Cape of Good Hope.

A. Dark yellowish brown above, with faint traces of darker markings, brownish yellow beneath with a few dark dots, head marbled with dark brown. (*E. inornata*, Smith.)

a. ♀ (Sc. 29; V. 140; C. 26). Snow Mountains, near Graaf Reynet. Sir A. Smith [P.]. (Type.)

B. Brown above, with two dorsal series of dark brown, black-edged spots. (*V. atropoides*, Smith.)

a. ♀ (Sc. 27; V. 126; C. 20). 40 miles E. of Cape Town. Sir A. Smith [P.]. (Type.)
b. ♀ (Sc. 29, V. 131; C. 19). S. Africa.

5. Bitis cornuta.

Paterson, Narr. Journ Hott. Caffr. p. 161, pl. — (1789).
Vipera cornuta, *Daud Rept.* vi. p. 188 (1803); *Schleg Phys. Serp.* ii. p. 582, pl. xxi. figs 8 & 9 (1837); *Smith, Ill. Zool. S. Afr., Rept.* pl xxxii. (1843); *Strauch, Syn. Viper.* p. 100 (1869); *Boettg Ber. Senck. Ges.* 1887, p. 168
—— armata, *Smith, Edinb. N. Philos. Journ.* i 1826, p. 251.
—— lophophris, *Cuv. R. A.* 2nd ed ii. p. 92 (1829), *Smith, Ill. Zool. S Afr., Rept.* pl. xxxiii. (1843); *Jan, Icon. Gén.* 45, pl. v. fig. 2 (1874).
Cerastes cornuta, *Gray, Zool Miscell.* p. 70 (1842).
Clotho cornuta, *Gray, Cat.* p 27 (1849).
Cerastes lophophrys, *Dum. & Bibr.* vii. p. 1444, pl. lxxviii. *b.* fig. 4 (1854)

Nostrils turned upwards and outwards. Rostral small, twice to twice and a half as broad as deep, head covered with small, imbricate, strongly keeled scales, 12 to 17 across the vertex from eye to eye; two to five scales above the eye raised, horn-like; 12 to 14 scales round the eye; three or four series of scales between the eye and the labials; two or three series of scales between the supranasals; two or three series of scales between the nasal and the rostral; 12 to 15 upper labials; two or three lower labials in contact with the chin-shields. Scales in 25–29 rows, strongly keeled, outer row smooth or feebly keeled. Ventrals 120–152; anal entire; subcaudals 18–36, well developed in the males, scale-like and more or less distinctly keeled in the females. Greyish or reddish brown above, with dark brown spots, often edged with whitish, disposed in three or four longitudinal series, with or without light spots between them; head with more or less distinct symmetrical markings; an oblique dark streak from the eye to the mouth; yellowish white or brownish beneath, uniform or spotted with dark brown.

Total length 510 millim.; tail 35.
Cape Colony, Namaqualand, Damaraland.

a-b. ♀ (Sc. 27; V. 152; C. 24) & yg. (Sc. 25; V. 149; C. 29).	Cape of Good Hope.	Lord Derby [P.].
c. ♀ (Sc. 29, V. 137; C. 25).	Cape of Good Hope.	Sir A. Smith [P.].
d. ♂ (Sc. 27; V. 123; C. 30).	Cape of Good Hope.	— Ford, Esq. [P.].
e. ♂ (Sc. 25; V. 124; C. 25)	Knysna, Cape Colony.	Rev. G H. R. Fisk [P.].
f, g. ♀ (Sc. 26, 29; V. 124, 120; C. 23, 21).	S. Africa.	

6. Bitis caudalis.

Vipera ocellata (*non Latr.*), *Smith, Mag N H.* (2) ii 1838, p 92.
Cerastes ocellatus, *Smith, Ill. Zool. S. Afr., Rept.* pl. iv., text (1838).
Vipera caudalis, *Smith, op. cit.* pl vii. (1839); *Jan, Rev. & Mag Zool.* 1859, p. 155; *Strauch, Syn. Viper.* p. 106 (1869); *Boettg Ber. Senck. Ges.* 1886, p. 6, and 1887, p. 167, *Bocage, Herp. Angola*, p. 150 (1895).
Cerastes caudalis, *Gray, Zool. Miscell.* p. 70 (1842); *Dum & Bibr.* vii. p. 1446 (1854).
Vipera schneideri, *Boettg. Ber. Senck. Ges.* 1886, p. 8, pl. i. fig. 1.

Nostrils turned upwards and outwards. Rostral small, once and two thirds to twice and a half as broad as deep; head covered with small, imbricate, keeled scales, 12 to 16 across the vertex from eye to eye; a single, erect, horn-like scale usually present above the eye; 10 to 16 scales round the eye; two to four series of scales between the eye and the labials; two or three series of scales between the supranasals; two series of scales between the nasal and the rostral; 10 to 13 upper labials; two or three lower labials in contact with the chin-shields. Scales in 22–29 rows, strongly keeled, outer row smooth or faintly keeled. Ventrals 112–153; anal entire; subcaudals 18–33, well developed in the males, scale-like and more or less distinctly keeled in the females. Pale buff, reddish, or sandy grey above, with two series of brown spots with light centres, and frequently a vertebral series of narrower spots; the spots may be edged with yellow; yellowish white beneath, uniform or with small blackish spots on the sides.

Total length 360 millim.; tail 25.
S.W. Africa, from Angola to Namaqualand.

a-e. ♂ (Sc. 29, 26, 25; V. 134, 124, 145; C. 32, 23, 30), ♀ (Sc. 25; V. 153; C. 23), & yg. (Sc. 20; V. 130; C. 29).	S. Africa.	Sir A. Smith [P].
f-l, m-n. ♀ (Sc. 25, 27, 25; V. 112, 113, 118; C. 22, 22, 20) & yg.	Port Nolloth, Namaqualand.	Rev. G. H. R. Fisk [P.].

(Sc. 25, 27, 23, 25, 25;
V. 113, 112, 113, 113,
144, C. 20, 19, 22,
19, 20).
o–q. ♀ (Sc. 22, 25, 25;   Damaraland.
V 143, 136, 139; C.
28, 23, 25).
r. ♀ (Sc 27; V. 138;   Mossamedes.   Dr. Welwitsch [P.].
C. 21).
s–t. ♀ (Sc 23, 23; V.   Benguela.   J. J. Monteiro, Esq [P].
130, ?; C. 19, 18).

7. Bitis gabonica.

Cerastes nasicornis (*non Shaw*), *Hallow. Proc Ac Philad*. 1847,
  p. 319, pl. —.
Echidna gabonica, *Dum. & Bibr* vii. p. 1428, pl. lxxx. *b*. (1854).
Vipera rhinoceros, *Schleg Versl. Ak. Amsterd*. iii. 1855, p 316;
  Strauch, Syn. Viper. p. 91 (1869); *Bocage, Herp. Angola*, p 149
  (1895).
Echidna rhinoceros, *A. Dum. Rev. & Mag. Zool*. 1856, p. 559, and
  Arch. Mus. x 1859, p 220
Clotho rhinoceros, *Cope, Proc. Ac. Philad*. 1859, p. 340
Bitis rhinoceros, *Peters, Mon. Berl. Ac*. 1877, p. 618, and *Reise n.
  Mossamb*. iii. p. 146 (1882), *Buttikofer, Reiseb. Liberia*, ii. p 444,
  pl xxxii. (1890).

Nostrils directed upwards and outwards. Rostral very small, once and a half to twice and a half as broad as deep; head covered with small, moderately keeled scales, smallest on the vertex, 13 to 16 from eye to eye; 15 to 19 scales round the eye; four or five series of scales between the eye and the labials; a pair of more or less developed, compressed, erectile, triangular, sometimes bi- or tricuspid shields, in contact with each other, between the supranasals, forming a pair of nasal "horns"; four or five series of scales between the nasal and the rostral; 13 to 16 upper labials; four or five lower labials in contact with the chin-shields. Scales in 33–41 rows, strongly keeled, outer row smooth; lateral scales slightly oblique, pointing downwards. Ventrals 125–140; anal entire; subcaudals 17–33. Brown above, with a vertebral series of elongate, quadrangular, yellowish or light brown spots connected by hourglass-shaped dark brown markings; a series of crescentic or angular dark brown markings on each side; head pale above, with a dark brown median line; a dark brown oblique band behind the eye, widening towards the mouth; yellowish beneath, with small brown or blackish spots.

Total length 1170 millim.; tail 70.

Tropical Africa (West Africa, from Liberia to Damaraland; Zanzibar; Mozambique).

a. Yg. (Sc. 35; V. 128;   Coast of Guinea.   Sir A. Smith [P.].
C. 21).
b. Head of adult.   Oil River.   Sir H. H. Johnston [P.].
c. Head of adult.   Angola.   J. J. Monteiro, Esq [P].

d. ♀ (Sc. 37; V. 131; C. 17).	W. Africa.	Zoological Society.
e. Yg. (Sc. 33; V. 125; C. 18).	W. Africa.	
f. Ad., stffd.	W. Africa.	Zoological Society.
g. Hgr. ♀ (Sc. 41; V. 139; C. 23).	Ushambola, Zanzibar.	Sir J. Kirk [C.].
h. Skeleton of *f.*		

8. Bitis nasicornis.

Coluber nasicornis, *Shaw, Nat. Miscell.* iii. pl. xciv., *and Zool.* iii. p. 397, pl. civ. (1802).
Vipera nasicornis, *Daud. Rept.* viii. p. 322 (1803); *Reinh. Vidensk. Selsk. Skrift.* x 1843, p. 273, pl. iii. figs. 8–10; *Schleg. Versl. Ak. Amsterd.* iii. 1855, p. 315; *Strauch, Syn. Viper.* p. 88 (1869); *Jan, Icon Gén.* 45, pl. iv figs. 3 & 4 (1874)
Clotho nasicornis, *Gray, Zool Miscell.* p. 69 (1842), *and Cat.* p. 25 (1849), *Wolf, Zool. Sketches,* ii. pl. — (1865).
Vipera hexacera, *Dum. & Bibr.* vii. p. 1416, pl. lxxviii. *b.* fig. 2 (1854).
Echidna nasicornis, *Hallow. Proc. Ac Philad.* 1857, p. 62; *A. Dum. Arch. Mus* x. 1859, p. 220.
Bitis nasicornis, *Buttikofer, Reiseb. Liberia,* ii. p. 444 (1890).

Nostrils directed upwards and outwards. Rostral very small, once and a half to twice and a half as broad as deep; head covered with small strongly keeled scales, smallest on the vertex, 14 to 16 from eye to eye; 15 to 20 scales round the eye; four or five series of scales between the eye and the labials; two or three pairs of compressed, erectile, horn-like shields between the supranasals, usually separated in the middle by one or two series of small scales; one of these horn-like scales usually much developed; four to six series of scales between the nasal and the rostral; 15 to 18 upper labials; four to six lower labials in contact with the chin-shields. Scales in 35–41 rows, strongly keeled, outer row smooth or feebly keeled. Ventrals 124–140; anal entire; subcaudals 16–32. Purplish or reddish brown above, with pale olive and dark brown or black markings; a vertebral series of pale dark-edged spots, angularly notched in front and behind to receive a rhomboidal black spot; an arrow-headed dark brown yellow-and-black-edged marking on the head and nape, the point on the snout; sides of head dark brown, with a triangular light marking in front of the eye and an oblique light streak from behind the eye to the mouth; pale olive beneath, speckled and spotted with blackish, or blackish olive speckled with yellowish.

Total length 1250 millim.; tail 125.

West Africa, from Liberia to the Gaboon.

a. Hgr. (Sc. 37; V. 124; C. 19).	Gold Coast.	Sir A. Smith [P.].
b. Yg. (Sc. 35; V. 131; C. 21).	Ashantee.	Leyden Museum
c–e. Yg. (Sc. 37, 35, 35; V. 127, 128, 130; C. 31, 23, 22).	Fernando Po.	
f, g. ♂ (Sc. 35; V. 130; C. 32) & ♀ (Sc. 41; V. 137; C. 20).	Guinea.	

$h, i, k-l$ ♀ (Sc. 41; V. 132; C. 21), hgr. (Sc. 39; V. 128; C. 16), & yg (Sc 35, 35, V. 125, 132, C. 30, 29).		W. Africa.	Zoological Society.
m Skeleton.		Niger.	J. W. Crosse, Esq. [P.].

m. Skull of *g.*

5. PSEUDOCERASTES.

Cerastes, part., *Dum. & Bibr. Erp Gén.* vii. p. 1438 (1854).
Vipera, part., *Jan, Elenco sist. Ofid.* p. 120 (1863); *Strauch, Syn. Viper.* p. 21 (1869).

Head very distinct from neck, covered with small imbricate scales; eye small, with vertical pupil, separated from the labials by small scales; nostrils directed upwards and outwards, pierced between two small nasals, a large crescentic anterior and a small scale-like posterior; nasals separated from the rostral by small scales. Body cylindrical; scales keeled, in 23–25 rows, the keels club-shaped and not extending to the extremity of the scale; ventrals rounded. Tail moderate; subcaudals in two rows.

Persia.

1. Pseudocerastes persicus.

? Vipera cerastes, *Pall Zoogr. Rosso-As.* iii p. 48 (1811).
Cerastes persicus, *Dum. & Bibr* vii. p. 1443, pl. lxxviii. *b.* fig. 5 (1854); *Blanf. Zool. E. Pers* p. 429 (1876).
Vipera persica, *Jan, Rev. & Mag. Zool.* 1859, p. 153; *Strauch, Syn. Viper.* p. 103, pl. ii. (1869), and *Schl. Russ. R* p. 225 (1873).

Snout very short and broadly rounded. Upper head-scales small, imbricate, keeled; an erect horn-like tubercle above the eye, covered with several imbricate scales; 15 scales round the eye; three series of scales between the eye and the labials; one series of scales between the nasal and the rostral; 13 upper labials; four lower labials in contact with the chin-shields. Scales strongly keeled, in 23 or 25 rows. Ventrals 151–156; anal entire; subcaudals 43–49. Greyish or brownish above, with four series of large dark spots, the two median sometimes confluent and forming cross-bars; a dark streak on each side of the head from the eye to behind the gape; whitish beneath, dotted with dark, and with a lateral series of dark spots.

Total length 890 millim.; tail 110.

Persia.

6. CERASTES.

Aspis, part., *Laur. Syn. Rept* p 105 (1768).
Echidna (*non Forst.*), part., *Merr. Tent Syst. Amph.* p. 150 (1820); *Dum. & Bibr. Erp. Gén.* vii. p. 1420 (1854).
Cerastes, part., *Wagl. Syst. Amph.* p. 178 (1830); *Gray, Zool. Miscell.* p 70 (1842); *Dum. & Bibr. t. c* p 1438.
Vipera, part, *Schleg. Phys Serp.* ii. p. 573 (1837); *Jan, Elenco sist. Ofid* p 120 (1863); *Strauch, Syn. Viper.* p. 21 (1869).
Cerastes, *Gray, Cat. Sn* p. 27 (1849); *Bouleng. Trans. Zool. Soc* xiii. 1891, p. 154.

Head very distinct from neck, covered with small juxtaposed or feebly imbricate scales; eye moderate or small, with vertical pupil, separated from the labials by small scales, nostril directed upwards and outwards, in a small single or divided nasal. Body cylindrical; scales keeled, with apical pits, in 23–35 rows; dorsal scales forming straight longitudinal series, with club- or anchor-shaped keels not extending to the extremity of the scale; lateral scales smaller, oblique, pointing downwards, with serrated keels; ventrals with an obtuse keel on each side. Tail short; subcaudals in two rows.

North Africa, Arabia, Palestine.

1. Cerastes cornutus.

Coluber cornutus, *Linn. in Hasselq. Reise Palæst.* p 315 (1762).
—— cerastes, *Linn. S. N.* i. p. 376 (1766), *Ellis, Phil. Trans.* lvi. 1767, p. 287, pl. xiv.; *Shaw, Nat Miscell.* iv. pl. cxxii., and *Zool.* iii. p. 385, pl ciii (1802)
Cerastes cornutus, *Forsk. Descr. Anim.* p. ix (1775); *Bouleng. Trans. Zool. Soc* xiii 1891, p. 155; *Werner, Verh. zool.-bot. Ges. Wien,* xliv. 1894, p. 86.
Vipera cerastes, *Latr. Rept.* iii. p. 313, pl. —. fig 2 (1802); *Daud. Rept.* vi. p. 178, pl. lxxiv. fig. 1 (1803); *I. Geoffr. Descr. Egypte, Rept.* p. 155, pl. vi. fig. 3 (1827); *Schleg. Phys. Serp.* ii. p. 585, pl. xxi. figs. 12 & 13 (1837); *Strauch, Erp. Alg.* p. 72 (1862), and *Syn. Viper.* p. 108 (1869), *Jan, Icon. Gén.* 45, pl. v. fig. 1 (1874).
Cerastes hasselquistii, *Gray, Zool. Miscell.* p. 70 (1842), and *Cat.* p. 28 (1849); *Tristram, Faun Palest.* p. 147 (1884).
Echidna atricauda, part, *Dum. & Bibr.* vii. p. 1430 (1854).
Cerastes ægyptiacus, *Dum & Bibr.* t c p. 1440, pl lxxviii. *b*. fig. 3.
Vipera avicennæ, part., *Jan, l. c.* fig. 3.

Snout very short and broad. Rostral small, twice to thrice as broad as deep; head covered with small tubercularly keeled scales of unequal size above, 15 to 21 across from eye to eye; a large, erect, ribbed, horn-like scale often present above the eye; 14 to 18 scales round the eye; 4 or 5 series of scales between the eye and the labials; nostril in a single small shield, separated from its fellow by six to eight longitudinal series of scales and from the rostral by two or three (rarely one); 12 to 15 upper labials; three lower labials in contact with the chin-shields. Scales in 27–35 rows. Ventrals 130–165, with very feeble lateral keel; anal entire; subcaudals 25–42, the posterior usually more or less distinctly keeled. Pale yellowish brown or grey above, with or without brown spots, forming four or six regular longitudinal series, the two middle ones sometimes confluent, forming cross-bars; a more or less distinct oblique dark streak behind the eye; lower parts white; end of tail sometimes black.

Total length 720 millim.; tail 90.

Northern border of the Sahara, Egypt, Nubia, Arabia, Southern Palestine.

a. ♂ (Sc. 30; V. 133;   Biskra.   J. Brenchley, Esq. [P.].
    C. 20).

6. CERASTES. 503

b–g. ♂ (Sc. 31, 32; V. 144, 146; C. 42, 42), ♀ (Sc 33, 34; V. 151, 144; C. 36, 37), & hgr. (Sc. 32, 33; V. 143, 145; C. 34, 40) — Egypt. — J. Burton Esq. [P.]

h–i, k–l. ♂ (Sc. 31, 29; V. 144, 146; C. 37, 40) & ♀ (Sc. 33, 31; V 148, 148; C. 39, 37). — Egypt. — Sir J. G. Wilkinson [P.].

m. ♀ (Sc. 31; V. 144; C. 33). — S. of Suez Canal. — Dr. J. Anderson [P.].

n. Hgr. ♀ (Sc. 30, V. 148, C. 39). — Gizeh. — Dr. J. Anderson [P.].

o–p. ♂ (Sc. 33; V. 142; C. 38) & ♀ (Sc. 33; V. 151; C. 33). — Luxor. — Dr. J. Anderson [P.]

q. ♂ (Sc. 31; V. 145; C. 33). — Assouan. — Dr. J. Anderson [P.].

r. Yg. (Sc. 33, V. 148; C. 40). — Wadi Halfa. — Dr. J. Anderson [P.].

s. ♀ (Sc 33; V 144; C. 29). — Suakin. — Col Sir Holled Smith & Dr. J. Anderson [P.].

t. ♂ (Sc. 35; V. 140; C. 33). — Suakin. — Dr. Penton & Dr. J. Anderson [P.].

u. ♂ (Sc. 33; V. 141; C. 35). — Suakin. — Dr. J. Anderson [P.].

v. ♂ (Sc. 32; V. 140; C. 34). — Arabia.

w. ♂ (Sc. 33; V. 139; C. 33). — Mount Sinai.

x. ♀ (Sc. 35, V 155; C. 34) — Timahat, Midian. — Major Burton [P.].

y. Hgr. ♀ (Sc. 32; V. 164, C. 34). — Hadramaut. — Dr. J. Anderson [P.].

Skull of *h*.

2. Cerastes vipera.

Coluber vipera, *Linn. in Hasselq. Reise Palæst.* p. 314 (1762), *and S. N.* i. p. 375 (1766).
Aspis cleopatræ, *Laur. Syn. Rept.* p. 105 (1768).
Vipera ægyptia, *Latr. Rept.* iii. p 320 (1802).
—— ægyptiaca, *Daud. Rept.* vi. p. 212 (1803).
Cerastes ritchiei, *Gray, Zool. Miscell.* p. 70 (1842), *and Cat.* p. 28 (1849)
Echidna atricauda, part., *Dum & Bibr.* vii. p. 1430 (1854)
Vipera avicennæ, part., *Jan, Rev. & Mag. Zool.* 1859, p. 152, *and Icon Gén.* 45, pl. v. fig. 4 (1874).
—— avizennæ, *Strauch, Syn. Viper.* p. 113 (1869).
Cerastes vipera, *Bouleng. Trans Zool. Soc.* xiii. 1891, p. 155, pl. xviii. fig. 2; *Anders. Proc. Zool. Soc.* 1892, p. 23; *Werner, Verh. zool.-bot. Ges. Wien,* xliv. 1894, p. 86.

Snout very short and broad. Rostral small, twice to thrice as broad as deep; head covered with small, tubercularly keeled, unequal or subequal scales above, 9 to 13 across from eye to eye; no "horns"; 9 to 14 scales round the eye; 3 or 4 series of scales between the eye and the labials; nostril between two small shields, separated from their fellows by 5 or 6 series of scales and from the rostral by one or two; 10 to 12 upper labials; three lower labials in contact with the chin-shields. Scales in 23–27 rows. Ventrals 102–122, rather strongly keeled laterally; anal entire; subcaudals 18–26, small, and often more or less distinctly keeled. Yellowish, pale brown, or reddish above, with or without darker spots; end of tail often black; lower parts white.

Total length 340 millim.; tail 30.

Northern border of the Sahara, from Algeria to Egypt.

a–b. ♂ (Sc. 23, V. 107; C. 23) & ♀ (Sc. 23; V. 117, C. 22).	Duirat, S. Tunisia.	Dr. J. Anderson [P.]
c, d, e. ♂ (Sc. 25, 25; V. 105, 102; C. 22, 22) & ♀ (Sc. 25; V. 109; C. 19).	Tripoli.	T. Ritchie, Esq. [P.]. (Type of *C. ritchiei*.)
f. ♂ (Sc. 25; V. 119; C. 22).	Gizeh, Egypt.	Dr. J. Anderson [P.]
g. ♂ (Sc. 25, V. 111; C. 23).	Abu Roash, Egypt.	Dr. J. Anderson [P.].
h ♂ (Sc. 27; V. 117; C. 26).	Beni Hassan, Egypt.	Dr. J. Anderson [P.].
i–l. ♂ (Sc. 24; V. 107; C. 25) & ♀ (Sc. 23, 25; V. 110, 112; C. 21, 22).	Desert coast W. of Suez Canal.	Dr. J. Anderson [P.].

7. ECHIS.

Pseudoboa, part., *Schneid. Hist. Amph.* ii p. 281 (1801).
Scytale, part., *Daud. Hist. Rept.* p. 334 (1803).
Echis, part., *Merr. Tent. Syst. Amph.* p. 149 (1820); *Jan, Elenco sist. Ofid.* p. 122 (1863).
Echis, *Wagl. Syst. Amph.* p. 177 (1830); *Gray, Zool. Miscell.* p. 70 (1842), *and Cat. Sn.* p. 29 (1849); *Dum. & Bibr. Erp. Gén.* vii. p. 1447 (1854); *Gunth. Rept. Brit. Ind.* p. 396 (1864); *Strauch, Syn. Viper.* p. 116 (1869); *Bouleng. Faun. Ind., Rept.* p. 421 (1890), *and Trans. Zool. Soc.* xiii. 1891, p. 155.
Vipera, part., *Schleg. Phys. Serp.* ii. p. 573 (1837).
Toxicoa, *Gray, Cat.* p. 20.

Head very distinct from neck, covered with small imbricate scales; eye moderate, with vertical pupil, separated from the labials by small scales; nostril directed upwards and outwards, in a single or divided nasal. Body cylindrical; scales keeled, with apical pits, in 27–37 rows; dorsal scales forming straight longitudinal series; lateral scales smaller, oblique, pointing downwards, with serrated keels; ventrals rounded. Tail short; subcaudals single.

Africa north of the Equator, Southern Asia.

1. Echis carinatus.

Russell, Ind. Serp. i. pl ii. (1796).
Pseudoboa carinata, *Schneid. Hist. Amph.* ii. p. 285 (1801).
Boa horatta, *Shaw, Zool.* iii. p. 359 (1802).
Scytale bizonatus, *Daud. Rept* v. p 339, pl. lxx. fig. 1 (1803).
Vipera (Echis) carinata, *Merr. Tent.* p. 149 (1820).
Echis ziczac, *Gray, Ann. Philos.* 1825, p. 205.
Scytbale pyramidum, *I. Geoffr. Descr. Egypte, Rept.* p. 152, pl. vii. fig. 1 (1827), *and Suppl* pl. iv. fig. 1 (1829).
Echis arenicola, *Boie, Isis,* 1827, p. 558; *Gray, Cat.* p. 29 (1849); *Strauch, Syn. Viper.* p. 117 (1869), *and Schl. Russ. R.* p. 228 (1873); *Boettg. Zool. Jahrb.* iii. 1888, p. 949.
—— carinata, *Wagl. Syst. Amph.* p. 177 (1830); *Gray, Cat* p. 29; *Guichen. in Lefebvre, Voy. Abyss* vi. p. 215, *Rept.* pl. iii. (?), *Dum & Bibr.* vii. p. 1448, pl. lxxxi *b.* fig. 3 (1854); *Günth Rept. Brit Ind* p 397 (1864), *and Proc. Zool. Soc.* 1869, p. 502; *Anders. Proc Zool. Soc* 1871, p. 196; *Fayrer, Thanatoph. Ind.* pl. xii. (1874); *Blanf. Zool. E. Pers.* p. 430 (1876); *Theob. Cat Rept. Brit. Ind* p. 218 (1876); *Blanf. Journ. As. Soc. Beng.* xlviii. 1879, p 116; *Murray, Zool Sind,* p 388, pl. — (1884); *Bouleng. Faun. Ind., Rept.* p. 422, fig. (1890); *Matschie, Zool. Jahrb* v. 1890, p. 617; *Bouleng. Trans. Zool. Soc.* xiii. 1891, p 155.
—— pavo, *Reuss, Mus. Senck* i. 1834, p. 157.
—— varia, *Reuss, l. c.* p. 160, pl. vii fig. 2.
Vipera echis, *Schleg. Phys Serp.* ii p. 583, pl. xxi figs. 10 & 11 (1837), *and in Wagner, Reis Alg* iii. p. 131 (1841).
Echis frenata, *Dum. & Bibr. t c* p. 1449.
Toxicoa arenicola, *Gunth. Cat* p. 268 (1858).
Vipera carinata, *Jan, Rev. & Mag. Zool.* 1859, p. 153, *Strauch, Erp. Alg.* p. 73 (1862).
—— (Echis) superciliosa, *Jan, l. c.* p. 156, *and Prodr.* pl. E (1859).
Echis superciliosa, *Jan, Elenco,* p. 122 (1863).

Snout very short, rounded. Rostral once and a half to twice and a half as broad as deep; head covered with small, more or less strongly keeled scales; a narrow supraocular sometimes present, 10 to 15 scales across from eye to eye; 14 to 20 scales round the eye; two (rarely three or one) series of scales between the eye and the labials; nostril between two (rarely three) shields, in contact with the rostral; 10 to 12 upper labials; three or four lower labials in contact with the chin-shields. Scales in 27–37 rows. Ventrals 132–192; anal entire; subcaudals 21–48. Pale buff, greyish, reddish, or brown above, with one or three series of whitish dark-edged spots, the outer sometimes forming ocelli, a zigzag dark and light band may run along each side; a cruciform, ⅄-, ⅄-, or Y-shaped whitish marking often present on the head; lower parts whitish, uniform, or with brown dots, or with small round black spots.

Total length 720 millim.; tail 70.

Desert or sandy districts of Africa north of the Equator; Southern Asia, from Transcaspia and Arabia to India.

a, b. ♂ (Sc. 31, 29; V. 148, 145; C. 26, 29).   W. Africa.   Mr. Dalton [C.].

c. ♂ (Sc. 29, V. 163; C. 39).	Barbary.	
d, e, f. ♂ (Sc. 31, 31, 29; V. 168, 173, 167; C. ?, 37, ?).	Egypt.	Sir J. G. Wilkinson [P.].
g–h. Yg. (Sc. 30, 29; V. 167, 172; C. 36, 37).	Mokattam Hills, near Cairo.	Dr. J. Anderson [P.].
i. ♀ (Sc. 29; V. 184; C. 34).	Assiout, Egypt.	Dr. J. Anderson [P.].
k. ♂ (Sc. 27; V. 173; C. 41).	Dooroor, N. of Suakin.	Dr. J. Anderson [P.].
l–m. ♂ (Sc. 29; V. 180; C. 43) & ♀ (Sc. 31; V. 191; C. 33).	Suakin.	Col. Sir Holled Smith & Dr. J. Anderson, [P.].
n. ♀ (Sc. 30, V. 186, C. 36).	Suakin.	Dr. Penton & Dr. J. Anderson [P.].
o–q. ♀ (Sc. 33; V. 189; C. 38) & yg. (Sc. 31, 31; V. 187, 185; C. 36, 30).	Suakin.	Dr. J. Anderson [P.].
r. ♀ (Sc. 31; V. 171; C. 43).	Somaliland.	Capt. Cox [P.].
s. ♂ (Sc. 29; V. 159; C. 31).	Aden.	Col. Yerbury [P.].
t. ♂ (Sc. 27; V. 184; C. 48).	Hadramaut.	Dr. J. Anderson [P.].
u, v–x. ♀ (Sc. 31, 31, 32, 32; V. 165, 165, 166, 162, C. 30, 32, 32, 30).	Muscat.	A. S. G. Jayakar, Esq. [P].
y. ♀ (Sc. 35; V. 185; C. 32).	Ashkabad, Transcaspia.	Warsaw Mus. [E.].
z. ♀ (Sc. 35; V. 174; C. 37).	Chilgez, Afghanistan.	Dr. Aitchison [C.]; Afghan Boundary Comm.
α. ♀ (Sc. 37; V. 173; C. 34).	Between Nushki & the Helmand.	Dr. Aitchison [C.]; Afghan Boundary Comm.
β. ♀ (Sc. 37; V. 182; C. 32).	Nasirabad, Sistan.	Gen. Goldsmid [P.].
γ. ♀ (Sc. 37; V. 173; C. 37).	Kilsa-i-Futh, Sistan.	Gen. Goldsmid [P.].
δ. ♀ (Sc. 34; V. 172, C. 34).	Bushire, Persia.	Dr. Leith [P.].
ε–η. ♀ (Sc. 35, 34, 31; V. 170, 180, 172; C. 30, 31, 30).	Bushire.	E. Lort Phillips, Esq. [P.].
θ–ι. Hgr. (Sc. 33, 31; V. 187, 175; C. 32, 36).	Jask, S. Persia.	B. I. Ifinch, Esq. [P.].
κ–ν. Hgr. (Sc. 35, 31, 31, 33; V. 177, 178, 180, 180; C. 35, 33, 34, 28).	Jask.	S. Butcher, Esq. [P.].
ξ–π. ♀ (Sc. 31; V. 172; C. 30), hgr. (Sc. 31; V. 169; C. 28), & yg. (Sc. 33; V. 163, C. 29).	Muckberabad, Persia.	

ρ–σ. ♀ (Sc. 35, 31; V. 192, 174; C. 30, 32).	W. of Bampur, Baluchistan.	W. T. Blanford, Esq. [E].
τ–υ. ♀ (Sc. 31; V. 168; C. 31) & hgr. (Sc. 33; V. 163; C. 31).	Kurrachee.	Dr. Leith [P.].
φ. Hgr. (Sc. 31; V. 173, C 28).	Sind.	Dr. Leith [P.]
χ–ψ. ♀ (Sc. 35, 35; V. 184, 183; C. 31, 31).	Sind.	F. Day, Esq. [P.].
ω. ♀ (Sc. 33; V. 179; C. 34).	Deesa.	Dr. Leith [P.]
a'–c'. Hgr. (Sc. 31, 31; V. 153, 155, C. 28, 31) & yg. (Sc. 33; V. 163; C. 28).	Mahabuleshwar.	Dr. Leith [P.].
d'–g'. ♀ (Sc. 31; V. 171; C. 31) & yg. (Sc. 27, 27, 27; V. 137, 132, 139; C 25, 25, 25).	Deccan.	Col. Sykes [P.].
h'–i'. ♀ (Sc. 27, 29; V. 158, 149; C. 26, 23).	Anamallays.	Col Beddome [C.].
k'. ♂ (Sc. 29; V. 141; C. 28).	Madras.	T. C. Jerdon, Esq. [P.].
l'–m'. ♂ (Sc. 27; V 133; C. 28) & ♀ (Sc. 29; V. 143; C. 23).	India.	Dr. P. Russell.
n'. Skull.		

2. Echis coloratus. (PLATE XXV. fig. 1.)

Echis arenicola (*non Boie*), *Gunth. Proc. Zool. Soc.* 1864, p. 489.
—— colorata, *Gunth. Proc Zool. Soc.* 1878, p. 978, and 1881, p. 463; *Peracca, Boll. Mus. Torin.* ix 1894, no. 167, p. 16

Scales on the snout and vertex convex, smooth or obtusely keeled, 13 to 15 across from eye to eye; no supraocular shield, 17 to 22 scales round the eye; three or four series of scales between the eye and the labials; nostril in a single or divided nasal, which is separated from the rostral by a series of scales; 12 to 15 upper labials. Scales in 31–35 rows. Ventrals 174–205; anal entire, subcaudals 42–52. No cruciform light marking on the head.

Total length 750 millim.; tail 80.

Palestine, Arabia, Socotra.

a–b. ♀ (Sc. 35, 35, V. 192, 187; C. 46, 44).	Dead Sea.	Canon Tristram [C.].
c. ♀ (Sc. 35; V. 205; C. 45).	Jebel Sharr, Midian, 4500 feet.	Major Burton [P] (Type.)
d–e. Hgr. ♀ (Sc 35, 31; V. 190, 186; C.51, 50).	Hadramaut.	Dr. J. Anderson [P.].
f–g. ♂ (Sc. 35; V. 179; C 52) & yg. (Sc. 35; V. 174; C 49).	Muscat.	A. S. G. Jayakar, Esq. [P.].
h. ♀ (Sc. 35; V. 185; C. 44).	Socotra	Prof. I. B. Balfour [C.].

8. ATHERIS.

Chloroechis, *Bonap. Proc. Zool. Soc.* 1849, p. 145.—No proper definition.
Atheris, *Cope, Proc. Ac. Philad.* 1862, p. 337; *Peters, Mon. Berl. Ac.* 1864, p. 642; *Strauch, Syn. Viper.* p. 123 (1869).
Pœcilostolus, *Günth. Ann. & Mag. N. H.* (3) xi. 1863, p. 25.
Echis, part., *Jan, Elenco sist. Ofid.* p. 122 (1863).

Head very distinct from neck, covered above with imbricate scales; eye large, with vertical pupil, usually separated from the labials by small scales; nostrils lateral. Body slightly compressed; scales keeled, with apical pits, laterals more or less oblique and smaller than dorsals and than outer row; ventrals rounded. Tail moderate, prehensile; subcaudals single.

The supratemporal is very short and the quadrate long and slender.

Tropical Africa.

Synopsis of the Species.

I. No horn-like supraciliary scales.

9–11 scales across the crown, from eye to eye; 25–36 scales across the middle of the body.................... 1. *chlorechis*, p. 508.
7–8 scales across the crown; 15–25 scales across the middle of the body.. 2. *squamiger*, p. 509.

II. Several erect, horn-like supraciliary scales; 9–10 scales across the crown; 25 scales across the middle of the body.
3. *ceratophorus*, p. 510.

1. Atheris chlorechis.

Vipera chlorechis, *Schleg. Versl. Ak. Amst.* iii. 1855, p. 317.
Toxicoa chloroechis, *Cope, Proc. Ac. Philad.* 1859, p. 341.
Vipera (Echis) chloroechis, *Jan, Rev. & Mag. Zool.* 1859, p. 512.
Echis chloroechis, *Jan, Elenco,* p 122 (1863).
Atheris polylepis, *Peters, Mon. Berl. Ac.* 1864, p. 642; *Günth. Zool. Rec.* 1864, p. 125.
—— chloroechis, *Peters, l. c.* p. 645; *Strauch, Syn. Viper.* p. 126 (1869), *F. Müll. Verh. Nat. Ges. Basel,* vii. 1885, p. 696; *Boettg. Ber. Senck. Ges.* 1888, p. 93.

Rostral at least twice as broad as deep; head-scales strongly keeled, 9 to 11 across the crown from eye to eye; 15 to 17 scales round the eye; one or two series of scales between the eye and the labials; nasal entire or semidivided; 9 to 12 upper labials, two pairs of small chin-shields, the anterior in contact with the first or first and second lower labials; gular scales keeled. Scales strongly keeled, in 25–36 rows. Ventrals 154–165; anal entire; subcaudals 53–62. Green above, uniform or with small yellow spots, uniform yellowish or pale green beneath; end of tail yellowish or blackish.

Total length 520 millim.; tail 85.

West Africa, from Liberia to the Ogowe.

a. ♂ (Sc. 25; V 165; Lagos.
C. 62).
b. ♀ (Sc. 25; V. 157; Lambarene, Ogowe   Miss Kingsley [C.].
C. 55).   River.

2. Atheris squamiger.

Echis squamigera, *Hallow. Proc. Ac. Philad.* 1854, p. 193.
Toxicoa squamigera, *Cope, Proc. Ac Philad.* 1859, p 341.
Atheris squamatus, *Cope, Proc. Ac. Philad.* 1862, p. 337.
Pœcilostolus burtonii, *Gunth. Ann. & Mag. N. H.* (3) xi. 1863, p. 25.
Atheris burtonii, *Gunth. Proc. Zool Soc.* 1863, p. 16, pl. iii.; *Strauch, Syn. Viper.* p. 125 (1869).
—— squamigera, *Peters, Mon. Berl. Ac* 1864, p. 645; *Strauch, l. c.* p. 124; *Bocage, Jorn Sc. Lisb* xi. 1887, p. 189; *Boettg. Ber. Senck Ges* 1888, p. 90; *Bocage, Herp Angola,* p 152 (1895).
—— lucani, *Rochebr Bull. Soc. Philom.* (7) ix. 1885, p. 89.
? Atheris proximus, *Rochebr. l. c.* p. 90.
Atheris anisolepis, *Mocq Bull. Soc Philom.* (7) xi. 1887, p. 89 *.
—— læviceps, *Boettg. Zool. Anz.* 1887, p. 651, *and Ber. Senck. Ges.* 1888, p 92, pl. ii. fig. 7.
—— subocularis, *Fischer, Jahrb. Hamb. Wiss. Anst.* v. 1888, p 5, pls. i. fig. 2, & ii fig. 11.

Rostral at least thrice as broad as deep; head-scales strongly keeled, or smooth between the eyes, 7 or 8 across the crown from eye to eye; 10 to 15 scales round the eye; one or two series of scales between the eye and the labials; nasal entire or divided; 9 to 12 upper labials (fourth, in one specimen, entering the eye); a pair of small chin-shields, in contact with one, two, or three lower labials on each side; gular scales keeled. Scales strongly keeled, in 15–25 rows. Ventrals 153–173; anal entire; subcaudals 51–65. Olive above, uniform or with more or less regular, narrow, yellow cross-bands, or yellow with small green spots; pale olive beneath, marbled with darker or with yellowish spots or uniform yellow.

Total length 550 millim.; tail 100.

West Africa, from the Cameroons to Angola.

a. ♂ (Sc. 21; V. 163; Cameroons   Capt. Burton [C].
C. 56).   (Type of *P. burtonii*.)
b. ♂ (Sc. 15; V. 163; Cameroons.   Hr. J. Voss [C]; J. G.
C. 65).   Fischer Collection
                    (Type of *A. subocularis*)
c. ♀ (Sc. 17; V. 173; Mouth of the Loango. Mr. H. J. Duggan [C.].
C. 58).
d. ♂ (Sc. 17; V. 162; W. Africa.   Sir A. Smith [P.].
C. 63).
e. ♂ (Sc. 17; V. 157; W. Africa.   Dr. Günther [P.].
C. 55).
f. ♂ skeleton.   W. Africa.

---

* Types examined.

This species is nearly completely connected with the preceding, and may ultimately have to be united with it.

3. Atheris ceratophorus.

Atheris ceratophora, *Werner, Verh. zool.-bot. Ges. Wien,* xlv. 1895, p. 194, pl. v. fig. 1.

Rostral twice and a half as broad as deep; head-scales strongly keeled, 9 or 10 across the interorbital region; three erect, horn-like, supraciliary scales, the longest as long as the eye; 16 or 17 scales round the eye; two series of scales between the eye and the labials; nostril between two nasals; 10 or 11 upper labials; a pair of chin-shields in contact with four lower labials on each side; gular scales keeled. Scales strongly keeled, in 25 rows. Ventrals 142; anal entire; subcaudals 55. Dark olive above, with black spots forming more or less regular cross-bands; pale olive beneath, speckled with black.

Total length 210 millim.; tail 65.

East Africa.

a. ♀ (V. 142; C. 55).   Usambara.   Dr. F. Werner. (Type.)

9. ATRACTASPIS.

Atractaspis, *Smith, Ill. Zool S. Afr., Rept.* (1849); *Dum. & Bibr. Erp Gén.* vii. p. 1303 (1854); *Gunth. Cat. Col. Sn.* p. 239 (1858); *Jan, Rev. & Mag. Zool.* 1858, p. 518, *Cope, Proc. Ac. Philad.* 1859, p. 342; *Peters, Reise n. Mossamb.* iii. p. 141 (1882).
Brachycranion, *Hallow. Proc. Ac. Philad.* 1854, p. 99; *Cope, l. c.*
Eurystephus, *Cope, Proc. Ac. Philad.* 1862, p. 337.
Clothelaps, *Cope, Trans. Amer. Philos. Soc.* xviii. 1895, p. 211.

Poison-fangs enormously developed; a few teeth on the palatines, none on the pterygoids; mandible edentulous in front, with two or three very small teeth in the middle of the dentary bone. Head small, not distinct from neck, covered with large symmetrical shields; nostril between two nasals; no loreal; eye minute, with round pupil. Postfrontal bone absent. Body cylindrical, scales smooth, without pits, in 17 to 37 rows; ventrals rounded. Tail short; subcaudals single or in two rows.

Tropical and South Africa.

This genus is remarkable as presenting the most extreme specialization in the Viperine direction, the poison-fangs being as large in proportion as in any other form and the solid teeth on the palate and mandible, which are much reduced in number in many of the Crotalines, having almost disappeared.

Fig. 36.

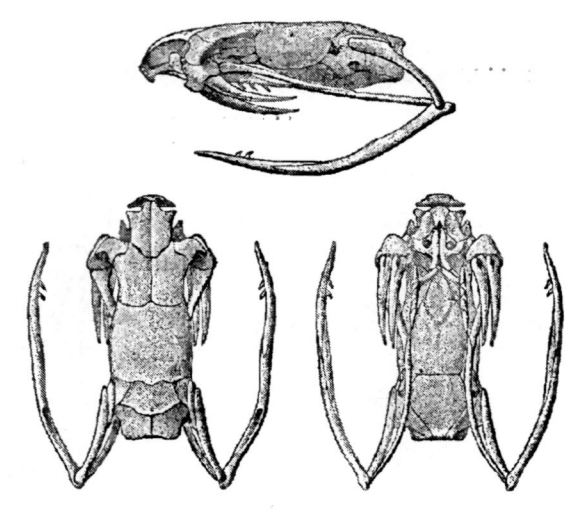

Skull of *Atractaspis aterrima*.

Synopsis of the Species.

I. Anal divided; subcaudals all or greater part divided.

    A. Six upper labials, fifth very large and forming a suture with the parietals; no præocular; frontal shorter than the parietals; scales in 17 rows; ventrals 167–174.
        1. *hildebrandtii*, p. 512.

    B. Five upper labials, fourth largest; postocular in contact with a large temporal; a præocular; frontal as long as, or slightly shorter than the parietals.

Scales in 19–21 rows; ventrals 200–230.   2. *congica*, p. 513.
Scales in 25–27 rows; ventrals 220–257.   3. *irregularis*, p. 513.

II. Anal entire; subcaudals all or part entire.

    A. Postocular in contact with a large temporal.

        1. Second lower labial very large, fused with the chin-shields; scales in 23–27 rows; ventrals 178–193; subcaudals 23–27 .... 4. *corpulenta*, p. 514.

2. Third lower labial very large.

    a. First lower labial in contact with its fellow behind the symphysial; scales in 19-23 rows.

Snout very prominent, cuneiform; rostral
with sharp horizontal edge; ventrals
227-248........................ 5. *rostrata*, p. 514.
Snout prominent, subcuneiform; ventrals
221-260........................ 6. *bibronii*, p. 515.
Snout rounded; ventrals 251-300 .... 7. *aterrima*, p. 515.

    b. Symphysial in contact with the chin-shields; scales in 31 rows; ventrals 240 .... 8. *dahomeyensis*, p. 516.

B. Temporals small, 2+3 or 4; fourth or fifth lower labial largest; ventrals 210-245; subcaudals 26-37.

    1. Scales in 23-25 rows.

Frontal slightly longer than broad, much
longer than the parietals .... 9. *micropholis*, p. 516.
Frontal once and two fifths as long as
broad, as long as the parietals ...... 10. *leucomelas*, p. 517.

    2. Scales in 29-37 rows .... 11. *microlepidota*, p. 517.

Atractaspis natalensis, Peters, Mon. Berl. Ac. 1877, p. 616, pl. —. fig. 3, is not included in this Synopsis. I am convinced it is identical with *Macrelaps microlepidotus*, Gthr. (*supra*, p. 255), and should be referred to the synonymy of that species.

1. Atractaspis hildebrandtii.

Atractaspis hildebrandtii, *Peters, Mon. Berl. Ac.* 1877, p. 616, pl. —. fig. 3.

    Snout rounded. Portion of rostral visible from above as long as, or a little shorter than, its distance from the frontal; suture between the internasals a little longer than that between the præfrontals; frontal once and a half as long as broad, much longer than its distance from the end of the snout, shorter than the parietals; no præocular; præfrontal entering the eye; a minute postocular; a large temporal, widely separated from the postocular; six upper labials, third and fourth entering the eye, fifth very large and forming a long suture with the parietal; first lower labial in contact with its fellow behind the symphysial; four lower labials in contact with the anterior chin-shields, which are followed by a second shorter pair. Scales in 17 rows. Ventrals 167-174; anal divided; subcaudals 22-28 pairs. Uniform dark brown.

    Total length 450 millim.; tail 53.

    East Africa.

    a. ♂ (V. 167; C. 28).   Mombasa.   H W. Lane, Esq. [C.].

2. Atractaspis congica.

Atractaspis aterrima (*non Gunth.*), *Bocage, Jorn. Sc Lisb* iv. 1873, p. 223.
—— congica, *Peters, Mon. Berl. Ac.* 1877, p. 616, pl. —. fig. 2, *Bocage, Jorn. Sc. Lisb.* x. 1887, p. 187, *and Herp. Angola*, p. 142 (1895).
—— irregularis, var. congica, *Boettg. Ber. Senck. Ges* 1888, p 87.

Snout very short, rounded. Portion of rostral visible from above about half as long as its distance from the frontal; suture between the internasals longer than that between the præfrontals; frontal slightly longer than broad, twice as long as its distance from the end of the snout, as long as the parietals; one præ- and one post-ocular; temporals 1+2, anterior very large and wedged in between the fourth and fifth labials; five upper labials, third and fourth entering the eye, fourth largest; first lower labial in contact with its fellow behind the symphysial; three lower labials in contact with the chin-shields, third extremely large. Scales in 19–21 rows. Ventrals 200–230; anal divided; subcaudals 19–23, a few of the anterior entire, rest in two rows. Uniform dark brown or black.

Total length 450 millim.; tail 35.

Congo, Angola.

a. ♂ (Sc. 19, V. 218, Pungo Andongo, Angola. Dr. Welwitsch [P]. C. 22).

3. Atractaspis irregularis.

Elaps irregularis, *Reinh. Vidensk. Selsk. Skrift.* x. 1843, p 264, pl iii. figs 1–3.
Atractaspis irregularis, *Jan, Rev. & Mag Zool* 1858, p. 518, and 1859, p. 511, *and Icon. Gén.* 43, pl iii. fig 1 (1873); *Peters, Mon Berl. Ac.* 1877, p. 616; *F. Müll. Verh. Nat. Ges Basel,* vi. 1878, p. 694, *Boettg Ber. Senck. Ges.* 1888, p. 87; *Gunth. Ann & Mag. N. H* (6) xv. 1895, p 527, *Bocage, Herp Angola*, p. 143 (1895).
—— corpulentus (*non Hallow.*), *Bocage, Jorn. Sc. Lisb* i. 1866, p. 49

Snout very short, rounded. Portion of rostral visible from above measuring two thirds to three fourths its distance from the frontal; suture between the internasals longer than that between the præfrontals; frontal as long as broad, much longer than its distance from the end of the snout, as long as or slightly shorter than the parietals; one præ- and one postocular; a very large temporal wedged in between the fourth and fifth upper labials, five upper labials, third and fourth entering the eye, fourth largest; first lower labial in contact with its fellow behind the symphysial; three lower labials in contact with the chin-shields, third extremely large. Scales in 25–27 rows. Ventrals 220–257, anal divided; subcaudals 22–28 pairs. Uniform dark brown or black.

Total length 560 millim.; tail 35.

West Africa, from the Gold Coast to the Congo; Central Africa.

a–b. Hgr. (Sc. 25; V. 220, 150 miles up the Niger.   W H. Crosse, Esq.
   237, C. 28, 26).   [P.].
c. ♀ (Sc. 27; V. 257, Wadelai.   Dr. Emin Pasha [P.].
   C 23)
d. Yg. (Sc. 25; V. 241, Uganda.   Mr. Baxter [C.].
   C. 22).

4. Atractaspis corpulenta.

Brachycranion corpulentum, *Hallow. Proc. Ac. Philad.* 1854, p. 99.
Atractaspis corpulentus, *Hallow. Proc. Ac. Philad.* 1857, p. 70;
   Günth. Cat. p. 239 (1858), and *Ann. & Mag. N. H.* (4) ix. 1872,
   p. 36, pl. iii. fig. F, *Mocq. Bull. Soc. Philom.* (7) xi. 1887,
   p. 87.
—— leucura, *Mocq. Bull. Soc. Philom.* (7) x. 1886, p. 14, pl. v.

Snout strongly projecting, cuneiform. Rostral large, its upper portion as long as its distance from the frontal; suture between the internasals a little shorter than that between the præfrontals*; frontal as long as broad, much longer than its distance from the end of the snout, as long as the parietals; one præ- and one postocular; temporals 1+3, anterior very large and wedged in between the fourth and fifth labials; five upper labials, third and fourth entering the eye, first lower labial in contact with its fellow behind the symphysial, second lower labial very large, fused with the chin-shields and also forming a suture with its fellow. Scales in 23–27 rows. Ventrals 178–193; anal entire, subcaudals 23–27, all entire or only a few divided. Uniform blackish brown; tail sometimes white.

Total length 345 millim.; tail 33.

West Africa (Liberia to Gaboon).

a. ♀ (Sc. 25; V. 178; C. 25).   Gaboon.

5. Atractaspis rostrata.

Atractaspis rostrata, *Günth. Ann. & Mag. N. H.* (4) i. 1868, p. 429,
   pl. xix. fig. I.
—— bibronii (*non Smith*), *Peters, Reise n. Mossamb* iii p. 142,
   pls. xix A. fig. 2 & xx. fig. 11 (1882).
? Atractaspis irregularis, *Pfeffer, Jahrb. Hamb. Wiss. Anst.* x. 1893,
   p. 19.

Snout very prominent, cuneiform. Rostral with sharp horizontal edge, the portion visible from above nearly as long as its distance from the frontal; suture between the internasals a little longer or a little shorter than that between the præfrontals; frontal a little longer than broad, longer than its distance from the end of the snout, as long as the parietals; one præ- and one postocular; a large temporal, wedged in between the fourth and fifth upper labials;

---

* The fusion of the internasals with the præfrontals, in the specimen described by Hallowell. is probably an individual anomaly

five upper labials, third and fourth entering the eye, fourth largest; first lower labial in contact with its fellow behind the symphysial; three lower labials in contact with the chin-shields, third extremely large. Scales in 23 rows. Ventrals 227-248; anal entire; subcaudals 19-24, single. Uniform dark brown or blackish.

Total length 600 millim.; tail 37.

East and Central Africa.

a-b. ♀ (V. 227, 244; C. 22, 19). Zanzibar. Sir J. Kirk [C.]. (Types.)
c. ♂ (V. 248, C. 24). L. Nyassa. Universities Mission.

6. Atractaspis bibronii.

Atractaspis bibronii, *Smith, Ill. Zool. S. Afr., Rept.* pl. lxxi. (1849); *Dum. & Bibr.* vii. p. 1304 (1854); *Bocage, Jorn. Sc. Lisb.* i 1866, p 227, *Bocage, Herp. Angola,* i p. 141 (1895).
—— inornatus, *Smith, l. c.*
—— irregularis (*non Reinh*), *Gunth. Cat.* p 239 (1858).
—— irregularis, var. bibronii, *Boettg. Ber. Senck Ges.* 1887, p 165

Snout prominent, subcuneiform. Portion of rostral visible from above as long as or a little shorter than its distance from the frontal; suture between the internasals nearly as long as that between the præfrontals, frontal as long as broad or slightly longer than broad, much longer than its distance from the end of the snout, as long as the parietals; one præ- and one postocular; a large temporal, wedged in between the fourth and fifth labials; five upper labials, third and fourth entering the eye, fourth largest; first lower labial in contact with its fellow behind the symphysial; three lower labials in contact with the chin-shields, third extremely large. Scales in 21-23 rows. Ventrals 221-260; anal entire, subcaudals 20-23, all or greater part single. Dark purplish brown above, yellowish or pale brown beneath

Total length 600 millim.; tail 25.

Eastern districts of Cape Colony, Natal, Namaqualand, Angola.

a. ♀ (Sc. 21, V. 260, C 20) Eastern districts of Cape Colony Sir A. Smith [P.]. (One of the types.)
b. ♂ (Sc 21, V. 222; C. 23). Durban, Natal. Col. Bowker [P.].
c. ♂ (Sc. 21; V. 221; C. 22) S. Africa.

7. Atractaspis aterrima.

Atractaspis bibronii (*non Smith*), *Jan, Rev. & Mag. Zool* 1859, p. 511, *and Icon Gén* 43, pl. iii fig. 2 (1873).
—— aterrima, *Gunth. Ann. & Mag N H* (3) xii. 1863, p. 363.

Snout rounded. Portion of rostral visible from above measuring one third to one half its distance from the frontal; suture between the internasals as long as or longer than that between the præfrontals; frontal as long as broad, longer than its distance from the end of the snout, shorter than the parietals, one præ- and one postocular; a large temporal, wedged in between the fourth and fifth labials; five upper labials, third and fourth entering the eye, fourth largest; first lower labial in contact with its fellow behind the symphysial; three lower labials in contact with the chin-shields, third extremely large. Scales in 19-21 rows. Ventrals 251-300; anal entire; subcaudals 18-24, single. Uniform dark brown or black.

Total length 650 millim.; tail 30
West and Central Africa.

a. Hgr. (Sc. 21; V 276; C. 18).	W. Africa.	Prof Grant [P.]. (Type.)
b. ♂ (Sc. 19; V 251; C. 22).	Ashantee.	Sir A. Smith [P.].
c. ♂ (Sc. 21; V. 256; C. 22).	Wegbe. Togoland.	W. G Innes, Esq. [C.].
d. ♂ (Sc. 21; V. 273; C. 23).	Lagos.	
e-f. ♀ (Sc. 19, V. 282; C. 19) & vg. (Sc. 19; V. 277; C. 24)	150 miles up the Niger.	W. H Crosse, Esq. [P.].
g. ♀ (Sc. 19; V. 300; C. 19).	Wadelai.	Dr. Emin Pasha [P.].
h. Skull of e.		

8. Atractaspis dahomeyensis.

Atractaspis dahomeyensis, *Bocage, Jorn Sc. Lisb* xi 1887, p. 196, and *Herp. Angola*, p 144 (1895).

Snout prominent and cuneiform, as in *A. rostrata*. One præocular; postocular absent, fused with the supraocular; a large anterior temporal; five upper labials, third and fourth entering the eye; symphysial in contact with the chin-shields; third lower labial very large. Scales in 31 rows Ventrals 240; anal entire; subcaudals 24, partly single, partly divided. Black above, brown beneath, the ventral shields edged with lighter.

Total length 490 millim.; tail 32.
Dahomey.

9. Atractaspis micropholis.

Atractaspis corpulentus (*non Hallow.*), *Günth. Ann. & Mag. N. H.* (3) xviii. 1866, p 29.

—— micropholis, *Günth. Ann & Mag. N. H.* (4) ix. 1872, p 36, pl iii. fig. E; *F. Müll. Verh Nat Ges Basel*, viii. 1887, p. 278.

Snout very short, prominent, cuneiform. Rostral large, the portion visible from above as long as its distance from the frontal; suture between the internasals as long as that between the præfrontals; frontal slightly longer than broad, much longer than its distance from the end of the snout, much longer than the parietals; one præ- and one postocular; temporals small, scale-like, 2+3 or 4; six upper labials, third and fourth entering the eye, fourth scarcely larger than third, fifth and sixth small, first lower labial forming a suture with its fellow behind the symphysial; three or four lower labials in contact with the chin-shields. Scales in 25 rows. Ventrals 210-215; anal entire; subcaudals 29-30, single. Uniform dark brown.

Total length 330 millim.; tail 28.

Cape Verd.

a. ♀ (V. 210; C 29). ——? Dr. St. George Mivart [P.]. (Type)

10. Atractaspis leucomelas.

Atractaspis leucomelas, *Bouleng Ann Mus Genova*, (2) xv. 1895, p. 16, pl. iv. fig. 2

Snout very short. Portion of rostral visible from above nearly as long as its distance from the frontal; suture between the internasals half as long as that between the præfrontals; frontal once and two fifths as long as broad, much longer than its distance from the end of the snout, as long as the parietals; one præ- and one postocular; temporals small, scale-like, 2+3; six upper labials, third and fourth entering the eye, fourth largest, first lower labial forming a suture with its fellow behind the symphysial; three lower labials in contact with the chin-shields. Scales in 23 rows. Ventrals 243; anal entire; subcaudals 27, nearly all single. Black above, with a white vertebral line, occupying one and two half rows of scales; ventrals and subcaudals, and four outer series of scales on each side, white; neck entirely black; head white, with a black blotch covering the nasals and the upper head-shields.

Total length 575 millim; tail 40.

Ogaden, Somaliland.

11. Atractaspis microlepidota.

Atractaspis microlepidota, *Gunth. Ann & Mag. N. H* (3) xviii. 1866, p. 29, pl vii fig 3, and (6) i. 1888, p. 332; *Bouleng. Ann. Mus. Genova*, (2) xv. 1895, p. 15

—— fallax, *Peters, Mon. Berl. Ac* 1866, p. 890, *and in Decken's Reise O.-Afr.* iii. p. 17, pl. i fig 3 (1869).

Snout very short, prominent, subcuneiform. Portion of rostral visible from above nearly as long as its distance from the frontal; suture between the internasals as long as that between the præfrontals; frontal a little longer than broad, much longer than its distance from the end of the snout, longer than the parietals; one præ- and one postocular; temporals small, 2+3 or 4; six upper labials, third and fourth entering the eye and largest; first lower labial in contact with its fellow behind the symphysial; three lower labials in contact with the chin-shields. Scales in 29-37 rows. Ventrals 212-245; anal entire; subcaudals 26-37, single. Uniform dark brown.

Total length 540 millim.; tail 45.

East and Central Africa.

a. ♀ (Sc. 29, V. 212; C. 26). ——? Dr. Günther [P.] (Type.)

b. ♀ (Sc. 37; V. 245; C. 28). L. Tanganyika. Sir J. Kirk [C].

Subfam. 2. CROTALINÆ.

Crotalini, *Oppel, Ordn. Rept.* p. 50, 1811.
Crotalidæ, part., *Gray, Ann. Philos.* 1825, p. 204.
Crotaloidea, *Fitzinger, Neue Classif. Rept.* p. 34, 1826.
Cophiadæ, *Boie, Isis,* 1827, p. 511.
Crotalina, *Bonaparte, Mem. Acc. Tor.* (2) ii. p. 393, 1840.
Crotalidæ, *Gray, Zool Miscell.* p. 47, 1842, *and Cat. Sn.* p. 3, 1849.
Crotaliens, *Duméril, Mém. Ac. Sc.* xxiii. p. 533, 1853; *Duméril & Bibron, Erp. Gén.* vii. p. 1451, 1854.
Crotalinæ, *Cope, Proc. Ac. Philad.* 1859, p. 334.
Crotalidæ, *Günther, Rept. Brit. Ind.* p. 383, 1864.
Crotalidæ, *Cope, Proc. Ac. Philad.* 1864, p. 231.
Teleuraspides, *Cope, Proc. Ac. Philad.* 1871, p. 205.
Bothrophes, *Schreiber, Herp. Eur.* p. 181, 1875.
Bothrophera, *Garman, N. Amer. Rept.* p. 104, 1883.
Crotalinæ, *Boulenger, Faun. Ind., Rept.* p. 418, 1890.
Crotalidæ (Cophiinæ, Crotalinæ), *Cope, Trans. Amer. Philos. Soc.* xviii. p. 212, 1895.

Fig. 37.

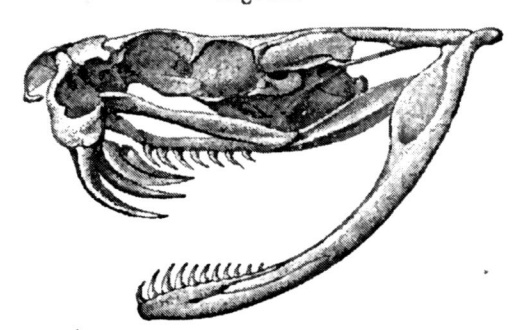

Skull of *Crotalus horridus*.

Synopsis of the Genera.

I. No rattle.

Upper surface of head covered with nine large symmetrical shields, the internasals and præfrontals sometimes broken up into scales.
10. **Ancistrodon**, p. 519.

Upper surface of head covered with scales or small shields.
11. **Lachesis**, p. 529.

II. Tail ending in a rattle.

Upper surface of head with nine large symmetrical shields.
12. **Sistrurus**, p. 569.

Upper surface of head covered with scales or small shields.
13. **Crotalus**, p. 572.

10. ANCISTRODON

Agkistrodon, *Palisot de Beauvois, Tr. Am. Philos Soc.* iv. 1799, p. 381; *Baird & Gir. Cat N. Am Rept.* p. 17 (1853); *Stejneger, Rep U.S Nat. Mus. f.* 1893, p 401 (1895).
Scytale, part, *Latr. Hist. Rept.* iii. p. 158 (1802); *Daud Hist. Rept.* v. p. 334 (1803).
Cenchris, *Daud. t. c.* p 356; *Wagl Syst. Amph* p 175 (1830); *Gray, Zool. Misc.* p 50 (1842), and *Cat. Sn.* p 15 (1849).
Cophias, part., *Merr Tent. Syst Amph.* p. 154 (1820).
Trigonocephalus (*non Opp*), *Kuhl, Isis*, 1822, p 473; *Fitzing. N. Classif. Rept.* p 34 (1826), *Wagl. l c* p 173; *Gray, ll cc.* pp. 50 & 14; *Dum. & Bibr. Erp. Gén.* vii. p 1488 (1854), *Jan, Elenco sist. Ofid.* p. 124 (1863); *Strauch, Schl Russ. R* p. 232 (1873).
Tisiphone, *Fitzing. l. c*; *Peters, Mon Berl Ac.* 1862, p. 673
Acontias (*non Cuv.*), *Troost, Ann Lyc. N York*, iii. 1836, p. 176.
Toxicophis, *Troost, l. c.* p. 190; *Baird & Gir. l. c* p. 19.
Trigonocephalus, part, *Schleg. Phys. Serp.* ii. p. 527 (1837).
Halys, *Gray, Cat.* p 14; *Peters, l. c.* p. 671; *Gunth. Rept Brit. Ind* p. 392 (1864).
Hypnale, *Gray, l. c.* p 15; *Peters, l. c.* p. 673; *Gunth l. c.* p. 394.
Leiolepis (*non Cuv.*), *Dum & Bibr Mém. Ac. Sc.* xxiii. 1853, p. 534, and *Erp Gén.* vii. p. 1499.
Ancistrodon, *Baird, Serp N York*, p 13 (1854); *Cope, Proc. Ac. Philad.* 1859, p 336; *Peters, l. c.* p. 671; *Bouleng. Faun. Ind., Rept.* p 423 (1890), *W. E Taylor, Amer. Nat.* 1895, p. 283.
Calloselasma, *Cope, Proc Ac. Philad* 1859, p 336, *Gunth. l c* p. 391

Upper surface of head with the nine normal shields, or internasals and præfrontals broken up into scales. Body cylindrical; scales smooth or keeled, with apical pits. Tail moderate or short; subcaudals single or in two rows.

Borders of the Caspian Sea; Asia; North and Central America.

Synopsis of the Species.

I. Scales in 21-27 rows; internasals and præfrontals well developed.

A. Scales keeled.

1. Anterior subcaudals single; second upper labial usually forming the anterior border of the loreal pit.

    a. Snout not produced.

No loreal, upper præocular in contact with the posterior nasal; third upper labial usually entering the eye; scales in 25 (rarely 27) rows; ventrals 130-147; subcaudals 33-51............ 1. *piscivorus*, p. 520.

A loreal, separating the upper præocular from the posterior nasal; eye separated from the labials by suboculars; scales in 23 (rarely 25) rows; ventrals 135-141; subcaudals 52-64....... 2. *bilineatus*, p. 521.

A loreal, usually separating the upper præocular from the posterior nasal; eye separated from the labials by suboculars; scales in 23 (rarely 25) rows; ventrals 145-155; subcaudals 31-52.......................... 3. *contortrix*, p. 522.

    b. Snout ending in a pointed appendage; scales in 21 rows; ventrals 162-166; subcaudals 58-60.
                        4. *acutus*, p. 524.

2. Subcaudals all paired; loreal pit separated from the labials; ventrals 137-174; subcaudals 31-55.

    a. Posterior labials distinct from the temporals.

Snout slightly turned up at the end; scales in 23 rows .... 5. *halys*, p. 524.
Snout not turned up; scales in 23 (rarely 21) rows .... 6. *intermedius*, p. 525.
Snout not turned up; scales in 21 (rarely 23) rows .... 7. *blomhoffii*, p. 525.

    b. Posterior labials fused with the temporals, snout slightly turned up; scales in 21 (rarely 23) rows.
                        8. *himalayanus*, p. 526.

B. Scales smooth, in 21 rows; ventrals 138-157, subcaudals 34-54 pairs .... 9. *rhodostoma*, p. 527.

II. Scales in 17 rows, more or less distinctly keeled; snout strongly turned up, covered above with small shields; ventrals 125-155; subcaudals 28-45 pairs. 10. *hypnale*, p. 528.

1. Ancistrodon piscivorus.

Crotalus piscivorus, part., *Lacép Serp.* ii. pp. 130, 424 (1789).
Scytale piscivora, part, *Latr. Rept.* iii. p 163 (1802); *Daud. Rept.* v. p. 344 (1802).
Coluber aquaticus, part., *Shaw, Zool.* iii. p. 425 (1802).
Acontias leucostoma, *Troost, Ann. Lyc. N. Y.* iii. 1836, p. 176.
Trigonocephalus cenchris, part, *Schleg. Phys. Serp.* ii. p. 553 (1837).
—— piscivorus, *Holbr. N. Am. Herp.* ii p. 63, pl. xiii. (1838), and 2nd ed. iii. p. 33, pl. vii. (1842); *Dum. & Bibr.* vii. p. 1491, pl lxxxii. *b.* fig. 2 (1854); *Jan, Icon. Gén* 46, pl. iv. (1874); *Bocourt, Miss. Sc. Mex., Rept.* pl. xxvii (1882).
Cenchris piscivorus, *Gray, Zool. Miscell.* p. 51 (1842), and *Cat.* p. 16 (1842).
Toxicophis piscivorus, *Baird & Gir. Cat. N. Am. Rept.* p. 19 (1853), and *Rep. Explor. Surv. R. R.* x. *Rept.* pl. xxv. fig. 13 (1859).
—— pugnax, *Baird & Gir. ll. cc.* p. 20, fig. 14, and *Rep U.S. Mex. Bound. Surv.* ii. *x. Rept.* p 15. pl. vi. (1859).

10. ANCISTRODON.

Ancistrodon piscivorus, *Cope, Proc. Ac. Philad* 1859, p 336, *Garm. N. Am Rept.* p. 121, pl. viii fig 2 (1883): *Cope, Proc. U.S. Nat. Mus.* xiv. 1892, p. 683.
—— pugnax, *Cope, Proc. Ac. Philad.* 1859, p. 336.
Agkistrodon piscivorus, *Jord. Man Vert N U S* 5th ed. p. 199 (1888); *Hay, Batr Rept. Ind.* p. 184 (1892), *Loennberg, Proc. U.S Nat. Mus.* xvii. 1894, p. 336; *Stejneger, Rep. U.S. Nat. Mus. f.* 1893, p. 406, pl. iv. (1895).

Snout rounded, not turned up, flat above, with sharp canthus. Rostral as deep as broad or slightly broader than deep; a pair of internasals and a pair of præfrontals; frontal as long as or a little shorter than its distance from the end of the snout, as long as or shorter than the parietals, which are usually followed by a pair of occipitals, no loreal; upper præocular in contact with the posterior nasal; two postoculars and one or two suboculars; 7 or 8 upper labials, second forming the anterior border of the loreal pit, third usually entering the eye. Scales strongly keeled, in 25 (rarely 27) rows. Ventrals 130–147; anal entire; subcaudals 33–51, all single or the posterior divided. Pale reddish brown to dark brown above, with more or less distinct dark brown or black cross-bands with broken outlines, or with alternating C-shaped dark markings each enclosing a central spot; a dark, light-edged band from the eye to the angle of the mouth; beneath yellowish, spotted with black, or black with or without lighter variegations.

Total length 1170 millim.; tail 200.

Eastern North America, from North Carolina and Indiana to Florida and Texas.

a, b ♂ (Sc. 27, 25; V. 146, 143, C. 49, 51).	Florida.	H. Hanauer, Esq [P.].
c, d ♂ (Sc 25; V. 134; C. 44) & ♀ (Sc. 25; V. 139; C. ?).	New Orleans.	H. Hanauer, Esq. [P].
e, f ♂ (Sc. 25; V. 141; C. 48) & yg. (Sc. 25; V. 132, C. 43).	New Orleans.	
g, h. ♂ (Sc. 25; V. 145; C. 43) & ♀ (Sc. 25, V. 143; C. 42)	Texas.	
i. ♂ (Sc. 25; V. 144; C. 47).	N. America.	Sir H Sloane [P.].
k. ♀ (Sc. 25, V. 137, C. 44).	N. America.	Dr. R. Harlan [P.].
l. ♂ (Sc. 25; V. 132; C. 41).	N. America.	Dr. Schaus [P.]
m ♀ (Sc. 25; V. 147, C. 48).	N. America.	Dr Gunther [P]
n–o. Yg (Sc. 25, V. 130, 131, C. 39, 39).	N. America.	Zoological Society.
p. Skull.	Charleston.	

2. Ancistrodon bilineatus.

Ancistrodon bilineatus, *Gunth Ann & Mag. N. H* (3) xii. 1863, p. 364; *Cope, Proc. Ac. Philad.* 1865, p 191, *F. Mull. Verh. Nat. Ges. Basel*, vi. 1878, p. 404, *Cope, Proc. U S. Nat. Mus.* xiv. 1892, p. 682; *Gunth. Biol. C.-Am., Rept.* p. 186, pl. lviii figs. A & B (1895).

Trigonocephalus bilineatus, *Bocourt, Miss. Sc. Mex., Rept.* pl. xxvii. fig. 1 (1882).

Snout obtusely pointed, not turned up, flat above, with sharp canthus. Rostral as deep as broad or slightly broader than deep; a pair of internasals and a pair of præfrontals; frontal shorter than its distance from the end of the snout, as long as or shorter than the parietals; upper præocular separated from the posterior nasal by a loreal; two postoculars and one or two suboculars, separating the eye from the labials; 8 or 9 (rarely 7) upper labials, second forming the anterior border of the loreal pit. Scales more or less strongly keeled, in 23 (rarely 25) rows. Ventrals 135–141; anal entire, subcaudals 52–64, anterior single, posterior divided, the divided shields usually more numerous than the single. Yellowish or reddish to dark brown above, with more or less distinct darker cross-bands or alternating transverse blotches with interrupted yellow edges; a vertical yellow, black-edged line on the rostral and symphysial shields, a fine yellow line round the snout on the canthus, continued behind the eye to the neck, and a broader yellow, black-edged streak on the upper lip from the anterior nasal to the last labial, brownish to blackish beneath, with white, black-edged markings.

Total length 1100 millim.; tail 200.

Mexico, Guatemala, Honduras.

a. Hgr. ♀ (Sc. 23, V. 141, C. 52).	Pacific Coast of Guatemala.	O Salvin, Esq. [C.]. (Type.)
b. ♂ (Sc. 23; V. 135; C. 61).	Belize.	P. L. Sclater, Esq. [P.].
c. ♀ (Sc. 25; V 140; C. 54).	Yucatan.	
d, e. Hgr. (Sc. 23, 23; V. 137, 137; C. 64, 62).	Presidio, nr. Mazatlan.	Hr. A. Forrer [C.].
f-g. ♂ (Sc. 23; V. 141; C. 59) & yg. (Sc. 24, V. 137; C. 55).	Tres Marias Ids, W. Mexico	Hr. A. Forrer [C.].

3. Ancistrodon contortrix.

Boa contortrix, *Linn. S. N.* i. p. 373 (1766).
Agkistrodon mokasen, *Pal. de Beauv. Tr. Amer. Philos. Soc.* iv. 1799, p. 370.
Scytale contortrix, *Latr. Rept.* iii. p. 159 (1802).
Cenchris mokeson, *Daud. Rept.* v. p. 358, pl. lx. figs. 3 & 4 (1802); *Harl. Med. Phys. Res.* p. 128 (1835).
Scytalus cupreus, *Rafin. Amer. Journ. Sc.* i. 1810, p. 84; *Harl. l. c.* p. 130.
Scytale mokeson, *Say, Amer. Journ Sc.* i. 1819, p 257.
Cenchris marmorata, *Boie, Isis,* 1827, p. 562.
? Acontias atrofuscus, *Troost, Ann. Lyc. N. Y.* iii. 1836, p. 181.
Trigonocephalus cenchris, part., *Schleg. Phys. Serp.* ii. p. 553, pl. xx. figs. 10 & 11 (1837).
—— contortrix, *Holbr. N. Am. Herp.* ii. p. 69, pl. xiv. (1838), and 2nd ed. iii. p. 39, pl. viii. (1842); *De Kay, N. Y. Faun.* iii. *Rept.*

10. ANCISTRODON.

p. 53, pl. ix fig. 18 (1842); *Dum. & Bibr.* vii p. 1404 (1854); *Jan, Icon Gén* 46, pl v. fig. 1 (1874); *Bocourt, Miss. Sc. Mex., Rept.* pl. xxvii. fig. 2 (1882).

Cenchris contortrix, *Gray, Zool. Miscell* p. 50 (1842), *and Cat.* p. 16 (1849).

? Trigonocephalus atrofuscus, *Holbr op cit* 2nd ed iii. p. 43, pl. ix.

? Cenchris atrofuscus, *Gray, Cat.* p. 16.

? Trigonocephalus histrionicus, *Dum. & Bibr. Mém Ac Sc* xxiii. 1853, p 534.

Agkistrodon contortrix, *Baird & Gir. Cat. N. Am. Rept.* p. 17 (1853); *Hay, Batr Rept. Ind* p. 123 (1892); *Stejneger, Rep. U.S. Nat. Mus. f.* 1893, p. 401, pl. iii (1895).

? Toxicophis atrofuscus, *Baird & Gir l c* p 150

Ancistrodon contortrix, *Baird, Serp. N. Y.* p. 13, pl. i. fig. 3 (1854); *Garm N. Am Rept.* p. 120, pl. viii. fig. 1 (1883), *Cope, Proc. U S Nat. Mus.* xiv. 1892, p 883.

? Ancistrodon atrofuscus, *Cope, Check-List N. Am. Rept.* p. 34 (1875).

Snout rounded or truncate, not turned up, flat above, with sharp canthus. Rostral once and one fourth to once and a half as broad as deep; a pair of internasals and a pair of præfrontals; frontal as long as or a little shorter than its distance from the end of the snout, usually longer than the parietals; loreal present, usually separating the upper præocular from the posterior nasal; two or three postoculars and one to three suboculars, separating the eye from the labials; 8 (rarely 9) upper labials, second usually forming the anterior border of the loreal pit. Scales strongly keeled, in 23 (rarely 25) rows. Ventrals 145-155; anal entire; subcaudals 31-52, anterior single, posterior divided. Yellowish, pinkish, or pale reddish brown above, with dark brown, reddish-brown, or brick-red cross-bars contracting in the middle; these bars sometimes broken up on the vertebral line and forming alternating triangles; a dark temporal streak sometimes present; yellowish or reddish beneath, more or less profusely speckled with grey or brown and with a lateral series of large blackish spots.

Total length 990 millim.; tail 110.

North America, from Massachusetts and Kansas to Northern Florida and Texas.

a. ♀ (V. 153; C. 46).	Pittsburg, Pennsylvania.	Christiania Mus.
b. ♂ (V. 155; C. 39).	New Harmony, Indiana	H. Hanauer, Esq. [P]
c. ♀ (V. 152 : C. 39)	Kansas.	
d. ♀ (V. 147; C. 45).	Arkansas.	Smithsonian Institution.
e. ♀ (V 151; C 43).	Louisiana.	
f. ♀ (V. 146; C. 42).	Fort Worth, Texas.	H. Hanauer, Esq. [P.]
g. ♂ (V. 145; C. ?).	Texas.	
h-i, k. ♂ (V 151, 153; C. 49, 47) & ♀ (V. 150, C. 46).	N. America.	Zoological Society.

4. Ancistrodon acutus.

Halys acutus, *Gunth. Ann. & Mag. N. H.* (6) i. 1888, p 171, pl. xii., and in *Pratt, Snows of Tibet*, p. 242 (1892).

Snout produced into a pointed dermal appendage directed forwards, covered above by the internasals, beneath by a separate shield above the rostral, which is as deep as broad or deeper than broad; upper head-shields finely granulate; frontal as long as or a little longer than the præfrontals, shorter than the parietals; upper præocular separated from the posterior nasal by a loreal; one postocular and one subocular, separating the eye from the labials; seven upper labials, second forming the anterior border of the loreal pit, third and fourth largest; three large lower temporals, anterior largest. Scales strongly and tubercularly keeled, in 21 rows. Ventrals 162–166; anal entire; subcaudals 58–60, mostly in pairs, 6 to 13 of the anterior single. Brown above, with blackish-brown X-shaped markings or alternating >-shaped ones; head dark brown above, yellow on the sides, with a black streak from the eye to the angle of the mouth; yellowish beneath, spotted with dark brown and with a lateral series of large black blotches.

Total length 1500 millim.; tail 200.

Upper Yang-tse, China.

a-c. ♂ (V. 165, 166, 162: C. 59, 60, 58).	Mountains North of Kiu Kiang.	A. E. Pratt, Esq. [C]. (Types.)	
d. ♂ (V 163, C. 58).	Ichang.	A. E. Pratt, Esq [C.]	

5. Ancistrodon halys.

Coluber halys, *Pall. Reise*, iii. p. 703 (1776).
Vipera halys, *Pall. Zoogr. Ross.-As.* iii. p. 49 (1811).
Trigonocephalus halys, *Licht. in Eversm Reise Orenb. Buch.* p. 147 (1823); *Eichw. Zool Spec* iii. p. 170 (1831), and *Faun. Casp.-Cauc.* p. 128, pl. xix (1841); *Dum. & Bibr.* vii. p. 1495 (1854); *Strauch, Schl. Russ. R* p. 231 (1873); *Jan, Icon Gén* 46, pl. vi. fig. 1 (1874), *Schreib Herp. Eur.* p 182, fig. (1875); *De Betta, Atti Ist Ven.* (5) vi. 1880, p. 388; *Boettg in Radde, Faun. Flor. Casp. Geb.* p. 74 (1886).
—— caraganus, *Eichw. Zool. Spec.* iii. p. 170.
Halys pallasii, *Gunth. Rept. Brit. Ind.* p. 392 (1864); *Blanf. Zool. E. Pers.* p. 430 (1876).

Snout obtusely pointed, slightly turned up at the end, with obtuse canthus. Rostral as deep as broad or slightly broader than deep; a pair of internasals and a pair of præfrontals; frontal as long as its distance from the end of the snout, as long as or a little shorter than the parietals, upper præocular separated from the posterior nasal by a loreal; one or two postoculars and a subocular; loreal pit separated from the labials; three large temporals, anterior largest; 7 or 8 upper labials, third entering the eye. Scales sharply keeled, in 23 rows. Ventrals 149–174, anal entire; subcaudals 31–44 pairs. Yellowish, greyish, reddish, or pale brown above, with darker spots or cross-bars with serrated edges; one or two lateral series of dark spots, a dark spot on the snout, a pair of spots on the vertex, and two pairs of oblique streaks on the back of the head; a dark, light-edged band on the temple; lips speckled with brown; lower parts whitish, more or less speckled with grey or brown.

Total length 490 millim.; tail 65.

From the borders of the Caspian Sea and the Ural River to the Upper Yenisei.

a. ♂ (V. 155; C. 37).	Mangyschlak.	St. Petersburg Mus. [E].
b. ♀ (V. 160; C. 38).	Anan, Mazandaran, Elburz Mts.	W. T. Blanford, Esq [E.].
c. ♂ (V. 154; C. 40).	Ai Dara, Transcaspia.	M. Eylandt [C.].
d. ♂ (V. 151; C. 38).	Varnoe, E. Turkestan.	St. Petersburg Mus. [E.]

6. Ancistrodon intermedius.

Trigonocephalus blomhoffii, part., *Schleg. Phys Serp.* ii. p. 552 (1837), *and Faun. Japon., Amph* p. 88 (1838)
—— intermedius, *Strauch, Trans. Assoc. Russ Nat. i. Zool. (Russian)*, p 295 (1868), *Schl. Russ. R.* p. 246 (1873), *and Voy. Przewalski, Rept.* p 52 (1876)
Halys intermedia, *Peters, Mon. Berl. Ac.* 1877, p. 736
Ancistrodon intermedius, *Bouleng. Ann. & Mag N H.* (6) v. 1890, p. 140.

Agrees in most respects with *A halys*, but the snout is not at all turned up at the end, as in *A. blomhoffii*.

Total length 750 millim.; tail 85.

Central Asia, Eastern Siberia, Mongolia, and Japan.

a. Hgr. (V. 161; C. 49).	Kunges, R. Ili, E. Turkestan	St. Petersburg Mus [E]
b. ♀ (V. 166, C. 45).	Smeinogorsk, Gov. Tomsk.	Dr. O. Finsch [C.].
c-d ♂ (V. 155, 156; C. 40, 40)	Chabarowka, Ussuri R.	Hr. Dorries [C.].
e. ♀ (V. 158; C. 39).	Ussuri R.	Warsaw Mus. [E.].
f-g Hgr. (V. 157, 164; C. 42, 44).	Tarim R, near Lob Nor	St George Littledale, Esq. [P.].

7. Ancistrodon blomhoffii.

Trigonocephalus blomhoffii, *Boie, Isis*, 1826, p 214; *Gray, Cat.* p. 14 (1849); *Dum. & Bibr* vii. p. 1496 (1854); *Strauch, Schl Russ R* p. 251 (1873), *and Voy Przewalski, Rept.* p. 52 (1876).
—— blomhoffii, part, *Schleg Phys Serp* ii. p 552, pl. xx. figs. 8 & 9 (1837), *and Faun. Japon., Amph.* p. 88, pl. vi. (1838).
—— affinis, *Gray, l c.*
—— blomhoffii, var. megaspilus, *Cope, Proc. Ac. Philad.* 1859, p 336.
Halys blomhoffii, *Gunth. Rept Brit. Ind.* p 393 (1864).
Ancistrodon blomhoffii, *Bouleng. Ann. & Mag. N. H.* (6) v. 1890, p. 140.

Closely allied to *A. halys*, with which it agrees in most respects, but snout not turned up at the end, and scales more strongly keeled, in 21 (exceptionally 23,—specs. *h, s*) rows. Upper labials constantly 7. Ventrals 137-166; subcaudals 29-55. Coloration very variable. Grey, brown, or red above, with large dark-edged spots disposed in pairs, opposite or alternating, or more or less regular dark cross-bands; a dark, light-edged temporal band; upper lip uniform yellowish or red; belly yellowish or red, more or less profusely speckled or spotted with blackish, or nearly entirely black.

Total length 720 millim.; tail 100.

Eastern Siberia, Mongolia, China, Japan, Siam.

a. ♂ (V. 140; C. 48).	Japan.	Leyden Museum.
b-c. ♀ (V. 145; C 47) & hgr ♂ (V. 142; C. 55).	Yokohama.	H.M.S. 'Challenger.'
d. ♀ (V. 142; C. 43).	Okinawa, Loo Choo Islands.	Mr. M. K. Rokugo [P.].
e-f, g. ♂ (V. 146; C. 46), hgr. (V. 138; C. 44), & yg. (V. 145; C. 45).	Tsu Sima, Loo Choo Islands.	Mr. Holst [C.].
h-i. ♂ (V. 151, 146, C. 40, 46).	Formosa.	R. Swinhoe, Esq [C.].
k-n ♀ (V. 142, 144; C ?, 32) & yg (V. 144, 141; C. 39, 32).	Hoi How, Hainan.	J. Neumann, Esq. [P.].
o-p. ♂ (V. 144, 144; C. 41, 35).	Hang-Chau, Prov. Che-Kiang.	J. J. Walker, Esq. [P.].
q. ♀ (V. 140; C. 30).	Ichang.	A. Henry, Esq. [P.].
r. ♂ (V. 143; C. 38).	Ichang.	R. Swinhoe, Esq. [C].
s. ♀ (V. 145, C. 31).	Ichang.	A. E. Pratt, Esq. [C.].
t-u. ♀ (V. 142, 138; C. 32, 29).	Mountains N. of Kiu Kiang.	A. E. Pratt, Esq. [C.].
v-w. ♀ (V. 138; C. 32) & yg. (V. 143; C. 31).	Mountains N. of Kiu Kiang	C. Maries, Esq. [C.].
x. ♂ (V. 137; C. 46).	——?	Sir E. Belcher [P.]. (Type of *T. affinis*.)

8. Ancistrodon himalayanus.

Halys himalayanus, *Günth. Rept. Brit Ind* p 393, pl xxiv. fig. A (1864); *Steindachn. Novara, Rept* p. 87 (1867); *Stoliczka, Journ. As. Soc. Beng.* xxxix. 1870, p 226; *Anders. Proc. Zool. Soc.* 1871, p. 196, and 1872, p. 401; *Fayrer, Thanatoph. Ind.* pl. xvi. (1874); *Theob. Cat. Rept. Brit. Ind.* p. 225 (1876), *Blanf Zool 2nd Yark. Miss, Rept.* p. 24 (1878).

Trigonocephalus himalayanus, *Strauch, Schl. Russ. R.* p. 234 (1873).
—— blomhoffii (*non Boie*), *Jan, Icon. Gén* 46, pl. v figs 4 & 5 (1874).

Ancistrodon himalayanus, *Bouleng. Faun. Ind., Rept* p. 424, fig. (1890).

Snout hardly turned up, with sharp canthus. Rostral as deep as broad, or a little broader than deep; a pair of internasals and a pair of præfrontals; upper præocular separated from the posterior nasal by a loreal; two postoculars, upper small, lower descending to below the eye, which it sometimes entirely separates from the labials; 5 to 7 upper labials, none entering the loreal pit, the penultimate and last very large, formed by fusion with the lower temporals. Scales sharply keeled, in 21 (rarely 23) rows. Ventrals 144–166; anal entire; subcaudals 35–51 pairs. Brown with black spots or transverse bands; sometimes with a light vertebral band with dark festooned borders; a black, light-edged band from the eye to the angle of the mouth; lower parts dark brown, or variegated with black and white.

Total length 590 millim.; tail 90.

Himalayas, 5000 to 10,000 feet; Khasi hills.

a	♂ (V. 162; C. 43)	Garwal, W. Himalayas.	Dr Cantor
b	♂ (V. 166, C. 50).	Garwal, W. Himalayas.	Messrs v. Schlagintweit [C.].
c–l.	♂ (V. 153, 153, 144; C. 44, 47, 47), ♀ (V. 157. C. 36), & yg. (V. 158, 153, 159, 160, 155, C. 40, 46, 39, 40, 47)	Himalayas.	T. C. Jerdon, Esq. [P.].
m–o	♂ (V. 153; C. 47), ♀ (V. 158; C. 36), & hgr. (V. 159; C. 39).	Khasi hills.	T. C. Jerdon, Esq [P].

(Types)

9. Ancistrodon rhodostoma.

Russell, Ind. Serp ii. pl. xxi. (1801).
Trigonocephalus rhodostoma, *Boie, Isis,* 1827, p. 561; *Schleg. Phys. Serp* ii p 547, pl xx figs 1–3 (1837), *and Abbild.* p. 140, pl xlix. (1844); *Gray, Cat.* p. 15 (1849); *Jan, Icon. Gén.* 46, pl vi. fig 2 (1874).
Leiolepis rhodostoma, *Dum & Bibr.* vii. p. 1500 (1854).
Tisiphone rhodostoma, *Peters, Mon Berl Ac.* 1862, p 673.
Calloselasma rhodostoma, *Gunth. Rept. Brit. Ind* p. 391 (1864).
Ancistrodon rhodostoma, *Boettg. Ber. Offenb Ver. Nat.* 1892, p. 135.

Snout pointed, somewhat turned up at the end. Rostral as deep as broad, or a little deeper than broad; a pair of internasals and a pair of præfrontals; frontal as long as or a little longer than its distance from the end of the snout, as long as or a little shorter than the parietals; upper præocular separated from the posterior nasal by a loreal, one or two postoculars and one subocular, separating the eye from the labials; loreal pit separated from the labials; 7 to 9 upper labials. Scales smooth, in 21 rows. Ventrals 138–157; anal entire; subcaudals 34–54 pairs. Reddish, greyish, or pale brown above, with large angular, dark brown, black-edged spots disposed in opposite pairs or alternating; a dark brown vertebral line; lips yellowish or pink, powdered with brown; a broad dark brown, black-edged band, festooned below, from the eye to the angle of the mouth, with a light band above it; yellowish beneath, uniform or powdered or spotted with greyish brown.

Total length 810 millim.; tail 90.

Java.

a. Hgr. ♂ (V. 148; C. 51).	Java.	Leyden Museum.
b-c. ♂ (V. 145; C. 46) & hgr. ♀ (V. 143; C. 34).	Java.	A. Scott, Esq. [P.].
d. ♀ (V. 156; C. 36).	Java.	
e-g. ♂ (V. 148; C 50) & ♀ (V. 154, 157; C. 34, 37).	Batavia.	R. Kirkpatrick, Esq. [P.].
h. ♂ (V. 149; C. 48).	Willis Mts., Kediri, Java, 5000 ft.	Baron v. Huegel [C.].
i. ♂ (V. 148; C. 50).	Siam (?).	

10. Ancistrodon hypnale.

Russell, Ind. Serp. ii. pl. xxii. (1801).
? Coluber nepa, *Laur. Syn. Rept* p. 97 (1768)
Cophias hypnale, *Merr Tent* p. 155 (1820).
Trigonocephalus hypnale, *Schleg Phys. Serp.* ii. p. 550, pl xx. figs. 6 & 7 (1837); *Gray, Cat* p 15 (1849); *Dum. & Bibr.* vii p. 1498 (1854); *Jan, Icon. Gén.* 46, pl. v. figs. 2 & 3 (1874).
Trimesurus ceylonensis, *Gray, Zool. Misc* p. 48 (1842).
Trigonocephalus halys, *Gray, Cat.* p. 14.
—— zara, *Gray, l. c.* p. 15.
Hypnale nepa, *Cope, Proc. Ac. Philad.* 1859, p. 335; *Gunth. Rept. Brit. Ind.* p 394 (1864); *Fayrer, Thanatoph. Ind.* pl xvii. (1874); *Theob. Cat. Rept. Brit. Ind* p. 226 (1876).
—— affinis, *Anders. Journ. As. Soc. Beng.* xl. 1871, p. 20.
Ancistrodon hypnale, *Bouleng. Faun. Ind., Rept* p. 424 (1890).

Snout more or less turned up at the end, with sharp canthus. Rostral as deep as broad, or deeper than broad; upper surface of snout covered with small shields, which are often irregular and scale-like; one or two postoculars and one or two suboculars; 7 or 8 upper labials, second entering the loreal pit, none entering the eye. Scales more or less distinctly keeled, in 17 rows. Ventrals 125-155; anal entire; subcaudals 28-45 pairs. Coloration very variable; upper parts brown, yellowish, or greyish, uniform or with blackish-brown alternating spots or cross-bands, frequently with small deep-black spots disposed in pairs; sides of head usually dark brown, edged above with a fine whitish line; sometimes a white, black-edged, longitudinal streak on each side of the neck; belly more or less closely powdered with dark brown.

Total length 480 millim.; tail 65.

Ceylon, and Western Ghats of India as far north as Bombay.

a. ♂ (V. 149; C. 43).	Ceylon.	Sir J. Banks [P.]
b. ♀ (V. 152; C. 36).	Ceylon.	R. Templeton, Esq. [P.].

11. LACHESIS.

c–d. ♀ (V. 144, 149; C. 36, 38).	Ceylon.	Capt. Gascoigne [P.].
e–f. ♂ (V. 125; C. ?) & ♀ (V. 128; C 28).	Ceylon.	Miss Layard [P.].
g, h. ♀ (V. 150, 141; C. 30, 36)	Ceylon.	
i–m, n–o. ♂ (V. 140; C. 46) & ♀ (V. 137, 138, 136, C. 35, 37, ?), hgr (V. 141; C. 37), & yg (V. 139; C. 44).	Anamallays.	Col. Beddome [C.].
p ♂ (V 140, C 43).	Belgaum	Dr. Leith [P].
q. ♂ (V. 144; C. 45).	—— ?	(Type of *T. zara.*
r–s, t. ♂ (V. 149, 148; C. ?, 45) & ♀ (V. 143, C 39).	—— ?	

11. LACHESIS.

Crotalus, part, *Linn. S N.* i. p. 372 (1766); *Schleg. Phys. Serp.* ii. p 555 (1837)

Scytale, part, *Latr. Hist. Rept.* iii. p. 158 (1802), *Daud. Hist. Rept.* v. p. 334 (1803).

Lachesis, *Daud. t c.* p. 349; *Wagl. Syst. Amph* p. 175 (1830), *Gray, Zool. Miscell.* p. 50 (1842); *and Cat. Sn.* p. 13 (1849); *Dum. & Bibr. Erp. Gén.* vii. p. 1483 (1854), *Peters, Mon. Berl. Ac.* 1862, p. 673; *Jan, Elenco sist. Ofid.* p. 124 (1863).

Trimeresurus, part, *Lacép. Ann du Mus* iv. 1804, p. 209.

Trigonocephalus, *Oppel, Ordn. Rept.* p. 50 (1811); *Peters, Mon. Berl Ac.* 1862, p 672

Cophias, part, *Merr. Tent. Syst. Amph.* p. 154 (1820)

Craspedocephalus, *Kuhl, Isis,* 1822, p. 472; *Gray, Ann. Philos.* 1825, p 205; *Fitzing N Class Rept* p. 34 (1826); *Gray, Cat.* p 4.

Bothrops, *Wagl. in Spix, Serp. Bras.* p. 50 (1824), *and Syst. Amph.* p. 174; *Gray, Zool. Miscell.* p. 47; *Dum. & Bibr t. c.* p. 1502; *Jan, l. c* p. 125

Megæra, *Wagl. Syst Amph* p. 174, *Gray, Zool. Miscell.* p. 49, *and Cat* p. 11; *Peters, l. c* p 671.

Atropos (non Oken), *Wagl. l. c.* p. 175; *Gray, ll. cc.* pp. 49, 12; *Dum. & Bibr. t. c* p 1517; *Peters, l c.*; *Jan, l. c.* p. 127.

Tropidolæmus, *Wagl. l. c.*; *Dum. & Bibr. t. c.* p. 1523; *Peters, l. c.*; *Jan, l c.*

Trigonocephalus, part., *Schleg. Phys. Serp.* ii. p. 527 (1837).

Trimesurus, *Gray, ll. cc.* pp 48, 7; *Peters, l. c.*

Parias, *Gray, Cat* p. 11.

Bothriechis, *Peters, Mon Berl. Ac.* 1859, p 278; *Cope, Proc. Ac. Philad* 1860, p. 345, and 1871, p. 207.

Teleuraspis, *Cope, Proc. Ac. Philad.* 1859, p. 338, 1860, p. 345, and 1871, p. 206.

Cryptelytrops, *Cope, Proc. Ac. Philad.* 1859, p 340.

Thamnocenchris, *Salvin, Proc. Zool. Soc.* 1860, p. 459

Bothriopsis, *Peters, Mon. Berl. Ac.* 1861, p. 359; *Cope, Proc. Ac. Philad* 1871, p. 208.

Trimeresurus, *Gunth. Rept. Brit Ind.* p. 384 (1864); *Bouleng. Faun. Ind., Rept.* p. 425 (1890).

Peltopelor, *Gunth. l. c.* p. 390.

Porthidium, *Cope, Proc Ac Philad.* 1871, p 207.
Atropophis, *Peters, Ann Mus. Genova*, iii. 1871, p 41.
Rhinocerophis, *Garman, Bull. Mus. Comp. Zool* viii. 1881, p. 85.
Ophryacus, *Cope, Bull. U S. Nat Mus.* no 32, 1887, p. 88
Thanatophis, *Posada-Arango, Bull. Soc Zool France*, 1889, p 343.

Upper surface of head covered with scales or small shields. Body cylindrical or compressed ; scales smooth or keeled, with or without apical pits. Tail moderate or short; subcaudals single or in two rows.

South-eastern Asia ; Central and South America.

Synopsis of the Species.

I. American species, with non-prehensile tail.

  A. Subcaudals all or greater part in two rows.

    1. Posterior subcaudals replaced by small scales ; upper head-scales granular, smooth or obtusely keeled ; supraocular shield narrow ; scales tubercularly keeled, in 35 or 37 rows ; ventrals 200–230 ; subcaudals 32–50.
                                    1. *mutus*, p. 534.

    2. No small scales under the tail ; upper head-scales imbricate or subimbricate ; supraocular large.

      a. Scales on the vertex and occiput more or less strongly keeled ; dorsal scales strongly keeled.

        α. Second upper labial forming the anterior border of the loreal pit.

          * Keels on the dorsal scales extending nearly to the extremity ; scales in 23–33 rows ; ventrals 180–240 ; subcaudals 46–70.   2 *lanceolatus*, p. 535.

          ** Keels on the dorsal scales much shorter than the scales

Scales in 25–29 rows ; ventrals 161–216 ; subcaudals 47–73 .... 3. *atrox*, p. 537.
Scales in 21–23 rows ; ventrals 156–172 ; subcaudals 58–64 .... 4. *pulcher*, p. 539.

          *** Keels on the dorsal scales extending nearly to the extremity ; scales in 21–23 rows ; ventrals 157–172 ; subcaudals 40–74.   6. *pictus*, p. 540.

        β. Loreal pit separated from the labials.

          * Keels on the dorsal scales much shorter than the scales ; scales in 23 rows ; ventrals 159–161 ; subcaudals 52–55 .... 5. *microphthalmus*,
                                                  [p. 540.

** Keels on the dorsal scales extending nearly to the extremity.

Scales in 29–35 rows; ventrals 167–188; subcaudals 31–51 .... 7. *alternatus*, p. 541.

Scales in 21–27 rows; ventrals 168–182; subcaudals 41–53 .... 8. *neuwiedii*, p. 542.

Scales in 23–25 rows; ventrals 149–160; subcaudals 30–38 .... 9. *ammodytoides*, p. 543.

    b. Upper head-scales all smooth; dorsal scales not strongly keeled; scales in 27 rows; ventrals 196; subcaudals 54 .... 10. *xanthogrammus*, [p. 543.

B. Subcaudals all or greater part single.

    1. Second upper labial forming the anterior border of the loreal pit; scales in 25–27 rows; ventrals 230–253; subcaudals 72–83 .. .. 11. *castelnaudi*, p. 544.

    2. Loreal pit separated from the labials.

        a. Supraocular narrow, separated from its fellow by 7–10 series of scales, scales in 23–27 rows; ventrals 121–134; subcaudals 26–36 .. 12. *nummifer*, p. 544.

        b. Supraocular large, separated from its fellow by 5–7 series of scales.

Snout not turned up; rostral not deeper than broad; scales in 21 rows; ventrals 135–142, subcaudals 22–34 .. 13. *godmani*, p. 545.

Snout turned up at the end; rostral once and one third to once and a half as long as broad; scales in 25–27 rows; ventrals 152–159, subcaudals 29–35. 14. *lansbergii*, p. 546.

Snout much produced above at the end; rostral once and two thirds to twice as deep as broad; scales in 23–25 rows; ventrals 132–150; subcaudals 27–38. 15. *brachystoma*, p. 547.

II. Asiatic species; subcaudals in two rows.

    A. Scales between the eyes smooth or obtusely keeled; gular scales smooth; first lower labial in contact with its fellow behind the symphysial.

        1. Scales in 21–25 (rarely 27) rows; ventrals 129–158; subcaudals 21–57; 5 to 9 series of scales between the supraoculars; tail not prehensile.

Supraoculars large, separated by 5 to 8 series of scales; scales smooth or feebly keeled; canthus rostralis obtuse .. .. 16. *monticola*, p. 548.

Supraoculars large, separated by 6 to 9 series of scales; scales strongly keeled; canthus rostralis sharp and raised.... 17. *okinavensis*, p. 549.

Supraoculars small, sometimes broken up, separated by 8 to 11 series of juxtaposed, convex scales; scales feebly keeled........................ 18. *strigatus*, p 549.

2. Scales in 27–37 rows, feebly keeled; ventrals 174–231; subcaudals 54–90; tail not prehensile.

Scales in 33–37 rows; ventrals 222–231; subcaudals 75–90; 8 or 9 upper labials .... 19. *flavoviridis*, p. 550.

Scales in 27–31 rows; ventrals 174–184; subcaudals 55–76; 13 upper labials . 20. *cantoris*, p. 551.

3. Scales in 21–27 rows, strongly keeled; ventrals 160–218; subcaudals 54–92; tail not or but slightly prehensile.

    a. 7 to 9 series of scales between the supraoculars; scales in 21 or 23 rows; ventrals 164–188; subcaudals 54–67.
                      21. *jerdonii*, p. 551.

    b. 10 to 15 series of scales between the supraoculars; scales in 23–27 rows.

Ventrals 183–218; subcaudals 72–92 .. 22. *mucrosquamatus*,
Ventrals 182–186; subcaudals 72–74; [p. 552.
supraocular large .... 23. *luteus*, p. 553.
Ventrals 160–182; subcaudals 55–76; supraocular very narrow, sometimes [p. 553.
broken up .... 24. *purpureomaculatus*,

4. Scales in 21 rows (rarely 19 or 23), smooth or feebly keeled; 7 to 13 series of scales between the supraoculars; tail more or less prehensile.

    a. Temporal scales smooth; subcaudals 53–82.

Ventrals 145–175; snout feebly prominent; supraocular narrow .... . 25. *gramineus*, p. 554.
Ventrals 170–187; snout prominent, obliquely truncate; supraocular narrow .... 26. *flavomaculatus*, p. 556.
Ventrals 180–191; supraocular large .. 27. *sumatranus*, p. 557.

    b. Temporal scales obtusely keeled; ventrals 138–158; subcaudals 44–58 .... 28. *anamallensis*, p. 558.

5. Scales in 13–19 rows; 3 to 5 series of scales between the supraoculars; tail prehensile.

Scales smooth or faintly keeled, in 17–19 rows; ventrals 145–170; subcaudals [p. 559.
53–67 .... 29. *trigonocephalus*,

Scales strongly keeled, in 13-15 rows;
 ventrals 134-143; subcaudals 48-56 . 30. *macrolepis*, p. 560.

B. Scales between the eyes smooth; gular scales smooth; first lower labial divided, the separate portion forming a pair of small additional chin-shields; scales feebly and obtusely keeled; ventrals 144-176; subcaudals 38-57; tail prehensile.

Scales in 21-23 rows; second upper labial usually not bordering the loreal pit; 12-14 series of scales between the supraoculars .... 31. *puniceus*, p. 560.

Scales in 19-21 rows; second upper labial bordering the loreal pit; 10-11 series of scales between the supraoculars .... 32. *borneensis*, p. 561.

C. Upper head-scales all strongly keeled; gular scales keeled; scales more or less distinctly keeled, in 19-27 rows; ventrals 127-154; subcaudals 45-55; tail prehensile.
33. *wagleri*, p. 562.

III. American species, with prehensile tail.

A. Subcaudals all or greater part in two rows.

Scales in 27-35 rows; ventrals 198-218; subcaudals 59-71 .... 34. *bilineatus*, p. 565.

Scales in 21 rows; ventrals 149-171; subcaudals 41-49; a horn-like scute above the eye...................... 35. *undulatus*, p. 565.

B Subcaudals all or greater part single.

1. Supraocular shield narrow, scales in 21-23 rows; ventrals 164-171; subcaudals 59-67.

Loreal pit separated from the labials; 9 upper labials .... 36. *lateralis*, p. 566.

Second labial forming the anterior border of the loreal pit; 10 or 11 upper labials........................ 37. *bicolor*, p. 566.

2. Supraocular shield large, separated from the eye by a series of pointed scales; scales in 19-25 rows; ventrals 138-162; subcaudals 47-62 ... 38. *schlegelii*, p. 567.

3. Supraocular shield large, bordering the eye; scales in 19 rows.

5 or 6 series of small scales between the supraoculars; ventrals 134-146; subcaudals 49-54 .... 39. *nigroviridis*, p. 568.

An enlarged frontal shield; ventrals 154-158; subcaudals 53-61....... 40. *aurifer*, p. 568.

1. Lachesis mutus.

Seba, Thes. ii pl. lxxvi fig. 1 (1735).
Crotalus mutus, *Linn. S. N.* i. p. 373 (1706); *Schleg. Phys. Serp.* ii. p. 570, pl. xx figs 19 & 20 (1837).
Boa muta, *Lacép. Serp.* ii. pp. 128 & 389 (1789).
Coluber crotalinus, *Gmel. S. N.* 1. p. 1094 (1789); *Shaw, Zool.* iii. p 400 (1802).
—— alecto, *Shaw, l. c.* p. 405.
Scytale catenata, *Latr. Rept.* iii. p. 162 (1802).
—— ammodytes, *Latr. t. c* p. 165; *Daud. Rept.* v. p. 347 (1803).
Lachesis mutus, *Daud t. c.* p. 351; *Dum. & Bibr.* vii. p. 1485 (1854); *Garm. N. Am. Rept.* p. 122 (1883); *Lacerda, Leçons Ven. Serp. Brés.* p. 5 (1884), *Gunth. Biol. C.-Am , Rept.* p. 188 (1895).
Trigonocephalus ammodytes, *Oppel, Ordn. Rept.* p. 66 (1811).
Cophias crotalinus, *Merr. Tent.* p 154 (1820).
Bothrops surucucu, *Wagl. in Spix, Serp. Bras.* p. 59, pl. xxiii (1824).
Lachesis rhombeata, *Wied, Abbild. Nat. Bras.* (1825).
Craspedocephalus crotalinus, *Gray, Ann. Philos.* 1825, p. 205.
Lachesis mutus, part, *Gray, Cat.* p. 13 (1849).
—— stenophrys, *Cope, Journ. Ac. Philad.* (2) viii. 1876, p 152.

Rostral as deep as broad or a little broader than deep; nasal divided; upper head-scales very small, granular, smooth or obtusely keeled; supraocular narrow; two or three scales separating the internasals in front; 10 to 15 scales on a line between the supraoculars, four or five series of scales between the eye and the upper labials; temporal scales obtusely keeled; 9 or 10 upper labials, second usually forming the anterior border of the loreal pit, third very large. Scales tubercularly keeled, feebly imbricate, in 35 or 37 rows. Ventrals 200-230; anal entire; subcaudals 32-50, all or greater part in pairs and followed by very small keeled scales covering the end of the tail. Yellowish or pinkish above, with a series of large rhomboidal dark brown or black spots enclosing smaller light spots; a black streak from the eye to the angle of the mouth.

Total length 1995 millim.; tail 170.

Central and Tropical South America.

a-b. Yg. (Sc. 37, 35; V. 202, 206; C. 36, 37).	Panama.	
c. ♂ (Sc. 37; V. 226; C. 36).	Demerara ?	Col. E. Sabine [P.].
d. ♀, head and tail (C. 36).	Surinam.	C. W. Ellascombe, Esq. [P.].
e. ♂ (Sc. 35; V. 223; C. 37).	Pernambuco.	W. A. Forbes, Esq. [P.].
f. ♂ (Sc. 35; V. 225; C. 34).	Bahia.	Dr. O. Wucherer [C.].
g. Ad., stffd.	Brazil.	Mrs. Parker [P.].
h. ♀ (Sc. 35; V. 225; C. 36)	Cajaria, N.E. Peru.	Mr. W. Davis [C.]; Messrs. Veitch [P.].
i. ♀ (Sc. 35; V. 226; C. 35)	Bolivia.	M. Suarez [P.].

2. Lachesis lanceolatus.

Moreau de Jonnès, Monogr. Trigonoc. des Antilles (1816).
? Vipera cærulescens, *Laur. Syn. Rept.* p 101 (1768)
? Coluber glaucus, *Gmel S. N.* i. p. 1092 (1788)
? Coluber ambiguus, *Gmel t c* p. 1104.
Coluber lanceolatus, *Lacép. Serp* ii. pp. 80, 121, pl. v. fig. 1 (1789).
—— tigrinus, *Lacép. t. c* pp. 82, 136.
—— brasiliensis, *Lacép. t. c.* pp. 98, 119, pl. iv. fig. 1.
Vipera lanceolata, *Latr Rept.* iii. p. 325 (1802); *Daud. Rept.* vi. p. 28 (1803).
—— brasiliensis, *Latr. op. cit.* iv. p. 7; *Daud. t. c.* p. 86.
Coluber megæra, *Shaw, Zool* iii. p. 406 (1802).
? Vipera weigelii, *Daud. t c.* p 60.
Trigonocephalus lanceolatus, *Oppel, Ordn. Rept.* p 66 (1811); *Schleg. Phys. Serp.* ii. p. 536, pl xix. figs. 3 & 4 (1837); *Rufz, Enquête Serp. Martin.* (1843); *Garm. Proc. Amer. Philos. Soc.* xxiv. 1887, p. 285, *W. Duncan, Proc. Bristol Natur. Soc.* (2) vi. 1889, p. 44.
—— tigrinus, *Oppel, l. c.*
Cophias lanceolatus, *Merr. Tent.* p. 155.
—— atrox (*non L*), *Wied, Reise n. Bras.* ii. p. 243 (1821).
—— holosericeus, *Wied, l. c*, *and Beitr.* i. p. 490 (1825).
Bothrops furia, *Wagl. in Spix, Serp. Bras* p. 52, pl xx. (1824).
—— leucostigma, *Wagl. l. c.* p 53, pl. xxi. fig. 1
Cophias jararacca, *Wied, Beitr.* i. p. 470, *and Abbild.* (1825).
Craspedocephalus lanceolatus, *Fitzing. N. Class. Rept.* p. 62 (1826); *Gray, Cat.* p 5 (1849).
—— jararaca, *Fitzing. l c.*
—— weigelii, *Fitzing. l. c.*
Trigonocephalus jararaca, *Schleg. l. c.* p. 532, pl. xix. figs. 1 & 2.
Bothrops megæra, *Gray, Zool. Miscell.* p. 47 (1842).
—— subscutatus, *Gray, l. c.*
—— sabinii, *Gray, l. c*
—— cinereus, *Gray, l. c.*
Craspedocephalus atrox, part., *Gray, Cat.* p. 6.
Bothrops lanceolatus, *Dum. & Bibr.* vii. p. 1505 (1854), *Rufz, Enquête Serp Martin* 2nd ed. (1859); *Jan, Icon. Gén.* 47, pl. i. fig. 1 (1875), *A. E. Brown, Proc Ac. Philad* 1893, p. 435.
—— jararaca, *Dum. & Bibr. t. c* p. 1509; *Jan, l. c* pl iii figs. 1 & 2; *Lacerda, Leç. Ven. Serp Brés.* p. 10 (1884); *F. Müll. Verh. Nat. Ges. Basel*, vii. 1885, p. 699; *A. E. Brown, l. c.*
Craspedocephalus brasiliensis, *Wucherer, Proc. Zool. Soc.* 1863, p. 52.
Bothrops atrox, var. dirus, *Jan, l. c* pl. ii. fig 1.
—— brasiliensis, *Cope, Journ. Ac. Philad.* (2) viii. 1876, p. 182.
Trigonocephalus atrox, *Garm. N Am Rept.* p. 124 (1883).
Bothrops jararacussu, *Lacerda, l. c* p. 8.
—— atrox septentrionalis, *F Müll. l. c.*
Trigonocephalus caribbæus, *Garm. Proc. Amer. Philos. Soc.* xxiv. 1887, p. 285.
Bothrops glaucus, *Vaill. Bull. Soc. Philom.* (7) xi. 1887, p. 48.
—— atrox, part., *Gunth. Biol. C.-Am*, *Rept.* p. 187 (1895)

Snout rounded or obtusely pointed, with sharp, slightly raised canthus. Rostral as deep as broad; nasal divided; upper head-scales small, imbricate, more or less strongly keeled, in 5 to 10 longitudinal series between the supraoculars, which are large; a pair of large internasals, usually forming a suture with each other, and a large canthal; two or three postoculars and one, two, or three suboculars, separated from the labials by one or two series of scales; temporal scales keeled; seven or eight upper labials, second forming the anterior border of the loreal pit. Scales in 23–33 rows, sharply keeled. Ventrals 180–240; anal entire; subcaudals 46–70, all or greater part in two rows. Coloration very variable: grey, brown, yellow, olive, or reddish above, uniform or with more or less distinct dark spots or cross-bands, or with dark triangles on the sides inclosing pale rhombs; a dark streak from the eye to behind the angle of the mouth; lower parts yellowish, uniform or powdered or spotted with brown, or brown with light spots.

Total length 1600 millim.; tail 190.

Tropical America.

a–b.	♀ (Sc. 27; V. 209; C. 62) & hgr (Sc. 27; V. 208; C. 61).	Atoyac, Guerrero.	Mr. H. H. Smith [C.], F. D. Godman, Esq. [P.].
c.	Yg. (Sc. 29; V. 212; C. 62).	Teapa, Tabasco.	F. D. Godman, Esq. [P.].
d	♂ (Sc. 25; V. 214; C. 67).	Tehuantepec.	M. F. Sumichrast [C.].
e, f, g.	♀ (Sc. 27, 27, 27; V. 220, 213, 221; C. 58, 57, 60).	Mexico.	Mr. Hugo Finck [C.].
h, i, k.	♂ (Sc 27, V. 210; C. ?) & yg. (Sc. 27, 25, V. 208, 196; C. 70, 69).	Mexico.	
l.	♂ (Sc. 25; V. 212; C. 62)	Pacific Coast of Guatemala.	O Salvin, Esq. [C.].
m.	Yg (Sc. 25; V. 195, C. 71).	Vera Paz.	O. Salvin, Esq. [C.].
n.	Yg. (Sc. 25; V. 189 C. 71).	Stann Creek, Brit. Honduras.	Rev. J. Robertson [C.].
o.	Yg. (Sc. 27; V. 210; C. 69).	Honduras.	
p.	♀ (Sc. 33; V. 226; C. 61).	Guadeloupe.	
q.	♀ (Sc. 27, V. 211; C. 65).	Dominica.	G. A. Ramage, Esq. [C.].
r, s, t.	Hgr. (Sc. 30, 31, 29; V. 217, 220, 212; C. 67, 69, 65).	Martinique.	
u.	♀ (Sc. 27; V. 213; C. 67).	St. Lucia.	Lady Wood [P.].
v.	Hgr. (Sc. 25; V. 200; C. 67).	St. Lucia.	Zoological Society.
w–y	♂ (Sc. 23; V. 191; C. 60), hgr (Sc. 23; V. 196; C. 62), & yg. (Sc. 25; V. 196; C. 54).	Venezuela.	
z.	♀ (Sc. 25; V. 197; C. 62).	Caracas.	
a.	♀ (Sc. 29; V. 214; C. 65).	Berbice.	Col Sabine [P.]. (Type of B. subscutatus.)

β, γ, δ. ♀ (Sc. 29; V. 211; C 66) & hgr. (Sc. 26, 27; V. 204, 211; C. 71, 63)   Demerara.   Col Sabine [P]. (Types of *B. sabinii*.)

ε. Yg. (Sc 25; V. 197; C 64)   Demerara.   Dr. Hancock [P.].

ζ. ♀ (Sc. 25; V. 190; C. 52).   Para.   R. Graham, Esq. [P.].

η. ♀ (Sc. 25; V. 203; C 64).   Pernambuco.   W A. Forbes, Esq. [P.].

θ ♂ (Sc. 23; V. 194; C. 57).   Rio Janeiro.   Mr. Fry [P].

ι ♂ (Sc. 23; V. 205; C. ?).   Rio Janeiro.   Haslar Collection.

κ–μ. ♂ (Sc. 23; V. 197, C. 60), ♀ (Sc. 25; V 206; C 64), & yg. (Sc 25; V 190; C. 63).   Porto Real, Prov. Rio Janeiro.   M. Hardy du Dréneuf [C.].

ν, ξ, ο. ♀ (Sc. 23, V. 216; C. 61) & hgr. (Sc. 23, 25; V. 204, 206, C. 66, 51).   Brazil.   Lord Stuart de Rothsay [P.].

π. ♀ (Sc. 23; V. 195; C. 54).   Madre de Dios, Bolivia.

ρ. Hgr. (Sc. 25, V. 194; C. 74).   Pampa del Sacramento, Peru.   Mr W. Davis [C.]; Messrs. Veitch [P.].

σ–τ. Yg. (Sc. 23, 25; V. 207, 180, C. 58, 66).   W. Ecuador.   Mr. Fraser [C.].

υ. Yg. (Sc. 27; V. 181; C. 71)   Ecuador.

φ. Hgr. (Sc 33; V. 229; C. 58).   ——?   E. MacLeay, Esq. [P.]. (Type of *B. cinereus*.)

χ. ♂ (Sc. 31; V. 225; C. 69).   ——?   (Type of *B. megæra*.)

ψ. Skeleton.   Martinique.
ω. Skeleton.   S. America
a'. Skull.   S. America.
b'. Skull.   C. America.

This species may have to be united with the following. The only character by which I have distinguished the two, viz., the length of the keel on the dorsal scales, is not dependent on age or sex, as had been supposed. Some specimens of *L. lanceolatus*, however, approach *L. atrox* in the swelling of the scales at the base of the keels, and are thus intermediate between the two supposed species. It is also not impossible that two or three species are confounded here under *L. lanceolatus*, but I have been unable to trace any limits or to find any correlation between the modifications in scaling and coloration.

3. Lachesis atrox.

Coluber atrox, *Linn. Mus. Ad. Frid* pl xxii. fig. 2 (1754), *and S. N.* i. p 383 (1766).

Vipera atrox, *Laur. Syn. Rept.* p. 103 (1768).

Cophias atrox, *Merr. Tent.* p. 154 (1820).
Bothrops megæra, *Wagl. in Spix, Serp. Bras.* p. 60, pl. xix. (1824).
—— tessellatus, *Wagl. l. c.* p. 54, pl. xxi. fig. 2.
—— tæniatus, *Wagl. l. c.* p. 55, pl. xxi. fig 3.
Craspedocephalus atrox, *Fitzing. N Class Rept.* p 62 (1826); *Wucherer, Proc. Zool Soc.* 1863, p. 51
Trigonocephalus atrox, *Schleg. Phys. Serp.* ii. p. 535, pl xix. figs. 5 & 6 (1837).
Craspedocephalus atrox, part., *Gray, Cat.* p. 6 (1849).
Bothrops affinis, *Gray, l. c.* p. 7.
—— atrox, part., *Dum. & Bibr* vii. p. 1507 (1854); *Gunth. Biol. C.-Am, Rept* p. 187 (1895).
—— atrox, *Jan, Arch. f. Nat.* 1859, p. 275, *A. E. Brown, Proc. Ac. Philad.* 1893, p 434.
Trigonocephalus asper, *Garm. N. Am. Rept.* p 124 (1883).

Snout obtusely pointed, with sharp, slightly raised canthus. Rostral as deep as broad or a little deeper than broad; nasal divided; upper head-scales small, imbricate, more or less strongly keeled, in 5 to 9 longitudinal series between the supraoculars, which are large; a pair of large internasals, forming a suture with each other, and a large canthal; two postoculars and one, two, or three suboculars, separated from the labials by one series of scales; temporal scales keeled; seven (rarely eight) upper labials, second forming the anterior border of the loreal pit. Scales in 25 to 29 rows, strongly keeled, the keels on the posterior part of the back very high, swollen in the middle, and much shorter than the scale. Ventrals 161–216; anal entire; subcaudals 47–73 pairs. Brown above, with more or less distinct dark, light-edged cross-bands or triangles with the apices approximating on the vertebral line; a more or less distinct dark streak from the eye to the angle of the mouth; belly yellowish white, much speckled and blotched with brown, or brown spotted with yellowish white.

Total length 1110 millim.; tail 180.

From Central America to Peru and Northern Brazil.

a. Hgr. (Sc. 25; V. 216, C. 60).	Coban, Guatemala.	F. Sarg, Esq. [O.].
b. ♂ (Sc. 25, V. 201; C. 65).	Matagalpa, Nicaragua.	Dr. E. Rothschuh [C.].
c. Yg. (Sc. 27; V. 197; C. 70).	Chontalez, Nicaragua	R A. Rix, Esq. [C.]; W. M. Crowfoot, Esq. [P.].
d–e. ♂ (Sc. 27; V. 202; C. 72) & yg. (Sc. 27; V. 195; C 65).	Chiriqui.	J. G. Champion, Esq. [C.]; F. D. Godman, Esq [P.].
f–g. Yg. (Sc. 26, 27; V. 204, 190; C. 62, 69).	Carthagena, Colombia.	Capt. Garth [P.].
h–i. Yg. (Sc. 25, 27; V. 210, 187; C. 77, 64).	Rosario du Cucuta, Colombia.	Mr. O. Webber [C.].
k. Yg. (Sc. 27; V. 200, C. 58).	Bogota	C. Laverde, Esq. [P.].
l–m. ♀ (Sc. 26, 27; V. 196, 195; C. 65, 58).	W. Ecuador.	Mr. Fraser [C.].

n–o Yg. (Sc. 25, 25 ; V. 194, 200 ; C. 61, 62).	Canelos, Ecuador.	Mr. Buckley [C.].
p. Yg (Sc. 25 ; V. 200, C. 68).	Pebas, Peru	Mr. Hauxwell [C.]
q, r–v. ♂ (Sc. 27 ; V. 196 ; C. 70) & yg. (Sc. 25, 27, 27, 27, 25 ; V. 203, 195, 187, 194, 185 ; C. 75, 60, 74, 63, 63).	Moyobamba, Peru.	Mr. A. H. Roff [C.].
w. ♂ (Sc. 25 ; V 196, C. 69).	Pozuzu, Peru.	H. J. Veitch, Esq. [P.]
x. Yg. (Sc. 25 ; V. 186 ; C. 63).	Sarayacu, Peru	Mr. W Davis [C.]; Messrs. Veitch [P.].
y. Yg (Sc. 25 ; V. 185 ; C. 66).	Cayaria, Peru.	Mr. W. Davis [C.]; Messrs Veitch [P.].
z Hgr. (Sc 27 ; V 190 ; C. 67).	Demerara.	Lieut. Friend [P].
a. ♂ (Sc. 27 ; V. 193 ; C. 68).	Demerara.	Mr. Snellgrove [C.].
β–γ. ♂ (Sc 25 ; V. 196 ; C. 65) & ♀ (Sc. 25 ; V. 198, C. 59).	Berbice.	Lady Essex [P.]
δ, ε–κ. ♂ (Sc. 25 ; V. 183 ; C 71) & yg (Sc. 27, 27, 27, 25, 25, 25 ; V. 185, 190, 194, 183, 182, 176 ; C. 73, 61, 59, 70, 70, 69).	Berbice.	
λ–μ. ♂ (Sc. 25 ; V. 161 ; C. 47) & ♀ (Sc. 27 ; V. 200 ; C. 58).	Brit. Guiana	Demerara Mus [P.].
ν Yg (Sc. 27, V. 177 ; C. 66).	Para.	

4. Lachesis pulcher.

Trigonocephalus pulcher, *Peters, Mon Berl Ac.* 1862, p. 672.

Snout broad, rounded, with sharp, slightly raised canthus. Rostral as deep as broad or slightly deeper than broad; nasal divided; upper head-scales imbricate, largest and smooth on the snout, obtusely keeled and in 5 to 7 longitudinal series between the large supraoculars, with strong, short keels on the occiput; a pair of large internasals and a large canthal; two postoculars and a subocular, separated from the labials by one series of scales; temporal scales keeled; seven upper labials, second forming the anterior border of the loreal pit. Scales in 21 or 23 rows, strongly and tubercularly keeled, the keels much shorter than the scales. Ventrals 156–172, anal entire; subcaudals 58–64 pairs. Olive-grey above, with brown, light-edged cross-bands which are continuous, or broken on the vertebral line and alternating; a light streak from the eye to behind the angle of the mouth; belly closely powdered with brown, with darker and lighter spots on the sides.

Total length 685 millim.; tail 115.

Andes of Ecuador.

a. Hgr. ♀ (Sc. 23, V. 156, C. 58).	Quito.	
b. ♀ (Sc. 23 ; V. 158 ; C. 64).	Intac.	Mr. Buckley [C].

5. Lachesis microphthalmus.

Bothrops microphthalmus, *Cope, Journ. Ac. Philad.* (2) viii. 1876, p. 182.

Snout short, rounded, with distinct canthus; eye very small. Rostral slightly deeper than broad; nasal divided; upper head-scales imbricate, smooth or obtusely keeled on the snout and vertex; supraoculars large, separated in the middle by five or six series of scales; scales on back of head smaller, with a short keel (or smooth); loreal pit separated from the labials; 7 upper labials, third and sixth or seventh largest. Scales in 23 rows; dorsals tubercularly keeled, the keel not reaching the extremity of the scales and terminating in an enlargement, which, on the posterior part of the body, is a prominent tubercle. Ventrals 159-161; anal entire; subcaudals 52-55 pairs. Yellowish brown or pale olive above, with dark brown triangles on the sides, the apices meeting or approaching on the vertebral line; posteriorly, the united triangles forming cross-bands; a yellowish band, edged with dark brown below, extending from the eye to the side of the neck; belly dark brown with some yellowish spots, or yellow anteriorly, gradually darkening to black on the tail.

Total length 630 millim.; tail 100.

Peru, Ecuador.

a. ♂ (V. 161; C. 55).   Guayaquil.   Mr. Fraser [C.].

6. Lachesis pictus.

Lachesis picta, *Tschudi, Faun. Per., Herp.* p. 61, pl. x. (1845); *Gray, Cat.* p. 13 (1849).

Bothrops pictus, *Jan, Elenco,* p 126 (1863), *and Icon Gén.* 47, pl. iii. fig. 3 & pl. iv. fig. 2 (1875).

Snout obliquely truncate, with sharp raised canthus all round. Rostral as deep as broad or a little deeper than broad; nasal divided; upper head-scales small, juxtaposed or subimbricate, largest and smooth on the snout, feebly keeled and in 5 to 7 longitudinal series between the supraoculars, which are large; a pair of small internasals, in contact with each other; two series of scales between the eye and the labials; temporal scales feebly keeled; 8 or 9 upper labials, second entering the loreal pit, third and fourth largest. Scales strongly keeled, in 21 to 23 rows. Ventrals 157-172; anal entire; subcaudals 40-74 pairs. Pale brown above, with a dorsal series of large black-edged brown spots which may be confluent and form an undulous or zigzag band; sides with small black spots; a dark streak behind the eye and a vertical bar below the eye; yellowish beneath, dotted or spotted with brown.

Total length 310 millim.; tail 43.

Peru.

a. Hgr. (Sc. 23 , V. 157 ; C. 45).   Lima.   Christiania Mus.
b, c. Yg. (Sc 22 ; V. 167 ; C. 42)   Lima.   Prof. W. Nation [P.].
 & head and tail (C. 40) of ♀.

7. Lachesis alternatus.

Craspedocephalus brasiliensis (*non Lacép*), *Gray, Cat.* p. 5 (1849).
Bothrops alternatus, *Dum. & Bibr.* vii. p. 1512, pl. lxxxii. fig. 1 (1854); *Guichen. in Casteln. Anim. Nouv. Amér. Sud, Rept.* p 76 (1855); *Jan, Icon Gén.* 47, pl. vi. fig. 1 (1875); *Bouleng. Ann. & Mag. N. H.* (5) xviii. 1886, p. 438.
Trigonocephalus alternatus, *Jan, Rev. & Mag. Zool.* 1859, p. 155
Bothrops atrox, part., *Hensel, Arch. f. Nat.* 1868, p. 334

Head narrow, elongate ; snout obtusely pointed, with sharp canthus. Rostral as deep as broad or a little deeper than broad ; nasal divided ; upper head-scales small, imbricate, strongly keeled, in 10 to 13 longitudinal series between the supraoculars, which are rather narrow ; a pair of large internasals, in contact with each other, each followed by a canthal ; two or three postoculars and one or two suboculars, separated from the labials by two series of scales ; loreal pit separated from the labials by small scales ; temporal scales keeled ; 8 or 9 upper labials, second small. Scales very strongly keeled, in 29–35 rows. Ventrals 167–181 ; anal entire ; subcaudals 34–51 pairs   Brown above, very elegantly marked with opposite or alternating pairs of large C-shaped, dark brown markings edged with black and yellow and separated by narrow interspaces of the ground-colour ; a series of smaller spots on each side ; head dark brown above, with a 人-shaped light marking, the transverse branch between the eyes, and a light line from the canthus rostralis to the angle of the mouth ; rostral and anterior labials white, the former with a dark brown vertical bar ; chin and throat with dark longitudinal streaks ; belly whitish, spotted with brown or black tail with two dark streaks below.

Total length 1190 millim. ; tail 110.

Southern Brazil, Paraguay, Uruguay, Argentina.

a, b. ♀ (Sc 29, 32 ; V. 188, 178 ; C. 34, 32). Brazil.
c, d–e. ♂ (Sc. 31 ; V. 179 ; C 42) & yg. (Sc 29, 33 ; V. 174, 176 ; C. 45, 38). S. Lorenzo, Rio Grande do Sul. Dr. H. v. Ihering [C.].
f. Hgr. (Sc 29 ; V. 180, C 42). Paraguay Prof Grant [P]
g. ♀ (Sc. 35 ; V. 181, C. 34). Asuncion, Paraguay. Dr. J. Bohls [C.].
h ♂ (Sc. 31 ; V. 167 ; C 41) Rosaria, Argentina. E W White, Esq. [C.].
i. ♀ (Sc. 33 ; V. 178 ; C. 41) Argentina Zoological Society

8. Lachesis neuwiedii.

Bothrops neuwiedi, *Wagl. in Spix, Serp. Bras* p. 56, pl. xxii. fig. 1 (1824); *Jan, Arch. f. Nat.* 1859, p. 275.
—— leucurus, *Wagl. l. c.* fig. 2.
Trigonocephalus neuwiedii, *Jan, Rev. & Mag. Zool.* 1859, p. 154.
Bothrops diporus, *Cope, Proc. Ac. Philad.* 1862, p. 347, *Boettg. Zeitschr. ges. Naturw.* lviii. 1885, p. 239; *Bouleng. Ann. & Mag. N. H.* (5) xviii. 1886, p. 438.
—— atrox, part., *Hensel, Arch. f. Nat.* 1868, p. 334.
Trigonocephalus (Bothrops) pubescens, *Cope, Proc. Amer. Philos. Soc.* xi 1869, p 157.
Bothrops urutu, *Lacerda, Leç. Ven. Serp. Brés.* p 11, pl. i. (1884).
—— atrox meridionalis, *F. Müll Verh. Nat. Ges. Basel*, vii. 1885, p. 699.

Snout obtusely pointed, with strong, slightly raised canthus. Rostral as deep as broad; nasal divided; upper head-scales small, imbricate, strongly keeled, largest on the snout; supraocular large, separated from its fellow by 6 to 9 longitudinal series of scales; internasals large and in contact with each other; a large canthal; two or three postoculars and a subocular, which is separated from the labials by two or three series of scales; loreal pit separated from the labials; temporal scales keeled; 8 or 9 upper labials. Scales very strongly keeled, in 21–27 rows. Ventrals 168–182; anal entire; subcaudals 41–53. Yellowish or pale brown above, with dark brown, black-edged spots; the spots on the back forming a single series or a double alternating series; a lateral series of small spots; a dark spot on the snout, a pair of dark bands from the vertex to the nape, and another from the eye to the angle of the mouth; all these markings may have a fine yellow edge; yellowish beneath, more or less profusely dotted or powdered with brown and largely spotted on the sides.

Total length 770 millim.; tail 120.

Brazil, Paraguay, Argentina.

a–b, c–f. ♂ (Sc. 25, 25; V. 171, 176; C. 50, 50), ♀ (Sc 25, V. 169; C. 47), & yg. (Sc 25, 25, 27; V. 173, 182, 170; C 42, 43, 49).	S. Lorenzo, Rio Grande do Sul.	Dr. H. v. Ihering [C.].
g–h. ♀ (Sc. 25; V. 177; C. 41) & hgr. (Sc. 27; V 179; C. 47).	Asuncion, Paraguay.	Dr. J. Bohls [C.].
i–k. ♂ (Sc. 21; V. 174; C. 53) & ♀ (Sc. 25; V. 177; C. 41)	Paraguay.	
l. ♂ (Sc. 25; V 176; C. 47).	Cordoba.	E. W. White, Esq. [C.].

9. Lachesis ammodytoides.

Bothrops ammodytoides, *Leybold, Escurs. Pamp. Argent.* p 80 (1873);
Berg, An. Soc Arg (5) xix 1885, p 236, *F. Mull. Verh. Nat. Ges. Basel*, viii. 1887, p. 284.
Rhinocerophis nasus, *Garm. Bull. Mus. Comp. Zool.* viii. 1881, p 85
Bothrops nasus, *Berg, Act Ac. Cordoba*, v. 1884, p. 96.
—— patagonicus, *F. Mull. Verh. Nat Ges. Basel*, vii 1885, p. 697.

Snout turned up and produced in a low wart, as in *Vipera latastii*. Rostral once and a half as deep as broad; nasal divided; upper head-scales small, imbricate, keeled; supraocular large, separated from its fellow by 8 or 9 series of scales; two series of scales between the eye and the labials; temporal scales keeled; 9 or 10 upper labials, second separated from the loreal pit, third and fourth largest. Scales very strongly keeled, in 23 or 25 rows. Ventrals 149–160; anal entire; subcaudals 30–38 pairs. Pale brown above, with large square dark brown black-edged spots or cross-bands which may alternate and form a zigzag band; a dark streak behind the eye; belly yellowish, dotted with brown.

Total length 460 millim.; tail 55
North-eastern Patagonia and Argentina.

a. ♂ (Sc. 23; V. 156, C. 37). Rio de Cordoba, E. Fielding, Esq. [P.].
                                     Argentina.
b ♀ (Sc 23; V. 149; C. ?). —— ? Haslar Collection.

10. Lachesis xanthogrammus.

Trigonocephalus xanthogrammus, *Cope, Proc. Ac. Philad.* 1868, p 110.
? Bothrops quadriscutatus, *Posada-Arango, Bull. Soc. Zool. France*, 1889, p. 345.

Head elongate; snout short. Rostral deep; nasal divided, upper head-scales all smooth, in 9 or 10 longitudinal series between the large supraoculars; four elongate shields in a row on the end of the snout; 7 upper labials, second forming the anterior border of the loreal pit. Scales not strongly keeled, in 27 rows. Ventrals 196; subcaudals 54. Very dark olive above, with a yellow zigzag line on each side from the head to the base of the tail, the apices of the open Λ's usually meeting on the vertebral line, enclosing dorsal rhombic spaces and lateral triangles; top of head black, with a pair of undulating yellow bands from the nape meeting in a Λ on the vertex; a bright golden band round the end of the snout, involving the greater part of the supraocular shields, and extending to the nape, bounded below by a black band from the eye to the angle of the mouth; labials bright yellow, ventral shields black, paler in the middle, with yellow triangular spots at their extremities.

Total length 1530 millim.; tail 190.
Pallatanga, E. Ecuador; Andes of Colombia (?).

11. Lachesis castelnaudi.

Bothrops castelnaudi, *Dum. & Bibr.* vii. p. 1511 (1854), *Guichen. in Casteln. Anim. Nouv. Amér. Sud, Rept.* p 75, pl. xv. (1855); *Steind. Sitzb. Ak. Wien*, lxii. i. 1870, p. 349.
Atropos castelnautii, *Dum. & Bibr.* ix. p. 388 (1854).
Trigonocephalus castelnaudi, *Jan, Rev. & Mag. Zool.* 1859, p. 155.
Bothriechis castelnaui, *Cope, Proc. Ac. Philad.* 1860, p. 345.
Bothriopsis quadriscutatus, *Peters, Mon. Berl. Ac.* 1861, p. 359; *R. Blanch. Bull. Soc. Zool. France*, 1889, p. 348.
—— castelnavii, *Cope, Proc. Ac. Philad.* 1871, p. 209.
Thanatophis castelnaudi, *Posada-Arango, Bull Soc. Zool. France*, 1889, p. 343.
? Thanatophis montanus, *Posada-Arango, l. c.* p. 344.

Head narrow and elongate; snout rounded, with well-marked canthus. Rostral as deep as broad; nasal divided; upper head-scales small, juxtaposed, smooth or feebly keeled on the snout and vertex; supraoculars very large, separated by five longitudinal series of scales; a pair of large internasals, in contact with each other, and a large canthal; two or three postoculars and a sub-ocular, separated from the labials by one series of scales; temporal scales keeled; 7 upper labials, second forming the anterior border of the loreal pit. Scales strongly keeled, in 25 or 27 rows. Ventrals 230–253, anal entire; subcaudals 72–83, all or greater part single. Greyish or brown above, with dark or light-edged crossbands or transverse series of spots; head above with dark spots, one of which occupies the middle of the snout; a dark band from the eye to the angle of the mouth; belly brown or blackish, speckled and spotted with yellow.

Total length 1220 millim.; tail 180.

Brazil, Ecuador, Eastern Peru.

a. ♂ (Sc. 27; V. 246; C. 81).	Moyobamba, Peru.	Mr. A H. Roff [C].
b-c. Yg. (Sc 25, 27; V. 243, 230; C. 83, 73).	Sarayacu, Ecuador.	Mr. C. Buckley [C.].

12. Lachesis nummifer.

Atropos nummifer, *Rupp Verz. Senck. Mus., Amph.* p. 21 (1845)
Lachesis mutus, part., *Gray, Cat.* p. 13 (1849).
Atropos mexicanus, *Dum. & Bibr* vii. p 1521, pl lxxxiii. b. (1854).
Teleuraspis nummifer, *Cope, Proc. Ac. Philad* 1859, p. 339; *Gunth. Ann. & Mag. N. H.* (3) xi. 1863, p. 25, pl. iii. fig. C.
Trigonocephalus nummifer, *Jan, Rev. & Mag. Zool.* 1859, p 155.
Bothriechis nummifera, *Cope, Proc. Ac. Philad.* 1860, p. 345; *Günth. Biol. C.-Am., Rept.* p. 191 (1895).
—— mexicanus, *Cope, Proc. Ac Philad.* 1861, p 294.
Bothrops nummifer, *Jan, Elenco*, p. 126 (1863), and *Icon. Gén.* 47, pl. v. fig. 2 (1875).
—— affinis, *Bocourt, Ann. Sc. Nat.* (5) x. 1868, p. 201.
Bothriopsis affinis, *Cope, Proc. Ac. Philad.* 1871, p 209.
—— mexicanus, *Cope, l. c.*
Bothriechis nummifera, var. notata, *Fisch. Arch. f. Nat.* 1880, p. 222, pl. viii. figs. 10–12.

Bothrops mexicanus, *F. Müll. Verh. Nat. Ges. Basel*, vii. 1882, p. 154.
Trigonocephalus affinis, *Garm. N. Amer. Rept.* p. 125 (1883).
Thanatophis nummifer, *Posada-Arango, Bull. Soc. Zool. France*, 1889, p. 343.

Snout broad, rounded, with moderately marked canthus. Rostral as deep as broad or a little broader than deep; nasal divided, sometimes separated from the rostral by a series of small scales; upper head-scales imbricate, strongly keeled, 7 to 10 in a series between the supraoculars, which are very narrow and sometimes broken up; no enlarged internasals; three or four series of scales between the eye and the labials; temporal scales strongly keeled; loreal pit separated from the labials by small scales; 10 or 11 upper labials, fourth and fifth largest. Scales in 23–27 rows, strongly keeled, tubercularly on the back in the adult. Ventrals 121–134; anal entire; subcaudals 26–36, all or greater part single. Pale brown above, with a dorsal series of dark brown, black-edged, rhomboidal spots, which may be confluent and form a zigzag band; a lateral series of dark brown or black spots or vertical bars; a dark brown streak on the side of the head, from the eye to the angle of the mouth; whitish beneath, uniform or spotted with dark brown.

Total length 800 millim.; tail 90.

Mexico and Central America.

a–c. ♂ (Sc. 25; V. 131; C. 35), ♀ (Sc. 23; V. 134, C. 26), & hgr. (Sc. 23; V. 132, C. 32).	Mexico.	Mr. H. Finck [C.].
d. Hgr. (Sc. 25; V. 128; C. 32).	Teapa, Tabasco.	F. D. Godman, Esq. [P.].
e. Hgr. (Sc. 25, V. 133; C. 31).	Huatuzco, Vera Cruz	F. D. Godman, Esq. [P.]
f–i. ♀ (Sc. 27, 27; V. 129, 128; C. 33, 32) & hgr. (Sc. 25, 27; V. 121, 125; C. 35, 33)	Vera Paz, low forest.	O. Salvin, Esq. [C.].
k–l ♀ (Sc. 27, 25; V. 129, 129; C. 32, 30).	Hacienda, Rosa de Jericho, Nicaragua, 3250 ft.	Dr. E. Rothschuh [C.].
m. ♀ (Sc 25; V. 130; C. 32).	Matagalpa, Nicaragua.	Dr. E. Rothschuh [C.].
n. ♀ (Sc. 25, V. 126; C. 28).	Monte Redondo, Costa Rica.	Mr C F. Underwood [C.]

13. Lachesis godmani.

Bothriechis godmanni, *Gunth. Ann. & Mag N. H* (3) xii 1863, p 364, pl. vi. fig. G, *and Biol. C.-Am., Rept.* p. 190, pl. lvii. fig. A (1895).
Bothrops brammianus, *Bocourt, Ann. Sc Nat.* (5) x. 1868, p 201.
Bothriopsis godmanni, *Cope, Proc Ac Philad* 1871, p. 208.
Bothrops (Bothriopsis) godmanii, *F. Müll. Verh Nat. Ges. Basel*, vi 1878, p. 402, pl. iii. fig. B.

Bothriechis scutigera, *Fisch. Arch. f. Nat.* 1880, p 218, pl. viii. fig. 8 & 9.
—— trianguligera, *Fisch. Oster-Progr. Akad. Gymn. Hamburg*, 1883, p. 13.
Bothriopsis scutigera, *Cope, Bull. U.S. Nat. Mus.* no. 32, 1887, p 88
—— trianguligera, *Cope, l. c.*

Snout broad, rounded, with well-marked canthus. Rostral as deep as broad or a little broader than deep; nasal divided; upper head-scales imbricate, feebly or moderately keeled, subequal or with a few enlarged shield-like ones on the vertex; 5 to 7 scales in a transverse series between the supraoculars, which are large; two series of scales between the eye and the labials; temporal scales keeled; loreal pit separated from the labials by small scales; 9 or 10 upper labials, the three anterior smallest. Scales strongly and sharply keeled, in 21 rows. Ventrals 135–142; anal entire; subcaudals 22–34, single. Brown above, with or without a dorsal series of large darker spots and two lateral series of dark brown or blackish alternating spots, the lower on the ventrals and lost on the anterior half of the body; a dark streak from the eye to a little beyond the angle of the mouth; belly yellowish, more or less speckled or spotted with grey or blackish.

Total length 610 millim.; tail 60.

Guatemala.

a. ♀ (V. 142; C. 28).	Totonicapam.	O. Salvin, Esq [C.]. (Type.)
b–e. ♂ (V. 138, 135; C. 27, 28) & ♀ (V. 140, 143; C. 22, 26).	Volcan de Fuego.	O. Salvin & F. D. Godman, Esqs. [P.].

14. Lachesis lansbergii.

Trigonocephalus lansbergii, *Schleg Mag. de Zool* 1841, *Rept* pl. i.
Teleuraspis lansbergii, *Cope, Proc. Ac Philad.* 1859, p 339.
Bothrops lansbergi, *Jan, Elenco*, p. 127 (1863), *and Icon. Gén* 47, pl. iv fig. 1 (1875), *Bocourt, Journ. de Zool.* v. 1876, p 410.
—— ophryomegas, *Bocourt, Ann. Sc. Nat.* (5) x 1868, p. 201.
Porthidium lansbergii, *Cope, Proc. Ac. Philad.* 1871, p. 207
Bothriopsis ophryomegas, *Cope, l. c.* p. 208.
Bothriechis lansbergii, part., *Gunth. Biol. C.-Am., Rept.* p. 190 (1895).
—— ophryomegas, *Gunth. l c.* p 191.

Snout pointed, with sharp canthus, turned up at the end, as in *Vipera aspis* Rostral once and one third to once and a half as deep as broad; nasal divided or semidivided; a pair of raised internasals; upper head-scales small, imbricate, strongly keeled; supraoculars large, separated by 5 to 7 series of scales; two or three series of scales between the eye and the labials; temporal scales keeled; 8 to 10 upper labials, none bordering the loreal pit, fifth, fourth and fifth, or fifth and sixth largest. Scales strongly keeled, in 25 to 27 rows. Ventrals 152-159; anal entire; subcaudals 29-35, single. Yellowish brown, pale brown, or grey above, with a dorsal series of large dark brown black-edged rhomboidal or squarish spots, usually divided by a narrow yellow or orange vertebral line, sides of head blackish; belly powdered with brown, with or without whitish spots.

Total length 575 millim.; tail 70.

From Southern Mexico to Colombia, Venezuela, and Brazil

a ♀ (Sc 25, V. 152, C. 35)		Yucatan.	
b-d. Hgr (Sc 26, 25, 27; V. 159, 155, 155; C. 32, 34, 29).		Chiriqui.	F D Godman, Esq. [P.].
e, f ♂ (Sc. 25, 25, V. 153, 152; C.?, 35).		Carthagena, Colombia.	Capt. Garth [P.].

15. Lachesis brachystoma.

Teleuraspis castelnaui, var. brachystoma, *Cope, Proc. Ac Philad.* 1859, p. 339.
Bothriechis brachystoma, *Cope, Proc Ac Philad.* 1861, p. 295.
Bothrops lansbergii (*non Schleg.*), *Gunth Ann. & Mag. N. H.* (3) xii 1863, p 350; *F. Mull. Verh. Nat. Ges. Basel,* vi. 1878, p. 703.
—— nasutus, *Bocourt, Ann. Sc. Nat.* (5) x. 1868, p. 202, *and Journ. de Zool* v. 1876, p 410
Porthidium nasutus, *Cope, Proc Ac. Philad.* 1871, p. 207, *and Proc. Amer Philos Soc.* xviii. 1879, p 271
Bothriopsis brachystoma, *Cope, l. c* p. 208
—— proboscideus, *Cope, Journ. Ac Philad.* (2) viii. 1876, p 150, pl. xxvii fig 3.
Bothrops brachystoma, *Bocourt, Journ. de Zool.* v. 1876, p. 410.
Thanatophis sutus, *Posada-Arango, Bull. Soc. Zool. France,* 1889, p. 344
Bothriechis lansbergii, part., *Gunth. Biol C-Am., Rept.* p 190 (1895).

Closely allied to the preceding, but snout much produced above, as in *Vipera latastii*, and rostral once and two thirds to twice as deep as broad. Scales in 23 (rarely 25) rows. Ventrals 132-150; subcaudals 27-38.

Total length 500 millim; tail 50.

Southern Mexico and Central America.

a. ♂ (V. 144, C. 38).	Tehuantepec.	M Sumichrast [C].
b-c. ♂ (V. 139; C. 36) & ♀ (V. 142; C. 30).	Vera Paz, low forest.	O. Salvin, Esq. [C.].
d-f. ♀ (V. 139, 133; C. 28, 28) & hgr. (V. 136; C. 33).	Hacienda Rosa de Jericho, Nicaragua, 3250 ft.	Dr E Rothschuh [C.].
g Hgr. (V. 137; C. 28).	Chontalez, Nicaragua.	
h Hgr (V 142, C. 27).	Colombia.	Mr. F. A. Simons [C.].

16. Lachesis monticola.

Parias maculata, *Gray, Ann. & Mag. N. H.* (2) xii. 1853, p. 392 (*nec Gray*, 1842).
Trimeresurus monticola, *Gunth. Rept. Brit. Ind.* p. 388, pl. xxiv. fig. B (1864); *Stoliczka, Journ. As. Soc. Beng.* xl. 1871, p. 445; *Fayrer, Thanatoph. Ind.* pl. xv. (1874); *Theob. Cat. Rept. Brit. Ind.* p. 220 (1876); *Anders An. Zool. Res. Yunnan*, p. 832, pl. lxxvi. figs. 4 & 5 (1879); *Boulenq. Faun. Ind., Rept.* p. 426 (1890); *Gunth in Pratt, Snows of Tibet*, p. 241 (1892).
—— convictus, *Stoliczka, Journ As. Soc Beng* xxxix 1870, p. 224, pl. xii. fig. 1; *Anders. Proc. Zool Soc* 1871, p. 196.
—— monticola, part., *Anders. l. c.* p. 194

Snout very short; eye very small. Rostral as deep as broad, or a little broader than deep; nasal divided or semidivided; upper head-scales small, subimbricate, smooth; supraocular large; internasals separated from each other by one to three scales, rarely in contact; 5 to 8 scales in a transverse line between the supraoculars; 3 or 4 rows of scales between the eye and the labials; 8 or 9 upper labials, second usually forming the anterior border of the loreal pit; temporal scales smooth. Scales feebly keeled, in some specimens almost smooth, in 21 to 25 rows (rarely 27). Ventrals 132–158; anal entire; subcaudals 21–57 pairs. Brown or yellowish above, with one or two dorsal series of large squarish dark brown spots, and a lateral series of smaller spots, head dark brown above, pale brown or yellowish on the sides, with a dark brown temporal streak, lower parts whitish, spotted or powdered with brown, the brown spots sometimes confluent into two stripes.

Total length 740 millim.; tail 115.

Tibet, Himalayas (2000–8000 feet), hills of Assam, Burma, and the Malay Peninsula; Pinang, Singapore, Sumatra.

a–b. ♂ (Sc 25; V. 151, 158; C 46, 40).	Kia-tiang-fu, 1070 ft., Prov Sze-Chuen	A. E. Pratt, Esq [C.]
c. ♂ (Sc. 23; V. 140; C. 43).	Nepaul	B H. Hodgson, Esq. [P.]. ⎫ (Types)
d Yg. (Sc. 23; V. 147; C. 47).	Sikkim.	Sir J. Hooker [P.]. ⎬
e. ♀ (Sc. 25; V. 152, C. 38).	Darjeeling	E. Blyth, Esq. [P.].
f–l. ♂ (Sc. 23; V. 141; C 44), ♀ (Sc. 23; V. 144; C 36), & yg. (Sc. 21, 23, 24, 22; V. 146, 145, 137, 141; C. 40, 49, 36, 45).	Darjeeling.	T C Jerdon, Esq. [P].
m, n–p. ♂ (Sc. 23, 23; V. 141, 148; C. 33, 36), hgr. ♀ (Sc. 23; V 148; C 35), & yg. (Sc. 23; V. 149; C. 38).	Darjeeling.	W. T. Blanford, Esq. [P.].
q, r. ♀ (Sc. 25; V. 151; C. 38) & yg. (Sc. 21; V. 143, C. 49).	Himalayas.	Col. Beddome [C.]

s. ♀ (Sc. 23; V. 142; C. 36)   Mt Mooleyit, 4500 ft. Col Beddome [C.].

t–v. ♂ (Sc. 25, V. 152, C 49), ♀ (Sc. 27; V. 150, C. 40), & yg. (Sc. 25; V. 144; C. 48).   Toungyi, Shan States, Lieut. Blakeway [C]. 5000 ft.

w. Yg (Sc 23, V. 147; C 45)   Toungyi, Shan States E. W. Oates, Esq [P.].

x. ♀ (Sc. 23; V. 134; C. 24).   Singapore.

17. Lachesis okinavensis. (PLATE XXV. fig. 2.)

Trimeresurus okinavensis, *Bouleng. Ann. & Mag. N. H.* (6) x. 1892, p. 302.

Snout short, obliquely truncate, with sharp raised angle all round; eye rather small. Rostral deeper than broad; nasal divided; upper head-scales small, subimbricate, smooth on the snout and vertex; 6 to 9 scales in a transverse series between the supraoculars, which are large, larger than the eye; a pair of scales separating the internasals in front; three series of scales between the eye and the labials; temporal scales obtusely keeled; 7 or 8 upper labials, second entering the loreal pit, third largest. Scales strongly keeled, in 21 or 23 rows. Ventrals 129–130; anal entire; subcaudals 43–47 pairs. Brown above, with darker cross-bands or alternating large quadrangular blotches, upper surface of head dark brown, sides blackish, with a lighter streak along the temple; lower parts brown, with a series of blackish blotches on each side, partly on the ventrals, partly on the two lower rows of scales.

Total length 350 millim.; tail 60.

Okinawa, Loo Choo Islands.

a–b. ♀ (V. 130, 129, C 43, 47).   Okinawa.   Mr. Holst [C.]. (Types)

18. Lachesis strigatus.

Trimesurus strigatus, *Gray, Zool. Miscell* p. 49 (1842), *and Cat* p. 10 (1849); *Gunth. Rept. Brit. Ind* p 389, pl. xxiv fig. D (1864); *Fayrer, Thanatoph. Ind* pl. xvi (1874); *Theob. Cat. Rept. Brit Ind.* p. 224 (1876), *Bouleng. Faun. Ind, Rept.* p. 427 (1890).

Atropos darwini, *Dum. & Bibr.* vii. pp. 1518 & 1520 (1854).

Trigonocephalus (Cophias) neelgherriensis, *Jerdon, Journ. As. Soc. Beng.* xxii. 1851, p 524

—— darwini, *Jan, Rev & Mag Zool* 1859, p. 155.

Bothrops darwini, *Jan, Elenco,* p. 126 (1863).

Rostral broader than deep; nasal entire; upper head-scales small, smooth, juxtaposed; supraocular small, sometimes broken up; no enlarged internasals; 8 to 11 scales in a transverse line between the supraoculars; two or three small postoculars and a subocular, which is separated from the labials by one or two series of scales; the shield forming the anterior border of the loreal pit distinct from the second labial; 9 or 10 upper labials. Scales feebly keeled, in 21 rows. Ventrals 136-145; anal entire; subcaudals 31-40 pairs. Brown above, with dark brown spots, those of the median series often confluent into a zigzag band; a more or less distinct ∩-shaped light marking on the nape; a dark temporal band; belly whitish, spotted or marbled with grey or black; end of tail yellow or reddish.

Total length 480 millim.; tail 55.

From the Bombay hills to the Anamallays and Nilgherries.

a-b ♂ (V. 136, 145; C. 39, 40).	Madras Presidency.	T. C. Jerdon, Esq. [P.]. (Types)
c. ♀ (V. 139; C. 31).	Deccan.	Col. Sykes [P.]
d. ♀ (V. 138; C. 34).	Anamallays, 4700 ft.	W. Davison, Esq [P].
e. ♀ (V. 137; C. 32).	Nilgherries.	Lord Dormer [P].
f, g-h. ♂ (V. 142; C. 39), ♀ (V. 137, C. 32), & yg. (V. 136; C 37).	Nilgherries.	Col. Beddome [C].

19. Lachesis flavoviridis.

Bothrops flavoviridis, *Hallow Proc. Ac. Philad.* 1860, p. 492; *Bouleng Proc Zool Soc.* 1887, p 149.
Trimeresurus riukianus, *Hilgend. Sitzb Ges Nat. Fr. Berl.* 1880, p. 118, pl. —. figs. 6-10, *Fisch. Jahrb. Hamb. Wiss. Anst.* v. 1888, p. 20.
—— flavoviridis, *Bouleng Faun. Ind*, *Rept.* p. 425 (1890).

Rostral as deep as broad or broader than deep; nasal divided or semidivided; upper head-scales very small, flat, juxtaposed, smooth; supraocular large, one to four scales separating the internasals in front; 7 to 12 scales on a line between the supraoculars; one to three small postoculars and a subocular, which is in contact with the third labial or separated by one series of scales: temporal scales smooth; 8 or 9 upper labials, second forming the anterior border of the loreal pit. Scales rather feebly keeled, in 33 to 37 rows. Ventrals 222-231; anal entire; subcaudals 75-90 pairs. Pale brownish or greenish yellow above, with black marblings or a dorsal series of dark rings or rhombs enclosing light spots of the ground-colour; head with longitudinal black streaks disposed symmetrically; belly yellowish or greenish white, with more or less distinct dark spots or variegations.

Total length 1215 millim.; tail 220.

Loo Choo Islands.

a-b. ♀ (Sc. 35, 37; V. 225, 225; C. 80, 76)	Okinawa.	Dr. J. G. Fischer.
c-d. ♂ (Sc. 35; V. 231; C 90) & yg. (Sc. 33; V. 229; C. 79).	Okinawa.	Mr. Holst [C.].
e-f, g. ♂ (Sc. 33; V. 223; C. 80) & yg. (Sc. 35, 35; V. 222, 230, C. 83, 75).	Loo Choo Is.	H. Pryer, Esq. [P.].

20. Lachesis cantoris.

Trigonocephalus cantori, *Blyth, Journ. As. Soc. Beng.* xv. 1846, p. 377.
Trimeresurus viridis, var cantori, *Blyth, Journ As. Soc. Beng.* xxix. 1860, p. 110.
—— labialis, *Steindachn. Novara, Rept.* p. 86, pl iii figs. 1 & 2 (1867); *Theob Cat. Rept Brit. Ind.* p. 221 (1876).
—— cantoris, *Stoliczka, Journ As Soc. Beng* xxxix. 1870, p. 222, pl. xii. figs. 3 & 4; *Theob. l. c.* p. 222, *Bouleng. Faun. Ind*, *Rept* p 428 (1890).

Rostral as deep as broad ; nasal divided ; upper head-scales very small, smooth, almost granular ; supraocular shields distinct, narrow, sometimes divided into two ; usually one or two scales between the internasals, 16 on a line between the supraoculars ; two small postoculars and a subocular, which is separated from the labials by two or three rows of scales ; 13 upper labials, first confluent with nasal, second forming the anterior border of the loreal pit ; third largest ; temporals small, feebly keeled. Scales rather feebly keeled, in 27 to 31 rows. Ventrals 174–184 ; anal entire ; subcaudals 55–76 pairs. Pale brown or dull green above, with small dark spots ; a whitish streak along the outer series of scales ; whitish or greenish beneath, uniform or with the base of the ventrals dark ashy or blackish.

Total length 1020 millim.; tail 140.

Andaman and Nicobar Islands.

a. ♀ (Sc 31; V. 178; C. 61).   Nicobars.

21. Lachesis jerdonii.

Trimeresurus jerdonii, *Gunth. Proc Zool. Soc* 1875, p. 233, pl. xxxiv., *Bouleng. Faun. Ind*, *Rept* p. 427 (1890).
—— xanthomelas, *Gunth. Ann. & Mag. N. H* (6) iv. 1889, p 221, and in *Pratt, Snows of Tibet*, p. 241, pl. i. fig. A (1892).

Rostral as deep as broad or a little deeper than broad ; nasal divided ; upper-head scales very small, smooth, juxtaposed ; supraoculars large, larger than the eye ; one or more scales between the internasals, 7 to 9 on a line between the supraoculars ; one or two small postoculars and a subocular, which is in contact with the third labial, and usually separated from the fourth by a series of small scales ; 7 or 8 upper labials, second forming the anterior border of the loreal pit, third and fourth large ; a series of large, smooth temporals above the labials. Scales strongly keeled, in 21 or 23 rows. Ventrals 164–188 ; anal entire ; subcaudals 54–67 pairs. Greenish yellow or olive above, mixed with black ; a dorsal series of transverse rhomboidal reddish-brown spots edged with black, head black above, with symmetrical yellow markings ; upper lip yellow, with one or more black spots, that on the second labial being constant; belly yellow, more or less profusely spotted or marbled with black.

Total length 930 millim., tail 145.

Khasi hills, Assam; Tibet; Upper Yang-Tse-Kiang.

a–c ♂ (Sc. 21, 21; V. 175, 173; C. 56, 58) & ♀ (Sc. 23; V. 164; C. ?).	Khasi hills.	T. C. Jerdon, Esq. [P.]. (Type.)
d. ♀ (Sc. 21; V. 175; C. 54).	Khasi hills.	Col. Beddome [O.].
e–i. ♂ (Sc. 22, 21; V. 183, 180; C. 67, 63) & ♀ (Sc. 21, 21, 21; V. 186, 187, 185; C. 58, 60, 55).	Ichang.	A. E. Pratt, Esq. [P.] (Types of *T. xanthomelas*.)
k. ♂ (Sc. 21; V. 188; C. 54).	Kia-tiang-fu, Prov. Sze-Chuen, 1070 ft.	A. E. Pratt, Esq. [C.].

22. Lachesis mucrosquamatus.

Trigonocephalus mucrosquamatus, *Cantor, Proc. Zool. Soc.* 1839, p. 32.

Craspedocephalus elegans, *Gray, Cat.* p. 7 (1849).

Trimeresurus mucrosquamatus, *Günth. Rept. Brit. Ind.* p. 390 (1864); *Swinhoe, Proc. Zool. Soc.* 1870, p. 411, pl. xxxi., *Theob. Cat. Rept. Brit. Ind.* p. 224 (1876); *Fischer, Jahrb. Hamb. Wiss. Anst.* v. 1888, p. 21; *Bouleng. Faun. Ind., Rept.* p. 428 (1890).

Rostral slightly broader than deep; nasal divided or semidivided; upper head-scales extremely small, granular, smooth or obtusely keeled; supraocular large, or rather narrow; 2 or 3 scales separating the internasals in front; 10 to 15 scales on a line between the supraoculars; three to five minute postoculars and a subocular, which is separated from the labials by one, two, or three series of scales; temporal scales smooth; 7 to 11 upper labials, second forming the anterior border of the loreal pit. Scales strongly keeled, in 25 or 27 rows. Ventrals 183–218; anal entire; subcaudals 72–92 pairs. Brownish grey above, with a dorsal series of large blackish spots and a lateral series of smaller ones; a blackish streak from the eye to the angle of the mouth; lower parts brownish, spotted with white.

Total length 1050 millim.; tail 210.

Formosa; Naga hills, Assam.

a. ♂ (Sc. 25; V. 200; C. 92).	Takow, Formosa.	R. Swinhoe, Esq. [C.].
b. ♀ (Sc. 27; V. 214; C. 76).	Formosa.	R. Swinhoe, Esq [C.].
c. Yg. (Sc. 27; V. 211; C. 80).	C. Formosa.	Mr. Holst [C.].
d. Yg. (Sc. 27; V. 210; C. 90).	S. Formosa.	Dr. J. G. Fischer
e,f. ♂ (Sc. 25; V. 187; C. 76) & yg. (Sc. 25; V. 183; C. 72)	—— ?	Sir E. Belcher [P.].

23. Lachesis luteus.

Trimeresurus luteus, *Boettg. Jahresb. Offenb. Ver. Nat.* 1895, p. 111.

Rostral broader than deep; nasal divided; upper head-scales very small, flat, juxtaposed, smooth on the snout and vertex; supraocular large; no internasals; 12 or 13 scales on a line between the supraoculars; two or three small postoculars and a subocular, which is separated from the labials by two series of scales; temporal scales keeled, 7 or 8 upper labials, second forming the anterior border of the loreal pit, third and fourth large. Scales strongly keeled, in 23 or 25 rows. Ventrals 182–186; anal entire; subcaudals 72–74. Yellow above, with a dorsal series of rhomboidal dark, black-edged spots partly confluent into a zigzag band; a lateral series of small spots; a blackish streak on each side of the head behind the eye; yellowish beneath, spotted and clouded with grey.

Total length 945 millim.; tail 164.

Loo Choo Islands.

24. Lachesis purpureomaculatus.

Trigonocephalus purpureomaculatus, *Gray, Ill. Ind Zool.* i pl. lxxxi. (1832).

Trimesurus purpureus, *Gray, Zool Misc.* p 48 (1842), *and Cat.* p 8 (1849)

—— carinatus, *Gray, ll. cc.*

Trigonocephalus puniceus (non *Boie*), *Cantor, Cat. Mal. Rept.* p 122 (1847).

Trimesurus bicolor, *Gray, Ann & Mag N. H* (2) xii. 1853, p. 392.

Cryptelytrops carinatus, *Cope, Proc. Ac Philad.* 1859, p. 340.

Trimeresurus porphyraceus, *Blyth, Journ As Soc Beng.* xxix 1861, p 110; *Theob. Journ Linn Soc* x. 1868, p. 64; *Stoliczka, Journ As. Soc Beng.* xxxix. 1870, p 218; *Theob. Cat. Rept Brit. Ind* p 222 (1876)

—— carinatus, *Gunth Rept Brit Ind.* p. 386 (1864); *Stoliczka, l c* p. 217; *Fayrer, Thanatoph. Ind* pl. xiii. (1874), *Theob. Cat. Rept. Brit. Ind.* p. 221.

—— purpureus, *Gunth. l c.* p. 387.

—— andersonii, *Theob Cat Rept. As Soc. Mus* 1868, p. 75; *Stoliczka, l c.* p 216, *and Journ As Soc. Beng* xl 1871, p 443; *Fayrer, l c* pl. xv.; *Theob. Cat. Rept. Brit. Ind* p 224.

—— obscurus, *Theob. Cat Rept As. Soc. Mus* 1868, p. 76.

—— monticola, part, *Anders Proc Zool. Soc* 1871, p 194

—— purpureomaculatus, *Bouleng Faun Ind, Rept.* p 429 (1890), *and Proc Zool. Soc.* 1890, p. 36; *W. Sclater, Journ. As. Soc. Beng.* lx. 1891, p. 248

Rostral as deep as broad; nasal entire; upper head-scales very small, juxtaposed, convex or obtusely keeled; supraocular very narrow, sometimes broken up, internasals small, separated from each other by one or two scales; 12 to 15 scales in a transverse line between the supraoculars; two or three small postoculars and a subocular, which is separated from the labials by two or three series of scales; 11 to 13 upper labials, the fourth and succeeding small, the first usually fused with the nasal, the second (usually) forming the anterior border of the loreal pit, temporal scales keeled. Scales strongly keeled, in 25 or 27 rows. Ventrals 160–182; anal entire; subcaudals 55–76 pairs. Tail slightly prehensile. Dark purplish brown above, uniform or variegated with pale green; flanks usually pale green or spotted with pale green, or with a series of pale spots on the outer series of scales; olive or greenish white below, uniform or spotted with black; some specimens uniform green.

Total length 980 millim.; tail 150.

Himalayas, Bengal, Assam, Burma, Malay Peninsula, Andamans, Nicobars, Pinang, Sumatra.

A. Uniform purplish brown to blackish above.

a.	♀ (Sc 27, V 163; C. 59).	Singapore.	Gen. Hardwicke [P.]. (Type)
b	♂ (Sc 27; V. 162; C.75).	Singapore.	Dr. Dennys [P.].
c	♂ (Sc. 25, V. 160; C. 74).	Singapore.	Dr Collingwood [P.].
d.	♀ (Sc. 27; V 174; C. 57).	Pinang.	Dr. Cantor.
e.	♂ (Sc. 25; V. 160, C. 76).	India.	J. Inskip, Esq [P.] (Type of *T. carinatus*)

B. Dark purplish brown or blackish, variegated with pale green.

a.	♀ (Sc. 27; V 178, C 63).	Pinang	Dr. Cantor
b.	♀ (Sc. 25; V. 170, C 58).	Yumeekee, Mergui.	Dr. J. Anderson [P.].

C. Uniform green above.

a.	♀ (Sc. 25, V. 168; C. 61).	Sikkim.	Sir J. Hooker [P.] (Type of *T. bicolor*.)
b-c.	♀ (Sc. 25; V. 162; C. 59) & yg. (Sc. 25; V. 163; C. 66.)	Rangoon.	W. Theobald, Esq [C.].
d	Hgr. (Sc. 25; V. 160; C. 56).	Pegu.	W. Theobald, Esq [C.].
e.	♀ (Sc. 25; V. 164; C. 52).	Toungoo.	E. W. Oates, Esq [P].

25. Lachesis gramineus.

Russell, Ind. Serp. i pl. ix. (1796) & ii pl. xx. (1801)
Coluber gramineus, *Shaw, Zool* iii. p 420 (1802).
Vipera viridis, *Daud. Rept.* vi p. 112 (1803).
Trimeresurus viridis, *Lacép. Ann. du Mus.* iv. 1804, p. 209, pl. lvi. fig. 2; *Gray, Cat.* p. 7 (1819), and *Ann. & Mag. N. H.* (2) xii. 1853, p. 391.
Cophias viridis, *Merr. Tent.* p. 155 (1820).
Trigonocephalus viridis, *Schleg. Phys. Serp* ii. p 344, pl xix. figs. 12 & 13.
—— erythrurus, *Cantor, Proc. Zool. Soc.* 1839, p. 31.

11. LACHESIS.

Trimesurus albolabris, *Gray, Zool. Miscell.* p. 48 (1842), *and Cat.* p. 8.
Trigonocephalus gramineus, part, *Cantor, Cat. Mal. Rept.* p 119 (1847).
Trimesurus elegans, *Gray, Ann. & Mag. N H.* (2) xii 1853, p. 391
Bothrops viridis, *Dum & Bibr.* vii. p. 1512 (1854).
Trimeresurus gramineus, *Gunth. Rept. Brit. Ind.* p 385 (1864), *Stoliczka, Journ. As. Soc. Beng* xxxix 1870, p 216, *Anders. Proc Zool. Soc* 1871, p. 194; *Theob Cat. Rept. Brit. Ind* p. 219 (1876), *Anders. An. Zool. Res. Yunnan,* p. 828 (1879); *Boettg. Ber. Senck. Ges.* 1887, p. 50; *Bouleng. Faun. Ind, Rept.* p. 429 (1890), *W. Sclater, Journ As Soc. Beng.* lx. 1891, p 248; *Boetty Ber. Senck. Ges.* 1894, p 135.
—— erythrurus, *Gunth. l. c.* p. 386; *Stoliczka, l. c.* p. 217; *Fayrer, Thanatoph. Ind.* pl. xiv. (1874); *Theob l. c.* p. 220, *F. Mull. Verh. Nat. Ges. Basel,* viii 1887, p 280
—— mutabilis, *Stoliczka, l. c* p. 219, pl. xii. fig. 5, *Theob l. c* p. 223.

Snout with distinct canthus; eye small or rather small. Rostral as deep as broad or a little broader than deep; nasal usually entire; upper head-scales small, smooth, imbricate or subimbricate, 8 to 13 in a transverse series between the supraoculars, which are narrow (rarely divided); internasals in contact or separated by one or two scales; two or three postoculars and a subocular; latter sometimes in contact with the third labial; usually one or two, rarely three, series of scales between the subocular and the labials; temporal scales smooth; 8 to 12 upper labials, second forming the anterior border of the loreal pit, third largest. Scales nearly smooth or more or less distinctly keeled, in 21 (rarely 19 or 23) rows Ventrals 145–175, anal entire; subcaudals 53–75. Tail more or less distinctly prehensile. Bright green above, rarely olive or yellowish, with or without ill-defined blackish cross-bands; usually a light, white or yellow streak along the outer row of scales; end of tail often yellow or red; lower parts green, yellow, or whitish.

Total length 870 millim ; tail 150.

South-eastern Asia.

a–b Hgr ♂ (V. 161; C. 75) & hgr ♀ (V. 162; C. 49)	Ladak.	— Strachey, Esq. [P].
c. ♂ (V. 167; C. 76).	Bimtal, 4400 ft.	Dr Cantor
d–e. ♀ (V. 164; C. 58) & hgr. ♀ (V. 159; C. 61).	Darjeeling.	W. T. Blanford, Esq. [P.].
f–h, i ♂ (V. 165, 164, C. ?, 64), ♀ (V 161; C. 58), & yg. (V 147; C 65).	Darjeeling.	T C. Jerdon, Esq.[P.].
k. ♂ (V. 157; C. 57)	Sikkim.	Sir J. Hooker [P.].
l. Yg. (V. 168; C. 61).	Sikkim.	Sir J Hooker [P] (Type of *T. elegans.*)
m–n. ♂ (V. 158, 166; C 62, 59).	Himalayas	Col. Beddome [C.].
o. Hgr ♀ (Sc. 19, V. 149; C. 56).	Khasi hills	Dr. Griffith.

p. ♂ (V 161; C. 60).	Khasi hills.	T. C. Jerdon, Esq [P.]
q. Yg (V. 169; C. 64).	Ganges Delta.	Dr. Cantor. (Type of *T. erythrurus*)
r. Head of adult.	Ganjam.	Col. Beddome [C.].
s, t Hgr. ♂ (V. 171, 172; C. 70, 70).	Matheran, Bombay.	Dr. Leith [P.].
u. Hgr. ♂ (V. 154; C. 63).	Mudmalley, Wynad	Col. Beddome [C.]
v. Hgr. ♂ (V. 145; C. 53)	Brumagherry hills.	Col. Beddome [C.].
w. Yg. (V. 175; C. 56).	Cuddapa hills.	Col. Beddome [C.].
x. Yg. (V. 170; C. 59).	Shevaroy hills.	Col. Beddome [C.]
y. ♂ (V. 169; C. 67).	Near Ningpo.	
z-δ, ε-ζ. ♂ (V. 163, 159, 156, 162, 155, 152, 151; C. 67, 71, 68, 68, 65, 66, 60).	Formosa.	R. Swinhoe, Esq. [C.].
η ♂ (V. 162; C. 70).	Hong Kong	H M S. 'Challenger.'
θ. ♀ (V. 164; C 51)	Hong Kong.	J. Bowring, Esq. [P.].
ι-κ. Hgr. ♂ (V. 154; C. 60) & ♀ (V. 160; C. 47).	China	J. Reeves, Esq [P.]. (Types of *T. albolabris*)
λ, μ. ♂ (V. 167; C. 71) & ♀ (V. 168; C. 63).	Lao Mts.	M. Mouhot [C.].
ν ♀ (V. 170; C 53).	Pachebon.	M. Mouhot [C.]
ξ. Hgr. ♀ (C. 158; C. ?).	Siam.	M. Mouhot [C.].
o. ♀ (V. 162; C. 52).	Siam.	W. H. Newman, Esq. [P.]
π. Yg. (V. 162; C. 66).	Toungyi, S. Shan States	E. W. Oates, Esq. [P.].
ρ, σ. ♀ (V. 158; C. 59) & hgr. ♀ (V. 164; C. 51).	Moulmein, Tenasserim	R C Beavan, Esq. [P.].
τ. Hgr. ♂ (V 159, C. 72).	Mergui	Prof. Oldham [P.].
υ-φ ♂ (V. 165; C. 72) & ♀ (V. 166; C. 58).	Pinang.	Dr. Cantor.
χ. ♂ (V. 161, C. 71).	Sumatra.	H. O. Forbes, Esq. [P.].
ψ-ω. ♂ (V. 162; C. 73) & ♀ (V. 163; C. 51).	Java.	G. Lyon, Esq. [P.].
a'-c'. ♂ (V. 162, 160; C. 65, 73) & hgr. ♀ (V. 164; C. 62).	Java.	
d'. ♀ (V 158; C. 59).	Java.	
e'. ♀ (V. 163, C. 58).	Timor.	
f'. Skull.	Siam.	

26. Lachesis flavomaculatus. (PLATE XXV fig. 3)

Megæra flavomaculata, *Gray, Zool. Miscell.* p. 49 (1842).
—— ornata, *Gray, l. c.*
—— variegata, *Gray, l. c.* p. 50.
Parias flavomaculatus, *Gray, Cat.* p. 11 (1849).
—— ornata, *Gray, l. c.*
—— variegata, *Gray, l. c.*
Trimeresurus flavomaculatus, *Günth. Proc. Zool. Soc.* 1879, p. 79.
—— schadenbergi, *Fisch. Jahrb. Wiss. Anst. Hamb.* ii. 1885, p 116

Snout with strong canthus, obliquely truncate, more prominent than in *L. gramineus*; eye small. Rostral as deep as broad; nasal entire or divided; upper head-scales small, smooth, imbricate, 8 to 10 in a transverse series between the supraoculars, which are narrow; two or three scales separating the internasals in front; two or three postoculars and a subocular, which is in contact with the third or third and fourth labials; temporal scales smooth; 9 to 11 upper labials, second forming the anterior border of the loreal pit, third largest. Scales smooth or feebly keeled, in 21 rows. Ventrals 170–187; anal entire; subcaudals 55–73. Tail prehensile. Bright green or olive above, uniform or spotted or barred with reddish brown; a series of bright yellow or salmon-pink spots on the outer row of scales; green, olive, or greenish yellow beneath; end of tail sometimes red.

Total length 1060 millim.; tail 160.

Philippine Islands.

a, b. ♂ (V. 184, C. 63) & hgr. ♂ (V. 178, C 65)	Philippines.	H Cuming, Esq [C.]. (Types.)
c. Hgr. ♂ (V. 182; C. 73).	Philippines	H Cuming, Esq [C.]. (Type of *M. ornata*)
d. Yg. (V. 178; C. 61).	Philippines.	H. Cuming, Esq [C.]. (Type of *M. variegata*.)
e. ♂ (V. 173, C. 64).	Placer, N.E. Mindanao.	A. Everett, Esq. [C.].
f–i. ♀ (V. 187; C 56) & yg. (V. 170, 181, 177; C 61, 55, 61).	Luzon.	Dr. A. B. Meyer [C.].

L. flavomaculatus should perhaps be regarded as a variety of *L. gramineus*.

27. Lachesis sumatranus.

Coluber sumatranus, *Raffles, Trans. Linn Soc.* xiii 1822, p. 334.
Trigonocephalus formosus, *Schleg. in Temm. Verh. Nat. Gesch. Nederl Ind., Rept.* p. 52, pl vii (1844).
Bothrops formosus, *Jan, Elenco*, p. 126 (1863), *and Icon. Gén.* 47, pl. v. fig. 1 (1875), *Modigliani, Ann. Mus Genova*, (2) vii. 1889, p. 121.
Trimeresurus formosus, *Bouleng. Ann & Mag. N. H.* (5) xvi. 1885, p. 388
Bothrops sumatranus, *v. Lidth de Jeude, Notes Leyd. Mus.* viii. 1886, p 52, pl ii. fig. 6.
—— hageni, *v. Lidth de Jeude, l. c.* p. 53.

Head rather elongate. Rostral as deep as broad or a little broader than deep; nasal entire or divided; upper head-scales rather large, flat, smooth, imbricate or subimbricate, largest on the snout, 4 to 9 in a transverse series between the supraoculars, which are large; two or three postoculars and a subocular, which is in contact with the third or third and fourth labials; temporal scales smooth; 9 to 11 upper labials, second forming the anterior border of the loreal pit, third largest. Scales feebly keeled, in

21 rows. Ventrals 180-191; anal entire; subcaudals 58-82. Tail prehensile. Bright green above, the scales usually black-edged, with or without black cross-bands; two series of small whitish spots may be present along the back; a more or less distinct whitish or yellow streak usually present on each side, along the outer row of scales; ventrals yellowish or green, with or without fine black edges, end of tail red.

Total length 1100 millim.; tail 180.

Singapore, Sumatra, Borneo, Palawan.

a, b ♀ (V. 187; C 69) & hgr ♂ (V. 180; C. 77).	Singapore.	Dr. Dennys [P.].
c. ♂ (V. 180; C. 76).	Deli, Sumatra.	Mr Iversen [C.].
d. Yg (V. 186; C. 67).	E Coast of Sumatra.	Mrs. Findlay [P.]
e-h. ♂ (V. 189, C. 72) & ♀ (V. 190, 191, 188, C 66, 66, 63)	Nias.	Hr. Sundermann [C.].
i Yg. (V 187; C. 58).	Mt Duht, Sarawak.	C. Hose, Esq. [C.].
k. Yg. (V. 187, C. 82).	Palawan	A. Everett, Esq. [C]

28. Lachesis anamallensis.

? Trigonocephalus (Cophias) malabaricus, *Jerdon, Journ. As Soc. Beng.* xxii. 1854, p. 523.
? Trigonocephalus (Cophias) wardii, *Jerdon, l. c* p 524
Trimeresurus anamallensis, *Gunth. Rept. Brit. Ind.* p. 387, pl. xxiv. fig. C (1864); *Fayrer, Thanatoph. Ind.* pl xiv (1874); *Theob. Cat. Rept Brit Ind.* p. 220 (1876), *F. Müll. Verh. Nat Ges. Basel*, vii. 1884, p 290; *Bouleng. Faun. Ind, Rept.* p 430 (1890), *Boettg. Ber Offenb Ver. Nat.* 1892, p. 92.

Rostral slightly broader than deep; nasal entire; upper head-scales small, smooth or obtusely keeled, imbricate; supraocular shield rather large, broken up into two or three; internasals in contact or separated by one scale; 7 to 9 scales on a line between the supraoculars; two or three postoculars and a subocular; the latter shield separated from the fourth and succeeding labials by two rows (rarely one) of scales; 9 or 10 upper labials, second forming the anterior border of the loreal pit, third largest; temporal scales obtusely keeled. Scales feebly keeled, in 21 (rarely 19, spec. i) rows. Ventrals 138-158; anal entire; subcaudals 44-58 pairs. Tail prehensile. Green, olive, yellowish, or reddish brown above with more or less well-defined black or reddish-brown spots; usually a series of yellow spots along each side of the belly, and a black temporal band; lower parts pale green, olive or yellow, or brown with yellow spots; tail usually black and yellow.

Total length 730 millim.; tail 110.

Anamallay and Nilgherry hills, S. India.

a-b, c, d, e, f, g. ♂ (V. 158, 148; C. 50, 56), ♀ (V. 150, 145, 149; C. ?, 53, 51), & yg. (V. 143, 149; C. 49, 47)	Anamallays.	Col. Beddome [C.]. (Types)

h–m. ♂ (V 155, 143, 149; C 58, 53, 55) & ♀ (V. 152, 139, C. 47, 52).	Anamallays.	Col. Beddome [C.].
n. Yg. (V. 145, C. 49).	Nilgherries.	Col Beddome [C].
o ♀ (V 138; C. 44).	Wynad.	Col. Beddome [C.].

29. Lachesis trigonocephalus.

Coluber capite-triangulatus, *Lacép. Serp* ii pp 112, 132, pl. v. fig 2 (1789).
Vipera trigonocephala, *Daud. Rept* vi. p. 173 (1803).
Cophias trigonocephalus, *Merr Tent.* p 156 (1820).
—— nigromarginatus, *Kuhl, Beitr* p 90 (1820).
Trigonocephalus nigromarginatus, *Schleg Phys Serp* ii p 541, pl xix figs 14 & 15 (1837).
Megæra trigonocephala, *Gray, Zool. Miscell.* p 49 (1842), *and Cat.* p 12 (1849).
—— olivacea, *Gray, ll. cc.*
Bothrops nigromarginatus, *Dum & Bibr.* vii p 1515 (1854)
Trimeresurus trigonocephalus, *Günth. Rept Brit Ind.* p 390 (1864); *Theob. Cat. Rept. Brit. Ind.* p. 223 (1876); *Bouleng. Faun. Ind.*, *Rept.* p. 431 (1890), *Boettg. Ber Offenb. Ver. Nat.* 1892, p. 93.

Snout very short. Rostral broader than deep, nasal entire or semidivided; upper head-scales smooth, imbricate; internasals large, in contact with each other, sometimes fused to one shield; supraocular large, divided into two; 4 to 6 scales in a transverse series between the supraoculars; two or three small postoculars and a subocular, the latter shield usually separated from the labials by one series of scales; 9 or 10 upper labials, second forming the anterior border of the loreal pit. Scales smooth or faintly keeled, in 17 or 19 rows. Ventrals 145–170, the last notched or divided into two; anal entire; subcaudals 53–67 pairs. Tail prehensile. Green above, uniform or with black markings, which may form wavy dorsal bands; a black temporal streak; upper surface of head with or without a network of black bands; ventrals yellowish, uniform or green at the base, end of tail usually black.

Total length 790 millim.; tail 130.
Ceylon.

a–d ♂ (Sc. 17; V. 153; C. 60) & ♀ (Sc. 19, 17, 17; V 152, 149, 148, C. 53, 58, 59).	Ceylon	R. Templeton, Esq. [P].
e. ♀ (Sc. 19; V. 153; C. 55).	Ceylon.	Capt Gascoigne [P.].
f. Hgr. (Sc. 17; V. 149, C. 54)	Ceylon.	B. H. Barnes, Esq. [P.].
g–h. ♀ (Sc 19, 19; V 146, 150, C. 55, 60).	Ceylon.	Miss Layard [P.]
i–k, l, m. ♀ (Sc. 19, 19, 19; V. 147, 147, 152, C 58, 55, 56) & hgr. (Sc. 17; V. 147; C. 60)	Ceylon.	

n–o. ♂ (Sc. 17; V. 145; C. 59) & yg. (Sc. 19, V. 145; C. 58).	Punduloya, 4000 ft.	E. E. Green, Esq. [P.].
p–q ♂ (Sc. 17; V 157; C. 68) & ♀ (Sc. 19; V. 144; C. 56).	——?	(Types of *M. olivacea*.)
r. Skull.	Ceylon.	Miss Layard [P.].

30. Lachesis macrolepis.

Trimeresurus macrolepis, *Beddome, Madras Quart Journ. Med. Sc.* 1863; *Bouleng. Faun. Ind., Rept.* p 431 (1890), *Boettg. Ber. Offenb Ver. Nat.* 1892, p. 93.
Peltopetor macrolepis, *Gunth. Rept Brit. Ind.* p. 391, pl. xxiii. fig. C (1864); *Theob Cat Rept. Brit. Ind.* p. 225 (1876).

Rostral a little broader than deep; nasal entire or divided; upper head-scales very large, imbricate, smooth; supraoculars very large, separated anteriorly by one scale, posteriorly by three; internasals in contact or separated by one scale, two postoculars and a subocular, the latter in contact with the third and fourth labials; 7 or 8 upper labials, the second forming the anterior border of the loreal pit. Scales very large, keeled, outer much smaller than dorsals, in 13 to 15 rows. Ventrals 134–143; anal entire; subcaudals 48–56 pairs. Tail prehensile. Uniform bright green or olive above; a whitish line along the outer row of scales, pale greenish beneath.

Total length 680 millim.; tail 120.

Anamallay and Pulney hills, S. India.

a, b, c. ♂ (Sc 13, 13; V. 134, 138; C. 53, 56) & yg. (Sc. 15; V. 135; C 52).	Anamallays	Col. Beddome [C.]. (Types.)
d. ♀ (Sc. 15; V. 140; C. 48).	Malabar.	Col. Beddome [C.].

31. Lachesis puniceus.

Cophias punicea, *Boie, Isis,* 1827, p. 561.
Trigonocephalus puniceus, *Schleg. Phys. Serp.* ii. p. 545, pl. xix. figs 10 & 11 (1837), *and Abbild.* p. 118, pl xxxviii. (1844).
Atropos acontia (*non Laur*), *Gray, Zool Miscell.* p. 49 (1842), *and Cat.* p. 13 (1849).
—— puniceus, *Dum. & Bibr* vii. p. 1519 (1854).
Atropophis puniceus, *Peters, Ann Mus. Genova,* iii. 1871, p. 41.
—— borneensis, part., *F. Mull. Verh. Nat. Ges. Basel,* viii. 1887, p. 282.
Trimeresurus puniceus, *Boettg. Ber. Offenb Ver. Nat.* 1892, p. 136.

Snout short, obliquely truncate, with sharp raised angle all round; eye rather small. Rostral as broad as deep or a little deeper than broad; upper head-scales small, juxtaposed or subimbricate, smooth on the snout and vertex; 12 to 14 scales in a transverse series between the supraoculars, which are narrow or broken up into pointed, erect scales; two pairs of internasals; two to four postoculars and one or two suboculars, separated from the labials by two or three series of scales; temporal scales smooth or obtusely keeled; 10 to 12 upper labials, second usually separated from the shield in front of the loreal pit, third largest; first lower labial divided into two, forming a pair of additional chin-shields behind the symphysial. Scales in 21 or 23 rows, dorsals feebly and obtusely keeled. Ventrals 144–176; anal entire, subcaudals 38–57. Tail prehensile. Grey, brown, or red above, with more or less distinct dark spots sometimes confluent to form a wavy dorsal band; a light streak on each side of the head, behind the eye; belly powdered with dark brown, usually with a lateral series of yellowish-white spots; end of tail red or reddish.

Total length 640 millim.; tail 90.

Sumatra, Java, Borneo, Natuna Islands.

a.	Hgr (Sc. 21; V 150, C 38).	Java.	Leyden Museum
b–d	♂ (Sc. 23, 23; V. 172, 176; C. 56, 57) & ♀ (Sc. 23, V. 162; C. 46).	Willis Mts., Kediri, Java, 5000 ft.	Baron v. Huegel [C].
e–f.	♂ (Sc 23; V. 166; C 56) & ♀ (Sc 23, V. 166; C. 43).	Borneo.	Sir H. Low [P.].
g.	Yg. (Sc. 21, V. 162; C. 49).	Great Natuna Id.	C. Hose, Esq [C]
h.	♀ (Sc. 21; V. 150; C. 38)	Pulu Laut, Natuna Ids.	C. Hose, Esq. [C.].

32. Lachesis borneensis.

Atropophis borneensis, *Peters, Ann. Mus Genova*, iii 1871, p. 41.
—— borneensis, part, *F. Mull. Verh. Nat. Ges. Basel*, viii. 1887, p. 283
Bothrops sandakanensis, *v. Lidth de Jeude, Notes Leyd. Mus.* xv. 1893, p 256, fig.

Closely allied to the preceding, but snout more prominent, strongly raised above the nostrils, upper head-scales larger (10 or 11 between the supraoculars), and second upper labial forming the anterior border of the loreal pit. Scales in 19 or 21 rows. Ventrals 152–168; anal entire; subcaudals 43–65.

Total length 770 millim.; tail 105.

Borneo, Sumatra.

a	♀ (Sc 21; V. 162; C. 48).	Pankalan Ampat, Sarawak.	Rajah Brooke [P.].
b–c	♂ (Sc. 21; V 166; C. 53) & ♀ (Sc. 21; V. 161, C. 45).	Baram R., Sarawak.	C. Hose, Esq [P.].
d, e	Hgr (Sc. 21, V. 157; C. 56) & yg (Sc. 19; V. 152, C. 43).	Mt. Dulit, Sarawak.	C. Hose, Esq [C.].
f.	♂ (Sc. 21; V. 168; C. 65).	Paitan, N. Borneo.	A. Everett, Esq. [C.]

33. Lachesis wagleri.

Seba, Thes. ii. pl. lxviii. fig. 4 (1735).
Cophias wagleri, *Boie, Isis,* 1827, p. 561.
Trigonocephalus wagleri, *Schleg. Phys. Serp.* ii. p. 542, pl. xix. figs. 16-18 (1837).
Trimesurus maculatus, *Gray, Zool. Miscell.* p. 48 (1842), *and Cat.* p. 8 (1849); *Motley & Dillwyn, Nat. Hist. Labuan,* p. 43 (1855).
—— subannulatus, *Gray, ll. cc.* pp. 48 & 9; *Motley & Dillwyn, l. c.* p. 44, pl. —.
—— philippensis, *Gray, ll cc.* pp. 48 & 10.
—— sumatranus (*non Raffles*), *Gray, ll cc.* pp. 48 & 10.
Trigonocephalus sumatranus, *Cantor, Cat Mal. Rept.* p. 121, pl. xl. fig. 9 (1847).
Trimesurus formosus (*non Schleg*), *Gray, Cat.* p. 10.
Tropidolæmus hombroni, *Guichen. in Dumont d'Urville, Voy. Pôle Sud, Zool., Rept.* p. 23, pl. ii. fig. 2 (1853); *Dum. & Bibr.* vii. p. 1527 (1854); *Peters, Mon. Berl. Ac.* 1867, p 29
—— wagleri, *Dum. & Bibr. t. c.* p. 1524; *F. Müll. Verh. Nat. Ges. Basel,* vii. 1883, p. 290.
Trigonocephalus hombroni, *Jan, Rev. & Mag Zool.* 1859, p. 155
Tropidolæmus subannulatus, *Peters, Mon. Berl. Ac.* 1861, p. 691.
——, philippinensis, *Peters, l c*
Trimeresurus wagleri, *Gunth. Rept. Brit. Ind.* p. 388 (1864); *Stoliczka, Journ. As Soc. Beng.* xlii. 1873, p. 126; *Blanf. Proc. Zool. Soc.* 1881, p. 224.
—— subannulatus, var. immaculatus, *Peters, Ann. Mus. Genova,* iii 1872, p. 42.
Tropidolæmus subannulatus, var. celebensis, *Peters, Mon. Berl. Ac.* 1872, p. 584
Bothrops wagleri, *F. Müll. Verh. Nat. Ges. Basel,* vii. 1882, p. 155; *v. Lidth de Jeude, Notes Leyd. Mus.* viii. 1886, p. 44.
Tropidolæmus sp., *F. Müll. Verh. Nat. Ges. Basel,* viii. 1887, p. 281.

Head very broad, little longer than broad; snout very short and broad, with more or less distinct canthus; eye very small. Rostral as deep as broad or a little broader than deep; nasal entire; upper head-scales small, strongly imbricate, keeled; supraocular usually narrow or broken up into scales; 7 to 13 scales across between the supraoculars; internasals more or less developed or indistinct; one, two, or three postoculars and a subocular; latter separated from the labials by one or two series of scales, rarely in contact with the third labial; temporal scales keeled; 8 to 10 upper labials, second not entering the loreal pit, third very large, gular scales obtusely keeled. Scales more or less distinctly keeled, in 19 to 27 rows. Ventrals 127-154; anal entire; subcaudals 45-55. Tail prehensile. Green, with darker or lighter markings, black and yellow, or nearly entirely black.

Total length 980 millim.; tail 150.

Malay Peninsula and Archipelago.

A. Green above, with white cross-lines edged behind with blue or purple, or with two dorsal series of small spots or cross-bars of the same colour; a white line on each side of the head, passing through the eye, edged below with blue or purple; belly white or pale green, with or without black edges to the ventrals; end of tail usually red or reddish brown. — (*C. wagleri*, Boie.)

a. Yg. (Sc 25; V. 145; C. 49). Thaiping, Perak. L Wray, Esq [P.].

b Yg. (Sc. 23; V. 142; C.?). Pinang. Dr. Cantor.

c. Hgr. ♂ (Sc. 23; V. 151; C 46). Singapore. Gen. Hardwicke [P.]. (Type of *T. maculatus*.)

d Yg. (Sc. 21; V. 146; C 50). Singapore. Capt. Gascoigne [P].

e. ♀ (Sc. 23; V 137; C. 51). Sumatra. Leyden Museum.

f. Yg. (Sc. 21; V. 146; C. 54). E. Coast of Sumatra. Mrs. Findlay [P.].

g, h, i–k. ♀ (Sc. 25, 25; V. 148, 141, C. 50, 48) & yg. (Sc. 23, 21, V. 154, 145; C. 55, 53). Labuan. L. L. Dillwyn, Esq. [P.].

l. Hgr. ♂ (Sc. 21; V. 146; C 51). Sarawak. Sir J. Brooke [P.].

m, n Yg. (Sc. 21, 21; V 146, 143; C. 51, 50). Sarawak. Sir H. Low [P.].

o. Yg (Sc. 25; V. 141; C 53). Borneo. Gen. Hardwicke [P.].

p. Hgr. ♀ (Sc. 25; V 145, C. 48). Borneo.

q Hgr. ♂ (Sc. 23; V. 143, C. 50). Mt Dulit, Sarawak. C. Hose, Esq. [C.].

r. Yg (Sc. 23; V. 147; C 50). Sandakan, Brit. N. Borneo. Douglas Cator, Esq. [P.].

s. Yg. (Sc. 25; V. 140; C. 52). Sinkawang, Borneo. Dr. Bleeker. (*Tropidolæmus schlegeli*, Blkr)

t. Hgr. ♂ (Sc. 21, V. 152, C. 53). Sirhassen, Natuna Ids. A. Everett, Esq. [C.].

u–v. ♀ (Sc. 25, V. 140; C. 49) & yg (Sc 24; V. 138; C. 49). Palawan. A. Everett, Esq. [C.].

w. Hgr. ♀ (Sc. 23, V. 141; C. 49). Puerta Princesa, Palawan. A Everett, Esq. [C.].

x–y. Hgr. ♀ (Sc 23, 22; V 131, 139, C. 49, 45). Butuan, N. Mindanao. A. Everett, Esq. [C.].

z–β. Yg (Sc 20, 21, 22; V 130, 127, 130; C. 45, 46, 47). Albay, S. E. Luzon. Whitehead Exped.

γ–δ. ♀ (Sc. 25, V. 141; C 47) & yg. (Sc. 23; V. 135, C 47). Philippines. H. Cuming, Esq [C.]. (Types of *T. subannulatus*.)

ε ♀ (Sc. 23, V. 142; C. 47). Celebes. Leyden Mus.

B. Green above, with small black spots or cross-bands; a black streak on each side of the head, passing through the eye; yellow beneath, with or without black edges to the ventrals,

2 o 2

with a series of small black spots on each side; end of tail red. (*T. hombroni*, Guich.)

a. Hgr. ♂ (Sc. 10; V. 134; C. 47).	Philippines.	H Cuming, Esq. [C.]. (Type of *T philippensis*)
b. ♀ (Sc. 25; V. 146; C. 48).	Sangir Ids.	Dr. A. B. Meyer [C.].

C. Yellowish green above, the scales edged with dark bottle-green; dark cross-bands of the latter colour: some specimens dark bottle-green above, with scattered yellowish-green dots; ventrals yellow, edged with dark green, with a series of round dark green spots on each side, or dark green with yellow spots; end of tail dark green or blackish.

a. ♀ (Sc. 25; V. 146; C. 50).	Borneo.	Sir E. Belcher [P.].
b, c. ♀ (Sc. 25, 25; V. 138, 144; C. 47, 49).	Sarawak.	Sir J. Brooke [P.].
d. ♀ (Sc 25; V. 143; C. 51).	Sarawak.	Sir H. Low [P.].
e. ♀ (Sc. 27; V. 148; C. 52).	Rejang R., Sarawak.	Brooke Low, Esq. [P.].
f, g, h. ♀ (Sc. 27, 25, 25, V. 149, 144, 144, C. 49, 48, 51).	Baram R., Sarawak	C. Hose, Esq. [C.].

D. Green above, with the scales black-edged, with bright yellow black-edged cross-bands, or black with yellow cross-bands; head black, spotted with yellow; belly bright yellow or yellow and green, ventrals black-edged; end of tail black.

a. ♀ (Sc. 23; V. 146; C. 50).	Pinang.	Dr. Cantor.
b. ♀ (Sc. 26; V. 145; C. 52).	Pinang.	Capt. Hay [P.].
c. ♀ (Sc. 25; V. 145; C. 53).	Malacca.	D. F A. Hervey, Esq. [P.]
d, e. ♀ (Sc. 26, 25, V. 143, 143; C. 54, 49).	Singapore.	Gen. Hardwicke [P.]
f. ♀ (Sc. 25; V 144; C. 49).	Singapore.	Dr Dennys [P.].
g ♀ (Sc. 25; V. 148; C. 48).	Deli, Sumatra.	Mr. Iversen [C.].
h. Hgr. ♀ (Sc. 25; V. 143; C. 52).	E. Coast of Sumatra.	Mrs. Findlay [P.].
i. Hgr ♀ (Sc. 25; V. 140; C. 55).	Great Natuna Id.	C. Hose, Esq. [C.].
k. ♀ (Sc. 25; V. 144; C. 51).	——?	Zoological Society.

E. A fifth, most remarkable colour-variety has lately been discovered at Minahasa, Celebes, by the Drs Sarasin.—Green above, with large brick-red, black-edged spots; white beneath, with black spots and marblings powdered with brick-red; end of tail red.

34. Lachesis bilineatus.

Cophias bilineatus, *Wied, Beitr. Nat Bras.* i p. 483, *and Abbild.* (1825).
Trigonocephalus bilineatus, *Schleg. Phys. Serp* ii. p. 540, pl. xix. figs 7 & 8 (1837); *Peters, Mon. Berl. Ac.* 1862, p. 673.
Craspedocephalus bilineatus, *Gray, Cat.* p. 7 (1849).
Bothrops bilineatus, *Dum. & Bibr.* vii p. 1514 (1854), *Jan, Icon. Gén.* 47, pl. i figs 2 & 3 (1875).
Trigonocephalus (Bothrops) arboreus, *Cope, Proc. Amer. Philos. Soc.* xi. 1869, p. 157.

Snout rounded, with sharp, somewhat raised canthus. Rostral as deep as broad; nasal divided or semidivided; upper head-scales small, imbricate, keeled, 5 to 8 in a transverse series between the supraocular shields, which are very large; internasal shields large and in contact with each other, followed by a large canthal; two or three postoculars and one or two suboculars, separated from the labials by one series of scales; temporal scales keeled; 7 or 8 upper labials, second forming the anterior border of the loreal pit. Scales strongly keeled, in 27–35 rows. Ventrals 198–218; anal entire, subcaudals 59–71, all or greater part in pairs. Tail prehensile Green above, uniform or speckled with black; a yellow lateral streak or series of spots running along the outer row of scales; belly white; end of tail reddish.

Total length 840 millim.; tail 125.

Brazil, Bolivia, Peru, Ecuador.

a.	♂ (Sc. 29; V. 211, C. 68)	Bahia.	Dr. Wucherer [C.].
b.	♀ (Sc 33; V. 207; C. 59).	Bahia.	Zoological Society.
c.	♀ (Sc. 29; V. 193; C. 65).	Campolican, Bolivia.	
d.	♀ (Sc. 27, V. 205; C. 68).	Moyobamba, Peru.	Mr. A. H. Roff [C.].
e.	Yg (Sc. 27, V. 201; C. 66).	Canelos, Ecuador.	Mr. C. Buckley [C.].
f.	♀ (Sc 27; V. 201; C 62).	W. Ecuador.	Mr. Fraser [C].

35. Lachesis undulatus.

Trigonocephalus (Atropos) undulatus, *Jan, Rev. & Mag. Zool.* 1859, p. 157, *and Prodr.* pl E (1859)
Atropos undulatus, *Jan, Elenco,* p. 127 (1863).
Teleuraspis undulatus, *Garm. N. Am. Rept.* p. 126 (1883).
Ophryacus undulatus, *Cope, Bull. U.S. Nat. Mus.* no. 32, 1887, p 88
Bothrops undulatus, *Gunth. Biol. C.-Am., Rept.* p. 187 (1895).

Snout short, rounded, with well-marked canthus. Rostral once and a half to twice as broad as deep, nasal divided; upper head-scales very small, juxtaposed or subimbricate, 14 to 20 across from eye to eye; no supraocular shield, but a long erect horn-like scute above the eye; internasals small; some of the scales on the canthus rostralis raised, forming a serration; three series of scales between the eye and the labials; loreal pit separated from the labials by small scales; temporal scales keeled; 11 upper labials. Scales in 21 rows, dorsals strongly or very strongly keeled. Ventrals 149-171; anal entire; subcaudals 41-49 pairs. Tail prehensile. Olive or brown above, sometimes speckled with black, with a dorsal series of large rhomboidal dark spots or an undulous or zigzag band; a light, dark-edged streak from the eye to above the angle of the mouth; belly yellowish or brownish, speckled or powdered with blackish; a more or less distinct series of light spots along each side close to the ventrals.

Total length 570 millim.; tail 75.

Mexico.

a. Yg. (V. 149; C. 42).   Orizaba.
b-c. ♀ (V. 166, C. 45)   Omilteme, Guerrero.   Mr H. H. Smith [C.];
   & yg. (V. 163; C. 49).   F. D. Godman, Esq.
                                                [P]
d. ♂ (V. 150; C. 41).   Oaxaca.   M. Sallé [C.].

36. Lachesis lateralis.

Bothriechis lateralis, *Peters, Mon. Berl. Ac.* 1852, p 674
Bothrops lateralis, *F. Mull. Verh Nat. Ges Basel*, vi. 1878, p. 401.

Snout rounded, with moderately marked canthus. Rostral much broader than deep; nasal divided; upper head-scales moderate, imbricate, keeled, largest on the snout and vertex, 7 across between the supraoculars, which are narrow; internasals small, with smaller scales between them; two series of scales between the eye and the labials; temporal scales keeled; 9 upper labials, second forming the anterior border of the loreal pit, fourth and fifth largest. Scales rather strongly keeled, in 21 or 23 rows. Ventrals 171; anal entire; subcaudals 59, single. Tail prehensile. Green above and below, with a yellow line running along the outer row of scales; back with some black-and-yellow short cross-bars.

Total length 485 millim.; tail 75.

Costa Rica.

a. Hgr (Sc 23; V 171;   Costa Rica.   O. Salvin, Esq. [C.].
   C. 59).

37. Lachesis bicolor.

Bothrops bicolor, *Bocourt, Ann. Sc. Nat.* (5) x. 1868, p. 201;
   F. Mull Verh Nat. Ges. Basel, vii. 1882, p 155
—— (Bothriechis) bernouillii, *F. Mull Verh. Nat Ges. Basel*, vi.
   1878, p. 399, pl. iii fig A.
Bothriechis bicolor, *Günth. Biol. C.-Am., Rept.* p. 189 (1895).

Closely allied to *L. lateralis*, but upper head-scales smaller (10 or 11 longitudinal series between the supraoculars), and 10 or 11 upper labials not very unequal in size, the second not entering the loreal pit. Scales in 21 rows. Ventrals 164-167; subcaudals 62-67, single. Uniform green above, yellowish beneath.

Total length 375 millim.; tail 60.
Guatemala

a. Yg. (V 166; C. 67).   S. Augustin, W.   Paris Mus. [E].
                         Guatemala   (One of the types.)

38. Lachesis schlegelii.

Trigonocephalus schlegelii, *Berthold, Abh. Ges. Wiss. Gotting* iii. 1846, p 13, pl. i figs 5 & 6
Lachesis nitidus, *Gunth Proc. Zool Soc* 1859, p 414, pl. xx. fig. C.
Teleuraspis schlegelii, *Cope, Proc. Ac. Philad.* 1859, p. 338, *and Journ. Ac. Philad* (2) viii. 1876, p. 149, pl. xxvii. fig. 2, *R. Blanch. Bull. Soc. Zool. France*, 1889, p. 348.
—— nitida, *Cope, Proc. Ac. Philad.* 1860, p. 345.
Bothrops schlegelii, *Jan, Elenco*, p 127 (1863), *and Icon. Gén.* 47, pl. vi. fig. 2 (1875)
—— (Teleuraspis) nigroadspersus, *Steind. Sitzb. Ak. Wien*, lxii. i. 1870, p. 348, pl. viii
Teleuraspis nigroadspersus, *Garm. N. Am Rept.* p. 126 (1883).
Thanatophis torvus, *Posada-Arango, Bull. Soc. Zool. France*, 1889, p. 345.
Bothriechis schlegelii, *Gunth. Biol. C.-Am., Rept.* p. 189 (1895).

Snout rounded, with sharp canthus. Rostral as deep as broad or broader than deep; nasal entire or semidivided; upper head-scales more or less strongly keeled, rarely smooth on the snout and vertex; a large supraocular shield, separated from the eye by small scales, two or three of which may be enlarged, erect, and horn-like; 5 to 9 longitudinal series of scales between the supraoculars; two or three series of scales between the eye and the labials; temporal scales keeled; 8 or 9 upper labials, second forming the anterior border of the loreal pit, third or fourth largest. Scales more or less strongly keeled, in 19–25 rows. Ventrals 138–162; anal entire; subcaudals 47–62, single. Tail prehensile. Coloration very variable. Green or olive above, speckled or spotted with black, or with pinkish, reddish, or purplish, black-edged spots or cross-bars; a series of yellow spots usually present on each side close to the ventral shields; belly yellow, spotted with green, or green speckled with black and yellow, or variegated yellow, olive, purple, and black; end of tail usually red.

Total length 600 millim.; tail 115.
Central America, Colombia, Ecuador.

a. Hgr. (Sc. 21; V. 159; Guatemala.   F. D. Godman, Esq.
   C. 62).   [P.].
b-d. ♂ (Sc. 21, 23; V. 157, Hacienda Rosa de Dr. E. Rothschuh
   155; C. 57, 56) & ♀   Jericho, Nicaragua [C.].
   (Sc. 23; V. 154; C. 50).
e. Hgr. (Sc. 23; V. 155, Matagalpa, Nicaragua. Dr E. Rothschuh
   C. 60).   [C.].
f-h. Hgr. (Sc. 23; V. 147; Chontalez, Nicaragua. R. A. Rix, Esq. [C.];
   C. 49) & yg (Sc. 25, 25,   W. M Crowfoot,
   V. 151, 150, C. 48, 54).   Esq. [P.].

i, k-l. Hgr (Sc. 23; V. 157; C. 49) & yg. (Sc. 25, 23; V. 145, 148; C. 51, 50).	Costa Rica.	
m. Hgr. (Sc. 21; V. 138; C. 47).	Chiriqui.	J. G. Champion, Esq. [C.]; F. D. Godman, Esq [P.].
n. Hgr. (Sc. 23; V. 151; C. 59).	W. Ecuador.	Mr. Fraser [C.]. (Type of *L. nitidus*.)
o-p. ♀ (Sc. 21; V. 140; C. 58) & hgr. (Sc 23; V. 140; C. 53).	Bologna, Ecuador.	E. Whymper, Esq. [C.].
q, r-s. ♂ (Sc. 19; V. 145, C. ?) & ♀ (Sc. 21, 21; V. 144, 143; C. 62, 62).	Quito.	

39. Lachesis nigroviridis.

Bothriechis nigroviridis, *Peters, Mon. Berl. Ac.* 1859, p. 278, pl. —. fig. 4, *Cope, Journ. Ac. Philad.* (2) viii. 1876, p. 150.
Bothrops nigroviridis, *F Müll Verh Nat. Ges. Basel*, vi. 1878, p. 401.

Snout short, rounded, with sharp canthus. Rostral as broad as deep or a little broader than deep; nasal entire or semidivided; upper head-scales flat and imbricate, largest and smooth on the snout and vertex; 5 to 7 longitudinal series of scales between the supraoculars, which are large and sometimes broken up into two; internasals small, two postoculars and a subocular, separated from the labials by one series of scales; temporal scales obtusely keeled; 9 to 11 upper labials, second only exceptionally forming the anterior border of the loreal pit. Scales rather feebly keeled, in 19 rows. Ventrals 134–146; anal entire; subcaudals 49–54, single. Tail prehensile. Green or olive above, speckled and spotted with black; a black streak on each side of the head, from the canthus rostralis, over the outer border of the supraocular shield, to a little beyond the angle of the mouth; upper surface of head sometimes with black longitudinal streaks; yellowish beneath, some or all of the shields black-edged.

Total length 535 millim.; tail 90.

Costa Rica.

a-c. ♂ (V 142, 134; C. 50, 54) & ♀ (V. 141, C. 50).	Rio Frisio.	Mr. Rogers [C.]; F. D. Godman, Esq. [P]
d-e. ♂ (V. 146; C. 53) & ♀ (V. 146; C. 49).	Irazu.	F. D Godman, Esq. [P.].

40. Lachesis aurifer.

Thamnocenchris aurifer, *Salvin, Proc. Zool. Soc.* 1860, p. 459, pl. xxxii. fig. 1.
Bothriechis aurifer, *Cope, Proc. Ac Philad.* 1871, p. 207.
Bothrops aurifer, *F. Müll. Verh Nat. Ges. Basel*, vi 1878, p. 401.

Snout short and broad, with well-marked canthus. Rostral broader than deep; nasal entire or semidivided; upper head-scales imbricate, large, shield-like and smooth or feebly keeled on the snout and vertex; an enlarged frontal, separated from the large supraocular by a series of two or three smaller shields; internasals small; two postoculars and a subocular, separated from the labials by one series of scales; temporal scales keeled; 9 or 10 upper labials, second forming the anterior border of the loreal pit. Scales rather strongly keeled, in 19 rows. Ventrals 154-158; anal entire; subcaudals 53-61, single. Tail prehensile. Green above, with more or less distinct, scattered yellow spots; a more or less distinct black streak on the temple; greenish yellow beneath.

Total length 825 millim.; tail 145.

Guatemala.

a. ♀ (V. 154; C 53).	Coban, Vera Paz	O. Salvin, Esq. [C]. (Type.)
b ♂ (V. 158; C. 61).	Coban.	O Salvin, Esq. [C].

12. SISTRURUS.

Crotalus, part, *Linn. S N* i. p. 372 (1766); *Schleg. Phys Serp* ii. p. 555 (1837), *Dum. & Bibr. Erp. Gén.* vii. p. 1453 (1854), *Jan, Elenco sist Ofid.* p. 123 (1863).

Crotalophorus (*non Houtt.*), *Gray, Ann Philos.* 1825, p. 205, *and Cat. Sn* p. 17 (1849); *Cope, Proc. U.S. Nat. Mus.* xiv. 1892, p 684

Caudisona (*non Laur.*), *Fitzing. N. Class. Rept.* p 34 (1826); *Wagl. Syst. Amph* p. 176 (1830); *Gray, Zool. Miscell.* p. 51 (1842).

Sistrurus, *Garm. N. Am. Rept.* p. 110 (1883), *and Science*, xix. 1892, p. 290, *Stejneger, Rep. U.S. Nat. Mus. f.* 1893, p. 410 (1895); *W. E. Taylor, Am. Nat.* 1895, p. 283.

Head very distinct from neck, covered above with nine large symmetrical shields; eye moderate or small, with vertical pupil. Body cylindrical; scales keeled, with apical pits; ventrals rounded. Tail short, ending in a segmented, horny, sound-producing apparatus or rattle; subcaudals all or greater part single.

North America East of the Rocky Mountains, Mexico.

Synopsis of the Species.

Rostral as deep as broad or deeper than broad; loreal separating the upper præocular from the posterior nasal; canthus rostralis sharp.	1. *miliarius*, p. 569.
Rostral as deep as broad or deeper than broad; upper præocular in contact with the posterior nasal; canthus rostralis sharp	2. *catenatus*, p. 570.
Rostral broader than deep; loreal separating the upper præocular from the posterior nasal; canthus rostralis obtuse	3. *ravus*, p. 571.

1. Sistrurus miliarius.

Crotalus miliarius, *Linn S. N.* i. p 372 (1766); *Daud Rept.* v. p. 328 (1803), *Say, Amer. Journ. Sc.* i. 1819, p. 263; *Harl Journ. Ac. Philad.* v. 1827, p. 371, *and Med. Phys. Res.* p. 134 (1835)

Schleg. Phys. Serp. ii. p. 560, pl. xx. figs. 17 & 18 (1837); *Holbr. N. Amer. Herp.* ii. p. 73, pl. xv. (1838); *Dum. & Bibr.* vii. p. 1477 (1854); *Baird, Rep. U.S. Explor. Surv. R. R.* x., *Rept.* pl. xxiv. fig. 7 (1859), *Garm. N. Am. Rept* p 119 (1883).

Crotalophorus miliarius, *Gray, Ann Philos* 1825, p 205; *Holbr N. Am. Herp.* 2nd ed iii. p. 25, pl. iv. (1842); *Baird & Gir. Cat.* *N Am Rept.* p. 11 (1853), *Cope, Proc. U.S. Nat. Mus.* xiv. 1892, p. 685.

Caudisona miliaria, *Fitzing. N Class. Rept.* p 63 (1826).

Crotalophorus miliarius, part., *Gray, Cat.* p 17 (1849).

Sistrurus miliarius, *Garm. l. c.* p. 177; *Stejneger, Rep. U.S. Nat Mus. f.* 1893, p. 418, pl. vii (1895).

Snout with sharp canthus. Rostral as deep as broad or a little deeper than broad; frontal as long as its distance from the end of the snout, shorter than the parietals; upper præocular separated from the posterior nasal by a loreal; eye separated from the labials by one or two series of scales; temporal scales keeled; 9 to 11 upper labials. Scales strongly keeled, in 21 or 23 rows. Ventrals 127–139; anal entire; subcaudals 27–36; rattle short, 10 being the highest number of segments on record. Greyish, yellowish, or brown above, the vertebral line often orange; one or two dorsal series of large dark, black-edged spots, or a series of narrow crossbars, and one or two lateral series of smaller spots; two undulating dark stripes from between the eyes to the occiput, the space between them usually orange; a dark temporal streak with a light streak below it extending from below the centre of the eye to the angle of the mouth; whitish beneath, speckled and spotted with dark brown or black.

Total length 520 millim.; tail 70.

South-eastern North America, from North Carolina to Texas.

a. ♂ (Sc. 23; V. 137; C. 36).	Orlando, Florida.	
b. Hgr. ♀ (Sc. 23; V. 138; C. 30)	Louisiana.	Smithsonian Institution.
c. Hgr. ♂ (Sc. 21; V. 127, C. 34).	Louisiana.	M. Sallé [C.].
d. ♀ (Sc 23; V. 132; C 33).	Texas.	
e, f. ♂ (Sc. 23; V. 139; C. 35) & ♀ (Sc 23; V. 134; C. 30).	N. America.	Dr. R. Harlan [P.].
g. Yg. (Sc. 23, V. 139, C. 33).	N America.	Lord Orkney [P.].
h. ♂ (Sc. 23, V. 135, C. 32).	N. America.	College of Surgeons
i. ♂ (Sc. 21; V. 127; C. 36)	N. America.	

2. Sistrurus catenatus.

Crotalinus catenatus, *Rafin. Amer. Monthly Mag.* iv. 1818, p. 41 *.

Crotalus tergeminus, *Say, in Long's Exped. Rocky M.* i p. 499 (1823), *Harl. Proc. Ac. Philad.* v. 1827, p 372, and *Med. Phys. Res* p. 135 (1835); *Dum. & Bibr.* vii. p. 1479, pl lxxxiv. b. fig. 5 (1854)

—— messasaugus, *Kirtland, in Mather's Sec. Rep. Geol. Surv. Ohio,* p. 100 (1838).

---

* I have not been able to refer to this paper.

Crotalophorus tergeminus, *Holbr. N. Am. Herp.* 2nd ed. iii. p. 29, pl. v. (1842); *Gray, Cat.* p 18 (1849); *Agassiz, Lake Superior*, p. 381, pl. vi. figs. 6–8 (1850); *Baird & Gir. Cat. N. Am. Rept.* p 14 (1853); *Wied, N. Acta Ac. Leop.-Carol.* xxxii. i. 1865, no. 8, p. 74
—— kirtlandii, *Holbr. t. c.* p. 31, pl vi.; *Gray, l. c.*; *Baird & Gir. l. c.* p. 16.
—— miliarius, part, *Gray, l. c.* p 17.
—— consors, *Baird & Gir. l c.* p. 12, *and Rep U.S. Explor. Surv. R. R.* x, *Rept.* pl. xxiv. fig. 8 (1859).
—— edwardsii, *Baird & Gir ll. cc.* p. 15, pl. xxv. fig. 10, *and Rep. U.S. Mex. Bound. Surv*, ii *Rept.* p. 15, pl. v. fig 1 (1859), *Dugès, Naturaleza*, iv. 1877, p. 27.
—— massasauga, *Baird, Serp. N. York*, p. 12 (1854).
Crotalus miliarius, vars edwardsii and tergeminus, *Jan, Elenco*, p. 124 (1863), *and Icon Gén* 46, pl iii. figs. 4 & 6 (1874).
Caudisona edwardsii, *Cope, Check-list N. Am. Rept.* p. 34 (1875).
—— tergemina, *Cope, l. c.*
Crotalus catenatus, *Garm N. Am Rept.* p. 118, pl ix. fig. 2 (1883).
Sistrurus catenatus, *Garm. l. c.* p. 176, *Hay, Batr. & Rept. Ind.* p. 126 (1892); *Stejneger, Rep U.S. Nat. Mus. f.* 1893, p. 411, pl. v. (1895).
Crotalophorus catenatus, *Cope, Proc. U.S. Nat. Mus.* xiv. 1892, p. 685.

Distinguished from the preceding in having the upper præocular in contact with the posterior nasal above the loreal, which is very small; two or three series of scales between the eye and the labials; temporal scales smooth; 11 to 14 upper labials. Scales in 23 or 25 rows. Ventrals 136–153; subcaudals 20–31. A dark spot on the parietal shields, between the two occipito-nuchal stripes: a light streak from the loreal pit to the angle of the mouth; dorsal spots usually larger than in *S. miliarius*, transversely elliptic or reniform.
Total length 680 millim.; tail 80.

Great Lakes district; United States East of the Rocky Mountains and West of the Mississippi; Northern Mexico.

a ♀ (Sc 25; V. 143; C 22). Canada. J Cruickshank, Esq [P].
b. ♂ (Sc. 25; V 139; C. 28). Illinois. Smithsonian Instit.
c. ♀ (Sc. 25; V. 148; C. 22). N. America.
d. ♂ (Sc. 25; V. 146, C. 31). ——?

3. Sistrurus ravus.

Crotalus ravus, *Cope, Proc. Ac. Philad.* 1865, p. 191.
Caudisona rava, *Cope, Check-list N. Am. Rept.* p. 31 (1875).
Crotalus miliarius, var. ravus, *Garm N. Am. Rept.* p. 120 (1883)
Crotalophorus ravus, *Cope, Proc Amer. Philos Soc* xxii. 1885, p. 382, *and Proc. U.S. Nat. Mus.* xiv. 1892, p. 684.

Canthus rostralis rounded. Rostral broader than deep, recurved above; temporal scales smooth; 11 or 12 upper labials. Scales in 21 or 23 rows, the keels on the median dorsal scales thick. Ventrals 147; subcaudals 26. Yellowish brown, with a dorsal series of deep brown spots, longer than broad, and a series of transverse dark bars on each side opposite to the dorsal spots; head without markings; a brown nuchal spot, forked in front; belly yellowish, thickly variegated with blackish brown.

Total length 200 millim.; tail 22.

Vera Cruz, Mexico.

13. CROTALUS.

Crotalus, part, *Linn. S. N* i. p. 372 (1766); *Schleg Phys. Serp.* ii. p. 555 (1837), *Dum. & Bibr. Erp. Gén.* vii. p. 1453 (1854); *Jan, Elenco sist. Ofid.* p. 123 (1863).
Caudisona, *Laur. Syn. Rept.* p. 92 (1768).
Crotalinus, *Rafin. Amer Monthly Mag* iii 1818, p. 416.
Crotalus, *Gray, Ann. Philos.* 1825, p. 205, *Fitzing. N. Class. Rept.* p. 34 (1826), *Wagl. Syst Amph* p. 176 (1830); *Gray, Zool. Miscell.* p. 51 (1842), *and Cat Sn* p. 19 (1849); *Cope, Proc U.S. Nat. Mus.* xiv. 1892, p. 686, *Stejneger, Rep. U.S. Nat. Mus. f.* 1893, p. 421 (1895).
Uropsophus, *Wagl. l. c.*, *Gray, ll. cc.* pp. 51, 18.
Aploaspis, *Cope, Proc. Ac. Philad.* 1866, p. 310.
Æchmophrys, *Coues, Wheeler's Surv. W. 100th Merid.* v. p. 609 (1875).

Head very distinct from neck, covered above with scales or small shields; eye moderate or small, with vertical pupil. Body cylindrical; scales keeled, with apical pits, ventrals rounded. Tail short, ending in a segmented, horny, sound-producing apparatus or rattle; subcaudals all or greater part single.

America, from Southern Canada and British Columbia to Southern Brazil and Northern Argentina.

Synopsis of the Species.

I. Supraocular shield not produced into a horn-like process.

   A. Eye separated from the labials by three to five rows of scales.

      1. Rostral as deep as broad or deeper than broad, in contact with the nasal.

         a. Upper surface of snout covered with one pair of internasals and one pair of præfrontals (with occasionally one or two small scales between them); scales in 23–31 rows; ventrals 160–199. .... 1. *terrificus*, p. 573.

         b. Upper surface of snout with several small shields or scales; scales in 23–29 rows; ventrals 165–197.

            α. Supraocular shields transversely striated, as broad as or slightly narrower than the space between them.

Two or three series of small shields between the supraoculars, which are in contact with four or five shields in addition to the præ- and postoculars .... 2. *scutulatus*, p. 575.

Three to ten series of scales between the supraoculars, which are in contact with six to eleven scales in addition to the præ- and postoculars .... 3. *confluentus*, p. 576.

    β. Supraocular shields smooth, much narrower than the space between them.

Two pairs of internasals; rostral deeper than broad .... 4. *durissus*, p. 578.
One pair of internasals; rostral as deep as broad .... 5. *horridus*, p. 578.

    2. Rostral broader than deep, in contact with the nasal; scales in 23 or 25 rows; ventrals 166-181.
                                                 6. *tigris*, p. 580.

    3. Rostral broader than deep, separated from the nasal by scales; scales in 25 rows; ventrals 178-198.
                                                7. *mitchelli*, p. 580.

B. Eye separated from the labials by one or two rows of scales.

    1. Upper præocular normal, separated from the nasal by a loreal; rostral as deep as broad.

Two internasals; scales in 21-25 rows; ventrals 142-184 .... 8. *triseriatus*, p. 581.
Four internasals; scales in 27-30 rows; ventrals 123-151 .... 9. *polystictus*, p. 582.

    2. Upper præocular divided into two by a vertical suture; rostral broader than deep; scales in 21-23 rows; ventrals 153-169 .... 10 *lepidus*, p. 582.

II. Supraocular produced into a horn-like process. scales in 21 or 23 rows; ventrals 146 .... 11. *cerastes*, p. 583.

1 Crotalus terrificus.

    Seba, Thes. ii pl. xcv figs 1 & 2, & pl xcvi. fig. 1 (1735).
    ? Crotalus dryinas, *Linn S N.* i p 372 (1766).
    Caudisona terrifica, *Laur. Syn Rept.* p. 93 (1768); *Cope, Proc. Ac. Philad.* 1866, p. 308.
    ? Caudisona dryinas, *Laur. l. c.* p. 94.
    Caudisona orientalis, *Laur. l c.*
    Crotalus boiquira, part, *Lacép Serp.* ii. pp. 130, 190 (1789).
    —— durissus, var., *Shaw, Zool.* iii pl. xc. (1802)
    —— horridus (*non L*), *Latr Rept* iii. p 186 (1802); *Daud. Rept.* v p 311, pl lxix fig. 1 (1803); *Harl. Proc. Ac. Philad* v. 1827, p 370; *Wied, Abbild. Nat Bras.* (1827); *Schleg. Phys. Serp.* ii. p. 561, pl. xx. figs. 12-14 (1837), *Dum & Bibr* vii. p 1472, pl. lxxxiv. *b* fig 2 (1854), *Hensel, Arch. f. Nat.* 1868, p. 338, *Jan, Icon. Gén* 46, pl iii. figs 1 & 2 (1874); *Peracca, Boll. Mus. Torino*, x. no. 195, 1895, p. 22.
    —— cascavella, *Wagl in Spix, Serp. Bras.* p. 61, pl. xxiv. (1824).

Crotalus horridus, part., *Gray, Cat.* p. 20 (1849).
—— molossus, *Baird & Gir. Cat N. Am. Rept.* p. 10 (1853), *and Rep. U.S Mex. Bound. Surv*, ii. *Rept* pl. ii. (1859); *Garm. Bull. Essex Instit.* xix. 1883, p. 123; *Cope, Proc. U.S. Nat. Mus* xiv. 1892, p. 688; *Stejneger, Rep. U.S. Nat. Mus. f.* 1893, p. 424 (1895).
—— ornatus, *Hallow. Proc. Ac. Philad.* 1854, p. 192, *and Rep. U.S. Surv. R. R.* x., *Parke's Rep.* p. 23, pl. ii. (1859).
—— durissus (*non* L.), *Cope, Proc. Ac. Philad* 1850, p. 337; *Garm. N. Am. Rept.* p. 111 (1883); *Cope, Proc. US. Nat. Mus.* xiv. 1892, p. 688
Caudisona basilisca, *Cope, Proc. Ac. Philad.* 1864, p. 166, and 1866, p. 308.
—— durissa, *Cope, Proc. Ac. Philad.* 1866, p. 308.
—— molossus, *Cope, l. c.*
Crotalus rhombifer (*non Latr.*), *Dugès, Naturaleza,* iv. 1877, p. 22.
—— basiliscus, *Cope, Proc. Amer. Philos. Soc.* xxii. 1885, p. 180; *Dugès, Naturaleza,* (2) i. 1888, p. 133; *Cope, Proc. U.S. Nat. Mus.* xiv. 1892, p. 688.
—— terrificus, *Cope, Proc. US. Nat Mus.* xiv. 1892, p 688.
—— horridus, var. unicolor, *v. Lidth de Jeude, Notes Leyd. Mus.* ix. 1887, p. 133.

Snout very short, with obtuse canthus. Rostral as deep as broad or a little deeper than broad, in contact with the anterior nasal; upper surface of snout covered by a pair of internasals and a pair of præfrontals, rarely with one or two small shields between them; scales between the supraoculars often more or less enlarged or shield-like, in two to five longitudinal series; three or four series of scales between the eye and the upper labials; latter, 12 to 17. Scales in 23 to 31 rows, dorsals very strongly keeled. Ventrals 160–199; anal entire; subcaudals 18–30. Brown above, with a series of darker, light-edged rhombs, often lighter in the centre, in contact with one another or narrowly separated, or with decussating yellow lines; occiput and neck with or without two more or less distinct dark parallel stripes; a dark streak from the eye to the angle of the mouth, and often another from the loreal pit to below the eye or beyond; the markings sometimes indistinct; yellowish white beneath, uniform or spotted with brown; tail usually brown or blackish.

Total length 1320 millim.; tail 130.

Arizona, New Mexico, and Texas to Southern Brazil and Northern Argentina.

A. Stripes on the neck absent or ill-defined.

a–b. Hgr. (Sc. 27, 27; V 188, 191, C. 24, 30).	Presidio, W. Mexico.	Hr. A. Forrer [C.].; F. D Godman, Esq [P.].
c, d. ♂ (Sc. 27, 23, V. 173, 170; C. 24, 26).	City of Mexico.	Mr. Doorman [C.].
e. Hgr. (Sc. 29; V. 182; C. 27).	Mezquital del Oro, Zacatecas.	Dr A. C. Buller [C.].
f–h. ♂ (Sc. 25; V. 170; C. 24) & hgr (Sc. 25, 25; V. 173, 174; C. 18, 18).	S. Mexico.	F. D. Godman, Esq. [P.]

13. CROTALUS. 575

i. ♂ (Sc. 27; V. 170;   Mexico.   M. Sallé [C].
   C. 27).
k. ♀ (Sc. 29; V. 181;   Venezuela.
   C. 22).

         B. Stripes on the neck well-marked.

a–d. ♀ (Sc. 29; V.   Omilteme, Guerrero.   F. D. Godman, Esq.
   182; C. 23) & yg   [P.].
   (Sc 29, 27, 29; V.
   180, 183, 170; C. 30,
   22, 29).
e. Yg. (Sc. 27; V.   Yucatan.
   187; C. 23).
f. ♂ (Sc. 31; V. 181;   S Mexico.   F. D Godman, Esq.
   C. 28).   Esq. [P.].
g. Hgr. (Sc. 29, V.   Mexico.
   172; C. 23)
h–i. Yg. (Sc. 31; V.   Berbice.
   176, C. 23) & head
   of adult.
k. ♂ (Sc. 30; V. 185;   Pernambuco.   W. A. Forbes, Esq.
   C 25).   [P.].
l Yg (Sc. 27; V.171;   S. José dos Campos,   Mr. A. Thomson [P.].
   C. 21)   Prov. S. Paulo.
m. Yg (Sc 27; V.175;   Brazil.
   C. 29).
n. Hgr. (Sc. 29; V.   Asuncion, Paraguay.   Dr. J. Bohls [C.].
   178, C. 30).
o. Yg. (Sc 27; V 187;   Campolican, Bolivia.
   C. 22).
p. Skeleton.   ———?   Zoological Society.

2. Crotalus scutulatus.

Caudisona scutulata, *Kennicott, Proc. Ac. Philad.* 1861, p. 207;
   Cope, Proc. Ac. Philad 1866, p. 309
Crotalus adamanteus scutulatus, *Cope, Check-list N. Am Rept.*
   p. 33 (1875), *Garm. N. Am. Rept.* p. 113 (1883): *Cope, Proc.*
   Amer Philos Soc. xxiii. 1886, p. 287, *and Proc. U.S. Nat. Mus*
   xiv. 1892, p 689.
—— scutulatus, *Cope, Proc. Ac. Philad.* 1883, p. 11.
—— atrox, var., *Stejneger, Rep. U S. Nat. Mus. f.* 1893, p. 438
   (1895)
—— salvini, *Günth. Biol. C.-Am, Rept.* p. 193, pl. lix fig. A
   (1895).

Canthus rostralis distinct. Rostral as deep as broad, in contact with the anterior nasal, upper surface of head with small shields; two pairs of internasals and two pairs of præfrontals; two or three series of shields between the supraoculars; supraoculars transversely striated, not broader than their distance from each other, in contact with four or five shields in addition to the præ- and postoculars, three or four series of scales between the eye and the labials; 13 to 16 upper labials. Scales in 25 or 27 rows, dorsals striated and strongly keeled. Ventrals 167–170, anal entire; subcaudals 18–20.

Yellowish or greyish brown above, with a series of large dark brown light-edged rhombs; a yellowish streak from the canthus rostralis along the supraciliary border to the middle of the temple: an oblique dark streak below the eye; uniform yellowish white beneath.

Total length 760 millim.; tail 65.

Arizona, New Mexico, Texas, North Mexico.

a. Yg (Sc. 27; V. 167, C. 18). Duval Co., Texas. W. Taylor, Esq. [P.].

b. ♀ (Sc. 25; V. 170; O. 20). Huamantla, Mexico, 8000 ft. T. M. Rymer Jones, Esq. [P.]. (Type of *C. salvini*.)

3. Crotalus confluentus.

? Crotalinus viridis, *Rafin. Am. Monthly Mag* iv. 1818, p. 41 *.
Crotalus confluentus, *Say, in Long's Exped. Rocky Mount.* ii. p. 48 (1823); *Baird & Gir. Cat N Am. Rept.* p. 8 (1853), and in *Marcy's Explor. Red Riv.* p. 217, pl. i. (1853); *Dum & Bibr.* vii. p. 1475, pl. lxxxiv. *b*. fig 4 (1854); *Baird, Rep. U S Expl Surv. R. R* x, *Rept* p 40 (1859); *Cope, Proc Ac Philad* 1859, p 337; *Garm. N. Am. Rept.* p. 114 (1883); *Stejneger, N. Am. Faun.* no. 5, p. 111 (1891); *Cope, Proc. U.S. Nat Mus.* xiv. 1892, p. 691; *Stejneger, Rep U.S. Nat. Mus* f. 1893, p 440 (1895).
—— oregonus, *Holbr N. Am. Herp.*, 2nd ed. iii. p. 21, pl. iii. (1842); *Garm N Am. Rept.* p. 173.
—— lucifer, *Baird & Gir. Proc Ac. Philad.* 1852, p. 177, and *Cat.* p. 6, *Girard, U S Explor. Exped, Herp.* p 187, pl. xv. figs. 1-6 (1858); *Baird, Rep. U.S. Expl. Surv R. R* x., *Williamson's Rep.* p 10, pl. xi. (1859); *Cope, Proc. Ac. Philad.* 1859, p 337; *Lord, Natur. Vanc Isl* ii. p 303 (1866); *Garm l c* p 114; *Stejneger, N. Am. Faun.* no 5, p. 111, and *Rep. U.S. Nat. Mus* f. 1893, p. 445.
—— lecontei, *Hallow. Proc. Ac. Philad.* 1852, p. 180, and *Rep. U.S. Surv. R. R* x., *Williamson's Rep.* p. 18, pl iii. (1859).
—— atrox, *Baird & Gir. Cat.* pp. 5 & 156; *Baird, Rep. U S. Mer. Bound Surv*, ii. *Rept.* p. 14, pl. i. (1859); *Stejneger, Rep. U.S. Nat. Mus.f.* 1893, p. 436.
—— adamanteus, var. atrox, *Jan, Rev. & Mag. Zool.* 1859, p. 153, and *Icon. Gén.* 46, pl. ii. fig. 1 (1874); *Garm. l. c.* p. 113; *Cope, Proc. U S Nat. Mus.* xiv. 1892, p. 690.
—— adamanteus, var confluentus, *Jan, Rev. & Mag. Zool* 1859, p. 153
Caudisona atrox, var. sonorensis, *Kennicott, Proc. Ac. Philad.* 1861, p 206
Crotalus durissus (non L.), *Wied, N. Acta Ac. Leop.-Carol.* xxxii. i. 1865, no. 8, p 65
Caudisona confluenta, *Cope, Proc. Ac. Philad* 1866, p. 309.
—— lucifer, *Cope, l. c.*
—— atrox, *Cope, l. c.*
Crotalus confluentus pulverulentus, *Cope, Proc. Ac Philad.* 1883, p. 11, and *Proc. U.S. Nat. Mus.* xiv. 1892, p. 691.
—— exsul, *Garm. l. c.* p. 114.
—— adamenteus ruber, *Cope, Proc. U.S. Nat. Mus.* xiv. 1892, p. 690.

---

* I have not been able to refer to this work.

Snout with obtuse canthus. Rostral as deep as broad or a little deeper than broad, in contact with the anterior nasal; upper head-scales small, striated; supraoculars transversely striated, as broad as or slightly narrower than the space between them, which is filled by 3 to 10 longitudinal series of scales; each supraocular in contact with 6 to 11 scales in addition to the præ- and postoculars; three or four series of scales between the eye and the labials; 13 to 18 upper labials. Scales striated and strongly keeled, in 25 to 29 rows. Ventrals 168–197; anal entire; subcaudals 17–34. Yellowish, greyish, or pale brown above, with a dorsal series of large brown or red spots, usually edged with darker and lighter and commonly rhomboidal or transversely elliptic in shape; a light streak or triangular marking across the supraocular shield; a more or less distinct dark, light-edged streak from the eye to the mouth; yellowish beneath, uniform or spotted with brown.

This species may be divided into two principal varieties, which are not definable by any structural characters that I know of, viz.:—the typical form, with a dark temporal band extending to the commissure of the mouth; and the Texan *C. atrox*, in which a dark band descends obliquely from the eye to the mouth far in advance of the commissure.

Total length 1520 millim.; tail 140.

Western North America, from British Columbia to South California, eastwards to Assiniboia, Dakota, Nebraska, Kansas, and Western and Southern Texas; Northern Mexico.

a. ♀ (Sc. 25; V. 183; C. 20).		Duval Co., Texas.	W. Taylor, Esq [P.].
b. Ad., skin (Sc. 27; V. 185; C. 25).		Texas.	Smithsonian Instit.
c. ♀ (Sc 27; V. 187; C. 21).		Nebraska.	Smithsonian Instit.
d, e, f ♂ (Sc 25; V 175; C. 23) & ♀ (Sc. 25, 25, V. 183, 175; C. 17, 17)		Brit. Columbia.	J. K. Lord, Esq. [P.].
g. ♂ (Sc. 25; V. 173, C. 22).		Coronado Ids., off San Diego, California.	Prof Eigenmann [E.].
h. ♀ (Sc. 25; V. 181; C. 20).		California.	Christiania Mus.
i. Hgr (Sc. 25; V. 176; C 18).		California.	Lord Walsingham [P.]
k. ♂ (Sc. 27, V. 174; C. 26).		California.	Haslar Collection.
l, m. ♂ (Sc. 25; V. 168; C. 20) & ♀ (Sc. 25; V.?; C. 17)		W. Coast of N. America.	Sir E. Belcher [P.].
n-o. ♀ (Sc 27; V. 190, C. 22) & yg. (Sc. 27; V.172; C.25).		N. America.	
p. ♀ (Sc 25; V. 182; C. 24).		——?	Zoological Society.

4. Crotalus durissus.

Linn. Amœn. Acad. i. p. 500 (1749).
Crotalus durissus, *Linn. S. N.* i. p. 372 (1766); *Shaw, Zool.* iii. p. 333, pl. lxxxix. (1802).
—— adamanteus, *Pal. de Beauv. Trans. Amer. Philos. Soc.* iv. 1799, p. 368, pl. —; *Say, Amer. Journ. Sc.* i. 1819, p 263; *Holbr. N. Am. Herp.* ii. p. 77, pl. xvi (1838), and 2nd ed. iii. p. 17, pl. ii. (1842), *Baird & Gir. Cat. N. Am. Rept.* p. 3 (1853), and *Rep. U.S. Surv. R. R.*, x. *Rept.* pl xxiv. fig. 2 (1859), *Jan, Icon. Gén.* 46, pl. ii. fig. 2 (1874); *Garm N Am. Rept.* p. 112 (1883); *Cope, Proc. U.S Nat. Mus.* xiv. 1892, p. 689; *Stejneger, Rep. U.S Nat. Mus f.* 1893, p. 433, pl. x. (1895).
—— rhombifer, *Latr. Rept.* iii. p. 197 (1802); *Daud. Rept.* v. p. 323, pl lx. figs. 22 & 23, & pl. lxix. fig. 2 (1803); *Dum. & Bibr* vii. p. 1470, pl. lxxxiv. b. fig. 3 (1854).
—— horridus, part., *Harl. Med. Phys. Res.* p. 133 (1835).
—— terrificus (non Laur.), *Leconte, Proc. Ac. Philad.* 1853, p. 419; *Cope, Proc. Ac. Philad.* 1859, p. 337.
Caudisona adamantea, *Cope, Proc Ac. Philad.* 1866, p. 309.

Canthus rostralis obtuse. Rostral deeper than broad, in contact with the anterior nasal; upper surface of snout covered with scales or small irregular shields; 7 or 8 longitudinal series of scales between the supraoculars, the width of which is much less than the interspace between them; three or four series of scales between the eye and the labials; 13 to 16 upper labials. Scales in 25–29 rows, dorsals strongly keeled. Ventrals 169–181; anal entire; subcaudals 24–32. Pale greyish or brownish above, with a dorsal series of large blackish rhombs, usually with lighter centres, edged with yellowish; snout blackish, with a yellowish cross-line between the eyes, yellowish margins to the rostral shields, and a yellowish vertical streak between the rostral and the nostril, on the anterior nasal and first upper labial; a broad blackish band, edged with yellowish above and beneath, extends from the supraocular, over the eye, to the four or five last upper labials; end of tail usually black; yellowish beneath, more or less spotted with brown or black.

The largest species of the genus, reaching a length of 8 feet.

South-eastern United States from North Carolina to the Florida Keys and the Mississippi River.

a. Yg. (Sc. 29; V. 181; C. 24). Orlando, Florida.
b. Yg. (Sc. 29; V 171; C. 30). United States. Smithsonian Institution.
c. Skull. N. America.

5. Crotalus horridus.

Catesby, Nat. Hist. Carol. i. pl. xli. (1743).
Crotalus horridus, *Linn. Mus. Ad. Frid.* p 39 (1754), and *S. N.* i. p. 372 (1766); *Leconte, Proc. Ac. Philad.* 1853, p. 417; *Cope, Proc. Ac. Philad.* 1859, p. 338; *Garm. N. Am. Rept.* p. 115,

13. CROTALUS.

pl. ix. fig. 1 (1883); *Cope, Proc. U S Nat Mus* xiv 1892, p 693; *Hay, Batr. Rept Ind* p. 128 (1893); *Steyneger, Rep U.S. Nat. Mus. f.* 1893, p 426, pl. ix (1895)

Crotalophorus horridus, *Houtt. Linn Nat. Hist* vi. p. 309 (1764).
Caudisona durissus (*non L.*), *Laur. Syn. Rept* p. 93 (1768).
Crotalus boiquira, part., *Lacép. Serp.* ii. pp. 130, 190, pl. xviii. fig. 1 (1789).
—— boiquira, *Pal. de Beauv Trans. Amer. Philos. Soc.* iv. 1799, p 368, pl —
—— durissus, *Latr. Rept.* iii. p. 190 (1802); *Daud. Rept.* v. p. 304, pl. lxviii. (1803), *Hari l Proc. Ac. Philad.* v. 1827, p. 368, *and Med. Phys Res* p. 132 (1835); *Schleg. Phys. Serp* ii. p. 565, pl xx. figs 15 & 16 (1837), *Storer, Rep Rept Massach.* p. 233 (1839); *Holbr N. Am. Herp* ii. p 81, pl xvii. (1838), *and 2nd ed* iii. p 9, pl. i. (1842); *De Kay, N. York Faun.* iii. p. 55, pl. ix. fig 19 (1842), *Baird & Gir. Cat. N. Am. Rept.* p. 1 (1853); *Baird, Serp N. York.* p. 9, pl. i fig. 1 (1854), *Dum & Bibr.* vii p 1465, pl. lxxxiv. *b.* fig. 1 (1854), *Jan, Icon Gén* 46, pl i. (1874).
—— atricaudatus, *Latr. t. c.* p. 209; *Daud. t. c.* p 316.
Crotalinus cyanurus, *Rafin. Amer. Monthly Mag.* iii. 1818, p. 446 *.
Caudisona horrida, *Flem. Philos Zool* ii p. 294 (1822); *Cope, Proc Ac Philad.* 1866, p 309
Uropsophus durissus, *Gray, Cat.* p. 19 (1849).
Crotalus horridus, part , *Gray, l. c.* p. 20.

Snout with obtuse canthus Rostral as deep as broad, in contact with the anterior nasals and a pair of rather large internasals; a large shield between the internasal and supraocular; middle of snout with scales or small shields; supraoculars considerably narrower than the space between them, which is covered by 3 to 8 longitudinal series of small scales; three or four series of scales between the eye and the labials; 12 to 16 upper labials. Scales in 23–29 rows, dorsals very strongly keeled. Ventrals 165–178; anal entire; subcaudals 19–29. Greyish brown above, usually with a rusty vertebral stripe and V- or M-shaped blackish crossbands; head uniform above, with a more or less distinct dark band from the eye to the angle of the mouth; usually a pair of roundish or triangular dark spots on the nape; neck with elongate spots or interrupted stripes; yellowish beneath, uniform or speckled or spotted with blackish; end of tail blackish.

Total length 1340 millim., tail 135.

United States, from Massachusetts and Iowa to Northern Florida and Texas.

a. ♂ (Sc 25; V 178; C 29)   New Orleans
b. Yg. (Sc. 25, V. 170; C. 24).   Texas.
c. Yg (Sc. 25; V. 177; C. 21).   Arkansas.
d. ♀ (Sc. 29, V. 176; C. 24)   N America.   Sir H. Sloane [P.].

---

* I have not been able to verify this reference.

e. ♂ (Sc. 23; V. 167; C. 24).		N. America.	College of Surgeons.
f. ♂ (Sc. 25; V. 173, C. 28).		N. America.	
g. Skull.		N. America.	

6. Crotalus tigris.

Crotalus tigris, *Kennicott, Rep. U.S. Mex. Bound. Surv.* ii., Rept. p 14, pl. iv (1859); *Garm. N. Am. Rept.* p. 117 (1883); *Cope, Proc. U.S. Nat. Mus.* xiv. 1892, p 689, *Stejneger, N. Am Faun.* no. 7, p. 214 (1893), *and Rep. U.S. Nat. Mus. f.* 1893, p. 449 (1895).

Caudisona enyo, *Cope, Proc. Ac. Philad.* 1861, p. 293, and 1866, p. 309.

—— tigris, *Cope, Proc. Ac. Philad.* 1866, p. 309.

Crotalus enyo, *Cope, Check-list N. Am. Rept.* p 33 (1875), *and Proc. U S. Nat. Mus* xiv. 1892, p. 689.

—— oregonus, var. enyo, *Garm. l. c.* p. 174

Snout with distinct canthus. Rostral broader than deep, in contact with the anterior nasal and a pair of internasals; a large shield on each side between the internasal and the supraocular; middle of snout covered with small smooth or obtusely keeled scales; supraoculars narrower than the space between them, which is occupied by six longitudinal rows of keeled scales; three series of scales between the eye and the labials; 13 to 15 upper labials. Scales in 23 or 25 rows, dorsals strongly keeled. Ventrals 166-181; anal entire, subcaudals 26-46. Yellowish or pale brown above, with a dorsal series of brown, dark-edged spots, widening to cross-bands posteriorly; sides with smaller dark spots; head with small dark spots and a dark streak from the eye to the angle of the mouth; yellowish beneath, scantily spotted with brown.

Total length 380 millim., tail 50.

Southern California, Lower California, Nevada, Colorado, Arizona, Northern Mexico.

a. Yg. (Sc. 25; V. 181, C. 46).		Ventanas, Durango	Hr. A. Forrer [C.].

7. Crotalus mitchelli.

Caudisona mitchellii, *Cope, Proc. Ac. Philad.* 1861, p. 293, and 1866, p. 310.

—— pyrrha, *Cope, Proc. Ac. Philad.* 1866, p. 308.

Crotalus mitchellii, *Cope, Wheeler's Rep Surv. W. 100th Mer.* v. p. 535 (1875), *and Proc. U.S. Nat. Mus.* xiv. 1892, p. 689; *Van Denburgh, Proc. Cal. Acad.* (2) iv. 1894, p. 450; *Stejneger, Rep. U S. Nat. Mus. f.* 1893, p. 454, pl. xvii. (1895).

—— pyrrhus, *Cope, Wheeler's Rep.* p. 535, pl. xxii., *and Proc. U S. Nat. Mus.* xiv. 1892, p. 689; *Stejneger, W. Amer. Scient.* vii. 1891, p. 165.

—— confluentus, var. pyrrhus, *Garm. N. Am. Rept.* p. 173 (1883).

—— oregonensis, var. mitchellii, *Garm. l. c.*

Snout without canthus. Rostral broader than deep, separated from the anterior nasal by scales; upper head-scales small, striated; supraoculars striated; three series of scales between the eye and the labials; 14 to 16 upper labials. Scales in 25 rows, striated, dorsals strongly keeled. Ventrals 178-198; anal entire; subcaudals 24-26. Greyish yellow to salmon-red above, finely punctulated with brown, with a dorsal series of transverse darker spots; yellowish beneath.

Total length 1020 millim.; tail 90.

Desert Regions of Southern California, Lower California, and Arizona.

8. Crotalus triseriatus.

Uropsophus triseriatus, *Wagl. Syst. Amph* p. 176 (1830).
Crotalus lugubris, part., *Jan, Rev. & Mag. Zool.* 1859, p. 156, *and Prodr.* pl E (1859).
—— intermedius, *Trosch in Mull. Reise Mexico*, iii. p. 613 (1865); *Fischer, Abh. Nat. Ver. Bremen*, vii 1882, p 230, pl. xiv. figs 1-4
Caudisona triseriata, *Cope, Proc. Ac. Philad.* 1866, p. 309.
—— lugubris, *Dugès, Naturaleza*, iv. 1876, p. 25.
—— triseriatus, *Cope, Proc Amer Philos Soc.* xxii 1885, p. 179, *and Proc. U S Nat. Mus.* xiv. 1892, p. 689
—— omiltemanus, *Gunth. Biol. C-Am*, *Rept.* p. 192, pl. lviii fig C (1895).
—— pallidus, *Gunth l. c.* p. 193, pl. lix. fig. B.

Canthus rostralis distinct. Rostral as deep as broad, well visible from above, in contact with the anterior nasals and a pair of internasals; internasal separated from the supraocular by a large shield; one to five small smooth shields on the middle of the snout; supraoculars as broad as the space between them, which is occupied by three to five longitudinal series of scales; one or two series of scales between the eye and the labials; 9 to 13 upper labials. Scales in 21 to 25 rows, dorsals strongly keeled. Ventrals 142-184; anal entire; subcaudals 22-30. Olive or brown above, with a vertebral series of rather small dark brown spots with a fine black-and-light edge; sides with two or three series of smaller spots; upper surface of head with or without small dark spots; a dark, light-edged band from the eye to the angle of the mouth or beyond; yellowish beneath, spotted or speckled with dark brown, or dark grey-brown powdered with whitish. Spec. *c* pale brown above, with mere traces of darker markings, yellowish beneath.

Total length 530 millim.; tail 55.
Mexico.

a. ♀, head and neck and tail (Sc 25; C. 25).	La Cumbre de los Arrastrados, Jalisco, 8500 ft.	Dr. A. C. Buller [C.].
b. Yg (Sc 23; V. 149; C. 24).	La Laguna, Juanacatlan, Jalisco	Dr A. C Buller [C.].
c. ♂ (Sc. 25, V. 149; C. 29).	City of Mexico.	Mr Doorman [C.] (Type of *C. pallidus*.)

d. ♀ (Sc. 23; V. 147, C. 24). Orizaba, Vera Cruz.

e-f. ♀ (Sc. 21; V. 184; C. 19) & yg. (Sc. 21; V. 177; C. 24). Omilteme, Guerrero. Mr. H. H. Smith [C.]; F. D. Godman, Esq. [P].
(Types of *C. omiltemanus*.)

g. ♀ (Sc. 23; V. 142, C. 30). S. Mexico. F. D. Godman, Esq. [P.].

h. Yg. (Sc. 21; V. 150; C. 25). Mexico. M. Sallé [C.]

9. Crotalus polystictus.

Crotalus lugubris, part., *Jan, Rev. & Mag. Zool.* 1859, p. 156.
Caudisona polysticta, *Cope, Proc. Ac. Philad.* 1865, p 191, and 1866, p. 309.
Crotalus lugubris, var. multimaculata, *Jan, Icon. Gén.* 46, pl. iii. fig. 3 (1874).
—— jimenezii, *Dugès, Naturaleza*, iv. 1876, p. 23, pl. i figs. 18–20.
—— polystictus, *Cope, Proc. Amer. Philos. Soc.* xxii. 1885, p 179; *Dugès, Naturaleza*, (2) 1. 1888, p 134, *Cope, Proc. U.S. Nat. Mus.* xiv. 1892, p. 689; *Gunth. Biol. C.-Am, Rept* p. 192 (1895).

Closely allied to *C. triseriatus*, but four internasals, 14 or 15 upper labials, and scales in 27 to 30 rows. Ventrals 123–151; subcaudals 18–23. Elegantly marked with six or seven longitudinal series of alternating elongate dark brown, black-and-white edged spots separated by narrow interspaces of the yellowish-brown ground-colour; a pair of diverging dark bands on the top of the head, divided by a light line across the supraocular shields, an oblique dark band below the eye and another from the eye to the angle of the mouth; these dark bands separated by narrow pinkish-white streaks; pinkish or yellowish beneath, spotted with dark brown.

Total length 600 millim.; tail 60.

Tableland of Mexico.

10. Crotalus lepidus.

Caudisona lepida, *Kennicott, Proc Ac. Philad.* 1861, p. 206.
Aploaspis lepida, *Cope, Proc. Ac. Philad.* 1866, p 310.
Crotalus lepidus, *Cope, Proc. Ac. Philad.* 1883, p. 13; *Garm. N. Am. Rept.* p. 117 (1883); *Cope, Proc. U.S. Nat. Mus.* xiv. 1892, p. 689, *Stejneger, Rep. U.S. Nat. Mus. f.* 1893, p. 452, pl. xvi. (1895).
—— palmeri, *Garm. Bull. Essex Inst.* xix. 1887, p. 124.

Canthus rostralis obtuse. Rostral broader than deep, in contact with the nasal, which is semidivided; upper surface of snout with eight small smooth shields; supraoculars as broad as the space between them, which is occupied by three series of scales; upper præocular divided vertically; two series of scales between the eye and the labials; 12 upper labials. Scales in 21 or 23 rows, dorsals strongly keeled. Ventrals 153–169; anal entire; subcaudals 24–31. Brown or greenish grey above, with distant dark brown or jet-black light-edged cross-bands narrowing on the sides; two dark spots or a V- or heart-shaped black marking on the nape, a dark streak behind the eye present or absent, beneath dirty white spotted with brown.

In *C. palmeri*, Garm., which appears to be based on a colour variation of this species, the markings are much effaced on the body and altogether absent on the head.

Total length 350 millim.; tail 60.

Western Texas, New Mexico, Arizona, North Mexico.

a. ♂ (Sc. 23; V. 169; C. 31). Milpas, Durango. Hr. A. Forrer [C.].

11. Crotalus cerastes.

Crotalus cerastes, *Hallow. Proc. Ac. Philad* 1854, p. 95, *and Rep. U S. Surv. R. R. x., Williamson's Rep.* p 17, pl iv. fig. 1 (1859), *Kennicott, Rep. U.S. Mex. Bound. Surv.* ii. *Rept.* p. 14, pl. iii. (1859); *Cope, Proc. Ac. Philad.* 1859, p. 337; *Jan, Icon. Gén.* 46, pl. iii. fig. 5 (1874); *Garm. N. Am Rept.* p. 116 (1883); *Cope, Proc. U.S. Nat. Mus* xiv 1892, p 689; *Stejneger, N. Am. Faun.* no. 7, p. 216 (1893), *and Rep. U.S. Nat. Mus. f.* 1893, p. 450, figs. (1895).

Caudisona cerastes, *Cope, Proc Ac. Philad.* 1866, p. 309, and 1867, p 85.

—— (Æchmophrys) cerastes, *Coues, Wheeler's Surv. W. 100th Mer.* v. p. 609 (1875).

Canthus rostralis rounded. Rostral as broad as deep or a little broader than deep, in contact with the nasal, which is single; snout and vertex covered with small scales; supraocular produced into a raised horn-like process; two or three series of scales between the eye and the labials: 11 to 13 upper labials. Scales in 21 or 23 rows, dorsals feebly keeled, each scale along the middle of the back with a central tubercular swelling. Ventrals 146; anal entire; subcaudals 17. Yellowish above, with a dorsal series of rather indistinct brown blotches; a narrow brown streak from the eye to the angle of the mouth.

Total length 250 millim.; tail 20.

Desert regions of Southern California, Nevada, Arizona, and Utah.

ADDENDA AND CORRIGENDA.

VOL I.

Page 6. Add a species:—

4 a. Helminthophis ternetzii

Rostral two fifths the width of the head, extending nearly to the level of the eyes, forming a broad, straight suture with the frontal, which is about thrice as broad as long; eye scarcely distinguishable through the ocular; two superposed præoculars and a subocular; four upper labials, first largest, second and third in contact with the lower præocular, third and fourth in contact with the subocular. Diameter of body 52 times in the total length; tail nearly twice as long as broad, ending in a spine. 22 scales round the body. Olive above and beneath; head and anal region yellowish.

Total length 335 millim.

Paraguay.

a. Ad.   Paraguay.   Dr C. Ternetz [C.].

Add:—   Page 15. Typhlops lineatus.

Typhlops lineatus, *Boettg in Semon, Zool. Forsch* v. pp. 121 & 125 (1894).

Werner, Verh. zool.-bot. Ges. Wien, xlvi. 1896, p. 13, distinguishes a var. *sumatranus* (an sp. n.?) with 24 series of scales.

Add:—   Page 16. Typhlops braminus.

Typhlops braminus, *Boettg. l. c.* p. 122.

tt–uu. Ad.   Singapore.   H. N. Ridley, Esq [P.].
vv–ww. Ad.   Labuan.   A. Everett, Esq. [C.].

Page 17. Add a species:—

4 a. Typhlops diversus.

Typhlops diversus, *Waite, Proc. Linn. Soc. N. S. W.* (2) ix. 1894, p. 10, pl. i. figs. 4–6.

Snout rounded; nostrils lateral. Rostral nearly half the width of the head, extending almost to the level of the eyes; nasal incompletely divided, the fissure extending from the anterior edge of the præocular to slightly beyond the nostril; præocular narrower than the ocular, in contact with the second and third labials; eye distinct; internasal, supraoculars, and parietals larger than the scales on the body; four upper labials   Diameter of body 67 times in the total length; tail a third longer than broad, terminating in a very minute spine. 20 scales round the body. Light horn-colour throughout, slightly darker on the dorsal surface.

Total length 212 millim.

Mowen, Queensland.

Add:—	Page 18. **Typhlops beddomii.**	
o–q. Ad. & hgr.	Tinnevelly hills.	Col. Beddome [C].

Add:—	Page 26. **Typhlops thurstonii.**	
c. Hgr	Nellambur.	G. E. Mason, Esq [P.].

Add:—	Page 28. **Typhlops reticulatus.**	
g. Ad.	Asuncion, Paraguay.	Dr. J Bohls [C.].
h. Ad.	Charobamba, Bolivia.	

Add:—	Page 31. **Typhlops lumbricalis.**	
t–u. Ad.	Antigua, W I.	F. Watts, Esq. [P.].

Page 32. Add a species:—

37 *a* Typhlops batillus.

Typhlops batillus, *Waite, Proc. Linn. Soc N S. W* (2) ix 1894, p. 9, pl. i figs. 1–3.

Snout prominent, much depressed and shovel-shaped; nostril lateral, close to the rostral. Head-shields granulated above and below; rostral half the width of the head, extending almost to the level of the eyes; nasal completely divided, the fissure much curved and extending from the second labial; præocular smaller than the ocular, in contact with the second and third labials; eye very distinct; internasal, supraoculars, and parietals larger than the scales on the body; four upper labials. Diameter of body 53 times in the total length; tail longer than broad, terminating in a blunt spine. 24 scales round the body. Tawny above, the edges of the scales forming longitudinal lines, lighter beneath.

Total length 230 millim.

Wagga Wagga, New South Wales.

Add:—   Page 34. **Typhlops ligatus.**

Typhlops ligatus, *Waite, Rec. Austral. Mus.* ii 1893, p. 57.

Add:—   Page 34. **Typhlops polygrammicus.**

Typhlops nigrescens, *Waite, Rec. Austral. Mus.* ii. 1893, p. 57, pl. xv. fig. 5.
—— ruppellii, *Waite, l. c.* fig. 6.
—— polygrammicus, *Waite, Proc. Linn. Soc. N.S.W.* (2) ix. 1894, p. 13.

The differences between *T. nigrescens* and *T. rueppelli* are probably sexual.
This species reaches a length of 717 millim.

Add:—   Page 36. **Typhlops wiedii.**

Typhlops wiedii, *Waite, Proc. Linn. Soc. N. S. W.* (2) ix. 1894, pl. i. figs. 7–9; *Boettg. in Semon, Zool. Forsch.* v. p. 117 (1894).

Page 36. Add a species:—

49 a. **Typhlops nigricauda.**

Typhlops nigricauda, *Bouleng. Proc. Zool. Soc.* 1895, p. 867, pl. xlix. fig. 1.

Snout very prominent, rounded; nostrils inferior. Rostral broad, more than half the width of the head, extending to the level of the eyes; nasal incompletely divided, the cleft proceeding from the second labial; præocular present, narrower than the nasal or the ocular, in contact with the second and third labials; eye distinguishable; præfrontal and supraoculars considerably enlarged; four upper labials. Diameter of body 70 to 80 times in the total length; tail a little longer than broad, ending in a spine. 18 scales round the body. Brown above, yellowish below; end of snout yellow; tail black.

Total length 315 millim.
Northern Australia.

a. Ad.	Daly River.	Dr. Dahl [C.].	Christiania Museum. (One of the types.)

Add:—   Page 38. **Typhlops obtusus.**

d. Ad.   Zomba, Brit. C. Africa.   Sir H. H. Johnston [P.].

Page 39. Add a species:—

57 a. **Typhlops boulengeri.**

Typhlops boulengeri, *Bocage, Jorn Sc Lisb.* (2) iii. 1893, p. 117, and *Herp. Angola,* p. 64 (1895).

Snout very prominent, rounded; nostrils inferior. Rostral large, more than half the width of the head, extending to between the eyes, the portion visible from below nearly as long as broad; nasal semidivided, the cleft proceeding from the first labial; præocular present, much narrower than the nasal or the ocular, in contact with the second and third labials; eyes distinct; præfrontal and supraoculars large; four upper labials. Diameter of body 29 or 30 times in the total length; tail broader than long, ending in a spine. 28 scales round the body. Pale olive, above with black longitudinal lines running between the scales.

Total length 180 millim.

Angola.

a. Ad.	Quindumbo.	M. d'Anchieta [C.]. Prof. Barboza du Bocage [P.]. (One of the types.)

Page 40. Add a species :—

61 *a*. Typhlops mandensis.

Typhlops mandensis, *Stejneger, Proc. U.S. Nat. Mus.* xvi. 1894, p 725.

Apparently nearly related to *T. hallowelli*. Snout not hooked, with obtusely angular horizontal edge; nostrils inferior, just below the edge. Rostral large; nasal large, semidivided, the cleft proceeding from the first labial; præocular present, narrower than the nasal or the ocular; eyes not distinguishable; præfrontal, frontal, and interparietal of equal size, much larger than the scales on the body; supraoculars and one pair of parietals larger still, four upper labials. Diameter of body 23 times in the total length; tail exceedingly short, much broader than long. 34 scales round the body. Uniform pale greenish grey above, pale buff beneath.

Total length 135 millim.

Island of Manda, north of Lamu, E. Africa.

Add :— Page 40. **Typhlops anchietæ.**

Typhlops anchietæ, *Bocage, Herp Angola*, p. 63 (1895).

Add :— Page 43. **Typhlops punctatus.**

Typhlops punctatus, *Bocage, Herp Angola.* p. 65 (1895).

aa. Ad. (A, *c*).	Mkonumbi, E. Africa.	Dr. J. W. Gregory [P.].
bb. Ad (B, *a*).	Leikipia, E. Africa.	Dr. J. W. Gregory [P.]

Add :— Page 44. **Typhlops bibronii.**

k. Ad.	Middelburg, Transvaal	D. Draper, Esq. [P.].

Page 44. Add a species:—

67 a. Typhlops hottentotus.

Typhlops hottentotus, *Bocage, Jorn. Sc. Lisb* (2) iii. 1893, p. 117, and *Herp Angola*, p. 69 (1895)

Closely allied to *T. schlegelii*, but snout less prominent; rostral narrower behind; præocular narrower and in contact with the second labial only; nasal narrower than the ocular; and scales in 36 rows. Dark olive-brown above, almost black, with a few scattered small yellow spots; lower part yellow, with olive-brown spots.

Total length 328 millim.

Humbe, Angola.

Add:—   Page 45. Typhlops schlegelii.

d. Hgr.   Leikipia, E Africa.   Dr J. W. Gregory [P.].

Add:—   Page 45. Typhlops delalandii.

m. Ad.   Rustenburg, Transvaal.   Mr. W. Ayres [C.].

Add:—   Page 46. Typhlops humbo.

Typhlops humbo, *Bocage, Herp. Angola*, p. 66 (1895).

c Ad   Quissange, Angola.   Prof. B. du Bocage [P.].

Add:—   Page 46. Typhlops mucruso.

Typhlops petersii (*non Steind.*), *Bocage, l c* p 68.

n. Ad. (A).   Zanzibar.   F Finn, Esq [P].
o–p Ad. & hgr. (A). Fwambo, Brit. C. Africa. E Carson, Esq. [C.].
q. Ad (A).   Zomba, Brit. C. Africa. Sir H H Johnston [P.].
r. Hgr. (B).   Quissange, Angola.   Prof B du Bocage [P.].

Add:—   Page 47. Typhlops anomalus.

Typhlops anomalus, *Bocage, l. c.* p. 20.

a. Ad.   Quindumbo, Angola.   Prof. B. du Bocage [P.].

Page 48. Add a species:—

75 a Typhlops proximus.

Typhlops proximus, *Waite, Rec. Austral. Mus.* ii. 1893, p. 60, pl. xv. figs. 3 & 4.

Snout very prominent, with sharp horizontal edge and inferior nostrils. Rostral large, its upper part a little more than half the width of the head, extending almost to the level of the eyes, its lower part longer than broad; nasal semidivided, the cleft proceeding from the first labial and extending to the upper surface of the snout; præocular narrower than the ocular; eyes distinct; parietals as large as supraoculars; four upper labials. Diameter of body 35 times in the total length; tail not longer than broad, ending in a small spine. 20 scales round the body. Brownish olive to greyish brown above, each scale margined with yellow; lower surfaces yellow.

Total length 405 millim.

New South Wales and Victoria.

Add:— Page 49. **Typhlops unguirostris.**

Typhlops unguirostris, *Waite, Proc Linn. Soc. N. S W.* (2) ix. 1894, p. 11; *Bouleng. t c.* p 719.

The specimen referred to *T. unguirostris* belongs to a distinct species:—

78 a. **Typhlops waitii.**

Typhlops waitii, *Bouleng. l. c* p. 718.

ʳ Nasal cleft proceeding from the second labial (from the first in *T. unguirostris*); 22 scales round the body (24 in *T. unguirostris*).

Add:— Page 49. **Typhlops affinis.**

Typhlops affinis, *Waite, l. c* p 11; *Bouleng l. c* p. 719.

Page 52. Add a species:—

85 a. **Typhlops somalicus.**

Typhlops somalicus, *Bouleng Proc Zool. Soc* 1895, p. 536, pl. xxx. fig. 1

Snout very prominent, obtusely pointed, with sharp cutting edge and inferior nostrils. Head-shields granulated; rostral very large, its upper portion a little longer than broad, its lower portion as broad as long; nasal completely divided, the cleft proceeding from the second labial; præocular present, nearly as large as the ocular, in contact with the second and third labials; ocular in contact with the third and fourth labials; eyes not distinguishable, præfrontal and supraoculars transversely enlarged. Diameter of body 90 times in total length; tail a little broader than long, ending in a small spine. 24 scales round the body. Pale olive, head yellowish.

Total length 450 millim.

Western Somaliland.

a. Ad.　　　　　Beearso.　　　　　Dr. Donaldson Smith [P.].
　　　　　　　　　　　　　　　　　　　　　　(Type.)

Page 52. Add a species:—

85 b. Typhlops præocularis.

Typhlops præocularis, *Stejneger*, Proc. U.S Nat. Mus xvi. 1894, p. 709.

Snout very prominent and pointed, but not hooked, with sharp cutting edge; nostrils inferior, between two large nasals almost at the point where the internasal suture joins the rostral: rostral very large, about two thirds the width of the head, the portion visible from below broader than long; a præocular, not in contact with the labials; no suboculars; ocular in contact with nasal below præocular, reaching lip behind second labial; eyes indistinguishable; four upper labials. Diameter of body at the middle 67 times in the total length, the body growing thicker posteriorly; tail very short, wider than long, ending in a spine. 24 or 26 scales round the body. Uniform pale brownish grey.

Total length 340 millim.

Leopoldville or Stanley Pool, Congo.

Page 53. Add a species:—

87 a. Typhlops bisubocularis.

Typhlops bisubocularis, *Boettg.* Zool. Anz. 1893, p. 336.

Very closely allied to *T. andamanensis*, but anterior upper head-scales broader and nearly twice as long as the scales on the body. Diameter of body 44 times in total length; length of tail once and a half its width. Dark grey, the scales with lighter edges, snout, chin, end of tail, and a pair of anal spots white.

Total length 131 millim.

Western Java.

Add:— Page 55. **Typhlops lumbriciformis.**

b. Ad. Fwambo, Brit. C. Africa. E. Carson, Esq. [C.].

Add.— Page 56. **Typhlops unitæniatus.**

b. Hgr. Kibroezi, E. Africa. Dr. J. W. Gregory [P.].

Add:— Page 57. **Typhlophis squamosus.**

a. Ad. Para. Dr. E. A. Góldi [P.].
b. Ad. Brazil.

Add:— Page 62. **Glauconia rostrata.**

Stenostoma rostratum, *Bocage*, Herp. Angola, p. 62 (1895).

Page 63. **Glauconia albifrons.**

For "Stenostoma melanosterna" read "S. melanoterma."
Add:—

| ζ. Ad. | Asuncion, Paraguay. | Dr J Bohls [C.]. |
| η Ad | Yungas, Bolivia. | |

Add:— Page 65. **Glauconia dulcis.**

| f. Ad. | Tampico, Mexico | F. D Godman, Esq. [P]. |

Add:— Page 65. **Glauconia narirostris.**

| b. Ad. | Lower Niger. | H. W. Crosse, Esq [P.]. |

Page 66. Add a species:—

14 a. **Glauconia nursii.**

Glauconia nursii, *Anders Rept Hadramut & Arab.* p. 64 *.

Snout rounded; supraocular present, nearly as large as the frontal, rostral broader than the nasal, reaching nearly the level of the eyes; nasal completely divided; ocular bordering the lip, between two labials, the first of which is very small; five lower labials. 14 scales round the body. Diameter of body 50 times in the total length, tail 10 times. Pale brownish above, white beneath.
Total length 250 millim.
Southern Arabia.

| a–b. Ad. | Aden. | Capt. Nurse [P.]. (Types.) |

Add:— Page 67. **Glauconia nigricans.**

| g–h. Ad. & hgr | Umfuli R, Mashonaland. | G. A. K. Marshall, Esq. [P]. |

Add:— Page 68. **Glauconia scutifrons.**

Stenostoma scutifrons, *Bocage, Herp. Angola*, p. 71 (1895).

Add:— Page 70. **Glauconia humilis.**

Rena humilis, *Stejneger, N. Am. Faun.* no. 7, pt. ii. 1893, p. 203.

| c Ad. | S. Bernardino, California. | |
| d. Ad. | S. Jose del Cabo, Lower California. | |

Add:— Page 80. **Liasis papuanus.**

| b. Yg. (Sc. 65; V. 364; C. 82). | Fergusson Id., D'Entrecasteaux Group, Brit. New Guinea. | Mr. Meek [C.]. |

---

* Not yet published.

Add :— Page 84. **Python amethystinus.**

q Yg. (Sc. 53; V. 328; C. 106). Trobriand Ids., Brit. New Guinea. Mr. Meek [C.].

Add :— Page 86. **Python reticulatus.**

o. Yg. (Sc. 75; V. 311; C. 95). Great Natuna Id. A. Everett, Esq. [C.].

Add :— Page 86. **Python sebæ.**

Python liberiensis, *Hallow. Proc. Ac. Philad.* 1845, p 249, and 1857, p. 66.
—— natalensis, *Bocage, Herp. Angola*, p 72 (1895).

m. Yg. (Sc. 85; V. 273; C. 72). Lower Niger. H W. Crosse, Esq. [P.].

Add :— Page 88. **Python anchietæ.**

Python anchietæ, *Bocage, Herp. Angola*, p 73, pl. ix. fig. 1 (1895).

Add :— Page 89. **Python regius.**

l. ♂ (Sc. 57; V. 200; C ?). Lower Niger. H W. Crosse, Esq. [C.].

Add :— Page 90. **Chondropython viridis.**

Chondropython viridis, *Boettg. in Semon, Zool. Forsch.* v. p. 120, pl. v. fig. 3 (1894).

Add :— Page 91. **Aspidites melanocephalus.**

Aspidites melanocephalus, *Boettg. l. c.* p. 119.

Add :— Page 92. **Aspidites ramsayi.**

Aspidites ramsayi, *Waite, Proc Linn. Soc N. S W.* (2) ix. 1895, p. 715, pl. l.

Add :— Page 92. **Calabaria reinhardti**

h. Head and tail. Nr. Mangala, Upper Congo. J. H. Weeks, Esq. [P.].

Add :— Page 94. **Epicrates cenchris.**

Coluber tamachia, *Scopoli, Delic. Faun Flor. Insubr.* iii. p. 38, pl xix. fig. 1 (1788).
Boa liberiensis, *Hallow. Proc. Ac. Philad.* 1854, p. 100, and 1857, p. 66.
Epicrates cupreus, *A E. Brown, Proc Ac Philad.* 1803, p. 430.

y. ♀ (B. Sc. 52; V. 237; C. ?). Panama. Christiania Mus

ADDENDA AND CORRIGENDA.

Page 96. Add a species:—

1 a. **Epicrates crassus.**

Epicrates crassus, *Cope, Proc. Ac. Philad.* 1862, p. 349.

Head-shields as in *E. cenchris*; twelve upper labials, sixth and seventh entering the eye. Form thick and stout. Scales in 39 rows. Leather-brown above, with three rows of darker spots on each side; a series of pale oval spots on each side of the vertebral line; a dark, light-edged stripe on each side of the anterior third of the body; a median and two temporal brown bands on the head. Total length 910 millim.; tail 85.

Cadosa, Parana River.

Add.—   Page 96. **Epicrates angulifer.**

a. ♀ (Sc. 62; V. 275; C. 45).   Cuba.   Christiania Mus.

Add:—   Page 98. **Epicrates fordii.**

d. ♀ (Sc. 35; V. 249; C. 76).   S. Domingo.

Add:—   Page 99. **Corallus cookii.**

Xiphosoma hortulana, *A. E. Brown, Proc. Ac. Philad.* 1893, p. 430
—— ruschenbergeri, *A. E. Brown, l. c.* p. 431.

q–t. Ad. & hgr. (Sc. 39, 43, 39, 41, V. 265, 264, 270, 270, C. 113, 101, 104, 108).   Id. of Grenada.   Mr. H. H. Smith [C], F. D. Godman, Esq. [P.].

Add:—   Page 102. **Corallus hortulanus.**

k. Hgr. (Sc. 59; V. 279; C. 109).   R. Ucayale.   Dr. E. A. Goldi [P.].

Add:—   Page 102. **Corallus annulatus.**

Xiphosoma annulata, *A. E. Brown, Proc. Ac. Philad.* 1893, p. 431.

Add:—   Page 103. **Corallus caninus.**

k. Hgr. (Sc. 67; V. 193; C. 64).   Para.   Dr. E. A. Goldi [P.].
l. Hgr. (Sc. 77, V. 195; C. 69).   Beni R., Bolivia.

Add:—   Page 109. **Enygrus carinatus.**

r. ♀ (A. Sc. 35; V. 175; C. 39).   Trobriand Ids., Brit. New Guinea.   Mr. Meek [C.]
v–ϕ. ♀ (C. Sc. 33, 35; V. 171, 173; C. 41, 39).   Trobriand Ids., Brit. New Guinea.   Mr. Meek [C.]

Add :— Page 109. **Enygrus asper.**

d. ♀ (Sc. 35; V. 138; C 16). Stephansort, N. Guinea.

Add :— Page 111. **Ungalia melanura.**

Ungalia melanura, *A. E. Brown, Proc. Ac. Philad.* 1893, p. 429

Add — Page 112. **Ungalia maculata.**

Ungalia maculata, *Cope, Proc. Ac. Philad.* 1894, p. 436.
—— hætiana, *Cope, l. c.*

l ♂ (Sc. 27; V. 186; C. 35)   Hayti   Christiania Mus

Page 116. Add a species :—

2. Eunectes notæus.

Eunectes notæus, *Cope, Proc. Ac Philad.* 1862, p. 70.

Rostral considerably broader than deep; thirteen to fifteen upper labials; no scales between the suboculars and the labials. Scales in 45 to 49 rows. A dark broad stripe originating between the orbits and extending to the nape, followed by a series of large transverse blackish spots, which extend to the end of the tail; two dark stripes on each side of the head, and a lateral series of blackish vertical bars. Otherwise as in *E. murinus.*
Total length 1850 millim.; tail 230. Grows to 3000 millim.
Paraguay and Bolivia.

a Hgr. (Sc. 49; V. 231; C. 54).   Bolivia.   M. Suarez [P.].

Add :— Page 118. **Boa occidentalis.**

b. ♀ (Sc. 75; V. 250; C. 44).   Paraguay.   Zoological Society.
13 of the subcaudals are divided. Total length 2730 millim

Add :— Page 119. **Boa imperator.**

Boa imperator, *Dugès, La Naturaleza,* (2) ii. 1893, p. 300, pl. xiii.

p. Yg. (Sc. 75; V. 245; C 56)   Brit Honduras   F. D. Godman, Esq. [P.]

Add :— Page 120. **Boa dumerilii.**

d. Yg. (Sc. 63; V. 223; C. 32).   Madagascar.   Mr. Last [C].

Add :— Page 120. **Boa madagascariensis.**

e. ♀ (Sc 60; V. 223; C. 33).   Madagascar.   Christiania Mus.

Add :—   Page 122. **Bolieria multicarinata.**

c. ♂ (Sc. 53; V. 196;   Mauritius.   Capt. Stokes [C.]; Col-
C 107).   lege of Surgeons [E]

Add :—   Page 125 **Eryx thebaicus.**

l ♂ (V. 179; C 24)   Fayoum.   Dr J. Anderson [P.].
m–n. Hgr (V 188, 182;   Suakin.   Dr Penton & Dr. J.
C. 24, 24).   Anderson [P.].
o Hgr. (V 171, C. 21).   Between W Shebeli & Juba R., Gallaland.   Dr Donaldson Smith [C].
p Hgr. (V 165; C. 20).   Lake Stephanie.   Dr. Donaldson Smith [C].

Add :—   Page 125. **Eryx jaculus.**

Eryx jaculus, *Méhely, Zool. Anz.* 1894, p. 93.

e. ♀ (V 197; C. 18).   Beltim, Delta.   Dr. J. Anderson [P.].

Add :—   Page 129. **Lichanura trivirgata.**

α ♂ (Sc. 41, V. 238; C 45)   San Diego, California   Christiania Mus.

9 scales round the eye; 13-14 upper labials. Uniform brown above, grey beneath.

Add :—   Page 130. **Charina bottæ.**

Charina plumbea, *Stejneger, N Am Faun* no 7, pt ii p. 203 (1893).

e Yg (Sc 49, V 208, C. 34)   San Francisco.   Christiania Mus

Anterior nasal fused with internasal, anterior præfrontal distinct; a small azygous shield between the internasals; loreal distinct, fifth upper labial entering the eye.

f ♂ (Sc. 47, V. 200, C. 35).   San Francisco   Christiania Mus.

Anterior nasal, internasal, and anterior præfrontal fused; no azygous præfrontal; loreal distinct; fourth and fifth upper labials entering the eye.

Add .—   Page 134. **Ilysia scytale.**

o–p Ad (V 229, 223,   Para.   Dr. E. A. Goldi [P].
C. 12, 18).

Add .—   Page 137 **Cylindrophis maculatus.**

h–k. ♀ (V. 190; C. 5)   Ceylon   Miss Layard [P].
& hgr (V. 180, 206,
C. 5, 4)

ADDENDA AND CORRIGENDA.

Add:— Page 141. **Rhinophis oxyrhynchus.**

d. ♀ (V. 225; C. 5). Ceylon. Dr. Bowles [P.]

Page 142. Add a species:—

4 a. Rhinophis fergusonianus.

Snout acutely pointed; rostral rounded, as long as its distance from the posterior extremity of the frontal; latter shield a little longer than broad. Diameter of body 46 times in the total length. 15 scales round the middle of the body, 19 behind the head. Ventrals 188; subcaudals 4. Caudal disk longer than the shielded part of the head. Blackish above; yellowish beneath, with black spots forming a zigzag band anteriorly.
Total length 320 millim.; tail 9.
Travancore.

a. ♀ (V. 188; C. 4). Cardaman Hills. H. S. Ferguson, Esq. [P.].

Add:— Page 143. **Rhinophis travancoricus.**

Rhinophis travancoricus, *Bouleng. Journ Bombay N. H. Soc.* 1892, p 318, pl —.

b. ♀ (V. 134; C. 6). Peermad, Travancore H. S. Ferguson, Esq [P.].

Add:— Page 155. **Silybura ellioti.**

w-x. ♀ (V. 165, 176; C. 6, 8). Foster Hill Rise, Nilgherries. W. M. Daly, Esq [P.]

Add.— Page 156. **Silybura myhendræ.**

c. ♀ (V. 144; C 7). Neduvangaud, Travancore. H. S Ferguson, Esq. [P.]

Add:— Page 157. **Silybura madurensis.**

e-g. ♂ (V. 142; C. 9) & ♀ (V. 143, 142; C. 7, 7). High Range, Travancore. H. S. Ferguson, Esq. [P.].
h-k. ♂ (V. 149; C 8) & ♀ (V. 148, 150, C. 7, 7). Peermad, Travancore. H. S. Ferguson, Esq. [P.].
l. ♂ (V. 140; C. 9). Alleppy, low country, Travancore. H. S. Ferguson, Esq. [P.].

Add:— Page 159. **Silybura brevis.**

w. ♂ (V. 132; C. 10). High Range, Travancore. H. S. Ferguson, Esq. [P.].
x ♀ (V. 132, C. 9). Peermad, Travancore. H. S. Ferguson, Esq. [P].
y. ♀ (V. 135; C. 9). Brumagherries, N. Wynad, 200 ft. G. E Mason, Esq. [P.].

Add :— Page 169. **COLUBRIDÆ**.

Calamariidæ, Lycodontidæ, Colubridæ, Xenodontidæ, Natricidæ,- *Cope, Am. Nat* 1893, p. 479.

Add :— Page 173. **Acrochordus javanicus**.

Coluber oularsawa, *Bonnat. Encycl Méth., Ophiol.* p. 26 (1789).

Add :— Page 174. **Chersydrus granulatus**.
u. Several specs.   Pinang   Dr Cantor.

Add :— Page 177. **COLUBRINÆ**.

Calamariidæ, Oligodontinæ, Lycodontinæ, Boodontinæ, part., Xenodontinæ, Pseudaspidinæ, Natricinæ, *Cope, Am. Nat.* 1893, p 480

Add :— Page 183. **Polyodontophis sumichrasti**.

Ablabes sumichrasti, *Gunth. Biol. C.-Am., Rept.* p. 105 (1893).

Add :— Page 184. **Polyodontophis collaris**.

Polyodontophis collaris, *Bouleng. Ann Mus. Genov.* (2) xiii. 1893, p. 322.

Add :— Page 186. **Polyodontophis geminatus**.

n ♀ (**B** V. 165, C ?).   Sarawak.   A. Everett, Esq. [C.].
o Hgr (**B.** V. 162, C. 130).   Muching, Sarawak.   Rajah Brooke [P.].

E. No light stripes, head dark brown above, with a black nuchal collar.

p ♀ (V. 183, C. 118).   Kina Balu, N. Borneo.   A Everett, Esq. [C.]

Page 186. Add a species :—

6 *a*. Polyodontophis bivittatus.

Polyodontophis bivittatus, *Bouleng. Ann. & Mag. N. H.* (6) xiv. 1894, p. 82

Rostral twice as broad as deep, just visible from above; internasals shorter than the præfrontals; frontal once and two thirds as long as broad, longer than its distance from the end of the snout, shorter than the parietals; loreal as deep as long, one præocular, two postoculars, both in contact with the parietal; temporals 2 + 2, the lower anterior wedged in between the sixth and seventh labials; eight upper labials, third, fourth, and fifth entering the eye; four lower labials in contact with the anterior chin-shields, which are as long as the posterior. Scales in 17 rows. Ventrals 153–155, anal divided; subcaudals —? (tail mutilated). Black above, with two white streaks commencing on the parietal shields and running along the sixth series of scales and the adjoining halves; a white crossbar on the forehead, occupying the anterior two thirds of the frontal and supraocular shields; a series of white spots along the upper lip; lower parts white, with a black dot or spot at the outer end of each shield.

Total length 490 millim.

Palawan.

a–b. ♂ (V. 153, 155; C. ?)　　　Palawan.　　　A. Everett, Esq. [C.]. (Types.)

Add:—　　Page 187. Polyodontophis subpunctatus.

n–p. ♂ (V. 157; C. 60), ♀ (V. 176; C. 53), & yg. (V. 163; C. 52).　　　Ceylon.　　　Miss Layard [P.].

Add:—　　Page 188. Polyodontophis sagittarius.

i. ♀ (V. 236; C. 54)　　　Bengal?　　　Dr. Cantor.

Page 189. Add a species:—

11. Polyodontophis venustissimus.

Henicognathus venustissimus, *Gunth. Biol C.-Am., Rept.* p. 144, pl. li. fig. C (1894).

Snout much flattened; rostral much broader than deep, visible from above; internasals shorter than the præfrontals; frontal longer than its distance from the end of the snout, a little shorter than the parietals; loreal as long as deep or a little longer than deep; one præ- and two postoculars; temporals 2+3; nine upper labials, fourth, fifth, and sixth entering the eye; four lower labials in contact with the anterior chin-shields, which are as long as or a little longer than the posterior. Scales in 17 rows. Ventrals 137–142; anal divided. Crimson above, each scale with a black dot, with black cross-bands edged with yellow; some of the cross-bands broken on the vertebral line and alternating; snout and occiput black, vertex yellow; labials, loreal, and præocular yellow; dark streaks radiating from below the eye; white beneath, with blackish dots on the sides; each subcaudal with a large black spot*.

Total length 430 millim., without tail.

Nicaragua.

a–b. ♂ (V. 142, 137; C. ?).　　Hacienda Rosa de　　Dr. E. Rothschuh
　　　　　　　　　　　　　　Jericho, Nicaragua.　　[C.]. (Types.)

Page 189. Add a genus:—

6 a. LIOPHIDIUM.

Maxillary teeth 25, small, closely set, the three posterior feebly enlarged; mandibular teeth small, equal. Dentary bone completely

---

* The coloration is described from the specimens when quite fresh.

detached from the articular posteriorly. Head small, not distinct from neck; eye small, with round pupil; nostril between two nasals and the internasal. Body cylindrical; scales smooth, without pits, in 17 rows, ventrals rounded. Tail rather short, subcaudals in two rows. Hypapophyses developed throughout the vertebral column.

Madagascar.

1. Liophidium trilineatum.

Snout much depressed, slightly projecting. Rostral small, broader than deep, just visible from above; internasals shorter than the præfrontals, frontal nearly twice as long as broad, scarcely broader than the supraocular, longer than its distance from the end of the snout, shorter than the parietals; loreal longer than deep; one præ- and two postoculars, temporals 1+2; eight upper labials, fourth and fifth entering the eye, four lower labials in contact with the anterior chin-shields, which are as long as the posterior. Scales in 17 rows. Ventrals 145; anal divided; subcaudals 57. Grey above, dotted with black, with three black longitudinal lines, the lateral on the third row of scales, and extending to the nostril after passing through the eye; head with dark brown variegations; upper labials white, the anterior edged with black; lower parts white, dotted with black on the sides.

Total length 330 millim.; tail 80.

Madagascar.

a ♂ (V. 145, C. 57).   S.W. Madagascar.   Mr. Last [C.].

Add :—   Page 189. **DROMICODRYAS.**

Lianthera, *Cope, Am. Nat.* 1893, p. 482.

Add :—   Page 190. Dromicodryas bernieri.

L. Yg. (V 184; C. 99)   Sahambendrana.   M. Majastre [C.].

Add :—   Page 191. Xenochrophis cerasogaster.

i. ♀ (V. 147, C. 71).   Bengal ?   Dr. Cantor.

Add :—   Page 192. **TROPIDONOTUS.**

Tropinotus, *Kuhl, Isis,* 1822, p. 473.
Hemigenius, *Dugès, Proc. Amer Philos. Soc* xxv. 1888, p. 182.
Diplophallus, *Cope, Am Nat* 1893, p 483
Ceratophallus, *Cope, l c*
Tropidonotus, *Bocourt, Miss. Sc. Mex., Rept.* p. 750 (1893).
Regina, *Bocourt, l.c.* p. 747.
Thamnophis, *Bocourt, l c* p 754.
Eutænia, *Bocourt, l. c* p. 760.
Trimerodytes, *Cope, Proc. Ac Philad* 1894, p. 426 (1895)
Seminatrix, *Cope, Am. Nat.* 1895, p. 678.

Add :— Page 201. **Tropidonotus leptocephalus.**

Eutænia leptocephala, *Bocourt, Miss. Sc. Mex., Rept.* p. 763, pl. lvi. fig. 5 (1893)
? Thamnophis parietalis, *Stejneger, N. Am. Faun.* no. 7, pt. ii p. 214 (1893).

Add :— Page 202. **Tropidonotus vagrans.**

Thamnophis vagrans, *Stejneger, N. Am. Faun.* no. 7, pt. ii. p. 213 (1893).
Eutænia vagrans, *Bocourt, Miss. Sc. Mex., Rept.* p. 783, pl. lviii. fig. 2 (1893).

s. ♀ (Sc. 23; V. 154; C. 68).   S. Diego, California.   Christiania Mus

Add :— Page 203. **Tropidonotus chrysocephalus.**

Eutænia chrysocephala, *Bocourt, Miss. Sc. Mex , Rept* p. 762, pl lvii fig. 1 (1893)

e Yg. (V. 152, C. 68).   Jalapa.   Mr. Hoege [C.].

Page 203. Add a species :—

3 *a.* Tropidonotus godmani.

Tropidonotus godmani, *Gunth. Biol. C.-Am , Rept.* p. 133 (1893).

Eye moderate. Rostral broader than deep, visible from above; internasals as long as broad or broader than long, shorter than the præfrontals; frontal once and a half to once and two thirds as long as broad, longer than its distance from the end of the snout, as long as or a little shorter than the parietals; loreal a little longer than deep, one præ- and three (rarely four) postoculars; temporals 1+2; seven upper labials, third and fourth entering the eye; five lower labials in contact with the anterior chin-shields, which are shorter than the posterior. Scales in 17 rows, strongly keeled. Ventrals 134–149; anal entire; subcaudals 61–81. Olive or brown above, with a yellowish vertebral line, one scale wide, and a light lateral streak on the second and third rows of scales; some black spots or bars on the neck; a black nuchal collar; upper lip pale, with black lines on the sutures between the labials; greyish or pale olive beneath.

Total length 600 millim.; tail 160.

Mexico.

a–g. ♂ (V. 148, 146, 146, 146; C. 80, 74, 81, 78) & ♀ (V 142, 145, 134; C. 66, 73, 61).   Omilteme, Guerrero.   Mr. H. H. Smith [C.]; F. D Godman, Esq [P.]. (Types)
h–k. Yg. (V. 149, 141, 145; C. 73, ?, 81).   Omilteme, Guerrero.   Mr. H. H. Smith [C.]; F. D. Godman Esq. [P.].

Add :— Page 203. **Tropidonotus scaliger.**

Eutænia scalaris, part., *Bocourt, Miss. Sc. Mex., Rept.* p. 768, pl. lvi. fig. 6 (1893).

Add — Page 204. **Tropidonotus scalaris.**

Eutænia scalaris, part., *Bocourt, l. c*

Page 206. **Tropidonotus ordinatus, var. sirtalis.**
Add :—

Eutænia sirtalis, *Bocourt, Miss. Sc. Mex., Rept.* p. 765, pl. lv. fig. 4 (1893).
Thamnophis ordinatus obscurus, *Rhoads, Proc. Ac. Philad.* 1895, p 387.

Page 208. **Tropidonotus ordinatus, var. infernalis.**
Add:—

Eutænia infernalis, *Bocourt, l. c.* p. 771, pl lv. fig. 2.
Thamnophis infernalis, *Stejneger, N. Am. Faun.* no. 7, pt. ii. p. 210 (1893)
—— elegans, *Stejneger, l c* p. 211.

δ ♀ (V. 158 ; A 2 ; C. 85)   California.   Christiania Mus.

Page 209. **Tropidonotus ordinatus, var. eques.**
Add :—

Tropidonotus eques, *Wiegm. Arch. f. Nat.* 1835, p. 282.
Eutænia pulchrilata, *Bocourt, l. c.* p. 767, pl. lvii. fig. 4.
—— cyrtopsis, *Bocourt, l. c.* p. 774, pl. lv. fig. 5.
—— cyrtopsis, var. fulvus, *Bocourt, l. c.* p. 777, pl. lvii. fig. 2.

y. Yg. (V. 141 ; C. 75).   Omilteme, Guer-   Mr. H. H Smith [C.],
                            rero.   F. D. Godman, Esq. [P.].

Page 209. **Tropidonotus ordinatus, var. sumichrasti.**
Add .—

Eutænia cyrtopsis, var. sumichrasti, *Bocourt, l. c* p. 775, pl lvii fig. 3.

Page 210. **Tropidonotus ordinatus, var phenax.**
Add :—

Eutænia cyrtopsis, var. phenax, *Bocourt, l. c.* p. 778.

Page 210. **Tropidonotus ordinatus, var. couchii.**
Add :—

Thamnophis couchii, *Stejneger, l. c.* p. 212.

Page 210. **Tropidonotus ordinatus, var. hammondii.**
Add :—

Thamnophis hammondii, *Stejneger, l c.*

Page 210. **Tropidonotus ordinatus, var marcianus.**

Add :—

Eutænia marciana, *Bocourt, l. c.* p. 784, pl. lix. fig. 1 (1895).

Page 211. **Tropidonotus ordinatus, var. radix.**

Add :—

Eutænia radix, *Bocourt, l. c.* p 781, pl. lviii. fig 3 (1895)

Page 212. **Tropidonotus ordinatus, var. macrostemma.**

Add :—

Eutænia megalops, *Bocourt, l. c.* p 786, pl. lix. fig. 2 (1895).
—— macrostemma, *Bocourt, l. c.* p. 788, pl. lix. fig. 3.

Page 212. *For* "Tropidonotus ordinatus, var. butleri," *read* :—

6 a. **Tropidonotus butleri.**

And add :—

Thamnophis butleri, *Stejneger, Proc. U.S. Nat. Mus.* xvii. 1895, p. 593.

Eye small. Temporals 1+1.

Add :— Page 212. **Tropidonotus saurita.**

Thamnophis saurita, *Bocourt, Miss. Sc. Mex., Rept.* p 754, pl. lv. fig 6, & pl. lvi. figs. 2-4 (1893).

Page 214 (*see* p. 418). **Tropidonotus præocularis.**

Add :—

Eutænia præocularis, *Bocourt, Miss. Sc. Mex., Rept.* p. 770, pl lvi. fig. 7 (1893).

Add :— Page 216. **Tropidonotus picturatus.**

Tropidonotus mairii, *Gray, in Grey's Trav. Austral.* ii. p. 442 (1841).

t. Yg. (V. 150 ; C. 72).	Herbert R.	J. A Boyd, Esq. [P.].
u. Yg. (V. 146; C. 65).	Daly R., N. Australia.	Dr. Dahl [C] Christiania Mus.
v. ♀ (V. 142 ; C.?).	Fergusson Id , Brit New Guinea.	Mr. Meek [C.]
w-y. ♂ (V. 152 ; C. 69), ♀ (V. 153 ; C. 73), & yg. (V. 152; C. 75)	Trobriand Ids., Brit. New Guinea.	Mr. Meek [C.].

Page 216. Add a species :—

11 a. **Tropidonotus punctiventris.**

Tropidonotus punctiventris, *Boettg Zool. Anz* 1895, p 129.

Allied to *T. picturatus*, but temporals 2+3, and nine upper labials, fourth, fifth, and sixth entering the eye. Scales in 15 rows, all strongly keeled. Ventrals 162; anal divided; subcaudals 74. Dark olive-grey above, with darker spots disposed quincuncially; lips white, the anterior labials black-edged, belly white, greyish behind, with about six longitudinal series of black dots.

Total length 461 millim.; tail 116.

Halmaheira.

Add:—   Page 216. **Tropidonotus truncatus.**

Styporhynchus truncatus, *Boettg. Zool. Anz.* 1895, p. 131

a–b ♂ (V. 142; C.?) & ♀   Halmaheira   Prof. Kukenthal [C.];
(V 149; C.?).   Senckenberg Mus. [E.].

Add:—   Page 217. **Tropidonotus fuliginoides.**

Mizodon fuliginoides, *Bocage, Herp. Angola*, p. 75 (1895).

l ♀ (V. 128; A. 1, C ?)   Mouth of the Loango.   Mr. H. J. Duggan [C].

Add:—   Page 218. **Tropidonotus variegatus.**

a ♀ (V. 134; C.?)   Lower Niger.   H W. Crosse, Esq [P]

Add:—   Page 219. **Tropidonotus natrix.**

Tropidonotus natrix, *Tomasini, Wiss. Mitth. aus Bosn u. Herzeg.* ii. p. 636 (1894); *Durigen, Deutschl. Amph. u. Rept.* p. 274, pl. vii. fig. 2 (1894).

A. Typical Form.

ζ ♂ (V. 169; C.?).   Newby Bridge, N. Lancashire.   Mr J. Paul [P].
η. ♀ (V. 167, C. 57).   Houffalize, Belgium.   Mlle L. Héger [P.].
θ. Yg. (V. 163; C. 63).   Freiburg, Baden.   G A Boulenger, Esq. [P].
ι Yg (V 172, C. 62)   Vienna.   Herr F. Henkel [E]
κ. ♂ (V. 176; C. 65)   Brasso, Hungary.   Prof. v. Méhely [C]
λ–ν. ♂ (V. 180; C. 54)   Pisa.   Prof. Della Torre
  & ♀ (V. 169, 171;   [E.].
  C. 56, 57).
ξ ♀ (V. 168; C. 54).   Sicily.   Christiania Mus.

C. (*C. persa.*)

n. ♀ (V. 176; C. 60).   Admont, Upper Styria.   Herr F. Henkel [E.].
o. ♀ (V. 166, C. 61).   Carinthia.   Herr F Henkel [E.].
p–q. ♂ (V. 184; C. 75)   Zara, Dalmatia   Herr Spada Novak
  & ♀ (V 176; C 65).   [C.].
r–t. ♂ (V. 187; C. 75)   Salonica.   J. Southgate, Esq.
  & yg. (V. 172, 176;   [P.].
  C. 58, 60).
u–w. ♂ (V. 171, 170;   Alexandretta.   Hr. Rolle [C.]
  C. 70, 71) & ♀ (V. 166;
  C. 50).

D. (*C. scutatus.*)

c. ♂ (V. 180; C. 69).   Pressbaum, nr. Vienna.   Hr. F. Henkel [E.].

F. Uniform black above, with a bright yellow collar.

a. ♀ (V. 174; C. 50).   Copenhagen.

Add:— Page 222. **Tropidonotus conspicillatus.**

e. ♀ (V. 145; C. 48).   Sarawak.   Rajah Brooke [P.]
f. Yg. (V. 152; C. 53).   Tandjong, S.E. Borneo.
g. ♂ (V. 138; C. 54).   Great Natuna Id.   C. Hose, Esq [C.].

Add:— Page 225. **Tropidonotus trianguligerus.**

w. ♀ (V. 136; C. 81).   Kina Balu, N. Borneo.   A. Everett, Esq [C.].

Add:— Page 226. **Tropidonotus melanogaster.**

Eutænia melanogaster, *Bocourt, Miss. Sc. Mex., Rept.* p 779, pl. liii. fig. 4, & pl. lv. fig. 3 (1893).

Add:— Page 227. **Tropidonotus olivaceus.**

Coronella olivacea, *Pfeffer, Jahrb Hamb. Wiss Anst* x. 1893, p 79.
Mizodon olivaceus, *Bocage, Herp Angola*, p. 74 (1895).

o–r. ♀ (V. 139, C. ?) & hgr. (V. 140, 141, 144, C. 75, ?, 59).   Zomba, Brit. C Africa.   Sir H. H. Johnston [P.].
s. ♀ (V. 136; C. 67).   Fwambo, Brit. C. Africa.   E. Carson, Esq. [C].
t. Hgr. (V. 136; C. 78).   Milangi, Brit. C. Africa.   Sir H. H. Johnston [P.].
u. Hgr. (V. 137; C. ?).   Ngatana, E. Africa.   Dr. J W Gregory [P].

Add:— Page 228. **Tropidonotus pygæus.**

Contia pygæa, *Loennberg, Proc. U.S. Nat. Mus.* xvii 1894, p. 323.
Seminatrix pygæus, *Cope, Am. Nat.* 1895, p. 678.

Add:— Page 230. **Tropidonotus sancti-johannis.**

o. ♂ (V. 139; C. 86).   Shillong, Assam.   H. M. Phipson, Esq. [P.].
p. ♂ (V. 145; C. ?).   Benares.   S. Flower, Esq [P].

Add:— Page 231. **Tropidonotus piscator.**

Bothrodytes piscator, *Cope, Tr. Am. Philos. Soc.* xviii. 1895, p. 216.

A.

β–γ, δ. ♀ (V. 143, 144; C. 68, ?) & yg. (V. 146; C. 71).   Peermad, Travancore.   H. S. Ferguson, Esq. [P.].
ε. ♂ (V. 135; C. 86)   Benares   S. Flower, Esq. [P]

B.

| *aa.* Hgr ♀ (V 141; C.70) | Swatow, China. | Christiania Mus |
| *bb* Yg. (V. 125; C. 77). | Pinang. | S. Flower, Esq.[P.]. |

C.

| *aa.* ♀ (V. 142; C. 78). | Java. | Christiania Mus |

Add.—   Page 233. **Tropidonotus annularis.**

i. ♀ (V. 149; C. 60).   Da-laen-saen, S W of Ningpo.   J. J. Walker, Esq [P.].

Add:—   Page 234. **Tropidonotus tessellatus.**

Tropidonotus tessellatus, *Fitzing. Beitr. Landesk. Oesterr.* i. p. 326 (1832); *Steind. Novara, Rept.* p. 66 (1867); *Durigen, Deutschl. Amph. u. Rept.* p. 295, pl vii. fig. 1 (1894)
Natrix hydrus, *Cope, Tr Am. Philos. Soc.* xviii. 1895, p. 216

ι. ♂ (V 161; C ?)	Zara, Dalmatia.	Dr. F. Werner [E.].
κ. ♀ (V. 165; C. 58).	Travnik, Bosnia	Dr. F. Werner [E.].
λ. ♀ (V. 168; C. 56).	Smyrna.	F. Holmwood, Esq [P.].
μ–ξ. Yg. (V.169,165,168, C. 61, 69, 63).	Jerusalem.	Canon Tristram [E.].
ο. ♂ (V. 167; C. 53).	Fao, Persia	W. Cumming, Esq. [P].
π. ♀ (V. 168; C. 57).	Beltim, Delta	Dr. J. Anderson [P.].

Add:—   Page 237. **Tropidonotus viperinus.**

| β. ♀ (V 151; C. 58). | Seville. | Prof. Calderon [E.]. |
| γ. Hgr. (V. 150; C. 50). | Cintra. | Col. Yerbury [P.]. |

Add:—   Page 237. **Tropidonotus validus.**

Tropidonotus quadriserialis, *Bocourt, Miss Sc. Mex., Rept.* p 752, pl. liv. fig. 6 (1893)

k. Yg (V. 139; C 74)   S. José del Cabo, Lower California.

Add:—   Page 239. **Tropidonotus compressicauda.**

Natrix compressicauda, *Loennberg, Proc. U.S. Nat. Mus* xvii. 1894, p. 330.
—— compressicauda tæniata, *Cope, Am. Nat* 1895, p 676

Add:—   Page 239. **Tropidonotus septemvittatus.**

Regina leberis, *Bocourt, Miss. Sc. Mex., Rept.* p. 747, pl. lii. fig. 1, & pl liii fig. 8 (1893).
Natrix septemvittata, *Cope, Tr. Am. Philos Soc.* xviii 1895, p 216.
—— leberis, *Rhoads, Proc. Ac. Philad.* 1895, p. 390.

Add :—   Page 240. **Tropidonotus rigidus.**

Regina rigida, *Bocourt, Miss. Sc. Mex., Rept.* p. 748, pl. liii fig 7 (1893).

Add :—   Page 242 **Tropidonotus anoscopus.**

a. ♂ (V. 144, C. ?).   —— ?   Christiania Mus.

Add :—   Page 242 **Tropidonotus fasciatus.**

Tropidonotus rhombifer, *Bocourt, Miss. Sc. Mex, Rept.* p. 751, pl. liv. fig 5 (1893).
—— anomalus, *Werner, Zool. Anz.* 1893, p. 362.
Natrix fasciata, *Loennberg, Proc. U.S. Nat. Mus.* xviii. 1894, p. 331.
—— fasciata pictiventris, *Cope, Am Nat.* 1895, p. 677.
—— sipedon, *Rhoads, Proc. Ac. Philad.* 1895, p. 387.

A. Forma typica.

r. ♂ (Sc. 25; V 143; C. 69).   Wisconsin.   Christiania Mus
s. Yg. (Sc. 23; V. 132; C. 68)   Alabama   Christiania Mus.

D. Var. *rhombifer*.

e. ♂ (Sc. 27; V. 146; C. 75).   New Orleans.   Christiania Mus.

Add :—   Page 244. **Tropidonotus cyclopium.**

Natrix cyclopion, *Loennberg, Proc. US. Nat. Mus.* xvii 1894, p. 332.

Add :—   Page 245. **Tropidonotus taxispilotus.**

Natrix taxispilota, *Loennberg, l c.* p. 332.

e. Yg. (Sc. 31; V. 138; C. 75).   Pensacola, Florida.   Christiania Mus.

Page 246. Add a species :—

47a. **Tropidonotus variabilis.**

Hemigenius variabilis, *Dugès, Proc. Amer. Philos Soc.* xxv. 1888, p. 182, fig.; *Bocourt, Miss. Sc. Mex., Rept.* p. 741, pl liii fig. 5 (1893).

Posterior maxillary teeth abruptly enlarged. Eye moderate. Rostral broader than deep, visible from above; internasals shorter than the præfrontals; frontal once and a half as long as broad, longer than its distance from the end of the snout, shorter than the parietals; loreal as long as deep; two præ- and two postoculars; temporals 1 + 2; seven upper labials, third and fourth entering the eye; four lower labials in contact with the anterior chin-shields, which are longer than the posterior. Scales in 15 rows, strongly keeled, outer row faintly keeled. Ventrals 122–130; anal divided; subcaudals 43–48. Olive-grey above, with small black spots; upper surface of head speckled with black, back of head nearly entirely black; pale olive beneath, speckled with blackish on the sides.

Total length 290 millim.; tail 65.

Mexico.

a. ♂ (V. 129; C 48).   Guanajuato.   Dr A. Dugès [C.]; Paris Museum [E].

Add :—   Page 246. **Tropidonotus sexlineatus.**

m Hgr ♂ (V. 153; C. 163).   Madagascar.   Christiania Mus.

Add :—   Page 247. **Tropidonotus dolichocercus.**

b. ♀ (V. 162, C 111).   Ambohimitombo forest, Madagascar.   Dr. Forsyth Major [C]

Page 248. Add a species —

51 a. **Tropidonotus balteatus.**

Trimerodytes balteatus, *Cope, Proc. Ac Philad.* 1894, p 426 (1895).

Internasals longer than broad; præfrontals fused to a single shield, frontal little longer than broad; loreal deeper than long, one præ- and two or three postoculars; temporals 1+2; nine upper labials, fourth and fifth or fifth and sixth entering the eye; six lower labials in contact with the anterior chin-shields, which are shorter than the posterior. Scales smooth, feebly keeled on the tail, in 19 rows. Ventrals 202; anal divided; subcaudals 84 Black, with white or pale yellow rings; labials and oculars with yellow centres; a yellow line from near the angle of the mouth to near the middle line above; a pair of yellow spots on the parietal shields near the common suture.

Total length 377 millim.; tail 80.

Hainan.

Add :—   Page 249. **Tropidonotus tigrinus.**

Bothrodytes tigrinus, *Cope, Tr. Am. Philos Soc.* xviii 1895, p. 216

t–u Yg. (V. 151, 153; C. 64, ?).   Chefoo

v. Hgr. ♀ (V. 161, C.71).   Chimabara, Japan   Mr Holst [C.]

Add :—   Page 252. **Tropidonotus ceylonensis.**

Bothrodytes ceylonensis, *Cope, Tr Am. Philos Soc.* xviii. 1895, p. 215.

ADDENDA AND CORRIGENDA.

Add :— Page 253. **Tropidonotus stolatus.**

Natrix stolata, *Cope, l. c.* p. 216.

Add :— Page 253. **Tropidonotus beddomii.**

n-p. ♂ (V. 143; C. 75) Peermad, Travancore. H. S. Ferguson, Esq.
& ♀ (V. 143, 142 ; [P.].
C. 62, 65).

Add :— Page 255. **Tropidonotus vittatus.**

Ceratophallus vittatus, *Cope, Tr. Am. Philos. Soc.* xviii. 1895, p 216

Add :— Page 255. **Tropidonotus nigrocinctus.**

Tropidonotus nigrocinctus, *Bouleng. Ann. Mus. Genova,* (2) xiii 1893, p. 322.

Add :— Page 256. **Tropidonotus subminiatus.**

x. ♂ (V. 163; C. 75). Nampandet, Shan States, 2000 ft. E. W. Oates, Esq. [P.]
y. ♀ (V. 163; C. 88). North Chin hills, Upper Burma. E. Y. Watson, Esq. [P.]

Add :— Page 257. **Tropidonotus spilogaster.**

Bothrodytes spilogaster, *Cope, Tr. Am. Philos. Soc.* xviii. 1895, p. 216.

g. ♀ (V. 152; C. 97) Highlands of Lepauto, N. Luzon. Whitehead Expedition.
h-i ♀ (V. 147, 146 ; C. ?, 82). Cape Engano, N. Luzon. Whitehead Expedition.

Add :— Page 259. **Tropidonotus chrysargus.**

z-α. Yg. (V. 148, 155 ; C. 85, 82). Balabac. A. Everett, Esq. [C.].
β-γ. Yg. (V. 153, 176, C. 85, 80). Palawan. A. Everett, Esq. [C.].
δ. Hgr ♂ (V. 143; C. 72). Sarawak Rajah Brooke [P.].

Add :— Page 260. **Tropidonotus monticola.**

g. ♂ (V. 137 ; C. 91) Peermad, Travancore, 3300 f. H. S. Ferguson, Esq [P.].

Add :— Page 260. **Tropidonotus maculatus.**

d ♂ (V. 140; C. ?). Labuan. A Everett, Esq. [C.].
e. ♀ (V. 148; C. 102). Mt. Mulu, Sarawak, 1000 ft. C. Hose, Esq. [C.].

ADDENDA AND CORRIGENDA.

f. ♀ (V. 155; C. ?)   Sarawak.   Rajah Brooke [P.].
g ♀ (V. 140; C. ?).   Spitang R., N. Borneo   A. Everett, Esq. [C.].
h. Yg. (V. 141; C. 117).   Great Natuna Id.   C. Hose, Esq. [C.].

Add:—   Page 261. **Tropidonotus saravacensis.**

g. ♀ (V 147; C. 74)   Kuching, Sarawak   Rajah Brooke [P.].

Add:—   Page 263. **Tropidonotus flavifrons.**

b. Yg. (V. 149, C. 102).   Penriser hills, Sarawak.   A. Everett, Esq. [C.].
c, d–e, f–h. ♂ (V. 147, 146; C 101, 101), ♀ (V. 153; C. 94), & yg. (V 153, 153, 153; C. 98, 87, 93).   Kina Balu.   A. Everett, Esq. [C.].

Page 265. Add a species :—

75. Tropidonotus halmahericus.

Tropidonotus (Macropophis) halmahericus, *Boettg. Zool. Anz* 1895, p. 130.

Allied to *T. hypomelas* and *T. dendrophiops*, but scales in 15 rows and ventrals 172–180. Head uniform black above, lower halves of labials white; body reddish white with black spots, or barred black and red anteriorly, black, uniform or with two series of round reddish-white spots posteriorly; belly white anteriorly, gradually darkening to black posteriorly.

Total length 1115 millim., tail 305.

Halmaheira.

a. ♀ (V. 172; C. ?).   Halmaheira.   Prof. Kukenthal [C.]; Senckenberg Mus [E.]. (One of the types)

Add.—   Page 266. **Macropisthodon flaviceps.**

o. ♀ (V. 129; C. 59).   Kuching, Sarawak.   Rajah Brooke [P.].

Add:—   Page 267. **Macropisthodon rhodomelas.**

h. Yg. (V. 124; C. 58)   Sarawak.   A Everett, Esq [C.].
i. Yg (V. 132, C 55).   Singapore.   H. N. Ridley, Esq. [P.].

Add:—   Page 267. **Macropisthodon plumbicolor.**

Tropidonotus plumbicolor, *Werner, Verh. zool.-bot. Ges Wien*, 1893, p. 350.

Young specimen, from Ceylon, with 21 rows of scales.

Page 268. Add a genus :—

11 *a.* COMPSOPHIS.

Compsophis, *Mocquard, CR. Soc. Philom.* 1894, no 17, p. 8.

Posterior maxillary teeth largest, separated from the rest by an interspace; anterior mandibular teeth longer than the posterior. Head distinct from neck; eye rather large, with round pupil; nasal single. Body short, rounded; scales smooth, without pits, in 19 rows. Tail moderate; subcaudals in two rows.

Madagascar.

1. Compsophis albiventris.

Compsophis albiventris, Mocq. l. c.

Rostral much broader than deep; internasals as long as the præfrontals; frontal once and a half as long as broad, longer than its distance from the end of the snout, shorter than the parietals; loreal deeper than long; one præ- and two postoculars; temporals 1+2; seven upper labials, third and fourth entering the eye; four lower labials in contact with the anterior chin-shields. Scales in 19 rows. Ventrals 148; anal entire; subcaudals 41. Uniform dark brown above, white beneath; a yellowish-white spot on each temple, and a small yellowish-white spot on each of the six last upper labials.

Total length 167 millim.; tail 28.

Ambre Mt.

Add:— Page 274. **Helicops bicolor.**

Helicops bicolor, *Bocage, Herp. Angola,* p. 76 (1895).

Add:— Page 275. **Helicops septemvittatus.**

Limnophis septemvittatus, *Bocourt, Miss. Sc. Mex., Rept.* p. 809, pl. lx. fig. 1 (1895).

Add:— Page 275. **Helicops allenii.**

Liodytes allenii, *Loennberg, Proc. U.S. Nat. Mus.* xvii. 1894, p. 330.

Add:— Page 281. **Hydræthiops melanogaster.**

Hydræthiops melanogaster, *Bocage, Herp. Angola,* p. 77 (1895).

Add:— Page 282. **Tretanorhinus variabilis.**

Tretanorhinus variabilis, *Bocourt, Miss. Sc. Mex., Rept.* p. 793, pl. lii. figs. 2 & 3 (1895).
—— variabilis, var. cubanus, *Bocourt, l. c.* p. 795, pl. lii. fig. 3.

d–e. ♂ (V. 152, 156; C. 66, 65). Cuba.

Add:— Page 282. **Tretanorhinus nigroluteus.**

Tretanorhinus nigroluteus, *Bocourt, l. c.* p. 798, pl. liv. fig. 1.
—— lateralis, *Bocourt, l. c.* p. 800, pl. lii. fig. 4.

Add :— Page 283 **Tretanorhinus mocquardii.**

Tretanorhinus mocquardi, *Bocourt, l. c.* p. 797, pl. lii. fig. 5.

Add :— Page 285. **Opisthotropis typica.**

a–c. ♂ (V. 184; C. 85) & ♀   Kina Balu.   A. Everett, Esq. [C.].
(V. 175, 174, C. 77, 76).

Præfrontals sometimes united.

Add :— Page 286. **Ischnognathus kirtlandii.**

Natrix kirtlandii, *Cope, Trans Amer. Philos. Soc.* xviii. 1895, p. 215.

Add :— Page 286. **Ischnognathus dekayi.**

Storeria dekayi, *Bocourt, l. c* p 742, pl liii fig 1; *Loennberg, Proc. U.S. Nat. Mus.* xvii 1894, p. 332.

o–p. ♂ (V. 133; C 53) &   Orizaba.   F. D. Godman, Esq.
♀ (V. 143; C. ?).   [P].

Loennberg records a specimen with 15 rows of scales.

Page 287. Add a species :—

2 *a.* **Ischnognathus victa.**

Storeria victa, *Hay, Science,* xix. 1892, p. 199.

Allied to *I. dekayi.* No loreal; scales in 15 rows; ventrals 146; anal entire; subcaudals 60.
Oklawaha River, Florida.

Page 287. **Ischnognathus occipitomaculata.**
Add :—

Storeria occipitomaculata, *Bocourt, l. c.* p. 745, pl. liii. fig. 6; *Loennberg, l. c.* p. 333.

Add :— Page 288. **Ischnognathus storerioides.**

Tropidonotus storerioides, *Bocourt, l. c.* p. 750.

p. ♂ (V. 127; C. 45).   Jalisco, N. of R. de   F. D. Godman, Esq.
                            Santiago.   [P]
q. ♀ (V. 131; C. 40).   Amula, Guerrero.   Mr H. H Smith [C.]; F. D. Godman, Esq. [P.].
r. ♂ (V. 125; C. 48).   Popocatepetl, 9000 ft.   Mr H. H Smith [C.]; F. D. Godman, Esq. [P.].

Add:— Page 291. **Haldea striatula.**

d. ♀ (V. 127; C. 37). Raleigh, N. Carolina. Messrs. Brimley [C.].

Add:— Page 294. **Streptophorus atratus.**

A. (*S. lansbergi.*)
h. ♀ (V. 146; C. 51). Trinidad. F. W. Urich, Esq. [P.].

B. (*S. atratus.*)
c. ♀ (V. 151; C. 49). Buenaventura, Colombia. Mr. W. F. H. Rosenberg [P.].

C. (*S. maculatus.*)
f. Yg. (V. 139, C. 48). Irazu, Costa Rica. F. D. Godman, Esq. [P.].

D. (*S. sebæ.*)
aa. Hgr (V. 148; C. 63). Hacienda Rosa de Jericho, Nicaragua, 3250 ft. Dr. E. Rothschuh [C.].

Add:— Page 297. **Hydrablabes præfrontalis.**

a. ♂ (V. 202; C. 72). Kina Balu. A. Everett, Esq. [P.].

Add:— Page 300. **Trachischium monticola.**

k. Hgr. (V. 120, C. 40). Naga hills. Dr. Cantor. (Type.)

Page 301 (*see* p. 419). **Trirhinopholis nuchalis.**
Add:—

Trirhinopholis nuchalis, *Bouleng. Ann. Mus. Genova*, (2) xiii. 1893, p. 323.

b-c. ♀ (V. 140, 140; C. 27, 24). Karin hills. M. L. Fea [C.].

Add:— Page 303. **Oxyrhabdium leporinum.**

c. ♂ (V. 167; C. 48). Highlands of Lepauto, N. Luzon. Whitehead Exped.

Add:— Page 304. **Xylophis perroteti.**

k. ♀ (V. 141; C. 10). High Range, Travancore. H. S. Ferguson, Esq. [P.].

Add:— Page 308. **Achalinus rufescens.**

b. ♂ (Sc. 23; V. 137; C. 70). Hong Kong, 1700 ft. J. J. Walker, Esq. [P.].

ADDENDA AND CORRIGENDA. 613

Add:—   Page 309. **Achalinus braconnieri.**

c. Yg. (V. 180; C. 48).   Mainland opposite   J. J. Walker, Esq. [P.].
                      Chusan Islands.

Add:—   Page 313 **Aspidura trachyprocta.**

i-m. ♂ (V. 142, 141; C. 23, 23),   Ceylon.   Miss Layard [P.].
♀ (V. 147; C. 17), & yg.
(V. 147; C. 14).

Add:—   Page 315. **Pseudoxyrhopus microps.**

Pseudoxyrhopus tritæniatus, *Mocquard, C.R. Soc. Philom.* 1894, no. 9, p. 4.

Page 315. Add a species:—

2 *a*. Pseudoxyrhopus ambreensis.

Pseudoxyrhopus ambreensis, *Mocquard, C.R. Soc. Philom.* 1894, no. 9, p. 4, *and Bull. Soc. Philom.* (8) vii. 1895, p. 123.

Rostral much broader than deep, visible from above, frontal a little longer than broad; loreal small; one præ- and two postoculars; seven upper labials, third and fourth entering the eye. Scales in 21 rows. Ventrals 147; anal divided; subcaudals 49 pairs or more. Uniform brown above, sandy grey beneath; a white line round the upper lip, along the upper border of the labials.

Total length 296 millim.

Ambre Mt., Madagascar.

Page 316. **Pseudoxyrhopus quinquelineatus.**
Add:—

c. ♀ (V. 148; C. 52).   Madagascar.   L. Greening, Esq. [P.].

Page 317. Add a species:—

4 *a*. Pseudoxyrhopus occipitalis.

Snout rounded, feebly projecting. Rostral broader than deep, just visible from above; internasals much shorter than the præfrontals; frontal once and one third as long as broad, longer than its distance from the end of the snout, shorter than the parietals; loreal longer than deep; one præ- and two postoculars; temporals 1+2; seven upper labials, third and fourth entering the eye; four lower labials in contact with the anterior chin-shields, which are a little larger than the posterior. Scales in 17 rows. Ventrals 183; anal divided; subcaudals 64. Pale brown above, scales edged with lighter, with two darker longitudinal streaks; crown and nape blackish brown, occiput and sides of head yellowish white; lower parts uniform white.

Total length 310 millim.; tail 70.

Madagascar.

a. Hgr. (V. 183; C. 64).   S.W. Madagascar.   Mr. Last [C].

Add :—   Page 317. **Lycognathophis sechellensis.**

Lycognathophis seychellensis, *Stejneger, Proc. U.S. Nat. Mus.* xvi. 1894, p. 726.

Page 320. Add a genus :—

38 *a*. MICROPISTHODON.

Micropisthodon, *Mocquard, C.R. Soc. Philom.* 1894, no. 17, p. 7.

Maxillary teeth 12; posterior maxillary and mandibular teeth shortest. Head not distinct from neck; eye rather large, with round pupil; nasal entire. Body slender, slightly compressed; scales narrow, smooth, oblique, with apical pits, in 17 rows; ventrals rounded. Tail long; subcaudals in two rows.

Madagascar.

1. Micropisthodon ochraceus.

Micropisthodon ochraceus, *Mocq. l c* p. 8.

Rostral large, twice as broad as deep; internasals a little shorter than the præfrontals; frontal as long as its distance from the end of the snout; supraoculars longer than the frontal, nearly as long as the parietals; loreal longer than deep; one or two præ- and two or three postoculars, temporals 2+2; eight upper labials, fourth and fifth entering the eye; four lower labials in contact with the chin-shields, which are short. Scales in 17 rows, very finely striated. Ventrals 145; anal divided; subcaudals 133. Light ochraceous brown above, with fine darker dots and small spots, two black lines on the neck, converging behind.

Total length 687 millim.; tail 260.

Nossi Bé.

Page 324. Add a species :—

2 *a*. Gonionotophis klingii.

Gonionotophis klingi, *Matschie, Sitzb. Ges. Naturf Fr.* 1893, p. 172.

Rostral hardly visible from above, internasals much broader than long; præfrontals a little longer than broad; frontal as long as its distance from the rostral, shorter than the parietals; loreal more than twice as long as broad; one præ- and two postoculars; temporals 2+2; seven upper labials, fourth and fifth entering the eye; five lower labials in contact with the anterior chin-shields, which are longer than the posterior. Scales very strongly keeled, in 19 rows. Ventrals 170; anal entire; subcaudals 92. Blackish brown above, each scale light-edged; yellowish beneath.

Total length 420 millim.; tail 125.

Togoland, W. Africa.

Page 326. Add a genus:—

42 a. GLYPHOLYCUS.

Glypholycus, *Gunth. Proc. Zool. Soc.* 1893, p. 629 (1894).

Dentition as in *Lamprophis* and *Bothrolycus*. Head rather small and depressed; eye small, with round pupil, nostril valvular, directed upwards; a longitudinal groove on each side of the head, separating the labials from the shields above. Body elongate, cylindrical; scales smooth, without pits, in 23 or 25 rows; ventrals rounded. Tail moderate; subcaudals in two rows. Hypapophyses developed throughout the vertebral column.

Central Africa.

1. Glypholycus bicolor.

Glypholycus bicolor, *Gunth. l. c.* fig.

Rostral much broader than deep, just visible from above; internasals longer than broad, very narrow in front, shorter than the præfrontals; eyes and nostrils directed upwards; nasal semidivided; frontal small, about once and a half as long as broad, as long as its distance from the rostral, much shorter than the parietals; loreal at least twice as long as deep; one præ- and two postoculars; temporals 1+2; eight upper labials, fourth entering the eye; four lower labials in contact with the anterior chin-shields, which are much longer than the posterior. Scales in 23 (rarely 25) rows. Ventrals 155–184; anal entire; subcaudals 56–69. Dark brown above; two outer rows of scales and lower parts whitish, a brown line along the meeting edges of the subcaudals.

Total length 530 millim., tail 140.

Lake Tanganyika.

a–f. ♂ (Sc. 23, 23, 25, 23, 23; V. 159,155,158,160, 158; C. 63, ?, ?, 65, 69) & ♀ (Sc. 23, V. 184; C. 56).	Lake Tanganyika.	E. Coode-Hore, Esq [P.]. (Types.)

Add:—   Page 327. **Cyclocorus lineatus.**

f. ♀ (V. 137; C. 44).	Placer, N.E Mindanao.	A. Everett, Esq.[C.].
g. ♀ (V. 167, C. ?).	Highlands of Lepauto, N. Luzon.	Whitehead Exped.
h. ♀ (V. 153; C.?).	Isabella, N.E. Luzon.	Whitehead Exped.
i. ♀ (V. 149; C. 45).	Albay, S. Luzon.	Whitehead Exped.

Add :—   Page 327. BOODON.

Theleus, Cope, Am. Nat. 1893, p. 482.

Add :—   Page 332. Boodon lineatus.

Borædon lineatus, Stejneger, Proc. U.S. Nat. Mus. xvi. 1894, p. 727 ; *Bocage,* Herp Angola, p. 78 (1895).

o-ϕ. ♀ (Sc. 29, 31, 29; V. 225, 228, 219; C. 49, 48, 51) & yg. (Sc. 29, 27, 31, 29; V. 220, 201, 212, 208; C ?, 62, 66, 63).	Zomba, Brit. C. Africa.	Sir H. H. Johnston [P.].
w-bb. Hgr. (Sc. 27; V. 188; C. 67) & yg. (Sc 27; V. 198, 190; C. 50, 53)	Ngatana, E. Africa.	Dr. J. W. Gregory [P.].
cc. ♀ (Sc. 33; V. 249; C. 52)	Mt. Maka, Kapti Plains.	Dr. J. W. Gregory [P.].
dd-ee. Yg. (Sc. 31, 29, V. 229, 215; C. 55, 64).	Bolama, Senegambia.	R. Kitching, Esq. [P.]
ff. Ad., head and neck.	Uganda.	Scott Elliot, Esq [P.]
gg. Yg. (Sc. 31; V. 220; C. 55).	Uganda.	F. J. Jackson, Esq. [P.].

Add —   Page 336. Boodon olivaceus.

m-o. ♂ (Sc. 25, 27, V 198, 180; C. 55, 52) & yg. (Sc. 25; V. 183; C. 53).	Mouth of the Loango.	Mr. H. J. Duggan [C.].

Add :—   Page 338. Lycophidium laterale.

Lycophidium laterale, Bocage, Herp. Angola, p. 82 (1895).

Add :—   Page 339. Lycophidium capense.

Lycophidium capense, Bocage, Herp. Angola, p. 339 (1805).

i. ♂ (A. V. 192; C. 41).	East London, Cape of Good Hope.	H. S. Thorne, Esq [P.].
k-l, m. ♂ (B. V. 100, 186; C. 46, 47) & yg (A V. 194; C. 38).	Zomba, Brit. C. Africa.	Sir H. H. Johnston [P.].
n. ♂ (B V. 180; C. 37).	Kariti, E. Africa.	Dr. J. W. Gregory [P.].
o. Yg. (B. V. 163, C. 36).	Mkonumbi, E. Africa.	Dr. J. W Gregory [P.]
p. Yg. (B. V. ?, C. 36).	N. Giriama, E. Africa.	Dr. J W. Gregory [P.].
q. ♂ (B. V. 180; C. 34).	Ugogo.	Mr. Baxter [C.].
r. ♂ (C. V. 181; C. 33).	Caconda, Angola.	Prof. B. du Bocage [P.].

Add.— Page 340 **Lycophidium irroratum.**

Alopecion (Lycodon) nigromaculatus, *Peters, Mon. Berl. Ac.* 1863, p. 288.

h–l ♂ (V. 168; C. 34), ♀ (V. 165, 169; C. 36, 32), & hgr. (V. 169; C. 41).	Niger.	W. H. Crosse, Esq. [P.].

Add :— Page 342. **Lycophidium semicinctum.**

B. (Var. *albomaculata*.)

e–h. ♂ (V. 190, 188; C. 46, 47), ♀ (V. 200; C. 36), & yg. (V. 189; C. 47).	Bissao.	V. H. Cornish, Esq. [P.].
i–k. ♂ (V. 190; C. 47) & ♀ (V. 205, C. 34).	Bolama, Senegambia.	R. Kitching, Esq. [P.].

The ♀ from Bolama measures 630 millim.

D. (Intermediate between B and C.)

a ♂ (V. 199; C. 55).	Niger.	W. H. Crosse, Esq. [P.].

Add.— Page 344. **Hormonotus modestus.**

e–f. ♀ (B. V. 234, 231; C. ?, 83).	Mouth of the Loango.	Mr H. J. Duggan [C.].

Add :— Page 345. **Simocephalus capensis.**

? Simocephalus guirali, *Bocage, Herp. Angola*, p. 84 (1895).

b, c. ♂ (V. 212; C. 54) & ♀ (V. 222; C. 47)	Zomba, Brit. C. Africa.	Sir H. H. Johnston [P.].

Add :— Page 346. **Simocephalus guirali.**

c. Hgr. ♀ (V. 246; C. 64).	Mouth of the Loango.	Mr. H. J. Duggan [C]

Page 347. Add two species :—

3 *a*. **Simocephalus chanleri.**

Simocephalus chanleri, *Stejneger, Proc. U.S. Nat. Mus.* xvi. 1894, p. 726.

Rostral visible from above, its depth two thirds its width; internasals slightly broader than long, two thirds the length of the præfrontals; frontal as long as broad, much shorter than the parietals; loreal as long as deep; one præ- and three postoculars; temporals 1+2; seven upper labials, third and fourth entering the eye; five lower labials in contact with the anterior chin-shields, which are considerably larger than the posterior. Scales in 15 rows, all strongly keeled. Olive-grey above, yellowish beneath.

Island Manda, N. of Lamu, E. Africa.

3 b. Simocephalus crossii.

Simocephalus crossii, *Bouleng. Ann. & Mag. N. H.* (6) xvi. 1895, p. 33.

Eye moderately large. Rostral much broader than deep, just visible from above; internasals broader than long, two thirds the length of the præfrontals; frontal as long as broad, as long as its distance from the end of the snout, much shorter than the parietals; loreal deeper than long; one præ- and two postoculars; temporals 2+3; seven upper labials, third and fourth entering the eye; four lower labials in contact with the anterior chin-shields, which are short, like the posterior. Scales strongly keeled, in 17 rows. Ventrals 234; anal entire; subcaudals 53. Blackish above and on the outer end of the ventrals, yellowish white beneath.

Total length 410 millim.; tail 50.

Niger.

a. ♀ (V. 234; C. 53).	Lower Niger.	W. H. Crosse, Esq. [P.]. (Type.)

Add :—   Page 351. **Lycodon jara.**

h. ♀ (V. 183; C. 68).	Bengal?	Dr. Cantor.

Add :—   Page 354. **Lycodon aulicus.**

D.

kk–ll ♂ (V. 100; C. 72) & ♀ (V. 106; C. 55).	Luzon.	A. Everett, Esq. [C.].

Add :—   Page 357. **Lycodon stormi.**

a. ♀ (V. 220; C. 73).	Buol, Celebes.	Drs. P & F. Sarasin [P.].

Add :—   Page 357. **Lycodon albofuscus.**

c. Hgr. (V. 234; C. 177).	Rejang R., Sarawak.	Rajah Brooke [P.].

Add :—   Page 358. **Lycodon fasciatus.**

c. Hgr. ♀ (V. 201; C. 74).	Shillong, Assam.	H. M. Phipson, Esq. [P.].

Add :—   Page 360. **Lycodon subcinctus.**

m. ♀ (V. 207; C. 65).	Muching, Sarawak.	Rajah Brooke [P.].
n. Yg. (V. 205; C. 67).	Sandakan, N. Borneo.	Douglas Cator, Esq. [P.].

Add :— Page 361. **Dinodon rufozonatus.**

Dinodon rufozonatus, *Boettg. Ber. Offenb. Ver. Nat.* 1895, p. 108 (Loo Choo Ids.).

Add :— Page 363. **Dinodon septentrionalis.**

Dinodon septentrionalis, *Bouleng. Ann. Mus. Genova,* (2) xiii 1893, p. 324.

e. Hgr. (A. V. 210; C. 87)   Cobapo, Karin hills.   M. L. Fea [C.]

Add :— Page 364. **STEGONOTUS.**

Stegonotus, *Cope, Proc. Ac Philad* 1865, p. 197.

Add :— Page 367. **Stegonotus modestus.**

m. Yg. (V. 193; C. 76).   Trobriand Ids.   Mr. Meek [C.].

Page 367. Add two species :—

3 a. Stegonotus guentheri.

Stegonotus guentheri, *Bouleng. Ann. & Mag. N. H.* (6) xvi. 1895, p. 31.

Rostral much broader than deep, the portion visible from above measuring one fourth to one third its distance from the frontal; internasals shorter than the præfrontals, frontal as long as broad, as long as its distance from the rostral, much shorter than the parietals; loreal about twice as long as deep; one præ- and two postoculars; temporals 1+2; eight upper labials, fourth and fifth entering the eye; four or five lower labials in contact with the anterior chin-shields, which are longer than the posterior. Scales in 15 rows. Ventrals 180-197; anal entire; subcaudals 75 pairs. Black or blackish brown above, turning to pale brown on the sides; upper lip and lower parts white.

Total length 1150 millim.; tail 230.

S.E. New Guinea.

a–c ♂ (V. 197; C. ?) & ♀   Fergusson Id.   Mr Meek [C.].
(V. 180, 193; C. 75, ?).   (Types.)

3 b. Stegonotus reticulatus.

Stegonotus modestus (*non Schleg.*), *Boettg. in Semon, Zool. Forsch.* v. p. 120 (1894)

——— reticulatus, *Bouleng. Ann. & Mag. N. H.* (6) xvi. 1895, p. 31.

Rostral much broader than deep, the portion visible from above measuring one fifth to one fourth its distance from the frontal; internasals shorter than the præfrontals; frontal as long as broad, as long as its distance from the rostral, much shorter than the parietals; loreal once and a half to twice as long as deep; two præ- and two postoculars; temporals 2+3; eight upper labials, fourth and fifth entering the eye; four or five lower labials in contact with the anterior chin-shields, which are as long as or a little longer than the posterior. Scales in 17 rows. Ventrals 200-203; anal entire; subcaudals 75-78 pairs. Pale greyish brown above, white on the sides, each scale edged with black; head uniform black above; lower parts white.

Total length 1140 millim; tail 250. The largest specimen, with mutilated tail, measures 1080 millim. from snout to vent.

S.E. New Guinea.

a–b. ♀ (V. 203, 201; C. ?, 78).	Fergusson Id.	Mr. Meek [C.]. (Types.)
c. ♂ (V. 200; C. 75).	New Guinea.	

Add :—   Page 369. **DRYOCALAMUS.**

Hemidipsas, *Günth. Cat. Col. Sn.* p. 181 (1858).

Add :—   Page 371. **Dryocalamus subannulatus.**

Hemidipsas ocellata, *Günth. Cat.* p. 182 (1858).

c. ♀ (V. 225; C. 88).	——?	Zoological Society. (Type of *H. ocellata*.)
d. ♀ (V. 232; C. 95).	Singapore.	H. N. Ridley, Esq. [P.].

Add :—   Page 373. **Dryocalamus tristrigatus.**

b. ♂ (V. 231; C. 93).	Claudetown, Baram R., Sarawak.	C. Hose, Esq. [C.]
c. ♂ (V. 229; C. 96).	Mt. Mulu, Sarawak, 2000 ft.	C. Hose, Esq. [C.].
d. ♂ (V. 231; C. 93).	Labuan.	A. Everett, Esq. [C.].
e. ♀ (V. 219; C. 91).	Great Natuna Id.	C. Hose, Esq. [C.]

Add :—   Page 373. **PSEUDASPIS.**

Ophirhina, *Bocage, Jorn. Sc. Lisb.* viii. 1882, p. 300.

Add :—   Page 373. **Pseudaspis cana.**

Coluber elegantissimus, *Laur. Syn. Rept.* p. 96 (1768).
—— ocellatus, *Gmel. S. N.* i. p. 1113 (1788).
Ophirhina anchietæ, *Bocage, l. c.*
Coronella cana, *Günth. Ann. & Mag. N. H.* (6) xv. 1895, p. 525.
Pseudaspis cana, *Bocage, Herp. Angola*, p. 100, pl. x. (1895).

s. Yg. (Sc. 25; V. 186; C. 57).	Caconda, Angola.	Prof. B. du Bocage [P.].
t. Yg. (Sc. 27; V. 194; C. 48).	S. Africa.	Christiania Museum.

u–v. ♀ (Sc. 29, 27; V. 206, 207, C. 50, ?).		Victoria West.	Rev. G. H. R. Fisk [P].
w. ♂ (Sc. 27; V. 183; C. 50).		Zomba, Brit. C. Africa.	Sir H. H. Johnston [P.].
x. ♂ (Sc. 27; V. 185; C. 50).		Chiradzulu, Brit. C. Africa	Sir H. H. Johnston [P.].

Add :— Page 377. **Zaocys carinatus.**

Zaocys carinatus, *Bouleng. Ann. Mus. Genova*, (2) xiii. 1893, p. 324

Add .— Page 378. **Zaocys fuscus.**

f–g. ♂ (V 193, 196; C. 163, 169).	E coast of Sumatra.	Mrs. Findlay [P.].
h. ♂ (V. 188; C. ?).	Mt. Mulu, Sarawak, 2000 ft.	C Hose, Esq. [C].
i. ♂ (V. 194; C. ?).	Great Natuna Id.	C. Hose, Esq. [C].

Add :— Page 379. **ZAMENIS.**

Hemidryas, *Peters & Doria, Ann. Mus. Genova*, xiii. 1878, p. 394.
Acanthocalyx, *Cope, Trans. Amer. Philos. Soc.* xviii. 1895, p. 204.
Tylanthera, *Cope, l. c.* p. 205.

Add :— Page 383. **Zamenis dipsas.**

Ahætulla (Hemidryas) dipsas, *Peters & Doria, l. c.* p. 392, fig.

Add :— Page 385. **Zamenis korros.**

q. ♂ (V. 162; C. 127).   Taipang, Perak.   S. Flower, Esq. [P.].

Add :— Page 386. **Zamenis mucosus.**

ζ. Yg. (V. 191; C. 107).   Toungoo.   E. W. Oates, Esq. [P.].

Add :— Page 387. **Zamenis constrictor.**

Zamenis stejnegerianus, *Cope, Am. Nat* 1895, p. 678.
―― conirostris, *Cope, l. c.* p. 879.

s. ♀ (V. 178; C. 85)   S. Francisco.   Christiania Museum.

Eight upper labials and two superposed loreals.

Add :— Page 388. **Zamenis lineatus**

Zamenis flavigularis, part., *Gunth. Biol. C.-Am., Rept.* p. 120 (1894).

Add :— Page 389. **Zamenis mentovarius.**

Zamenis flavigularis, part., *Gunth. l. c.*

Add:— Page 390. Zamenis flagelliformis.

Bascanium flagellum frenatum, *Stejneger, N. Am. Faun.* no. 7, pt. ii. p. 208 (1803).
—— flagellum, *Stejneger, Proc. U.S Nat. Mus.* xvii. 1895, p. 595.

Add:— Page 391. Zamenis tæniatus.

Zamenis semilineatus, *Gunth. Biol. C.-Am., Rept.,* p. 121, pl. xlvi. fig. A (1894).
—— ornatus, *Gunth. l. c.* p. 122, pl. xlvi. fig. B.
—— lateralis fuliginosus, *Cope, Am. Nat.* 1895, p. 679.

Add:— Page 392. Zamenis pulcherrimus.

Drymobius lemniscatus, *Cope, Trans. Amer Philos. Soc.* xviii. 1895, p. 203.

Add:— Page 392. Zamenis mexicanus.

Bascanium mexicanum, *Cope, l. c.* p. 203.

Add:— Page 394. Zamenis grahamiæ.

h. Yg. (V. 179; C. 108). Amula, Guerrero. Mr. H. H. Smith [C.]; F. D. Godman, Esq. [P.].

Var. hexalepis.

Salvadora grahamiæ hexalepis, *Stejneger, N. Am. Faun.* no. 7, pt. ii. p. 205, pl. iii. fig. 2.

In this form the eye is sometimes separated from the labials by a series of suboculars.

Add:— Page 394. Zamenis spinalis.

e. Yg. (V. 206; C. 90). Chefoo.

Add:— Page 395. Zamenis gemonensis.

Zamenis gemonensis, *Minà-Palumbo, Nat. Sicil.* xii. 1892, p. 55; *Tomasini, Wiss Mitth aus Bosn u. Herzeg.* ii. p. 624 (1894); *Méhely, Zool. Anz.* 1804, p. 84.

A.

w. Hgr. ♀ (Sc. 19; V. 170; C. 93). Dalmatia. Christiania Mus.
x. Yg. (Sc. 19; V. 209; C. ?) Sicily. Christiania Mus.

B. (Var. *caspius.*)

d. ♂ (Sc. 19; V. 197; C. 107). Salonica. J. Southgate, Esq [P.].

ADDENDA AND CORRIGENDA. 623

Add :— Page 397. **Zamenis dahlii.**

Zamenis dahlii, Tomasini, Wiss. Mitth. aus Bosn. u. Herzeg. ii. p. 627 (1894).

m. Hgr. (V. 210 ; C. 112). Mt. Tabor. Canon Tristram [E.].

Add :— Page 398. **Zamenis rhodorhachis.**

Zamenis ladacensis, var *subnigra, Boettg. Zool. Anz.* 1893, p. 118.
—— *rhodorhachis, Anders. Proc. Zool. Soc.* 1895, p. 654.

γ. Yg (V. 229 ; C. 129). Zaila, Somaliland. Capt. Nurse [P.].

Add :— Page 399. **Zamenis ventrimaculatus.**

Acanthocalyx ventrimaculatus, Cope, Trans. Amer. Philos. Soc. xviii. 1895, p. 215.

Page 401. Add two species :—

17 a. Zamenis rogersi.

Zamenis rogersi, Anders. Ann. & Mag. N. H. (6) xii. 1893, p. 439.

Allied to *Z. rhodorhachis* and *Z. ventrimaculatus*, but rostral about half as deep as broad. Ventrals 197–201; anal divided; subcaudals 95–105. Pale sandy, with a dorsal series of large, light-edged dark spots, alternating on each side with a series of smaller spots; sides of head and neck orange; a dark oblique streak below the eye and an oblique band on the temple; uniform white beneath.
Total length 830 millim.; tail 215.
Lower Egypt.

a. Yg. (V. 198 ; C. 95).	Desert east of Helouan, near Cairo.	Dr. J. Anderson [P.].	
b. ♂ (V. 197 ; C. 105).	Beltim, Delta.	Dr. J. Anderson [P.].	(Types.)
c. ♀ (V. 201 ; C. 96).	Suez.	Dr. J. Anderson [P.].	

17 b. Zamenis brevis.

Zamenis brevis, Bouleng. Ann. Mus. Genova, (2) xv. 1895, pl. iii. fig. 3.

Snout obtuse, feebly projecting. Rostral once and a half as broad as deep, the portion visible from above measuring one fourth its distance from the frontal; internasals as long as the præfrontals; frontal broader than the supraocular, once and two fifths as long as broad, longer than its distance from the end of the snout, shorter than the parietals; loreal as long as deep, one præocular, not in contact with the frontal, with a subocular below it; two post-oculars; temporals 2+2; nine upper labials, fifth and sixth entering the eye; four or five lower labials in contact with the anterior chin-shields; posterior chin-shields as long as the anterior and separated from each other by two or three series of scales. Scales smooth, in 19 rows. Ventrals obtusely angulate laterally, 159; anal divided; subcaudals 76. Pale greyish above, with four longitudinal series of pale grey-brown spots, the two vertebral series formed of larger spots which are partly confluent; a blackish spot below the eye; lower parts white.

Total length 200 millim.; tail 47.

Ogaden, Somaliland

Page 402. Add a species:—

19 a. Zamenis smithii.

Zamenis smithi, *Bouleng. Proc. Zool. Soc.* 1895, p. 536, pl. xxx. fig. 2.

Snout obtuse, feebly projecting Rostral once and a half as broad as deep, the portion visible from above measuring one fourth its distance from the frontal, internasals as long as the præfrontal; frontal broader than the supraocular, once and two fifths as long as broad, longer than its distance from the end of the snout, shorter than the parietals; loreal longer than deep; one præocular, in contact with the frontal, with one or two suboculars below it, two postoculars; temporals 2+2; nine (exceptionally ten) upper labials, fifth and sixth (or sixth and seventh) entering the eye: four or five lower labials in contact with the anterior chin-shields, posterior chin-shields as long as or longer than the anterior and separated from each other by two series of scales. Scales smooth, in 21 rows. Ventrals very obtusely angulate laterally, 171–185; anal divided, subcaudals 100. Uniform pale buff above, pinkish on the sides; a greyish blotch below the eye and another across the temple; white beneath.

Total length 560 millim.; tail 170.

Western Somaliland and Gallaland.

a. ♂ (V. 171; C. 100).	Webi Shebeli.	Dr. Donaldson Smith [P.]. (One of the types)
b. ♂ (V. 171; C. ?).	W. of Juba R.	Dr. Donaldson Smith [C.].

Add :—   Page 403. Zamenis florulentus.

Tylanthera florulenta, *Cope, Trans. Amer. Philos. Soc.* xviii. 1895, p. 215.

u. ♂ (V. 215; C. ?).	Mandara, near Alexandria.	Dr. J. Anderson [P.].
v. ♀ (V. 217; C. 99).	Beltim, Delta.	Dr. J. Anderson [P.].

Add :—   Page 404. Zamenis gracilis.

? *Coluber cinereus*, *Linn. Mus. Ad. Frid.* p. 37, pl. xxiii. fig. 2 (1754).

Add :— Page 405. Zamenis ravergieri.

Zamenis ravergieri, *Méhely, Zool Anz.* 1894, p. 85, *Peracca, Boll. Mus. Torino,* ix. 1894, no. 167, p. 11.

Add :— Page 407. Zamenis nummifer.

Zamenis nummifer, *Peracca, l. c.* p 12

s. ♂ (Sc. 23; V. 203, C. ?).		Beltim, Delta.	Dr. J. Anderson [P.]
t–u. Yg. (Sc. 25; V. 210, 213; C. 83, 84)		Helouan, near Cairo.	Dr. A. Fényes [P.].

Add :— Page 409. Zamenis algirus.

Zamenis algirus, *Werner, Verh. zool.-bot. Ges Wien,* xliv. 1894, p. 84.

f–h ♀ (Sc. 25; V 225; A. 2; C. 97), hgr. (Sc. 25; V. 215, A. 2; C. 98), & yg. (Sc. 25, V 216, A. 1; C 100).	Between Batna and Biskra	
i Yg. (Sc. 25; V. 222; A. 2, C. 90).	Sfax, Tunisia	Christiania Mus.

Add — Page 409. Zamenis hippocrepis.

Zamenis hippocrepis, *Minà-Palumbo, Nat. Sicil.* xii. 1892, p 80.

q. ♀ (Sc. 27; V. 237; C. 97)   Seville   Prof. Calderon [E.].

Add :— Page 411. Zamenis diadema.

Zamenis diadema, *Peracca, Boll. Mus Torino,* ix 1894, no 167, p. 12.

π. ♀ (Sc. 29, V. 242; C 75).   Fayed, Egypt   Dr J. Anderson [P]

Add :— Page 413 Zamenis microlepis.

Zamenis microlepis, *Werner, Verh. zool.-bot. Ges Wien,* xlv 1895, p. 18, pl. iii. fig 4

VOL. II.

Add :— **Page 8. DRYMOBIUS**

Cacocalyx, *Cope, Proc. Ac. Philad.* 1894, p. 427.

Add :— **Page 13. Drymobius boddaertii.**

B.
c ♂ (V 173 ; C. 100)   Monte Redondo, Costa   Mr. Underwood [C.]
                        Rica.

Add :— **Page 15. Drymobius rhombifer.**

h. Yg. (V. 154 ; C. 86)   Chiriqui   J. G Champion, Esq. [C.],
                                     F. D. Godman, Esq. [P.]

Add :— **Page 15 Drymobius bivittatus.**

b. Hgr. ♂ (V. 145 ; C. 122).   Cali, Colombia,   Mr. W. F. H Rosenberg
                               3200 ft.   [O.].

Add :— **Page 15. Drymobius dendrophis.**

Drymobius paucicarinatus, *Cope, Proc Ac. Philad.* 1894, p 202.
Crossanthera melanotropis, *Cope, l. c.* p. 203.

Add :— **Page 17. Drymobius margaritiferus**

Masticophis margaritiferus, *Cope, Proc. Amer. Philos Soc.* xi. 1869, p. 162.

Add :— **Page 19. Phrynonax sulphureus.**

? *Seba, Thes.* ii. pl. lxvii. fig 3 (1735)
? Coluber caracaras, *Gmel. S N.* i p. 1117 (1788).

Add :— **Page 20. Phrynonax pœcilonotus.**

d-e ♂ (V. 202, 199 ;   Buenaventura, Colombia.   Mr W. F. H. Rosen-
C. 125, 122).   berg [C.].

Add :— **Page 22. Phrynonax fasciatus.**

d. Hgr (V. 201 ; C. 130).   Buenaventura, Colombia.   Mr. W. F. H. Rosen-
                                                      berg [C.].
e. Yg. (V. 201 ; C. 110).   Larecaja, Bolivia.
f. Yg. (V. 195 ; C. 113).   Aschiquiri, Bolivia

Add :— **Page 22. Phrynonax eutropis.**

Phrynonax eutropis, *Boettg Bull. Trinid. Club,* ii. 1894, p. 85.
Trinidad.

ADDENDA AND CORRIGENDA.

Add:—   Page 24. **COLUBER.**

Aepidea, *Hallow. Proc. Ac. Philad.* 1860, p. 488.
Leptophidium, *Hallow. l. c.* p 498.
Epiglottophis, *Cope, Trans Amer Philos. Soc.* xviii. 1895, p. 204.

Add:—   Page 32 **Coluber corais**
C.
d. ♂ (V. 189; C. 67).   N. Carolina.   H. Hanauer, Esq. [P].

Add:—   Page 38. **Coluber triaspis.**
e. Hgr. (Sc. 35; V. 266, C. 87).   Yucatan.

Add:—   Page 39. **Coluber guttatus.**

Callopeltis guttatus, *Loennberg, Proc. U S. Nat Mus.* xvii. 1894, p 326

Add:—   Page 47. **Coluber tæniurus.**

Coluber tæniurus, *Boettg. Ber Senck. Ges* 1894, p. 144

Add —   Page 50. **Coluber obsoletus.**

Coluber obsoletus, *Rhoads, Proc. Ac. Philad* 1895, p. 391.

Add:—   Page 54. **Coluber longissimus.**
p. ♂ (Sc. 23; V. 219;   Kaposvar, Hungary.   Prof. L v Méhely [E]
C. 79).

Page 56. Add a species:—

29 a. Coluber schmackeri.

Coluber schmackeri, *Boettg Ber. Offenb Ver Nat* 1895, p 108.

Allied to *C. moellendorffii,* but præocular not reaching the frontal, and scales perfectly smooth. Rostral broader than deep, nine or ten upper labials, fifth and sixth or sixth and seventh entering the eye. Scales in 27 rows. Ventrals 260; anal divided, subcaudals 104. Greenish grey above, with a dorsal series of W- or X-shaped blackish markings; tail with four black stripes, yellowish beneath, spotted and mottled with blackish.
Total length 2080 millim., tail 445.
Loo Choo Islands.

Add:—   Page 57. **Coluber oxycephalus.**

Aepidea robusta, *Hallow Proc. Ac Philad* 1860, p. 488

o. Yg (Sc. 25, V. 236,   Catanduanes Id., S E.   Whitehead Exped.
C 129).   Luzon
p ♀ (Sc 25; V. 247,   Great Natuna Id   C Hose, Esq. [C.]
C. 132).

Add:— Page 59. **Coluber quadrivirgatus.**

Leptophidium dorsale, *Hallow Proc. Ac. Philad.* 1860, p. 498.

Add:— Page 63. **Coluber erythrurus.**

A.
h. Yg (V. 211; C. 92). Albay, S Luzon. Whitehead Exped
i. Hgr (V 225; C. 94). Tavi-Tavi, Sooloo Ids A. Everett, Esq. [C.]

Add:— Page 73. **Herpetodryas carinatus.**

Zaocys tornieri, *Werner, Verh. zool.-bot. Ges. Wien,* 1896, p. 15, pl. 1 fig. 1.

A.
e. ♂ (V. 159; C. 129). Para Dr. E. A. Goldi [P].
f. ♂ (V. 149; C. 111). Buenaventura, Colombia. Mr. W F.H Rosenberg [C]

In the latter specimen, the lateral scales and the outer ends of the ventrals, on the anterior half of the body, vermilion red.

C.
n. ♂ (V. 185; C. 177). R. Ucayale. Dr. E A Goldi [P.]

Add:— Page 76. **Herpetodryas fuscus.**

F. Brick-red above, bright orange beneath.

a. ♂ (V. 163; C. 114). Para. Dr. E. A. Goldi [P.].

Add:— Page 76. **Herpetodryas melas.**

a. ♀ (V. 154; C.?). Matagalpa, Nicaragua. Dr E. Rothschuh [C.].

Add:— Page 79. **Dendrophis pictus.**

π. ♂ (V. 172; C. 149). Albay, S. Luzon. Whitehead Exped.
ρ. ♀ (V. 173; C.?). Tavi-Tavi, Sooloo Ids A. Everett, Esq. [C.].
σ. ♀ (V. 176; C 140) Great Natuna Id. C. Hose, Esq. [C.].
τ. ♀ (V. 156; C. 138). Tandjong, S.E. Borneo.

Add:— Page 80. **Dendrophis calligaster.**

Dendrophis punctulatus, part., *Boettg. in Semon, Zool. Forsch.* v. p. 120 (1894).

E.
n–q. ♂ (V. 182, 181; C. 144, 141) & ♀ (V. 188, 184; C. 146, ?) Fergusson Id., Brit New Guinea Mr. Meek [C.]
r–s. ♀ (V. 187, 181; C. 146, 146). Trobriand Ids., Brit. New Guinea Mr Meek [C.].

Add :— Page 83. **Dendrophis punctulatus.**

Elaps lewisii, *Gray, in Grey's Trav. Austral.* ii. p 444 (1841)
Dendrophis bilorealis, *Macleay, Proc. Linn. Soc. N. S W* viii. 1883, p 435, & ix 1884, p 549.
—— punctulatus, *Boettg in Semon, Zool Forsch.* v. p. 110 (1894).

C. Black above, olive or blackish beneath, with the exception of the chin and throat, which are white; ventral keels whitish. (*D. bilorealis*, Macleay.)

a. ♀ (V. 201; C. 120). Queensland. Christiania Mus.

Add :— Page 84. **Dendrophis formosus.**

Dendrophis pictus, *Boettg. in Semon, op. cit* p. 123.

g. ♀ (V. 185; C 144) Sandakan, N Borneo. Douglas Cator, Esq. [P.]
h Hgr. (V. 183; C. 144) Tandjong, S.E. Borneo.

Add :— Page 86. **Dendrophis lineolatus.**

Dendrophis punctulatus, part., *Boettg. in Semon, op cit.* p. 120.

k-o ♂ (V 202, 201; C. 137, 133), ♀ (V. 196; C. 143), hgr. (V. 195, C 139), & yg. (V. 202; C. ?). Fergusson Id., Brit. New Guinea. Mr. Meek [C.]

Page 86. Add a species :—

8 a. **Dendrophis meeki.**

Dendrophis meeki, *Bouleng. Ann & Mag. N. H.* (6) xvi 1895, p. 32.

Maxillary teeth 32 or 33. Eye very large, as long as its distance from the centre or the anterior border of the nostril. Rostral nearly twice as long as deep, just visible from above; internasals as long as the præfrontals; frontal once and one third to once and a half as long as broad, as long as its distance from the end of the snout, much shorter than the parietals; loreal once and two thirds or twice as long as deep; one præ- and two postoculars; temporals 2+2 or 3; eight or nine upper labials, fourth and fifth or fourth, fifth, and sixth entering the eye; five lower labials in contact with the anterior chin-shields, which are shorter than the posterior. Scales in 13 rows, vertebrals about as large as outer. Ventrals 170-178, anal divided; subcaudals 139-147. Dark olive above; upper lip white, sharply limited above by a black line passing through the eye; lower parts pale olive, more or less freckled with darker.

Total length 1160 millim., tail 420.

Fergusson Id., British New Guinea.

a-d. ♂ (V. 174; C 147) & ♀ (V. 175, 178, 170, C. 141, 146, 139). Fergusson Id Mr Meek [C.] (Types)

Add :—   Page 89. **Dendrelaphis tristis.**

s Hgr. (V. 176 ; C. 130).   Ceylon.   Dr. Bowles [P].
Loreal absent on the left side

Add :—   Page 89. **Dendrelaphis caudolineatus.**

Dendrophis picta, *Motley & Dillwyn, Nat. Hist Labuan,* p. 46, pl. — (1855).

z ♀ (V. 180 ; C. 106)   Sandakan, N. Borneo   Douglas Cator, Esq [P.]

Add :—   Page 91. **Dendrelaphis terrificus.**

e. ♀, head & tail.   Albay, S. Luzon.   Whitehead Exped

Add :—   Page 91. **Dendrelaphis modestus.**

c-d. ♀ (V. 186, 190 ; C. ?, 121).   Halmaheira.   Prof. Kükenthal [C.] ; Senckenberg Mus. [E.].
e. Hgr. (V. 185 ; C. 121)   Batjan   Prof. Kükenthal [C.] ; Senckenberg Mus [E]

Page 91. Add a species :—

6. Dendrelaphis papuensis.

Dendrelaphis papuensis, *Bouleng. Ann. & Mag. N. H.* (6) xvi. 1895, p. 409.

Maxillary teeth 21 or 22. Eye as long as its distance from the nostril. Rostral broader than deep, visible from above, internasals as long as the præfrontals ; frontal once and a half to once and two thirds as long as broad, as long as its distance from the end of the snout, a little shorter than the parietals ; loreal elongate ; one præ- and two postoculars ; temporals 2+2 ; eight upper labials, fourth and fifth entering the eye ; five or six lower labials in contact with the anterior chin-shields, which are shorter than the posterior. Scales in 13 rows. Ventrals 185–190 ; anal divided ; subcaudals 119–126. Olive-brown above, head and neck dark, blackish ; a black streak on each side of the head and neck, passing through the eye ; upper lip white ; vertebral scales on anterior part of body lighter, edged with whitish in front ; ventrals and subcaudals pale olive.

Total length 1050 millim.; tail 310.

Trobriand Ids , British New Guinea.

a-e. ♂ (V 190 ; C. 119) & ♀ (V. 188, 188, 185, 185 ; C. ?, 124, 125, 126)   Trobriand Ids.   Mr. Meek [C.]. (Types.)

Add :— Page 93. **Chlorophis ornatus.**

Philothamnus ornatus, *Bocage, Herp. Angola*, p. 93, pl. xii. fig 1 (1895).

Add.— Page 94. **Chlorophis neglectus.**

m–n ♂ (V 149; C 97) & ♀ (V. 155; C. 84).	Zomba, Brit C. Africa.	Sir H. H. Johnston [P].
o ♂ (V. 152; C. 87).	Mandala, Brit. C. Africa.	Scott Elliot, Esq [P.].
p. ♀ (V. 163; C. ?).	Witu, E. Africa.	F J. Jackson, Esq. [P.]

Add — Page 95. **Chlorophis heterolepidotus.**

Chlorophis gracillimus, *Gunth. Ann. & Mag. N. H.* (6) xv. 1895, p 528.
Philothamnus heterolepidotus, *Bocage, Herp. Angola*, p. 88 (1895).

Add :— Page 96 **Chlorophis irregularis.**

? Coluber cæsius, *Cloquet, Dict Sc. Nat.* xi. p. 201 (1818).
Chlorophis guentheri, *Gunth. l. c*
—— shirana, *Gunth l c*
Philothamnus irregularis, *Bocage, l. c* p. 85, pl. xii. fig. 2 (1895)

y. ♀ (V 162, C. 112)	Mandala, Brit. C. Africa	Scott Elliot, Esq. [P.].
z–γ. ♀ (V. 171; C 102) & yg (V. 170, 158, 175 : C. 108, 123, 117).	Lower Niger	W. H. Crosse, Esq. [P.].

Add :— Page 98. **Chlorophis heterodermus.**

Philothamnus heterodermus, *Bocage, l. c.* p. 89.

l. Hgr. ♀ (V. 157, C. 80) Lower Niger. W. H. Crosse, Esq. [P.].

Add :— Page 99. **Philothamnus semivariegatus.**

Philothamnus kirkii, *Gunth. Ann. & Mag. N. H.* (6) xv. 1895, p. 528.
—— bocagii, *Gunth. l. c.*
—— semivariegatus, *Bocage, l. c.* p. 90, pl xiii fig 2

a. ♂ (V. 189, C. 157). Upper Shiré R. Sir H. H. Johnston [P.]

Add :— Page 101. **Philothamnus dorsalis.**

Philothamnus dorsalis, *Bocage, l. c* p 92, pl xiii. fig. 1.

f ♂ (V 167; C. 126) Lower Congo Rev. J. Pinnock [C.].

Add :— Page 103. **Gastropyxis smaragdina.**

q. ♂ (V. 162, C. 157). Lower Niger. W. H. Crosse, Esq. [P.].

Page 104. Add a genus:—

69 a. RHAMNOPHIS.

Rhamnophis, *Günth. Ann. & Mag. N. H.* (3) ix. 1862, p. 129, and *Zool Rec* 1864, p 122.
Crypsidomus, *Günth. Proc. Zool Soc.* 1864, p 309.

Maxillary teeth 20 to 23, the three last longest and separated from the rest by an interspace; anterior mandibular teeth feebly enlarged. Head rather short, distinct from neck; eye very large, with round pupil. Body compressed; scales very narrow, smooth or keeled, with apical pits, disposed obliquely, in 17 or 19 rows, vertebral row enlarged; ventrals obtusely keeled laterally. Tail long; subcaudals in two rows.

Tropical Africa.

Might be united with *Thrasops*.

1. Rhamnophis æthiops.

Rhamnophis æthiopissa, *Günth. Ann. & Mag N. H.* (3) ix. 1862, p. 129, pl. x.
Crypsidomus æthiops, *Boettg. Ber Senck. Ges.* 1888, p. 64.
Chrysidomus æthiops, *Matschie, Zool. Jahrb.* v. 1890, p. 616.

Rostral much broader than deep, visible from above; internasals as long as the præfrontals, frontal bell-shaped, little longer than broad, as long as or a little longer than its distance from the end of the snout, as long as or a little shorter than the parietals; a pair of very large occipitals may be present; loreal nearly twice as long as deep; one præocular, in contact with or narrowly separated from the frontal; two postoculars; temporals 1 or 1+2; eight upper labials, fourth and fifth entering the eye; four or five lower labials in contact with the anterior chin-shields, which are shorter than the posterior Scales smooth, in 17 rows. Ventrals 158–179; anal divided; subcaudals 140–158. Black above, each scale with a green streak; head pale olive, the shields spotted and edged with black; yellowish or pale olive beneath, outer ends of ventrals green, edged with black; subcaudals with three black streaks.

Total length 1500 millim.; tail 530.

Guinea.

a. Hgr. (V. 175; C. 152).	W. Africa.	(Type.)
b. ♀ (V. 158; C. 140).	Liberia.	Dr. Büttikofer [C.]
c. Hgr. (V. 159; C. ?).	Sierra Leone.	Sir A. Kennedy [P.].
d. ♀ (V. 179; C. 158).	Fernando Po.	Dr. Statham [P.].
e. ♂ (V. 169; C. 141).	Gaboon.	

2. Rhamnophis jacksonii.

Thrasops jacksonii, *Günth. Ann. & Mag N. H.* (6) xv. 1895, p. 528

Differs from the preceding in the larger rostral, which is but little broader than deep, the shorter loreal, three postoculars,

temporals 1+1, and scales keeled, in 19 rows   Ventrals 198; subcaudals 138.   Uniform black above and beneath.
Total length 1670 millim. ; tail 500.
East Africa.

a. Ad., skin (V. 198, C. 138).   Kavirondo.   F. J. Jackson, Esq. [P.]. (Type.)

Add :—   Page 111. **Leptophis bilineatus.**

f. ♂ (V. 153 ; C. 148).   Buenaventura, Colombia.   Mr. W. F. H. Rosenberg [C.]

Page 111. Add a species :—

8 *a*. **Leptophis ultramarinus.**

Leptophis ultramarinus, *Cope, Proc Ac. Philad.* 1894, p. 203.

Eye as long as its distance from the rostral. Præocular reaching the frontal; two postoculars, temporals 1+2; eight upper labials; posterior chin-shields a little longer than the anterior. Scales in 15 rows, five median rows keeled. Ventrals feebly angulate, 168; anal divided; subcaudals 176. Uniform ultramarine-blue above, silvery white below and on the outer scales and upper lip
Total length 1050 millim. ; tail 425.
Pazu Azul, Costa Rica.

Add .—   Page 111. **Leptophis occidentalis.**

Leptophis occidentalis, *Bocourt, Miss. Sc Mex., Rept.* pl. lxiii. fig. 1 (1895).

k. ♀ (V. 181 ; C. 176).   Brit. Honduras.

Add ·—   Page 112. **Leptophis nigromarginatus.**

Leptophis nigromarginatus, *Bocourt, l c.* p. 826, pl. lxiii. fig 3

i ♀ (V. 150, C. 134).   Rio Ucayale   Dr. E A Göldi [P.]

Add :—   Page 113. **Leptophis liocercus.**

Leptophis ahætulla, *Bocourt, l c.* p. 821, pl. lxii fig. 2.
—— liocercus, *Bocourt, l. c.* p 823, pl. lxii. fig 3.
—— marginatus, *Bocourt, l c* p. 824, pl. lxiii fig 4.

o–p, q–r ♂ (V. 161, 149; C. 146, 126) & ♀ (V. 175, 151; C. 156, 134).   Rio Ucayale.   Dr. E A Göldi [P.].

Add :—   Page 118. **DROMICUS.**

Monobothris, *Cope, Amer Nat.* 1894, p. 841.
Halsophis, *Cope, Trans. Amer. Philos. Soc.* xviii. 1895, p. 201.

Add :— Page 122. **Dromicus sanctæ-crucis.**

e–h. ♂ (V. 173, 176; C. ?, 121), Moua. Hr W. Wolterstorff [P.].
♀ (V. 177; C. 113), & yg.
(V. 170, C. 123).

Add :— Page 126. **LIOPHIS.**

Opheomorphus, *Fitzing. in Tschudi, Faun. Per., Herp.* p 50 (1846)
Echinanthera, *Cope, Amer. Nat.* 1894, p 841.

Add :— Page 129. **Liophis triscalis.**

Seba, Thes. ii. pl. lii. fig. 4, & pl xvii fig. 1 (1735)
Coluber corallinus, *Linn Mus. Ad. Frid* p. 33 (1754).

Add :— Page 136. **Liophis viridis.**

f. ♂ (V. 165, C. 68). Pernambuco W. A. Forbes, Esq [P.].

Add :— Page 136. **Liophis typhlus.**

Philodryas crassifrons (*non Cope*), *Boettg. Zeitschr f. Naturw.* lviii 1885, p 235

l. ♀ (V. 165, C. ?). Paraguay.

Add :— Page 143. **Liophis flavilatus.**

Rhadinæa flavilatus, *Cope, Trans. Amer. Philos. Soc.* xviii. 1895, pp 202 & 217.

Add :— Page 147. **Xenodon colubrinus.**

t. ♂ (V. 143, C. ?). Hacienda Rosa de Jericho, Dr. E. Rothschuh
Nicaragua. [C.].

Add :— Page 155. **Heterodon platyrhinus.**

Heterodon platyrhinus, *Rhoads, Proc. Ac Philad.* 1895, p. 393.

Page 158. **Aporophis lineatus.**

Erase from the synonymy :—

Lygophis dilepis, *Cope*,

and add :—

Coluber atratus, part., *Gmel. S. N.* i. p. 1103 (1788).
Aporophis lineatus, *Peracca, Boll. Mus. Torino,* x. 1895, no. 195, p. 16.

Page 158. Add a species :—

1 *a.* **Aporophis dilepis.**

Lygophis dilepis, *Cope, Proc. Ac. Philad.* 1862, p. 81.
Aporophis dilepis, *Cope, Proc. Amer. Philos. Soc.* xxii. 1885, p. 191;
Peracca, Boll Mus Torino, x. 1895, no. 195, p. 15.

Closely allied to *A. lineatus.* Agreeing in the number (19) of rows of scales and in the coloration; differing in the shorter tail (4–4¼ times in the total length). Ventrals 165–179; subcaudals 71–93. Yellowish olive above, with a reddish-brown, black-edged vertebral stripe three scales wide, and a narrower, black lateral stripe; three and a half outer rows of scales, upper lip, and lower parts uniform yellow.

Total length 490 millim.; tail 120.

Paraguay.

a. ♂ (V. 179; C. 71).   Rio Apa, N. Paraguay.   Dr. Borelli [C.]; Turin Mus. [E.].

Add :—   Page 160. **RHADINÆA.**

Tæniophallus, *Cope, Trans Amer. Philos. Soc.* xviii. 1895, p. 201.

Add.—   Page 171   **Rhadinæa genimaculata.**

c. ♂ (V. 207; C. 71).   Marajo, nr. Para   Dr. E A Goldi [P.]

Add :—   Page 172. **Rhadinæa serperastra.**

a Yg (V. 169; C 60).   La Palma, Costa Rica   Mr. Underwood [C.].

Add :—   Page 174. **Rhadinæa undulata.**

Tæniophallus nicagus, *Cope, Trans Amer. Philos Soc.* xviii. 1895, p. 217.

Add :—   Page 176. **Rhadinæa occipitalis.**

g–h ♂ (V 162, 165; C. 77, 79)   Yungas, Bolivia.

Add :—   Page 179   **Rhadinæa vittata.**

n Hgr., **A.** (V. 165; C. 85).   Omilteme, Guerrero   F D. Godman, Esq. [P.].
o Yg., **B.** (V. 164; C. 116).   Omilteme, Guerrero.   F. D Godman, Esq. [P.]
p Hgr, **C.** (V 180; C. 111).   S. Mexico   F. D. Godman, Esq. [P.].
q. Yg., **C.** (V. 150; C. 130).   Mezquital del Oro, Zacatecas.   Dr A. C Buller [C].

Page 179. Add a species :—

24 *a.* Rhadinæa pulveriventris.

Eye rather small. Rostral twice as broad as deep, just visible from above; internasals broader than long, much shorter than the præfrontals; frontal once and three fourths as long as broad, longer than its distance from the end of the snout, shorter than the parietals; loreal longer than deep, one præ- and two postoculars;

temporals 1+2; eight upper labials, fourth and fifth entering the eye; five lower labials in contact with the anterior chin-shields, which are shorter than the posterior. Scales in 17 rows. Ventrals 132; anal divided; subcaudals 66. Reddish brown above; a black lateral line between the fourth and fifth rows of scales, edged above with yellowish on the anterior part of the body; this line widens on the neck and head, and, passing through the eye, joins its fellow on the end of the snout; upper lip white; belly pinkish yellow, finely speckled all over with blackish.

Total length 430 millim.; tail 140
Costa Rica.

a. ♀ (V. 132; C 66)   Azahar de Cartago.   Mr Underwood [C.].

Add :—   Page 182. **Urotheca lateristriga.**

e. Yg. (V. 135; C. 117)   Costa Rica.
f-g. ♂ (V. 132, 134;   La Palma, Costa Rica   Mr. Underwood [C.].
C. 91, 101).

Add :—   Page 183. **Urotheca elapoides.**

Erythrolamprus venustissimus, spec. *w*, *Gunth. Cat.* p. 48 (1858).

k. ♂, **A.** *a.* (V. 128; C. 102).   Mexico.   Mr. H. Finck [C.].
l. ♀, **A.** *b.* (V. 134, C. ?).   Atoyac, Guerrero.   F D Godman, Esq [P]
m. Yg, **A.** *b* (V. 124; C. 114).   Belize.
n. ♀, **A.** *b.* (V. 133; C. ?)   Para.   J P G. Smith, Esq. [P.].
o. ♀, **C.** 6 broad black rings on the body (V. 134; C. ?).   Yucatan.

Add :—   Page 184. **Urotheca bicincta.**

d. Yg. (Sc. 19; V. 179, C. 74).   Para   Dr. E A. Goldi [P].

Add :—   Page 185. **Trimetopon gracile.**

c. ♂ (V. 132, C. 63).   Turrialba, Costa Rica.   Mr Underwood [C.].

Page 185. Add a species :—

2. Trimetopon pliolepis.

Trimetopon pliolepis, *Cope, Proc Ac. Philad.* 1894, p. 201.

Apparently closely allied to, and possibly identical with, *T. gracile.* The only important difference seems to be in the number of rows of scales, viz 17 instead of 15. Ventrals 154; subcaudals 69. Coloration more obscure.

Total length 287 millim; tail 76.
San José, Costa Rica.

Add :— Page 186. **Dimades plicatilis.**

Pseuderyx plicatilis, *Bocourt, Miss. Sc. Mex , Rept.* p 802, pl. lx. fig 7 (1895).
—— plicatilis, var. anomalolepis, *Bocourt, l. c.* p 804, pl. lx. fig 6

Page 186. Add a species:—
2. **Dimades mimeticus.**

Pseudoeryx mimeticus, *Cope, Proc. Amer. Philos. Soc.* xxiii. 1886, p. 95.

Head-shields as in *D. plicatilis.* Ventrals 163; subcaudals 35. Dorsal region brown for a width of five and two half rows of scales, sides on the third and fourth, and half of the second and fifth rows, marked with a black band, which extends from the eye to the end of the tail and is edged with yellow above; a yellow band from the eye to the angle of the mouth; lips black, yellow-spotted; below yellow with two small brown spots on each ventral shield and one on each caudal.
Total length 490 millim.; tail 56.
Mamoré R , Eastern Bolivia.

Add :— Page 187. **Hydrops triangularis.**

Pseuderyx triangularis, *Bocourt, Miss Sc Mex , Rept.* p 806, pl lx. fig. 5 (1895).

Add :— Page 187. **Hydrops martii.**

Pseudoeryx callostictus, *Cope, Proc. Amer. Philos. Soc* xxiii 1886, p. 103.
Pseuderyx martii, *Bocourt, l. c.* p. 805, pl. lx. fig. 4.

Add :— Page 192. **Coronella austriaca.**

Coronella austriaca, *Sarauw, Natur. og Mennesk* xii. 1894, p. 379.
Loennberg, Biol. Centralbl xv. 1895, p. 672, figs.

bb ♀ (V. 178; C. 41).   Brasso, Hungary.   Prof L. v. Méhely [E.].
cc. ♂ (V. 174, C. 58).   Friesach, Carinthia.   Hr F. Henkel [E.]

Add .— Page 194. **Coronella amaliæ.**

n ♀ (V. 185; C. 57).   Oran.   M Doumergue [E].

In the shape of the rostral intermediate between *C. girondica* and *amaliæ* Snout pointed and very prominent.

Add :— Page 197. **Coronella regularis.**

b–d ♂ (V. 181, C. 66),   Lower Niger   W. H. Crosse, Esq. [P.].
♀ (V 180; C. 68), &
yg (V. 182, C. 68)

Add:— Page 197. **Coronella getula.**

Lampropeltis getulus, *Loennberg, Proc. U.S. Nat. Mus.* xvii. 1894, p. 324.

Page 198. **Coronella getula, C.**

Erase " *C. californiæ.*"
And add:—

g. Yg. (Sc. 23; V. 230; C. 47).		S. Bernardino, California.	Mr. R Douglas [C.]

Add:— Page 204. **Coronella micropholis.**

A.

h. ♀ (Sc. 21; V. 202; C. 43).		Guayaquil	Mr Fraser [C].

B.

u. ♀ (Sc. 21; V. 229; C. 58).		Matagalpa, Nicaragua.	Dr. E Rothschuh [C.].
v ♀ (Sc. 21; V. 224; C. 47).		Bebedero, Costa Rica	Mr. Underwood [C.].
w. Hgr. (Sc. 19; V. 215; C. 45).		Cali, Colombia, 3200 ft.	Mr. W. F. H. Rosenberg [C.].
x. Yg. (Sc. 21; V. 221; C. 44).		Zaruma, Ecuador.	Mr Gunter [C.]

Add:— Page 205. **Coronella doliata.**

Osceola elapsoidea, *Loennberg, Proc. U S Nat. Mus.* xvii. 1894, p. 325

Add.— Page 206. **Coronella punctata.**

Diadophis punctatus, *Loennberg, l. c.* p. 325

Add:— Page 208. **Coronella amabilis.**

g. ♀ (V. 207; C. 54).		S. Bernardino, California.	Mr. R. Douglas [C]

Page 208. Add a species :—

17 *a*. **Coronella arnyi.**

Diadophis arnyi, *Kennicott, Proc. Ac. Philad.* 1859, p 99.
—— punctatus, var. arnyi, *Garm. N. Am. Rept.* p. 72 (1883).

Agrees with *C. regalis* in the number (17) of scales, with *C. punctata* in the low number of ventrals (142-161).
Kansas, Missouri.

a-b. ♂ (V. 142, C. 35) & ♀ (V. 161; C. 40)		St. Louis Co., Missouri.

Add :—   Page 208. **Coronella regalis.**

Erase "*Diadophis arnyi*" from the synonymy.

Page 211. Add a genus .—

89 *a*. DREPANODON.

Clœlia (*non Fitz*), *Jan, Elenco sist Ofid* p 92 (1863)
Drepanodon, *Peracca, Boll Mus Torin.* xi. 1896, no. 231, p. 3.

7 to 10 small maxillary teeth increasing in length, followed, after an interspace, by two large, compressed teeth ; mandibular teeth subequal. Head distinct from neck ; eye moderate, with vertically elliptic pupil. Body cylindrical ; scales smooth, with or without apical pits, in 15 (or 17) rows; ventrals rounded. Tail moderate ; subcaudals in two rows.

South America.

1 Drepanodon anomalus.

Clœlia anomala, *Jan, l c, and Icon. Gén.* 35, pl. i. fig. 4 (1870).
Oxyrhopus anomalus, *Boettg. Zool. Anz* 1891, p. 347.
Drepanodon anomalus, *Peracca, l. c.* p 3.
—— stigmaticus, *Peracca, l. c.* p. 5.

Rostral broader than deep, just visible from above; internasals half as long as the præfrontals ; frontal slightly longer than broad, as long as its distance from the end of the snout, as long as or slightly shorter than the parietals; loreal very small or absent; one præ- and two postoculars ; temporals 1+2 or 2+2 ; six upper labials, third and fourth entering the eye : three or four lower labials in contact with the anterior chin-shields ; posterior chin-shields as long as or shorter than the anterior. Scales in 15 rows. Ventrals 150–169 ; anal entire; subcaudals 67–77. Yellowish above, each scale with a black terminal dot, upper surface of head and nape black, with a whitish collar ; uniform yellowish white beneath.

Upper Amazon.

2. Drepanodon ? flavitorques.

Liophis flavitorques, *Cope, Proc Ac. Philad* 1868, p. 307.

Rostral projecting and well visible from above ; frontal very broad, with a long produced posterior angle ; loreal deeper than long ; one præ- and two postoculars ; temporals 1+2 ; seven upper labials, third and fourth entering the eye ; chin-shields short. Scales in 17 rows. Ventrals 188 ; anal divided ; subcaudals 105. Uniform dark brown above, with a broad yellow half-collar crossing the posterior half of the parietal shields and two rows of scales ; below dirty yellowish.

Total length 440 millim ; tail 140.

Magdelen River, Colombia.

Add :—   Page 214. Cemophora coccinea.

Cemophora coccinea, *Loennberg, Proc. U.S. Nat. Mus.* xviii. 1894, p. 321.

Add :—   Page 218. Simotes purpurascens.

Simotes purpurascens, *Bouleng. Ann. Mus. Genova,* (2) xiv. 1894, p. 616
Djeraulax purpurascens, *Cope, Trans. Amer. Philos. Soc* xviii. 1895, p 200.

Add :—   Page 222. Simotes formosanus.

c–d. ♂ (V. 172 ; C. 48)　　C. Formosa.　　Mr. Holst [C.].
 & yg. (V. 162, C. 46)

Add :—   Page 222. Simotes violaceus.

Holarchus dolleyanus, *Cope, Proc. Ac. Philad.* 1894, p. 423, pl. x. fig. 1 (1895).

Add :—   Page 224. Simotes octolineatus.

B.

e. ♂ (V. 155, C. 47).　　Taiping, Perak　　S Flower, Esq. [P.]

Vertebral line scarlet, others white.

D. Intermediate between B & C.

a–b. ♂ (V. 161, 161 ;　　Sandakan, N. Borneo.　　Douglas Cator, Esq
 C. 44, 43).　　　　　　　　　　　　　　　　　　　　[P.].

Add :—   Page 225. Simotes phænochalinus.

f. ♀ (V. 162 ; C. 35).　　Mt. Benguet, N.　　Whitehead Exped
　　　　　　　　　　　Luzon
g. Yg (V. 156 ; C. 38).　　Isabella, N.E Luzon.　　Whitehead Exped.

Add :—   Page 239. Oligodon everetti.

b–c. ♂ (V. 138 ; C. 65)　　Tandjong, S.E Borneo.
 & ♀ (V. 145 ; C. 61).

Add :—   Page 242. Oligodon sublineatus.

p. ♀ (V. 161 ; C. 27).　　Punduloya.　　E E. Green, Esq. [P]

Page 245. Add a species :—

16 a. Oligodon schadenbergii.

Oligodon schadenbergi, *Boettg. Abh Mus Dresd* 1894–95, no 7, p. 4 (1895).

Near *O vertebralis*, but snout shorter and blunter, frontal twice and a half to thrice as broad as the supraocular, loreal smaller, and suture between the internasals shorter than that between the præfrontals Scales in 15 rows. Ventrals 145-147; anal divided; subcaudals 38-39. Dark grey above, with very small white, black-edged spots; head-markings as in *O. vertebralis*; orange beneath. Total length 310 millim.; tail 52.

Busuanga, Calamianes, Philippines.

Add :— Page 248. **Prosymna frontalis.**

Prosymna frontalis, *Bocage, Herp Angola*, p. 98, pl. xi. fig. 2 (1895).

Add .— Page 248. **Prosymna ambigua.**

Prosymna ambigua, *Bocage, l. c.* p. 99, pl. xi. fig. 1

Add :— Page 249. **Prosymna meleagris.**

c–d. ♀ (V 148; C. 34) Wegbe, Togoland. W. G. Innes, Esq. [C.].
& yg. (V. 149; C. 31)

Add :— Page 249. **LEPTOCALAMUS.**

? Enulius, *Cope, Proc. Amer. Philos Soc.* xi. 1871, p. 558.

Add ·— Page 250. **Leptocalamus torquatus.**

? Enulius murinus, *Cope, l. c., Günth. Biol. C.-Am, Rept.* p. 157 (1895).
Enulius torquatus, *Cope, Proc. Ac Philad.* 1894, p. 205.

b. ♂ (V. 181; C. 103). Guatemala. L. Greening, Esq. [P.].
c ♀ (V. 209; C. 85). L. Nicaragua. Rev. G. E. Henderson [P.].

Add :— Page 251. **Leptocalamus sclateri.**

b. ♂ (V. 132, C.?). Guasimo, Costa Rica. Mr. Underwood [C.].

Add :— Page 254. **Scaphiophis albopunctatus.**

b. ♂ (Sc. 24, V. 194; Ugogo. Mr. Baxter [C.].
C. 72).

Add :— Page 258. **Contia æstiva.**

Opheodrys æstivus, *Bocourt, Miss. Sc. Mex., Rept.* p. 817, pl. lxi. fig. 3 (1895)

Add :— Page 259. **Contia vernalis.**

Cyclophis vernalis, *Bocourt, l. c.* p. 815, pl. lxi. fig. 2.

Page 259. Contia agassizii.

Is an Opisthoglyphous Snake. See this volume, p. 126 (*Pseudablabes agassizii*).

Page 261. Contia collaris.

Add:—

l-m. ♂ (Sc. 17; V. 171, C. 62) & ♀ (Sc. 17, V. 176; C. 57).   Tiflis.   Tiflis Mus. [E.].

n-o ♂ (Sc. 15; V. 150; C. 58) & ♀ (Sc. 15; V. 157; C 54).   Aresh, Gov. Elizabethpol.   Tiflis Mus. [E.].

p. ♀ (Sc. 17; V. 160; C. 59).   Mt. Hermon, Palestine.   Turin Mus. [E.].

Page 273. Add a genus:—

101 *a*. SYMPHIMUS.

Symphimus, *Cope, Proc. Amer. Philos. Soc.* xi 1869, p. 150.

Apparently agreeing with *Chilomeniscus*, but rostral shield not prominent.

Mexico.

1. Symphimus leucostomus.

Symphimus leucostomus, *Cope, l. c*

Snout obtusely pointed. Rostral as deep as broad, scarcely visible from above; suture between the internasals as long as that between the præfrontals; frontal longer than broad, with concave sides, much shorter than the parietals; one præ- and one or two postoculars; temporals 1+2; seven upper labials, third and fourth entering the eye; anterior chin-shields a little longer than the posterior. Scales in 15 rows. Olive-grey above, with a light brown vertebral stripe three scales wide; lips light yellow; belly dirty white.

Total length 800 millim.; tail 250.

Chihuiatan, Tehuantepec.

Page 276. Homalosoma lutrix.

Add:—

p-u. ♂ (V. 119, 116, 113; C. 27, 31, 34) & ♀ (V. 134, 122, 126; C. 23, 19, 22).   Uganda.   F. J. Jackson, Esq. [P.].

The head-shields vary considerably, and *H. shiranum* should be united with *H. lutrix*.

Add :—   Page 277. ABLABES.

Phragmitophis, *Gunth Ann. & Mag. N. H* (3) ix. 1862, p. 53.
Entechinus, *Cope, Proc. Ac. Philad.* 1894, p. 427 (1895).

Page 279. Add a species :—

1 *a*. Ablabes herminæ.

Ablabes herminæ, *Boettg. Ber. Offenb. Ver. Nat.* 1895, p. 110.

Snout pointed. Rostral small, a little broader than deep, just visible from above; nasal divided; eye small; suture between the internasals more than half as long as that between the præfrontals; frontal as long as its distance from the end of the snout, much shorter than the parietals; loreal nearly twice as long as deep; one præ- and two postoculars; temporals 1+2, eight upper labials, fourth and fifth entering the eye; four lower labials in contact with the anterior chin-shields, which are a little longer than the posterior. Scales in 17 rows, smooth, faintly keeled towards the base of the tail. Ventrals 163; anal divided; subcaudals 58. Grey above, white beneath, the grey extending to the sides of the belly; back dotted with black; some of the scales black-edged; upper lip yellowish white, the shields finely edged with grey.

Total length 580 millim.; tail 107.

Loo Choo Islands.

Add .—   Page 281. Ablabes tricolor.

Phragmitophis tricolor, *Gunth. Ann. & Mag. N. H.* (3) ix 1862, p. 126.

h. ♀ (V. 154; C.?).   Singapore.   H. N Ridley, Esq. [C.].

Add :—   Page 284. Ablabes longicauda.

Ablabes longicauda, *Werner, Verh. zool.-bot. Ges. Wien*, xlvi. 1896, p. 17.

Add :—   Page 287. Grayia smythii.

Grayia smythii, *Gunth. Ann. & Mag N. H.* (6) xv. 1895, p. 525.
—— triangularis, *Bocage, Herp Angola*, p. 102 (1895).
—— ornata, *Bocage, l. c.* p. 104

n. Head and tail, bad state.   Uganda.   Scott Elliot, Esq. [P.].

Page 288. Add a genus :—

105 *a*. OLIGOLEPIS.

Oligolepis, *Bouleng. Ann & Mag N. H.* (6) xvi. 1895, p. 171.

Maxillary teeth 30, small, closely set, equal; mandibular teeth equal. Head distinct from neck; eye large, with round pupil.

Body cylindrical; scales finely striated, without pits, oblique, in 13 rows; ventrals rounded. Tail rather long; subcaudals in two rows. East Africa.

1. Oligolepis macrops.

Oligolepis macrops, *Bouleng. l. c.*

Eye nearly as long as the snout. Rostral nearly twice as broad as deep, just visible from above; internasals broader than long, a little shorter than the præfrontals; frontal once and a half as long as broad, longer than its distance from the end of the snout, slightly shorter than the parietals; loreal twice as long as deep; one præ- and two postoculars; temporals 1+2; nine upper labials, fifth and sixth entering the eye; five lower labials in contact with the anterior chin-shields, which are shorter than the posterior. Scales in 13 rows on the body, in 4 rows on the tail. Ventrals 148; anal divided; subcaudals 75. Olive above, with rather irregular light cross-bars; upper lip and lower parts white.

Total length 215 millim.; tail 57.

East Africa.

a. Yg. (V. 148; C. 75).   Usambara.   (Type.)

Add:— Page 290. **Abastor erythrogrammus.**

Duberria ancoralis, *Berthold, Abh. Ges. Wiss. Gotting.* i. 1843, p. 66, pl i. figs. 9 & 10.
Homolopsis parviceps, *Blyth, Journ. As. Soc. Beng.* xxiii. 1854, p. 301.

Add:— Page 291. **Farancia abacura.**

Homolopsis crassa, *Blyth, l. c.* p. 300.

Add:— Page 293. **Petalognathus nebulatus.**

Sibon nebulatus, *Fitzing. N. Class. Rept.* p. 60 (1826).
? Leptognathus affinis, *Fischer, Verh. Nat. Ver. Bremen*, (2) iii. 1879, p. 78, pl. i. fig. 1.

κ. ♀ (V. 170; C. 83). Atoyac, Guerrero. Mr. H. H. Smith [C.]; F. D. Godman, Esq. [P.].

Add:— Page 294. **TROPIDODIPSAS.**

Dipeltophis, *Cope, Bull. U.S. Nat. Mus.* no. 32, 1887, p. 58

Add:— Page 295. **Tropidodipsas philippii.**

Dipeltophis albocinctus, *Cope, l. c.* p. 91.

Add :—   Page 296. **Tropidopisas sartorii.**

? Leptognathus semicinctus, *Bocourt, Bull. Soc. Philom* (7) viii. 1884, p. 139.

Add :—   Page 299. **Dirosema psephotum.**

a. ♀ (V. 164 ; C. 66).   La Palma, Costa Rica.   Mr. Underwood [C.].

Add :—   Page 306. **Atractus bocourti.**

b. ♂ (V. 190 ; C. 36).   Canelos, Ecuador.   Mr Buckley [C.].
c. ♂ (V. 189 ; C. 35).   Paitanga, Ecuador.   Mr. Buckley [C.].
d-e. ♂ (V. 166 ; C 30) & ♀ (V. 182 ; C. 24).   Yurimaguas, Huallaga R.   Dr. Hahnel [C.].

Add :—   Page 307. **Atractus maculatus.**

c-d. ♂ (V. 166, 165 ; C. 32, 34).   Charobamba, Bolivia.
e. ♀ (V. 165 ; C. 33).   Aschiquiri, Bolivia.
f-g. Yg. (V. 164, 162 ; C. 31, 31).   Yungas, Bolivia.

Add :—   Page 312. **Atractus emmeli.**

a. ♀ (V. 161 ; C. 16).   Para.   Dr. E. A. Goldi [P.].
b-d. ♂ (V. 158 ; C. 27) & ♀ (V. 185, 183 ; C. 24, 26).   Charobamba, Bolivia.
e. ♂ (V. 167 ; C. 27).   Yungas, Bolivia.
f. ♀ (V. 181 ; C. 21).   Campolican. Bolivia.

Page 312. Add a new species :—

19 *a*. **Atractus boettgeri.**

Snout rounded. Rostral a little broader than deep, just visible from above; internasals very small; præfrontals a little longer than broad; frontal once and a half as long as broad, shorter than the præfrontals, much shorter than the parietals; loreal twice and a half as long as deep; two postoculars; temporals 1+1 or 2; six upper labials, third and fourth entering the eye; four or five lower labials in contact with the single pair of chin-shields, which are elongate and separated from the symphysial. Scales in 15 rows. Ventrals 177; anal entire; subcaudals 20. Uniform dark brown above; belly yellowish white, spotted with black; subcaudals black.
Total length 350 millim.; tail 22.
Bolivia.

a. ♀ (V. 177 ; C. 20).   Yungas.

Add :—   Page 317. **Geophis semidoliatus.**

k. ♀ (V. 168 ; C. 24).   Orizaba.

Add:— Page 320. **Geophis hoffmanni.**

h–i. ♀ (V. 140, 144; C. 32, 36).   La Palma, Costa Rica.   Mr. Underwood [C.].

k. ♀ (V. 124; C. 28).   Monte Redondo, Costa Rica.   Mr. Underwood [C.].

Add:— Page 325. **STILOSOMA.**

8 strong, subequal maxillary teeth.

Add:— Page 325. **Stilosoma extenuatum.**

Stilosoma extenuatum, *Loennberg, Proc. U S. Nat. Mus.* xvii. 1894, p 323, figs

a. ♂ (V. 258; C. 40).   Orange Co., Florida.   Dr. E. Loennberg [P.].

Add:— Page 329. **Pseudorhabdium longiceps.**

m. ♀ (V. 140; C. 20).   Sarawak.   Rajah Brooke [P.].

Add:— Page 334. **Calamaria vermiformis.**

A.

c–d. ♀ (V. 167; C. 22) & yg. (V. 188; C. 15)   Tandjong, S.E. Borneo.

e. Hgr. ♀ (V. 149; C. 21).   Great Natuna Id   C. Hose, Esq. [C.].

E.

f. ♀ (V. 184; C. 16)   Kina Balu.   A. Everett, Esq. [C.].

Add:— Page 335. **Calamaria baluensis.**

b–d. ♂ (V. 190, 187, C. 29, 27) & ♀ (V. 206; C. 24).   Kina Balu.   A. Everett, Esq. [C.].

Add:— Page 338. **Calamaria bitorques.**

f. ♀ (V. 177; C. 15).   Cape Engano, N. Luzon.   Whitehead Exped.

Page 340. Add a species:—

12 *a.* **Calamaria mindorensis.**

Calamaria mindorensis, *Bouleng. Ann. & Mag. N. H.* (6) xvi. 1895, p. 481.

Rostral a little broader than deep, visible from above; frontal longer than broad, twice as broad as the supraocular, shorter than the parietals; a præ- and a postocular; diameter of the eye equal to its distance from the mouth; five upper labials, third and fourth entering the eye; symphysial in contact with the anterior chin-shields, two pairs of chin-shields in contact with each other Scales in 13 rows. Ventrals 193; anal entire; subcaudals 15. Brown above, with longitudinal series of black dots; a yellow spot on each side of the neck; a white spot on each scale of the outer row; upper lip and lower parts yellowish; a black spot at the outer end of each ventral; a black line along the middle of the tail.

Total length 240 millim.; tail 13.

Mindoro, Philippine Islands.

a. ♀ (V. 193; C. 15)   Mindoro   A. Everett, Esq. [C.].   (Type.)

Add :—   Page 340. **Calamaria virgulata.**

Calamaria modesta, var. bogorensis, *Boettg in Semon, Zool. Forsch.* v. p. 125 (1894)

Page 343. Add two species :—

18 *a.* Calamaria brookii.

Calamaria brookii, *Bouleng. Ann. & Mag. N H.* (6) xv. 1895, p. 331.

Rostral as deep as broad, the portion visible from above half as long as its distance from the frontal; frontal once and one fourth as long as broad, much shorter than the parietals, thrice as broad as the supraocular; a præocular and a postocular; diameter of the eye equal to its distance from the mouth; five upper labials, third and fourth entering the eye; first pair of lower labials forming a suture behind the symphysial; two pairs of chin-shields, in contact with each other. Scales in 13 rows. Ventrals 147; anal entire; subcaudals 23. Tail obtusely pointed. Yellowish brown above, with five black stripes, the median the broadest and occupying one scale and two halves, head marbled with black; a black nuchal collar; two similar black bars on the tail, one at the base, the other near the end; outer row of scales, ventrals, and subcaudals yellowish white, the upper third of the outer scale black, otherwise unspotted.

Total length 220 millim.; tail 23.

Borneo.

a. ♂ (V. 147, C. 23).   Matang.   Rajah Brooke [P.].

18 *b.* Calamaria brachyura.

Calamaria brachyura, *Bouleng Ann. & Mag. N. H.* (6) xvi. 1895, p. 481

—— anceps, *Werner, Verh. zool.-bot. Ges. Wien,* xlvi. 1896, p. 18.

Rostral a little broader than deep, visible from above; frontal longer than broad, more than twice as broad as the supraocular, shorter than the parietals; one præ- and one postocular; diameter of the eye equal to its distance from the mouth; five upper labials, third and fourth entering the eye, fourth smallest; first lower labial in contact with its fellow behind the symphysial; two pairs of chin-shields in contact with each other. Scales in 13 rows. Ventrals 201–210; anal entire; subcaudals 9. Dark grey-brown above, with six black longitudinal lines, which disappear on the anterior half of the body; two outer rows of scales black and white; a narrow yellow cross-band on the nape; head black above, with a small yellow spot on each præfrontal and parietal shield; upper lip white; lower parts white, with a black spot at the outer end of each ventral shield; a black line along the middle of the tail.

Total length 275 millim.; tail 8.

North Borneo.

a. ♀ (V. 201, C. 9).   Kina Balu.   A. Everett, Esq [C.].   (Type.)

Add:—   Page 347. **Calamaria borneensis.**

d. ♂ (V. 152; C. 22).   Sarawak   Rajah Brooke [P.].

Add:—   Page 350. **Calamaria melanota.**

e. Yg. (V. 182; C. 16).   Tandjong, S.E. Borneo.

Add:—   Page 355. **Dasypeltis scabra.**

Dasypeltis scabra, var. fasciolata, *Peters, Mon. Berl. Ac.* 1868, p. 451.
—— fasciolata, *Boettg. Ber. Offenb. Ver. Nat* 1885, p. 14.
—— scabra, *Bocage, Herp. Angola,* p. 106 (1895).

B.

o. ♂ (Sc. 23; V. 229; C. 83).   Freetown, Sierra Leone.   R. Dinzey, Esq. [P.].
p. Yg. (Sc. 23; V. 203; C. 54).   Uganda.   F. J. Jackson, Esq. [P.].

F.

i. ♂ (Sc. 23; V. 224; C. 54).   Lower Congo.   Rev. G. Pinnock [C.].

VOL. III.

Add :— Page 68. **Dipsadomorphus pulverulentus.**

h. ♀ (V. 249 ; C ?).   Wegbe, Togoland.   W. G. Innes, Esq [C.].

Add :— Page 91. **Leptodira hotambœia.**

b. Yg (Sc. 21 ; V. 161 ; C. 42).   Uganda.   F. J. Jackson, Esq. [P.].

Add :— Page 119. **Hemirhagerrhis kelleri.**

d. ♀ (V 147 ; C. 67).   Uganda.   F. J. Jackson, Esq. [P.].

Add :— Page 121. **Tomodon ocellatus.**

Pelias trigonatus, *Leybold, Escurs. Pamp. Argent.* p. 82 (1873)

Add :— Page 140. **Trimerorhinus tritæniatus.**

r. ♀ (V. 169 ; C. 63).   Uganda.   F. J. Jackson, Esq. [P.].

Add :— Page 257. **Aparallactus jacksonii.**

b. ♀ (V. 148 ; C. 33).   Uganda.   F. J. Jackson, Esq. [P.].
Total length 245 millim. ; tail 35.

Add — Page 263. **Elapops modestus.**

m. ♂ (V. 138 , C. 44).   Wegbe, Togoland.   W. G. Innes, Esq. [C].

Add :— Page 379. **Naia nigricollis (F. typica).**

k. ♀ (Sc. $\frac{25}{23}$; V. 204 , C. 59).   Wegbe, Togoland.   W. G Innes, Esq. [C.].

ALPHABETICAL INDEX

TO THE THREE VOLUMES.

abacura (Farancia), ii. 291; iii 644
abacurum (Calopisma), ii. 291.
abacurus (Coluber), ii. 291.
abacurus (Farancia), ii. 291.
abacurus (Helicops), ii. 291.
abacurus (Hydrops), ii. 291.
Abastor, ii 289
abbreviatus (Hydrophis), iii 301
Ablabes, i. 181, 297, 300, 318, ii. 9, 25, 160, 188, 255, 277, iii 643.
Ablabophis, i 318
abnorma (Coronella), ii. 203.
aboma (Boa), i 94.
abyssina (Dasypeltis), ii. 355.
abyssinicum (Homalosoma), ii 276.
abyssinicum (Lycophidium), i 342.
abyssinicus (Rachiodon), ii. 355.
Acalyptophis, iii. 269.
Acalyptus, iii 269
acanthias (Elapomorphus), iii. 250, 251, 252.
acanthias (Miodon), iii 250
acanthias (Urobelus), iii. 250
Acanthocalyx, iii. 621.
Acanthophallus, ii. 144.
Acanthophis, iii. 354.
acanthophis (Ophryas), iii 355
acanthophis (Vipera), iii. 355.
accedens (Elapomorphus), iii. 240.

accedens (Typhlops), i. 17.
Achalinus, i 308
Achirina, ii 255
acontia (Atropos), iii. 560.
Acontias, iii. 519.
Acontiophidæ, i. 169, 177.
Acontiophis, i 414
acontistes (Coluber), i. 395
Acrantophis, i. 116, 414
Acrochordidæ, i. 169, 172
Acrochordiens, i. 172.
Acrochordina, i 169, 172.
Acrochordinæ, i 172.
Acrochordus, i 173.
aculeata (Boa), iii 356.
acuminata (Dryiophis), iii. 192.
acuminatus (Coluber), iii. 192.
acuminatus (Oxybelis), iii. 192
acuta (Psammophis), iii. 147, 148.
acuta (Rhagerrhis), iii 148.
acuticauda (Typhlops), i. 26.
acutirostre (Lycophidium), i. 338.
acutus (Ancistrodon), iii. 524.
acutus (Cerberus), iii 16.
acutus (Gryptotyphlops), i 56.
acutus (Halys), iii 524.
acutus (Ogmius), iii. 229.
acutus (Onychocephalus), i 56.
acutus (Psammophis), iii 148

acutus (Rhamphiophis), iii. 148.
acutus (Typhlops), i. 56
adamantea (Caudisona), iii 578.
adamanteus (Crotalus), iii 575, 576, 577.
Adelophis, i. 285.
Adelphicos, ii 300
Ademophis, iii 400
adnexus (Tretanorhinus), i. 282.
adspersus (Dromicus), ii. 120.
adspersus (Lycodon), i. 356.
Æchmophrys, iii 572
ægyptia (Vipera), iii 503.
ægyptia (Walterinnesia), iii. 392.
ægyptiaca (Coronella), ii. 192.
ægyptiaca (Vipera), iii. 503
ægyptiacus (Cerastes), iii. 502.
ægyptiacus (Dipsas), iii 52.
æmula (Procinura), iii 212.
æmulus (Scolecophis), iii. 212
æneus (Dryinus), iii. 192.
æneus (Dryiophis), iii. 192.
æneus (Oxybelis), iii. 192.
æneus (Xenodon), ii 150.
Aepidea, iii. 627
æqualis (Elapochrus), ii. 183.
æqualis (Liophis), ii. 183.
æqualis (Pleiocercus), ii. 182.

ner (Coluber), iii 6.
aer (Homalopsis), iii. 6.
aer (Hypsirhina), iii. 7.
æruginosus (Leptophis), ii. 107.
æruginosus (Philothamnus), ii. 107.
æsculapii (Callopeltis), ii 53.
æsculapii (Coluber), ii 52, 357; iii 141, 200.
æsculapii (Elaphis), ii 52.
æsculapii (Erythrolamprus), iii. 200.
æsculapii (Natrix), iii. 200.
æsculapii (Zamenis), ii. 52
æstiva (Contia), ii. 258, iii. 641.
æstivus (Coluber), ii. 258.
æstivus (Cyclophis), ii. 258; iii. 641
æstivus (Dryophylax), iii. 128
æstivus (Herpetodryas), ii. 15, 258, iii. 128.
æstivus (Leptophis), ii 258.
æstivus (Liopeltis), ii. 258.
æstivus (Opheodrys), ii. 258.
æstivus (Philodryas), iii 128.
æstivus (Phyllophilophis), ii 258
æstivus (Tropidodryas), iii. 128.
æthiopissa (Rhamnophis), iii 632.
æthiops (Chrysidomus), iii 632.
æthiops (Crypsidomus), iii. 632.
æthiops (Rhamnophis), iii 632.
affine (Stenostoma), i. 62.
affinis (Bothriopsis), iii. 544
affinis (Bothrops), iii. 544.
affinis (Dromicus), ii. 172, 173.
affinis (Drymobius), ii. 14.
affinis (Elaps), iii 423.
affinis (Glauconia), i. 62.
affinis (Herpetodryas), ii. 14

affinis (Hypnale), iii. 528
affinis (Hypsiglena), ii. 210.
affinis (Leptodira), iii. 95
affinis (Leptognathus), iii 644.
affinis (Oligodon), ii 236.
affinis (Pituophis), ii. 69.
affinis (Platurus), iii. 307.
affinis (Pseudonaja), iii. 326.
affinis (Rhadinæa), ii. 172
affinis (Simotes), ii. 218
affinis (Tachymenis), iii. 119
affinis (Trigonocephalus), iii. 525, 545.
affinis (Typhlops), i. 49; iii. 589.
affinis (Uropeltis), i. 137.
agamensis (Calamaria), ii 343
agassizii (Ablabes), ii. 259
agassizii (Coluber), ii. 65
agassizii (Contia), ii 259; iii. 126, 642.
agassizii (Eirenis), ii. 259
agassizii (Helicops), i. 282
agassizii (Nerodia), i. 243
agassizii (Pseudablabes), iii 126
agassizii (Rhinechis), ii. 65
agilis (Coluber), iii 200.
Agkistrodon, iii. 519.
aglæope (Elaps), iii. 423.
Aglypha, i 170
Aglyphodontes, i 71, 131, 167, 169, iii. 438.
Agrophis, ii. 360.
Ahætulla, ii. 77, 91, 98, 102, 105, 111.
ahætulla (Ahætulla), ii. 113.
ahætulla (Coluber), ii. 78, 113.
ahætulla (Leptophis), ii. 78, 113.
ahætulla (Natrix), ii. 78.
ahætulla (Thrasops), ii. 113.
Ailurophis, iii. 47.

Aipysurus, iii 303
albertisii (Liasis), i 80.
albicans (Boa), i. 87.
albifrons (Dipsadomorus), iii. 451.
albifrons (Glauconia), i. 63, iii. 591.
albifrons (Leptognathus), iii. 451.
albifrons (Stenostoma), i 63
albifrons (Typhlops), i. 63.
albirostris (Helminthophis), i. 6
albirostris (Liotyphlops), i. 6
albirostris (Rhinotyphlops), i 6
albiventer (Ablabes), i. 299.
albiventer (Calamaria), ii. 336.
albiventer (Changulia), ii 336.
albiventer (Simotes), ii. 229.
albiventris (Coluber), ii. 99
albiventris (Compsophis), iii 610.
albiventris (Liophis), ii. 130.
albocincta (Coronella), ii. 220.
albocinctus (Dipeltophis), iii 644.
albocinctus (Leptognathus), ii. 295
albocinctus (Ophis), iii. 90
albocinctus (Simotes), ii. 218, 220
albofusca (Leptodira), iii. 95.
albofuscus (Coluber), iii. 95.
albofuscus (Lycodon), i. 357; ii 618
albofuscus (Ophites), i. 357.
albofuscus (Sphecodes), i. 357.
albolabris (Trimesurus), iii 555.
albomaculata (Hypsirhina), iii. 11.
albomaculata (Lycophidium), i. 341; 617.
albomaculatus (Homalopsis), iii. 11.

ALPHABETICAL INDEX. 653

albomaculatus (Leptophis), i. 258
albopunctatus (Scaphiophis), ii. 254.
albostolatus (Erythrolamprus), iii. 201.
albovariata (Dendrophis), ii. 96
albovariata (Philothamnus), ii. 96.
albus (Brachyorrhus), i. 305.
albus (Coluber), i. 305.
Alecto, iii. 332, 348, 351.
alecto (Coluber), iii. 534.
algira (Periops), i. 408.
algirus (Zamenis), i. 408, iii 625
alkeni (Calamaria), ii. 333
alleghaniensis (Coluber), ii 50.
alleghaniensis (Elaphis), 40, 50
alleghaniensis (Pantherophis), ii 50
alleghaniensis (Scotophis), ii 50
allenii (Helicops), i. 275, iii. 610.
allenii (Liodytes), i 275, iii 610.
Allophis, ii. 25
Alluaudina, iii 26, 38
almadensis (Liophis), ii. 134
almadensis (Natrix), ii 134.
Alopecion, i. 327, 336.
Alopecophis, ii 25
alpestris (Coluber), ii. 46
alpinus (Coluber), ii. 192.
Alsophis, ii 118
alternans (Brachyorrhos), iii 4.
alternans (Coluber), ii 131.
alternans (Eurostus), iii 4.
alternans (Hypsirhina), iii. 4
alternans (Leptognathus), iii. 456.
alternans (Miralia), iii. 4.
alternatus (Bothrops), iii 541.
alternatus (Coryphodon), ii 11.

alternatus (Drymobius), ii. 11
alternatus (Lachesis), iii 541.
alternatus (Trigonocephalus), iii. 541.
alticolus (Liophis), ii 130.
alticolus (Opheomorphus), ii 130
altirostris (Elaps), iii 427.
aluensis (Typhlops), i 27.
amabilis (Coronella), ii. 207; iii 638.
amabilis (Diadophis), ii. 207
amabilis (Dromicus), ii. 158
amabilis (Simotes), ii 221.
amaliæ (Coronella), ii 193, 359, iii. 637.
amaliæ (Rhinechis), ii. 193
Amastridium, ii 352.
amaura (Lampropeltis), ii 203
ambigua (Prosymna), ii 248, iii 641.
ambiguus (Coluber), iii. 535.
ambiniger (Rhynchonyx), iii 237.
ambinigra (Apostolepis), iii 237.
Amblycephalus, iii. 438, 439, 440
Amblymetopon, ii. 270
Amblyodipsas, iii. 244, 245
amboinense (Rhabdosoma), ii. 237
ambreensis (Pseudoxyrhopus), iii 613.
amethystina (Boa), i. 83.
amethystinus (Liasis), i. 83, 85.
amethystinus (Python), i. 83; iii. 592.
ammodytes (Cobra), iii. 485
ammodytes (Coluber), iii. 485
ammodytes (Echidna), iii. 485.
ammodytes (Rhinechis), iii. 485.
ammodytes (Scytale), iii. 534.

ammodytes (Trigonocephalus), iii 534
ammodytes (Vipera), iii. 484, 485
ammodytoides (Bothrops), iii. 543
ammodytoides (Lachesis), iii 543.
amœna (Calamaria), ii. 324
amœna (Carphophiops), ii. 324
amœna (Celuta), ii 324
amœnus (Aporophis), ii. 160
amœnus (Brachyorrhos), ii 324.
amœnus (Carphophis), ii. 324
amœnus (Coluber), ii. 324
amœnus (Enicognathus), ii. 160
Amphiardis, i. 290
Amphibola, i. 169
Amphiesma, i 193, 265
Amphiophis, iii. 124, 152
Amplorhinus, iii 124
anaconda (Boa), i. 115
anamallensis (Lachesis), iii. 558
anamallensis (Lycodon), i. 351.
anamallensis (Trimeresurus), iii 558
anceps (Calamaria), iii. 647.
anchietæ (Naia), iii. 387
anchietæ (Onychocephalus), i. 40; iii 587
anchietæ (Ophirhina, iii. 620.
anchietæ (Python), i. 88, iii. 592.
anchietæ (Typhlops), i. 40
Ancistrodon, iii 519
ancoralis (Duberria), iii. 644.
ancoralis (Elaps), iii 432
ancoralis (Simotes), ii. 225.
ancorus (Xenodon), ii 225
andamanensis (Dendrophis), ii. 78.
andamanensis (Typhlops), i 52
andersoni (Amblycephalus), iii. 444.

andersonii (Calamo-
hydrus), i. 284.
andersonii (Opistho-
tropis), i. 284.
andersonii (Pareas), iii.
444.
andersonii (Trimere-
surus), iii. 553.
andiana (Leptognathus),
iii. 452
andreæ (Liophis), ii. 140.
andrei (Leptognathus),
iii. 453.
Angiostomata, i 3, 131
angolensis (Amphiophis),
iii. 170.
angolensis (Causus), iii
468.
angolensis (Chlorophis),
ii 95
angolensis (Dromophis),
iii 170
angolensis (Onychocepha-
lus), i 42.
angolensis (Philotham-
nus), ii. 95.
angolensis (Psammophis),
iii. 170
Anguiformes, i. 3, 131.
anguiformis (Boa), i.
127
anguiformis (Clothonia),
i. 127.
anguiformis (Eryx), i.
127.
anguillæformis (Aipy-
surus), iii. 304
anguillæformis (Thalas-
sophis), iii. 304
angulata (Dipsas), iii.
75.
angulata (Homalopsis),
i. 278.
angulatus (Coluber), i
278
angulatus (Dipsadomor-
phus), iii. 75.
angulatus (Helicops), i.
278.
angulatus (Uranops), i
278
angulifer (Alsophis), ii.
120.
angulifer (Dromicus), ii.
120.
angulifer (Epicrates), i.
96; iii. 593.
angulifera (Dinodipsas),
iii. 470.
angusticeps(Chloroechis),
iii. 437.

angusticeps (Contia), ii.
262.
angusticeps (Dendraspis),
iii. 435, 436, 437.
angusticeps (Diemenia),
iii. 323.
angusticeps (Dinophis),
iii. 437
angusticeps (Naja), iii.
437.
angusticeps (Onycho-
cephalus), i. 50
angusticeps (Tropido-
notus), i 215, 234,
270
angusticeps (Typhlops), i.
50
angustirostris (Eutainia),
i 210
angustirostris (Xenodon),
ii 146.
Anholodon, iii. 446
Anilios, i. 7.
Anilius, i. 133, 134
Anisodontiens, iii 1, 26.
anisolepis (Atheris), iii.
509
anisolepis (Himantodes),
iii. 84.
annectens (Dipsadomor-
phus), iii 71.
annectens (Doliophis),
iii 402.
annectens (Pituophis), ii
67
annellatus (Elaps), iii
418.
annularis (Bungarus), iii.
365
annularis (Callophis), iii.
398.
annularis (Galedon), ii.
296
annularis (Tropidonotus),
i 224, 233
annulata (Anguis), i. 133.
annulata (Coronella), ii.
203.
annulata (Demansia), iii.
325
annulata (Dipsas), iii. 93,
95, 97.
annulata (Eteirodipsas),
iii. 93, 97.
annulata (Lampropeltis),
ii. 201, 203.
annulata (Leptodira), iii.
93, 95, 97.
annulata (Leptognathus),
iii. 457.
annulata (Naja), iii. 376.

annulata (Sibon), iii. 93,
95, 97.
annulata (Silybura), i.
158.
annulata (Tantilla), iii.
217
annulata (Vermicella), iii.
407.
annulatum (Homalo-
cranium), iii. 217.
annulatum (Sibon), iii.
93, 95
annulatum (Tropido-
clonium), ii 296.
annulatum (Xiphosoma),
i 102, iii. 593
annulatus(Aipysurus), iii.
304.
annulatus (Chersydrus),
i. 174.
annulatus (Coluber), iii.
95, 97
annulatus (Corallus), i.
102, iii. 593
annulatus (Diadophis), i.
189.
annulatus(Dipsas), iii 95.
annulatus (Elapoides), i.
359.
annulatus (Emydocepha-
lus), iii. 304.
annulatus(Enicognathus),
i 189.
annulatus (Geophis), ii.
296.
annulatus (Henico-
gnathus), i. 189
annulatus (Heterodon),
ii 155.
annulatus (Hydrophis),
iii 288.
annulatus (Leptogna-
thus), iii. 457.
annulatus (Ophibolus), ii.
201, 203.
annulatus (Polyodonto-
phis), i. 189.
annulatus (Polyodontus),
iii 302.
annulifer (Alopecion), i.
331
annulifer (Boa), i 94.
annulifer (Simotes), ii.
226
annulifera (Naja), iii.
374.
annulifera (Tropido-
dipsas), ii 297
Anodon, ii. 353.
anomala (Clœlia), iii.
639

anomala (Coronella), ii. 165
anomala (Hydrophis), iii. 269
anomala (Rhadinæa), ii. 165
anomala (Storeria), i. 287.
anomala (Uriechis), iii. 262
Anomalepis, i 58.
Anomalochilus, i. 134.
Anomalodon, i 268.
anomalolepis (Pseuderyx), iii 637.
anomalolepis (Spilotes), ii 23.
anomalus (Alsophis), ii. 125.
anomalus (Aparallactus), iii 262
anomalus (Apocophis), ii 165
anomalus (Drepanodon), iii 639
anomalus (Dromicus), ii. 125
anomalus (Elaps), iii. 417.
anomalus (Onychocephalus), i 47
anomalus (Oxyrhopus), iii 639.
anomalus (Thalassophis), iii 269
anomalus (Tropidonotus), iii. 606.
anomalus (Typhlops), i. 47, iii. 588.
anomalus (Zamenis), ii 125.
Anoplodipsas, iii 81.
Anoplophallus, ii 353.
anoscopus(Natrix), i 242.
anoscopus (Tropidonotus), i 242, iii. 606.
anostomosatus (Coluber), i 230
antarctica (Acanthophis), iii. 355
antarctica (Boa), iii 355.
antarcticus (Acanthophis), iii 355
anthicum (Bascanium), i. 395.
anthracops (Leptognathus), ii. 297
anthracops (Tropidodipsas), ii. 297.
antillensis (Alsophis), ii. 123.

antillensis (Dromicus), ii. 122, 123.
antillensis (Psammophis), ii 122, 123.
antinorii (Dendraspis), iii. 437.
Antiochalina, i. 169.
antonii (Rhinochilus), ii. 213
Aparallactus, iii. 255.
aphanospilus (Simotes), ii. 225.
apiata (Stenorhina), iii. 230.
apiatus (Elaps), iii 423.
Aploaspis, iii. 572.
Aplopeltura, iii 439
Aporophis, ii. 157, 160
Apostolepis, iii 232
approximans (Dipsas), iii. 97
Aprotérodontes, i. 93.
Aprotérodontiens, i. 71, 131
aquatica (Boa), i. 115.
aquaticus (Coluber), iii. 520
arabicus (Coluber), i. 219.
araramboya(Xiphosoma), i. 102.
arboreus (Bothrops), iii. 565.
arboreus (Trigonocephalus), iii. 565
arcticeps (Calamaria), ii. 341
arcticeps (Silybura), i. 156, 157.
arctifasciatus (Dipsas), iii. 43.
arctifasciatus (Heterurus), iii. 43
arctifasciatus(Stenophis), iii 43.
arctiventris (Calamaria), ii. 274.
arctiventris (Coluber), ii. 274.
arctiventris (Duberria), ii 274.
arctiventris (Homalosoma), ii. 274.
arcuatus (Bungarus), iii 368.
arenarius (Onychocephalus), i 49
arenarius (Typhlops), i. 49.
arenarius (Zamenis), i 413

arenicola (Echis), iii. 505, 507.
arenicola (Toxicoa), iii. 505.
argentatus (Coluber), iii 190
argentea (Dryiophis), iii. 190
argenteus (Coluber), iii 190
argenteus (Oxybelis), iii 190.
argonauta(Tyria), ii 260
argus (Coluber), i. 82.
argus (Leptognathus), iii. 458.
argus (Morelia), i. 82
argus (Spilotes), ii 20.
Argyrophis, i 7
arietans (Bitis), iii. 493.
arietans (Clotho), iii. 494.
arietans (Echidna), iii. 494
arietans (Vipera), iii. 494.
Arizona, ii. 25
arizonæ (Coluber), ii 66
armata (Vipera), iii. 497
armillatum (Homalocranium), iii. 215, 220.
arnensis (Coluber), ii. 229.
arnensis (Simotes), ii. 229, 359
arnyi (Coronella), iii. 629
arnyi (Diadophis), ii. 208, iii 638
arnyi (Liophis), ii. 208.
Arrhyton, ii 251.
articulata (Leptognathus), iii 458
aruanus (Dipsas), iii. 75.
aruensis (Dendrophis), ii 80.
aruensis(Lycodon), i 366
asclepiadeus (Coluber), ii 52.
asiana (Zamenis), i. 395.
Asinea, i. 71, 169
asper (Enygrus), i 109, iii 594
asper (Erebophis), i 109
asper (Trigonocephalus), iii. 538
aspera (Hydrophis), iii 295
aspera (Natrix), i 278.
asperrimus (Tropidonotus), i 232.

ALPHABETICAL INDEX.

Aspidelaps, iii. 388, 390, 465.
Aspidiotes, i. 91.
Aspidites, i. 91.
Aspidoboa, i. 81.
Aspidoclonion, iii. 365.
Aspidopython, i. 81.
aspidorhyncha (Diemenia), iii. 326.
Aspidorhynchus, i. 7.
Aspidura, i. 309, 310.
Aspis, iii 372, 501.
aspis (Coluber), iii 476, 481, 484.
aspis (Vipera), iii. 481, 484, 487.
assimilis (Apostolepis), iii 234.
assimilis (Dipsadoboa), iii 82.
assimilis (Elapomorphus), iii. 234.
assimilis (Helicops), i. 277.
assimilis (Hoplocephalus), iii. 343.
assimilis (Psammophylax), iii. 118.
Asthenodipsas, iii. 440
Asthenognathus, iii. 446
astreptophorus (Tropidonotus), i 220.
Astrotia, iii. 285.
ater (Alsophis), ii. 121.
ater (Amhos), i 53.
ater (Bothrolycus), i. 326.
ater (Dromicus), ii. 121
ater (Hoplocephalus), iii. 351.
ater (Oxyophis), ii. 121.
ater (Tropidonotus), i 215, 219
ater (Typhlops), i 53
ater (Zamenis), ii. 139.
aterrima (Atractaspis), iii. 513, 515.
Atheris, iii. 508
atmodes (Heterodon), ii. 155.
Atomarchus, i. 193.
Atomophis, iii. 127.
atra (Anguis), i. 133.
atra (Diemenia), iii. 323
atra (Naja), iii. 380.
atra (Natrix), ii. 121.
atra (Opisthotropis), i. 284.
atra (Vipera), iii. 482.
Atractaspididæ, iii. 464.
Atractaspidinæ, iii. 464.

Atractaspis, iii. 510.
Atractocephalus, i. 305.
Atractus, ii 300.
atrata (Eutainia), i. 201.
atrata (Ninia), i 293.
atratus (Coluber), i. 293; iii 634.
atratus (Streptophorus), i. 293; iii. 612.
atratus (Neusterophis), i. 227
Atretium, i 272
atricauda (Echidna), iii. 502, 503
atricaudatus (Crotalus), iii 579.
atriceps (Homalocranium), iii. 226.
atriceps (Hydrophis), iii. 281.
atriceps (Urrechis), iii. 260.
atrocincta (Calamaria), iii 211.
atrocinctum (Homalocranium), iii 211.
atrocinctus (Coluber), iii. 200.
atrocinctus (Scolecophis), iii 211.
atrofrontalis (Elaps), iii. 398.
atrofuscus (Ancistrodon), iii 523
atrofuscus (Acontias), iii. 522.
atrofuscus (Cenchris), iii. 523.
atrofuscus (Trigonocephalus), iii. 523.
atropoides (Vipera), iii. 496.
atropohos (Pseudelaps), iii. 317.
Atropophis, iii. 530.
Atropos, iii 529.
atropos (Bitis), iii. 495.
atropos (Clotho), iii. 496.
atropos (Cobra), iii 495.
atropos (Coluber), iii. 495
atropos (Echidna), iii. 496.
atropos (Vipera), iii. 496.
atropurpureum (Tetragonosoma), i. 356.
atropurpureus (Lycodon), i. 356
atrostriata (Dendrophis), ii. 85.

atrovirens (Coluber), i. 395
atrovirens (Tyria), i 395.
atrovirens (Zamenis), i. 395.
atrox (Bothrops), iii 535, 538, 541, 542.
atrox (Caudisona), iii. 576.
atrox (Coluber), iii. 537.
atrox (Oophias), iii. 535, 538.
atrox (Craspedocephalus), iii. 535, 538.
atrox (Crotalus), iii. 575, 576.
atrox (Lachesis), iii. 537.
atrox (Trigonocephalus), iii. 535, 538.
atrox (Vipera), iii. 537.
Aturia, iii. 271, 285.
atypicus (Leptognathus), iii. 463.
atypicus (Pseudoparcas), iii. 463
audax (Coluber), iii 57.
audax (Dipsas), iii. 57.
audax (Hormonotus), i. 343.
audax (Lycodon), iii. 57.
aulicus (Chamætortus), iii 98.
aulicus (Coluber), i. 352.
aulicus (Lycodon), i 349, 352, iii 618.
aurantiaca (Boa), i. 102.
aurata (Dryiophis), iii. 192.
aurata (Eutænia), i. 208.
auratus (Dryinus), iii 192
aureus (Plectrurus), i. 162.
auribundus (Spilotes), ii. 33.
auriculatus (Tropidonotus), i. 261
aurifer (Bothriechis), iii. 568
aurifer (Bothrops), iii. 568.
aurifer (Lachesis), iii. 568.
aurifer (Thamnocenchris), iii. 568.
aurigulum (Bascanium), i. 301.
aurigulus (Drymobius), i. 301.
auritus (Coluber), iii. 161.
aurolineatus (Coluber), i 236.
aurora (Cerastes), i. 321.

ALPHABETICAL INDEX.

aurora (Coluber), i. 321.
aurora (Coronella), i. 321
aurora (Duberria), i. 321.
aurora (Lamprophis), i. 321.
auspex (Constrictor), i. 117.
australis (Aipysurus), iii. 305.
australis (Anilios), i 35
australis (Boa), i. 105.
australis (Brachyurophis), iii 363.
australis (Cerberus), iii. 18.
australis (Coronella), ii. 168
australis (Enygrus), i 105.
australis (Homalopsis), iii. 18.
australis (Naja), iii. 330.
australis (Pseudechis), iii. 329, 330
australis (Rhynchelaps), iii 363
australis (Simotes), iii 363.
australis (Tropidonotus), i 215
australis (Typhlops), i. 35.
australis (Zamenophis), i. 365
austriaca (Coronella), ii. 53.
austriacus (Coluber), ii. 191
austriacus (Zacholus), ii 192
avicennæ (Vipera), iii. 502, 503
Azémiophides, i 71, 131.
Azemiops, iii. 470
azureus (Chondropython), i. 90.

bachmanni (Coronella), iii. 103, 107
badia (Calamaria), ii 308, 309
badium (Rhabdosoma), ii. 307, 308
badius (Atractus), ii 308
badius (Brachyorrhos), ii 308.
badius (Geophis), ii 308.
bahiensis (Natrix), i. 409.
bairdi (Coluber), ii. 40
bairdi (Lycodon), iii 172.

VOL. III.

bairdi (Salvadora), i. 393.
bairdii (Phimothyra), i. 393
baliocoryphus (Elaps), iii. 427.
baliodeira (Coronella) ii. 283.
baliodeirus (Diadophis), ii. 283.
baliodirus (Ablabes), ii. 283
baliogaster (Helicops), i. 276.
baliolum (Homalosoma), ii. 282.
balteata (Coronella), ii 197.
balteatus (Trimerodytes), iii. 607
balteatus (Tropidonotus), iii. 607
baluensis (Calamaria), ii 335, iii 646.
bancana (Dipsas), iii 74.
barbarus (Coluber), i. 407.
barmanus (Typhlops), i. 22.
barnesii (Dipsadomorphus), iii. 73
barnesii (Dipsas), iii 73
baroni (Dromicus), i 247.
baroni (Philodryas), iii 136
baronis-mulleri (Tropidonotus), i 226
barrowii (Onychophis), i. 42.
barthii (Polemon), iii. 251, 254
Bascanion, i 379
basilisca (Caudisona), iii. 574
basiliscus (Crotalus), iii. 574.
basimaculatus (Typhlops), i 28
batesii (Chrysenis), i 102.
batesii (Elaps), iii. 416.
batillus (Typhlops), iii. 585
batjanensis (Coluber), i. 368.
batjanensis (Lielaphis), i. 368.
batjanensis (Stegonotus), i. 368.
beauperthuisii (Erythrolamprus), iii 201.
beccarii (Calamaria), ii. 343.

beckeri (Pseudoelaps), iii. 325.
beddomii (Silybura), i 153, 154.
beddomii (Simotes), ii. 229
beddomii (Tropidonotus), i 252, iii 608.
beddomii (Typhlops), i. 18, iii. 585
belcheri (Aturia), iii. 296.
belcheri (Distira), iii 296
belcheri (Hydrophis), iii. 296
bellii (Ahætulla), ii 78.
bellii (Bucephalus), iii 187.
bellii (Herpetæthiops), ii. 97.
bellii (Leptophis), [iii. 165.
bellii (Python), i 89
bellona (Churchillia), ii. 69
bellona (Pituophis), ii. 69
Bellophis, ii 188
bellulus (Tropidonotus), i. 224.
bellyi (Alluaudina), iii 38
bengalensis (Coluber), i. 230
bengalensis (Enhydrina), iii 302
bengalensis (Eryx), i. 124.
bengalensis (Falconeria), i 291.
bengalensis (Hydrophis), iii 302
benjaminsii (Calamaria), ii 347.
bennetti (Hypsirhina), iii 8
berdmorii (Pareas), iii. 444, 445.
Bergenia, iii 229.
bernardi (Elaps), iii. 423.
bernieri (Dromicodryas), i. 189, iii. 599.
bernieri (Herpetodryas), i. 189, 190
bernouilli (Bothriechis), iii 566
bernouilli (Bothrops), iii 566.
bernouilli (Leptognathus), ii. 296
bernouilli (Tropidodipsas), ii. 296.
bertholdi (Dipsas), iii. 81.

2 U

bertholdi (Elaps), iii. 362.
bertholdi (Rhynchelaps), iii 362.
bertholdi (Vermicella), iii 362
bertholdi (Xenodon), ii. 146.
berus (Coluber), iii. 476
berus (Pelias), iii. 473, 476.
berus (Vipera), iii 473, 475, 476, 482, 484.
betsileana (Dipsas), iii 44.
betsileanus (Stenophis), iii. 44.
bianconii (Typhlops), i. 41.
bibroni (Elaps), iii 399
bibronii (Atractaspis), iii. 514, 515
bibronii (Calloplis), iii 399
bibronii (Enygrus), i 105, 106.
bibronii (Onychocephalus), i. 44
bibronii (Typhlops), i 44; iii 587.
bicarinata (Natrix), ii. 73
bicarinatus (Coluber), ii 73
bicarinatus (Heterolepis), i 346
bicarinatus (Notopsis), i. 111
bicatenata (Silybura), i. 158.
bicatenatus (Simotes), ii. 219.
bicincta (Urotheca), ii 184; iii 636
bicinctum (Bascanium), i. 390.
bicinctus (Coluber), ii. 184.
bicinctus (Leiosophis), ii 184.
bicinctus (Liophis), ii. 184.
bicinctus (Xenodon), ii. 184
bicolor (Ablabes), i 301
bicolor (Argyrophis), i. 24.
bicolor (Bothriechis), iii. 566.
bicolor (Bothrops), iii. 566.
bicolor (Calamaria), i. 301; ii. 342.

bicolor (Coluber), ii. 131, 168; iii. 89.
bicolor (Dirosema), ii. 298.
bicolor (Fordonia), iii 22
bicolor (Geophis), ii 298.
bicolor (Gerarda), iii 20
bicolor (Glauconia), i. 69
bicolor (Glypholycus), iii. 615.
bicolor (Grotea), i. 301.
bicolor (Helicops), i 274, iii. 610
bicolor (Heterurus), iii 82.
bicolor (Hydrophis), iii. 267.
bicolor (Hydrus), iii 267
bicolor (Lachesis), iii 566
bicolor (Leptognathus), iii 460
bicolor (Limnophis), i. 274
bicolor (Liophis), ii 168.
bicolor (Loxocemus), i. 74.
bicolor (Neopareas), iii 460
bicolor (Onychocephalus), i. 48.
bicolor (Pelamis), iii 267.
bicolor (Pseudocyclophis), i 301.
bicolor (Rhabdops), i. 301.
bicolor (Rhinhoplocephalus), iii. 353.
bicolor (Stenostoma), i. 69
bicolor (Trimesurus), iii. 553
bicolor (Typhlops), i. 48
bicolor (Xenocalamus), iii. 248.
bifasciatus (Streptophorus), i 292
bifossatus (Coluber), ii. 10
bifossatus (Drymobius), ii. 10
bifrenalis (Dendrophis), ii 80, 358
bifrenatus (Helicops), i. 282.
bilineata (Diplotropis), ii. 111.
bilineata (Glauconia), i. 70
bilineata (Hypsirhina), iii 7.

bilineatum (Melanophidium), i 164
bilineatum (Stenostoma), i 70
bilineatus (Adeniophis), iii 404
bilineatus (Ancistrodon), iii. 521
bilineatus (Bothrops), iii. 565
bilineatus (Callophis), iii. 404
bilineatus (Coluber), i. 219, 253.
bilineatus (Cophias), iii. 565
bilineatus (Craspedocephalus), iii 565
bilineatus (Doliophis), iii 404.
bilineatus (Drymobius), ii 11.
bilineatus (Elaphis), ii. 59.
bilineatus (Elapomorphus), iii 243
bilineatus (Elaps), i 253.
bilineatus (Enicognathus), ii 173.
bilineatus (Herpetodryas), ii 11.
bilineatus (Lachesis), iii. 565
bilineatus (Leptophis), ii 111, 358, iii 633.
bilineatus (Masticophis), i. 391
bilineatus (Phalotris), iii. 243.
bilineatus (Platyplecturus), i 165
bilineatus (Psammophis), iii. 162.
bilineatus (Trigonocephalus), iii. 521, 565.
bilineatus (Typhlops), i. 70
biloreolis (Dendrophis), iii 628.
bimaculata (Furina), iii. 406
bimaculata (Tantilla), iii. 227.
bimaculatum (Brachysoma), iii. 406
bimaculatum (Homalocranium), iii 227.
bimaculatus (Pseudelaps), iii 406
binatus (Coluber), iii. 200

ALPHABETICAL INDEX. 659

binotatus (Simotes), ii. 235, 243.
bipartitus (Typhlops), i. 37
bipes (Coluber), i. 219.
bipræocularis (Boodon), i. 332
bipræocularis (Oxyrhopus), iii. 101.
bipræocularis (Xenodon), ii. 146.
bipunctata (Coronella), iii. 208
bipunctata (Tachymenis), iii 208
bipunctatum (Lycophidion), i. 350.
bipunctatus (Coluber), i. 206, 350
bipunctatus (Coniophanes), iii. 208.
bipunctatus (Diadophis), ii. 285
bipunctatus (Erythrolamprus), iii 208.
bipunctatus (Tropidonotus), i 205, 206, 207
bipunctiger (Elaps), iii. 409.
biscutata (Dipsas), iii. 54, 55.
biscutata (Eutænia), i. 202
biscutatum (Sibon), iii. 54, 55, 56.
biscutatus (Dipsadomorphus), iii 54.
biscutatus (Eteirodipsas), iii. 54, 55.
biscutatus (Trimorphodon), iii 54.
bisecta (Natrix), i 243
bisectus (Tropidonotus), i. 243.
biserialis (Herpetodryas), ii 119.
biserialis (Orophis), ii. 120
biseriata (Psammophylax), iii 138
biseriatus (Psammophis), iii 168
bishopii (Hydrophis), iii. 292
bistrigatus (Ablabes), i. 188.
bistrigatus (Cynophis), ii. 36
bistrigatus (Polyodontophis), i 188.

bisubocularis (Typhlops), iii. 590.
Bitia, iii. 24.
bitin (Coluber), iii. 493.
Bitis, iii 492
bitis (Coluber), i 101
bitis (Vipera), i 101
bitorquata (Alecto), iii. 349.
bitorquata (Coronella), ii. 196.
bitorquatum (Meizodon), ii. 196
bitorquatus (Hoplocephalus), iii. 349.
bitorquatus (Oligodon), ii. 237.
bitorquatus (Oxyrhopus), iii. 104
bitorquatus (Tachymenis), iii 104.
bitorques (Calamaria), ii. 338, iii. 646.
bituberculata (Distira), iii 296
bituberculatus (Hydrophis), iii. 296
bituberculatus (Onychocephalus), i. 48.
bituberculatus (Typhlops), i. 48
bivirgatus (Adeniophis), iii. 400
bivirgatus (Callophis), iii. 400
bivirgatus (Doliophis), iii. 400.
bivirgatus (Elaps), iii. 400.
bivittata (Natrix), i 239.
bivittatum (Arrhyton), ii. 252
bivittatus (Drymobius), ii. 15; iii. 626
bivittatus (Leptophis), ii 15
bivittatus (Polyodontophis), iii. 597.
bivittatus (Python), i. 86, 87.
bivittatus (Thamnosophis), ii. 15
bizona (Erythrolamprus), iii 201
bizonatus (Scytale), iii 505.
blackmanni (Cacophis), iii. 319
blakewayi (Plagiopholis), i 301.

blandingii (Boiga), iii. 78.
blandingii (Dipsadomorphus), iii. 77.
blandingii (Dipsas), iii. 77.
blandingii (Toxicodryas), iii. 78.
blanfordii (Glauconia), i. 66.
blanfordii (Hypsirhina), iii 10
blanfordii (Typhlops), i. 39.
blomhoffii (Ancistrodon), iii. 525
blomhoffii (Halys), iii. 525.
blomhoffii (Trigonocephalus), iii. 525, 526
blumenbachii (Coluber), i. 385.
blumenbachii (Coryphodon), i. 385.
blumii (Calamaria), iii. 239.
blumii (Elapomorphus), iii. 239
Blythia, i. 313
blythii (Rhinophis), i. 144, 146
Boa, i. 93, 99, 104, 110, 115, 116, 121.
boa (Amblycephalus), iii. 439.
boa (Dipsas), iii 440.
boa (Haplopeltura), iii. 439.
boa (Nardoa), i. 76
boa (Tortrix), i. 76.
Boædon, i 327.
boæformis (Cerberus), iii 16.
boæformis (Elaps), iii. 16.
boæformis (Homalopsis), iii 16
Boæidæ, i 71
Boæides, i 93
bocagii (Ahætulla), ii 99.
bocagii (Aspidelaps), iii. 377
bocagii (Philothamnus), ii. 99, iii 621
bocagii (Psammophis), iii 161
bocourti (Atractus), ii 306, iii. 645
bocourti (Homalocranium), iii. 224.
bocourti (Zamenis), i. 394.

2 U 2

ALPHABETICAL INDEX.

bocourtii (Elaps), iii. 420.
bocourtii (Hypsirhina), iii 10.
boddaertii (Coluber), ii. 11
boddaertii (Drymobius), ii 11, 357, iii 626
boddaertii (Eudryas), ii 12
boddaertii (Herpetodryas), ii. 11.
Boédoniens, i 177
boettgeri (Atractus), iii. 645
boettgeri (Callophis), iii. 395
boettgeri (Piesigaster), i 97.
boettgeri (Typhlops), i. 39
bogorensis (Calamaria), ii 340
Boidæ, i 71, 131.
boiei (Trimeresurus), iii 387
Boiga, iii 58, 59
boiga (Coluber), ii 113
boii (Dendrophis), ii 88.
Boina, i 93.
Boinæ, i. 93.
boiquira (Crotalus), iii. 573, 578
Bolieria, i. 121.
bolivianus (Philodryas), iii. 132
Boodon, i 327, iii 616.
Boodontinæ, iii. 597
boops (Dipsas), iii 73.
bora (Python), i 87.
borneensis (Atropophis), iii 560, 561.
borneensis (Calamaria), ii 347, iii. 648.
borneensis (Lachesis), iii. 561.
bor ensis (Pythonopsis), iii 12.
borneensis (Rabdosoma), iii. 5.
Bothriechis, iii. 529.
Bothriophis, iii 141.
Bothriopsis, iii 529.
bothriorhynchus (Typhlops), i. 23
Bothrodytes, i. 193
Bothrolycus, i 325.
Bothrophera, iii. 518.
Bothrophes, iii 518
Bothrophthalmus, i 324.
Bothrops, iii. 529.

bottæ (Charina), i. 130, iii. 595.
bottæ (Pseudoeryx), i. 130.
bottæ (Tortrix), i. 130.
boulengeri (Elapechis), iii 361.
boulengeri (Elapsoidea), iii 361
boulengeri (Geodipsas), iii 32
boulengeri (Homalocranium), iii 221
boulengeri (Tachymenis), iii. 32.
boulengeri (Typhlops), iii 586
Boulengerina, iii 357.
bourcieri (Dromicus), ii 174
boydii (Dipsas), iii 67
boylii (Lampropeltis), ii. 197
boylii (Ophibolus), ii 197.
Brachyaspis, iii 353
brachycephalum (Catostoma), ii. 299.
brachycephalum (Dirosema), ii. 299.
brachycephalus (Choristodon), i 401
brachycephalus (Colobognathus), ii 299
brachycephalus (Elapoides), ii 299
Brachycranion, iii 510.
Brachyophis, iii 254
brachyops (Charina), i 131.
Brachyorrhos, ii 300
brachyorrhos (Calamaria), i 305, ii 218.
brachyorrhos (Scytale), i. 311.
Brachyorrhus, i. 305
brachyorrhus (Aspidura), i. 311, 313
Brachyruton, iii. 99.
Brachysoma, iii 313, 315, 405.
brachystoma (Bothriechis), iii. 547.
brachystoma (Bothriopsis), iii. 547.
brachystoma (Bothrops), iii. 547.
brachystoma (Eutænia), i 418.
brachystoma (Lachesis), iii. 547.

brachystoma (Teleuraspis), iii. 547.
brachyura (Calamaria), iii 647
brachyura (Coronella), ii. 206
brachyura (Vipera), iii. 494.
Brachyurophis, iii. 361.
brachyurum (Amphiesma), i. 267.
brachyurus (Coluber), i. 305
brachyurus (Opheomorphus), ii 136
brachyurus (Zamenis), ii. 206
braconnieri (Achalinus), i. 309 ; iii 613
braconnieri (Enicognathus), i. 187
braconnieri (Ophielaps), i 309
braconnieri (Xenopholis), iii 232
bramicus (Argyrophis), i 16.
braminus (Coluber), i 230
braminus (Eryx), i. 16
braminus (Typhlops), i. 16, iii. 584
brammianus (Bothrops), iii 545
bransbyi (Hoplocephalus), iii 335
brasiliæ (Coluber), iii. 380.
brasiliensis (Bothrops), iii 535
brasiliensis (Coluber), iii. 535.
brasiliensis (Craspedocephalus), iii 535, 541.
brasiliensis (Naja), iii 380.
brasiliensis (Vipera), iii. 535.
breitensteini (Python), i 89
breve (Homalocranium), iii 225.
brevicauda (Glauconia), i 67.
brevicauda (Liopeltis), ii 259
brevicauda (Oligodon), ii 240.
brevicauda (Stenostoma), i 67.

ALPHABETICAL INDEX. 661

breviceps (Coluber), ii. 149
breviceps (Dasypeltis), ii 355
breviceps (Dendrophis), ii 86.
breviceps (Liophis), ii. 164.
breviceps (Ophiomorphus), ii. 164.
breviceps (Rhadinæa), ii. 164
brevifacies (Leptognathus), iii. 452.
brevifacies (Tropidodipsas), iii. 452.
brevifrenum (Rhabdosoma), ii 302
brevirostris (Dromicus), ii 174.
brevirostris (Dryophis), iii. 190
brevirostris (Geophis), i. 303.
brevirostris (Oxybelis), iii. 190.
brevirostris (Psammophis), iii 166.
brevirostris (Stenognathus), i. 303
brevis (Calamaria), ii 348.
brevis (Coronella), iii. 175
brevis (Dipsas), iii 458
brevis (Hydrophis), iii. 301.
brevis (Leptognathus), iii. 457.
brevis (Sibybura), i. 158
brevis (Typhlogeophis), ii 351.
brevis (Zamenis), iii 623.
brocki (Tropidonotus), i 245
bronni (Loxocemus), i. 74
bronni (Plastoseryx), i. 74
brookii (Calamaria), iii. 647
brookii (Hydrophis), iii. 282
broughami (Silybura), i. 152.
browni (Phyllorhynchus), i. 417.
brownii (Acanthophis), iii. 355
brownii (Lytorhynchus), i. 417.

brugmansii (Distira), iii. 292
brugmansii (Hydrophis), iii 292.
brunnea (Eutænia), i. 202.
brunneus (Bothrophthalmus), i. 324.
brunneus (Drymobius), ii. 16.
brunneus (Herpetodryas), ii. 15.
brunneus (Masticophis), ii. 15.
brussauxi (Gonionotophis), i. 323
brussauxi (Gonionotus), i. 323.
bubalina (Dipsas), iii 72
buccata (Homalopsis), iii. 14
buccata (Vipera), iii. 14.
buccatus (Coluber), iii 14
bucculenta (Ungalia), i. 112.
bucephala (Dipsas), iii. 461.
Bucephalus, iii. 186.
bucephalus (Bungarus), iii. 461.
bucephalus (Coluber), iii. 461
bucephalus (Dipsadomorus), iii. 461
bucephalus (Leptognathus), iii 461
buchholzi (Onychocephalus), i. 41
buchholzi (Typhlops), i 41.
buckleyi (Elaps), iii. 416.
Bungaroidea, i. 169
bungaroides (Alecto), iii. 348
bungaroides (Bungarus), iii 370
bungaroides (Elaps), 370.
bungaroides (Hoplocephalus), iii 348.
bungaroides (Naja), iii. 348.
bungaroides (Xenurelaps), iii. 370
Bungarus, iii 83, 365, 460.
bungarus (Naia), iii 386.
bungarus (Trimeresurus), iii 386
burmeisteri (Dryophylax), iii 135
burmeisteri (Philodryas), iii 135.

burtonii (Atheris), iii. 509.
burtonii (Pœcilostolus), iii 509.
butleri (Eutænia), i. 212.
butleri (Thamnophis), iii. 602.
butleri (Tropidonotus), i. 212; iii. 602.

Cacocalyx, iii. 626.
cacodæmon (Coluber), ii. 154
Cacophis, iii 315.
Cadmus, i. 373
cæca (Letheobia), i 55
cæcatus (Typhlops), i 32
cæcus (Coluber), iii 380.
cæcus (Onychocephalus), i. 55
cæcus (Typhlops), i. 55.
cæcutiens (Elapomorphus), iii 252.
cærulea (Anguis), i. 133.
cærulea (Enhydris), iii 6
cærulea (Pseudoboa), iii 368
cærulescens (Coluber), ii. 96
cærulescens (Enhydris), iii. 275.
cærulescens (Hydrophis), iii. 275
cærulescens (Hydrus), iii. 275.
cærulescens (Oxybelis), iii 190
cærulescens (Vipera), iii 535.
cæruleus (Bungarus), iii. 368, 370.
cæruleus (Coluber), iii. 476
cæruleus (Dromicus), ii. 11.
cæruleus (Drymobius), ii. 12
cæruleus (Hapsidophrys), ii 103
cæsar (Xenurophis), ii. 288.
cæsius (Coluber), iii 631.
cahirinus (Coluber), i. 402.
cairi (Glauconia), i. 65.
cairi (Stenostoma), i. 65.
Calabaria, i 92
Calamaria, i. 290, 305, 306, 310, ii. 188, 233, 255, 273, 300, 324, 330, iii 210, 212, 232, 238.

ALPHABETICAL INDEX.

calamaria (Ablabes), ii. 282.
calamaria (Anguis), ii 345.
calamaria (Cyclophis), ii. 232
Calamaridæ, i. 177; iii. 26, 597.
Calamariens, i. 177.
Calamarina, i 169
calamarina (Tantilla), iii. 227.
Calamarinæ, i 177; iii 26.
calamarinum (Homalocranium), iii 227.
calamarius (Coluber), ii. 345.
Calamelaps, iii 245
Calamohydrus, i. 283
Calamophis, i. 305
Calechidna, iii. 492
californiæ (Coluber), ii 197
californiæ (Coronella), ii 197
californiæ (Ophibolus), ii. 197
californiæ (Ophis), ii 197.
callicephalus (Coluber), ii 34.
callicephalus (Coronella), ii 34
calligaster (Ablabes), ii. 198
calligaster (Callophis), iii 393
calligaster (Coluber), ii. 198.
calligaster (Contia), ii. 164
calligaster (Coronella), ii 198
calligaster (Dendrophis), ii 80; iii 628
calligaster (Elaps), iii. 393
calligaster (Hemibungarus), iii. 393.
calligaster (Lampropeltis), ii 199
calligaster (Ophibolus), ii 199.
calligaster (Rhadinæa), ii. 164
calligaster (Scotophis), ii 40.
callilæma (Dromicus), ii. 142.
callilæma (Natrix), ii. 142.
callilæmus (Liophis), ii. 142.

Calliophis, iii. 396.
Callirhinus, iii 127.
callistus (Tropidonotus), i 263
Callopeltis, ii. 24
Callophis, iii. 392, 396, 400
Calloselasma, iii. 519
callostictus (Hydrops), ii 187.
callostictus (Pseudoeryx), iii. 637
calonota (Furina), iii. 407
calonotos (Brachysoma), iii 407
calonotos (Furina), iii 407.
Calonotus, ii 160.
calonotus (Neelaps), iii 407
calonotus (Pseudelaps), iii 407.
Calopisma, ii 186, 289, 290.
Campylodon, iii 20.
cana (Coronella), i. 373, iii 620
cana (Duberria), i 373.
cana (Ficimia), ii. 272.
cana (Pseudaspis), i. 373; iii 620.
cana (Ungalia), i. 114.
canarica (Silybura), i 160
canaricus (Plectrurus), i 160.
canaricus (Pseudoplectrurus), i. 160
canariensis (Leptophis), iii 178
cancellatum (Dinodon), i 361.
candidissimus (Coluber), iii. 374
candidus (Bungarus), iii. 368, 370
candidus (Cerastes), iii. 374.
candidus (Coluber), iii. 368
caniilatus (Tachymenis), iii 133
canina (Boa), i 102.
caninana (Natrix), ii. 23
caninum (Xiphosoma), i. 102.
caninus (Boa), i. 102.
caninus (Corallus), i. 102; iii. 593
caninus (Draco), i 102.
cantori (Hydrus), iii. 299.

cantori (Trigonocephalus), iii. 551.
Cantoria, iii 23
cantoris (Coluber), ii 35
cantoris (Hydrophis), iii 281
cantoris (Lachesis), iii. 551
cantoris (Trimeresurus), iii. 551.
canula (Homalocranium), iii 222.
canula (Tantilla), iii. 222.
canulum (Homalocranium), iii 222.
canum (Gyalopion), ii. 272
canus (Coluber), i 373
capense (Bœdon), i 332
capense (Lycophidium), i. 338, 339, iii 616.
capensis (Aparallactus), iii 259
capensis (Bucephalus), iii. 187.
capensis (Elapomorphus), iii 259
capensis (Heterolepis), i. 345.
capensis (Lycodon), i 339.
capensis (Naia), iii. 376, 389.
capensis (Onychocephalus), i 16
capensis (Simocephalus), i. 345, iii. 616.
capensis (Thelotornis), iii. 185.
capensis (Uriechis), iii. 259, 260, 261.
capistrata (Natrix), ii 121
capistrata (Tantilla), iii. 215
capistratus (Coluber), ii. 10
capite-triangulatus (Coluber), iii 559
capucinus (Lycodon), i 352.
caracaras (Coluber), iii. 626.
caraganus (Trigonocephalus), iii. 524
carbonaria (Zamenis), i. 395
carbonarius (Coluber), i. 395.

caribbæus (Trigonocephalus), iii. 535
carinata (Aspidura), i. 310
carinata (Boa), i. 107
carinata (Caudoia), i. 107.
carinata (Cynophis), ii. 36
carinata (Dipsas), iii 415.
carinata (Echis), iii 505
carinata (Hurria), i. 358.
carinata (Pareas), iii. 443, 445
carinata (Phyllophis), ii. 55.
carinata (Pseudoboa), iii. 505.
carinata (Pythonodipsas), iii. 45
carinata (Tropidechis), iii. 350.
carinata (Vipera), iii. 505.
carinatus (Amblycephalus), iii 445
carinatus (Cercaspis), i. 359.
carinatus (Chironius), ii. 73.
carinatus (Coluber), ii. 73
carinatus (Coryphodon), i 216, 375, 376, 377.
carinatus (Cryptelytrops), iii 553
carinatus (Dipsas), ii 354
carinatus (Echis), iii. 505.
carinatus (Enygrus), i. 107, iii. 593
carinatus (Eumesodon), i 363
carinatus (Herpetodryas), ii 72, 73, 75, 76, iii 628
carinatus (Hoplocephalus), iii. 350
carinatus (Leptognathus), iii 445
carinatus (Lycodon), i. 358.
carinatus (Philodryas), iii 128.
carinatus (Trimesurus), iii 553
carinatus (Tropidechis), iii. 350.
carinatus (Zaocys), i. 377, iii. 621

carinicauda (Helicops), i. 276.
carinicaudus (Coluber), i. 276
carinicaudus (Helicops), i 276, 277.
carinicaudus (Homalopsis), i. 276
carneus (Coluber), iii. 49
carolinianus (Coluber), ii 39.
carpentariæ (Denisonia), iii 344
carpentariæ (Hoplocephalus), iii 344.
Carphophiops, ii 324
Carphophis, ii 288, 324.
Casarea, i 121.
cascavella (Crotalus), iii. 574.
caspia (Enhydris), i 233.
caspicus (Zamenis), i 395
caspius (Coluber), i 395.
caspius (Zamenis), i. 395.
castanea (Boa), i 87.
castelnaudi (Bothrops), iii. 544.
castelnaudi (Lachesis), iii. 544.
castelnaudi (Thanatophis), iii. 544
castelnaudi (Trigonocephalus), iii. 544.
castelnaui (Bothriechis), iii 544
castelnaui (Teleuraspis), iii. 544, 547.
castelnautii (Atropos), iii. 544.
castelnavii (Bothriopsis), iii. 544
Catachlæna, i 414
cataphronotus (Zamenis), i 394
catenata (Calamaria), ii. 351.
catenata (Scytale), iii. 534
catenatus (Crotalinus), iii. 570.
catenatus (Crotalophorus), iii 571.
catenatus (Crotalus), iii. 571
catenatus (Cyclophis), ii. 274
catenatus (Lycodon), i. 185.

catenatus (Sistrurus), iii. 570
catenifer (Coluber), ii 67.
catenifer (Pituophis), ii. 67, 69
catenifer (Simotes), ii. 218
catenularis (Coluber), iii. 63.
catesbæi (Dipsas), iii 449.
catesbyi (Ahætulla), ii. 115
catesbyi (Coluber), iii. 449
catesbyi (Dendrophis), ii 115
catesbyi (Dryiophis), iii. 191.
catesbyi (Heterodon), ii. 156.
catesbyi (Leptognathus), iii 449, 450.
catesbyi (Leptophis), ii 115
catesbyi (Stremmatognathus), iii. 449.
catesbyi (Uromacer), ii. 115
Cathetorhinus, i. 7.
Catodon, i. 59
Catodonta, i. 57.
Catodoniens, i. 57.
Catostoma, ii. 314.
caucasica (Coronella), ii. 192
caucasicus (Coluber), ii. 192
caudælineatus (Periops), i. 405
caudælineatus (Zamenis), i. 405, 407.
caudalis (Bitis), iii. 498.
caudalis (Cerastes), iii. 498
caudalis (Vipera), iii. 498.
cauda-schistosus (Coluber), i. 242
Caudisona, iii 569, 572.
caudolineata (Ahætula), ii 89
caudolineata (Dendrophis), ii. 89.
caudolineatus (Dendrelaphis), ii. 89, 358, iii 630
caudolineatus (Ithycyphus), iii. 34.
caudolineatus (Leptophis), ii. 89
caudolineolatus (Dendrophis), ii. 85.

Causidæ, iii. 465.
Causinæ, iii. 464.
Causus, iii. 465.
caymanus (Alsophis), ii. 120.
celæno (Tropidonotus), i. 237.
celebensis (Elaphis), ii. 62.
celebensis (Tropidolæmus), iii. 562.
celebicus (Styporhynchus), i. 216
celebicus (Tropidonotus), i. 216.
Celuta, ii. 324.
Cemophora, ii. 213.
cenchoa (Coluber), iii 84.
cenchoa (Dipsas), iii. 84.
cenchoa (Himantodes), iii. 84, 85, 86.
cenchria (Boa), i. 94.
cenchria (Epicrates), i. 94.
Cenchris, iii. 519.
cenchris (Boa), i. 94.
cenchris (Epicrates), i. 94; iii 592.
cenchris (Trigonocephalus), iii. 520, 522.
cenchrus (Coluber), ii. 166.
cencoalt (Bungarus), iii. 84.
Cephalolepis, i 57
cerasinus (Callophis), iii. 399
cerasinus (Elaps), iii. 399
cerasogaster (Psammophis), i. 191.
cerasogaster (Tropidonotus), i. 191.
cerasogaster (Xenochrophis), i. 191; iii. 599.
Cerastes, iii 492, 501
cerastes (Æchmophrys), iii. 583.
cerastes (Anguis), i. 125
cerastes (Caudisona), iii. 583.
cerastes (Coluber), iii 502.
cerastes (Crotalus), iii. 583.
cerastes (Eryx), i. 125.
cerastes (Vipera), iii. 501, 502.

cerastinus (Acanthophis), iii 355
Ceratophallus, iii 599.
ceratophorus (Atheris), iii. 510.
Cerberus, iii. 15.
cerberus (Coluber), iii. 16.
cerberus (Homalopsis), iii 16
Cercaspis, i 348
Cercocalamus, iii 255.
cervina (Coronella), iii. 57.
cervinus (Coluber), iii. 57.
cervinus (Lycognathus), iii. 57
cervone (Elaphis), ii. 46.
cetti (Natrix), i. 219.
ceylanicus (Coluburus), i. 158.
ceylanicus (PseudoTyphlops), i 158
ceylonensis (Aspidura), i. 310
ceylonensis (Bothrodytes), iii. 607.
ceylonensis (Dipsadomorphus), iii 66
ceylonensis (Dipsas), iii. 66, 69.
ceylonensis (Haplocercus), i 309
ceylonensis (Odontomus), i 370
ceylonensis (Trimesurus), iii 528.
ceylonensis (Tropidonotus), i 252; iii 607
ceylonica (Silybura), i 155, 158.
ceylonicus (Bungarus), iii. 366.
ceylonicus (Coloburus), i. 154.
ceylonicus (Plectrurus), i. 146.
ceylonicus (Siluboura), i. 154.
ceylonicus (Uropeltis), i 158.
chairecacos (Dendrophis), ii 88.
chalceus (Prymnomiodon), i. 192.
chalybæa (Geophis), ii. 317, 318, 319, 320, 321, 322.
chalybæum (Catostoma), ii. 318.

chalybæus (Elapoides), ii. 319
chalybæus (Hemiodontus), iii 22
chalybeus (Alopecophis), ii. 57
chalybeus (Geophis), ii. 318, 320.
Chamætortus, iii. 98.
chamissonis (Coronella), ii. 119.
chamissonis (Dromicus), ii. 119
chamissonis (Opheomorphus), ii. 120.
championi (Geophis), ii. 321.
chanleri (Simocephalus), iii 617.
charasii (Coluber), iii. 482.
Charina, i. 130
Charinidæ, i. 71.
Charinina, i. 93
Chatachlein, i 414.
Cheilorhina, ii 188
chelonicephalus (Aipysurus), iii 304.
chenonii (Dendrophis), ii 96.
chenonii (Leptophis), ii. 96.
chersæa (Vipera), iii. 476, 482.
chersea (Coluber), iii. 476, 482.
chersea (Pelias), iii. 473, 477.
cherseoides (Natrix), i. 235.
Chersodromus, i. 295.
chersoides (Tropidonotus), i. 236
Chersydrus, i 173.
chesnei (Coluber), i 399.
chiametla (Natrix), ii. 168
Chilabothrus, i 93
childreni (Liasis), i. 77, 418
chilensis (Coronella), iii. 118.
chilensis (Dipsas), iii. 118
chilensis (Mesotes), iii. 118.
chilensis (Tachymenis), iii. 118
Chilolepis, i. 379
Chilomeniscus, ii. 272.
Chilopoma, i. 193

chinensis (Hypsirhina), iii 8.
chinensis (Simotes), ii. 228
chinensis (Tropidonotus), i. 233
Chionactis, ii 255
Chironius, ii. 24, 71, 118.
chitalonensis (Dromicus), iii 207.
Chitulia, iii 285
chlorechis (Atheris), iii. 508
chloris (Herpetodryas), ii 279
chloris (Hydrophis), iii. 281, 284
chloris (Pelamis), iii. 284.
Chloroechis, iii. 508.
chloroechis (Atheris), iii. 508
chloroechis (Echis), iii. 508.
chloroechis (Toxicoa), iii. 508
chloroechis (Vipera), iii. 508.
chlorophæa (Hypsiglena), ii. 209
Chlorophis, ii. 91
Chlorosoma, ii 255, iii 127
chlorosoma (Coluber), ii. 38
chloroticum (Dendrophidium), ii 16.
chloroticus (Drymobius), ii. 16
Chondropython, i 90.
Chondropythonina, i 74.
Chondropythoninæ, i 74.
Chorisodon, iii 151.
Choristodon, iii 245.
chrysargoides (Amphiesma), i. 260
chrysargoides (Tropidonotus), i 260
chrysargum (Amphiesma), i. 258, 260
chrysargus (Tropidonotus), i. 252, 258, iii. 608
Chrysenis, i 99
chrysobronchus (Phrynonax), ii. 22.
chrysobronchus (Spilotes), ii 22
chrysocephala (Eutænia), i. 203, iii 600
chrysocephalus (Tropidonotus), i. 203, iii. 600.

chrysochlora (Chrysopelea). iii 198.
chrysochloros (Dendrophis), iii 196
chrysogaster (Homalochilus), i. 98.
Chrysopelea, iii. 149, 193, 195.
chrysopelcoides (Elaps), iii 409
chrysostictus (Tachynectes), i 280
chrysostoma (Rhadinæa), ii. 167.
Churchillia, ii. 25.
cincta (Carphophis), ii. 273
cinctus (Ablabes), ii 283
cinctus (Chilomeniscus), ii. 273.
cinerea (Boa), i. 87
cinereus (Alsophis), ii. 124.
cinereus (Bothrops), iii. 535
cinereus (Cerberus), iii 16, 18.
cinereus (Coluber), iii 624.
cinereus (Hydrus), iii 16.
cinereus (Simotes), ii. 222.
cinereus (Typhlops), i. 31
cinnamomea (Natrix), ii. 72
circinalis (Elaps), iii. 420, 423
cisticeps (Dipsadomorus), iii. 462.
cisticeps (Leptognathus), iii. 462
citrinus (Thrasops), i 317
Cladophis, iii 185
clarkii (Natrix), i 238
clarkii (Regina), i 238.
clarkii (Tropidonotus), i. 238
clathratus (Oxyrhopus), iii 107
clavata (Rhadinæa), ii. 177
clavatus (Dromicus), ii. 177.
Clelia, iii. 99.
cleopatræ (Aspis), iii. 503
clericus (Ophibolus), ii. 200.

cliffordii (Coluber), i. 411
cliffordii (Zamenis), i. 411
Cliftia, i 94.
clinacophorus (Coluber), ii 54.
Clœlia, iii. 212
clœlia (Brachyruton), iii. 109, 111
clœlia (Coluber), iii. 108.
clœlia (Lycodon), iii 109, 111, 112
clœlia (Oxyrhopus), iii. 108.
Clonophis, i. 285.
Clothelaps, iii 510.
Clotho, iii. 492
clotho (Cobra), iii 493.
clotho (Coluber), iii. 493.
clotho (Echidna), iii. 494
Clothonia, i 122
cobella (Coluber), ii. 166
cobella (Coronella), ii. 166
cobella (Elaps), ii 166
cobella (Liophis), ii. 166, 167
cobella (Ophiomorphus), ii. 166.
cobella (Rhadinæa), ii. 166.
Cobra, iii. 471, 492
coccinea (Cemophora), ii 214, iii 640.
coccinea (Coronella), ii. 205
coccinea (Lampropeltis), ii 205
coccineus (Coluber), ii. 214
coccineus (Elaps), ii 214.
coccineus (Heterodon), ii. 214
coccineus (Ophibolus), ii. 201
coccineus (Rhinostoma), ii 214
coccineus (Simotes), ii. 214.
cochinchinensis (Simotes), ii. 219
Cochliophagus, iii 446.
Cœlognathus, ii 25
Cœlopeltis, iii. 141, 144.
cognatus (Heterodon), ii. 155
colchica (Tropidonotus), i. 219.

ALPHABETICAL INDEX.

collare (Microsoma), iii. 250, 251.
collaris (Ablabes), i. 184, ii. 261.
collaris (Cercocalamus), iii. 260.
collaris (Coluber), ii. 260
collaris (Contia), ii. 260, iii 642
collaris (Coronella), ii. 261
collaris (Cyclophis), ii. 261.
collaris (Eirenis), ii 260, 261
collaris (Elaps), iii 393.
collaris (Eutænia), i. 209
collaris (Geoptyas), ii. 31
collaris (Hemibungarus), iii. 393.
collaris (Homalosoma), ii 262.
collaris (Hoplocephalus), iii 336.
collaris (Idiopholis), ii. 327
collaris (Liophis), ii 167.
collaris (Miodon), iii. 251.
collaris (Ophibolus), ii 200.
collaris (Polyodontophis), i 184 ; iii 597.
collaris (Psammophis), i. 184
collaris (Streptophorus), i 293.
collaris (Trimorphodon), iii 55.
collaris (Tropidonotus), i. 209
Colobognathus, ii. 314.
Coloburus, i 144.
Colophrys, ii. 314.
coloratus (Echis), iii 507
Colorhogia, ii. 251.
Coluber, i. 193, 373, 379 ; ii. 24 ; iii. 43, 99 ; 627
Colubridæ, i. 169, 177 ; iii. 438, 597.
Colubriens, i. 177.
Colubriformes, i. 169
colubrina (Anguis), i. 125.
colubrina (Dendrophis), iii 187.
colubrina (Dipsas), iii. 39.
colubrina (Eteirodipsas), iii 39.

colubrina (Tortrix), i 126.
Colubrinæ, i. 169, 177, iii 597
Colubrini, i. 71, 177 ; iii. 26.
colubrinus (Eryx), i. 125
colubrinus (Hydrophis), iii. 307, 308, 309.
colubrinus (Hydrus), iii. 308.
colubrinus (Platurus), iii. 308
colubrinus (Xenodon), ii. 146, 359, iii. 634.
Colubroidea, i. 169.
Comastes, ii 208.
communis (Coluber), i. 395.
communis (Vipera), iii 476, 482.
comorensis (Dipsas), iii. 42
comorensis (Heterurus), iii. 42.
comorensis (Typhlops), i. 21
compressicauda (Natrix), i. 239, iii 605
compressicauda (Nerodia), i. 238.
compressicauda (Tropidonotus), i. 238, iii. 605
compressus (Coluber), ii. 39, iii. 58
compressus (Dipsadomorphus), iii 57
compressus (Dipsas), iii 57.
compressus (Trypanurgos), iii. 58.
compsolæmus (Tropidonotus), i. 238.
Compsophis, iii. 609.
Compsosoma, ii 25
concinna (Eutainia), i. 208.
concinnus (Callophis), iii. 394
concinnus (Tropidonotus), i. 207, 243.
concolor (Aparallactus), iii 257.
concolor (Calamelaps), iii. 246
concolor (Choristodon), iii. 246.
concolor (Conophis), iii 122.
concolor (Hydromorphus), ii. 185.

concolor (Tropidonotus), i. 220.
concolor (Uriechis), iii 257.
concolor (Xenopeltis), i. 108.
condanarus (Psammophis), iii 155, 165.
condanurus (Coluber), iii 165
confinis (Scotophis), ii 49.
confluenta (Caudisona), iii. 576.
confluenta (Vipera), iii. 488.
confluentus (Crotalus), iii. 576, 580
confluentus (Erythrolamprus), iii. 201
congestus (Onychocephalus), i 42.
congica (Atractaspis), iii 513.
congicus (Onychocephalus), i 40
congicus (Typhlops), i. 40
conica (Boa), i 124.
conicus (Eryx), i. 124.
conicus (Gongylophis), i 124
Coniophanes, iii 199.
conirostris (Aporophis), ii. 135.
conirostris (Liophis), ii. 134.
conirostris (Lygophis), ii. 134.
conirostris (Zamenis), iii. 621.
conjuncta (Coronella), ii. 203
conjuncta (Glauconia), i. 67.
conjuncta (Lampropeltis), ii 197
conjuncta (Ungalia), i. 113
conjunctum (Stenostoma) i. 67.
conjunctus (Brachyorrhos), i. 306.
conjunctus (Psammodynastes), iii. 174.
conjunctus (Psammophis), iii 174
conjunctus (Tropidophis), i. 113.
Conocephalus, i. 290.
Conocerques, iii 310.

Conophis, iii. 122.
Conopsis, ii 255.
conradi (Typhlops), i. 33.
consors (Crotalophorus), iii 572
conspicillata (Coronella) ii. 51.
conspicillatus (Callopeltis), ii. 51.
conspicillatus (Coluber), ii 51.
conspicillatus (Elaphis), ii 51.
conspicillatus (Tropidonotus), i 222, iii 604.
Constrictor, i. 80, 116.
constrictor (Bascanion), i. 387
constrictor (Boa), i. 117, 118, 119.
constrictor (Coluber), i. 387, 389
constrictor (Coryphodon), i. 387, ii 31
constrictor (Zamenis), i. 387, iii 621.
Constrictores, i. 71.
constrictrix (Boa), i. 117.
Contia, ii. 255.
continentalis (Ungaliophis), i. 114.
contortrix (Agkistrodon), iii. 523.
contortrix (Ancistrodon), iii 522
contortrix (Boa), iii 522.
contortrix (Cenchris), iii. 523
contortrix (Scytale), iii. 522.
contortrix (Trigonocephalus), iii 522.
convictus (Trimeresurus), iii. 548.
cookii (Corallus), i 99
cooperi (Eutainia), i 201.
cooperi (Tropidonotus), i 201
copei (Adelophis), i. 289.
copei (Storeria), i. 289.
Cophiadæ, iii 518
Cophias, iii 519, 529
Cophiinæ, iii. 518.
copii (Aspidura), i 311.
copii (Cemophora), ii. 214
copii (Ischnognathus), i. 289
copii (Leptognathus), iii. 450.

Cora, i 285
corais (Coluber), ii. 31; iii. 627
corais (Spilotes), i. 389; ii. 31.
corallina (Anguis), i. 133, 135.
corallinus (Coluber), iii. 634.
corallinus (Elaps), iii. 416, 417, 420, 423, 429.
corallinus (Tortrix), i. 133
coralloides (Synchalinus), ii. 70.
coralliventris (Aporophis), ii 159
Corallus, i 99.
cornuta (Bitis), iii. 497.
cornuta (Cerastes), iii 497.
cornuta (Clotho), iii 497.
cornuta (Vipera), iii 497.
cornutus (Cerastes), iii 502
cornutus (Coluber), iii. 502
cornwallisius (Liasis), i 78
coronata (Alecto), iii 336.
coronata (Apostolepis), iii 233
coronata (Boa), iii. 111.
coronata (Calamaria), ii. 196
coronata (Coronella), ii. 196
coronata (Denisonia), iii. 335
coronata (Hydrophis), iii 279.
coronata (Pseudoboa), iii. 111.
coronata (Scytale), iii. 111, 112.
coronata (Tantilla), iii 218
coronatum (Homalocranium), iii. 218, 224.
coronatum (Scytale), iii. 111, 112, 113.
coronatus (Cerastes), ii. 23
coronatus (Coluber), ii. 23.
coronatus (Elapomorphus), iii 233
coronatus (Elaps), iii. 335.
coronatus (Hoplocephalus), iii. 336

coronatus (Hydrophis), iii. 279.
coronatus (Mizodon), ii. 196
coronatus (Olisthenes), iii 112.
coronatus (Oxyrhopus), iii. 111.
Coronella, i. 318, 320, 373; ii 25, 126, 160, 188, 214, 277, iii 88, 117, 124, 138, 175, 199.
coronella (Ablabes), ii 264
coronella (Calamaria), ii. 264
coronella (Coluber), ii 191
coronella (Contia), ii. 264
coronella (Homalosoma), ii 264.
Coronellæ, i 177, iii 26.
Coronellidæ, i 177, iii 26.
Coronellinæ, i. 177.
coronelloides (Homalosoma), ii 264
coronilla (Natrix), ii. 191.
coronoides (Denisonia), iii. 336
coronoides (Hoplocephalus), iii. 336
corpulenta (Atractaspis), iii 514.
corpulentum (Brachycranium), iii. 514
corpulentus (Atractaspis), iii 513, 514, 516.
Coryphodon, i 374, 379, ii 7, 9, 188
Coryphodontiens, i. 177.
Cosmiosophis, ii 180
couchii (Eutainia), i 210
couchii (Nerodia), i 243
couchii (Thamnophis), iii 601
couchii (Tropidonotus), i. 210; iii 601.
couperi (Coluber), ii. 31
couperi (Georgia), ii 31
couperi (Spilotes), ii. 31.
Craspedocephalus, iii. 529.
crassa (Homolopsis), iii. 644.
crassa (Nardoa), i. 78
crassatus (Onychocephalus), i. 47
crassatus (Typhlops), i. 47

crassicaudatum (Rhabdosoma), ii 304, 310.
crassicaudatus (Atractus), ii. 310.
crassicollis (Hydrophis), iii. 295.
crassifrons (Philodryas), iii. 129, 634
crassum (Ophthalmidion), i 28.
crassus (Epicrates), iii. 593.
crassus (Simotes), ii 219.
crawshayi (Naja), iii 378
Crealia, i 144
crebripunctatus (Elaps), iii. 423
crebripunctatus (Tropidonotus), i. 262.
crista-galli (Langaha), iii 37
crococatus (Typhlops), i 27.
Crossantbera, ii. 9.
crossii (Simocephalus), iii. 618.
crossii (Typhlops), i. 52.
Crotalidæ, iii 518.
Crotaliens, iii 518.
Crotalina, iii. 518.
Crotalinæ, iii 518
Crotalini, iii. 518.
Crotalinus, iii. 572.
crotalinus (Coluber), iii. 534.
crotalinus (Cophias), iii. 534
crotalinus (Craspedocephalus), iii. 534
Crotaloidea, iii 518
Crotalophorus, iii. 569.
Crotalus, iii 529, 569, 572.
Crotaphopeltis, iii 88.
cruciatum (Rhabdion), ii. 245.
crucifer (Coluber), iii. 169.
crucifer (Psammophis), iii. 169
cruentatus (Coluber), ii. 41.
cruentatus (Simotes), ii. 231
Crypsidomus, iii. 632
Cryptelytrops, iii. 529.
Cryptodacus, ii. 251
cubæ (Typhlops), i 31.
cubanus (Tetranorhinus), iii. 610.
cubanus (Tropidonotus), i. 282.

cubensis (Dromicus), ii. 140.
cucullata (Coronella), iii. 175
cucullata (Diemansia), iii. 317
cucullata (Furina), iii. 325.
cucullatum (Lycodon), i. 365.
cucullatum (Petrodymon), iii. 317.
cucullatus (Coluber), iii. 175
cucullatus (Lielaphis), i. 365
cucullatus (Lycognathus), iii 175.
cucullatus (Macroprotodon), iii. 175
cucullatus (Psammophylax), iii 175.
cucullatus (Stegonotus), i. 365.
cuculliceps (Leptognathus), ii 296.
cuculliceps (Tropidodipsas), ii. 206
cumingi (Onychocephalus), i. 51.
cumingii (Onychophis), i. 51.
cumingii (Typhlops), i. 51.
cuneiformis (Cadmus), i. 373
cuneirostris (Typhlops), i. 32
cupreum (Rhinostoma), ii 247
cupreus (Coluber), ii. 191.
cupreus (Epicarsius), i. 95
cupreus (Epicrates), i. 95, iii 592.
cupreus (Leptophis), ii. 109
cupreus (Pseudechis), iii. 329.
cupreus (Scytalus), iii. 522
cupreus (Thrasops), ii. 109.
cursor (Coluber), ii. 139.
cursor (Dromicus), ii. 139, 140
cursor (Herpetodryas), ii. 139, 140
cursor (Liophis), ii. 139.
Cursoria, i. 122.

curta (Alecto), iii. 335, 351.
curta (Aspidobon), i. 89.
curta (Brachyaspis), iii. 353
curta (Hydrophis), iii 300
curta (Naja), iii 353
curta (Unguaha), i 113
curticeps (Cylindrophis), i. 137.
curtus (Enhydris), iii 300.
curtus (Hoplocephalus), iii 351, 353
curtus (Hydrus), iii. 300.
curtus (Lapemis), iii. 300.
curtus (Python), i. 89.
curtus (Typhlops), i 34.
curvirostris (Coluber), i. 404.
curvirostris (Typhlops), i. 48
Cusoria, i 122
cuvieri (Calamaria), ii. 344
cyanea (Dipsas), ii. 72.
cyaneus (Dipsadomorphus), iii 72
cyanocincta (Distira), iii. 294
cyanocincta (Hydrophis), iii. 292, 295.
cyanocinctus (Enhydris), iii 295.
cyanocinctus (Hydrophis), iii 294.
cyanocinctus (Hydrus), iii 295.
cyanopleurus (Aporophis), ii. 142.
cyanurus (Crotalinus), iii. 579.
Cyclagras, ii 144, 180.
cyclides (Thamnophis), i. 209.
Cyclocorus, i 326
Cyclophiops, ii. 277.
Cyclophis, ii. 255, 277.
cyclopion (Tropidonotus), i. 243, 244.
cyclopium (Natrix), i. i 244; iii 606.
cyclopium (Nerodia), i. 244
cyclopium (Tropidonotus), i. 244; iii. 606.
cyclops (Helicops), i. 279.
cyclura (Coronella), ii. 219.

ALPHABETICAL INDEX. 669

cyclurus (Simotes), ii. 219
Cylindrophis, i. 134.
cynodon (Dipsadomorphus), iii. 78.
cynodon (Dipsas), iii. 64, 73, 78, 80
cynodon (Eudipsas), iii. 79
cynodon (Opetiodon), iii. 79
Cynophis, ii. 24.
Cyrtophis, iii. 390
cyrtopsis (Eutainia), i. 209, iii. 601.
cyrtopsis (Thamnophis), i. 209.

Daboia, iii. 471.
dæmelii (Denisonia), iii. 339
dæmelii (Hoplocephalus), iii. 339
dahlii (Psammophis), i. 397.
dahlii (Tyria), i. 397
dahlii (Zamenis), i. 397, 403; iii. 623
dahomeyensis (Atractaspis), iii. 516
Dapatnaya, i. 140
darnleyensis (Dendrophis), ii. 80
darnleyensis (Lycodon), i. 365
darwini (Atropos), iii. 549.
darwini (Bothrops), iii. 549
darwini (Trigonocephalus), iii. 549
darwiniensis (Hydrelaps), iii. 270.
darwiniensis (Pseudechis), iii. 330
Dasypeltinæ, ii. 353
Dasypeltis, ii. 353
daudinii (Clelia), iii. 108
daudini (Pseudoeryx), ii. 186
davidi (Coluber), ii. 56
davidi (Tropidonotus), ii. 56
davidsoni (Plecturus), i. 162.
davisonii (Dryocalamus), i. 372
davisonii (Hydrophobus), i. 372

davisonii (Plecturus), i. 162.
davisonii (Ulupe), i. 372.
dayana (Cantoria), iii. 23
dayanus (Hydrophis), iii. 297
decalepis (Herpetodryas), ii. 75
decemlineata (Contia), ii. 260
decemlineatus (Ablabes), ii. 260.
decemlineatus (Eirenis), ii. 260.
decipiens (Ablabes), ii. 181
decipiens (Erythrolamprus), iii. 204.
decipiens (Tachymenis), iii. 204
decorata (Coronella), ii. 174, 176
decorata (Rhadinæa), ii. 176, 359
decoratus (Diadophis), ii. 176, 178
decoratus (Elaps), iii. 419.
decorosus (Ophthalmidion), i. 38
decorosus (Typhlops), i. 38
decorus (Ahætulla), ii. 78.
decorus (Coluber), ii. 78
decosteri (Elapechis), iii. 360
decosteri (Elapsoidea), iii. 360.
decurtata (Phimothyra), i. 417
decurtata (Salvadora), i. 417
decurtatus (Lytorhynchus), i. 417
decurtatus (Phyllorhynchus), i. 417
decussata (Anguis), i. 136.
decussata (Homalopsis), iii. 4
decussatus (Elaps), iii. 431.
defilippii (Causus), iii. 469
defilippii (Heterodon), iii. 469
defilippii (Oxyrhina), ii. 269
degener (Opisthoplus), iii. 121
degenhardtii (Calamaria), iii. 229

degenhardtii (Stenorhina), iii. 229
Deirodon, ii. 353
dekayi (Ischnognathus), i. 286, 287, iii. 611.
dekayi (Storeria), i. 286; iii. 611
dekayi (Tropidonotus), i. 286.
dekayi (Typhlops), i. 45.
delalandii (Typhlops), i. 45; iii. 588
Demansia, iii. 320
Dendraspididæ, iii. 310
Dendraspidinæ, iii. 310.
Dendraspis, iii. 434
Dendrechides, iii. 310.
Dendrelaphis, ii. 87.
Dendroechis, iii. 434
Dendrophidæ, i. 177, iii. 26
Dendrophidium, ii. 9.
dendrophila (Boiga), iii. 70
dendrophila (Dipsas), iii. 70.
dendrophilum (Triglyphodon), iii. 70
dendrophilus (Dipsadomorphus), iii. 70
dendrophiops (Tropidonotus), i. 264
Dendrophis, ii. 71, 77, 87, 98, 102, 105, 115; iii. 186, 195.
dendrophis (Dendrophidium), ii. 15.
dendrophis (Drymobius), ii. 15, 357, iii. 626
dendrophis (Herpetodryas), ii. 14, 15.
Denisonia, iii. 332.
dennysi (Simotes), ii. 218.
deppei (Elaphis), ii. 66
deppei (Pituophis), ii. 66
deppei (Spilotes), ii. 67.
deppei (Tantilla), iii. 222
deppii (Coluber), ii. 66
deppii (Elapochrous), ii. 182
deppii (Homalocranium), iii. 222
depressirostris (Leptophis), ii. 107.
depressirostris (Philothamnus), ii. 107
depressus (Typhlops), i. 33
deserti (Vipera), iii. 488
deserticola (Pituophis), 68.

dhara (Coluber), iii 52.
dhumna (Coluber), i. 385.
dhumnades (Coluber), i. 375
dhumnades (Coryphodon), i. 376.
dhumnades (Zaocys), i 375.
Diacrantériens, i. 177.
diadema (Brachysoma), iii. 319, 406.
diadema (Calamaria), iii. 319
diadema (Catachlæna), i. 415
diadema (Chatachlein), i. 415.
diadema (Coluber), i 399, 411
diadema (Furina), iii. 319
diadema (Heterodon), i. 415.
diadema (Hydrophis), iii. 284.
diadema (Lytorhynchus), i. 415.
diadema (Pseudelaps), iii 319
diadema (Simotes), i. 415.
diadema (Zamenis), i. 411, iii. 625
diademata (Ninia), i. 292.
diadematus (Streptophorus), i 292.
Diadophis, ii. 160, 188, 277.
Diaphorotyphlops, i 7
diardi (Typhlops), i. 22.
diasu (Chionactis), ii. 268.
diastema (Elaps), iii. 423
diastema (Liophis), ii. 183.
dichroa (Herpetodryas), ii. 30.
dichromatus (Typhlops), i 29.
dichrous (Coluber), ii. 30.
dicranta (Erythrolamprus), iii. 201.
Dicraulax, ii. 215
Diemansia, iii. 315, 320.
Diemenia, iii. 320.
dightoni (Dipsas), iii. 69.
dightonii (Dipsadomorphus), iii. 62
digitalis (Colubor), iii. 101.

dilepis (Aporophis), ii. 158; iii 634
dilepis (Lygophis), ii. 158; iii. 634.
Dimades, i 272; ii. 185.
dimidiata (Calamaria), ii. 333
dimidiata (Glauconia), i. 64.
dimidiata (Leptognathus), iii. 549.
dimidiatum (Pilidion), i 25
dimidiatum (Stenostoma) i 64
dimidiatus (Elapochrus), ii. 183
dimidiatus (Elapomoius), iii 238
dimidiatus (Elapomorphus), iii 238
dimidiatus (Leptognathus), iii 459.
dimidiatus (Mesopeltis), iii 459
dimidiatus (Pliocercus), ii. 183.
dimidiatus (Rhinocalamus), iii. 247.
dimidiatus (Tropidonotus), i 274.
dindigalensis (Silybura), i. 152
dinga (Onychocephalus), i 45
dinga (Typhlops), i. 45.
Dinodipsas, iii 466.
Dinodon, i. 360
Dinophis, iii 434.
dione (Cœlopeltis), ii. 44.
dione (Chironius), ii. 44.
dione (Coluber), ii. 44.
dione (Elaphis), ii 44, 46.
Dipeltophis, iii. 644
Diplophallus, iii. 599.
Diplotropis, ii. 105.
diplotropis (Ahætulla), ii. 110
diplotropis (Hapsidophrys), ii. 110.
diplotropis (Leptophis), ii. 110.
diporus (Bothrops), iii. 542.
Dipsadidæ, i 177; iii. 26, 438
dipsadides (Hypaspistes), i 84.
Dipsadiens, iii. 26.

dipsadina (Ungalia), i 112.
Dipsadinæ, iii 26
Dipsadoboa, iii. 39, 81.
Dipsadomorphinæ, iii 26
Dipsadomorphus, iii. 53, 59.
Dipsadomorus, iii. 446, 460.
Dipsas, ii 292; iii 38, 39, 47, 53, 58, 59, 82, 83, 88, 115, 117, 124, 138, 439, 440, 446, 460
dipsas (Ahætulla), iii. 621.
dipsas (Hemidryas), iii. 621.
dipsas (Herpetodryas), i. 383.
dipsas (Tropidonotus), i. 223, 258
dipsas (Zamenis), i. 383; iii 621
Dipsina, iii. 144
Diroseina, ii. 298.
Dirrbox, iii 127.
dirus (Bothrops), iii 535.
discolor (Hypsiglena), ii. 211.
discolor (Leptodira), ii. 211.
dispar (Dryophis), iii 179.
dispar (Tragops), iii 179.
disparilis (Diaphorotyphlops), i 53.
disparilis (Typhlops), i. 53
Dispholidus, iii. 186.
dissimile (Stenostoma), i. 70.
dissimilis (Glauconia), i. 70
dissoleucus (Elaps), iii. 422
distans (Elaps), iii. 423.
distanti (Glauconia), i 62.
Disteira, iii 271, 285, 302
Distichurus, iii. 465.
distinctus (Bothriopsis), iii. 142
distinctus (Tropidophis), i. 112.
Distira, iii. 285.
Ditypophis, iii 46.
divaricatus (Elaps), iii. 423.
diversus (Typhlops), iii. 584.

divmiloqua (Boa), i 118, 119.
divmiloquus (Constrictor), i 118
docilis (Diadophis), ii 207, 208
doliata (Coronella), ii. 200, 201, 203, 205; iii 638
doliata (Disteira), iii. 276, 289.
doliata (Hydrophis), iii. 276, 278, 298
doliata (Lampropeltis), ii. 201
doliatus (Coluber), ii. 131, 205
doliatus (Ophibolus), ii. 200, 201, 203, 205
doliatus (Ophiomorphus), ii. 132
doliatus (Oxyrhopus), iii. 57, 106.
dolichocephalum (Catostoma), ii. 320.
dolichocephalus (Colobognathus), ii 320
dolichocephalus (Elapoides), ii 320.
dolichocephalus (Geophis), ii 320
dolicocercus (Dromicus), i 246.
dolichocercus (Tropidonotus), i 246, iii 607.
Doliophis, iii 399
dolleyanus (Holarchus), iii. 640
domesticus (Coluber), i. 409
domicella (Coluber), iii. 409
dora (Coluber), i 230.
dorbignyi (Apostolepis), iii 236
dorbignyi (Calamaria), iii 236
dorbignyi (Heterodon), ii 151
dorbignyi (Lystrophis), ii. 151, iii 114
dorbignyi (Oxyrhopus), iii 103.
doriæ (Ablabes), ii 279
doriæ (Cyclophiops), ii. 279
doriæ (Homalophis), iii. 12, 13.
doriæ (Hypsirhina), iii 13.
doriæ (Psammophis), iii. 151.

dorri (Periops), i 410.
dorri (Zamenis), i 410.
dorsale (Gonyosoma), i. 398.
dorsale (Leptophidium), iii 628
dorsale (Oligodon), ii. 234
dorsalis (Ahætulla), ii 101.
dorsalis (Alecto), iii 343.
dorsalis (Dromicus), ii. 119
dorsalis (Drymobius), ii. 12.
dorsalis (Elaps), ii 241, iii 410
dorsalis (Eutainia), i. 207
dorsalis (Homorelaps), iii 410.
dorsalis (Ialtris), iii 137
dorsalis (Leptophis), ii 101.
dorsalis (Liophis), ii. 170
dorsalis (Oligodon), ii 241.
dorsalis (Ophiomorphus), ii 170.
dorsalis (Pelias), iii 477.
dorsalis (Philodryas), iii 137.
dorsalis (Philothamnus), ii. 101, iii. 631
dorsalis (Pœcilophis), iii 410
dorsalis (Pseudoxenodon), i 271
dorsalis (Tropidonotus), i. 207, 271.
dorsata (Clœlia), iii. 215.
dorsatus (Tomodon), iii. 121
dorsopictus (Pareas), iii. 442
dorsuale (Xiphosoma), i. 101.
dougesii (Diadophis), ii. 208.
Draco, i. 93, 99, 115, 116
drapiezii (Dipsadomorphus), iii 74
drapiezii (Dipsas), iii 74
drapiezii (Triglyphodon), iii 74
Drepanodon, iii 639.
dromiciformis (Coniophanes), iii. 205

dromiciformis (Erythrolamprus), iii. 205.
dromiciformis (Tachymenis), iii. 205.
Dromicodryas, i. 189, iii 599.
Dromicus, ii 9, 118, 126, 157, 160, iii. 633.
Dromophis, iii. 149.
drozii (Streptophorus), i 293.
drummondi (Farancia), ii 291.
Dryadidæ, i 177, iii. 26
drymas (Caudisona), iii 573
drymas (Crotalus), iii. 573
Drymus, iii. 177, 189.
Dryiophidæ, iii. 26.
Dryiophis, iii 35
Drymobius, i 379, ii. 8, 25, iii 626.
Dryocalamus, i 369
Dryophidinæ, iii. 26
Dryophilidæ, i. 177; iii. 26
Dryophiops, iii 193.
Dryophis, iii 177, 185, 189, 193
Dryophylax, iii. 34, 115, 127, 149
Duberria, i. 320, 373, ii. 273, iii. 99, 212
duberria (Coluber), ii. 274
duberria (Elaps), ii 274.
dubium (Geophidium), ii 322.
dubium (Rhabdosoma), ii. 308
dubium (Xenodon), ii 243
dubius (Acrochordus), i. 173
dubius (Geophis), ii. 322, 323
duboisi (Atractus), ii. 310
duboisi (Rhabdosoma), ii. 310
duboisii (Aipysurus), iii. 305.
duceboracensis (Liasis), i. 84.
dugesi (Elapoides), ii. 317
dugesii (Catodon), i. 70.
dugesii (Geophis), ii. 317.
dugesii (Rena), i. 70

ALPHABETICAL INDEX.

dugesii (Siagonodon), i. 70
dulce (Stenostoma), i. 65
dulcis (Glauconia), i 65; iii 591.
dulcis (Leptotyphlops), i. 65.
dulcis (Rena), i. 65.
dumerilii (Calamaria), ii. 343
dumerilii (Acrantophis), i. 120.
dumerilii (Boa), i 120, iii. 594
dumerilii (Coronella), i. 227.
dumerilii (Dendrophis), ii. 8
dumerilii (Disteira), iii. 289
dumerilii (Dromicus), ii. 181
dumerilii (Elaps), iii 419
dumerilii (Leptognathus), ii 296.
dumerilii (Meizodon), i. 227
dumerilii (Stegonotus), i 368.
dumerilii (Urotheca), ii. 181
dumfriesiensis (Coluber), ii 205
dupeni (Silibura), i 150.
durissa (Caudisona), iii. 574, 578
durissus (Crotalus), iii. 573, 576, 577, 579.
durissus (Uropsophus), iii. 579.
dussumieri (Boa), i. 121.
dussumieri (Casarea), i. 121.
dussumieri (Eurostus), iii. 19
dussumieri (Hypsirhina), iii. 19.
dussumieri (Leptoboa), i. 121.
dysopes (Diadophis), ii. 206.

Echidna, iii. 471, 492, 501.
Echidnoides, iii. 471.
Echinanthera, iii 634.
Echis, iii. 504, 508
echis (Vipera), iii. 488, 505
edwardsii (Caudisona), iii. 571.

edwardsii (Crotalophorus), iii. 571.
edwardsii (Crotalus), iii. 571.
effrene (Tetragonosoma), i 356.
effrenis (Lycodon), i. 356
Eirenis, ii 255.
eiseni (Ophibolus), ii 197.
Elachistodon, iii 263.
Elachistodontinæ, iii. 263
elaiocroma (Ficimia), ii. 271.
Elapechis, iii 358
Elaphis, ii. 24
elaphis (Coluber), ii 45.
elaphis (Natrix), ii 46
elaphoides (Coluber), i. 234.
elaphoides (Tropidonotus), i 234.
Elapida, iii. 310.
Elapidæ, iii. 310.
elapiformis (Cantoria), iii 23
elapiformis (Hemiodontus), iii 23
elapiformis (Hydrodipsas), iii. 23.
Elapinæ, iii 310
Elapocephalus, iii 239, 320
Elapochrous, ii 180.
Elapocranium, iii 320.
Elapognathus, iii 356
Elapoides, i 306; ii 314.
elapoides (Calamaria), i. 307.
elapoides (Hoplocephalus), iii. 347.
elapoides (Liophis), ii 183
elapoides (Lycophidium), i 343
elapoides (Micropechis), iii 347
elapoides (Pliocercus), ii. 182.
elapoides (Urotheca), ii. 182, 359; iii. 636
Elapomoius, iii. 237.
Elapomorphus, iii. 231, 232, 237, 238, 255.
Elapops, iii. 262.
Elaposchema, iii. 248
Elapotinus, iii. 244.
Elaps, iii 315, 320, 332, 361, 390, 392, 396, 399, 405, 408, 411

elaps (Atractus), ii 302
elaps (Geophis), ii 302
elaps (Hamadryas), iii. 386.
elaps (Naja), iii. 347, 386.
elaps (Ophiophagus), iii. 347, 386
elaps (Rhabdosoma), ii. 302.
elaps (Trimeresurus), iii. 347
Elapsoidea, iii. 358
elapsoidea (Calamaria), ii. 205.
elapsoidea (Osceola), ii. 205, iii. 638
elapsoideus (Lampropeltis), ii. 205.
elegans (Arizona), ii 66.
elegans (Aturia), iii 278.
elegans (Boa), i. 101.
elegans (Coluber), iii 167.
elegans (Coronella), i 175, 196
elegans (Craspedocephalus), iii 552
elegans (Cursoria), i 128.
elegans (Cusoria), i. 128
elegans (Dabota), iii. 490
elegans (Dendrophis), ii. 86
elegans (Dromicus), iii. 133
elegans (Dryophylax), iii. 133.
elegans (Echidna), iii. 490.
elegans (Elaps), iii 418.
elegans (Enicognathus), ii. 173.
elegans (Eryx), i 128.
elegans (Eutainia), i. 202, 208.
elegans (Himantodes), iii. 85
elegans (Hydrophis), iii. 276, 278.
elegans (Leptognathus), iii. 452.
elegans (Lygophis), iii. 133
elegans (Macrosoma), iii. 167.
elegans (Ophthalmidion), i 37.
elegans (Philodryas), iii. 133.
elegans (Pityophis), ii. 66.

elegans (Psammophis), iii. 167.
elegans (Rhinechis), ii. 66
elegans (Tachymenis), iii. 133.
elegans (Thamnophis), iii. 601.
elegans (Trimesurus), iii. 555.
elegans (Tropidonotus), i. 208.
elegans (Typhlops), i. 37.
elegans (Vipera), iii. 490
elegans (Virginia), ii. 289.
elegantissimus (Coluber), iii 620.
elegantissimus (Zamenis), i 402.
elliott (Halys), i. 267.
elliotti (Hydrophis), iii 290.
elliotti (Oligodon), ii 242.
elliotti (Silybura), i. 153, 154, 155, 158, iii 596.
elliotti (Trigonocephalus), i 267.
elongata (Cantoria), iii. 23.
elongata (Dasypeltis), ii. 355.
emini (Ahætulla), ii 92
emini (Chlorophis), ii 92
emini (Glauconia), i. 64
emmeli (Atractus), ii. 311, iii. 645
emmeli (Geophis), ii. 311.
emoryi (Coluber), ii 40.
emoryi (Natrix), ii 40.
emoryi (Scotophis), ii. 40.
emunctus (Helminthophis), i 7.
emunctus (Idiotyphlops), i. 6
emunctus (Typhlops), i 6
Emydocephalus, iii. 303.
enganensis (Coluber), ii. 63
Enhydrina, iii 302.
Enhydris, iii. 271, 285, 300.
enhydris (Homalopsis), iii 7.
enhydris (Hydrus), iii 6
enhydris (Hypsirhina), iii. 6, 8.
VOL. III.

Enicognathus, i. 181, ii. 160.
ensifera (Langaha), iii. 36.
Entechinus, iii 643
Enulius, ii 249, iii. 641
enydris (Boa), i. 101.
Enygrus, i 104, 109
enyo (Caudisona), iii 580
enyo (Crotalus), iii. 580.
Epanodontiens, i 3.
ephippicus (Chilomeniscus), ii. 273.
ephippifer (Elaps), iii. 423
Epicrsius, i. 94
Epicrates, i. 93.
Epictia, i 59
Epiglottophis, iii 627.
epinephelus (Liophis), ii. 137
episcopa (Contia), ii 265, 266.
episcopum (Homalosoma), ii 265
episcopum (Lamprosoma), ii 265
epistema (Elaps), iii. 423
eques (Boa), i 119.
eques (Coluber), i. 209.
eques (Tropidonotus), i. 209, iii 601
erebennus (Spilotes), ii 31
Erebophis, i 104
eremita (Coluber), ii. 44.
Erpetodryas, ii. 71
Erpeton, iii 25
erpeton (Rhinopirus), iii. 25.
Eryces, i 93
Erycidæ, i. 71
Erycides, i 74, 93.
Erycina, i. 93
erythrogaster (Bothriophis), i 395.
erythrogaster (Coluber), i 242, 395
erythrogaster (Nerodia), i 243
erythrogaster (Tropidonotus), i. 242.
erythrogastra (Calopeltis), i. 395
erythrogrammum (Calopisma), ii 290.
erythrogrammus (Abastor), ii 290, iii. 644.
erythrogrammus (Coluber), ii. 290

erythrogrammus (Helicops), ii. 290
erythrogrammus (Homalopsis), ii 290.
erythrogrammus (Hydrops), ii 290.
Erythrolamprinæ, iii. 26.
Erythrolamprus, iii. 99, 199
erythronota (Apostolepis), iii. 236.
erythronotus (Elapomorphus), iii 236, 237.
erythrurum (Compsosoma), ii 62.
erythrurus (Coluber), ii. 62, 358, iii. 628.
erythrurus (Plagiodon), ii 62
erythrurus (Trigonocephalus), iii 554.
erythrurus (Trimeresurus), iii 555.
Eryx, i 122
eryx (Tortrix), i 124, 126, 127.
Eryxina, i 93
eschrichtii (Aspidorhynchus), i. 42
eschrichtii (Ophthalmidion), i 42
eschrichtii (Typhlops), i 32, 41, 42
Eteirodipsas, iii 38, 53, 88
Eudipsas, iii. 58
Eudryas, ii 9.
Eugnathiens, i. 177.
Eugnathus, i 327
Eumesodon, i 360.
Eunectes, i. 116
Euophrys, iii. 127
euphæus (Olisthenes), iii 112
euphratica (Daboia), iii. 488.
euphratica (Vipera), iii. 488
euproctus (Typhlops), i. 16.
Eurostus, iii 2, 19
Euryphohs, ii 277
Eurystephus, iii 510.
Eurystomata, iii. 310, 463
euryxanthus (Elaps), iii. 415
euryzona (Elapochrus), ii 182
euryzona (Urotheca), ii. 182

2 x

euryzonus (Pliocercus), ii 182.
Eutainia, i. 193.
eutropis (Phrynonax), ii. 22; iii. 626
evansii (Coronella), ii 199
evansii (Ophibolus), ii. 199.
everetti (Doliophis), iii 404
everetti (Calamaria), ii. 340
everetti (Oligodon), ii. 239, iii. 640.
excipiens (Typhlops), i. 56.
exigua (Boa), i. 102
exiguus (Dromicus), ii. 126.
exiguus (Typhlops), i 31
eximia (Coronella), ii. 200.
eximius (Coluber), ii. 197, 200
eximius (Ophibolus), ii. 200
exocœti (Typhlops), i. 36.
Exorhina, ii 255.
exsul (Crotalus), iii. 576.
extenuatum (Stilosoma), ii 325; iii 646
eydouxii (Aipysurus), iii. 304
eydouxii (Tomogaster), iii 304.

faireyi (Eutainia), i. 213.
Falconeria, i. 290.
fallax (Atractaspis), iii 517.
fallax (Dipsas), iii. 48, 50.
fallax (Stenostoma), i 63
fallax (Tarbophis), iii. 48
fallax (Tropidonotus), i. 219
familiaris (Eryx), i 126.
Farancia, ii 290
fasciata (Anguis), i. 133.
fasciata (Boa), iii. 365.
fasciata (Clitulia), iii. 275
fasciata (Contia), ii. 262.
fasciata (Dendrophis), ii. 85
fasciata (Dipsas), iii. 78.
fasciata (Disteira), iii. 281.
fasciata (Farancia), ii. 291.
fasciata (Geophis), ii 296.
fasciata (Higina), ii. 187
fasciata (Hydrophis), iii. 277, 279, 281.
fasciata (Leptognathus), ii. 294
fasciata (Liopala), iii. 281.
fasciata (Natrix), i. 243; iii. 606
fasciata (Naja), iii. 380, 386.
fasciata (Nerodia), i 242
fasciata (Potamophis), i 174.
fasciata (Pseudoboa), iii. 365.
fasciata (Tropidodipsas), ii. 294, 295, 296
fasciata (Vermicella), iii 364
fasciatum (Alopecion), i. 342
fasciatum (Lycophidium), i 342
fasciatus (Ablabes), ii. 262
fasciatus (Acrochordus), i 174
fasciatus (Bungarus), iii. 365, 366
fasciatus (Chersydrus), i. 174
fasciatus (Chilomeniscus), ii 273
fasciatus (Coluber), i. 242.
fasciatus (Cyclophis), ii. 262.
fasciatus (Dasypeltis), ii 354
fasciatus (Dipsadomorus), iii. 452.
fasciatus (Eirenis), ii. 262.
fasciatus (Elapoides), ii. 296
fasciatus (Elapoidis), i. 293.
fasciatus (Hipistes), iii. 24.
fasciatus (Hydrophis), iii. 281, 302
fasciatus (Hydrus), iii 281
fasciatus (Lepidocephalus), i. 362.
fasciatus (Lycodon), i. 358, iii 618
fasciatus (Oligodon), ii. 243.
fasciatus (Ophiophagus), iii. 347.
fasciatus (Ophites), i 358.
fasciatus (Pelamis), iii. 281.
fasciatus (Phrynonax), ii. 21; iii 626.
fasciatus (Platurus), iii. 307, 308.
fasciatus (Spilotes), ii 21, 22
fasciatus (Tropidonotus), i 238, 242, iii. 606
fasciolata (Alecto), iii. 351.
fasciolata (Dasypeltis), iii 648
fasciolata (Tyria), i. 404.
fasciolatus (Coluber), i. 404
fasciolatus (Coryphodon), i 404
fasciolatus (Dinophis), iii 436
fasciolatus (Dryophis), iii. 182.
fasciolatus (Rhinelaps), iii 364
fasciolatus (Rhynchelaps), iii. 364
fasciolatus (Simotes), ii. 219.
fasciolatus (Tragops), iii. 182
fasciolatus (Zamenis), i. 404.
favæ (Atractus), ii. 313
favæ (Calamaria), ii 313.
favæ (Rhabdosoma), ii 313
fayreriana (Hydrophis), iii. 301
feæ (Azemiops), iii. 471
fedtschenkoi (Zamenis), i. 405.
Ferania, iii 2.
Feranoides, iii. 2
fergusonianus (Rhinophis), iii 596.
fergusonii (Odontomus), i 371
ferox (Diemenia), iii. 332.
ferox (Hypsirhynchus), ii 117.
ferox (Pseudechis), iii 332
ferox (Tropidonotus), i. 241.
ferruginea (Dipsas), iii. 172
ferruginosus (Coluber), ii. 191

ALPHABETICAL INDEX. 675

Ficimia, ii. 270.
filholii (Labionaris), iii. 313
filiformis (Elaps), iii. 430.
filiformis (Typhlops), i. 29
fischeri (Dipsas), iii. 78
fischeri (Platurus), iii 307.
fischeri (Tropidodipsas), ii 296
fischeri (Zamenis), ii 195.
fiskii (Lamprophis), i. 322
fissidens (Coniophanes), iii 207.
fissidens (Coronella), iii. 206, 207.
fissidens (Erythrolamprus), iii. 207.
fissidens (Tachymenis), iii. 206, 207.
fitzingeri (Elaps), iii. 423.
fitzingeri (Glauconia), i. 66
fitzingeri (Oxyrhopus), iii 108.
fitzingeri (Siphlophis), iii 108.
fitzingeri (Stenostoma), i. 66
fitzingeri (Zacholus), ii. 192
flagelliforme (Bascanium), i 390.
flagelliformis (Drymobius), i 390.
flagelliformis (Herpetodryas), i 390.
flagelliformis (Masticophis), i. 390
flagelliformis (Natrix), i. 389; iii 191.
flagelliformis (Oxybelis), iii 191.
flagelliformis (Psammophis), i. 390.
flagelliformis (Zamenis), i 389, iii. 622
flagellum (Bascanium), iii. 622.
flagellum (Coluber), i 389.
flagellum (Denisonia), iii. 340.
flagellum (Hoplocephalus), iii 340
flammigerus (Brachyorrhos), ii 308
flava (Echidna), iii 376.
flava (Naia), iii. 376.

flava (Vipera), iii. 376
flavescens (Callopeltis), ii. 52.
flavescens (Coluber), ii. 52.
flavescens (Dipsadomorphus), iii 77
flavescens (Dipsas), iii. 72, 77.
flavescens (Elaphis), ii. 53
flavescens (Heleophis), iii 21.
flavescens (Phyllosira), ii. 75.
flavescens (Triglyphodon), iii. 77.
flavescens (Tropidonotus), i 234
flavescens (Typhlops), i. 21.
flaviceps (Ablabes), i 185.
flaviceps (Ademophis), iii. 400
flaviceps (Amphiesma), i. 266
flaviceps (Bungarus), iii. 371
flaviceps (Calamaria), ii 333.
flaviceps (Doliophis), iii. 400
flaviceps (Elaps), iii. 400.
flaviceps (Enicognathus), i 185.
flaviceps (Macropisthodon), i 266, iii 609
flaviceps (Megærophis), iii 371.
flaviceps (Tropidonotus), i 266.
flavifrenatus (Aporophis), ii 158.
flavifrenatus (Dromicus), ii. 158
flavifrenatus (Lygophis), ii. 158.
flavifrons (Tropidonotus), i 263, iii 609
flavigastra (Pappophis), iii 75.
flavigularis (Dendrophis), ii 105.
flavigularis (Herpetodryas), i 390, 391
flavigularis (Masticophis), i. 390.
flavigularis (Psammophis), i 390.
flavigularis (Thrasops), ii. 105, 358.

flavigularis (Zamenis), iii. 621.
flavilabris (Eutænia), i. 212
flavilatus (Dromicus), ii. 143.
flavilatus (Liophis), ii. 143, iii 634.
flavilatus (Rhadinæa), iii. 634
flavipunctatum (Amphiesma), i. 231.
flavipunctatus (Tropidonotus), i 231.
flavirufus (Coluber), ii 39.
flavirufus (Natrix), ii 39.
flavitorquata (Apostolepis), iii 234
flavitorques (Drepanodon), iii. 639.
flavitorques (Liophis), iii. 639.
flaviventer (Typhlops), i. 25.
flaviventris (Bascanion), i. 387.
flaviventris (Coluber), i. 387
flaviventris (Coryphodon), i 387
flaviventris (Geoptyas), ii. 31.
flaviventris (Liophis), ii. 167.
flavolineatus (Herpetodryas), ii. 73
flavomaculata (Megæra) iii. 556
flavomaculatus (Lachesis), iii 556
flavomaculatus (Parias), iii. 556.
flavomaculatus (Trimeresurus), iii 556
flavoterminatus (Helminthophis), i 5.
flavoterminatus (Idiotyphlops), i. 5.
flavoterminatus (Typhlops), i. 5
flavotorquatus (Elapomorphus), iii. 234
flavoviridis (Bothrops), iii. 550
flavoviridis (Lachesis), iii. 550.
flavoviridis (Trimeresurus), iii 550.
flexuosus (Coluber), iii. 141.

floridanus (Coluber), ii 40.
florulenta (Tylanthera), iii 624.
florulentus (Coluber), i. 402.
florulentus (Zamenis), i. 402, 408, iii. 624.
forbesii (Simotes), ii 225.
fordei (Cacophis), iii 318.
fordii (Chilabothrus), i. 98.
fordii (Epicrates), i 98; iii 593.
fordii (Onychophis), i 45.
fordii (Pelophilus), i 98.
fordii (Pseudelaps), iii. 318
Fordonia, iii. 21.
formosa (Coronella), ii. 203.
formosa (Dendrophis), ii. 84.
formosa (Duberria), iii. 106.
formosana (Dinodon), i. 361.
formosanus (Simotes), ii. 222, 359, iii 640
formosissimus (Constrictor), i 117
formosus (Bothrops), iii. 557.
formosus (Coluber), iii. 106.
formosus (Dendrophis), ii 84.
formosus (Leptophis), ii. 78
formosus (Lycodon), iii. 103, 104, 106.
formosus (Megærophis), iii 371.
formosus (Oxyrhopus), iii. 106
formosus (Trigonocephalus), iii. 557.
formosus (Trimeresurus), iii. 557.
formosus (Trimesurus), iii. 562.
fornasinii (Typhlops), i. 38
forsteni (Dipsadomorphus), iii 80.
forsteni (Dipsas), iii. 80
forsteni (Rhabdion), ii. 328.
forsteni (Rhabdophidium), ii. 328.
forsteni (Triglyphodon), iii. 80.

forsteri (Natrix), ii. 136.
Fowlea, i. 193.
foxii (Bascanion), i. 387.
francisci redi (Vipera), iii 481.
franklinii (Onychophis), i 45.
fraseri (Elaps), iii 432
fraseri (Homalocranium), iii 215.
fraseri (Liophis), ii 131
freminvilli (Dryophylax), iii. 133
freminvilhi (Philodryas), iii 133.
freminvillii (Stenorhina), iii 229
fremontii (Bascanion), i. 387.
frenata (Ahætulla), ii 116
frenata (Denisonia), iii. 338
frenata (Echis), iii. 505.
frenata (Leptodira), iii. 92.
frenatum (Bascanium), iii 622
frenatum (Gonyosoma), ii 58
frenatum (Sibon), iii. 92.
frenatus (Ablabes), ii. 280
frenatus (Coluber), ii 58.
frenatus (Cyclophis), ii 280.
frenatus (Dromicus), ii. 181.
frenatus (Herpetodryas), ii. 58.
frenatus (Hoplocephalus), iii. 338
frenatus (Leptophis), ii. 141.
frenatus (Uromacer), ii. 116
frontalis (Contia), ii. 270.
frontalis (Denisonia), iii. 340
frontalis (Elaps), iii. 427, 429
frontalis (Ficimia), ii. 270
frontalis (Geagras), ii. 270.
frontalis (Helminthophis), i. 5.
frontalis (Hoplocephalus), iii. 340.
frontalis (Hydrophis), iii. 276.

frontalis (Prosymna), ii. 248; iii 641.
frontalis (Pseudoficimia), ii 270.
frontalis (Temnorhynchus), ii 247, 248.
frontalis (Toluca), ii. 270.
frontalis (Typhlops), i 5.
fronticinctus (Dryophis), iii 179.
fronticinctus (Tragops), iii 179.
fruhstorferi (Tetralepis), i. 320.
fugax (Coluber), ii 52
fugitivus (Coluber), ii. 139
fugitivus (Dromicus), ii. 139, 140, 141
fugitivus (Liophis), ii. 139.
fula-fula (Naia), iii 391.
fulgidus (Coluber), iii. 191.
fulgidus (Dryophis), iii. 191.
fulgidus (Oxybelis), iii. 181, 191.
fuliginoides (Coronella), i 217
fuliginoides (Mizodon), iii 603.
fuliginoides (Tropidonotus), i. 217, iii 603
fuliginosus (Aipysurus), iii 305.
fuliginosus (Boodon), i. 334
fuliginosus (Lycodon), i. 334
fuliginosus (Zamenis), iii. 622.
fulvia (Vipera), iii 423.
fulviceps (Rhadinæa), ii. 179
fulvicollis (Microsoma), iii 252
fulvius (Coluber), iii. 422.
fulvius (Elaps), iii. 415, 422
fulvivittis (Diadophis), ii. 178
fulvivittis (Dromicus), ii. 178
fulvivittis (Rhadinæa), ii. 178
fulvum (Arrhyton), ii. 252.
fulvus (Eutænia), iii. 61.

fumiceps (Scolecophis), iii. 226.
fumigatus (Helicops), i. 279.
funereus (Alsophis), ii. 142
furcata (Grayia), ii. 287.
furcata (Hypsirhina), iii. 7.
furcata (Vipera), iii 401.
furcatus (Callophis), iii. 402
furcatus (Dendrophis), iii 159
furcatus (Elaps), iii. 401.
furcatus (Psammophis), iii. 164.
furia (Bothrops), iii. 535.
Furina, iii. 315, 320, 405.
fusca (Ahætula), ii. 82.
fusca (Calabaria), i 92
fusca (Calamaria), i 297.
fusca (Cliftia), i. 95
fusca (Dendrophis), ii. 82, iii. 67.
fusca (Dipsas), iii. 67, 73, 78.
fusca (Passerita), iii. 183.
fusca (Rhadinæa), ii 169.
fusca (Stephanohydra), iii 305.
fuscum (Homalocranium), iii. 220.
fuscum (Ophthalmidion), i. 30.
fuscum (Trachischium), i. 297.
fuscum (Triglyphodon), iii 77.
fuscus (Ablabes), i 297.
fuscus (Aipysurus), iii. 305.
fuscus (Coluber), ii. 11, 75; iii. 141.
fuscus (Coryphodon), i. 378.
fuscus (Dendrophis), ii. 82
fuscus (Dipsadomorphus), iii 67
fuscus (Elapoides), i. 307.
fuscus (Elaps), iii. 380
fuscus (Geophis), ii. 322
fuscus (Herpetodryas), ii 73, 75; iii 628.
fuscus (Hoplocephalus), iii. 351
fuscus (Lamprophis), i. 322.
fuscus (Liasis), i. 322.

fuscus (Liophis), ii 169.
fuscus (Opheomorphus), ii. 169
fuscus (Rhabdodon), iii. 141.
fuscus (Typhlops), i 30
fuscus (Zaocys), i 378, iii 621.
fusiformis (Oxyorrhos), i. 306

gabina (Natrix), i. 234
gabinus (Coluber), i 233.
gabonensis (Elapomorphus), iii. 252
gabonensis (Miodon), iii 252
gabonica (Bitis), iii. 499
gabonica (Echidna), iii 499
gabonicus (Elapomorphus), iii 252
gabonicus (Urobelus), iii 252.
gaimardi (Dipsas), iii. 41, 42.
gaimardi (Heterurus), iii. 41, 42
gaimardii (Stenophis), iii. 42.
galathea (Coluber), i. 349.
galathea (Lycodon), i. 349
Galeodon, ii. 294.
Galeophis, iii 127.
gallicus (Coluber), ii 192.
gammiei (Lycodon), i. 358
gammiei (Ophites), i 358.
garmani (Leptognathus), iii 453.
gastrodelus (Elaps), iii. 393
gastrogramma (Calamaria), ii. 349
Gastropyxis, ii. 102
gastrosticta (Elaps), iii. 420.
gastrosticta (Helicops), i. 276.
gastrostictus (Dendrophis), ii. 86
gastrotænia (Rhabdion), i. 305
Geagras, ii. 326.
gemianulis (Callophis), iii 393.
gemianulis (Hemibungarus), iii 393
geminatus (Ablabes), i. 185.

geminatus (Coluber), i 185.
geminatus (Enicognathus), i. 185
geminatus (Herpetodryas), i 185.
geminatus (Lycognathus), iii. 57.
geminatus (Polyodontophis), i. 185, iii. 597.
gemmicincta (Dipsas), iii. 70
gemmicinctum (Triglyphodon), iii 70.
gemmistrata (Dipsas), iii. 86.
gemmistratus (Himantodes), iii. 86.
gemonensis (Natrix), i. 395.
gemonensis (Zamenis), i 395, iii 622
genimaculata (Liophis), ii 170.
genimaculata (Lygophis), ii 170
genimaculata (Rhadinæa), ii 170, iii 635
gentilis (Coronella), ii 201.
gentilis (Ophibolus), ii. 201.
Geodipsas, iii. 32.
geometricum (Boædon), i. 329, 332
geometricus (Boodon), i. 329, 332
geometricus (Eugnathus), i 329.
geometricus (Lycodon), i. 329, 332
Geophidium, ii. 314.
Geophis, i. 303, ii. 314.
Geoptyas, ii. 25.
Georgia, ii 25.
Gephyrinus, iii. 177.
Gerardia, iii. 20.
gerrardi (Mytilia), i. 142.
Gerrhopilus, i 7.
Gerrhosteus, iii. 231.
gervaisii (Calamaria), ii. 338
getula (Coronella), ii. 197; iii. 638.
getula (Lampropeltis), ii. 197; iii 638.
getulus (Coluber), ii. 197.
getulus (Coronella), ii. 197.
getulus (Herpetodryas), ii. 197.

getulus (Ophibolus), ii. 197.
giardi (Grayia), ii. 288.
gigas (Boa), i. 115.
gigas (Cyclagras), ii 144.
gigas (Leiosophis), ii. 144
gigas (Xenodon), ii. 144.
gilberti (Nardoa), i. 77.
girardi (Philothamnus), ii 102
girondica (Coronella), ii. 194.
girondicus (Coluber), ii. 194.
glaber (Heterolepis), i. 344
glabra (Herpetodryas), ii 75
Glaniolestes, ii. 286.
Glaphyrophis, iii. 199.
glaphyros (Tropidonotus), i. 211.
glaucoides (Coluber), i. 395
Glauconia, i 59
Glauconiidæ, i. 57.
Glauconiinæ, i. 57
glaucus (Bothrops), iii. 535.
glaucus (Coluber), iii. 535.
globiceps (Boiga), iii. 78.
globiceps (Dipsas), iii 78.
Glyphodon, iii 313, 315.
Glyphodonta, i. 169.
Glypholycus, iii 615.
godeffroyi (Distira), iii. 291.
godeffroyi (Hydrophis), iii. 291.
godmani (Bothriopsis), iii. 545.
godmani (Bothrops), iii. 545.
godmani (Coronella), ii. 180.
godmani (Geophis), ii. 322
godmani (Lachesis), iii. 545.
godmani (Rhadinæa), ii. 179.
godmani (Tropidonotus), iii. 600.
godmanni (Henicognathus), ii. 179.
godmanni (Bothriechis), iii 545.
godmanni (Dromicus), ii. 179.

gokool (Dipsadomorphus), iii. 64.
gokool (Dipsas), iii. 64.
goldii (Naia), iii. 387.
Gongylophis, i 122
Gonionotophis, i 323.
Gonionotus, i. 175, 323.
Gonyophis, ii 70
Gonyosoma, ii 24.
goudoti (Ithycyphus), iii 34
goudoti (Dryophylax), iii. 34
goudotii (Glauconia), i. 64
goudoti (Herpetodryas), iii 34
goudoti (Philodryas), iii 34
goudoti (Stenostoma), i 64.
gouldi (Alecto), iii. 342.
gouldi (Denisonia), iii. 342.
gouldi (Elaps), iii. 342
gouldi (Hoplocephalus), iii. 342
grabowskii (Calamaria), ii. 336.
grabowskyi (Elaphis), ii. 47
gracile (Homalocranium), iii 228
gracile (Stenostoma), i. 69.
gracile (Trimetopon), ii 184; iii. 636
gracilis (Ablabes), ii 184.
gracilis (Callophis), iii. 396.
gracilis (Chilabothrus), i 98
gracilis (Dendrophis), ii. 82
gracilis (Disteira), iii 280
gracilis (Dryocalamus), i. 371
gracilis (Elaps), iii 396.
gracilis (Enhydris), iii. 280.
gracilis (Epicrates), i. 98.
gracilis (Hydrophis), iii. 280, 281, 285.
gracilis (Hydrophobus), i. 371.
gracilis (Hydrus), iii. 280, 281.
gracilis (Leipython), i 80.
gracilis (Leptophis), ii 103.
gracilis (Liopala), iii. 280.
gracilis (Microcephalophis), iii. 280.

gracilis (Odontomus), i. 371.
gracilis (Tantilla), iii 228.
gracilis (Tropidonotus), i. 234.
gracilis (Tyria), i. 404.
gracilis (Zamenis), i. 404; iii 624.
gracillima (Ahætulla), ii. 95
gracillima (Calamaria), ii. 350.
gracillima (Dipsas), iii. 87.
gracillimus (Chlorophis), iii. 631.
gracillimus (Himantodes), iii. 87.
gracillimus (Typhlocalamus), ii. 350.
græca (Elaphis), ii. 46.
grahami (Tropidonotus), i. 225, 240.
grahami (Zamenis), i. 393; iii 622.
grahamiæ (Phimothyra), i 393
grahamiæ (Salvadora), i. 393, iii. 622.
grahami (Natrix), i. 240.
grahami (Regina), i. 240.
graminea (Eutæma), i. 206.
gramineum (Gonyosoma), ii 59.
gramineus (Coluber), ii. 554
gramineus (Lachesis), iii. 554.
gramineus (Trigonocephalus), iii. 555.
gramineus (Trimeresurus), iii 555.
grammophrys (Erythrolamprus), iii. 204.
grammophrys (Tachymenis), iii. 204
grandis (Distira), iii. 293.
grandis (Rhinophis), i. 148.
grandis (Silybura), i. 148.
grandis (Uropeltis), i. 139.
grandisquamis (Herpetodryas), ii 76
grandisquamis (Spilotes), ii 76
grandoculis (Asthenognathus), ii. 459.
grandoculis (Dendrophis), ii. 84.
grandoculis (Leptognathus), iii. 459.

ALPHABETICAL INDEX. 679

granosa (Hydrophis), iii. 288
grantii (Gonionotophis), i 324.
grantii (Gonionotus), i. 324
grantii (Simocephalus), i. 324.
granulatus (Acrochordus), i 174
granulatus (Chersydrus), i 174
granulatus (Hydrus), i. 174
granulatus (Pelamis), i. 174
granuliceps (Dipsas), iii. 41.
granuliceps (Heterurus), iii 41.
granuliceps (Stenophis), iii 41.
graphicus (Coluber), ii. 137.
gravenhorstii (Elaps), iii 415
grayi (Calamaria), ii. 338.
grayi (Enicognathus), i 187.
Grayia, ii. 286
gregorii (Dendrophis), ii. 82
greineri (Ablabes), i 366.
gronoviana (Natrix), i. 219.
gronovianus (Coluber), i 219.
Grotea, i. 300.
groutii (Stenostoma), i 68
Gryptotyphlops, i 7.
guatemalensis (Peropodum), i 114
gueinzii (Simocephalus), i. 345.
guentheri (Aparallactus), iii. 259.
guentheri (Aspidura), i. 312
guentheri (Atractus), ii. 305.
guentherii (Cacophis), iii 325
guentheri (Chlorophis), iii 631.
guentheri (Elapechis), iii. 359.
guentheri (Elapsoidea), iii. 359
guentheri (Erythrolamprus), iii. 201.

guentheri (Geophis), ii. 305.
guentheri (Helminthophis), i 6.
guentheri (Hydrophis), iii 280. 288
guentheri (Naia), iii 388.
guentheri (Onychocephalus), i. 20.
guentheri (Philothamnus), ii 96
guentheri (Phrynonax), ii 20
guentheri (Plecturus), i 162.
guentheri (Silybura), i. 147.
guentheri (Stegonotus), iii. 619.
guentheri (Stenophis), iii 40
guentheri (Tarbophis), iii. 52.
guentheri (Trachischium), i 298.
guentheri (Typhlops), i 20.
guentheri (Xenodon), ii 147
guerini (Oxyrhopus), iii 113
guerini (Phimophis), iii 113.
guerini (Rhinostmus), iii 113.
guianense (Rhinostoma), iii 114
guianensis (Heterodon), iii. 114.
guineensis (Coluber), iii. 409.
guiralii (Heterolepis), i 346.
guiralii (Simocephalus), i. 346, iii. 617.
guiraonis (Dipsas), iii. 75
guiraonis (Eudipsas), iii 75
gularis (Enygrus), i 109.
gularis (Trachyboa), i. 109.
guntheri (Rhinostoma), iii. 114
guttata (Hydrophis), iii. 288
guttatus (Boodon), i 331.
guttatus (Callopeltis), iii. 627
guttatus (Coluber), i. 402, ii. 39, 198, iii. 627
guttatus (Elaphis), ii 40, 49.

guttatus (Lycodon), i 331.
guttatus (Lycophidium), i 340
guttatus (Scotophis), ii 40.
guttulatum (Rhabdosoma), ii. 298
gutturalis (Bucephalus), iii. 187.
gutturalis (Naja) iii. 376
Gyalopion, ii 270.

habeli (Dromicus), ii 119
hæmachates (Aspidelaps), iii. 389
hæmachates (Coluber), iii. 389
hæmachates (Naja), iii. 389
hæmachates (Sepedon), iii 389
hæmachates (Vipera), iii. 389.
hæmatois (Pityophis), ii 67.
Hæmorrhois, i 379.
hætiana (Ungalia), i. 112, iii 594
hageni (Bothrops), iii. 557
hageni (Hypsirhina), iii. 12.
haie (Naia), iii. 374, 376, 378, 387
hainanensis (Simotes), ii. 359
haje (Coluber), iii 374
haje (Vipera), iii. 374
Haldea, i. 290.
hallowelli (Tantilla), iii. 228.
hallowelli (Typhlops), i. 40.
halmahericus (Macropophis), iii. 609.
halmahericus (Tropidonotus), iii 609
Halsophis, iii 633.
Halys, iii. 519.
halys (Ancistrodon), iii. 524.
halys (Coluber), iii. 524.
halys (Trigonocephalus), iii. 524, 528.
halys (Vipera), iii. 524.
Hamadryas, iii 372.
hammondii (Dinophis), iii. 435
hammondii (Eutainia), i. 210.
hammondii (Thamnophis), iii. 601.

hammondii (Tropidonotus), i 210, iii. 601.
hannah (Hamadryas), iii. 386.
Haplocercus, i 309
Haplopeltura, iii. 439
Hapsidophrys, ii 102, 103.
hardwickii (Enhydris), iii 301.
hardwickii (Homalopsis), iii 14
hardwickii (Hydrophis), iii. 301.
hardwickii (Hypsirhina), iii 5
hardwickii (Lapemis), iii. 301.
harperti (Virginia), ii. 289.
harpertii (Carphophis), ii 289.
harriettæ (Cacopsis), iii. 318
harriettæ (Pseudelaps), iii. 318
hasselquistii (Cerastes), iii 502.
hassoltii (Chrysopelea), iii. 199.
haydenii (Eutainia), i. 211.
haydenii (Tropidonotus), i. 211.
heathii (Drymobius), ii 11.
heathii (Herpetodryas), ii 11.
hebe (Coluber), i. 404.
hebe (Lycodon), i 352.
hedemanni (Tachyplotus), iii. 12.
Helerionomus, i. 80
helena (Coluber), ii. 36, 357.
helena (Cynophis), ii. 36.
helena (Dendrophis), ii 88
helena (Herpetodryas), ii. 36.
helena (Plagiodon), ii 36.
helenæ (Carphophiops), ii. 325.
helenæ (Carphophis), ii. 325.
helenæ (Celuta), ii. 324.
Heleophis, iii. 20
Helicops, i 272, 281, ii 185, 289.
Helicopsoides, i. 283.
helluo (Anguis), i 126.
Helminthoelaps, iii 396, 399.
Helminthophis, i. 4.

helveticus (Coluber), i. 219
Hemibungarus, iii 392.
Hemidipsas, iii. 620
Hemidryas, iii 621
Hemigenius, iii. 599.
Hemiodontus, iii 21, 23.
Hemirhagerrhis, iii. 119.
hemprichii (Elaps), iii 421
Hemicognathus, i. 181.
henshawi (Eutænia), i. 210
heraldica (Vipera), iii. 495
Herbertophis, i 364.
herbeus (Coluber), iii. 129
hermanni (Coluber), ii 65
hermiæ (Ablabes), iii. 643
Herpetæthiops, ii 91
Herpetodryas, i. 181, 189, 364, 374, 379, ii. 8, 24, 71, 126, 157, 188, 256, 277, iii 34, 127.
Herpeton, iii 25.
herpeton (Homalopsis), iii 25
Herpetoreas, i. 193.
herzi (Simotes), ii 43
hessei (Elapsoidea), iii. 360
hessii (Elapechis), iii 360.
heteraspis (Eurostus), iii. 12
heterochilus (Elaps), iii. 414.
heteroderma (Ahætulla), ii 97.
heterodermus (Chlorophis), ii 97, 358, iii. 631.
heterodermus (Philothamnus), ii. 95, iii. 631.
Heterodon, i 268, 414, ii. 153, 213, 253
heterodon (Coluber), ii. 154, 156
Heterodonta, i. 169
heterolepidota (Ahætulla), ii. 95.
heterolepidota (Leptophis), ii 95
heterolepidotus (Chlorophis), ii 95, 358, iii. 631.
heterolepidotus (Philothamnus), ii. 95, iii. 631.
Heterolepis, i. 343, 344.
Heteronotus, ii. 286.

Heterophis, iii 466
heterozonus (Elaps), iii. 417.
Heterurus, iii. 39, 81, 88.
heterurus (Homalocephalus), i 315.
heterurus (Ophis), iii. 89
heterurus (Pseudoxyrhopus), i 315
heterurus (Stegonotus), i 367.
hewstoni (Platyplecturus), i. 166.
hexacera (Vipera), iii 500.
hexagonata (Dipsas), iii 65, 66.
hexagonotus (Dipsadomorphus), iii 65.
hexagonotus (Dipsas), iii. 65
hexagonotus (Ptyas), ii 8
hexagonotus (Xenelaphis), ii. 8.
hexahonotus (Coluber), ii 8
hexahonotus (Xenelaphis), ii 8
hexalepis (Phimothyra), i 393
hexalepis (Salvadora), iii. 622
hexanotus (Coryphodon), ii 8
hieroglyphica (Boa), i 86.
hieroglyphicus (Python), i. 86
hierosolimitana (Psammophis), iii 157.
Higina, ii 186.
hildebrandtii (Ablabes), iii. 125.
hildebrandtii (Atractaspis), iii. 512.
hildebrandtii (Hemirhagerrhis), iii 125
himalayanus (Ancistrodon), iii. 526.
himalayanus (Halys), iii. 526.
himalayanus (Trigonocephalus), iii 526.
himalayanus (Tropidonotus), i. 251.
himalayanus (Zamenis), i 248
Himantodes, iii 83.
Hipistes, iii. 24.
hippocrepis (Cœlopeltis), i 409.
hippocrepis (Coluber), i. 409

hippocrepis (Dipsas), iii. 90.
hippocrepis (Elaps), iii 423
hippocrepis (Heterurus), iii 90
hippocrepis (Natrix), i. 409
hippocrepis (Periops), i. 409.
hippocrepis (Tyria), i. 409
hippocrepis (Zamenis), i. 407, 409; iii 625
hippus (Coluber), i. 230
hispanica (Coronella), ii. 194.
histricus (Heterodon), ii. 152
histricus (Lystrophis), ii 152
histrionicus (Trigonocephalus), iii 523
hitambœia (Coluber), iii. 89.
hitambœia (Crotaphopeltis), iii 90
hodgsonii (Coluber), ii 35.
hodgsonii (Compsosoma), ii 35.
hodgsonii (Spilotes), ii 35.
hœvenii (Calamaria), ii. 337.
hoffmanni (Coloboganathus), ii 319
hoffmanni (Elapoides), ii. 319
hoffmanni (Geophis), ii 319; iii 646
hoffmanseggii (Dipsas), iii. 72.
hohenackeri (Coluber), ii. 42
Holarchus, ii. 215.
holbrookii (Elaphis), ii 50
holbrookii (Nerodia), i. 243.
holdsworthii (Hydrophis), iii 297.
Holochalina, i. 169, iii. 310, 463.
holochlorus (Herpetodryas), ii 75
holochrous (Coluber), i 366
Holodonta, i. 71.
Holodontes, i. 74.
Holodonticns, i. 71, 131, 167.

Hologerrhum, iii. 33.
holosericeus (Cophias), iii 535
Holuropholis, i 327.
Homalocephalus, i. 314.
Homalochilus, i 94.
Homalocranium, iii 210, 212.
Homalophis, iii. 2
Homalopsidæ, iii 1
Homalopsinæ, i. 177, iii 1
Homalopsis, i. 272, ii. 185, 186, 289, 290, iii. 2, 13, 15, 21, 25, 209.
Homaloselaps, iii. 405.
Homalosoma, ii. 233, 255, 273, 277
hombroni (Trigonocephalus), iii. 562
hombroni (Tropidolæmus), iii 562
homeyeri (Ablabes), iii. 170
homolepis (Rhinophis), i. 142.
Homorelaps, iii 408.
Homoroselaps, iii 408
Hoplocephalus, iii 332, 348, 351, 353.
hoplogaster (Ahætulla), ii. 93.
hoplogaster (Chlorophis), ii 93.
hoplogaster (Philothamnus), ii. 93.
horatta (Boa), iii 505.
Hormonotus, i. 343
horneri (Herpetodryas), i. 378
horrida (Caudisona), iii. 579
horridus (Coluber), iii. 14
horridus (Crotalophorus), iii. 579.
horridus (Crotalus), iii. 573, 578.
horsfieldii (Argyrophis), i 22
horsfieldii (Typhlops), i. 22
horstokii (Lycodon), i. 339.
horstockii (Lycophidium), i 337, 339, 341.
hortulana (Boa), i. 99, 101
hortulanum (Xiphosoma), i 99, 101; iii. 593.
hortulanus (Coluber), i. 101.

hortulanus (Corallus), i 99, 101; iii 593
hortulanus (Draco), i 101
Hortulia, i 81.
hotambœia (Coronella), iii. 89, 649.
hotambœia (Leptodira), iii. 89.
hottentotus (Typhlops), iii. 588
houttuynii (Python), i. 86.
hugyi (Vipera), iii 482.
humberti (Enicognathus), i 186
humberti (Ablabes), i. 186.
humbo (Onychocephalus), i. 46.
humbo (Typhlops), i. 46; iii 588
humile (Stenostoma), i. 70
humilis (Glauconia), i. 70, iii. 591.
humilis (Rena), i 70, iii. 591.
Hurria, iii. 59, 327.
hybridus (Coluber), i. 219
hybridus (Hydrophis), iii 274.
hybridus (Tropidonotus), i 219
Hydrablabes, i. 296.
Hydræthiops, i 280.
Hydrelaps, iii 270.
Hydri, iii 264.
Hydridæ, i 169, 172, iii. 1, 264.
hydrina (Homalopsis), iii 24
hydrinus (Hipistes), iii. 24
Hydrocalamus, iii 209.
Hydrodipsas, iii. 23
hydroides (Bitia), iii 24
Hydromorphus, ii. 185
Hydrophidæ, i 172, 177; iii. 1, 264
Hydrophinæ, iii 264
hydrophilus (Coluber), i. 233
Hydrophis, iii 266, 268, 271, 285, 300, 302, 303, 306
Hydrophobus, i 369
Hydrops, ii 186
Hydrus, i 173, iii. 2, 15, 266, 271, 285, 306
hydrus (Coluber), i. 233.

hydrus (Natrix), iii 605.
hydrus (Tropidonotus), i.
233.
hygeæ (Elaps), iii 409.
hygeiæ (Coluber), iii. 409.
hygiæ (Pœcilophis), iii.
409
Hypaspistes, i 81
Hypnale, iii 519.
hypnale (Ancistrodon),
iii. 528
hypnale (Boa), i 102.
hypnale (Cophias), iii.
528.
hypnale (Trigonocephalus), iii. 528.
hypoconia (Tachymenis),
iii. 116
hypomelas (Tropidonotus), i 264.
Hypotropis, iii 303.
Hypsiglena, ii 208
Hypsirhina iii. 2 19.
hypsirhinoides (Tytleria),
i 352.
Hypsirhynchus, ii 117.
Hypsiscopus, iii. 2.

Ialtris, iii 137.
iberus (Tarbophis), iii. 49.
iberus (Trigonophis), iii.
49
ibibe (Coluber), i. 206.
ibibiboca (Coluber), iii.
196.
ibibiboca (Elaps), iii 428.
Idiopholis, ii. 327.
Idiotyphlops, i. 4.
ignita (Coronella), ii. 176.
ignita (Rhadinæa), ii
176.
ignitus (Dromicus), ii.
176.
iheringi (Elapomorphus),
iii 242
iheringii (Coronella), ii.
172.
ikaheka (Coluber), iii.
347.
ikaheka (Diemenia), iii.
347.
ikaheka (Micropechis),
iii. 347.
ikaheka (Ophiophagus),
iii. 347.
ikaheka (Trimeresurus),
iii. 316, 347.
illyrica (Vipera), iii 485.
Ilysia, i. 133, 134.
Ilysiidæ, i 131.
Ilysioidea, i. 131.

Imantodes, iii. 83.
Imbricatæ, i 3, 131, 167.
imerinæ (Liophis), i 316
imerinæ (Pseudoxyrhopus), i 316
immaculatus (Oxyrhopus), iii. 101.
immaculatus (Trimeresurus), iii. 562.
imperator (Boa), i 119,
iii 594.
imperator (Elaps), iii.
416, 418
imperialis (Coniophanes),
iii 206.
imperialis (Erythrolamprus), iii. 206
imperialis (Rhadinæa),
iii 206.
imperialis (Tachymenis),
iii. 206.
imperialis (Tæniophis),
iii 206
inæquifasciata (Leptognathus), iii. 455.
inæquifasciatus (Cochliophagus), iii 455, 456.
inæquifasciatus (Leptognathus), iii 455
inconspicuus (Typhlops),
i. 16.
inconstans (Dromicus),
ii. 121.
indica (Dipsas), iii. 461.
indica (Hypsirhina), iii.
4
indica (Rachitia), iii 4.
indicus (Dipsadomorus),
iii 461.
indicus (Leptognathus),
iii. 461.
indicus (Psammophis),
iii. 165.
indicus (Tortix), i 127.
indicus (Xylophis), i. 304.
infernalis (Boodon), i.
330
infernalis (Coluber), i.
207
infernalis (Eutainia), i.
207, iii. 601.
infernalis (Thamnophis),
iii. 601.
infernalis (Tropidonotus),
i. 201, 207.

inflata (Vipera), iii. 494.
infralineata (Geodipsas),
iii 32.
infralineatus (Tachymenis), iii. 32.
infrasignatus (Ptyas), i.
247
infratæniatus (Helicops),
i 276
infuscatus (Bothrophthalmus), i. 324.
ingens (Naja), iii. 386.
inornata (Bitis), iii 496
inornata (Boa), i. 97.
inornata (Chitulia), iii;
290.
inornata (Clotho), iii 496
inornata (Coronella), ii.
195
inornata (Echidna), iii.
496.
inornata (Vipera), iii. 496.
inornata (Virginia), i
290
inornatus (Amphiardis),
i. 290
inornatus (Atractaspis),
iii. 515
inornatus (Chilabothrus),
i 97, 112.
inornatus (Dasypeltis),
ii. 354
inornatus (Dipsas), iii 90.
inornatus (Dryophylax),
iii 136.
inornatus (Eirenis), ii.
260.
inornatus (Epicrates), i.
i. 97.
inornatus (Himantodes),
iii 88.
inornatus (Lamprophis),
i. 321.
inornatus (Philodryas),
iii. 136.
inornatus (Potamophis),
i. 291
inornatus (Pseudoxenodon), i. 272.
inornatus (Rachiodon),
ii. 355
inornatus (Stenophis), iii.
42.
inornatus (Typhlops), i.
54.
inornatus (Uromacer), ii.
116.
inornatus (Xenodon), i.
272
insigniarum (Eutænia), i.
212.

ALPHABETICAL INDEX. 683

insignitus (Cœlopeltis), iii. 142.
insignitus (Coluber), iii. 141
intermedia (Langaha), iii. 37.
intermedia (Halys), iii. 525.
intermedia (Typhlops), i. 42.
intermedius (Ancistrodon), iii. 525.
intermedius (Crotalus), iii. 581.
intermedius (Dendraspis), iii. 437.
intermedius (Psammophis), iii 162
intermedius (Pityophis), ii 37.
intermedius (Trigonocephalus), iii. 525
intermedius (Tropidonotus), i. 210.
intestinalis (Adeniophis), iii 402
intestinalis (Aspis), iii. 401.
intestinalis (Callophis), iii 402, 404
intestinalis (Doliophis), iii. 401
intestinalis (Elaps), iii. 401, 404.
intricatus (Erythrolamprus), iii. 201.
intumescens (Coluber), iii 494
Iobola, iii 310, 463
iowæ (Tropidoclonium), i. 289.
iphisa (Coluber), iii 409.
iris (Calamaria), ii. 344.
irregularis (Ahætulla), ii. 92, 94, 96
irregularis (Atractaspis), iii. 513, 514, 515.
irregularis (Boiga), iii. 75.
irregularis (Chlorophis), ii. 96, iii. 631.
irregularis (Coluber), ii 96, iii. 75.
irregularis (Dipsadomorphus), iii. 75
irregularis (Dipsas), iii. 75.
irregularis (Elaps), iii. 513
irregularis (Philothamnus), ii. 96, 99, iii. 631

irregularis (Psammophis), iii. 161.
irregularis (Triglyphodon), iii. 75
irregularis (Xenodon), ii. 150
irrorata (Metoporhina), i 340.
irroratum (Lycophidium), i 340, 342; iii 617.
irroratus (Coluber), i. 340
isabella (Wenona), i 130.
isabellina (Phayrea), iii. 165.
Ischnognathus, i. 285
Isodonta, i 71, 169.
Isodontiens, i 177.
isolepis (Xenodon), ii 136
Isoscelis, ii. 300.
isozona (Contia), ii. 266.
isozonus (Elaps), iii 427.
isthmica (Boa), i 119
isthmicus (Atractus), ii. 307
italica (Coronella), ii. 192.
Ithycyphus, iii. 34.

jacksoni (Lycophidium), i 340
jacksonii (Aparallactus), iii 256, 649
jacksonii (Causus), iii. 468
jacksonii (Rhamnophis), iii 632.
jacksonii (Thrasops), iii. 632
jacksonii (Uriechis), iii. 256
jaculus (Anguis), i. 125.
jaculus (Eryx), i 125, 128, iii. 595
jaculus (Tortrix), i. 126.
jægeri (Coronella), ii. 170
jægeri (Rhadinæa), ii. 170
jagori (Typhlops), i. 18.
jagori (Eurostus), iii. 6.
jagori (Hypsirhina), iii. 6
jakati (Aspidopython), i. 84.
jamaicensis (Anguis), i 31.
jamesonii (Dendraspis), iii. 435, 436
jamesonii (Elaps), iii. 436.

jamesonii (Naja), iii 435.
jamesonii (Python), i 85.
jamnæticus (Feranoides), iii 11
jani (Arizona), ii. 66.
jani (Galeophis), iii 134.
jani (Homalocranium), iii. 220.
jani (Prosymna), ii 249.
jani (Liophis), ii. 359.
janseni (Coluber), ii. 57, 357
jansenii (Gonyosoma), ii. 57, 357
janthinus (Coluber), iii. 129.
japonicus (Callophis), iii. 395.
japonicus (Dinodon), i. 363.
japonicus (Hemibungarus), iii. 395
japonicus (Ophites), i. 363
jara (Coluber), i. 350.
jara (Leptorhytaon), i. 350
jara (Lycodon), i 350, iii. 618.
jararaca (Bothrops), iii. 535
jararaca (Craspedocephalus), iii. 535
jararaca (Trigonocephalus), iii 535.
jararacca (Cophias), iii. 535.
jararacussu (Bothrops), iii 535
jardinii (Bucephalus), iii. 187.
jaspidea (Dipsas), iii. 73.
jaspideum (Triglyphodon), iii 73
jaspideus (Dipsadomorphus), iii 73.
jauresi (Tropidonotus), i. 206
javanica (Calamaria), ii. 347
javanica (Potamophis), i. 173
javanicum (Xenoderma), i 175.
javanicus (Acrochordus), i 173
javanicus (Coluber), i 85.
javanicus (Enicognathus), i 185.
javanicus (Tragops), iii. 179, 180.

javanicus (Xenodermus), i. 175.
jayakari (Eryx), i. 129
jayakari (Hydrophis), iii. 298.
jerdoni (Typhlops), i. 19, 418.
jerdonii (Distira), iii. 299.
jerdonii (Hydrophis), iii. 299.
jerdonii (Kerilia), iii 299.
jerdonii (Lachesis), iii. 551
jerdonii (Trimeresurus), iii. 551.
jimenezii (Crotalus), iii. 582.
joberti (Enicognathus), ii. 174.
jobiensis (Brachyorrhos), i 306
jobiensis (Calamophis), i. 305
johnii (Boa), i. 127.
johnii (Clothonia), i. 127
johnii (Eryx), i. 127
jugularis (Coluber), i. 395.
jukesii (Hypotropis), iii 305
juliæ (Aporophis), ii. 139.
juliæ (Dromicus), ii 139
juliæ (Liophis), ii 139
junceus (Tropidonotus), i. 224, 258.

kaouthia (Naja), iii 380.
karelinii (Coluber), i. 401
karelinii (Tyria), i. 401
karelinii (Zamenis), i. 401.
Katophis, i. 193.
katowensis (Dendrophis), ii. 80.
kelleri (Hemirhagerrhis), iii. 119, 649.
kennerlyi (Heterodon), ii. 156
kennicottiana (Stenorhina), iii. 229.
kennicottii (Tropidonotus), i 203
kentii (Neospades), iii. 20.
Kerilia, iii. 285.
keyensis (Liclaphis), i. 365.
keyensis (Lycodon), i. 365.
khasiensis (Stoliczkaia), i. 176
khasiensis (Tropidonotus), i. 223.

kingii (Hydrophis), iii 276
kirkii (Ahætulla), ii. 99.
kirkii (Philothamnus), iii 631.
kirtlandii (Cladophis), iii. 185
kirtlandii (Olonophis), i. 286
kirtlandii (Crotalophorus), iii. 571
kirtlandii (Dryiophis), iii 185.
kirtlandii (Ischnognathus), i. 286, 419; iii. 611.
kirtlandii (Leptophis), iii. 185
kirtlandii (Natrix), iii. 611.
kirtlandii (Oxybelis), i. 185.
kirtlandii (Regina), i. 286.
kirtlandii (Thelotornis), iii 185.
kirtlandii (Tropidoclonion), i. 286
kirtlandii (Tropidonotus), i 286
klingii (Gonionotophis), iii 614
korros (Coluber), i. 384.
korros (Coryphodon), i 384
korros (Ptyas), i 377, 384.
korros (Zamenis), i. 384; iii 621
kraalii (Typhlops), i. 30
krait (Pseudoboa), iii. 368
kraussi (Onychocephalus), i 42.
kraussii (Typhlops), i. 42.
kraussii (Ophthalmidion), i. 42.
krefftii (Cacophis), iii. 318.
krefftii (Pseudelaps), iii. 318
kubingii (Pseudoelaps), iii. 325
kuhlii (Brachyorrhos), i. 305.

labialis (Alecto), iii 336.
labialis (Hoplocephalus), iii. 336
labialis (Oxyrhopus), iii. 107.
labialis (Trimeresurus), iii. 551.

Labionaris, iii. 312
labiosa (Ninia), i. 293
labiosus (Streptophorus), i. 293
labuanensis (Simotes), ii. 218
lacepedei (Hydrophis), iii. 289.
lacertina (Cœlopeltis), iii. 142
lacertina (Natrix), iii 141.
lacertinus (Malpolon), iii. 141.
lacertinus (Psammophis), iii. 142
Lachesis, iii. 529
lachesis (Cobra), iii. 493.
lachrymans (Dromicus), ii 174
lachrymans (Lygophis), ii 174
lachrymans (Rhadinæa), ii. 174.
lacrymans (Coluber), iii. 157.
lacrymans (Psammophis), iii. 157.
lactea (Stenorhina), iii. 229
lactea (Vipera), iii 409.
lacteus (Aspidelaps), iii 409.
lacteus (Cerastes), iii 409.
lacteus (Coluber), iii 409.
lacteus (Elaps), iii. 409.
lacteus (Homorelaps), iii 409
lacteus (Pœcilophis), iii. 409.
ladacensis (Zamenis), i. 398, iii. 622
lætus (Coluber), ii. 40
lætus (Diadophis), ii. 208.
lætus (Liophis), ii. 208.
lætus (Scotophis), ii. 49.
læviceps (Atheris), iii. 509.
lævicollis (Coluber), ii. 73.
lævis (Acanthophis), iii. 355
lævis (Aipysurus), iii. 304, 305.
lævis (Amblycephalus), iii. 441.
lævis (Boa), iii. 351.
lævis (Coluber), ii. 191, 286.
lævis (Coronella), ii. 192, 194; iii. 175.

ALPHABETICAL INDEX. 685

lævis (Dipsas), iii. 441
lævis (Drymobius), ii 11
lævis (Herpetodryas), ii. 11
lævis (Hydrophis), iii. 290
lævis (Leptognathus), iii. 441.
lævis (Pareas), iii. 441.
lævis (Thamnodynastes), iii. 116.
lævis (Zacholus), ii. 192.
lævissima (Natrix), i 226.
lævissima (Neusterophis), i 226
lævissimus (Tropidonotus), i. 226.
lagoensis (Ahætulla), ii. 100
lagoensis (Philothamnus), ii 100.
lalandii (Dispholidus), iii 187
lalandii (Onychophis), i. 45.
lalandii (Typhlops), i 45.
lambda (Trimorphodon), iii 54
Lampropeltis, ii. 188.
Lamprophis, i. 318, 320, 343.
Lamprosoma, ii. 255.
lanceolata (Vipera), iii. 535.
lanceolatus (Bothrops), iii 535.
lanceolatus (Coluber), iii. 535
lanceolatus (Cophias), iii. 535.
lanceolatus (Craspedocephalus), iii 535.
lanceolatus (Lachesis), iii. 535.
lanceolatus (Trigonocephalus), iii. 535.
Langaha, iii 35.
langaha (Amphisbæna), iii 36.
langaha (Dryiophis), iii. 36
langsdorffii (Elaps), iii. 416.
lankadivana (Dapatnaya), i 141.
lansbergi (Streptophorus), i. 293
lansbergii (Bothriechis), iii. 546, 547.
lansbergii (Bothrops), iii. 546, 547.

lansbergii (Lachesis), iii. 546.
lansbergi (Ninia), i 293.
lansbergii (Porthidium), iii 546
lansbergii (Teleuraspis), iii 546
lansbergii (Trigonocephalus), iii. 546.
laoensis (Lycodon), i 354.
lapemidoides (Distira), iii. 297.
Lapemis, iii 300
lapemoides (Aturia), iii. 297
lapemoides (Hydrophis), iii 297
larvata (Naja), iii 380.
latastii (Vipera), iii 484.
laterale (Bascanium), i. 391.
laterale (Lycophidium), i. 338, iii 616.
lateralis (Ahætulla), i. 248
lateralis (Bothriechis), iii 566
lateralis (Bothrops), iii. 566.
lateralis (Calamaria), ii. 342.
lateralis (Coniophanes), iii. 206.
lateralis (Glaphyrophis), iii. 206.
lateralis (Lachesis), iii 566.
lateralis (Leptophis), i. 247, 248, 391
lateralis (Macrocalamus), ii 327
lateralis (Philothamnus), i. 248.
lateralis (Thamnosophis), 247, 248.
lateralis (Tretanorhinus), i. 282, iii 610.
lateralis (Tropidonotus), i. 248, 249
lateralis (Zamenis), iii. 622.
lateristriga (Clotho), iii. 494.
lateristriga (Dromicus), ii. 181.
lateristriga (Liophis), ii. 181.
lateristriga (Urotheca), ii. 181, iii 636.
lateritia (Tachymenis), iii. 205.

lateritius (Coniophanes), iii 205.
lateritius (Erythrolamprus), iii. 205.
Laticauda, iii 306
laticaudatus (Coluber), iii 307
laticaudatus (Platurus), iii 307, 308
laticeps (Homalocranium), iii 219
laticeps (Pappophis), iii. 75
laticeps (Tantilla), iii. 219
laticollaris (Elaps), iii. 423.
latifascia (Dipsas), ii 55.
latifasciata (Hydrophis), iii 279
latifasciata (Hypsiglena), ii 211.
latifasciatus (Dipsadomorphus), iii 71
latifasciatus (Hydrophis), iii 279
latifrons (Atractus), ii. 303
latifrons (Geophis), ii. 303
latifrontalis (Atractus), ii 304
latifrontalis (Geophis), ii 304.
latirostris (Philodryas), iii 129
lativittatus (Dirrhox), iii. 132.
latonia (Coluber), iii 390
laureata (Rhadinæa), ii. 179
laureatus (Dromicus), ii. 179.
leachii (Anilios), i. 31.
leberis (Coluber), ii 154.
leberis (Natrix), i 239
leberis (Regina), i 239; iii. 605
leberis (Tropidonotus), i. 237, 238, 239
lebetina (Vipera), iii. 487.
lebetinus (Coluber), iii. 487.
lecomtei (Oxybelis), iii. 185.
lecontei (Crotalus), iii. 576.
lecontii (Rhinochilus), ii. 212.
Leiolepis, iii 519.
Leionotus, i 210, ii 286.

Leiopython, i 76
Leioselasma, iii. 285.
Leiosophis, ii. 144, 180.
leithii (Psammophis), iii. 155, 157
lemniscata (Natrix), iii. 430.
lemniscata (Vipera), iii. 430.
lemniscatus (Boodon), i. 329.
lemniscatus (Coluber), iii. 430.
lemniscatus (Drymobius), iii 622
lemniscatus (Elapomorphus), iii 241
lemniscatus (Elaps), iii. 421, 423, 427, 428, 439.
lemniscatus (Phalotris), iii. 242
lentiferus (Himantodes), iii. 86.
lentiginosum (Rhinobothryum), iii. 82
lentiginosus (Coluber), iii. 82
lenzi (Typhlops), i. 16
leonis (Coronella), ii. 199
leopardina (Coronella), ii 192
leopardina (Dimades), i 278
leopardina (Homalopsis), i 278.
leopardina (Natrix), ii.41.
leopardina (Psammophis), iii 162
leopardinus (Callopeltis), ii. 41.
leopardinus (Coluber), ii. 41.
leopardinus (Helicops), i. 278
lepida (Aploaspis), iii. 582
lepida (Apostolepis), iii. 241
lepida (Gaudisona), iii. 582.
Lepidocephalus, i 360
Lepidognathus, i 283
lepidus (Crotalus), iii 582.
lepidus (Elapomorphus), iii 241.
leporinum (Oxyrhabdium), i. 303, iii. 612.
leporinum (Rhabdosoma), i 302, 303.
leprieurii (Helicops), i. 277, 278.

leprosus (Coluber), ii. 52.
Leptoboa, i. 121.
Leptocalamus, ii. 249; iii. 641
leptocephala (Eutainia), i 201; iii. 600
leptocephalus (Trimeresurus), iii 328
leptocephalus (Tropidonotus), i. 201, 418; iii. 600
Leptodira, iii. 88.
leptodira (Hydrophis), iii 285
Leptognathiens, i. 177, ii. 353, iii. 438.
Leptognathinæ, iii 438
Leptognathus, iii. 440, 446, 460, 462.
Leptophidium, iii. 627
Leptophis, i. 193, 379, ii 9, 77, 87, 91, 102, 105, 255
Leptorhytaon, i. 348.
Leptotyphlops, i 59.
Letheobia, i 7
leucobalia (Fordonia), iii. 21.
leucobalia (Hemiodontus), iii 22
leucobalia (Homalopsis), iii 21.
leucocephala (Boiga), iii. 57.
leucocephala (Calamaria), ii 344
leucocephala (Dipsas), iii. 57
leucocephala (Xenopeltis), i 168.
leucocephalus (Cephalolepis), i 57.
leucocephalus (Coluber), iii. 57.
leucocephalus (Eudipsas), iii. 58.
leucocephalus (Lycognathus), iii. 57
leucocephalus (Oxyrhopus), iii. 58, 106
leucogaster (Calamaria), ii. 341.
leucogaster (Liophis), ii 163.
leucogaster (Rhadinæa), ii. 163.
leucomelas (Alsophis), ii 123
leucomelas (Atractaspis), iii. 517.

leucomelas (Dromicus), ii. 123
leucomelas (Himantodes), iii 84.
leucomelas (Leptognathus), iii. 453
leucomelas (Tropidonotus), i 266
leucomelas (Typhlops), i. 18
leucopilus (Coronella), i. 318.
leucoproctus (Typhlops), i 20
leucosticta (Naja), iii 377
leucostigma (Bothrops), iii. 535
leucostoma (Acontias), iii 520
leucostomus (Leptognathus), ii. 296.
leucostomus (Symphimus), iii 642.
leucura (Atractaspis), iii. 514
leucurus (Bothrops), iii 543
levingii (Silybura), i 152
lewisii (Elaps), iii 629
Lianthera, iii. 599.
Liasis, i 76, 81
liberiensis (Boa), iii. 592.
liberiensis (Onychocephalus), i. 42
liberiensis (Python), iii. 592
liberiensis (Typhlops), i 42
Lichanura, i. 129.
lichensteinii (Aspidelaps), iii. 470.
lichensteinii (Causus), iii. 470.
lichensteinii (Coluber), ii. 10
liebmanni (Chersodromus), i 295
Lioelaphis, i. 364.
ligatus (Typhlops), i 34; iii 585
Ligonirostra, ii 246
limnæa (Vipera), iii 477.
Limnophis, i 272
lindheimeri (Coluber), ii. 50.
lindheimeri (Pantherophis), ii 50.
lindheimeri (Scotophis), ii. 50
lindsayi (Aturia), iii. 281.

lindsayi (Hydrophis), iii. 281
lineata (Boa), iii 368
lineata (Hapsidophrys), ii 104.
lineata (Maticora), iii 401.
lineata (Storeria), i 289
lineata (Tachymenis), iii. 123
lineata (Toluca), ii 269
lineata (Typhlina), i. 15
lineaticollis (Arizona), ii 64.
lineaticollis (Coluber), ii. 64
lineaticollis (Pituophis), ii 64
lineatum (Boædon), i 332
lineatum (Homalocranium), iii 219
lineatum (Pilidion), i 15.
lineatum (Rhabdosoma), ii 312
lineatum (Tropidoclonion), i 289
lineatum (Typhlinalis), i 15.
lineatus (Aparallactus), iii. 261.
lineatus (Aporophis), ii. 158; iii 634
lineatus (Apostolepis), iii. 236
lineatus (Bascanion), i 388.
lineatus (Boodon), i. 331, 332, iii 616
lineatus (Bothrophthalmus), i 324
lineatus (Bungarus), iii. 368, 370.
lineatus (Coluber), ii. 158.
lineatus (Conophis), iii. 122
lineatus (Conopsis), ii. 268
lineatus (Cyclocorus), i. 327, iii 615.
lineatus (Cylindrophis), i 137.
lineatus (Dromicus), ii 141, 158, 170
lineatus (Dromophis), iii. 149.
lineatus (Dryophylax), iii 149
lineatus (Elaphis), i. 324.

lineatus (Geophis), ii. 312.
lineatus (Herpetodryas), ii 158
lineatus (Ischnognathus), i 289
lineatus (Lycodon), i 327
lineatus (Lygophis), ii. 158.
lineatus (Metopophis), iii 261
lineatus (Microps), i. 289.
lineatus (Philodryas), iii. 149
lineatus (Psammophis), iii. 122.
lineatus (Tomodon), iii. 122
lineatus (Tropidonotus), i 262.
lineatus (Typhlops), i 15, iii 584
lineatus (Uriechis), iii. 261
lineatus (Zamenis), i. 388; iii 621.
lineofasciatus (Helicops), i 281
lineolata (Dendrophis), ii 80, 85
lineolata (Eutænia), i. 202
lineolatum (Taphrometopon), iii. 151
lineolatus (Coluber), iii 151.
lineolatus (Dendrophis), ii 80, 85, iii. 629.
lineolatus (Sphenocalamus), ii. 326
lineolatus (Typhlops), i 42.
linnæi (Calamaria), ii 336, 345, 349
liocercus (Ahætulla), ii. 111, 113.
liocercus (Coluber), ii. 113.
liocercus (Dendrophis), ii 111, 113
liocercus (Leptophis), ii. 111, 113, iii 633
Liodytes, i 272
Lioheterodon, i. 268.
Lionima, iii 212.
Liopala, iii 271.
Liopeltis, ii 255, 257.
Liophallus, iii 59
Liophidium, iii 598.

Liophis, ii 118, 126, 160, 180
Liotyphlops, i 4
lippicus (Geophis), ii 188
lippicus (Sympholis), ii. 188.
Lisalia, i 76
Lissophis, i 336.
liura (Silybura), i. 149
lividum (Lycodon), i. 366
lividus (Bungarus), iii 370
lividus (Lielaphis), i 366
lividus (Pseudylocodon), i 366
longicauda (Ablabes), ii. 284, iii 643.
longicauda (Coronella), i. 217.
longicauda (Glauconia), i. 66
longicauda (Meizodon), i. 217
longicauda (Stenostoma), i 66
longicaudata (Grayia), ii. 288
longicaudatum (Rhabdosoma), ii 313.
longicaudatus (Geagras) ii 250
longiceps (Atractus), ii 305
longiceps (Calamaria), ii. 329
longiceps (Hydrophis), iii 275.
longiceps (Oxycalamus), ii 329
longiceps (Pseudorhabdium) ii 329, iii. 646
longiceps (Rhabdosoma), ii 305
longifrenatus (Philothamnus), ii 96.
longifrons (Psammophis), iii 165.
longifrontale (Homalocranium), iii 218
longissima (Natrix), ii. 52
longissimus (Ophthalmidion), i. 33
longissimus (Callopeltis), ii 53.
longissimus (Coluber), ii 52, 357; iii. 627
longissimus (Typhlops), i. 33.

ALPHABETICAL INDEX.

lophophris (Vipera), iii. 497.
lophophrys (Cerastes), iii 497
loreata (Hydrophis), iii. 301.
loreata (Rhadinæa), ii. 179.
loreatus (Lapemis), iii 301.
lovii (Calamaria), ii. 350.
Loxocemi, i. 74.
Loxocemina, i. 74.
Loxocemus, i. 74.
Loxodon, i. 413
lubrica (Naja), iii 390.
lubrica (Natrix), iii 390.
lubricus (Aspidelaps), iii. 390.
lubricus (Elaps), iii 390.
lubricus (Hydrops), iii. 210
lubricus (Pelagophis), iii. 306
lucani (Atheris), iii. 509.
lucifer (Caudisona), iii. 576.
lucifer (Crotalus), iii. 576.
lugubris (Crotalus), iii. 581, 582
lumbricalis (Anguis), i. 21, 31.
lumbricalis (Typhlops), i. 21, 27, 31; iii 585.
lumbriciformis (Letheobia), i. 54.
lumbriciformis (Onychocephalus), i 54.
lumbriciformis (Typhlops), i 54, iii 590
lumbricoidea (Calamaria), ii. 333, 344.
lunulata (Tropidodipsas), ii. 21
lunulata (Vermicella), iii 407.
lunulatus (Aparallactus), iii. 258.
lunulatus (Phrynonax), ii 21
lunulatus (Spilotes), ii 21.
lunulatus (Uriechis), iii. 258
luteostriatus (Coluber), i. 395.
lutescens (Naja), iii. 380
luteus (Lachesis), iii 553
luteus (Trimeresurus), iii. 553.

lutrix (Coluber), ii 274.
lutrix (Homalosoma), ii. 274, 275, iii. 642
luzonensis (Zaocys), i. 377
Lycodon, i 327, 336, 348, 360, 364, 369, iii. 56, 99.
Lycodoniens, i. 177
Lycodontidæ, i 177, iii. 597.
Lycodontiens, i 177.
Lycodontinæ, i. 177; iii. 597.
Lycodryas, iii 44.
Lycognathophis i 317.
Lycognathus, iii 56, 58, 175
Lycophidium, i 336
Lygophis, iii. 127
lyrophanes (Lycodon), iii. 56.
lyrophanes (Trimorphodon), iii. 56
Lystrophis ii 151
Lytorhynchus, i. 414.

macclellandii (Callophis), iii. 398, 402.
macclellandii (Elaps), iii. 398
macclellanii (Pituophis), ii 69
macfarlani (Distira), iii. 294
mackloti (Liasis), i 79
macleayi (Hypsirhina), iii 9
macleayi (Pseudoferania), iii. 9.
Macrelaps, iii 255.
Macrocalamus, ii 327.
macrocercus (Dromicus), i. 246
macrolepis (Glauconia), i. 69
macrolepis (Lachesis), iii. 560.
macrolepis (Peltopelor), iii 560
macrolepis (Silybura), i. 159.
macrolepis (Stenostoma), i. 69
macrolepis (Trimeresurus), iii. 560.
Macrophis, ii 286
macrophthalma (Herpetodryas), ii. 73
macrophthalmus (Tropidonotus), i. 251, 270.

macrophthalmus (Xenodon), i. 251, 270, 271.
Macropisthodon, i. 265.
Macropophis, i 264
Macroprotodon, iii. 175
Macrops, ii 71.
macrops (Dendrophis), ii. 85
macrops (Oligolepis), iii. 644.
macrops (Pseudoxenodon), i. 270
macrops (Tropidonotus), i 270.
macrorhina (Dipsas), iii. 83
macrorhinum (Rhinobothryum), iii 82
macrorhynchum (Stenostoma), i. 61
macrorhynchus (Glauconia), i. 61.
macrorhynchus (Silybura), i 153.
macroscelis (Cylindrophis), i. 137.
Macrosoma, iii 167.
macrostemma (Eutainia), i. 211, iii 602
macrostemma (Tropidonotus), i. 211; iii. 602.
Macrostomata, i 71, 169.
macrurus (Calamaria), ii. 344.
macrurus (Onychocephalus), i. 32.
macularius (Amblycephalus), iii. 444.
macularius (Pareas), iii. 444.
maculata (Anguis), i. 136.
maculata (Cylindrophis), i 136
maculata (Denisonia), iii. 341
maculata (Dipsadoboa), iii. 43
maculata (Ficimia), ii. 268.
maculata (Hydrophis), iii. 267
maculata (Hypsirhina), iii. 8, 10.
maculata (Ilysia), i 136.
maculata (Isoscelis), ii. 306
maculata (Naja), iii 380.
maculata (Oxyrhina), ii. 268.
maculata (Parias), iii 548.
maculata (Silybura), i 149.

ALPHABETICAL INDEX. 689

maculata (Ungalia), i. 112, 113, iii 594
maculatum (Nymphophidium). i. 371.
maculatum (Rhabdosoma), ii. 305, 306, 307, 308.
maculatus (Anoplophallus), ii 353
maculatus (Atractus), ii 306, iii 645.
maculatus(Chilabothrus), i 98.
maculatus (Coluber), i. 405, ii. 39.
maculatus (Conopsis), ii. 268
maculatus (Corallus), i. 101.
maculatus (Cyclochorus), iii 33
maculatus (Cylindrophis), i 136, iii. 595.
maculatus (Distichurus), iii. 467.
maculatus (Eryx), i. 127.
maculatus (Hoplocephalus), iii 341
maculatus (Leionotus), i 112.
maculatus (Megalops), ii 353
maculatus (Oxyrhopus), iii 110
maculatus (Stenophis), iii. 43.
maculatus (Streptophorus), i 293
maculatus (Tortrix), i 136
maculatus (Trimesurus), iii. 562
maculatus (Tropidonotus), i 225, 258, 260, iii 608.
maculatus (Tropidophis), i. 112, 113
maculiceps (Callophis), iii. 397
maculiceps (Elaps), iii 397
maculivittis (Alsophis), ii 11
maculivittis (Dromicus), ii. 11.
maculolineata (Calamaria), ii 336.
maculosa (Calamaria), ii 345
maculosa (Hypsirhina), iii. 10.
VOL. III.

maculosus (Lasis), i. 77.
madagascariensis (Anomalodon), i 269
madagascariensis (Boa), i 120, iii 594.
madagascariensis (Corallus), i. 103.
madagascariensis (Dromicus), i 248
madagascariensis (Heterodon), i. 269.
madagascariensis (Langaha), iii. 36
madagascariensis (Lioheterodon), i 269.
madagascariensis (Mimophis), iii 171.
madagascariensis (Pelophilus), i 120
madagascariensis (Sanzinia). i. 103
madagascariensis (Typhlops), i. 25
madagascariensis (Xiphosoma), i 103.
madarensis (Vipera), i. 101.
madcnsis (Tropidonotus), i. 256
maderensis (Coluber), i 191.
madurensis (Platyplectrurus), i 166.
madurensis (Silybura), i. 156, iii 596
maeoticus(Coluber), ii 44.
magnus (Lycodon), i. 365.
mahfalensis (Mimophis), iii. 171
mahfalensis (Psammophis), iii. 171.
Mainophis, i 305
mairii (Tropidonotus), iii. 602.
majalis (Leptophis), ii 258
majalis (Philophyllophis), ii. 258
major (Ablabes), ii. 279.
major (Atractus), ii. 307.
major (Cyclophis), ii. 279.
major (Distira), iii. 289.
major (Hydrophis), iii. 289
major (Hydrus), iii. 288, 289
major (Trimorphodon), iii. 54.

malabaricus (Cophias), iii. 558.
malabaricus (Cynophis), ii 36
malabaricus (Elaps), iii. 394.
malabaricus (Herpetodryas), ii. 36
malabaricus (Trigonocephalus), iii 558
malaccana (Asthenodipsas), iii 442.
malaccanus(Amblycephalus), iii 442
malayana (Callophis), iii. 402
malayanus (Adeniophis), iii 402.
malignus (Coluber), i 349
malignus (Lycodon), i. 349
Malpolon, iii. 141.
mamillaris (Anguis), iii. 277
mamillaris (Hydrophis), iii. 277
mancus(Leptophis), ii 88
mandarinus (Coluber), ii. 62
mandensis(Typhlops), iii. 587.
maniar (Dendrophis), ii. 88
manillensis (Elaphis), ii 62.
Manolepis, iii 120.
maregravii (Elaps), iii. 419, 423, 427, 428, 432.
marciana (Eutainia), i. 210; iii 602.
marcianus (Tropidonotus), i 210; iii 602
margaritatum (Gonyosoma), ii 71.
margaritatus (Gonyophis), ii 71
margaritifera (Calamaria), ii. 336
margaritiferus (Coryphodon), ii 196.
margaritiferus (Dromicus), ii 17
margaritiferus (Drymobius), ii. 17, iii 626.
margaritiferus (Herpetodryas), ii. 17
margaritiferus (Leptophis), ii. 17.
margaritiferus (Masticophis), iii 626

2 Y

margaritiferus (Thamnophis), ii. 17.
margaritophora (Calamaria), ii. 336.
margaritophorus (Aipysurus), iii. 304.
margaritophorus (Amblycephalus), iii. 445.
margaritophorus (Leptognathus), iii. 445.
margaritophorus (Pareas), iii. 445.
marginatus (Helicops), i. 281.
marginatus (Leptophis), ii. 112; iii 633.
marginatus (Thrasops), ii 113.
marmorata (Cenchris), iii. 522.
maroccanus (Macroprotodon), iii. 175.
martapurensis (Calamaria), ii. 344.
martensii (Tropidonotus), i. 221.
martii (Calopisma), ii. 187.
martii (Homalopsis), ii. 187.
martii (Hydrops), ii. 187; iii 637.
martii (Pseuderyx), iii. 637.
massasauga (Crotalophorus), iii 571.
mastersii (Hoplocephalus), iii 336.
Masticophis, i. 379.
Maticora, iii 399.
mattazoi (Elaps), iii 362.
Maudia, i 160.
maura (Hypsirhina), i. 340.
mauritanica (Bitis), iii. 488.
mauritanica (Clotho), iii. 488.
mauritanica (Echidna), iii 488.
mauritanica (Vipera), iii. 488.
mauritanicus (Macroprotodon), iii. 175.
maurus (Coluber), i 235.
maurus (Epicrates), i. 94.
maximiliani (Coluber), iii. 57.
mayottensis (Ablabes), i. 183.

mayottensis (Enicognathus), i. 183.
mayottensis (Polyodontophis), i. 183.
mechovii (Xenocalamus), iii. 248.
medici (Dipsas), ii. 355.
Meditoria, i. 7.
medusa (Tropidonotus), i. 238.
meeki (Dendrophis), iii. 629.
Megablabes, i. 379.
Megaera, iii 529.
megaera (Bothrops), iii. 535, 538.
megaera (Coluber), iii 535.
Megaerophis, iii 365.
megalolepis (Spilotes), ii. 24.
Megalops, ii. 353.
megalops (Eutainia), i. 212, iii 602.
megaspilus (Trigonocephalus), iii 525.
Meizodon, ii. 188.
melanauchen (Enicognathus), ii. 175.
melanauchen (Rhadinaea), ii. 175.
melanichnus (Alsophis), ii. 122.
melanis (Vipera), iii. 476.
melanis (Coluber), iii. 476.
melanocephala (Calamaria), iii. 215.
melanocephala (Coronella), ii. 246.
melanocephala (Duberria), iii. 215.
melanocephala (Rhadinaea), i 100.
melanocephala (Tachymenis), iii. 205.
melanocephala (Tantilla), iii. 215.
melanocephalum (Homalocranium), iii. 215, 218, 220.
melanocephalum (Homalosoma), ii 246.
melanocephalus (Ablabes), i 185.
melanocephalus (Aspidiotes), i. 91.
melanocephalus (Aspidites), i 91; iii. 592.
melanocephalus (Cathetorhinus), i. 15.

melanocephalus (Coluber), iii. 215.
melanocephalus (Dromicus), ii. 173.
melanocephalus (Elaps), iii. 215.
melanocephalus (Enicognathus), i 186, ii. 172, 174.
melanocephalus (Erythrolamprus), iii. 205.
melanocephalus (Hydrophis), iii 283.
melanocephalus (Lycodon), i. 185.
melanocephalus (Oligodon), ii. 246.
melanocephalus (Polyodontophis), i. 185.
melanocephalus (Rhynchocalamus), ii. 246.
melanocephalus (Typhlops), i. 15.
melanocrotaphus (Oxyropus), iii 90.
melanogaster (Crealia), i. 146.
melanogaster (Eutaenia), i 226, iii. 604.
melanogaster (Hydraethiops), i 281, iii 610.
melanogaster (Mytilia), i 146.
melanogaster (Rhinophis), i. 146.
melanogaster (Silybura), i. 146, 151.
melanogaster (Tropidonotus), i 225; iii 604.
melanogenys (Elaps), iii. 427.
melanogenys (Oxyrhopus), iii 105.
melanogenys (Sphenocephalus), iii. 105.
melanoleuca (Naia), iii. 376.
melanoleucus (Coluber), ii 68.
melanoleucus (Pituophis), ii. 68.
melanolomus (Masticophis), ii 11.
melanolomus (Zamenis), ii 12.
melanonotus (Liophis), ii. 134.
Melanophidium, i 163.
melanopleurus (Phalotris), iii 242.

melanorhynchus (Calamaria), ii 333
melanosoma (Distira), iii. 291
melanosoma (Hydrophis), iii 291
melanostigma (Dendrophis), ii 99
melanostigma (Dromicus), ii 142.
melanostigma (Liophis), ii 142
melanostigma (Natrix), ii 142
melanota (Calamaria), ii. 349, iii 648
melanotænia (Elaps), iii. 403
melanotænia (Eutænia), i 211
melanoterma (Stenostoma), i. 63, iii 591
melanotropis (Coluber), ii 33
melanotropis (Crossanthera), iii 626
melanotropis (Dendrophidium), ii 33
melanotropis (Elaphis), ii 33
melanotus (Coluber), ii. 134
melanotus (Cylindrophis), i 135.
melanotus (Dromicus), i 248, ii. 134.
melanotus (Elaps), iii. 433
melanotus (Liophis), ii 134.
melanotus (Triglyphodon), iii 71.
melanozostus (Bothrophthalmus), i 324
melanozostus (Tropidonotus), i 230
melanura (Boa), i 111
melanura (Denisonia), iii. 345.
melanura (Ungalia), i. 111, iii. 593
melanurum (Compsosoma), ii 60, 62
melanurus (Coluber), ii. 60; iii 397
melanurus (Elaphis), ii. 60, 62
melanurus (Elaps), iii. 397
melanurus (Hoplocephalus), iii 345.

melanurus (Hydrophis), iii 273
melanurus (Spilotes), ii. 31, 35, 60, 62.
melanurus (Tropidophis), i 111
melas (Herpetodryas), ii 76, iii 628.
meleagris (Calamaria), ii. 249.
meleagris (Lycophidium), i 337.
meleagris (Opheomorphus), ii 132.
meleagris (Prosymna), ii. 249, iii. 641
meleagris (Temnorhynchus), ii 249
mentalis (Boodon), i. 335.
mentalis (Dromicus), iii. 137.
mentalis (Elaps), iii. 432.
mentalis (Hydrophis), iii. 289
mentovarium (Bascanium), i. 389
mentovarius (Coluber), i 389.
mentovarius (Coryphodon), i 389.
mentovarius (Zamenis), i 389, iii 621.
meridionalis (Bothrops), iii 542
meridionalis (Coluber), ii 194.
meridionalis (Coronella), ii. 194
merremi (Boa), i 101.
merremii (Coluber), ii 168.
merremii (Coronella), ii. 131, 168.
merremii (Liophis), ii. 131, 138, 168, 169
merremii (Ophiomorphus), ii 168, 169
merremii (Ophis), ii 150
merremii (Rhadinæa), ii. 168.
merremii (Xenodon), ii. 150.
mesomelana (Regina), i 226
mesomelanus (Tropidonotus), i. 225.
Mesopeltis, iii. 446.
Mesotes, iii. 115, 117.
messasaugus (Crotalus), iii 570

Metoporhina, i. 336.
mexicana (Ahætulla), ii. 108.
mexicana (Anomalepis), i. 59.
mexicana (Boa), i. 119.
mexicana (Coronella), ii. 201.
mexicana (Phimothyra), i. 392
mexicana (Salvadora), i. 392
mexicania (Bergenia), iii. 229.
mexicanum (Bascanium), iii 622.
mexicanum (Homalocranium), iii 215.
mexicanus (Anomalepis), i. 59.
mexicanus (Atropos), iii. 544.
mexicanus (Bothriechis), iii. 544
mexicanus (Bothriopsis), iii. 545.
mexicanus (Bothrops), iii 545.
mexicanus (Cerastes), ii. 33
mexicanus (Chilomeniscus), iii. 230.
mexicanus (Coluber), i. 392
mexicanus (Elapomorphus), iii. 215
mexicanus (Hapsidophrys), ii. 108
mexicanus (Leptophis), ii 108
mexicanus (Lytorhynchus), i 392
mexicanus (Masticophis), i 392
mexicanus (Ophibolus), ii. 201
mexicanus (Pituophis), ii. 66, 69
mexicanus (Thrasops), ii. 108
mexicanus (Zamenis), i. 392; iii 622
meyerinkii (Simotes), ii. 224
michahelles (Xenodon), ii. 65.
michoacanense (Homalocranium), iii 211
michoacanensis (Contia), iii. 211

2 y 2

ALPHABETICAL INDEX.

michoacanensis (Elapomorphus), iii. 211.
michoacanensis (Elaps), iii. 423.
michoacanensis (Scolecophis), iii. 211.
Micrelaps, iii. 248
microcephala (Hydrophis), iii. 280.
microcephala (Thalassophis), iii 280
Microcephalophis, iii. 271.
microcephalum (Rhabdosoma), i. 304.
microcephalus (Geophis), i 304
Microdromus, iii. 212.
microlepidota (Atractaspis), iii 517
microlepidota (Diemenia), iii. 332
microlepidotus (Macrelaps), iii 255, 512
microlepidotus (Pseudechis), iii. 332
microlepidotus (Urυechis), iii 255.
microlepis (Cerberus), iii. 18.
microlepis (Loxodon), i 413
microlepis (Rhinophis), i 143
microlepis (Spalerosphis), i 413
microlepis (Zamenis), i. 413; iii 625.
Micropechis, iii 346
Microphis, iii 229
micropholis (Atractaspis), iii. 516.
micropholis (Coronella), ii 203, iii 638.
micropholis (Lampropeltis), ii 203
microphthalma (Amblyodipsas), iii. 244.
microphthalma (Calamaria), iii 244
microphthalmus (Bothrops), iii. 540.
microphthalmus (Lachesis), iii. 540.
Micropisthodon, iii. 614.
Microps, i. 285
microps (Coronella), i. 316.
microps (Pseudoxyrhopus), i. 315, iii 613.

microrhynchum (Rhabdosoma), ii 308.
Microsoma, iii. 249
microstomus (Typhlops), i 53
Micrurus, iii. 411
mikani (Leptognathus), iii 452, 453, 456.
mikanii (Anholodon), iii. 453
mikanii (Dipsas), iii. 453.
milberti (Erythrolamprus), iii 201.
miliaria (Caudisona), iii. 570.
miliaris (Anguis), i. 125.
miliaris (Coluber), ii. 168.
miliaris (Tortrix), i. 126.
miliarius (Crotalophorus), iii 570, 571.
miliarius (Crotalus), iii. 569, 571.
miliarius (Sistrurus), iii. 570.
mimeticus (Dimades), iii. 637.
mimeticus (Pseudoeryx), iii. 637.
Mimophis, iii. 171
mimus (Opheomorphus), ii 164
mimus (Rhadinæa), ii. 164.
minax (Natrix), i 219
mindorensis (Calamaria), iii. 646.
miniata. (Tantilla), iii. 222.
miniatum (Homalocranium), iii 222.
miniatus (Coluber), iii 35
miniatus (Dryophylax), iii. 35.
miniatus (Ithycyphus), iii. 35.
miniatus (Philodryas), iii 35.
minor (Elapognathus), iii 356.
minor (Hoplocephalus), iii. 356.
minuta (Vipera), iii 488.
minutus (Coluber), i. 219.
Miodon, iii 249.
miolepis (Calamelaps), iii. 246.
miolepis (Dromicus), ii. 175.

mipartitus (Elaps), iii. 431.
Miralia, ii. 2
mirus (Typhlops), i 52.
mitchelli (Caudisona), iii. 580
mitchelli (Crotalus), iii. 580
mite (Homalosoma), ii. 267
mitis (Contia), ii 267.
M-nigrum (Coluber), ii. 131.
mocquardii (Tetranorhinus), i. 283, iii 611.
modesta (Ahætulla), ii 107
modesta (Boa), i 101
modesta (Cacophis), iii. 324.
modesta (Calamaria), ii. 340; iii 647.
modesta (Contia), ii 261.
modesta (Coronella), ii. 260.
modesta (Diemenia), iii. 324
modestum (Brachyrhyton), i 366.
modestum (Lycodon), i. 366
modestum (Oxyrhabdium), i. 302
modestum (Rhabdosoma), i 302, 303
modestus (Ablabes), ii 260, 261, 262.
modestus (Amblycephalus), iii. 444
modestus (Atractus), ii. 304.
modestus (Boodon), i 344.
modestus (Bothrophthalmus), i 324
modestus (Cyclophis), ii. 261.
modestus (Dendrelaphis), ii. 91; iii. 630
modestus (Diadophis), ii. 208
modestus (Elapops), iii. 262, 649.
modestus (Euophrys), iii. 131.
modestus (Geophis), i. 302
modestus (Helicops), i 277.
modestus (Heterodon), i. 269.

modestus (Homalosoma), ii 260.
modestus (Hormonotus), i. 343; iii 617.
modestus (Lamprophis), i. 343.
modestus (Leptophis), ii. 107.
modestus (Lielaphis), i. 366, 367.
modestus (Lioheterodon), i 269
modestus (Lycodon), i 365, 366
modestus (Oligodon), ii. 238
modestus (Pareas), iii. 414.
modestus (Philothamnus), ii 107.
modestus (Stegonotus), i. 366
modestus (Stenognathus), i 302, 303
modestus (Tropidonotus), i. 229.
moellendorffii (Amblycephalus), iii. 443.
moellendorffii (Coluber), ii 56
moellendorffii (Cynophis), ii 56
moellendorffii (Pareas), iii. 443
moesta (Geophis), ii. 319.
moesta (Helicops), i 277.
moesta (Tantilla), iii. 225
moestum (Homalocranium), iii. 225
moestum (Rhabdosoma), ii. 319
moestus (Geophis), ii. 319.
moestus (Tropidonotus), i. 274.
moilensis (Coelopeltis), iii. 143.
moilensis (Coluber), iii. 143
mokasen (Agkistrodon), iii 522
mokeson (Cenchris), iii. 522
mokeson (Scytale), iii 522.
moliniger (Psammophis), i 189.
molorchinus (Philodryas), iii. 134.

molossus (Caudisona), iii. 574.
molossus (Coluber), ii. 39.
molossus (Crotalus), iii. 574.
molurus (Coluber), i 87.
molurus (Homalopsis), iii 14, 16.
molurus (Python), i. 87, 418
moniliger (Coluber), iii 161
moniliger (Psammophis), ii 261, iii 156, 157, 161, 164, 169
monilis (Coluber), iii. 14.
monilis (Homalopsis), iii. 14.
Monobothris, iii 633.
monochrous (Calamaria), ii. 340
monozona (Erythrolamprus), iii 201
monspeliensis (Coluber), iii. 142.
monspessulana (Coelopeltis), iii. 141.
monspessulanus (Coluber), iii 141
montanta (Vipera), iii. 496.
montanum (Pilidion), i 137.
montanus (Thanatophis), iii 544
monticola (Amblycephalus), iii 443.
monticola (Calamaria), i. 299.
monticola (Cyclophis), i. 299
monticola (Dipsas), ii. 280, iii 443.
monticola (Lachesis), iii. 548.
monticola (Pareas), iii. 443
monticola (Trachischium), i. 299, iii. 612
monticola , (Trimeresurus), iii. 548, 553
monticola (Tropidonotus), i 259; iii 608.
monticolus (Coluber), ii. 229
moreleti (Tropidonotus), i. 111.
moreleti (Ungalia), i 111.
Morelia, i 81.

mormon (Coluber), i. 387.
mormon (Masticophis), i. 387.
mortoni (Tropidonotus), i 267
mortuarius (Coluber), i. 230, 241.
mortuarius (Helicops), i. 241.
mortuarius (Tropidonotus), i 230, 241
mosis charas (Vipera), iii. 481.
mossambica (Naja), iii. 378.
mossambica (Dasypeltis), ii. 355.
mossambica (Psammophis), iii 162
mossambicus (Onychocephalus), i 41
mossambicus (Typhlops), i 41
mucosa (Natrix), i 385
mucosus (Coluber), i 385.
mucosus (Ptyas), i 385.
mucosus (Zamenis), i. 385, iii. 621
mucronatus (Typhlops), i. 37.
mucrosquamatus (Lachesis), iii. 552
mucrosquamatus (Trigonocephalus), iii. 552
mucrosquamatus (Trimeresurus), iii 552.
mucruso (Onychocephalus), i 46
mucruso (Typhlops), i. 46, iii. 588.
muelleri (Demansia), iii 316
muelleri (Denisonia), iii. 337.
muelleri (Diemenia), iii. 316
muelleri (Elaps), iii. 316.
muelleri (Eryx), i 128.
muelleri (Gongylophis), i 128
muelleri (Hoplocephalus), iii 337
muelleri (Micrelaps), iii. 249
muelleri (Platurus), iii. 309
muelleri (Pseudelaps), iii. 316.
muelleri (Stegonotus), i. 367

mulleri (Typhlops), i. 25.
mulleri (Herpetodryas), i. 367.
mulleri (Lycodon), i. 368.
mulleri (Odontomus), i. 368.
multicarinata (Bolieria), i. 122, iii. 595.
multicarinatus (Platygaster), i. 122.
multicinctum (Rhabdosoma), ii. 308.
multicinctus (Bungarus), iii. 368.
multicinctus (Dipsadomorphus), iii. 71.
multicinctus (Ophibolus), ii. 197.
multifasciata (Coronella), ii. 202.
multifasciata (Dipsas), iii. 69.
multifasciatus (Dipsadomorphus), iii. 69.
multifasciatus (Elaps), iii. 431.
multifasciatus (Mesopeltis), iii. 459.
multifasciatus (Oxyrhopus), iii. 101.
multifasciatus (Petalognathus), iii. 459.
multifasciatus (Simotes), ii. 222.
multilineata (Hypsirhina), iii. 10.
multilineatus (Dromicus), ii. 181.
multilineatus (Onychocephalus), i. 50.
multilineatus (Typhlops), i. 50.
multimaculata (Boiga), iii. 64.
multimaculata (Coronella), iii. 125, 148.
multimaculata (Dipsas), iii. 63.
multimaculata (Dipsina), iii. 148.
multimaculata (Eutænia), i. 214.
multimaculata (Lycophidium), i. 339.
multimaculata (Rhagerrhis), iii. 148.
multimaculatus (Amplorhinus), iii. 125.
multimaculatus (Atomarchus), i. 214.

multimaculatus (Crotalus), iii. 582.
multimaculatus (Dipsadomorphus), iii. 63.
multimaculatus (Psammophylax), iii. 125.
multimaculatus (Rhamphiophis), iii. 148.
multimaculatus (Tropidonotus), i. 214.
multipunctata (Calamaria), ii. 345.
multisectus (Homalochilus), i. 96.
multistratus (Ophibolus), ii. 201.
multistriata (Lampropeltis), ii. 201.
multocarinata (Eryx), i. 122.
murina (Boa), i. 115.
murinus (Enulius), ii. 250, iii. 641.
murinus (Eunectes), i. 115.
murorum (Natrix), i. 219.
muta (Boa), iii. 534.
mutabilis (Coluber), ii. 37.
mutabilis (Natrix), ii. 37.
mutabilis (Scotophis), ii. 37.
mutabilis (Trimeresurus), iii. 555.
mutitorques (Geophis), ii. 304.
mutitorques (Rhabdosoma), ii. 304.
mutus (Crotalus), iii. 534.
mutus (Lachesis), iii. 534, 544.
mycterizans (Coluber), iii. 182.
mycterizans (Dryinus), iii. 182.
mycterizans (Dryophis), iii. 182.
mycterizans (Passerita), iii. 183, 184.
myhendræ (Silybura), i. 156; iii. 596.
myopica (Glauconia), i. 69.
myopicum (Stenostoma), i. 69.
myriolepis (Lichanura), i. 129.
Myron, i. 272, iii. 19.

mystacina (Leptodira), iii. 92.
mystacinum (Sibon), iii. 92.
Mytilia, i. 140, 144.

Naja, iii. 327, 346, 348, 372, 388, 390, 465.
naja (Coluber), iii. 380.
naja (Vipera), iii. 380.
najadum (Tyria), i. 397.
Najidæ, iii. 310.
Najinæ, iii. 310.
napei (Lycodon), i. 349.
Nardoa, i. 75, 76.
narduccii (Elaps), iii. 433.
narirostre (Stenostoma), i. 65.
narirostris (Glauconia), i. 65, iii. 591.
nasale (Catostoma), ii. 318.
nasale (Rhabdosoma), ii. 318.
nasalis (Causus), iii. 468.
nasalis (Cyclophis), ii. 282.
nasicornis (Bitis), iii. 500.
nasicornis (Cerastes), iii. 499.
nasicornis (Clotho), iii. 500.
nasicornis (Coluber), iii. 500.
nasicornis (Echidna), iii. 500.
nasicornis (Vipera), iii. 500.
nasicus (Heterodon), ii. 156.
nasua (Vipera), iii. 114.
nasus (Bothrops), iii. 543.
nasus (Conopsis), ii. 268.
nasus (Coutia), ii. 268.
nasus (Ficimia), ii. 268.
nasus (Rhinoccrophis), iii. 543.
nasuta (Langaha), iii. 36.
nasuta (Meditoria), i. 31.
nasutus (Anguis), i. 27.
nasutus (Bothrops), iii. 547.
nasutus (Coluber), iii. 182.
nasutus (Dryinus), iii. 180, 182.

ALPHABETICAL INDEX. 695

nasutus (Dryophis), iii. 183.
nasutus (Manolepis), iii. 120.
nasutus (Porthidium), iii. 547
nasutus (Tomodon), iii. 120.
nasuum (Rhinostoma), iii 114
natalensis (Ahætulla), ii. 94.
natalensis (Atractaspis), iii 512.
natalensis (Chlorophis), ii 94
natalensis (Dendrophis), ii. 94.
natalensis (Hortulia), i. 86.
natalensis (Philothamnus), ii. 94.
natalensis (Python), i 86, iii. 592.
Natricidæ, i 177, iii. 597.
Natricinæ, iii 597.
Natrix, i. 192', ii. 24, 25
natrix (Coluber), i 219.
natrix (Tropidonotus), i. 219, 419, iii 603
nattereri (Coluber), iii 116
nattereri (Dipsas), iii 116
nattereri (Heterodon), ii. 152.
nattereri (Philodryas), iii. 134.
nattereri (Thamnodynastes) iii 116.
nattereri (Tropidonotus), iii 116
nauii (Coluber), ii 45
Nauticophes, iii. 264.
nebulatus (Cerastes), ii 293.
nebulatus (Coluber), ii. 293.
nebulatus (Dipsas), ii 293
nebulatus (Leptognathus), ii 293, iii 644.
nebulatus (Petalognathus), ii 293.
nebulatus (Sibon), iii. 644.
nebulosus (Cyclophis), ii. 278.
nebulosus (Coluber), ii. 192
Neelaps, iii 405.

neelgherriensis(Cophias), iii 549.
neelgherriensis (Trigonocephalus), iii. 549.
neglecta (Ahætulla), ii 94
neglectus (Chlorophis), ii 94; iii 631
neglectus (Dendraspis), iii. 436.
neglectus (Periops), i 407
neglectus (Philothamnus), 94
neglectus (Zamenis), i. 407.
Neopareas, iii 446.
Neospades, iii 19.
neovidii (Xenodon), ii. 148
nepa (Coluber), iii 39, 528
nepa (Hypnale), iii. 528
Nerodia, i. 193
neumayeri (Coluber), iii. 142.
Neusterophis, i 193.
neuwiedii (Bothrops), iii. 542
neuwiedii (Elapomorphus), iii. 253.
neuwiedii (Lachesis), iii 542
neuwiedii (Microsoma), iii. 253.
neuwiedii (Miodon), iii. 253
neuwiedii(Oxyrhopus),iii. 112
neuwiedii (Pseudoboa), iii 112
neuwiedii (Scytale), iii. 112, 113
neuwiedii (Trigonocephalus), iii 542
neuwiedii (Urobelus), iii. 253
neuwiedii (Xenodon), ii. 148.
newtoni (Onychocephalus), i 55.
newtonii (Typhlops), i. 55
nicaga (Rhadinæa), ii. 174.
nicagus (Lygophis), ii. 174.
nicagus (Tæniophallus), iii 635
nicobariensis (Ablabes), ii 285

nicobariensis (Tropidonotus), i. 192
niger (Elapechis), iii. 359
niger (Hapsidophrys), ii 105
niger (Heterodon), ii 155
niger (Nerodia), i. 243.
niger (Ophibolus), ii 197.
niger (Scytale), ii 154
niger (Tropidonotus), i. 242
nigra(Elapsoidea),iii.359
nigra (Hydrophis), iii 274
nigra (Naja), iii. 376, 380
nigra (Pseudohaje), iii 388.
nigra (Silybura), i. 151.
nigra (Tropidonotus), i. 219
nigrescens (Anilios), i 34.
nigrescens (Callophis), iii 394.
nigrescens (Demisonia), iii. 343
nigrescens (Hemibungarus), iii. 394
nigrescens (Hoplocephalus), iii 343
nigrescens (Typhlops), i. 35, iii 586.
nigricans (Chersodromus), i 295.
nigricans (Glauconia), i. 67, iii 591
nigricans (Stenostoma), i. 67
nigricans (Typhlops), i. 67
nigricauda (Typhlops), iii 586.
nigricaudus (Allophis), ii 58
nigricaudus (Elaphis), ii 58
nigriceps (Aparallactus), iii. 260
nigriceps (Dipsadomorphus), iii. 72
nigriceps (Dipsas), iii 72.
nigriceps (Hoplocephalus), iii, 342
nigriceps (Tantilla), iii. 226.
nigriceps (Uriechis), iii. 260
nigricollis (Coluber), ii. 260.

nigricollis (Naia), iii 378, 649.
nigroadspersus (Bothrops), iii 567
nigroadspersus (Teleuraspis), iii. 567
nigro-alba (Calamaria), ii. 344.
nigroalbus (Typhlops), i. 24.
nigrocincta (Hydrophis), iii 273, 283, 292.
nigrocincta (Elaps), iii. 423.
nigrocinctus (Enhydris), iii 277.
nigrocinctus (Hydrophis), iii. 273, 277.
nigrocinctus (Hydrus), iii. 277, 283, 299.
nigrocinctus (Tropidonotus), i. 255; iii. 608.
nigrofasciata (Leptodira), iii. 92
nigrofasciatum (Sibon), iii. 92.
nigrofasciatus (Coluber), iii. 200
nigrofasciatus (Philothamnus), ii. 99.
nigrofasciatus (Psammophis), ii 34.
nigrolateris (Eutænia), i. 210.
nigrolineata (Apostolepis), iii 235
nigrolineatus (Elapomorphus), iii. 235.
nigrolineatus (Onychocephalus), i 42.
nigrolutea (Regina), i 282.
nigroluteus (Helicops), i 282.
nigroluteus (Tretanorhinus), i. 282; iii. 610.
nigromaculatus (Alopecion), iii. 617.
nigromaculatus (Elaps), iii 396
nigromaculatus (Lycophidium), i. 340
nigromarginata (Ahætulla), ii 112.
nigromarginata (Dipsas), iii. 72
nigromarginatus (Bothrops), iii 559
nigromarginatus (Coluber), i. 376.

nigromarginatus (Cophias), iii 559
nigromarginatus (Leptophis), ii. 112, iii. 633.
nigromarginatus (Trigonocephalus), iii. 559.
nigromarginatus (Zaocys), i 376.
nigrostriata (Denisonia), ii. 343
nigrostriatus (Hoplocephalus), iii. 343
nigrotæniatus (Adeniophis), iii. 402.
nigrotæniatus (Callophis), iii 402
nigroterminata (Apostolepis), iii 235.
nigroviridis (Bothriechis), iii. 568.
nigroviridis (Bothrops), iii. 568.
nigroviridis (Lachesis), iii. 568.
nigrum (Boædon), i. 331.
nilgherriensis (Silybura), i. 156, 157, 158
Ninia, i 291.
nitida (Ahætulla), ii 100, 101
nitida (Silybura), i. 151.
nitida (Teleuraspis), iii. 567
nitidus (Lachesis), iii. 567.
nitidus (Philothamnus), ii 100.
nivea (Naja), iii. 376.
nivea (Vipera), iii 374.
niveus (Coluber), iii 374.
non naja (Naja), iii 380.
notæus (Eunectes), iii. 594.
notata (Bothriechis), iii. 544.
notatum (Microsoma), iii. 252
notatus (Miodon), iii. 252.
Notechis, iii. 351
Nothopidæ, i. 169, 172.
Nothopsis, i. 176.
Notophis, i 110.
notospilus (Oligodon), ii. 239.
notostictus (Psammophis), iii 156.
nototænia (Amphiophis), iii. 125.
nototænia (Amplorhinus), iii 125
nototænia (Coronella), iii 125.

nototænia (Hemirhagerrhis), iii 125.
nototænia (Psammophylax), iii. 125
nototænia (Tachymenis), iii. 125.
novæ-hispaniæ (Coluber), ii. 33.
nuchalis (Diemenia), iii. 326
nuchalis (Dipsas), iii 66.
nuchalis (Herpetodryas), ii. 15.
nuchalis (Pseudonaja), iii. 326
nuchalis (Trirbinopholis), i 419; iii 612.
nuchalis (Tropidonotus), i. 218.
nummifer (Atropos), iii. 544.
nummifer (Bothrops), iii. 544.
nummifer (Coluber), i. 407.
nummifer (Lachesis), iii. 544.
nummifer (Teleuraspis), iii 544.
nummifer (Thanatophis), iii 545
nummifer (Trigonocephalus), iii 544
nummifer (Zamenis), i. 407; iii 625.
nummifera (Bothriechis), iii. 544
nuntius (Dromicus), ii. 181.
nursii (Glauconia), iii. 591.
nuthalli (Coluber), ii. 47.
nyassæ (Simocephalus), i. 347
nyctenurus (Elaphis), ii. 64.
Nympha, i. 369.
nympha (Coluber), i. 370.
nympha (Dryocalamus), i 370
nympha (Hydrophobus), i. 370.
nympha (Lycodon), i. 370
nympha (Odontomus), i. 370
Nymphophidium, i. 369.

oatesii (Eryiophis), iii. 185

oatesii (Typhlops), i. 23.
oaxaca (Bascanion), i. 386
oaxaca (Coryphodon), i 386.
oaxacæ (Zamenis), i. 386.
obliquus (Tropidonotus), i. 243.
obscura (Eutænia), i. 207.
obscura (Hydrophis), iii 281.
obscuro-striata (Calamaria), i. 297.
obscuro-striatum (Trachischium), i 298.
obscurus (Hydrophis), iii 284, 294.
obscurus (Pelamis), iii. 284
obscurus (Simotes), ii. 219
obscurus (Trimeresurus), iii 553
obsoleta (Georgia), ii 31
obsoletus (Coluber), ii 31, 50.
obsoletus (Elaphis), ii 50
obsoletus (Scotophis), ii. 50
obsoletus (Spilotes), ii 31
obtrusus (Mesotes), iii. 116.
obtusa (Coronella), ii. 171.
obtusa (Rhadinæa), ii 171.
obtusa (Vipera), iii 487
obtusirostris (Corallus), i 101
obtusus (Coluber), iii 52.
obtusus (Onychocephalus), i. 38.
obtusus (Tarbophis), iii. 52
obtusus (Telescopus), iii. 52
obtusus (Typhlops), i. 38, iii. 586.
occidentalis (Abætulla), ii 111
occidentalis (Boa), i 118; iii. 594.
occidentalis (Drymobius), ii 17
occidentalis (Leptophis), ii. 111, iii 633.
occidentalis (Thrasops), ii. 111.

occipitale (Lamprosoma), ii 266.
occipitale (Rabdion), iii. 319.
occipitale (Rhinostoma), ii 266
occipitalis (Ablabes), ii. 206.
occipitalis (Calamaria), ii 342.
occipitalis (Chionactis), ii. 266
occipitalis (Contia), ii. 266
occipitalis (Diadophis), ii 206
occipitalis (Elaps), iii. 407.
occipitalis (Enicognathus), ii. 175.
occipitalis (Furina), iii 407.
occipitalis (Herpetodryas), ii 30
occipitalis (Natrix), iii. 108.
occipitalis (Ophibolus), ii. 203.
occipitalis (Pseudoxyrhopus), iii 613
occipitalis (Rhadinæa), ii. 175, iii 635
occipitalis (Vermicella) iii 407
occipito-album (Rhabdosoma), ii 310.
occipito-albus (Atractus), ii. 310.
occipitoluteum (Brachyruton), iii 110.
occipitoluteus (Oxyrhopus), iii 110.
occipitomaculata (Storeria), i. 287; iii 611.
occipitomaculatus (Coluber), i 287.
occipitomaculatus (Ischnognathus), i 287, iii. 611.
ocellata (Calechidna), iii. 496
ocellata (Cenchris), i. 107
ocellata (Coluber), i 397.
ocellata (Echidna), iii. 496
ocellata (Eutænia), i. 209.
ocellata (Hemidipsas), iii 620
ocellata (Hydrophis), iii. 290.

ocellata (Leptodira), iii. 94.
ocellata (Natrix), i. 235.
ocellata (Silybura), i. 150
ocellata (Tyria), i 397
ocellata (Vipera), iii 482, 487, 498
ocellatus (Cerastes), iii. 498.
ocellatus (Coluber), iii. 620
ocellatus (Erythrolamprus), iii 201.
ocellatus (Psammophylax), iii 138
ocellatus (Tomodon), iii. 121, 649.
ocellatus (Tropidonotus), i 236.
ocellatus (Xenodon), ii. 150.
ochracea (Dipsas), iii. 65.
ochracea (Silybura), i. 150.
ochraceus (Micropisthodon), iii 614.
ochrorhynchus (Hypsiglena), ii 209
octolineata (Coronella), ii 224
octolineata (Dendrophis), ii 89
octolineatus (Coluber), ii. 224
octolineatus (Elaps), ii 224.
octolineatus (Simotes), ii. 224; iii 640.
Ocyophis, ii. 118.
Odontomus, i. 369
Ogmius, iii. 228
Ogmodon, iii. 312
okinavensis (Lachesis), iii. 549.
okinavensis (Trimeresurus), iii. 549
oldhami (Chlorophis), ii. 93
oldhami (Cyclophis), ii. 93
olfersii (Coluber), iii 129.
olfersii (Dryophylax), iii. 129.
olfersii (Herpetodryas), iii. 129
olfersii (Philodryas), iii. 129.
Oligodon, ii. 233
oligodon (Calamaria), ii. 237.

Oligodonta, i 169.
Oligodontidæ, i. 177.
Oligodontinæ, iii. 597
Oligolepis, iii. 643
oligozona (Coronella), ii. 203.
Olisthenes, iii 99.
olivacea (Ablabes), i 300.
olivacea (Abætula), ii 82.
olivacea (Boodon), i. 335, iii. 616
olivacea (Coronella), i 217, 227, iii 604
olivacea (Demansia), iii. 323
olivacea (Dendrophis), ii. 82.
olivacea (Diemenia), iii 323
olivacea (Ficimia), ii. 270, 271.
olivacea (Megæra), iii. 559
olivacea (Mizodon), i. 227
olivaceus (Holuropholis), i. 335.
olivaceus (Homalopsis), iii. 7.
olivaceus (Leptophis), i. 383
olivaceus (Liasis), i. 78, 79.
olivaceus (Lycodon), iii 323.
olivaceus (Megablabes), i. 383.
olivaceus (Mizodon), iii. 604.
olivaceus (Onychocephalus), i. 50
olivaceus (Onychophis), i 50.
olivaceus (Pseudocyclophis), i 300
olivaceus (Rhabdops), i. 300
olivaceus (Trimesurus), iii 336
olivaceus (Tropidonotus), i 227, iii. 604
olivaceus (Typhlops), i. 50.
olivaceus (Zamenis), i. 383.
omiltemana (Geophis), ii. 299.
omiltemanum (Dirosema), ii. 299.
omiltemanus (Crotalus), iii. 581
omiltemanus (Dromicus), ii. 178.

Onychocephalus, i. 7
Opetiodon, iii. 59
Ophibolus, ii 188
Ophielaps, i 308
Ophiomorphus, ii. 160, iii 634
Ophiophagus, iii. 373.
ophiophagus (Hamadryas), iii 386
ophiophagus (Trimeresurus), iii. 347, 386.
Ophirhina, iii 620
Ophis, ii 144.
ophiteoides (Lycodon), i. 356
Ophites, i 348
ophrias (Boa), 118.
Ophryacus, iii 530.
Ophryas, iii. 354.
ophryomegas (Bothriechis), iii 546
ophryomegas (Bothriopsis), iii 546
ophryomegas (Bothrops), iii 546.
Ophthalmidion, i 7
Opisthiodon, i 295
Opisthoglypha, iii. 1
Opisthoglyphes, i 169.
Opisthotropis, i 283.
Opisthoplus, iii. 120.
Oplocephalus, iii 348.
Opotérodontes, i. 3, 57.
oppeln (Tropidonotus), i. 236.
orbiculata (Boa), i 87.
orbignyi (Apostolepis), iii 236
orbignyi (Elapomorphus), iii 236
orcuttii (Lichanura), i. 129
ordinata (Boa), i. 87.
ordinata (Eutainia), i. 206
ordinatus (Coluber), i. 205, 206, 286
ordinatus (Python), i 87.
ordinatus (Tropidonotus), i 201, 202, 205, 206, 207, 208, iii. 600.
ordinoides (Eutainia), i. 208.
oreas (Leptognathus), iii. 453
oregonensis (Crotalus), iii. 580
oregonus (Crotalus), iii. 576, 580
orientalis (Caudisona), iii 573.

orientalis (Coronella), ii. 167
orientalis (Ophites), i. 363.
orientalis (Tropidonotus), i. 249
ornata (Aturia), iii 290.
ornata (Boa), i 124.
ornata (Chrysopelea), iii. 196, 198
ornata (Dendrophis), iii 196, 198
ornata (Denisonia), iii 341.
ornata (Dipsas), iii 81.
ornata (Distira), iii 290.
ornata (Eutainia), i. 207.
ornata (Ficimia), ii. 271.
ornata (Grayia), iii 643.
ornata (Hydrophis), iii. 290.
ornata (Hypsiglena), ii. 211.
ornata (Liophis), ii 138.
ornata (Megæra), iii 556.
ornata (Parias), iii. 556
ornata (Pelamis), iii 267.
ornata (Tyria), iii 196
ornaticeps (Diemenia), iii. 324.
ornaticeps (Elapocephalus), iii 324
ornaticeps (Elapocranium), iii 324
ornatissimus (Elaps), iii. 420
ornatum (Bascanium), i. 391.
ornatum (Xiphosoma), i. 101.
ornatus (Ablabes), i 185.
ornatus (Chlorophis), ii. 93, iii. 631.
ornatus (Coluber), ii. 139, 196
ornatus (Comastes), ii. 211.
ornatus (Crotalus), iii. 574.
ornatus (Dromicus), ii. 139
ornatus (Elaps), iii 319
ornatus (Enicognathus), i. 185
ornatus (Glyphodon), iii. 319
ornatus (Hoplocephalus), ii. 341
ornatus (Leptophis), iii. 196, 198
ornatus (Liophis), ii. 13

ornatus (Macrophis), ii. 287
ornatus (Masticophis), i. 391
ornatus (Philothamnus), ii 93, iii 631
ornatus (Tropidonotus), i 238
ornatus (Zamenis), iii 622
Orophis, ii 118.
ortonii (Boa), i. 119.
ortonii (Leptophis), ii 114.
Osceola, ii 188
oular-awa (Coluber), iii 597
ovivorus (Coluber), ii. 291.
owenii (Ablabes), ii 282.
oxiana (Naja), iii. 380.
oxiana (Tomyris), iii 380.
Oxybelis, iii 184, 189.
Oxycalamus, ii 328.
Oxycéphaliens, iii 26
oxycephalum (Gonyosoma), ii. 57.
oxycephalum (Pseudorhabdium), ii 329
oxycephalum (Rhabdosoma), ii 329.
oxycephalus (Coluber), ii. 56, 357, iii. 627.
oxycephalus (Herpetodryas), ii 57
oxycephalus (Oxycalamus), ii 329
Oxyorrhos, i. 305.
Oxyrhabdium, i 302
Oxyrhina, ii 255
Oxyrhopus, iii 56, 58, 99
oxyrhyncha (Ahætulla), ii 117
oxyrhyncha (Leptophis), ii 117
oxyrhynchus (Cœlopeltis), iii 146.
oxyrhynchus (Dryinus), iii 183.
oxyrhynchus (Psammophis), iii 146.
oxyrhynchus (Pseudo-Typhlops), i. 141.
oxyrhynchus (Rhagerrhis), iii 146
oxyrhynchus (Rhamphiophis), iii. 146
oxyrhynchus (Rhinophis), i 141, iii. 596
oxyrhynchus (Typhlops), i. 141

oxyrhynchus (Uromacer), ii 117
pachycercos (Hydrophis), iii 297.
pachycercus (Distira), iii 297
pachyura (Contia), ii. 267.
pacifica (Leptodira), iii 91
pacificum (Sibon), iii 91.
pacificus (Hydrophis), iii. 278
pallasii (Halys), iii 524.
pallida (Dipsas), iii 75.
pallida (Letheobia), i 54
pallida (Tantilla), iii 217.
pallidiceps (Denisonia), iii 344
pallidiceps (Hoplocephalus), iii 314, 349.
pallidus (Crotalus), iii. 581.
pallidus (Diadophis), ii. 206.
pallidus (Typhlops), i. 54.
palmarum (Coluber), ii. 354
palmarum (Dasypeltis), ii 355.
palmeri (Crotalus), iii 582.
palpebrosa (Boa), iii 355
palustris (Hydrus), i 230
pammeces (Typhlops), i. 16.
pannonicus (Coluber), ii 52
pantherinus (Coluber), ii 10, 40
pantherinus (Coryphodon), ii. 10
pantherinus (Drymobius), ii 10
pantherinus (Ptyas), ii 10.
Pantherophis, ii 25
Pappophis, iii 59.
papuæ (Dendrophis), ii 86
papuanus (Liasis), i 80; iii 591.
papuanus (Pseudechis), iii 331
papuensis (Dendrelaphis), iii. 630
papuensis (Diemenia), iii 322.

papuensis (Fordonia), iii. 23
par (Denisonia), iii 345
par (Hoplocephalus), iii. 345.
paradisi (Chrysopelea), iii 196.
paradoxa (Acontiophis), i 415
paradoxus (Lytorhynchus), i 145.
Parageophis, ii 314
parallelus (Ophibolus), ii. 200
parallelus (Periops), i 411
parallelus (Tropidonotus), i 223
pardalinus (Elaphis), ii. 39
pardalis (Boa), i. 112, 113.
pardalis (Ungalia), i. 112, 113
pardalis (Uropeltis), i. 139
Pareas, iii 440.
Paréasiens, i. 177, iii. 438
Parias, iii 529.
Pariaspis, iii. 262
parietalis (Coluber), i. 206
parietalis (Eutainia), i. 207
parietalis (Thamnophis), iii 600.
parietalis (Tropidonotus), i. 207
parreysii (Elaphis), ii. 46.
parviceps (Homolopsis), iii 644
parvifrons (Dromicus), ii 141.
parvifrons (Liophis), ii 141
parvus (Lycodon), i. 366.
Passerita, iii 177
patagonicus (Bothrops), iii 543
patagoniensis (Callirhinus), iii. 131
patagoniensis (Dirrhox), iii. 131.
patagoniensis (Pseudophis), iii 131
paucicarinatus (Drymobius), iii. 626.
paucisquamis (Philodryas), iii 126.

pavimentata (Calamaria), ii. 348.
pavimentatus (Streptophorus), i. 293
pavo (Echis), iii 505.
pavonina (Dipsas), iii. 450
pavonina (Leptognathus), iii. 450.
pavoninus (Dryophis), iii. 183
pavoninus (Leptognathus), iii. 449, 450.
pealii (Tropidonotus), i. 214
peguensis (Fowlea), i. 228.
Pelagophis, iii 303.
pelamidoides (Hydrophis), iii 301, 305.
pelamidoides (Pelamis), iii 301.
Pelamis, iii 266, 271, 285, 300
pelamis (Hydrophis), iii 267.
Pelias, iii. 471
pelias (Vipera), iii 477
Pelophilus, i. 116.
Peltopelor, iii. 529
pentalineatus (Callophis), iii. 394.
percarinatus (Drymobius), ii. 16
perditus (Typhlops), i. 28.
perfuscus (Dromicus), ii. 133
perfuscus (Liophis), ii. 133
peringueyi (Bitis), iii. 495
peringueyi (Vipera), iii. 495
Periops, i. 379.
periops (Ablabes), i. 296, 297.
periops (Hydrablabes), i. 296
permixta (Alecto), iii. 344
pernambucense (Homalocranium), iii. 215.
peronii (Acalyptophis), iii. 269.
peronii (Acalyptus), iii. 269.
peronii (Python), i 82
Peropoda, f. 71.
Peropodes, i. 71.
Peropodum, i. 114.

perroteti (Dryophis), iii. 178.
perroteti (Geophis), i. 304.
perroteti (Platypteryx), i 304
perroteti (Plecturus), i. 161
perroteti (Psammophis), iii. 178
perroteti (Tragops), iii. 178
perroteti (Tropidococcyx), iii. 178.
perroteti (Xylophis), i. 304, iii. 612.
persa (Coluber), i 219.
persa (Tropidonotus), i 219.
persica (Contia), ii. 263.
persica (Vipera) iii. 501.
persicus (Cerastes), iii. 501.
persicus (Cyclophis), ii. 263.
persicus (Pseudocerastes), iii 501
persicus (Pseudocyclophis), ii. 263
persicus (Tropidonotus), i. 219.
persicus (Typhlops), i 21
persicus (Zamenis), i 400.
persimilis (Liophis), ii. 173.
personata (Leptodira), iii. 95.
personatum (Sibon), iii. 93.
personatus (Coluber), i. 395
personatus (Elaps), iii. 398.
peruana (Ophis), iii. 118.
peruvianum (Rhabdosoma), ii 305.
peruvianus (Atractus), ii. 305.
peruvianus (Coluber), iii. 70
peruvianus (Tachymenis), iii 118
peruvii (Coluber), iii 380.
petalarius (Coluber), i. 395, iii. 101.
Petalognathus, ii 292.
petersii (Elapops), iii. 262
petersii (Geophis), ii. 321
petersii (Helminthophis), i. 6.

petersii (Liasis), i. 85
petersii (Onychocephalus), i 46.
petersii (Silybura), i 148.
petersii (Tropidonotus), i. 210.
petersii (Typhlops), i. 29, 46, iii. 588
pethola (Coluber), iii 101
petiti (Rhoptrura), i 92
petolarius (Coluber) iii 101.
petolarius (Lycodon), iii. 101
petolarius (Oxyrhopus), iii. 101, 103
Petrodymon, iii 315
phænochalinus (Simotes), ii. 224, iii. 640.
Phalotris, iii. 239
Phayrea, iii 152
phenax (Eutænia), i. 210, iii. 601
phenax (Tropidonotus), i. 210; iii 601.
phenops (Stenostoma), i. 63
philippensis (Trimesurus), iii 562
philippii (Leptognathus), ii. 295
philippii (Tropidodipsas), ii. 295; iii 644
philippina (Callophis), iii. 404
philippina (Dipsas), iii 77.
philippina (Dryophiops), iii. 195.
philippinensis (Dendrophis), ii. 90.
philippinensis (Tropidolæmus), iii. 562.
philippinica (Calamaria), ii 338
philippinum (Hologerrhum), iii 33.
philippinus (Adeniophis), iii. 404.
philippinus (Dipsadomorphus), iii 77.
philippinus (Doliophis), iii. 404.
philippinus (PseudoTyphlops), i 139
philippinus (Rhinophis), i. 141
philippinus (Typhlops), i. 141.
philippinus (Uropeltis), i. 139.

phillipsii (Coluber), iii 161.
phillipsii (Psammophis), iii 161.
Philodryadinæ, iii. 26.
Philodryas, iii 34, 127, 137, 149
Philothamnus, ii. 91, 98.
Phimophis, iii 99
Phimothyra, i 379.
phipsoni (Hydrophis), iii. 295
phipsonii (Silybura), i. 155
phocarum (Coronella), i. 373
Phragmitophis, iii 643
phrygia (Boa), i 85.
Phrynonax, ii 18
Phyllophilophis, ii 255
Phyllophis, ii. 25.
phyllophis (Coluber), ii. 55.
Phyllorhynchus, i. 414.
Phyllosira, ii 71
Phytolopsis, iii 2
piceivittis (Coniophanus), iii 209.
piceivittis (Erythrolamprus), iii 209
piceivittis (Tachymenis), iii. 209
piceum (Bascanium), i. 390
piceus (Spilotes), ii 30
pickeringii (Coluber), ii. 75
pickeringii (Eutainia), i 208.
picta (Ahætulla), ii 78
picta (Dendrophis), ii 78, 80, 89, 90, iii. 630.
picta (Silybura), i. 156
picteti (Elapotinus), iii 245.
pictiventris (Leptognathus), iii. 459.
pictiventris (Natrix), iii. 606
picturatus (Tropidonotus), i. 215, 219, iii. 602.
pictus (Bothrops), iii. 540.
pictus (Coluber), ii 46, 78
pictus (Dendrophis), ii 78, 88, 358, iii 628, 629.
pictus (Glaphyrophis), iii. 208
pictus (Lachesis), iii 540.

pictus (Leptophis), ii. 78, 88
pictus (Psammodynastes), iii 174.
pictus (Psammophis), iii. 174
Piesigaster, i. 94.
pileatus (Coluber), iii. 129.
Pilidion, i. 7
piscator (Bothrodytes), iii 604.
piscator (Enhydris), i. 230.
piscator (Hydrus), i 230
piscator (Tropidonotus), i 230, 232, iii 604
piscivora (Scytale), iii. 520
piscivorus (Agkistrodon), iii 520.
piscivorus (Ancistrodon), iii 520.
piscivorus (Cenchris), iii. 520.
piscivorus (Crotalus), iii 520
piscivorus (Toxicophis), iii. 520.
piscivorus (Trigonocephalus), iii 520
Pituophis, ii 24.
Plagiodon, ii 25.
Plagiodontiens, i 177.
Plagiopholis, i 301.
planiceps (Coluber), iii 226.
planiceps (Homalocranium), iii. 226
planiceps (Rhinophis), i. 141.
planiceps (Simotes), ii 232.
planiceps (Tantilla), iii. 226
Plastoseryx, i 78.
platura (Anguis), iii 267.
platura (Hydrophis), iii. 267
platurinus (Lycodon), i 359
Platurus, iii. 306.
platurus (Hydrus), iii. 267.
platurus (Pelamis), iii. 267
platycephalus (Typhlops), i. 30
Platyceps, i. 379.
platyceps (Amphiesma), i. 258.

platyceps (Tropidonotus), i 248
Platycerques, iii 264.
Platycranion, iii 210
Platygaster, i 121.
Platyplectrurus i 165.
Platypteryx, i. 303
Platyrhinens, iii 1.
platyrhinus (Heterodon), ii 154, 156.
Plectrurus, i. 160.
pleii (Dromicus), ii. 11, 142
pleii (Drymobius), ii. 12.
pleuralis (Natrix), i 243.
pleurostictus (Elaphis), ii 66.
pleurostictus (Pituophis), ii 67.
plicatile (Calopisma), ii. 186
plicatilis (Cerastes), ii 186
plicatilis (Coluber), ii 186
plicatilis (Dimades), ii. 186, iii. 637
plicatilis (Elaps), ii 186
plicatilis (Homalopsis), ii. 186, 290.
plicatilis (Pseuderyx), iii. 637.
Phocercus, ii 180
pholepis (Trimetopon), iii 636
plumbea (Charina), i. 130, iii. 595
plumbea (Duberria), iii. 109
plumbea (Homalopsis), iii. 5.
plumbea (Hydrophis), iii. 298.
plumbea (Hypsirhina), iii 5.
plumbea (Katophis), i. 215
plumbea (Wenona), i. 130.
plumbeater (Elapops), iii. 262
plumbeatra (Pariaspis), iii 262.
plumbeum (Brachyruton), iii. 109, 111.
plumbeus (Coluber), iii 5, 108.
plumbeus (Eurostus), iii 5
plumbeus (Gonionotus), i. 175.

plumbeus(Herbertophis), i 368.
plumbeus (Oxyrhopus), iii 109.
plumbeus (Stegonotus), i. 368
plumbiceps (Coronella), ii. 195.
plumbicolor (Macropisthodon), i 267; iii 609.
plumbicolor (Tropidonotus), i. 267; iii. 609
plutonia (Eutænia), i 202
plutonius (Coluber), ii. 23.
pœcilocephalus(Coluber), ii 46.
pœcilogaster (Coluber), i. 242
pœcilogyrus (Coluber), ii. 131.
pœcilogyrus (Liophis), ii. 131.
pœcilolæmus (Coronella), ii. 168.
pœcilonotus (Phrynonax), ii 20, iii. 626.
pœcilonotus (Spilotes), ii. 20, 21.
Pœcilophis, iii. 408
pœcilopogon (Coronella), ii 173.
pœcilopogon (Rhadinæa), ii 173.
pœcilostictus (Liophis), iii 131
Pœcilostolus, iii. 508
pœcilostoma (Coluber), ii 19.
pœcilostoma (Spilotes), ii. 19
pœcilostomus (Lygophis), iii 133
poensis (Boodon), i. 335.
poensis (Simocephalus), i. 346.
pœppigii (Geophis), ii. 310
pœppigii (Rhabdosoma), ii. 316.
Pogonaspis, iii. 212.
pogonias (Tropidonotus), i. 243.
poitei (Herpetodryas), ii 15.
Polemon, iii. 253.
polychroa (Dendrophis), ii. 78.
polygrammicus (Argyrophis), i 34.

polygrammicus (Typhlops), i 34, iii. 586.
polyhemizona (Ablabes), ii. 8
polylepis (Ahætulla), ii. 21.
polylepis (Atheris), iii. 508
polylepis (Calamelaps), iii. 246.
polylepis (Dendraspis), iii. 437.
polylepis (Helicops), i 280
polylepis (Hypsirhina), iii 9
Polyodontophis, i 181.
Polyodontus, iii 302
polyodontus(Hydrophis), iii. 274.
polysticta (Caudisona), iii. 582.
polysticta (Leptodira), iii. 95
polystictus (Crotalus), iii. 582
polyzona (Coronella), ii. 203
polyzona (Lampropeltis), ii 203
polyzonus (Ophibolus), ii. 203.
ponticus (Coluber),i 233; ii 192.
porcatus (Coluber), i. 242.
porcatus (Tropidonotus), i. 242.
porphyraceus (Ablabes), ii 34
porphyraceus (Coluber), ii 34
porphyraceus (Trimeresurus), iii. 553.
porphyrea (Naja), iii.329.
porphyreus (Coluber), iii. 328.
porphyreus (Hurria), iii. 328
porphyreus (Trimeresurus), iii. 329.
porphyriaca (Duberria), iii. 328
porphyriaca (Naja), iii. 328.
porphyriacus (Coluber), iii 328.
porphyriacus (Pseudechis), iii. 328, 330.
porphyricus (Trimeresurus), iii. 328.

porrectus (Cœlopeltis), iii 146.
porrectus (Typhlops), i. 19.
Porthidium, iii. 530
portoricensis (Alsophis), ii 122
Potamophidæ, i. 177, iii. 26
Potamophis, i. 173, 290.
præfrontalis (Ablabes), i. 297
præfrontalis (Hydrablabes), i 297; iii 612.
prælongus (Acanthophis), iii 353.
prælongus (Typhlops), i. 28.
præocularis (Eutænia), i. 418; iii 602.
præocularis (Tropidonotus), i 418, iii 602
præocularis (Typhlops), iii 590.
præoculum (Homalocranium), iii 226
præornata (Chrysopelea), iii 150.
præornata (Dendrophis), iii. 150
præornatus (Dromophis), iii. 150.
præornatus (Oxyrhopus), iii. 150
præscutata (Disteira), iii. 298.
præstans (Leptophis), ii. 111.
præstans (Thrasops), ii. 111
prakkii (Calamaria), ii. 337
prasina (Liophis), ii. 135.
prasinus (Coluber), ii 59.
prasinus (Dryinus), iii. 180
prasinus (Dryophis), iii. 180.
prasinus (Tragops), iii. 181
preissi (Typhlops), i 35.
prester (Coluber), iii. 476.
prester (Pelias), iii 477
prester (Vipera), iii. 476, 482.
prevostiana (Gerardia), iii. 20.
prevostianum (Campylodon), iii 21

prevostianus (Coluber), iii. 20.
prevostianus (Homalopsis), iii 20
prionotus(Herpetodryas), i. 185.
problematicus (Hydrophis), iii. 301.
Probletorhinidæ, i. 177; iii 26
proboscideus (Bothriopsis), iii 547
proboscideus (Rhinaspis), ii. 253.
Procinura, iii. 210
producta (Cœlopeltis), iii. 143
producta (Rhagerhis), iii. 143
propinquus (Hydrophis), iii 300.
propinquus (Oligodon), ii. 240.
prosopeion (Coronella), i. 371.
prosopis (Gerrhosteus), iii. 232.
Prosymna, ii. 246
protenus (Dromicus), ii. 141.
Proterodon, i. 360.
Proteroglypha, i.169, iii. 264
Protéroglyphes, i. 169
proterops (Coniophanes), iii. 206.
proterops (Erythrolamprus), iii 206.
proterops (Rhadinæa), iii 206.
protervus (Hydrophis), iii. 289.
proxima (Eutainia), i 213
proxima (Thamnophis), i. 213.
proximus (Atheris), iii. 509.
proximus (Coluber), i. 212
proximus(Tropidonotus), i 213.
proximus (Typhlops), iii 588
pryeri (Tropidonotus), i. 250.
Prymnomodon, i. 192.
Psammodynastes, iii. 172.
Psammophidæ, iii. 26.
psammophideus (Philodryas), iii. 132

Psammophidinæ, iii. 26
psammophidius (Pseudelaps), iii 322.
Psammophis, i. 189, 317, 379; ii 188, iii 122, 141, 149, 151, 152, 172, 177
psammophis (Demansia), iii 322
psammophis (Diemenia), iii 322.
psammophis (Elaps), iii. 322
psammophis (Herpetodryas), i 390.
psammophis (Pseudelaps), iii. 322
Psammophylax, iii. 117, 124, 138, 175.
psephota (Geophis), ii 299
psephotum (Catostoma), ii 299.
psephotum (Dirosema), ii. 299, iii 645
psephotus (Elapoidis), ii 299.
Pseudablabes, iii. 126
Pseudaspidinæ, iii 597.
Pseudaspis, i 373, iii 620
Pseudechis, iii 327
Pseudelaps, iii. 315, 320, 361, 405
Pseudoboa, iii. 99, 365, 504
pseudoboiga (Hurria), iii 75
Pseudocerastes, iii. 501.
Pseudocyclophis, i. 300, ii. 255.
Pseudodipsas, ii. 208.
pseudodipsas (Dendrophis), iii 187.
Pseudoeryx, i 130, 272, ii 185, 289
pseudo-eryx (Bolyeria), i 122
pseudo-eryx (Tortrix), i. 122
Pseudoferania iii. 2
Pseudoficimia, ii. 255
pseudogetulus (Coronella), ii. 197
Pseudohaje, iii 373.
Pseudolycodon, i 364
Pseudonaja, iii. 320
Pseudopareas, iii. 462.
Pseudoplecturus, i. 160.
Pseudorhabdium, ii. 328.
Pseudo-Typhlops, i 139, 140, 144

Pseudoxenodon, i 270.
Pseudoxyrhopus, i. 314.
Psilosoma, ii 255.
psyches (Elaps), iii. 426
psyches (Vipera), iii. 426.
Ptyas, i 379
pubescens (Bothrops), iii. 542
pubescens (Trigonocephalus), iii 542.
publia (Ficimia), ii 271
pugnax (Ancistrodon), iii. 521
pugnax (Toxicophis), iii. 520.
pulchella (Coronella), ii. 165
pulchella (Daboia), iii 490.
pulchellus (Diadophis), ii. 207
pulcher (Alsophis), ii 11.
pulcher (Chondropython), i 90
pulcher (Conophis), iii. 123
pulcher (Heterodon), ii. 153
pulcher (Lachesis), iii. 539
pulcher (Liophis), ii 165.
pulcher (Psammophis), iii. 169.
pulcher (Tomodon), iii. 123
pulcher (Trigonocephalus), iii. 539.
pulcherrimus (Drymobius), i 392
pulcherrimus (Masticophis), i. 392.
pulcherrimus (Zamenis), i 392, iii 622
pulchra (Pseudoficimia), ii. 270.
pulchriceps (Masticophis), ii. 11.
pulchrilatus (Eutænia), i. 209, iii 601.
pullata (Tyria), ii 23
pullatus (Coluber), ii 23, 33.
pullatus (Spilotes), ii. 23
pulneyensis (Plecturus), i 147.
pulneyensis (Rhinophis), i. 147.
pulneyensis (Silybura), i. 147.

pulveriventris (Rhadinæa), iii. 635.
pulverulenta (Dipsas), iii. 68.
pulverulenta (Psammophis), iii 172.
pulverulentus (Crotalus), iii 576.
pulverulentus (Dipsadomorphus), iii. 68, 649
pulverulentus (Dryinus), iii. 184
pulverulentus (Dryophis), iii. 184.
pulverulentus (Psammodynastes), iii 172, 174.
punctata (Calamaria), ii. 206
punctata (Coronella), ii. 206, iii 638.
punctata (Crotaphopeltis), iii 91.
punctata (Denisonia), iii. 341.
punctata (Hypsirhina), iii 12.
punctata (Leptodira), iii. 91.
punctata (Morelia), i. 82
punctata (Onychophis), i 42
punctata (Phytolopsis), iii. 12.
punctata (Psammophis), iii 157.
punctata (Pythonopsis), iii. 12.
punctata (Silybura), i. 154
punctatissima (Dipsas), iii. 117.
punctatissima (Natrix), iii. 117
punctatissimus (Sibon), iii. 117
punctatissimus (Thamnodynastes), iii. 116, 117
punctatolineata (Cyclophis), ii. 261.
punctatolineatus (Aparallactus), iii. 261
punctatostriatus (Enicognathus), i. 227
punctatovittatum (Rhabdosoma), ii. 312.
punctatum (Melanophidium), i 164.
punctatus (Ablabes), ii. 206.
punctatus (Acontias), i. 42.

punctatus (Coluber), ii. 206.
punctatus (Diadophis), ii. 206, 207, 208; iii. 638.
punctatus (Elaps), iii 409.
punctatus (Leptophis), ii 99
punctatus (Philothamnus), ii. 99.
punctatus (Psammophis), iii 157.
punctatus (Pseudoxyrhopus), i 317.
punctatus (Python), i 82.
punctatus (Rhinophis), i 141.
punctatus (Typhlops), i. 42, iii. 587.
punctatus (Xenodon), i 317.
punctigularis (Coniophanes), iii 207
punctiventris (Tropidonotus), iii. 602.
punctulata (Dendrophis), ii. 82
punctulatus (Coronella), ii. 220.
punctulatus (Dendrophis), ii 80, 82, 85; iii 628, 629.
punctulatus (Leptophis), ii 82
punctulatus (Psammophis), iii 159
punctulatus (Simotes), ii. 220
punctulatus (Tropidonotus), i. 228.
punicea (Cophias), iii. 560
puniceus (Atropophis), iii 560
puniceus (Atropos), iii. 560.
puniceus (Lachesis), iii. 560
puniceus (Trigonocephalus), iii 553, 560
puniceus (Trimeresurus), iii 560.
purpurans (Ablabes), ii. 167.
purpurans (Diadophis), ii. 167.
purpurans (Liophis), ii. 168
purpurans (Rhadinæa), ii. 167
purpurascens (Dicraulax), iii. 640.

purpurascens (Passerita), iii 184
purpurascens (Simotes), ii. 218, 220, 225, 226, iii. 640
purpurascens (Xenodon), ii. 218, 220.
purpureocauda (Ablabes), ii. 267.
purpureomaculatus (Lachesis), iii. 553
purpureomaculatus (Trigonocephalus), iii. 553.
purpureomaculatus (Trimeresurus), iii 553.
purpureus (Trimesurus), iii 553.
pustulatus (Thrasops), ii 105.
putnami (Dromicus), iii. 120.
putnami (Manolepis), iii. 120.
putnami (Ocyophis), iii. 120.
putnami (Philodryas), iii 120
putnami (Liophis), ii 139
pygæa (Contia), i. 228; iii 604
pygæus (Seminatrix), iii. 604
pygæus (Tropidonotus), i 228, iii 604.
pygmæus (Liophis), ii. 129
pyramidum (Scythale), iii 505
pyromelanus (Ophibolus), ii 202
pyrrha (Caudisona), iii. 580.
pyrrhocryptus (Elaps), iii 429
pyrrhomelas (Ophibolus), ii 202.
pyrrhopogon (Coluber), ii 73
pyrrhus (Crotalus), iii. 580
Python, i. 80
Pythones, i 74.
Pythonia, iii. 13.
Pythonidæ, i. 71.
Pythonides, i. 74.
Pythoniens, i. 71.
Pythonina, i 74.
Pythoninæ, i 74
pythonissa (Coluber), iii. 6
Pythonodipsas, iii. 45

Pythonoidea, i. 71.
Pythonopsis, iii 2

quadrangularis (Ficimia), ii 272
quadrangularis (Geophis), ii. 320.
quadricarinatus (Erpetodryas), ii 72.
quadrifasciatus (Coluber), ii 61
quadrilineata (Coronella), ii. 41.
quadrilineata (Eirenis), ii 260
quadrilineata (Liophis), ii 130
quadrilineata (Psammophis), iii 165
quadrilineatum (Boædon), i. 332
quadrilineatus (Ablabes), ii. 41
quadrilineatus (Callopeltis), ii 41
quadrilineatus (Coluber), ii 41, 45
quadrilineatus (Dromicodryas), i 190
quadrilineatus (Elaphis), ii 46
quadrilineatus (Herpetodryas), i 190.
quadrilineatus (Simotes), ii 227
quadrimaculata (Calamaria), ii 348, 349
quadriscutatus (Bothriopsis), iii 544
quadriscutatus (Bothrops), iii 543
quadriserialis (Regina), i. 237
quadriserialis (Tropidonotus), i 237, iii. 605.
quadristriatus (Coluber), ii 45.
quadrivirgatum (Adelphicos), ii. 312.
quadrivirgatum (Boædon), i 331
quadrivirgatum (Compsosoma), ii. 59.
quadrivirgatus (Atractus), ii 312
quadrivirgatus (Coluber), ii 59; iii 628
quadrivirgatus (Elaphis), ii 59.
quadrivirgatus (Elaps), iii 400.

VOL. III.

quadrivittatum (Boædon), i. 332.
quadrivittatus (Coluber), ii. 50
quadrivittatus (Elaphis), ii 50.
quaterradiatus (Coluber), ii 45
quaterradiatus (Elaphis), ii 46
quatuorlineatus (Coluber), ii 45, 53
quincunciatus (Comastes), ii 210
quincunciatus (Tropidonotus), i. 230, 231, 232, 257
quinque (Tropidonotus), ii. 61
quinquelineata (Apostolepis), iii 235
quinquelineata (Coronella), ii 178.
quinquelineata (Rhadinæa), ii 178.
quinquelineata (Stenorhina), iii 229
quinquelineatus (Herpetodryas), ii 11.
quinquelineatus (Liophis), i. 315.
quinquelineatus (Microphis), iii 229.
quinquelineatus (Peudoxyrhopus), i. 315, iii. 613
quinquestriatus (Ablabes), ii 284
quinquevittatum (Calopisma), iii 210
quinquevittatus (Homalopsis), iii 210
quinquevittatus (Hydrocalamus), iii 210
quinquevittatus (Hydrops), iii. 210.

Rabdion, ii 328
rabdocephalus (Coluber), ii. 146, 150
Rabdosoma, ii. 300, 314.
Rachiodon, ii. 353.
Rachiodontidæ, ii 353
Rachitis, iii. 2.
raddii (Vipera), iii. 487
radiatum (Compsosoma), ii. 61
radiatus (Coluber), ii 61.
radiatus (Elaphis), ii 62.
radiatus (Spilotes), ii 62

radix (Eutainia), i. 211; iii. 602.
radix (Tropidonotus), i. 211; iii 602
raffravi (Atractocephalus), i 306
raffreyi (Scaphiophis), ii. 254.
rakosiensis (Vipera), iii. 473.
ramsayi (Aspidiotes), i 92.
ramsayi (Aspidites), i 92; iii 592.
ramsayi (Denisonia), iii. 338
ramsayi (Furina), iii 324
ramsayi (Hoplocephalus), iii 338
raninus (Coluber), ii 134
rappi (Hydrophis), iii. 292.
rappii (Ablabes), ii. 282.
rappii (Drymobius), ii 11.
rappii (Herpetodryas), ii. 11
rava (Caudisona), iii 571.
ravergieri (Coluber), i. 405
ravergieri (Zamenis), i 405, 407, iii. 625
ravus (Crotalophorus), iii 571
ravus (Crotalus), iii 571.
ravus (Sistrurus), iii 571.
rebentischii (Calamaria), ii. 343
rectangulus (Coluber), i. 230
redi (Coluber), iii 481.
redi (Vipera), iii 482
redimita (Colorhogia), ii. 252
redimita (Geophis), ii 326.
redimitum (Arrhyton), ii. 252
redimitus (Cryptodacus), ii 252
redimitus (Geagias), ii. 326.
regalis (Coronella), ii 208, iii 639
regalis (Diadophis), ii. 208
regalis (Dipsas), iii 78
regalis (Liophis), ii 208.
regia (Boa), i 88
regia (Cenchris), i. 88
regia (Hortulia), i 89
Regina, i 193, iii 599.
reginæ (Coluber), ii 137.

2 z

reginæ (Coronella), ii. 138.
reginæ (Liophis), ii. 130, 132, 137, 142, 175.
reginæ (Typhlops), i. 35.
regius (Python), i 88, iii. 592.
regularis (Coronella), ii. 196, iii 637.
regularis (Dipsadomorphus), iii. 71.
regularis (Meizodon), ii. 196.
· reinhardti (Calabaria), i. 92; iii 592.
reinhardti (Philodryas), iii. 129.
reinhardti (Rhoptrura), i. 92.
reinhardtii (Eryx), i. 92
reinwardti (Calopisma), ii 291.
reinwardtii (Homalopsis), ii. 291
reinwardtii (Hydrops), ii 291.
reissii (Drymobius), ii 11.
reissii (Herpetodryas), ii. 11.
Rena, i 59.
renardi (Pelias), iii. 475.
renardi (Vipera), iii 475.
resimus (Causus), iii. 468.
resimus (Heterophis), iii. 468
resplendens (Cylindrophis), i. 135.
reticulare (Compsosoma), ii 35.
reticularis (Coluber), ii. 31, 35
reticularis (Spilotes), ii. 35.
reticulata (Anguis), i 27.
reticulata (Blythia), i. 314.
reticulata (Boa), i. 85
reticulata (Calamaria), i. 314, ii. 345
reticulata (Demansia), iii. 322.
reticulata (Dendroechis), iii. 435.
reticulata (Diemenia), iii. 322
reticulata(Herpetodryas), ii. 11.
reticulata (Tantilla), iii. 224.
reticulatum (Homalocranium), iii. 224.

reticulatus (Argyrophis), i 28.
reticulatus (Atractus), ii. 311
reticulatus (Coluber), i. 234; ii 260
reticulatus (Elaphis), ii. 67
reticulatus (Elapomorphus), iii 241.
reticulatus (Geophis), ii. 311.
reticulatus (Lycodon), iii 322
reticulatus (Phalotris), iii 242
reticulatus (Pituophis), ii 68.
reticulatus (Python), i. 85, iii. 592.
reticulatus (Stegonotus), iii 619.
reticulatus (Typhlops), i. 27, iii. 585
reuteri (Typhlops), i 16.
revoili (Brachyophis), iii. 254.
rex-serpentum (Constrictor), i 117.
rhabdocephalus (Xenodon), ii 146, 148, 150.
Rhabdodon, iii. 141
Rhabdophidium, ii. 328.
Rhabdops, i. 300.
Rhabdosoma, i 302, 303.
Rhachiodontinæ, ii 353
Rhadinæa, ii 160; iii. 635.
Rhagerhis, iii 141.
Rhamnophis, iii 632.
Rhamphiophis, iii. 144.
Rhamphostoma, i. 59.
Rhegnops, ii 300
Rhinaspis, ii. 253, iii. 471
Rhinechis, ii 24.
Rhinelaps, iii. 361.
Rhinhoplocephalus, iii. 352
Rhinobothryum, iii. 82.
Rhinocalamus, iii. 247.
Rhinocerophis, iii. 530.
Rhinochilus, ii 212.
rhinoceros (Clotho), iii. 499.
rhinoceros (Echidna), iii. 499
rhinoceros (Vipera), iii 499
rhinomegas (Coluber), ii. 40.
Rhinophidæ, i. 137.

Rhinophis, i. 140.
Rhinopirus, iii. 25
rhinopoma (Dipsas), iii. 50.
rhinopoma (Tarbophis), iii. 50.
Rhinosimus, iii 99.
Rhinostoma, ii. 246, 253, iii 114.
rhinostoma (Furina), iii. 363.
rhinostoma (Heterodon), ii 253.
rhinostoma (Simophis), ii. 253
rhinostomus (Pseudoelaps), iii. 363
Rhinotyphlops, i 4.
rhodogaster (Ablabes), i. 183
rhodogaster (Alecto), iii. 336.
rhodogaster (Colophrys), ii 317.
rhodogaster (Enicognathus), i 182, 183.
rhodogaster (Geophis), ii. 317.
rhodogaster (Herpetodryas), i 182
rhodogaster (Polyodontophis), i. 182.
rhodomelas(Amphiesma), i 266
rhodomelas (Macropisthodon), i. 266, iii. 609.
rhodomelas (Tropidonotus), i 266.
rhodomelas (Xenodon), i. 267.
rhodopleuron (Chrysopelea), iii 195.
rhodopleuron (Dendrophis), iii. 195
rhodorhachis (Zamenis), i. 398; iii. 623.
rhodostoma (Ancistrodon), iii 527
rhodostoma (Calloselasma), iii 527.
rhodostoma (Leiolepis), iii. 527.
rhodostoma (Tisiphone), iii. 527.
rhodostoma (Trigonocephalus), iii 527.
rhombeata (Boa), i. 85.
rhombeata (Cœlopeltis), iii. 138
rhombeata (Coronella), iii. 138.

rhombeata (Dipsas), iii. 138
rhombeata (Lachesis), iii. 534.
rhombeata (Naja), iii. 467.
rhombeatus (Aspidelaps), iii. 467.
rhombeatus (Causus), iii. 467
rhombeatus (Coluber), iii. 138.
rhombeatus (Lycognathus), iii. 58.
rhombeatus (Oxyrhopus), iii. 58.
rhombeatus (Psammophylax), iii. 125, 138
rhombeatus (Sepedon), iii. 467.
rhombeatus (Trimerorhinus), iii 138.
rhombifer (Coryphodon), ii. 14
rhombifer (Crotalus), iii. 574, 578.
rhombifer (Drymobius), ii. 14, 357; iii 626
rhombifer (Nerodia), i. 243.
rhombifer (Oxyrhopus), iii 103.
rhombifer (Spilotes), ii 14.
rhombifer (Tropidonotus), i. 242; iii 606
rhombifer (Zamenis), ii. 14
rhombifera (Leptodira), iii 93.
rhombifera (Natrix), i. 243
rhombiferum (Sibon), iii. 93.
rhombomaculata (Coronella), ii 198.
rhombomaculata (Lampropeltis), ii. 199.
rhombomaculatus (Ophibolus), ii. 198
Rhoptrura, i 92.
Rhynchelaps, iii. 361
Rhynchocalamus, ii 233.
Rhynchoelaps, iii. 361.
Rhynchonyx, iii 232.
rhynchops (Cerberus), iii. 16.
rhynchops (Homalopsis), iii 16.
rhynchops (Hydrus), iii. 16.

rhynchops (Python), iii. 16
riccioli (Coluber), ii. 194.
riccioli (Coronella), ii. 194.
riccioli (Zamenis), ii. 194
richardi (Ahætula), ii. 113
richardii (Coluber), ii. 113
richardii (Typhlops), i. 31.
richardsoni (Myron), iii. 20.
ridgewayi (Lytorhynchus), i 415.
rigida (Natrix), i. 240.
rigida (Regina), i. 240; iii 606.
rigidus (Coluber), i 240
rigidus (Tropidonotus), i. 240, iii 606.
riisii (Elaps), iii 420.
rijersmæi (Alsophis), ii 124.
riparius (Onychocephalus), i 46.
riparius (Typhlops), i. 46
ritchiei (Cerastes), iii. 503
riukianus (Trimeresurus), iii 550
robusta (Aepidea), iii. 627.
robusta (Distira), iii. 292
robusta (Hydrophis), iii 292
robusta (Mainophis), i. 305.
rodriguezii (Elaphis), ii. 39.
roelandti (Calamaria), ii. 344.
rogersi (Zamenis), iii. 623.
rohdii (Rhinaspis), ii. 254.
rohdii (Simophis), ii. 254.
romanus (Coluber), ii. 52
rosaceus (Coluber), ii. 49.
rosenbergii (Coronella), i. 366
roseofusca (Lichanura), i. 129.
rostrale (Rhabdosoma), ii. 323.
rostralis (Anguis), i. 27.
rostralis (Elapoides), ii. 323.

rostralis (Geophis), ii. 323.
rostrata (Atractaspis), iii. 514.
rostrata (Glauconia), i. 62; iii. 590.
rostratum (Stenostoma), i. 62; iii 590.
rostratus (Anguis), i. 27.
rostratus (Causus), iii. 469.
rostratus (Heterophis), iii. 469.
rostratus (Rhamphiophis), iii. 146.
rothi (Ablabes), ii. 262.
rothi (Contia), ii 262
rothi (Eirenis), ii 262
ruatanus (Elaps), iii. 423.
rubellum (Stenostoma), i. 65.
rubens (Coluber), ii. 194.
ruber (Crotalus), iii 576.
rubescens (Chrysopelea), iii 194, 195, 196
rubescens (Diadophis), ii. 120
rubescens (Dipsas), iii. 194
rubescens (Dryophiops), iii 194.
rubescens (Dryophis), iii. 194.
rubescens (Leptophis), iii. 194
rubinianum (Rabdosoma), ii 308
rubra (Tantilla), iii. 219
rubricatum (Sibon), iii. 94
rubriceps (Elaphis), ii. 40.
rubriventer (Cyclophis), i. 300.
rubriventer (Trachischium), i. 300.
rubriventris (Coluber), ii 42
rubrolineata (Silybura), i. 155
rubromaculata (Silybura), i. 157.
rubropunctata (Dipsina), iii. 146.
rubropunctatus (Rhagerrhis), iii 146.
rubropunctatus (Rhamphiophis), iii. 146.
rubrum (Homalocranium), iii. 219
rufa (Anguis), i. 135.

2 z 2

rufa (Cylindrophis), i. 135.
rufa (Ilysia), i 135
rufa (Tortrix), i. 135.
rufescens (Achalinus), i 308, 309; iii 612.
rufescens (Coluber), iii 89.
rufescens (Coronella), iii. 90.
rufescens (Crotaphopeltis), iii 90.
rufescens (Heterurus), iii 90
ruficauda (Anilios), i 29.
ruficauda (Typhlops), i 29.
ruficeps (Homalocranium), iii. 223.
ruficeps (Pogonaspis), iii. 223
ruficeps (Tropidonotus), i 253
rufiventris (Alsophis), ii 124
rufiventris (Dromicus), ii. 124
rufodorsatus (Ablabes), ii. 43
rufodorsatus (Coluber), ii. 43
rufodorsatus (Dromicus), iii 133.
rufodorsatus (Tropidonotus), ii 43
rufopunctata (Eutænia), i 214
rufopunctatum (Chilopoma), i. 214
rufopunctatus (Tropidonotus), i 214
rufotorquatum (Amphiesma), i. 266
rufozonatus (Dinodon), i 361
rufozonatus (Lycodon), i 361.
rufula (Coronella), i. 318.
rufulus (Ablabes), i. 318.
rufulus (Ablabophis), i. 318.
rufulus (Lamprophis), i. 318.
rufulus (Tragops), iii 185.
rufus (Coluber), iii 380.
rufus (Cylindrophis), i. 135.
rufus (Eryx), i 135.
rufus (Liophis), ii. 129.

rugosa (Opisthotropis), i. 284.
rugosum (Trachischium), i 297.
rugosus (Lepidognathus), i. 284.
rugosus (Nothopsis), i 176
ruhstrati (Ophites), i. 363.
rupestris (Coluber), iii. 141
ruppelli (Typhlops), i. 35, iii 586
ruschenbergeri (Xiphosoma), i. 99, iii 593
russelii (Coronella), ii. 229.
russelius (Coluber), ii. 229.
russellianus (Dryinus), iii 183
russellii (Coluber), iii. 490
russellii (Daboia), iii. 490.
russellii (Disteira), iii. 302
russellii (Echidna), iii. 490
russellii (Simotes), ii. 229
russellii (Tortrix), i. 16
russellii (Typhlops), i. 16, 56.
russellii (Vipera), iii. 490
rusticus (Oxyrhopus), iii 111.
rutiloris (Eutænia), i 213.
rutilus (Lygophis), ii. 165.

sabini (Bothrops), iii. 535
Sabrina, i 59.
sackenii (Eutainia), i. 213
saffragamus (Uropeltis), i. 139.
sagittaria (Calamaria), i. 186, 187.
sagittarius (Ablabes), i. 187.
sagittarius (Polyodontophis), i. 187; iii. 598.
sagittatus (Coluber), iii. 63
sagittifer (Chlorosoma), ii. 165

sagittifer (Liopeltis), ii. 165
sagittifera (Rhadinæa), ii 165.
sallæi (Geophis), ii 318
salomonis (Dendrophis), ii. 80
Salvadora, i. 379.
salvini (Crotalus), iii 575
salvinii (Spilotes), ii 33
samarensis (Naia), iii 385.
samarensis (Spilotes), i 367.
sanctæ-crucis (Dromicus), ii. 122; iii 634
sanctici ucis (Alsophis), ii. 122.
sancti-johannis (Lycodryas), iii 45
sancti-johannis (Tropidonotus), i 230; iii. 604.
sandakanensis (Bothrops), iii 561
sanguineus (Platyplectrurus), i 166
sanguineus (Plectrurus), i. 166
sanguineus (Rhinophis), i. 143
sanguineus (Teretrurus), i 166
sanguiventer (Hurriah), i 360
sanniola (Leptognathus), iii 459.
sanniolus (Mesopeltis), iii 459
sansibaricus (Philothamnus), ii 99
Sanzinia, i 99
sarasinorum (Agrophis), ii. 360.
saravacensis (Tropidonotus), i 260, 261, iii.609
sardus (Coluber), i 395.
sargi (Adelphicus), ii 313.
sargi (Ahætulla), ii. 111.
sargi (Leptophis), ii. 111.
sargi (Phocercus), ii 183.
sargi (Rhegnops), ii. 313.
sargi (Thrasops), ii. 111
sartorii (Leptognathus), ii 296
sartorii (Tropidodipsas), ii. 296, iii 645.
saturatus (Hapsidophrys), ii 110.

ALPHABETICAL INDEX. 709

saturatus (Leptophis), ii. 110
saturninus (Coluber), ii. 75
saurita (Coluber), i 212
saurita (Eutainia), i 213.
saurita (Thamnophis), iii. 602
saurita (Tropidonotus), i. 212; iii. 602.
sauritus (Leptophis), i 213
saurocephalus (Coluber), ii 149
sauromates (Coluber), ii 45, 52.
sauromates (Elaphis), ii. 46, 55.
sauromates (Tropidonotus), ii. 46.
savignyi (Tarbophis), iii 48.
savorgnani (Simocephalus), i. 345.
sayi (Coluber), ii 68.
sayi (Coronella), ii. 197.
sayi (Lampropeltis), ii 197
sayi (Ophibolus), ii 197.
sayi (Pituophis), ii 69.
scaber (Dasypeltis), ii. 354
scaber (Deirodon), ii.354.
scaber (Coluber), ii 354.
scaber (Rachiodon), ii. 354.
scaber (Tropidonotus), ii 354.
scabra (Dasypeltis), ii. 354, iii. 648.
scabricauda (Plectrurus), i. 166.
scalaris (Coluber), ii. 65
scalaris (Elapomorphus), iii. 232.
scalaris (Eutainia), i. 203, 204, iii. 601
scalaris (Helicops), i 279
scalaris (Hypsirhynchus), ii. 117
scalaris (Rhinechis), ii. 65
scalaris (Thamnophis), i. 204
scalaris (Tropidonotus), i. 204; iii 601.
scalaris (Xenopholis), iii. 232.
scaliger (Tropidonotus), i. 203; iii. 601.

Scaphiophis, ii 254.
schadenbergi (Geophis), i. 302.
schadenbergi (Trimeresurus), iii 556.
schadenbergii (Oligodon), iii 640
scheuchzeri (Scytale) i 135.
schinzi (Onychocephalus), i 47.
schinzi (Typhlops), i. 47.
schirazana (Periops), i. 411
schistaceum (Amphiesma), i 191
schistorhynchus (Platurus), iii 309.
schistosa (Enhydrina), iii 302
schistosa (Hydrophis), iii. 302
schistosa (Tantilla), iii. 221
schistosum (Atretium), i. 274
schistosum (Homalocranium), iii. 221
schistosus (Coluber), i 274
schistosus (Helicops), i. 274.
schistosus (Hydrophis), iii 274.
schistosus (Hydrus), iii. 302
schistosus (Pelamis), iii. 274.
schistosus (Pseudoeryx), i. 274
schistosus (Tropidonotus), i. 275.
schistosus (Tropidophis), i. 274
schizopholis (Astrotia), iii. 288
schizopholis (Hydrophis), iii 288
schlegeli (Leionotus), ii. 286.
schlegeli (Ablabes), ii. 282.
schlegeli (Bothriechis), iii 567
schlegeli (Bothrops), iii. 567
schlegeli (Calamaria), ii. 333, 345.
schlegeli (Diemenia), iii. 316

schlegeli (Hydrophis), iii. 290
schlegeli (Lachesis), iii. 567.
schlegeli (Nardoa), i. 76.
schlegeli (Onychocephalus), i 44, 45.
schlegeli (Rhinostoma) ii. 253
schlegeli (Teleuraspis), iii. 567
schlegeli (Thalassophis), iii. 290
schlegeli (Trigonocephalus), iii 567
schlegeli (Tropidolæmus), iii. 563
schlegeli (Typhlops), i. 44, iii. 588.
schmackeri (Coluber), iii. 627
schmidti (Streptophorus), i 293.
schmidti (Alecto), iii 335
schneideri (Homalopsis), iii 16.
schneideri (Python), i. 85.
schneideri (Typhlops), i. 27.
schneideri (Vipera), iii. 498
schneideriana (Hurria), iii 16.
schokari (Coluber), iii. 157
schokari (Dipsas), ii. 78, 88.
schokari (Psammophis), iii 157.
schotti (Masticophis), i. 391.
schotti (Philodryas), iii. 130
schottii (Bascanium), i. 391.
schottii (Dryophylax), iii. 130
schottii (Pseudophis), iii. 131.
schottii (Xenodon), iii. 130.
schrancki (Elaps), ii. 184.
schrenckii (Coluber), ii. 48
schrenckii (Elaphis), ii. 48
schyta (Vipera), iii 176.

sclateri (Leptocalamus), ii. 251; iii 641.
Scolécophides, i. 3, 57.
Scolecophidia, i. 3.
Scolecophis, iii. 210.
scolopax (Lycognathus), iii. 57.
scolopax (Oxyrhopus), iii. 57.
scolopax (Siphlophis), iii. 57.
scopinucha (Naja), iii. 380
scopolianus (Coluber), i 219.
scopolii (Coluber), ii. 52.
Scotophis, ii. 25
scriptus (Ablabes), ii. 284.
scurrula (Herpetodryas), ii. 75.
scurrula (Natrix), ii 75.
scutata (Eryx), i 125.
scutata (Hamadryas), iii. 351.
scutata (Laticauda), iii. 307, 308.
scutata (Naja) iii. 351.
scutatus (Aspidelaps), iii. 391.
scutatus (Coluber), i 219.
scutatus (Cyrtophis), iii. 390, 391.
scutatus (Notechis), iii 351.
scutatus (Platurus), iii. 308.
scutatus (Tropidonotus), i. 234.
scutellatus (Pseudechis), iii 331.
scutifrons (Glauconia), i. 68; iii. 591.
scutifrons (Stenostoma), i 68, iii 591.
scutigera (Bothriechis), iii. 546.
scutigera (Bothriopsis), iii. 546.
scutiventris (Elaps), iii. 433.
scutulata (Caudisona), iii 575.
scutulatus (Crotalus), iii. 575.
Scytale, iii 99, 504, 519, 520.
scytale (Anguis), i. 133, 135.
scytale (Aspidura), i. 311, 315
scytale (Boa), i. 115.

scytale (Calamaria), i. 311.
scytale (Ilysia), i. 133, iii. 595.
scytale (Torquatrix), i. 133.
scytale (Tortrix), i. 133.
Scytalidæ, iii 26.
Scytaliens, iii. 26.
Scytalinæ, iii. 26.
scytalinus (Scolecophis), iii. 109.
scytha (Coluber), iii. 476
sebæ (Coluber), i. 86.
sebæ (Hortulia), i 86.
sebæ (Ninia), i 293.
sebæ (Oxyrhopus), iii. 101.
sebæ (Python), i 86; iii. 592
sebæ (Streptophorus), i. 293
sebastus (Herpetodryas), ii. 75.
sechellensis (Lycognathophis), i. 317, iii 614
sellatus (Coluber), ii. 40.
sellmanni (Coluber), ii. 52.
semiannulata (Contia), ii. 268
semiannulata (Elapsoidea), iii. 359.
semiannulata (Leptodira), iii 51.
semiannulata (Sonora), ii. 268
semiannulatus (Crotaphopeltis), iii 51.
semiannulatus (Tarbophis), iii. 51.
semiannulatus (Telescopus), iii. 51.
semiannulus (Lycophidium), i. 339.
semiaureus (Ophiomorphus), ii 169
semicarinatus (Ablabes), ii 278.
semicarinatus (Dinodon), i 362.
semicarinatus (Eumesodon), i. 362
semicarinatus (Eurypholis), ii. 278.
semicincta (Tantilla), iii. 219.
semicincta (Ungalia), i. 113.
semicinctum (Homalocranium), iii. 219.

semicinctum (Lycophidium), i. 341; iii. 617.
semicinctus (Heterodon), ii 153
semicinctus (Leptognathus), iii. 645.
semicinctus (Lystrophis), ii. 153
semicinctus (Tropidonotus), i 215.
semidoliatum (Catostoma), ii. 316
semidoliatum (Rabdosoma), ii 316
semidoliatus (Elapoides), ii. 316.
semidoliatus (Geophis), ii. 316; iii. 645.
semifasciata (Brachyurophis), iii. 363
semifasciata (Compsosoma), i 400
semifasciata (Eutainia), i. 207.
semifasciatum (Aspidoclonion), iii. 368
semifasciatus (Bungarus), iii. 368.
semifasciatus (Coluber), i. 400.
semifasciatus (Himantodes), iii. 86.
semifasciatus (Hydrophobus), i 370.
semifasciatus (Lycodon), iii. 101.
semifasciatus (Oxyrhopus), iii. 101
semifasciatus (Platyceps), i 399.
semifasciatus (Rhynchelaps), 363
semifasciatus (Simotes), ii 222.
semilineata (Natrix), ii. 138
semilineatum (Bascanium), i 391.
semilineatus (Zamenis), iii. 622.
semimaculata (Ablabes), ii. 261
Seminatrix, iii 599.
semiornata (Coronella), ii. 195, 359.
semipartitus (Elaps), iii 431.
semivariegata (Ahætulla), ii. 99
semivariegata (Dendrophis), ii. 99.

semivariegatus (Philothamnus), ii 99, iii 631.
semizonata (Homalopsis), iii 14.
semizonata (Pythonia), iii. 14.
semperi (Distira), iii. 292.
semperi (Hydrophis), iii. 292.
sennaariensis (Eryx), i. 125
seoanei (Vipera), iii. 477.
Sepedon, iii. 388.
septemstriata(Glauconia), i. 71.
septemstriatum (Stenostoma), i. 71.
septemstriatus(Catodon), i. 71
septemstriatus (Siagonodon), i. 71.
septemstriatus (Typhlops), i 71.
septemvittata (Natrix), iii. 605.
septemvittatum (Calopisma), i. 275.
septemvittatus (Coluber), i 239.
septemvittatus(Helicops), i. 275; iii. 610
septemvittatus (Limnophis), i 275, iii. 610
septemvittatus (Tropidonotus), i. 239, 419; iii. 605.
septentrionale (Sibon), iii. 93, 94.
septentrionalis (Bothrops), iii. 535.
septentrionalis (Calamaria), ii 349.
septentrionalis(Dinodon), i. 363; iii 619.
septentrionalis (Dipsas), iii. 93.
septentrionalis (Eteirodipsas), iii. 93.
septentrionalis (Leptodira), iii. 93.
septentrionalis(Lycodon), i. 363.
septentrionalis (Ophites), i 363
seriatus(Coluber), ii 290.
serpentinus (Coluber), ii. 166.
serperastra (Ablabes), ii. 172.
serperastra (Rhadinæa), ii. 172, iii. 635.

serra (Dryophylax), iii. 134.
serra (Herpetodryas), iii. 134.
serra (Philodryas), iii. 134
serra (Tropidodryas), iii. 134.
severa (Vipera), iii. 494.
severus (Cerastes), ii. 149
severus (Coluber), ii. 149.
severus (Xenodon), ii. 146, 148, 149, 150.
sexcarinata (Natrix), ii. 72.
sexcarinatus (Herpetodryas), ii. 72.
sexfasciata (Tantilla), iii. 223
sexfasciatum (Homalocranium), iii. 223.
sexlineata (Coronella), ii. 43.
sexlineatus (Ablabes), ii. 43.
sexlineatus (Dromicus), i. 246.
sexlineatus (Tropidonotus), i. 246, iii. 607.
sexscutatus (Leptognathus), ii 296.
seychellensis (Boodon), i. 329.
seychellensis (Psammophis), i. 317.
seychellensis (Tropidonotus), i. 317.
shavii (Pelamis), iii. 289.
shirana (Ahætulla), ii. 96
shirana (Chlorophis), iii. 631.
shiranum (Homalosoma), ii. 276; iii. 642.
shortii (Silybura), i 158.
Siagonodon, i. 59
siamensis (Calamaria), ii. 348.
siamensis (Coluber), iii. 409.
siamensis (Naja), iii 380.
siamensis (Typhlops), i. 24.
sibilans (Coluber), iii. 161, 169.
sibilans (Psammophis), iii. 149, 156, 157, 160, 161, 164, 165, 166, 168.
sibiricum (Chorisodon), iii. 151.

Sibon, iii 88.
sibon (Coluber), ii 293.
sibonius(Alsophis),ii 123.
siculus (Coluber), i. 219.
sieboldi (Elapoides), ii. 318
sieboldii (Ferania), iii. 10, 11.
sieboldii (Herpetoreas), i 248.
sieboldii (Homalopsis), iii. 11.
sieboldii (Hypsirhina), iii. 11
sieboldii (Ninia), ii. 318.
sieboldii (Trigonurus), iii. 11.
signata (Alecto), iii. 338.
signata (Denisonia), iii. 338.
signata (Glauconia), i 64.
signatum (Stenostoma), i. 64
signatus (Coniophanes), iii. 205
signatus (Hoplocephalus), iii. 338.
signatus (Simotes), ii 226
sikkimensis (Tropidonotus), i. 270.
Siloboura, i. 144
silurophaga (Grayia), ii. 286.
Silybura, i. 144.
Simalia, i. 81.
simile (Brachysoma), iii. 319.
Simocephalus, i. 344.
simoni(Onychocephalus), i. 51.
simoni (Typhlops), i. 51.
Simophis, ii. 253
Simoselaps, iii. 361.
Simotes, i. 414, ii. 213, 214.
simplex (Lichanura), i. 129
simus (Coluber), ii 156.
simus (Heterodon), ii. 156.
sindanus (Psammophis), iii 157
sinensis (Ablabes), i 184.
sinkawangensis (Calamaria), ii. 343.
sipedon (Coluber), i. 242.
sipedon (Nerodia), i 242.
sipedon (Tropidonotus), i 242.

Siphlophis iii. 56, 99
sirtalis (Coluber), i. 206.
sirtalis (Eutainia), i. 205, 206, 208; iii. 601
sirtalis (Thamnophis), i. 207.
sirtalis (Tropidonotus), i. 201, 202, 205, 206, 207, 209, 210, 211, 237, iii 601.
Sistrurus, iii 569.
smaragdina (Ahætulla), ii. 103
smaragdina (Dendrophis), ii. 103
smaragdina (Gastropyxis), ii. 103, iii. 631.
smaragdina (Hapsidophrys), ii. 103
smaragdinus (Leptophis), ii 103.
smithii (Dipsas), ii 125.
smithii (Philothamnus), ii 99.
smithii (Typhlops), i. 45
smithii (Zamenis), iii 624.
smythii (Coluber), ii. 286.
smythii (Grayia), ii. 286, iii 643.
socotræ (Zamenis), i 408.
socotranus (Typhlops), i. 21.
Solenoglypha, iii 463.
Solénoglyphes, iii 463
somalicus (Typhlops), iii. 589.
somersetta (Naia), iii. 390.
sondaica (Naja), iii. 380.
Sonora, ii 255.
sonorensis (Caudisona), iii 576.
sordellii (Pseudoelaps), iii. 325.
spadiceus (Oxyrhopus), iii. 101.
Spalerosophis, i. 379
speciosus (Coluber), i 86.
spectabilis (Hoplocephalus), iii. 342.
Sphecodes, i 348
Sphenocalamus, ii. 326.
Sphenocephalus, iii. 99.
spilogaster (Bothrodytes), iii 608.
spilogaster (Ninia), i. 293.
spilogaster (Tropidonotus), i 257; iii. 608.
spiloides (Coluber), ii. 50.
spiloides (Elaphis), ii. 50.
spilonotus (Oligodon), ii. 243
Spilotes, ii 18, 23, 25.
spilotes (Echidna), i 82
spilotes (Morelia), i. 82.
spilotes (Python), i. 82.
spilotus (Coluber), i 82.
spinæpunctatus (Oligodon), i. 186
spinalis (Achalinus), i. 309.
spinalis (Coluber), i 394.
spinalis (Masticophis), i. 394.
spinalis (Zamenis), i. 394, iii. 622.
spiralis (Enhydris), iii 273
spiralis (Hydrophis), iii. 273
spiralis (Hydrus), iii 273.
spixii (Coluber), ii. 75.
spixii (Elaps), iii. 427.
spixii (Helicops), i 280
spixii (Micrurus), iii. 427.
splendens (Liophis), ii. 182
splendida (Dipsas), iii 86
splendida (Lampropeltis), ii. 197.
splendida (Leptodira), iii. 93
splendidus (Ophibolus), ii 197
splendidus (Simotes), ii. 217.
sputatrix (Naja), iii 380.
squamatus (Atheris), iii. 509.
squamiger (Atheris), iii. 509
squamigera (Atheris), iii. 509.
squamigera (Echis), iii. 509
squamigera (Toxicoa), iii. 509.
squamosus (Amblos), i. 57.
squamosus (Typhlophis), i. 57.
squamosus (Typhlops), i. 57; iii. 590.
squamulosus (Pseudoelaps), iii. 317
stahlknechtii (Calamaria), ii. 335
Stasiotes, ii. 213.
Stegonotus, i 364; iii 619.

stejnegerianus (Zamenis), iii 621.
Sténocéphalene, iii. 26.
stenocephalus (Psammophis), iii 156.
Stenognathus, i. 302.
Stenophis, iii 39.
stenophrys (Lachesis), iii. 534.
stenophthalmus (Heterolepis), i. 347
stenophthalmus (Simocephalus), i. 347.
Stenorhina, iii. 229.
stenorhynchus (Geophis), i. 304
stenorhynchus (Xylophis), i 304.
Stenostoma, i. 59.
Stenostoma, i 57.
Stenostomidæ, i. 57
Stephanohydra, iii 303
stephensii (Hoplocephalus), iii. 350.
stewartii (Hydrophis), iii 297.
stictogenys (Diadophis), ii. 207.
stigmaticus (Drepanodon), iii 639.
Stilosoma, ii 325; iii. 646.
stokesii (Distira) iii. 288.
stokesii (Hydrophis), iii. 288.
stokesii (Hydrus), iii 288.
stolata (Natrix), iii 608
stolatum (Amphiesma), i 253
stolatus (Coluber), i. 253.
stolatus (Tropidonotus), i. 253, iii 608.
stoliczkæ (Ablabes), ii. 281.
Stoliczkaia, i. 175.
Storeria, i 285.
storerioides (Ischnognathus), i 288; iii. 611.
storerioides (Natrix), i. 288.
storerioides (Storeria), i. 288.
storerioides (Tropidoclonium), i. 288
storerioides (Tropidonotus), iii. 611
stormi (Lycodon), i. 357, iii. 618.
stormei (Boulengerina), iii. 357.
straminea (Carphophis), ii. 273.

ALPHABETICAL INDEX. 713

stramineus (Chilomeniscus), ii. 273.
stratissima (Leptognathus), iii 85.
Stremmatognathus, iii 446.
Streptophorus, i 291.
striata (Coronella), i 361
striata (Leioselasma), iii 294
striaticeps (Teleolepis), iii 134.
stricticollis (Hydrophis), iii. 284
striatula (Calamaria), i 291
striatula (Haldea), i. 291; iii. 612
striatula (Potamophis), i. 291.
striatula (Virginia), i 291.
striatulus (Coluber). i. 291
striatulus (Conocephalus), i. 291.
striatus (Coluber), i. 349.
striatus (Enhydris), iii. 295.
striatus (Epicrates), i 96
striatus (Eumesodon), i 361.
striatus (Homalochilus), i 96
striatus (Hydrophis), iii. 290.
striatus (Hydrus), iii. 292, 295.
striatus (Lycodon), i. 349.
strigatus (Lachesis), iii. 549
strigatus (Tachymenis), iii. 116.
strigatus (Thamnodynastes), iii. 116.
strigatus (Tomodon), iii. 116
strigatus (Trimesurus), iii. 549.
strigilatus (Homalochilus), i 96
striolatus (Dendrophis), ii. 85.
striolatus (Tropidonotus), i. 231.
striolatus (Typhlops), i. 22
stuhlmanni (Ligonirostra), ii. 248.
stumpffi (Dromicus), i. 247.

stumpffi (Tropidonotus), i. 247
Stypocemus, i 193.
Styporhynchus, i. 193.
subæqualis (Dipsas), iii 88.
subæqualis (Himantodes) iii. 88.
subalbidus (Coluber), iii. 14.
subannulata (Hydrophis), iii 295
subannulatum (Nymphophidium), i. 371.
subannulatus (Dryocalamus), i. 371, iii 620
subannulatus (Hydrophobus), i 371.
subannulatus (Leptognathus), ii. 294
subannulatus (Odontomus), i. 371.
subannulatus (Trimesurus), iii 562.
subannulatus (Tropidodipsas), ii. 295.
subannulatus (Tropidolæmus), iii 562.
subcarinatus (Dendrophis), ii 91
subcarinatus (Simotes), ii 226
subcincta (Distira), iii. 292
subcinctus (Hydrophis), iii. 292.
subcinctus (Lycodon), i. 359; iii 619.
subcinctus (Ophites), i. 359
subfasciata (Hydrophis), iii 302
subfasciatus (Liophis), ii. 132
subfasciatus (Rachiodon), ii 355
subfuscus (Lycodon), i 356.
subgriseus (Oligodon), ii. 243
sublævis (Hydrophis), iii. 283, 292.
sublineatus (Liophis), ii. 132
sublineatus (Oligodon), ii. 242; iii 640.
sublutescens (Coryphodon), ii. 8.
submarginatus (Oxyrhopus), iii. 104
subminiatum (Amphiesma), i. 256.

subminiatus (Tropidonotus), i 256, iii 608
subnigra (Zamenis), iii. 623
suboccipitalis (Hoplocephalus), iii 339
suboculare (Bascanium), i 389.
subocularis (Atheris), iii. 509
subocularis (Dendrelaphis), ii 89.
subocularis (Dendrophis), ii 89
suborbitalis (Spilotes), i 389.
subpunctatus (Oligodon), i 186
subpunctatus (Oxyrhopus), iii 103
subpunctatus (Polyodontophis), i 186, iii 598.
subquadratus (Oligodon), ii. 237.
subradiatum (Compsosoma), ii 64
subradiatus (Coluber), ii 64
subradiatus (Elaphis), ii. 62, 64.
subradiatus (Tropidonotus), ii 15
subscutatus (Bothrops), iii 535.
substolatum (Amphiesma), i 260
subtæniatus (Psammophis), iii 160
sulcans (Hoplocephalus), iii 349
sulcatus (Typhlops), i. 31.
sulphurea (Natrix), ii. 19.
sulphureus (Phrynonax), ii. 19, iii 626.
suluensis (Callophis), iii. 402
sumatrana (Calamaria), ii. 333, 339.
sumatrana (Naja), iii. 386.
sumatranus (Bothrops), iii 557
sumatranus (Coluber), iii 557
sumatranus (Dendrophis), iii. 194.
sumatranus (Elaphis), i. 307
sumatranus (Elaps), iii. 402.

sumatranus (Lachesis), iii. 557.
sumatranus (Trigonocephalus), iii. 562.
sumatranus (Trimesurus), iii. 562.
sumatranus (Typhlops), iii. 584.
sumichrasti (Ablabes), iii 597
sumichrasti (Conophis), iii 123.
sumichrasti (Eutænia), i. 209 ; iii. 601
sumichrasti (Geagras), ii. 250
sumichrasti (Henicognathus), i 183
sumichrasti (Leptocalamus), ii. 250.
sumichrasti (Loxocemus), i. 74.
sumichrasti (Polyodontophis), i. 183 ; iii 597.
sumichrasti (Rhadinœa), i. 183.
sumichrasti (Tropidonotus), i 209 , iii. 601.
sundanensis (Tropidonotus), i 225, 260
sunderwallii (Elaps), iii. 360.
sundevalli (Temnorhynchus), ii. 247.
sundevallii (Elapechis), iii. 360
sundevallii (Elapsoidea), iii. 360.
sundevallii (Glauconia), i 68
sundevallii (Prosymna), ii. 247.
sundevallii (Stenostoma), i. 68.
superba (Denisonia), iii. 335
superbus (Hoplocephalus), iii. 335, 356.
superciliaris (Vipera), iii 491.
superciliosa (Diemenia), iii 325.
superciliosa (Echis), iii 505.
superciliosa (Vipera), iii. 505.
superciliosus (Acalyptus), iii 269.
superciliosus (Enygrus), i. 107.
superciliosus (Pseudoelaps), iii. 325.

supracinctum (Homalocranium), iii 219.
surgens (Tropidonotus), i 274.
surinamensis (Coluber), i. 278
surinamensis (Elaps), iii. 414.
surucucu (Bothrops), iii. 534
suspectus (Xenodon), ii. 147.
suta (Denisonia), iii 339.
sutherlandi (Brachysoma), iii. 320.
sutherlandi (Pseudelaps), iii. 320.
sutus (Hoplocephalus), iii. 339.
sutus (Thanatophis), iii. 547
swinhonis (Simotes), ii. 222.
swinhonis (Tropidonotus), i. 218.
Symphimus, iii 642.
Sympholis, ii 188.
Synchalinus, ii. 70
Syncrantérieus, i 177.
syriaca (Tarbophis), iii. 48, 49.
syriacus (Typhlops), i. 21
syspylus (Ophibolus), ii. 201.

Tachymenis, iii. 47, 117, 124, 199.
Tachynectes, i 272.
Tachyplotus, iii. 2.
taczanowskyi (Ungalia), i 111.
tænia (Tropidonotus), i. 207.
tæniata (Coronella), iii. 175.
tæniata (Leptophis), i. 390.
tæniata (Natrix), iii. 605.
tæniata (Rhadinœa), ii. 178.
tæniata (Tachymenis), iii. 209.
tæniata (Tantilla), iii. 217.
tæniatum (Arrhyton), ii. 252.
tæniatum (Bascanium), i. 391.
tæniatum (Homalocranium), iii. 217.

tæniatus (Bothrops), iii. 538
tæniatus (Conophis), iii. 124.
tæniatus (Dromicus), ii. 178.
tæniatus (Drymobius), i. 391.
tæniatus (Elapocephalus), iii. 239.
tæniatus (Lycognathus), iii. 175
tæniatus (Nasticophis), i. 391.
tæniatus (Philodryas), iii 124.
tæniatus (Simotes), ii. 227.
tæniatus (Zamenis), i. 390 ; iii. 622.
tæniogaster (Liophis), ii. 166.
tæniolata (Coronella), ii. 174.
tæniolata (Rhadinæa), ii. 174.
tæniolatus (Enicognathus), ii. 174.
Tæniophallus, iii 635.
Tæniophis, ii. 118
tæniurus (Aporophis), ii. 130.
tæniurus (Coluber), ii. 47 , iii 627
tæniurus (Elaphis), ii 47.
tæniurus (Liophis), ii. 130, 138
tæniurus (Oligodon), ii. 360.
tamachia (Coluber), iii. 592.
tantalus (Tropidonotus), i 234.
Tantilla, iii. 212.
tantillus (Tæniophis), ii. 119.
Taphrometopon, iii 151.
taprobanica (Hydrophis), iii 295
Tarbophis, iii 47.
tatarica (Boa), i. 126.
tau (Trimorphodon), iii. 56.
taxispilota (Natrix), i. 245 ; iii. 606.
taxispilota (Nerodia), i. 245.
taxispilotus (Tropidonotus), i. 245 , iii. 606.
taylori (Contia), ii. 265.
teberana (Eryx), i. 126.
Teleolepis, iii. 127.

ALPHABETICAL INDEX. 715

Telescopus, iii. 47.
Teleuraspides, iii. 518.
Teleuraspis, iii. 529.
temminckii (Calamaria), ii. 333.
temminckii (Dromicus), ii. 119.
temminckii (Liophis), ii. 119.
temminckii (Psammophis), ii. 119.
temminckii (Typhlops), i. 29.
Temnorhynchus, ii. 246.
templetonii (Mytilia), i. 144
templetonii (Oligodon), ii. 241, 259
temporalis (Dromicus), ii. 143.
temporalis (Hoplocephalus), iii. 353.
temporalis (Hydrophis), iii. 292.
temporalis (Liophis), ii. 143.
temporalis (Ophibolus), ii. 200
tenasserimensis (Zaocys), i. 378.
tenere (Elaps), iii. 423
tentaculatum (Herpeton), iii. 25.
tentaculatus (Erpeton), iii. 25.
tenue (Ophthalmidium), i. 16
tenuiceps (Ablabes), i. 299.
tenuiceps (Calamaria), i. 299.
tenuiceps (Trachischium), i. 299
tenuicollis (Onychocephalus), i. 37.
tenuicollis (Ophthalmidion), i. 37.
tenuicollis (Typhlops), i. 37.
tenuicula (Rena), i. 70.
tenuiculum (Stenostoma), i. 70
tenuis (Typhlops), i. 16, 19, 28.
tenuissima (Dipsas), iii. 86.
tenuissimus (Himantodes), iii. 86
tephropleura (Tropidonotus), i. 237.
Teretrurus, i. 165.
tergemina (Caudisona), iii. 571.

tergeminus (Crotalophorus), iii. 571
tergeminus (Crotalus), iii. 570.
tergeminus (Oxyrhopus), iii. 104, 105.
ternatea (Boa), i. 94.
ternetzii (Helminthophis), iii. 584.
terrifica (Caudisona), iii. 573.
terrificus (Crotalus), iii. 573, 578.
terrificus (Dendrelaphis), ii. 90; iii. 630.
terrificus (Dendrophis), ii. 90
tessellata (Coronella), i. 233
tessellata (Dipsas), iii. 80
tessellata (Natrix), i. 234.
tessellata (Sabrina), i. 63.
tessellatum (Triglyphodon), iii. 80
tessellatum (Typhlops), i. 63.
tessellatus (Ablabes), ii. 11.
tessellatus (Bothrops), iii. 538.
tessellatus (Coluber), i. 233.
tessellatus (Dinodon), i. 364.
tessellatus (Lycodon), i. 351.
tessellatus (Ninia), i. 293.
tessellatus (Proterodon), i. 364.
tessellatus (Rhinochilus), ii. 213.
tessellatus (Streptophorus), i. 293.
tessellatus (Tropidonotus), i. 233, 236, iii. 605.
testaceus (Coluber), i. 389.
testaceus (Coryphodon), i. 386, 387.
testaceus (Drymobius), i. 390.
Tetracheilostoma, i. 59.
Tetragonosoma, i. 348.
tetragonus (Coluber), ii. 274.
Tetralepis, i. 319.
tetratænia (Ademophis), iii. 400.
tetratænia (Elaps), iii. 400.
tetratænia (Herpetodryas), ii. 15.

tetrazona (Erythrolamprus), iii 201.
tettensis (Onychocephalus), i. 41.
tettensis (Psammophis), iii. 166
tettensis (Typhlops), i. 41.
texana (Hypsiglena), ii. 209.
texensis (Diadophis), ii. 207.
textilis (Coronella), iii. 175.
textilis (Diemenia), iii. 325
textilis (Furina), iii. 325.
textilis (Lycognathus), iii. 175.
textilis (Pseudoelaps), iii. 325.
thalassina (Boa), i 102.
Thalassophis, iii. 266, 268, 271, 285, 303.
Thamnocenchris, iii. 529.
Thamnodynastes, iii. 115.
Thamnophis, i. 193, iii. 599
Thamnosophis, i. 193; ii. 9.
Thanatophides, iii. 463.
Thanatophis, iii 530.
thebaicus (Eryx), i 125; iii. 595.
thebaicus (Gongylophis), i. 125.
Theleus, iii. 616.
Thelotornis, iii. 184.
theobaldi (Simotes), ii. 230.
theobaldianus (Typhlops), i 26.
thepassi (Elaps), iii. 401.
thermalis (Coluber), i. 395.
thomensis (Philothamnus), ii 101.
thominoti (Rhinochilus), ii. 213.
thraso (Coluber), ii. 155.
Thrasops, ii 104, 105.
thurstonii (Typhlops), i. 26, iii. 585.
tigrina (Coronella), ii 199; iii 138
tigrinum (Amphiesma), i. 249.
tigrinus (Bothrodytes), iii. 607
tigrinus (Coluber), iii. 138, 535.
tigrinus (Heterodon), ii. 155.

tigrinus (Trigonocephalus), iii 535.
tigrinus (Tropidonotus), i. 249; iii 607.
tigris (Caudisona), iii. 580.
tigris (Crotalus), iii. 580.
tigris (Python), i. 87.
timorensis (Python), i 85.
timoriensis (Liasis), i. 85
Tisiphone, iii. 519
togoensis (Psammophis), iii 147
togoensis (Rhamphiophis), iii 147
Toluca, ii. 255
Tomodon, iii 115, 120, 122.
Tomogaster, iii 303.
Tomyris, iii 372.
tornieri (Zaocys), iii. 628
torquata (Contia), ii. 266
torquata (Coronella), i. 183.
torquata (Demansia), iii. 323
torquata (Diemenia), iii. 323.
torquata (Hypsiglena), ii. 209, 210, 359.
torquata (Leptodira), ii. 210
torquata (Natrix), i. 219.
Torquatrix, i 133, 135.
torquatum (Pseudorabdion), ii 329.
torquatum (Rabdion), ii 329.
torquatum (Rabdosoma), ii. 309
torquatus (Atractus), ii · 309.
torquatus (Coluber), i 219, ii. 206.
torquatus (Enulius), iii. 641.
torquatus (Hydrophis), iii. 283.
torquatus (Leptocalamus), ii. 250, iii 641.
torquatus (Leptognathus), iii 452
torquatus (Opisthiodon), i. 295
torquatus (Polyodontophis), i. 183.
torquatus (Simotes), ii. 232
torquatus (Tropidonotus), i 258.
torresianus (Typhlops), i. 34.
tortor (Acanthophis), iii. 328.
Tortricidæ, i. 131, 167.

Tortriciens, i. 131.
Tortricina, i. 131.
Tortrix, i. 1, 75, 121, 122, 133, 134, 167.
torva (Vipera), iii. 477.
torvus (Thanatophis), iii 567.
Toxicoa, iii 504
Toxicodryas, iii 59.
Toxicophis, iii. 519
trabalis (Coluber), i. 395; ii 44, iii. 151
trabalis (Hæmorrhois), i. 395.
trabalis (Zamenis), i. 395.
Trachischium, i 297.
Trachyboa, i 109
trachyceps (Hydrophis), iii. 295.
trachyprocta (Aspidura), i. 313, iii 613.
transversa (Nerodia), i. 243.
transversus (Tropidonotus), i 242
travancoricus (Cercaspis), i. 355.
travancoricus (Lycodon), i 355.
travancoricus (Oligodon), ii 236
travancoricus (Rhinophis), i 143; iii 596.
travancoricus (Teretrurus), i. 166.
trevelyana (Dapatnaya), i 142
trevelyanus (Rhinophis), i 142
triangula (Lampropeltis), ii. 200.
triangularis (Coronella), ii 286
triangularis (Elaps), ii. 187.
triangularis (Grayia), ii. 287; iii 648
triangularis (Heteronotus), ii. 286
triangularis (Hydrops), ii. 187, 359; iii 637.
triangularis (Pesuderyx), iii. 637.
trianguligera (Bothriechis), iii. 546
trianguligera (Bothriopsis), iii 546.
trianguligerus (Tropidonotus), i. 224; iii. 604.
triangulum (Ablabes), ii. 198, 200
triangulum (Coluber), ii. 200.

triangulum (Coronella), ii 200
triangulus (Ophibolus), ii. 199, 200, 201
triaspis (Coluber), ii. 37, iii 627.
triaspis (Natrix), ii. 37.
Tricheilostoma, i. 59
tricinctus (Liophis), ii 183
tricolor (Ablabes), ii. 281, iii. 643
tricolor (Cylophis), ii 281.
tricolor (Elapomorphus), iii 241.
tricolor (Herpetodryas), ii. 281.
tricolor (Liopeltis), ii 281.
tricolor (Phalotris), iii. 241.
tricolor (Phragmitophris), iii. 643
trifrenatus (Leptophis), i. 385.
trigeminus (Oxyrhopus), iii. 104.
Triglyphodon, iii 59.
trigonata (Dipsas), iii. 63.
trigonatus (Coluber), iii. 62
trigonatus (Dipsadomorphus), iii 62, 64, 69
trigonatus (Pelias), iii. 649.
trigonocephala (Megæra), iii. 559
trigonocephala (Vipera), iii 559.
Trigonocephalus, iii 519, 529
trigonocephalus (Cophias), iii 559
trigonocephalus (Lachesis), iii. 559.
trigonocephalus (Trimeresurus), iii. 559.
Trigonophis, iii 47.
Trigonurus, iii. 2.
trigrammus (Psammophis), iii. 159.
trilamina (Echidnoides), iii. 477.
trilamina (Vipera), iii. 477
trilineata (Eutænia), i 208.
trilineata (Herpetodryas), i 189, 190.
trilineata (Hypsirhina), iii. 7.
trilineatum (Homalocranium), iii. 217.

trilineatum (Liophidium), iii 599
trilineatus (Atomophis), iii 135.
trilineatus (Atractus), ii 312
trilineatus (Elapomorphus), iii. 243
trilineatus (Elaps), iii. 401.
trilineatus (Herpetodryas), iii. 135
trilineatus (Leptocalamus) iii 217.
trilineatus (Oligodon), ii. 238
trilineatus (Platyplectrurus), i 165
trilineatus (Plecturus), i 165.
trilineatus (Psammophylax), iii 138
trilineatus (Simotes), ii 238
trilobus (Onychocephalus), i 38
trimaculata (Vipera), iii. 397
trimaculatus (Callophis), iii. 397.
trimaculatus (Elaps), iii 397
Trimeresurus, iii. 327, 346, 373, 529.
Trimerodytes, iii 599
Trimerorhini, i 177, iii. 26
Trimerorhinus, iii. 138.
Trimesurus, iii. 529
Trimetopon, ii. 184.
Trimorphodon, iii 53
trinoculus (Coluber), iii. 490.
trinotatus (Simotes), ii 218
Tripeltis, ii 233
tripudians (Naia), iii. 380, 385, 386
Trirhinopholis, i. 419
triscalis (Coluber), ii. 129.
triscalis (Dromicus), ii. 129
triscalis (Liophis), ii 129, iii 634.
triseriata (Caudisona), iii 581.
triseriatus (Coluber), iii. 490.
triseriatus (Crotalus), iii 581

triseriatus (Uropsophus), iii. 581.
triste (Brachysoma), iii 314
tristis (Coluber), ii. 88.
tristis (Dendrelaphis), ii. 88, 358, iii. 630
tristis (Elaps), iii 423
tristis (Glyphodon), iii. 314
tristrigatus (Dryocalamus), i. 372, iii. 620.
tritænia (Coronella), iii. 139
tritæniata (Rhagerrhis), iii 139
tritæniatus (Psammophylax), iii 139
tritæniatus (Pseudoxyrhopus), iii 613.
tritæniatus (Trimerorhinus), iii 139, 649
trivirgata (Charina), i 129
trivirgata (Lichanura), i 129, iii 595
trivirgatum (Rhabdosoma), ii 312
trivirgatus (Psammophis), iii. 159.
trivirgatus (Xenopeltis), i 137.
trivittatum (Homalocranium), iii 217
trivittatus (Helicops), i. 276
trivittatus (Myron), i. 276
trivittatus (Tropidonotus), i 208
tropica (Storeria), i 287.
Tropidechis, iii. 350
Tropidoclonion, i 285
Tropidoclonium, ii 294
Tropidococcyx, iii. 177.
tropidococcyx (Dryiophis), iii. 178.
Tropidodipsas, ii. 294, iii. 644
Tropidogeophis, ii. 294.
Tropidolæmus, iii. 529.
Tropidonophis, i. 193, 272.
Tropidonotus, i. 191, 192, 265, 270, 272, 317, ii 9, 353, iii. 599.
Tropidophis, i. 110.
Tropidophorus, i 193
Tropinotus, iii. 599.
truncatus (Argyrophis), i 16

truncatus (Styporhynchus), i 216.
truncatus (Tropidonotus), i 216, iii 603
Trypanurgos, iii. 58.
tschudii (Elaps), iii 422.
tuberculata (Distira), iii 293
tuberculata (Hydrophis), iii 293
tuberculatus (Emydocephalus), iii 304.
tumboensis (Dipsas), iii. 78
turcica (Boa), i. 125
turcicus (Eryx), i 126
turgida (Leptognathus), iii 456.
twiningi (Eutænia), i. 211
Tylanthera, iii. 621.
Typhlina, i 7.
Typhlinalis, i. 7.
Typhlocalamus, ii 330.
Typhlogeophis, ii 351.
Typhlopes, i 3.
Typhlophis, i. 57.
Typhlopidæ, i. 3
Typhlopiens, i 3
Typhlopina, i. 3
Typhlopoidea, i 137.
Typhlops, i 7, 59
Typhlopsidæ, i 3, 57.
typhlus (Coluber), ii. 136.
typhlus (Liophis), ii 135, 136; iii 634.
typhlus (Opheomorphus), ii. 136
typhlus (Xenodon), ii. 136.
typica (Opisthotropis), i. 285, iii 611
typicus (Helicopsoides), i 285.
typus (Anodon), ii. 354.
typus (Bucephalus), iii. 187.
typus (Dispholidus), iii. 187
Tyria, i 379, ii 23, 24; iii. 195.
tyria (Coluber), i 407.
tyrolensis (Coluber), i. 219
tytleri (Tropidonotus), i. 231
Tytleria, i 348

ultramarinus (Leptophis), iii 633
Ulupe, i 369.

umbratus (Coluber), i. 230
umbratus (Tropidonotus), i 224, 231.
undecimstriata (Epictia), i 63.
undecimstriatus (Typhlops), i 63.
undulata (Rhadinæa), ii. 174, iii 635
undulatus (Atropos), iii. 565.
undulatus (Bothrops), iii 565
undulatus (Coluber), iii. 174.
undulatus (Dromicus), ii. 174
undulatus (Lachesis), iii. 565.
undulatus (Ophryacus), iii 565.
undulatus (Teleuraspis), iii 565
undulatus (Trigonocephalus), iii. 565.
Ungalia, i 110.
Ungaliophis, i. 114.
unguiculata (Rhagerrhis), iii 146
unguirostris (Onychocephalus), i. 49.
unguirostris (Typhlops), i. 49; iii 589.
unicolor (Amblyodipsas), iii 245
unicolor (Bœdon), i. 334
unicolor (Calamaria), iii. 245
unicolor (Calamelaps), iii 245
unicolor (Cerberus), iii. 16
unicolor (Crotalus), iii. 574.
unicolor (Dipsadoboa), iii. 81.
unicolor (Dromicus), ii. 120.
unicolor (Fordonia), iii. 22
unicolor (Geophis), ii. 250.
unicolor (Leptocalamus), ii. 250.
unicolor (Lycodon), i. 352.
unicolor (Naja), iii 380.
unicolor (Rachiodon), ii. 355.

unicolor (Xenopeltis), i 168, 334.
unilineatus (Onychocephalus), i. 15
unilineatus (Typhlops), i. 15.
unimaculata (Mytilia), i. 141.
unitæniatus (Letheobia), i 55
unitæniatus (Typhlops), i. 55, iii. 590
univirgata (Callophis), iii. 398.
univirgatus (Elaps), iii. 398
univittatum (Rabdosoma), ii. 305
Upérolissiens, i. 137.
upsilon (Sibon), iii 55
upsilon (Trimorphodon), iii. 55
Uræus, iii. 372
Uranops, i. 272
Uriechis, iii. 235.
Urobelus, iii. 249
Uromacer, ii 115
Uropeltacea, i. 137.
Uropeltidæ, i. 137.
Uropeltis, i 132, 144.
Uropsophus, iii. 572.
urosticta (Athætulla), ii. 115.
urostictus (Leptophis), ii. 115.
Urotheca, ii. 180
ursinii (Pelias), iii. 473.
ursinii (Vipera), iii 473.
urutu (Bothrops), iii. 542.
usta (Natrix), i. 259
ustus (Tropidonotus), i. 238.

vagrans (Eutainia), i. 202; iii. 600.
vagrans (Thamnophis), iii. 600
vagrans (Tropidonotus), i. 202, iii. 600.
vagus (Leptognathus), iii. 462.
vagus (Pareas), iii. 462
vagus (Pseudopareas), iii. 462.
vaillanti (Calamelaps), iii 249.
vaillanti (Elaposchema), iii. 249.
vaillanti (Micrelaps), iii. 249.

vaillanti (Simotes), ii. 228.
valakadien (Enhydrina), iii. 302.
valakadyn (Hydrus), iii. 302
valeriæ (Virginia), ii. 289
valida (Dipsas), iii. 78
valida (Natrix), i. 237
valida (Regina), i. 237.
validus (Tropidonotus), i 237; iii. 605
varia (Echis), iii. 505.
variabilis (Calamaria), ii. 333
variabilis (Coluber), ii. 23.
variabilis (Fordonia), iii. 22
variabilis (Helicops), i. 282.
variabilis (Hemigenius), iii. 606
variabilis (Psammophylax), iii 140
variabilis (Spilotes), ii. 23, 33.
variabilis (Stenophis), iii. 43.
variabilis (Tretanorhinus), i. 282; iii 610
variabilis (Trimerorhinus), iii 140
variabilis (Tropidonotus), iii 606.
varians (Conopsis), ii. 268.
varians (Ogmius), iii. 229.
varians (Oxyrhina), ii. 268.
variegata (Alecto), iii. 348.
variegata (Dipsas), iii. 51.
variegata (Ficimia), ii. 271.
variegata (Leptognathus), iii 451.
variegata (Megæra), iii. 556.
variegata (Morelia), i. 82.
variegata (Pariаs), iii. 556.
variegatum (Alopecion), i 332
variegatum (Amblymetopon), ii. 271.
variegatum (Homalosoma), ii. 276.

variegatus (Dipsadomorus), iii. 451.
variegatus (Heleionomus), i. 86
variegatus (Hoplocephalus), iii. 349.
variegatus (Leptognathus), iii 451.
variegatus (Mizodon), i. 217.
variegatus (Tarbophis), iii. 51
variegatus (Tropidonotus), i. 217; iii. 603.
varium (Rabdosoma), ii 309
varius (Leptophis), i. 246.
varius (Onychocephalus), i. 46.
varius (Typhlops), i. 46.
veliferum (Amastridium), ii 352.
venenosi (Colubriformes), i 169.
ventralis (Boodon), i. 331
ventralis (Stenorhina), iii. 229.
ventrimaculata (Leptognathus), iii 454.
ventrimaculata (Tyria), i. 400.
ventrimaculatus (Acanthocalyx), iii. 623
ventrimaculatus (Leptognathus), iii. 454.
ventrimaculatus (Zamenis), i. 398, 399, 401, 403, 404; iii. 623.
ventromaculatus (Coluber), i 399.
venustissima (Coronella), iii 200.
venustissimus (Coluber), iii 200.
venustissimus (Elaps), iii. 200
venustissimus (Erythrolamprus), iii. 201; iii. 636.
venustissimus (Henicognathus), iii. 598.
venustissimus (Polyodontophis), iii. 598.
venustus (Coluber), i. 287.
venustus (Oligodon), ii. 235.
venustus (Simotes), ii. 235.

verecundus (Liophis), ii. 134.
Vermicella, iii. 405.
vermicularis (Argyrophis), i. 21.
vermicularis (Typhlops), i. 21, 418.
vermiculata (Cœlopeltis), iii. 142.
vermiculaticeps (Coronella), ii. 177.
vermiculaticeps (Rhadinæa), ii 177
vermiculaticeps (Tæniophis), ii. 177.
vermiculatus (Coluber), iii 141.
vermiforme (Homalocranium), iii. 225.
vermiformis (Calamaria), ii. 333, iii. 646
vermiformis (Carphophiops), ii. 324
vermiformis (Lioninia), iii 225
vermiformis (Tantilla), iii. 225.
vermis (Carphophiops), ii. 325
vermis (Celuta), ii. 324
vernalis (Chlorosoma), ii. 258.
vernalis (Coluber), ii 258.
vernalis (Contia), ii. 258, iii. 641
vernalis (Cyclophis), ii. 258, iii. 641
vernalis (Herpetodryas), ii. 258
vernalis (Liopeltis), ii. 259.
versicolor (Calamaria), ii. 345.
versicolor (Coluber), i. 411, ii 149, 191.
versicolor (Epicrates), i. 96.
versicolor (Periops), i. 411.
versicolor (Zamenis), i. 411.
vertebralis (Coluber), ii. 67.
vertebralis (Oligodon), ii. 245.
vertebralis (Pituophis), ii 66, 67, 68.
vertebralis (Simotes), ii. 245
verticalis (Onychocephalus), i. 32.

verticalis (Typhlops), i 32
vestigiatus (Hoplocephalus), iii 335.
vetustus (Bascanion), i. 387.
vibakari (Tropidonotus), i. 221.
vicina (Chrysopelea), iii. 195.
victa (Storeria), iii. 611.
victus (Ischnognathus), iii. 611.
vidua (Eutænia), i. 208.
viduus (Conophis), iii. 123
viguieri (Leptognathus), iii. 457.
vilkinsonii (Trimorphodon), iii 55.
villarsii (Cheilorhina), ii 188
vincenti (Herpetodryas), ii. 73.
violacea (Cantoria), iii. 23
violacea (Coronella), ii. 222.
violacea (Oxybelis), iii. 185.
violaceus (Coluber), ii. 137.
violaceus (Erythrolamprus), iii 207.
violaceus (Simotes), ii. 222, iii 640
Vipera, iii 354, 471, 492, 501, 504
vipera (Cerastes), iii. 503
vipera (Coluber), iii. 476, 503
Viperida, iii. 465.
Viperidæ, iii. 463, 464.
Vipériens, iii. 464
Viperiformes, iii 463.
Viperina, iii 463, 464.
viperina (Boa), i. 124
viperina (Distira), iii. 298
viperina (Hydrophis), iii. 298
viperina (Natrix), i. 236.
viperina (Thalassophis), iii. 298.
Viperinæ, iii 464.
viperinus (Coluber), i. 219, 235
viperinus (Dromicus), ii. 174.

ALPHABETICAL INDEX.

viperinus (Psammophylax), iii 125
viperinus (Tropidonotus), i 234, 235; iii 605.
Viperoidea, i. 169, iii. 464
virens (Coluber), iii. 141
virgata (Tantilla), iii. 223.
virgatum (Homalocranium), iii 223
virgatus (Boodon), i. 331.
virgatus (Cœlopeltis), i 331.
virgatus (Coluber), ii 54.
virgatus (Elaphis), ii. 47, 54
virgatus (Microdromus), iii 223
Virginia, ii. 288.
virginica (Coronella), iii. 89
virgulata (Calamaria), ii 338, 340, iii 647.
viride (Gonyosoma), ii. 57.
viridicyanea (Liophis), ii. 132.
viridiflavus (Coluber), i. 395
viridiflavus (Zamenis), i 395
viridis (Anoplodipsas), iii. 82
viridis (Boa), i. 90
viridis (Bothrops), iii. 555.
viridis (Bucephalus), iii. 187
viridis (Chondropython), i. 90; iii. 592
viridis (Chrysopelea), iii. 195
viridis (Cophias), iii. 554
viridis (Crotalinus), iii. 576
viridis (Dendraspis), iii 435.
viridis (Dendrophis), ii. 75
viridis (Leptophis), iii. 435
viridis (Liophis), ii. 134; iii 634
viridis (Naja), iii. 374.
viridis (Ophiomorphus), ii. 135.
viridis (Trigonocephalus), iii. 554.
viridis (Trimeresurus), iii. 551, 554

viridis (Vipera), iii. 554.
viridis (Xenodon), i. 267.
viridissimus (Coluber), iii 129
viridissimus (Dryophylax), iii. 129.
viridissimus (Herpetodryas), iii. 129.
viridissimus (Philodryas), iii 129
visoninus (Adelphicus), ii 313.
visoninus (Rhegnops), ii. 313.
vitellinus (Dryophilax), iii 133
vitellinus (Philodryas), iii. 133
vitianus (Ogmodon), iii. 313.
vittata (Natrix), i. 255.
vittata (Rhadinæa), ii. 178.
vittatum (Arrhyton), ii. 252
vittatum (Rhinostoma), iii 115
vittatus (Ablabes), i 375.
vittatus (Atractus), ii 304
vittatus (Ceratophallus), iii. 608
vittatus (Coluber), i 255; ii. 134.
vittatus (Conophis), iii. 123.
vittatus (Cryptodacus), ii. 252.
vittatus (Dryophis), iii. 192.
vittatus (Enicognathus), ii 176, 178
·vittatus (Liophis), ii. 134.
vittatus (Rhynchonyx), iii. 237.
vittatus (Spilotes), i 252.
vittatus (Tomodon), iii. 123
vittatus (Tropidonotus), i. 255, iii. 608.
vivax (Ailurophis), iii. 48.
vivax (Coluber), iii 48.
vivax (Ditypophis), iii. 46.
vivax (Tachymenis), iii. 48, 49.
vivax (Tarbophis), iii. 48, 49, 50.
V-nigrum (Naja), iii 467.

vossi (Gonionotus), i. 323
vossii (Alopecion), i 344
vossii (Boodon), i 344.
vossii (Gonionotophis), i. 323
vudii (Alsophis), ii. 120.
vulgaris (Coluber), i. 395
vulgaris (Natrix), i. 219
vulgaris (Vipera), iii 482.
vulneratus (Coluber), ii 59
vulpinus (Coluber), ii 49.
vulpinus (Elaphis), ii. 49.
vulpinus (Scotophis), ii. 49
vultuosa (Ialtris), iii. 137.

waandersii (Oligodon), ii. 245
waandersii (Pareas), iii. 79.
waandersii (Rabdion), ii. 245.
wagleri (Bothrops), iii. 562.
wagleri (Cophias), iii. 562
wagleri (Helicops), i 282.
wagleri (Lachesis), iii. 562
wagleri (Liophis), ii 134.
wagleri (Trigonocephalus), iii. 562.
wagleri (Trimeresurus), iii. 562.
wagleri (Tropidolæmus), iii. 562.
wagneri (Homalocranium), iii. 218.
waitii (Hoplocephalus), iii 349.
waitii (Typhlops), iii 589
walkeri (Tropidonotus), i 238.
walteri (Contia), ii 263.
walteri (Pseudocyclophis), ii 263
Walterinnesia, iii 392
wardii (Cophias), iii. 558
wardii (Trigonocephalus), iii. 558
warro (Cacophis), iii. 320
warro (Pseudelaps), iii. 320
weberi (Anomalochilus), i. 134.

ALPHABETICAL INDEX. 721

weigelii (Craspedocephalus), iii 535
weigelii (Dipsas), iii 84
weigelii (Vipera), iii 535.
welwitschii (Dendraspis), iii. 436
Wenona, i 130.
werneri (Aparallactus), iii 257
westermanni (Elachistodon), iii. 264.
westermanni (Onychocephalus), i. 56
whymperi (Coronella), ii 174.
wiedii (Typhlops), i 36, iii 586.
wieneri (Eteirodipsas), iii 97
wilderi (Typhlops), i. 7
wilkesii (Pituophis), ii 67.
woodfordii (Denisonia), iii 346
woodfordii (Hoplocephalus), iii. 346.
woodhousii (Nerodia), i 243
woodhousii (Tropidonotus), i. 243.
wood-masoni (Silybura), i 147.
woodmasoni (Simotes), ii 223.
wuchereri (Dromicus), ii. 175.
wuchereri (Elapomorphus), iii 240, 241.
wuchereri (Lygophis), ii 175
wynadense (Melanophidium), i 163

wynandensis (Plecturus), i. 163.

xanthina (Daboia), iii. 488.
xanthina (Vipera), iii 487, 488
xanthogaster (Coluber), ii 46
xanthogrammus (Lachesis), iii 543
xanthogrammus (Trigonocephalus), iii 543.
xanthomelas (Trimeresurus), iii 551.
xanthozona (Dryophis), iii 180
xanthozonius (Tragops), iii 181
xanthurus (Spilurus), ii 31
Xenelaphis, ii 7
Xenocalamus, iii. 247
Xenochrophis, i 191
Xenodermina, i. 172.
Xenodermus, i 175
Xenodon, i 265, 270, ii 24, 126, 144, 151, 180, 214, iii 127
Xenodontidæ, iii 597.
Xenodontinæ, iii. 597
Xenopeltidæ, i. 167
Xenopeltis, i. 167
xenopeltis (Tortrix), i 168.
Xenopholis, iii. 231.
Xenurelaps, iii 365.
Xenurophis, ii 288
Xiphosoma, i. 99
Xylophis, i 303
Xyphorhynchus, iii 35

Y (Pseudoelaps), ii 200.

y-græcum (Liophis), ii 135.
y-græcum (Lygophis), ii. 135
yucatanense (Sibon), iii. 95
yucatanensis (Leptodira), iii 95
yunnanensis (Atretium), i. 274.
yunnanensis (Elaphis), ii. 47.

Zacholus, ii. 188.
Zamenis, i 379, ii 24; iii 621.
Zamenophis, i 364
Zaocys, i 374
Zapyrus, i 374
zara (Trigonocephalus), iii 528.
zebrina (Geophis), ii. 308
zebrinum (Rabdosoma), ii 306, 307,
zebrinus (Rhegnops), ii 308.
zebrinus (Tropidonotus), i. 258.
zeylonicus (Coluber), iii 57.
ziczac (Echis), iii. 505
zonata (Coronella), ii 202
zonatus (Bellophis), ii 202
zonatus (Coluber), ii 202.
zonatus (Elaps), iii 211
zonatus (Ophibolus), ii 203
zonatus (Scolecophis), iii 211
zonatus (Zacholus), ii. 202

VOL III 3 A

LIST OF PLATES.

Plate I.

Fig. 1. *Hypsirhina indica*, Gray, p. 4. Upper and lower views of head and anterior part of body.
   1 a. —— ——. Upper view of head. ×2.
   1 b. —— ——. Side view of head ×2.
  2. *Hypsirhina chinensis*, Gray, p. 8. Upper and lower views of head and anterior part of body.
   2 b. —— ——. Side view of head. ×1½.

Plate II.

Fig. 1. *Cerberus australis*, Gray, p. 18.
  2. —— *microlepis*, Blgr., p. 18.
   Upper and lower views of head and anterior part of body, and side view of head.

Plate III.

Fig. 1. *Geodipsas infralineata*, Gthr., p. 32. Upper and side views of head and anterior part of body, and lower view of middle of body.
  2. *Lycodryas sancti-johannis*, Gthr., p. 45. Upper and side views of head and anterior part of body.
  3. *Dipsadomorphus nigriceps*, Gthr., p. 72. Upper view of head and anterior part of body, and side view of head.

Plate IV.

Fig. 1. *Stenophis guentheri*, Blgr., p. 40.
    2. —— *maculatus*, Gthr., p. 43.
    3. —— *variabilis*, Blgr., p. 43.
    3 a. —— ——. Young.
    4. —— *betsileanus*, Gthr., p 44.
        Upper and side views of head and anterior part of body.

Plate V.

Fig. 1. *Himantodes inornatus*, Blgr., p. 88. Upper and lower views of head and anterior part of body, and side view of head.
    2. *Leptodira nigrofasciata*, Gthr., p. 92. Upper view of head and anterior part of body.
    2 a. —— ——. Upper view of head. ×2.
    2 b. —— ——. Side view of head. ×2.
    3. *Rhinostoma vittatum*, Blgr, p. 115. Upper and side views of head and anterior part of body.

Plate VI.

Fig. 1. *Oxyrhopus bitorquatus*, Gthr., p. 104. Young (type). Upper view of head and anterior part of body.
    1 a. —— ——. Adult, from Moyobamba. Upper and side views of head and anterior part of body.
    1 b. —— ——. Adult, from Sarayacu. Upper view of head and anterior part of body.
    2. *Oxyrhopus maculatus*, Blgr., p. 110. Upper view of head and anterior part of body.
    2 a. —— ——. Side view of head.

Plate VII.

Fig. 1. *Tachymenis affinis*, Blgr., p. 119.
    2. *Ialtris dorsalis*, Gthr., p. 137.
        Upper, lower, and side views of head and anterior part of body.

Plate VIII.

Fig 1. *Psammophis bocagii*, Blgr., p. 161. Upper and side views of head and anterior part of body, and upper view of middle of body

2. ——— *longifrons*, Blgr., p. 165. Upper and side views of head and anterior part of body.

Plate IX.

Fig. 1. *Philodryas bolivianus*, Blgr., p. 132. Upper and side views of head and anterior part of body.

2. *Dryophiops philippina*, Blgr., p. 195. Upper, lower, and side views of head and anterior part of body.

3. *Homalocranium longifrontale*, Blgr., p. 218. Upper and side views of head and anterior part of body, and upper and side views of head. × 1½.

Plate X.

Fig. 1. *Apostolepis quinquelineata*, Blgr., p. 235. Upper view of head and anterior part of body, and of posterior part of body and tail.

1 a ——— ———. Upper view of head × 4
1 b. ——— ———. Side view of head. × 4.
1 c. ——— ———. Lower view of head. × 4.

2. *Apostolepis nigroterminata*, Blgr., p. 235. Upper view of head and anterior part of body, and of posterior part of body and tail

2 a. ——— ———. Upper view of head. × 3.
2 b. ——— ———. Side view of head. × 3.
2 c. ——— ———. Lower view of head. × 3.

3. *Elapomorphus trilineatus*, Blgr., p. 243. Upper, side, and lower views of head and anterior part of body.

Plate XI.

Fig. 1. *Aparallactus werneri*, Blgr., p. 257.
2. ——— *guentheri*, Blgr., p. 259.
3. ——— *anomalus*, Blgr., p. 262.

Upper and side views of head and anterior part of body, and upper (*a*) and side (*b*) views of head. × 2

Plate XII

Fig. 1 *Hydrelaps darwiniensis*, Blgr , p. 270. Upper and lower views of head and anterior part of body, side view of tail, and enlarged (×1½) side view of head.

2. *Hydrophis pacificus*, Blgr., p. 278. Upper and side views of head and anterior part of body, side view of middle of body, and side view of tail.

Plate XIII.

Hydrophis latifasciatus, Gthr., p. 279. Upper, side, and lower views of head and anterior part of body, side view of middle of body, and side view of tail.

Plate XIV.

Hydrophis cantoris, Gthr., p. 281. Upper, side, and lower views of head and anterior part of body, side view of middle of body, and side view of tail.

Plate XV.

Hydrophis melanocephalus, Gray, p. 283. Upper, side, and lower views of head and anterior part of body, side view of middle of body, and side view of tail

Plate XVI.

Distira grandis, Blgr., p. 293. Upper, side, and lower views of head and anterior part of body, and side view of posterior part of body

Plate XVII.

Fig. 1. *Distira macfarlani*, Blgr., p. 294.

2. *Distira belcheri*, Gray, p. 296.

Upper, side, and lower views of head and anterior part of body, side view of middle of body, and side view of tail.

Plate XVIII

Fig. 1. *Glyphodon tristis*, Gthr., p. 314.
2. *Diemenia olivacea*, Gray, p. 323.
3. *Denisonia dæmelii*, Gthr., p. 339.
4. —— *punctata*, Blgr., p. 341.
5. *Bungarus bungaroides*, Cantor, p. 370.
Upper and side views of head and anterior part of body.

Plate XIX.

Fig. 1. *Tropidechis carinatus*, Gthr., p. 350. Upper and side views of head and anterior part of body.
2. *Elapognathus minor*, Gthr., p. 356. Upper, lower, and side views of head and anterior part of body.
3. *Bungarus ceylonicus*, Gthr., p. 367. Upper view of head and anterior part of body.

Plate XX.

Fig. 1. *Elapechis niger*, Gthr., p. 359. Upper, lower, and side views of head and anterior part of body.
2. *Naia goldii*, Blgr, p. 387. Upper, lower, and side views of head and anterior part of body, and side view of middle of body.

Plate XXI.

Naia guentheri, Blgr., p. 388. Upper, lower, and side views of head and anterior part of body.

Plate XXII.

Fig. 1. *Elaps buckleyi*, Blgr., p. 416.
2. —— *anomalus*, Blgr., p. 417.
3. —— *fraseri*, Blgr, p. 432.
4. —— *mentalis*, Blgr., p. 432.
Upper and lower views of head and anterior part of body, and enlarged (×2) side view of head.

Plate XXIII.

Fig. 1. *Amblycephalus monticola*, Cantor, p. 443.
    2. *Leptognathus andiana*, Blgr., p. 452.
    3. —— *elegans*, Blgr., p. 452.

        Upper and side views of head and anterior part of body, lower view of head, and enlarged view of dorsal scales in the middle of the body.

Plate XXIV.

Fig. 1. *Leptognathus leucomelas*, Blgr., p. 453.
    2. —— *ventrimaculata*, Blgr., p. 454.

        Upper, lower, and side views of head and anterior part of body.

Plate XXV.

Fig. 1. *Echis coloratus*, Gthr., p. 507. Upper and side views of head and anterior part of body.
    2. *Lachesis okinavensis*, Blgr., p. 549. Upper and side views of head and anterior part of body.
    3. —— *flavomaculatus*, Gray, p. 556. Upper and side views of head.

PRINTED BY TAYLOR AND FRANCIS, RED LION COURT, FLEET STREET

BRIT.MUS.N.H.   Pl. I.

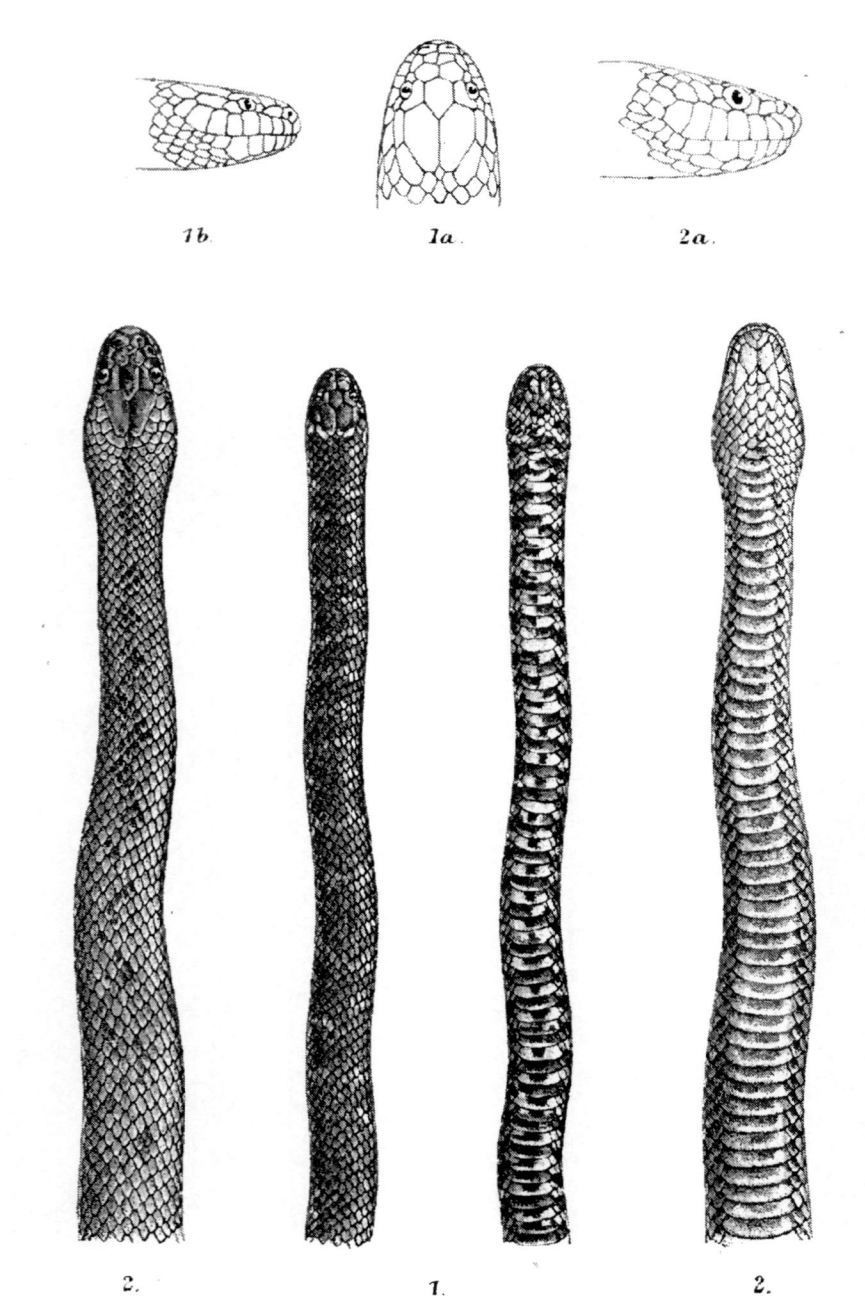

1b.   1a.   2a.

2.   1.   2.

J. Green & R.E.M. del et lith.   Mintern Bros. imp.

1. Hypsirhina indica.   2. Hypsirhina chinensis.

BRIT. MUS. N.H.   Pl. II.

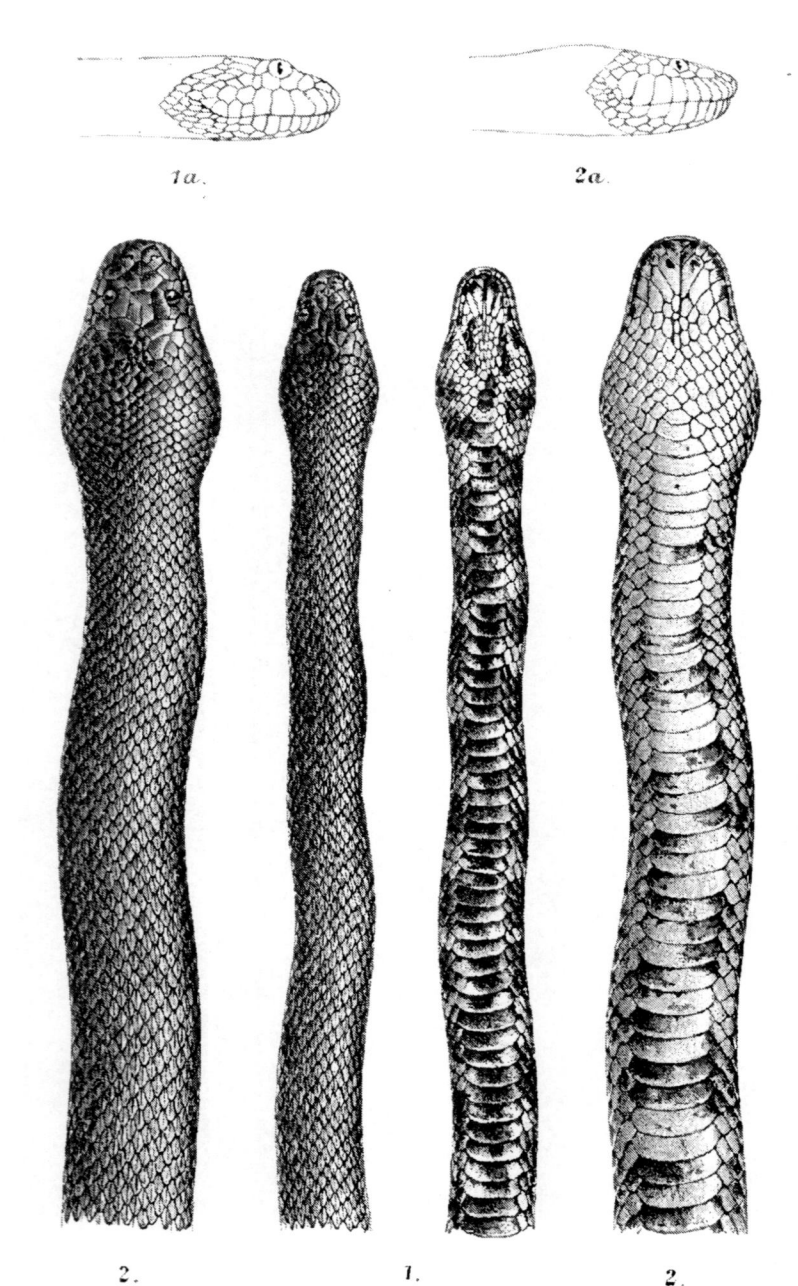

1a.   2a.

2.   1.   2.

J. Green & R. I. M...   ...t. Bros. imp.

1. *Cerberus australis*.   2. *Cerberus microlepis*.

BRIT. MUS. N. H.   Pl. III.

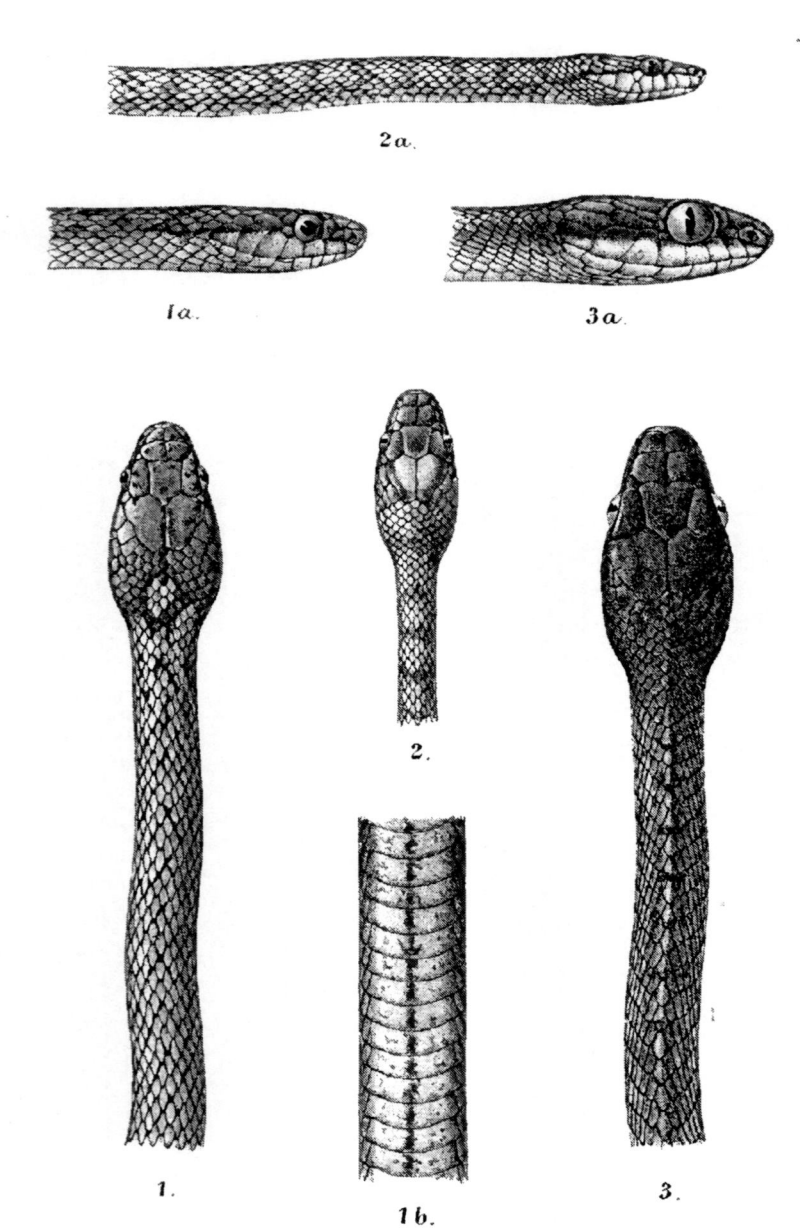

J Green del. et lith.   Mintern Bros. imp.

1. Geodipsas infralineata   2. Lycodryas sancti-johannis.
3. Dipsadomorphus nigriceps.

BRIT. MUS. N. H.   Pl. IV.

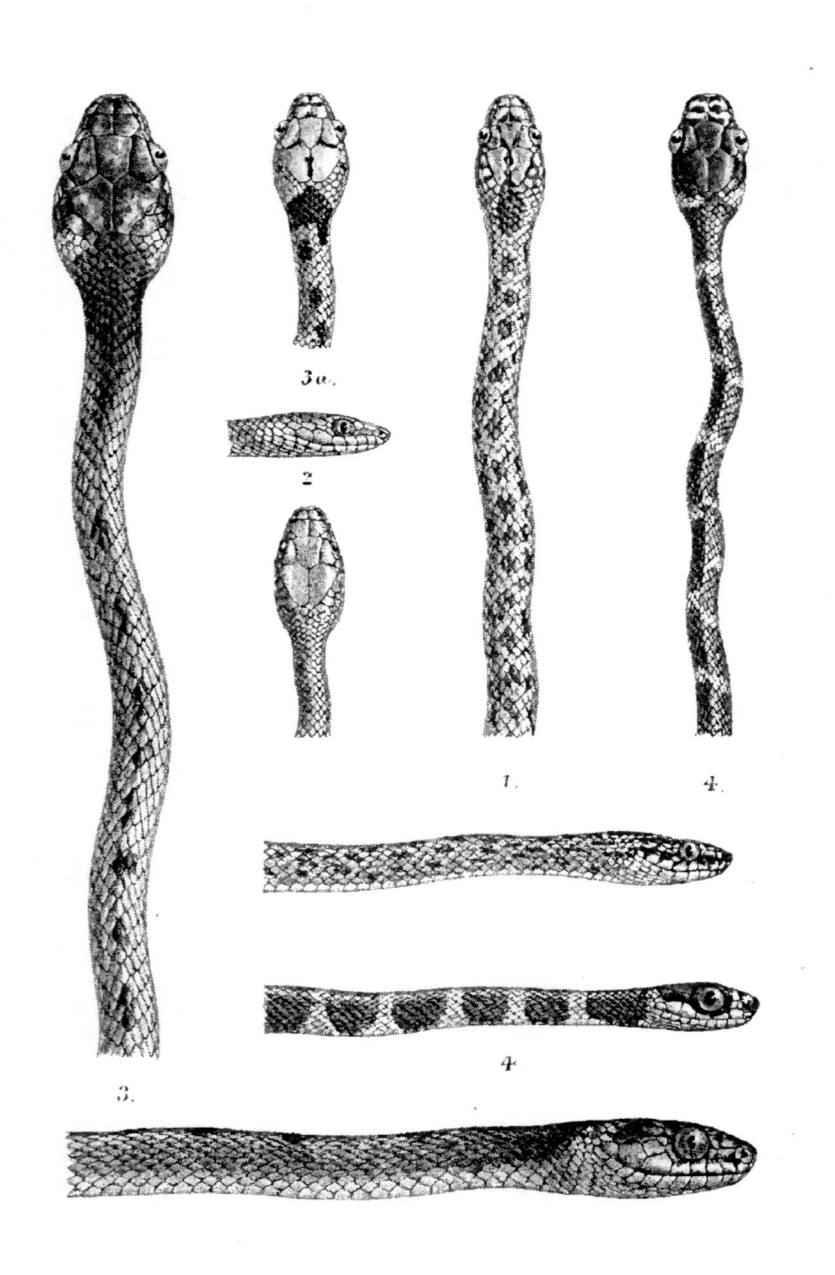

J. Green & R.E.M. del.   Mintern Bros. imp.

1. Stenophis guentheri.   2. Stenophis maculatus.
3. Stenophis variabilis.   4. Stenophis betsileanus.

BRIT. MUS. N. H. Pl. V.

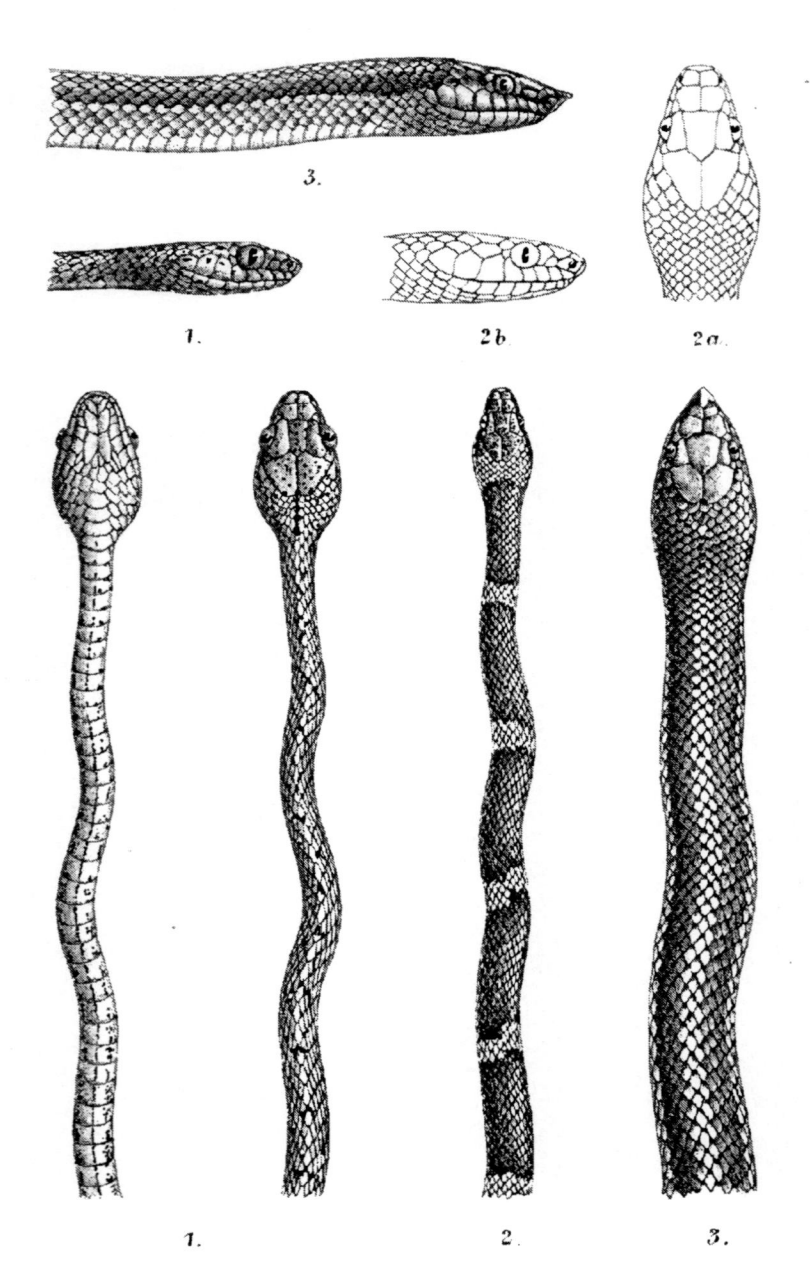

J. Green & R.E.M del. et lith. Mintern Bros. imp.

1. Himantodes inornatus. 2. Leptodira nigrofasciata.
3. Rhinostoma vittatum.

BRIT. MUS. N.H. Pl. VI.

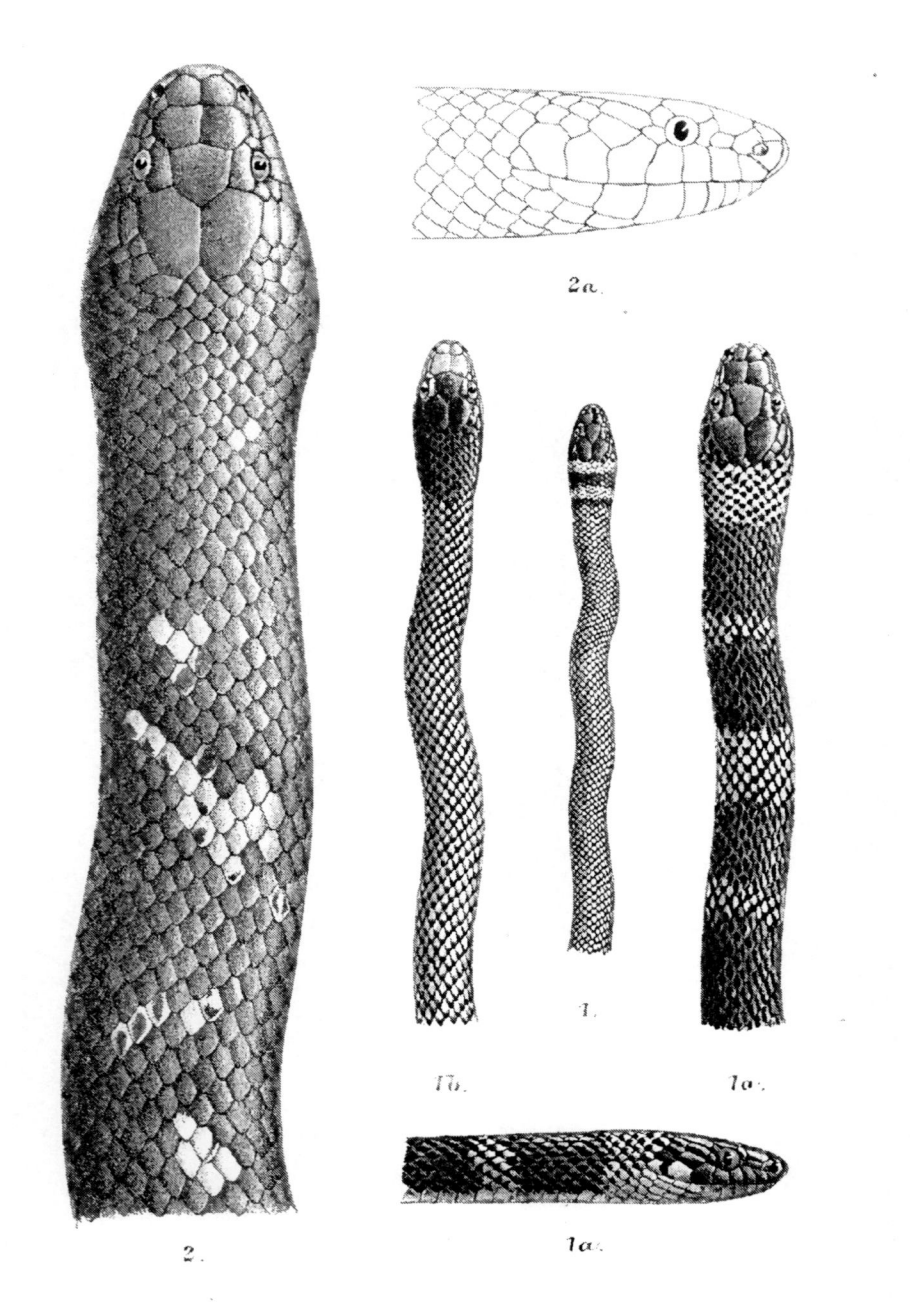

J. Green. del. et lith.. Mintern Bros. imp.

1. *Oxyrhopus bitorquatus.* 2. *Oxyrhopus maculatus.*

BRIT.MUS.N.H.　　　　　　　　　　　　　　　　　　Pl. VII.

2.　　　　　　　　　1.　　　　　　　　2.
J. Green & R.M del et lith.　　　　　　　Mintern Bros. imp.

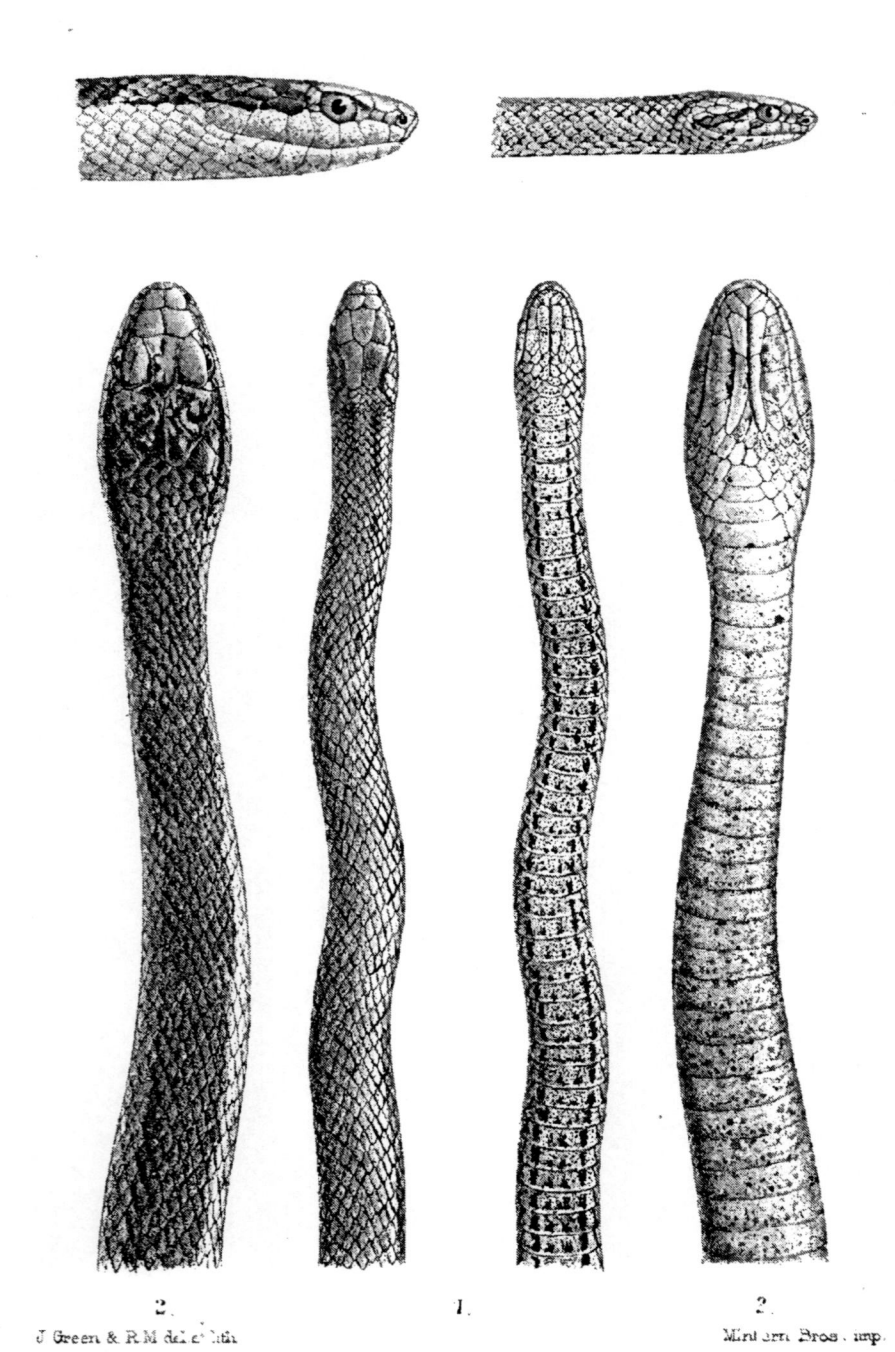

1. *Tachymenis affinis.*　　2. *Ialtris dorsalis.*

BRIT. MUS. N. H.   Pl. VIII.

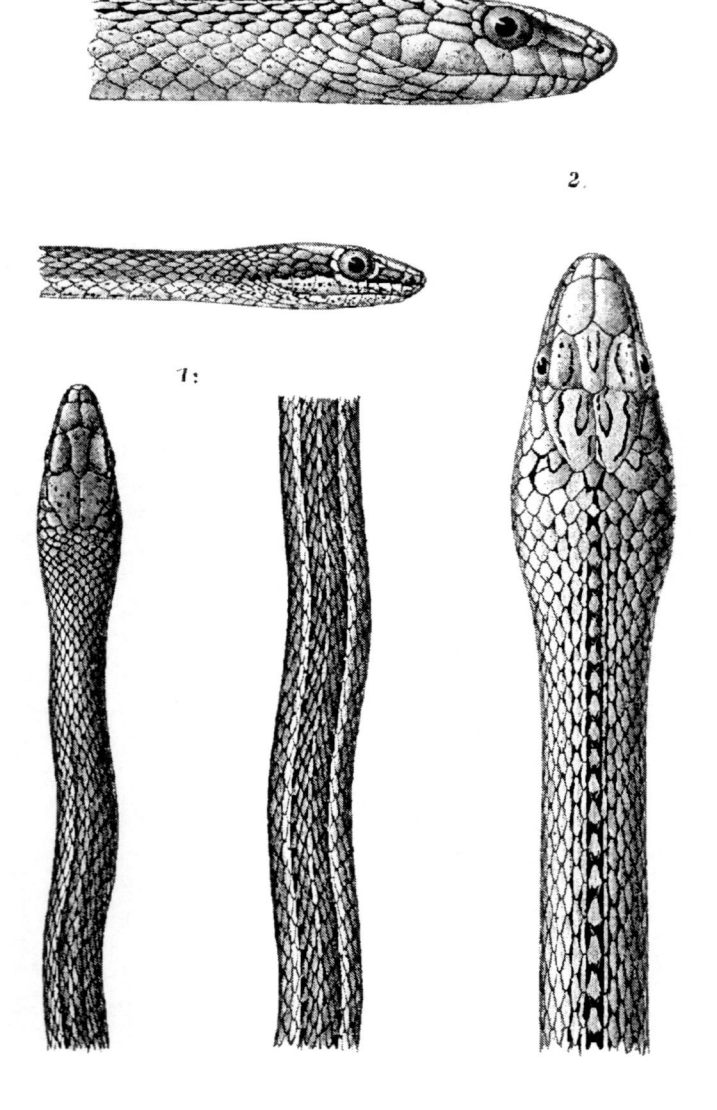

J. Green del et lith.   Mintern Bros. imp.

1. Psammophis bocagii.   2. Psammophis longifrons.

BRIT. MUS. N.H. Pl. IX.

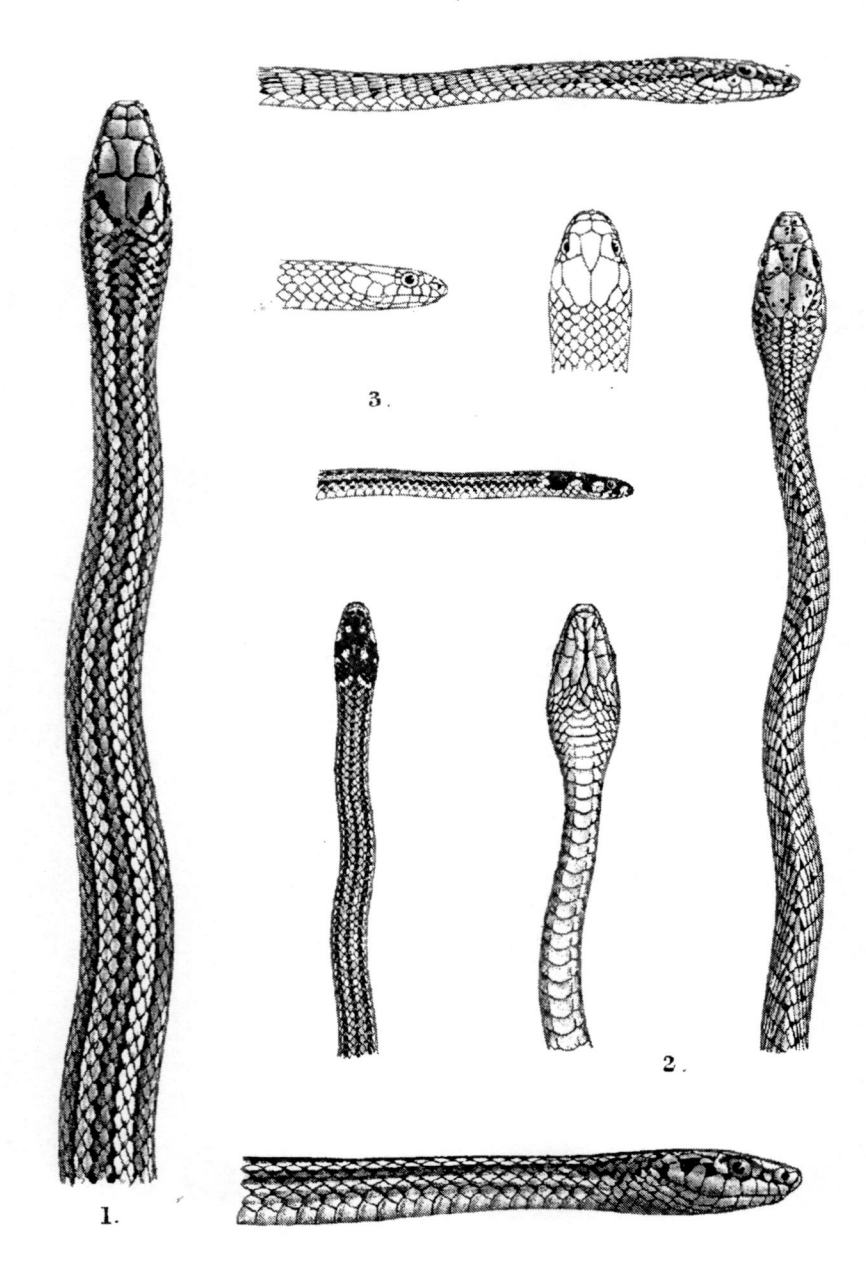

J. Green del. et lith. Mintern Bros. imp.

1. Philodryas bolivianus.   2. Dryophiops philippina.
3. Homalocranium longifrontale.

BRIT. MUS. N.H.
Pl. X.

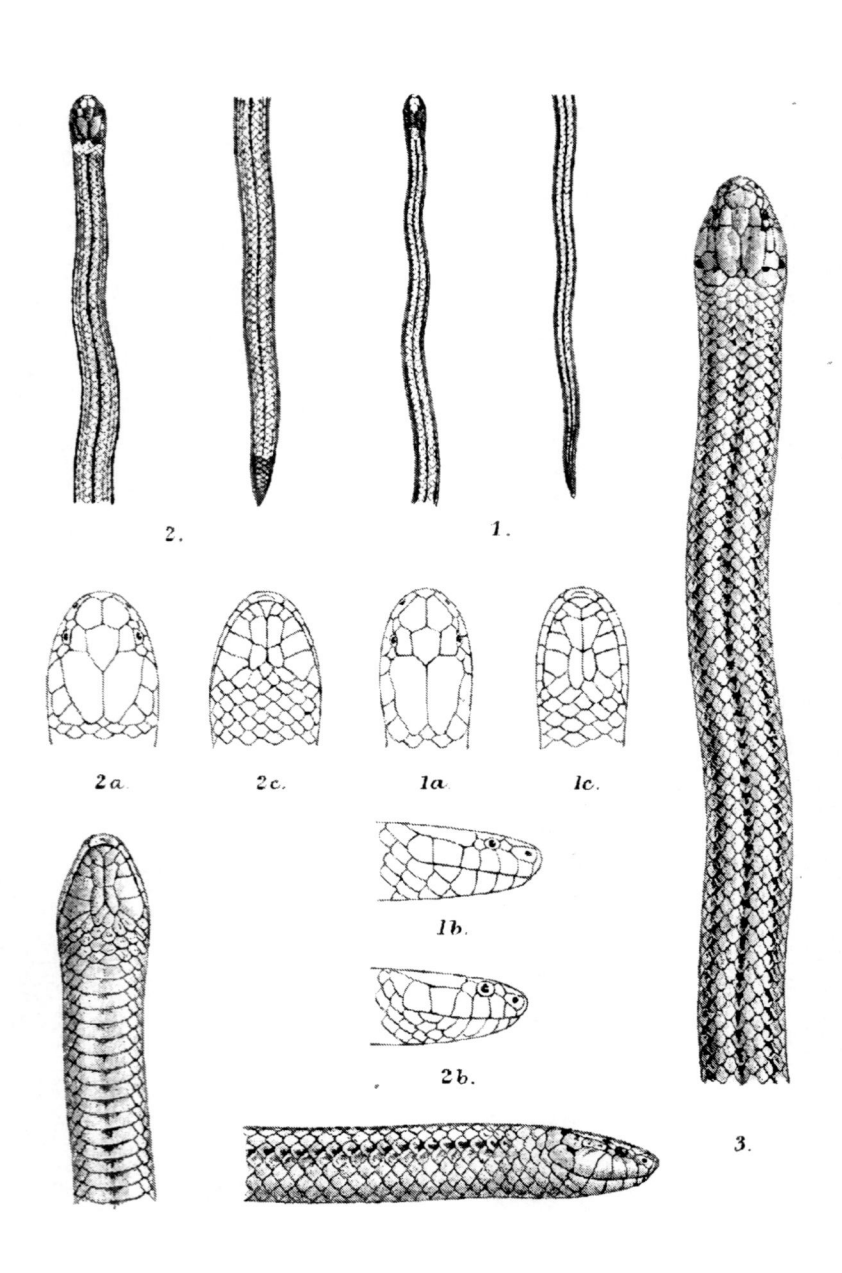

J. Green & R. M. del. et lith.
Mintern Bros. imp.

1. Apostolepis quinquelineata. 2. Apostolepis nigroterminata.
3. Elapomorphus trilineatus.

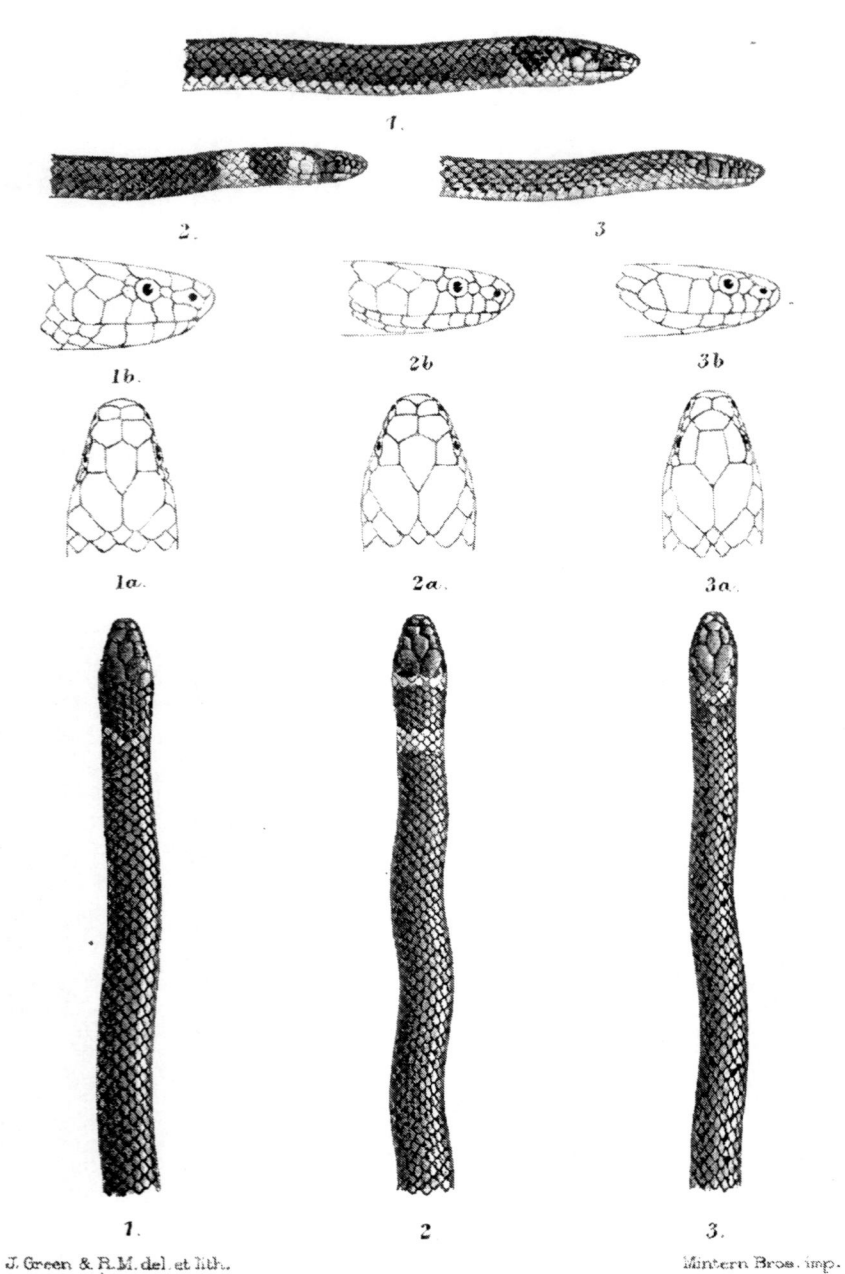

1. Aparallactus werneri. 2. Aparallactus guentheri.
3. Aparallactus anomalus.

BRIT MUS. N H.   PL. XII.

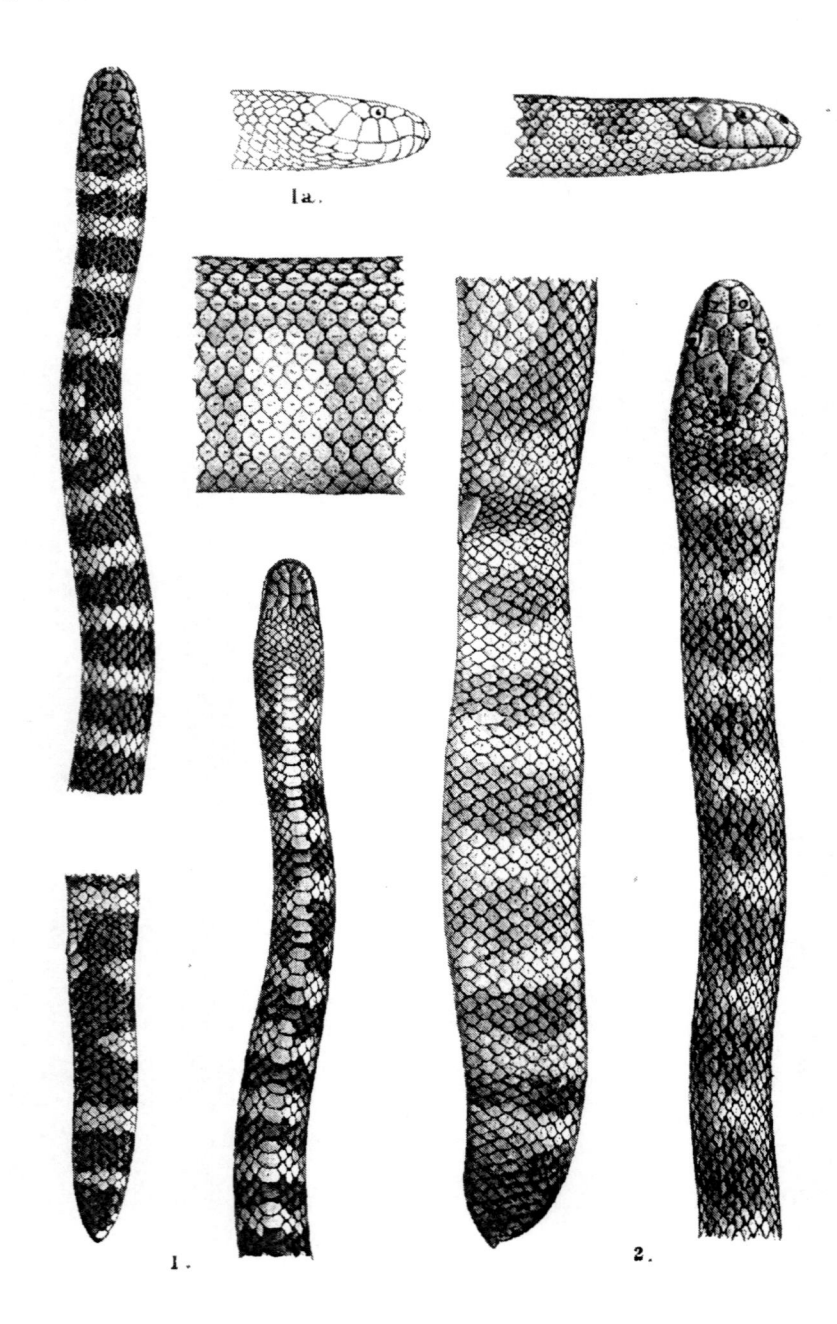

1a.

J. Green del et lith.   Mintern Bros. imp.

1. *Hydrelaps darwiniensis*. 2. *Hydrophis pacificus*.

BRIT. MUS. N.H.   Pl. XIII.

J. Green & R. F. M. del. et lith.   Mintern Bros. imp.

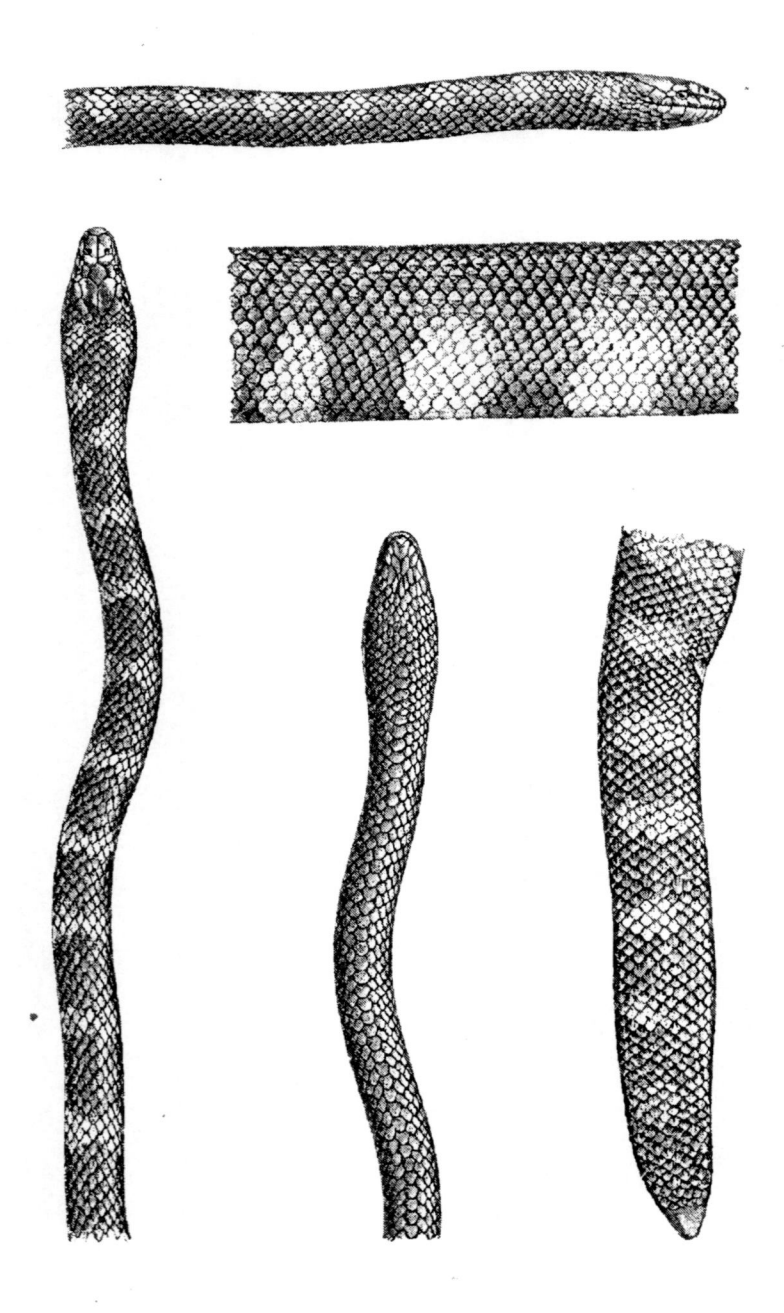

Hydrophis latifasciatus.

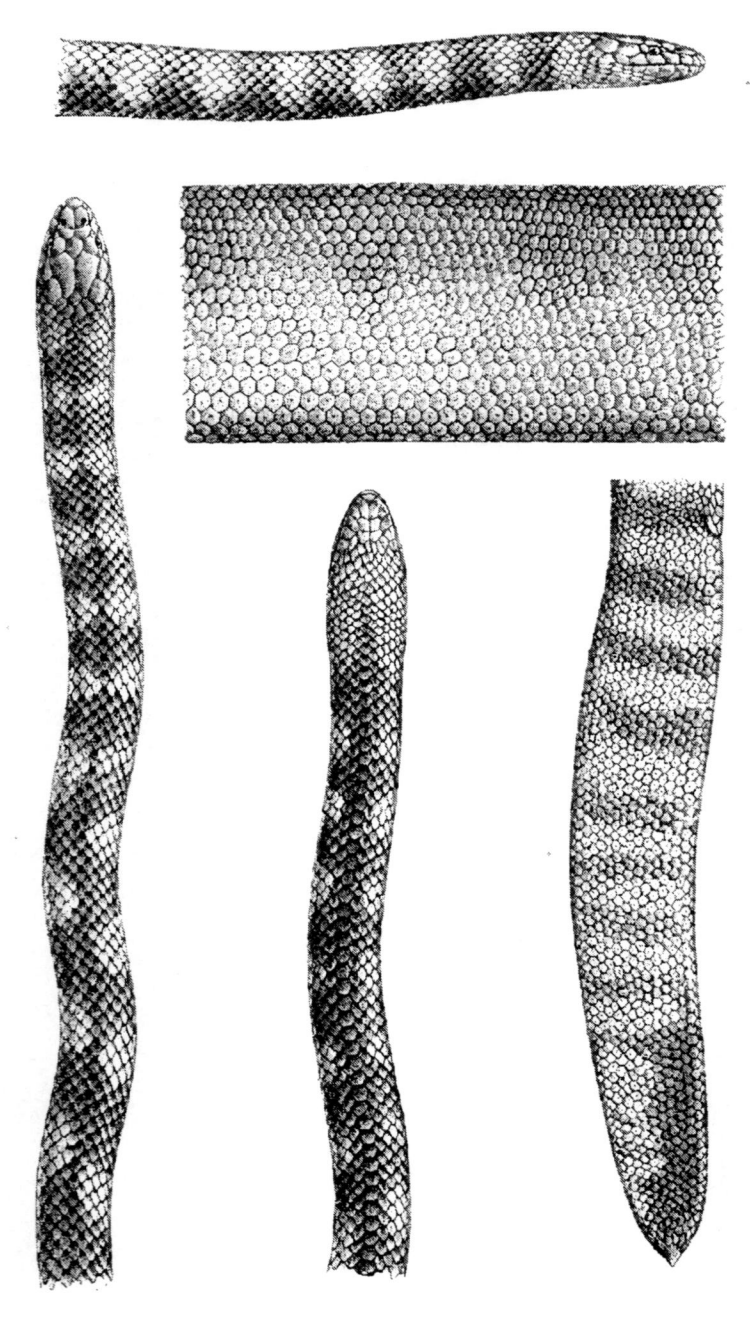

BRIT. MUS. N H.　　　　　　　　　　　　　　　　Pl. XIV.

Hydrophis cantoris.

J. Green del. et lith.　　　　　　　　　　　Mintern Bros. imp.

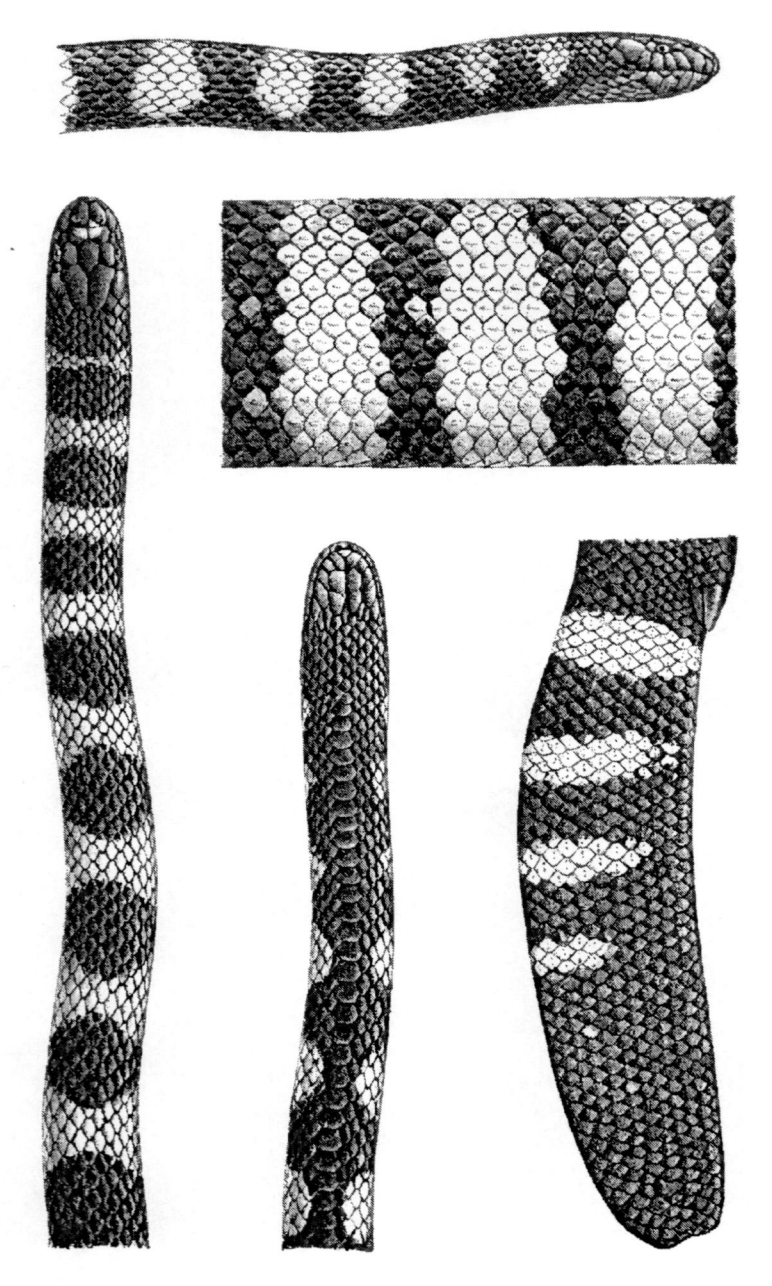

BRIT. MUS. N. H. Pl. XV.

J. Green del. et lith. Mintern Bros. imp.

Hydrophis melanocephalus.

BRIT. MUS. N.H.
PL. XVI.

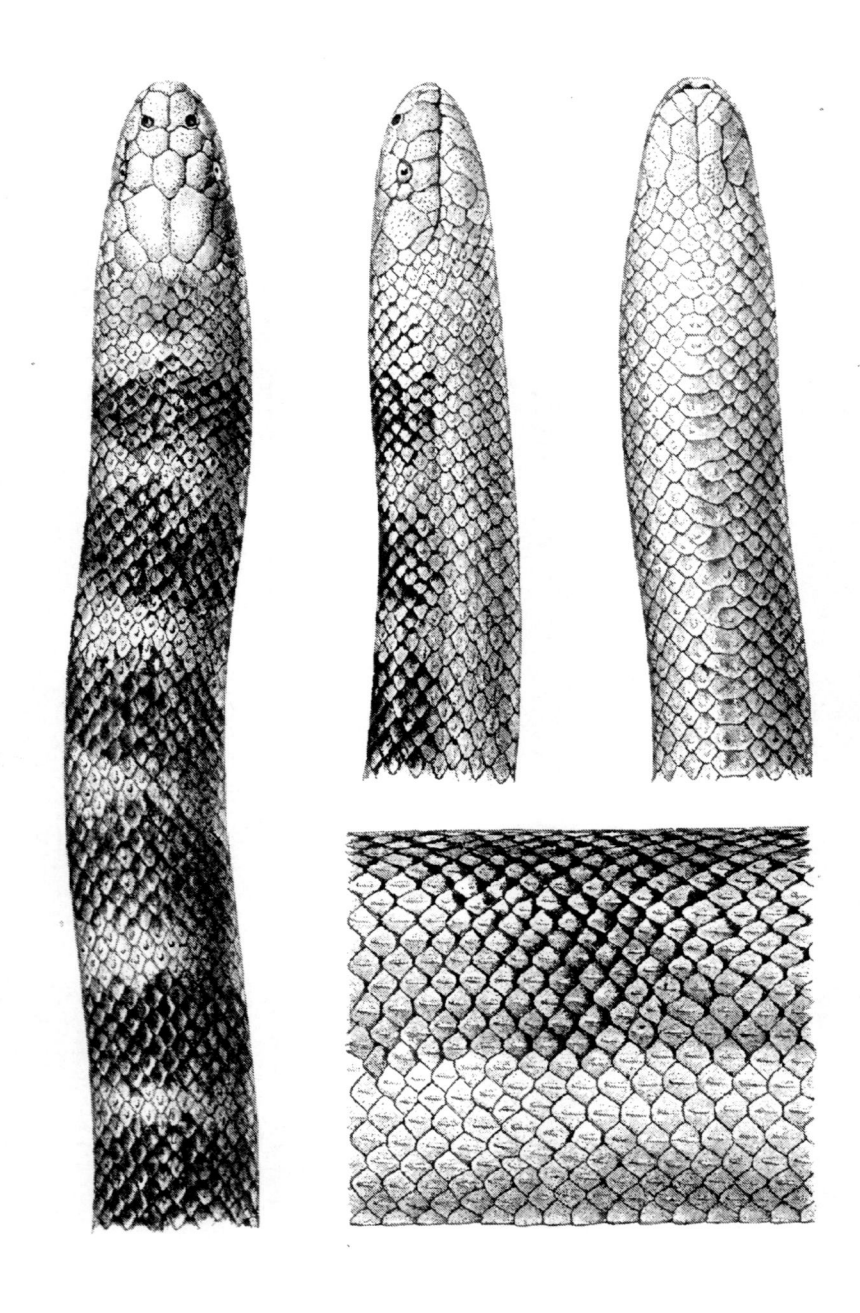

J. Green & R.E.M. del. et lith.
Mintern Bros. imp.

Distira grandis.

BRIT MUS.N.H. *Pl. XVII*

1.

2.

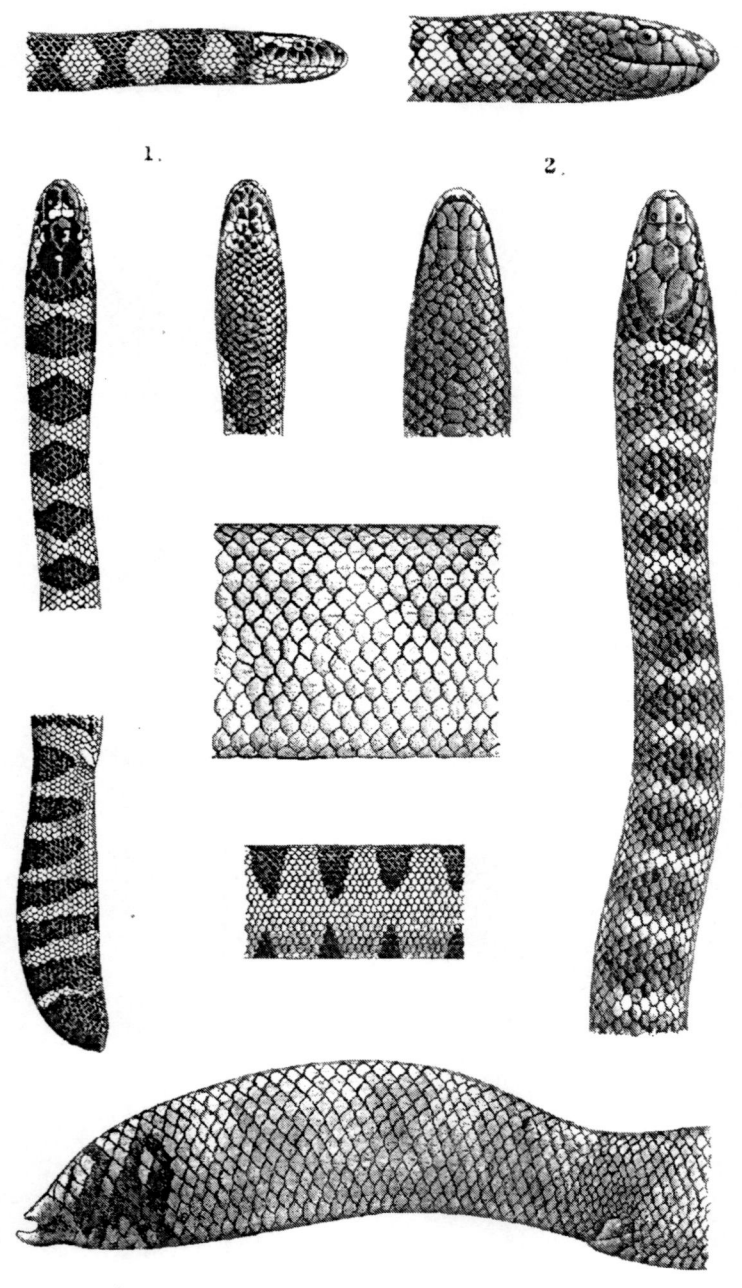

J. Green del. et lith.   Mintern Bros. imp.

1. Distira macfarlani.   2. Distira belcheri.

BRIT. MUS. N. H.
Pl. XVIII.

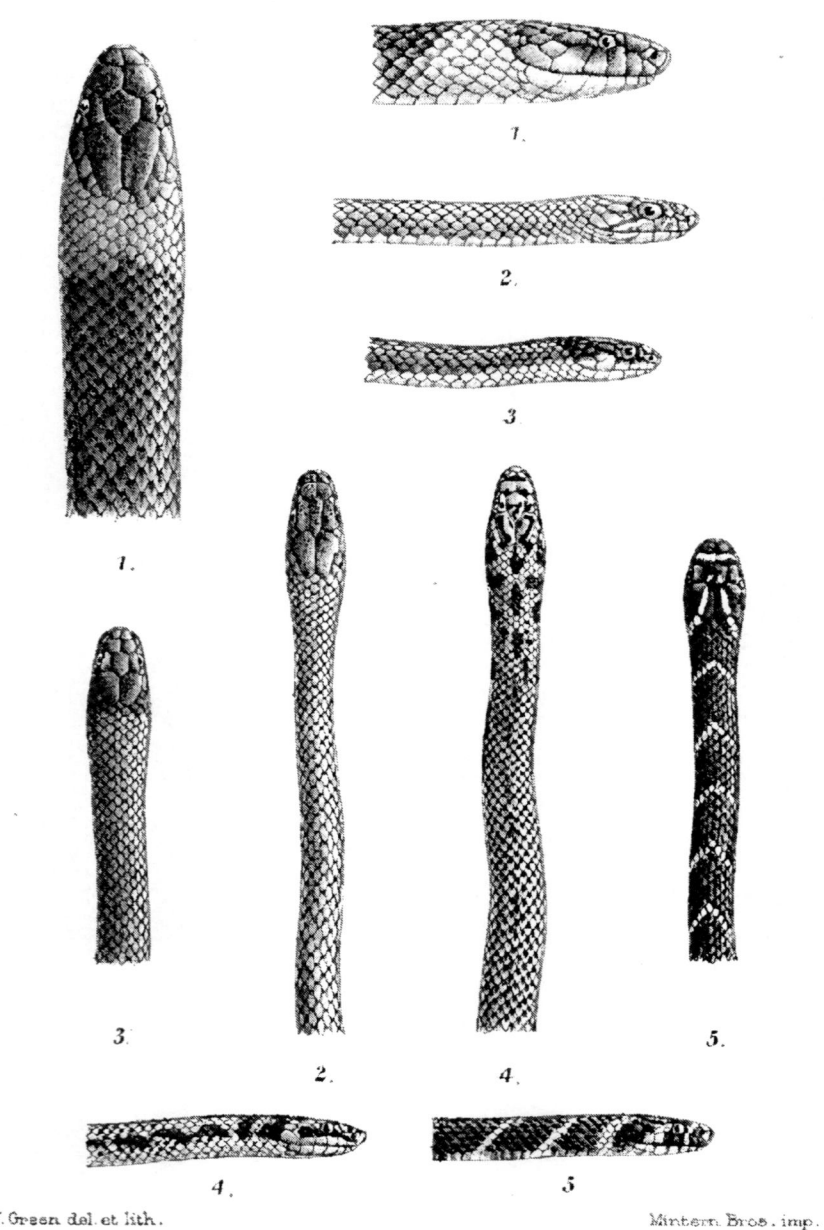

J. Green del. et lith.
Mintern Bros. imp.

1. Glyphodon tristis.   2. Diemenia olivacea.
3. Denisonia dæmelii.   4. Denisonia punctata.
5. Bungarus bungaroides.

BRIT. MUS. N.H.
Pl. XIX.

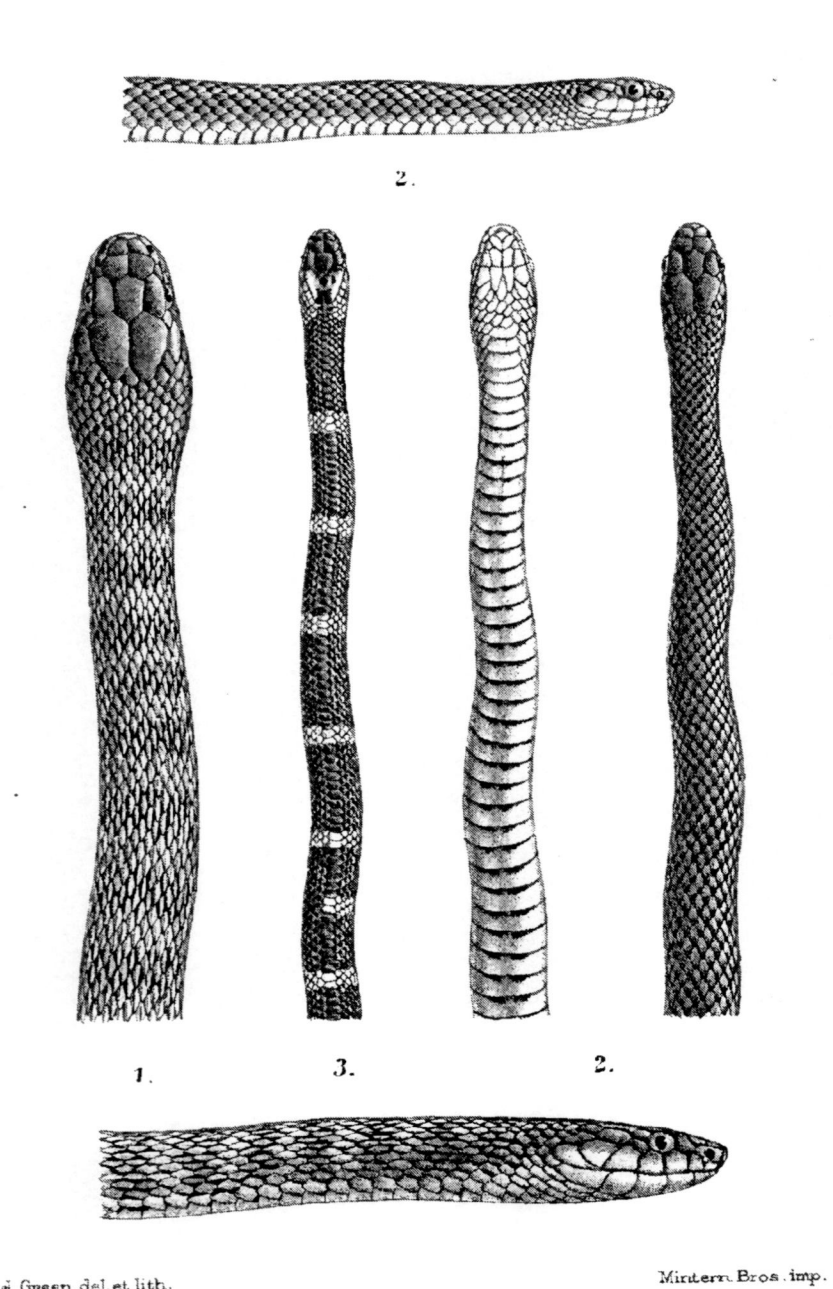

J. Green del. et lith.   Mintern Bros. imp.

1. *Tropidechis carinatus.*   2. *Elapognathus minor.*
3. *Bungarus ceylonicus.*

BRIT. MUS. N.H. PL. XX.

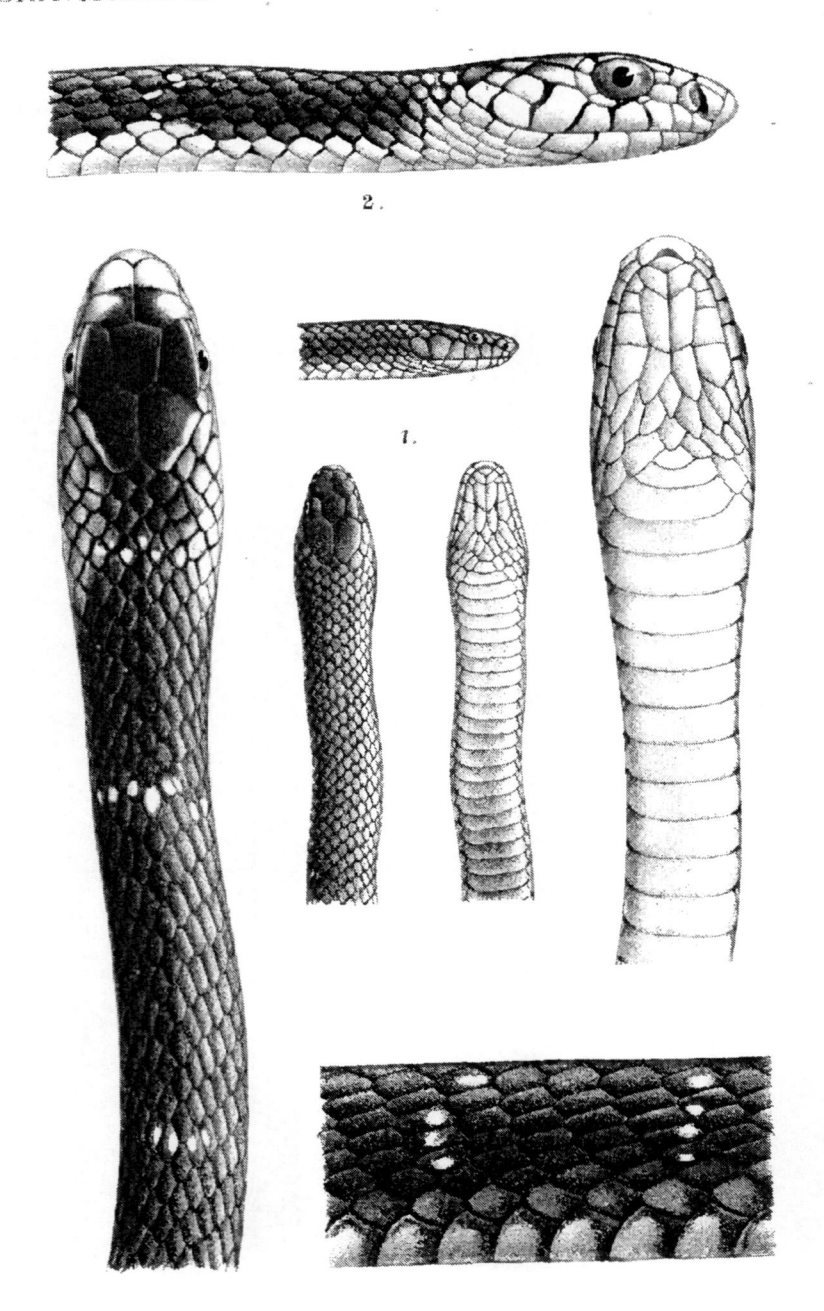

J. Green del. et lith.   Mintern Bros. imp.
1. *Elapechis niger*.   2. *Naia goldii*.

BRIT. MUS. N. H.   Pl. XVI.

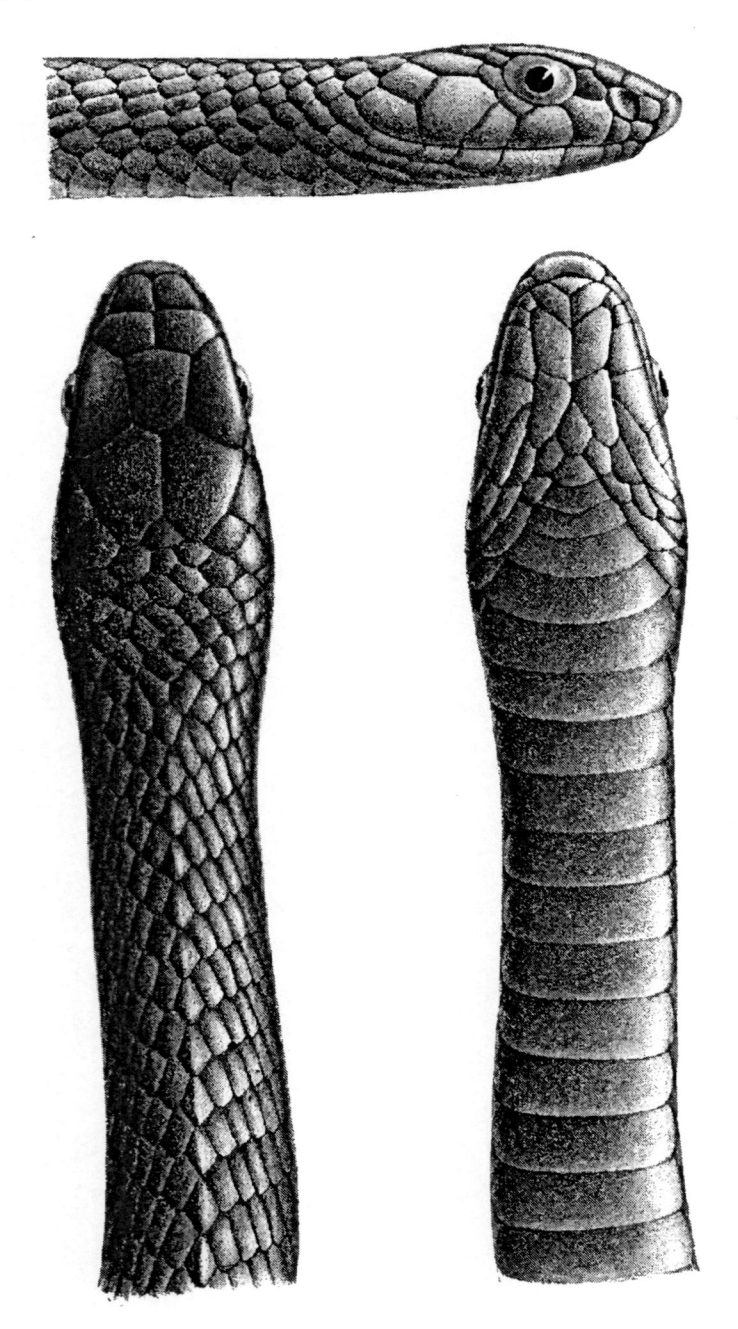

J. Green del. et lith.   Mintern Bros. imp.

Naia guentheri.

BRIT. MUS. N. H.   Pl. XXII.

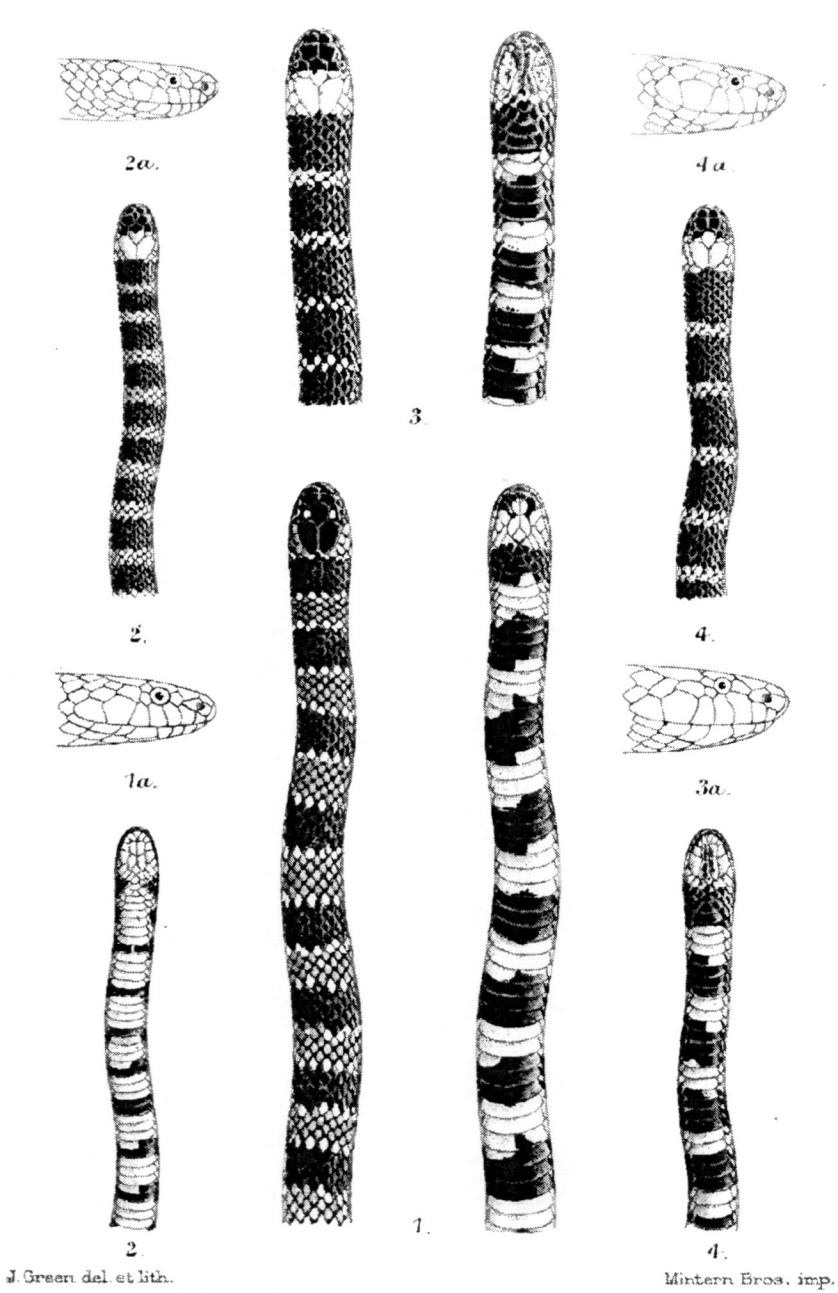

1. Elaps buckleyi. 2. Elaps anomalus.
3. Elaps fraseri. 4. Elaps mentalis.

BRIT. MUS. N.H.

Pl. XXIII.

J. Green del. et lith.

Mintern Bros. imp.

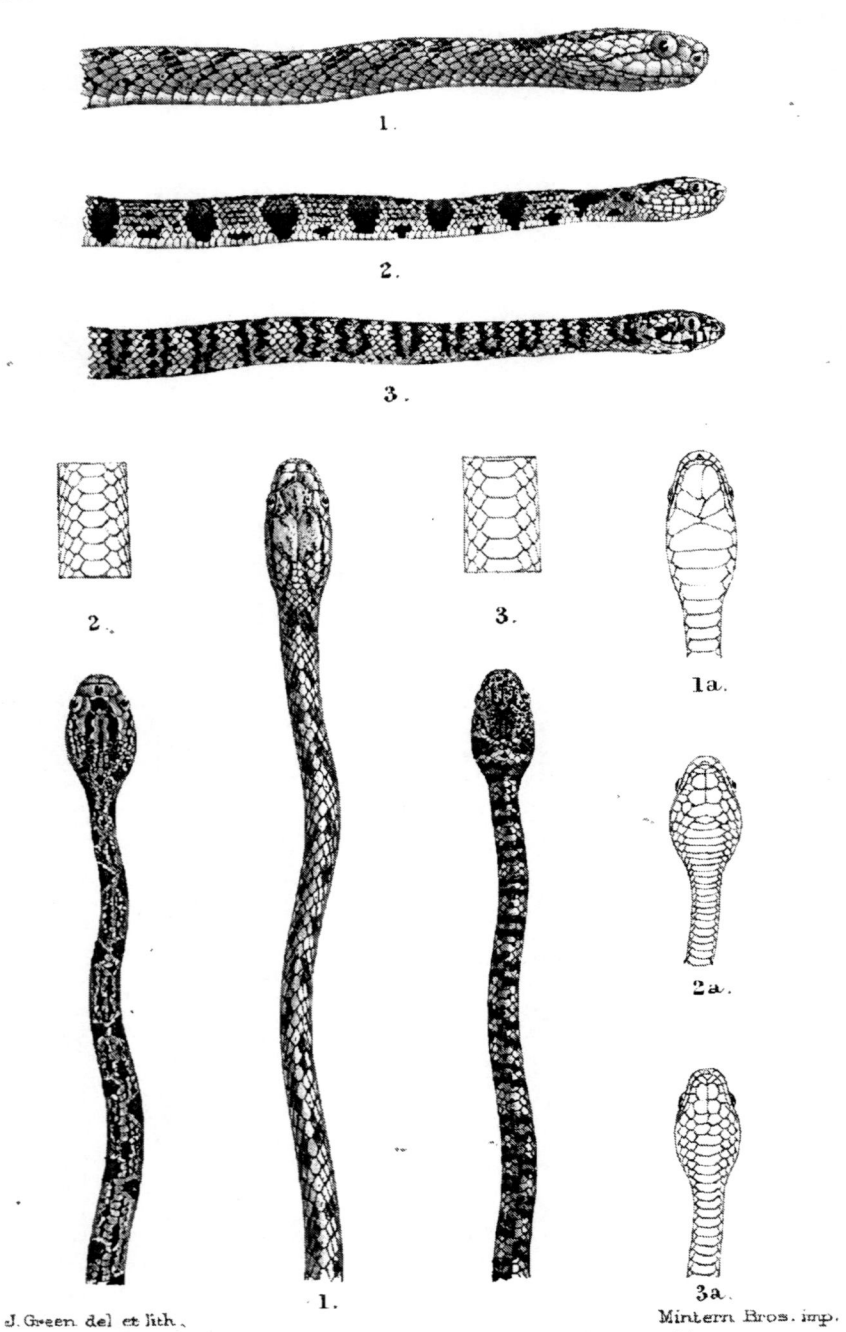

1. Amblycephalus monticola.   2. Leptognathus andiana.
3. Leptognathus elegans.

BRIT. MUS. N.H.   Pl. XXIV.

2.

2.   1   2.

J. Green del. et lith.   Mintern Bros. imp.

1. Leptognathus leucomelas.   2. Leptognathus ventrimaculata.

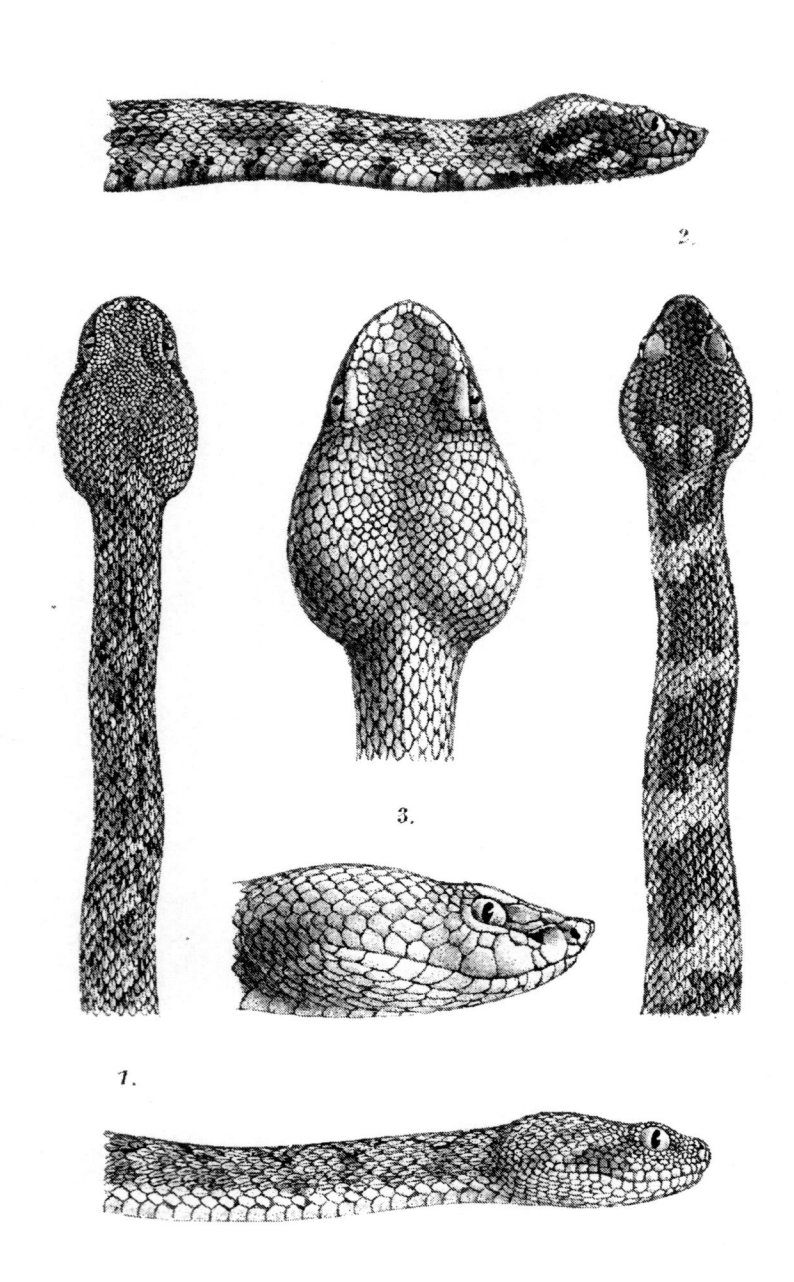

BRIT. MUS. N. H. Pl. XXV.

I. Green del. et lith. Mintern Bros. imp

1. Echis coloratus. 2. Lachesis okinavensis.
3. Lachesis flavomaculatus.

LIST OF THE CURRENT

NATURAL HISTORY PUBLICATIONS OF THE TRUSTEES OF THE BRITISH MUSEUM.

The following publications can be purchased through the Agency of Messrs. LONGMANS & CO., 39, *Paternoster Row;* Mr. QUARITCH, 15, *Piccadilly;* Messrs KEGAN PAUL, TRENCH, TRÜBNER & Co., *Paternoster House, Charing Cross Road;* and Messrs. DULAU & CO, 37, *Soho Square;* or at the NATURAL HISTORY MUSEUM, *Cromwell Road, London, S W.*

Catalogue of the Specimens and Drawings of Mammals, Birds, Reptiles, and Fishes of Nepal and Tibet. Presented by B H Hodgson, Esq, to the British Museum. 2nd edition By John Edward Gray. Pp. xii., 90. [With an account of the Collection by Mr Hodgson.] 1863, 12mo. 2s. 3d.

Report on the Zoological Collections made in the Indo-Pacific Ocean during the voyage of H.M.S. "Alert," 1881-2 Pp. xxv., 684 54 Plates. 1884, 8vo.

Summary of the Voyage	- By Dr. R. W. Coppinger.
Mammalia	„ O. Thomas
Aves	„ R. B. Sharpe.
Reptilia, Batrachia, Pisces	„ A. Gunther.
Mollusca	„ E. A Smith.
Echinodermata	„ F. J Bell.
Crustacea	„ E. J. Miers.
Coleoptera	„ C O. Waterhouse.
Lepidoptera	„ A. G. Butler.
Alcyonaria and Spongiida	„ S. O Ridley.

1*l*., 10s.

MAMMALS.

List of the Specimens of Mammalia in the Collection of the British Museum. By Dr. J E. Gray, F.R S. Pp. xxviii, 216. [With Systematic List of the Genera of Mammalia, Index of Donations, and Alphabetical Index.] 1843, 12mo. 2s. 6d

List of the Osteological Specimens in the Collection of the British Museum By John Edward Gray. Pp. xxv., 147. [With Systematic Index and Appendix.] 1847, 12 mo. 2s.

Catalogue of the Bones of Mammalia in the Collection of the British Museum. By Edward Gerrard. Pp. iv., 296 1862, 8vo. 5s.

Catalogue of Monkeys, Lemurs, and Fruit-eating Bats in the Collection of the British Museum By Dr. J. E Gray, F.R.S., &c. Pp. viii., 137. 21 Woodcuts. 1870, 8vo. 4s

Catalogue of Carnivorous, Pachydermatous, and Edentate Mammalia in the British Museum. By John Edward Gray, F R S., &c. Pp. vii, 398. 47 Woodcuts. 1869, 8vo. 6s. 6d

Catalogue of Seals and Whales in the British Museum. By John Edward Gray, F.R.S., &c. 2nd edition. Pp. vii., 402. 101 Woodcuts. 1866, 8vo. 8s.

——— Supplement. By John Edward Gray, F.R.S., &c. Pp vi, 103 11 Woodcuts 1871, 8vo 2s. 6d.

List of the Specimens of Cetacea in the Zoological Department of the British Museum. By William Henry Flower, LL.D, F.R S, &c. [With Systematic and Alphabetical Indexes.] Pp. iv, 36. 1885, 8vo. 1s. 6d.

Catalogue of Ruminant Mammalia (*Pecora*, Linnæus) in the British Museum By John Edward Gray, F.R.S., &c Pp. viii., 102. 4 Plates 1872, 8vo. 3s. 6d.

Catalogue of the Marsupialia and Monotremata in the Collection of the British Museum. By Oldfield Thomas. Pp. xiii, 401. 4 coloured and 24 plain Plates. [With Systematic and Alphabetical Indexes.] 1888, 8vo. 1l. 8s.

BIRDS.

Catalogue of the Birds in the British Museum:—
  Vol. VI. Catalogue of the Passeriformes, or Perching Birds in the Collection of the British Musuem. *Cichlomorphæ*: Part III, containing the first portion of the family Timeliidæ (Babbling Thrushes). By R. Bowdler Sharpe. Pp xiii, 420. Woodcuts and 18 coloured Plates. [With Systematic and Alphabetical Indexes.] 1881, 8vo. 1l.

  Vol. VII. Catalogue of the Passeriformes, or Perching Birds, in the Collection of the British Museum. *Cichlomorphæ*: Part IV., containing the concluding portion of the family Timeliidæ (Babbling Thrushes). By R. Bowdler Sharpe. Pp xvi, 698. Woodcuts and 15 coloured Plates. [With Systematic and Alphabetical Indexes.] 1883, 8vo. 1l. 6s.

  Vol. VIII. Catalogue of the Passeriformes or Perching Birds, in the Collection of the British Museum. *Cichlomorphæ*: Part V., containing the families Paridæ and Laniidæ (Titmice and Shrikes); and *Certhiomorphæ* (Creepers and Nuthatches). By Hans Gadow, M.A., Ph.D. Pp. viii., 386 Woodcuts and 9 coloured Plates. [With Systematic and Alphabetical Indexes 1883, 8vo. 17s.

Catalogue of the Birds in the British Museum—*continued.*
  Vol. IX. Catalogue of the Passeriformes, or Perching Birds, in the Collection of the British Museum. *Cinnyrimorphæ*, containing the families Nectariniidæ and Meliphagidæ (Sun Birds and Honey-eaters). By Hans Gadow, M.A., Ph.D. Pp. xii., 310. Woodcuts and 7 coloured Plates. [With Systematic and Alphabetical Indexes.] 1884, 8vo. 14s.

  Vol. X. Catalogue of the Passeriformes, or Perching Birds, in the Collection of the British Museum. *Fringilliformes*: Part I., containing the families Dicæidæ, Hirundinidæ, Ampelidæ, Mniotiltidæ, and Motacillidæ. By R. Bowdler Sharpe. Pp. xiii., 682. Woodcuts and 12 coloured Plates. [With Systematic and Alphabetical Indexes.] 1885, 8vo. 1l. 2s.

  Vol. XI. Catalogue of the Passeriformes, or Perching Birds, in the Collection of the British Museum. *Fringilliformes*: Part II., containing the families Cœrebidæ, Tanagridæ, and Icteridæ. By Philip Lutley Sclater, M.A., F.R.S. Pp. xvii., 431. [With Systematic and Alphabetical Indexes.] Woodcuts and 18 coloured Plates. 1886, 8vo. 1l.

  Vol. XII. Catalogue of the Passeriformes, or Perching Birds, in the Collection of the British Museum. *Fringilliformes*. Part III., containing the family Fringillidæ. By R. Bowdler Sharpe. Pp. xv., 871. Woodcuts and 16 coloured Plates. [With Systematic and Alphabetical Indexes.] 1888, 8vo. 1l. 8s.

  Vol. XIII. Catalogue of the Passeriformes, or Perching Birds, in the Collection of the British Museum. *Sturniformes*, containing the families Artamidæ, Sturnidæ, Ploceidæ, and Alaudidæ. Also the families Atrichiidæ and Menuridæ. By R. Bowdler Sharpe. Pp. xvi, 701. Woodcuts and 15 coloured Plates. [With Systematic and Alphabetical Indexes.] 1890, 8vo, 1l. 8s.

  Vol. XIV. Catalogue of the Passeriformes, or Perching Birds, in the Collection of the British Museum. *Oligomyodæ*, or the families Tyrannidæ, Oxyrhamphidæ, Pipridæ, Cotingidæ, Phytotomidæ, Philepittidæ, Pittidæ, Xenicidæ, and Eurylæmidæ. By Philip Lutley Sclater, M.A., F.R.S. Pp. xix., 494. Woodcuts and 26 coloured Plates. [With Systematic and Alphabetical Indexes.] 1888, 8vo. 1l. 4s.

  Vol. XV. Catalogue of the Passeriformes, or Perching Birds, in the Collection of the British Museum. *Tracheophonæ*, or the families Dendrocolaptidæ, Formicariidæ, Conopophagidæ, and Pteroptochidæ. By Philip Lutley Sclater, M.A., F.R.S. Pp. xvii., 371. Woodcuts and 20 coloured Plates. [With Systematic and Alphabetical Indexes.] 1890, 8vo. 1l.

Catalogue of the Birds in the British Museum—*continued.*

Vol XVI. Catalogue of the Picariæ in the Collection of the British Museum. *Upupæ* and *Trochili*, by Osbert Salvin. *Coraciæ*, of the families Cypselidæ, Caprimulgidæ, Podargidæ, and Steatornithidæ, by Ernst Hartert. Pp xvi., 703. Woodcuts and 14 coloured Plates. [With Systematic and Alphabetical Indexes.] 1892, 8vo. 1*l*. 16*s*.

Vol. XVII. Catalogue of the Picariæ in the Collection of the British Museum. *Coraciæ* (contin.) and *Halcyones*, with the families Leptosomatidæ, Coraciidæ, Meropidæ, Alcedinidæ, Momotidæ, Totidæ, and Colildæ, by R Bowdler Sharpe. *Bucerotes* and *Trogones*, by W. R. Ogilvie Grant. Pp. xi., 522. Woodcuts and 17 coloured Plates. [With Systematic and Alphabetical Indexes.] 1892, 8vo. 1*l*. 10*s*

Vol. XVIII. Catalogue of the Picariæ in the Collection of the British Museum. *Scansores*, containing the family Picidæ. By Edward Hargitt. Pp. xv., 597. Woodcuts and 15 coloured Plates. [With Systematic and Alphabetical Indexes] 1890, 8vo. 1*l*. 6*s*.

Vol. XIX. Catalogue of the Picariæ in the Collection of the British Museum. *Scansores* and *Coccyges :* containing the families Rhamphastidæ, Galbulidæ, and Bucconidæ, by P. L. Sclater ; and the families Indicatoridæ, Capitonidæ, Cuculidæ, and Musophagidæ, by G. E. Shelley. Pp. xii., 484 . 13 coloured Plates. [With Systematic and Alphabetical Indexes.] 1891, 8vo. 1*l*. 5*s*.

Vol XX Catalogue of the Psittaci, or Parrots, in the Collection of the British Museum. By T Salvadori. Pp xvii , 658: woodcuts and 18 coloured Plates [With Systematic and Alphabetical Indexes.] 1891, 8vo. 1*l* 10*s*.

Vol. XXI. Catalogue of the Columbæ, or Pigeons, in the Collection of the British Museum. By T. Salvadori Pp xvii., 676: 15 coloured Plates. [With Systematic and Alphabetical Indexes.] 1893, 8vo 1*l*. 10*s*.

Vol. XXII. Catalogue of the Game Birds (*Pterocletes, Gallinæ, Opisthocomi, Hemipodii*) in the Collection of the British Museum. By W. R. Ogilvie Grant. Pp. xvi., 585 : 8 coloured Plates. [With Systematic and Alphabetical Indexes.] 1893, 8vo. 1*l*. 6*s*.

Vol. XXIII. Catalogue of the Fulicariæ (Rallidæ and Heliornithidæ) and Alectorides (Aramidæ, Eurypygidæ, Mesitidæ, Rhinochetidæ, Gruidæ, Psophiidæ, and Otididæ) in the Collection of the British Museum. By R. Bowdler Sharpe. Pp. xiii, 353 : 9 coloured Plates. [With Systematic and Alphabetical Indexes.] 1894, 8vo. 20*s*.

List of the Specimens of Birds in the Collection of the British Museum. By George Robert Gray :—

Part III., Section I. Ramphastidæ. Pp. 16. [With Index.] 1855, 12mo. 6*d*.

List of Specimens of Birds in the British Museum—*continued*
 Part III., Section II. Psittacidæ Pp. 110. [With Index.] 1859, 12mo. 2s.

 Part III., Sections III and IV. Capitonidæ and Picidæ. Pp. 137. [With Index] 1868, 12mo. 1s. 6d.

 Part IV. Columbæ. Pp 73. [With Index.] 1856, 12mo. 1s 9d

 Part V. Gallinæ. Pp. iv., 120. [With an Alphabetical Index.] 1867, 12mo. 1s. 6d.

Catalogue of the Birds of the Tropical Islands of the Pacific Ocean in the Collection of the British Museum. By George Robert Gray, F.L.S, &c Pp 72. [With an Alphabetical Index.] 1859, 8vo. 1s. 6d.

REPTILES.

Catalogue of the Tortoises, Crocodiles, and Amphisbænians in the Collection of the British Museum. By Dr. J. E. Gray, F R.S., &c. Pp. viii., 80. [With an Alphabetical Index.] 1844, 12mo. 1s.

Catalogue of Shield Reptiles in the Collection of the British Museum. By John Edward Gray, F.R.S., &c. :—
 Appendix. Pp 28. 1872, 4to. 2s. 6d.

 Part II. Emydosaurians, Rhynchocephalia, and Amphisbænians Pp. vi., 41. 25 Woodcuts 1872, 4to 3s. 6d

Hand-List of the Specimens of Shield Reptiles in the British Museum By Dr. J. E. Gray, F.R.S, F.L.S., &c. Pp. iv., 124. [With an Alphabetical Index.] 1873, 8vo. 4s.

Catalogue of the Chelonians, Rhynchocephalians, and Crocodiles in the British Museum (Natural History). New Edition. By George Albert Boulenger. Pp x., 311. 73 Woodcuts and 6 Plates [With Systematic and Alphabetical Indexes.] 1889, 8vo. 15s

Catalogue of the Specimens of Lizards in the Collection of the British Museum. By Dr. J. E. Gray, F.R.S., &c. Pp xxviii., 289 [With Geographic, Systematic, and Alphabetical Indexes.] 1845, 12mo. 3s. 6d.

Catalogue of the Lizards in the British Museum (Natural History). Second Edition. By George Albert Boulenger :—
 Vol. I. Geckonidæ, Eublepharidæ, Uroplatidæ, Pygopodidæ, Agamidæ Pp. xii., 436 32 Plates. [With Systematic and Alphabetical Indexes.] 1885, 8vo. 20s.

 Vol. II Iguanidæ, Xenosauridæ, Zonuridæ, Anguidæ, Anniellidæ, Helodermatidæ, Varanidæ, Xantusiidæ, Teiidæ, Amphisbænidæ Pp. xii., 497. 24 Plates. [With Systematic and Alphabetical Indexes.] 1885, 8vo 20s.

Catalogue of the Lizards in the British Museum—*continued*.
  Vol. III. Lacertidæ, Gerrhosauridæ, Scincidæ, Anelytropidæ, Dibamidæ, Chamæleontidæ Pp. xii., 575. 40 Plates. [With a Systematic Index and an Alphabetical Index to the three volumes.] 1887, 8vo. 1*l*. 6*s*.

Catalogue of the Snakes in the British Museum (Natural History). By George Albert Boulenger, F.R.S. :—
  Vol. I, containing the families Typhlopidæ, Glauconiidæ, Boidæ, Ilysiidæ, Uropeltidæ, Xenopeltidæ, and Colubridæ aglyphæ, part. Pp xiii., 448: 26 Woodcuts and 28 Plates. [With Systematic and Alphabetical Indexes] 1893, 8vo. 1*l*. 1*s*.

  Vol. II., containing the conclusion of the Colubridæ aglyphæ Pp xi., 382: 25 Woodcuts and 20 Plates. [With Systematic and Alphabetical Indexes] 1894, 8vo. 17*s* 6*d*.

Catalogue of Colubrine Snakes in the Collection of the British Museum. By Dr Albert Gunther. Pp. xvi., 281 [With Geographic, Systematic, and Alphabetical Indexes.] 1858, 12mo. 4*s*.

BATRACHIANS.

Catalogue of the Batrachia Salientia in the Collection of the British Museum. By Dr Albert Günther. Pp. xvi., 160. 12 Plates. [With Systematic, Geographic, and Alphabetical Indexes.] 1858, 8vo. 6*s*.

Catalogue of the Batrachia Gradientia, s Caudata, and Batrachia Apoda in the Collection of the British Museum. Second Edition. By George Albert Boulenger. Pp. viii., 127. 9 Plates. [With Systematic and Alphabetical Indexes] 1882, 8vo. 9*s*.

FISHES.

Catalogue of the Fishes in the Collection of the British Museum. By Dr. Albert Günther, F.R.S., &c. :—
  Vol. VII. Physostomi (Heterophygii, Cyprinidæ, Gonorhynchidæ, Hyodontidæ, Osteoglossidæ, Clupeidæ, Chirocentridæ, Alepocephalidæ, Notopteridæ, Halosauridæ). Pp. xx, 512 Woodcuts. [With Systematic and Alphabetical Indexes] 1868, 8vo. 8*s*.

  Vol. VIII. Physostomi (Gymnotidæ, Symbranchidæ, Murænidæ, Pegasidæ), Lophobranchii, Plectognathi, Dipnoi, Ganoidei, Chondropterygii, Cyclostomata, Leptocardii Pp xxv, 549. [With Systematic and Alphabetical Indexes] 1870, 8vo. 8*s* 6*d*.

Catalogue of the Fishes in the British Museum. Second edition. Vol. I. Catalogue of the Perciform Fishes in the British Museum. Vol. I. containing the Centrarchidæ, Percidæ, and Sciranidæ (part). By George Albert Boulenger, F.R.S. Pp. xix., 394. Woodcuts and 15 plates. [With Systematic and Alphabetical Indexes.] 1895, 8vo. 15s.

List of the Specimens of Fish in the Collection of the British Museum. Part I. Chondropterygii. By J. E. Gray. Pp. x., 160. 2 Plates. [With Systematic and Alphabetical Indexes.] 1851, 12mo. 3s.

Catalogue of Fish collected and described by Laurence Theodore Gronow, now in the British Museum. Pp. vii., 196. [With a Systematic Index.] 1854, 12mo. 3s. 6d.

Catalogue of Lophobranchiate Fish in the Collection of the British Museum. By J. J. Kaup, Ph.D., &c. Pp iv., 80. 4 Plates. [With an Alphabetical Index.] 1856, 12mo. 2s.

MOLLUSCA.

Guide to the Systematic Distribution of Mollusca in the British Museum. Part I. By John Edward Gray, Ph.D, F.R.S, &c. Pp. xii., 230. 121 Woodcuts. 1857, 8vo. 5s.

List of the Shells of the Canaries in the Collection of the British Museum, collected by MM. Webb and Berthelot. Described and figured by Prof. Alcide D'Orbigny in the "Histoire Naturelle des Iles Canaries." Pp. 32. 1854, 12mo. 1s.

List of the Shells of Cuba in the Collection of the British Museum, collected by M. Ramon de la Sagra. Described by Prof. Alcide d'Orbigny in the "Histoire de l'Ile de Cuba." Pp 48. 1854, 12mo. 1s.

List of the Shells of South America in the Collection of the British Museum. Collected and described by M. Alcide D'Orbigny in the "Voyage dans l'Amérique Méridionale." Pp. 89. 1854, 12mo. 2s.

Catalogue of the Collection of Mazatlan Shells in the British Museum, collected by Frederick Reigen. Described by Philip P. Carpenter. Pp. xvi., 552. 1857, 12mo. 8s.

List of Mollusca and Shells in the Collection of the British Museum, collected and described by MM. Eydoux and Souleyet in the "Voyage autour du Monde, exécuté pendant les années "1836 et 1837, sur la Corvette 'La Bonite,'" and in the "Histoire naturelle des Mollusques Ptéropodes." Par MM. P. C. A. L. Rang et Souleyet. Pp. iv., 27. 1855. 12mo. 8d.

Catalogue of the Phaneropneumona, or Terrestrial Operculated Mollusca, in the Collection of the British Museum. By Dr L. Pfeiffer. Pp. 324. [With an Alphabetical Index.] 1852, 12mo. 5s.

8   LIST OF PUBLICATIONS OF THE

Nomenclature of Molluscous Animals and Shells in the Collection of the British Museum. Part I. Cyclophoridæ. Pp. 69. [With an Index] 1850, 12mo 1s 6d

Catalogue of Pulmonata, or Air Breathing Mollusca, in the Collection of the British Museum Part I . By Dr. Louis Pfeiffer. Pp, iv., 192. Woodcuts. 1855, 12mo. 2s. 6d

Catalogue of the Auriculidæ, Proserpinidæ, and Truncatellidæ in the Collection of the British Museum. By Dr. Louis Pfeiffer. Pp. iv , 150. Woodcuts 1857, 12mo. 1s. 9d.

List of the Mollusca in the Collection of the British Museum. By John Edward Gray, Ph.D , F.R.S , &c.
    Part I. Volutidæ. Pp. 23. 1855, 12mo. 6d
    Part II. Olividæ. Pp. 41. 1865, 12mo. 1s.

Catalogue of the Conchifera, or Bivalve Shells, in the Collection of the British Museum. By M. Deshayes :—
    Part I. Veneridæ, Cyprinidæ, Glauconomidæ, and Petricoladæ. Pp. iv., 216. 1853, 12mo. 3s.
    Part II. Petricoladæ (concluded); Corbiculadæ. Pp. 217-292. [With an Alphabetical Index to the two parts.] 1854, 12mo. 6d.

BRACHIOPODA

Catalogue of Brachiopoda Ancylopoda or Lamp Shells in the Collection of the British Museum. [*Issued as* "Catalogue of the Mollusca, Part IV"] Pp iv., 128. 25 Woodcuts. [With an Alphabetical Index] 1853, 12mo. 3s.

POLYZOA.

Catalogue of Marine Polyzoa in the Collection of the British Museum. Part III. Cyclostomata. By George Busk, F.R.S. Pp. viii., 39. 38 Plates. [With a Systematic Index.] 1875, 8vo. 5s

CRUSTACEA.

Catalogue of Crustacea in the Collection of the British Museum. Part I Leucosiadæ. By Thomas Bell, V.P.R S , Pres L.S., &c. Pp. iv , 24. 1855, 8vo. 6d.

Catalogue of the Specimens of Amphipodous Crustacea in the Collection of the British Museum. By C. Spence Bate, F.R.S., &c Pp. iv., 399. 58 Plates. [With an Alphabetical Index.] 1862, 8vo. 1l. 5s

ARACHNIDA.

Descriptive Catalogue of the Spiders of Burma, based upon the Collection made by Eugene W. Oates and preserved in the British Museum. By T. Thorell. Pp xxxvi., 406 [With Systematic List and Alphabetical Index.] 1895, 8vo. 10s. 6d.

MYRIOPODA

Catalogue of the Myriapoda in the Collection of the British Museum. By George Newport, F.R S., P.E.S., &c. Part I. Chilopoda Pp iv., 96. [With an Alphabetical Index] 1856, 12mo 1s 9d.

INSECTS.

Coleopterous Insects.

Nomenclature of Coleopterous Insects in the Collection of the British Museum:—

Part IV. Cleridæ. By Adam White Pp. 68. [With Index.] 1849, 12mo 1s. 8d.

Part V. Cucujidæ, &c. By Frederick Smith. [*Also issued as* "List of the Coleopterous Insects Part I"] Pp. 25. 1851, 12mo. 6d

Part VI. Passalidæ. By Frederick Smith. Pp. iv, 23. 1 Plate [With Index.] 1852, 12mo. 8d

Part VII. Longicornia, I. By Adam White. Pp. iv, 174. 4 Plates. 1853, 12mo. 2s. 6d.

Part VIII. Longicornia, II. By Adam White. Pp 237. 6 Plates. 1855, 12mo 3s 6d

Part IX. Cassididæ. By Charles H. Boheman, Professor of Natural History, Stockholm. Pp. 225. [With Index.] 1856, 12mo. 3s.

Illustrations of Typical Specimens of Coleoptera in the Collection of the British Museum Part I. Lycidæ By Charles Owen Waterhouse Pp. x., 83. 18 coloured Plates. [With Systematic and Alphabetical Indexes.] 1879, 8vo 16s

Catalogue of the Coleopterous Insects of Madeira in the Collection of the British Museum. By T. Vernon Wollaston, M A., F L.S Pp. xvi, 234: 1 Plate [With a Topographical Catalogue and an Alphabetical Index] 1857, 8vo. 3s.

Catalogue of the Coleopterous Insects of the Canaries in the Collection of the British Museum. By T. Vernon Wollaston, M A., F L.S Pp. xiii., 648 [With Topographical and Alphabetical Indexes.] 1864, 8vo 10s. 6d.

Catalogue of Halticidæ in the Collection of the British Museum. By the Rev. Hamlet Clark, M.A., F.L.S. Physapodes and Œdipodes. Part I. Pp. xii., 301. Frontispiece and 9 Plates. 1860, 8vo. 7s.

Catalogue of Hispidæ in the Collection of the British Museum. By Joseph S. Baly, M E S., &c. Part I. Pp. x., 172. 9 Plates. [With an Alphabetical Index.] 1858, 8vo. 6s

Hymenopterous Insects.

List of the Specimens of Hymenopterous Insects in the Collection of the British Museum. By Francis Walker, F L.S. :—
    Part II. Chalcidites. Additional Species. Appendix. Pp. iv., 99-237. 1848, 12mo. 2s.

Catalogue of Hymenopterous Insects in the Collection of the British Museum. By Frederick Smith. 12mo.:—
    Part I. Andrenidæ and Apidæ. Pp. 197. 6 Plates. 1853, 2s. 6d.
    Part II. Apidæ. Pp. 199-465. 6 Plates. [With an Alphabetical Index.] 1854, 6s.
    Part III. Mutillidæ and Pompilidæ. Pp 206. 6 Plates. 1855, 6s.
    Part IV. Sphegidæ, Larridæ, and Crabronidæ. Pp. 207-497. 6 Plates. [With an Alphabetical Index.] 1856, 6s
    Part V. Vespidæ Pp 147. 6 Plates. [With an Alphabetical Index.] 1857, 6s.
    Part VI Formicidæ. Pp. 216 14 Plates [With an Alphabetical Index.] 1858, 6s.
    Part VII. Dorylidæ and Thynnidæ. Pp. 76. 3 Plates. [With an Alphabetical Index.] 1859, 2s.

Descriptions of New Species of Hymenoptera in the Collection of the British Museum. By Frederick Smith. Pp. xxi, 240 [With Systematic and Alphabetical Indexes.] 1879, 8vo. 10s.

List of Hymenoptera, with descriptions and figures of the Typical Specimens in the British Museum. Vol. I., Tenthredinidæ and Siricidæ By W. F. Kirby. Pp. xxviii, 450. 16 Coloured Plates. [With Systematic and Alphabetical Indexes.] 1882, 8vo. 1l. 18s.

Dipterous Insects.

List of the Specimens of Dipterous Insects in the Collection of the British Museum. By Francis Walker, F.L.S. 12mo.:—
    Part IV. Pp. 689-1172. [With an Index to the four parts, and an Index of Donors.] 1849. 6s.
    Part VII. Supplement III. Asilidæ. Pp. ii. 507-775. 1855. 3s. 6d.

Lepidopterous Insects.

Illustrations of Typical Specimens of Lepidoptera Heterocera in the Collection of the British Museum :—
    Part III. By Arthur Gardiner Butler. Pp. xviii, 82. 41-60 Coloured Plates. [With a Systematic Index.] 1879 4to. 2l. 10s

Illustrations of Typical Specimens of Lepidoptera Heterocera
—*continued*.
> Part V. By Arthur Gardiner Butler. Pp. xii, 74. 78–100 Coloured Plates. [With a Systematic Index.] 1881, 4to. 2*l*. 10*s*.
>
> Part VI. By Arthur Gardiner Butler. Pp. xv., 89 101–120 Coloured Plates. [With a Systematic Index.] 1886, 4to. 2*l*. 4*s*.
>
> Part VII. By Arthur Gardiner Butler. Pp. iv., 124. 121–138 Coloured Plates [With a Systematic List.] 1889, 4to. 2*l*.
>
> Part VIII. The Lepidoptera Heterocera of the Nilgiri District By George Francis Hampson. Pp. iv., 144. 139–156 Coloured Plates. [With a Systematic List.] 1891, 4to. 2*l*.
>
> Part IX. The Macrolepidoptera Heterocera of Ceylon. By George Francis Hampson. Pp. v., 182 157–176. Coloured Plates. [With a General Systematic List of Species collected in, or recorded from, Ceylon] 1893, 4to. 2*l*. 2*s*.

Catalogue of Diurnal Lepidoptera of the family Satyridæ in the Collection of the British Museum. By Arthur Gardiner Butler, F.L S., &c Pp. vi., 211. 5 Plates. [With an Alphabetical Index.] 1868, 8vo 5*s*. 6*d*.

Catalogue of Diurnal Lepidoptera described by Fabricius in the Collection of the British Museum. By Arthur Gardiner Butler, F.L S , &c. Pp. iv , 303. 3 Plates. 1869, 8vo. 7*s*. 6*d*.

Specimen of a Catalogue of Lycænidæ in the British Museum. By W. C. Hewitson. Pp. 15. 8 Coloured Plates. 1862, 4to. 1*l*. 1*s*.

List of Lepidopterous Insects in the Collection of the British Museum. Part I. Papilionidæ. By G. R. Gray, F L S Pp. 106. [With an Alphabetical Index] 1856, 12mo. 2*s*.

List of the Specimens of Lepidopterous Insects in the Collection of the British Museum. By Francis Walker. 12mo. :—
> Part VI. Lepidoptera Heterocera Pp. 1258–1507. 1855, 3*s*. 6*d*.
> Part X Noctuidæ Pp. 253–491 1856, 3*s*. 6*d*.
> Part XII. ——— Pp. 765–982 1857, 3*s*. 6*d*.
> Part XIII. ——— Pp. 983–1236 1857, 3*s*. 6*d*.
> Part XIV. ——— Pp. 1237–1519. 1858, 4*s*. 6*d*.
> Part XV. ——— Pp. 1520–1888. [With an Alphabetical Index to Parts IX –XV.] 1858, 4*s*. 6*d*.
> Part XVI. Deltoides. Pp. 253. 1858, 3*s* 6*d*.
> Part XIX. Pyralides. Pp. 799–1036. [With an Alphabetical Index to Parts XVI.–XIX.] 1859, 3*s*. 6*d*.
> Part XXI. Geometrites. Pp 277–498. 1860, 3*s*.
> Part XXII. ——— Pp. 499–755. 1861, 3*s*. 6*d*.
> Part XXIII. - —— Pp. 756–1020. 1861, 3*s*. 6*d*.

List of Specimens of Lepidopterous Insects—*continued*
  Part XXIV. ——— Pp. 1021–1280. 1862, 3s. 6d.
  Part XXV ——— Pp. 1281–1477. 1862, 3s.
  Part XXVI. ——— Pp 1478–1796. [With an Alphabetical Index to Parts XX.–XXVI.] 1862, 4s. 6d.
  Part XXVII. Crambites and Tortricites. Pp 1–286. 1863, 4s
  Part XXVIII. Tortricites and Tineites. Pp. 287–561. 1863, 4s.
  Part XXIX. Tineites. Pp 562–835 1864, 4s
  Part XXX ——— Pp 836–1096. [With an Alphabetical Index to Parts XXVII–XXX.] 1864, 4s.
  Part XXXI. Supplement. Pp. 1–321. 1864, 5s.
  Part XXXII. ——— Part 2 Pp. 322–706. 1865, 5s.
  Part XXXIII. ——— Part 3. Pp 707–1120. 1865, 6s.
  Part XXXIV. ——— Part 4. Pp. 1121–1533. 1865, 5s. 6d.
  Part XXXV. ——— Part 5. Pp 1534–2040. [With an Alphabetical Index to Parts XXXI.–XXXV] 1866, 7s.

Neuropterous Insects.

Catalogue of the Specimens of Neuropterous Insects in the Collection of the British Museum By Francis Walker. 12mo :—
  Part I. Phryganides—Perlides. Pp iv., 192 1852, 2s. 6d.
  Part II. Sialidæ—Nemopterides. Pp. ii., 193–476, 1853, 3s. 6d.
  Part III. Termitidæ—Ephemeridæ. Pp. ii, 477–585 1853, 1s. 6d.
Catalogue of the Specimens of Neuropterous Insects in the Collection of the British Museum. By Dr. H. Hagen. Part I. Termitina. Pp. 34. 1858, 12mo. 6d.

Orthopterous Insects

Catalogue of Orthopterous Insects in the Collection of the British Museum. Part I. Phasmidæ. By John Obadiah Westwood, F L.S., &c. Pp. 195. 48 Plates. [With an Alphabetical Index.] 1859, 4to. 3l.
Catalogue of the Specimens of Blattariæ in the Collection of the British Museum. By Francis Walker, F.L.S., &c Pp. 239 [With an Alphabetical Index.] 1868, 8vo. 5s. 6d.
Catalogue of the Specimens of Dermaptera Saltatoria [Part I.] and Supplement to the Blattariæ in the Collection of the British Museum. Gryllidæ. Blattariæ. Locustidæ. By Francis Walker, F.L.S., &c Pp 224. [With an Alphabetical Index.] 1869, 8vo 5s.

Catalogue of the Specimens of Dermaptera Saltatoria in the Collection of the British Museum. By Francis Walker, F L S., &c.—

    Part II. Locustidæ (continued). Pp. 225-423. [With an Alphabetical Index.] 1869, 8vo 4s 6d.

    Part III. Locustidæ (continued) —Acrididæ. Pp. 425-604 [With an Alphabetical Index.] 1870, 8vo. 4s.

    Part IV. Acrididæ (continued) Pp. 605-809 [With an Alphabetical Index.] 1870, 8vo. 6s.

    Part V. Tettigidæ.—Supplement to the Catalogue of Blattariæ.—Supplement to the Catalogue of Dermaptera Saltatoria (with remarks on the Geographical Distribution of Dermaptera) Pp. 811-850, 43; 116. [With Alphabetical Indexes.] 1870, 8vo. 6s.

Hemipterous Insects

List of the Specimens of Hemipterous Insects in the Collection of the British Museum. By W S. Dallas, F.L.S. Part II. Pp. 369-590. Plates 12-15. 1852, 12mo. 4s.

Catalogue of the Specimens of Heteropterous Hemiptera in the Collection of the British Museum. By Francis Walker, F.L.S., &c. 8vo :—

    Part I. Scutata. Pp. 240. 1867. 5s.
    Part II. Scutata (continued) Pp. 241-417. 1867. 4s.
    Part III. Pp. 418-599. [With an Alphabetical Index to Parts I., II., III, and a Summary of Geographical Distribution of the Species mentioned] 1868. 4s. 6d
    Part IV. Pp. 211. [Alphabetical Index.] 1871   6s
    Part V. Pp. 202. ——————— 1872.   5s.
    Part VI Pp. 210. ——————— 1873   5s.
    Part VII. Pp. 213 ——————— 1873.   6s.
    Part VIII Pp. 220. ——————— 1873.   6s. 6d.

Homopterous Insects.

List of the Specimens of Homopterous Insects in the Collection of the British Museum. By Francis Walker. Supplement. Pp. ii , 369. [With an Alphabetical Index.] 1858, 12mo 4s. 6d.

VERMES

Catalogue of the Species of Entozoa, or Intestinal Worms, contained in the Collection of the British Museum By Dr. Baird. Pp. iv, 132. 2 Plates [With an Index of the Animals in which the Entozoa mentioned in the Catalogue are found; and an Index of Genera and Species.] 1853, 12mo 2s.

ANTHOZOA.

Catalogue of Sea-pens or Pennatulariidæ in the Collection of the British Museum. By J. E. Gray, F.R.S., &c. Pp. iv, 40. 2 Woodcuts. 1870, 8vo. 1s. 6d.

Catalogue of Lithophytes or Stony Corals in the Collection of the British Museum. By J. E. Gray, F.R.S., &c. Pp. iv., 51. 14 Woodcuts. 1870, 8vo. 3s.

Catalogue of the Madreporarian Corals in the British Museum (Natural History). Vol. I. The Genus Madrepora. By George Brook. Pp. xi, 212. 35 Collotype Plates. [With Systematic and Alphabetical Indexes, Explanation of Plates, and a Preface by Dr. Gunther.] 1893, 4to 1l 4s.

BRITISH ANIMALS.

Catalogue of British Birds in the Collection of the British Museum. By George Robert Gray, F.L.S., F.Z.S., &c. Pp. xii., 248. [With a List of Species.] 1863, 8vo. 3s 6d.

Catalogue of British Hymenoptera in the Collection of the British Museum. Second edition. Part I. Andrenidæ and Apidæ. By Frederick Smith, M.E.S. New Issue. Pp xi.; 236. 11 Plates [With Systematic and Alphabetical Indexes.] 1891, 8vo. 6s.

Catalogue of British Fossorial Hymenoptera, Formicidæ, and Vespidæ in the Collection of the British Museum. By Frederick Smith, V.P.E.S. Pp 236. 6 Plates. [With an Alphabetical Index.] 1858, 12mo. 6s.

A Catalogue of the British Non-parasitical Worms in the Collection of the British Museum. By George Johnston, M.D., Edin., F.R.C.L. Ed., LL.D. Marischal Coll. Aberdeen, &c. Pp 365. Woodcuts and 24 Plates. [With an Alphabetical Index.] 1865, 8vo 7s.

Catalogue of the British Echinoderms in the British Museum (Natural History). By F. Jeffrey Bell, M.A. Pp xvii, 202. Woodcuts and 16 Plates (2 coloured). [With Table of Contents, Tables of Distribution, Alphabetical Index, Description of the Plates, &c.] 1892, 8vo. 12s. 6d.

List of the Specimens of British Animals in the Collection of the British Museum, with Synonyma and References to figures. 12mo.:—

> Part I. Centroniæ or Radiated Animals. By Dr. J. E. Gray. Pp. xiii., 173. 1848, 4s.
>
> Part IV. Crustacea. By A. White. Pp. iv., 141. (With an Index.) 1850, 2s. 6d.
>
> Part V. Lepidoptera. By J. F. Stephens. 2nd Edition. By H. T. Stainton and E. Shepherd. Pp. iv, 224. 1856, 1s. 9d
>
> Part VI. Hymenoptera. By F. Smith. Pp 134. 1851, 2s.
>
> Part VII. Mollusca, Acephala, and Brachiopoda. By Dr. J. E. Gray. Pp iv., 167. 1851. 3s. 6d.

List of the Specimens of British Animals—*continued*
  Part VIII. Fish. By Adam White. Pp. xxiii, 164. (With Index and List of Donors.) 1851, 3s 6d.
  Part IX. Eggs of British Birds. By George Robert Gray. Pp. 143. 1852, 2s. 6d.
  Part XI. Anoplura or Parasitic Insects. By H. Denny. Pp. iv, 51. 1852, 1s.
  Part XII. Lepidoptera (continued.) By James F. Stephens. Pp iv., 54. 1852, 9d.
  Part XIII. Nomenclature of Hymenoptera. By Frederick Smith. Pp. iv., 74. 1853, 1s 4d.
  Part XIV. Nomenclature of Neuroptera. By Adam White. Pp. iv, 16. 1853, 6d.
  Part XV. Nomenclature of Diptera, 1. By Adam White. Pp. iv., 42. 1853, 1s.
  Part XVI. Lepidoptera (completed). By H T. Stainton. Pp. 199. [With an Index.] 1854, 3s.
  Part XVII Nomenclature of Anoplura, Euplexoptera, and Orthoptera. By Adam White. Pp. iv., 17. 1855, 6d.

PLANTS.

A Monograph of Lichens found in Britain: being a Descriptive Catalogue of the Species in the Herbarium of the British Museum. By the Rev. James M. Crombie, M A., F.L.S, F.G.S., &c Part I. Pp. viii., 519; 74 Woodcuts. [With Glossary, Synopsis, Tabular Conspectus, and Index.] 1894, 8vo. 16s.

A Monograph of the Mycetozoa : being a Descriptive Catalogue of the Species in the Herbarium of the British Museum By Arthur Lister, F.L.S. Pp. 224. 78 Plates and 51 Woodcuts. [With Synopsis of Genera and List of Species, and Index.] 1894, 8vo. 15s.

List of British Diatomaceæ in the Collection of the British Museum. By the Rev. W. Smith, F.L.S., &c. Pp. iv., 55. 1859, 12mo. 1s.

FOSSILS.

Catalogue of the Fossil Mammalia in the British Museum (Natural History) By Richard Lydekker, B.A , F.G.S. :—
  Part I. Containing the Orders Primates, Chiroptera, Insectivora, Carnivora, and Rodentia. Pp xxx., 268. 33 Woodcuts. [With Systematic and Alphabetical Indexes.] 1885, 8vo. 5s
  Part II. Containing the Order Ungulata, Suborder Artiodactyla Pp xxii, 324 39 Woodcuts [With Systematic and Alphabetical Indexes.] 1885, 8vo. 6s.
  Part III. Containing the Order Ungulata, Suborders Perissodactyla, Toxodontia, Condylarthra, and Amblypoda. Pp.

Catalogue of the Fossil Mammalia—*continued.*
>xvi, 186. 30 Woodcuts. [With Systematic Index, and Alphabetical Index of Genera and Species, including Synonyms.] 1886, 8vo 4s.
>
>Part IV Containing the Order Ungulata, Suborder Proboscidea Pp. xxiv, 235. 32 Woodcuts [With Systematic Index, and Alphabetical Index of Genera and Species, including Synonyms] 1886, 8vo 5s.
>
>Part V. Containing the Group Tillodontia, the Orders Sirenia, Cetacea, Edentata, Marsupialia, Monotremata, and Supplement Pp. xxxv., 345. 55 Woodcuts. [With Systematic Index, and Alphabetical Index of Genera and Species, including Synonyms] 1887, 8vo. 6s.

Catalogue of the Fossil Birds in the British Museum (Natural History). By Richard Lydekker, B.A. Pp. xxvii, 368. 75 Woodcuts. [With Systematic Index, and Alphabetical Index of Genera and Species, including Synonyms] 1891, 8vo. 10s. 6d.

Catalogue of the Fossil Reptilia and Amphibia in the British Museum (Natural History). By Richard Lydekker, B A., F.G.S.:—

>Part I. Containing the Orders Ornithosauria, Crocodilia, Dinosauria, Squamata, Rhynchocephalia, and Proterosauria. Pp. xxviii, 309. 69 Woodcuts [With Systematic Index, and Alphabetical Index of Genera and Species, including Synonyms.] 1888, 8vo. 7s. 6d.
>
>Part II. Containing the Orders Ichthyopterygia and Sauropterygia Pp. xxi., 307. 85 Woodcuts. [With Systematic Index, and Alphabetical Index of Genera and Species, including Synonyms.] 1889, 8vo. 7s. 6d
>
>Part III. Containing the Order Chelonia. Pp xviii., 239. 53 Woodcuts. [With Systematic Index, and Alphabetical Index of Genera and Species, including Synonyms.] 1889, 8vo 7s. 6d.
>
>Part IV. Containing the Orders Anomodontia, Ecaudata, Caudata, and Labyrinthodontia; and Supplement Pp. xxiii, 295 66 Woodcuts. [With Systematic Index, Alphabetical Index of Genera and Species, including Synonyms, and Alphabetical Index of Genera and Species to the entire work.] 1890, 8vo. 7s. 6d

Catalogue of the Fossil Fishes in the British Museum (Natural History). By Arthur Smith Woodward, F.G.S, F.Z.S.:—

>Part I. Containing the Elasmobranchii. Pp. xlvii., 474. 13 Woodcuts and 17 Plates [With Alphabetical Index, and Systematic Index of Genera and Species.] 1889. 8vo 21s
>
>Part II. Containing the Elasmobranchii (Acanthodii), Holocephali, Ichthyodorulites, Ostracodermi, Dipnoi, and Teleostomi (Crossopterygii and Chondrostean Actinopterygii). Pp. xliv, 567 58 Woodcuts and 16 Plates. [With Alphabetical Index, and Systematic Index of Genera and Species.] 1891, 8vo 21s

Catalogue of the Fossil Fishes—*continued*.
- Part III. Containing the Actinopterygian Teleostomi of the Orders *Chondrostei* (concluded), *Protospondyli*, *Aetheospondyli*, and *Isospondyli* (in part). Pp. xlii., 544. 45 Woodcuts and 18 Plates. [With Alphabetical Index, and Systematic Index of Genera and Species.] 1895, 8vo 21s.

Systematic List of the Edwards Collection of British Oligocene and Eocene Mollusca in the British Museum (Natural History), with references to the type-specimens from similar horizons contained in other collections belonging to the Geological Department of the Museum. By Richard Bullen Newton, F.G.S.. Pp. xxviii., 365. [With table of Families and Genera, Bibliography, Correlation-table, Appendix, and Alphabetical Index.] 1891, 8vo. 6s.

Catalogue of the Fossil Cephalopoda in the British Museum (Natural History). By Arthur H. Foord, F.G.S. :—
- Part I. Containing part of the Suborder Nautiloidea, consisting of the families Orthoceratidæ, Endoceratidæ, Actinoceratidæ, Gomphoceratidæ, Ascoceratidæ, Poteriioceratidæ, Cyrtoceratidæ, and Supplement Pp. xxxi., 344. 51 Woodcuts. [With Systematic Index, and Alphabetical Index of Genera and Species, including Synonyms.] 1888, 8vo. 10s. 6d.
- Part II. Containing the remainder of the Suborder Nautiloidea, consisting of the families Lituitidæ, Trochoceratidæ, Nautilidæ, and Supplement. Pp. xxviii., 407. 86 Woodcuts. [With Systematic Index, and Alphabetical Index of Genera and Species, including Synonyms] 1891, 8vo. 15s.

A Catalogue of British Fossil Crustacea, with their Synonyms and the Range in Time of each Genus and Order. By Henry Woodward, F.R.S. Pp. xii., 155. [With an Alphabetical Index.] 1877, 8vo. 5s.

Catalogue of the Blastoidea in the Geological Department of the British Museum (Natural History), with an account of the morphology and systematic position of the group, and a revision of the genera and species. By Robert Etheridge, jun., of the Department of Geology, British Museum (Natural History), and P. Herbert Carpenter, D.Sc., F.R.S., F.L.S., (of Eton College). [With Preface by Dr. H. Woodward, Table of Contents, General Index, Explanations of the Plates, &c.] Pp. xv., 322. 20 Plates. 1886, 4to. 25s.

Catalogue of the Fossil Sponges in the Geological Department of the British Museum (Natural History). With descriptions of new and little known species. By George Jennings Hinde, Ph.D., F.G.S. Pp. viii., 248. 38 Plates. [With a Tabular List of Species, arranged in Zoological and Stratigraphical sequence, and an Alphabetical Index.] 1883, 4to. 1l. 10s.

Catalogue of the Fossil Foraminifera in the British Museum (Natural History). By Professor T. Rupert Jones, F.R.S., &c. Pp. xxiv., 100. [With Geographical and Alphabetical Indexes.] 1882, 8vo. 5s.

Catalogue of the Palæozoic Plants in the Department of Geology and Palæontology, British Museum (Natural History). By Robert Kidston, F.G.S. Pp. viii., 288. [With a list of works quoted, and an Index.] 1886, 8vo. 5s.

Catalogue of the Mesozoic Plants in the Department of Geology, British Museum (Natural History).: The Wealden Flora. By A. C. Seward, M.A., F.G.S., University Lecturer in Botany, Cambridge.

    Part I. Thallophyta—Pteridophyta. Pp. xxxviii., 179 : 17 Woodcuts and 11 Plates. [With Preface by Dr. Woodward, Alphabetical Index of Genera, Species, &c., Explanations of the Plates, &c.] 1894, 8vo. 10s.

    Part II. Gymnospermæ. Pp. viii., 259. 9 Woodcuts and 20 Plates [With Alphabetical Index, Explanations of the Plates, &c.] 1895, 8vo. 15s.

GUIDE-BOOKS.

(To be obtained only at the Museum.)

A General Guide to the British Museum (Natural History), Cromwell Road, London, S.W. [By W. H. Flower.] With 2 Plans, 2 views of the building, and an illustrated cover. Pp. 80. 1895, 8vo. 3d.

Guide to the Galleries of Mammalia (Mammalian, Osteological, Cetacean) in the Department of Zoology of the British Museum (Natural History). [By A. Gunther.] 5th Edition. Pp. 126. 57 Woodcuts and 2 Plans. Index. 1894, 8vo. 6d.

Guide to the Galleries of Reptiles and Fishes in the Department of Zoology of the British Museum (Natural History). [By A. Gunther.] 3rd Edition. Pp. iv., 119. 101 Woodcuts and 1 Plan. Index. 1893, 8vo. 6d.

Guide to the Shell and Starfish Galleries (Mollusca, Echinodermata, Vermes), in the Department of Zoology of the British Museum (Natural History). [By A. Gunther.] 2nd Edition. Pp. iv., 74. 51 Woodcuts and 1 Plan. 1888, 8vo. 4d.

A Guide to the Exhibition Galleries of the Department of Geology and Palæontology in the British Museum (Natural History), Cromwell Road, London, S.W. [New Edition. By Henry Woodward.]—

    Part I. Fossil Mammals and Birds. Pp. xii., 103. 119 Woodcuts and 1 Plan. 1890, 8vo. 6d.

    Part II. Fossil Reptiles, Fishes, and Invertebrates. Pp. xii., 109. 94 Woodcuts and 1 Plan. 1890, 8vo. 6d.

Guide to the Collection of Fossil Fishes in the Department of Geology and Palæontology, British Museum (Natural History), Cromwell Road, South Kensington. [By Henry Woodward.] 2nd Edition. Pp. 51. 81 Woodcuts. Index. 1888 8vo. 4*d*.

Guide to Sowerby's Models of British Fungi in the Department of Botany, British Museum (Natural History). By Worthington G. Smith, F.L S. Pp 82. 93 Woodcuts. With Table of Diagnostic Characters and Index. 1893, 8vo. 4*d*.

Guide to the British Mycetozoa exhibited in the Department of Botany, British Museum (Natural History). By Arthur Lister, F.L.S. Pp 42. 44 Woodcuts. Index. 1895, 8vo. 3*d*

A Guide to the Mineral Gallery of the British Museum (Natural History) [By L. Fletcher] Pp 32. Plan. 1895, 8vo. 1*d*.

An Introduction to the Study of Minerals, with a Guide to the Mineral Gallery of the British Museum (Natural History), Cromwell Road, S.W. By L. Fletcher. Pp. 120. With numerous Diagrams, a Plan of the Mineral Gallery, and an Index. 1895, 8vo. 6*d*.

The Student's Index to the Collection of Minerals, British Museum (Natural History). [New Edition.] Pp. 33. With a Plan of the Mineral Gallery. 1895, 8vo. 2*d*

An Introduction to the Study of Meteorites, with a List of the Meteorites represented in the Collection. [By L. Fletcher.] Pp. 94. [With a Plan of the Mineral Gallery, and an Index to the Meteorites represented in the Collection.] 1894, 8vo. 6*d*.

An Introduction to the Study of Rocks. [By L. Fletcher.] Pp. 118. [With plan of the Mineral Gallery, table of Contents, and Index.] 1895, 8vo. 6*d*.

W. H. FLOWER,
Director.

British Museum
(Natural History),
Cromwell Road,
London, S.W.

December 1st, 1895.

Lightning Source UK Ltd.
Milton Keynes UK
UKOW012313180213

206470UK00008B/1028/P